S0-AXE-857

PSYCHOLOGY

SECOND EDITION

PSYCHOLOGY

SECOND EDITION

Camille B. Wortman
University of Michigan

Elizabeth F. Loftus
University of Washington

Mary E. Marshall

Alfred A. Knopf
NEW YORK

THIS IS A BORZOI BOOK PUBLISHED BY ALFRED A. KNOPF, INC.

Second Edition
98765432
Copyright © 1985, 1981 by Alfred A. Knopf, Inc.

All rights reserved under International and Pan-American Copyright Conventions. No part of this book may be reproduced in any form or by any means, electronic or mechanical, including photo-copying, without permission in writing from the publisher. All inquiries should be addressed to Alfred A. Knopf, Inc., 201 East 50th Street, New York, N.Y. 10022. Published in the United States by Alfred A. Knopf, Inc., New York, and simulta-neously in Canada by Random House of Canada Limited, Toronto. Distributed by Random House, Inc., New York.

Library of Congress Cataloging in Publication Data

Wortman, Camille.
  Psychology.

  Bibliography: p.
  Includes indexes.
  1. Psychology.   I. Loftus, Elizabeth F., 1944–
II. Marshall, Mary E.   III. Title.
BF121.W67   1985   150   84-14384
ISBN 0-394-33189-3

Manufactured in the United States of America
Text design: John Lennard
Cover sculpture: Jose De Rivera, Construction #107
(1969), Hirshhorn Museum and Sculpture Garden,
Smithsonian Institution.

Preface

THE GOALS OF THIS BOOK

Although this second edition of *Psychology* includes much that is new, our basic goals remain the same as in the first edition. We strive to integrate theories and research with real-life applications so as to make the study of psychology both interesting and meaningful to students. We also strive to encourage critical thinking about psychological ideas and findings by stressing the kinds of critical questions that scientific researchers ask. A desire to strengthen these two aspects of our book guided much of our efforts in revising the first edition.

Integrating Theory, Research, and Applications

As we noted in the preface to the first edition, there seems to be a tension between the basic science that instructors want to teach and the practical information that students want to learn. Different texts have dealt with this problem in different ways. Some have taken a strong research orientation, with little apparent concern for readability or student interest. Others have chosen to be research-oriented in some parts of the book but to intersperse these parts with separate sections on applications and other high-interest topics. This second approach has become increasingly popular in recent years. Many authors have filled their texts with an array of "special features"—cartoons, newspaper clippings, boxed inserts of various kinds, even stories and vignettes. Indeed, many current books seem to be based on the assumption that the only way to make scientific content palatable to students is to offer them a panoply of gimmicks and titillating topics. It was because of our belief that psychology can be exciting and engaging without recourse to gimmicks or sacrifice of scientific integrity that we originally decided to write this book.

Our aim in the second edition, as in the first, has been to integrate conceptually sophisticated theories and research with applications and topics of current concern to students. We feel that separate boxes, vignettes, and other added-on features have several serious drawbacks. For one thing, they disrupt the flow and coherence of a chapter, often making it hard for readers to grasp how topics interrelate. For another, such added-on extras are based on the erroneous assumption that students need a breather from their toils as they wearily plod through scientific material. For those who disagree with this assumption we offer an alternative view: By fully interweaving theories and research with applications, *all* of introductory psychology can be made fascinating and meaningful to students.

The second edition of *Psychology* includes many new efforts to carry out this integration. Our section on affirmative action in Chapter 17 is one good example. In it we relate social psychological theories and findings to the problem of equalizing opportunities for minority groups. Attribution theory, self-perception theory, the principle of psychological reactance, and Sherif's work on cooperation and intergroup tolerance are all shown to shed light on this critical issue. Similarly, in Chapter 6, our discussions of ways to improve long-term recall and study habits are integrated with current theories and research on how human memory works. In these and many other instances students can clearly see that scientific findings often have direct application to matters of practical importance in everyday life.

Encouraging Critical Thought

There is more to a good text than integration of theory, research, and applications. In planning our approach to writing this book, we asked ourselves the following question: How can this text enhance the long-run impact of a student's first (and often only) psychology course? One of the most difficult problems we as instructors have faced is that no matter how carefully and thoroughly we present material, the details of specific experiments seem to fade from students' memories after the term is over. We gave this problem a great deal of thought during the initial stages of this book. The conclusion we came to is that retention of specific facts is not as important as acquiring an understanding of what the science of psychology is all about. For this reason we have made every effort to emphasize the *process* of scientific inquiry. Repeatedly we focus on how psychologists develop testable hypotheses, how they gather and interpret data, and how they arrive at conclusions. We try to show how early studies form the foundation for later research, which in turn often refines our understanding by ruling out alternative explanations.

We believe that this emphasis on the process of science has two important benefits. First, it conveys much of the excitement of doing scientific work. Second, and even more important, it gets students to think critically about psychological information by encouraging them to ask questions about how "facts" are obtained. In this way we hope to promote a healthy skepticism toward ideas derived from poor research methods. Such skepticism is very valuable in today's society, where people are exposed to a barrage of popular "psychologizing"—everything from tests in the Sunday supplement to evaluate one's marriage, to the numerous "self-improvement" books that line drugstore shelves. We have tried to provide students with the critical skills needed to question the validity of this popularized psychology. We hope that these skills will remain with them long after their introductory course.

Of course, the goal of teaching students to think critically is not an easy one. How, specifically, have we tried to accomplish it?

Repeated Evaluation of Research Findings.
For one thing, we have devoted an early chapter of the book (Chapter 2) to a careful consideration of how psychologists define research objectives, select a method of inquiry, gather and interpret their data, rule out alternative explanations, and deal with the ethical dilemmas that research sometimes poses. We then carry these themes throughout the book by repeatedly encouraging students to evaluate the theories and research we present. For example, under-

graduates are often impressed by Rosenhan's study in which normal people who entered mental hospitals posing as schizophrenics failed to be detected as normal by the hospital staffs. Many introductory texts stop with a brief summary of Rosenhan's findings. This book, in contrast, encourages critical thought by guiding readers through an analysis of what the Rosenhan study does and doesn't prove. Similarly, some texts that present Klaus and Kennell's theory of early mother–infant bonding do little more than describe these researchers' experimental results. This book, in contrast, goes much further, encouraging students to identify some of the flaws in Klaus and Kennell's experiment, discussing the problems that other researchers have had replicating it, and leading students to consider the dangers of premature conclusions when doing scientific work.

Comparing Empirical Data with Common-Sense Ideas.
A second technique we use to develop critical thinking is to contrast "common sense" myths about psychology with what empirical data reveal. One of the frustrating things about teaching introductory psychology is the large number of students who believe that psychology is nothing more than "common sense." We try to show that while empirical data sometimes support our common-sense notions, they often do not. For instance, common sense leads us to believe that the more motivated people are, the better they will perform on a task. Drawing from theoretical and empirical work, we demonstrate in Chapter 11 how simplistic this assumption is. Similarly, common sense also tells us that a good way to help prevent depressed people from attempting suicide is to stop them from talking about the subject of death. In Chapter 15 we counter this popular misconception. We present data which show that letting despondent people discuss their suicidal wishes may actually help them overcome self-destructive thoughts. By highlighting such discrepancies between common sense and empirical findings, we hope to emphasize that people cannot trust their intuitions when it comes to human behavior. A careful evaluation of available evidence is always essential.

In-Depth Sections.
Finally, a third and very important way we encourage critical thinking is through the section in each chapter labeled "In Depth." In these sections we explore in detail how psychologists have investigated a particular research question—how

they developed their initial hypotheses, designed studies to test them, interpreted the findings, and modified their conclusions in light of new information or criticisms raised by others.

Some of our In-Depth sections present a critical discussion of one research program, chosen both for its importance in the field and for its intrinsic interest to students. For example, in the chapter on cognition and problem solving (Chapter 7) we investigate Kahneman and Tversky's program of research on how people judge uncertain odds. Here we examine the fascinating finding that reliance on decision-making heuristics often leads people astray. At the same time, we encourage students to evaluate whether and how such cognitive strategies affect their own decisions, and we lead them to consider the extent to which Kahneman and Tversky's results can be generalized outside the laboratory.

Some chapters contain In-Depth sections that concentrate not on a single research program but on a single critical issue, investigating how different researchers have shed light on it. For instance, in the motivation chapter (Chapter 11) the In Depth explores obesity. We review the theoretical and empirical work of Schachter, Nisbett, Rodin, Herman and Polivy, and others, with particular attention to how these investigators have influenced one another's work. In the process, we touch on the psychological principles underlying many current weight-reducing diets, why they so often fail in the long run, and even whether some obese people should diet at all. We also examine exercise as an alternative to constant dieting, especially in light of recent evidence linking regular exercise to increased metabolic rate. Throughout, the reader is led to see that the problem of significant, permanent weight loss is a complex one to which there are seldom simple answers. The many other In-Depth sections included in this book are listed in the table of contents.

WHAT'S NEW IN THIS EDITION?

Although the second edition of *Psychology* continues to emphasize the themes present in the first edition, we incorporated much new material when revising the book. Here we can review only the highlights of the many improvements we have made.

Concepts Are Better Tied Together Throughout the Book

In this edition we have tried to stress that the various subfields in psychology are not mutually independent. Increasingly, researchers in different areas are sharing data and insights, which often makes concepts presented in one part of the book relevant to concepts in another. We have made every effort to tie these interrelated concepts together so as to enrich students' overall understanding. Consider, for instance, the concept of a limited human capacity for processing information. This idea is introduced in Chapter 4, which deals with sensation and perception. In Chapter 6 we pick up the thread again when discussing the limitations of human memory. The same idea appears again in Chapter 7, where we examine how people go about solving problems and making decisions. Still later, in Chapter 17, on social psychology, we relate the very same idea to social cognition, especially to how people employ schemas in forming impressions of others. In this way we hope that students will perceive some of the important consistencies in how we humans think and act.

Important New Research Has Been Added

So much is happening in all the subfields of psychology that textbook writers face a real challenge in deciding what new information to include. In this edition we have added exciting new research findings in every chapter of the book. For instance, in Chapter 3 we describe some of the latest methods for mapping the human brain, especially for tracking down the roles that neurotransmitters play in controlling human behavior. In Chapter 6 we explore recent findings on state-dependent memory, including a current theory about why this phenomenon occurs. In Chapter 10 we examine some of the latest techniques for managing stress, raising the question of why these approaches are effective. In Chapter 12 we look at recent studies on the subject of sleep, including ones designed to see if we can actually control our dreams. In Chapter 15 we take up some of the latest insights into the causes of psychological disorders, especially depression and schizophrenia. And in Chapter 18 we investigate the most recent evidence concerning whether TV violence promotes aggression in children. This, of course, is just a sampling of the new research added. A look through individual chapters will reveal the scope of our updating.

Discussions of Major Theories Have Been Strengthened

We have made every effort to strengthen our discussions of important psychological theories. This effort begins in Chapter 1, where we have tried to present the major schools of psychological thought in ways that will be both clear and interesting to students. In this chapter we have also stressed how the major schools of thought developed in response to one another, and how each now provides important insights into human behavior. In later chapters we continue these themes when presenting psychological theories. In Chapter 8, for instance, we discuss recent alternatives to Piaget's theories, and we attempt to show how these newer outlooks sometimes complement Piaget's. Similarly, in Chapter 13, we try to show how theories of personality have influenced one another and how each fits together important pieces of the puzzle of human behavior. In this way we hope that students will be able to place opposing views in proper perspective and avoid becoming confused when no one view turns out to be "right."

Many New In-Depth Sections Have Been Added

Instructors and students alike responded very favorably to the In-Depth sections in our first edition. In this edition, therefore, we have retained the best of the old, while creating many new In Depths on important research topics. The new additions are: an In Depth on how researchers have gone about investigating the hazards of smoking (Chapter 2); an In Depth on subliminal perception and its limitations (Chapter 4); an In Depth on the impact of early day care on emotional development (Chapter 8); an In Depth on why some children have problems learning to read (Chapter 9); an In Depth on self-esteem and how it affects behavior (Chapter 13); and an In Depth on the consequences of affirmative action programs (Chapter 17). In addition, we have heavily revised the In Depths retained from the first edition, in order to

incorporate new research findings. The result is an overall strengthening of this very popular feature.

New Learning Aids Have Been Added

Several new learning aids have been added to this edition. An outline of text headings now introduces each chapter so that students can see at a glance what material will be covered and how major topics relate to one another. The suggested readings at the end of each chapter have been extensively revised, and each reading is now annotated so that students will be better able to select among them. Our end-of-book glossary has been greatly expanded, and a separate index of names is now included in addition to a thorough index of subjects.

Visual Features Have Been Changed

Finally, in this second edition we took special care with the design of the book. The text is now printed in two columns, with slightly larger type for easier reading. Many of the illustrations have also been changed, and much attention has been given to selecting diagrams and photos that reinforce and clarify points made in the text.

ACKNOWLEDGMENTS

Our publisher has made many resources available to us to enhance the quality of this book. One is the text *Psychology Today*, which is owned by Random House/ Alfred A. Knopf and to which Elizabeth Loftus was a contributor. The ability to draw on materials and illustrations from this text has been of great value, especially in developing Chapters 3, 8, 9, and 12.

When this edition of the book was in first-draft form, a number of reviewers were immeasurably helpful in offering their criticisms and thoughtful ideas for improvement. We are especially grateful to Alan G. Glaros of Wayne State University for his comments on Chapters 15 and 16. The following people also provided valuable insights:

David Barkmeier
Northeastern University

Major Johnston Beach
United States Military Academy

Norma Benimoff
Camden County College

Philip G. Benson
Auburn University

Ilene L. Bernstein
University of Washington

John Best
Eastern Illinois University

Ross Buck
University of Connecticut

John L. Caruso
Southeastern Massachusetts University

Douglas Chatfield
Texas Technical University

Eva Conrad
San Bernardino Valley College

Ronald Finke
State University of New York at Stony Brook

Donald Forsyth
Virginia Commonwealth University

Russell G. Geen
University of Missouri—Columbia

Richard A. Griggs
University of Florida

Carlos V. Grijalva
University of California at Los Angeles

Joseph C. Hammock
University of Georgia

Richard Harris
University of New Mexico

Walter G. Klopfer
Portland State University

Frank Kodman
Murray State University

Janet M. Kulberg
University of Rhode Island

Wesley Lynch
Montana State University

Michael McCloskey
Johns Hopkins University

Captain Gerald Mitchell
United States Military Academy

Gregory L. Murphy
Brown University

Nora Newcombe
Temple University

Ronald Nowaczyk
Clemson University

Major Timothy R. O'Neill
United States Military Academy

Charlotte J. Patterson
University of Virginia

Norman Poppel
Middlesex County College

Milton Rosenbaum
University of Iowa

Paul Rosenfeld
Pennsylvania State University

David Schroeder
University of Arkansas

Kimron Shapiro
Pennsylvania State University

Susan A. Shodahl
San Bernardino Valley College

Abigail Stewart
Boston University

Helen Tager-Flusberg
University of Massachusetts

Elaine Walker
Cornell University

Benjamin Wallace
Cleveland State University

Joel Warm
University of Cincinnati

Susan Warner
University of Arizona

Keith Wollen
Washington State University

The people at Random House/Knopf with whom we worked put enormous care, skill, and effort into this project. The following people deserve our special thanks for making the second edition a reality: Elaine Romano, who coordinated development of the manuscript and whose talent and intelligence made a difficult job far easier; Cecilia Gardner, who did excellent work supervising the copy-editing process and illustration program and overseeing production; Mary Falcon and Suzanne Thibodeau, who helped shape and articulate many of the ideas for the second edition; Rochelle Diogenes, who coordinated the reviewing process; Virginia Joyner, Betty Gatewood, John Sturman, and Barbara Salazar, talented freelance editors who helped the book along its way; John Lennard, who devised the book's attractive new design; Stacey Alexander, who supervised the production process; and Kathy Bendo and Barbara Salz, who worked on photo research and selection. Of course, our thanks go to our husbands once again for their understanding and support during the many months when the book consumed so much of our time.

CBW
EFL
MEM

About the Authors

Camille B. Wortman is professor of psychology at the University of Michigan, Ann Arbor. A social psychologist, her major research interests include reactions to uncontrollable outcomes and undesirable events, causal attribution, and reactions to stress and victimization. Wortman graduated summa cum laude from Duke University in 1969, and received her Ph.D. from Duke in 1972. Prior to joining the Michigan faculty in 1979, she was a member of the psychology faculty at Northwestern University for seven years. The introductory psychology course that she taught there was so successful that a lottery for enrollment had to be instituted because of student demand. In recognition of her excellence in undergraduate teaching, she won the Distinguished Teaching Award at Northwestern University. Since receiving her degree, Wortman has published numerous articles in every major journal in her field. She has also contributed chapters to a large number of edited books including the *Advances in Experimental Social Psychology, New Directions in Attribution Research,* and *Advances in Environmental Psychology* series. On the basis of her research, Wortman received the American Psychological Association's Distinguished Scientific Award for an Early Career Contribution to Psychology.

Elizabeth F. Loftus is professor of psychology at the University of Washington, Seattle. A specialist in learning and memory, she has been nationally recognized for her research on eyewitness testimony. Her book on the subject, *Eyewitness Testimony,* was published by Harvard University Press in 1979 and won an APA National Media Award, Distinguished contribution, in 1980. Another book, *Eyewitness Testimony: Psychological Perspectives,* which she co-edited, was published in 1984. *Memory* appeared in 1980; *Essence of Statistics* and *Mind at Play,* both co-authored, appeared in 1981 and 1983, respectively. Loftus received her B.A. with highest honors in mathematics and psychology from UCLA in 1966, and an M.A. (1967) and Ph.D. (1970) in psychology from Stanford University. In 1982 she received an honorary doctor of science degree from Miami University of Ohio. She has been a visiting instructor at Harvard University and the National Judicial College, and was assistant professor at the New School for Social Research before moving to the University of Washington. Loftus was a Fellow at the Center for Advanced Study in the Behavioral Sciences, Stanford, 1978–79. She has published numerous articles, and travels extensively to present papers at college and university colloquia and to the legal profession. She has twice been the APA nominee for the NSF Waterman Award for outstanding contributions to science. Loftus has served as president of the Western Psychological Association (1984) and of the Psychology and Law Division of the American Psychological Association (1985).

Mary E. Marshall, until she became a psychology writer in 1979, was manager of special projects at the college department of Random House. During her ten years in college publishing, she supervised the development of introductory texts such as *Psychology Today, Abnormal Psychology* (2d and 3d eds.), and *Understanding Psychology* (2d ed.). Marshall is a graduate with distinction of Connecticut College, Phi Beta Kappa and magna cum laude.

Contents

part 1

THE SCIENCE OF PSYCHOLOGY

We begin with a discussion of psychology
as an activity—its scope and its methods.
Chapter 1 explores the dimensions of
psychology: what psychologists do and the
areas to which their activities are applied.
Chapter 2 examines the methods
psychologists use and the structure of
psychological research.

1

THE DIMENSIONS OF PSYCHOLOGY

Bruce Nauman, *Untitled*, 1978.

Psychology as a Vocation and a Perspective

When you hear the word *psychology*, what comes to mind? Do you imagine a laboratory in which rats are run through mazes, pigeons peck at keys, and dogs salivate at the sound of a bell? Does the word conjure up images of a therapist listening to a client's problems, analyzing dreams, or providing expertise on how to raise children? These are common preconceptions about **psychology,** which can be defined as the study of behavior and mental processes. How accurate are they? Certainly these two images provide only a limited picture of what this book is all about. Yet each touches on an important aspect of the subject you are about to explore. *Psychology is a science*, a set of procedures for systematically observing facts about behavior and for organizing these facts into generalizations, or laws, that seek to explain why human beings and other animals act as they do. In addition, *psychology is a means of promoting human welfare*, a body of information that can be applied to help solve a variety of individual and group problems.

DEFINING PSYCHOLOGY

Psychology Is a Science

The hallmark of science is reliance on empirical data— that is, on information that has been systematically observed, measured, and recorded—and a true psychologist will rely on these rather than informal observation, casual assumptions, or common sense. Although the latter may serve us well in everyday life, even "obvious" common-sense notions can sometimes be incorrect. Suppose, for example, that you are teaching elementary mathematics. You are concerned about some students in your class who tend to perform poorly in math and who give up as soon as a problem seems difficult. How can you help these students? Common sense suggests that you might build their confidence by assigning them many easy problems, thus ensuring success. But you would have no way of being *sure* that this method would work unless you tested it scientifically.

Psychologist Carol Dweck (1975) decided to do just that. She had doubts about the common-sense tactic of giving children who quit when threatened with failure many easy problems to raise their confidence. In some of her earlier research, Dweck had found that children whose performance deteriorates under failure usually explain their failure in terms of things they cannot change, such as innate lack of ability (Dweck and Reppucci, 1973). Such children feel helpless in problem-solving situations. They believe that there is no reason to keep trying, since nothing they do will make any difference. Dweck suspected that if these children were taught to attribute their failure to something they *could* influence, they might persist longer at problems and experience more success. To test her hypothesis, Dweck chose twelve children known to behave helplessly in the face of failure. She divided the children into two groups and gave them twenty-five days of special training with math problems. Children in one group, the "success only" condition, were assigned only easy problems to solve. Those in the other group, the "attribution retraining" condition, also received some easy problems. But they were given some very difficult problems as well and thus deliberately induced to fail. Each time a child failed, he or she was encouraged to attribute failure to lack of effort—something that could be controlled. ("You should have tried a little harder.") At the end of the training, both groups were tested on new arithmetic problems. The "success only" students continued to give up after each failure. But the students who had had attribution retraining improved in their reaction to failure. As Dweck predicted, they persisted longer at the problems and performed much better than they had initially. Studies such as Dweck's, which use the methods of science, have provided important generalizations about many aspects of behavior—including some that contradict widely held beliefs.

Yet some people still question whether behavior, especially human behavior, is accessible to scientific inquiry. One recent critic of psychology and the other social sciences is William Proxmire, chairman of the Senate subcommittee that oversees the National Science Foundation (NSF). Senator Proxmire believes that certain human behaviors are too individual, too unpredictable to be studied scientifically. One of his targets several years ago was an NSF-funded grant for research on love. Proxmire argued:

I object to this not only because no one—not even the National Science Foundation—can argue that falling in love is a science; not only that even if they spend $84 million or $84 billion they wouldn't get an answer that anyone would believe. I am against it because I don't want the answer. I believe that 200 million other Americans want to leave some things in life a mystery, and right at the top of the things we don't want to know is why a man falls in love with a woman and vice versa. (National Science Foundation Funded Projects, 1975.)

Psychologists, of course, disagree. They believe that it is possible and desirable to conduct rigorous scientific research on human behavior—even on aspects of it as complex and multifaceted as love. (In Chapter 17 we will discuss psychological research on love, including those research projects that Senator Proxmire criticized.) Psychologists doubt that human behavior is such a mystery that it cannot be understood. They believe that there are patterns underlying human thought and actions, just as there are patterns underlying all phenomena in the physical universe. These patterns can be understood by careful observation and measurement of the ways people respond under various conditions. This is not to deny that research in psychology can be challenging. Often it is a complicated matter even to identify the variables under study. In a study of love, for example, we might have to figure out how to measure such variables as how deeply in love two people are, how similar their atti-

In the view of psychologists, even a subject as complex and variable as romantic love can be studied scientifically. *(Patrick Ward/Stock, Boston.)*

tudes are, how much contact they have had before marriage, and how much their parents have interfered in the relationship. But even though it is frequently more difficult to quantify and measure variables in the social sciences than in the physical sciences, it is not impossible to do so. From a large number of observations, psychologists can generalize about how people typically behave in a given situation. On the basis of these generalizations, they can make predictions about how a person might act in a slightly different but related situation. By testing these predictions, psychologists can further evaluate their initial generalizations, modifying them as evidence demands. This, in essence, is the process of science, and psychologists argue that it can be applied to human behavior just as it can be applied to the study of atoms and molecules, celestial bodies, or any aspect of the living world.

Psychology vs. Common Sense. If psychology is a science, why do people sometimes fail to regard it as such? One important reason is that, unlike such "hard" sciences as chemistry and physics, psychology deals with everyday human concerns—childhood development, motivation, learning, personality, and the like. People naturally have ideas about such topics, and they sometimes may think that they know as much about such matters as the experts do—or even more. Although few people would claim to know more than chemists or physicists do about their fields, many people fancy themselves knowledgeable in psychology. Even much of the specialized vocabulary of psychology has become a part of everyday life, and people who have never sat in a psychology class or read a book on the subject are quick to use such terms as "ego," "paranoid," "fixated," "traumatized," and "neurotic."

But psychology is not just common sense. As we just saw, psychological research often contradicts popular explanations about behavior. Most college students, for instance, assume that the more highly motivated a person is, the better he or she will be at solving a complex problem (Vaughan, 1977). Psychologists have found, however, that when people perform any complex task, either mental or physical, very high levels of motivation usually have a detrimental effect. The highly motivated person tries to attend to too many details at once, becomes confused, and so fails to find a solution. Apparently there is an optimum motivation level for efficient problem solving that varies with the complexity of the task. This

optimum motivation level also varies with the personality of the individual, as we will discuss in Chapter 11.

Consider another example in which psychological research contradicted what "everyone knows." Is the following statement true or false? To change a person's negative behavior toward members of ethnic minorities, that person's prejudiced attitudes must first be changed (Vaughan, 1977). The overwhelming majority of people (you too?) accept this commonsense notion, yet psychologists have challenged it. In an experiment conducted many years ago, psychologist Richard LaPiere (1934) traveled around the United States with a Chinese couple, expecting to encounter anti-Oriental attitudes that would make it difficult for them to find places to eat and sleep. But this was not the case. "In something like ten thousand miles of motor travel," LaPiere wrote, "twice across the United States, up and down the Pacific Coast, we met definite rejection from those asked to serve us just once" (LaPiere, 1934, p. 233). Judging from the courteous reception of the innkeepers and tradespeople LaPiere and his companions encountered, one might conclude that Americans at that time were almost entirely free of prejudice against Orientals. This, however, was far from true. LaPiere followed up his travels by writing a letter to each of the 251 establishments he and his Chinese friends had visited, asking whether they would provide food or lodging to Orientals. Of the 128 who responded, more than 90 percent answered with a flat no. This study provides suggestive evidence that people do not necessarily act on their attitudes. In Chapter 17, where this study is critically evaluated and more recent experiments are presented, we will explore the conditions under which people behave in ways that are inconsistent with their attitudes.

That psychology sometimes contradicts intuitive judgment about human behavior is an important theme of this book. As you read the text and learn more about the discipline of psychology, you may be surprised to learn just how many of the "facts" about human nature that you accept as valid fail to hold up under scientific scrutiny.

Psychology as an Ongoing Science. As we mentioned above, observation and measurement are sometimes difficult in psychology, given the nature of its subject matter: behavior and mental processes. Psychologists can't dismantle the human organism to find out what makes it tick. Studying people often takes ingenuity. Psychologists routinely rise to this challenge, devising experiments to investigate very slippery questions.

Consider, for example, the question of why people sometimes fail to help a stranger in distress. This is an important problem. We have all heard stories of city dwellers hurrying past a person who has collapsed in the street or ignoring the victim of assault who calls for help. In 1964 this kind of behavior made headlines when a young woman was brutally stabbed to death while on her way home from her night-shift job in a middle-class neighborhood of Queens, a borough of New York City. At least thirty-eight people witnessed the crime from their apartment windows, but no one offered assistance, beyond shouting at the man to "leave that girl alone." Only one person called the police, and he delayed so long in doing so that they arrived to find the woman already dead.

Were these people heartless and uncaring, made callous by the anonymity of city life? How would you go about answering this question? Bystanders who ignore the victim of a crime or a medical emergency are seldom available for interviewing after the event. And could you even trust that the explanations they gave for their own behavior were accurate? How, then, could you investigate this question, short of rushing to the scene of an emergency in progress with your note pad and tape recorder?

Faced with this problem, psychologists John Darley and Bibb Latané decided to stage some simulated emergencies under controlled conditions so that they could observe and record bystander response (Darley and Latané, 1968; Latané and Darley, 1968). In one experiment, smoke began pouring into a room where subjects were filling out a questionnaire; in another, subjects heard someone in the next room crash to the floor and moan in pain (actually a tape-recorded performance); in a third, a fellow subject was heard having a violent seizure (also simulated); in still another, the experimenter pretended to be severely shocked by electrical equipment while subjects looked on. Concerned with dispelling possible aftereffects of these alarming situations, the researchers were careful to debrief subjects after each of these experiments was concluded. The subjects were told that the emergencies were not real, and the investigators explained why it was necessary to stage an emergency in order to test their hypotheses. The investigators also took time to explain why they were interested in this aspect of human behavior and to discuss the entire experi-

ence with the subjects. As it turned out, Darley and Latané made some surprising discoveries, which we will discuss later in this chapter.

Darley and Latané's studies were initially quite novel. But very quickly they attracted attention, and soon other researchers were raising questions that Darley and Latané had overlooked. These other researchers set up their own experiments to test slightly different hypotheses, and so our knowledge of how people respond in emergency situations has grown enormously. Even today, however, we still do not have all the answers about this fascinating subject. This is what we mean by saying that psychology is an *ongoing* science. No matter how much we currently know about any given topic, there is always something more to be learned.

If we still have more to learn about bystander intervention in emergencies, we certainly have more to learn about the physiological side of psychology—particularly about the workings of the human brain. Our brains are involved in every action we take, from breathing to reading a textbook. In studying the relationship between the brain and behavior, however, psychologists have faced an obvious problem: it is unethical to tamper with a normal human brain simply to observe the effects. As a result, most of what we have learned about the brain so far has come from research done with other animals. But there is still the problem of how, technically speaking, one goes about exploring the brain of a living organism. This problem baffled scientists for many generations. It is only with twentieth-century advances in technology that probing a living, functioning brain has come within the scientist's reach.

One approach is to stimulate activity in the brain with mild electrical currents (mild enough to cause no damage or pain). José Delgado, for example, has investigated the brains of rats, cats, monkeys, and other animals in this way, and he has made some fascinating discoveries. In one dramatic study, Delgado implanted electrodes in a Spanish bull that had been specially bred for ferocity. He then climbed into a ring with this animal and waved a red cape at it. It began to charge, but as it raced headlong toward Delgado, the researcher pressed a button on a radio transmitter in his hand. The bull stopped dead in its tracks (Delgado, 1969).

Psychologists have learned a great deal about the brain's organization and functions from experiments such as this one. And they have been able to apply what they have learned to several human disorders. Delgado, for example, was a pioneer in the application of electrode implants in humans in order to diagnose and treat involuntary movements, persistent pain, epilepsy, and some cases of schizophrenia and extreme anxiety (Scarf, 1970). More recently, researchers exploring the electrochemistry of the brain developed tests that can help to detect learning disorders in children, early indications of senility among the elderly, and certain psychological disorders by pinpointing abnormal electrical activity in the brain (Restak, 1979). We will say much more about these procedures and their applications in Chapter 3, which is devoted to the brain.

We have described just a few examples of the imaginative and diligent detective work that psychological research can entail. Throughout this book we will emphasize the theme of psychology as a creative, ongoing science. You will learn much more about how psychologists formulate their theories, develop strategies for tracking down information, and systematically test alternative possibilities, thereby constantly adding to our knowledge. This theme will be especially apparent in the sections of subsequent chapters that are labeled In Depth. In these sections we will take a close look at particularly intriguing research problems, the ways investigators have tackled them, and the discoveries they have made. As you will see, few scientific questions are ever fully and unequivocally answered. The findings of one investigator inevitably lead to new problems, new directions, new possibilities. This is what makes the science of psychology so dynamic and exciting for researchers and students alike: there is always more to learn.

Psychology Is a Means of Promoting Human Welfare

The application of psychological findings to a variety of human problems is in keeping with the major goals of the American Psychological Association (APA), the principal professional organization for American psychologists. According to the bylaws of the APA, its primary aims are the advancement of "scientific interests and inquiry, and the application of research findings to the promotion of the public welfare" (APA, 1968, p. xii).

The deliberate use of research findings to solve some practical problem or to improve the quality of human life is generally called **applied science. Basic science,** in contrast, aims at understanding a subject without regard to whether that understanding will have immediate practical effects. The work of José Delgado, the psychologist we mentioned earlier who implanted electrodes in animals' brains to see how the brain affects behavior, is an example of basic research. In contrast, a researcher seeking to find ways to use mild electrical stimulation of the brain to treat severe epilepsy would be engaged in applied science. At times basic and applied research cannot be distinguished so neatly. Psychologists sometimes discover a new "basic" fact about their subject when they are working on an "applied" problem, and vice versa.

Some people have difficulty seeing the eventual benefits of basic scientific research. Consequently, they are quick to label many such studies a frivolous waste of money, a criticism that is usually groundless. But why does the public so readily jump to this conclusion? One reason is lack of understanding about how science progresses. What may seem at first a trivial finding can turn out to provide a small but vital clue in a larger and more important puzzle. The progress of science, in other words, is largely incremental. Without the many small contributions to scientific knowledge accumulated over years of basic research, great breakthroughs in applied science— the first human heart transplant, the first landing of human beings on the moon—would never have been possible.

Another reason for underestimation of the practical value of basic research is that the full implications of a particular study are seldom spelled out for the public. Several years ago, for example, a great public outcry arose over government funding of a study of the sexual behavior of the screwworm fly. It's easy to laugh at such a research project, and many people did. But closer examination shows that the study did have merit. The larvae of the screwworm fly are deadly to cattle and other domesticated animals, and this study provided the information needed to develop a means of controlling these pests. Apparently the female screwworm fly mates only once in her lifetime. If sterile males are released into breeding areas, the screwworm fly population can be efficiently controlled. Clearly this basic research had great benefits to both livestock breeders and consumers.

Similar misunderstandings have plagued other kinds of research. Consider, for example, a study of the hearing problems of pigs. Should deafness in pigs really concern scientists, when so many more urgent problems need attention? Once again, this is a narrow view. The study of pigs has helped researchers develop a way to diagnose hearing problems in babies early enough so that they can be corrected (Walgren, 1982).

One problem in judging basic research is that it is usually difficult for people to predict the ultimate value of a particular investigator's work. Many years ago, for instance, the work of B. F. Skinner, who eventually became one of the most influential psychologists in the twentieth century, was attacked as frivolous. Skinner was interested in the effects of rewards and punishments on an organism's behavior. He conducted a great number of experiments with animals—rewarding a pigeon with a food pellet whenever it pecked a key, for example, to see what effect this reward would have on the bird's subsequent behavior. Seemingly simple experiments like this enabled Skinner to develop the theory for which he ultimately became famous. Yet his first book, *The Behavior of Organisms* (1938), sold a mere eighty copies in its first four years in print. Much of the resistance to Skinner's early work was due to the belief that his findings had limited application. How likely was it, critics asked, that an organism as complex as a human being would respond to rewards and punishments in the same predictable way that a pigeon does?

Applied research in the past several decades has challenged Skinner's early critics. People seem to be every bit as susceptible to rewards and punishments as lower animals are. Psychologist Nathan Azrin, for instance, who worked under Skinner as a graduate student, has divided his very productive career between basic research on learning and applied research into how the principles of reward and punishment can be used to solve human problems. Azrin began his applied work by designing procedures to teach severely retarded people to feed and dress themselves, to use the toilet, and to stop such negative behaviors as bed wetting and sprawling on the floor. These training programs proved so successful that Azrin soon expanded his efforts to alleviate common problems among normal children and adults. He has developed widely accepted therapies for problems as diverse as stuttering, nail biting, alcoholism, and marital discord. We will say much more about such practical applications of learning theory in Chapters 5 and 16.

Besides doing research, both basic and applied, psychologists are involved in promoting human welfare more directly. They do so by working as counselors and clinicians in many settings: schools, hospitals, places of employment, community health centers, and private offices. Many students who take psychology courses in college do so because they are attracted to the idea of helping other people. We will discuss several of these careers in more detail a bit later in this chapter.

PSYCHOLOGY YESTERDAY AND TODAY

We have described at some length what psychology is. But you may still feel that you don't fully understand what psychology is "about." Before we can go on to consider the various topics that psychologists study, however, we need to look briefly at the discipline's past.

Psychology's Roots

Few things can be fully understood without some sense of where they came from and how they developed, and this is certainly true of psychology. A hundred years ago, when psychology first began to be thought of as a separate discipline, its subject matter and research methods were far narrower than they are today. Psychology has grown enormously in its brief history. Perhaps the best way to appreciate this impressive growth is to examine the ideas and accomplishments of some of the people who have contributed most to it. We begin in the newly founded psychology laboratory of Professor Wilhelm Wundt at the University of Leipzig, Germany. The year is 1879.

Wundt Studies Conscious Experience. Wilhelm Wundt (1832–1920), in creating a laboratory for the sole purpose of exploring the workings of human

consciousness, is generally considered to have launched psychology as a science and a discipline (Boring, 1957). Wundt was conscious of his pioneering status. His work was, as he put it, "an attempt to mark out a new domain of science . . . still at its first beginnings" (quoted in Mueller, 1979). Wundt was impressed with the analytical approach then being taken by scientists in other fields. Chemists had identified the atom as the fundamental unit of matter and were busy exploring the ways in which atoms combine with one another. Similarly, biologists had discovered that the cell is the basic unit of life and were beginning to understand how cells interact in living organisms. Wundt wondered if human consciousness could also be analyzed into its constituent parts and the ways these parts combine to form the organization, or structure, of the mind. Convinced that the answer was yes, he set out to undertake such an analysis in a systematic way. Since Wundt was concerned with identifying the structure of the mind, his approach came to be known as **structuralism.**

Wundt's first challenge was developing some way to investigate consciousness. How was such a private world to be explored scientifically? Wundt's answer was a technique called **introspection,** a very precise and systematic form of self-observation. Introspection as Wundt used the term did not mean mere contemplation or reflection, but a process that might be thought of as putting one's own mental activity under a microscope. Wundt thought that careful training could enable a person to adopt an extremely detached way of looking at his or her mental experiences. Thus, properly trained, one could look at an apple and see not an apple but a somewhat spherical reddish object with an indentation at either end, a somewhat shiny surface, and a small, irregularly cy-

lindrical brownish extension protruding slightly from one end—and so on, in minute detail. Wundt trained his students in this kind of meticulous observation of awareness, and after much careful laboratory study, he concluded that conscious experience consists of three basic elements: sensations (the perception of external stimuli impinging on the body), images (experiences produced by the mind alone), and feelings (the emotional aspects of consciousness). All awareness, Wundt argued, consists of some combination of these three elements.

One frustrating aspect of Wundt's theory, critics found, was its peculiar resistance to confirmation or attack. If you searched your own consciousness and arrived at conclusions different from Wundt's, who could say who was right? Because consciousness is such a personal realm, there is no way to compare your mental processes with those of other people. Thus the question of whether Wundt's ideas were right turned out to be unanswerable: his theories could be neither proved nor disproved.

A second problem with Wundt's approach was that introspection could be done only by trained observers. Thus no insight into the consciousness of children, retarded or disturbed persons, or animals was possible, since these subjects lack the ability to practice Wundt's highly disciplined technique.

Despite the imperfections of his theories, Wundt is usually considered to be the father of experimental psychology. He conducted systematic studies of the mind, in a laboratory designed specifically for that purpose, and published what was probably the first psychology journal. He also trained his students well. They started new laboratories throughout Europe. One student, Edward Titchener, a British psychologist, brought the new discipline to the United States. But most important, Wundt helped place psychology on a firm scientific footing by insisting that the discipline adopt the careful, rigorous methods of other sciences.

The Functionalists Broaden the Definition of Psychology.
To understand the next development in psychology, we must first consider the work of a great scientist in another discipline, Charles Darwin (1809–1882). Darwin's famous theory of biological evolution is set forth in his books *On the Origin of Species* (1859) and *The Descent of Man* (1871). Backed by biological evidence collected over many years, he proposed that all living organisms are descended from simpler forms of life. Human beings, in other words,

Wilhelm Wundt (1832–1920) *(The Bettmann Archive.)*

are not above nature, as theologians of the time believed. Instead, they are part of nature, related through ancestry to every other living thing but most closely to the great apes—chimpanzees, gorillas, and orangutans. Darwin's ideas sparked an explosive controversy that has still not completely subsided. Thoughtful people everywhere were forced to revise their conceptions of humanity's place in the biological world.

Darwin's theory had a special impact on psychology. First, it challenged the belief that the human brain was solely an organ of the intellect: if the human species shared a common ancestor with the apes, and ultimately all other living things, then surely we share some inherited characteristics—notably instinctive drives—with our animal relations. These innate behaviors thus became a topic of interest and importance to psychologists, as we shall see.

But Darwin was to have still another impact on psychology through his theory that species evolve through a process of *natural selection*. The members of most species vary with respect to certain inherited physical characteristics—hair and eye color in human beings, for example. Some of these variations, such as keen vision, are *adaptive*; members of the species who possess such a trait are better able to survive and produce offspring. Therefore, they come to form a greater proportion of the population of the species. If Darwin was correct, psychologists began to theorize, then our psychological characteristics also must have some adaptive *functions*. Thus, after Darwin, many psychologists began to consider the adaptive functions of psychological processes, and the school known as **functionalism** was born. Functionalism, unlike structuralism, had no one "father." Many psychologists in Europe and in the United States were beginning to adopt the functionalist point of view. Here we shall consider only one of the most important and influential of the functionalists, William James (1842–1910).

James was the eldest son in a prominent New England family and the brother of the novelist Henry James. He originally wanted to be a painter, but at his father's urging he abandoned his ambition and chose a scientific education instead, entering Harvard to study medicine. But James began to be dissatisfied with scientific study and, suffering poor health and growing self-doubt, he contemplated suicide. Fortunately for psychology, he completed his studies at Harvard, where he became an instructor in anatomy

William James (1842–1910). *(Culver Pictures.)*

and physiology. His experiences in medicine had made him curious about the relationship between the mind and the body, and this curiosity led him to begin work on a psychology text—the first ever to be published on this new and growing science.

In his book *The Principles of Psychology* (1890), James took issue with Wundt and the structuralist point of view. Breaking down consciousness into its simple elements, he said, "taxes patience to the utmost." Not only were such "experiments" as describing an apple in painfully tiny detail tedious, they also produced an artificial view of human thought. To James, consciousness did not resemble marbles in a jar—a collection of separate items such as sensations, images, and feelings; rather, it was like the waters of a stream—fluid, ever-changing, defying analysis such as Wundt's. According to James, this "stream of consciousness" was what was important, for somehow it had helped us survive. It was "mind" as a process that had had adaptive value for our species, and *how* our minds had helped us survive was the appropriate subject matter for psychology.

James's *Principles of Psychology*, which took him twelve years to write and runs to 1377 pages, is filled with provocative insights about such subjects as our habits and emotions. We shall consider one of James's theories, on human emotion, in Chapter 10.

The Behaviorists Focus on Observable Behavior. Directly opposed to both structuralism and functionalism were a group of psychologists who came to be known as **behaviorists.** These researchers, led by the brilliant but brash young scholar John B. Watson (1878–1958), argued that subjective reports of conscious experience simply are not science. By definition, they maintained, science relies only on data that can be empirically measured. Thus, if psychology was to be a science, it must stop trying to study what goes on in people's heads. Instead, it must be limited to the study of observable behavior.

This narrower definition of psychology led the early behaviorists into a new kind of research. They began to investigate how diverse environmental stimuli can produce particular responses. The work of Watson and his associates was strongly influenced by the pioneering studies of the great Russian physiologist Ivan Pavlov (1849–1936). In a now-famous experiment, Pavlov rang a bell a few seconds before he gave a dog some meat, a stimulus to which the dog responded by salivating profusely. After repeating this procedure many times, Pavlov found that the dog would salivate on hearing the bell alone, even if given no food. The concept of the **conditioned response**— a learned response to a previously neutral stimulus— was born. Like all behaviorists, Pavlov was accounting for present behavior (salivation) in terms of an association (bell and food) that the organism had learned in the past.

Watson took the extreme position that *all* behavior represents learned responses to particular environmental stimuli. He rejected the notion of innate, or inherited, differences in ability or temperament. He believed that by controlling environmental stimuli, he could shape an infant's character into anything one might wish. "Give me a dozen healthy infants, well-formed, and my own specified world to bring them

John B. Watson (1878–1958). *(Culver Pictures.)*

up in," Watson boasted, "and I'll guarantee to take any one at random and train him to become any type of specialist I might select—doctor, lawyer, artist, merchant-chief, and yes, even beggar-man and thief, regardless of his talents, penchants, tendencies, abilities, vocations, and race of his ancestors" (Watson, 1924, p. 82). Perhaps fortunately for the babies, Watson never got the chance to do this experiment.

In 1920, Watson's academic career came to an unfortunate end when he was forced to resign his position at Johns Hopkins University because he had divorced his wife to marry one of his former students. He did a number of odd jobs for a time, including selling coffee from door to door and clerking in a department store. Eventually he became vice-president of a New York City advertising agency. Yet his point of view and his writings continued to influence psychologists long after his departure from academia (McKinney, 1976).

Other American psychologists were also influential in developing behaviorist thought. One of these was E. L. Thorndike (1874–1949), who conducted a series of experiments with cats. Each cat was placed in a wooden box that was secured on all sides. The cat tried to escape by grabbing at a mesh of wires, a lever, a string, or some other object attached to the inside of the box. One of these attachments would open a door, and the cat could escape and receive some food. Although the cat's first successful responses were largely a matter of chance, after several attempts its movements became centered in the area of the release mechanism, and eventually it performed the correct response as soon as it was placed in the box. As Thorndike wrote,

> Starting, then, with its store of instinctive impulses, the cat hits upon the successful movement, and gradually associates it with the sense-impressions of the interior of the box until the connection is perfect, so that it performs the act as soon as confronted with the sense-impression. . . . Never will you get a better psychological subject than a hungry cat. (Quoted in Diamond, 1974.)

On the basis of his work with cats, Thorndike is credited with the discovery of *trial-and-error learning,* in which an animal learns to choose the one response out of many that will satisfy a need. This type of learning emphasizes the importance of rewards. Thorndike argued that if an animal comes to associate a particular response with a reward, that response will be strengthened and will increase in frequency. Conversely, if an animal comes to associate a particular response with punishment, that response will weaken and will decrease in frequency.

The contemporary American psychologist B. F. Skinner (1904–   ), like both Watson and Thorndike, spent a good part of his career studying animal behavior. (We mentioned his experiments with pigeons earlier in this chapter.) But Skinner has also gone far beyond either of his predecessors in arguing that behaviorism's insights can and should be applied to society as a whole. His widely read and highly controversial novel *Walden Two* (1948b) portrays a behaviorist utopia: a small community in which people are trained from birth to be productive and satisfied citizens. For example, through the application of rewards and punishments, children would be taught to appreciate the arts and sciences and to shun excessive materialism and the destruction of the environment. Skinner believes that this type of society is essential to the survival of the human species in light of the seemingly insurmountable problems that confront us today.

To those who are appalled by the social control this kind of society would involve, Skinner replies that we who supposedly live in a free society are already controlled. But the control is not planned, and much of it takes place in ways we are not aware of—through advertising, for example. In his utopia, in contrast, control is open and aboveboard, planned by parents, teachers, and others for the good of all. You will probably want to make up your own mind when you read more about behaviorism in Chapter 5.

Even if behaviorist techniques are never used on society at large, however, they have proved very useful in treating some psychological disorders (recall the work of Nathan Azrin, mentioned earlier). And many people now toilet-train their children, lose weight, quit smoking, and otherwise change their behavior by using Skinner-inspired methods.

The Gestaltists Look at the Whole. The behaviorists were not the only psychologists to react to the ideas of the structuralists and functionalists. At about the same time that Watson was launching behaviorism in America, three German psychologists, Max Wertheimer (1880–1943), Kurt Koffka (1886–1941), and Wolfgang Köhler (1887–1967), were developing **gestalt psychology.** The gestaltists believed that it was impossible to divide mental life into elements, as

Wundt had attempted to do. As Wertheimer wrote in 1923,

> I look out my window and see a house, some trees, the sky. On theoretical grounds I could say: There are 327 brightnesses and color-tones. But do I experience 327? No. (Quoted in Lowry, 1982.)

The various pieces of information picked up by the sense organs are inevitably brought together by the mind, and then something new emerges. This something, the *Gestalt* (the German word for "form" or "pattern"), is different from and more valuable than the individual elements that make it up. In other words, the gestaltists believed that "the whole is greater than the sum of its parts." A film, for example, is made up of many still photos, each slightly different from the others. When we put them together in rapid succession, however, we see not a series of still photos, but *motion.*

The gestaltists, although sharply critical of introspection of the kind advocated by Wundt, did not agree with the behaviorists that psychology must be limited to the study of observable behavior. What went on within the mind was critical, in their view. This they often demonstrated by appealing to people's subjective experiences. They noted, for example, that we recognize a tune even when it is played in another key, although all of its notes—or constituent elements, as Wundt might call them—have changed. The gestaltists also performed experiments to show how the mind works. Köhler, for example, did an experiment in which hens were trained to eat grain only from a dark gray sheet of paper, not from a lighter gray sheet (if they approached the latter, they were shooed away). Eventually they learned to avoid the lighter gray paper and eat only from the darker one. Then the papers were changed: the lighter gray sheet was replaced with a sheet still darker than the original dark gray sheet. The hens now pecked not at the sheet they had learned to eat from, but at the new, extra-dark sheet. They had learned not simply to choose a certain shade; they had learned to choose the darker of two shades. This choice requires the consideration of a whole situation (gestalt), not merely the repetition of a particular learned response.

When the Nazis came to power in Germany, many of the gestalt psychologists fled to the United States, where they continued to study how the mind organizes information. Their work became a foundation for research into thinking, problem solving, sensation, and perception. We will be mentioning it again in Chapters 4 and 7.

Today, many psychologists agree with the basic gestalt idea that what goes on within a person's mind while learning and responding is extremely important to understanding behavior. These processes of thought are called **cognitions,** and a great many psychologists are now involved in studying them. In fact, some psychologists initially trained in the behaviorist tradition have broken with the views of Skinner and his followers precisely over the importance of cognitions in explaining human actions. Disagreement between the behaviorist and the cognitive perspectives has arisen in many areas of psychology that we will be exploring later, including learning, personality, and the treatment of people with psychological problems.

Freud Starts Psychologists Probing the Unconscious.

No discussion of psychological thought is complete without mention of the remarkably imaginative Viennese physician Sigmund Freud (1856–1939). Freud, who was a specialist in disorders of the nervous system, observed that many of his patients had nothing physically wrong with them, even though they had symptoms of physical illness (headaches, exhaustion, insomnia, and so forth). He theorized that mental conflicts were actually behind these symptoms—conflicts that had been pushed out of normal awareness and into a part of the mind Freud called **the unconscious.** Freud was impressed with the results that another Viennese doctor, Josef Breuer, had obtained in his treatment of a woman

Sigmund Freud (1856–1939). *(Culver Pictures.)*

suffering from apparent paralysis. Breuer found that if he hypnotized the woman, she was able to discuss the psychological roots of her disorder quite freely, and after such discussion her condition tended to improve. Freud became convinced that if unconscious conflicts could be brought into a patient's awareness, they would lose their power to control that person's life.

One of Freud's challenges was how to uncover the unconscious conflicts that underlay his patients' problems. Although he started by using hypnosis, he became dissatisfied with this technique, which often failed to reach deeply enough into a person's buried memories. Eventually he developed a method called **free association,** in which the patient was asked to recline comfortably on a couch and say whatever came to mind, no matter how irrelevant or foolish it sounded. The patient's apparently random talk, Freud believed, would eventually contain themes related to the unconscious conflict. Freud also encouraged patients to talk about their dreams, because he believed that dreams were full of symbolic hints as to what was really bothering the dreamer. With these verbal clues, Freud helped his patients interpret and understand their symptoms. He called his approach to treatment **psychoanalysis,** and today there are still some therapists who adhere to Freud's traditional methods. Many modern-day followers of Freud, however, have substantially modified his original methods, as you will see in Chapter 16, which deals with contemporary psychotherapy.

Freud took extensive, meticulous notes during all his treatment sessions. He gradually developed an elaborate theory of personality development and structure based on his observations. For instance, Freud found that when a patient's unconscious was probed for critical events that had initiated psychological problems, the most significant memories were usually those of some forbidden sexual impulse during childhood. Freud took this as evidence that human beings, like other animals, are driven by powerful biological urges, especially sexual ones. In humans, however, such urges often conflict with society's moral standards, so people must somehow learn to restrict and inhibit them. A major part of this learning, according to Freud, takes place during childhood, when the rules of society are first imposed on people. Thus, in Freud's view, psychological problems arose when early conflicts between society's demands and innate biological urges were never satisfactorily resolved. In the Victorian age in which Freud wrote, his stress on childhood sexuality was often seen as shocking, and today many criticize Freudian theory for being hard to verify scientifically. Nevertheless, psychology owes Freud a debt for calling attention to the frequent importance of early life events in the formation of adult personality.

Like the behaviorists, Freud believed that many of our actions are determined by forces beyond our control. In contrast to the behaviorists, however, he did not focus on the power of rewards and punishments, but rather on how biological urges are accommodated or frustrated during childhood. To Freud, we humans are not rational creatures possessed of free will. Instead, we are creatures driven by powerful instincts beyond our conscious awareness. A vast part of "who we are," Freud argued, always remains buried in the unconscious—unless it is uncovered by psychoanalysis. This stress on unconscious motivations is one of Freud's most important contributions. It has had a profound impact not only on psychology, but also on twentieth-century philosophy, art, and literature.

The Phenomenologists Question Determinism.

The deterministic views of behaviorists and Freudians flourished in the early part of this century, but soon a reaction against them began to set in. By the 1930s and 40s some psychologists had begun to fashion a new perspective on human beings. These theorists were in part influenced by a philosophical approach called phenomenology—the study of how people subjectively experience phenomena. In sharp contrast to behaviorists, this new group of psychologists firmly believed that a person's subjective experiences are critical to understanding why that person acts in particular ways. Hence, this new school of psychological thought came to be called the **phenomenological approach.**

As we said, the phenomenologists were strongly opposed to the determinism implicit in both behaviorism and the Freudian view. They took issue with the suggestion that people are often shaped by forces beyond their control. To the phenomenologists, people have the power to carve their own fates; they are free to become whatever they are capable of being. The phenomenologists, in fact, saw a striving for psychological growth and self-fulfillment as the fundamental motivation underlying human behavior. Many felt that Freudian theory placed too much

stress on instinctual urges that propel people toward selfish, often aggressive acts. Central to the phenomenological perspective was an emphasis on the positive side of human nature—the side that is creative and constructive and that seeks to build caring relationships with others. In later chapters we will be exploring the contributions of several contemporary phenomenological thinkers, including Abraham Maslow, a noted personality theorist, and Carl Rogers, a widely influential psychotherapist.

Although the views of phenomenologists have sometimes been criticized as vague and unscientific, they have nevertheless had a strong impact on modern-day thinking. The stress on fulfilling individual potential, on establishing close relationships with others, and on fashioning lives that are meaningful strikes a responsive chord in contemporary society, where huge bureaucracies and anonymous urban living seem to threaten our fundamental humanness. In fact, today's proliferation of group therapies aimed at helping people to grow psychologically and experience more joy in their lives is part of a human potential movement influenced to a great extent by phenomenological thinkers.

Building on the Past. As we have suggested in this

brief overview of the history of psychological thought, many of the ideas of the early researchers have since been rejected or modified. Yet their theories have served to inspire further study. Wundt's notions about the organization of consciousness, for instance, have long since been abandoned, but psychology still owes him a debt for launching the discipline as a science. The functionalists drew attention to the importance of mental life in adapting to the environment. This insight led, in turn, to a focus on learning as a means of adaptation. Behaviorists have further enhanced our understanding of learning, although most contemporary psychologists, like the gestaltists before them, are unwilling to rule out cognitions—or processes of thought—as a subject for scientific inquiry. Freud has also made a significant contribution, despite extensive criticism and modification of his ideas. He gave psychology the very important understanding that some of our motivations may be hidden from conscious awareness. Finally, the phenomenologists, while also criticized by many, have reemphasized the uniqueness of individuals and the human potential for freedom of choice. As you read more about psychology in subsequent chapters, you will see how today's psychologists are building on these fundamental ideas.

Contemporary Fields of Specialization

Fifty years ago, a single diligent scholar could conceivably stay abreast of most developments in psychology. The discipline was still young and its subject matter fairly narrow. Today this situation has changed. With the diversity of subjects under study, one person would be overwhelmed by the volumes of reading needed to keep up with all the latest findings in the discipline. Psychologists have necessarily become specialists, just like their colleagues in every other modern science. To get an idea of the diversity that exists in psychology today, consider some of the topics discussed at a recent meeting of the American Psychological Association. Psychologists explored subjects as varied as brain function in gifted children; the underlying causes of intense sensation seeking; food additives and hyperactivity; teacher diagnosis of learning disabilities; alcohol use among elementary-school children; male-female differences in verbal assertiveness; programs for preventing and stopping smoking; approaches to treating depressed children; stress and coping in surgical patients; workplace design and worker behavior; amphetamine effects on the brain; the psychology of dieting, depression, and overeating; and the family life of pathological gamblers. Clearly such a range of topics is too broad for any one person to master.

Because of the enormous scope of psychology, we will not even attempt to describe all aspects of it here. But we do want to acquaint you with some of the main fields of specialization and the kinds of research they encompass.

Experimental and Physiological Psychology. If you are like most people, you've had the frustrating experience of having a word on the tip of your tongue. The word is tantalizingly close, yet it won't come to mind. At such times you probably run through a list of possible responses until the desired word eventually pops into your mind. But how did you find it? Did you search for the word by sound? By meaning? In some other way? The answers to such questions provide important clues to the way information is "filed" in the brain. When you consider that a person stores and retrieves literally millions of facts over a lifetime, you begin to realize how incredibly efficient this filing system must be. As you will see in Chapter 6, psychologists Roger Brown and David McNeill (1966) devised a very clever way of creating the tip-of-the-tongue phenomenon in the laboratory in order to investigate the organization of memory. Their findings, and those of other researchers, have provided some intriguing insights into the way that the human information-processing system works.

The organization of memory is just one of an enormous number of problems that **experimental psychologists** investigate. Unfortunately, the term *experimental psychology* is a bit of a misnomer. It implies that this field is defined strictly by the use of experimentation as a data-gathering technique. Experimental psychologists *do* rely largely on laboratory experiments, but this fact alone is insufficient to distinguish them from their colleagues in other fields. Researchers in many areas of psychology also use controlled experiments. So to define experimental psychology we must

Experimental psychologists who work with animals try to find parallels between the behavior of their subjects and that of humans. This psychologist has found that rats, like many people, enjoy a cocktail after a hard day and that "rat drinking patterns often mimic those of harried executives." *(UPI.)*

look as much to its subject matter as to its methods. The experimental psychologist usually studies one of several "basic" behavioral processes—basic in the sense that they are shared by a variety of animal species. These processes include sensation, perception, learning, memory, problem solving, communication, emotion, and motivation. To understand what a broad and rich field of investigation this is, consider some discoveries that experimental psychologists have made.

- In the area of perception, Blakemore and Cooper (1970) have helped to demonstrate the startling degree to which early life experiences shape the way we see the world. They exposed newborn kittens to severely restricted visual stimuli, such as an environment containing only horizontal patterns. Within a few weeks, the kittens were functionally blind to vertically oriented objects. Apparently the development of normal visual capabilities depends in part on growing up in a visually normal world. We will discuss the link between perception and early life experiences in more detail in Chapter 4.
- In the area of learning, John Garcia has found that when a rat learns to associate the taste of a particular food with illness, it develops a remarkably strong aversion to that food (Garcia and Koelling, 1966). (You may have acquired this kind of aversion yourself if you once ate a food that made you violently sick.) Garcia's discovery has had practical applications. For instance, ranchers can now protect their sheep from attack by wolves by feeding the wolves sheep flesh laced with a substance that produces nausea. Why are such associations learned so quickly and so intensely? Garcia's answer is discussed in Chapter 5.
- In the area of motivation, a number of researchers have shown that obese animals, including humans, are extremely sensitive to external eating cues (Decke, 1971; Schachter, 1971a, 1971b). They will gorge themselves on a good-tasting meal but shun food that is bland or slightly bitter. They will eat every last morsel of food that is placed within sight and easy reach, but if securing food involves any degree of effort, the obese subject suddenly becomes indifferent. (These findings suggest some ways in which dieters can help themselves stick to their regimen—by not keeping the refrigerator full of tempting foods, for example.) Some possible causes for this odd pattern of eating will be explored in Chapter 11.

Researchers who study the underlying biological bases of behavior are called **physiological psychologists.** When asking questions about perception, learning, motivation, and other basic processes, physiological psychologists search for answers in how the organs of the body work. How can environmental stimuli permanently affect an animal's visual capabilities? The secret is found in the development of the animal's brain. Why are learned taste aversions so persistent? The answer probably lies in the structure of the nervous system among animals with diverse diets. Why would obese people be such choosy eaters? Once again the ultimate control mechanisms are located somewhere in the brain. Thus, physiological psychologists examine how the body's two principal communication networks—the nervous system and the endocrine glands—are related to all our behaviors.

Because most experimental and physiological psychologists are engaged in research, they are often affiliated with colleges and universities, as Table 1.1 indicates. Almost as many of these specialists, however, work in private industry. Pharmaceutical companies, for instance, hire such psychologists to assess the effects of newly developed drugs. In fact, as scientists learn more about the way the brain and nervous system function, **psychopharmacology** (the study of the relationship between drugs and behavior) is a rapidly growing field. Other experimental psychologists may work in clinical settings where they help to develop treatment programs. An experimental psychologist, for example, might be involved in training people with chronic pain to lead more productive lives (Woods, 1976).

Personality Psychology. If a person is independent, self-reliant, and assertive (traits we usually consider "masculine"), is it likely that he or she is also affectionate, gentle, compassionate, and sensitive (traits we usually consider "feminine")? Even in today's world, many people still maintain that these traits do not mix. They see masculinity and femininity as polar opposites. Yet psychologist Sandra Bem has gathered impressive evidence that this common assumption is wrong. Some men and women are truly androgynous: they successfully combine both masculine and feminine traits. (The term *androgyny* comes from the Greek combining form *andr-*, from *aner*, man, and *gyne*, woman.) Bem argues that such people are far more adaptable than those who conform to masculine or feminine stereotypes. They can behave either assertively and independently or compassion-

TABLE 1.1 FULL-TIME EMPLOYMENT SETTINGS OF 1980 PSYCHOLOGY DOCTORATE RECIPIENTS, BY SUBFIELD

SUBFIELD	TOTAL NUMBER OF SURVEY RESPONDENTS	COLLEGES/ UNIVERSITIES	INDEPENDENT PRACTICE	HEALTH-CARE SETTINGS	BUSINESS, GOVERNMENT, AND NONPROFIT SETTINGS	SCHOOLS AND OTHER EDUCA-TIONAL SETTINGS	OTHER SETTINGS
Experimental	76	38.2%	0.0%	7.9%	35.5%	1.3%	17.1%
Social	95	36.8	2.1	5.3	32.6	0.0	23.2
Industrial/ organizational	44	27 3	0.0	6.8	52.3	0.0	13.6
Developmental	97	40.2	1.0	26.8	12.4	4.1	15.5
Educational	102	24.5	3.9	17.6	9.8	23.5	20.6
School	103	8.7	3.9	14.6	3.9	64.1	4.9
Clinical	590	8.6	8.8	62.5	2.9	3.9	13.2
Counseling	208	13.5	6.3	50.5	7.7	6.3	15.9

Source: Joy Stapp and Robert Fulcher, "The Employment of 1979 and 1980 Doctorate Recipients in Psychology," *American Psychologist*, 1982, *37* (11), 1180–1181.

ately and affectionately, depending on the demands of the situation (Bem, 1974, 1975).

Bem's research is an important example of the kinds of issues **personality psychologists** explore. Personality psychology is concerned with explaining individual differences in behavior. To what extent is one person more aggressive than another, more manipulative, more outgoing, more obedient to authority? And how can we account for any differences in personality that researchers might observe? Is there something "inside" that makes us think, feel, and act in distinctive ways? Are we driven by biological forces? Do we inherit personality traits? Or do "outside" factors—our experiences and personal histories, our culture, the times in which we live, the unique, immediate situation—largely shape the ways in which we respond? How, in other words, does personality develop? And perhaps most important, does personality change over time? These are the central questions that personality psychologists ask. We will investigate them in detail in Chapters 8 and 13.

Social Psychology. Earlier we mentioned the innovative methods of psychologists John Darley and Bibb Latané in their study of bystander apathy. These researchers staged a series of simulated emergencies—fires, accidents, robberies, medical catastrophes—in order to see whether unsuspecting witnesses would offer assistance. Their findings were somewhat disturbing: willingness to help was *not* related to individual personality traits. A genuinely kind and sensitive person could ignore a stranger in apparent trouble as surely as a callous person could. The factor that *did* influence the way onlookers responded was the situation in which they found themselves. Bystanders were far more likely to seek or provide assistance in an emergency when they were alone than when they were in groups. Surprisingly, the presence of other people actually appears to inhibit the helping response. We will suggest some reasons for this phenomenon in Chapter 18.

You may be thinking that the powerful influence of other people revealed in Darley and Latané's research must be unique to emergency situations. If so, you are wrong. **Social psychologists** have shown repeatedly that our behavior is not just the result of our personalities and predispositions. Environmental factors, especially the presence of others, greatly influence what we think, say, and do. This finding sheds light on many incidents that would otherwise be difficult to explain. How could a company of American soldiers have massacred nearly five hundred civilians, most of them women and children, at the Vietnamese village of My Lai? Social psychologist Stanley Milgram (1963) has demonstrated the incredible extent to which average people will inflict severe pain on their fellow human beings if an authority figure requires them to do so. How can intelligent, well-informed adults make decisions that are so terrible, so poorly thought out, that any casual observer could point out

The research of social psychologists provides useful insights into such questions as why passers-by help—or fail to help—strangers in emergencies. *(Arnold J. Saxe.)*

their flaws? Social psychologist Irving Janis (1972) believes they may be victims of "groupthink." In a small, closely knit group, he argues, the pressures for conformity and unanimity can become so great that members can no longer appraise alternatives realistically. In Chapters 17 and 18 we will explore these and many other examples of how our perceptions, beliefs, motivations, and behaviors are influenced by situational factors, especially by the actions of other people. This is the unique and fascinating perspective of social psychology.

Social psychologists, like experimental psychologists, work largely in two settings: in colleges and universities (around 37 percent) and in business, government, and nonprofit agencies (around 33 percent).

Industrial and Organizational Psychology.

Work: it is what most of us do at least half our waking hours for more than forty years. How can these thousands of hours on the job be made more pleasurable, more productive, more personally rewarding and satisfying? These are some of the questions of interest to

industrial psychologists and **organizational psychologists,** who are concerned with the relationship between people and their work.

Psychology's interest in the workplace is not new. It began years ago with the use of intelligence and aptitude tests to help screen job applicants. But in recent decades the application of psychology to work-related problems has expanded enormously. One sizable challenge has been improving worker morale, and thus business productivity. To this end, some industrial psychologists have designed job-enrichment programs, to ensure that jobs are not so repetitive and routine that workers become bored and perform poorly. Besides creating job-enrichment programs, industrial psychologists may design training programs for employees, administer various kinds of counseling programs, and set up performance evaluation systems. Of those psychologists employed in business, many work in a subfield known as **personnel psychology,** which is concerned with hiring, assigning, and promoting employees. One important task of personnel psychologists is supervising the selection of new employees, through interviews, testing, and so on. As Table 1.1 shows, more than half of the people in industrial psychology work in business and industry, government agencies, research and consulting firms, and independent or group practices.

Developmental Psychology. Everyone knows that a great deal of development—intellectual, social, and emotional, as well as physical—takes place as children grow older. But what is less obvious is the degree to which the human newborn enters the world prepared to begin this long developmental journey. Contrary to what your grandparents or even your parents may have believed, babies are capable of seeing and hearing from the moment of birth. Almost immediately they begin to process information about their new environments. By the age of only six months, researchers have demonstrated, babies can recognize familiar objects that they haven't seen for up to a day (Weizmann, Cohen, and Pratt, 1971). Apparently, a young infant's capacity for learning and memory is far better than most people imagine (Nelson and Ross, 1980). No wonder that by the end of the first year of life children have made great developmental progress. They show many quite mature emotions (anger, fear, joy, anxiety, surprise), love to interact socially in games of give and take, and understand that people and things often respond predictably when acted upon (Izard, 1978).

Developmental psychology is the branch of the discipline that is concerned with describing and explaining the systematic changes that occur in human beings throughout the life cycle, from conception to death. The capabilities of babies, a growing subject of research, is just one of many topics that developmental psychologists study. In fact, virtually every field of psychology—from sensation and perception to learning and memory, thinking and problem solving, emotion and motivation, personality and social interaction—can be studied from a developmental perspective. How do newborn infants perceive the world? What motivates them to learn and to explore? Why will a four-year-old tell you that a lump of clay grows "bigger" as it is rolled into a snake, whereas an adult can easily see that the quantity of the clay does not change with a simple change in shape? What about intellectual skills in adulthood? Do memory, learning, and problem-solving abilities decline in old age? How did you develop your unique personality, your customary ways of interacting with other people? Are there any basic differences in personality

between males and females, and if so, how can these differences be explained? The answers to these and many other questions are explored in Chapter 8.

Developmental psychologists work in a variety of settings, as Table 1.1 suggests. Most, however, find careers either in colleges and universities or in health-care settings. In addition to doing academic research, developmental psychologists may be involved in evaluating children who are not developing normally, and advising parents as to how they can help.

Educational and School Psychology. The formal educational process is such an important part of twentieth-century life that it is not surprising to find psychologists who specialize in analyzing and improving it. The factors that contribute to good and bad teaching are not just a matter of common sense. To understand how true this statement is, consider a clever experiment performed by three psychologists studying the topic of teacher evaluation (Naftulin, Ware, and Donnelly, 1973). These researchers had a professional actor give a lecture to an audience of psychologists, psychiatrists, social workers, and educators. The actor was instructed to deliver his lecture in a captivating style and with great enthusiasm—but the speech was totally without substance. It was filled with non sequiturs and invented words, circular reasoning and self-contradictions. Surprisingly, all four groups in the audience rated this charming but double-talking teacher quite favorably. Apparently student ratings of a teacher's effectiveness may have little relation to the teacher's knowledge and scholarly ability. The highly rated teacher, some psychologists argue, is simply an exceptionally good talker (Kulik and McKeachie, 1975). Such findings have important implications for the role of student evaluations in determining faculty salaries and promotions.

Research into the factors that contribute to a positive student evaluation is just one of many issues that **educational psychologists** investigate. Educational psychologists are concerned with all psychological aspects of the learning process. What factors affect a student's performance in the classroom? How important is motivation? IQ? Personality? The use of rewards and punishments? The size of the class? The expectations of the teacher? The way in which student and teacher interact? How can a student's performance best be evaluated?

Given their field of study, you might expect educational psychologists to work primarily in colleges and universities. Actually, as Table 1.1 shows, only about 25 percent do so. Nearly as many work in schools and an increasingly large number work in health-care settings, where they are often concerned with planning and supervising "special" education—classes for learning-disabled children, for example. Of those who work in private industry, government, nonprofit agencies, and large school systems, many are engaged in developing test materials, planning and evaluating training, and setting up training systems.

In contrast to educational psychology, **school psychology** is a strictly applied field. More than half the school psychologists in this country work in elementary and secondary schools. They may be involved in training teachers to deal better with difficult students, in counseling such students and their parents, in administering standardized tests and interpreting the results, and in assessing students' learning difficulties.

Clinical and Counseling Psychology. Some years
ago, eight men and women presented themselves at the admitting offices of twelve mental hospitals in five states. All, they said, were troubled by a similar symptom: they claimed to hear voices whispering the words "hollow," "empty," and "thud." All were diagnosed as psychotic and admitted to the hospital wards. Then a curious thing happened. These patients reported no further symptoms. In fact, they behaved normally in every way; they were models of courtesy and cooperation. Within one to seven and a half weeks their psychoses were judged to be "in remission" (temporarily abated), and each was released from the hospital. In reality, these eight patients were not psychotic at all. They were people from various walks of life who had agreed to take part in a psychological experiment. The experiment involved trying to get admitted to a mental hospital on the basis of a fictitious symptom and then seeing how the hospital staff would react to subsequently normal behavior. The startling finding was that not one staff member at any of the twelve hospitals ever gave a hint that he or she suspected the fraud. Quite the contrary: they sometimes interpreted perfectly rational behavior as pathological because such interpretations supported the original diagnosis that these people were severely disturbed.

This provocative study, conducted in the early 1970s (Rosenhan, 1973), rekindled a long-standing controversy among **clinical psychologists,** who spe-

cialize in the diagnosis and treatment of behavior disorders. How accurate are professional diagnoses of abnormal behavior if eight normal people can be mistakenly labeled psychotic? And if diagnostic procedures are unreliable, of what value are they? As you will see in Chapter 15, which begins a detailed discussion of clinical psychology, strong arguments have been raised on both sides of this important issue.

Clinical psychology, of course, involves much more than diagnosis. It also involves investigation into the causes of behavior disorders and into how such disorders can best be treated. Here, too, clinical psychologists frequently disagree. Are behavior disorders the result of unresolved conflicts and unconscious motivations, as Freud proposed? Or are they learned responses that can be unlearned with proper training? Is there a biological basis to many psychopathologies, and if so, what might the underlying disorder be? As you will discover in Chapter 16, different answers to these questions have given rise to a wide variety of treatment programs for problems as diverse as phobias, depression, paranoia, and drug dependence.

Given the problems with which clinical psychologists are concerned, it is not surprising that more than half are employed in hospitals, clinics, and private practice. There they often work closely with two other specialists in the mental-health field: the psychiatrist and the psychoanalyst. Unlike clinical psychologists, who have earned a Ph.D. and have completed specialized training in diagnosis and psychotherapy, **psychiatrists** first earn an M.D. and complete a medical internship, as other physicians do. Then, during a three-year residency program in psychiatry, nearly always in a hospital, they receive specific training in the treatment of mental disorders. As physicians, psychiatrists can prescribe drugs and use other medical procedures that clinical psychologists cannot. Some psychiatrists go on to become **psychoanalysts,** practitioners of the form of therapy originally developed by Freud. To become a psychoanalyst, psychiatrists must extensively study psychoanalytic theory, undergo psychoanalysis themselves, and analyze clients under the supervision of an experienced analyst. Psychoanalytic institutes that provide such training are found in several major cities.

Whereas clinical psychologists generally treat people with serious psychological disorders, **counseling psychologists** usually help those with milder problems of social and emotional adjustment. Some counseling psychologists specialize in particular areas, such as marriage and family life. They may also help normally adjusted people with such tasks as setting vocational goals. As Table 1.1 suggests, about half of all counseling psychologists, like their colleagues in clinical psychology, now work in health-care settings.

Trends Among the Subdisciplines. During the past decade, certain of the psychological specialties have experienced considerable growth, while others have declined. The boom has been largely in two areas: clinical and counseling psychology. These two specialties now account for three out of five new Ph.D.s in psychology. Fields that have experienced slower growth are developmental, educational, and school psychology. In contrast, two other specialties—physiological and experimental psychology—have declined, especially the latter. To some extent, these developments reflect students' desire to "go where the jobs are." As college and university positions are increasingly difficult to secure, graduate students have chosen training that will prepare them to work in health care, school systems, and private business (Syverson, 1982).

Emerging Fields of Specialization. In addition to the areas we have discussed so far, psychologists are increasingly developing specialties in less traditional fields. One such field is **environmental psychology,** the study of the relationship between human beings and all aspects of their environment. The growth of environmental psychology in recent years has been prompted by public concern that conditions of modern urban civilization, such as high-density housing, have caused the quality of life to decline. One recent study by Baum, Aiello, and Calesnick (1978), for instance, focused on the social effects of dormitory design on college students. The researchers found that dorms built to cluster a small number of students around a shared area were better than long-corridor dorms in fostering cooperation. Residents of long-corridor dorms tended to display competitive behavior or to withdraw from social interaction because they felt they had less control over their environment. Environmental psychologists have also helped answer such questions as: What are the effects of excessive noise, heat, chemical pollutants, and overcrowding on human welfare, and how can these problems be alleviated? What can be done to encourage people to use mass transportation and to

conserve energy in other ways? Because of their applied focus, environmental psychologists are often found outside traditional departments of psychology. They may be employed by a government agency, such as the Department of Transportation or the Department of Energy; they may serve as consultants to city planners in large metropolitan areas; or they may teach and conduct research at a school of architecture.

Another growing field is **forensic psychology,** the application of psychological principles to the problems of law enforcement and the courts. Today forensic psychologists perform a variety of tasks. In urban police departments, for example, they evaluate officers who have emotional problems, help select psychologically stable recruits, analyze clues in order to construct personality profiles of those responsible for crimes, and help train police to handle crowd control, hostage crises, suicide threats, family violence, and any other situation that requires an understanding of personality variables and reactions to stress. Forensic psychologists are also found in correctional institutions, where they counsel and advise inmates and provide psychotherapy to those who have severe emotional problems. Another area where the skills of the forensic psychologist are employed is the court system. Here these specialists are often called on to determine the competency of a defendant to stand trial and to consult with judges and attorneys regarding the psychological aspects of a case. Because of the very specialized focus on forensic psychology, programs designed exclusively to train people in this field have now begun to appear.

Opportunities for psychologists are also expanding in the field of **health and health care.** For years scientists have known that emotional stress is related to such conditions as ulcers and heart disease. Now they are beginning to realize that the mind may play a role in many other physical disorders, from the common cold to cancer. In fact, some researchers suspect that psychological factors may be involved in the onset and progress of all diseases, as you will learn in Chapter 10. If this is so, then psychologists can obviously make an important contribution to modern health care and disease prevention. They can identify the psychological factors related to disease, for example, and devise ways to test individuals for susceptibility to illness. They can add to our current understanding of just how a psychological factor, such as stress or depression, can have a deleterious effect on the body.

Forensic psychologists may work in prisons where they counsel inmates, using a variety of treatment techniques. Here a forensic psychologist and a case worker, using the family approach, meet with an inmate and his wife. *(Courtesy, C. Scott Moss, Ph.D.)*

They can identify the psychological and social factors that motivate people to engage in unhealthful behaviors, such as smoking and overeating; to ignore the signs of disease until a condition is far advanced; or to neglect medical treatment once an illness has been diagnosed. They can help identify the most effective psychological strategies for coping with serious disease or disability, for recent research suggests that a person's psychological response to catastrophe has a significant impact on his or her recovery. New programs to train psychological researchers and practitioners specifically in the health field will undoubtedly develop in the coming years.

A final emerging field of specialization in psychology is **program evaluation.** Logic suggests that not all government programs designed to alleviate social problems are effective. Yet until recently no systematic effort was made to determine which programs were working and which were not, and which among those that appeared to be working were most cost-effective. Clearly such efforts are needed to avoid wasteful spending and to accomplish our national aims. Thus the field of program evaluation came into being. Many observers feel that psychologists can make a unique contribution to program evaluation. With their extensive training in experimental methods, psychologists have the skills needed to measure and compare both the variables that go into a particular program and its results. Until now, relatively few psychologists were involved in program evaluation, and they were involved in only a few areas, such as education. But in the years ahead, more psychologists will undoubtedly be finding jobs in this important field, working on problems as diverse as health care, employment, transportation, energy conservation, and the rehabilitation of criminals.

PSYCHOLOGY AS A VOCATION AND A PERSPECTIVE

To prepare for a career in many of the fields discussed in the previous sections, a person must earn a doctoral degree. Traditionally, this has meant a Doctor of Philosophy (Ph.D.) in psychology. Candidates for a Ph.D. generally participate for four to six years in a university graduate program that involves broad exposure to the theories and findings of psychology, special focus on one subfield, and extensive training in research methods. In addition, each Ph.D. candidate must complete an original research project under the direction of experienced researchers on the graduate faculty and submit his or her findings as a doctoral dissertation.

In the past a person who had just received a Ph.D. in psychology usually went to work at a college or university in a teaching and/or research position. Today, however, this traditional pattern is changing as the number of psychology doctorates grows more rapidly than positions available in academia. Since 1970 the rate of growth of new doctorates in psychology has been more rapid than the rate of growth of doctorates in all other disciplines combined (Syverson, 1982). At the same time, undergraduate enrollments have started to level off and will continue to decline throughout the 1980s. Naturally, a decrease in the number of college students is bound to affect the number of faculty positions, even in such a field as psychology, which is one of the most popular undergraduate majors. As a result of these factors, a growing number of people with psychology doctorates are seeking employment outside of academia—in government agencies, industry, private practice, and nonprofit organizations, such as hospitals and clinics (Stapp and Fulcher, 1982). This trend is expected to continue, with more and more psychologists working in health care and rehabilitation, counseling, services for children and the aged, and other nonacademic settings. Fortunately, because there is substantial demand for psychologists in these other fields, employment opportunities for psychology Ph.D.s are better than they are for people with doctorates in many other disciplines (Syverson, 1982).

As more psychologists seek employment outside academia, there is a growing concern that the traditional Ph.D. program is not adequately preparing students for nonacademic careers. Many graduate departments of psychology are therefore beginning to add courses in such fields as environmental psychology, psychology and health, and program evaluation. In addition, some schools offer an alternative doctoral degree, called the Doctor of Psychology (Psy.D.), for those who are interested in such applied vocations as psychotherapy and forensic psychology. The major difference between the Ph.D. in psychology and the Psy.D. is that the latter places greater emphasis on practical experience than on research methodology. The Psy.D. does not, for example, require a research-oriented dissertation, as the Ph.D. does. Instead, most Psy.D. candidates conduct a doctoral project related to their future profession.

Although a doctoral degree is a prerequisite for certain careers in psychology, a master's degree is adequate training for others. These careers include teaching at some two-year colleges; certain jobs in industrial and environmental psychology; work as a school psychologist; and employment in various capacities in mental health and rehabilitation facilities. A Master of Arts (M.A.) in psychology usually requires from one to two years of graduate work in a department of psychology plus successful completion of a master's thesis based on original research. But master's degrees with a focus on psychology can also be earned in other departments. A person can obtain a degree in educational psychology, for instance, from a department of education, or a degree in industrial psychology from a school of business.

What about the student who earns a bachelor's degree in psychology? Some of these graduates will find employment directly related to psychology—as welfare case workers, for example, or in rehabilitation programs, correctional institutions, or community mental health centers—though not, of course, as therapists. Others will find that a major in psychology is indirectly related to many other careers. A person who finds a job in advertising, for instance, will probably consider courses in social psychology, human motivation, and human learning invaluable. Similarly, a person who enters the field of personnel management will make much use of information gained from courses on personality and individual differences and on assessment and testing. Psychological knowledge also has important applications in such careers as teaching, social work, nursing, business, engineering, and law.

But the value of psychology to the college student is not only vocational. Even if you take no psychology courses beyond this one, you will still learn much about yourself and others from this broad introduction to psychological findings and principles. How can I improve my memory? My study habits? How can I get my father to stop smoking? When people pressure me to do something I would rather not do, why do I sometimes go along? Whenever I babysit for my infant nephew, he cries continually unless I hold him. What can I do to change his behavior? I get so tense when I sit down to take an exam that my mind goes completely blank. Is there a way I can get over this? Answers to these and many other questions of great personal interest are contained in this book.

Finally, the study of psychology has the important benefit of giving you a perspective for evaluating new psychological findings reported in newspapers and in magazines, on television, and in popular books. Consider, for example, a startling news item widely publicized several years ago. A team of medical researchers in England had found that chronic marijuana use was associated with cerebral atrophy, a wasting away of the brain (Campbell et al., 1971). This conclusion was based on brain X rays of ten habitual marijuana users compared with brain X rays of nonusers the same age. On the surface, this evidence may strike you as very convincing. But consider some questions that a critical psychologist might ask. What evidence is there that the cerebral atrophy did not occur *before* the marijuana smokers started using the drug? And if there is good evidence to rule out this possibility, could the brain damage be due to some other cause? As it turned out, the conclusion of the study was suspect. Of the ten marijuana users with wasted brain tissue, all had also used the hallucinogen LSD, some more than twenty times; eight had used amphetamines, another powerful drug; and several had frequently taken sedatives, barbiturates, heroin, or morphine. In addition, one young man had a medical history of convulsive seizures, and four had suffered substantial head injuries in the past (Kolodny, 1974). Thus there was very good reason to believe that the cerebral atrophy revealed by the brain X rays might have been caused by some factor other than marijuana.

This example nicely illustrates the perspective of the behavioral scientist. A good scientist is an incurable doubter. He or she is always asking: What is the evidence and how reliable is it? Was this study designed and carried out carefully enough? Were all other possible influences controlled before conclusions were drawn? Are alternative interpretations of the data possible, and if so, what additional information is needed to rule them out? Exposure to the methods of psychology will help you develop this questioning approach yourself. By the end of this course, you should share with the psychologist a healthy skepticism of the sweeping generalizations and psychological cure-alls you read and hear about. This newly acquired outlook should make you a more sophisticated consumer of information that can greatly affect your life.

SUMMARY

1. Psychology is, first of all, a science, and like all sciences, it relies on empirical data—information that has been systematically observed, measured, and recorded—to test its predictions formally. In psychology these predictions concern human behavior itself, for psychologists believe that there are patterns underlying human behavior, and that they can be understood.

2. The second dimension of psychology is its use as a means of promoting human welfare. Sometimes this application is a direct one, resulting from the deliberate use of research findings to solve a practical problem or to improve an aspect of human life. That kind of use is known as **applied science.** More often, it is the result of the application of knowledge acquired for its own sake, or **basic science.**

3. The founder of psychology is generally considered to be Wilhelm Wundt, who in the late nineteenth century created a laboratory to explore the workings of human consciousness. His movement came to be known as **structuralism.** Wundt's process of **introspection,** by which he concluded that conscious experience consists of three fundamental elements—sensations, images, and feelings—could not be subjected to proof because of personal differences in each person's explorations of his or her own consciousness.

4. Charles Darwin's ideas about evolution sparked psychologists' investigation into the adaptive functions of psychological processes, thus launching the movement called **functionalism.** The functionalists, whose leading exponent was William James, saw mental life as a stream of consciousness and the mind's activities as more important than its structure, as Wundt had believed. The aim of mental life was to help the organism adapt to and cope with its environment.

5. The **behaviorist** researchers insisted that psychology rely only on data that can be empirically measured. Their concern with the study of how environmental stimuli can produce responses led to the pioneering work of Ivan Pavlov. In his famous experiment with dogs, he initiated the concept of the conditioned reflex, a learned response to a previously neu-

tral stimulus. In the United States, the ability to control responses by manipulating rewards and punishments was first delineated by John B. Watson and more recently refined by B. F. Skinner. Although the behaviorist viewpoint has been criticized, especially in recent years, it has led to some quite effective treatments for various psychological disorders.

6. In contrast to Wundt's emphasis on the isolated elements of mental life and the behaviorists' focus on measurable behavior, the **gestaltists** stressed the organized whole. They maintained that what emerges from perception of individual pieces of information is a whole that is greater than the sum of its parts. Every stimulus has meaning only within the context of surrounding events. This emphasis on context and pattern formed the basis for the modern study of perception.

7. Today, most psychologists agree that we cannot ignore the processes going on within the minds of people, even though such processes are often hard to study objectively, as behaviorists have pointed out. Without some investigation into human thought, or **cognition,** we would restrict our knowledge of many fundamental aspects of human behavior—especially such aspects as problem solving, decision making, and communication. Thus, cognitive processes have now become a very important area of psychological investigation.

8. The Viennese physician Sigmund Freud emphasized the role of the unconscious in the development of personality. He felt that many physical disorders are the result of unconscious conflicts that can be deprived of their power to dominate a person's life if they are brought into awareness. Freud's method of treatment, called **psychoanalysis,** involved the use of **free association,** in which patients suffering from neurotic symptoms attempted to bring unconscious conflicts to the surface by discussing everything that came to their minds, including dreams. While few psychologists wholly accept Freud's ideas today, his influence on twentieth-century thought has been profound.

9. Phenomenologists have reacted against the determinism of both the behaviorist and the Freudian perspectives. They maintain that people are free to become whatever they are capable of being. The **phenomenological approach,** although sometimes criticized as unscientific, has had a substantial impact on contemporary society.

10. Psychology has branched into so many areas that its practitioners have been forced—like those of every other science—to become specialists. **Experimental psychology** relies largely on laboratory experiments to investigate the behavioral processes, such as sensation, perception, and learning, which are basic to many animal species. Researchers who study the underlying physical bases of behavior are called **physiological psychologists.** Pharmaceutical companies employ such psychologists to assess the effects of new drugs, and **psychopharmacology**—the study of the relationship between drugs and behavior—is a growing field.

11. Measuring and explaining individual differences in behavior is the focus of **personality psychology.**

12. Taking a different perspective, **social psychologists** look at the influence of the presence and actions of other people on what we think, say, and do.

13. **Industrial** and **organizational psychology** are growing specialties that focus on the relationship between individuals and their work. A closely related field, **personnel psychology,** is concerned with hiring, assigning, and promoting employees.

14. **Developmental psychology** is the branch of the discipline that focuses on describing and explaining the systematic changes that occur in human beings throughout the life cycle.

15. Psychologists who specialize in all the psychological aspects of the learning process are called **educational psychologists. School psychologists,** in contrast, work in the strictly applied field of assessing children with emotional or learning difficulties and making recommendations as to how these students may best be helped.

16. **Clinical psychologists** specialize in the diagnosis and treatment of behavior disorders. **Counseling psychologists** usually help those with much milder problems of social and emotional adjustment.

17. Besides the specialties we have listed, psychologists are beginning to explore new fields, such as en**vironmental psychology, forensic psychology, health and health care,** and **program evaluation.**

SUGGESTED READINGS

AMERICAN PSYCHOLOGICAL ASSOCIATION. *Careers in psychology.* Washington, D.C.: American Psychological Association, 1983.

A useful booklet describing current career opportunities and educational requirements in various fields of specialization. A copy can be obtained by writing the American Psychological Association, 1200 Seventeenth St. NW, Washington, D.C. 20036.

BORING, E. G. *A history of experimental psychology.* 2d ed. New York: Appleton-Century-Crofts, 1950.

This challenging volume is considered a definitive source on the history of psychology as a scientific discipline.

FREUD, SIGMUND. *An outline of psychoanalysis.* Rev. ed. Lytton Strachey, tr. and ed. New York: Norton, 1970 (paperback; originally published 1940).

An overview of Freud's explorations of human feelings and behavior.

JAMES, WILLIAM. *The principles of psychology.* Fredson Bowers and Frederick Burkhardt, eds. Cambridge, Mass.: Harvard University Press, 1983 (originally published 1890).

A paperback edition of the first major classic work in psychology, which is very readable and remains influential.

ROBINSON, D. N. *An intellectual history of psychology.* Rev. ed. New York: Macmillan, 1981.

An exceedingly readable account of the philosophical and ideological roots of psychology, from Hellenist Greece to the present.

SCHULTZ, DUANE. *A history of modern psychology.* 3d ed. New York: Academic Press, 1981.

The development of psychology over the past hundred years, including brief biographies of major figures.

SKINNER, B. F. *Science and human behavior.* New York: Free Press, 1965 (originally published 1953).

A classic presentation of the behaviorist view of the effect of reinforcement on behavior.

WATSON, R. E. *The great psychologists: From Aristotle to Freud.* 4th ed. Philadelphia: Lippincott, 1978.

A discussion of the contributions made to the birth and growth of psychology by important historical figures in the field; includes brief biographies.

2

THE METHODS OF PSYCHOLOGY

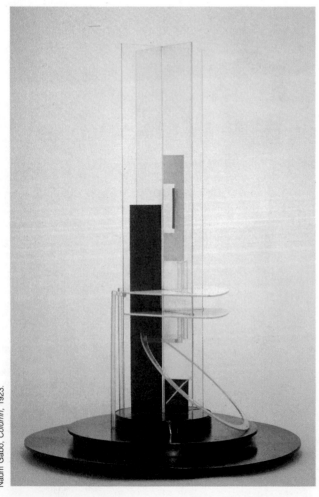

Naum Gabo, *Column*, 1923.

Demand Characteristics

Drawing Premature Conclusions

The Ethics of Research in Psychology

Some questions about human behavior are asked by virtually everyone. Why did I perform so poorly on yesterday's exam even though I *knew* the information? How can I convince my friends who are smokers that they should give up cigarettes? Why do some people seem to be constantly dieting and yet never lose any weight? What causes irrational fears in people, such as a fear of germs or a fear of closed-in places? Why do I sometimes go along with others' opinions even though I really disagree? These are the same kinds of questions that professional psychologists ask. The difference between you and them lies in how the answers are sought.

Consider a question that psychologist Elliot Aronson once asked—probably along with thousands of other people. The year was 1961. President John F. Kennedy had just embroiled the nation in a disastrous attempt to overthrow Communist Cuba using an invasion force of American-trained Cuban exiles. The ill-conceived mission was a colossal failure. In just three days the Cuban army had destroyed American supply ships and captured or killed all the invading troops. One would have thought that JFK's public popularity would plummet. Historically, Americans are not very tolerant of such gigantic presidential blunders. Yet shortly after the Cuban fiasco Kennedy's popularity actually rose. The question Elliot Aronson asked was "Why?"

Like many other observers, Aronson proposed an answer. Perhaps, he reasoned, before this foreign policy blunder Kennedy had seemed *too* perfect. He was intelligent, handsome, urbane, and wealthy, a charming and witty conversationalist. Even his political opponents found his accomplishments impressive: a Harvard graduate, a war hero, an influential sena-

tor, he had won the nation's highest political office at the age of only forty-three. Maybe a display of fallibility would not hurt such a person. Maybe it would even make him seem more human and therefore more likable. This is precisely the kind of theory that any armchair observer might propose. But unlike the armchair theorist, Aronson did not stop there.

Aronson's next step was to conduct a study to test his proposed explanation (Aronson, Willerman, and Floyd, 1966). He had college students listen to tapes of other students presumably trying out for a TV program called "The College Quiz Bowl." In some cases, the candidate on the tape was a near-perfect person—Aronson's experimental JFK. He was bright, versatile, a high achiever, who answered almost all of the game-show questions right. In other cases, however, the candidate was an average person—a second-string athlete with an only fair scholastic record who tended to answer the questions wrong. For each of these candidates Aronson then introduced the critical "blunder" factor. Some of the time the interview proceeded routinely, with the candidate first briefly telling about himself and then answering the trial questions. But other times the candidate committed a major gaffe midway through the interview by spilling a cup of coffee all over his new suit. Thus each of Aronson's listeners heard one of four tapes: a "perfect" person who blundered, a "perfect" person who did not, an average person who blundered, or an average person who did not. Afterward the listeners were asked to rate how much they liked the candidate they had heard. As Aronson expected, the "perfect" person who had shown a bit of fallibility by blundering was liked significantly better than his nonblundering counterpart. In contrast, the same blunder committed by an average person tended to brand him as incompetent and much less likable.

This is not to say that Aronson had unequivocally solved the puzzle of the rise in Kennedy's popularity after the Cuban fiasco. But he *had* gathered concrete evidence consistent with his "perfect person" theory. This is what separates the trained scientist from the average observer. Scientists are never content with mere speculation. They always demand hard data on which to base their conclusions. In the following sections we will describe many of the procedures that psychologists use to gather and analyze such data. A knowledge of these procedures is of great value to everyone. Psychologists have much to say about important issues, from child care to education to mental health to race relations and sex roles. The more you

know about the methods they use to arrive at their conclusions, the better able you will be to understand and evaluate what they say.

But perhaps you feel that scientific methods are far too dry and complicated to be of interest to you. Many introductory psychology students draw this hasty conclusion, only to find out later how mistaken they were. As you become more familiar with the field of psychology you will find that psychological investigation has all the fascination of solving a complex mystery. It begins with the same puzzling questions, proceeds to the same tentative conclusions, involves the same imaginative suppositions, logical reasoning, and carefully conducted tests as does detective work. And the eventual findings are always highly rewarding because they shed light on a person of great intrinsic interest—yourself.

GATHERING DATA

Imagine that you are a psychologist interested in determining people's attitudes toward smoking. You want to find out what percentage of smokers intend to go on smoking indefinitely, what percentage hope to quit someday, what percentage hope to quit in the near future, and what percentage are trying to quit right now. How would you go about conducting your research? Now suppose your interest shifts to the problem of which method of quitting smoking is more effective—cutting down slowly or stopping "cold turkey." Would you use your previous approach to answer this new question? Probably not. The research method a psychologist uses to gather data depends in part on the nature of the question being asked. Each method is better suited to some questions than to others. You will see this quite clearly in the sections that follow, which discuss specific research methods in detail. But first we should say a word about a task common to almost all psychological research—the task of drawing a sample.

Sampling

The saying "You don't have to eat the whole ox to know that the meat is tough" could have been coined by psychologists doing scientific research. Their

problem is that few questions about human behavior permit them to study every single person they are trying to generalize about. The number of people who would have to be considered is usually far too large. But fortunately, researchers almost always have an alternative. They can select a segment of all the people in a given population and draw their conclusions on the basis of this **sample.** In a sense, they are tasting just parts of the ox to determine its overall tenderness.

The size of a sample is extremely important, however. A poll intended to reflect the opinions of all the Democrats in the United States could not sample only five people. Given the millions of Americans who can be considered Democrats, such a small sample is very likely to produce bias. Suppose, for example, that just by chance one of these people had highly atypical views—views shared by only a tiny minority of Democrats. In a sample of five, this person's opinions would represent a full 20 percent of the total. The larger the sample, the greater the likelihood that such inadvertent biases will be balanced out.

Another requirement of a good sample is that the members be randomly selected. A **random sample** is one in which everyone in the total population has an equal chance of being included. Suppose you wanted to draw a random sample of the student body at your

Figure 2.1A Can you spot the errors in the sampling techniques described here? The answers can be found in Figure 2.1B on the next page.

1. A senator is interested in whether his constituents favor the death penalty. His staff reports that letters about the death penalty have been received from 458 constituents and that 398 favor it.

2. A cookie manufacturing company wants to know what percentage of Dallas residents make cookies from scratch. A sample of 1,000 residential addresses is chosen and interviewers call these households during regular working hours on weekdays.

3. A newspaper is interested in finding out what proportion of drivers in the city wear seat belts. Some reporters go to a Ford Motor Company plant and record the number of employees who fasten their seat belts when they leave work.

university. You could obtain from the administration a list of all currently enrolled students and select, say, every fifth name. Depending on the total size of the student population, this technique would probably provide a sample that was representative along many dimensions. For instance, the sample would probably closely reflect the total student body in terms of attitudes toward a campus issue such as the lengthening of the midsemester recess. If 60 percent of all students at the university supported this change, close to 60 percent of those in your sample probably would do so as well.

Sometimes, however, a psychologist wants to make certain that a sample includes members of specific subgroups. To understand why, consider again our earlier sampling of American Democrats. It is widely known that the views of southern Democrats frequently differ from those of their northern counterparts. So a good sample of all Democrats would probably have to include appropriate numbers from each regional subgroup. The goal here is to create what is called a **representative sample**—that is, a sample in which critical subgroups are represented according to their incidence in the population as a whole. Public opinion pollsters routinely construct their samples in this manner. They include certain proportions from each sex, each ethnic minority, each age group, each geographic region, and so forth, so that the end results accurately reflect all people in the nation.

Failure to construct a truly representative sample was the cause of a famous polling error. In 1936 a poll of more than two million people taken by *Literary Digest* magazine predicted an overwhelming victory for the Republican presidential candidate, Alf Landon, over the Democratic incumbent, Franklin Roosevelt. Yet Roosevelt won by a landslide. The problem was that the magazine had polled people whose names appeared in telephone directories and on lists of automobile owners. In those days—this was during the Depression—people who had telephones and cars could be counted among the affluent, and like the affluent today, they were likely to vote Republican. Thus, even though many people were sampled in the survey, they did not represent the population as a whole, and the survey results were consequently misleading (Gallup, 1978). Figure 2.1 describes some

other sampling approaches that contain significant flaws. Can you determine what the weakness in each one is?

Although all psychologists recognize the advantages of forming their generalizations on the basis of truly representative samples, those who conduct laboratory research are seldom able to meet this sampling ideal. An example will illustrate why. Suppose you are a social psychologist interested in why people sometimes seek the companionship of others and at other times prefer to be alone. To investigate this question you could design an experiment in which you created various conditions that you suspect might promote human affiliation and then observe how subjects reacted in each one. But what are your chances of persuading hundreds of people from every part of the country and from all age brackets, ethnic groups, and social strata to come to your laboratory just to participate in your research? Your chances are slim. Although such a procedure would increase the representativeness of your sample, you will undoubtedly have to content yourself with a more homogeneous sample found closer to home.

Like most experimental psychologists who study human beings, you will probably use students from your own university (often those taking introductory psychology) or perhaps residents from the surrounding community solicited in newspaper advertisements. True, this sample may not precisely mirror the human population as a whole. But in doing laboratory research one must weigh ideal sampling proce-

WHAT'S WRONG:

1. People who write to their representatives in Congress tend to have strong opinions. The opinions of this group are often systematically different from those of the population as a whole.

2. This sampling technique tends to exclude working people, whose responses may be very different from those given by people at home on weekdays. Thus the sample is not representative.

3. People who work for an auto company are probably not representative of all people on an issue having to do with cars. They may, for example, be more safety conscious than the average driver.

Figure 2.1B

dures against the difficulties of finding any subjects at all. Does this sampling dilemma call into question the results of most experimental work with humans? No, it does not. It simply means that researchers must sometimes be cautious in generalizing from their findings to the behavior of all people everywhere.

Research Methods

In general, psychological research is intended to accomplish one or more of three basic goals: to *describe* behavior, to *explain* its causes, and to *predict* the circumstances in which that behavior might occur again. Each of the various data-gathering methods we are about to describe is more useful for achieving some of these aims than others. Observation in a natural setting, for example, allows researchers to describe behavior and to generate possible explanations, but it does not allow them to test their hypotheses about why certain responses occur. Surveys also allow researchers to describe human behavior, including people's attitudes and feelings. But they, too, are not very useful for determining causes. An experiment, in contrast, allows explanations to be tested under controlled conditions and so helps to pinpoint cause, but it may not reveal the complexities of behavior as it occurs in the real world. Different research methods, then, often complement one another, and together they can enrich our understanding of many psychological issues.

The Experiment. Many psychologists prefer to use an **experiment** whenever the question they are investigating allows. The main advantage of the experiment over other data-gathering methods is that it permits the researcher to control conditions and so rule out—to as large an extent as possible—all influences on subjects' behavior except the factors being examined. This goal motivated Aronson's choice of the experimental method to test the "perfect person" theory we described earlier. The experiment he designed enabled him to recreate only those factors he believed had caused the sudden rise in Kennedy's popularity, while excluding all the additional factors found in real life which could provide alternative explanations. In this way, psychologists can more clearly infer cause-and-effect relationships from results. The experimental method has one potentially important disadvantage, however. The elimination of all extraneous influences occasionally creates such an unnatural situation that one wonders if the results are applicable to behavior in real life.

The basic procedures in an experiment are best explained by means of a specific example. Consider the social-psychological question we raised earlier: Under what conditions are people more likely to want to be with others rather than to be alone? Of the many experiments that have been conducted on this topic, we will focus on a classic one performed some twenty-five years ago by Stanley Schachter (1959). Schachter was one of the first psychologists to suggest that the desire to affiliate does not depend simply on individual personality traits. Affiliation, he proposed, also depends on the situations in which people find themselves, and among the situations most conducive to affiliation are those that arouse fear. This was Schachter's **hypothesis,** the proposition or belief that he set out to test.

Schachter's first step was to design an experiment in which subjects would experience fear. How could this goal be accomplished? The method Schachter chose was devious but highly effective. He arranged for a number of students who had volunteered to participate in an experiment to be met at the laboratory door by a white-coated man who identified himself as Dr. Gregor Zilstein, of the medical school's Department of Neurology and Psychiatry. Surrounded by an impressive array of electrical equipment, Dr. Zilstein told the students that they were part of a very important study on the physiological effects of electric shock. Each of them would undergo a series of shocks while pulse rate, blood pressure, and other physical reactions were recorded. The shocks, the doctor warned in an ominous tone, would be extremely painful, for only intense shock could provide the information required. But, he added with a tight smile, they would cause no permanent tissue damage.

The students who encountered this diabolical doctor composed what is called the **experimental group.** An experimental group consists of those subjects who experience the experimental condition—in this case exposure to a fear-arousing situation. But usually experiments must also have a **control group** to provide a source of comparison. Control subjects experience all the conditions the experimental subjects do *except* the key factor the psychologist is evaluating. Thus in Schachter's experiment the control subjects were also greeted at the door by a white-coated doctor who told them that they were about to participate in an experiment on the effects of electric shock; but this time, instead of grimly warning the subjects of impending pain, the doctor assured them in a kindly manner that the shocks would produce only a mild, not unpleasant, tingling sensation.

Note that, as in all experiments, placement of subjects in either the experimental or the control group was done completely at random. This is a way of compensating for the fact that experimenters cannot possibly control for everything about their subjects. In this study, for instance, some people may have been generally outgoing, while others were more socially withdrawn. Schachter could certainly not erase such tendencies in his subjects by the stroke of some magic experimental wand. But he could make sure that all of the extroverts (the outgoing individuals) did not end up in one group while all of the introverts (shy people) ended up in the other. The ideal would be for each type of person to be placed in both conditions in roughly equal proportions. In this way, any biases they might impose would balance each other out. This is where random assignment of subjects comes in. When a sample is sufficiently large, random assignment ensures a good "shuffling," so to speak, not just in regard to introversion and extroversion, but also in regard to any other extraneous factors that might otherwise alter the results. Consequently, any observed differences in the behavior of the two groups are not likely to have been caused by systematic differences in the subjects placed in each one.

Now that Schachter had created appropriate experimental and control groups, one last step remained. He had to give his subjects the opportunity to affiliate with others in order to observe the effects, if any, of fear. So after Dr. Zilstein had finished describing the upcoming experiment, he announced that everyone must wait ten minutes while the experimental equipment was prepared. Each subject was given the choice of waiting alone in a private room or waiting in a classroom with other subjects. These choices, of course, provided the real experimental data. Once the subjects had expressed their preferences, the experiment ended and no shocks were ever given.

The results of Schachter's pioneering study are shown in Figure 2.2. They indicate that the tendency to affiliate does indeed seem to increase in fear-arousing circumstances. Subjects in the experimental condition (where the doctor's words were ominous and his smile sadistic) were much more likely to want to wait with others than were subjects in the control condition (where the doctor's words were reassuring and his manner kindly). Thus Schachter's hypothesis that fear can promote affiliation was supported by his data.

But note that these findings do not begin to answer all the important questions about the human motivation to affiliate. Are there other situations that can also encourage affiliation? And exactly why, in Schachter's study, did fear induce a preference for waiting with other people? Did Schachter's fearful subjects simply want to be distracted? Did they want to express their anxious feelings to a sympathetic ear? Or might they be looking for a chance to compare their own emotions with those of others in the same predicament? Only additional research addressed specifically to such questions could help provide the necessary answers. Like a full understanding of any aspect of human behavior, a full understanding of human affiliation can be gained only from a large

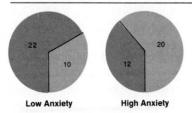

Figure 2.2 The results of Schachter's 1959 experiment testing the effects of anxiety on affiliation.

Low Anxiety   High Anxiety

22   10   20   12

● Subjects who chose to be alone or did not care
● Subjects who chose to affiliate

number of studies that build and expand on one another.

For our purposes, however, the important thing about Schachter's experiment is not the follow-up studies it generated but rather the fact that his basic procedures conformed to those required in all experimental work. An experiment is a controlled method of exploring the relationship between **variables**—that is, between factors capable of change. The factor that the experimenter deliberately manipulates is called the **independent variable.** In Schachter's study the independent variable was the degree to which the doctor behaved in a way that might induce fear. The **dependent variable** is what is expected to change when the independent variable is manipulated. In Schachter's experiment the dependent variable was the choice between waiting alone and waiting with other subjects.

It may help you to keep these terms straight if you remember that the words "independent" and "dependent" refer to the relationship between the variables. Changes in the independent variable are manipulated by the experimenter and are not controlled by changes in the dependent variable. Changes in the dependent variable, however, *depend* on changes in the independent variable if the experimenter's hypothesis is correct. It is also helpful to know that an experimental hypothesis can always be phrased as an "if/then" statement. The variable that follows the word "if" is the independent variable; the variable that follows the word "then" is the dependent variable. For Schachter's experiment the "if/then" statement would be: "*If* a subject is exposed to a fear-arousing situation, *then* under these conditions the desire to affiliate with other subjects should increase over normal levels." Such a statement emphasizes that a cause-and-effect relationship occurs in only one direction. Change in the independent variable causes change in the dependent variable, and not vice versa. Because an experiment provides this means of establishing causality, it is the data-gathering method of choice for many psychologists.

Quasi-Experimental Designs. Sometimes, however, psychologists cannot study a cause-and-effect question by means of a true experiment. Certain variables, for one reason or another, cannot be experimentally manipulated. A person's biological sex may have a profound effect on his or her behavior, for instance, but it simply cannot be varied at a researcher's will. As a result, the effects of biological sex cannot be experimentally separated from the learning experiences associated with being a male or a female. Other factors too are beyond a researcher's control, although for different reasons. A psychologist interested in how much the death penalty deters people from committing murder, for example, would certainly have difficulty arranging a true experiment. Death penalties are imposed and lifted through changes in public attitudes, not through experimental whim.

In still other cases an experiment is ruled out because manipulating the variable of interest would raise serious ethical problems. A psychologist might suspect, for instance, that overly harsh or overly lax parental discipline leads to juvenile delinquency, but he or she could hardly conduct an experiment to find out. To do so the psychologist would have to persuade one group of parents to be extremely strict with their children from birth and another group to be extremely lenient. When the children grew to be teenagers, the experimenter could then count the instances of delinquent behavior. Obviously, few parents would agree to this procedure, and even if they did, such tinkering with people's lives would be unacceptable for moral reasons.

How, then, can questions of this sort be investigated? One possibility is to wait for "experimental" and "control" groups to form naturally—that is, in real life. This approach creates a research design that approximates that of a true experiment. But because the investigators have far less control over variables than they do in true experiments, and because they cannot assign subjects randomly to conditions, such studies are called **quasi-experiments** (*quasi* means resembling but not identical with).

There are several types of quasi-experimental designs (Campbell and Stanley, 1963). In the **time series** design, a researcher repeatedly observes or measures the dependent variable both before and after the independent variable changes. This design has been used to determine the effect of the death penalty on the homicide rate. In one study the homicide rate in Sweden between 1754 and 1921, when the death penalty was in effect, was compared with the homicide rate between 1921 and 1942, when the death penalty was abolished (Schuessler, 1952). Since the number of murders fluctuated greatly from one year to the next but with little apparent change over time, the data suggested that the death penalty does not serve as a deterrent. The time series design was also used to evaluate the effectiveness of a prolonged crackdown on speeding in the state of Connecticut after a record number of traffic deaths in the year 1955. Figure 2.3 shows that the highway fatality rate did indeed drop in 1956 and continued to fall over the next three years. Of course, in order to label the crackdown a success, one has to be certain that this decline is larger than what might have occurred by chance. Because the 1955 fatality rate was so unusually high, it is likely that traffic deaths would have dropped anyway, with or without the crackdown. Using complex statistical procedures to compensate for this fact, researchers were able to conclude that even when a natural decline was taken into account, the crackdown was still effective (Campbell, 1978).

There are problems with drawing causal inferences from quasi-experimental data, however. At the heart of these problems lies the fact that a quasi-experiment does not provide the powers of control that a true experiment does. Consider a times series, for instance. Perhaps before the independent variable changed people were systematically influenced by

Figure 2.3 When the number of traffic deaths in Connecticut peaked at 324 in 1955, state officials instituted a crackdown on speeding. The dramatic drop in fatalities between 1955 and 1956 does not indicate, however, that the crackdown caused the decline. Decreases in accidents had been registered in 1952 and 1954 as well without the crackdown, and a decline could have been expected in 1956 following the unusually high fatality rate in 1955. But the continued decline in deaths from 1955 to 1959 may indicate that the prolonged crackdown had a genuine effect. *(After Campbell and Ross, 1968.)*

one set of factors, whereas afterward they were influenced by another set. To use our Connecticut example, perhaps 1956 was also the year when car makers introduced important new safety features (seat belts, padded dashboards, more shatter-resistant windshields, and so forth). If so, then loss of life on the highway could have dropped for reasons that had nothing to do with the crackdown on speeding. In a true experiment, of course, any such systematic differences between the subjects and their automobiles would be balanced out through random assignment to experimental and control conditions. But in a quasi-experiment researchers lack this power to shuffle subjects at will. Their only alternative is to try to take all additional variables into consideration, but this is often difficult to do. Something important may easily be overlooked. As a result, quasi-experiments should be used to investigate causal relationships only when true experiments are not feasible (Campbell, 1971).

Unfortunately, quasi-experimental designs are sometimes used when better alternatives are available, and people not aware of their shortcomings may draw invalid inferences. Suppose, for example, you are an aspiring lawyer and you see an advertisement for an expensive year-long program that claims to improve test scores on the qualifying entrance exam for law school. The advertisement says that students who have taken the course show an average gain of fifty points on their scores. On the basis of this evidence, should you sign up for the course? This type of quasi-experimental design, in which people first are tested, participate in treatment, and then are retested, is fraught with problems. The students may do better on the second test not because of the special course but because of what they learned in their college classes over the intervening year. Furthermore, students may do better on the second test because of "practice effects"—because they are more familiar with the test and therefore more relaxed. A better way to determine the effectiveness of the training program would be to conduct a true experiment, in which students are randomly assigned to the treatment or to the no-treatment (control) condition, and in which performance of both groups is measured both at the beginning and at the end of the experiment.

Correlational Research. Another approach that can be used when a true experiment is not feasible is **correlational research.** Suppose an investigator wants to determine the extent to which two variables—parental discipline and juvenile delinquency—are related. The investigator might select a number of children at random and interview their parents to determine the severity of discipline in the home. The researcher might ask such questions as "How often do you spank your child?" and "What would you do if your child told a lie?" On the basis of each parent's responses, he or she could then be assigned a severity-of-discipline score. The children's behavior could next be assessed, perhaps with the help of school or court records, to see which ones had committed delinquent acts, and how frequently. Finally, the researcher could calculate a numerical value called a **correlation coefficient,** which would indicate the strength and direction of the relationship between discipline and delinquency.

We will have more to say about correlation coefficients later in this chapter. For now we simply point out that the results of correlational studies vary widely. In some instances the relationship between the two variables under investigation turns out to be close and positive—in other words, a high rank on one is accompanied by a high rank on the other. There is a strong **positive correlation,** for example, between IQ scores and academic performance. People who score high on IQ tests tend to get high grades. In other instances, the relationship between the two variables is close but negative—a high rank on one is accompanied by a low rank on the other. There is a strong **negative correlation,** for example, between musical ability and tone deafness (inability to distinguish the pitch of musical notes). The more difficulty a person has perceiving pitch, the less likely he or she is to be able to play a musical instrument well. In still other instances, little or no relationship, positive or negative, exists between two variables. There is no relationship, for example, between eye color and academic success, or between hair color and tone deafness.

Correlations allow psychologists to make predictions about behavior. If you know that a woman has a high IQ, you can predict that she is likely to get good grades. If you know that a man is tone deaf, you can predict that he is not likely to play a piece of music that you would care to hear. Note that in either case your prediction, although probable, could ultimately prove wrong, for very few relationships are perfectly correlated.

It is very important to realize that although a cor-

relational study can show that two variables are related, it cannot establish that one factor *causes* the other. A third factor, related to each of the other two, may also be involved. Consider a study of motorcycle accidents the army once conducted. They attempted to correlate the number of accidents a person had with such variables as income and age. The best predictor of whether a person had been involved in a motorcycle accident turned out to be the number of tattoos that person had! Obviously, tattoos do not cause motorcycle accidents, nor does being in a motorcycle accident prompt a person to get tattooed. Instead, some third factor, perhaps a desire for risk or personal display, probably caused both tattooing and dangerous operation of a motorcycle.

Assessing whether causality exists between two correlated factors is seldom this easy, however. Often two factors that logically *might* be causally connected turn out not to be. This is where the need for experiments comes in. Only through experiments or very well-constructed quasi-experimental designs can researchers demonstrate cause-and-effect relationships.

The Survey. In all correlational studies the initial data about the variables being considered must be collected by some means. Frequently this means is a **survey.** A survey is an attempt to estimate the opinions, characteristics, or behaviors of a particular population by investigation of a representative sample. Researchers conducting a survey gather the data of interest to them through interviews, questionnaires, or sometimes public records. Interviews have the advantage of letting the researchers see or speak with their subjects and of allowing them to modify their questions when clarification is needed. Questionnaires, on the other hand, take less time to administer and so are particularly useful when information must be gathered from a large number of people.

Although survey findings may later be used to seek correlations between factors, they are also of great interest in their own right. Probably the most famous survey in this century is the one that resulted in the Kinsey reports, published in 1948 and 1953. Alfred Kinsey and his staff interviewed more than ten thousand men and women about their sexual behavior and attitudes—a radical thing to do at the time. Kinsey found, among other things, that behaviors often labeled abnormal, such as masturbation, homosexual activity, and oral-genital sex, were much more common than most people supposed. Of course, in conducting a survey on sexual practices, one must be careful that the people who are questioned are truly representative of the population as a whole. Often people who eagerly volunteer to participate in such research differ in significant ways from the average person. The investigators must therefore be especially cautious about how they draw their sample (Rosenthal and Rosnow, 1975).

Many other factors contribute to a survey's validity. One is the wording of the questions. Leading questions can completely bias the results. Even very subtle changes in wording can alter a person's responses. Elizabeth Loftus (1975) found that subjects who were asked, "Do you get headaches frequently and if so how often?" reported an average of 2.2 headaches a week, whereas subjects asked "Do you get headaches occasionally and if so how often?" reported a weekly average of 0.7 headache. Even when a question is neutrally worded, people can still give misinformation. Some people invariably answer yes just to be agreeable; others seem to have a built-in tendency to say no. If a survey contains questions that reflect on ability or character, people frequently present themselves in a more favorable light than is warranted (Cannell and Kahn, 1968; Myers and Ridl, 1979). Similarly, if a survey covers a touchy area, such as race relations, people are likely to claim that they believe what they think they *ought* to believe. The characteristics of the person doing the questioning can also make a difference. In one study conducted in the late 1960s, a time of great racial conflict, black residents of Detroit were asked if they felt they could trust most whites. When the interviewer was white, 35 percent of respondents answered yes to this question, but when the interviewer was black, only 7 percent gave a yes response (Moore, 1979).

Psychologists conducting surveys must be careful to guard against such inadvertent biases. When it is suspected that some characteristic of an interviewer (such as his or her race) might encourage "polite" lying, this trait must be taken into account when interviewers and respondents are paired. Alternatively, a mail questionnaire might be used. Steps can also be taken to counteract potential problems with the wording of survey questions. A researcher can include several differently worded questions on the same topic and see how consistent a person's answers are. In answer to one question, for example, a man may respond that he has no objection to homosexuality, yet when questioned later about his own experi-

ence with homosexual acts he may emphatically report that he has never engaged in them and certainly never intends to. In such a case psychologists would have reason to suspect that this man's true attitude toward homosexuality may be somewhat more negative than his first response implied. This kind of careful construction of a survey greatly increases the likelihood that the findings will accurately reflect what people really think and do.

Naturalistic Observation. As careful as researchers may be in gathering data through surveys or by means of experiments, sometimes the very act of filling out a questionnaire or being in a laboratory changes the way a subject is inclined to feel or behave. Imagine investigating the effects of alcohol on social aggressiveness by means of an experiment. Even if you tried to design a laboratory to look just like a bar, as at least one researcher and his colleagues have actually done (Marlatt and Nathan, 1978; Collins and Marlatt, in press), could you completely rule out the possibility that subjects were controlling their behavior because they knew they were being watched? Probably not. The only way around this problem would be to do your observing in a natural setting where the drinkers did not know they were being studied. The cardinal rule of such **naturalistic observation** is that the investigator stay out of the way.

Many questions lend themselves to naturalistic observation. A social psychologist might use this method to study leadership roles in a small group. A developmental psychologist might use it to study the way four-year-olds interact in a preschool classroom. Such observation is sometimes done through a one-way window so that the presence of the psychologist cannot interfere with routine behavior. Alternatively, psychologists sometimes use a form of naturalistic observation known as **participant observation,** in which they join an existing group in order to record thoughts and feelings accessible only to group members. In one such study three social psychologists joined a secretive group that predicted that a great flood would end the world at a certain time on a certain day (Festinger, Riecken, and Schachter, 1956). By becoming members of this doomsday group the psychologists were able to be present when the fateful moment came and went, and to observe the way in which disconfirmation of the prophecy influenced behavior. Contrary to what might be expected, the group did not disband after the prediction was

A one-way window is useful in naturalistic observation. The subjects, seeing only a mirror on their side of the window, behave more naturally than they probably would in the presence of the researchers. *(Bohdan Hrynewych/Southern Light.)*

proved false. Instead, members became less secretive, publicizing the view that their belief had saved the world, in an attempt to attract new believers.

In observational research it is very important to develop ways of recording data in order to avoid completely subjective interpretations. How do we know, for example, that members of the doomsday group became less secretive after disconfirmation of their prophecy? We know because the researchers kept careful records of what they saw and heard. Such records can take the form of written notes, tape recordings, or ratings on evaluation forms. Such records help other researchers to detect biases and idiosyncratic interpretations.

Although naturalistic observation is extremely valuable for investigating many types of questions, it also has its limitations. The main problem is that a researcher has no way of controlling the situation and so cannot test cause-and-effect hypotheses. If the psychologists in our hypothetical barroom study, for example, observe that customers get rowdier as they drink more, is it necessarily the alcohol that is inducing their behavior? What if, as the evening wears on,

the bar becomes packed with people? Perhaps increased aggressiveness is due less to the amount of alcohol consumed than to the extent of crowding. As we saw earlier, the degree to which a particular factor is causally related to another can be inferred only through an experiment or a very well-constructed quasi-experimental design.

The Case Study. Most of the data-gathering methods we have discussed so far involve collection of information from a representative sample of people ideally chosen at random from a much larger population. But some things of interest to psychologists occur too rarely to be studied in this way. Consider the psychological disorder commonly called multiple personality, in which a single individual has two or more highly distinct personalities, at least one of which is typically unaware of the thoughts and actions of the others. Because only a very small number of multiple personalities has ever been reported, psychologists cannot study the nature and possible causes of the condition by means of, say, correlational research. Instead, they must rely on intensive investigation of the few people known to have the disorder. Such in-depth analysis of a single individual is called a **case study.** In this instance, a case study would involve probing the past of the disturbed person to discover any unusual factors that might have contributed to the condition.

In other instances, psychologists conducting a case study may know the unusual factors that pertain to a particular person but not know exactly what influences those factors have on behavior. Their occurrence is simply far too rare. Case studies of people with localized damage to the brain often fall into this category. Brenda Milner (1966), for example, once studied a young man whom she referred to by his initials, H. M. In an effort to relieve the severity of H. M.'s steadily worsening epileptic seizures, doctors removed a specific portion of his brain—a procedure that had not been tried before in the treatment of epilepsy. The surgery helped the seizures, but it had a terrible side effect: H. M. could remember nothing new. As soon as he shifted his attention from a new piece of information, H. M. would lose all recollection of it. People he had just met would seem complete strangers to him five minutes later, and he could flip through the same magazines again and again without finding their contents familiar. Interestingly, however, H. M.'s recall of things learned *before* the operation was as good as ever. As we will see in Chapter 6, this and similar case studies provide strong evidence that human memory consists of a short-term and a long-term component, and that what was surgically destroyed in H. M.'s brain was the mechanism for transferring information from one system to the other.

In much the same way, studies of children who have been raised in near-total isolation from other human beings provide important insights into the way the use of language develops. One such child was Genie, a girl who from the age of one to the age of thirteen had been imprisoned alone in a small room in her parents' house (Curtiss, 1977; Pines, 1981). During the day she was harnessed in a sitting position, and at night she was often bound within a cage-like crib. Her psychotic father beat her whenever she made noise, and he forbade her mother ever to talk to the child. When authorities finally discovered Genie, she was a frail, pitiful creature who was unable to stand erect and had no ability to speak. Through much subsequent training, she gradually acquired some language. Yet even after years, many principles of grammar eluded her. Does Genie's slow and difficult progress acquiring language provide evidence that language must be learned during a critical period early in life? As you will discover in Chapter 9, the answer is far from simple. But the case study of Genie has given psychologists some important clues.

Case studies, then, not only provide a wealth of descriptive information about a particular psychological phenomenon; they may also suggest important principles underlying that behavior. In the hands of a brilliant psychologist the case study method may be a powerful tool indeed. Sigmund Freud's theory of personality, described in Chapter 13, was based on case studies of the patients who came to him for treatment. Similarly, Jean Piaget's theory of intellectual development in childhood, described in Chapter 8, began with intensive observation of his own three children as they were growing up. As insightful as they may be, however, case studies can never *prove* that suspected principles of behavior actually operate. Still, subsequent researchers can learn much by attempting to corroborate the patterns of behavior observed in case study investigations.

Measurement Tools and Approaches

In discussing the data-gathering methods that psychologists use, we have not had a chance to say very much about the way variables are measured. Yet careful measurement is just as important to the success of a psychological study as careful selection of a research approach. If results cannot be accurately measured— if they cannot be quantified in some way—then they cannot be meaningfully compared. In the following sections we will explore the three major approaches to measurement that psychologists employ: self-reports, behavioral measures, and physiological assessments. We will also explore a special problem of measurement that developmental psychologists often face, the problem of assessing behavioral change over time.

How Different Variables Are Measured. In many of the studies we discussed earlier, researchers assessed the variables of interest by means of **self-reports.** Subjects were asked how they thought, felt, or were inclined to act in a given situation, and their responses were recorded and tallied. Self-reports, of course, form the basis of all surveys, and they figure prominently in many other types of research. In Stanley Schachter's classic study of affiliation, for example, both the assessment of how fear-inducing the experimental condition was (the sadistic Dr. Zilstein and his painful electric shocks) and the assessment of whether subjects wished to wait by themselves or with others were gathered through self-reports.

But however useful self-reports may be in many kinds of studies, they do have limitations. If you were interested in measuring social aggression in a barroom, for example, it is unlikely that you would set about the task by questioning all the patrons about their aggressive feelings. To do so would almost certainly influence the very phenomenon you were trying to measure, as many drinkers would become annoyed at your inquisitiveness. A more reliable approach would be to use what psychologists call **behavioral measures**—that is, objective, quantifiable assessments of how people actually behave. In this case, you might try unobtrusively to count the number of verbal or physical acts of aggression that occurred in the bar during a given period of time. Such unobtrusive behavioral measures are also useful when it is suspected that subjects might distort their answers to questions in order to present themselves in a more favorable light. Thus counting the number of empty bottles would probably be a more accurate way of determining how much alcohol people had consumed than would asking them outright to specify how many drinks they had had (Webb et al., 1966).

Often the tendency to misreport what we ourselves have done or are likely to do is not at all conscious. We may honestly maintain that we would act one way and then behave quite differently when a real-life test arises. This was demonstrated in an alarming study of obedience to authority conducted by Stanley Milgram (1963). Subjects were ordered to deliver increasingly painful electric shocks to a supposed fellow subject as part of a bogus learning experiment. Milgram used a behavioral measure in his study—the number of shocks that each subject was willing to deliver. He found that a surprisingly large percentage of people delivered the maximum voltage (despite the victim's convincing screams of protest) simply because a stern experimenter told them that they must. Before conducting this experiment, Milgram asked people how they thought they would react if they were a subject in it. Most people said that neither they nor anyone else would administer painful shocks to another person. In short, people were completely incapable of pre-

dicting how they would behave. This important study and the controversy it has generated are discussed more fully in Chapter 18. The point here is that without behavioral measures psychologists would have little idea how strong certain tendencies are in human beings.

But although behavioral measures often have advantages over self-reports, they have some limitations of their own. In and of themselves they may give little insight as to *why* an observed behavior has occurred. In Milgram's study, for instance, we are left with an important question: What motivated subjects to go along with the experimenter? The simple act of delivering the shocks provides no real answers. Further experiments would have to be conducted in order to find out. In addition, behavioral measures are inappropriate for studying certain topics, such as sexual fantasies (too mental) or people's sexual practices (usually considered too private to be observed). Finally, behavioral measures are often more troublesome to collect than subjective ratings, questionnaires, and other kinds of self-reports. Such potential drawbacks will usually be weighed in a researcher's final choice of measurement techniques.

Physiological measures are a third kind of assessment that have pros and cons. Their great value lies in providing objective data on things that are difficult to measure precisely in other ways. Consider the problem of determining when subjects in studies on sleeping are actually asleep. You certainly cannot rely on self-reports in this instance. Nor can you trust to simple observations of behavior, such as the fact that subjects have closed their eyes. Fortunately, a physiological recording called the electroencephalogram (EEG) helps researchers out. By measuring the brain's electrical activity, it allows psychologists to tell which of several stages of sleep or wakefulness a person is in. Similarly, psychologists studying emotion can usually learn more about the strength of an emotional response by measuring changes in heart rate, respiration, and galvanic skin response (a measure of the electrical conductivity of the skin, which increases when a person perspires) than they can by simply observing outward behavior or eliciting a subjective report. One problem, however, is the difficulty of interpreting the nature of an emotion detected in this way. If a person shows an increased heart rate or galvanic skin response (GSR), how is an experimenter to know for sure whether he or she is frightened, excited, or sexually aroused? Behavioral and self-report data can add important dimensions in this case.

Figure 2.4 (A) When asked to assign numbers to their feelings of fear (with 1 meaning the time of least fear and 10 meaning the time of most fear), novice parachutists reported most fear at the "ready" signal just before the jump. Experienced parachutists said their fear was nearly at its lowest at this time. (B) Physiological measures indicated that both groups became more aroused right up to the time of the jump. Fenz and Epstein suggest that the experienced parachutists had learned to inhibit their subjective experience of fear in response to the first signs of physiological arousal. *(After Fenz and Epstein, 1967.)*

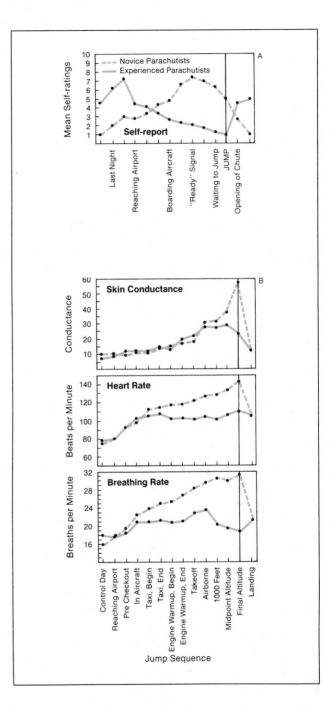

Physiological measures of emotion are especially useful when subjects are not willing to admit to particular feelings, or when they are not even consciously aware that those feelings exist. This can be seen in a study of fear in skydivers conducted by Fenz and Epstein (1967). They asked novice and experienced divers to rate on a ten-point scale the intensity of their fear at various stages in the jump sequence. As Figure 2.4 shows, the novices reported that fear steadily increased until the "ready" signal, after which it dropped off. The experienced jumpers, in contrast, reported a very different pattern. They said that fear gradually decreased from a high point the morning of a jump to the moment the parachute opened, after which a sudden rush of fear occurred. Interestingly, the subjective ratings of the experienced divers did *not* correspond to their patterns of physiological arousal. Heart rate, respiration, and GSR tended to increase for novice and experienced jumpers alike right up to the moment of the jump. Fenz and Epstein speculated that perhaps the experienced jumpers had learned to inhibit the subjective experience of fear in response to the first signs of physiological arousal. In any case, self-reports and physiological measures *together* were needed to give a full and accurate picture.

Such multiple measures are advantageous in many other kinds of studies because they help to guard against inadvertent biases. In fact, psychologists are increasingly using within a single study all three of the measurement techniques we have discussed. Wortman and her colleagues (1980) did this in a recent study of effective coping with permanent paralysis. They assessed coping in a variety of ways, including self-reports (the patients' own subjective ratings of how well they felt they were doing), behavioral measures (such as attendance at therapy sessions and other voluntary activities), and physiological measures (such as measurements of sleep disturbances).

Each type of measurement helped to compensate for any limitations in the others.

Assessing Behavioral Change Over Time. One special measurement problem psychologists sometimes face is that of assessing behavioral change over a relatively long period of time. Imagine, for example, that you are trying to find out whether dependent children grow up to be dependent adults. You might randomly select a group of adults, assess each person's degree of dependency, and then try to discover, by reconstructing their biographies, how dependent they were as children. But this approach would probably require you to rely on people's memories to some extent, and memories of events that happened years ago are notoriously unreliable. A more accurate way to answer the same question would be to conduct what is called a **longitudinal study,** a study in which the same group of people is examined over a number of years. Thus you might select a group of children, assess each one's current level of dependency, and assess it again every few years as the children grow up.

Longitudinal studies are the most reliable method available for assessing long-term change or stability in human behavior. But longitudinal studies are also time-consuming. An alternative approach that psychologists sometimes take is to study a population cross-sectionally by age. In a **cross-sectional study,** the population is divided into subgroups on the basis of certain criteria (in this case age), the subgroups are randomly sampled, and the members of each sample are then surveyed, tested, or observed. If you were conducting a cross-sectional study of intelligence by age, for instance, you would administer an IQ test to people of various ages—some ten years old, some fifteen, some twenty, and so forth—and then draw conclusions about intelligence through the life cycle on the basis of the results. Such studies usually show that the high point of intellectual development is somewhere around age thirty, after which intelligence consistently declines.

There is a serious problem with cross-sectional studies of intellectual development, however. The older people sampled have had very different educations and life experiences from the younger ones, and this age-related difference in intellectual stimulation can easily influence the test results. In fact, longitudinal studies of intelligence over the life span have shown this factor to be highly significant. When psychologists examine the same people at different points in their lives, they generally find that some measures of intellectual performance either increase or stay the same until the age of fifty or sixty (Baltes, Reese, and Nesselroade, 1977). Thus longitudinal studies have in some instances provided data quite different from those collected when a population is studied cross-sectionally by age.

This does not mean that the longitudinal approach is always preferred, however. Both longitudinal and cross-sectional studies have certain advantages and limitations that make each more or less useful in answering particular types of research questions. A combination of the two methods is probably ideal. Cross-sectional research is less expensive, the data can be gathered in a much shorter time, and a larger number of subjects can usually be studied. When cross-sectional studies are used for preliminary investigations, they can often provide important directions for later, more extensive longitudinal research. You will meet the complementary use of these two approaches again in our unit on human development.

in depth Exploring the Hazards of Smoking

So far in this chapter we have presented a series of descriptions of the data-gathering methods that psychologists use, as well as their measurement techniques. Now it is time to step back and actually use what you have learned in an effort to solve an important real-life problem. Imagine that you are a doctor living in the 1920s. Like many others in the medical field, you suspect that smoking may be hazardous to human health. In particular, you are concerned about a possible causal relationship between smoking and lung cancer. How would you begin to gather scientific evidence that might back up your suspicions?

A logical place to start might be with correlational data. Certainly if smoking caused lung cancer, there would have to be a strong positive correlation between the incidence of this disease and the use of cigarettes by patients. Not surprisingly, a number of physicians in the 1920s did indeed conduct such research (Brown, 1978). In 1927, for instance, a British physician named F. E. Tulecote published his professional finding that in nearly every case of lung cancer he had ever treated the victim was a habitual smoker. A few years later two other doctors provided a more precise statistic (Arkin and Wagner, 1936, cited in Brown, 1978). Their research showed that of 135 patients suffering from lung cancer, fully 90 percent were chronic smokers.

The inferences we can draw from such findings are limited, however, as you already know. Although correlational studies demonstrate that smoking and lung cancer often go together, they in no way show that smoking is *causing* the cancer. Perhaps some third factor, not yet identified, is encouraging the onset of both. Extreme nervousness, for instance, might induce both a tendency to smoke heavily and a tendency to produce some body chemical that irritates cells, increasing the likelihood of malignancy. If so, then smoking really has nothing to do with the development of cancer. They are two simultaneous but independent processes. Here we see again the major limitation of correlational research. You simply cannot demonstrate causal relationships on the basis of correlational data alone.

What, then, must researchers do to show a causal link? Like many other medical professionals in the 1930s and 1940s, you might argue that what is needed is a true, carefully controlled experiment. Such a study would involve the random assignment of a large number of young people to either a smoking or a nonsmoking condition. Then each subject's health would be monitored over many years. But how, in all good conscience, could you ever conduct such a study? Remember that you are dealing with a substance suspected of causing a potentially fatal disease. On ethical grounds this experiment would have to be ruled out, and some morally acceptable alternative would have to be found instead. If you were a medical researcher during this era, what alternative methodology might you propose? On the basis of what you learned earlier in this chapter, you might very well design some kind of quasi-experiment—a study in which you took advantage of "experimental" and "control" groups that had formed naturally through personal choice. This, in fact, is what many mid-century investigators of smoking resourcefully decided to do.

The earliest such studies were retrospective ones, or studies that looked backward in time (Brown, 1978). The researchers began with a sample of current lung cancer patients and then collected information about their smoking histories. Next, these histories were compared with those of a control group. Members of the control group were similar to the cancer patients along many potentially relevant dimensions—age, sex, place of residence, type of occupation, and so forth—but they differed in that they were *not* suffering from any lung disease. If the researchers found that the cancer patients, on average, smoked significantly more than their healthy counterparts, they would have additional evidence that smoking is linked to lung cancer. And, in fact, studies

designed in this manner found just that. Could scientists now conclude that smoking *causes* cancer?

Unfortunately, they could not, as you may have already guessed. The quasi-experimental design we have just described has many potential weaknesses. Recalling our discussions earlier in this chapter, can you suggest what some of those weaknesses are? With a little thought you can probably come up with several. For one thing, when researchers select people for a comparable control group, it is very easy to introduce an inadvertent bias in favor of nonsmokers. Suppose physicians supplied candidates from their files of patients not suffering from lung cancer. If they knew the purpose of the proposed study, might they not unconsciously lean toward people who had never or seldom smoked? And what about the problem of relying strictly on self-reports? Might not lung cancer patients, looking back regretfully over their lives, tend to portray themselves as heavier smokers than they actually were? The opposite might be true of people who were healthy. Might not their very healthiness prompt them to underestimate how long and frequently they had actually smoked? This tendency would be especially likely if they or even the researchers interviewing them knew the purpose of the study. Such strong and persuasive criticisms forced scientists to search for other, less questionable research methods. Once again try to place yourself in their position and see what alternative research design you might devise.

One solution researchers came up with consisted of **prospective studies**—that is, studies that followed subjects forward through time (Brown, 1978). Smokers and nonsmokers, none of whom were being treated for serious illnesses, were selected from the larger population. Then health records for these people were collected over the ensuing years. Such an approach was certainly more time-consuming than the retrospective research of the past, but it also reduced some of the problems encountered in the earlier retrospective investigations. Note that this prospective research design more closely approximates the setup of a true experiment. Nevertheless, it is still a quasi-experiment because subjects are not randomly assigned to each group. Instead, they are self-assigned—that is, people themselves are deciding whether to smoke or not.

The data collected from such prospective quasi-experiments weighed heavily against smoking. One study conducted in England followed 40,000 smokers and nonsmokers over a number of years, while an even larger study in the United States followed 200,000 people (Hammond and Horn, 1954; Doll and Hill, 1956). Each found the rate of death due to lung cancer to be an alarming 24 times greater in heavy smokers than in people who did not smoke at all. Moreover, the same studies revealed unexpected connections between smoking and other types of illness. In particular, death from heart and circulatory system diseases was found to be over one and a half times greater in the sample of heavy smokers than in the sample of nonsmokers. This was the first time research had been designed which enabled such comparative death rates to be calculated. The statistics gave even the staunchest supporters of smoking reason to pause (Brown, 1978).

But some investigators were still not satisfied. After our earlier discussion of quasi-experimental data, you can probably suggest why. The doubters rightly argued that there could very well be important, systematic differences between the smoking and the nonsmoking groups—differences that had nothing directly to do with the use or nonuse of cigarettes but that were causally linked to susceptibility to disease. As we suggested earlier, for instance, people who smoke, in general, might be more nervous than nonsmokers, and this nervousness might generate excessive amounts of hormones, which in turn could tend to irritate the body. Alternatively, perhaps smokers, on average, are psychologically inclined to eat more poorly and get less exercise than nonsmokers are. Couldn't such factors make them more vulnerable to disease? Or maybe a certain biological makeup simply predisposes a person toward both cigarette addiction and a tendency to develop lung and heart problems. The point is that the quasi-experimental studies that researchers had conducted so far did not enable such feasible possibilities to be ruled out.

At this point it might seem as if research into the hazards of smoking had reached a stalemate. On the one hand, quasi-experimental designs by their very nature made it difficult for researchers to infer causal

relationships with any confidence. True experiments were better suited to this task. Yet in this case true experiments could not be conducted for ethical reasons. What, then, could investigators do?

Fortunately, new methodology came to the rescue (Brown, 1978). After much effort, researchers finally devised ways to simulate human smoking in laboratory animals. As a result, they were now able to conduct true experiments—that is, they could randomly assign some animal subjects to be smokers and others to be nonsmokers and then record the incidence of disease that developed in each. Food, exercise, and all other possibly relevant factors could be held constant. Moreover, scientists no longer had to rely on the potentially biased self-reports submitted by human subjects. They could note precisely how many cigarettes an experimental animal smoked each day. The results of these studies suggested that, in animals at least, smoking was indeed a cause of lung cancer. At the same time, researchers also devised more sophisticated quasi-experiments—studies in which alternative causes of lung, heart, and vascular disease were taken into account. These investigations provided stronger and stronger evidence that cigarettes were indeed causally related to some very serious human illnesses. Finally, in 1964, the accumulated evidence was so convincing that the United States Surgeon General issued his now famous report declaring cigarette smoking to be potentially hazardous to health (Public Health Service, 1964).

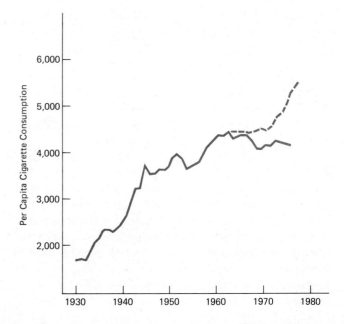

Figure 2.5 Cigarette consumption increased almost continuously from 1930 to 1964. Consumption began to decline after the government began an antismoking campaign in 1964. Without that campaign, cigarette consumption would have been nearly 42 percent higher per person in 1978, as shown by the difference between the end points of the dashed and solid lines. *(After Warner, 1981.)*

The rest of the story is well known. Cigarette manufacturers were required by law to place warnings on their packages and advertisements. Cigarette ads were totally banned from television, in order to decrease children's exposure to them. Strong antismoking campaigns were launched by the American Cancer Society, the National Lung Association, and other health-oriented groups. Subsequent reports issued by the Surgeon General declared the dangers of cigarettes with even stronger wording. Figure 2.5 shows that since 1964 annual cigarette consumption per person in the United States has dropped far below what it would have been without such active antismoking efforts (Warner, 1981).

Research into the hazards of smoking still goes on today. Recent studies tie smoking to a long list of medical problems. There is even evidence that passive smoking (inadvertently inhaling the cigarette smoke of others) can be detrimental to health (Public Health Service, 1982). Scientists are now trying to discover how each of these apparent effects of smoking actually operates. Often the answers lie in complex biochemical processes that can be identified only through highly sophisticated research techniques. Thus current findings are generating new questions and new approaches to their answers. This pattern in which new knowledge is gradually built on old occurs in all types of scientific research. You will encounter numerous examples of it throughout the rest of this book.

ANALYZING DATA

In previous sections of this chapter we have focused primarily on how psychologists gather their data. But almost inevitably we have been forced to touch also on the closely related topic of data analysis. Usually such analysis involves some form of **statistics**—mathematical methods for assessing data and presenting them in summary form. There are two main kinds of statistics: descriptive and inferential. A student of psychology should have at least some knowledge of each.

Descriptive Statistics

Psychologists doing research typically collect numerical information. Looking at these data in their initial, unorganized state can be a bewildering experience for a person with an untrained eye. But by using various procedures for presenting quantitative information, psychologists can summarize even vast amounts of data in forms that are brief, meaningful, and easy to grasp. These various procedures are collectively called **descriptive statistics.** In this section we will show how descriptive statistics enable researchers to accomplish two important goals: to specify at a glance how scores in a sample are distributed, and to convey in a shorthand way how closely two factors are related.

Describing Distributions of Scores. Suppose a congresswoman wants to find out the things that are bothering people in her district. She also wants to know if blue-collar and white-collar workers are concerned about largely the same or largely different issues. As you learned earlier in our discussion of research methods, a survey is ideally suited to these types of questions. So our congresswoman asks two psychologists to conduct a survey for her.

The psychologists compose a questionnaire containing forty-five questions that can be answered yes or no; for example, "I am dissatisfied with the quality of education in my local schools" and "I am displeased with the job the police force is doing." They then administer the survey to fifty blue-collar workers selected at random from a representative sample of neighborhoods within the congresswoman's district. The responses show that some blue-collar workers are dissatisfied with many things, while others are dissatisfied with only a few. No one, however, is unhappy about more than thirty-six items on the questionnaire, and no one complains about fewer than eleven. The scores therefore spread between 11 and 36, and so are said to have a **range** of 25 (36 − 11 = 25). The researchers now construct a **histogram**—that is, a graph of the **frequency distribution** in which the data are arranged in a way that shows the number of instances (the frequency) of each score. This histogram is shown in Figure 2.6A. They then administer the questionnaire to fifty white-collar workers, tabulate their scores, and construct another

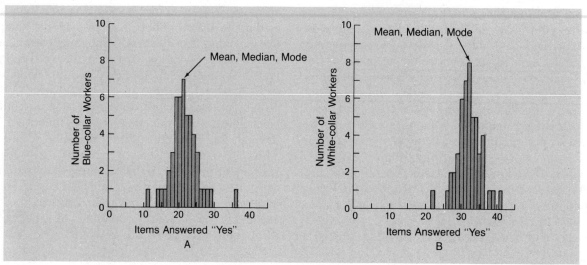

Figure 2.6 Two frequency distributions. In each figure, the vertical scale shows the frequency with which a score on the horizontal scale was observed. (A) The distribution of the scores from an imaginary group of blue-collar workers on an imaginary questionnaire. (B) The distribu-tion of the scores of an imaginary group of white-collar workers on the same test. Note that these normal distribu-tions are similar in range but different in their averages, and that mean, median, and mode—the three measures of central tendency—are the same in each distribution.

histogram, shown in Figure 2.6B. This is a first step toward a meaningful organization of the data.

Measures of Central Tendency. The next step is to choose some method of calculating the central tendencies of the two distributions. A **central tendency** is a middle value of a set of scores. There are several middle values that psychologists might calculate, one of which is the arithmetic average, or **mean**. To find the mean, you merely add all the scores and then divide by the number of people who took the test. As Figure 2.6 shows, the mean score was 21 for blue-collar workers and 32 for white-collar workers.

The other two measures of central tendency labeled in these graphs are the median and the mode. The **median** is the score that falls in the exact middle of a distribution of numbers that are arranged from highest to lowest. For example, the median of the set of numbers 84, 84, 78, 77, 70, which represent the height, in inches, of five players on a hypothetical basketball team, is 78. The **mode** is the score that is most frequently obtained in a distribution, in this case 84. The mean is 78.6. The mean, median, and mode are often different, as in this case, but that is not always so. Note that in each graph in Figure 2.6 the mean, the median, and the mode are equal.

When plotted as a line graph instead of a histogram, some distributions result in a curve with a characteristic "bell" shape, like the one in Figure 2.7. This is called a **normal curve,** and the distribution in this case is called a **normal distribution.** Normal curves are most nearly approximated when a very large number of randomly selected subjects are measured regarding some trait for which individuals vary from a maximum to a minimum, with smooth gradations in between. If, for instance, you were to administer an IQ test to a random sample of 100,000 Americans

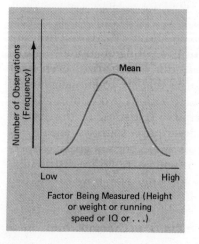

Figure 2.7 The "bell" shape of an ideal normal distribution of frequencies. The highest point of the normal curve represents the mean.

Figure 2.8 The distribution of incomes in an imaginary company. Note that the shape of this distribution is completely different from the shapes in Figure 2.7. Note also that the mean, median, and mode are not identical in this distribution. Frequency distributions of this kind—and of many other kinds—occur often in psychology.

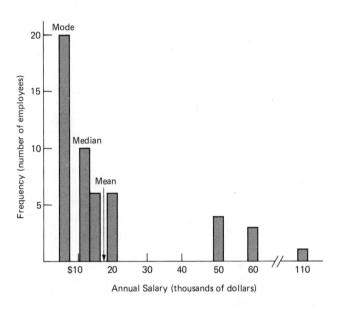

and you plotted the frequency of each score obtained, you would be very likely to get a curve much like the one in Figure 2.7. A large proportion of scores would fall relatively close to the mean, a much smaller proportion would be a moderate distance away from it, and only a very small percentage of all the scores obtained would be extremely far from the average. Note, however, that just by looking at a curve and observing it to have a roughly bell shape you cannot tell for sure whether it represents a normal distribution. Normal curves are formed only when very specific percentages of all the scores collected fall within specific units of deviation from the mean. In psychological research few distributions have these exact characteristics.

Those distributions that are not normal are skewed. In such cases the mean, median, and mode are not equal. How, then, does a psychologist decide which measure of central tendency to use? The answer depends in part on the exact way in which the scores are distributed.

Suppose someone told you that the mean income at a certain company was $19,000 a year. What would this suggest to you? Look at Figure 2.8, the salary distribution for a hypothetical firm employing fifty people. The president of the company earns $110,000 a year; he pays three executives $60,000 and four executives $50,000 each; six supervisors earn $20,000 each and six salespeople earn $15,000 each; the remaining thirty manual and clerical workers all earn $12,000 or less. The mean of all fifty salaries is $19,000, but this is not really a fair representation of the actual distribution of incomes. It seems too high. In this case, a better measure of central tendency would be the median, the salary level at which the number of people who earn more than this amount and the number who earn less are the same. This level is $12,000. Because the mode, or most frequent salary, is only $6,500, it is as misleading an indicator of overall distribution as the mean.

Why would anyone go to the trouble of calculating a measure of central tendency? Beyond the goal of organizing a mass of data into a meaningful and useful form, psychologists want to be able to describe their data in simple, quantitative statements. Being able to locate a point of central tendency helps accomplish this aim. It is much easier, for example, to tell someone that the median salary earned at a particular company is $12,000 than it is to say, "One person earns $110,000, three people earn $60,000, four people earn $50,000 . . . " Central tendencies, then, like other statistical tools, provide a kind of quantitative shorthand.

Measures of Variability. But a measure of central tendency such as the mean, median, or mode actually supplies only a limited amount of information. It does not tell the whole story. To describe a distribution of numbers more fully, psychologists also need information about the **dispersion** of scores. Are scores clustered closely together or are they widely spread out? To understand why this question is important, imagine that you are about to visit a foreign country and hear that the mean monthly rainfall there is five inches. Does this information tell you what kind of weather to expect? Clearly it does not, for you also need to know the extent to which rainfall at different times of year varies from this mean. The statistical techniques for expressing this information are called **measures of variability.**

The range, mentioned earlier, is one measure of variability. But it can sometimes be deceptive. A single extreme score can dramatically alter a range. The salary range at our hypothetical company, for example, was $103,500 ($110,000 − $6,500), but suppose high profits allowed the president to take a raise of $20,000 a year. The range would leap to $123,500, even though the amount of variation among the remaining forty-nine salaries stayed exactly the same. Clearly it would be helpful to have a more sensitive measure of variability—one that takes into account all the scores in a given set of data, not just the outermost extremes.

The **standard deviation** is such a measure of variability. It indicates the average extent to which all the scores in a particular set vary from the mean. The more dispersed scores are, the more the individual scores tend to deviate from the mean and the greater the standard, or average, deviation. If, on the other hand, scores are clustered around the mean, the average deviation is small. Which of the following sets of scores would you guess has a greater standard deviation?

Group A: 52 65 78 95 100   (mean = 78)
Group B: 85 89 91 97 98   (mean = 92)

If you guessed Group A, you are correct. Its standard deviation is 17, while that for Group B is 5. Table 2.1 explains the steps involved in calculating the standard deviation. The important point to remember is that a standard deviation measure tells you immediately whether a set of scores varies widely or only narrowly from the mean. The greater the standard deviation, the wider the variation.

Correlation Coefficients. Earlier in this chapter, when we discussed correlational research, we said that psychologists assess the strength of a correlation (the degree of relatedness between two variables) by calculating what is called a correlation coefficient. Now we are ready to describe this statistical tool in more detail. A correlation coefficient is a number ranging from −1, which indicates a perfect negative correlation, through 0, which indicates no correlation, to +1, which indicates a perfect positive correlation. Thus the closer a correlation coefficient is to +1 or −1, the stronger the relationship—positive or negative—between the two variables.

It is important to remember that a correlation coefficient of, say, −.65 is just as strong as a correlation

TABLE 2.1 CALCULATING THE STANDARD DEVIATION

Step 1: Calculate how much each score deviates from the mean:

Group A (mean: 78)					Group B (mean: 92)				
Value	52	65	78	95	100	Value	85	89	93	97	98
Deviation from mean	−26	−13	0	+17	+22	Deviation from mean	−7	−3	+1	+5	+6

Step 2: To get rid of the minus signs, square each deviation:

Group A					Group B				
Deviation	−26	−13	0	+17	+22	Deviation	−7	−3	+1	+5	+6
Deviation squared	676	169	0	289	484	Deviation squared	49	9	1	25	36

Step 3: Find the mean of the squared deviations:

Group A	Group B
$\dfrac{676 + 169 + 0 + 289 + 484}{5} = 324.2$	$\dfrac{49 + 9 + 1 + 25 + 36}{5} = 24$

Step 4: To convert the squared figures back into the same units as the original values, find the square root of the mean deviations. This is the standard deviation.

Group A	Group B
$\sqrt{324.2} = 18$	$\sqrt{24} = 5$

coefficient of +.65. The strength of a correlation is determined not by the sign of its coefficient (+ or −) but by the absolute value of the coefficient. To test your understanding of this potentially confusing point, suppose that researchers at a certain university find that grade point average and number of traffic violations have a correlation of −.42, while grade point average and running speed have a correlation of +.26. Which relationship is stronger? In this fictitious example, a stronger correlation exists between traffic violations and grade point average than between running ability and grade point average, because 42 is larger than 26. Note that the minus sign in front of .42 has nothing to do with the strength of the relationship being measured. It simply indicates that the relationship is negative: as traffic violations *increase,* grade point average *declines,* and vice versa.

To summarize, correlational studies are a way of discovering the extent to which two variables are related, and the correlation coefficient is a quantitative means of expressing this relationship. At one extreme, a correlation coefficient of 0 indicates that there is no relationship between the variables in question: they vary independently of one another. At the other extreme, a correlation coefficient of −1 or +1 indicates that a perfect relationship exists: if you know the quantitative change in one variable, you can precisely state the accompanying change in the other. Most of the relationships that psychologists study fall somewhere between these extremes.

Inferential Statistics

Descriptive statistics enable researchers to convey the highlights of their findings with only a few words and figures. They can reduce a mass of numerical data to a form that is more manageable and easier to understand. But often the investigators' task is not over when they have finished "describing" their data. Many times the goal of research is to explore hypotheses, and for this purpose psychologists must turn to **inferential statistics.**

Inferential statistics provide ground rules or conventions for determining what conclusions can legitimately be drawn from data. Remember that researchers begin with a hypothesis—a conjecture that, under certain circumstances, people (or animals) will behave in a certain way. They then collect quantifiable data (scores, ratings, behavioral measures, and so on)

about the way people in a sample do behave under those specific circumstances. Next they summarize their data by means of descriptive statistics, like those discussed in the preceding section. But now they must also make use of inferential statistics to infer (draw a reasonable conclusion as to) whether the data clearly support their original hypothesis. Were the results due primarily to chance, or was there indeed a significant pattern or relationship?

Probability. You undoubtedly know that the odds of getting heads on any given toss of an unbiased coin are 50-50—that is, a head will probably turn up half the time. Now suppose that out of 100 tosses of a coin it lands heads up 53 times. Is the coin biased? What if it lands heads up 79 times? Statisticians have determined the probability of obtaining any given result with any given number of tosses of an unbiased coin. Thus they can tell you how often in, say, 100 tosses one can expect to obtain 28, 53, 79, or any other number of heads from 0 to 100.

Probability is a complex area of mathematics that is frequently misunderstood. Our intuitions about "what the chances are" are not always correct. Assume, for example, that you have tossed a coin ten times and that it has landed heads up each time. You are about to toss it again. What do you predict will occur on this next toss? There are three possibilities: (1) another head will turn up; (2) a tail will turn up; or (3) the odds are still even (.50), so it is impossible to tell. If you predicted that a tail would turn up, you committed a common error known as the "gambler's fallacy." There is no reason to expect that the probability of a tail turning up is any better than even, no matter how many times a head has already appeared. Indeed, the prediction that a head will turn up again probably has more merit than the prediction that a tail will turn up, for it appears that the coin you have been dealing with may, for some reason, be a biased one.

If the probability of getting a head on a single toss of a coin is 1 out of 2, how do you determine the probability of getting several heads in a row? This is done by multiplying the odds for getting one event (one head) by the odds for getting each subsequent one. The probability of getting two heads in a row, therefore, is $1/2 \times 1/2$, or 1/4. For four heads in a row, the odds would by 1/16 ($1/2 \times 1/2 \times 1/2 \times 1/2$). The probability that a coin will come up heads ten times in a row is 1/2 raised to the tenth power, which

Many people believe that the longer they lose at gambling, the better their odds of winning become. This belief that a win must eventually come up is the "gambler's fallacy." The fact is that the odds are exactly the same with each pull of the handle or roll of the dice. *(Aton Reininger/Contact Press Images.)*

is 1/1024. That is, the odds against this event occurring by chance with a fair coin are 1,024 to 1, which is why you might begin to suspect in such a case that the coin is biased and that your coin-tossing results are not a matter of chance. What are you doing when you form this suspicion is making a judgment about the meaning of an event (ten heads in a row) based on the odds of its occurring purely by chance. Because the likelihood of a chance occurrence is so slim, you might favor some alternative explanation. This is exactly the kind of logic that psychologists employ when they use inferential statistics to judge the significance of their data.

Statistical Significance. The crux of the problem psychologists face is that the influence of chance can never be eliminated. Whenever a researcher conducts an experiment there will invariably be some difference, based strictly on chance, between the performance of one group and the performance of another. If you gave a vision test to one hundred people with brown hair, for instance, and gave the same test to one hundred blonds, you might find that the blonds, on average, had slightly better eyesight. Now vision undoubtedly has nothing to do with the color of a person's hair, so we can assume that this observed difference was caused entirely by chance. This means that if you ran the same test again with a different group of subjects, you would be just as likely to get the opposite results. But how do you assess the influence of chance on a relationship that is far more plausible? Clearly what is needed is a statistical test to help us decide when a given difference in performance is reliable—that is, when we can expect it to occur again

and again under the same circumstances. Such a test is called a measure of **statistical significance.**

An example will help clarify the importance of being able to calculate statistical significance. Suppose that an experimental group of rats has been given an injection of caffeine, the stimulant in coffee. On the average, these rats learn to run a maze in thirty trials. A control group of animals is injected with a **placebo** (a substance that has no physiological effect) to ensure that the two groups will not perform differently merely because one has received an injection and the other has not. The control group learns to run the same maze in an average of thirty-eight trials. Is the difference between thirty and thirty-eight trials large enough to enable the experimenter to conclude that the caffeine increased the speed with which the experimental animals learned the maze, or might these results have occurred merely by chance?

Psychologists and other scientists have adopted an arbitrary convention for making such decisions. By various methods they calculate the probability that the outcome of the study could have occurred by chance alone. If this probability is quite low, say .05 (5 times out of 100), they then have good reason to reject the "chance" explanation and to conclude instead that the independent variable under consideration caused the results. In this instance the researchers would report that the data had attained the .05 level of statistical significance. Some investigators choose more stringent levels, say .01 (1 time out of 100). In each case, however, the investigator computes the probability that the results occurred solely by chance. Only if that probability is low does the researcher assert that the results support the hypothesis.

SOME PITFALLS IN PSYCHOLOGICAL RESEARCH

Good research is difficult in any scientific field. It requires a broad knowledge of available tools and approaches for collecting and analyzing data, as well as careful attention to the details of carrying out these tasks. At the same time, good research demands creativity in asking the initial questions and in putting together an effective research strategy. And it also demands a wariness regarding the various traps into which eager investigators can stumble. In this section we take a look at three of the most common pitfalls in psychological research.

The Self-Fulfilling Prophecy

The term **self-fulfilling prophecy** refers to the fact that the expectations of investigators can influence their findings. In psychology, as in other fields, people tend to find what they are looking for. More than that, they may even tend unwittingly to *create* what they seek. If, for example, a researcher conducting an interview smiles faintly when a subject's response corroborates the theory under investigation, this inadvertent act can easily affect the subject's answers to subsequent questions. If this seems difficult to believe, consider the following real-life experiment.

Robert Rosenthal (1966) told a group of elementary-school teachers that certain pupils had obtained high scores on some special tests and so were sure to show unusual intellectual development during the school year. Actually, these potential "late bloomers" were no different from other pupils who had not been so labeled. Later in the year, the teachers rated the "late bloomers" as more interested, more curious, and happier than other students. And when all the children were given IQ tests at the end of the year, those who had been labeled late bloomers showed a significantly greater gain in IQ than did their classmates, as Figure 2.9 indicates. As you can see, this effect occurred primarily with first- and second-grade children, perhaps because their teachers had not yet had a chance to formulate contradictory opinions about these relative newcomers to the school. In this case, of course, it was the teachers, not the experimenter, who fulfilled the prophecy of academic success through their differential treatment of the supposed late bloomers. But an experimenter, even one who is fully aware that self-fulfilling prophecies can occur, can also sometimes unintentionally create the expected results.

One way for a researcher to avoid self-fulfilling prophecies is to employ a procedure known as the **double-blind technique,** in which neither the experimenter nor the subjects know who has been assigned to the experimental group or who is acting as a control. (This procedure differs from the **single-blind technique,** in which the experimenter knows who is

Figure 2.9 Teachers in each of the six grades of an elementary school were led to believe that certain of their pupils had been discovered to be "late bloomers" on the basis of a special test and would show great academic gains during the year. In fact, the pupils were selected at random. Intelligence tests were given both at the beginning and at the end of the school year. This histogram shows the relative IQ gains during the year of the control group (pupils not expected to be "late bloomers" by their teachers) and the experimental group (pupils who were expected to be late bloomers). Both groups gained in the lower grades, but the experimental group gained more. In the upper grades, however, there was little effect, perhaps because the teachers already had strong expectations about the pupils on the basis of their performances in earlier grades. *(After Rosenthal, 1966.)*

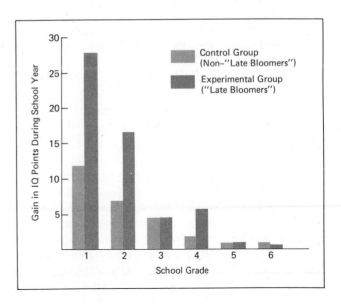

in which group but the subjects do not.) In an experiment testing the effects of a tranquilizing drug, for example, the experimental group would be given the tranquilizer and the control group would receive a placebo, perhaps in the form of a sugar pill. Only some outside party, such as the pharmacist who supplied the pills, would know which group received which kind of pill. The pharmacist would not give that information to the experimenter until after the effects of drug and placebo on the two groups of subjects had been recorded. In other types of studies similar techniques can be used. Psychologists looking for a possible positive correlation between IQ and psychological adjustment, for example, would assess psychological adjustment first, without knowing their subjects' IQ scores. In this way they could avoid seeing better adjustment in high-IQ subjects than was actually present.

Demand Characteristics

Even if a researcher employs the double-blind technique, there is still a possibility that subjects will invalidate research findings by trying to behave like "good" subjects. Most students who volunteer for an experiment want to do well at the experimental task, so they search for clues as to what the experiment is about. The clues they uncover have been called **demand characteristics,** because subjects feel that these clues *demand* certain "correct" responses on their part (Orne, 1962). An example will illustrate the distorting effects demand characteristics can have.

Suppose you have volunteered for a psychological experiment. When you arrive at the laboratory, a researcher tells you that the study involves memory of fast-moving events. She shows you a series of slides depicting successive stages in an automobile accident and then asks you twenty questions about them. One of the questions is: "Did another car pass the red Datsun while it was stopped at the stop sign?" This question puzzles you. The sign you remember seeing at the corner was a yield sign, not a stop sign. You conclude that the experimenter must be trying to trick you. But why? Later you believe you detect the experimenter's intentions. She shows you several pairs of very similar slides and asks which of each pair you saw previously. One pair shows the Datsun stopped at an intersection with either a stop sign or a yield sign at the corner. "Aha!" you say to yourself. "She expects me to choose the stop sign! Well, perhaps I should.

After all, I'd hate to ruin her experiment." If you select the stop sign knowing full well it is the wrong sign, you have succumbed to demand characteristics. In doing so, you have obviously misled the experimenter and have probably made it more difficult for her to interpret the results correctly.

How can researchers counteract demand characteristics? One approach is to question subjects carefully after an experiment to see if demand characteristics influenced them. At the end of an experiment on memory similar to the one just described, Loftus and her colleagues (1978) revealed their true purpose. They told subjects that they were trying to determine the effects of false information on eyewitness testimony by showing slides of an automobile accident and later asking questions about them. One of those questions, the researchers confessed, may have contained false information about the traffic sign located at the intersection. Would the subjects now please indicate which sign they *really* remembered seeing? In this way, Loftus and her colleagues were able to get some idea of the extent to which demand characteristics had influenced their results. The conclusion they drew at the end of this procedure? Demand characteristics had affected subjects' responses hardly at all.

There are problems with this end-of-experiment questioning, however. Sometimes even the most careful and sensitive questioning may not reveal the real reasons behind a person's behavior. Subjects may be unwilling to admit to reasons that place them in an unflattering light, or they may be only vaguely aware of the complex motivations that prompted a particular response.

There are several ways of minimizing the problem of demand characteristics. One way is to try to conceal the true purpose of the experiment through deception. In the study by Milgram described earlier, subjects were led to believe that the experiment concerned the effect of punishment on learning. The real question, of course, was whether subjects would obey an authority figure even if to do so meant delivering painful electric shocks to a fellow subject. The use of deception in psychological research is highly controversial, however. Another way to reduce the effects of demand characteristics is to automate an experiment as much as possible in order to avoid personal sympathy or hostility toward the experimenter. A researcher, for example, might avoid face-to-face contact with subjects by using tape-recorded instructions and anonymous responses. A third approach is to increase the use of unobtrusive measures. If subjects are not aware that a particular behavior is being recorded, they are unlikely to distort it. In fact, behavioral measures in general may be less influenced by demand characteristics than are verbal self-reports. White subjects may *report* that they are not prejudiced against blacks, but they may reveal negative attitudes by refusing to spend a weekend escorting black students around campus (Marlowe, Frager, and Nuhall, 1965).

Drawing Premature Conclusions

During the course of their training, psychologists are taught to anticipate and overcome the kinds of methodological problems we have been describing. Despite an investigator's efforts, however, errors and oversights sometimes occur. This is why it is essential to avoid drawing firm conclusions on the basis of a single study, or even several studies. Yet the temptation to do so is often powerful, as the following example illustrates.

In the early 1970s two pediatricians, Marshall Klaus and John Kennell, decided to test an intriguing hypothesis they had been thinking about. They questioned the wisdom of standard hospital procedures for newborn infants and their mothers. The new mother was given a glimpse of her baby at the time of delivery, and then the child was whisked away to be medically examined and ministered to. Klaus and Kennell were aware that in some animal species contact during the period immediately after birth is often critical for the development of a normal mother-infant bond. If a ewe is separated from her lamb immediately after giving birth, for instance, and then the two are reunited several hours later, the mother will often reject the infant even though she would have readily nurtured it earlier (Collias, 1956). Klaus and Kennell wondered if such a sensitive period might also occur in humans. If it did, then existing hospital procedures were less than ideal for encouraging strong mother-infant bonds.

To test their hypothesis, Klaus and Kennell created experimental and control groups. The control group consisted of fourteen mothers and their firstborn infants who underwent routine hospital care. The mothers were briefly shown their infants right after delivery and during the next three days saw their babies every four hours for routine feedings. The fourteen mothers in the experimental group were allowed a private hour with their infants right after de-

livery. During the rest of their stay, the experimental mothers were given an extra five hours each day with their babies. Klaus and Kennell found that, a month after the baby's birth, mothers in the experimental group on average were more attentive toward their infant in a routine medical exam, more inclined to look at and fondle the baby, and more reluctant to leave the child with a babysitter than control mothers were (Klaus et al., 1972). Even when the child was a year old the experimental mothers seemed more concerned and attentive in certain situations than did control mothers (Kennell et al., 1974).

These findings made nationwide headlines, and the two pediatricians went on to write a popular book in which they claimed that optimal later development depended on bonding in the first minutes and hours of life (1976). Concerned parents pressured the medical establishment to change hospital procedures; by the late 1970s it had become standard practice for parents to be given time alone with their just-born infants so that proper bonding could occur. But what about the parents who for various reasons were denied this opportunity? Perhaps they adopted their baby. Perhaps special medical treatment after birth required the baby to be isolated. Some of these parents began to worry that they had irreversibly missed one of the most important foundations for a close parent-child relationship.

It was not long, however, before other researchers began to point to serious problems in Klaus and Kennell's original study. For one thing, doctors and nurses at the hospital where the study had been conducted might have biased the results by inadvertently giving the experimental women more encouragement as new mothers. And what about the size of the samples—fourteen women and infants in each group? With samples this small it is certainly possible for systematic differences to exist between experimental and control subjects just by chance. The experimental mothers, for example, might have been more attentive because of preexisting personality traits, or because their infants' temperaments just happened to elicit such responses. Questions of this kind prompted several psychologists to try to replicate Klaus and Kennell's findings.

Replication is an essential part of scientific research. Other investigators reconstruct the basic features of the original study and see if the results are similar. In the case of early mother-infant bonding, other researchers' results did not always conform to Klaus and Kennell's findings. Sometimes no significant differences between experimental and control groups could be discovered. Other investigators did find some differences, but not always the same ones that Klaus and Kennell had found. In most cases any observed differences between experimental and control mothers were very few. This pattern led to the suspicion that perhaps the differences were due simply to chance. Certainly the combined evidence showed that the universal importance of early mother-infant contact claimed by its proponents was far from an established fact (Lamb and Hwang, 1982).

The history of research into early mother-infant bonding underscores the importance of avoiding premature conclusions. Even when the results of a new study sound convincing, people must be careful to place these findings in their proper perspective. Additional investigations are essential to verify the initial results. And even if a given study is successfully replicated, many questions remain. Are there particular circumstances under which the experimental outcomes are more likely? Are there other ways in which the current findings might be reasonably interpreted? Such constant questioning is fundamental to scientific work.

THE ETHICS OF RESEARCH IN PSYCHOLOGY

At several points in this chapter we have said that certain research could not be conducted for ethical reasons. We noted, for example, that severely disciplining a group of children from birth to adolescence in order to assess the relationship between harsh child rearing and delinquency would be out of the question. Such an experiment could obviously cause irreparable harm. So could a true experiment investigating the effects of smoking on human health. Those assigned to the experimental group—the ones required to smoke a certain number of cigarettes each day—would be asked to do something that could lead to a fatal illness. But the propriety of other psychological studies is not always so clear-cut. See for yourself by considering the following three examples.

Suppose you are a clerk in a shoestore. At the busiest time of day a woman with a heel missing from one of her shoes approaches you, wanting a new pair of shoes. You show her pair after pair but she curtly rejects each one. Would you feel annoyed or harassed to discover later that the woman was actually a psychologist who wanted to observe your reaction? Suppose now that you are a homemaker. A man phones one morning claiming to represent a consumer group. He interviews you about the soap products

In studying diabetes, this researcher has induced obesity in rats. Such experimental manipulation would be unethical if conducted with human subjects. *(Richard Howard.)*

you use, allegedly for a report in a public-service magazine. Several days later the same man calls again wanting to know if five or six other men could come to your home to "classify" all of the products you buy. If you found out later that this caller was a psychologist studying people's willingness to agree to such requests, would you feel that your privacy had been invaded? Suppose finally that you are riding on a New York subway and the passenger beside you collapses at your feet, blood trickling from his mouth. This incident severely upsets you. If you subsequently learned that the victim was a confederate in an experiment designed to investigate bystander apathy, would you feel that this deception was justified?

These are all actual experiments that psychologists have performed (Schaps, 1972; Freedman and Fraser, 1966; Piliavin and Piliavin, 1972). As you can see, whether they were right or wrong is not easy to say. The crux of the problem is that psychologists have an obligation to find answers to important questions about human behavior, but they also have an obligation to protect the dignity and welfare of the people who participate in their research. These two obligations can sometimes conflict. When they do, how can a researcher decide whether or not to proceed with a particular investigation?

The American Psychological Association (1981) has helped to answer precisely this question by issuing ethical guidelines for studies involving human subjects. These guidelines require, among other things, that researchers avoid all procedures that would in any way cause lasting harm to people. "Harm" includes psychological as well as physical injury. Subjects should not, for instance, leave an experiment feeling degraded and manipulated. If they do, their rights as participants have been violated. Whenever the possibility of some physical or mental discomfort exists, the researcher should inform subjects of this fact and secure their consent before proceeding. If for some reason it is essential to deceive subjects, the researcher must later explain why this concealment was necessary. A subject's participation in any study, of course, must always be voluntary. It should not be made a requirement for passing a psychology course, or in any other way coerced. And if a subject decides to withdraw from a study for any reason, his or her decision must be respected. Finally, subjects in psychological studies have a right to privacy. The researcher should not reveal participants' identities when presenting a study's findings unless the participants themselves willingly authorize such disclosure.

The American Psychological Association is not the only organization that is concerned about the ethics of psychological research. The federal government also requires that all research sponsored by U.S. government grants be reviewed for ethical standards by a panel of qualified people. In fact, most universities today require that *all* research involving human subjects receive the approval of such a review board, and strict standards also exist for the care and treatment of animal subjects.

The decision as to whether a particular study conforms to ethical principles is, of course, a complex one. In the 1960s and early 1970s, the decision was usually made by weighing possible risks to subjects against the value of the information to be gained. By the late 1970s, however, the tide had turned toward more stringent standards, and researchers have become extremely sensitive to ethical considerations that go far beyond the question of whether subjects will be directly harmed (Davidson, 1982). Some psychologists worry that the increasing regulations and concerns about ethics may make it difficult for them to conduct meaningful research (Kimmel, 1979). But all agree that researchers have a responsibility to design their studies in ways that will safeguard the rights of participants.

SUMMARY

1. In order to answer the questions they ask, psychologists use a variety of research methods. Which method is used depends in part on the goal of the research. Because it would be impossible to observe all the people relevant to any question about human behavior, psychologists almost always rely on a **sample,** or selected segment, of the data potentially available. In a **random sample,** every member of the total population has an equal chance of being included. In a **representative sample,** people belonging to groups that contain specific characteristics are randomly selected in proportion to their numbers in the population as a whole.

2. The **experiment** is a method favored by many researchers because it permits them to rule out to as large an extent as possible all influences on subjects' behavior except the factors being examined. The researcher works with two groups of subjects—the **experimental group,** which experiences the experimental condition, and the **control group,** which does not. All experimenters set out to test a **hypothesis,** or proposition. To do so they explore the relationship between **variables,** or factors that can change. The variable that the experimenter deliberately manipulates is called the **independent variable.** The one that is expected to change when the independent variable changes is called the **dependent variable.**

3. Sometimes psychologists use **quasi-experimental designs** to try to infer causal relationships. The researchers take advantage of "experimental" and "control" groups that have formed naturally in real life. But because the investigators have little or no control over variables, and because they cannot assign subjects randomly to conditions, quasi-experiments should be used to explore causes only when true experiments are not feasible.

4. **Correlational research** allows psychologists to determine the extent to which two variables are related to each other. A **positive correlation** means that a high incidence of one variable tends to be accompanied by a high incidence of the other, while a **negative correlation** means that a high incidence of one variable tends to be accompanied by a low incidence of the other. Both the direction and the strength of a correlation are indicated by a numerical value called the **correlation coefficient.**

5. One way to collect data for a correlational study is by means of a **survey**—an attempt to estimate the opinions, characteristics, or behaviors of a population by investigation of a representative sample. Interviews, questionnaires, or public records may provide the information of interest.

6. In order to avoid the biasing effects that may flow just from the formal environment of a laboratory, psychologists sometimes use **naturalistic observation**—that is, observation in a setting where the subjects are naturally found. In **participant observation,** not only is the setting natural, the researchers actually join an existing group to record thoughts and feelings accessible only to group members.

7. A **case study,** or in-depth analysis of an individual, can be used when the population of such individuals is not large enough to permit a sample to be drawn.

8. Psychologists use a variety of tools for measuring individual differences. Such tools include **self-reports, behavioral measures,** and **physiological assessments.**

9. Sometimes psychologists want to know how behavior changes over time. For this purpose they may use either a **longitudinal study,** in which the same group of people is examined at intervals over a period of years, or a **cross-sectional study,** in which people of different ages are simultaneously assessed. The longitudinal approach is more reliable, but it is extremely time-consuming.

10. To interpret the data they have collected, psychologists use **statistics**—mathematical methods for assessing and presenting data in summary form. Statistics may be descriptive or inferential. **Descriptive statistics** enable investigators to present their findings with a few words and figures. One goal is to convey in a shorthand manner how scores in a sample are distributed. Sometimes the **frequency distribution** is plotted on a graph called a **histogram.** In order to compare two histograms, researchers compare **central tendencies,** or middle values, of the two sets of scores. The **mean,** the **median,** and the **mode** are all measures of central tendency.

11. Psychologists also need ways of describing the variability in a set of data. The **range** is the distance between the highest and lowest scores. A more sensitive measure is the **standard deviation,** which indicates the average extent to which all the scores in a particular set vary from the mean.

12. **Inferential statistics** enable researchers to conclude whether their data tend to support their original hypothesis, or whether the results could have occurred by chance alone. They use measures of **probability** to answer this question. Only when results are **statistically significant** is the explanation of chance rejected.

13. Use of the research methods and statistical techniques we have described does not guarantee that psychologists will avoid problems that can invalidate their studies. Among possible pitfalls is the **self-fulfilling prophecy,** the fact that the investigators'

expectations can influence their findings. To avoid this pitfall, psychologists may use the **double-blind technique,** in which neither the researcher nor the subjects know who has been assigned to experimental or control conditions.

14. Another problem arises when subjects search for **demand characteristics,** or clues to the responses they think the researcher wants. Although demand characteristics and their biasing effect can seldom be eliminated entirely, they can be minimized in a variety of ways.

15. A third pitfall in psychological research is the temptation to draw premature conclusions on the basis of a single study. In order to be accepted as valid, research findings must be capable of **replication**—that is, essentially the same results must be obtained by other investigators who repeat the original study under similar conditions.

16. Psychologists follow strict ethical guidelines in conducting research with human subjects. The subjects have a right to know beforehand what a study entails and a right to decline to participate. Researchers must also make sure that their subjects are in no way harmed by their participation, and that their identities are not divulged without their consent.

SUGGESTED READINGS

ANDERSON, B. F. *The psychology experiment.* 2d ed. Belmont, Calif.: Brooks-Cole, 1971.

Written expressly for the nonscientist, this book presents the principles of the scientific method in a way that enables the reader to incorporate them into day-to-day thinking.

McINNIS, R. G. *Research guide for psychology.* Westport, Conn.: Greenwood Press, 1982.

A book about sources of information that may be useful in solving particular research problems in psychology. This guide contains more than 1,200 substantive and bibliographic information sources, each of which is annotated to explain its content, emphasis, and potential usefulness for the researcher.

MOORE, D. S. *Statistics: Concepts and controversies.* San Francisco: Freeman, 1979.

A book that focuses on statistical ideas and their impact on public policy and everyday life. The author deals with the interaction of statistics and society as well as with the concepts of statistics itself, discussing, for example, opinion polls in the political process, the ethics of experimentation with human subjects, and the use and misuse of IQ scores.

NEALE, J. M., AND LIEBERT, R. M. *Science and behavior.* 2d ed. Englewood Cliffs, N.J.: Prentice-Hall, 1980.

A broad general introduction to social science research methodology. A primary aim of the book is to explain the logic of science, as well as to offer details about its methods.

ROWNTREE, D. *Statistics without tears.* New York: Scribner's, 1981.

An introduction to the main concepts and terminology of statistics, providing the reader with an understanding of the topics before presenting the associated calculations. Essential concepts are explained through words and diagrams rather than by means of formulas and equations.

SCHUTTE, J. G. *Everything you always wanted to know about elementary statistics (but were afraid to ask).* Englewood Cliffs, N.J.: Prentice-Hall, 1977.

Using a question-and-answer format, the author introduces topics through analogies and metaphors, when possible. The concepts are rooted in everyday experience.

STERNBERG, R. J. *Writing the psychology paper.* Woodbury, N.Y.: Barron's Educational Series, 1977.

Scientific work has little value unless it is communicated effectively to others. This book offers standardized procedures that a writer can follow to produce readable papers.

2

BIOLOGICAL AND PERCEPTUAL PROCESSES

The biological and perceptual aspects of our functioning are discussed in Part 2. Chapter 3 describes communication within the nervous system, as the brain mediates behavior. Chapter 4 focuses on sensation and perception: how we perceive—and therefore experience—the world around us.

3

BIOLOGICAL FOUNDATIONS OF BEHAVIOR

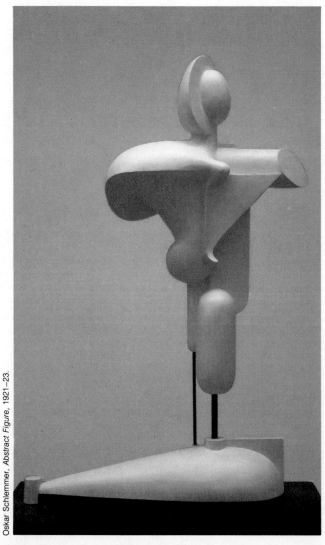

Oskar Schlemmer, *Abstract Figure*, 1921–23.

At birth the baby boy looked perfectly normal, but by age 6 months unusual symptoms had begun to appear. The child could not sit up unsupported, and he began to make strange movements of his hands, arms, feet, and legs. By age three he could not yet speak and appeared severely retarded. But the worst symptom of all was his self-mutilation. When he was not hitting or biting other people and inanimate objects, he would turn these compulsive tendencies toward himself. Incessantly he would bite his lips and fingers and bang his head against furniture and walls. For his own safety he had to be constantly restrained. Although this is an extremely rare set of symptoms, it is not unprecedented. About 1 in every 50,000 male children is afflicted with this disorder, called the Lesch-Nyhan syndrome. What could possibly prompt such bizarre behavior? It is only in the last several decades that scientists have come to learn that it is caused by the absence of a single body chemical, the lack of which has a devastating effect on the development and functioning of the brain (Rodgers, 1983; Reed, 1975).

The question of why people behave as they do has puzzled scholars for centuries. The Greek philosopher Aristotle believed that the heart controlled behavior, while others suggested that the various bodily fluids were responsible. A great many centuries passed before the brain was identified as the principal organ involved. But this insight alone did not begin to uncover the mysteries of how the brain works. For a long time people assumed that the brain was a unitary organ, with a totally homogeneous interior. Then, in the early eighteenth century, a Viennese anatomist named Franz Joseph Gall meticulously dissected the brains of humans and various other animals. He came to the essentially accurate conclusion that the brain is composed of a large number of interconnected substructures, and that different areas of the brain are related to different behavioral processes. Unfortunately, Gall's pioneering research did not stop there. He went on to propose that one could predict a person's behavioral tendencies by analyzing the size and shape of the skull. Gall reasoned that the more a person expressed a certain behavior, the more the associated region of the brain (and the skull encasing it) would increase in size, much as a muscle develops with repeated use. So he set about concocting an elaborate "map" of the human brain, based on comparisons of the head shapes of people who displayed various traits and talents. (See Figure 3.1.) Subsequent efforts to assess people's natures by "reading" the bumps on their heads came to be called **phrenology.** Gall's reputation never quite recovered from his association with this ludicrous practice (Fowler and Fowler, 1969; Broad, 1983).

In the century and a half since Gall's day we have acquired much more reliable data about the relationship between the brain and behavior. We know that damage to certain parts of the brain can disrupt muscle movement and perception and produce a host of specific behavioral disturbances, such as hypersexuality, overeating, inability to awaken from sleep (or to fall asleep in the first place), inability to remember anything new, inability to control aggression, inability to use or to understand speech, and so on

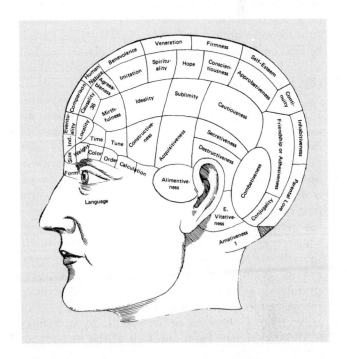

Figure 3.1 Franz Joseph Gall believed that the shape of the skull revealed the shape of the brain beneath it. Traits considered to be specifically "human" (such as logical thinking ability) were thought to be located in the front part of the brain, because this part was much larger in human beings than in other animals. Other, more "animal" traits such as amativeness (sexual behavior) were thought to be located toward the bottom and rear of the brain, since these areas appeared to be quite similar in many animals. According to Gall's "science" of phrenology, when the area of the skull presumably corresponding to the trait of, say, "causality" was very large in a particular individual, this meant the person was capable of deep and powerful reasoning. If this area was small, the individual was thought to be lacking in this trait.

through a long list of disorders. Likewise, mild electrical stimulation of various parts of the brain may cause changes in eating, drinking, sleeping, mating, aggression, and many other behaviors. Equally exciting has been the discovery in recent decades of an ever-growing number of special brain chemicals that are intimately tied to the functioning of the nervous system. We now know that many drugs and toxins have their effects by changing, inhibiting, or mimicking the way these natural brain chemicals work. Yet even with all these discoveries, we still have penetrated only a small fraction of the many secrets locked within the brain's complex labyrinth of some 100 billion cells.

This chapter invites you to take a look inside that labyrinth to understand how the brain and its related biological systems carry out their functions. This area is the province of **physiological psychologists,** who specialize in learning how biological processes are related to an organism's actions and experiences. We begin by discussing some basic features of the body's two communication networks: the nervous system, of which the brain is a part, and the endocrine system, which consists of hormone-secreting glands. Together these two systems are responsible for integrating and regulating all signals and responses in the body. We then focus on the brain and how its various structures are related to aspects of behavior. In the process, we explore the major techniques for studying brain function and some of the interesting findings they have revealed. And finally, we look at the brain's role in such complex behaviors as learning, remembering, and problem solving. As you will see, how the brain performs these activities is still largely a mystery.

THE NERVOUS SYSTEM

Consisting of billions of interconnected cells that radiate throughout the body, the human nervous system is one of the most complex creations in the living world. Consciously running such a vast and intricate network is inconceivable (Thomas, 1974). Hundreds of billions of tiny atoms and molecules would have to be shuttled back and forth across cell membranes at a split second's notice. Cellular factories would have to be kept constantly busy churning out all the chemicals needed to carry out the nervous system's work. These chemicals would have to be delivered to precisely the right locations and used at just the right moments. Error, indecision, napping on the job could have disastrous consequences. With such precise and ceaseless demands on the human nervous system, it is reassuring that the system operates so automatically, without our conscious awareness, let alone our conscious control. Yet we *can* consciously use the brain, a central part of the nervous system, to explore this remarkable network and understand its complex workings.

The cells of the human nervous system are highly specialized. **Receptor cells,** embedded in the sense organs, are specialized to receive various types of stimulation from the environment. **Effector cells** are specialized to contract muscles and stimulate glandular secretions. **Neurons,** or nerve cells, are specialized to conduct signals from one part of the body to another. Neurons connect receptor cells to effector cells and integrate and coordinate their activities. During each waking second, a person's eyes, ears, and other sense receptors send approximately 100 million messages to the brain. To perform even such a simple behavior as swinging a tennis racket, the brain must issue millions of commands to the muscles. In this section we will be most concerned with neurons, which form the major part of the nervous system. We begin with a description of the nervous system as a whole before turning to the structure and operation of the neuron, its basic unit.

Divisions of the Nervous System

Most of the body's neurons are found in the brain and spinal cord, which lie within the bony casings of the skull and spinal column. These parts of the nervous system are called the **central nervous system** because they provide the ultimate control center for all human behavior, from simple reflexes to abstract reasoning. Branching out from the central nervous system and leading to all parts of the body is the **peripheral nervous system.** The peripheral nervous system conveys signals from the body's sensory receptors to the central nervous system and transmits messages

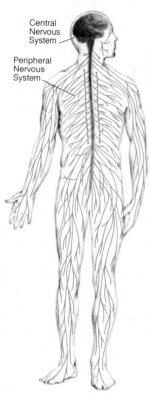

Central Nervous System

Peripheral Nervous System

Figure 3.2 The central nervous system (CNS) and the peripheral nervous system (PNS) in the human body. Both of these systems are made up of billions of nerve cells, or neurons, each of which is capable of transmitting a train of electrochemical signals in one direction. In the CNS, these neurons form an immensely complex network that organizes, stores, and redirects vast quantities of information. In the PNS, neurons in every pathway carry information either from receptors (such as the sense organs) toward the CNS or away from the CNS to effectors (in the muscles, for example). There is a close match between information going to the CNS and information coming from it. Every muscle, for example, not only receives from the CNS directions to contract or relax but also sends back information about its present state of contraction or relaxation.

your somatic nervous system. These are activities that we usually think of as being under voluntary control. The **autonomic nervous system,** in contrast, controls the visceral muscles (blood vessels, heart, intestines) and the glands. Autonomic activity is usually classified as involuntary because it occurs more or less automatically. Most people do not consciously control the contractions of their digestive tract, for instance, or the beating of their heart. There is evidence, however, that people can learn to influence such "involuntary" autonomic activities when appropriate feedback is available. Thus cardiac patients have sometimes learned to lower their heart rate and reduce their blood pressure voluntarily. Research on this procedure, called biofeedback, is discussed more fully in Chapters 10 and 12.

The autonomic nervous system itself has two divisions: the **sympathetic** and the **parasympathetic.** With few exceptions, any given visceral muscle or gland in the body is supplied with nerves by both of these divisions. This is called **dual control.** In general, these two divisions can be viewed as working antagonistically—that is, they tend to have broadly opposite effects.

The sympathetic system is usually involved in mobilizing the body's resources. In an emergency or a stressful situation, it responds by increasing blood sugar, raising heart rate and blood pressure, and inhibiting digestive processes. The parasympathetic division, in contrast, dominates under conditions of relaxation and tends to conserve the body's energy. After you eat a large meal, for example, your parasympathetic system works to aid digestion, at the same time decreasing heart rate and blood flow to the

back out to the muscles and glands. The interrelationship of the central and peripheral nervous systems is shown in Figure 3.2.

The peripheral nervous system can be further subdivided into the somatic and the autonomic divisions. The **somatic nervous system** controls the skeletal muscles—that is, the muscles that move the bones. When you raise an arm or wriggle a toe, you are using

Figure 3.3 Diagram of the relationship among the parts of the nervous system.

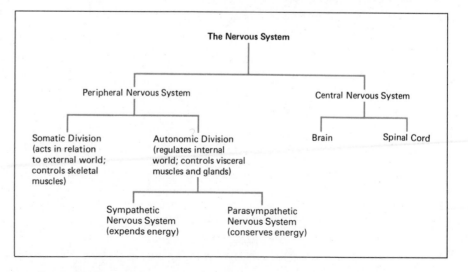

The Nervous System

Peripheral Nervous System

Central Nervous System

Somatic Division (acts in relation to external world; controls skeletal muscles)

Autonomic Division (regulates internal world; controls visceral muscles and glands)

Brain

Spinal Cord

Sympathetic Nervous System (expends energy)

Parasympathetic Nervous System (conserves energy)

skeletal muscles. The actions of the sympathetic and parasympathetic divisions, of course, do not always divide as neatly as these brief descriptions suggest. Often the effects of one influence the effects of the other. Thus, if you received distressing news while eating a meal, the sympathetic system would quickly exert itself, causing you to experience nausea and loss of appetite. Then, too, many behaviors require a combination of sympathetic and parasympathetic activity. Sexual arousal, for instance, is mediated by the parasympathetic division, but orgasm is a sympathetic response. A schematic diagram showing how the various parts of the nervous system are related is presented in Figure 3.3.

Neurons and Reflex Arcs

Neurons are the building blocks of the nervous system. All the tissues we call **nerves** are simply bundles of many neurons. These cells transmit messages in the form of electrochemical impulses from one part of the body to another. There are many billions of neurons in the human body, and even the simplest action, such as blinking your eyes, involves many thousands of neurons all working together.

The vast majority of neurons are located in the brain, with the rest distributed throughout the spinal cord and the peripheral nervous system. Although all

neurons appear to operate in much the same way, their sizes and shapes depend on their locations in the nervous system. Despite this variation, most neurons have three major regions: the **cell body,** which contains the cell nucleus and all the other life-sustaining systems of the cell, and two types of fibers that branch out from the cell body—the numerous and relatively short **dendrites** and the long **axon**—both of which are part of the neuron's communications equipment. (See Figure 3.4.)

Neurons are categorized according to the structures between which they conduct messages. As Figure 3.5 illustrates, **sensory neurons** carry information from the sense organs to the brain and spinal cord, while **motor neurons** carry signals from the brain and spinal cord to the muscles and glands. **Interneurons** connect neurons to other neurons and integrate the activities of the sensory and motor neurons. It is the relationships among interneurons that somehow become translated into thoughts, feelings, perceptions, and memories. In humans, interneurons are much more numerous than sensory and motor neurons. It has been estimated that for every motor neuron there are more than 4,000 interneurons.

Neurons share the central nervous system with tissue called **glia,** consisting of cells that are usually smaller than neurons but about ten times more numerous. *Glia* means "glue," and the word precisely describes one of the functions that the glial cells serve: they surround the neurons and hold them in place. In addition, the glial cells also appear to carry nutrients to the neurons, to remove their waste prod-

Figure 3.4 The major regions of a typical neuron.

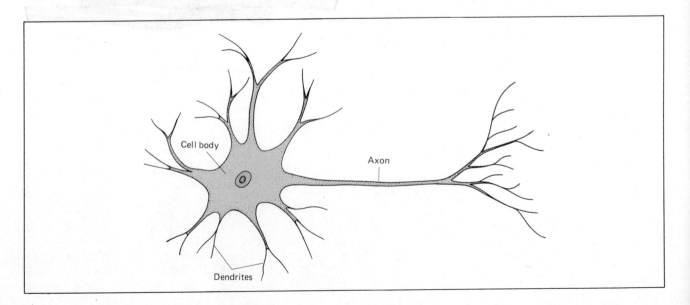

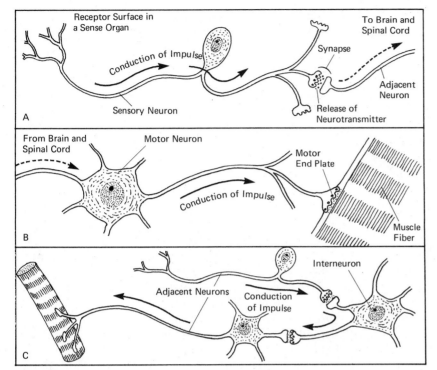

Figure 3.5 The three types of specialized neurons. (A) A sensory neuron. (B) A motor neuron. The motor end plate releases a neurotransmitter that can change the electrical state of the muscle it is connected to. (C) An interneuron. The interneurons either inhibit or excite the motor neurons that supply opposing muscles. Their action on the motor neurons is based on the input they receive from sensory neurons. For example, in order for the pain reflex to occur, the interneuron must receive information from a sensory neuron, which causes the interneuron to send inhibitory impulses to the connecting motor neuron. This motor neuron, in turn, inhibits the appropriate extensor muscle, thereby permitting withdrawal of the arm from a painful stimulus. (*Adapted from Williams and Warwick, 1975.*)

ucts, to repair damaged neurons, and to provide a barrier that protects the neurons from certain substances in the bloodstream. They may also play a role in the propagation of nerve impulses. The glia, then, is extremely important in enabling neurons to carry out their work. But the neurons themselves play the major role in behavior.

The cell body is the life-support center of the neuron and provides the energy for its activities. The dendrites, which can be thought of as the "antennae" of the neuron, have specialized areas for receiving messages transmitted by other neurons. (Parts of some cell bodies and axons have such specialized receiving areas as well.) Neural messages usually travel in only one direction: from the dendrites to the cell body and down the length of the axon, the cell's "outgoing message line." When the messages reach the end of the axon, they activate the muscle fibers, glandular cells, or other neurons with which the axon connects.

The simplest set of connections between neurons is the **reflex arc,** which links a sensory input to a motor response. Reflex arcs are located throughout the nervous system, but those that occur within the spinal cord, with no direct relay to the brain, have been the most systematically studied.

One well-known spinal reflex arc is the knee jerk, which is elicited by a tap on the tendon below the kneecap. It involves only two kinds of neurons: the sensory neurons that convey to the spinal cord information about stimulation of the tendon, and the motor neurons that stimulate the muscle groups in the thigh to contract, causing a kick. This two-neuron reflex arc is illustrated in part A of Figure 3.6. Most reflexes, however, are more complicated than the two-neuron knee jerk. Part B of Figure 3.6 diagrams a pain withdrawal reflex, which involves three kinds of neurons, the extra neurons in this chain being interneurons, which connect the other two kinds. When you pull back a foot after stepping on a thorn, for example, these interneurons also pass information to your other leg, prompting your body weight to shift automatically.

Although spinal reflexes can take place without control by the brain, this does not mean that the brain is uninvolved in them. The painful stimulation that triggers a withdrawal reflex, for instance, must travel to the brain in order to be experienced as pain. This trip takes time, so the subjective feeling of pain often takes place after we have begun to perform the reflexive response. You probably can recall an occasion when you touched a very hot object, withdrew your

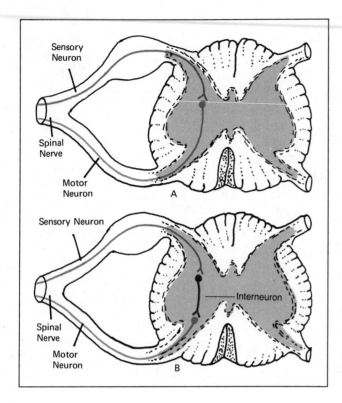

Figure 3.6 (A) A diagram of a two-neuron reflex arc, such as the one present in the knee-jerk reflex. This is the simplest form of reflex arc. (B) A diagram of a three-neuron reflex arc. The pain reflex, which causes a quick withdrawal from the painful stimulus, is an example of this type of reflex arc. It involves one set each of motor and sensory neurons (as in the two-neuron reflex arc), but in addition, an interneuron is present in the gray matter of the spinal cord. The extra neuron means that the information now crosses two synapses. (*Gardner, 1975.*)

hand, and only then became aware of the pain. The neurons that travel the length of the spinal cord and lead to and from the brain also permit some voluntary control over reflexes. You can demonstrate such control by having someone tap the tendon below your kneecap to elicit the knee-jerk reflex. Then have the person tap in the same place while you concentrate on preventing the response. The pathways that link the brain to the spinal cord should enable you to hold your leg steady.

You can appreciate the importance of these neural pathways by considering what happens to a paraplegic—a person whose spinal cord has been severed and hence cut off from its link to the brain. Paraplegics have no sensation in the lower part of their bodies, and they cannot move their legs voluntarily. Since the nerves in the spinal cord are not capable of regeneration, this condition is permanent. The reflexes controlled by the isolated spinal cord still operate, however, so a paraplegic continues to show the knee-jerk reflex if his or her leg is tapped. But unlike people with an intact spinal cord, paraplegics are not able consciously to prevent the knee jerk. Nor can they feel the leg kick. In fact, they would not even know that their leg had moved unless they were watching it.

A similar process occurs with sexual behavior, which can also be controlled reflexively by the spinal cord. If their genitals are directly stimulated, most male paraplegics are capable of erection and ejaculation, but they experience none of the local sensations that normally accompany these responses.

We have discussed spinal reflex arcs in some detail because they provide a relatively simple model of reflex action. But reflex systems are by no means confined to the spinal cord. They are present throughout the nervous system and are involved in a large number of complex behaviors. Even a seemingly simple reflex, such as dilation of the pupil of the eye, can be linked to many neural pathways. At the most basic level, pupil dilation is a reflex reaction to a sudden reduction of light. The dimmed lighting is sensed by receptor cells in the eye, and the message is routed through sensory neurons, interneurons, and motor neurons until it reaches the appropriate muscles in the iris (the colored portion of the eye that surrounds the pupil). This you may have already known. But did you know that pupil dilation is also triggered by emotional arousal, and by the performance of various mental activities that seem to have no emotional overtones?

These facts were confirmed by psychologist Eckhard Hess, who studied pupil response extensively (Hess, 1965). In many of his earliest experiments, Hess had subjects peer into a box that had a projection screen at the rear. A motion picture camera recorded the size of a subject's pupils while various slides were displayed. Hess found that pupils tend to dilate in response to pleasant or interesting visual stimuli (such as a nude of the opposite sex) and to constrict in response to unpleasant ones (such as a picture of a crippled child). People in many Eastern cultures apparently have recognized this pattern for centuries. A Chinese jade merchant will usually observe the dilation of customers' pupils to judge their interest in a particular stone and to estimate the price they might be willing to pay. This is one reason why they may stand at a closer conversational distance than most Westerners find comfortable: pupil response is difficult to scrutinize much beyond two feet (Hall, 1979).

The pupils also dilate extensively when people taste a food they particularly like or listen to a piece of music they find especially pleasing. Moreover, pupil dilation occurs in situations seemingly unrelated to pleasure. If you were asked to solve a mental arithmetic problem, for instance, your pupils would steadily enlarge while you were computing the answer and then rapidly constrict once you announced the solution. The maximum size your pupils reached would be closely correlated with the problem's difficulty. Such findings show how complex the circuitry of the human nervous system is and how even a seemingly simple reflex can be triggered by many nerve networks.

How Neural Signals Are Transmitted

The Role of Action Potentials. Although we have talked about reflex arcs at some length, we have not yet explained how the neurons involved in such systems actually transmit their messages. For many years scientists recognized that nerve signals were electrical in nature, but the details of neural activity remained a mystery until researchers had the technology to measure the responses of a single nerve cell. These measurements revealed that neural impulses are conducted by means of an electrochemical process. The fluids in the body contain ions—electrically charged molecules or atoms. The nerve cell membrane selectively regulates the passage of particular ions into and out of the cell. In its resting state, the membrane allows potassium (K^+) and chloride (Cl^-) ions to enter the cell, but excludes sodium (Na^+) ions. As a result, the cell becomes **polarized**—negatively charged inside and positively charged outside. This electrical imbalance across the cell membrane is known as the **resting potential.** If a stimulus affects the cell with enough intensity, the membrane temporarily becomes permeable to a sudden inrush of sodium ions, which causes the cell's polarity to change at the point of stimulation. For an instant the cell interior becomes positive and the exterior negative. This abrupt change, called the **action potential,** is conducted down the length of the axon much as a spark travels down a fuse. But the neuron, in contrast to a fuse, very quickly restores itself, and so is able to conduct a burst of many action potentials in rapid succession.

The velocity at which action potentials travel ranges from about 1 to 400 meters per second—that is, from about 2 to nearly 900 miles an hour. The exact speed depends on the properties of the various axons. One important property is the presence of the **myelin sheath,** a fatty whitish substance wrapped around an axon. (Myelinated axons form the **white matter** of the nervous system; nonmyelinated axons, dendrites, and cell bodies form the **gray matter.**) The sheath serves as insulation and thereby increases the speed at which neural impulses can travel by as much as five times the velocity along nonmyelinated structures. Because the myelin sheaths perform such a key function, it is not surprising that extensive damage to them severely hinders the workings of the nervous system. The disease called multiple sclerosis, for example, is caused by progressive destruction of myelin in the spinal cord and brain. The myelin is replaced by a hard, intermeshing plaque, and the axons that lie within it can no longer conduct nerve impulses. The results are lack of coordination and progressive loss of muscle control. Scientists do not yet know what initiates multiple sclerosis, but they suspect that a virus may be involved and that the destruction of the myelin may be a tragic side effect of the body's efforts to combat this invader (Morell and Norton, 1980).

How is a neural message coded in action potentials? The *nature* of a message is determined in large part by the particular pathway along which it travels. Stimulation of the visual nerves, for example, produces a visual sensation. When you close your eyelids and rub your eyes, you often stimulate your visual nerves and perceive splashes of color. Similarly, stimulation of the nerves leading from your tongue, nasal membranes, and inner ears produces the sensations of taste, smell, and hearing, respectively. The *strength* of a message is primarily conveyed by the axon's rate of firing: the more intense a stimulus, the higher the firing rate. Some neurons can generate as many as a thousand action potentials per second. Also, as stimuli increase in intensity, many more neurons fire.

The Role of Neurotransmitters. We have said that when action potentials reach the end of an axon they stimulate the muscle fibers, glandular cells, and other neurons with which that axon connects. But we have not yet explained how this communication is possible, given that every axon is physically separated from adjacent cells by tiny gaps called **synapses.** The answer lies in chemical substances known as **neurotransmitters,** which are stored at the terminals, or endings, of each axon. When action potentials reach an axon terminal, they stimulate the release of these neurotransmitters, which diffuse across the synapse and activate receptor sites on the adjacent cell.

Figure 3.7 illustrates this general process, although it cannot show several important details. First, a typical neuron has between 1,000 and 10,000 synaptic connections on its surface, not the two shown here (Stevens, 1979). Neuroscientists seldom venture a guess as to the total number of synapses in a human brain, but 100 *trillion* would not be out of the question (Hubel, 1979). Second, the receptor sites on a "receiving" neuron are activated because the molecular structure of the incoming neurotransmitter "fits" them, much as a key fits a lock. Different neurotransmitters have different molecular structures, so those that activate one group of receptors do not activate others. Different neurotransmitters also carry different messages. Some are *excitatory,* making nerve impulses more likely, while others are *inhibitory,* making nerve impulses less likely.

You might think that the nervous system could make do with just two transmitters, one to excite and one to inhibit. But this is not the case. In recent years scientists have isolated quite a number of neurotransmitters, and undoubtedly many more are still to be discovered. Some experts think there may be several hundred (Snyder, 1980). Why so many chemical transmitters? No one knows for sure. At this point, researchers are concerned primarily with identifying these substances, mapping the locations of their receptor sites, and discovering the behavioral processes in which they are involved. Table 3.1 summarizes some of their findings.

Consider acetylcholine, or ACh, one of the best understood of the neurotransmitters. It is found in various parts of the peripheral nervous system (especially the parasympathetic division), in the spinal cord, and in specific regions of the brain. In the peripheral nervous system it activates receptor sites embedded in both muscles and glands. For instance, ACh carries messages across the synapses between motor neurons and skeletal muscles, where it has an excitatory effect. Thus it is instrumental in making skeletal muscles contract.

Identification of the roles that neurotransmitters play at various receptor sites has provided important insights into the way certain drugs produce their effects. Curare, the poison that South American Indians use on their arrows, appears to occupy the receptor sites that ACh molecules normally activate and so prevents ACh from functioning. The result is complete paralysis. The lethal poison botulin, which develops in improperly preserved food, also causes paralysis through its effects on ACh synapses, but these effects are quite different from those of curare. Botulin appears to block the release of ACh from axon terminals. Interestingly, the venom of the black widow spider has the opposite effect: it causes a continuous flood of ACh into neuromuscular synapses. The result is violent and uncontrollable muscle contraction. In Chapter 12 we will explore the relationships between various neurotransmitters and the ef-

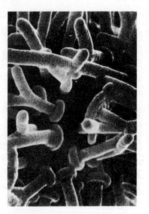

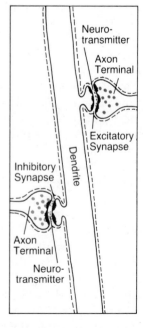

Figure 3.7 An electron micrograph and a diagram of the structures at the synapse. When an action potential reaches the end of the axon of a neuron, small amounts of neurotransmitter are released and diffuse across the synapse to activate the dendrites of another neuron. The substances from some neurons are excitatory in their effect, the substances from others are inhibitory.

TABLE 3.1 NEUROTRANSMITTERS

Transmitter	Location	Suspected Effects
Acetylcholine (ACh)	Brain, spinal cord, peripheral nervous system, especially the target organs of the parasympathetic nervous system	Deficiency: paralysis (curare and botulin poison); Alzheimer's disease Excess: violent muscle contraction (venom of black widow spider)
Norepinephrine (NE)	Brain, target organs of sympathetic nervous system	Deficiency; depression
Serotonin	Brain	Deficiency: depression
Dopamine (DA)	Brain	Deficiency: muscular rigidity and uncontrollable tremors (Parkinson's disease) Excess: symptoms of schizophrenia
Gamma-amino butyric acid (GABA)	Brain	Deficiency: mental deterioration (Huntington's chorea)
Enkephalins and endorphins	Brain, spinal cord	Fighting pain

fects of certain psychoactive drugs, such as mescaline, LSD, and amphetamines or "speed."

Scientists are compiling an ever-growing list of neurotransmitters, each associated with specific neural pathways, behavioral functions, and psychological states. Abnormalities in the activities of neurotransmitters have been implicated in many serious disorders. As you will see in Chapter 15, for instance, low levels of the neurotransmitters norepinephrine and serotonin seem to be related to depression, while overactivity of the neurotransmitter dopamine may be involved in the symptoms of schizophrenia. In fact, the drugs called phenothiazines, which are widely used to treat schizophrenia, are believed to inhibit the action of dopamine receptors in certain parts of the brain. In other brain regions, degeneration of dopamine-releasing neurons is related to the muscular rigidity and uncontrollable tremors of Parkinson's disease (Kety, 1979). Deficiencies of another neurotransmitter, called GABA for short, have been found in the brains of people afflicted with Huntington's chorea, a neurological disorder marked by total mental deterioration beginning in middle age (Iversen, 1979). And a form of senility that sometimes develops in the elderly, called Alzheimer's disease, has also been linked to deficits of a neurotransmitter, in this case acetylcholine. Neurons that normally release acetylcholine in a particular brain center undergo massive degeneration in severely senile patients (Whitehouse et al., 1982).

Such insights provide important clues to possible treatments for these and other disabling, even fatal disorders. For instance, a major breakthrough in the treatment of Parkinson's disease has recently emerged from the knowledge that this disorder is linked to deficiencies in the neurotransmitter dopamine. Although dopamine molecules are too large to cross the membrane barrier separating brain tissue from the bloodstream, a substance from which dopamine is constructed, called L-dopa, *can* diffuse from the blood into the brain. So doctors are now treating Parkinson's disease by administering large doses of L-dopa, with very impressive results (Kety, 1979). Even more dramatic is the fact that very recently doctors have actually implanted healthy dopamine-producing tissue in the brain of a man suffering from acute Parkinson's disease. Although it is too early to evaluate this pioneering experiment fully, the man's condition seems to have improved somewhat. Researchers have hopes that in another five to ten years, such brain implants may become an accepted part of medical practice. In work with laboratory animals, scientists have already had some success correcting neurotransmitter-related disorders—from memory loss to hyperactivity to lack of muscular control—by means of brain grafts that produce the deficient chemical (Kolata, 1982).

The number of substances suspected of being neurotransmitters has increased greatly in recent years with the discovery of a whole new class of brain chemicals called **neuropeptides.** Many of these chemicals were first identified as hormones elsewhere in the body, serving a variety of functions unrelated to nerve cell communication. Among the newest and most fascinating of the neuropeptides are the **enkephalins** and **endorphins.** These chemicals, which occur naturally within the central nervous system, bear a striking resemblance in molecular structure to morphine and other opium-based narcotics. (The term *endorphin* is simply a contraction of "endogenous morphine," a morphine made in the body.) Opiates, in fact, bind to the same neural receptor sites to which enkephalins and endorphins bind; this is how opiates have their pain-killing effects (Snyder,

1980). Apparently the enkephalins serve as our bodies' natural pain fighters, among several other suspected functions. When exposed to painful stimuli, such as electric shocks, we produce increased amounts of them (Bolles and Fanselow, 1982). There is now evidence that certain substances and procedures whose effectiveness as pain relievers was previously unexplained, such as placebos and acupuncture, may work by triggering release of these chemicals into the nervous system (Fields, 1978). It has even been speculated that the pain caused by running may stimulate the flow of endorphins and thereby produce the feeling of euphoria commonly called the "runner's high." Some researchers have thought that the pain relief sometimes obtained through hypnosis may also be mediated by these opiate-like chemicals. But recent studies suggest that some other natural pain-regulating system, still to be identified, is probably involved instead (Watkins and Mayer, 1982). Thus we have much more to learn about the way our bodies sense and cope with pain. The more we discover about the roles that neurotransmitters play in this and other processes, the more incredibly intricate the human nervous system seems.

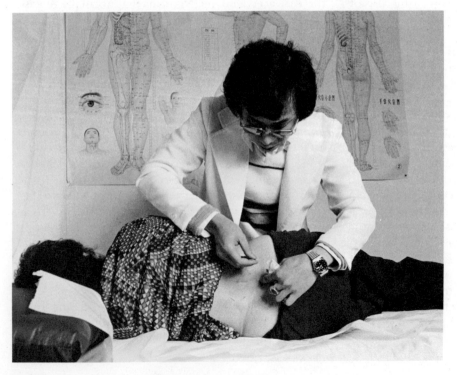

Acupuncture is an ancient Chinese method of anesthesia. When needles are inserted into the skin at specific sites identified in charts like the ones shown here, pain is relieved in certain other parts of the body. It is believed that acupuncture stimulates release of the body's own pain-relieving chemicals. (*Charles Kennard/Stock, Boston.*)

THE ENDOCRINE SYSTEM

The complex network of billions of cells that makes up the nervous system enables the human body to respond to a vast range of situational demands. And the speed with which it does so is remarkable. Because a nerve impulse can travel through the body in a mere thousandth of a second, we can pull back a hand from a hot surface almost instantaneously. Not all situations necessitate such quick responses, however. For those in which speed is not so crucial, such as sexual arousal and physical growth, the endocrine system provides a more economical and comprehensive means of internal communication.

The endocrine system is a chemical communications network: its messengers are chemical substances called **hormones,** which are produced by the **endocrine glands** and secreted into the bloodstream. (See Figure 3.8.) Although these hormones circulate throughout the body, each has its effects only at specific **target organs.** Hormone action, in other words, is highly selective.

Do not make the mistake of thinking that the endocrine system is completely divorced from the nervous system. The two are constantly interacting, and their effects are closely coordinated. In fact, some of the substances originally identified as hormones (such as norepinephrine) are now known to be, or suspected of being, neurotransmitters as well. The process of evolution is apparently very opportunistic. A substance that serves one function in a certain physiological system may later be adapted to a different function in yet another system (Iversen, 1979).

Probably the most influential gland in the human body is the **pituitary,** a structure only about half an inch (a little more than a centimeter) in diameter, which lies at the base of the brain just below a region called the hypothalamus. Despite its small size, the pituitary controls a wide range of body functions. Consequently, it has often been called the "master gland."

The pituitary is divided into two distinct lobes, the anterior and the posterior. The posterior lobe, which is attached directly to the hypothalamus by a small stalk, releases two hormones. One stimulates muscular contraction in the uterus (and so is involved in both female orgasm and childbirth) as well as the release of milk from the mammary glands. The other acts to decrease the amount of water that the kidneys excrete. The anterior pituitary lobe produces at least six hormones. Of particular importance is **growth hormone,** which plays a key role in a child's physical development. If a severe deficit of growth hormone occurs during childhood, a person will become a midget. If, in contrast, an excess of growth hormone is produced at an early age, a child will become a giant. Some pituitary giants have grown to heights of nearly nine feet. When such glandular oversecretion begins in adulthood, a person does not suddenly resume growing, for only a few adult tissues are sensitive to growth hormone—namely, the bones of the face, fingers, and toes. Thus adults with excessive output of growth hormone develop a condition called acromegaly, in which the hands, feet, and facial features become grossly enlarged and distorted. In addition to growth hormone and another hormone that stimulates the production of milk in females, the anterior pituitary secretes four hormones that regulate the output of other endocrine glands. One affects the thyroid gland; another affects the cortex of the adrenal glands; and two affect the output of the sex glands, or gonads.

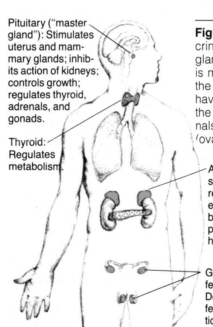

Pituitary ("master gland"): Stimulates uterus and mammary glands; inhibits action of kidneys; controls growth; regulates thyroid, adrenals, and gonads.

Thyroid: Regulates metabolism.

Figure 3.8 The endocrine glands. The glands whose activity is most important in the regulation of behavior are the pituitary, the thyroid, the adrenals, and the gonads (ovaries or testes).

Adrenals: Active in stress reaction; help regulate water and mineral concentrations and blood sugar supply; produce some sex hormones.

Gonads (ovaries in female, testes in male): Develop male and female sex characteristics; maintain reproductive organs.

Giantism is the result of the pituitary gland's overproduction of growth hormone in childhood. This sixteen-year-old Chinese girl, Zing Qin Lian, is believed to be the tallest female in the world. She is 7 feet 10½ inches tall and weighs 324 pounds. Her normal-sized sister and mother must help her walk because her legs cannot support the weight of her torso. (*Liu Heung Sh'ing 1980/Contact Press Images.*)

The **thyroid gland** is located in the neck, on either side of the windpipe and esophagus (the tube that carries food to the stomach). Under the influence of the thyroid-stimulating hormone that the pituitary secretes, the thyroid produces several hormones of its own. One of these hormones is **thyroxin,** which plays an important role in regulating the body's metabolism. Too much thyroxin speeds up metabolism and leads to a condition called hyperthyroidism. The victim suffers from weight loss, an elevated body temperature, profuse sweating, intense thirst, accelerated heart rate, general excitability, and often difficulty in sleeping. The opposite disorder—too little thyroxin, or hypothyroidism—slows metabolism and creates a range of related symptoms including obesity, a slowed heartbeat, lowered body temperature, re-

duced sweat gland activity, physical lethargy, and lack of mental alertness. Hypothyroidism can have far more devastating effects in infants. If untreated in newborns, it leads to a condition called cretinism, which is characterized by severely retarded mental and physical development.

The **adrenals** are a pair of glands that lie just above the kidneys. Each adrenal actually consists of two glands, an inner region called the medulla and an outer region called the cortex. The adrenal medulla produces the hormones **epinephrine** and **norepinephrine** (also called adrenalin and noradrenalin). They play a role in the body's reaction to stress. Suppose you are severely frightened or subjected to intense pain. The outpouring of epinephrine from your adrenal medulla increases your heartbeat and blood pressure, releases more sugar into your bloodstream, accelerates your rate of breathing, and increases the flow of blood to your skeletal muscles, among other things. (Norepinephrine has very similar effects.) These changes help prepare you to deal with the threat you face. You may have noticed that these responses closely parallel those produced by activation of the sympathetic nervous system. When the body's resources must be mobilized in emergency situations, the activities of the nervous system and the endocrine system greatly overlap.

The other portion of the adrenal glands, the adrenal cortex, is probably the most diversified hormone factory in the body. It produces at least fifty hormone-like chemicals, and perhaps many others that scientists have not yet identified. Some of these chemicals help regulate the supply of sugar in the blood; others help regulate the relative concentrations of minerals and water in the body; still others act as sex hormones, chiefly the male hormones, called **androgens.** Gross overproduction of adrenal androgens in women can promote the growth of facial and chest hair, a deepening of the voice, and the development of muscular arms and legs.

The final set of endocrine glands we will consider are the sex glands, or **gonads.** These glands secrete hormones very similar in structure and function to the sex hormones that the adrenal cortex produces, although in much larger amounts. The female gonads, or ovaries, are located on either side of the uterus. They secrete the hormones **estrogen** and **progesterone,** which are involved in the development of female secondary sex characteristics at puberty as well as in the onset of the menstrual cycle. The male gonads, or testes, are located in the scrotal sac. The testes secrete the hormone **testosterone,** which is involved in, among other things, the development of male sex characteristics and the regulation of sperm production.

Some research suggests that the higher levels of testosterone and other androgens in males than in females may contribute to the generally higher level of aggression commonly displayed by males. When researchers injected pregnant monkeys with testosterone, they found that the female offspring were more inclined than normal young females to engage in aggressive, rough-and-tumble play (Young, Goy, and Phoenix, 1964). Similarly, a study of young girls who had been exposed to high levels of male sex hormones before birth (often as a result of abnormal functioning of their adrenal glands) revealed that they, too, exhibited more "masculine" behavior. They preferred active outdoor sports to quiet indoor activities, usually chose boys as playmates, and picked fights somewhat more frequently than hormonally normal girls (Ehrhardt and Baker, 1973). From these and similar findings, some psychologists suspect that the sex hormones present before birth may influence a person's readiness to respond aggressively to certain situations later in life (Maccoby and Jacklin, 1974).

One must be very cautious in drawing such inferences from these kinds of studies, however. Female monkeys exposed to testosterone before birth look quite unusual, because the testosterone has stimulated development of malelike external genitals. So their appearance may elicit certain responses from other monkeys, which in turn shape their behavior (Lips, 1978). Similarly, it is hard to separate the effects of girls' early hormonal excesses from their learning experiences after birth. Such girls also are born with "masculinized" external genitals, which have to be surgically corrected, and most receive lifelong hormone therapy to counteract the effects of their malfunctioning adrenal glands. They and their parents are therefore constantly reminded that they are different from other girls. Might not this fact affect the way the girls are raised and the way they come to think of themselves? This is a limitation of such quasi-experimental research, which we talked about in Chapter 2. It is sometimes difficult to rule out all the other factors that may be causing the results. We will say more about the challenge of explaining observed differences in the behaviors of men and women when we discuss human development in detail later in this book.

Speculation that a link exists between prenatal androgens and a readiness to respond aggressively in certain situations underscores the close connection between the endocrine and nervous systems. Researchers who adopt this view are proposing that the presence of testosterone in the bloodstream of a human embryo affects the way that neural pathways in the brain develop. Whether this is true or not, the fact remains that an intricate interaction does exist between the workings of our endocrine glands and our nervous system. In fact, the region of the brain called the hypothalamus is itself a source of hormones. The hormones of the posterior pituitary are all produced in the hypothalamus, with the posterior pituitary simply serving as a storehouse and distribution center. In addition, the hypothalamus secretes into the bloodstream substances that trigger release of anterior pituitary hormones, which in turn regulate the output of other endocrine glands. And the influence between the nervous and endocrine systems works in the opposite direction as well: the hormones that the endocrine glands secrete affect neural activity, including secretions from the hypothalamus. Thus the communication networks of the human body are intimately interconnected, with the brain having the ultimate task of maintaining equilibrium. The brain, in short, is the body's master control center. We will spend the rest of this chapter exploring it.

MASTER CONTROL CENTER: THE BRAIN

The brain is a voracious energy consumer. Although its mere three pounds contribute only about 2 percent to total body weight, it uses a full 20 percent of all the energy-sustaining oxygen that is not exhaled. (In fact, when the vital flow of oxygen to the brain is temporarily reduced, we quickly feel faint and may lose consciousness.) This enormous consumption of energy is necessary for the brain to carry out its work. The brain is the ultimate regulator of everything we do. Our abilities to walk, talk, eat, sleep, dream, think, plan, and remember all arise from its elaborate operations.

The human brain is composed of numerous substructures with interrelated functions. The brain can generally be described, however, as consisting of three overlapping regions: the central core, the limbic system, and the cerebral hemispheres and cortex. Each of these regions represents a stage in the brain's long evolution.

The Central Core

The central core of the human brain is sometimes called the "old brain," because in appearance and function it is highly similar to the brains of more primitive animals. In fact, the central core of the brain varies little among vertebrates, or animals that have backbones. The central core includes several structures that together carry out the functions most basic to survival, such as sleeping and waking, respiration, and feeding. The structures that make up the central core of the brain are shown in Figure 3.9.

They include the brainstem, the cerebellum, the thalamus, and the hypothalamus.

The Brainstem. As the spinal cord enters the skull, it swells and forms a knobby extension known as the **brainstem.** The first structure of the brainstem is the **medulla.** The medulla plays a critical role in many autonomic activities, such as circulation and breathing, and it is also involved in chewing, salivation, and facial movements. Above and extending forward from the medulla is the **pons** (meaning "bridge"), which connects the two halves of the cerebellum lying above it. The pons transmits motor information from the higher brain areas and the spinal cord to the cerebellum, and it is vital in integrating movements between the right and left sides of the body.

In the upper portion of the brainstem is a small structure called the **midbrain.** All neural information passing back and forth between the brain and the spinal cord must pass through the midbrain. The midbrain contains important centers for visual and auditory reflexes. The "startle" reflex to sudden intense stimuli, for example, is controlled by the midbrain. In

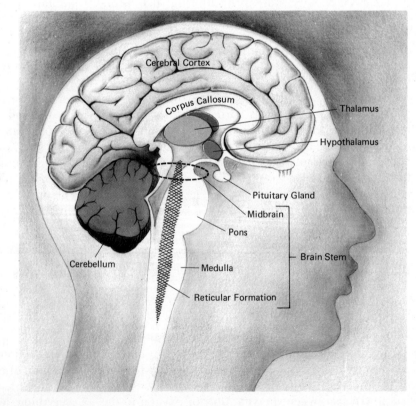

Figure 3.9 The structures composing the central core of the brain. (This illustration shows the right hemisphere of the brain as it would appear if the head were sliced exactly in half from front to back.) The structures represented in this figure are the first to receive incoming information, and they regulate the most fundamental processes of the body. The reticular formation, which controls the most general responses of the brain to sensory input, is located in the area that connects the brain to the spinal cord and to the rest of the nervous system. The thalamus has a central location in the brain, and the hypothalamus is attached to the pituitary gland, which controls the activity of the other endocrine glands. A few brain structures that evolved more recently than the central core are also shown here. Note particularly the corpus callosum, the large band of nerve fibers that connects the two hemispheres of the cerebral cortex.

species whose auditory and visual reflexes are essential to survival, these areas of the midbrain are relatively large. Birds that sight, track, and capture prey in flight, for instance, have very prominent and bulging visual areas in the midbrain. In contrast, bats, which use sound rather than sight to locate their prey, have small visual midbrain areas but very prominent auditory ones.

The midbrain contains a part of the **reticular formation,** a complex network of crisscrossing neural fibers and cell bodies that extends from the spinal cord up through the core of the brainstem into the thalamus. It appears to function as a sentry system, arousing the higher brain when information related to survival must be processed and permitting periods of sustained attention. The reticular formation also appears to help screen extraneous sensory input, especially during sleep. Damage to the reticular formation usually disrupts the natural sleep-waking cycle and can even result in an almost permanent coma-like state of sleep (Magoun, 1963).

The Cerebellum.

To the rear of the brainstem and slightly above the medulla is the **cerebellum.** This name, which means "little brain," derives from the fact that the cerebellum is divided into two hemispheres and so looks like a miniature version of the higher brain. The cerebellum's chief function is to coordinate voluntary movement of the skeletal muscles and to regulate physical balance. Motor commands that originate in the higher brain are processed by the cerebellum before being transmitted to the muscles. At the same time, the cerebellum receives continuous information from the muscles about their tension and position. The cerebellum reconciles any differences in these messages to produce a smooth and balanced motor response (Eccles et al., 1967). Damage to the cerebellum may cause ataxia, a condition characterized by drunken movements, severe tremors, and a lack of balance. A person who has ataxia lacks the control needed for even simple reaching movements. He or she may accidentally hit a friend in the stomach while trying to reach out and shake the friend's hand.

The Thalamus.

At the top of the brainstem and deeply embedded within the central mass of the cerebral hemispheres is a pair of connected egg-shaped structures collectively called the **thalamus.** The word *thalamus* comes from the Greek word for inner chamber: the thalamus forms part of the walls of a small central cavity in the brain. Early brain anatomists believed that all brain processes emanated from the clear fluid that fills this central inner chamber. Unfortunately, they mistakenly emphasized the cavity (or ventricle) rather than its walls (the thalamus) as being of special interest in understanding human behavior.

The thalamus is a crucial link between the cerebral hemispheres and the sense organs. It acts partly as a relay station, sorting information from the sensory receptors and routing it to appropriate areas of the higher brain. In addition, the thalamus interrelates information coming from various areas of the cerebral hemispheres, processes that information, and sends it to the cerebellum and medulla. Thus it performs a major integrative role in connecting one area of the brain to another.

The Hypothalamus.

The **hypothalamus** is a small structure (about as big as the tip of your index finger) located just below the thalamus. It is an important center for regulating the body's internal environment, as we mentioned in our discussion of the endocrine system. The hypothalamus monitors internal changes and initiates appropriate responses to maintain balance within the body. It performs these functions in two ways. First, it sends electrochemical signals to the entire autonomic nervous system, triggering the sympathetic or the parasympathetic division into action. Second, through release of hormones it directly influences the pituitary gland, which in turn regulates the functioning of other endocrine glands. The behaviors most profoundly influenced by the hypothalamus are those related to basic survival: feeding, sexual function, internal temperature regulation, and emotional and physiological responses to stress.

An example of the hypothalamus' internal regulatory function is the control of body temperature. When a warm-blooded animal is exposed to cold, signals from the hypothalamus cause the blood vessels in the skin to contract, reducing heat loss from the surface of the body. Other hypothalamic signals instruct the pituitary gland to produce a thyroid-stimulating hormone, which activates the thyroid gland to produce the hormone thyroxin. Thyroxin, in turn, causes a general increase in body metabolism so that more heat is produced to compensate for the external cold. At higher levels, thyroxin induces the shivering response in the skeletal muscles, causing even more heat production. Conversely, when a warm-blooded animal is exposed to a hot environment, the hypothalamus mobilizes the body to cool itself by dilating the blood vessels in the skin, by sweating, and by reducing the metabolic rate. Thus certain areas of the hypothalamus act as a kind of thermostat to maintain optimal body temperature. Other hypothalamic areas play similar roles in controlling many other bodily functions. You will learn about the involvement of the hypothalamus in the regulation of hunger in Chapter 11, on motivation.

The Limbic System

Above the central core lies the **limbic system,** so named because it forms the innermost border of the cerebral hemispheres (*limbic* means "bordering"). The limbic system contains several highly interrelated structures, among them the **hippocampus,** the **amygdala,** and the **septal area.** These structures form a loop around the top of the central core and are closely connected with the hypothalamus and the inner surface of the cerebral cortex. Figure 3.10 shows the structure of the limbic system.

The limbic system has also been called the "nose brain," because its original function was presumably to analyze olfactory information and so allow an animal to identify food and potential mates and to avoid predators. It also appears to be closely involved with behaviors that satisfy certain motivational and emotional needs, such as feeding, fighting, fleeing, and mating (MacLean, 1958). Damage to various parts of the limbic system, for example, can produce gross changes in aggressiveness. Such ordinarily intractable wild animals as the lynx have become very tame following certain types of limbic system damage. Conversely, such tame animals as domestic cats have become quite savage after sustaining other kinds of limbic system injury. Disruption of the limbic system can also produce marked changes in sexual and feeding behavior (Klüver and Bucy, 1939). Each of these classes of behavior has emotional components, and each involves a choice as to whether to approach or avoid things. The limbic system seems to provide one basis for making such approach-avoidance decisions.

In 1954 James Olds and Peter Milner accidentally discovered that rats will quickly learn to press a lever in order to receive mild electrical stimulation in certain parts of the limbic system. The pleasure apparently provided by stimulation of these regions seems to be intense. A hungry rat hurrying to the feeding tray will stop in its tracks to receive such stimulation, and it will remain in the same spot as long as the stimulation continues, even when food is only inches away. When allowed to stimulate their own limbic system pleasure centers by pressing a bar that connects the current, rats have been known to press frenetically thousands of times an hour, until they collapse in exhaustion. What could the nature of such intense pleasure be? Humans who have undergone pleasure-center stimulation (usually during treatment of some neurological disorder) report that they experience a rush of extremely "good" feelings, feelings that some have compared with the buildup to an orgasm. Exactly how stimulation of these pleasure centers is related to such behaviors as feeding and mating, which are also influenced by the limbic system, is still largely unknown.

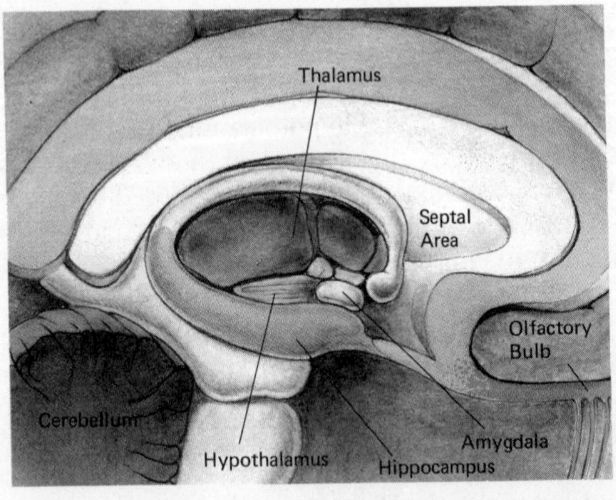

Figure 3.10 A schematic diagram of the limbic system. Structures within this system play a significant role in a variety of emotional behaviors. Damage to various regions of the limbic system may cause wild animals to become tame or tame animals to become vicious. Other limbic lesions may radically alter sexual and feeding behavior. The olfactory bulb (responsible for the sense of smell) is closely associated with other limbic structures, suggesting the importance of this sense to several limbic system functions.

The Cerebral Hemispheres and Cortex

The **cerebral hemispheres** are the two large structures that lie above the brain's central core, one on the left side, the other on the right. Because of their prominence, most people think of them as "the brain." The cerebral hemispheres constitute about 85 percent of the human brain's total weight, and they are involved in the processes of learning, speech, reasoning, and memory, so important to human behavior.

In addition to including much of the limbic system, which we have already discussed, the cerebral hemispheres are surrounded by a thin layer of gray matter called the **cortex** (the term means "bark" or "outer covering"). The cortex is the most recent evolutionary development of the nervous system. It is only about two millimeters (one-twelfth of an inch) thick, but it has so many convolutions that it accommodates more than 9 billion neurons. If the human cortex were flattened out, its area would be about 2.5 square feet.

The external surface of the cortex has certain characteristic "landmarks." The most prominent are the two deep fissures that subdivide each hemisphere

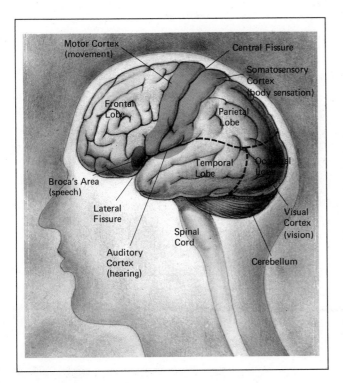

into its principal areas, or lobes. As Figure 3.11 shows, the **central fissure** separates the frontal lobe from the parietal lobe, while the **lateral fissure** marks the top boundary of the temporal lobe. Demarcations between the occipital lobe and its neighboring lobes are much less distinct.

As the name implies, the **frontal lobe** is located at the front of each hemisphere. The area of this lobe next to the central fissure is concerned primarily with the regulation of voluntary movements and so is called the **motor cortex.** An area of the left frontal lobe is involved in the use of language. In 1861 the French physician Paul Broca discovered that damage to this part of the left hemisphere affected the ability to speak. Broca's discovery was one of the first indications that different parts of the brain might be involved in different types of behavior—that is, that the brain might show some **localization of function.** Some early brain anatomists believed that the prefrontal area of the frontal lobe (the area to the left of the motor cortex in Figure 3.11) was the repository of intellectual ability. Most modern researchers reject this notion, however, for some people perform just as well on intelligence tests after massive amounts of prefrontal tissue have been removed. The behavioral defects resulting from damage to the prefrontal area, it now appears, include the abilities to order stimuli, sort out information, and maintain attention to a particular task in the face of distraction, but not the kind of intellectual abilities measured by IQ tests (Milner, 1964).

The **parietal lobe** contains the so-called **somatosensory cortex,** the primary receiving area for the skin senses and for the sense of body position. Damage to the somatosensory cortex generally impairs the sense of touch. Damage to parts of the parietal lobe on the right hemisphere disrupts spatial organization and may distort perception of personal body image.

The areas of auditory reception are located in the **temporal lobe** of each hemisphere, as are certain areas for the processing of visual information. In a series of studies with epileptic patients who underwent brain surgery, Canadian neurosurgeons Wilder

Figure 3.11 An external view of the left hemisphere of the cerebral cortex. The diagram shows the two major fissures, the four lobes, and several other cortical regions whose functions are relatively well known.

Penfield and Theodore Rasmussen (1950) elicited some dramatic responses by applying electrical stimulation to certain points on the temporal lobe during the operation. At some locations stimulation caused complex auditory or visual hallucinations. At others it seemed to reactivate past sensations with such vividness that the patients felt as though they were reliving the experience rather than merely remembering it. One woman heard a familiar song so clearly that she thought a record was being played in the operating room. More will be said about Penfield's work later in this chapter.

The **occipital lobe,** located at the back of each hemisphere, is particularly concerned with the reception and analysis of visual information. Sensory receptors in the eye transmit their information to the occipital lobe via the optic nerve and thalamus. In humans, injury to this portion of the cortex can produce blind spots in the visual field.

This brief review of the brain's principal lobes suggests that physiological psychologists have had the greatest success in identifying cortical regions with motor and sensory functions. The motor cortex and the somatosensory cortex, for example, are extremely well defined, and their organizations have been quite precisely mapped. (See Figure 3.12.) This mapping reveals that the amount of cortex concerned with movement or touch in a particular body part depends not on the size of that part but rather on its degree of motor control or sensitivity to stimulation. The fingers, for example, which can make very precise movements, have much larger representation in the motor cortex than does the trunk of the body. Similarly, the lips, which can also make fine movements and are extremely sensitive to touch, have a very large representation in the somatosensory cortex. It is interesting that these two areas are related to the two behavioral capacities that best distinguish humans from other animals—the use of tools and speech. In marked contrast to the precision with which researchers have defined the brain's motor and sensory areas, no locations have yet been found to be associated exclusively with learning, memory, and intelligence. About three-quarters of the cortex, however, is *not* devoted to a motor or sensory function. Undoubtedly these areas, called the **association cortex,** participate in more abstract mental processes. As we will see in the concluding section of this chapter, learning and remembering appear to involve cells in many parts of the cortex.

Figure 3.12 (A) A diagram representing the location and amount of cortical space devoted to the motor capacities of various body parts. Areas of the body capable of the most complex and precise movements take up the largest quantities of space in the motor cortex. For example, the eyelid and eyeball (capable of many precise movements), have a larger representation than the face. (B) A diagram representing the location and amount of cortical space devoted to the sensory capacities of various body parts. In the sensory realm, those organs capable of the highest sensitivity have the largest representations in the somatosensory cortex. (Penfield and Rasmussen, 1950.)

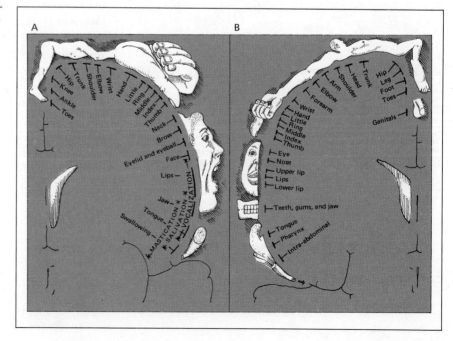

STUDYING BRAIN–BEHAVIOR RELATIONSHIPS

We have said a great deal about the fact that different parts of the brain are involved in different kinds of behavior. But we have not yet explained in any detail how these relationships were discovered. Exactly how have scientists managed to learn what they now know about the complex workings of the brain?

Research Methods

Over the years, investigators have developed a variety of research methods. Some have observed brain-damaged people or people who have undergone neurosurgery, and made inferences accordingly. Others have manipulated the brains of laboratory animals and traced the resulting effects. Still others have employed sophisticated electronics to eavesdrop on the brain's electrical activity. And some are now using chemical and other types of labeling techniques to map the brain's pathways quite precisely.

Clinical Observations. The oldest method of mapping the brain involves careful observation of behavioral deficits in people with localized brain damage due to head injuries, tumors, or strokes (the blockage or rupturing of blood vessels on the brain's surface, which cuts off the supply of oxygen and nutrients to that area). Nineteenth-century medical practitioners noticed, for instance, that damage to certain brain areas typically caused very specific disorders— blindness, deafness, paralysis of a certain body part, speech difficulties, and so forth—depending on the brain region involved. The theories of brain organization developed from these early insights helped to guide later research on brain–behavior relationships.

And the usefulness of clinical findings has certainly not ended. Brain-damaged patients continue to provide clues about the organization of our mental processes. Some of the most fascinating things about these clues are the surprises that they bring. Sometimes pieces of information that you would think would be processed through exactly the same neural pathways turn out to be processed through significantly different routes. People with extensive damage to the un- dersides of both occipital lobes, for example, are often afflicted with the inability to identify familiar faces. Even when shown pictures of their own family members, they simply cannot say who they are. Yet the same people can identify pictures of animals or objects with virtually no hesitation or error (Geschwind, 1979). Equally surprising is the person with brain damage to the left hemisphere who has completely lost the ability to read words (a condition called alexia) but retains the ability to read numbers. Such a person might be able to interpret the symbols MIX as meaning 1,009 in Roman numerals, yet be totally unable to see them as an English word (Gardner, 1975). Similarly, Oriental patients with pure alexia can sometimes read ideographs (characters that represent an entire idea or object) even though they cannot read words in which letters are used to represent speech sounds (Gardner, 1982). Such unexpected clinical findings remind us that, ironically, the logic of the human brain's organization does not necessarily conform to the logic of the human minds that analyze it.

Brain Stimulation. Because neural activity is electrochemical, it can be induced by tiny amounts of electrical stimulation applied to nerve tissue. Scientists have taken advantage of this fact in their efforts to explore the brain. Some of these efforts have been part of attempts to cure neurological disorders. Neurosurgeon Wilder Penfield, for example, whose work we mentioned earlier (Penfield and Rasmussen, 1950), used electrical stimulation quite successfully to locate the sites of focal epilepsy. Focal epilepsy is a disease in which a small abnormal area of the brain periodically irritates surrounding tissues until nerve cells fire uncontrollably. The result is an epileptic seizure. In severe cases of focal epilepsy, doctors sometimes recommend surgical removal of the diseased area. But how can this area be found? Penfield's approach, innovative for its time, was to apply a weak electrical current to various portions of the brain and to ask the unanesthetized patient what sensations were being produced. If the person experienced the precise feelings he or she always experienced just before a seizure, Penfield knew that he had probably located the focal region.

Over the course of many operations, Penfield kept careful records of the particular points on the brain that evoked particular responses. Stimulation of the part of the frontal lobe next to the central fissure, for example, produced muscle movements on the opposite side of the body, whereas stimulation of areas in the left hemisphere either caused people to emit sounds or prevented them from speaking. Stimulation of the somatosensory cortex caused patients to claim that they had been touched somewhere on the body, the exact location corresponding to a specific location in the brain. The most intriguing aspect of Penfield's work was his claim that stimulation of certain points on the temporal lobe seemed to evoke remarkably vivid memories, sometimes apparently dredged from the very distant past. Whether the temporal lobe is indeed a storehouse of past events remains open to question, however. Penfield's patients were epileptics whose brains were in certain respects abnormal. This fact raises some doubt about the extent to which his findings can be generalized. In addition, Penfield never investigated each patient's history to check the accuracy of the memories he or she claimed to retrieve. We will say more about this criticism of Penfield's results in Chapter 6, which deals with memory.

Penfield's efforts to map the brain were largely incidental to his primary goal, locating diseased tissue. Brain stimulation has also been used on laboratory animals, however, for the sole purpose of identifying the brain's control centers. In the laboratory, researchers have used both electrical and chemical techniques. When chemicals are employed, the investigator implants a small hypodermic needle into an animal's brain so that the tip touches the area to be manipulated. Then the researcher delivers a tiny amount of a chemical through the needle. This approach has generated many interesting findings. Various chemicals applied to the hypothalamus, for example, have been shown to affect feeding and drinking (Grossman, 1960), and sexual behavior can be stimulated or inhibited by minute amounts of specific hormones applied to hypothalamic regions (Fisher, 1956). Since the brains of the animals used in such research are organized very similarly to the human brain, information gleaned in this way is often directly relevant to human functioning.

In addition to their enormous value in charting the brain, electrical and chemical stimulation techniques are providing new means of treating certain medical disorders. An electrical current delivered through electrodes implanted in specific areas of the brain, for example, seems to provide temporary relief from pain. Consequently, electrical stimulation is now sometimes used to relieve the intolerable pain experienced by patients who have terminal cancer and other serious illnesses. It is believed that the pain relief obtained in this manner may be linked to release of the body's own natural pain-killing brain chemicals, the endorphins, which we talked about earlier. In some cases, electrodes implanted in the brain are activated by the patients themselves. This approach has been used to help control narcolepsy, a disorder in which a wide-awake person suddenly loses all muscular control and lapses into sleep. Narcoleptic patients being treated in this way push the button of a self-stimulator attached to an appropriate area of the brain whenever they feel an attack coming on. Undoubtedly the most controversial application of brain stimulation is its use with mental patients. A number of psychiatrists have turned to brain stimulation to reduce violent aggression in patients for whom no other method of restraint has been successful. This application has raised substantial concern among people who fear the potential abuse of brain stimulation as a method of mind control (Valenstein, 1973).

Brain Lesions. Like brain-stimulation techniques, brain-lesion techniques are used to determine which of an organism's behaviors a particular brain region is involved in. A **lesion** is produced in laboratory animals by surgical destruction or removal of a small area of the brain. After the surgery, the researchers carefully assess changes or deficits in the animal's behavior. The results of brain stimulation procedures and lesion procedures are related. In general, if electrical stimulation of a certain area *increases* a certain type of behavior, lesions in that area will *decrease* the behavior. Conversely, if stimulation tends to block a behavior when it is normally appropriate, lesions may cause the behavior to occur more vigorously.

Brain lesion and stimulation techniques have been used together to increase our understanding of the brain's control over eating. Investigators have found that stimulation of the lateral part of the hypothalamus will cause an animal to eat voraciously, even if it has just consumed a full meal. In other words, the animal behaves as if it were hungry even though it has no immediate biological need for food (Miller, 1957). It would seem, then, that the lateral hypothalamus is

After destruction of the ventromedial area of the hypothalamus, the rat shown here has overeaten to such an extent that it weighs 1,080 grams. (The dial has gone beyond the 1,000-gram capacity of the scale and registers an additional 80 grams.) A normal rat would weigh about 320 grams. (Courtesy, Dr. Neal Miller.)

in some way involved with an animal's ability to recognize when it is hungry, and brain-lesion techniques have supported this conclusion. When an animal's lateral hypothalamus is selectively destroyed with a strong electrical current, it will not eat unless it is force-fed. Most animals, if well cared for, will eventually overcome this dysfunction and begin to eat again. This partial recovery may take months, however, and the animals will always be underweight and show other permanent feeding problems (Epstein, 1971).

Lesions in the ventromedial (lower middle) area of the hypothalamus have an effect opposite to that caused by lateral hypothalamic lesions. That is, they prompt animals to overeat to the point of obesity (Hetherington and Ranson, 1940). A rat may eat enough to triple its normal weight, as shown in the accompanying photograph. When this area in a normal animal is stimulated with a mild electrical current, the animal will stop eating even if it is starving. Thus it appears that this area of the hypothalamus is related to an animal's ability to recognize when it is full.

We will say a great deal more about the control of eating behavior in Chapter 11, on motivation. The important point here is that much of what we know about the brain's role in regulating hunger comes from the combined use of brain stimulation and lesion techniques. These techniques have also been used to analyze many other kinds of brain–behavior relationships.

Recording Electrical Potentials. You may already know that scientists can trace the electrical signals of a human brain by taking an electroencephalogram, or EEG. In a typical EEG procedure, electrodes are attached to various areas of the scalp, and the voltage emitted by the brain beneath causes a pen to record its patterns on rolling graph paper. A standard EEG, as you will learn later in this book, is useful in many types of psychological investigation. It has serious limitations, however, for a researcher who wants to determine how a particular stimulus—such as a flash of light or a mild shock to the fingers—

affects electrical activity in the brain. The problem is that the brain emits a mass of electrical signals. How is the researcher to distinguish the specific electrical response evoked by the stimulus in question? One solution is quite simple. Researchers present the stimulus many times and use a computer to average out the responses recorded from the brain. Over a large number of trials, electrical activity unrelated to the stimulus will be sometimes negative and sometimes positive, and so will average to zero. What emerges, then, is the **evoked potential**—the pattern of electrical activity *caused* by the stimulus.

Evoked potential technology has helped scientists to chart many reactions in the brain. When the notes of the musical scale are played to a subject, for example, evoked potentials arise in a rather orderly fashion along the auditory cortex. Low notes produce potentials at one end of the region, high notes at the other end, and middle notes in between (Woolsey, 1961). Similar kinds of detailed arrangements have been found for other sensory areas.

Evoked potentials are not always produced by specific sensory stimuli, however. In the process of analyzing and coping with more general events in the environment, the brain routinely evokes its own potentials. If you were listening to a repetitive series of sounds and they suddenly and unpredictably stopped, for instance, your brain would register its surprise by emitting a large, positive electrical wave beginning three-tenths of a second after the sounds ceased (Restak, 1979). Alternatively, if you read a sentence that ended with a word that did not fit in the context, your brain would reveal its effort to make sense out of nonsense with a negative voltage beginning four-tenths of a second after you encountered the troublesome word. Researchers are now discovering that a wide variety of other mental processes are accompanied by their own characteristic patterns of electrical activity (Ritter et al., 1982; Renault et al., 1982). These patterns, called **event-related potentials** to distinguish them from electrical potentials evoked by external stimuli, are illustrated in Figure 3.13. It is not difficult to imagine the important diagnostic tools that such patterns could provide. Scientists working in this area have already developed tests to help spot learning disabilities in children, early signs of senility among the elderly, and various types of mental disorders—all by locating abnormalities in event-related potentials (Restak, 1979).

The electrical potentials we have discussed so far are measured by recording electrodes placed on the surface of the scalp or the brain. Consequently, they

involve electrical activity in a *group* of neurons. But modern technology has also made it possible to record the electrical response of a *single* neuron, which at its widest has a diameter of only about one-thousandth of an inch. Such single-unit recording is accomplished with the use of a microelectrode that is placed into or very close to an individual nerve cell. The single-unit recording technique has provided some important insights into the functional organization of the brain. When researchers inserted microelectrodes and took recordings from the optic nerve of a frog, for example, they discovered cells that increase firing *only* when dark spots move across the visual field—a useful adaptation for a creature whose primary food consists of flying insects (Lettvin, 1959). The high degree of stimulus-response selectivity that many neurons exhibit is believed to provide a foundation for the very precise behavioral and perceptual capabilities that many animals display.

Labeling Techniques. In the past decade or so whole new lines of brain research have become possible with the development of various novel methods for labeling the brain's neural pathways. Some of these techniques involve the use of chemicals. For instance, researchers can now inject experimental animals with radioactively labeled amino acids that are incorporated into a neurotransmitter or with a neurotransmitter that has been given fluorescent proper-

Figure 3.13 Scientists using a computer can filter out "noise" in the brain and isolate electrical changes related to specific thoughts on graphed readouts. This graph contrasts the brain waves produced by a normal sentence and by a nonsense sentence. Notice the high peak the brain registers after the final word of the nonsense sentence. (*Adapted from The New York Times, March 1, 1980, p. C1.*)

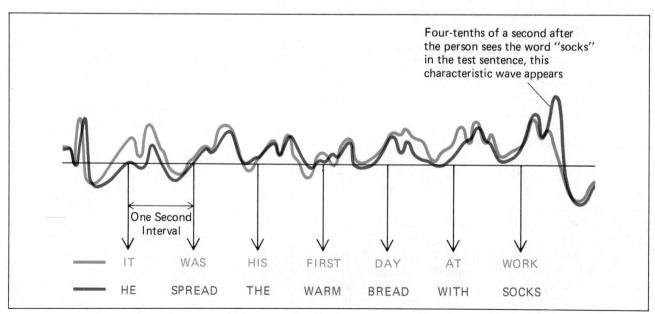

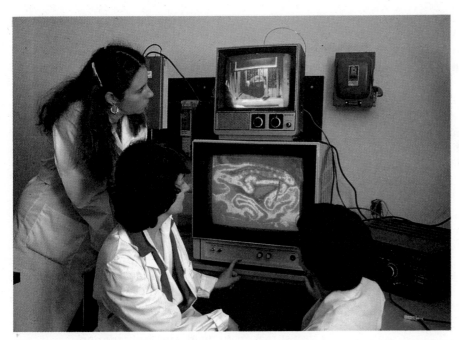

Chemical labeling techniques enable these researchers to view the metabolic activity taking place in the brain of a monkey (bottom screen) that is performing a task similar to the one being performed by the monkey shown on the top screen. (*Roe Di Bona.*)

ties. The labeled brain chemical is then selectively taken up by the axons that normally contain that neurotransmitter. Later, when thin sections of brain tissue are placed on radiation-sensitive film or viewed under a fluorescent microscope, the researchers obtain a picture of how the various cells using that neurotransmitter interconnect. As a result of such techniques, we now know a great deal about the distribution within the brain of several neurotransmitters.

In addition to mapping the pathways of neurotransmitters, chemical labeling techniques are also used to map the patterns of brain activity that accompany various types of behavior (see the accompanying photograph). One such method takes advantage of the fact that the more a particular brain cell participates in controlling a thought or action, the more sugar it absorbs from the bloodstream, because sugar is the brain cell's fuel. Under normal circumstances, of course, absorbed sugar is broken down almost as soon as it is taken up, in order to release energy. But researchers have found that if they inject into the blood a radioactive substance very similar chemically to sugar, it will be taken up by neurons just as regular sugar is, but it will not be "burned" away. Instead, this radioactive substance will accumulate in the brain cells. Most important, the amount absorbed by differ-

ent brain cells while an animal is performing some experimental task provides a measurable record of the extent to which those cells are involved in controlling that behavior. Thus a researcher might flash a light previously paired with a mild electric shock and then observe which parts of an animal's brain are thereby activated. The latest technology (called PET, for positron emission tomography) even allows researchers to trace the path of the radioactive substance from *outside* the skull.

Another revolutionary procedure for examining neural activity is the CAT scan (computerized transaxial tomography). Researchers pass an X ray beam through the brain and by means of detectors on the skull record the amount of radiation not absorbed by brain tissue. The X ray beam is then moved one degree and the procedure is repeated, 180 times in all. The resulting data are processed by computer to provide what amounts to a three-dimensional cross section of the brain. The CAT scan is especially useful in diagnosis. Within 25 minutes a neurologist can examine a brain for tumors, lesions, and the effects of strokes and head injuries, without the need for exploratory surgery (Kolb and Whishaw, 1980).

The CAT scan does have some disadvantages, however. It uses X rays, which are potentially hazardous, and it reveals only density. Another new diagnostic technique, called NMR (for nuclear magnetic resonance), apparently overcomes these problems. NMR makes use of magnetic fields, which are not known to be harmful, and can provide sensitive data about the chemical contents and environments of cells. The technique involves studying the effects of alternate magnetic fields on the nuclei of cells, which release signals that are analyzed by computer and displayed as an image or as chemical data. This method is still in its experimental stages, but some observers believe it will revolutionize medicine. It can be used to detect cancer, diagnose strokes, examine blood vessels, and evaluate the effects of drugs, as well as to provide precise information about brain and body relationships (Edelson, 1983).

in depth Exploring the Two Sides of the Brain

As our discussion of research methods has suggested, different approaches to the study of brain–behavior relationships often complement each other, and together they expand our understanding of how the brain works. You can see this even more clearly if we explore in depth how researchers have gone about investigating a question that has fascinated psychologists for over a century: Are the two sides of the brain exact duplicates of one another? Or does each control its own specialized functions?

Curiosity about this subject reaches back to the early nineteenth century, when doctors began to notice that damage to one side of the brain often produces numbness or paralysis on the *opposite* side of the body. This observation led to the basic concept of *contralateral control*—the idea that the left hemisphere of the brain controls the right side of the body, while the right hemisphere controls the left side. But because the body is essentially symmetrical, and because the brain looks symmetrical too, most early-nineteenth-century physiologists assumed that each side of the brain controls exactly the same functions as the other. The two hemispheres, in short, were seen as paired duplicates that formed a single system, much like the kidneys or the lungs.

One of the first indications that the two hemispheres might be organized differently came in the early 1860s, when the French physician Paul Broca

found that a specific area of the left frontal lobe was involved in the human ability to speak. Broca's view was based on numerous autopsies of patients who had suffered speech defects after damage to the left frontal lobe. Broca was struck by the fact that damage to the right frontal lobe in precisely the same location had no effect on language ability. Soon additional evidence that the left hemisphere is indeed the brain's "language center" began to pile up. The German neurologist Carl Wernicke, for instance, discovered a portion of the left temporal lobe which has come to be called Wernicke's area. Whereas damage to Broca's area often results in speech that is labored and fragmented (much like a slow, cryptic telegram), damage to Wernicke's area often results in fluent speech that gives a superficial impression of proper grammatical form but is curiously devoid of meaning (Geschwind, 1979). Such early clinical findings quickly led to the view that the left side of the brain houses most of the higher intellectual functions (such as speaking and writing) that make us distinctively human.

What about the right hemisphere? Was it grossly deficient in comparison with the left? Many researchers assumed so until well into the twentieth century. The principal reason was that people with damage to the right side of the brain did not seem to suffer serious intellectual impairments. Gradually, however, this viewpoint changed as more careful testing revealed that the right hemisphere is also specialized for certain cognitive functions. In one extensive study of more than 200 brain-damaged patients, those with injury to the right hemisphere tended to have trouble filling in missing parts to a pattern, assembling various kinds of puzzles, and manipulating geometric shapes (Weisenberg and McBride, 1935). Other investigations showed that right-hemisphere damage was sometimes linked to distortions in depth and distance perception and the ability to orient oneself in space. People with tumors or lesions in certain parts of the right hemisphere, for instance, sometimes have trouble finding their way around a place they have lived in for many years. These discoveries were slow in coming probably because such cognitive deficits are more subtle than speech disturbances, and because a fairly large portion of the right hemisphere must be injured before impairments are apparent. By the 1930s, at any rate, scientists were acknowledging the right hemisphere's special role in tasks involving form, distance, and spatial relationships. But the right brain's functions were still widely considered to be "lower order" ones.

Unfortunately, there were limits to what could be deduced about right and left brain specializations from clinical studies alone. The fact that damage to a certain part of one hemisphere impairs a particular cognitive function does not necessarily mean that the damaged region is the sole site for control of that behavior. It might simply be a key part in a much more diffuse set of neural circuits that extends to the opposite side of the brain as well. But how could researchers investigate such possibilities? One opportunity arose quite unexpectedly with the introduction of a surgical treatment for severe and intractable epilepsy. This technique involved the cutting of the large cable of nerve cells (the *corpus callosum*) that connects the two cerebral hemispheres. With the hemispheres thus separated, the random neural firing that causes epileptic convulsions is confined to the side of the brain where it begins, and the severity of a seizure is greatly reduced. Psychologists interested in how the two cerebral hemispheres are specialized saw here a chance for some very important research.

One of the pioneers in research on "split-brain" patients, as they came to be called, was psychologist Roger Sperry, who has since won a Nobel Prize for his work in this field. When Sperry and his colleagues tested their first split-brain subjects, the results were startling indeed. Imagine yourself in their laboratory observing a middle-aged female subject sitting at a table with a screen in front of her, her eyes fixed on a dot at the screen's center. (See Figure 3.14.) A projector behind the screen flashes a picture for a fraction of a second to the left or the right visual field. Since the left visual field sends messages to the right side of the brain, while the right visual field sends messages to the brain's left side, this procedure is a way of ensuring that visual images are projected to one cerebral hemisphere only as long as the subject has no time to shift her gaze. (See Figure 3.15.) Suppose that a picture of a spoon is flashed to the right side of the screen. The experimenter asks the subject what she saw, and the subject quickly answers, "A spoon." So far, so good. But when a picture of a spoon is flashed to the left side of the screen, the woman reports that she sees nothing. When she is asked to use her left hand to identify the object among those out of sight behind the screen, however, her left hand unhesitingly selects the spoon. It almost seems as if the left hand has a mind of its own, quite apart from the woman's conscious awareness.

An explanation of what is happening here requires an understanding of the tasks for which the two cere-

Figure 3.14 Experimental apparatus used for testing split-brain patients. When a picture of an object is presented on a screen in one half of the visual field, this information is transmitted exclusively to the opposite hemisphere. Normally this information is first received by the hemisphere opposite the visual half-field in which the image was presented, and then this information is transmitted to the other hemisphere. In split-brain patients the hemispheres are disconnected, and therefore their independent functions can be studied. If a picture of a spoon was presented in the right half of the visual field (transmitted to the left hemisphere), and a patient was asked to identify verbally the object she saw, she would readily say, "Spoon." If, however, the same picture was presented in the left half of the visual field (transmitted to the right hemisphere), the patient would be unable to name the object, because speech mechanisms are found only in the left hemisphere in most people. Although the right hemisphere cannot name the object, it "knows" what the object is. The left hand, which sends its touch information primarily to the right hemisphere, is able to pick the spoon from several objects hidden behind a screen, as illustrated here. (*After Springer and Deutsch, 1981.*)

bral hemispheres are specialized. When the spoon was flashed to the right side of the screen, its image was sent to the brain's left hemisphere. Since the left hemisphere is the one proficient at speech, the woman could verbally identify the object. When the picture of a spoon was flashed to the left side of the screen, in contrast, the image was sent to the brain's right hemisphere, the one *not* adept at language. This is why the woman verbally reported seeing nothing. The side of her brain with the capacity for speech had in fact seen nothing. The right hemisphere, however, had recognized the spoon and could identify it if allowed to do so through touch rather than words. But because the right hemisphere controls the left side of the body, the woman had to use her left hand for this task.

Split-brain subjects, then, have two cerebral hemispheres that cannot communicate directly. Outside the laboratory, fortunately, this loss of direct communication is seldom a handicap. In everyday situations split-brain patients can readily send visual information to both cerebral hemispheres at once just by shifting their eyes. Still, a few common tasks are more difficult for split-brain subjects. One is linking a new name to a new face. The learning of names is basically a left-hemisphere specialty, while the recognition of

faces is a right-hemisphere specialty. An absence of direct communication between the two hemispheres seems to make the combined process difficult (Levy, Trevarthen, and Sperry, 1972).

The existence of split-brain subjects allowed researchers to establish in greater detail those tasks at which the right and left hemispheres excel. Of particular interest were the capabilities of the right hemisphere, for so long considered the lesser of the two sides of the brain. Investigators discovered that the right hemisphere's abilities were more impressive than had previously been believed. This was strikingly demonstrated in a film that Roger Sperry and his colleague Michael Gazzaniga made of a split-brain patient in their laboratory (described in Springer and Deutsch, 1981). The subject, W. J., is given a set of four blocks, each of which has two white surfaces, two red surfaces, and two surfaces diagonally divided into red and white halves. W. J.'s task is to use the blocks to duplicate a series of simple geometric patterns, like the one in Figure 3.16. Starting with his left hand (controlled by the right side of the brain), W. J. moves along confidently, duplicating the patterns with little effort. When he is asked to switch to his right hand (controlled by the left side of the brain), his performance plummets. The right hand moves slowly and hesitantly, making many mistakes. At one point the left hand reaches toward the blocks, apparently to help the awkward right hand out. The experimenter moves the left hand back down to W. J.'s lap, and the right hand continues along in its sadly inept fashion.

Such experiments with split-brain patients lead many researchers to believe that it is a mistake to think of the right hemisphere as always cognitively inferior to the left (Sperry, 1982). It seems more accurate to say that each has its own specialized mode of perceiving and thinking about information. The left hemisphere is more analytic, and more likely to process things sequentially. The right hemisphere is better at focusing on spatial relationships and at processing inputs as wholes (Levy, 1974).

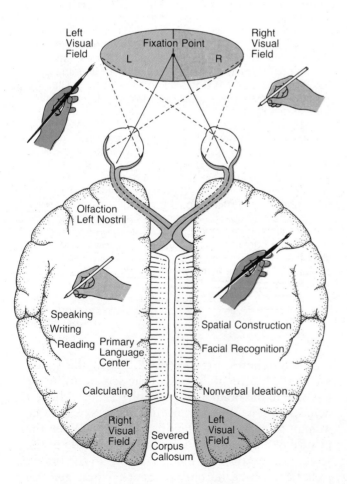

Figure 3.15 This schematic drawing of the brain from above shows the complementary dominance of the cerebral hemispheres for different tasks. For most people, the left hemisphere, which is specialized for writing, language, and analytical tasks, is dominant. The right hemisphere seems to be specialized for spatial, pattern, and musical recognition.

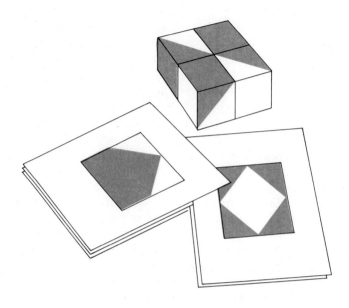

Figure 3.16 Researchers Roger Sperry and Michael Gazzaniga gave a split-brain patient a set of four blocks with differently colored and patterned surfaces and asked him to arrange the blocks so as to match patterns on cards. The patient could accomplish the task easily with his left hand, but not with his right—an indication of the right hemisphere's superior spatial ability. (*After Springer and Deutsch, 1981.*)

same pair of scissors was flashed to the left hemisphere, the subject would tend to match it by function rather than form (the needle and thread rather than the crossed utensils). In short, each side of the brain appeared to have its own preferred mode of information processing—one more analytic, the other more visual and holistic.

Such findings have led to much speculation about the way a normal brain works. Robert Ornstein, a psychologist who has studied human consciousness extensively, argues that coexisting in each of us are two distinct minds: the left logical and analytical, the right intuitive and artistic (Ornstein, 1977). The impression that the mind is unitary, Ornstein proposes, may simply be an illusion produced by constant and instantaneous communication between hemispheres across the corpus callosum. Others, however, are highly skeptical of this viewpoint. They maintain that such speculations are largely inferred from observations of split-brain subjects, whose condition is far from normal. The only way we can discover how the

This basic dichotomy can be seen in an interesting experiment with split-brain subjects performed by Jerre Levy and Colwyn Trevarthen, two of Roger Sperry's former students (Levy and Trevarthen, 1976). They flashed pictures of everyday objects (Figure 3.17) to the left or the right of a screen while the split-brain patient looked straight ahead. After each picture the subject was asked to select a "similar" one from an array of drawings. Among these other drawings were one that was similar to the original picture in function and another that was similar to it in appearance. How do you think each side of the subject's brain reacted? When a picture of, say, a pair of open scissors was projected to the right hemisphere, the subject would usually select the "match" by form rather than function (the crossed fork and spoon rather than the needle and thread). But when the

Figure 3.17 When split-brain subjects in Levy and Trevarthen's study (1976) were presented with one of the objects shown here and were asked to match it with one of the other objects, their responses tended to vary depending on the brain hemisphere to which the objects were presented. The right hemisphere usually matched objects by their appearance (matching the eyeglasses with the needle and thread positioned as shown here, for instance), while the left hemisphere was more likely to match objects by their function (matching the eyeglasses with the hat, both being items that people wear).

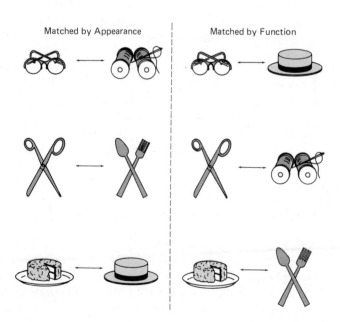

Matched by Appearance   Matched by Function

two cerebral hemispheres contribute to *normal* human thought, these critics say, is to investigate the activities of a normal, intact human brain.

This requirement has proved far easier to demand than to carry out. But fortunately, some of the latest techniques for investigating the brain's activities have finally brought it within our reach. For instance, neuroscientists now have equipment that can map the blood flow in a person's brain on a video monitor while that person is performing various tasks. Since blood flow increases as brain cells become more active, overall blood-flow patterns are good indicators of which brain regions are most involved in various kinds of behavior. Using this approach, one group of researchers found that blood flow to the left hemisphere is indeed greater than blood flow to the right when a person is engaged in a verbal task. Conversely, when a person is engaged in a visual perception task (such as trying to identify pictures that are drawn with very few lines), blood flow to the right hemisphere is greater than to the left (Risberg et al., 1975). Such research indicates clearly that the two sides of the brain are unequally involved in certain behaviors and abilities.

We must be careful not to overstate this basic conclusion, however. An equally striking thing about such studies is the degree to which they show the involvement of *both* cerebral hemispheres in any activity a person may be engaged in (Lassen, Ingvar, and Skinhoj, 1978). Thus when a person is reading or speaking, behaviors often labeled "left-hemisphere activities," blood-flow monitoring reveals that the right hemisphere is intimately involved as well. This fact makes it clear that the two sides of the brain do not function as independent units in normal human beings. Each hemisphere does not turn on for some tasks and off for others, while its partner either sits idly by or moves in to assume control. Although opposite sides of the brain and specific areas within each side are more prominently involved in some tasks than in others, human thought and behavior are made possible by activation of many quite widely distributed brain regions (Gazzaniga and Ledoux, 1978; Springer and Deutsch, 1981; Kinsbourne, 1982). This is particularly true in regard to such complex processes as reasoning and memory, as you will see in the following section.

THE BRAIN'S ROLE IN COMPLEX BEHAVIORS

Scientists still know very little about the way such complex processes as learning, memory, perception, and reasoning are related to brain activity. Yet these processes are the very ones of greatest interest to psychologists. All we know for sure is that none of them is isolated in any one area of the brain. Almost everything we do, in fact, appears to involve activity in most or all of the brain. A famous physiological psychologist, Karl Lashley, called this the **principle of mass action.**

Mass Action and Learned Behavior

Lashley attempted to locate specific areas of the cortex that were responsible for the learning and remembering of particular behaviors. In one set of experiments, rats were trained in mazes after lesions has been made in several cortical areas of their brains.

The locations of the lesions overlapped considerably, so that no area of the cortex was left unexplored. Lashley found that no lesion completely obliterated the rats' ability to learn a maze, although all of the lesions interfered with learning to some extent. He found in addition that the degree to which learning was retarded by a lesion was directly related to the lesion's size: the larger the lesion, the greater the learning deficit. This was particularly true in regard to the learning of the more complex mazes. On the basis of these findings, Lashley came to an important conclusion: the learning of a specific task does not appear to be localized in any particular cortical area. Instead, the entire cortex seems to be involved in learning and memory (Lashley, 1929).

This view has been bolstered by more recent research. Consider psychologist E. Roy John's investigation of the brain's electrical activity during learning and performance. John presented a cat with a flashing light while he recorded the electrical waves from the animal's brain. Soon the waves in the visual region of the cat's cortex started to follow the same frequency pattern as the light. John called these waves "labeled rhythms" because in a very real sense they bore the light's imprint. Next John assigned meaning to the light. Whenever the cat saw the light flash, it had to jump a hurdle to avoid a shock. What change, if any, did this innovation produce in the brain's electrical activity? It caused the labeled rhythms to spread to other regions. Sometimes the rhythms would arise spontaneously when the light was turned off and the cat was only expecting it to flash. In such instances, the animal would often leap the hurdle several times, as though performing trial runs. John concluded that in observing these labeled rhythms he was observing the effects of memory formation. Significantly, these effects were spread throughout the brain (John, 1976).

The Principle of Multiple Control

We have seen that the performance of any specific behavior is likely to involve most or all of the brain. The complementary principle also seems to be true—that is, a specific part of the brain is likely to be involved in the performance of many types of behavior. This is called the **principle of multiple control.** The cortex, for example, has been shown to influence behaviors ranging from complex intellectual processes to sexual and feeding behavior, sleeping and waking cycles, and simple spinal reflexes. Thus the cortex is involved not only in the "higher" behaviors but in other activities as well. Similarly, the lateral hypothalamus is involved in many behaviors other than feeding. Rats with lesions in the lateral hypothalamus, for example, show deficits in certain learning situations in addition to exhibiting severe loss of appetite (Teitelbaum, 1971).

Thus the principles of mass action and multiple control tell us that the brain is a highly integrated unit. Although this remarkable organ is composed of billions of discrete neurons, all organized into functionally distinct substructures, in the final analysis it operates as an inseparable whole. To understand brain–behavior relationships, therefore, not only must we examine the activities of neurons and the workings of the brain's major parts, we must also explore how the brain functions as a complete and unified system.

SUMMARY

1. The human nervous system, an intricate communications network that radiates throughout the body, consists of billions of interconnected, highly specialized cells. **Receptor cells,** embedded in sense organs, receive various types of stimulation from the environment. **Effector cells** cause muscles to contract and glands to secrete. **Neurons,** or nerve cells, connect receptor cells to effector cells, integrating and coordinating their activities.

2. Most of the body's neurons are found in the **central nervous system,** which consists of the brain and spinal cord. Branching out from the central nervous system to all parts of the body is the **peripheral nervous system.** Its two divisions, the **somatic** and the **autonomic,** are related to control of the skeletal muscles and control of the internal organs, respectively. The autonomic system can be further subdivided into **sympathetic** and **parasympathetic** components. The first is involved in mobilizing the body's resources, while the second is involved in conserving them.

3. Most neurons have three structural components: the **cell body,** containing the nucleus; relatively short **dendrites,** along which impulses travel to the cell body; and a long **axon,** along which impulses travel away from the cell body to muscle fibers, glandular cells, and other neurons. The simplest set of neural connections is a **reflex arc,** in which a sensory input is linked to a motor response.

4. Nerve impulses are transmitted by means of an electrochemical process. The electrical part of the process involves a sudden change in the cell's electrical potential. In the state known as the **resting potential,** the nerve cell membrane is negatively charged inside and positively charged outside. It is said to be **polarized.** When the cell is stimulated, this polarity is

abruptly reversed, giving rise to an **action potential,** which rapidly travels down the length of the axon.

5. Every axon is physically separated from adjacent cells by a gap called a **synapse.** When an action potential reaches the end of an axon, a chemical called a **neurotransmitter** is released from the axon terminal and diffuses across the synapse to activate receptor sites on the adjacent cells. Depending on the chemistry of the neurotransmitter and the nature of the receptor site activated, the message conveyed may be excitatory or inhibitory. Scientists are compiling an ever-growing list of neurotransmitters, each associated with specific neural pathways, behavioral functions, and psychological states.

6. The body's second major communications network, which closely interacts with the nervous system, is the **endocrine system.** Its messengers are chemicals called **hormones,** which circulate in the bloodstream and have their effects on specific **target organs.** The endocrine system affects physical growth, metabolism, reproductive functioning, and other physiological processes.

7. The brain is the body's master control center because it ultimately regulates all behavior. It consists of three overlapping regions, each representing a consecutive stage in the brain's evolution. The **central core,** or "old brain," is involved in the control of functions most basic to survival, such as sleeping, waking, respiration, and feeding. Its major areas include the **brainstem,** the **cerebellum,** the **thalamus,** and the **hypothalamus.** Above the central core lies the **limbic system,** which is involved in the regulation of behaviors that satisfy emotional and motivational needs, such as fighting, fleeing, and mating. Among its highly interrelated structures are the **hippocampus,** the **amygdala,** and the **septal area.** The two large structures at the top of the brain are collectively called the **cerebral hemispheres.** Covered by a thin outer layer called the **cortex,** the cerebral hemispheres are involved in the processes of learning, speech, reasoning, and memory.

8. Researchers have developed a variety of techniques to study brain–behavior relationships. Some have observed brain-damaged people or people who have undergone neurosurgery in order to link injury in some brain region to a particular behavioral deficit. Electrical or chemical stimulation of the brain has also helped to clarify the role of certain brain areas in specific feelings and actions. So has the technique of making brain lesions in experimental animals by surgically destroying a small area of brain tissue. Scientists are employing sophisticated electronic equipment to monitor the brain's electrical activity. They are also using various labeling techniques to map the brain's numerous pathways.

9. Many research methods have been used in the study of the two sides of the brain. The basic question scientists are trying to answer is to what extent the cerebral hemispheres are specialized for different functions. By the mid-twentieth century clinical observations and work with split-brain patients had helped to establish that the left side of the brain is the major center for language abilities, while the right side of the brain is important in visual and spatial tasks. This basic dichotomy can be easily exaggerated, however. Except in people who have had their cerebral hemispheres surgically separated, the two sides of the brain do not function as independent units. Both are involved to some extent in virtually every kind of behavior.

10. Two complementary principles help to sum up what we know about the working of the brain as a unified system. The **principle of mass action** states that almost all human behaviors appear to involve activity in most or all of the brain. The **principle of multiple control** says that a specific part of the brain is likely to be involved in many types of behavior.

SUGGESTED READINGS

ADLER, N. T. *Neuroendocrinology of reproduction: Physiology and behavior.* New York: Plenum, 1981.

An excellent introduction to the methods, problems, and data of reproductive behavior. Includes the basic chemistry, research techniques, and historical background needed to understand this interesting subject.

BLAKEMORE, C. *Mechanics of the mind.* New York: Cambridge University Press, 1977.

A good introduction to physiological psychology presented in an attractive paperback.

SCHNEIDER, A. M., AND TARSHIS, B. *An introduction to physiological psychology.* 3d ed. New York: Random House, 1985.

A highly readable introductory textbook for the student without a strong background in biology or physiology. Biological and physiological material is presented in the context of behavior.

SPRINGER, S. P., AND DEUTSCH, G. *Left brain, right brain.* San Francisco: Freeman, 1981.

An up-to-date discussion of 100 years of research into the nature of hemispheric differences in both humans and animals. Findings are presented on asymmetry in brain-damaged, split-brain, and normal subjects, and the implications for human behavior are explored.

4

SENSATION AND PERCEPTION

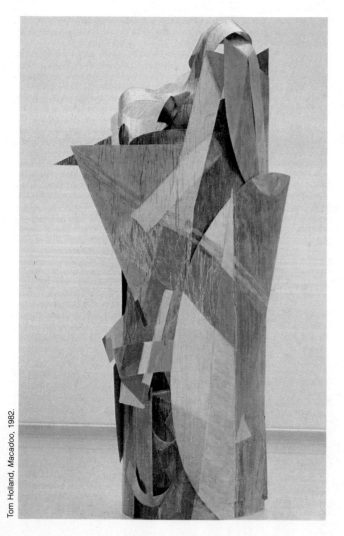

Tom Holland, *Macadoo*, 1982.

The Development of Perceptual Processes
Evidence for the Influence of Learning
Evidence for Inborn Mechanisms
The Interactionist View

You live in the midst of a barrage of physical stimuli. Light waves from the sun and other sources bombard your eyes. Pulses of air molecules, called sound waves, impinge on your ears. Vaporized molecules from thousands of substances assail the sensitive membranes of your nose. The human sensory organs are intricately designed to detect and discriminate among these stimuli, thus giving you windows to the outside world. But how accurately do you sense and perceive your surroundings? Are there certain stimuli you are unable to detect? Do you ever perceive things that are not really there or misperceive things that are? Are your sensations and perceptions in some respects different from those of other people? Psychologists who study sensation and perception seek to answer such questions, and equally important, they seek to explain just why we perceive things in the ways that we do.

Traditionally, psychologists have thought of sensation and perception as two distinguishable processes. **Sensation** is essentially the process whereby stimulation of receptor cells in various parts of the body (the eyes, ears, nose, mouth, and surface of the skin) sends nerve impulses to the brain, where these impulses register as a touch, a sound, a taste, a splash of color, and so forth. **Perception,** in contrast, is the process whereby the brain interprets the sensations it receives, giving them order and meaning. Thus, hearing sounds and seeing colors may be largely sensory processes, but following a melody and detecting depth in a two-dimensional painting are largely perceptual ones. We say *largely,* of course, because in everyday life it is almost impossible to separate sensation from perception. As soon as the brain receives sensations, it automatically interprets or perceives

them, and without sensations of some kind, perception could not occur. This is why some contemporary psychologists contend that the distinction between sensation and perception is not as useful as it has traditionally been considered. Both processes, they correctly stress, are part of a single information-processing system.

One fact that has repeatedly emerged from the scientific study of sensation and perception is that each organism's view of the world is to some extent unique. This fact will be immediately clear if we compare our own sensory and perceptual capabilities with those of other species. Consider the ability to detect sounds. Many animals can hear sounds far too high-pitched or low-pitched for humans to detect. A dog's range of hearing is more than twice that of ours, and so is a cat's. Bats are virtuosos at the detection of high-pitched sounds. In fact, they depend on such sounds for navigation. A bat sends out a shrill stream of ultrasonic cries, listens for the echoes bouncing off surrounding objects, and so locates those objects in space. But even though a flying bat is constantly emitting powerful noises, it seems virtually soundless to us because the human ear is tuned too low to detect most of its cries. Interestingly, from a bat's perspective we humans also appear mute, for the sounds we normally make are just below the pitch level that will stimulate a bat's hearing.

Sensory and perceptual capabilities, then, clearly vary among species, but do they also vary among members of the same species? The answer is a qualified yes. Although members of the same species usually experience the world in very similar ways, some sensory and perceptual differences do exist. Consider an example in taste detection. We all know that some people like their coffee black, while others insist on adding a great deal of sugar and cream. Although a number of factors may contribute to these different taste preferences, one thing is certain: most people who use lots of sugar and cream in their coffee find the taste of black coffee extremely bitter. How, they wonder, could anyone drink such bitter-tasting stuff? One answer is that the black-coffee drinkers do not perceive coffee as being particularly bitter. There are, in fact, genetic differences in taste receptors that make some people less sensitive to coffee's bitter flavor. We will return to this subject later when we discuss the physiology of taste. For now the important point to remember is that two people sitting side by side can, under certain circumstances, experience the world in significantly different ways.

A basic cause underlying all the sensory and perceptual differences we have mentioned so far is variation in the way that sensory-perceptual systems are structured. The function of any physiological mechanism is inseparably linked to its structure. Your fingers' ability to turn the pages of this book, for example, is governed largely by the structure of your hands. Because your thumb can rotate forward and touch any of your other four fingers, you are able to manipulate very small and delicate objects, such as a sheet of paper a fraction of a millimeter thick. This link between structure and function will be seen again and again as we explore the workings of our major sensory organs and examine the role of the brain in perceptual processing. But first let us briefly consider the general relationship between physical stimuli in the external world and the subjective sensations they create in us.

STIMULI, SENSATIONS, AND PERCEPTIONS

If a tree falls in a forest where no one is present to hear, does it nevertheless make a sound? This question, frequently debated in the intellectual salons of eighteenth-century Europe, is perplexing at first because it clouds the distinction between a physical stimulus (sound waves produced by a falling tree) and a subjective sensation (hearing a crash). The two, of course, are not synonymous. A **stimulus** is any form of energy (sound waves, light waves, heat, pressure) to which an organism is capable of responding. A sensation is a response to that energy by a sensory system. Stimuli and sensations, then, have a cause-and-effect relationship.

Most sensory systems respond to differences in both the quality and the quantity of stimuli. The *quality* of a stimulus refers to the kind of sensation it produces. Color is a quality related to visual stimulation; musical pitch is a quality related to auditory stimulation. *Quantity,* in contrast, refers to the amount of stimulation present. Thus brightness represents the perceived quantity of light and loudness the perceived quantity of sound.

Remember, though, that such characteristics as color, brightness, pitch, and loudness are simply ways in which an individual *experiences* a stimulus. They are not necessarily completely accurate reflections of the physical properties that the stimulus has. In analyzing the relationship between what a person senses and what a stimulus is physically like, psychologists study three basic things: the quantity of a stimulus needed for a person to sense it in the first place; the ratio between the magnitude of the stimulus and the magnitude of the corresponding sensation; and the factors that reduce or increase sensory capacities. Let us consider some basic concepts that have emerged from the study of each of these topics.

Some Basic Sensory Concepts

Absolute Thresholds. How much light must be present before a person sees it? How much pressure must be applied to the skin before a person feels it? The answers to these questions involve the concept of **absolute threshold:** the minimum stimulus necessary to produce a detectable sensation.

How do psychologists measure absolute thresholds? A person's absolute threshold for light might be measured in the following manner. The subject enters a completely dark room and, after being given time to adapt to the dark, watches for a light on the wall. The psychologist, using a specially designed instrument, projects a very dim beam and gradually increases its intensity until the person says, "I see it." Generally this procedure will be repeated several times. An individual's absolute threshold is the lowest intensity of light that the person is able to see 50 percent of the time.

Under ideal conditions, our senses have very low absolute thresholds—that is, we experience sensations when we are exposed to very small amounts of stimulation. Human vision, for example, is keen enough to see the flame of a single candle from a distance of several miles on a clear, moonless night. Similarly, the human sense of smell is sensitive enough to detect the musky odor of mercaptan, the scent that makes skunks so unpopular, at concentrations as low as 1 part mercaptan to 50 trillion parts of air (Geldard, 1972). But in a natural setting ideal conditions seldom exist. Thus if we want to determine how well our senses *normally* operate, we must consider them under less than ideal circumstances.

Several factors regularly serve to limit our sensory capacities. One is the existence of irrelevant, competing stimuli, often referred to as background **noise.** You can probably think of many occasions when your ability to detect a particular sound was hampered by auditory noise—as when you tried to hear what someone was saying at an especially loud party. But "noise" can affect other senses as well. An inexperienced person viewing a radar screen, for example, usually has great difficulty distinguishing the blips made by an airplane from those made by stormy weather, a form of visual noise. In much the same way, you would be hard pressed to smell the fragrance of a delicate flower in a smoke-filled room.

Lack of prior information about a stimulus also hinders the ability to detect it. A sound, for instance, is more difficult to hear when you do not know what its qualities will be or when to expect it (Swets and Sewall, 1961; Scharf, 1970). Similarly, a touch is more difficult to feel when you do not know where on your body it is going to occur (Meyer, Gross, and Teuber, 1963). The same is true of visual stimuli. A moving target is harder to spot if you do not know at what speed it will be traveling or in which direction (Sekuler and Ball, 1977). Stimulus uncertainty, then, is a second factor that can reduce performance on sensory tasks.

A third factor is motivation. Sometimes people are inclined to set rather stringent criteria for determining when a stimulus has occurred. People who fear illness, for instance, may ignore the sensations associated with it until a condition is far advanced. Such people are highly motivated *not* to perceive these stimuli. Other people are simply conservative in acknowledging weak sensory stimuli. There is evidence, for instance, that the elderly, because they are usually more conservative than the young, are also more cautious in reporting stimulus detection. In one experiment, subjects aged sixty-five to seventy-seven were significantly more reluctant to say that they had heard a very faint sound (one just at the edge of their auditory thresholds) than were subjects aged eighteen to twenty-one.

Thus many factors influence the ability to detect sensory stimuli. Psychologists have tried to summarize these various influences on the basis of an approach called **signal detection theory.** According to signal detection theory, some of these influences pertain to the stimulus itself (How intense is it? How muffled by background noise?), while others pertain to the sensory system on which that stimulus impinges (Is the sensory system sensitive or is it somehow impaired?). Equally important is the motivation of the person. What criteria does the person use in deciding whether to ignore faint or ambiguous stimuli? The probability that the stimulus will occur may be important. So may the rewards or punishments associated with detecting a sensation. In short, the absolute threshold for any given stimulus varies greatly with the circumstances. It is never a firmly fixed value.

Sensory Ratios. In addition to their interest in absolute thresholds and the factors that affect them, psychologists are interested in **sensory ratios**—the relationship between the intensity of a stimulus and the intensity of its resulting sensation. As you change the settings on a three-way light bulb from 50 to 100 to 150 watts, do you experience the same increase in brightness between 50 and 100 watts as you do between 100 and 150? Since the fixed increase in the number of watts suggests that you should, psychologists' findings may surprise you.

Research in this area began in the mid-nineteenth century, when Ernst Weber discovered that although people can perceive small changes in a weak stimulus,

You will need three quarters, two envelopes, and your shoes. Take one quarter and put it in an envelope and put the remaining two quarters in the other. If you now gently lift each envelope and put it down (use the same hand), it is quite easy to distinguish the heavier envelope. Now insert one envelope into one of your shoes and the other envelope into your second shoe, and lift them one at a time. The weight difference should be almost imperceptible.

Figure 4.1 A demonstration of Weber's law for the perception of heaviness. Note that changes in an intense stimulus must be large before they can be noticed, while small changes in a weaker stimulus are easily distinguished. (*From Coren, Porac, and Ward, 1978, p. 32.*)

they notice only large changes in a strong stimulus. You can experience this phenomenon yourself, as Figure 4.1 demonstrates. After further study, Weber's brother-in-law, Gustav Fechner, specified the nature of this relationship more precisely (Fechner, 1860). Fechner noted that the amount by which a stimulus must be increased to produce a "just noticeable difference" is always a constant proportion of the initial stimulus intensity. In honor of his brother-in-law, Fechner called this **Weber's law.**

The proportional increase in the initial stimulus needed to create a just noticeable difference varies with the kind of stimulus involved. For weight, the proportion is about 1 to 50. This means that the average person will just notice a difference when a single pound is added to a backpack initially weighing fifty pounds; but *two* pounds must be added to a backpack weighing 100 pounds in order for a difference to be detected. (In both cases the *proportional* increase remains constant.) The proportions for some other sensations are 1 to 10 for auditory tones, 1 to 7 for skin pressure, and 1 to 5 for the saltiness of a liquid. Although Weber's law does not hold true under all circumstances, it is a useful approximation.

An important question still remained, however. What exactly was the relationship between any given increase in stimulation and the corresponding increase in sensation? S. S. Stevens (1957, 1962) helped to provide the answer. According to **Stevens' power law,** the magnitude of a sensation is essentially equal to the intensity of the initial stimulus raised to some power, or mathematical exponent. As Weber's law

implied, that exponent varies with the type of stimulus. For some stimuli the exponent is less than 1, meaning that the perceived increase in sensation will be proportionally less than the actual increase in the stimulus. When the volume of a sound is increased threefold, for example, it usually sounds only twice as loud; and to double the perceived brightness of a light, it must usually be increased eightfold. For both hearing and vision, then, the magnitude of the sensation increases more slowly than the magnitude of the stimulus. For some sensory judgments, however, the Stevens exponent is greater than 1, meaning that the perceived increase in sensation will be greater than the actual increase in the stimulus. A twofold increase in the intensity of an electric shock to the fingers, for instance, produces about a tenfold increase in perceived pain.

Sensory Adaptation. All sensory systems display **sensory adaptation**—reduced ability to provide information after prolonged, constant stimulation. When you enter a room with a distinctive odor, the smell may be very noticeable at first, but soon it will appear to fade away. This effect is due to sensory adaptation, a form of adjustment. Some senses, such as smell and touch, adapt quite quickly, while others, such as pain, adapt very slowly. All, however, do adapt.

Sensory adaptation occurs because the sense receptors in your body are designed to be maximally sensitive to *changes* in stimulation. This makes sense. We do not need to be constantly reminded, for example, that our shoes are securely on our feet. Thus when you stimulate the touch receptors in your foot's skin by putting on a shoe, and that pressure is held constant, the rate at which nerve impulses are generated steadily declines. This same adaptive process occurs in the visual receptors of the eyes. In fact, if you were truly able to stare at something, it would gradually disappear. Fortunately, you cannot lock your gaze onto a single point. Whenever you try to do so, your eyes involuntarily move very tiny amounts at a rapid rate, thus shifting the light image to many visual receptor cells. These involuntary movements prevent any single group of cells from so adapting to an unchanging light stimulus that vision fades away.

Because sensory adaptation affects sensitivity to stimuli, it can change the sensation produced by any given amount of stimulation. You can experience this effect with a simple experiment. Place one hand in ice-cold water and the other in bearably hot water.

After your hands have adapted to these two temperatures, plunge them into a bucket of warm water. What temperature does this water feel? Oddly, it feels both hot (to the hand that has been in cold water) and cold (to the hand that has been in hot water), even though you know it is neither.

This example of a perceptual distortion caused by sensory adaptation reinforces an important point raised at the beginning of this chapter: the way we view the world is not always an accurate reflection of the physical stimuli that exist there. Note, however, that distortions in perception are not necessarily caused by abnormalities in sensory processing, as many people assume. They are frequently caused by the use of normal sensory systems in unusual situations. We will say more about this later when we explain the reasons for certain visual illusions.

So far we have focused on sensations above a person's absolute threshold. But what about stimuli of even lower intensity—those a particular person has *never* reported perceiving? Is it possible that a person's brain might still detect these very faint stimuli at some subconscious level? This brings us to the realm of **subliminal perception**—the brain's ability to register a stimulus presented so briefly or weakly that it cannot be consciously perceived. This phenomenon is very controversial.

---

in depth Studying Subliminal Perception

In the summer of 1957 a marketing executive named James Vicary conducted a 6-week study that was soon to ignite an explosion of interest in subliminal perception. The site of the study was an unimposing movie theater in Fort Lee, New Jersey, just across the Hudson River from New York City. What Vicary did was very simple, and some might even think ludicrous. He superimposed on the regular film some verbal messages that appeared so briefly they could not be consciously detected. One message told the unsuspecting movie-goers, "Eat popcorn " while the other instructed them, "Drink Coke." According to Vicary, popcorn sales surged upward by an impressive 58 percent, and Coke sales rose by a very respectable 18 percent (Morse and Stoller, 1982).

Vicary's study made national headlines. Many people were outraged at such underhanded practices. They lobbied politicians to outlaw subliminal adver-

tising and worried about the dangers of subliminal political propaganda. (Remember that this was an era in which communist infiltration was dreaded.) But other Americans could not resist the temptation to try out their own subliminal messages (Moore, 1982). One radio station in Seattle launched a subliminal campaign against its archrival, television, by broadcasting such subaudible slurs as "TV's a bore." A few department stores in Toronto even played subliminal antishoplifting messages over their public address systems. As shoppers browsed through kitchenware and tried on shoes, a subaudible voice repeatedly warned them, "If you steal, you'll get caught." Many psychologists were fascinated. Some were eager to find out if subliminal perception was even possible, let alone whether such perceptions could actually influence behavior.

Studies conducted by many psychologists over the intervening years suggest that, under carefully controlled circumstances, a person may in fact detect certain kinds of stimuli without conscious awareness. Signal detection researchers have sometimes found this to be true. When they ask subjects to express the degree of their confidence that a very weak stimulus was or was not presented, a person's confidence is directly related to the intensity of the stimulus—even for stimuli that the subject reports *not* detecting (Swets, 1961; Green and Swets, 1966). On some level, therefore, the subject must be registering the "undetected" stimuli. Additional evidence comes from studies by William Bevan (1964). He has found that when people are given mild electric shocks to the wrist and asked to judge their severity, they tend to describe the shocks as significantly more intense when brief subliminal shocks are administered before each test shock. It is as if the subjects' brains are subconsciously adding up the subliminal shocks *plus* the consciously perceived one and reporting the total sensation.

Still more support for subliminal perception can be found in recent work by Robert Zajonc and his colleagues. In one study they took advantage of the fact that repeated exposure to a stimulus often breeds liking for it, an effect we will talk about further in Chapter 17. They presented subjects with a series of various-shaped polygons, each for only a single thousandth of a second. Later they showed the subjects the same polygons plus new ones, giving them as long as they needed to rate each one both for liking and for recognition. Significantly, most subjects tended to like the previously seen polygons better than the ones they had never seen before, even though they could not consciously distinguish between the "old" and the "new" (Kunst-Wilson and Zajonc, 1980). Once again it appears that at some level subjects are processing subliminal information.

But it is one thing to say that subliminal perception may be possible and quite another to assert that such perceptions can actually direct behavior, as proponents of subliminal advertising have claimed. What evidence is there that subliminal messages can prompt people to do things that they otherwise would not do? The evidence is extremely sparse and very much open to question. One of the few studies appearing to support this view was conducted several decades ago by psychologist Marvin Zuckerman (1960). Zuckerman projected onto a screen a series of thirty pictures about which subjects were to write descriptive stories. For the first ten pictures, experimental and control subjects were treated exactly alike. The pictures were displayed individually and the subjects wrote a story after viewing each one. This procedure established a baseline level of writing for each group. Then Zuckerman accompanied the next ten pictures presented to the experimental subjects (but not to the controls) with the subliminal message "Write more." Finally, Zuckerman accompanied the last ten pictures flashed to his experimental subjects with the subliminal instruction "Don't write." Zuckerman found that the experimental subjects *did* write more than the baseline level during the second condition, and they decreased their level of writing slightly during condition three. He interpreted this finding to mean that the experimental subjects had indeed followed his subliminal directives.

But other interpretations of Zuckerman's results are also possible (Moore, 1982). It seems that even from the beginning Zuckerman's experimental subjects were more enthusiastic writers than his control subjects were. During the baseline condition, they spontaneously wrote much more about each picture than those in the control group did. Later, in condition two, they *did* increase their levels of output, as a subliminal perception interpretation would predict, but so did the control subjects who received no subliminal "Write more" message. Thus the fact that the experimental subjects increased the extent of their writing significantly more than the control subjects may simply have been a product of their natural enthusiasm for writing. Finally, the small drop in writing output shown by the experimental subjects in condition three may have been nothing more than a

"wearing out" effect. If you had written twenty stories as diligently as you could, it wouldn't be surprising if you found yourself writing a bit less in the next ten. In short, Zuckerman's findings by no means strongly support the power of subliminal instructions to direct behavior. This interpretation may help explain why no other researchers appear to have replicated his results (Moore, 1982).

What about the Vicary study mentioned at the beginning of this section? Didn't it provide some convincing evidence that people sometimes follow what subliminal messages tell them? The answer here is no, not really. When you look carefully at the study's design, you will find it has serious flaws. Vicary's research is an example of a quasi-experiment, discussed in Chapter 2. As we pointed out there, a quasi-experiment does not provide the powers of control that a true experiment does. Perhaps other factors were systematically influencing Coke and popcorn sales after Vicary introduced his subliminal messages. Maybe the weather grew hotter and people were thirstier. Or perhaps some lengthy movies were shown during that six-week period, so that people simply got hungrier as they were watching the shows. If so, purchases of Coke and popcorn might have risen for reasons that had nothing to do with Vicary's subliminal ads. Since Vicary apparently made no effort to take such additional influences into account, we simply cannot conclude that subliminal advertising caused his reported effects.

And even if Vicary's study had been more carefully constructed, there would still be reasons to doubt any positive effects of subliminal advertising (Moore, 1982). For one thing, people have quite variable sensory thresholds, so it is difficult to pick a single stimulus intensity that will be below threshold for an entire theater audience, yet not so far below that it has no effect whatsoever on the senses. In addition, it is not easy to display subliminal stimuli in a barrage of consciously perceived ones. On a motion picture screen, the ongoing movie will almost inevitably overpower any fleeting subliminal ad (Dixon, 1971). Finally, people are not robots. Even if they did detect a subliminal message, there is no reason to think that even a sizable minority would automatically follow its directives. People are not that easy to sway with overt advertising. Why would they be so much more susceptible to weak and fleeting ads? Thus there are many compelling reasons that most psychologists agree that subliminal advertising is probably not an effective method of persuasion.

in depth

THE HUMAN SENSES

Our eyes, ears, nose, tongue, and skin are the organs that link us to the outside world via the familiar senses of sight, hearing, smell, taste, and touch. But a human being possesses considerably more senses than just these basic five. The skin alone contains receptors for at least five sensations, and an organ in the inner ear gives us a sense of balance and equilibrium. In addition, sensory systems related to muscles and joints provide awareness of body position and movement, and many other internal receptors supply the brain with vital information about blood chemistry and temperature. Although the following discussion is restricted to the classic five senses, plus a number of other skin sensations, those omitted are no less important to normal human functioning.

Vision

Vision is the richest of the human senses. Our eyes receive light from surrounding objects and translate it into nerve impulses that travel to the brain. When they reach their destination, we experience the vast array of shapes, colors, textures, and movements that make up our visual world. To understand how this remarkable system works, you must first know something about the basic stimulus for vision—light.

The Nature of Light. Light is a form of electro-magnetic radiation, which itself is a form of energy. Several hundred years ago Sir Isaac Newton proposed that light behaves as if it were a stream of tiny particles. Modern physicists call these subatomic particles of light radiation **photons.** An important characteristic of light is that it travels in wavelike patterns rather than in straight lines. Different streams of light have somewhat different **wavelengths**—that is, different distances between the crest of one wave and the crest of the next—as illustrated in Figure 4.2. These varying wavelengths of light (usually measured in billionths of a meter, or nanometers) determine the colors we see. The brightness of any color is determined by the **intensity** of light—that is, by how densely the photons in the light wave are packed.

Figure 4.2 shows that the light energy to which our eyes are sensitive is just one small part of the total electromagnetic spectrum. This spectrum also includes longer wavelengths, such as radio and infrared waves, as well as shorter wavelengths, such as ultraviolet rays, X rays, and gamma rays. It is no evolutionary accident that many animals see by using the same narrow band of electromagnetic radiation that we do. Basically, living things use the radiation that is available to them, and a large portion of the sun's energy that strikes the surface of the earth is in the range we call "visible." If our eyes were structured just a little differently, however, we might see some parts of the electromagnetic spectrum now invisible to us. People

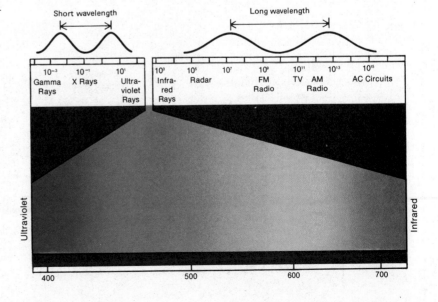

Figure 4.2 The spectrum of electromagnetic energy. Electromagnetic energy comes to us in varying wavelengths. The very short wavelengths at the left of the scale and the very long ones at the right are not registered as light. The small portion of the spectrum to which the human eye is sensitive is shown expanded. The scale on the large spectrum is a logarithmic scale of wavelength: each step on the scale corresponds to a tenfold increase in the wavelength of the electromagnetic radiation.

who have had the lenses within their eyes removed because they have become clouded by cataracts see slightly more ultraviolet light than normal people do because the eyes' lenses absorb a great deal of ultraviolet radiation.

Structure of the Visual System.

Our visual system begins with the eye, through which light enters. The structure of the human eye is shown in Figure 4.3A. Light passes first through a tough, transparent window, called the **cornea,** which covers the front of the eyeball. Because the cornea is deeply curved, it bends the rays of incoming light and helps to focus them. Behind the cornea is a pouch of liquid (the aqueous humor) that helps maintain the cornea's rounded shape. To its rear lies the **iris,** a ring of pigmented tissue that gives the eye its color (brown-eyed people have pigmentation that blue-eyed people lack). Contraction and relaxation of muscle fibers in the iris close and open the **pupil,** the opening in the center of the eye, which appears black. In this way the amount of light entering the eye is regulated. You can observe the action of your own iris by turning on a bright bulb in a dimly lit room and watching your pupil in a mirror. It will rapidly close to a very small hole, thus reducing the amount of light that is able to pass through the pupil to the lens behind it. The **lens** is a transparent, elastic structure that allows the eye to adjust its focus in accordance with an object's distance. This adjustment is accomplished by **ciliary muscles,** which change the shape of the lens, flattening it to focus on more distant objects and allowing the lens to become more spherical to focus on near

objects. The incoming light is then projected through the liquid that fills the center of the eyeball (the vitreous humor) and onto the **retina,** the eye's light-sensitive inner surface.

You can easily see the intimate relationship of the eye's structure and function by considering some of the visual malfunctions caused by structural defects. With aging, for instance, the lens of the eye typically loses much of its elasticity and so does not easily assume a convex shape when the ciliary muscles relax. As a result, elderly people have difficulty focusing on near objects. This is why they tend to hold books and newspapers at a much greater distance than younger people do, sometimes at a full arm's length. Another structural defect of the lens usually associated with aging is the formation of cataracts, which cause the lens to become somewhat opaque. As a result, less light passes through it and visual images appear fuzzy and dim. When this condition becomes severe, the affected lens is often surgically removed, as we mentioned earlier. The patient then either wears a special contact lens or glasses to compensate for the lost lens or has an artificial lens implanted in the eyeball. An understanding of these and other structural defects has provided great insight into the normal functioning of a healthy human eye.

So far we have simply followed the movement of light into the eye and onto the light-sensitive surface called the retina. But how is the light then transformed into visual experiences registered by the brain? The answer lies in a network of millions of nerve cells. The outermost layer of each retina contains two types of receptor cells, the rods and the

Figure 4.3 The structure of the eye and the transduction of light energy into an electrical signal. (A) A cross section of the human eye. Note that the lens transmits an inverted image onto the retina. (B) The detailed structure of a small portion of the retina close to the fovea. Arrows on the figure indicate the passage of neural impulses from the receptor cells through bipolar cells and ganglion cells to the optic nerve on their way to the brain.

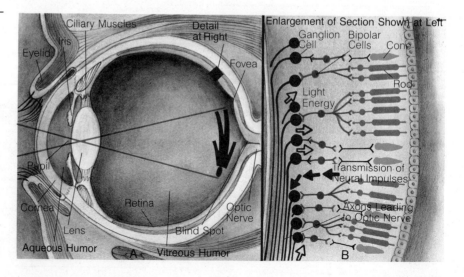

Figure 4.4 Although you are usually unaware of it, the blind spot is literally blind. To demonstrate this fact to yourself, hold this figure at arm's length, cover your left eye, and focus on the center of the X. Slowly move the figure toward you, staring continuously at the X. At some point, you will no longer be able to see the red spot. This is the point at which the red spot's image has fallen on the blind spot in your right eye. The red spot will reappear if you move the figure even closer.

cones. When a receptor cell absorbs light energy, the cell generates a small electrical signal. The strength of this signal is determined by the amount of light energy absorbed. As Figure 4.3B shows, the receptor cells then stimulate the neighboring **bipolar cells,** which in turn stimulate the neighboring **ganglion cells.** The ganglion cells form fibers of the **optic nerve,** which carries visual information from the eye to the brain for interpretation.

If we trace the path of each optic nerve to the brain, we find that the area of the retina through which the optic nerve leaves each eye contains no receptor cells. Consequently, this area is aptly named the **blind spot.** Using Figure 4.4, you can demonstrate to yourself that the image of an object that falls on the blind spot is completely invisible. Why, then, do we not see "holes" in our visual field? One reason is that the blind spot in each eye is off center, so one eye can usually see what the other does not. Also, because the eyes are constantly moving, the brain can readily fill in missing visual information.

Another feature of the optic nerve's pathway to the brain is the crossover point, called the **optic chiasma,** where the nerves from each retina meet and then split. Fibers from the left half of each eye go to the left hemisphere of the cerebral cortex, and fibers from the right half of each eye go to the right hemisphere. As a result, if damage occurs to the visual cortex of one hemisphere, only one side of each eye is affected.

Abnormal pressure on the optic nerve is responsible for the disease called glaucoma, which primarily strikes people over forty. The buildup of pressure

begins in the aqueous humor when fluid does not return to the bloodstream as quickly as it is produced. The fluid accumulates, exerting pressure on the lens and in turn on the vitreous humor and the retina. At first this pressure shuts off messages in the nerve fibers that carry information about peripheral stimuli, thus causing what is called "tunnel vision." If the disease remains untreated, it will eventually cause total blindness. Glaucoma, in fact, is one of the most common causes of blindness among the elderly.

Beyond the optic chiasma the optic nerve fibers form several pathways through the brain. The most important is the one that leads first to an area of the thalamus that serves as a relay station. From there the nerve network radiates out and travels to the visual cortex, located at the very back of the brain. It is here that the nerve impulses initiated when light hits the retina begin to give rise to the visual sensations we call sight. How this actually happens is still not fully understood. But scientists have discovered important pieces of the puzzle, especially in the last several decades.

How Light Becomes Sight. As the starting point in the visual nerve network leading to the brain, the receptor cells in the retina play a vital role. So let us examine their structure and function in greater detail. Rods and cones are so named because of their characteristic shapes. **Rods** are long thin cells; **cones** are more bulbous, tapering nearly to a point at one end. Each serves a different visual function. Simply stated, the rods mediate nighttime or low-light-intensity vision and the cones mediate daytime or high-light-intensity vision. The cones are also the primary mechanism for color vision (although some data suggest that rods can contribute to color vision as well) (McKee, McCann, and Benton, 1977; Sandberg, Berson, and Effron, 1981). Thus we see little color by moonlight because there is not enough light to stimulate the cones, but we can see shades of light and dark because moonlight *is* intense enough to stimulate the rods. A rod, in fact, is capable of responding to a single photon of light (O'Brien, 1982). Cones, however, provide a much sharper image than rods do. This is why objects lit by moonlight, although visible, may appear coarse and ill defined.

Rods and cones are not evenly distributed over the surface of the retina. Cones are far less numerous than rods (there are about 5 million of them in each human retina, compared with about 120 million rods). But the cones are highly concentrated in and near the center of the retina, an area known as the **fovea.** In Latin the word *fovea* means "small pit," and this is exactly how the fovea of your eye appears—a pitlike depression about 1.5 millimeters in diameter. Many thousands of cones are packed into the fovea. In fact, this area contains no rods at all. When you want to inspect something closely, you look at it with your foveal cones because they provide your sharpest, most detailed vision. Not only are the cones very dense there, they are also heavily exposed to light, since the blood vessels and nerve cells that cover all rods and cones form only a thin layer over the fovea. In addition, many cones in the fovea are connected to their own bipolar cells, which in turn are connected to their own ganglion cells. Thus a majority of foveal cones have their own private "lines" to the brain. Many rods, in contrast, may be connected to a single bipolar cell, which in turn may be one of many such cells connected to a single ganglion. As a result, the signals from rods are usually blended, giving rise to visual images that are not particularly distinct.

The rods are densest a short distance to either side of the fovea. Since these regions have relatively few cones, they tend to be very insensitive to color. You can verify this for yourself by first looking straight ahead and then noting the colors of the objects at the sides of your visual field. They will probably appear much duller than they do when you look at them directly. The portions of the retina to either side of the fovea are very sensitive to movement and dim light, however. This is why, if you want to view a faint star, you tend to look at it out of the corner of your eye.

Regardless of their location, all photoreceptors, whether rods or cones, convert light into electrical signals by means of chemical reactions. These reactions involve light-sensitive pigments. The pigment contained in the rods is called **rhodopsin,** or "visual red," because of its deep-red color. When light strikes a rod, it changes the chemical structure of rhodopsin

by bleaching it (Wald, 1968). This bleaching, in turn, generates neural activity that, after some transformations, travels to the brain. Similar processes take place in the cones, although different pigments are involved.

Because light breaks it down, rhodopsin must continually be regenerated if the rods are to function. In very bright light, the speed of rhodopsin's synthesis cannot keep pace with the speed of its breakdown, and the pigment becomes depleted. Rhodopsin will replenish itself in the dark, but this process takes time. In humans, full recovery of the rods' rhodopsin supply can take up to about half an hour, depending on the intensity and duration of light to which the eye was previously exposed. This is why you have difficulty seeing when you first enter a dark room from bright sunlight: your supply of rhodopsin has not yet had a chance to replenish itself.

Although most people's rods gradually become quite sensitive to dim illumination, some people have persistent difficulty adapting to the dark. This condition, known as night blindness, can be caused by several factors, but perhaps the most common is an inability to metabolize or store vitamin A, which is needed for rhodopsin production. For this reason an increase in vitamin A consumption is often prescribed for night blindness.

Some of the most fascinating physiological discoveries in recent decades have been those regarding the firing of nerve cells in the visual system in response to stimulation of the rods and cones. In 1981 psychologists David Hubel and Torsten Wiesel at Harvard University won a Nobel Prize for their work in this area (Hubel and Wiesel, 1959, 1965a, 1965b, 1968, 1979). Hubel and Wiesel found that each of the millions of neurons in the visual cortex of a higher mammal seems to be activated by a very specific visual stimulus. Some visual cortex neurons respond only to lines of a particular width, oriented at a particular angle, and in a particular part of the visual field. Others also respond to lines of a certain width and orientation, but moving, not stationary, and often traveling in a particular direction. Still others respond not only to a line's width, orientation, and position or direction, but to its length as well.

Such findings have led to speculation that these stimulus-specific cortical neurons—or "feature detectors," as they are often called—perform an early step in the brain's analysis of visual patterns and forms. Imagine yourself looking at a triangle, for instance. It can certainly be thought of as a collection of lines in various orientations relative to one another. It is tempting to surmise that other areas of the brain take this collection of lines and angles registered in the visual cortex and abstract the form "triangle" from it. Unfortunately, the process by which the brain synthesizes separate features into unified visual wholes is still almost entirely unknown. One thing that is almost certain is that this process takes place not in the visual cortex but in some "higher" brain regions to which visual information is subsequently passed (Hubel and Wiesel, 1979).

Understanding Color Vision.

We have talked about the way light eventually gives rise to the forms and patterns that we see. But as everyone knows, the perception of forms is not all there is to human visual abilities. We humans can also see a wide range of colors—about 200 distinguishable shades in all (Coren, Porac, and Ward, 1978). This wide range of colors helps give our visual world its impressive richness. Yet the colors we see are not inherent in the objects around us. They are simply products of the human visual system's response to light of different wavelengths. If you are presented with a wavelength of 480 nanometers, you will see it as a deep blue. If you are shown a wavelength of 700 nanometers, you will perceive it as a vibrant red. But exactly how does your

visual system translate these different wavelengths into the sensations of different colors?

Theories of color vision were proposed long before scientists knew much about the way the visual system works. One of the earliest was given the name **trichromatic** (or three-color) **theory.** It was first advanced by Thomas Young, an Englishman, at the turn of the nineteenth century, and then was reformulated some fifty years later by the German physiologist Hermann von Helmholtz. Proponents of the trichromatic theory reasoned that color vision is probably not explained by the existence in our eyes of separate receptors for each of the approximately 200 colors we are able to discriminate. If this were the case, relatively few receptors would be activated for each color we perceive, and our color vision would not be as sharp and clear as it is. But if there are not 200 different kinds of color vision receptors, how can we possibly see this many shades? The answer given by the trichromatic theory is that we do so by "mixing" colors. In fact, by mixing just three colors of light (blue, green, and red) it is possible to make *every* color on the visible spectrum. Thus three different kinds of cones would be all that the eye needs—one set sensitive to short-wave light (the blue band), another sensitive to medium-wave light (the green band), and a third sensitive to long-wave light (the red band). The many colors we see would simply be caused by differ-

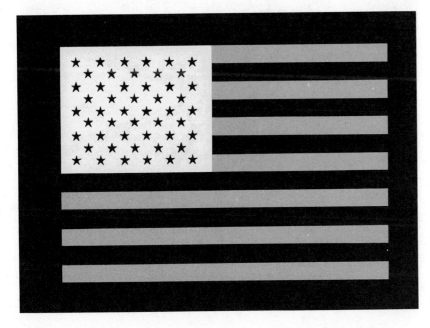

Figure 4.5 Reverse American flag that can be used to demonstrate the phenomenon of afterimages.

ent relative activations of these three types of cones.

But other scientists were not satisfied with the trichromatic theory. One of the things that bothered them was its inability to explain color afterimages. An **afterimage** is a visual impression that persists after removal of the stimulus that originally caused it. An example is produced by Figure 4.5. Rest your eyes for a few minutes and then stare intently at the lower right-hand star in the flag for forty-five seconds. Now transfer your gaze to a white surface, such as a blank sheet of paper. You should see an American flag in its correct colors—blue instead of yellow, red instead of green, and white instead of black. Similarly, a person usually reports seeing yellow shortly after a brief flash of an intense blue light, and green after a brief flash of red light. Why does our visual system produce these sensations?

The **opponent-process theory** of color vision provided one answer. It was first proposed by another German physiologist, Ewald Hering, in the latter half of the nineteenth century, and has subsequently been revised and updated (Hurvich and Jameson, 1957).

Basically, the opponent-process theory argues that there are four primary colors, not three, as the trichromatic theory claims. These primary colors are red, green, blue, and yellow. We speak of red-green and blue-yellow as being *complementary*, meaning that when lights of these paired colors are mixed we see a colorless gray or white. (In fact, as Figure 4.6 shows, the true complementary for red is a blue-green and for blue is a yellow-red, but for convenience we refer to the pairs as red-green and blue-yellow.) Presumably these color pairs are linked in the brain to form "opponent systems." One opponent system contains cells that are excited by red and inhibited by green. This system also contains cells that are excited by green and inhibited by red. A second opponent system responds in the same manner to blue and yellow: some of its cells are excited by blue and inhibited by yellow, while others are excited by yellow and inhibited by blue. (A third opponent system, responding essentially to light and dark, is said to enable the perception of brightness.)

Given this scheme, we can explain color after-

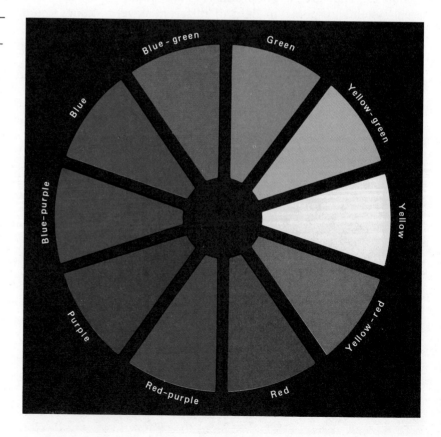

Figure 4.6 The color wheel. Any two colors that are opposite each other are complementaries; that is, combining them produces gray or white. Thus, when red is mixed with its opposite (really a bluegreen, not a pure green), we see a grayish-white color.

images. When you look at the green stripes in Figure 4.5, you are stimulating the green response in your red-green opponent color system. Soon, however, this response adapts and becomes less vigorous, a process we described earlier in this chapter. You then shift your gaze to a white surface. Normally you see this surface as white because the light reflected from it stimulates equally your red and green responses, giving rise to a colorless sensation. But because your green response in a striped pattern has been depressed through adaptation, your red response dominates and you see a set of red stripes. In much the same way, the opponent-process theory explains why we never speak of seeing a greenish red or a yellowish blue. These color pairs are wired as opposites in the brain—when simultaneously stimulated in normal circumstances, they produce a sensation of white.

The trichromatic theory and the opponent-process theory were originally proposed as competing explanations of how we see colors. Recent evidence suggests, however, that they are not mutually exclusive. Both seem to have validity, but at different levels of the visual system. At the lowest level—the level of the receptor cells—the trichromatic theory appears to apply best. Researchers have identified three types of cones, each containing a slightly different form of a light-sensitive pigment called **iodopsin.** This pigment, not to be confused with the reddish rhodopsin contained in the rods, is purple. Each form of iodopsin responds to a different band of light waves: the first a short-wave band, the second a medium-wave band, and the third a long-wave band (Wald, 1964; MacNichol, 1964; Mollon, 1982). These somewhat overlapping bands are shown in Figure 4.7. Beyond the cones, however, an opponent-process system comes into play. Investigators have found ganglion cells, cells in the thalamus, and also cells in the visual cortex that respond as predicted by the opponent-process model (Daw, 1968; De Valois, Abramov, and Jacobs, 1966). Exactly how these various systems are interrelated is still largely unknown, however. Much more research is needed—especially about the way colors are registered in the visual cortex and beyond—

before the process of color vision can be fully understood.

We should not leave the subject of color vision without some mention of the abnormality commonly called color blindness. Actually, there are several kinds of color blindness, each caused by a particular defect in the visual system, especially in the composition of iodopsin, the visual pigment in the cones. A person with normal color vision, as we said earlier, has three distinct forms of iodopsin, each maximally sensitive to certain wavelengths of light. Such a person is called a normal **trichromat.** A very few people, in contrast, are totally color blind. They see the world in shades of gray, like the pictures on a black-and-white television. Some people have no iodopsin and see only through their rods. Not surprisingly, such people do not see well in extremely bright light. Similar to the visual world of those who lack iodopsin is the visual world of those who have only one form of this pigment. These people are called **monochromats,** and they, too, cannot distinguish one color from another.

More common is partial color blindness caused by a lack or loss of one of the three visual pigments normally found in the cones (Mollon, 1982). Such a person is called a **dichromat.** Most dichromats are red-

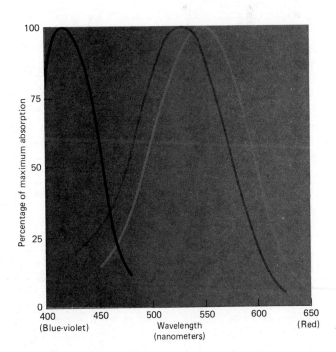

Figure 4.7 While all cones are sensitive to a broad range of wavelengths, each cone is maximally sensitive to a certain band of light waves, as these three curves show.

A   B   C   D

green blind; that is, they cannot see red or green. Although blue-yellow blindness also occurs, it is far less common. Finally, some people have three cone pigments but one of them is abnormally structured—typically one in the red-green range. In vision tests, these people require unusually large amounts of the affected color to produce a "mixed" hue. Psychologists often refer to such a person as color "weak." The photograph above shows how the world appears to people with various kinds of color vision abnormalities.

You should not conclude that all people who have none of the abnormalities mentioned see colors in exactly the same way. Research suggests that they do not. In fact, whole groups of people who share certain slight variations in the eye's structure or chemistry may see their own somewhat unique color spectrums. Marc Bornstein (1973) has noticed, for instance, that societies whose languages lack separate color terms for blue and green are often found at high altitudes or near the equator, regions where sunlight striking the earth contains a large amount of ultraviolet radiation. Significantly, people native to these regions tend to have quite dark pigmentation in both skin and eyes (Coon, 1966; Silvar and Pollack, 1967). These dense pigments filter out harmful ultraviolet radiation and so provide a kind of protective shield (Judd and Wyszecki, 1963). But coincidentally they also absorb significant amounts of light in the

The same scene as perceived by a person with normal vision and by people with three kinds of color blindness. (A) The scene as people with normal vision see it. (B) The experience of a person who is red-green blind; he or she sees everything in shades of blue and yellow. (C) Someone who is blue-yellow blind sees the world in shades of red and green. (D) The scene as experienced by a monochromat.

adjacent portion of the electromagnetic spectrum—that is, light in the range of 410 to 430 nanometers, or much of what we call blue (Thompson, 1951). As a result, these people tend to confuse blue with the adjacent color on the visible spectrum, green. This confusion, Bornstein argues, may underlie the fact that their languages often make no distinction between these two colors. Although this theory is still speculative, it is a fascinating argument in support of the idea that differences in biological makeup may give human beings slightly different sensory perspectives on the world.

Hearing

Waves of Sound. Whereas visual receptors in the eyes convert light waves into neural signals, auditory receptors in the ears convert waves of sound. Sound waves are caused when changes in the pressure of the atmosphere cause air molecules to vibrate. When you turn on a radio, for example, the amplifier makes the speaker vibrate. The vibrating speaker alternately pushes against the air in front of it, compressing it, and pulls away from the air, allowing it to become less dense, or rarefied. These waves of compressed and rarefied air molecules then strike the eardrum, pushing and pulling it in the same pattern as the vibrating speaker, although with much less intensity. Other sound-producing stimuli—a rustling piece of paper, a honking horn, a vibrating set of vocal cords—create sound waves in essentially the same way.

The number of compression-rarefaction cycles that occur per second determines a sound wave's **frequency.** (Sound waves are measured in cycles per second, or hertz, abbreviated Hz.) Frequency corresponds to the pitch we hear: the higher the frequency, the higher the pitch. The human ear is sensitive to frequencies from about 16 Hz to 20,000 Hz. Since human voices range from 100 Hz to 3,500 Hz, we can easily hear them. In fact, our ears are most sensitive to sounds in the frequency range of human speech. This is a good example of how two of our physiological systems—speech and hearing—have coevolved, thus facilitating communication. Frequencies outside our range, in contrast, are inaudible to us. You cannot hear the sound made by a dog whistle because it is above 20,000 Hz, but dogs can hear it because their auditory systems are sensitive to these higher frequencies.

The intensity of a sound wave, the amount of pressure it exerts, corresponds to its **amplitude**—that is, to the distance of its peaks and valleys from a baseline of zero. The greater the amplitude of a wave, the louder it sounds to a listener. Amplitude is usually expressed in a unit of measurement called a decibel. Normal conversation takes place at about 50 to 60 decibels, but humans can also hear sound of much lower amplitude. It has been calculated that a person can actually hear the sound of one air molecule striking the eardrum. This feat can be accomplished only under ideally quiet circumstances, however. Normally, background noise makes such acute hearing impossible. At the other extreme, sounds above 120 decibels are likely to be painful to the human ear, and people who are frequently exposed to such sounds can suffer permanent hearing loss through damage to delicate portions of the inner ear. Rock musicians, for example, sometimes become partially deaf, as do workers constantly exposed to the roar of heavy machinery.

Basic Workings of the Auditory System.

The human ear is a masterpiece of engineering. Into a space of about one cubic inch are packed all the amplifying mechanisms needed to make audible the buzz of a tiny mosquito or the splash of a single drop of falling water. To understand how the ear works, we must understand the structure and function of its three interrelated parts: the outer, the middle, and the inner ear. (See Figure 4.8.)

Sound is funneled into the outer ear through the **pinna,** the skin-covered cartilage visible on the outside of the head. From the pinna, sound travels down the **auditory canal,** a passageway about an inch long sealed off at its inner end by the thin membrane called the **eardrum.** Because of its long, narrow shape, the auditory canal resonates as sound passes through it, and so the sound is amplified. It has been calculated that for frequencies between 2,000 and 5,500 Hz, the pressure exerted at the eardrum is about twice that exerted at the entrance to the auditory canal.

The eardrum responds to changes in air pressure by moving in and out. Its movement, however, is extremely slight. When you listen to a normal speaking voice, your eardrum vibrates only about 100 millionths of a centimeter. Nevertheless, this is enough to set into motion three tiny, interconnected bones on the inner side of the eardrum in the area known as the middle ear. These bones, called the **hammer,** the **anvil,** and the **stirrup** because of their distinctive shapes, are positioned and linked in such a way that movement of the eardrum moves the hammer, which in turn moves the anvil, which in turn moves the stirrup, which ultimately presses against the **oval window,** a membrane stretching across an opening to the inner ear. The hammer, the anvil, and the stirrup are the smallest bones in the human body, no bigger than the letters on this page.

But why are these bones needed? Why isn't the ear constructed so that sound energy passes directly from the eardrum to the inner ear? The answer lies in the fact that the inner ear is filled with liquid, and liquid is much more difficult to compress than air. Consequently, the pressure that sound waves typically exert on the eardrum must be substantially amplified if the liquid in the inner ear is to be set in motion. Motion is

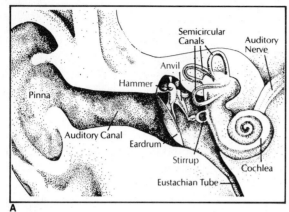

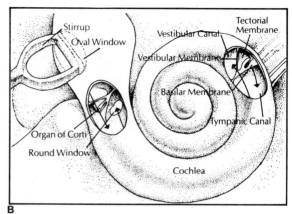

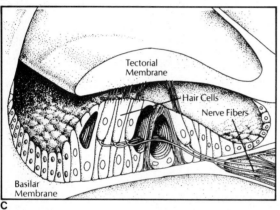

Figure 4.8 The hearing process. (A) Cross-section showing the outer, middle, and inner ear. Sound waves pass through the auditory canal and are transformed into mechanical vibration by the eardrum. The three small bones—hammer, anvil, and stirrup—amplify this motion and transmit it to the oval window of the cochlea, which is depicted in B. The motion of the oval window sends pressure waves through the fluid in the cochlea in the directions shown by the arrows. (C) Closeup cross section of the hair cells positioned between two membranes, within the cochlea. Waves in the cochlear fluid cause the basilar membrane to vibrate, which in turn disturbs the hair cells, the receptor cells of hearing.

initiated in two ways. First the bones of the middle ear act as a series of levers, each one increasing the pressure on the next. In addition, the fact that the oval window is up to thirty times smaller than the eardrum means that the pressure per square millimeter it receives is likewise increased. The end result is that the pressure exerted by the stirrup on the oval window can be up to ninety times greater than the pressure that the original sound wave exerted on the eardrum.

This amplified pressure is then transmitted to the fluid in the spiral-shaped part of the inner ear called the **cochlea.** The cochlea is divided into several canals separated by membranes. Within the central canal is a string of many thousands of receptors, called **hair cells** because of their long hairlike projections. The hair cells are positioned between two membranes, one of which, called the **basilar membrane,** is quite elastic, and the other of which, the **tectorial membrane,** is relatively rigid. Movement of the fluid in the inner ear pushes the basilar membrane, which in turn pushes the hair cells against the tectorial membrane,

bending and rubbing them in the process. This movement of the hair cells triggers neural impulses. These impulses travel via the adjacent auditory nerve to the brainstem, and from there ascend through the thalamus to the auditory cortex, where the perception of sounds begins.

Theories of Pitch Detection.

How the brain distinguishes tones of different pitches is not yet fully understood. Just as with color vision, there are two classic theories, both dating back to the nineteenth century. One was first proposed by Hermann von Helmholtz, the physiologist who helped formulate the trichromatic theory. He and others argued that each pitch we hear depends on which part of the basilar membrane a given sound wave vibrates the most. This view is aptly called the **place theory** of pitch.

In support of the place theory is the finding that sound waves of different frequencies do indeed vibrate the basilar membrane in a nonuniform manner (Békésy, 1959). High-frequency waves have their maximum effect on the region near the oval window, while mid-frequency waves have their maximum effect near the cochlea's inner lip. Moreover, when small groups of neurons leading from different parts of the basilar membrane are electrically stimulated, people hear sounds of different pitches (Simmons et al., 1965). As you would expect, damage to selected portions of the basilar membrane tends to affect only certain tones. With age, for instance, many people gradually lose their sensitivity to high-frequency tones, so that by the age of seventy they cannot hear frequencies greater than 6,000 Hz. This high-tone hearing loss among the elderly is caused by deterioration of receptor cells close to the oval window.

Unfortunately, however, vibration of the basilar membrane does not occur in such a completely tidy fashion as the place theory predicts. Particularly troublesome is the fact that low-frequency sound waves tend to vibrate the membrane fairly uniformly across its surface. The second major theory of pitch detection overcomes this problem by assuming that the exact location of the basilar membrane's vibration is not especially important. Instead, the **frequency theory** argues that the basilar membrane vibrates in exactly the same frequency pattern (the same number of cycles per second) as the original sound wave, thus causing neural impulses to fire in that pattern too. These different patterns of neural firing in turn determine the pitches we hear.

The frequency theory has problems of its own, however. Remember from Chapter 3 that each time a nerve impulse travels down an axon, the cell must have a brief time to restore its firing potential before another impulse can be triggered. This fact imposes a limit on the number of nerve impulses a single cell can transmit in any given period. A thousand impulses per second is probably the maximum. How, then, can the rate of firing of the auditory nerves mimic the frequencies of many of the sound waves that hit our ears? As we said earlier, the human auditory system is capable of detecting frequencies of up to 20,000 cycles per second. No single nerve cell could possibly fire this rapidly.

Although this problem at first seemed perplexing, Ernest Wever and Charles Bray (1937) ultimately proposed an answer, which they called the **volley principle.** It is based on the assumption that the frequency of neural firing which the brain detects is determined not by the rate of firing of single neurons, but rather by *groups* of neurons. Think of the audi-

tory nerve as consisting of squads of rifle-firing soldiers (related groups of neurons). Each soldier must take time to reload after firing, and so can fire only a small number of shots in any given period. But if the squad of soldiers fires in a volley pattern, so that some are always firing while others are reloading, the group as a whole can substantially increase the total number of shots per time unit. The neurons of the auditory system, Wever and Bray argued, operate in much the same fashion. This theory explains why they can in fact follow sound frequencies above 1,000 Hz—up to a rate of about 4,000 cycles per second.

Thus both the place theory and the frequency theory help explain how we perceive pitch. Many physiologists believe that the two probably operate together to give us our powers of pitch discrimination. For sounds of intermediate and high frequencies, the place theory seems to apply. The location of maximum vibration on the basilar membrane does indeed change as the sound frequencies in this range are altered. In fact, for higher frequencies, there seems to be a one-to-one correspondence between the area of the basilar membrane being displaced and the area of the auditory cortex being activated. At lower frequencies, however, vibration of the basilar membrane is too diffuse to support the place theory. In this range, the frequency theory provides a better explanation of pitch perception. But note that there seems to be a lower-intermediate frequency range in which *both* mechanisms may operate. This may help explain why our pitch perception is so acute for sounds within this range—a range that corresponds to the frequency levels of normal human speech.

The Skin Senses

The skin contains receptors for at least five sensations: touch, pressure, warmth, cold, and pain. As Figure 4.9 illustrates, these receptors have different structures, and they lie at different depths in the body tissue. All connect with neurons that transmit information, usually first to the spinal cord and then through the thalamus to the somatosensory area of the cortex.

Scientists do not yet have a clear picture of the relationships between these various types of receptors embedded in our tissues and the various skin sensations that we feel. The receptors around the roots of hair cells seem to produce the sensation of touch on

Figure 4.9 A cross-sectional diagram of human skin. Different kinds of receptors have been identified near the surface of the skin, but there is considerable uncertainty about their functions. Meissner's corpuscles are believed to be pressure sensitive. Pacinian corpuscles may be additional receptors for "deep" pressure. Free nerve endings may be important in the sensation of pain. It is speculated that Krause bulbs are responsive to cold and Ruffini endings responsive to warmth.

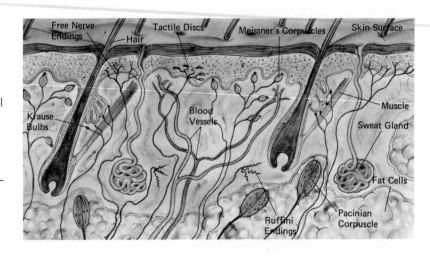

the skin's surface, as do the Meissner's corpuscles, which are abundant in hairless areas, such as the fingertips, palms, and lips. Lying below these two surface receptors are the Pacinian corpuscles, which seem to respond to pressure within muscles and internal organs. The receptors believed to be responsible for the sensations of warmth and cold are the Ruffini endings and the Krause bulbs, respectively. Interestingly, the sensation of heat can be produced by the simultaneous activation of warm and cold receptors (the "cold" receptors responding to extreme heat as well as to cold). Researchers once believed that free (in contrast to encapsulated) nerve endings were associated with the sensation of pain only. But the cornea of the eye, which contains almost nothing but free nerve endings, is responsive to pressure and temperature as well as to pain (Geldard, 1972). Thus to understand pain, as to understand any other sensation, we must look beyond the various neural receptors.

Any explanation of pain must be able to account for all of this sensation's unusual characteristics. Sometimes, for instance, people continue to experience pain after its original cause has disappeared. Sufferers of neuralgia (an infection of the peripheral nervous system) sometimes complain of persistent pain even after the infection has cleared up. Related to this phenomenon is referred pain—the sensation of pain in one location in the absence of any direct stimulation of that site. People suffering from angina pectoris report pain extending from the chest to the forearm, though the pain is thought to originate in the heart (Barlow and Mollon, 1982). In addition, psychological and emotional factors can alter the experience of pain, magnifying or inhibiting it. When

people are anxious, for example, they often report more discomfort from a painful stimulus than they do in a more relaxed mood (Merskey, 1973). Likewise, strong emotions can sometimes make us forget about pain. Soldiers in the heat of battle have been known to suffer quite severe wounds and hardly know it until after the fighting has died down. In fact, the modern approach to childbirth is based on the assumption that people can consciously reduce pain by intensely concentrating on other things. Millions of women trained in natural childbirth attest that this strategy works (Coren, Porac, and Ward, 1979). How can such phenomena be explained?

One very influential model that can account for all of these factors is the **gate-control theory** (Melzack and Wall, 1965). It argues that the neurons that carry messages of pain up the spinal cord to the brain receive input from several different types of peripheral nerve fibers. Some (often called C fibers) are small in diameter and relatively slow in conducting, while others (often called A fibers) are large in diameter and relatively fast in conducting. Within a region of the spinal cord are certain interneurons that serve as "gate cells." These cells are inhibited by activation of the C fibers and excited by activation of the A fibers. Most important, the activity of these interneurons is tied to responses in the pain pathway leading to the brain. When the interneurons are excited, they block the transmission of pain messages up the spinal cord. Thus high activation of the A fibers relative to the C fibers can actually close the pain "gate," causing the brain to sense little or no pain.

You can easily see how this theory could explain some of pain's unusual features. Persistent pain after a wound or infection has healed, for instance, may be caused by damage to the *A* fibers. Because the *A* fibers involved can no longer stimulate the interneurons and close the pain gate, the person feels pain chronically. In a somewhat similar fashion, psychological and emotional factors from higher brain centers are assumed to send messages downward through the spinal cord to affect the activities of the interneurons, thus accentuating or reducing pain sensations.

The gate-control theory of pain is still controversial. Some researchers have found that the peripheral nerve fibers and spinal cord neurons presumably involved in it do not operate in precisely the ways the gate-control theory predicts (Whitehorn and Burgess, 1973). Yet therapeutic treatments based on gate-control theory have often been quite successful. Electrical stimulation of *A* fibers, for example, has been found to relieve pain in chronic pain sufferers for up to thirty minutes (Wall and Sweet, 1967). It has even been suggested that gate-control theory may explain how acupuncture works. With acupuncture, pain is alleviated when small needles are inserted into various points on the body, sometimes heated, twirled, or electrically stimulated. Acupuncture has been used successfully instead of anesthetics in major surgery (Hilgard, 1975). Perhaps this practice activates the *A* fibers and closes the pain gate. Much more research needs to be done, however, before this and other mysteries of pain and its relief are solved.

The Chemical Senses: Smell and Taste

The human senses of smell and taste are closely related. Not only do both respond to the chemical composition of stimuli, but they are very close together physically. This is why we often confuse or blend their separate sensations. When describing how food "tastes," we usually include its odor, which circulates from the back of the mouth up into the nasal cavity. The intimate relationship that usually exists between taste and smell is most noticeable when the sense of smell is temporarily blocked. Try biting into an apple and then a raw potato while holding your nose. You will probably have difficulty distinguishing between the two tastes. And for the same reason food has a flat, uninteresting flavor when you have a bad head cold. Despite this close interaction, however, taste and smell are distinct senses, so we will consider each separately.

Smell. The sense of smell, or **olfaction,** is commonly considered to be one of the "lower" senses, probably because it contributes less to reasoning and memory, our "higher" mental functions, than vision and hearing do. This lesser importance is reflected in the human brain. Relatively speaking, our olfactory regions are much smaller than those of lower animals, which depend more heavily on odors for information about their environments. Nevertheless, the sense of smell can be vital to our survival. A primary function of smell for humans seems to be to warn us of potentially toxic substances that we may eat or inhale. In addition, the ability to detect odors is a major basis for one of life's greatest pleasures, eating, a pleasure that is backed by a multimillion-dollar spice and condiment industry. As we will see later, loss or distortion of our sense of smell can be a very disturbing experience.

Smell requires that vaporized molecules of a substance enter the nasal passages and contact the **olfactory membranes** that line the roofs of these cavities. Often we make this happen deliberately, by sniffing. Research shows that people have their own distinctive styles of sniffing in order to detect an odor, and that these sniffing styles probably maximize vapor contact with the olfactory membranes given the shape of the person's nose (Laing, 1982). Within the olfactory membranes are millions of receptor cells, each with hairlike projections reaching out into the circulating air. When molecules of certain airborne substances contact these receptors, nerve impulses are generated. These impulses travel directly to the **olfactory bulbs** at the forward base of the cerebral hemispheres. From there nerve signals are relayed to various other parts of the brain, where the odor is consciously perceived and analyzed.

Most odors to which human beings are sensitive are organic compounds, but little else is known about why people can smell some volatile substances (substances capable of releasing molecules into the air) and not others. Nor is much known about why certain groups of odors smell alike. One theory is that the quality of an odor is related to the size and shape of the molecules that give rise to it (Amoore, Johnston, and Rubin, 1964). Molecules of various sizes and shapes are presumed to fit into slots on the receptor cells, much as keys fit into locks. In support of this theory, researchers have shown that people's judgments about the similarities among odors are related to measures of molecular similarity (Amoore and Venstrum, 1967). Unfortunately, this relationship between chemical structure and type of odor sensed does not hold for all substances, so we still are uncertain about the physical basis of different kinds of smells.

Taste. Compared with our sense of smell, our sense of taste seems quite restricted. Although we can easily detect and identify odor sources from substantial distances, taste sources must be placed in the mouth to be perceived. In addition, we perceive fewer distinct tastes than odors. Most people can discriminate among hundreds of odors, yet they appear to sense only four basic categories of taste: sweet, sour, salty, and bitter. Other taste sensations are generally regarded as mixtures of these four or as some combination of taste and smell (Bartoshuk, 1971).

Yet even though we can detect only four basic categories of taste, the receptors in our organs of taste, the **taste buds,** are highly sensitive to these four categories. A salty or sweet solution applied to the tongue for only a tenth of a second is enough to trigger an appropriate taste sensation (Kelling and Halpern, 1983). Figure 4.10 shows that different areas of the tongue are especially sensitive to one or more of the four basic taste qualities. The front of the tongue is particularly sensitive to sweet and salty, the sides to sour, the back to bitter. To a remarkable extent these various receptor sites operate independently. This is why, even though a food has a mixture of taste qualities, we can still identify its component tastes.

The fact that we detect each of the four basic tastes somewhat independently also means that each can be selectively suppressed or distorted. Cocaine is one drug that temporarily suppresses all tastes, but it always eliminates them in a particular order: bitter disappears first, then sweet, then salty, and finally sour (Moncrieff, 1966).

Sometimes a person's sense of taste may become permanently distorted. Consider the well-documented case of a restaurant owner known as Rudy C. (see, for example, Roueché, 1977). After recovering from a brief bout of flu, Rudy found that everything tasted like rotting garbage. He could manage to eat only bland foods, such as boiled potatoes and milk. His sense of smell was affected, too, and this severely restricted his activities. He could not work because his

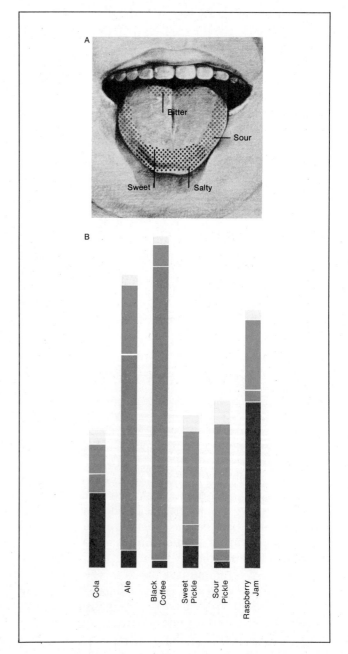

Figure 4.10 (A) A map of the human tongue showing the areas of maximum sensitivity to the four fundamental kinds of taste sensation. (B) The tastes of six foods analyzed into the four components of taste shown in A. The length of the colored bars indicates the amount of each component judged to be present in the taste of the food by subjects in a psychophysical experiment. (*Data from Beebe-Center, 1949.*)

restaurant kitchen stank of burning plastic; he could not relax in his back yard because his lawn had an overpowering odor of green grass; he could not even sleep because his pillow had a terrible stench of dirt. Rudy's affliction was finally diagnosed as hypogeusia, a condition that involves loss of taste discrimination, sometimes accompanied by distortions of smell. Doctors have found that hypogeusia can often be cured or substantially alleviated by heavy doses of zinc or copper, minerals that people with hypogeusia seem to lack.

How do the taste buds function in a normal person? The upper surface of a normal human tongue, where the taste buds are most concentrated, contains about 10,000 of these structures, mostly grouped in hill-like projections known as **papillae.** It is the papillae that make the top of your tongue appear bumpy. With time, liquids washing over the tongue can gradually erode the papillae, thus decreasing the number of functioning taste buds. This is one reason why taste acuity tends to diminish in old age. The taste buds themselves are actually embedded beneath the surface of the papillae, with access to the outside through a tiny hole, or taste pore. Each taste bud contains receptor cells, which are connected to nerve fibers that carry taste information to the brain. How these nerves function is not completely understood. In several animal species, the individual nerve fibers respond to more than one kind of taste stimulus. This fact suggests that the neural code for different tastes may be based on different patterns of activity in the thousands of nerve fibers leading from the tongue. An alternative possibility is that each nerve fiber carries a message regarding only one of the basic taste sensations.

The sense of taste is an excellent illustration of the fact that different people sometimes perceive the world in very different ways. You have undoubtedly known people whose taste preferences do not precisely match your own. Does the person who heaps four teaspoons of sugar into a cup of coffee taste what you would taste if you took a sip of this sweet brew? There is a good possibility that he or she does not. This person may well be more sensitive to the bitter taste of coffee than other people are, thus requiring more sugar to compensate. The fact that such differences in taste sensitivity do exist has been demonstrated in the laboratory. About a third of the human population, for example, is insensitive to a normally very bitter-tasting substance called phenylthiocarbamide, or PTC. The cause appears to be a genetically determined absence of one of two tongue receptor sites for bitter taste. Interestingly, this same physical trait also seems to make people who cannot taste PTC insensitive to the bitter taste of the relatively small amount of caffeine in coffee (Bartoshuk, 1974). The sensations we experience, then, are always the products of our individual sensory systems, and these systems can in some ways vary from one person to the next.

PERCEIVING A COMPLEX WORLD

Earlier we defined perception as the process whereby the brain interprets the sensations it receives, giving them order and meaning. We also pointed out that in everyday life it is hard to separate sensation from perception because the two are so closely linked. But some stimuli help us to make this distinction. Look, for example, at Figure 4.11. From a sensory perspective the drawing really amounts to just three solid circles with a wedge missing from each one, plus three roughly 45-degree angles. Yet we perceive much more in it than this. A white fan-shaped figure seems to project forward at the center of the drawing, as if it were partially covering a triangle and

Figure 4.11 Subjective contours. The brain seeks to tie the components of an incomplete picture together by creating the perception of contours that complete the picture. (*After Kanizsa, 1976.*)

three complete circles. The shape appears to have distinct contours, even though in reality you know that none exist. This perception is called a **subjective contour**—a line or shape that appears to be present but is not physically there (Kanizsa, 1976). Subjective contours are one result of the brain's automatic attempts to understand and give meaning to visual images. Although you are seldom aware of it, the brain is constantly interpreting sensory data in such ways. These fascinating processes, and the explanations for them, are the subject of the rest of this chapter.

Some Perceptual Processes

Over the years psychologists have studied many perceptual processes. Of great interest to a group of researchers known as gestalt psychologists was the way the brain orders sensory stimuli and perceives them as unified wholes. Other psychologists have been concerned with other kinds of perceptions. Some have investigated **perceptual constancies**—the tendency of the brain to see the world as consisting of objects with stable properties even though the images we receive of them are constantly changing. Still others have been intrigued by **depth perception**—the brain's tendency to see the world in three dimensions

although the images that strike our retinas are in two dimensions only. In the following sections we will explore all three of these aspects of perception.

Gestalt Principles. The gestalt movement began in Germany in the early twentieth century. Such psychologists as Max Wertheimer, Kurt Koffka, and Wolfgang Köhler believed that it is impossible to understand perception simply by analyzing each of the many sensations registered in the brain when we see, hear, smell, taste, or touch something. Often, the gestalt psychologists argued, our perceptions are *more* than the sensations that give rise to them. These investigators called a meaningful pattern that the brain constructs from bits and pieces of sensory information a ***Gestalt,*** which in German means "pattern" or "whole," and thus the movement got its name. The photograph below shows an example of the gestalt concept. This figure consists of just a series of black blotches, but we see it as more than that. Because of the way the blotches are organized, we perceive the form of a spotted dog sniffing in a seemingly wooded area. This image is a gestalt, a perceptual whole, which goes beyond the parts that compose it.

The early gestalt psychologists were mainly interested in determining the "rules" that the brain uses to

A stable differentiation of the elements of this picture into figure and ground is difficult at first, and would probably be impossible if you had no previous knowledge of or experience with Dalmatian dogs. The knowledge that there is a Dalmatian dog in this picture, however, makes it possible to differentiate one set of spots as figure and the other spots as undifferentiated ground. (*R. James.*)

order sensory information into wholes. So in their research they typically presented people with various stimuli—often dots or musical tones—and asked them to describe what they saw or heard. From their data they developed principles related to the perception of gestalts. Two of their major concepts are *perceptual grouping* and *figure and ground.*

Perceptual grouping is one way of forming relationships among sensory stimuli. Several principles of grouping are illustrated in Figure 4.12. In part A, dots of equal size are evenly spaced across a field, and we perceive no stable distinguishing pattern. In part B, the spacing between the dots has been changed so that we see them as forming four parallel lines. This effect demonstrates the principle of **proximity:** stimuli that are close together tend to be seen as a group. In part C, the dots in part B have been slightly rearranged so that we now perceive two curved lines. In this case, the principle of **continuity** overrules the influence of proximity: dots that form a single, continuous grouping are seen as a gestalt. Another organizing principle, illustrated in part D, is **similarity.** Here we perceive an *X* in the original pattern of A because the dots that form the *X* are similar in shade.

These principles of grouping apply not only to vision but to other senses as well. Consider a musical composition. The notes of a melody are automatically grouped according to their proximity in time. However, in a composition that includes two melody lines played simultaneously—a Bach fugue, for example—the principle of continuity overrides that of proximity. Notes of the separate melodies are *not* perceived as a single gestalt.

Various psychologists have suggested that all these principles of grouping can be integrated under a single concept: **simplicity** (Attneave, 1954; Hochberg, 1964). Simple patterns are more easily perceived than complex ones, whether the simplicity is a result of proximity, continuity, similarity, or some other principle of perceptual organization. Thus, despite conflicting cues and possible interpretations, Figure 4.13 is seen as two interlocking circles, by far the simplest way to perceive it.

Another basic perceptual principle extensively studied by gestalt psychologists is the division of stimuli into figure and ground. When we look at a scene with any detail, we automatically separate it into regions that represent objects, or **figure,** and regions that represent spaces between objects, or **ground.** This ability to distinguish objects from space does not

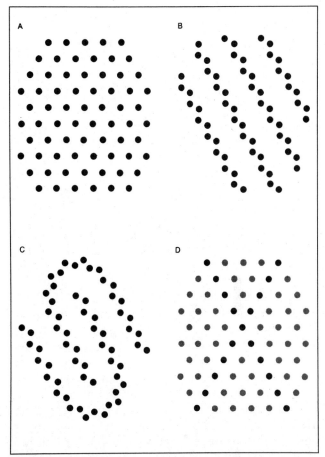

Figure 4.12 A demonstration of some of the gestalt principles of organization. The pattern of evenly spaced identical dots in A is not easily organized. It is seen either as an undifferentiated field or as a set of unstable overlapping patterns. In B a stable perception of parallel lines emerges because of the *proximity* of some dots to others. When some of these lines are made *continuous* with one another in C, dots that are physically quite distant from one another are seen as belonging to a single curved line. In D a very stable organization emerges suddenly because some dots have been made *similar* to one another and different from the rest.

seem to depend on past experience. When people who have been blind from birth are given sight through surgery, they very quickly are able to separate figure from ground (Senden, 1960). When stimuli are very ambiguous, however, experience does help in this process. Your knowledge of what a dog looks like, for instance, is an enormous aid in perceiving the forms in the photograph opposite. In fact, without such knowledge, this perception would be almost impossible.

Figure 4.13 An illustration of the perceptual tendency toward simplicity. Despite conflicting cues, this figure is seen as two intersecting circles. The circle is among the simplest of perceived forms and provides by far the simplest means of interpreting this pattern.

Figure and ground are ambiguous in the photograph because the blotches are vague and the contours ill defined. In other cases figure-ground ambiguity is caused by the fact that the picture is essentially reversible. Examine Figure 4.14. Is this a white vase against a black background or two black facing profiles against a white background? Depending on your perspective, it may be either, and most people can easily switch from one perception to the other. Interestingly, if you were to draw a small line anywhere on the white portion of this figure, the clarity of that line would vary greatly as you reversed figure and ground. A line drawn on what is currently figure would be distinct and very noticeable, but just by switching your perspective and making this area ground you would make the same line appear to recede and fade (Wong and Weisstein, 1982). This is because the brain emphasizes figure at the expense of ground.

Our tendency to distinguish figure from ground is not limited to vision. When we follow someone's voice at a noisy party, that voice becomes the figure and all other sounds become ground. If we shift our attention to another voice, the second voice replaces the first as figure. Similarly, if we walk into a kitchen filled with unfamiliar cooking odors and suddenly recognize the aroma of brewing coffee, that odor becomes a figure, reducing the other odors to ground.

Perceptual Constancy. In addition to the principles of perceptual organization analyzed by gestalt psychologists, we routinely impose order on sensory information in other ways. One, which we introduced earlier, is our tendency to maintain perceptual constancy. When you walk toward a tree, for instance,

the image that the tree casts on your retinas steadily enlarges, its colors become more distinct, and the details of the branches and trunk sharpen. Yet you do not perceive the tree as suddenly growing bigger, changing color, or acquiring details before your eyes. Even when large changes occur in the sensory information received from objects, we tend to ignore these moment-to-moment changes in favor of a view of the world that is constant and predictable. Thus, although the image of a departing car rapidly becomes smaller, we do not perceive the car as actually shrinking, and when it turns a corner, and we view it from the side instead of from the rear, we do not think it has literally changed its shape. How does the brain maintain such perceptual constancies in a world of ever-changing stimuli?

Let us consider size constancy. An object's distance and the size of the image it projects on the retina are inversely related: the greater the distance, the smaller the projected image. This relationship, moreover, has a ratio of 1 to 1. When an object's distance from the eye is doubled, for instance, its projected size is halved. The brain takes these facts into account when judging true size. If a tree 200 feet away looks about half the size of a tree 100 feet away, a person will automatically perceive them as being nearly the same height.

This size analysis can operate effectively, however, only if distance cues are clear. If they are not, a person can easily be fooled about an object's real size. The reverse, of course, is also true: if an object is not the size you expect it to be, you can easily misjudge its distance from you. The Allies took advantage of this

Figure 4.14 The reversible vase-face. This drawing is a classic demonstration of figure-ground ambiguity. What you perceive as figure and as ground depends on a number of factors, including your expectation.

fact during their invasion of Normandy in World War II. In the early-morning twilight they dropped two-foot-tall dummies of paratroopers onto fields away from the planned landing site on the coast. When the dummies hit the ground, the impact set off a series of small explosions, simulating rifle fire. In the poor light and general confusion, German observers thought the dummies were real paratroopers attacking from a substantial distance. Only when the Germans responded and moved close enough to see the dummies did they realize that the dummies' small size had misled them about distance. In the meantime, the Allies had gained extra time for their landing.

Depth Perception. What the Allies had actually done in this case was to take advantage of the fact that relative size has an important influence on the perception of depth. Depth perception is simply the ability to tell how far away an object is. Because the images cast on the retina are in two dimensions, not three, depth perception cannot be explained by the eye's anatomical structure. Instead, depth perception, like perceptual constancy, must be an outcome of the way the brain organizes and gives meaning to sensory information. Let us examine some of the ways this process works.

First, depth perception is partly the result of the fact that the brain receives visual input from two eyes rather than one. Since the eyes are set apart from each other, each views the world from a slightly different angle, so that the two retinas receive slightly different images. This difference in retinal images is called **binocular disparity.** You can demonstrate binocular disparity to yourself by holding a finger in front of you and looking at it with one eye at a time. The image registered by the right eye will be slightly left of center, while that registered by the left eye will be slightly right of center. Now line up your finger with some other object that is farther away, and look at both your finger and that object with one eye at a time. As you switch from eye to eye, your finger will seem to jump back and forth in relation to the more distant object because the binocular disparity of far objects is less than that of near ones. The brain uses such binocular disparity cues to help judge distances. In some way that is not yet completely understood, the information from our two eyes combines, perhaps in the visual cortex, to give a sense of depth.

It is not necessary to have two eyes to perceive depth, however. Several monocular cues—that is, cues potentially available to one eye only—augment depth perception. One of these cues is **motion parallax,** the differences in the relative movements of retinal images that occur when we change position. An easy way to demonstrate motion parallax is to look toward two objects, one very near you and the other some distance away, and move your head back and forth. The near object will seem to move more than the far object. Because of this disparity, when you look out the side window of a car as you drive along a highway, nearby trees seem to zip by while distant mountains may not appear to move at all. We use such differences in apparent movement between near and far objects to help perceive depth.

Other monocular depth cues do not depend on movement. One, mentioned earlier, is **relative size.** When we think that objects are the same size, the one that casts the smaller retinal image is perceived to be farther away. Another monocular cue to depth is **linear perspective,** produced by the apparent convergence of parallel lines as they recede into the distance. **Texture gradient** also influences depth perception. In a highly textured scene, such as the one in the photograph below, the near stones appear coarser in texture and the more distant ones finer. Then, too, we judge distance by the **partial overlap** of objects. When one object appears to cover another, we perceive the object that is covered as farther away.

An example of texture gradient as a cue to depth perception. (© *Frank Siteman/Stock, Boston.*)

Perceptual Illusions

Usually the perceptual processes we have been discussing serve us quite well. But when these processes are applied in unusual circumstances, they can sometimes give rise to **perceptual illusions**—that is, perceptions not in accord with the true characteristics of objects—because our perceptual processes have been fooled.

Illusions of this sort provide important insights into the way our perceptual processes normally operate. At first glance this may seem a contradiction. How can illusions shed light on normal perceptual functioning? To help answer this question, examine the room shown below, known as the Ames room after its inventor, Adelbert Ames. Using one eye only, the viewer peers into the room through a small hole in the front wall, thus eliminating the depth cues normally provided by binocular disparity. Since the viewer cannot move his or her position, depth cues from motion parallax are also eliminated. The observer therefore relies mainly on linear perspective to judge the shape and depth of the room. But linear perspective is distorted by, among other things, the way the "windows" are painted on the rear wall. These windows are really trapezoids (taller on the left side than on the right), but they appear to be rectangular because they parallel an angled rear wall and a downward-sloping floor. The viewer receives the impression of a normal rectangular room in which each of the two women stands at an equal distance from the peephole. Thus, when you perceive the woman on the right as gigantic in comparison with the woman on the left, it is not because your normal powers of perception have broken down. You are applying the perceptual processes that successfully serve you in everyday life to a stimulus purposely designed to produce perceptual error.

To understand this important point more fully, study Figure 4.15, which illustrates two other illusions apparently caused by a misapplication of perceptual processes related to size constancy.

Such illusions are of more than simply theoretical interest. They can be applied quite purposefully to create a desired effect. A motorist driving at a constant speed over evenly spaced horizontal lines, for example, will become accustomed to the constant amount of time it takes to drive from one line to the next. If the lines are spaced progressively closer together, even though the motorist continues at the same constant speed, he or she will experience the illusion that the car's speed is increasing and will slow down to compensate (Denton, 1971). This technique has been used to induce drivers to slow down when leaving high-speed roads and when approaching toll booths.

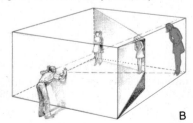

The Ames room. The illusion is produced by trapezoidal windows that run parallel to the sloping floor, making the room look rectangular (A). In B the actual construction of the room is compared with the way the room is perceived. The brain infers that both women standing against the back wall are at the same distance from the eye and interprets the difference between the size of their images as a real difference in size. (*Photo by Robert Berger, reprinted with permission of* Science Digest © *Hearst Corporation.*)

A

B

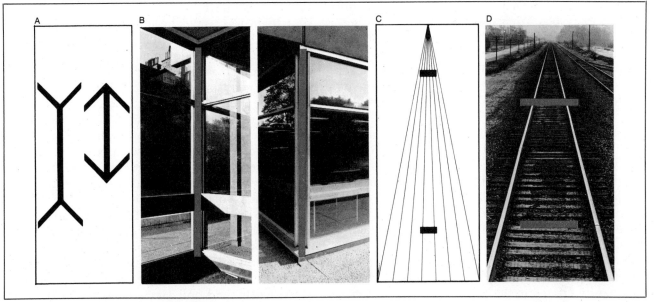

Figure 4.15 Two famous illusions and possible explanations of the way they work. The vertical lines of the figures in the Müller-Lyer illusion (A) are identical in length, but they do not appear to be. An explanation for this illusion, suggested in B, is that the arrow markings on the lines in A cause them to be perceived as three-dimensional objects that have corners. The corners seem to induce a size-constancy effect: The vertical line that appears to be distant is perceived as larger. The horizontal lines in the Ponzo illusion (C) are also identical in length. As the photograph in D suggests, this figure, too, could easily be perceived as three-dimensional, and again size constancy would cause the apparently more distant "object" to be scaled up in apparent size relative to the "nearer object" (*After Gregory, 1970*).

The Development of Perceptual Processes

We have talked a great deal about the ways in which we perceive the world. But we have not yet raised the question of how these perceptual processes develop. Historically, there have been two rather extreme lines of thought on this issue. The first, called the **empiricist viewpoint,** argues that perceptual processes are largely a matter of learning. Babies, it claims, enter the world with little or no ability to see form, depth, perceptual constancies, and so forth. To them the world is "one great blooming, buzzing confusion," as psychologist William James (1890) once put it. Only

gradually do infants learn to infer the perceptions we take for granted on the basis of the kinds of cues we discussed in the previous sections. On the opposite side of this controversy is the **nativist viewpoint,** which holds that not all of perception can be accounted for by learning. Perceptual processes also arise quite automatically from the ways in which our sensory systems work. As we will discuss in more detail later, the current perspective in psychology holds that neither of these traditional viewpoints is adequate in itself. Only through the interaction of inherited biological factors and experience do our perceptual processes unfold. This is why traditionally both the empiricists and the nativists have been able to muster impressive evidence in support of their views.

Evidence for the Influence of Learning. When you are shown a black-and-white photograph, do you have any problem seeing it as a representation of the real world? Of course not. In fact, so lifelike does the picture look that it is hard to believe that anyone could fail to perceive its various forms. It may therefore surprise you to learn that in cultures where people have no experience with photographs, a black-and-white picture may be completely meaningless. One group of anthropologists, for instance, reported that when a woman of the African San people was shown a photo of her son, she had great difficulty perceiving the image (Segall, Campbell, and Herskovitz, 1966). What she was accustomed to seeing dramatically influenced what she in fact saw.

Other perceptions are also shaped by cultural experiences. You had no trouble seeing the Müller-Lyer illusion in Figure 4.15, for example, partly because Western culture affords you numerous opportunities to view right angles, both in real life and on the printed page. People who have not had this experience are much less susceptible to the illusion. The Zulus of southern Africa traditionally grow up in an environment characterized by roundness and lack of "carpentered" corners. Unlike us, they live in round, packed-mud houses with cone-shaped thatched roofs. As a result, while Westerners learn to use the angles in the Müller-Lyer illusion to infer distance, Zulus make no such automatic inference (Segall, Campbell, and Herskovitz, 1966). Significantly, however, Zulus who have migrated to the cities and live in Westernized environments come to see this illusion readily.

Further evidence for the influence of learning on perception comes from the phenomenon of **illusion decrements**—the fact that the longer you scan certain illusion-producing stimuli, the less strongly you experience the illusion. Consider again the Müller-Lyer illusion. If you were to scan Figure 4.15A for a full five minutes, the illusory elongation of the left-hand line relative to the right would probably decrease by about 40 percent (Coren and Girgus, 1972,

1978). This effect would result from the fact that your brain was using the information you received from the figures to correct the perceptual error. In short, you would be learning how to look at these stimuli and perceive their true length. In a sense you would be reversing the previous learning that gave rise to the illusion in the first place.

Studies of young animals raised in restricted visual environments also lend support to the importance of learning to perception. In one early study, R. Held and A. Hein (1963) raised kittens in the dark until they were two to three months old, then began to expose them to visual stimuli in the experimental apparatus shown in Figure 4.16. As you can see, two kittens were placed simultaneously in the same circular chamber, but only one was allowed to walk normally (led by a rotating harness); the other was carried in a small carriage and denied the use of its legs. Later, when Held and Hein tested the animals for depth perception, they found that the "carried" animal had significant depth impairment. The development of normal depth perception, they concluded, is greatly facilitated by the chance to learn about the visual world while the individual actively moves in it. In much the same way, human infants who are given ample opportunity to reach for and manipulate objects tend to develop accurate reaching behavior somewhat earlier than more restricted babies do (White, 1971).

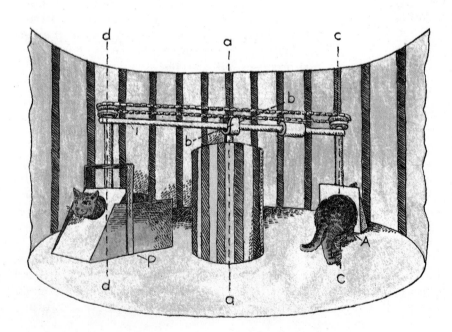

Figure 4.16 Apparatus used in the experiment by Held and Hein. Although the "passive" kitten on the left receives about the same amount of visual stimulation as the "active" one on the right, it does not develop depth perception, while the active kitten does. Feedback from self-induced movement seems to be an important element in learning how to see things in depth. (*After Held and Hein, 1963.*)

The visual cliff apparatus. An infant who can crawl may cross the glass surface over the "shallow" side but is unlikely to venture out over an edge that appears to be a sudden drop or to cross the surface over the "deep" side. *(Courtesy, Dr. Richard Walk.)*

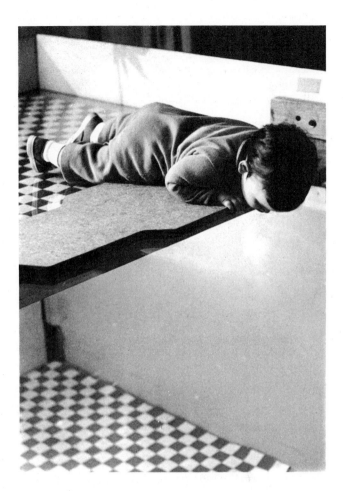

Evidence for Inborn Mechanisms.

Studies such as those just discussed clearly demonstrate an important influence of learning on perception. But is *most* of what we perceive simply a product of our various experiences? This is the point on which many psychologists have taken issue with the strict empiricist view. James Gibson, for instance, has persuasively argued that many kinds of perception do not require elaborate inferences by the brain on the basis of past learning (Gibson, 1950, 1966, 1979). Instead, perception is a *direct* outcome of the way our sensory systems work.

Some of the evidence in support of this viewpoint comes from research with infants. This research shows that babies have the ability to see form, depth, and perceptual constancies at impressively early ages. Psychologists have tested young infants for depth perception, for instance, by means of a clever apparatus called the visual cliff, designed by Eleanor Gibson and Richard Walk (1960). As the photograph shows, it consists of a large glass table with a checkerboard pattern beneath. On one side of the table the pattern is directly against the glass, while on the other side it is several feet below, giving the impression of a cliff. When babies two and three months old are placed face down on the table's "deep" side, their heart rates increase significantly, suggesting that they perceive the cliff (Campos, Langer, and Krowitz, 1970). Because infants this young have not yet had a great deal of visual experience, especially the "active" kind Held and Hein found important, it seems likely that their ability to perceive depth in this instance is not just a product of learning. Instead, depth perception may to some extent emerge "automatically" as a child's visual system matures.

Additional evidence that certain aspects of perception may be built into our sensory systems comes from studies that use visual illusions to which not everyone is susceptible. If you follow the instructions for viewing the painting shown on the next page, for instance, you may think you see the spiral rotating—or you may not. Apparently it all depends on how your sensory-perceptual system is structured. About 60 percent of people perceive the illusion of strong clockwise rotation, while the other 40 percent perceive either a counterclockwise motion or no motion at all (Fraser and Wilcox, 1979). Even more important, about 90 percent of all identical twins (that is, twins who developed from the same fertilized egg and therefore have identical genetic makeups) perceive the stimulus in exactly the same manner. Only about 50 percent of other brothers and sisters share the same way of seeing the spiral. This is strong evidence that some aspects of perception are heavily influenced by inherited biological factors, as well as by learning and experience.

The Interactionist View.

As we mentioned earlier and will discuss more fully in Chapter 8, on human development, most psychologists now believe it is fruitless to try to argue that any aspect of behavior is

Under proper conditions, this painting by Alex Fraser produces an illusion of rotary motion in some people. To see if you perceive the illusion, stand about two feet from the drawing and gaze at a point about five to ten inches below the edge of the spiral. It may help to move your gaze slowly along a horizontal line. If you are like most people, you will see the spiral rotating clockwise. (*Courtesy, Alex Fraser, F.A.A., University of Cincinnati.*)

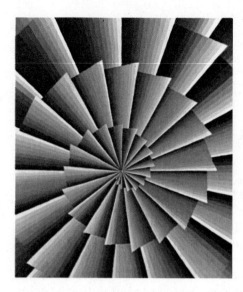

entirely a product of biological inheritance or entirely a product of experience. Instead, the contemporary developmental perspective is that the way we come to think and act is the outgrowth of heredity and environment working together. This view applies to the development of perception, as it does to every other human trait. What we consciously see, hear, feel, and so forth is partly the result of the way our sensory systems are programmed by inheritance and partly the result of what we have learned through exposure to our worlds.

This crucial interaction between heredity and experience is vividly demonstrated by research into the development of the visual cortex. Remember from our earlier discussion that in virtually all higher species, cells in the visual cortex respond only to very specific stimuli. In the adult cat, for example, some cells respond only to lines or edges oriented at a particular angle; others respond only to objects moving in a particular direction. In addition, some cells in the adult cat's visual cortex are driven only by the left eye, others are driven only by the right, and many others (often called binocular cells) are driven by both eyes. Investigation of the visual cortex of newborn kittens shows that some of the cells at this early stage of life are likewise tuned to very specific stimuli, although others are more broadly sensitive to all visual inputs (Wiesel and Hubel, 1965). This finding suggests that within the womb, in the absence of any visual experience, the visual cortex is genetically programmed to begin taking on its adult structure. An intriguing question for psychologists has therefore been to what extent the development of a fully mature visual cortex is simply programmed genetically, and to what extent it can be influenced by early life experiences.

The answer, of course, is that an infant's genetic program and its visual environment closely interact. In one experiment, for instance, R. Blake and H. V. B. Hirsch (1975) denied newborn kittens the simultaneous use of both eyes. On one day they cov-

ered the left eye with an opaque contact lens; on the next they covered the right eye, continuing in this manner over a period of several months. At the end of this period the experimental kittens had difficulty perceiving depth. What had happened to them? The answer lies in the visual cortex. The experimental treatment had prompted the development of two distinct sets of cells, one set activated by the left eye, the other by the right. This pattern is quite different from that found in the visual cortex of a normal adult cat, where most cells receive impulses from both eyes. Such binocular cells, it seems, are essential for normal depth perception, and they do not develop as they should without normal two-eyed visual experience early in life.

Perhaps you are thinking that this experiment, however fascinating, is rather remote from conditions in the real world. Under normal circumstances, you may be reasoning, babies are hardly ever denied the simultaneous use of both eyes. Or are they? Consider the child who is born with misaligned eyes. Because the two eyes do not cooperate normally, the infant gets little experience using both eyes together. Thus, if this condition is not corrected by the age of about five, few binocular cells will be found in the cortex, for much the same reason that they were absent in Blake and Hirsch's kittens. The result is impaired depth perception (Banks, Aslin, and Letson, 1975).

In addition to emphasizing the critical interaction of heredity and environment in the development of perception, such research stresses another important theme of this chapter. This is the fact that perceptual processing can vary from one person to the next. Some of these variations may arise largely from differences in visual experience, while others may be more genetically based. But whatever the cause, the end result is that each of us constructs a perceptual world that is in certain ways unique.

SUMMARY

1. **Sensation** is the process whereby stimulation of receptor cells in various parts of the body sends nerve impulses to the brain, where they register as a touch, a sound, a taste, a splash of color, and so forth. **Perception** is the process whereby the brain interprets the sensations it receives, giving them order and meaning.

2. In analyzing the relationship between what a person senses and what a stimulus is physically like, psychologists study three basic things: the quantity of a stimulus needed for a person to sense it (known as the person's **absolute threshold**), the ratio between the intensity of a stimulus and the intensity of its resulting sensation (known as a **sensory ratio**), and the factors that reduce or increase sensory capacities, one of which is **sensory adaptation.**

3. People have long been fascinated by **subliminal perception**—the apparent ability of the brain to register a stimulus presented so briefly or weakly that it cannot be consciously perceived. There is evidence that, in carefully created laboratory situations, subliminal perception may in fact occur. But the extent to which such perceptions actually influence behavior is highly controversial and very much open to question.

4. The sensation of sight begins when light waves pass through the eye's **cornea, pupil,** and **lens** and strike the light-sensitive surface called the **retina,** at the back of the eyeball. Here receptor cells convert light energy into nerve impulses, which travel via the **optic nerve** to the brain, where they give rise to the perceptions of shape, color, depth, texture, movement, and so forth. Little is known about exactly how these perceptual processes occur. One early stage takes place in the visual cortex, which consists of cells that are activated by highly specific visual stimuli, such as lines in a particular orientation.

5. The receptors in the eyes are of two kinds, **rods** and **cones.** Both convert light into electrical signals by means of chemical reactions involving light-sensitive pigments. Rods mediate low-light-intensity vision, while cones mediate high-light-intensity sight. Cones also trigger the perception of color. Scientists do not yet fully understand how color vision occurs. Part of the answer lies in the fact that our cones contain three different forms of pigment, each maximally sensitive to light of different wavelengths. According to the **trichromatic theory** of color vision, the many colors we see are caused by different relative activations of these three types of cones. This explanation alone, however, has proved incomplete. Investigators have also found that nerve cells in the visual system respond in an opponent on-off fashion to complementary color pairs, thus providing support for what is called the **opponent-process theory.**

6. Sound waves travel down the **auditory canal** to the **eardrum,** which responds to changes in air pressure by moving in and out. Its movements set in motion three tiny bones called the **hammer, anvil,** and **stirrup,** which amplify the pressure exerted on the **oval window** leading to the inner ear. Within the inner ear's spiral-shaped **cochlea** are thousands of receptors called **hair cells,** which trigger nerve impulses when they are bent and rubbed by movement of the **basilar membrane.** These impulses then travel via the **auditory nerve** to the brain, where the perception of sound occurs.

7. There is still debate over how sound waves of different frequencies are translated into the perception of different pitches. According to the **place theory,** each pitch depends on which part of the basilar membrane a given sound wave vibrates the most. According to the **frequency theory,** pitch depends on the patterns with which auditory nerve cells fire, these patterns presumably matching the frequencies of the original sound waves. Both these theories appear to have merit.

8. The skin senses include touch, pressure, warmth, cold, and pain. From receptors lying at different depths in the body tissue, these sensations are transmitted to the brain. Understanding how pain occurs is particularly difficult because of this sensation's unusual characteristics. Not only does pain sometimes occur when there seems to be no physiological cause for it, but emotions can greatly enhance or reduce pain sensations. The **gate-control theory** of pain holds that gate cells in the spinal cord serve to block or release the transmission of pain messages to the brain.

9. The closely linked senses of smell and taste both respond to the chemical composition of stimuli. Smell, or **olfaction,** occurs when vaporized molecules of a substance enter the nasal passages and contact receptor cells in the **olfactory membranes,** which in turn send neural messages to the brain. Different areas of the tongue are especially sensitive to one or more of the four basic taste qualities we perceive: sweet, sour, salty, and bitter. **Taste buds,** grouped on the upper surface of the tongue in hill-like projections called **papillae,** contain receptor cells connected to nerve fibers that carry taste information to the brain.

10. The brain plays a vital role in perception by organizing and giving meaning to the information our senses gather. According to gestalt psychologists, the brain is constantly organizing pieces of information into meaningful patterns, called *gestalts*. Two major ways it does this is through **perceptual grouping** and through division of stimuli into **figure** (objects) and **ground** (spaces between objects). Another way that we routinely impose order on sensory information is through **perceptual constancy,** the tendency of the brain to see the world as consisting of objects with stable properties even though the images we receive of them are constantly changing. A third important perceptual process is **depth perception,** the brain's tendency to see the world in three dimensions although the images that strike our retinas have only two dimensions. Depth is perceived binocularly partly as a result of **binocular disparity.** Monocular depth cues include **motion parallax, linear perspective, texture gradients,** and **partial overlap** of objects.

11. When perceptual processes are applied in unusual circumstances, they can sometimes give rise to **perceptual illusions.** Such illusions provide important insights into the way our perceptual processes normally work.

12. There is evidence that both learning and heredity contribute to the perceptions we experience. The contemporary view in psychology is that these two factors are constantly interacting.

SUGGESTED READINGS

COREN, S., PORAC, C., AND WARD, L. *Sensation and perception.* New York: Academic Press, 1979.

A textbook covering a wide range of topics. Taste, smell, and touch are covered, as well as vision and audition.

GREGORY, R. L. *Eye and brain: The physiology of seeing.* New York: McGraw-Hill, 1973.

A lively and highly readable introduction to the area of visual perception.

LEVINE, M. W., AND SHEFNER, J. *Fundamentals of sensation and perception.* Reading, Mass.: Addison-Wesley, 1981.

A textbook that focuses on the processes involved in vision and audition.

LUDEL, J. *Introduction to sensory processes.* San Francisco: Freeman, 1978.

This introductory book on the senses does not assume any prior knowledge either of sensory anatomy and physiology or of perception. It is clearly written and beautifully illustrated.

part 3

LEARNING AND INFORMATION PROCESSING

This section examines thinking. Chapter 5 focuses on learning and the influences that can affect it. How is what we learn stored, and how is it retrieved? Chapter 6 looks at the area of memory and forgetting. Cognition and problem solving are the subjects of Chapter 7: How does thinking proceed?

5

LEARNING

Seymour Lipton, *Loom*, 1965.

Psychologists have been interested in uncovering the basic principles of learning almost from the inception of the discipline. Their interest has been spurred not just by a desire to know how learning takes place but by the hope of applying their discoveries to human problems. In a classic application of learning theory, for example, Mary Cover Jones (1924), a pioneer in this field, attempted to reduce a child's fear of animals. The subject, a thirty-four-month-old boy named Peter, was afraid of rabbits in particular and of furry objects in general, including fur coats, feathers, cotton, and wool. Jones began her treatment by putting a caged rabbit in Peter's room while he was eating, being careful to keep it at a good distance so as not to upset the child. The cage was then moved closer by stages, always at mealtime, and at last, when Peter had become familiar with his new companion, the rabbit was allowed to leave the cage. By this time Peter had entirely overcome his fear—not only of the rabbit but of other furry objects as well—and even expressed affection for the animal. Thus Jones had demonstrated that the pairing of a pleasant activity (eating) with an aversive stimulus (the rabbit) could eliminate a strong fear.

Jones (1974) became interested in the learning approach to changing behavior while working as a graduate student under John B. Watson, the psychologist credited with founding the behaviorist movement in America, and Watson had much to say about the causes and cures of phobias (or irrational fears) such as Peter's. He argued that most human phobias could arise from pairings of previously neutral stimuli with intrinsically fear-arousing events. Such learned responses, Watson claimed, would be very strong and enduring, even likely to persist indefinitely. As you will discover later in this chapter, many contemporary psychologists take issue with Watson's viewpoint, and criticize some of his experimental work for serious methodological flaws (Harris, 1979; Samelson, 1980). Nevertheless, the fact that Watson's and Jones's ideas captured such enormous interest attests to the great importance that psychologists give to the task of understanding human learning.

And no wonder learning has such a prominent place in the discipline of psychology. Learning has an impact on almost everything we think and do. What causes you to perceive depth when you view converging lines on a two-dimensional drawing? Why is it that women in general are more emotionally expressive than men? What accounts for the fact that identical twins can develop quite different personalities? Why do people sometimes persist in behaviors that undermine their own happiness? Why are we sometimes so attracted to another person that we say we are in love? All these and many other questions about human behavior can be explained at least in part by learning.

THE NATURE OF LEARNING

Since learning is a mental activity and not something that can be seen, how do psychologists know when learning has occurred? As you learned in Chapter 1, this was a question that particularly concerned such early behaviorists as Watson, who strongly maintained that subjective reports of mental experiences could not be considered reliable scientific data. The solution the founders of behaviorism advocated, and which has influenced research ever since, is that learning can only be inferred from observation of changes in a subject's *performance*. Performance is something that we can objectively measure. Therefore, a psychologist can set up various situations conducive to learning and measure a subject's performance in each one. To the extent that the situations are carefully controlled, changes in performance can be said to reflect differences in learning.

An example will help clarify the way this process works. Suppose researchers present an eight-year-old boy with a game they have devised that resembles billiards. The object of the game is to launch a ball from a spring-loaded tube so that it hits various targets placed on a billiard table. The ball cannot be shot directly at each target but must instead be ricocheted off one of the table's walls so that it hits the target on the rebound. The boy starts off by angling the launching tube at random, so that he succeeds in hitting his targets only occasionally, by pure chance. But gradually, through trial and error, he begins to aim the launcher more accurately, until eventually he can hit almost any target on the table with just a single shot. From this measurable change in performance the researchers are justified in concluding that learning has probably occurred.

But inferring learning from changes in performance is not as simple as this example implies. Performance may be influenced by many factors other than learning. Physical maturation alone produces some changes in behavior, and behavior is also affected by emotion, motivation, health, and fatigue. Thus, if a football player performs better this week than last, we cannot infer that his improvement is necessarily due to the learning of some new skill. He may have had a cold the previous week or a fight with the team manager, or this week's game may be especially important to him. Similarly, if performance changes for the worse, we cannot automatically conclude that something learned has been forgotten. When our young boy begins to shoot the billiard balls haphazardly after a period of near-perfect scoring, it may simply be that he has grown bored with the game. These additional influences on performance make the task of inferring learning more difficult than it seems at first glance.

Given that learning can only be inferred from performance yet performance is influenced by other things, how do psychologists define learning? A good definition of learning must make several points. First,

it must specify that learning is not necessarily reflected in performance—that learning is merely a *potential* for performance. Second, it must differentiate learning from all the other factors that can possibly influence behavior. To distinguish learning from factors that affect us only temporarily, such as emotion or fatigue, learning can be labeled a *relatively permanent* change in performance potential. And to distinguish learning from physically based factors, such as maturation or illness, learning can be designated as a change in performance potential that results from *experience*. Putting all these elements together, we have the following definition: **Learning** is a relatively permanent change in performance potential that arises from experience (Kimble, 1961).

Such a definition, of course, is quite general. It says nothing about how learning actually takes place. This is the subject we will be exploring in the remainder of this chapter. As you will see, there are actually several different types of learning, each involved in the acquisition of specific kinds of information. *How* we learn, in other words, depends in large part on *what* we are learning.

Perhaps one of the simplest kinds of learning is acquiring the knowledge that things in our environment exist and differ from one another. We accomplish this task by examining novel stimuli with our senses. Most unfamiliar, unusually intense, or unexpected stimuli tend to produce what is called an **orienting reflex,** a response that involves a whole chain of activities—looking, listening, touching, sniffing—designed to enable us to find out what the new stimulus is about. But as we repeatedly encounter the same stimulus, the orienting reflex gradually disappears. The unfamiliar has become commonplace, and we tend to ignore it. Thus, when your car first develops a peculiar rattle, you are likely to pay it close attention. But as time goes by, you may seldom hear the noise, not because it has stopped but because you have become **habituated,** or accustomed, to it. If you become habituated to a stimulus, that means you must have learned something about it. In the case of the rattle, you have "learned" not to be bothered by it.

But even very simple organisms are capable of learning far more than this about the things around them. Animals also learn that certain events are associated with one another. Psychologists call this **associative learning.** Suppose your rattling car suddenly acquires a new sputtering sound. A few seconds after this noise begins, the engine stalls and is very difficult to start again. If thereafter you experience a feeling of anxiety as soon as you hear your finicky engine cough, psychologists would say that you have learned an association between the sputter and the stall and that the anxiety you feel is a **classically conditioned response.** Classical conditioning is a very basic kind of learning, and with just a moment's thought you can probably identify many instances of it. A simple example is that of the dog who learns to cringe and whine whenever it hears the approaching footsteps of its cruel, abusive master. We will say much more about this pervasive form of learning in a later section of this chapter.

Another kind of associative learning is equally pervasive. Individuals are continually discovering that their own actions have both positive and negative consequences, and these consequences, in turn, affect behavior. Thus you may find that if you hit the accelerator every time your car emits its sputter, you can avoid the frustration of stalling in the middle of the road. Psychologists would say that the lurching style of driving you are sure to develop is an **operantly conditioned response.** It is due to a learned association between a particular action (quick pressure on the gas pedal) and a desirable consequence (an engine that does not stall). Clearly, a great deal of our behavior takes place in very similar ways. A child learns to be helpful around the house because that behavior brings him praise and affection. A student learns to study regularly because that behavior earns her good grades. After discussing classical conditioning, we will investigate how such operantly conditioned responses are formed and maintained.

Some psychologists have taken the position that virtually all learning can be explained by classical and operant conditioning. Others argue that while these two forms of learning are important, much of human learning does not fall neatly into either category. Various kinds of **cognitive learning,** they contend, are also crucial to us. By cognitive learning we mean learning that involves the formation of concepts, schemes, theories, and other mental abstractions. This, you will recall, is an area of learning that the behaviorists rejected as too vague and subjective for scientific study. To cognitive psychologists, however, the thought processes going on in a person's mind are just as important as the overt behaviors we can see.

To get a better idea of the aspects of learning on which cognitive psychologists focus, let us return briefly to our earlier example of researchers studying a young boy's mastery of their billiard-type game. Cognitive psychologists would be interested not only in the steadily improving accuracy of the boy's performance but also in the child's improved understanding of how the task should be approached. This particular experimental game, in fact, was devised by the famous cognitive psychologist Jean Piaget to examine how a child's ways of thinking and learning mature (Inhelder and Piaget, 1958). Piaget found that by adolescence a child is able to abstract the general principle behind the game's aiming strategy: the fact that the angle at which the ball hits a wall of the table will always be equal to the angle at which it ricochets. Thus, in mastering the game, the child is learning more than just a set of behaviors. He or she is also learning an underlying rule. We will conclude this chapter with a similar look at learning from the cognitive psychologist's perspective. First, however, our attention turns to classical and operant conditioning.

CLASSICAL CONDITIONING

A famous experiment in classical conditioning was performed by John B. Watson and Rosalie Rayner, one of his students (Watson and Rayner, 1920). Unfortunately, it is somewhat infamous as well, since it involved teaching a previously healthy, normal child to be fearful. Not surprisingly, many psychologists have since condemned experimentation of this sort as highly unethical.

In any event, Watson and Rayner decided to teach their subject, an eleven-month-old boy who is always referred to as "little Albert," to fear a harmless laboratory rat. At the beginning of the experiment he was clearly not afraid of the animal; he enjoyed watching it and even tried to play with it. But his enjoyment quickly changed after Watson and Rayner set to work. Every time they presented the rat to little Albert, one

Every pet owner knows something about classical conditioning. The sight of food will produce expressions of pleasurable anticipation in the animal, but when food is repeatedly preceded by the sight or sound of a can opener, the animal will begin to respond to that neutral stimulus alone. (*Peter Vandermark/Stock, Boston.*)

Perhaps the best-known example of classical conditioning is the conditioned salivation response, studied by the great Russian physiologist Ivan Pavlov. Pavlov's international reputation grew out of his research on the physiology of digestion, which earned him one of the first Nobel prizes in medicine. His work was characterized by both extraordinary ingenuity and total dedication. One story has it that Pavlov even refused extra food rations during the hard times of the Russian Revolution until additional food was also made available to his famous experimental dogs.

Like many great discoveries, Pavlov's discovery of classical conditioning was largely accidental. At the time, he was studying how the mouth prepares itself for food by secreting saliva, which contains digestive enzymes. In a series of experiments with dogs (1927), Pavlov found that the mouth also secretes saliva when food is merely seen or smelled. He called this salivation "psychic secretion" because it occurred in anticipation of food, *before* food was actually presented. Pavlov also found that when a dog first sees an unfamiliar food, it does not salivate. Only when the animal learns that particular sights, odors, or other stimuli are associated with a desirable food will psychic secretions occur. These discoveries provided the foundation for Pavlov's subsequent investigations into classical (sometimes called Pavlovian) conditioning.

Establishing a Classically Conditioned Response

Pavlov's experimental apparatus is illustrated in Figure 5.1. Before the experiment began, each dog underwent minor surgery: a tube was inserted in its cheek so that saliva would flow from the duct in the animal's salivary gland into a glass container. The mechanical device shown on the far left of the drawing kept track of the number of drops secreted. In front of the dog was a food tray from which the animal could eat when food was made available. In his studies Pavlov presented a stimulus—say, a tone—and several seconds later dropped food into the dog's

of them would strike an iron bar with a hammer just behind the child's ear. This terrible noise made little Albert jump, wail, and try to bury his face in the mattress on which he sat. After seven pairings of these two stimuli, little Albert began to respond with fear to the sight of the rat alone, in the absence of the loud noise. And his fear appeared to generalize to other furry objects—a rabbit, a dog, a sealskin coat, even, it seemed, to a bearded Santa Claus mask.

We have said that little Albert's fear of furry white rats was classically conditioned, but what exactly happens when a classically conditioned response is formed? Basically, a neutral stimulus (in this case a laboratory rat) is repeatedly paired with another stimulus (a loud noise) that evokes a response (fear). Eventually, the neutral stimulus alone comes to elicit the response—the rat alone evokes fear.

Figure 5.1 The apparatus used in early studies of classical conditioning. Saliva dropping from a tube inserted into the dog's cheek strikes a lightly balanced arm, and the resulting motion is transmitted hydraulically to a pen that traces a record on a slowly revolving drum. Pavlov's discovery of conditioned salivation was an accidental by-product of his research into the activity of the digestive system.

tray. The dog picked up its food and salivated as the food entered its mouth. As the pairing of the tone and the food continued, the previously neutral stimulus, the tone, began to elicit salivation. Eventually the tone alone was enough to elicit this response. The outcome of one such classical conditioning experiment is shown in Figure 5.2.

Let us summarize Pavlov's findings again. When a stimulus that has no effect on the salivary response, such as the sound of a tone, repeatedly occurs just before food is presented, the tone itself gradually comes to elicit salivation. In Pavlov's terms, the food in the mouth is the **unconditioned stimulus** (UCS), which elicits the **unconditioned response** (UCR) of salivation. The word *unconditioned* indicates that the connection between this particular stimulus and response does not have to be learned. The new stimulus that comes to elicit salivation, in contrast, is called the **conditioned stimulus** (CS), and the animal's saliva-

tion response to it is called the **conditioned response** (CR). The word *conditioned* indicates that this new response is learned through an association. Thus the end result of a classical conditioning experiment is that a conditioned stimulus produces a response similar to the one produced by an unconditioned stimulus. This process is shown in Figure 5.3.

Pavlov found that a large number of auditory, visual, or tactile sensations—including the ticking of a metronome, the flash of a light, or a brush on the skin—can serve as conditioned stimuli for salivation. He also found that, using procedures similar to those just described, he could condition responses other than salivation. Consider the eye blink, for instance. It is used in many classical conditioning experiments with humans, although it was not specifically studied by Pavlov. An eye blink can easily be evoked by a puff of air directed at someone's eye. If a bell is rung immediately before each puff of air occurs, and if this

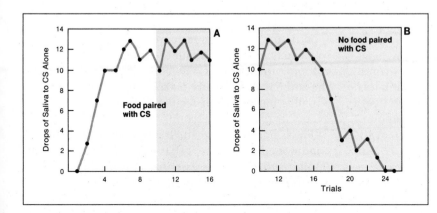

Figure 5.2 (A) Acquisition of a conditioned response. On early test trials—with the tone alone—there is little salivation. Later in the series the tone alone (CS) elicits considerable salivation. A conditioned response (CR) has been acquired. (B) Extinction of a conditioned response. When the tone–food pairings are eliminated, the amount of salivation (CR) to the tone alone (CS) drops steadily until the relationship between the CS and the CR is destroyed.

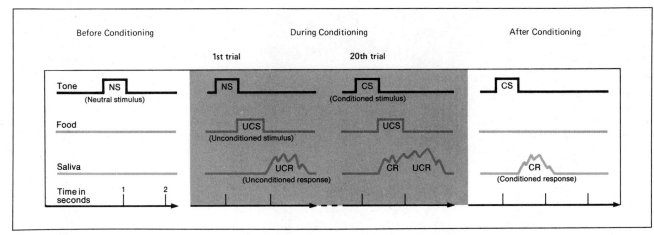

Figure 5.3 The relationship of events in classical conditioning (from left to right). *Before conditioning*—A stimulus such as a tone that elicits no salivary response can be described as a neutral stimulus (NS) with respect to salivation. *During conditioning*—The neutral stimulus, the tone, is paired with an unconditioned stimulus (UCS), food, which elicits the unconditioned response (UCR) of salivation. Repeated pairing of the tone and the food begin to elicit salivation in response to the tone as well as to the food. Because the previously neutral tone is no longer neutral, but capable of calling forth salivation, the tone itself becomes a conditioned stimulus (CS), and the salivation it elicits now becomes a conditioned response (CR). *After conditioning*—Finally, a test with the tone alone is sufficient to elicit salivation.

pairing is repeated several times in succession, the subject will probably learn to blink at the sound of the bell alone, as though in anticipation of the puff. The eye blink, in other words, will be elicited by a stimulus that does not normally evoke it. Blinking in response to the bell has been classically conditioned.

This tendency to react to a previously neutral stimulus, now a CS, as though it were the UCS Pavlov called **stimulus substitution.** In our examples, Pavlov's dogs responded to a tone as though it were food and a person responded to the ringing of a bell as though it were a puff of air directed at the eye.

CS-UCS Contingencies. A strong classically conditioned response can be established and maintained only if certain requirements are met. One is that a **contingency** must exist between the presentation of the conditioned stimulus and the appearance of the unconditioned stimulus (Rescorla, 1967). By contingency we mean a relationship between the two variables such that the occurrence of one seems to depend

on the occurrence of the other. For this reason, the CS in a typical conditioning experiment is presented slightly in advance of the UCS. Pavlov, for example, presented the tone (CS) five seconds before the food (UCS), and in some cases the tone continued until the food was given. If, in contrast, this order of presentation is reversed and the food is given *before* the tone, the animal is not likely to learn to salivate at the tone because it does not signal that food is about to arrive. This presentation of the UCS before the CS is called **backward conditioning,** and it is usually ineffective in establishing a classically conditioned response. For much the same reason, simultaneous presentation of the CS and the UCS is also a difficult way to produce classical conditioning.

If the existence of a contingency between the CS and the UCS is necessary for classical conditioning to occur, it is not surprising that many conditioning failures will result when these two events are presented randomly in time—that is, when there is no consistent relationship between them. If the tone is presented five seconds before the food, then five seconds after the food, then ten seconds before the food, and so on, the animal learns that the tone is not related to the food in any systematic fashion. In fact, such inconsistency may make it difficult to establish a conditioned response to the same CS in later experiments, because the animal has already learned that this particular stimulus has not been related systematically to other events in the past (Rescorla, 1967).

Thus, one requirement for establishing classically conditioned responses is that in most classical conditioning situations it is essential that the conditioned and the unconditioned stimuli occur close together in time; otherwise the subject may fail to perceive the relationship between them. In addition, the CS and the UCS must usually be paired several times in succession to establish a strong conditioned response. So basic are these requirements in most of the classical conditioning experiments psychologists have conducted that many researchers once believed they constituted universal "rules" of conditioning. Findings in the last several decades, however, have uncovered some intriguing exceptions to these traditionally accepted rules, as you will see in the following section.

in depth The Garcia Effect

The time is the mid-1950s. Just a decade earlier physicists working to develop an atomic bomb had succeeded in tapping the secrets of nuclear fission. But how serious were the hazards posed by nuclear wastes and fallout? Many concerned scientists were anxious to find out. Among them was a psychologist named John Garcia.

In the course of his investigation into the effects of radiation on living organisms, Garcia made a puzzling discovery (Garcia et al., 1956). Rats placed in a radiation chamber once a week and exposed to moderate levels of radiation for eight hours progressively lowered their intake of water, as though for some reason they were learning *not* to drink. Yet when the rats were returned to their home cages, they drank as usual. It was only the water in the radiation chamber that they refused to touch. In fact, when they were in the chamber they avoided water even when no radiation was actually given. What could explain this strange behavior? Garcia suspected that it must reflect some kind of associative learning. But what specific stimuli were involved?

Later Garcia believed that he had deduced the answer. This behavior, he proposed, was essentially a case of classical conditioning. The water bottles in the radiation chamber were made of plastic, while the water bottles in the home cages were made of glass. Apparently the plastic bottles imparted a peculiar taste to the water. It was this taste that served as the conditioned stimulus. The unconditioned stimulus was stomach upset caused by exposure to radiation. Irradiation of almost any animal, be it a rat, a mon-

key, or a human being, generally causes severe illness. The plastic-tasting water, then, had been repeatedly paired with stomach upset. Soon the taste of the water alone was enough to evoke nausea and strong avoidance behavior.

Garcia's next step was to conduct controlled experiments to test this hypothesis. He spiked water with various novel flavors and administered various kinds of illness-inducing agents. As predicted, the rats did seem to acquire a classically conditioned taste aversion after the pairing of a new flavor with severe stomach upset. Furthermore, such learning seemed to occur with remarkable speed and to have remarkable persistence. In one of Garcia's experiments, a single pairing of salty water with illness was enough to cause the rats to shun salty water when they encountered it again more than a month later (Garcia, Hankins, and Rusiniak, 1974).

But why, Garcia wondered, had the rats developed an aversion specifically to the water? Why hadn't they developed an aversion to the sight of the experimental chamber as well? After all, it, too, had been associated with illness. Yet experiments showed that it was extremely difficult to get a rat to avoid the *place* where it had become ill, even though that place was readily distinguishable (Garcia, Kimeldorf, and Hunt, 1961). What could be going on here? Was there something special about the link between a certain cue and a certain consequence that made an association between them somehow easier or more difficult to learn? If so, this linkage contradicted one of the basic assumptions about classical conditioning prevalent at the time—the assumption, dating back to Pavlov, that an unconditioned or nonvoluntary response could become conditioned with equal ease to virtually *any* formerly neutral stimulus. Garcia's work suggested that this long-held belief might be false. The nervous system of an organism might be structured in such a way as to facilitate the learning of certain contingencies and hinder the learning of others.

To investigate this intriguing possibility, Garcia and his colleague Robert Koelling designed a clever experiment in which various kinds of stimuli were paired with various aversive outcomes (Garcia and Koelling, 1966). One group of rats was presented with saccharin-flavored water, and as soon as the animals drank it they either received a foot shock or were induced to become ill (by radiation poisoning or injection of a toxin). Another group of rats was presented with water that, when sipped through a drinking tube, set off an impressive display of flashing lights and loud noises. Drinking this "bright, noisy water" was again followed by either a foot shock or an induced illness.

The results of this experiment are shown in Table 5.1. As you can see, whether a rat subsequently avoided the water to which it had been exposed depended on the water's characteristics and what happened after the animal drank it. An aversion developed when saccharin-flavored water was paired with illness and when bright, noisy water was paired with shock. But no aversion resulted when these stimuli were paired in the opposite way—that is, saccharin water with shock and bright, noisy water with illness. Garcia concluded that the ease with which an animal learns a given association seems to depend on some intrinsic relationship between the cue (the CS) and its consequence (the UCS).

Why should this be the case? Garcia believes that the answer lies in the evolutionary history of the species. He argues that natural selection has favored a nervous system that allows rapid learning of contingencies that are common in a given animal's habitat and that are crucial to its survival. Consider the dietary practices of a rat. These animals are opportunistic foragers: they eat virtually anything they can find. Such a strategy has obvious advantages in expanding the supply of available food. But it also involves some risks. It greatly increases the likelihood that a rat will become poisoned by eating something toxic. So any rat whose nervous system is "programmed" to remember foods previously associated with illness will clearly have a better chance of surviving to reproduce. In this way, a "built-in" facility for learning to avoid dangerous foods may have evolved. Therefore, it makes sense that taste but not noise would work as a conditioned stimulus for illness.

This evolutionary perspective helps explain why learned taste aversions violate another traditional rule of classical conditioning—that the UCS must follow the CS within a matter of seconds if learning is to occur. Even in his earliest experiments, Garcia noticed that a fairly substantial delay could occur between the taste of a novel flavor and the onset of illness, yet the animal would still develop an aversion to that flavor. How prolonged could the separation between the CS and the UCS be? Subsequent research showed that it could be very long indeed. In one experiment Garcia found that if delays of up to seventy-five minutes occurred between intake of saccharin-

TABLE 5.1 RESULTS OF THE BRIGHT, NOISY WATER EXPERIMENT

		RESULTS	
		Illness	**Shock**
Cues	Taste	Avoid	—
	Audio-visual	—	Avoid

Source: From "Relation of cue to consequence in avoidance learning" by J. Garcia and R. A. Koelling, *Psychonomic Science,* 1966, *4,* 123–124.

flavored water (the CS) and illness due to injection of a toxic drug (the UCS), a strong taste aversion to saccharin would still be learned (Garcia, Ervin, and Koelling, 1966). Other studies have shown that the lapse between the two can be even longer—anywhere from three to twelve hours, depending on the circumstances (Kalat and Rozin, 1971; Andrews and Braveman, 1975). Furthermore, in many cases tastes intervening between the CS and the UCS do not prevent a strong aversion to the CS from forming provided that the flavor of the CS is novel and salient enough (Revusky and Bedharf, 1967). Such findings are understandable if you assume that organisms have biological predispositions to learn adaptive behaviors. In nature, substantial time gaps often occur between ingestion of a toxin and the subsequent feeling of illness, so any organism capable of learning despite such gaps would clearly have a survival advantage.

During a year spent at the University of Utah, Garcia began a line of research that would put his discoveries to very practical use. He and several colleagues started to investigate learned taste aversions in carnivorous predators, such as coyotes and wolves, which plague sheep ranchers in the West (Gustavson et al., 1974). They found that just one or two meals of sheep flesh tainted with lithium chloride (a chemical that causes severe nausea) were enough to make a coyote refuse to attack lambs. When presented with a lamb, these formerly fierce animals often ran away and retched. Subsequent field studies showed that when similarly tainted bait was scattered around a sheep range, the number of attacks on lambs dramatically decreased. Thus Garcia and his colleagues had found a way to reduce losses to sheep ranchers without killing off the large predators otherwise important to the balance of nature on the ranges.

Do humans also have a built-in facility for learning tastes related to illness? Casual observation suggests that they may. Most of us know at least one person who claims to loathe the very sight of a certain food that was once associated with nausea. Psychologists have seldom investigated these responses in controlled experiments, however. One of the few such studies conducted to date focused on learned taste aversions in children who were receiving chemotherapy for cancer. It is well known that cancer patients often suffer serious loss of appetite. Could this symptom be due to a pairing of food with the severe stomach upset caused by many drugs used in cancer treatment?

Ilene Bernstein (1978) set out to explore this possibility. She took forty-one young cancer patients aged two to sixteen and randomly assigned them to three groups. The patients in group 1, the experimental group, were given a dish of Mapletoff, a novel-flavored ice cream, fifteen minutes to one hour before receiving treatment with a drug that would make them feel ill. The patients in group 2 received no ice cream, but they, too, underwent illness-inducing chemotherapy. Finally, the patients in group 3 ate the Mapletoff but did not subsequently become ill, either because they received no drug treatment or because the drug they were given did not cause nausea. Four and a half months later all the patients were offered two kinds of ice cream: Mapletoff and another unusual flavor called Hawaiian Delight. Only 25 percent of those in group 1, for whom Mapletoff had previously been paired with illness, said that they preferred the Mapletoff. And as expected, these patients ate substantially less Mapletoff than Hawaiian Delight when given a choice of eating as much of either flavor as they wished. This was not true of control subjects in groups 2 and 3. In these groups, 66 and 50 percent of the patients preferred the Mapletoff. Bernstein concluded that humans, like many other species, seem readily to acquire aversions to novel tastes paired with illness.

In a follow-up study, Bernstein, Webster, and Bernstein (1982) extended their earlier findings with ice cream, noting that patients also form aversions to familiar foods eaten before chemotherapy. Interestingly, however, they discovered that this aversion was less marked in subjects who had received a novel-flavored ice cream along with their usual diets. In

other words, these patients associated their uncomfortable side effects at least partly with the test ice cream, while a second group of patients who received no ice cream with their meal had only their normal diets to focus on. This finding suggests that eating problems among cancer patients may be mitigated simply by exposing them to a novel-tasting food. On the other hand, patients in a third group, who ate little or nothing before chemotherapy, were far less likely to develop food aversions of any kind, suggesting that pretherapeutic fasting might be another useful approach.

Extinction of a Classically Conditioned Response

Once a classically conditioned response has been established, can we expect it to be maintained indefinitely? That depends in part on the way the conditioned stimulus and the unconditioned stimulus are related in the future. Pavlov found that a conditioned response will persist only if the conditioned and unconditioned stimuli continue to be paired at least occasionally. If occasional pairing does not occur, the conditioned response will gradually disappear. For example, if a dog has been trained to salivate in response to a tone paired with food, and then the tone is repeatedly presented without the food, the number of drops of saliva will gradually decline toward zero, as shown in Figure 5.2B. This slow weakening and eventual disappearance of the conditioned response is called **extinction** (see Figure 5.4).

You have undoubtedly experienced the extinction of classically conditioned responses yourself. Think of something you feared as a very young child but no longer fear today. This change may well be an example of extinction. Many small children come to fear the dark, for instance, because of its association with unidentifiable sounds and eerie shadows. As they mature, however, they learn that the strange sounds are not followed by bad happenings. As a result, this classically conditioned fear is extinguished.

There is one catch to the extinction of classically conditioned fears, however. When the fear is so powerful that it prompts complete avoidance of the fear-provoking conditioned stimulus, the person may never have the chance to learn that this stimulus is normally quite harmless. If you were once terrified as

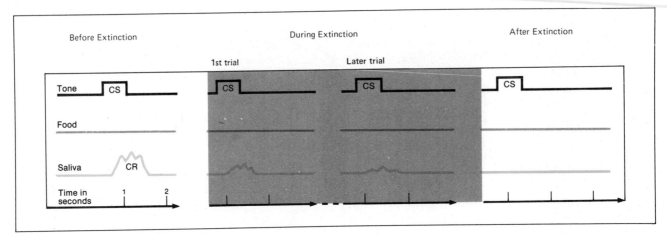

Figure 5.4 The relationship of events in the extinction of a classically conditioned response. The CS is presented repeatedly without the UCS. As a result, the CR gradually diminishes until it is no stronger than it was before conditioning.

a child by the bite of a ferocious dog, for instance, you may never allow yourself to get close enough to other dogs to discover that most are very friendly. As a result, your learned fear may persist. In much the same way, the learned taste aversions studied by Garcia could persist indefinitely because the animal would never venture to experience the conditioned stimulus again.

Applications of Classical Conditioning Principles

Pavlov's experiments in classical conditioning had an enormous impact on American psychology in general and on behaviorism in particular. John B. Watson was so impressed by Pavlov's work that he based most of his analysis of behavior on it. All learning, Watson argued, can be explained within the framework of classical conditioning. According to Watson his famous experiment with little Albert was a provocative demonstration of the far-reaching impact classical conditioning can have.

Today few psychologists (even behaviorists) would agree that all learning can be explained by classical conditioning. Some have also criticized the little Albert study for its reliance on only one subject and its lack of rigor in experimental procedures (Harris, 1979). Still, most psychologists believe that classical conditioning is indeed important in certain types of

learning. As we have seen, emotional responses are particularly susceptible to it. Suppose that in several consecutive arithmetic lessons a child is asked a question and does not know the answer. He experiences sweaty palms, a flushed face, halting speech, and a confused train of thought. In time, the very mention of arithmetic may cause the child to experience these same symptoms of anxiety. This response may be difficult to extinguish, for the very fact that the child becomes so physiologically aroused may cause him to perform poorly, thus maintaining the association.

Watson and his students (Jones, 1974) were among the first psychologists to study how much difficult-to-extinguish fears might be reduced or eliminated. The approach that proved to be most successful was the one pioneered by Mary Cover Jones. In a case like Peter's, the feared object would be paired with a pleasant experience, such as eating or receiving special attention from adults. As a result, the earlier negative reaction would gradually give way to a positive emotional response.

This technique is quite similar to those used today to treat people with strong, persistent, and debilitating phobias. Imagine a young woman for whom riding in an elevator is a terrifying experience. The moment she sets foot inside one, her heart pounds, her legs tremble, she feels queasy and has difficulty breathing. Such intense anxiety naturally imposes severe restrictions on her activities. She cannot live in a high-rise apartment, nor can she visit friends who do. She cannot even accept a job with a firm whose offices are located in a tall building. One very effective technique for reducing such a phobia is called **systematic desensitization.** It involves teaching a person to relax totally in the presence of the fear-arousing stimulus, thus introducing a response incompatible with anxiety. If this woman with an elevator phobia underwent systematic desensitization, she would be trained to relax all the muscles of her body while imagining a series of increasingly anxiety-arousing situations—approaching an elevator, seeing the doors open, stepping inside, watching the doors close behind her, and so forth. If she mastered this task, she might then attempt to remain relaxed during successive stages of an actual encounter with an elevator. By the end of the treatment, if it was successful, she would be able to lead a more normal life. Chapter 16 will say more about systematic desensitization, a form of behavior therapy based on classical conditioning principles.

In the case of systematic desensitization, classical conditioning principles are used to eliminate a previously learned response. But the principles of classical conditioning can also be used therapeutically to *instill* some desired behavior. Many years ago, for instance, Mowrer and Mowrer (1938) proposed a classical conditioning approach to getting young children with a bed-wetting problem to awaken when they are about to urinate, and to get up and use the bathroom. They designed a bed pad that causes a bell to ring the moment it is moistened with the slightest bit of urine. The bell serves as the unconditioned stimulus, which elicits the unconditioned response of waking up. The physical sensation of a full bladder therefore becomes the conditioned stimulus that repeatedly precedes the sound of the bell. In time the child should come to awaken at the bladder cues alone, as if in anticipation that the bell is about to ring. Research has demonstrated that this approach to bed-wetting is a very effective way to establish the desired alternative response (Ross, 1981; Wilson, 1982).

OPERANT CONDITIONING

Even before Pavlov's experiments in classical conditioning, the innovative and highly influential American psychologist Edward L. Thorndike was investigating another form of learning through association. Thorndike was interested in how the *consequences* of an organism's behavior can affect its behavior in the future. In one classic experiment, published as part of his doctoral dissertation, he placed a hungry cat in one of his famous "puzzle boxes" (1932). The box was designed in such a way that if the cat made a certain combination of moves, the door to the box would fly open, allowing the animal to escape. Upon emerging, the cat would be given a piece of fish to eat. Thorndike found that the cat's initial behavior in the box was erratic. It would scramble about and only accidentally make the correct responses. But as the cat was returned to the same box again and again, the animal gradually became more proficient at escaping, until it was eventually able to open the door almost immediately. Thorndike concluded that the cat had learned to escape because the escape response was associated with a desirable consequence—food. This relationship he summarized in the **law of effect.** It states that responses that lead to satisfying consequences will be strengthened and are likely to be repeated, whereas responses that lead to unsatisfying consequences will be weakened and are unlikely to be repeated. In this way Thorndike anticipated later studies on the effects of rewards and punishments on learning.

The Central Role of Rewards and Punishments

B. F. Skinner, the leading contemporary behaviorist, is interested in some of the same problems as Thorndike. Skinner has proposed that the basic mechanism for controlling human behavior is the **principle of reinforcement.** Our social environment, Skinner argues, is filled with positive and negative consequences that mold our behavior as surely as the piece of fish molded the behavior of Thorndike's cat. Our friends and families control us with their approval or disapproval. Our jobs control us by offering or withholding money. Our schools control us by passing or failing us, thus affecting our access to jobs. In short, in all areas of life our actions are shaped by pleasant and unpleasant consequences.

Learning either to make or to withhold a particular response because of its positive or negative consequences has come to be called **operant conditioning.** Important differences exist between classical and operant conditioning. One of the most basic is that classical conditioning usually applies to reflexes (or more generally to nonvoluntary behavior), whereas operant conditioning applies to voluntary behavior. **Operant behaviors** are actions that an organism emits spontaneously—that is, of its own accord. No particular stimulus, for instance, is needed to induce a rat to sniff and move about its cage. Such behavior is as natural to a rat as flying is to a bird or swinging through the trees is to a monkey. Psychologists say that the rat is "operating" on its environment, not responding involuntarily to a particular stimulus in it.

Operant behavior is influenced by some environmental factors—in particular by its own consequences. Consequences can either increase or decrease the frequency of a response. A consequence that produces repetition (increase in frequency) of the behavior that caused it is called **reinforcement** or **reward.** A consequence that produces suppression (decrease in frequency) of the behavior that caused it is called **punishment.** Note that whether a given consequence is reinforcing or punishing can vary from person to person. One child who hits another and makes him cry may be spurred on to increase this form of bullying, for example, whereas another child who experiences the same consequence may feel sorry and refrain from hitting others in the future. For the first child the consequence served as rein-

forcement; for the second it served as punishment. This example emphasizes why the behaviorists have carefully avoided defining reinforcement and punishment simply as "good" versus "bad" consequences. "Good" and "bad" are highly subjective terms, which depend on the individual's viewpoint. It is much more objective, the behaviorists argue, to define reinforcement and punishment in terms of their effects on subsequent behavior, because behavior (or performance) is something that an observer can measure.

After analyzing various consequences that serve to increase the frequency of a behavior, psychologists have drawn a distinction between positive and negative reinforcement. In **positive reinforcement,** the frequency of a response increases because that response is followed by a subjectively positive (pleasant) stimulus. When a hungry rat presses a lever and receives a pellet of food, lever pressing is being positively reinforced. In **negative reinforcement,** the frequency of a response increases because that response either removes some subjectively negative (painful or unpleasant) stimulus or enables the individual to avoid it. When a rat presses a lever that temporarily turns off an electric shock, lever pressing is being negatively reinforced. In both cases, however, the consequence of pressing the lever is reinforcing because it *increases* this particular response. (See Figure 5.5.)

Because negative reinforcement and punishment may both involve aversive stimuli (such as electric shock), they can easily be confused. The trick to keeping this distinction straight is to focus not just on the nature of the stimulus but also on whether that stimulus is being added to or removed from the environment and particularly on the resulting consequences

Figure 5.5 The relationship of events in operant conditioning (from left to right). Before conditioning, some particular response occurs infrequently. Then a food reinforcer is introduced as an immediate consequence of that response. The subsequent rate of responding increases markedly until the response occurs at a very high rate. If the food reinforcer is later stopped, responding will still continue, but only for a short period of time.

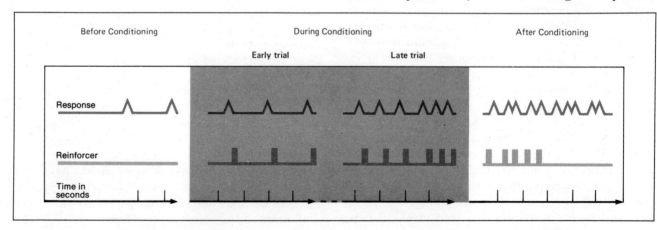

for the individual. When behavior is followed by the *appearance* of an unpleasant stimulus, punishment occurs. Punishment always tends to *decrease* the frequency of the response that provoked it. Thus when a boy is severely scolded for taking his little sister's favorite toy, his action is being punished and he is *less* likely to steal the toy again. In contrast, when a particular behavior is followed by the *removal* of an unpleasant stimulus, negative reinforcement occurs. Negative reinforcement always tends to *increase* the frequency of the response that preceded it. Thus when a boy gives his little sister back her favorite toy to get her to stop kicking him in the shin, his action is being negatively reinforced and he is *more* likely to return a toy when asked to do so in the future.

In these examples, a cause-and-effect relationship exists between a particular behavior (stealing a toy or giving it back) and the outcome associated with it (being scolded or obtaining relief from pain). That is to say, the behavior specifically *produces* the consequence. But although such cases are common, the apparent relationship may not in fact exist. Sometimes a behavior by mere chance happens to be followed by reinforcement or punishment. Although the relationship between the behavior and the consequence in such instances is purely accidental (*not* contingent), the individual sometimes mistakenly acts as though the behavior caused the consequence and so repeats or inhibits the response. Behavior that arises in this way can be called a form of **superstitious behavior.**

Skinner (1948a) produced superstitious behavior in pigeons by presenting them with a food reinforcer on a regular schedule, say every two minutes, regardless of what the pigeons were doing at the time. After a few hours every bird began to develop its own ritualistic, stereotyped behavior, such as bobbing its head, turning in circles, or hopping from side to side. Because this behavior had accidentally coincided with the presentation of a reward, the pigeon now performed it during the intervals between reinforcements, as though there were some contingency between the behavior and the arrival of food.

Human intelligence does not protect us from acquiring similar superstitious behaviors. Why does a gambler blow on the dice before every roll? Why does a football coach wear his "lucky" hat to every game? The reason probably is that at some time in the past these behaviors were accidentally linked with a winning streak. Because the behaviors were reinforced,

they tend to persist, even though no cause-and-effect relationship exists.

Establishing an Operantly Conditioned Response

We have said that though operant behavior is voluntary, its frequency is influenced by its consequences. Thus the general procedure for establishing an operantly conditioned response is to control the consequences of behavior by manipulating rewards and punishments.

One rule of operant conditioning is that the behavior and its consequences must be close enough together in time so that the individual can experience them near to one another. That is, the occurrence of the consequence must seem to depend on the performance of the behavior. When a substantial time gap intervenes between behavior and consequence, the relationship between them may become clouded and learning is more difficult. This is as true for humans as it is for other species. In fact, B. F. Skinner (1983) has argued that one reason why we humans go to war so readily is that the consequences of war (the massive death and destruction) occur a good deal later than the actions that precipitate them.

For operant conditioning of experimental animals in the laboratory, psychologists have created many devices to present rewards and punishments immediately after behavior. One of the best known is the **maze,** in which a hungry or thirsty animal learns to find its way along a complex path that leads to food or water. Another widely used apparatus is the **Skinner box,** or operant chamber, developed by B. F. Skinner (1938). A Skinner box provides a controlled setting in which a rat or other animal may be trained to press a bar or peck a disk for a reward in much the same way that a person pulls a lever to obtain food from a vending machine. The experimenter, of course, can vary the number of times the animal must press the bar to obtain the reward. The experimenter can also vary the type of consequence—from a positive reinforcer, such as food or water, to a negative reinforcer, such as cessation of electric shock. The basic features of a Skinner box are shown in the photograph on the next page.

One potential problem that researchers face in establishing a new operantly conditioned response is getting the experimental animal to perform that behavior in the first place. After all, one cannot reward

The operant chamber, or Skinner box. When the rat presses the bar just visible at right, a pellet of food drops into the tray. (*Ken Robert Buck/The Picture Cube.*)

behavior if it never occurs. Usually researchers circumvent this problem by selecting a behavior that the animal tends to do naturally. No special inducement is needed, for instance, to get pigeons to peck. They peck at virtually everything. So when a pigeon is placed in an operant chamber, it usually soon hits upon the button that the experimenter wants it to press. A food reward can then be delivered and the pigeon begins to learn the association between this behavior and its consequence.

But suppose an animal is slow at performing the particular behavior a psychologist wants to reinforce. Physically forcing the desired behavior would be ineffective because the animal would be too frightened to learn. Must the psychologist therefore wait for a fortuitous accident? To overcome the potential frustration of waiting for an animal to stumble onto the correct response, B. F. Skinner developed a technique called **shaping,** in which an animal is reinforced for displaying closer and closer approximations of the desired behavior.

To understand how shaping works, imagine that you are trying to get a reluctant rat, like the animal shown in Figure 5.6, to press a bar. You begin by reinforcing the first response that shows the rat is on the right track—in this case, approaching the bar. After a few reinforcements, the rat will interrupt its other activities to walk toward the bar. Now you withhold reinforcement until the rat not only approaches the bar but also rises slightly off the floor in front of it. At first you may reward the rat for merely lifting one paw, but gradually you reinforce it only if both paws are lifted high enough to reach the bar. Finally, you make the reward contingent on actually pressing the bar. When the animal learns this contingency, the desired behavior has been shaped, or produced

Figure 5.6 Shaping the bar-press response. A clicking noise first cues the rat to orient itself toward the food box and the bar. The rat is rewarded at first for any movements in the general vicinity of the bar, later only if it rises on its hind legs; and finally only when it places its forepaws on the bar. The weight of the paws activates an electric circuit that automatically dispenses food (reinforcer). The shaping process is now complete.

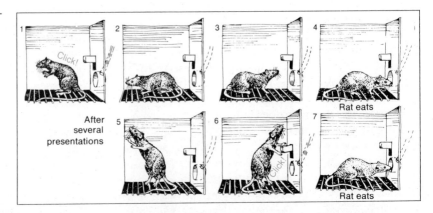

Shaping can be used to train animals to perform spectacular tricks, even those that seem to violate the most deep-seated reactions, such as fear of fire. (*Hank Morgan/Rainbow.*)

through a form of operant conditioning based on reinforcement of ever-closer approximations. Each successive approximation, however, must be only a small step beyond what the subject was previously doing; otherwise, the procedure will fail.

Shaping has been used to train performing animals to do complicated tricks. Chickens, for example, have been taught to play a simple Mozart piece on the piano. Shaping can be used to modify human behavior, too. It is the basic procedure recommended to parents in the popular book *Toilet Training in Less than a Day* (Azrin and Foxx, 1974). And even when not directly told to do so, parents often use shaping to guide their children's behavior. Consider how they teach a preschooler to write his or her name. At first they praise mere scribbles on the paper, but gradually only more accurately shaped letters are rewarded until eventually the child writes the name legibly. Another example of shaping is often seen in political campaigns. Voters' responses to a candidate's speeches (cheers and applause versus stony silence) prompt the candidate to stress very well-received viewpoints and to downplay very poorly received ones. So gradually the politician's words come to mirror more closely what people want to hear. Shaping also provides one important foundation for modern behavioral therapy. As you will see in Chapter 16, it has proved quite effective in treating a number of behavior disorders in adults (Lanyon and Lanyon, 1978; Wilson, 1982).

Maintaining an Operantly Conditioned Response

Once an operant response has been established, how can we make sure that it will last? The key to maintaining operant behavior is continued reinforcement, just as you might expect. But the full story about how best to keep it going is more complex than this. By altering the schedule on which reinforcement is delivered, an experimenter can alter both the frequency and persistence of virtually any operantly conditioned response.

Schedules of Reinforcement. Consider a man who hires himself out to plow fields. He can be paid in one of three ways: by the hour, by the number of acres plowed, or by a percentage of the farm's profits. Clearly, the method of payment can exert a powerful influence on the way this man works. If he is paid by the hour, he may work relatively slowly, especially if only a limited amount of work is available. If he is paid by the acre, he may set his plow shallowly so that he can work faster, and he may space his furrows farther apart. If he is paid a percentage of the profits, he may take care to cultivate the land as effectively as possible, perhaps by plowing the soil deeply to produce plants with a higher yield. Using psychological terms, we would say that each method of payment represents a different **schedule of reinforcement,**

and the plowman alters his behavior accordingly to produce the greatest reward. The same is true of people in other situations. At school, on the job, and in the laboratory, the prevailing schedule of reinforcement considerably controls behavior.

Psychologists have found that the most effective reinforcement schedule for establishing an operantly conditioned response is not the most effective for maintaining that response. New operant behavior is usually firmly established when reinforcement is provided each time the response occurs, as when a rat is given a food pellet every time it presses a bar. This is called a **continuous reinforcement schedule.** Once the behavior has been established, however, the best way to maintain it is to use a **partial reinforcement schedule.** Paradoxically, researchers have found that they induce more behavior per unit of reward when they withhold the reward some of the time than they do when they offer the reward every time the behavior occurs, as we shall see below.

One schedule of partial reinforcement is called a **fixed-ratio schedule.** On this schedule a behavior is rewarded after it occurs a specific number of times. A rat may be reinforced with a food pellet, for instance, for every twenty bar presses. This schedule is analogous to that of the plowman who is paid by the number of acres plowed. The rat performing on a fixed-ratio schedule tends to press the bar at a more rapid rate than it would if it were rewarded continuously. The relationship between work and reward is direct and explicit: the faster the rat works, the more it eats.

Another schedule of partial reinforcement is called a **fixed-interval schedule.** In this situation, the rat is rewarded for a bar press at the end of a fixed interval of time, say one minute, regardless of the number of presses it made in the interim. Thus the first correct response the rat makes after the fixed period triggers reinforcement. This schedule is somewhat analogous to that of a young woman whose mail delivery always comes at exactly noon. Although she is eager to see what the day's mail has brought, she soon learns not to visit her mailbox several times before noon. Once the letter carrier has appeared, she will then wait until the following day before checking the mailbox again. Similarly the rat, having received a reward, will tend to ignore the bar for a while and then gradually increase its bar pressing as the time of the next available reward approaches. A fixed-interval schedule, then, may yield a relatively low frequency of response because the total amount of work performed is unrelated to delivery of the reward.

In contrast to fixed-ratio and fixed-interval schedules, which establish regular and predictable relationships between behavior and reward, some partial reinforcement schedules are irregular and unpredictable. A reward may be given *on average* once every ten responses, for example, with reinforcement sometimes arriving after every response and at other times after twenty or thirty responses. This is called a **variable-ratio schedule.** Similarly, reinforcement may be given *on average* once every ten minutes, with the actual times ranging randomly from once every ten seconds to once every quarter hour. This is called a **variable-interval schedule.** How do you think such reinforcement patterns affect the frequency of behavior? Because variable-ratio and variable-interval schedules are unpredictable, they encourage a subject to test constantly for a reward. As a result, they tend to produce very high rates of response—higher than those associated with fixed reward schedules.

Variable-ratio schedules also result in behavior that is very resistant to extinction. To understand why, imagine yourself at a slot machine. Now slot machines are designed to make money, not to lose it, and most people are aware that in the long run the player is bound to lose. Yet, because the amount and schedule of reinforcement are so highly varied, slot machines have a compelling effect on behavior. People continue to harbor the hope that the next pull of the handle will bring the big jackpot. Consequently, they keep right on playing coin after coin. This would certainly not be the case if a slot machine paid off, say, on a fixed-interval schedule, so that the first response after a fixed period of time triggered a reward. Then people would only have to wait around for the fixed period to elapse, insert a coin, and collect the money. If no reward appeared, they would quickly conclude that the machine was broken and quit.

Because irregular schedules of reinforcement are so powerful, they can easily maintain undesirable responses unintentionally. Consider a tyrannical two-year-old who flatly refuses to go to bed. When his parents insist, he throws a colossal tantrum. Usually the parents try to ignore these outbursts and simply continue with bedtime preparations. But every so often the mother or father can stand the uproar no longer and the little boy is allowed to get his way "just this once." What is going on in this situation? The frustrated parents are unwittingly rewarding the two-year-old's negative behavior on a very effective variable-ratio schedule. To halt the child's bedtime rebellion, the parents must never again give in to his tantrums, no matter how ear-splitting they become (Tavris, 1982).

Stimulus Control. Besides controlling the vigor and frequency of operant responses, reinforcement has another important effect. It relates a particular behavior to stimuli associated with the learning situation. Suppose that a rat has been conditioned to press a bar for a reward whenever a bulb in a Skinner box lights up. In this case, the stimuli of a Skinner box and a lighted bulb have become associated with reinforcement and the behavior of bar pressing. Thus, whenever these stimuli are present, the rat is likely to press the bar. This is called **stimulus control.** The stimuli prevailing at the time of reinforcement have come to control the organism's response.

A human example may help to clarify the concept of stimulus control. Suppose you live in a university dormitory with poor plumbing. Because the cold-water pressure is low, flushing the toilet invariably reduces the amount of cold water being fed to the shower. So if you are unfortunate enough to be taking a shower when the toilet is used, the sound of the flush will probably send you fleeing from the shower stall to avoid the suddenly scalding water. What has happened psychologically here? First, you have acquired an operantly conditioned response: running from the stall to avoid a painful burn. Second, this behavior is under the control of a specific stimulus: the sound of the toilet being flushed. You flee only when you hear this cue.

This example also illustrates how classical and operant conditioning can be combined in a single learning situation. Your flight from the shower to avoid pain is an operantly conditioned response. But what about your reaction of fear to the sound of the flush? This response has probably been learned through classical conditioning. A previously neutral stimulus (the flushing toilet) has been repeatedly paired with a fear-arousing unconditioned stimulus (scalding water) until the flush alone comes to elicit fear. Thus it is not always easy to separate those aspects of a particular response that have been operantly conditioned from those that have been classically conditioned.

Extinction of an Operantly Conditioned Response

When an operantly conditioned response is no longer reinforced, it gradually decreases in frequency and eventually disappears. This extinction process is illustrated in Figure 5.7. For the rat in a Skinner box, bar pressing dies out after food pellets are no longer presented. For the rebellious two-year-old, the tantrums eventually decline once the parents refuse to give in to them. But note that although most behaviors that are no longer reinforced will *eventually* decline in frequency, the response tends to be executed more forcefully during the initial stages of extinction. If a pigeon that has been reinforced for pecking at a light has this reinforcement withdrawn, for example, the bird typically becomes agitated and tends to exaggerate the formerly rewarded response. Similarly, the child whose defiant screams are ignored will probably scream even more frantically before this response is extinguished.

If you think about such exaggeration of previously reinforced behavior, you can probably find instances of it in your own experience. Suppose your front

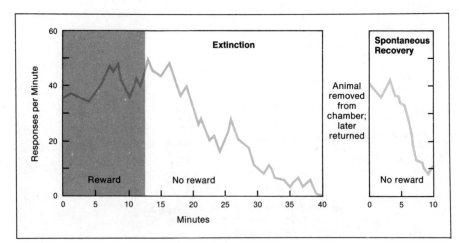

Figure 5.7 Extinction of an operantly conditioned response. Initially the animal's responding is reinforced. After 12½ minutes reinforcement is withheld, and responding steadily declines. After 40 minutes the animal is removed from the chamber. When it is returned, its response begins again at nearly the original rate, even though there is *no* reinforcement. This spontaneous recovery may result from an association between the chamber and being rewarded.

door, which usually works well, does not open one day. In psychological terms, the previously reinforced response of grasping the knob and turning it is no longer rewarded by entrance into the house. Before you give up on the door, however, your efforts to open it will probably become more forceful—you may rattle the knob, pound the door, and give it a good solid kick before finally going to another door.

Now suppose you have been away from home for several days. When you return, are you likely to try the front door again? Most people would. In the same way, if an animal is removed from an experimental chamber for a while after a response has been extinguished and then is put back in, the response will reappear. This phenomenon is called **spontaneous recovery.** During the period when the animal is away from the experimental apparatus, its behavior seems to recover spontaneously from the effects of extinction, at least to some extent. Perhaps the behavior reappears because the animal is responding once more to the stimuli associated with the chamber. In the past it was reinforced for a certain behavior when it was placed there. Why not this time?

Applications of Operant Conditioning Principles

In the last twenty years operant conditioning has gradually found its way out of the laboratory, with its experimental rats and pigeons, and into virtually every center of human life. Operant learning principles have been applied in schools, hospitals, prisons, rehabilitation centers, offices, factories, even our own homes. Two of the most important outcomes of this trend have been the educational method called programmed instruction and the therapeutic approach called behavior modification.

Programmed Instruction. However it is presented, whether by means of specially written textbooks or brightly colored graphics on a computer screen, **programmed instruction** always emphasizes reinforcement in the learning situation. The student is provided with immediate feedback for every response. Information is presented sequentially in small segments, and a student does not proceed to a new unit until he or she has demonstrated comprehension of the present one. Thus each student's progress through a program is paced according to his or her individual abilities. In this way, slow and fast learners alike receive a great deal of positive reinforcement. The aim is to encourage a sense of competence and to minimize the frustration and defeat that inevitably accompany frequent failure.

Programmed instruction also incorporates the principle of active repetition. Usually a program presents information with numerous examples. It also requires students to answer several questions about new material or to restate it in various ways before proceeding to the next segment. Programmed

By providing continual positive reinforcement, programmed instruction enables young children to achieve mastery over educational material at their own pace. (*Chuck O'Rear/West Light.*)

instruction offers students the advantage that, instead of proceeding in a linear fashion from step A to step B, they can branch off into remedial or supplementary lessons if their responses point to a need for such extra work. They can be directed back to the beginning of a sequence that is causing difficulty or, if they are fast learners, forward to a new sequence. The students, of course, are positively reinforced for each correct answer. In this manner, the correct response is strengthened, just as any response is strengthened when it is followed by reinforcement.

There are several methods for presenting programmed instruction. One is the programmed textbook. Another is the teaching machine, developed by B. F. Skinner in the 1950s. The most sophisticated method of programmed teaching is computer-assisted instruction (CAI). An advantage of this method is that it greatly increases the amount of branching that can be built into the system. In addition, the computer can maintain a record of each student's progress and use this information to structure subsequent work.

Some early critics of computer-assisted instruction predicted that this approach would prove to have only limited value in the classroom. The machines were too cold and impersonal, they argued. Students who were made to work with them for long periods would soon miss certain stimulating aspects of classroom instruction—the human interaction, the exchange of ideas, even the competition. But such early prophecies now appear to have been too negative. Early critics did not foresee the rapid development of microcomputers and their software, which now enable teaching programs to incorporate synthesized speech, sound effects, and color graphics as arresting as anything in a video space-wars game (Loftus and Loftus, 1983).

For more sophisticated users of computer-assisted instruction, mathematician Seymour Papert (1980) has devised a computer language called LOGO, which enables children to do some programming of their own. This gives students a chance to bring greater creativity to their work with computers and helps to motivate the more imaginative child. Besides, the experience of teaching a computer how to "think," Papert argues, encourages children actively to explore the way they themselves think—something that traditional classroom instruction has not always done.

Despite the obvious usefulness of computer-assisted instruction, many educators believe that it should serve only as a supplement to regular classroom teaching, not as a substitute for it. Even as supplements, computers are expensive to install and maintain; therefore, at least in the immediate future, they are likely to find only limited use in most schools.

Behavior Modification. The scene is an elementary school classroom. One boy of about ten takes out a large watch, places it in front of him, and selects some learning material from a nearby table. The material consists of a series of problems in addition. He works on the problems slowly. When he has finished he notes the time and summons the teacher. She corrects the material, smiles, and says, "Very good. You get ten tokens for this." The boy takes his tokens and crosses the hall to another room, where he trades them for a large candy bar. Smiling happily, he skips back to his ward in this institution for the mentally retarded. The boy's IQ when he came to the institution was extraordinarily low. Now he can perform tasks that no one then thought he could ever master.

This is an example of **behavior modification,** the conscious use of operant conditioning principles to change human behavior. The concept of behavior modification comes from B. F. Skinner's stress on behavior as the proper focus of psychological study. As early as the 1950s, Skinner argued that we must stop thinking of the behavioral aspects of psychological disorders as mere "symptoms" of some inner cause (Skinner, 1953). Instead, we must address the problem behaviors in their own right, for if we eliminate these behaviors, we effectively eliminate the problem. Very soon some of Skinner's students, armed with operant conditioning techniques, set out to apply this perspective outside the laboratory (Wilson, 1982).

Some of the earliest behavior modification programs involved the creation of so-called **token economies** in mental hospitals and other institutions for people with severe behavior problems. The boy we just described in an institution for the mentally retarded was participating in a token economy. As operant conditioning principles would prescribe, he was immediately reinforced for performing a relatively complex task—solving some arithmetic problems. His reward was a handful of tokens that could be exchanged at any time for more basic reinforcers, such as candy bars. Such token economies have proved quite successful in establishing positive behaviors in a variety of settings. We will discuss them in more detail in Chapter 16.

Since the earliest behavior modification programs,

learning principles have gradually been applied to the full range of everyday human problems. Behavioral therapists address themselves to matters as diverse as smoking, overeating, truancy, stuttering, shyness, poor study habits, volatile tempers, and lack of self-assertion. Operant conditioning techniques have even been used by employers to raise worker productivity and by government officials to stop littering in public parks. In all cases the procedure is much the same: trying to eliminate inadvertent rewards for the problem behavior and at the same time systematically reinforcing a more desirable alternative response. Thus a teacher trying to engage a shy boy in group activities would be careful not to give him attention when he withdrew from the class but instead would encourage and praise him whenever he interacted with others.

As you have seen, one way to reduce the frequency of a behavior is to eliminate any unintended rewards that may be supporting it, so that the behavior is gradually extinguished. Another way is actively to punish the undesirable response by introducing an aversive consequence. Punishment has been used therapeutically, for instance, to cure the disorder called writer's cramp, in which the hand of a person who writes for extended periods is afflicted with uncontrollable spasms. J. D. Sylvester and L. A. Liversedge (1960) designed writing equipment that delivered an electric shock each time a hand tremor occurred. Of the thirty-nine people they treated in this way, twenty-four improved enough to return to work. Therapists have used other forms of punishment to treat more severe behavior disorders, as we will discuss in Chapter 16.

Although punishment has been successful in helping to suppress certain maladaptive behaviors, it has important limitations as a method of behavior modification. For one thing, punishment may only temporarily discourage the behavior it is intended to eradicate. When the punisher is no longer present or the motivation to commit the act is extremely strong, the suppressed behavior may reappear. In addition, when punishment is harsh, it may create such anxiety that a "backfire" effect occurs. A child who is punished for stuttering by laughter and ridicule, for instance, is likely to stutter all the worse. Then, too, punishment can sometimes cause the punisher to become an "aversive stimulus," to be escaped from or avoided. Thus a child punished at school for truancy may come to dislike school even more—another example of a backfire effect. Finally, punishment may only indicate to a person what he or she is *not* to do. It does not in itself establish a positive response. Consequently, when one undesirable behavior is suppressed through punishment, another may appear in its place.

It seems, then, that punishment will probably be most effective when it is used in conjunction with positive forms of behavior modification. Punishment's greatest benefit is in preventing, even temporarily, some extremely undesirable behavior, so that a more acceptable response can then be rewarded and strengthened. In many instances, however, a negative behavior can be completely eliminated without resort to punishment. For example, a psychologist can determine whether the undesirable behavior is inadvertently being maintained by some reinforcer. Then, by eliminating the reinforcer, he or she can extinguish the response. Another technique that avoids punishment is to use positive reinforcement to condition behavior that is incompatible with the unwanted behavior. Thus, instead of attempting to eliminate a child's selfishness by using punishment, a parent or teacher can reinforce sharing and cooperation with others. Still another method is to try to avoid the need to punish incorrect behavior by ensuring from the start that only correct behavior occurs. But this technique usually requires careful initial shaping of behavior and elimination of all opportunities to perform undesirable responses. Outside the laboratory, such highly controlled conditions seldom if ever exist.

SHARED FEATURES OF CONDITIONING MODELS

So far we have focused on differences between classical and operant conditioning, differences that are important enough so that most psychologists consider these separate and distinct models of learning. There are, however, similarities between classical and operant conditioning. Consider the role of reinforcement. Reinforcement is clearly essential to establish and maintain operantly learned behavior. But it plays a part in classical conditioning as well. In Pavlov's experiments, for example, a hungry dog came to salivate at the sound of a tone, after which it received food. The food can be said to have served as a reinforcer because it increased the likelihood that the dog would salivate again when it heard the tone. And when the food was no longer presented, the conditioned response of salivation was gradually extinguished, just as an operantly conditioned response is extinguished after removal of the reinforcer. Another similarity between classical and operant conditioning lies in the fact that both involve stimulus control. In the classical conditioning model, the organism's behavior comes under the control of the conditioned stimulus (in Pavlov's experiments, the tone). In operant conditioning, the controlling stimuli are the salient cues associated with the learning situation (a lever, a light, a Skinner box, a maze, or what have you). Given these basic similarities, then, it is not surprising that some of the same principles apply to both classical and operant conditioning. Among these principles are those of stimulus generalization and discrimination.

Stimulus Generalization and Discrimination

Suppose that we have successfully trained a dog to salivate at the sound of a dinner bell. Can we also expect this animal to salivate if it hears a set of chimes, a ringing telephone, or high-pitched notes on a piano? Conversely, can we train this dog to salivate only when it hears a particular bell and to ignore all other bell-like stimuli? The first process is called **stimulus generalization**—performing a learned response in the presence of similar stimuli. The second is called **stimulus discrimination**—learning to make a particular response only to a particular stimulus. Both processes apply to operant as well as classical conditioning. In operant conditioning, it is the set of stimuli associated with the learning situation that the subject generalizes or discriminates. In classical conditioning, it is the conditioned stimulus (the CS).

Stimulus generalization is common in everyday life. Watson claimed that little Albert generalized his classically conditioned fear of rats to other furry animals and objects. In essentially the same way, a black person who has several hostile encounters with a white southerner may generalize these negative feelings to all white southerners or even to all whites. Operantly

conditioned responses can also be generalized. For instance, a person who has installed a smoke detector at home (the sound of which is a controlling stimulus for the operant behavior of escaping) may bolt for the front door when an alarm clock accidentally rings in the middle of the night. In such cases, of course, the generalizations are inappropriate. We might call them false alarms. But at other times generalization allows us correctly to apply information learned in one situation to new but similar conditions. Thus a person who has once slipped on an icy stairway learns to take great care on icy roads and sidewalks too. Without the ability to generalize in this fashion, people would profit very little from their past experiences.

Generally speaking, the more similar a subsequent stimulus is to that which prevailed during learning, the more likely it is that generalization will occur. Conversely, the less similar these two sets of stimuli are, the more likely it is that the individual will discriminate between them and withhold the conditioned response. In animal research, a procedure called **discrimination training** is often used to enhance such stimulus discrimination. Suppose an experimenter has trained a pigeon to peck at a yellow key in order to receive a food reward. How do you think the bird will respond if the experimenter suddenly presents it with a green key? As you may have guessed, the pigeon will probably peck at the green key as well, although not as frequently as it pecks at the yellow. To reduce the response to the green key still further, the experimenter could present the yellow key alternately with the green one but reward the pigeon only for pecking at the yellow. Soon the bird would learn to peck exclusively at the yellow key. Note that reinforcement and extinction have been used together to bring behavior under the control of a specific stimulus—in this case, a yellow key. A parallel procedure could easily be used in classical conditioning. If a particular bell was always followed by food and another bell was never followed by food, a dog would soon learn to salivate only at the sound of the first bell. In these examples, the yellow key and the distinctive-sounding bell are **discriminative stimuli.** They allow the subject to respond discriminatively because they provide specific information about when reinforcement will occur.

Psychologists can test the effectiveness of discrimination training by comparing the behavior of two subjects—one that has learned to respond only to the discriminative stimulus and one that has not. For in-

Through discrimination training—reinforcing only the appropriate response—the pigeon has learned to peck at a key of a certain color. (*Yale Joel/LIFE Magazine © 1950 Time, Inc.*)

stance, a pigeon trained to discriminate yellow from several other colors and another bird conditioned simply to peck at a yellow key might be given a test consisting of different-colored stimuli. The psychologist would then measure the number of responses each pigeon made to the various colors before key-pecking behavior was extinguished. Figure 5.8 shows the results of a typical experiment of this kind. The number of responses are plotted along the vertical axis, and the resulting curve is called a **generalization gradient.** The peak of the generalization gradient for each pigeon is at the color yellow—that is, the less similar the stimulus is to yellow, the less either bird responds. The pigeon that did not receive discrimination training, however, produces a wider and flatter generalization gradient than does the bird that was so

trained. In other words, the one without discrimination training responds more to colors other than yellow. This points up an important and well-documented finding: the effect of discrimination training is to sharpen and strengthen stimulus control.

Discrimination training has many practical applications. Through the use of this procedure, for instance, pigeons have been turned into very important members of certain air-sea rescue teams (Diamond, 1979). The pigeons are placed in special cages on the undersides of helicopters just before the rescue teams take off to locate survivors of a sinking vessel. The birds have been taught to peck at a button whenever they see the colors orange, yellow, and red (the colors of life vests, life rafts, and distress flares, respectively). Pecking this button turns on a light in the helicopter cockpit, alerting the pilot that a likely object has been spotted. A switch allows the pilot to reward the pigeon for its help with the delivery of some food. Because pigeons have much keener eyesight than humans, their success rate at detecting survivors is over twice that of helicopter crews. In trial runs the birds have correctly signaled the sighting of small, appropriately colored buoys from a height of 500 feet above the water and at a distance of a quarter of a mile. But without discrimination training, this innovative program would not be nearly so effective.

Stimulus discrimination can also be put to use to control human behavior. Sometimes our responses become a problem when they are performed in the wrong context—that is, when they are triggered by inappropriate cues in the environment. People who are overweight, for instance, often associate eating with all kinds of stimuli, such as watching television,

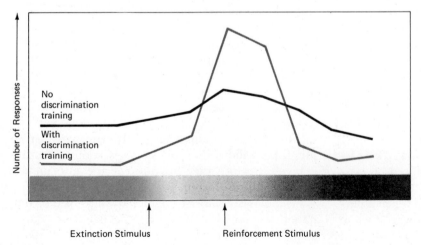

Figure 5.8 Graph showing generalization gradients for two pigeons in a test of color generalization. One pigeon had previously received discrimination training; the other had been rewarded for pecking at a yellow light but had seen no other colored lights before the generalization test. Discrimination training results in a much more sharply peaked generalization gradient. That is, the pigeon that had received discrimination training treated the colors as more distinct than did the pigeon without this training. Color difference exerted more control over its behavior.

reading a book, going to a movie, or sitting on a beach. One way to get them to decrease their eating behavior is to ask them to confine all eating to one specific location, usually the dining table. This location thereby becomes a discriminative stimulus. It is hoped that, through lack of reinforcement, all other environmental cues formerly associated with eating will gradually lose their power of control, until eventually the individuals feel the compulsion to eat primarily when they sit down to a meal. We will say more about this approach to behavior modification in Chapter 16, on psychological therapies.

Conditioned Reinforcers

Another basic concept that applies to both classical and operant conditioning is that of conditioned reinforcers. This concept is easiest to understand first in the context of operant conditioning. In most of the operant conditioning experiments we have discussed so far, the reinforcer that established and maintained the conditioned response was a **primary reinforcer,** such as food or water—something that satisfied some basic biological need. The effects of a primary reinforcer can generalize, however, to a secondary reinforcer. A **secondary or conditioned reinforcer** is a stimulus signaling that a primary reinforcer is on its way. The clicking sound of food being released into a food cup, for example, signals to a hungry rat that a primary reinforcer, food, will very soon appear. If this signal consistently precedes the arrival of food, it may itself acquire the power to reinforce a learned response.

In the world outside the laboratory, it is rare for a learned behavior to be immediately followed by a primary reinforcer. Usually some secondary reinforcer signals that primary reinforcement will eventually be forthcoming. Most people, for example, are paid for their work with money, a secondary reinforcer that can later be exchanged for primary reinforcers. If a currency should lose its value, however, it will also lose its power to maintain behavior. This is precisely what happened in Germany during the runaway inflation of the 1920s. When currency became worthless, people quickly stopped working for money and insisted on being paid directly in essential goods and services.

The power of conditioned reinforcers was demonstrated in an early series of experiments with chimpanzees (Wolfe, 1936). The chimps readily learned to perform tasks in order to obtain tokens that they could later use to buy food from a vending machine called a Chimp-O-Mat. The form of human behavior modification called the token economy clearly parallels this procedure. The most important conclusion stemming from research with the Chimp-O-Mat was that conditioned reinforcers—in this case the tokens—can bridge very long delays between the performance

A powerful conditioned reinforcer in human life is money. Wolfe (1936) showed in a series of experiments that chimpanzees, too, can learn to use "money." Chimps were conditioned to pull down a heavily weighted handle in order to obtain tokens (poker chips), which they could then use to buy peanuts or bananas from a Chimp-O-Mat. The value of the tokens to the chimps was evident from the fact that they would work for them and save them— and would sometimes try to steal them from one another. (*Yerkes Regional Primate Research Center, Emory University.*)

of a task and the arrival of a primary reinforcer, such as food. Without the tokens, even small delays between the response and the receipt of food made the chimpanzees reluctant to continue performing.

Behaviorists argue that conditioned reinforcers explain why people perform many of the activities they do. When each of a series of related responses is rewarded by a conditioned reinforcer, long sequences of behavior can be effectively maintained. Although people derive many kinds of satisfaction from their jobs, for instance, the behavior of working is maintained in part by the conditioned reinforcer of a paycheck. The behavior of going to the bank and cashing that paycheck is maintained by the conditioned reinforcer of obtaining paper money. The behavior of spending that money in the grocery store is maintained by the conditioned reinforcer of taking home a bagful of food. And finally, the behavior of cooking and serving a meal is maintained by the primary reinforcer of eating. Learning such a sequence of operant behaviors that eventually ends in a primary reward is often called **chaining.** Each link in the chain is presumably maintained by its own conditioned reinforcer.

Although conditioned reinforcement in everyday life is most obvious with operant conditioning, it can occur with classical conditioning too. Suppose a dog has been trained to salivate at the sound of a bell (the CS), which is always followed by food (the UCS, or primary reinforcer). Pavlov called this **first-order conditioning.** If the presentation of food is then eliminated and the sound of the bell is repeatedly paired with, say, a flashing light, the dog will soon salivate in response to the light alone. This Pavlov called **second-order conditioning.** The animal acts as if the light signaled that the bell was about to ring, the bell, in turn, being the previous signal for food. Thus, because the bell has come to mean that a primary reinforcer is about to arrive, it is able to serve as a conditioned reinforcer. In the same way, if Watson had repeatedly paired presentation of a white rat with, say, the sound of someone singing, little Albert might have developed a second-order conditioned fear of lullabies.

LEARNING AND COGNITION

The early behaviorists, such as Thorndike and Watson, explained the process of learning in a very mechanistic way. They argued that when an organism makes a response to a certain stimulus and that response is reinforced, a stimulus-response (or S-R) connection forms in the brain. Subsequent reinforcement of the same response strengthens this neural connection until eventually the behavior will almost always occur in the presence of the controlling stimulus. Thus the pigeon that pecks at a button as soon as it lights up, the dog that sits by the table just when dinner is served, and the person who answers the telephone whenever it happens to ring are simply exhibiting automatic stimulus-response patterns that in the past have been rewarded.

Many contemporary psychologists, however, strongly reject this argument because it ignores the mental activity going on inside the organism. They maintain that in almost any learned association important thought processes intervene between the stimulus and the response. This view has come to be called the **cognitive** (or "thinking") **approach** to learning. One of its earliest proponents was Edward Tolman, an American psychologist who worked at a time when psychology in this country was largely dominated by strict behaviorists. Tolman argued in favor of the then unorthodox notion that most animals capable of learning are adaptive, intelligent, creative organisms and that any explanation of learning must take these qualities into account. Tolman's professional career was spent at the University of California at Berkeley, and the mass of research that came from his laboratory there made Berkeley the center of cognitive psychology for years. Today the cognitive approach is highly influential in all areas of learning.

Explaining Associative Learning: The Cognitive View

Central to the cognitive interpretation of associative learning is a concern for the thought processes that may occur when conditioning takes place. Many cognitive psychologists, for example, now stress that what an organism learns during classical conditioning is an *expectation* that a previously neutral event, say a flashing light, will be followed by an unconditioned stimulus, such as food. It is this expectation that brings about the conditioned response. The cognitive view of classical conditioning seems to be supported by an interesting anecdote about one of Pavlov's experimental dogs that had been conditioned to respond to the ticking of a metronome. When the metronome was turned off, the dog planted himself in front of it and proceeded to whine and beg. If this story is true, more seems to be going on here mentally than the development of a mechanistic stimulus-response association.

Similarly, cognitive psychologists argue that what a rat acquires when it learns to run a maze is not necessarily a series of automatic movements controlled by specific stimuli but rather a "cognitive map" of the maze's spatial layout. This interpretation received some support from an ingenious experiment by one of Tolman's students (Macfarlane, 1930). He filled a maze with several inches of water and trained rats to swim to a goal box where they could hoist themselves out and obtain food. He then drained the maze and tested to see if the rats could still find their way to the goal. Now if what the rats had learned was simply a set of S-R associations, this change should severely disrupt the animals' performance. After all, the controlling stimulus was no longer the same (a body of water had been replaced by a dry chamber), and swimming and running do not involve anything like the same set of responses. But the rats negotiated the dry maze flawlessly. What they appeared to have acquired during their previous training was a mental map, or image, of the maze, which could be used to locate the goal regardless of changes in surrounding stimuli or in required muscular movements. Such findings seriously call into question the view that associative learning is strictly mechanistic.

Figure 5.9 Latent learning. Tolman and his colleagues argued that learning is a result of cognition—a thinking process that involves more than just the association of stimuli and responses through reinforcement. Support for this idea came from a series of experiments like the one shown here (Blodgett, 1929). Rats in group I were put in the complex maze once a day for nine consecutive days; they always found food at the maze's end. Group II rats were also put in the maze, but they were not rewarded until the seventh day. Group III found their first reward on day 3. Rats in II and III began by making many errors, but these dropped abruptly on the day *after* reward was first introduced. Thus, during *nonrewarded* trials the rats had been learning more than they had exhibited; reward improved performance, but did not determine it.

Learning Without Reinforcement

Bolstering the cognitive view of learning is the demonstration in recent years that learning can occur in the absence of reinforcement. Such learning presents some difficulty for a strict S-R model, according to which an association will not be established unless it is reinforced. Yet cognitive psychologists maintain that much of human learning takes place without the meting out of overt rewards or punishments. Two types of learning that fall into this category are latent learning and learning through observation.

Latent Learning. When an organism learns a new behavior but does not demonstrate this knowledge until an incentive to do so arises, the learning is called **latent.** In an early demonstration of latent learning, Tolman and Honzik (1930) permitted some rats to explore a maze in the absence of any reward. Mean-

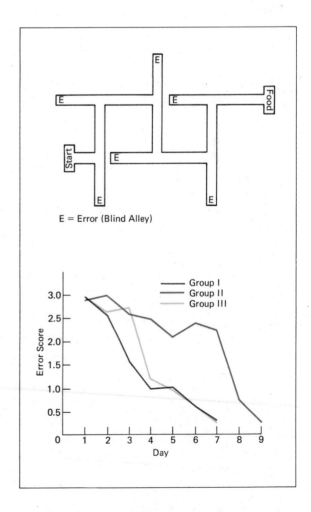

while, other rats were presented with food whenever they reached the goal box. As expected, the rewarded rats soon learned to run the maze quickly and without error. The unrewarded rats, in contrast, seemed to wander the maze aimlessly. When a food reward was subsequently given to the rats that had not previously been reinforced, however, their error rate fell very abruptly to the same level as that of the first group. (See Figure 5.9.) In fact, these formerly unrewarded rats mastered the maze more quickly than their continuously reinforced counterparts had done.

Tolman and Honzik concluded that the initially unrewarded group of rats had profited by their early explorations, but their learning remained latent until after a reward for reaching the goal box was introduced. This experiment provided support for Tolman's notion that learning is cognitive in nature, rather than a series of S-R connections stamped in by reinforcement. This viewpoint corresponds to much of our own experience. People, for example, can find their way without error from one part of a strange city to another simply on the basis of having once been given verbal instructions. Reinforcement and repeated practice are not essential for learning the specific route. Instead, the verbal instructions are stored in memory until the time comes to use them. Reinforcement, in effect, is not needed for learning to occur.

Observational Learning. The research on latent learning suggests that experimental animals acquire a great deal of information about their environments without being directly reinforced for it. Such information is amassed largely through casual observation—looking, listening, touching, and so forth—in the course of normal activities. The same is true of humans. But when it comes to human learning, a large proportion of the observations we make pertain to other people. What do we acquire from the act of observing what other people do? According to **social learning theory,** we acquire a wide variety of strategies, outlooks, and behaviors that we may imitate, avoid, or modify to our advantage. And once again, no particular reinforcement is needed to enable us to accumulate this information. We do so naturally in the course of cognitively processing what those around us do. This process of learning how we may fashion our own behavior by observing the behavior of others is called **observational learning.**

Note that social learning theorists do not say that rewards and punishments are unimportant to human behavior. They simply say that reinforcement is not essential for learning to occur. According to Albert Bandura (1977a), one of the leading proponents of this view, reinforcement is much more important in getting people to exhibit a newly learned behavior than it is in teaching that behavior in the first place. A little girl who observes her older brother building a playhouse enters this behavior into her repertoire of possible responses regardless of the outcome of her brother's actions. But if she also observes that her brother is warmly praised for his accomplishment, she will probably be even more inclined to build a similar playhouse in the future. Thus Bandura makes a sharp distinction between learning and performance. Learning involves the acquisition of new ideas and strategies, while performance involves action on the basis of these new cognitions. Reinforcement in Bandura's scheme mainly affects the likelihood of performance. Learning to him is a process independent of rewards.

Bandura also conceptualizes rewards and punishments differently than strict behaviorists do. To the behaviorist, a reward or punishment is a positive or negative stimulus in the external environment that impinges directly on the actor. To Bandura, rewards and punishments are defined more broadly than this. We are influenced, Bandura says, not only by the consequences of our own behavior but also by the consequences we see other people experiencing. Thus the little girl in the example above is likely to build a playhouse not because she herself has been rewarded for this action but because she has seen her brother praised for doing so. Bandura calls such "secondhand" consequences **vicarious reinforcement and punishment,** and he correctly points out that they can have very important effects on our behavior. In addition, Bandura stresses the importance of **intrinsic reinforcement and punishment.** By this term he means that our actions are regulated not just by the environmental consequences we observe but by our own reactions as well. These reactions are related to our internalized standards of behavior, against which we measure our own performance. If we exceed our own standards, we feel self-esteem, a powerful form of reinforcement; if we fall short of those standards, we feel self-reproach, a potent form of punishment.

But remember that, to Bandura, none of these various forms of reward and punishment are essential for the occurrence of learning. Learning to him is a change in acquired information (and hence in performance potential), which can occur just by virtue of the fact that one is an observer in the world. As you will discover in subsequent chapters, Bandura and others have conducted experiments showing that such observational learning can and does take place in the absence of reinforcement. In a typical study, groups of children observe a model who responds to a situation in some unusual way. Then the experimenter puts the children in a similar situation and notes the number of imitative responses they make. Such studies clearly demonstrate that children may learn and imitate a novel behavior with no external inducement at all. And even those who do not spontaneously mimic the model's actions still learn a new set of potential behaviors that they may act out at some time in the future.

One of Bandura's classic experiments, in which very young children learned a series of highly aggressive acts after observing an adult model, is discussed in Chapter 18. This study has led to increased concern over the influence of TV violence on what children learn through observation. Bandura reports that "children have been apprehended for writing bad checks to obtain money for candy, for sniping at strangers with BB guns, for sending threatening letters to teachers, and for injurious switchblade fights after witnessing similar performances on television" (1973, pp. 101–102). And it is not just children who are susceptible to the information about human behavior provided by our TV screens. Recent surveys show that adults who are heavy TV watchers (over four hours a day) often accept as valid the networks' portrayal of life in our society (Gerbner and Gross, 1976). They tend to believe, for instance, that American women are primarily homemakers; that the elderly are a very small segment of our population; that a large percentage of people are professionals, such as doctors and lawyers; and that the chances of being the victim of violent crime in this country are very, very high. Outside the world of prime-time television, not one of these things is statistically true. But observational learning gleaned through heavy TV watching seems to have helped make them reality in many people's minds.

Bandura and other social learning theorists point out that once such distorted beliefs are established, they tend to persist unless they are disconfirmed by contrary observations. And because people often see what they believe they will see, this disconfirmation process may never take place. The woman who fears she will be the victim of violent crime, for instance, tends to search out signs of bad intentions in all the strangers who approach her. As a result, she tends to see most strangers as far more threatening than they actually are. One way to help free this person of her distorted view of reality might be through a program of observational learning, in which it is repeatedly demonstrated that a walk on the streets seldom results in assault or robbery and that most strangers are not dangerous but are quite law-abiding citizens.

As you will learn in Chapter 16, psychologists have in fact developed forms of psychotherapy based on observational learning principles. Consider their treatment of phobias. The treatment rests on the belief that if people with phobias can observe someone else performing the activity that they so greatly dread, they are likely to develop confidence that they, too, can perform it without adverse effects (Bandura, 1977b). The most effective of the observational learning therapies appear to be those in which people are gradually encouraged to engage in the feared activity themselves after first watching others do so. In one study of people with snake phobias, for instance, subjects who first observed the therapist approach and handle snakes and then performed the same behaviors in progressively bolder steps were much more successful in overcoming their phobia than were subjects who simply watched a film of people handling snakes or who, while trying to remain relaxed, imagined themselves interacting with snakes (Bandura, Blanchard, and Ritter, 1969). Apparently disconfirmation of a false belief is more powerful when we demonstrate it to ourselves in real life. We will say more about observational learning approaches to the treatment of behavior disorders in Chapter 16.

At this point it seems clear that observational learning is very widespread and that cognitive forms of learning have great relevance to both human and animal behavior. Cognition is an almost constant part of human experience, and learning theories that do not consider the role of mental activity and knowledge seem to ignore a crucial facet of human life. Cognitive theories of learning contribute to many areas of psychology, including personality and social development, psychological disorders, and psychotherapy. This theoretical approach to human behavior will reappear in many of the following chapters. It provides the major foundation for the next chapter, which deals with memory.

SUMMARY

1. **Learning** is a relatively permanent change in performance potential that arises from experience. Psychologists infer learning by observing changes in performance. A new stimulus tends to evoke an **orienting reflex,** a chain of exploratory actions aimed at determining what the stimulus is about. One of the simplest kinds of learning is **habituation,** which occurs when a subject becomes accustomed to a repeated stimulus and ceases to respond to it. **Associative learning** is more complex, involving learned relationships between events. Two kinds of associative learning are **classical conditioning,** which involves nonvoluntary responses, and **operant conditioning,** which involves voluntary behavior. Some psychologists emphasize **cognitive learning**—that is, learning that entails active thinking and reasoning.

2. Pavlov discovered classical conditioning while studying the physiology of digestion. He found that the **unconditioned stimulus** (UCS) of food in a dog's mouth elicited the **unconditioned response** (UCR) of salivation. When the UCS (the food) was repeatedly preceded by a neutral stimulus—for example, the sound of a bell—the dog eventually salivated in response to the bell alone. The bell had therefore become a **conditioned stimulus** (CS), and the learned reaction to it was a **conditioned response** (CR).

3. To establish and maintain a classically conditioned response such as this one, the conditioned and unconditioned stimuli must be experienced relatively close together in time; also, the CS and UCS must continue to be paired at least occasionally. The weakening and eventual disappearance of a conditioned response when pairing is abandoned is called **extinction.**

4. Psychologists once believed that for classical conditioning to be established, the conditioned and unconditioned stimuli must occur close together and be paired at least several times in succession. But recent findings have revealed some exceptions to these traditionally held rules. Apparently, natural selection has favored a nervous system that allows easy learning of contingencies that are common in a given animal's habitat and are crucial to its survival. One example is learned taste aversions to foods paired with illness among animal species that tend to have very unselective diets.

5. Some psychologists have applied classical conditioning principles to the treatment of certain psychological disorders. For instance, the technique of **systematic desensitization,** developed from procedures for extinguishing classically conditioned responses, has been used to reduce human phobias.

6. According to Thorndike's **law of effect,** responses that result in satisfying consequences will be strengthened, while responses that lead to unsatisfying consequences are unlikely to be repeated. Learning either to make or to withhold a particular response because of its positive or negative consequences has come to be called **operant conditioning.** A consequence that increases the frequency of a behavior is called **reward** or **reinforcement.** A consequence that decreases the frequency of a behavior is called **punishment.** In **positive reinforcement** the frequency of a response increases because the response is followed by a positive stimulus. In **negative reinforcement** the frequency of a response increases because the response removes some negative stimulus. **Superstitious behavior** often occurs when a response is strengthened or weakened because it happens by chance to precede reinforcement or punishment.

7. In the laboratory, researchers have studied operant conditioning by manipulating rewards and punishments in such devices as the **Skinner box. Shaping**—a technique in which a subject is reinforced for displaying closer and closer approximations of a desired response—has been used to establish new behaviors in both humans and other animals.

8. Once established, an operantly conditioned response is maintained through reinforcement. The **schedule of reinforcement** controls the behavior to a great extent. A **continuous reinforcement schedule**—reinforcement each time the response occurs—is effective in establishing new behavior. A **partial reinforcement schedule**—withholding of the reward some of the time—is most effective for maintaining a behavior. Schedules of partial reinforcement include a **fixed-ratio schedule,** in which the subject is rewarded each time a specified number of responses are made, and a **fixed-interval schedule,** in which the subject is rewarded at the end of a fixed time interval regardless of the number of responses. Two schedules that result in high rates of response that are quite

resistant to extinction are the **variable-ratio schedule** and the **variable-interval schedule,** both of which derive their power from their unpredictability.

9. An operantly conditioned response gradually decreases and disappears when it is no longer reinforced. But sometimes a response (whether operantly or classically conditioned) will reappear after it seems to have been extinguished, a phenomenon called **spontaneous recovery.**

10. Operant conditioning principles have been applied in both **programmed instruction** and **behavior modification.** In the behavior modification approach called the **token economy,** desired behaviors are rewarded with the receipt of tokens that can then be exchanged for more basic reinforcers.

11. Classical and operant conditioning have several principles in common. Among these principles are those of **stimulus generalization** (performing a learned response in the presence of similar stimuli) and **stimulus discrimination** (learning to make a particular response only to a particular stimulus). In operant conditioning, it is the set of stimuli associated with the learning situation that the subject generalizes or discriminates. In classical conditioning, it is the conditioned stimulus (the CS).

12. The effects of **primary reinforcers** (those that satisfy biological needs) can generalize to **secondary or conditioned reinforcers** (those that signal that primary reinforcement is on its way). Learning a sequence of operant behaviors, each one maintained by its own conditioned reinforcer and eventually leading to a primary reward, is often called **chaining.** The concept of conditioned reinforcers also applies to classical conditioning. **First-order conditioning** occurs when a previously neutral stimulus is paired with a primary reinforcer. **Second-order conditioning** occurs when the resulting conditioned stimulus is paired with yet another originally neutral stimulus, which in turn comes to elicit the conditioned response.

13. Cognitive psychologists believe that important thought processes intervene between the stimulus and the response in most instances of associative learning. In particular, both humans and experimental animals tend to develop expectations that one event will be followed by another.

14. Cognitive psychologists also maintain that much of human learning does not depend on overt rewards or punishments. Two examples are **latent learning** (learning that occurs but is not demonstrated until there is an incentive) and **observational learning** (learning that results simply from observation of other people's behavior).

SUGGESTED READINGS

ADAMS, J. A. *Learning and memory: An introduction.* Homewood, Ill.: Dorsey Press, 1980.

This basic text describes experimental investigations of learning and memory. It presents findings on animal and human learning, as well as the theories that have been devised to explain them.

HERGENHAHN, B. R. *An introduction to theories of learning.* Englewood Cliffs, N.J.: Prentice-Hall, 1982.

An up-to-date text that contains in-depth discussions of the work and lives of leading learning theorists: Edward Thorndike, B. F. Skinner, Ivan Pavlov, Edwin Guthrie, William Estes, and others.

PAPERT, S. *Mindstorms.* New York: Basic Books, 1980.

In this remarkable book, Papert presents an exciting vision of education for the future—the collaboration of computers and children.

PAVLOV, I. P. *Conditioned reflexes.* New York: Oxford University Press. 1927.

The ideas of one of the pioneers in the field of learning research are presented in this work.

SKINNER, B. F. *The behavior of organisms.* New York: Appleton-Century-Crofts, 1938.

Skinner's ideas on operant conditioning are set forth in this work.

6
MEMORY AND FORGETTING

Arnaldo Pomodoro, *Sphere No. 6*, 1963.

Interference
Motivated Forgetting

How Much Do We Really Forget?

When psychologist Peter Polson first spotted waiter John Conrad in a Boulder, Colorado, restaurant, he was understandably impressed. Conrad had the uncanny ability to remember elaborate dinner orders without writing anything down. He once served a table of nineteen people without making a single mistake. Not only were all the meats, the vegetables, the salads, the dressings just as each customer had ordered, but Conrad remembered without hesitation precisely who got what. And this feat of gastronomic recall did not even begin to tap the outer limits of Conrad's memory capability. He maintains that he can remember orders for up to thirty dinners at a time before his powers of recall begin to break down (Singular, 1982).

For those of us who have trouble remembering where we left the car keys, John Conrad's feats of memory seem awesome indeed. It may therefore come as a surprise that his impressive accomplishments are well within the bounds of normal human memory. We are all endowed with a remarkable capacity for processing information, even though we seldom devote the time and energy to memorization that John Conrad has. Who were your closest friends

in high school? When was the American Revolution? In which state is Chicago? What is the melody of the "Star-Spangled Banner"? How does a Christmas tree smell? You immediately know the answers to these and hundreds of thousands of other questions. In its breadth and flexibility, the capacity of human memory far exceeds that of the most advanced computer.

Psychologists usually divide memory into three distinct types: sensory, short-term, and long-term. **Sensory memory** is the momentary lingering of sensory information after a stimulus has been removed. If you touch the palm of your hand with the point of a pencil, for instance, you continue to feel the sensation for several seconds after the point is withdrawn. This momentary storage of tactile information is just one example of sensory memory. Actually, we seem to have five separate forms of sensory storage, one for each of our five senses. We can store a great deal of information in such sensory memory systems, but only for an instant or so.

Short-term memory is far more durable than sensory memory. Many psychologists believe it contains the contents of our conscious awareness. It involves our deliberate thoughts about things we have just

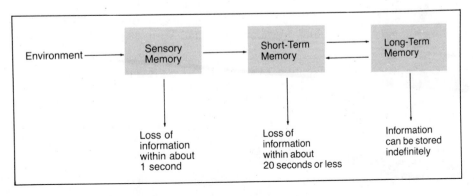

Figure 6.1 A diagram of the human memory system, showing the relationships among sensory memory, short-term memory, and long-term memory.

encountered, such as a phone number we have just looked up or a tune we have just heard. It is also the "active file" of information we have retrieved from long-term storage. When you think about what you did last week or repeat the lines of a memorized poem, you are reprocessing this information through short-term memory. As we will discuss in detail later, this storage system holds only a small amount of information at any one time, and its contents fade in about twenty seconds if they are not actively renewed.

Long-term memory, in contrast, can store things indefinitely without active effort. It can be thought of as our long-term library of information, and its capacity is believed to be virtually limitless. A diagram of the proposed relationships among sensory, short-term, and long-term memory is given in Figure 6.1.

Much of this chapter is devoted to a discussion of these three memory systems. We will be answering many questions you may already have about memory.

Why is it usually so difficult to remember a long string of numbers but so easy to remember a sentence with the same number of words? Why do some people seem to have remarkable powers of recall while others appear to be constantly forgetting? How can you improve your own memory? Next we will turn to the biological side of memory. How, we ask, does the human brain manage to store items in memory? Exciting recent findings in this area may provide a whole new dimension to our understanding of the way memory works. And finally, we will explore one of the most frustrating realities of daily life—the experience of forgetting. How much do we really forget? Is it possible that everything we have ever learned is still stored somewhere in memory and we just have to know how to retrieve it? These are some of the many issues we will raise in this chapter. We begin with the entry of new information into human memory by means of sensory storage.

SENSORY MEMORY

Glance very briefly at the pattern of letters and numbers in Figure 6.2. Then close your eyes and try to list out loud as many as you can. You will probably find that your powers of recall are rather disappointing. In fact, the results of many carefully controlled experiments indicate that most people can remember only about four or five of twelve unrelated items that

are flashed to them for just an instant. Yet such findings seem to contradict much of everyday experience. When we glance very quickly at something and then look away, most of us are left with the impression of a fairly complete and accurate image, however fleeting that image may be. If visual sensory memory is indeed rich, why in laboratory tests does it seem to be so poor?

This puzzle greatly intrigued a young psychology graduate student named George Sperling. Perhaps, Sperling reasoned, previous researchers had been testing visual sensory memory in the wrong way. So he set about to devise a new test (Sperling, 1960). He flashed a twelve-item pattern like the one in Figure 6.2, but he did not ask subjects to specify *all* the letters and numbers they had seen. Instead, on removing

Figure 6.2 When exposed to this array of unrelated items for a brief period, people typically recall no more than four or five of them. But if subjects are signaled immediately after the exposure to recall just one of the lines, they can almost always recall all four items correctly. This evidence suggests that people "read" the information from some sort of complete sensory image of the stimulus, which fades in the time it takes to say the names of a few of the letters and numbers in the image.

the pattern, he immediately sounded a high, medium, or low tone to indicate which line subjects should report. Under these conditions, subjects could correctly report almost all of the four items in *any* of the three rows. Sperling's research demonstrated that the ability to process information through the senses is indeed better than verbal reports suggest. The instant after we scan a multi-item pattern we usually retain a fairly complete image of it. This visual memory is fleeting, however; it lasts for only about a second. Consequently, during the time it takes to report four or five items, the remaining images fade from sensory memory.

We are seldom aware of the instantaneous decay of information entering sensory memory because new information is constantly following old. Only special circumstances can make us aware of how fragile sensory storage is. Old-time movies provide one demonstration. In today's movies the action seems smooth and realistic because the time lapse between frames is extremely brief—briefer than the duration of visual sensory storage. The result is a blending of successive images that gives the illusion of continuous motion. In contrast, when movies made early in this century are shown with a modern projector, the action seems jerky and unnatural. The reason is that too much time is left between frames, permitting the image of one frame to begin to fade from sensory storage before the next frame appears.

Physiological psychologists seek to learn where in the human nervous system sensory memories are stored. Apparently there are five separate storage systems, each corresponding to one of our five senses. But exactly where within our neurological mechanisms of sight, hearing, smell, taste, and touch are these lingering sensations held? Some researchers have claimed that visual images are probably stored in the retina's photoreceptors, the rods and cones we talked about in Chapter 4 (Sakitt, 1975, 1976). Others, however, are not so certain. They believe they have evidence that more central parts of the visual nervous system—parts located closer to the brain— may be involved as well.

One such piece of evidence comes from a fascinating study in which researchers asked subjects to look in turn at the four shapes shown in Figure 6.3A (McCloskey & Watkins, 1978). Each shape was made to move very rapidly back and forth behind a narrow slit cut into a dark surface. Because each shape was substantially wider than the slit through which it was viewed, the subjects could never see the entire shape at once. Yet when asked to reproduce on paper what they saw, they invariably drew a compressed version of the actual figure, squashed into the narrow opening. (See Figure 6.3B.) And this illusion occurred even when the subjects held their eyes stationary, and so were using only a single set of rods and cones. You can create this curious illusion for yourself by following the instructions in the figure caption. How can it be explained?

The psychologists who conducted this experiment argue that these illusory images are being held in visual sensory storage, the mechanism for which cannot be just the rods and cones alone. Remember that the

Figure 6.3 McCloskey and Watkins showed subjects figures like the ones reproduced in A. The figures were moved rapidly back and forth behind slits, represented by the parallel vertical lines. To perform this experiment yourself, cut a slit in a piece of cardboard; then quickly pass a figure placed beneath the cardboard back and forth so that the figure clears both sides of the slit. Despite the fact that subjects could see only part of a figure at a given instant, they could reproduce reasonable facsimiles of the whole figure, as shown in B. As the researchers explained, subjects held information in visual sensory memory until information appearing later could be integrated with it. *(After McCloskey and Watkins, 1978.)*

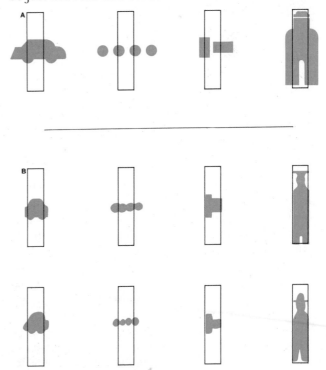

illusion occurs even when the subjects hold their eyes motionless, thus repeatedly using the same set of photoreceptor cells. How, then, can this limited number of receptor cells manage to retain consecutive pieces of the original figure and ultimately merge them into a whole? One would think that each piece

of subsequent information would immediately disrupt what a rod or cone was currently holding. A logical explanation is that visual sensory storage is carried out to some extent in a more central part of the visual nervous system—a part capable of simultaneously holding and integrating several visual images.

SHORT-TERM MEMORY

If sensory memories are so fleeting, what purpose do they serve? Apparently they provide a literal representation of events that perceptual and cognitive processes can then work on and encode into short-term memory. Obviously not all events warrant such processing. If we tried to scrutinize all the many sights, sounds, odors, tastes, and tactile sensations that bombard us from all sides, we would surely be overwhelmed. Some kind of selectivity is clearly essential. Two cognitive processes are crucial to getting the more interesting information into short-term memory—sensory gating and selective attention.

Instatement into Short-Term Memory

Sensory Gating. Your mind controls the "volume" of all incoming sensory information, often turning up the input from one sensory channel while turning down the inputs from others. When you read a very interesting book, for example, you may be only vaguely aware of surrounding sounds and odors. This selective control over sensory inputs is called **sensory gating.** By cutting down extraneous "noise" in the environment, sensory gating permits you to focus attention on the most important sensory channel at any given time. Information from the damped-down senses is not completely eliminated, however. If you suddenly detect a strange sound, or even an unexpected silence, your attention will probably shift from what you are seeing to what you are hearing. This indicates that you are still processing information from your turned-down senses to some extent; otherwise, you would not know when to shift your focus.

Actually, it should come as no surprise that we can focus attention on information entering one sensory

channel while still processing at least some input through the others. We all do this every day. When driving a car, for example, we routinely watch the road, listen to the radio, and perhaps even enjoy the taste of food at the same time. In the past many psychologists argued that people can perform several activities simultaneously only when some of them require little or no central processing by the brain. But this view has recently been challenged. Ulric Neisser and his colleagues (Hirst, Neisser, and Spelke, 1978) have trained subjects to read difficult encyclopedia articles at a normal speed and level of comprehension while simultaneously hearing, transcribing, and understanding the meaning of dictated sentences unrelated to those articles. Still, this skill is not acquired without many hours of practice. Under normal circumstances, people do tend to turn down extraneous sensory channels when they concentrate.

Selective Attention. In addition to damping down information entering competing sensory channels, we may also damp down some of the information entering the *same* sensory channel. This process is called **selective attention.** When you are carrying on a conversation at a crowded cocktail party, for example, your ears receive a great deal of extraneous information. You hear not only the person you are speaking with but the din of other voices, the clink of glasses, and perhaps the sound of music too. Yet despite this confusion of sounds, you somehow manage to follow your partner's conversation. You may think you accomplish this feat by completely ignoring all the peripheral sounds, but in fact you actually give them an elementary form of attention. In the same way that sensory gating does not completely eliminate information from your other senses, selective attention allows some processing of peripheral information entering a single sensory channel. For example, you may suddenly hear your name mentioned in one of the conversations you were "ignoring," showing that you were partly processing that conversation.

Psychologists have extensively studied this "cocktail party phenomenon." Cherry (1953) used a **dichotic listening** technique in which subjects wearing earphones simultaneously heard one message played into the left ear and a different message played into the right ear. Cherry instructed his subjects to "shadow" one of the messages—that is, to repeat it aloud as they heard it. (The subject's voice, like a shadow, trails along immediately behind the recorded message.) Later he tested to see if subjects could recognize or recall material from the nonshadowed message, the one that had entered the other ear. While the meaning of the message generally eluded the subjects, under most conditions they could detect the physical characteristics of the nonshadowed message, such as pitch and volume.

The same conclusion has been drawn from many subsequent studies in which this technique was used. It has been found, for instance, that subjects can correctly report whether a male or a female voice is speaking into the nonshadowed ear, and whether a speaker of the other sex replaces the original speaker midway (Moray, 1959). But they seldom notice a change in the language in which the nonshadowed message is spoken, and they generally fail to grasp the content even when the message is delivered in their own language. They do not even notice the difference between speech and nonsense syllables fed into the tuned-down ear. Such findings lend support to a theory of selective attention that holds that we discriminate among the physical aspects of different stimuli entering the same sensory channel, and it is these physical differences that guide our attention (Broadbent, 1958). Physical differences among voices—for example, pitch, volume, accent, and other qualities—allow you to attend to a single speaker even at a crowded party.

While this explanation seems logical, it is probably incomplete. Various other experiments in dichotic listening show that we sometimes do attend to conceptual information in the nonshadowed message. We are able, for instance, to react to words with special emotional significance in the nonshadowed message, such as those previously paired with mild electric shock (Corteen and Wood, 1972). Another experiment demonstrated that people instructed to listen to a message in only one ear will often involuntarily switch to listening to the other ear if the words needed to continue the message come on that side (Treisman, 1960). Selective attention, then, is probably based on both physical and conceptual information. At first we may attend to the physical characteristics of a message (where it comes from, what the voice qualities are), but we may then switch our attention to the message's content when we have gathered enough information to make sense of what is being said (Treisman, 1964).

Short-Term Storage

Once information has been attended to, it must be stored long enough to be useful—longer than the duration of our fragile sensory memories. After you look up a telephone number in a directory, for example, you must certainly retain it longer than a second, otherwise you would not be able to dial. You probably dial quickly, however, knowing that you will not remember the number very long without some special effort. Often you repeat the number several times, either aloud or mentally, while reaching for the phone. If you get distracted for a few seconds and interrupt this repetition, you will probably be forced to consult the directory again. This example illustrates a basic feature of short-term memory: information entering short-term memory is lost rather rapidly unless a person regards it as important enough to renew through **rehearsal.**

The rehearsal process usually involves some kind of speech—either overt, as when you repeat a telephone number aloud, or implicit, as when you repeat a number mentally. Rehearsal seems to maintain information in short-term memory in the following way: a person says the information aloud or silently, hears what is being said, and then re-stores it. Rehearsal, in other words, often maintains items in memory *acoustically*—it is the *sounds* of the items that are repeated and stored. Although rehearsal can also be visual, acoustic rehearsal (especially the silent, mental kind) seems to be more efficient (Weber and Castleman, 1970). Yet it can easily be disrupted either by external distractions (the sound of someone talking, for instance) or by internal events (such as thinking about your own telephone number while trying to remember a new one).

Exactly how long can new information stay in short-term memory without rehearsal? Studies yield figures under twenty seconds. For example, when researchers briefly show subjects a short series of consonants—say, CPQ—and then instruct them to count backward by threes from, say, 270 (267, 264, 261 . . .), the subjects are very likely to forget the letters within about twenty seconds (Peterson and Peterson, 1959). (See Figure 6.4.) The backward counting is an interfering task, a device psychologists use to prevent rehearsal. If the interfering task is ineffective and subjects manage to rehearse CPQ secretly while appearing to take a deep breath between counts, their memory of the letters will probably last longer. The exact duration depends on the amount of rehearsal they are able to squeeze in.

Other factors also affect the exact duration of short-term memory. For one thing, its duration depends on the degree to which new material just happens to be associated with information already held in *long*-term memory. Thus if CPQ happens to be a subject's initials, he or she is likely to recall them no matter how distracting an interfering task may be. In addition, the duration of short-term memory is affected by whether or not a person is *trying* to remember. If subjects who have viewed three consonants are then distracted by a backward-counting task when they do not expect ever to have to recall the letters again, those letters fade from short-term storage with astonishing speed—often within a mere two seconds (Muter, 1980). This finding suggests that the ability to retain new information in short-term memory depends on the way a person processes it in the first place. Information deemed insignificant is likely to evaporate almost immediately, whereas information one wants to remember has a better chance of being recalled despite a few seconds of distraction.

Just as important as the question of short-term memory's duration is the question of its capacity. How much information does short-term memory hold? In 1956 George Miller published a paper titled "The Magical Number Seven, Plus or Minus Two." In it he summarized the results of many experiments, all of which indicated that the majority of people can hold only between five and nine items in short-term memory. Most psychologists agree that the capacity of short-term memory is very near this range. Miller's estimate, in fact, may be a bit high.

At first researchers were puzzled by the ability of humans, despite the limited capacity of our short-term memories, to process large amounts of information. How, they wondered, can we read and comprehend even a very brief sentence if we are unable to handle more than seven letters at once? George Miller had an answer: We expand our relatively limited capacity by "chunking" information. We see groups of letters as words (small chunks), groups of words as phrases (larger chunks), and finally series of phrases as sentences. Short-term memory can hold only about seven chunks, but each chunk may be a complex item containing much information. In this manner we greatly increase the amount of information we can process at any one time.

Interestingly, the process of chunking uses material already stored in long-term memory to categorize new information entering short-term memory. The number 1492, for example, is easier to recall than the number 2769 (if you remember that 1492 is the year in which Columbus landed in America). What you have done is to use this "old" information to reduce your memory load to a single date instead of four separate digits. Conceivably you could hold in short-term memory a string of twenty-eight numbers if they could be chunked into seven familiar dates.

In one recent study, researchers showed that almost anyone can become a short-term memory virtu-

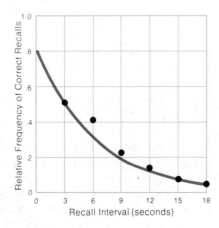

Figure 6.4 The results of Peterson and Peterson's (1959) experiment to measure the length of time that short-term memory lasts without the aid of rehearsal. Subjects were shown a three-consonant combination (CPQ, for example) that they were to remember; immediately after they saw it, they began to count backward by threes from some number supplied by the experimenter. The longer the subjects counted before being asked to recall the combination, the less likely they were to recall it correctly.

Figure 6.5A Study this arrangement of chess pieces for five seconds. Then turn to the empty chess board on the next page and try to reproduce the arrangement. The amount you are able to recall correctly represents approximately seven of the chunks you have developed for processing information about chess games.

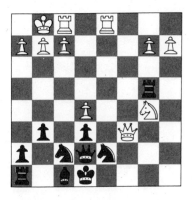

oso by means of appropriate chunking strategies (Ericsson et al., 1980). They began with a college student named Steve Faloon, who was of average intelligence and had ordinary short-term memory capacity (he could remember a string of approximately seven random digits). They then proceeded to give him repeated practice in the recall of random digits, until after twenty months Faloon could remember a staggering eighty random digits presented at the rate of one every second. The start of Faloon's phenomenal improvement lay in a clever chunking technique he devised. Faloon was an accomplished long-distance runner, and he hit upon the scheme of categorizing digits whenever possible according to running times. Thus he would encode into short-term memory the sequence 3492 as "3 minutes and 49.2 seconds, near the world record mile time." Several other strategies supplemented this initial one to give Faloon his impressive powers of recall. But note that his basic short-term memory *capacity* never really increased. When the researchers suddenly switched from presenting random digits to presenting random letters, Faloon's memory span plummeted from eighty back to seven. In short, what Faloon had improved was simply the skill with which he used his limited short-term memory capacity through learned techniques of chunking digits.

Chunks, of course, need not be verbal. Success at the following task requires visual chunking. First study the chessboard shown in Figure 6.5A for about five seconds, then turn the page and see how many pieces you can draw correctly on the empty board in

Figure 6.5B. If you are unfamiliar with the game of chess, your limit will probably be close to the magical number seven. In fact, you may recall far fewer than seven pieces because storing each one requires several items of information: what the piece looks like, the row in which it is located, and also its column. It may therefore surprise you to know that master chess players can reproduce the entire arrangement after just a five-second look. Does this mean that chess masters have exceptional memories? Once again research suggests not (De Groot, 1965; Simon and Gilmartin, 1973). When pieces are arranged on a chessboard in a random pattern, the chess master's memory is no better than anyone else's. But when pieces are arranged in a pattern that might possibly occur in a game between good players, the master can easily encode the pattern as a number of large chunks, making the entire arrangement well within the capacity of normal short-term memory. How many visual chunks are chess masters familiar with? Research shows that they can identify between 25,000 and 100,000 distinct groupings. Although this sounds like an astronomical number, it does not seem so unreasonable when you consider that an educated speaker of English has a vocabulary of about the same size.

LONG-TERM MEMORY

A few pages back we discussed the process of looking up a telephone number and holding it in short-term memory. This information remains available only as long as we repeat it to ourselves. If we are distracted for even a few seconds, the number is likely to evaporate. If this were the entire capacity of human memory, we would have to spend our days continually repeating our own names just to remember who we were. Obviously there is much more to memory than this short-term "holding pattern."

Figure 6.5B Turn to Figure 6.5A on the preceding page, if you have not already looked at it, and study it for five seconds. Then try to reproduce the arrangement shown there on this empty chess board. See the text for an explanation of the results.

Learning and intelligence are made possible through what is called long-term memory. Because of long-term memory, our experiences are not lost the moment we cease to think about them. Instead, we are able to retain the past and use it to shape the present. As the repository of all our accumulated knowledge, long-term memory must contain an extraordinary amount of information. Consider the hundreds, even thousands of facts you store away daily over a lifetime of some seventy years. Viewed in this light, the capacity of long-term memory seems almost beyond comprehension.

Long-Term Storage and Retrieval

The way information is transferred from short-term to long-term memory is not completely understood. Studies show that transfer depends in part on the amount of time we rehearse information: the longer the rehearsal, the more likely the transfer. But even more important is the *type* of rehearsal (Craik and Lockhart, 1972). When people simply repeat something to themselves without giving it any thought, as they tend to do when they rehearse a telephone number, they may maintain that information in short-term memory indefinitely, but they may not transfer it to long-term memory. In contrast, when people take a new piece of information and mentally do something with it—make an image of it, apply it to a problem, relate it to other things—it is more likely to be deposited in long-term storage.

We can see this in the case of Steve Faloon, the random digit recall wizard we talked about earlier. After an hour-long experimental session, Faloon could recall over 80 percent of all the number sequences he had seen that day. He could even recognize many of the sequences he had seen a week earlier (Ericsson et

al., 1980). Clearly, the way in which he chunked the digits and related them to meaningful things facilitated their transfer from short-term to long-term storage. The opposite kind of processing—processing that is shallow and inattentive—is undoubtedly the cause of many common memory lapses, such as the inability to recall a person's name just minutes after you have been introduced (Baddeley, 1982). In this case, you are probably so concerned about making appropriate small talk that you fail to think actively about the name you have just heard.

In some ways, our ability to *retrieve* items from long-term memory is even more impressive than our ability to store them in the first place. Consider, for example, the fact that most people can read at a steady rate of 300 to 600 words per minute—five to ten words per second. This skill requires an amazingly efficient system for retrieving the meanings of words. But because we are so accustomed to our remarkable powers of information retrieval—powers we call upon virtually every waking minute—we seldom stop to think how truly impressive they are.

Just how do we go about retrieving things from long-term memory? Psychologists have extensively studied two basic processes, recognition and recall, both of which involve a variety of mental operations (Brown, 1976). In **recognition** people decide whether they have ever encountered a particular stimulus before. Identifying a suspect in a police line-up is an example of recognition. **Recall,** in contrast, entails the retrieval of specific pieces of information, usually guided by retrieval cues. To ask a witness to a robbery "What did the thief look like? Do you remember what he was wearing?" is to demand that the person recall. The witness must search through his or her memory and come up with an appropriate description. Thus recognition and recall are different kinds of memory tasks. Nevertheless, the mental processes involved in them overlap substantially. Let us see how.

Recognition is essentially a matching process. We consider a given stimulus and decide whether it "matches" something already stored in memory. Many psychologists believe that in doing so we tend to evaluate not the object as a whole but instead its various components (Adams, 1980). If all the components match, the object is quickly recognized. If, however, some of the components match while others do not, we are left with a feeling of only vague familiarity. Such "partial matches" can easily occur when we meet a person again after a lapse of many years. Some of the old acquaintance's features immediately match our memory of them—the eyes and smile, for example—but others do not; body weight, perhaps (some fifteen pounds heavier), or amount of hair (decidedly thinner). The result is the uncomfortable feeling "Do I know you?" This same process of partial recognition may account for the phenomenon called *déjà vu*—the distinct feeling that something is familiar even though we have never encountered it before. In this case we may be partially matching a novel experience with a very similar but unidentifiable past event.

According to many psychologists, recall involves more mental operations than recognition does. When we try to recall something we must first search through long-term memory to find the appropriate information. Then we must determine, as in recognition, whether the information we come up with matches the correct response. If we think it does, we give the answer; if we think it does not, we search again.

Retrieval cues are especially important to the success of the search component of recall. In one experiment (Tulving and Pearlstone, 1966) subjects read lists of words that included both category names (animals, fruits, furniture, for example) and the name of one or more members of each category (dog, plum, chair). The subjects were asked to remember only the names of specific items, not the categories. When the time came to recall the words, half the subjects were given the category words as retrieval cues. These subjects remembered about 50 percent more words out of a list of forty-eight than subjects who were not given the categories to help them recall. Without adequate retrieval cues, therefore, things that are stored in memory may be difficult to find.

This fact should come as no surprise. We have all had the frustrating experience of knowing that something is stored somewhere in memory but of being unable to locate it quickly. One such familiar experience is what psychologists call the **tip-of-the-tongue phenomenon,** from the common experience of feeling that an answer is poised to emerge, but being unable to get it out. How do people pry these uncooperative facts loose? Usually they employ a variety of retrieval cues based on the bits of information about the target word they are able to recall. Suppose you were asked to remember the word for "a small Chinese boat propelled by a single oar over the stern and with the deck usually covered by a roof." You might

grope your way through a string of similar-sounding words—"Cheyenne . . . Siam . . . Saipan"—until you eventually arrived at the correct response, "sampan" (Brown and McNeill, 1966). Similarly, when shown a picture of Elliott Gould and asked to remember his name, you might first recall his profession and then one of his films: "Movie actor . . . starred in *Bob and Carol and Ted and Alice* . . . Elliott Gould!" (Yarmey, 1973). When we store information in long-term memory, therefore, we also seem to create a number of retrieval pathways to it. These cues typically involve both sounds (particularly the first letter) and associated facts and events. Try to recall the names of the people shown in the photographs on the following page and see what retrieval pathways you use.

Since recall always involves a search through memory to find the correct response, is recall necessarily more difficult than recognition? Frequently it is. As a student you have probably deduced this yourself. Most students find that tests consisting of multiple-choice or true-false questions (recognition tests) are substantially easier than those that require them to fill in the blanks (recall tests). Studies confirm that under ideal circumstances, our ability to recognize familiar stimuli can be impressive indeed. Haber and Standing (1969), for example, showed subjects more than 2,500 photographs of various scenes. The next day the subjects were able to recognize between 85 and 95 percent of these pictures. Our capacity to discriminate among stimuli is far from limitless, however. Much depends on the similarity between the initial stimulus and subsequent ones. If you were shown a scene of a crowded railroad station, and later shown an almost identical scene with one or two details changed, you would be very likely to say that the second picture was the same one you saw originally. The same holds true for recognizing other types of stimuli. Circumstances always determine the accuracy of memory, a point we will return to later.

Factors Affecting Long-Term Memory Performance

Most of us complain about our memories. We consider them unreliable and sometimes downright poor. We are annoyed when others' powers of recall seem to be much better than our own. What accounts for differences in long-term memory performance?

A   B   C

Do you know who these people are? Try to recall their
names and follow the retrieval pathways you use. *(A,
Christopher Brown/The Picture Group, B, AP/Wide World
Photos, C, U.P.I.)*

(A) Gloria Steinem, (B) Larry Hagman (C) Nell Carter.

Are there any factors that can enhance one's effectiveness on long-term memory tasks?

Use of Mnemonic Devices. Some simple techniques can greatly improve virtually anyone's powers
of long-term recall. A few such devices are listed in
Figure 6.6. Among them are a group of external aids
(calendars, diaries) and a group of internal aids
known as **mnemonic devices,** from the Greek word
mneme, "memory." The latter are especially useful in
enabling us to make better use of the memory capacities we have.

Many mnemonic devices simply involve clever ways
of organizing material when it is stored in long-term
memory. The **method of loci,** for example, involves
association of items to be remembered with a series of
places, or loci, that are already firmly fixed in memory. Suppose you had to learn, in chronological
order, the names of all the presidents of the United
States in the twentieth century. You would simply visualize a familiar place, say the house in which you
live, and imagine each president in a particular location. Teddy Roosevelt, carrying a big stick, might
greet you at the front door. Stout William Howard

Taft might be found talking to a thin, bespectacled
Woodrow Wilson in the entrance hall. On you would
go, through the living room, up the stairs, until you
finally came to the attic window, through which you
would spot a smiling Ronald Reagan sunning himself
on the roof.

One of the most famous memory whizzes of all
time—a Russian newspaper reporter named
Shereshevskii, who was studied for many years by
psychologist Aleksandr Luria—often used this system to remember long lists of unrelated words. When
each word was presented to him, he would form a
concrete image of it and place the image in a certain
location along Gorky Street in Moscow. Then, to recall the list, he simply took an imaginary walk down
Gorky Street, encountering each of his visual images
along the way. Luria (1968) claimed that with this system Shereshevskii could conjure up a string of fifty
words presented to him only once—even after an interval of fifteen years. A somewhat similar mnemonic
device is called the **key word system,** by which you
associate items to be learned with appropriate key
words that are easily visualized (see Figure 6.7).

Although the method of loci and the key word system are based primarily on organization, they also
employ imagery. Research shows that people can
remember verbal material better if they relate the
words to be learned to visual images of some kind
(Bower and Clark, 1969; Paivio, 1971). You would

1. **Shopping lists.**

2. **First-letter memory aids.** The first letters of "Richard of York gave battle in vain," for example, give the first letters of the colors of the rainbow.

3. **Diary.**

4. **Rhymes.** "In fourteen hundred ninety-two Columbus sailed the ocean blue," for example, helps you to remember the date 1492.

5. **The place method.** Items to be remembered are imagined in a series of familiar places. When recall is required, one "looks" at the familiar places.

6. **Writing on your hand** (or any other part of your anatomy or clothing).

7. **The story method.** Making up a story that connects items to be remembered in the correct order.

8. **Mentally retracing a sequence of events or actions** in order to jog your memory; useful for remembering where you lost or left something, or at what stage something significant happened.

9. **Alarm clock** (or other alarm device) for waking up only.

10. **Kitchen timer with alarm** for cooking only.

11. **Alarm clock** (or other alarm devices such as watches, radios, timers, telephones, calculators) used for purposes other than waking up or cooking.

12. **The keyword method.** "One is a bun, two is a shoe, three is a tree," etc., as a method of remembering lists of items in correct order (Figure 6.7).

13. **Turning numbers into letters.** For remembering telephone numbers, for example.

14. **Memos.** Writing notes and "To do" lists for yourself, for example.

15. **Face-name associations.** Changing people's names into something meaningful and matching them with something unusual about their faces. Red-bearded Mr. Hiles, for example, might be imagined with hills growing out of his beard.

16. **Alphabetical searching.** Going through the alphabet letter by letter to find the initial letter of a name. For example, does a particular person's name begin with A...B...?Ah, yes, C! C for Clark.

17. **Calendars, wall charts, year planners, display boards, etc.**

18. **Asking other people to remember things for you.**

19. **Leaving objects in special or unusual places** so that they act as reminders.

Figure 6.6 How many of these memory aids do you use and how frequently do you use them? Researcher John Harris (1980) distributed a questionnaire among university students and found that the devices used most frequently by that group were items 3, 8, and 13. *(After Baddeley, 1982.)*

probably have an easier time remembering that the French word *escargot* means "snail," for example, if you pictured a giant snail carrying a cargo of *S*'s on its back. This strategy would leave you with the paired images "*S*-cargo" and "snail." Studies show that this kind of interactive imagery is an especially effective mnemonic device for remembering pairs or clusters of words (Bower, 1972).

The waiter John Conrad we talked about earlier used imagery extensively to perform his feats of recall (Singular, 1982). For one thing, he always tried to make visual associations between customers' faces and the entrees they ordered. Thus a woman who or-dered chicken might be remembered for her thin, birdlike nose, while a man who ordered a rib-eye steak might be recalled for his beefy jowls.

Why is imagery such a powerful memory tool? No one knows for sure. One line of reasoning holds that having two different kinds of notes—verbal and visual—makes it twice as likely that we will remember (Paivio, 1971). More recent research, however, suggests that this explanation may not be quite accurate. High-imagery words have been found to improve memory even for subjects who have been totally blind since birth (Jonides, Kahn, and Rozin, 1975).

The use of visual imagery to remember things takes on special meaning for the extremely small number of people who can retain exact visual images after a stimulus has been removed. They are able to recall precise details apparently by "reading" the information off their visual images. In some children and a very few adults this phenomenon takes the form of

One is a bun.	Six is sticks.
Two is a shoe.	Seven is heaven.
Three is a tree.	Eight is a gate.
Four is a door.	Nine is a line.
Five is a hive.	Ten is a hen.

Figure 6.7 These are *key words* commonly used as aids in learning a series of items in order. Say that you want to remember to buy eggs, milk, candy, flowers, and a newspaper, in that order. First learn the rhyming key words that correspond to the numbers; then visually associate each shopping item with the appropriate key word. Thus you might imagine an egg on a bun, drinking milk from a shoe, pieces of candy hanging from a tree, flowers growing up a door. and a newspaper jammed into a hive.

eidetic imagery, images that persist with incredible clarity and detail for a minute or two before they fade (Haber, 1969, 1979). This phenomenon is different from what is known as "photographic memory," which is experienced by some adults. Such people have acute visual memories that do not fade but can be recalled at will (Neisser, 1976, p. 150).

One adult adept at eidetic imagery—a teacher at Harvard referred to as Elizabeth by the psychologist who studied her (Stromeyer, 1970)—could easily form an eidetic image of a 10,000-dot pattern after looking at it with only one eye for as little as a minute. When she was then asked to look at a companion pattern with the opposite eye and superimpose on it the first image, she would quickly perceive a "hidden" geometric figure projecting into space. With a longer look at the original pattern she could continue to conjure up its image even twenty-four hours after it had been formed. And one eidetic image didn't seem to interfere with others. In one experimental session, for instance, Elizabeth recalled images of four separate 10,000-dot patterns she had formed the previous day, superimposing them each in turn on a companion dot pattern and perceiving four different three-dimensional shapes. You can try this task for yourself by looking at the dot patterns in the photograph below. Don't be surprised if you fail. Adults with Elizabeth's ability are rare indeed. In fact, this experiment has never been replicated, and no theory at present can account for its results.

Reconstructing Context and Mood. Although few of us have such camera-like memories, we have at our disposal many very valuable memory aids. Reconstructing the context in which information was learned is one commonly used technique. If you were asked to recall the names of your high school classmates, how would you go about it? Research shows that you would probably reconstruct various scenes from your high school days—hockey practice, for example, or an after-school hangout—and then try to name all of the people you pictured present. This approach often enables people to remember the names of a large number of classmates even after many years (Williams, 1976).

Even information that seems impossible to retrieve may suddenly emerge through reconstruction. Suppose you were asked to recall what you were doing at

Can you form an eidetic image? To find out, take this test: Cover your left eye and with only your right eye carefully examine this 10,000-random-dot pattern. Scan the pattern for a few minutes, then close your eye and try to recall an image of it. At first you may be able to recall only part of the pattern. If you are able to form an image, keep scanning the pattern for about ten minutes or until you have a detailed eidetic image. Now close your right eye and open the left. Turn the page and look at the picture there. Keep your right eye closed and try to visualize the image on the previous page. If you are successful, you will see a figure float off the page toward you. *(Courtesy of Bela Julesz, Bell Telephone, Inc., from Stromeyer, 1970.)*

1:30 in the afternoon on April 27 two years ago. Your initial response to this question might be "Ridiculous!" But try breaking the problem down into smaller subproblems. What day of the week was it? Were you in school at the time? What courses were you taking? At what hour did each class meet? In this way, you could probably reconstruct the broad outline of that particular afternoon. Retrieval, then, can often be viewed as a problem-solving task in which the right answer comes from asking the right questions (Lindsay and Norman, 1977). You may want to try out your problem-solving ability on the questions in Figure 6.8.

Another technique is to relive the emotional state associated with the experience in which information was originally learned. Consider the case of Sirhan Sirhan, the man who assassinated Robert Kennedy. Sirhan was in a highly agitated state when he shot Kennedy in the midst of a crowd of campaign aides and reporters. Afterward he had no recollection of having committed the crime. Yet when under hypnosis he was placed back into the agitated state in which he had pulled the trigger, the events of the episode came flooding back in vivid detail (Diamond, 1969; Kaiser, 1970; Bower, 1981). Sirhan's was an extreme case of **state-dependent memory**—that is, a memory that is retrievable only in the psychological state in which it was originally stored.

Less extreme examples of state-dependent memory have been demonstrated in the laboratory. If subjects learn one list of words when happy and another list when sad (both emotions being induced through hypnosis), they can recall each list better when they return to the mood in which that list was initially learned (Bower, Monteiro, and Gilligan, 1978). The same is true for recall of personal experiences. Subjects in a happy mood find it easy to retrieve pleasant memories, whereas subjects in a sad mood find it easy to retrieve unpleasant ones (Teasdale and Fogarty,

1979; Bower and Gilligan, 1979). One explanation of such mood-dependent recall is based on a **network theory** of memory and emotion. There are many network models of memory, but one stresses that when information is stored in long-term memory it becomes linked to whatever strong emotion one may be feeling at the time. When that emotion is reactivated later, it tends to reactivate the memories to which it is tied. Thus it is likely that appropriate retrieval cues will call those memories to mind (Bower, 1981).

Use of Study Aids. Are there ways to improve our memories of what we study in school? An improved memory performance is of more than passing interest to many college students, who must make sense of quantities of assigned reading material and be able to recall key points when they are tested. Psychologists have conducted many studies of techniques that can enhance the effectiveness of studying. Out of these studies has emerged at least one highly recommended method of studying textbook material—the SQ3R method (Robinson, 1970). The five steps of this method—survey, question, read, recite, review—make maximum use of good memory concepts. Briefly, here is how it works:

1. SURVEY   Before reading a chapter, look over the headings and the introductory and summary paragraphs to familiarize yourself with the three to six main ideas of the chapter. Resist the temptation to read at this point; this survey should take no more than one minute.

2. QUESTION   Beginning with the first headed section, turn the head into a question. This technique allows you to focus on what is relevant in the section and to formulate an answer as you read.

3. READ   Read the first section to find the answer posed by the head. This type of reading is not passive; it requires concentration.

4. RECITE   After reading the first section, jot down a key phrase that sums up the major

In the classroom where you take psychology, how many desks are there?

On what day of the week and at what time was the TV show "Happy Days" shown in 1977?

On the average, how many cups of coffee (or glasses of milk) do you drink per week?

Figure 6.8 Retrieval problems that demonstrate the reconstructive nature of memory. If at first glance any of these questions seems impossible to answer, try anyway. You may be surprised at what you can recall if you put your mind to it.

points and answers the question. It is important that you use your own words and not simply copy out a sentence from the book. This type of recitation not only checks your comprehension of the material but also fixes the idea in your memory.

Steps 2, 3, and 4 should be repeated with every section of the chapter. After you have finished, your notes of key phrases provide you with an outline of the chapter that is invaluable in step 5.

5. REVIEW   Read the outline of notes to get an overview of the chapter and to make connections between major points. Test your comprehension by covering up the notes and trying to recall the key phrases for each section. This review should immediately follow the reading and should take no more than five minutes. Reread sections for which you could not recall key phrases. Subsequent reviews of the notes aid in fixing the material in memory.

Studies have shown that students who use the SQ3R method can significantly improve their reading rate, comprehension, and performance on tests (Robinson, 1970).

Long-Term Memory Distortions

Although there is much we can do to improve our powers of long-term recall, human memory is far from reliable. People commonly confuse what happened at one time with what happened at another. When memories are vague, people fill in the gaps with what they *believe* to be true. In short, the process of piecing together the past is often prone to distortion. This tendency to distort is one of the most fascinating aspects of the way we humans remember.

Preconceptions and Inferences. What causes memory distortions? The tendency to edit and embellish what we learn and recall seems to be a natural outcome of the way human memory works. Psychologist Frederic C. Bartlett set out to demonstrate that memory follows predictable patterns in a series of experiments that worked like the children's game of "telephone." He gave his first subject an Indian tribal legend to read. Briefly, the story tells of an Indian who joins a war party that he subsequently recalls as consisting of ghosts. During the fighting he does not think he has been shot, yet at sunrise at his house the next day he falls over dead. This basic theme was embellished by many details. The first subject told the story to another subject, who in turn told it to another, and so on down the line.

After many subjects and many renditions, the story became substantially changed. But Bartlett found that the changes were not haphazard. Several important patterns emerged. First, subjects tended to "flatten" details that did not fit within their existing viewpoints. By the time the tale was told by the tenth subject, for example, all references to ghosts had been eliminated. Bartlett argued that because the mystical references to ghosts were not easily assimilated into most subjects' existing concepts of life, warfare, and death, they tended to be dropped. For a somewhat similar reason other details tended to be sharpened. In the original story a second Indian declined to join the war party because his relatives would not know where he had gone. The tenth subject said the Indian refused because his elderly mother was dependent on him—an expansion that fits preexisting concepts of a son's responsibilities. Finally, many subjects added a moral to the story, because this kind of ending is typical of the folktales they were accustomed to.

Figure 6.9 The original figure used in the Allport and Postman experiment (1947).

The influence of expectations on memory storage and retrieval has been demonstrated many times since. In one experiment two psychologists showed subjects the scene from a subway car reproduced in Figure 6.9 (Allport and Postman, 1947). Among other things, it shows a black man apparently talking to a white man who is carrying a razor. The researchers asked one subject to describe the picture to a second subject, and so on until the description had passed through many people. Significantly, the razor tended to migrate from the white hand to the black hand. The common stereotype of blacks as more violent than whites influenced what subjects saw and recalled.

Bartlett was one of the first psychologists to propose that such distortions provide important clues to the way human memory works. Apparently people try to assimilate new information within the framework of their existing knowledge and beliefs. If we learn that an Indian goes into battle, for example, we try to fit this fact into our established notion of what Indian warfare is like. Information that does not conform to our expectations we may recast or simply drop. Thus the process of storing information in memory is one of active construction. So is the process of retrieving it. During retrieval we may actively construct fairly detailed accounts, guided by our existing concepts. If we know that a black man, a white man, and a razor appear together in a picture, and if we believe that blacks are generally more violent than whites, a logical inference is that the razor is in the black man's grasp.

The tendency of people to make many inferences on the basis of preconceptions can be illustrated in other ways. Look very briefly at the top drawing in Figure 6.10A. Then turn away and try to reproduce from memory this sketch of a pair of eyeglasses. If you are like most people, your drawing will look very similar to the one at the top of the left-hand column in Figure 6.10B. Although the original sketch consisted of two circles joined together by a short, straight stick, people who are told this is a representation of eyeglasses tend to connect two circles with a slightly curved and elevated line—much as we think eyeglasses should look. In contrast, people who are told that the same initial sketch is a picture of a dumbbell tend to reproduce the drawing as shown in the right-hand column of Figure 6.10B. Memory for visual material, in other words, is easily distorted by what we are *told* we see (Carmichael, Hogan, and Walter, 1932).

Findings such as these have enormously important

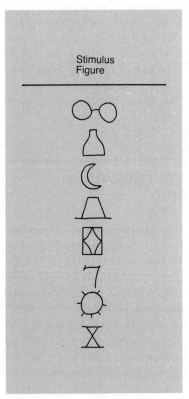

Stimulus
Figure

Figure 6.10A Carmichael, Hogan, and Walter (1932) designed an experiment to study the influence of set on perception. Subjects were shown these line patterns, which were described as drawings of various objects. When the subjects were asked to reproduce the patterns they had seen, they made the drawings shown in Figure 6.10B.

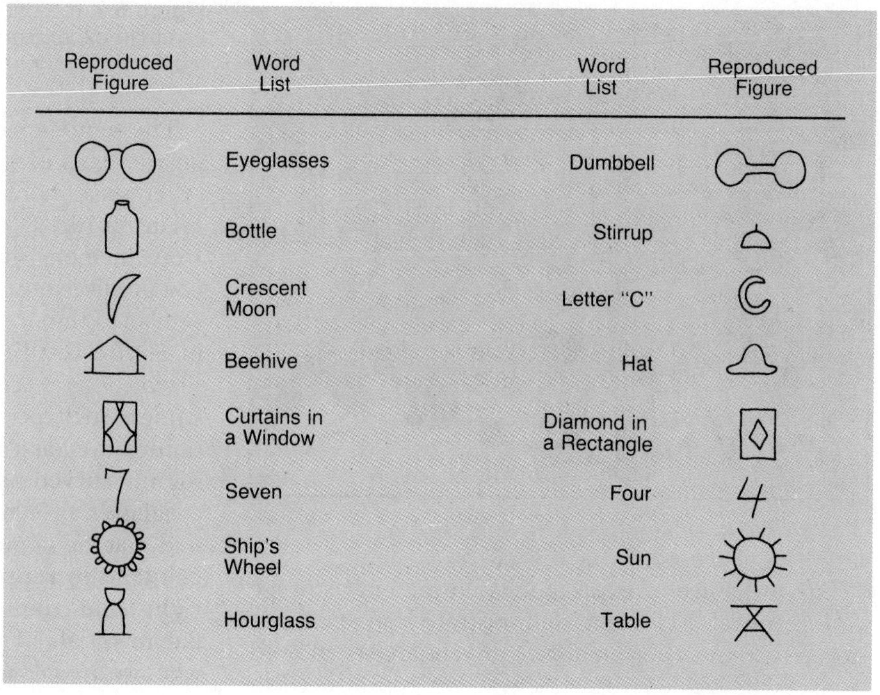

Figure 6.10B You can see how the naming of the patterns influenced the subjects' drawings. *(After Carmichael, Hogan, and Walter, 1932.)*

Reproduced Figure	Word List	Word List	Reproduced Figure
	Eyeglasses	Dumbbell	
	Bottle	Stirrup	
	Crescent Moon	Letter "C"	
	Beehive	Hat	
	Curtains in a Window	Diamond in a Rectangle	
	Seven	Four	
	Ship's Wheel	Sun	
	Hourglass	Table	

implications for the success of our legal system. A person who witnesses an accident or a crime will almost always be questioned before a trial takes place. Could something said during this initial interrogation alter the witness's later recollection of events? And if so, under what conditions are distortions most likely to occur? Recent research on the accuracy of eyewitness testimony provides some interesting answers (Loftus, 1979a).

in depth Studying Eyewitness Testimony

Much of the recent work in the area of eyewitness testimony has been conducted by Elizabeth Loftus, one of the authors of this book. Loftus began her investigation of this important topic with several questions in mind. Prior research had clearly suggested that human memory is a process of active construction, in both the storage and the retrieval stages. Yet the stimuli that subjects in these experiments had been asked to remember were unlike much of the information learned in everyday life. Many were verbal stimuli—word lists, sentences, at times brief stories. And those that were visual were almost always static, such as a simple picture of two circles connected by a stick. Loftus felt that such stimuli were not highly representative of the memories we most commonly form. In the world outside the laboratory, we are constantly processing information that is not only largely visual but also fast-moving and complex. Did past findings regarding memory apply to such events as well? In addition, Bartlett and other psychologists had stressed that new information instated into memory is assimilated within the framework of prior knowledge and beliefs. This was fine as far as it went. But what about the relationship between memory for a given experience and information acquired *after* that event? Is *subsequent* information also integrated into a person's existing memory structure?

This second question may sound abstract to you, but it is critical to the subject of eyewitness testimony. To understand why, imagine yourself in the following situation. It is nine o'clock on a rainy Christmas Eve, and you are hurrying home from some last-minute shopping. The streets are practically deserted, but ahead you spot a man with an armful of packages stepping off the curb into the crosswalk. Halfway across the street he drops a small box and bends to pick it up. Suddenly you see a car headed toward the

The critical slides used by Loftus, Miller, and Burns (1978) to test the accuracy of recollection. Half the subjects saw the picture with the stop sign at the corner and half saw the picture with the yield sign. *(Courtesy, Professor Elizabeth F. Loftus.)*

stooped figure. The next instant the car strikes the man, throwing him some twenty feet to the side of the road. You have witnessed a serious automobile accident.

Within a few minutes police and ambulance are at the scene and a young officer begins to ask you a series of questions. Where was the man standing when he was hit? From what direction did the car come? How fast was the car going when it ran the stop light at the crosswalk? Although you may not have noticed it, this last question presupposes a piece of information you did not actually witness—a red traffic light. You have no recollection of a traffic light. Do you think this subsequent information introduced by the police officer would alter the representation of the accident already in your memory? Research suggests that it very well might.

Loftus (1975) showed subjects a brief videotape of an automobile accident and then asked them questions about it. For half the subjects, one of the questions was: "How fast was the white sports car going while traveling along the country road?" For the other half, a similar question was: "How fast was the white sports car going when it passed the barn while traveling along the country road?" In fact, there was no barn in the film. Yet when the subjects were questioned again about the accident a week later, more

than 17 percent of those exposed to the false information about a barn answered yes to the question: "Did you see a barn?" In contrast, only about 3 percent of the other subjects answered yes to the same question. Apparently the assumption of a barn during the initial questioning caused many subjects to incorporate the nonexistent barn into their recollections of the event.

In this case the initial memory of an event is being *supplemented* with additional, false information. On a previously empty country landscape, subjects now imagine a barn. In a sense, their recollection of the facts is not so much altered as amplified—albeit incorrectly. An important question therefore remains. Can something said to a witness immediately after an incident actually *transform* that person's original memory of what occurred? Suppose that during our hypothetical Christmas Eve accident you did see the traffic light, but you remembered it as being green when the car crossed the intersection. Could the police officer's mention of a red light cause you later to recall the light as being red instead of green? Studies indicate that it could.

Loftus, Miller, and Burns (1978) showed subjects thirty color slides of successive stages in an automobile accident involving a red Datsun. The critical slide was of the Datsun stopped at an intersection before it eventually turned right and hit a pedestrian. Half the subjects saw a slide with a stop sign at the corner; half saw a slide with a yield sign. (These almost identical photographs are shown above.) Immediately after viewing the slide series, the subjects answered questions about it. One of the questions presupposed the existence of either a stop sign or a yield sign. For half the subjects the presupposed sign was consistent with what they had actually seen; for half it was inconsistent. The subjects then performed a distracting task for twenty minutes, after which a final recognition test began. The researchers showed the subjects fifteen pairs of slides and asked them to choose the one slide out of each pair that they had seen before. How do you think the subjects responded when they were shown two views of the intersection, one with a stop sign and one with a yield sign? When the critical question asked earlier had presupposed a traffic sign *consistent* with what the subjects had actually seen, they chose the correct sign 75 percent of the time. In contrast, when the earlier question presupposed an *inconsistent* traffic sign, the subjects chose the correct slide only 41 percent of the time. Thus presuppositions do indeed seem capable of *transforming* a witness's memory. The rate at which such transformations occur, moreover, can be substantially increased by a change in the timing of misinformation. If subjects are exposed to inaccurate information a week after they witness an accident, when the true details are more difficult to retrieve, they are susceptible to the misinformation 80 percent of the time (Loftus, Miller, and Burns, 1978).

Other experiments have shown that the more violent an event is, the more likely subjects are to incorporate subsequent misinformation into memory. Apparently, shocking events disrupt the ability to

form a strong memory, so subsequent misinformation is less likely to be conflicting (Loftus and Burns, 1982). Memory distortion has been not only demonstrated in the laboratory but documented in real life. Take the case several years ago of a Roman Catholic priest who stood trial for a series of armed robberies in the Wilmington, Delaware, area (Rodgers, 1982). A citizen notified police that Father Bernard Pagano looked remarkably like a sketch of the robber being circulated in the local media. The linkage of the crimes to a priest made some sense when one realized that this particular robber was dubbed the "gentleman bandit" because of his impeccably polite manners and well-groomed appearance. Seven eyewitnesses positively identified Father Pagano as the culprit. At his trial the prosecution's case seemed airtight. But then, in a turn of events that could have come from a television melodrama, the trial was abruptly halted when another man confessed to the robberies. He knew details about the crimes that only the true gentleman bandit could have known. The state dropped its charges against Father Pagano and his ordeal was finally over.

How could this case of widespread mistaken identity have happened? The two men are not obvious look-alikes. Apparently, before showing pictures of suspects to witnesses, the police had let it be known that the robber might be a priest. Since Father Pagano was the only suspect wearing a clerical collar, the witnesses' memories were strongly prejudiced against him. In one respect Father Pagano was lucky:

Father Bernard Pagano (right) was almost convicted of armed robbery when seven eyewitnesses mistook him for Ronald Clouser (left), the real culprit. *(U.P.I.)*

other people falsely accused of crimes have actually been convicted on the basis of mistaken identification, and some of them have spent many years in prison. Such cases are tragic testimony to the fallibility of eyewitness accounts.

An important issue for our legal system is the extent to which the memories of eyewitnesses are susceptible to modification. To what extent can a person's recollection of an event be shaped by subsequent information? The answer is, further than you might think. Even rather implausible false information can sometimes be added to memory. Loftus (1979a) has managed to get subjects to accept misleading suggestions as unlikely as a telephone booth in a farmyard. In all cases, however, people's susceptibility to implausible suggestions is substantially less than their susceptibility to plausible ones.

There appears to be a limit, then, as to how far our recollections can be swayed. Information to which we have committed ourselves is particularly resistant to change. If we publicly state that we remember a particular detail to be one way, it is unlikely that subsequent suggestions will cause us to change our minds (Loftus, 1977). In addition, we tend to resist information that blatantly contradicts a clearly perceived detail. In one experiment, for example, subjects viewed a series of slides showing the theft of a large, bright-red wallet from a woman's handbag. Few accepted the blatantly false suggestion that the wallet had in fact been brown (Loftus, 1979b). Resistance to misinformation is also increased when subjects are warned of possible distortion before a misleading message is presented (Greene, Flynn, and Loftus, 1982). Thus, although our memories may be malleable, they are not infinitely so. To most of us this is a reassuring thought.

in depth

THE RELATIONSHIP BETWEEN SHORT-TERM AND LONG-TERM MEMORY

We have talked in some detail about the nature of long-term memory, how the information in it is stored and retrieved, and how it can sometimes be distorted. But we have not yet discussed the relationship between long-term and short-term memory. Are these systems separate and distinct? Certainly there are significant differences between them. Consider short-term memory. Its duration is brief—under twenty seconds if information is not renewed by rehearsal. The capacity of short-term memory is also very limited—it can hold no more than nine items and perhaps as few as five. Long-term memory, in contrast, endures for many years. Some of our long-term memories never fade. Moreover, the capacity of long-term memory is virtually limitless. Even if a person lives to be a hundred, he or she can continue to store additional information. We are never forced to drop old memories in order to make room for new ones. These differences suggest that short-term and long-term memory are in fact separate systems. A number of laboratory and clinical findings strongly support this view.

Evidence for a Dual Memory

Studies involving what is known as **free recall** lend substantial support to the **dual memory view.** In a typical experiment, subjects are presented with a list of words, one at a time, and then asked to recall as many as they can in any order. The results are represented in Figure 6.11. This graph is called a **serial position curve,** because it shows the percentage of words, averaged over many trials, that subjects recall at each of the positions on the list. As you can see, memory for words at the end of the list is excellent, memory for words at the beginning is also good, but memory for words in the middle is weak. Those who believe that short-term and long-term memory are two distinct systems explain this pattern in the following way. The nearer a word is to the end of the list, they argue, the greater the likelihood that it is still in short-term storage. Such words would naturally be recalled very well. The words at the beginning of the list are also recalled quite well, but for a very different reason. Because subjects have had more time to re-

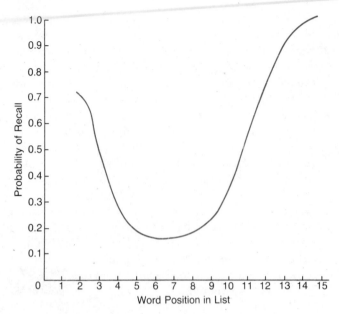

hearse and think about them, these items are more likely to have been transferred to long-term storage. In short, the shape of the curve reflects the existence of two separate memory "compartments."

A variation of the free-recall experiment just described provides further evidence in support of this view. As usual, subjects are presented with a list of words. This time, however, before they are given a chance to recall, they are asked to perform a distracting mental task, such as counting backward by threes from 100. If memory is a single system, this task should interfere equally with recall of *all* the words on the list—that is, the resulting curve should be virtually the same shape as the one in Figure 6.11, only lower on the graph. But this is definitely not the case. Generally speaking, such a task interferes with memory *only* for words at the end of the list, as shown in Figure 6.12. For those who adopt a dual memory view, this result is not the least bit surprising. The distracting mental task, they argue, uses short-term memory and so dislodges the words that were formerly held there. Words at the beginning of the list, on the other hand, should be affected hardly at all because they are stored in long-term memory.

The condition known as **anterograde amnesia** pro-

vides even more compelling evidence for a dual memory system. This form of amnesia affects memory only for new events. Things that were learned before the condition started are recalled perfectly. Neuropsychologist Brenda Milner (1966) studied a number of people with anterograde amnesia and has described in detail the case of one young man whom she referred to as H. M. This man, as we saw in Chapter 2, developed his tragic condition after radical brain surgery to relieve severe epileptic seizures. Although H. M. was actually twenty-nine at the time Milner interviewed him, he believed that he was twenty-seven—his age at the time of the operation. He could remember new experiences only as long as he paid attention to them. As soon as he shifted his attention, the memories were lost. As a result, he faced enormous problems in his daily life. When his family moved, for example, he was unable to remember the new address. Over and over he returned to the old house. For those who support a dual memory system, a very plausible explanation for H. M.'s condition is that the operation somehow destroyed the man's ability to transfer information from short-term to long-term memory. There must, they argue, be two types of memory, two separate and distinct systems.

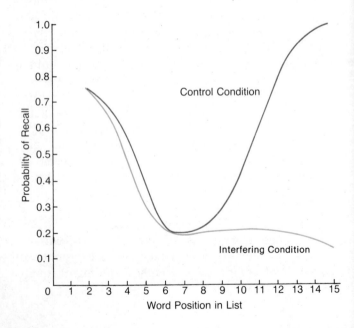

Figure 6.12 Results of a modified free-recall experiment. *(After Loftus and Loftus, 1976.)*

The Depth of Processing View

The dual memory view has received widespread support, but it is not without its critics. Some psychologists have argued that there is no need to assume the existence of two separate memory systems. The observed differences between short-term and long-term memory, they say, can be attributed simply to differences in the way information is processed, or encoded into memory. If, on the one hand, we process information "shallowly," say by repeating a telephone number several times, then instatement into memory will be weak, and forgetting will occur quickly. If, on the other hand, we process information "deeply"—for instance, by associating it with other facts we know—we are likely to remember it much longer. This argument is called the **depth of processing view.**

But what exactly constitutes shallow and deep processing? It seems reasonable to surmise that some kind of semantic processing (probing the meaning of a word) would be deeper, and therefore result in better retention, than visual or auditory processing (focusing on the look or sound of a word). Craik and Tulving (1975) designed a series of experiments to test this hypothesis. In one study they asked subjects one of several types of questions about each word on a list. Sometimes the question related to the *look* of the word—"Is it written in capital letters?" At other times the question pertained to the *sound* of the word—"Does it rhyme with weight?" And at still other times the question had to do with the *meaning* of the word—"Would it fit in the following sentence?" Thus the questions induced processing at one of three different levels: visual, auditory, semantic. The researchers then distributed another list of words and asked the subjects to check off all items that had appeared on the previous list. As expected, memory of a given word increased as processing went from visual to auditory to semantic. The greater the depth of processing, the better the retention.

The depth of processing view of memory is still relatively new, so its validity as a general theory remains to be demonstrated. Ultimately, however, it seems likely that physiological research will provide the final answer to the question of whether human memory is a dual or a unitary system. As you will see in the following section, the findings in this area to date seem to support the notion of a dual memory. Certainly the results of such depth of processing experiments as those by Craik and Tulving are not incompatible with this view. Shallow or deep processing of information held in short-term memory may determine what and how much gets transferred to long-term storage, as we suggested earlier in this chapter.

THE PHYSIOLOGY OF MEMORY

A central question about memory is how, physiologically, we manage to record information. The answer lies somewhere in the billions of interconnecting neurons that make up a human brain. But how this labyrinth of cells changes to form a memory trace remains a profound puzzle that scientists have only begun to solve.

Some of the earliest clues to the biological basis of memory came from clinical findings. In 1933, for instance, doctors recorded the case of a twenty-two-year-old man who was accidentally thrown from his motorcycle and received a severe blow to the head. When he regained consciousness, he insisted that the year was 1922 and that he was a boy of eleven. Gradually over the next ten weeks the young man recalled the past decade, beginning with the most distant years and working up to the most recent. But no matter how hard he tried, he could never remember the minutes before the critical accident (Baddeley, 1982). Such a condition, called **retrograde amnesia,** involves memory loss for only a segment of the past, not for new events. Retrograde amnesia is fairly common among people who receive severe blows to the head. This fact implies that information stored in short-term memory at the time the head injury occurs is held far more fragilely than information stored in long-term memory. This implication in turn suggests that long-term and short-term memory may involve different physiological mechanisms.

What could the fragile, short-term mechanism be?

The answer is far from clear. But many neurophysiologists believe that it somehow involves a temporary circulation of electrical impulses around complex loops of interconnected neurons. This theory is supported both directly and indirectly. Some indirect evidence is provided by the fact that any event that either suppresses neural activity (such as a blow to the head, carbon monoxide poisoning, or heavy anesthesia) or causes neurons to fire incoherently (such as electroconvulsive shock) can apparently erase information held in short-term memory. (As we will see later, these same factors also appear to interfere with the transfer of information from short-term to long-term memory.) More direct evidence comes from studies in which researchers have probed the brains of experimental animals with electrodes and found that different circulating patterns of electrical activity are indeed associated with attention to different stimuli (Vereano et al., 1970). How such activity relates to short-term memory, however, remains a mystery.

Whatever the basis of short-term memory is, the brain must ultimately have some means of transferring information from short-term to long-term storage. One thing that is certain is that this transfer process takes time. In a classic experiment, Duncan (1949) trained rats to run from a darkened compartment at the flash of a light in order to avoid an electric shock to their feet. After each training session, the rats were given electroconvulsive shock (ECS) administered through the ears. (Electroconvulsive shock involves the passage of enough electrical current through the brain to induce convulsions and unconsciousness.) The timing of the ECS varied among the rats. Some were shocked as soon as twenty seconds after training; others were shocked after intervals of as long as fourteen hours. As you might expect, the rats that received the ECS shortly after training showed almost no recollection of what they had previously experienced in regard to darkness and flashing lights. But significantly, the rats that had received ECS up to an hour after training *also* showed memory deficits. Thus it seemed to take nearly an hour for an experience to become firmly fixed in long-term memory. The idea that a series of solidifying events occurs when a memory is acquired is termed the **consolidation hypothesis.** If ECS is given *after* consolidation is complete—that is, after information is instated into long-term memory—little or no memory loss occurs.

Neurological Changes

Because most long-term memories are so impervious to head blows, ECS, and other factors that temporarily disrupt neural activity, scientists assume they must reflect relatively permanent alterations in the ways that neurons interconnect. Remember from Chapter 3 that electrochemical messages are transmitted from neuron to neuron across tiny junction gaps called synapses. Synapses, then, are the means by which neurons "communicate." Consequently, scientists believe that long-term memory must involve some sort of synaptic change. Such change could be either structural or chemical, or perhaps both. By structural change scientists mean a change in the size or the number of neural synapses. By chemical change they mean a change in the amount or the composition of the transmitter substances that carry neural impulses across synapses. The neural activity associated with short-term memory may itself be capable of initiating the physical changes that create long-term memory traces. Alternatively, neural activity may initiate only the first stage of consolidation into long-term memory.

Neuroscientists are just now beginning to piece together some of the neurological changes associated with memory. So far, their explorations have focused mainly on very simple animal species with very simple nervous systems, and on the most rudimentary processes of learning and memory, such as habituation to a repeated stimulus, which we talked about in Chapter 5 (Kandel, 1979). In more complex animals, with billions rather than thousands of nerve cells, memory capabilities are much more sophisticated and their underlying mechanisms much more difficult to pinpoint.

Research with rats, for instance, has so far uncovered only very broad changes in brain anatomy and physiology that seem to be associated with learning and memory. Consider what happens when baby rats from the same litter are placed in two radically different environments. One is an "enriched" environment consisting of wheels, ladders, slides, and a variety of other "toys" that the rats can explore and manipulate. The toys are changed frequently so as to ensure a continual barrage of new learning experiences. The remaining rats are placed in an "impoverished" environment that consists of an empty cage located in an isolated room. After nearly three months in their respective worlds, the young rats are killed and their brains compared. The differences are dramatic. The cerebral cortices of rats that have spent their days in the enriched setting are thicker, heavier, and endowed with more blood vessels. They also contain more of an enzyme related to the neurotransmitter acetylcholine (believed to be associated with memory) than do the cortices of the animals relegated to the impoverished environment (Rosenzweig, Bennett, and Diamond, 1972). What's more, subsequent research has revealed that rats raised in an enriched environment have a significantly greater number of dendrite spines on their cortical neurons; dendrite spines are the structures on a neuron where other neurons connect to form synapses (Globus et al., 1973). Such experiments clearly demonstrate that neural changes do result from different kinds of experience. But exactly how these changes may be related to memory formation remains unknown.

The Genetic Factor

Although scientists are still a long way from understanding the biological processes underlying memory, they think that these processes must somehow involve changes in the way an organism's genes are expressed. Genes, as you probably know, are tiny bits of matter contained in the nucleus of each of the body's cells; they provide the blueprints for all of the body's biochemical and anatomical features. The instructions coded in the genes are transported from the cell nucleus via various "messenger" molecules composed of ribonucleic acid (RNA). It seems likely, therefore, that if permanent changes take place in the brain when memory traces are formed, the quantity or the composition of RNA in those cells should also change.

Hydén and Egyhazi (1962) first found this to be true, and other researchers have since confirmed their findings. Victor Shashoua at Harvard University Medical School devised an imaginative technique for studying learning and RNA synthesis in goldfish (Shashoua, 1970). He attached a small piece of styrofoam to a fish's belly, causing the animal to float upside down. With great effort, the goldfish eventually learned to right itself and swim normally. Then it was killed and dissected. Analysis of the goldfish's brain showed significant changes in RNA compared with the RNA in the brain of a control fish spared this arduous learning experience. There is an important problem with such studies, however. They do not demonstrate conclusively that the observed changes in RNA are related to memory formation rather than to some other factor, such as stress or muscular activity, associated with the learning task.

The logical link between RNA synthesis and the development of long-term memory traces has intrigued many researchers. Some have even wondered if it might not be possible to transfer memory from one organism to another simply by injecting the RNA from the brain of a "trained" individual into the brain of a "naive" one. McConnell and his colleagues (1966) attempted to find out. They conditioned planarians (flatworms) to contract their bodies at the flash of a light by repeatedly pairing the light with an electric shock. (Planarians naturally contract when shocked but not usually when stimulated by light.) They then extracted RNA from the trained planarians and injected it into the untrained ones. The naive planarians contracted in response to light more often than control planarians did. McConnell speculated that specific memories might in fact be chemically transferrable, and this idea became widely publicized. Perhaps, science-fiction writers proposed, we might one day learn the theory of relativity simply by consuming some RNA from the brain of a theoretical physicist.

Memory transfer studies have many serious problems, however. One is the enormous difficulty of replicating them. At times researchers have been unable to reproduce even their own findings. In addition, because such large molecules as RNA cannot be absorbed into a cell, it is difficult to imagine how they might affect the brain cells of another organism. It is much more likely that the results obtained in certain memory transfer studies are caused instead by a chemical other than RNA (Ungar, 1970). Significantly, many of the RNA extracts used in such studies have also contained other substances. This other chemical might be one that somehow facilitates learning or simply enhances performance (McGaugh, 1966). In humans, for instance, the hormone vasopressin has been found to improve the ability to learn and remember things (Weingartner et al., 1981). Similar memory-enhancing substances might also exist in planarians. In any case, most scientists now agree that injecting RNA from the brain of one organism into the brain of another cannot in itself transfer specific memories.

The scientific investigation of memory and the brain has only begun. Even after the mechanisms of short-term and long-term storage are better understood, there are many other mysteries to unravel. Consider retrieval, for example. The average adult can quite quickly recall any one of many thousands of facts and experiences stored away in the brain. How is such remarkably efficient retrieval accomplished? Why do we not have to sort laboriously through an enormous number of episodes just to arrive at the memory of a single event? No one yet knows. Undoubtedly in the years ahead many fascinating discoveries will be made in this and other frontier areas of neurophysiology.

FORGETTING

Until now we have concentrated primarily on the successful side of human memory. We have seen that people can instate, store, and retrieve information from long-term memory with a reasonable degree of speed and accuracy, even if some distortions of memory occur. But what about the all-too-familiar process called forgetting? It, too, is of interest to psychologists.

Psychologist Marigold Linton (1978), frustrated by the undependability of her own memory, set out in the early 1970s to investigate the phenomenon of forgetting personal experiences. Following the lead of the nineteenth-century memory researcher Hermann Ebbinghaus (1885), Linton chose herself as the most willing and reliable subject available. For six years she recorded on file cards two or more distinct events that happened to her each day. The entries varied from such mundane occurrences as eating dinner at a Chinese restaurant to rather unusual happenings, such as an important job interview. Every month she tested her recall of the dates of some 150 events selected at random from the card file as well as some other information related to the events. The results were not encouraging. By the end of 1978, Linton had slowly but steadily forgotten almost a third of the events she had considered memorable six years earlier.

Theories of Forgetting

What are the reasons for this persistent forgetting? Psychologists have suggested three major causes: decay, interference, and motivation to forget. Although these explanations conflict with one another in several important ways, they are not entirely incompatible. A full account of forgetting should probably include all three.

Decay of Memory Traces. Perhaps the oldest theory of forgetting is that memories simply fade away, or decay, with the passage of time if they are not renewed through periodic use. This notion has a certain romantic appeal and tends to fit well with some of our personal experiences. The memory of a movie seen last week, for example, is usually stronger and more detailed than that of a movie seen last year. Nevertheless, some of the things we know about human memory appear to contradict **decay theory.** For one thing, not all long-term memories seem to dissipate with time. Motor skills, for instance, are particularly resistant to decay. An adult who has not ridden a bicycle in twenty years usually has no trouble demonstrating the skill to a child. Second, if long-term memories do in fact fade over the years, then the structural or chemical changes in the brain that originally encoded those memories must also break down in some way. As yet, however, we do not know why such a breakdown would regularly and spontaneously occur. The concept of decay, then, may be useful in explaining loss from fragile short-term memory, but its application to long-term memory is open to question.

Interference. The phenomenon of **interference** is another cause of forgetting. According to this view, memory of a year-old movie fades because of the unavoidable confusion that results when you subsequently encounter very similar experiences (other movies or television shows with similar characters and plots). Marigold Linton was surprised at how much of her forgetting was attributable to this kind of confusion. As a string of similar events in her life became longer (the sixth time she dined at a certain restaurant, or the twelfth time she attended a certain professional meeting), she found it increasingly difficult to distinguish one episode from another. The details of the separate episodes blended together, until none could be clearly recalled (Linton, 1982).

Interference may hinder recall of verbal information, too. You may have had this experience yourself when you studied for exams. If you have just memorized the names of various bones of the body for a test in human anatomy, for instance, reading about the related muscles could begin to confuse you. When information learned later interferes with information learned earlier, psychologists say that **retroactive interference** has taken place. (*Retro* means "backward in time.") Conversely, when material learned earlier interferes with recall of material learned later, **proactive interference** has occurred. (*Pro* means "forward in time.") You may have had this experience when you introduced someone by her maiden name, even though she has been using a married name for months.

Sleep seems to be one of the best temporary safeguards against interference. Research has shown that people forget substantially less if they sleep for several hours after learning than if they continue their waking activities. In one experiment, subjects who stayed awake for eight hours recalled only about 10 percent of material they had previously learned, whereas subjects who slept for eight hours remembered about 60 percent of the same material (Jenkins and Dallenbach, 1924). Presumably those who went to sleep were not subject to interference. These findings can be applied to your own study habits. Getting a good night's sleep after studying for an exam will probably increase your powers of recall in the morning.

Motivated Forgetting. It is not hard to believe that we sometimes forget because we *want* to. Such **motivated forgetting** is, in fact, the foundation of Freud's psychoanalytic theory. According to Freud, people often push unacceptable, anxiety-provoking thoughts and impulses into their unconscious so as to avoid confronting them directly. This psychological defense mechanism is called **repression.** Sirhan Sirhan's inability to remember shooting Robert Kennedy is probably an instance of repression. In fact, repression seems to be quite common among people who have committed violent crimes of great passion; it occurs in an estimated one out of three such cases (Bower, 1981).

Not all motivated forgetting is a defense mecha-nism against severe anxiety, however. Research shows that people generally tend to forget unpleasant experiences more readily than pleasant ones, even when the unpleasant events are not especially threatening. In one early experiment, students returning to college after Christmas vacation tended to remember more pleasant than unpleasant things about the holiday. And when the same students were unexpectedly interviewed again six weeks later, they remembered even fewer unpleasant holiday experiences in proportion to pleasant ones (Meltzer, 1930). Negative memories, it appears, are banished more readily than positive ones.

Part of this tendency to remember the past as better than it actually was may be motivated by a desire to enhance our own self-esteem. Research shows that people often remember themselves as having held more responsible, better-paying jobs than they actually had. They also recall donating more to charity, voting more frequently, and raising more intelligent children than objective records indicate (Cannell and Kahn, 1968). We tend, in other words, to edit our personal memories in order to cast ourselves in a more favorable light (Myers and Ridl, 1979). From this point of view, forgetting is partly self-serving.

How Much Do We Really Forget?

The theories of interference and motivated forgetting suggest an interesting possibility. Perhaps many of the things we fail to remember are not completely lost. Perhaps they lie somewhere in the recesses of the brain, awaiting the right retrieval cues to coax them to the surface. The notion that forgetting reflects a retrieval failure and not a permanent memory loss has widespread appeal. In an informal survey of people across the country, including many professional psychologists, 75 percent agreed with this point of view (Loftus and Loftus, 1980).

What is the basis of this conviction that memories are essentially indelible, even if many are difficult to retrieve? The evidence is quite intriguing. As we mentioned in Chapter 3, brain surgeon Wilder Penfield has found that people sometimes report vivid memories of apparently long-forgotten events when parts of the cerebral cortex are electrically stimulated (Penfield, 1969). When a mild electrical current was passed through a region of one patient's brain, for example, he claimed to hear an old tune being played. Another patient "relived" the birth of her child through brain stimulation. Yet another "revisited" the midway of a traveling circus. In these and other instances, Penfield reports, it is as though a former stream of consciousness is made to flow again with all the clarity of the original experience.

Other evidence also supports the belief that whatever enters long-term storage may well remain there for life. We have all experienced sudden recall of some long-forgotten detail from the past. You might be walking by the building where you attended grade school and unexpectedly remember an event that happened to you in the playground when you were very young. Similarly, many psychologists have been impressed with the apparent ability of people in a hypnotic trance to give detailed reports of events that occurred long ago. The hypnotist may ask a subject to describe his sixth birthday, and the subject complies with a detailed account of a party complete with cake, decorations, presents, and guests. People undergoing psychoanalysis also seem to dredge up deeply repressed happenings from the distant past. Surely these are strong indications that virtually everything we learn stays permanently locked away in memory. All we seem to need to recall them is the proper key.

As compelling as these findings may seem, however, all of them can be explained in other ways. Of the small percentage of Penfield's patients who actually experienced lifelike memories from brain stimulation, for example, some reported events as though they were observing them from the sidelines, much as we often do in dreams. Others recalled being in places where in all probability they had never really been. There is a good possibility, therefore, that many of Penfield's cases of memory "retrieval" did not involve accurate retrieval at all. Instead of "reliving" the past, these people may simply have been reconstructing it. Similarly, although hypnotized subjects are usually convinced that what they report is true, objective evidence often contradicts them. It can frequently be shown that the subject has committed an error called **confabulation.** When a person is unable to retrieve a certain item from memory, he or she manufactures something else that seems appropriate. Thus the man who is asked to remember his sixth birthday combines his recollections of several childhood parties and invents the missing details. The same may be true of many people who appear to recover memories through psychoanalysis.

The evidence for memory permanence, then, is not so strong as it appears at first glance. But this fact alone does not demonstrate that some memories are completely and irrevocably lost. Unfortunately, permanent forgetting is something that can never really be proved. The fact that we fail to retrieve a certain memory is not absolute proof that the memory trace no longer exists. Still, if we can show that rigorous efforts to dislodge the information are unsuccessful, we at least have a strong indication that complete memory loss *may* occur.

Loftus performed such rigorous tests in variations of the eyewitness testimony studies discussed earlier. First she subtly suggested to subjects that they had viewed a traffic sign other than the one they had actually seen. Most of the subjects incorporated the false information into their recollections of the picture in question. But was the correct information still stored somewhere in memory? Loftus tried to find out. She provided powerful incentives for correct responses—up to $25 in cash—and still most subjects clung to the misinformation. She offered them a second chance to give the correct response (out of three possible choices), but their performance on the second try was no better than sheer guesswork (Loftus, 1979a).

One recent study, however, does suggest that it is possible to recover the correct memory (Bekerian and Bowers, 1983). When subjects were shown the pairs of slides of the traffic accident in their *original* sequence (instead of in random order as in Loftus' studies), most of the subjects could recognize the critical slide (stop sign or yield sign) they had previously seen, despite intervening misinformation. The correct sequence apparently provided the retrieval cues necessary to dislodge the correct visual memory.

At this point, psychologists cannot say for sure whether all memories are permanent, or only some are, or no memories are permanent. More research is required before any firm conclusions can be drawn. Whether memories are permanent or not, the fact is we do forget and we can probably be grateful for this fact. Consider what life would be like if we *never* forgot. The remarkable Russian newspaper reporter studied by Aleksandr Luria had a so-called perfect memory (Luria, 1968). This man remembered everything in astonishing detail. Images of each experience haunted him for hours. Whatever he had seen, done, read, or heard—pleasant and unpleasant, trivial and important, from his earliest childhood to his old age—stayed in his memory, shifting, combining, piling up. He was left with a junk heap of impressions. Often he got confused and frustrated. The mere thought of such complete and total recall is probably enough to make most of us content to have an ordinary mem-

ory—one that lets us remember almost everything we want or need to recall while the rest is allowed to slip unobtrusively away.

SUMMARY

1. **Sensory memory** is the momentary lingering of sensory information after a stimulus has been removed. A person can store a great deal of information in sensory memory, but its duration is very brief—only a second or so.

2. **Short-term memory** is often considered "working" memory. Whatever you are actively thinking about at a given moment is held in this system.

3. Instatement of information into short-term memory must somehow be limited; otherwise we would surely be overwhelmed by sensory stimuli. One process that contributes to this screening of information is **sensory gating,** a turning up of one kind of sensory channel while others are simultaneously turned down. Another process crucial to the prevention of short-term memory overload is **selective attention,** a damping down of some of the information entering a given sensory channel while attention is directed to other information entering the same channel.

4. Once information is instated into short-term memory, it will fade in less than half a minute if it is not renewed by **rehearsal.** The rehearsal process usually involves some kind of speech, either overt (saying the information aloud) or implicit (repeating it mentally).

5. In addition to being of rather short duration, short-term memory is also quite limited in capacity: it seems to hold only between five and nine items. But through "chunking" (perceiving groups of related items as larger units) we can greatly increase the amount of information processed in short-term memory at any one time.

6. In contrast to short-term memory, **long-term memory** stores information indefinitely, and its capacity is essentially limitless. Successful transfer of information from short-term to long-term storage depends on both the amount and the type of rehearsal.

7. Retrieval from long-term memory is measured in two basic ways: **recognition** and **recall.** Recognition seems to involve a kind of matching process. We consider a given stimulus and decide whether it matches something already stored in memory. Recall appears to be somewhat more complex. It demands that we first search through memory and locate appropriate information before we test for a "match." This search is largely directed by retrieval cues. So when retrieval cues are weak, we may have difficulty recalling; one such experience is the **tip-of-the-tongue phenomenon.**

8. Several factors can affect performance on long-term memory tasks. One is the use of **mnemonic devices.** Most are clever ways of organizing information when it is stored in memory, and many make effective use of imagery. Some rare people, most of them young children, can form **eidetic images**—visual images of extraordinary clarity and detail. Reconstructing the context or the mood in which material was originally learned is another memory aid at our disposal. Our memory performance in schoolwork can be improved by study habits that make maximum use of good memory concepts.

9. One fascinating aspect of long-term memory is the extent to which it appears to involve a process of active construction. New information is assimilated within the framework of existing knowledge and beliefs, so that we tend to recast or dismiss facts that do not fit our expectations. At the same time, information acquired after an event has taken place can transform our memory of that experience. This process is especially important to keep in mind when we evaluate the accuracy of eyewitness testimony.

10. Many psychologists believe that long-term and short-term memory are two separate systems, a view that is supported by a number of laboratory and clinical findings. Other psychologists, however, argue that the apparent differences between long-term and short-term memory may instead be attributable to

differences in the "depth" with which people process, or encode, information. Although there is also evidence to support this **depth of processing view,** it is not incompatible with the idea of a **dual memory system.**

11. The ultimate answer to the question of whether human memory involves two separate systems may come from the study of the brain. Scientists still know very little about how, physiologically, our brains manage to store information. The current thinking is that short-term memory somehow involves a temporary circulation of electrical impulses around complex loops of neurons. Long-term memory, in contrast, is thought to involve some kind of permanent change—either structural or chemical, or both—in the way that neurons interconnect. What these changes are, however, remains a mystery.

12. In addition to studying memory, psychologists have also investigated the process of forgetting.

Three major causes of forgetting have been proposed. **Decay theory** suggests that memories simply fade away, or decay, with the passage of time if they are not renewed through periodic use. The concept of **interference** holds that forgetting is basically due to the confusion that results when we encounter very similar stimuli. Finally, forgetting may also be **motivated**—we may forget because we want to forget. A complete account of forgetting should probably include all three of these explanations.

13. Psychologists are not yet certain how much of what we learn over a lifetime is retained and how much is forgotten. Some have argued that we permanently retain almost everything we learn, but we often lack the retrieval cues needed to bring these memories to the surface. Others believe that at least a portion of the information we acquire is permanently altered or lost. Unfortunately, permanent forgetting may be a phenomenon that can never really be proved.

SUGGESTED READINGS

BADDELY, A. *Your memory: A user's guide.* New York: Macmillan, 1982.

A fascinating, authoritative handbook that blends up-to-date information with self-help so that readers learn not only how memory works but also what they can do to make it work better. Many aspects of memory—verbal, numerical, visual, and spatial—are presented in games that are entertaining as well as enlightening.

LOFTUS, E. F. *Eyewitness testimony.* Cambridge, Mass.: Harvard University Press, 1979.

This award-winning book describes a great deal of research on the subject of eyewitness testimony. The implications of eyewitness memory for the legal system are also discussed.

NEISSER, U. *Memory observed: Remembering in natural contexts.* San Francisco: W. H. Freeman, 1982.

A distinguished researcher looks at memory as it serves us in natural contexts such as recollections of childhood and eyewitness testimony. The book takes the view that progress in understanding human memory will require a new emphasis on observations made in the everyday world rather than in the psychology laboratory.

ZECHMEISTER, E. B., AND NYBERG, S. E. *Human memory: An introduction to research and theory.* Monterey, Calif.: Brooks/Cole, 1982.

A basic text on memory that covers sensory memory, short-term memory, long-term memory, and many other topics central to this field.

7

COGNITION AND PROBLEM SOLVING

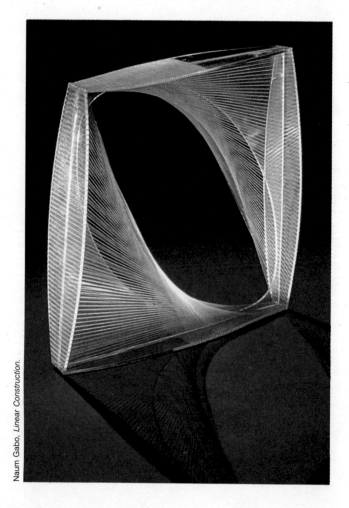

Naum Gabo, *Linear Construction.*

Two men play five games of checkers. There are no ties, yet each man wins the same number of games. How could this happen? If at first this situation sounds impossible, don't give up. Reread the first two sentences carefully and avoid drawing any hasty conclusions. If each man won the same number of games out of five and there weren't any ties, these two men couldn't possibly have been playing one another. The answer must be that they were playing *different* opponents.

The very fact that you can solve such a problem demonstrates that there is much more to human cognitive capabilities than learning and memory alone. Although you held in memory all the separate facts needed to arrive at the answer, you had to combine these facts in a certain way to find the correct response. This process of organizing information in our minds to help accomplish some desired end is the essence of what psychologists call **cognition,** or thought. In our ability to engage in complex thinking—to ponder, to reason logically, to draw conclusions, to have sudden bursts of creative insight—we humans are unparalleled in the living world.

Yet mental activities are highly subjective and therefore not easy to explore. If you were a researcher, how might you go about studying the workings of a human mind? In the early part of this century many psychologists used a method called **introspection.** A subject was typically given a question or problem and asked to describe in detail the thought processes that led to an answer. The results were believed to reveal much about the way the human mind operates. But other psychologists were critical of the introspection method. Behaviorists at the time were very skeptical that such a technique could ever provide reliable and meaningful data. All we can know about the introspections of others is what they *say,* the behaviorists objected. And people may not always describe their introspections accurately (Wessells, 1982). As a result, early behaviorists took the radical view that the study of human thought had no place within psychology. Psychology, they argued, should be confined to the study of processes that can be directly observed and measured. Contemporary psychologists agree, of course, that research must be scientific and objective. But they also believe that the mental activities that take place between an external stimulus and a person's response are far too important to be ignored. This is why interest in cogni-

tive processes has steadily grown in recent decades until today it is a major field of investigation.

The difficulty of studying human thought still remains, however. Even if we take great pains to ensure that people describe their thought processes fully and carefully, introspection may not always prove the best means of revealing those processes. The reason, rather surprisingly, is that we do not always have access to certain of our cognitions, no matter how hard we try.

Consider the results of a classic experiment conducted by Norman Maier (1931). From the ceiling of his laboratory he hung two long strings far enough apart so that a person could not hold the end of one and reach the other. Subjects were asked to figure out ways of tying the two strings together. They were allowed to use any object found in the laboratory, including pliers, clamps, extension cords, ringstands, and poles. Every time a subject came up with a solution, such as tying an extension cord to one string and pulling it toward the other, Maier would say, "Now do it another way." One solution was particularly elusive. This was the pendulum technique. When a pair of pliers or some other heavy object was tied to the end of one string, that string could be set swinging and grasped as it approached the other string. Although few subjects thought of this solution on their own, most were susceptible to a hint. When Maier saw that a subject was clearly stumped for another approach, he would walk by one of the strings and casually set it in motion. Within less than a minute the subject was busy constructing a pendulum. Yet when they were asked what caused the pendulum idea to occur to them, very few subjects mentioned Maier's hint. Most of their answers were vague: "It just dawned on me" or "It was the only thing left." Yet the hint had undeniably been influential. The unavoidable conclusion, then, was that thought processes were going on in these people's minds of which they were totally unaware.

Subsequent research has shown that this is not an isolated case. In a lengthy series of studies, Nisbett and Wilson (1977) found that subjects can easily make mistakes in assessing the impact that something has on their behavior, especially when that impact differs from what one would normally expect. Under these circumstances, people often maintain that a truly influential factor had no effect on them, or they insist that a noninfluential one was indeed important. Nisbett and Wilson argued that people tend to assess a factor as influential if logic or cultural norms suggest that it *should* be influential. In short, our estimates of the causes of our own behavior may be little more than judgments of what we consider plausible. Although we certainly are aware of the content of our thoughts at any given moment, we apparently have very limited access to the influences behind our thoughts.

While in many respects introspection is not a very reliable method of exploring cognitive processes, it has been useful in some research. Scientists who design machines capable of artificial intelligence value the types of information provided by introspective reports (Ericsson and Simon, 1980). Most psychologists who study cognition, however, prefer to focus on mental activities that have results they can observe and measure. In this chapter we will examine some of the results of these investigations. Because cognition is such a broad topic, including all the numerous activities of the mind, our focus must necessarily be limited. We will concentrate on three areas that psychologists have studied extensively: concept formation, problem solving, and decision making. In the process we hope to reveal some important generalizations about human thought. One is a curious paradox. Although the human brain is truly remarkable in the amount of information it can store and retrieve, and although the average person can solve problems of enormous complexity, the amount of information that can actually be processed at any one time is significantly restricted by the limited capacities of our short-term memories. You will see the impact of this restriction at many points in this chapter.

FORMING CONCEPTS

If you were asked what you saw in front of you at this moment, you would undoubtedly answer with a series of one- or two-word names: a book, a pen, a coffee mug, a lamp, a desk, a wall. The nature of these responses illustrates an important point about human cognition. Although the world consists of a multitude of objects and events, each in many ways unique, we tend to simplify and order our surroundings by classifying together those things that have common features. The mental constructs that enable us to make such classifications are called **concepts** (Anglin, 1977). A moment's reflection will reveal that your world is very neatly structured by hierarchies of concepts (Collins and Quillian, 1969). The object in your hand, for example, may be an instance of the concept *felt-tip pen*, which in turn is an instance of the more general concept *pen*, which in turn is an instance of the even broader concept *writing instrument*. In a similar manner, we classify and subclassify an enormous variety of other objects, qualities, and behaviors that possess shared characteristics.

It is difficult to overestimate the importance of concepts to cognitive processing. In a very real sense, concepts are the building blocks of thought. They enable us to impose structure and predictability on a world that might at first appear to be a welter of unrelated stimuli. With concepts we can take advantage of regularities. We need not treat everything we encounter as though it were completely novel and unique. It is an understanding of the concepts *stove* and *hot*, for example, that enables a child once burned by a stove to learn to avoid similar objects. It is your understanding of the concepts *student* and *professor* that guides your behavior in a college classroom. Through concepts, then, we form general rules that can be applied to particular situations. Such generalizations make complex thought possible.

Feature Analysis and Concept Formation

Suppose you encounter for the first time the object shown here. When you ask yourself, "What is that?" you are searching for a concept or set of concepts in which to place this unfamiliar thing. What does this search process entail? Many psychologists believe that we compare the salient features of the new stimulus with the features of a concept previously learned. If the two sets of features seem to match, at least along key dimensions, we label the stimulus an instance of the concept. The caption describes the thought proc-

In order to determine what an unfamiliar object is, we are likely to identify its salient features and then compare them with the features of an already familiar concept. Thus, we would note that the object shown here has legs, a seat, and what could be a back rest. These features match the concept of "chair"—and this is in fact a chair, designed by Heidi Wianecki. *(Courtesy of Whiteley Gallery, Los Angeles.)*

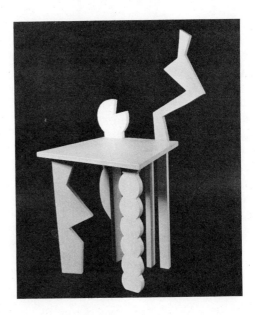

esses one might go through in an effort to pin a label on the object in the photograph.

But how do we arrive at the features that define a concept in the first place? Some researchers have suggested that we systematically test a series of hypotheses, guided by some overall strategy. You might, for example, begin with what is called a **global hypothesis:** when you first encounter a stimulus said to be an instance of an unfamiliar concept, you assume that all of its salient features are defining characteristics until proven otherwise. Suppose you are told that a housefly is an example of the concept *arthropod*, but you have no idea what traits qualify it as such. So you begin by hypothesizing that the concept *arthropod* includes any creature with all the basic features that a housefly possesses: external skeleton, segmented body, membranous wings, six legs, and two antennae. According to this definition, houseflies are classified as arthropods, as are mosquitoes, wasps, and other flying insects. But now someone tells you that an ant is also an arthropod. Your understanding of the concept must consequently change. Wings cannot be defining features. Through more experience with other examples of arthropods you gradually learn to eliminate from your definition all those features that can be varied and still yield an instance of the concept. This approach to concept formation is called a **focusing strategy** because you begin with a global hypothesis and gradually focus on the relevant characteristics.

Alternatively, you might arrive at an understanding of a concept by beginning with a much more limited hypothesis. You might begin to explore the concept *arthropod* with the tentative assumption that all six-legged creatures belong in this category. Then, as you discovered that spiders, centipedes, and lobsters are also arthropods, you would revise your hypothesis until you hit upon those attributes that together differentiate arthropods from other animals: an external skeleton, segmented body, and jointed legs. This approach is called a **scanning strategy,** because you

systematically scan a number of stimuli for potentially relevant features.

Early research suggested that people generally used some variation of either a focusing or a scanning strategy when they attempted to abstract the defining features of an unfamiliar concept (Bruner, Goodnow, and Austin, 1956). There are, however, age-related differences (Gholson, Levine, and Phillips, 1972). Because young children tend to be scanners, they often overextend concepts. When a toddler learns that *dog* is the word for the family pet, he or she may initially focus on Fido's abundant coat of fur and so for a time apply the concept not only to dogs but to all other furry creatures too. Adults, in contrast, often adopt a global focusing strategy, at least when they form new concepts in the laboratory. With this approach errors of underextension are more common. Of course, children also occasionally commit errors of underextension. After learning that the concept *telephone* refers to a boxlike object with dial and receiver that sits on a table or desk, a child may fail to recognize as an instance of this concept a phone of less traditional design.

Prototypes and Concept Formation

The **feature-based model** of concept formation we have been discussing assumes that each concept has a set of fairly unambiguous defining traits. But critics ask whether most of the concepts we use every day have defining features that are this clear-cut. Psychologist Eleanor Rosch (1978), among others, believes they do not. Granted, some concepts, such as *arthropod*, do have a set of clearly defined features that all instances of the class share. But try to list the defining features of such a concept as *furniture, candy*, or *fruit*. You will probably find this rather difficult. Although it is possible with careful thought to provide a definition for these and many other so-called **natural concepts,** we are unaccustomed to doing so.

Rosch proposes that we do not encode most natural concepts into memory in terms of a list of defining features. Instead, we encode them in terms of a **prototype**—that is, an example that best illustrates the concept—plus an implicit understanding of the degree to which stimuli can vary from the prototype and still be regarded as instances of the class. Rosch points out that this theory explains why some stimuli are considered better instances of a natural concept than others. You would probably agree, for example, that a robin or a sparrow is a better instance of the concept *bird* than a penguin or an ostrich. In fact, if you were asked for an example of the concept *bird*, a robin or a sparrow is very likely what you would say (Mervis, Catlin, and Rosch, 1976). According to Rosch, this is because robins and sparrows are very close to our prototypical birds, whereas penguins and ostriches are not. If natural concepts were learned only in terms of a list of defining features, Rosch asks, why isn't one example as good as another?

Rosch and others have gone on to perform many experiments believed to demonstrate that the prototype model of concept formation is closer than the feature-based model to the way we actually categorize things in everyday life. Figure 7.1 is drawn from one such study. You should be able to answer true or false to the questions in part A faster than to the questions in part B. Why? Rosch argues it is because the examples in part A are much closer to our prototypes for the concepts (*bird, fruit*, etc.) than are the examples in part B. As a result, we process the part A questions much more quickly. For them we do not have to stop and think to ourselves: How close is that to my prototype image of an *X*?

Rosch's prototype theory may not, in fact, be incompatible with feature-based theory. The prototype—or "best instance"—of a category is itself defined by a number of characteristic features. While we may not treat the features as definitions in the categorizing process, they clearly play a part in our analysis of natural concepts. Edward E. Smith and his colleagues (Smith, Shoben, and Rips, 1974; Smith and Medin, 1981) argue that people may divide the attributes of a concept into "defining" features, which are essential for membership in the category, and "characteristic" features, which many but not all instances of the concept possess. Thus a robin is considered a better example of a bird than a penguin because, although the penguin has all the defining features of a bird (two-legged, egg-laying vertebrate with bill, wings, and feathers), it lacks one of the most characteristic features of a bird: the ability to fly. It is possible, then, that the two views of the structure of concepts will be reconciled sometime in the future.

PART A

1. A sparrow is a bird.
2. An orange is a fruit.
3. A dog is a fish.
4. A hammer is a tool.
5. A bean is a vegetable.
6. A chair is an example of furniture.
7. A shirt is an example of clothing.

PART B

1. An ostrich is a bird.
2. A tomato is a fruit.
3. A whale is a fish.
4. A crane is a tool.
5. Rice is a vegetable.
6. A telephone is an example of furniture.
7. A bat is a bird.

Figure 7.1 Here are two sets of statements involving prototypes. Indicate whether each statement is true or false, and determine whether you take longer to respond to part A or part B. Your response time will probably be shorter for part A, for the reason explained in the text. *(From Matlin, 1983, p. 208.)*

SOLVING PROBLEMS

A knowledge of concepts and relationships among them makes problem solving possible. To understand why, observe the role that concepts play in solving the following puzzle. Take six matches of the same size and assemble them so that they form four equilateral triangles with every side equal to the length of one match. Most people find this task quite difficult. If you see the solution, it is undoubtedly because of your knowledge of the concepts *triangle* and *pyramid* and the way they relate to each other. Only by building a three-dimensional structure, as shown in Figure 7.2, can you perform the task described. The solutions to other problems likewise involve the use of some of the many concepts we have stored away in memory.

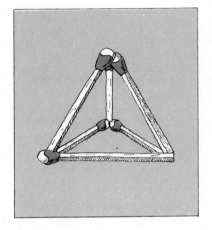

Figure 7.2 The match problem is solved by building a three-dimensional pyramid; most people assume that the matches must lie flat, as they were first perceived.

Stages in Problem Solving

For purposes of analysis, psychologists sometimes divide problem solving into three stages: initially assessing the problem, devising strategies for reaching a solution, and deciding when a satisfactory answer has been found. The demands of problems vary greatly, of course, so it is doubtful that precisely the same steps are involved in all the problems we encounter. Nevertheless, these three basic stages remain a useful way to organize a general discussion of problem solving (Posner, 1973).

Initially Assessing the Problem. No single aspect of problem solving has a greater impact on the speed and likelihood of a correct solution than the way the problem is initially assessed. Consider Figure 7.3. It shows a circle with a radius of five inches. In it is drawn a right-angled triangle, *xdl*. What is the length of side *l*, that is, of the triangle's hypotenuse? If you are searching your memory for the formula to calculate the length of a hypotenuse, stop. You are assessing the problem in a more difficult way than you need to. Instead of viewing figure *xdl* as a triangle, try viewing it instead as half a rectangle. Now the solution is probably obvious. Line *l* is one diagonal of a rectangle, the other diagonal extending from the center of the circle to the point where *x* and *d* meet—the radius of the circle. Since you know that the radius is five

inches long, *l* too must be five inches long. Thus what at first glance appeared to be a fairly difficult problem suddenly becomes much easier when it is perceived in a different manner.

Ironically, then, when you interpret a problem quickly and decisively, you may actually be hindering your ability to solve it. Once you have committed yourself to defining a problem in a certain way, you automatically structure available information accordingly, and your chances of seeing better alternatives are thus reduced. This is why psychologists who study problem solving often suggest that people avoid settling on a solution strategy as soon as they encounter a seemingly difficult problem. Instead, they should

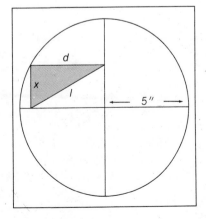

Figure 7.3 Problem illustrating the importance of the initial representation.

Exactly at sunrise one morning, a Buddhist monk set out to climb a tall mountain. The narrow path was not more than a foot or two wide, and it wound around the mountain to a beautiful, glittering temple at the mountain peak.

The monk climbed the path at varying rates of speed. He stopped many times along the way to rest and to eat the fruit he carried with him. He reached the temple just before sunset. At the temple, he fasted and meditated for several days. Then he began his journey back along the same path, starting at sunrise and walking, as before, at variable speeds with many stops along the way. However, his average speed going down the hill was greater than his average climbing speed.

Prove that there must be a spot along the path that the monk will pass on both trips at exactly the same time of day.

Figure 7.4 The Buddhist monk problem. Try to think of a visual representation of the situation described here. The answer is shown in Figure 7.13A, at the end of the chapter. *(From Matlin, 1983, pp. 227–228.)*

view the question from various angles, searching for different ways to perceive its requirements. Making notes about the problem, or drawing a simple sketch of it, can help. Figure 7.4 contains a problem that almost defies solution unless you assess the situation visually.

Of course, changing your perspective on a problem is not always easy. Many things can steer you toward an unproductive point of view. One is the fact that the critical aspects of a problem may sometimes be embedded in irrelevant information. Consider, for instance, this problem: "If you have black socks and brown socks in your drawer, mixed in the ratio of 4 to 5, how many socks will you have to take out to make sure of having a pair the same color?" (Sternberg and Davidson, 1982). If you failed to know right away that the answer is three, it was probably because that 4:5 ratio misdirected your attention. The ratio of black socks to brown socks is irrelevant information. If you

have taken out two socks already and they do not match, the third sock *must* match one of them. Thus irrelevant information may come to dominate our thinking and make flexible assessment of a problem harder.

Much the same thing can happen when we become locked into perspectives we have always held in the past. For example, people often perceive objects as having only their customary functions, even though a more flexible outlook may help to solve a problem. This tendency to overlook novel uses for things is called **functional fixedness.** Functional fixedness may help explain why people faced with Maier's problem of tying together two widely spaced strings seldom think of the pendulum solution. A pair of pliers or some other object likely to be found in a laboratory is not ordinarily used as a pendulum weight. Consequently, this alternative function is not likely to occur to people. Another problem whose solution

A problem used by Duncker (1945) to demonstrate functional fixedness: He gave subjects the materials shown and asked them to mount a candle on a wall so that it could be used to give light. Try to solve the problem yourself. (The use of the term "functional fixedness" gives you a clue to the solution of the problem that Duncker's subjects did not have.) The solution is given in Figure 7.13B.)

may be obscured by functional fixedness is illustrated in the photograph at the bottom of the facing page (Duncker, 1945). How would you use these materials to mount a single lighted candle on a vertical wooden wall? Because the candle and the matches are presented in their boxes, you may be encouraged to fixate on the familiar function of a box as a container. But a box can also serve as a platform on which to stand a candle, as illustrated in Figure 7.13B. If you were flexible in your assessment of this problem, you probably arrived at much the same solution.

Situational factors can often intensify functional fixedness. For example, if a person's attention is drawn to the customary function of an object just before the presentation of a problem in which that object must be used in a novel way, the likelihood of functional fixedness is increased (Birch and Rabinowitz, 1951). Subjects who had just finished wiring a switch or a relay into an electrical circuit were much less likely than control subjects to use a switch or a relay as a pendulum weight. Functional fixedness may also increase when people are required to refer to an object by its usual name, rather than by a nonsense label. This is because an object's name is often strongly associated with its customary function (Glucksburg and Danks, 1968). Perhaps, then, one way to "break" functional fixedness might be to analyze available tools visually, without referring to each by name. It might also be helpful to examine thoroughly the separate parts of all objects instead of perceiving them strictly as wholes.

Devising Solution Strategies. So far we have focused on problems that cease to be problems once they are perceived in the right way. The answers just leap to mind in a single burst of insight. Not all problems are simply a matter of proper perspective, how-

ever. Sometimes the information initially given must be supplemented or manipulated in some fashion before the final answer emerges. In such cases, we must devise strategies for carrying out the necessary operations. Psychologists have found that the strategy we select varies mainly with the type of problem we are facing.

Some problems can best be solved by a strategy called an **algorithm:** a precisely stated set of rules for solving problems of a particular kind. The formula πr^2, for example, is an algorithm for finding the area of a circle given its radius, whether the radius is measured in millimeters or in miles. As you might guess, the major advantage of an algorithm is that it guarantees success if it is applied in the right circumstances and followed correctly.

The use of algorithms is not always practical, however. Consider the task of rearranging the letters *bnirg* to form an English word. An algorithmic solution would be systematically to arrange the letters in all possible ways until a meaningful combination appeared. Obviously, this procedure could be enormously time-consuming, for five letters can be combined in a total of 120 ways. Most people, therefore,

Figure 7.5 Match your skill against that consummate expert in deductive problem solving, Sherlock Holmes. The case of Hilton and Elsie Cubitt began when client Hilton handed Sherlock the first hieroglyphic fragment. Several days later Sherlock received three more samples; shortly afterward the last example came. Sherlock rushed into action after seeing the last fragments and realizing that they were addressed to Elsie. Why? What message did these last figures contain? How would you solve this puzzle of the "dancing men"? What heuristics, or rules of thumb, might be helpful? Check your solution with the one explained in Figure 7.13C.

would follow a short-cut strategy. They would focus on letter combinations likely to appear in the English language, such as *br* at the beginning of a word or *ing* at the end. Using this approach, they would probably discover the word *bring* quite quickly (Bourne, Dominowski, and Loftus, 1979). A rule-of-thumb problem-solving strategy like this one is called a **heuristic.** Although heuristics do not guarantee success, they frequently pay off with very speedy solutions. This is why we tend to use them so often. In "The Adventure of the Dancing Men," Sherlock Holmes, the consummate expert in deductive problem solving, employed a heuristic strategy to decode the puzzling set of hieroglyphics shown in Figure 7.5, on the preceding page. Knowing that each man represents a letter, what heuristics would you use to decipher this cryptic five-part message?

The heuristics used for solving anagrams (scrambled word problems) or coded messages are very specific to these particular tasks. But there are also a number of very general heuristics that people commonly use in solving problems of all kinds (Newell and Simon, 1972). One is **subgoal analysis.** Consider a chess player. A person beginning a game of chess could never consider all of the 10^{120} play sequences that are theoretically possible. Even if the person could evaluate one play every micromillisecond (one-millionth of one-thousandth of a second), it would

still take billions upon billions of centuries to consider all the alternatives. Clearly a chess player must have some way of limiting his or her focus. The strategy seems to be to break down the problem of winning the game into a series of smaller problems, or subgoals, each of which is of manageable scope. For example, the player may first determine if the king is in danger of attack, and if so, concentrate on moves that protect the king. If, however, the king is safe, the player may proceed to the next most important subgoal: ensuring that all other major pieces are safe. If the other pieces do not need defending, the player may then work through a series of offensive subgoals. In this way the demands on the player's limited information-processing capabilities are substantially reduced, even though there is no guarantee that the player will spot the best move.

Subgoal analysis, of course, is not the only problem-solving strategy people use. Another general heuristic, often applied to problems with very specific goals, is **means-end analysis.** This strategy involves comparing one's current position with a desired end point and then trying to find a means of closing the gap between the two. To take a very simple example, if you had to get to work on a morning when your car broke down, means-end analysis would tell you that you had a distance of, say, five miles between you and your destination. You might cover this distance on

Figure 7.6 The water lily problem. Water lilies double in area every twenty-four hours. At the beginning of the summer there is one water lily on a lake. It takes sixty days for the lake to become covered with water lilies. On what day is the lake *half* covered? For the answer, see the text. *(After Sternberg and Davidson, 1982, p. 40.)*

foot, by bicycle, or by bus. Note, however, that means-end analysis has a built-in bias: it encourages you to focus on reducing the *existing* distance between where you are and where you want to be. If, alternatively, a problem can best be solved by first *increasing* the gap between your current state and your desired goal, means-end analysis may actually divert you from the optimum solution. Thus, if you employed a strict means-end analysis on the morning your car broke down, you might decide to walk toward your office to catch a bus that took a circuitous route instead of first heading in the *opposite* direction in order to catch a more direct bus. Keep the bias of means-end analysis in mind, because it may impede your efforts to solve a problem later in this chapter.

A third general heuristic is the **backward search,** in which a person begins at the end point of a problem and then works backward in order to discover the steps involved in getting there. Consider, for instance, the problem in Figure 7.6. If you try to work forward toward the answer, beginning with one water lily and doubling the area every twenty-four hours, you will remain hopelessly stumped. But now begin on the sixtieth day and work backward. The solution is simple. If the lake is completely covered on the sixtieth day, it must be *half* covered on the fifty-ninth. The backward search heuristic is most helpful in circumstances like these, where the end point in a problem is very clear-cut and specific (a lake totally covered with water lilies) while the starting point is surrounded by many options or questions (How big is a water lily? How big is the lake?). For this reason, you might also try a backward search when solving a maze puzzle, in which many paths lead away from the starting point yet only one path leads to the goal (Matlin, 1983).

Our brief discussion of selecting a strategy that you hope will lead to a solution points up a central dilemma in problem solving. Human information processing is substantially constrained by the limited capacity of active (short-term) memory, explored in Chapter 6. As a result, we must find ways of solving problems that avoid cognitive overload. One way to do so is to use a heuristic, such as one of the ones just described. But in using a heuristic there is always the risk that our attention will be drawn to inferior solutions or to no solution at all.

The tendency to use previously successful heuristics even when they no longer work was demonstrated in a classic experiment by Abraham Luchins (1946). If you had been a subject in one of his experiments, you would have been given a series of six problems like those in Figure 7.7. Each problem requires that you imagine three jars, labeled A, B, and C, with the capacities listed from left to right in each row of the table. Your task is to use these jars to measure out the amount of water shown at the far right. In problem 1, for example, you are to use jars with capacities of 21, 127, and 3 quarts to measure out 100 quarts. A moment's thought will probably give you the solution. You fill jar B (127 quarts), pour off enough to fill jar A (21 quarts), and then pour off enough to fill jar C (3 quarts) twice. You will be left with 100 quarts of water in jar B (127 quarts − 21 quarts − 2 × 3 quarts = 100 quarts). Now proceed to solve the remaining five problems.

If you breezed through problems 2 through 5 but were stumped by problem 6, you probably encountered the same obstacle that two-thirds of Luchins' subjects did. You became so accustomed to using the technique "jar B minus jar A minus twice jar C" that you failed to explore other possibilities. You employed a solution to an earlier problem to solve a current one because the two problems seemed analo-

Figure 7.7 Luchins' (1946) classic demonstration of set in problem solving. In each of the problems in this series you must work out how you could measure out the quantities of liquid indicated on the right by using jars with the capacities shown on the left. Try the series yourself before reading on. After solving the first five problems, nearly two-thirds of Luchins' subjects were unable to solve the sixth. The sixth problem actually requires a simpler strategy than the first five, and it would be easily solved were it not for the set established by the first five.

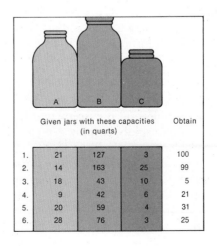

	Given jars with these capacities (in quarts)			Obtain
	A	B	C	
1.	21	127	3	100
2.	14	163	25	99
3.	18	43	10	5
4.	9	42	6	21
5.	20	59	4	31
6.	28	76	3	25

gous, or alike in their critical features. But in this case the analogy has led you astray because the demands of problem 6 are different from those of problems 1 through 5. Actually, the solution to problem 6 is extremely easy. You simply fill jar A and subtract jar C. Luchins found that almost anyone could solve this problem if he or she had not already learned the steps for solving the other five problems. But a subject who had acquired the B − A − 2C rule was very likely either to give up on problem 6 or to insist staunchly that the previously successful formula still worked— that 76 − 28 − 2(3) did in fact equal 25!

Pychologists call the common inclination to stick with a solution that has worked in the past, without considering other options, a **mental set.** Once locked into a mental set, a person tends to lose control over the outcome of problem-solving efforts. Sometimes unreflective transfer of a previously successful strategy will just by luck bring further solutions. At other times, however, such transfer will make it difficult for new problems ever to be solved.

Luchins' experiment emphasizes that flexibility is as important in the selection of problem-solving strategies as it is in the initial assessment of problems. A person must resist the tendency to stick with a previously successful tactic that is no longer proving productive. A number of psychologists have suggested ways of encouraging this flexibility. One is to get away from the problem for a while—that is, to seek a period of **incubation.** Does research confirm the idea that incubation facilitates problem solving? The limited evidence available suggests that under certain circumstances it may.

Consider the following problem:

> A man had four chains, each three links long. He wanted to join the four chains into a single closed chain. Having a link opened cost 2 cents and having a link closed cost 3 cents. The man had his chains joined into a closed chain for 15 cents. How did he do it? (Silveira, 1971)

See if you can solve this problem in a reasonable amount of time. Most people find it extremely difficult, perhaps because they rigidly employ a means-end analysis. If the problem is to join four chains into a single circular chain, disassembling one of the chains completely seems to be working in the wrong direction. Yet, as Figure 7.13D shows, this is the only way to produce the desired result by opening and closing only three links.

Jeanette Silveira (1971) presented this problem to subjects, allowing them work and incubation periods of varying lengths. She found that if a subject worked on the problem steadily for some time, a temporary break from it greatly increased the likelihood that he or she would later find the solution. What occurred during incubation that facilitated problem solving? One possibility is that subjects were simply given a rest and so were more energetic and persistent in their efforts. Then, too, a period of interruption may have enabled them to break free of inappropriate mental sets that were blocking more productive approaches. In short, subjects may have returned to the problem with a fresh eye. These two factors alone are enough to explain Silveira's results, but another factor may also have been at work. Subjects may have continued to search for the solution on an unconscious level, even though they were engaged in other cognitive tasks. The extent to which such unconscious processes actually contribute to creative insights is not yet known, but their possible role is highly intriguing (Posner, 1973). We will say more about unconscious processes later in this chapter, when we look at the way very creative people sometimes generate solutions.

Deciding When a Solution Is Satisfactory. For some problems the task of deciding when a solution is satisfactory poses no difficulty at all. Problems like the four-chain puzzle just described have very clearly defined goals that can be achieved in only one way. When that goal is reached, the problem is solved. No questions or doubts remain. Often the solution to such a problem occurs in a moment of what psychologists call **insight**—a rather sudden perception of the critical relationships. A less formal name for insight is the "Eureka!" or "Aha!" experience.

The gestalt psychologist Wolfgang Köhler conducted some of the earliest studies of insight. In one famous investigation in which chimpanzees were used as subjects, Köhler (1925) suspended a banana from the ceiling of a chimp's cage, out of the animal's reach. The cage also contained a number of boxes that the chimp could move and stack. Usually a chimp would try to reach the banana by jumping, climbing the bars of the cage, or using some other futile approach. When all such efforts failed, the animal often paused for a long while, as though studying the situation. Then suddenly it appeared to see the value of the boxes as a means of obtaining the fruit. Hurriedly

Wolfgang Köhler's classic work with chimpanzees. In this instance, the chimp seemed to have an "Aha!" experience when it realized the value of using objects as tools to achieve a goal, building a four-story structure out of boxes in order to obtain food that is hung out of immediate reach. *(From* The Mentality of Apes, *1925, by Wolfgang Köhler.)*

The solution must be understood in its entirety with no doubts or questions remaining. Thus, if you do the set of subtractions in Figure 7.8, you will soon realize that the answer is always the next highest odd number. But unless you understand precisely *why* this pattern occurs, you will not experience the insight phenomenon.

Unfortunately, the solutions to many problems are not as clear and final as those associated with insight. How, for example, would you determine when you had selected the "best" topic for a term paper? Or when you had made the "best" move in a game of chess? It is very difficult to say. But one thing that psychologists have learned about the termination of such problems is that people are often willing to settle for a less than optimum solution if finding the ideal solution places too great a demand on cognitive capacity (Posner, 1973). This concession makes sense. To function effectively, people must avoid cognitive overload, and one way to do so is to accept a solution that may not be perfect but is good enough. This is why a person sometimes returns to a previously rejected solution after devoting a great deal of time to a problem. Locating a better solution no longer seems worth the effort. We will say much more about the effects of our cognitive limitations on decision making in the final section of this chapter.

Highly Creative Problem Solvers

History tells us that the ancient Greek scientist Archimedes was a highly creative problem solver. When King Hiero suspected that his new crown had not been fashioned of pure gold, as he had ordered, but instead was a blend of gold and silver, Archimedes was asked to determine the truth. Archimedes knew how to calculate what an object of a particular volume would weigh if it was made of either gold or

the chimp would pile the boxes beneath the banana and climb them to reach the goal. From then on, the animal had little difficulty solving similar problems. Köhler used his findings as evidence that animals do not always solve problems through simple trial and error, as behaviorists at the time maintained. A cognitive restructuring of information is often at work, even when the problem solver is a chimp.

In describing the human experience of insight, Köhler stressed the enormous feeling of satisfaction it brings. A puzzle that moments earlier seemed impossibly difficult is suddenly seen in a new light and its solution is completely clear. Note that just solving a problem is not necessarily accompanied by insight.

1	4	9	16	25	36	49	64
0	1	4	9	16	25	36	49
1	3	5	7	9			

Figure 7.8 This subtraction problem illustrates the importance of insight in problem solving. Subtracting each successive square number from the next larger one produces the series of odd digits.

silver. But he had no idea how to measure the volume of the king's crown without first melting it down. Although he pondered this question diligently, he could not come up with an answer. Then one day while sitting down in his bathtub and observing the water rise, the solution just leapt to his mind. He could determine the volume of the crown by immersing it in water and measuring the amount of water it displaced!

Psychologists label Archimedes' solution *creative* because it meets several criteria. For one thing, it was novel. No one had ever thought of measuring volume in quite this way before. In fact, Archimedes had to break free from previous approaches to measurement that might otherwise have obstructed his thinking. Most creative solutions are likewise the product of clever cognitive restructuring (Newell, Shaw, and Simon, 1963). But in addition to being novel, Archimedes' solution was also practical. It was easy to measure volume by the method he had devised. This is another hallmark of creative problem solving. The answer one comes up with must not only be unusual, but it must be readily workable as well (Stein, 1956; Murray, 1959).

Exploring Creative Processes.

Some researchers are fascinated by the processes that lead to such creative solutions. Does the highly creative person's approach to problem solving differ from that of the average person? Psychologists do not yet have all the answers to this question. But on the basis of personal accounts by famous artists, writers, scientists, and the like, it appears that the problem-solving experiences of the highly creative are much like those of other people—just in some respects more intense.

Consider how the German chemist Friedrich August Kekulé (1829–1896) discovered the molecular structure of benzene, a highly volatile and flammable liquid often used as solvent. Until the mid-nineteenth century, chemists could not figure out why benzene had the chemical properties it did. The answer had to lie in the way that benzene's six carbon atoms and six hydrogen atoms were structured. But what that structure was remained a mystery. Then one evening Kekulé was busy writing a textbook when his thoughts began to wander from his work. As he tells the story:

I turned my chair to the fire and dozed. Again the atoms were gambolling before my eyes. This time the smaller groups kept modestly in the background. My mental eye . . . could now distinguish larger structures . . . all twining and twisting in snake-like motion. But look! What was that? One of the snakes had seized hold of its own tail, and the form whirled mockingly before my eyes. As if by a flash of lightning I awoke.

Kekulé had found the answer. The carbon atoms of benzene formed a closed ring, with a hydrogen atom attached to each one.

One striking aspect of Kekulé's experience is the suddenness and unpredictability with which the solution occurred. This is characteristic of many great creative insights, whether they are made by composers, writers, mathematicians, philosophers, or scientists. The answer often comes when the person is not deliberately trying to solve the problem. This common experience has led some psychologists to suggest that many creative inspirations may be largely the products of unconscious thought (Ghiselin, 1952).

But other psychologists maintain that such subconsciously generated insights, if they indeed occur, are not enough to explain creative processes. Other important factors also contribute. One is simply a broad knowledge of the subject in which a problem has arisen (Wood, 1983). There is little evidence that brilliant ideas just pop into the minds of people who have no background in the problem area. Creative solutions are far more likely with a solid information base on which to build.

Equally important seems to be a strong motivation and persistence at the problem-solving task (Gruber, 1981). Consider the outputs of some of the world's great creative artists. For Beethoven, composing music was a tortured process. He would agonizingly write, discard, and rewrite over and over again. Similarly, Thomas Mann, the Nobel Prize–winning author, struggled to turn out a meager three pages a day (Gardner, 1982). For these and many other creative geniuses, great works have been partly the products of sheer perseverance.

Yet another ingredient of creativity appears to be a conducive setting. In one study of more than a hundred scientists, for instance, those who scored high on tests of creativity tended to produce creative research only in a certain kind of working environment (Andrews, 1975). This environment provided a secure position for the scientist, gave him or her a chance to innovate without fear of ridicule in the event of failure, and offered the opportunity to work independently and to make decisions freely. Thus it seems that potentially creative people are most creative when their surroundings allow or encourage them to be so.

What Are Creative People Like?

In addition to exploring how creative solutions tend to come about, psychologists are also interested in discovering what highly creative people are like. The first step in determining their characteristics has been to devise tests of creativity itself. Unfortunately, the task has not proved easy, for it demands that psychologists pinpoint those cognitive abilities most important to creative outputs. Many such tests have been proposed, each one measuring slightly different aspects of creative thinking. Figure 7.9 shows sample items from two tests of creativity (Matlin, 1983). Unfortunately, neither of these tests has been found to correlate particularly well with real-life creativity (Hayes, 1978).

Mixed results in predicting creative individuals have been obtained with the Divergent Production Test, but scores on the Remote Associates Test (RAT) appear to bear little relation to creativity in real-life situations. While RAT scores do correlate highly with IQ, this is not what the test was devised to measure. Try these tests on yourself and others to see if people you think of as very creative do in fact score high.

Special cognitive abilities are not the only features that creative people seem to share. Although no single set of personality traits describes all creative people, some interesting general patterns do exist. For one thing, the creative person tends to show marked independence in judgment. If his or her views differ from those of other people, the creative person is often willing to stand alone as a minority of one. The less creative person, in contrast, is typically much more influenced by group pressure to conform (Bar-

Divergent Production Test

1. Many words begin with an L and end with an N. List as many words as possible, in a one-minute period, that have the form L _____ N. (They can have any number of letters in between the L and the N.)

2. Suppose that people reached their final height at the age of 2, and so normal adult height was less than 3 feet. In a one-minute period, list as many consequences as possible that would result from this change.

3. Here are four shapes. Combine them to make each of the following objects: a face, a lamp, a piece of playground equipment, a tree. Each shape may be used once, many times, or not at all in forming each object, and it may be expanded or shrunk to any size.

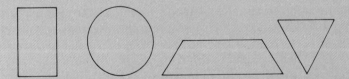

Remote Associates Test

4. For each set of three words, try to think of a fourth word that is related to all three words. For example, the words ROUGH, RESISTANCE, and BEER suggest the word DRAFT, because of the phrases ROUGH DRAFT, DRAFT RESISTANCE, and DRAFT BEER.

1. CHARMING	STUDENT	VALIANT
2. FOOD	CATCHER	HOT
3. HEARTED	FEET	BITTER

Figure 7.9 Sample items from two tests of creativity. The Divergent Production Test measures the ability to think of varied answers to a question—that is, to shift viewpoint repeatedly in order to solve a problem in many different ways. The Remote Associates Test measures the ability to see associations among ideas that ordinarily seem remote from one another. *(From Matlin, 1983, pp. 251–252.)*

Inkblots devised by Frank Barron (1958), with the "uncommon responses" given by creative subjects.

A small boy and his mother hurrying along on a dark windy day, trying to get home before it rains

Mexican in sombrero running up a long hill to escape from rain clouds

ron, 1958). The creative person also tends to show a rather unusual preference for the asymmetrical and complex. This difference in preference may be related to a talent highly creative people have for seeing a comprehensive, synthesizing order in what other people see as a confusing chaos. Consider the interpretations that two very creative people gave to the inkblots shown here. They are certainly notable for the total order they manage to impose on what to others may look simply like meaningless blotches. Thus the creative response to disorder, according to one researcher in this field, "is to find an elegant new order more satisfying than any that could be evoked by a simpler configuration" (Barron, 1958).

Does this mean that the highly creative person is more intelligent than others? Perhaps. As we mentioned before, some studies have shown that creative problem solving and intelligence do tend to go to-

gether (Guilford, 1967; Sternberg and Davidson, 1982). But note that intelligence is not enough to guarantee creative insights. While people who score high in creativity also tend to score high in intelligence, many intelligent people are not very creative (Roe, 1946, 1953; Wood, 1983).

Can people be trained to be creative? This has been a controversial topic in recent years. A number of creativity training courses have attempted to teach both adults and children how to generate new ideas for given situations. While various claims are made for the success of these programs, it appears that they succeed largely in improving performance on problems similar to those used in instruction. The learned problem-solving ability apparently does not generalize into more global skills. The successful problem-solving course focuses on specific knowledge and skills in a particular field (Mayer, 1983).

MAKING DECISIONS

Although creativity is a great asset in many kinds of problem solving, it does not necessarily help people make sound judgments in the hundreds of decisions they face every day. Granted, most such decisions involve simple, mundane choices—whether to carry an umbrella on a cloudy morning or which of several routes to take to work. But some decisions are far more complex and have a much greater impact on our lives. Such decisions as whether to get married, have children, go to graduate school, or change careers can greatly alter one's future. And political decisions made by voters and government officials can affect a nation, the world, even the course of history. The far-reaching importance of many decisions has helped fuel great interest in the processes by which human beings make choices. Bibliographies compiled in the past ten years list well over a thousand books and articles on decision making (Barron, 1974; Kleiter, Gachowetz, and Huber, 1976). In the following sections we will explore some of the highlights of this research.

Rational Models of Decision Making

Suppose you are faced with the following decision. Your friends are planning a weekend ski trip, but you have an exam scheduled for Monday morning. Although you have already studied, you are not certain how difficult the exam will be. And because it is early in the ski season, conditions on the slopes may be only fair. Should you go with your friends or not?

According to psychologists, two sets of variables will probably enter into your decision. One is the value you place on potential outcomes—often called their **utility.** How much pleasure will you derive from a weekend of fun and relaxation? How much satisfaction from doing well on your exam? How much annoyance will you feel if you miss this ski weekend? How much distress if you do poorly on the test? But estimates of utility, though important, are not really enough. In addition, you must also estimate the **probability** that each potential outcome will actually happen. What are the chances that insufficient snow will ruin the skiing? What are the odds that this particular instructor will give a difficult exam? Your decision, then, involves a combined evaluation of both utility and probability. This is true of most decisions regarding your own behavior.

If you were a completely rational creature, you might tackle this problem as a mathematician would. You would start by assigning a utility value to each potential outcome of forgoing additional studying and spending the weekend skiing. You might use a scale of, say, −10 to +10, negative numbers being assigned to unpleasant outcomes and positive numbers to pleasant ones. You would then multiply these figures by your estimated probability that each outcome will occur. Tallying up these figures would give you a plus or minus number—minus telling you to stay at home, plus telling you to go skiing.

How closely does this very rational approach match the way people actually make such decisions? Sometimes we may intuitively approximate this strategy, although we seldom make our calculations in a formal, mathematical way. Lee Beach and his colleagues, for instance, asked married couples who were contemplating having a child to assign relative utilities to a number of outcomes associated with parenthood. These outcomes included such things as opportunities for personal growth and maturity, changes in vocational or educational plans, changes in family finances, approval or disapproval of relatives and friends, changes in the quality of one's marriage, and so forth. The couples then estimated the probability that each outcome would actually take place if they decided to have a child. From these figures the researchers calculated an overall score that could be used to predict the likelihood that that particular couple would have a child in the next two years. This score proved reasonably accurate: it correctly predicted the decision to have or not to have a child more than 70 percent of the time (Beach, Campbell, and Townes, 1979). Thus, in this decision at least, both utility and probability seem to have been taken into account in much the way that a rational model would predict.

There is also evidence that, with proper guidance, people can learn to become more rational decision makers. One technique for making more rational choices is to fill out a simple balance sheet for each major alternative one faces. Figure 7.10 shows a balance sheet drawn up by a production manager who was trying to decide whether to stay in his present job. As you can see, the positive and negative consequences he anticipates from staying are divided into several categories: (1) tangible gains and losses for self; (2) tangible gains and losses for significant others; (3) self-approval or self-disapproval; and (4) social approval or disapproval. Psychologists Irving Janis and Dan Wheeler, who recommend the balance sheet as a decision-making aid, believe it helps people consider *all* the consequences related to a particular choice. As a result, they are less likely to encounter unpleasant surprises and are more likely to develop contingency plans in case negative outcomes do arise. Does such an approach really work? Research suggests that it may. In several large-scale studies of people making decisions of various sorts (high school

	Positive Anticipations	Negative Anticipations
Tangible gains and losses for *self*	1. Satisfactory pay. 2. Plenty of opportunities to use my skills and competencies. 3. For the present, my status in the organization is okay (but it won't be for long if I am not promoted in the next year).	1. Long hours. 2. Constant time pressures—deadlines too short. 3. Unpleasant paper work. 4. Poor prospects for advancement to a higher-level position. 5. Repeated reorganizations make my work chaotic. 6. Constant disruption from high turnover of other executives I deal with.
Tangible gains and losses for *others*	1. Adequate income for family. 2. Wife and children get special privileges because of my position in the firm.	1. Not enough time free to spend with my family. 2. Wife often has to put up with my irritability when I come home after bad days at work.
Self-approval or self-disapproval	1. This position allows me to make full use of my potentialities. 2. Proud of my achievements. 3. Proud of the competent team I have shaped up. 4. Sense of meaningful accomplishment when I see the products for which we are responsible.	1. Sometimes feel I'm a fool to continue putting up with the unreasonable deadlines and other stupid demands made by the top managers.
Social approval or disapproval	1. Approval of men on my team, who look up to me as their leader and who are good friends. 2. Approval of my superior who is a friend and wants me to stay.	1. Very slight skeptical reaction of my wife—she asks me if I might be better off in a different firm. 2. A friend in another firm who has been wanting to wangle something for me will be disappointed.

Figure 7.10 A production manager at a manufacturing plant who was trying to decide whether to remain in his present position drew up this grid, which lays out the pros and cons of staying. A grid such as this can be used for working out the alternatives in any important decision-making situation. *(After Janis and Mann, 1979.)*

seniors deciding where to go to college, adults deciding whether to start a diet and attend an exercise class), those who constructed a balance sheet before making a final choice expressed significantly fewer regrets later on (Janis and Wheeler, 1978).

Yet the very fact that such a technique is needed suggests that the decisions people make are not always sound. Studies show that people often ignore important information pertaining to a decision even though it is readily available. Research on consumer behavior, for example, indicates that shoppers motivated to buy the most economical product may still choose relatively expensive items despite the fact that unit prices are posted on grocery shelves (Russo, Krieser, and Miyashita, 1975). Even matters of personal safety are not exempt from poor decision mak-

ing. Residents of flood-plain areas, for instance, tend to ignore the hazards of living where they do. They often refuse to purchase flood insurance, and they frequently rebuild houses destroyed by a flood in exactly the same locations (Slovic, Kunreuther, and White, 1974). The question, of course, is why.

Part of the answer may lie in a person's emotional reaction to very difficult choices. When decisions must be made under unusual stress, critical faculties may be impaired. This is one reason why some people whose careers have been going poorly and whose jobs are in serious jeopardy fail to make the very rational decision either to improve their performance or to look for other work. Instead, they engage in wishful thinking that allows them to deny the severity of the threat. Janis and Wheeler (1978) call this **defensive avoidance.** Its most common symptoms are rationalization ("I've been under a lot of pressure lately"), procrastination ("I'll do something about it after next month's sales meeting"), and buck passing ("He deserves more blame than I do for missing that deadline").

Despite the undeniable toll that stress can take on sound decision making, much recent research shows that it is not the only factor that can lead people's judgment astray. Another is the persistent human tendency to restrict cognitive focus because of our limited capacity for processing and weighing information at any one time. Especially when a decision is fairly complex, we tend to simplify our choices by concentrating on a few of the relevant facts and largely ignoring the others. Often this approach serves us quite well. In a study of how highly skilled radiologists assess the malignancy of an ulcer, six relevant factors were available for assessment, but the radiologists tended to focus on only one or at most two of them (Hoffman, Slovic, and Rorer, 1968). If they used the other factors at all, it was only to make small adjustments in their diagnoses. Still, their assessments were correct most of the time.

Narrowing the range of relevant information is not always this successful, however. Sometimes it leads to choices that are less than ideal. Figure 7.11 allows you to demonstrate this to yourself. It offers you a choice between two games. In game 1, you have a 40 percent chance of winning $10 but also a 20 percent chance of losing $20. In game 2, you have a 90 percent chance of winning $10 but also a 40 percent chance of losing $25. Decide in the next 30 seconds which game you prefer to play, say, ten times in a row.

If you are like most people, you failed to multiply the probability of winning or losing by the amounts to be won or lost. Instead, you made a rough estimate of which game looked most favorable. Perhaps you reasoned that game 2's 90 percent chance of winning looked very good indeed. This game did involve a somewhat higher chance of losing, and the amount at

risk was also slightly higher. But overall, 90 percent odds in your favor were too good to pass up. If game 2 was indeed your choice, you have not made a good decision, as the caption to Figure 7.11 explains. In this case, narrowing your cognitive focus mainly to the probability of winning led to a decision that made little sense from a strictly logical point of view. In terms of your limited time, attention, and short-term memory, however, the strategy you used was quite understandable.

Interestingly, if the conditions of this choice had been somewhat different, you might have limited your cognitive focus in another way. Suppose the amount to be won had been quite large—say, more than $1,000. In this case, you might have discounted the probabilities and focused instead on the utility of winning that much money. This is why so many people buy tickets for million-dollar lotteries even though their chance of winning is minuscule. Similarly, when the amount a person risks losing is very large, the probabilities involved again tend to recede into the background. This may be why so many wage earners with dependent families purchase life insurance even though their chances of dying young are slim.

Many people find the tendencies we have been describing a bit disturbing. After all, we like to think of

Figure 7.11 Which of these two games should you play? A consideration of the probabilities of winning and losing should lead you to prefer game 1. In game 1, the odds are that you will break even: in ten tries, for example, you will probably win $40 and lose $40 (40% × 10 tries × $10 = 20% × 10 tries × $20). In game 2, however, you're likely to lose money: in ten tries, probability says you may win $90 but lose $100 (90% × 10 tries × $10 = $90; 40% × 10 tries × $25 = $100). *(After Slovic and Lichtenstein, 1968.)*

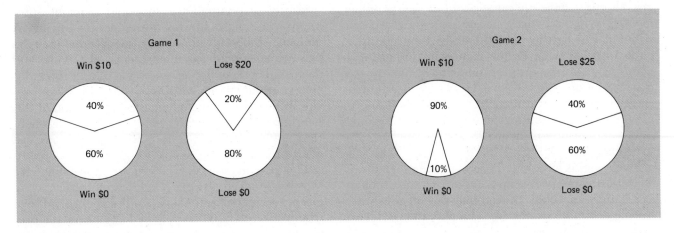

ourselves as rational decision makers. Yet studies show that our inclination to limit cognitive focus sometimes causes us to make serious mistakes. How common are the errors that our short-cut tactics can lead to? Might it be that our general sense of being competent decision makers is in many instances just an illusion? Such questions have recently generated heated controversy. On the one hand are those who emphasize the skill that people tend to show in making daily choices. On the other hand are those who stress the unperceived errors that our rule-of-thumb decision-making strategies can bring. So fascinating is this controversy, and so important to our lives, that we have decided to examine it in depth. Our exploration brings us to an issue we have not yet touched on, but one on which much current research centers. That issue can be stated simply: Exactly how good are we at judging uncertain odds?

in depth Are We Good at Judging Odds?

In June 1979 NASA informed the public that its seventy-nine-ton Skylab would probably fall out of orbit within a matter of weeks. But there was no great cause for worry, the space agency hastened to add. The odds were 151 to 1 *against* the plummeting Skylab causing harm to human beings. And the chance that the spacecraft would injure any given person was no less than 600 billion to 1. Most citizens undoubtedly breathed a sigh of relief. Such odds are astronomical, they reasoned; the chance that it will ever fall on me is almost nonexistent.

A desire to know the odds is common in everyday life. Should I have my car serviced or wait another month? What are the chances something will go wrong if I neglect it? Should I study this evening or go to a movie? What are the chances my instructor is planning a surprise quiz for tomorrow? Should I get married or stay single? What are the chances either choice will affect my career? In such matters the odds are uncertain. We must try to estimate them for ourselves. But as most of us are not statisticians, how do we go about it?

Psychologists have found that in making such probability estimates, people do *not* approach the problem as a statistician would. Instead they rely on heuristics, or rule-of-thumb strategies, to simplify the task. Two very common heuristics are representativeness and

availability. As you will see, when people overlook their limitations, both can lead to errors in judgment.

When Heuristics Lead Us Astray. Read the following description of a young man named Steve, who was picked at random from the population as a whole:

> Steve is very shy and withdrawn, invariably helpful, but with little interest in people, or in the world of reality. A meek and tidy soul, he has a need for order and structure, and a passion for detail. (Tversky and Kahneman, 1973, p. 1124)

Given this brief personality profile, what would you estimate the chances to be that Steve is engaged in each of the following occupations: salesman, airline pilot, librarian, physician? Write your answers, in percentages, on a sheet of paper before reading further.

How did you arrive at your probability estimates of Steve's line of work? If you are like most people, you relied on a heuristic called **representativeness.** You compared what you knew about Steve's personality with your understanding of what an "average" or "representative" salesman, pilot, librarian, or physician is like. The extent to which Steve matched each of these stereotypes determined your estimate of the probability that he was indeed employed in that particular occupation. The job to which you gave the highest probability was undoubtedly librarian. Salesman, on the other hand, probably scored close to zero.

There is no doubt that the representativeness heuristic is a useful device—as long as it does not blind you to other relevant information. The problem is that it sometimes does. What other factors, besides similarity to occupational stereotypes, might enter into your estimates of what Steve does for a living? A moment's thought will probably suggest that the relative proportion of salesmen, pilots, librarians, and doctors in the population as a whole should also influence your judgment. Did you consider this factor previously? Probably not. When asked a question of this type, most people employ the representativeness heuristic and completely ignore what statisticians call prior probabilities.

This remains so even when prior probabilities are specifically given. In one experiment subjects were given a series of personality profiles allegedly drawn from a group of 100 lawyers and engineers, the proportion of each being clearly stated (Kahneman and

Tversky, 1973). Logically, these proportions should have influenced the subjects' estimates that a given profile belonged either to a lawyer or to an engineer. But they did not. The subjects based their evaluations solely on the similarity between each profile and the personality stereotypes of people in those two occupations. Thus a particular profile was just as likely to be judged that of an engineer when only 30 percent of the group were engineers as when 70 percent were engineers. Prior probabilities were simply ignored in favor of the representativeness heuristic.

Some psychologists believe that the same judgmental bias may frequently influence decisions outside the laboratory. Most admissions boards of medical schools, for instance, place a great deal of importance on personal interviews with candidates. They are convinced that a variety of personality traits are representative of a "good" aspiring doctor. Yet there is no statistical evidence that a favorable admissions interview is any indication of subsequent success in medical school. Here, then, is a case where more reliable yardsticks, such as past academic performance and scores on entrance exams, are given less weight than they deserve in favor of a very intuitive assessment of representativeness (Nisbett and Ross, 1980). Much the same thing may happen when a judge tries to decide whether a man convicted of murder should be granted parole after twenty years in prison. If the man has a record of fights with other inmates and an uncooperative attitude toward guards, the judge may deny him his freedom even though statistics show that the vast majority of murderers who have served this much time do not go on to commit another crime. Here again we see the representativeness heuristic—a stereotyped image of the "unreformed" prisoner—causing prior probability to be ignored (Loftus and Beach, 1982).

And prior probability is not the only factor that the representativeness heuristic can prompt us to overlook. Consider the following problem:

> A game of squash can be played either to 9 or to 15 points. Holding all other rules of the game constant, if A is a better player than B, which scoring system will give A a better chance of winning? (Kahneman and Tversky, 1982)

When asked this question, most people maintain that the scoring system shouldn't matter. You may therefore be surprised to learn that this answer is incorrect. If you assumed that each type of game would be equally representative of the two players' respective skills, you overlooked an important fact learned in Chapter 2. The smaller the size of a sample, the greater the likelihood that just by chance it will fail to conform to expectations. Thus the shorter game offers player B a better chance of winning despite his lesser skill. It is the longer game that benefits player A. If you answered otherwise, it was probably because you overlooked the influence of sample size and misapplied the representativeness heuristic.

You can probably think of similar errors in everyday life. Here is just one example. Members of the United States Congress have been known to discount EPA mileage estimates, which are based on a sample of ten or more cars, when a fellow legislator reports a different mileage figure for his or her own car (La Breque, 1980). Clearly, information derived from a sizable sample should be considered more representative of a car's true performance than data obtained from one individual's experience. Yet in this case sample size is ignored completely and judgments are based instead on intuitive feelings about representativeness.

Although we use the representativeness heuristic in making many probability judgments, there are numerous situations in which this approach does not apply. For example, if you travel about 10,000 miles a year by car and are a driver of average skill, how would you estimate the probability that you will someday be involved in an automobile accident? In order to make such a judgment you would probably try to reconstruct the frequency of automobile accidents from past experience. Have you or has anyone you know ever been involved in a car accident? Have you ever witnessed a collision? How often do you hear about traffic accidents in the news? What you are doing here is assessing the probability of an uncertain event according to the ease with which instances come to mind. Events that are easy to remember are perceived as more frequent and therefore more probable than events that are difficult to remember. This approach is called the **availability** heuristic, and it makes a good deal of sense. In general, the present probability of an event is directly related to its frequency in the past, and the more often an event has been previously experienced, the easier it is to recall. But note the qualification "in general." Like any rule-of-thumb device, the availability heuristic has limitations that people sometimes ignore.

The basic problem is that some things come more readily to mind than others for reasons that have nothing to do with the frequency of past instances. A person who has just seen a highway accident is far more likely to remember it than a person who saw one ten years ago, for recency affects availability. There is some evidence that the vividness of an event has an effect as well (Thompson, Reyes, and Bower, 1979). You are much more likely to remember a five-car collision you witnessed yourself than one you merely read about in a newspaper. Familiarity, too, can make it easier to remember the things that we observe. For instance, when people are shown a list composed of an equal number of famous women and not-so-famous men, they later tend to describe it as consisting primarily of women (Tversky and Kahneman, 1973). The fame of the women apparently makes them easier to remember and so distorts perceptions concerning their relative frequency.

The availability heuristic is often used in making everyday judgments. Consider how we estimate the risks we face from diseases, accidents, natural disasters, and exposure to various toxins. The part played by the availability heuristic was indicated in a set of studies in which subjects were asked to estimate the likelihood of dying from an assortment of potential hazards (Slovic, Fischhoff, and Lichtenstein, 1976, 1980). The subjects greatly overestimated the risks from dangers that were both highly publicized and very dramatic—tornadoes, nuclear accidents, and homicides, for example. At the same time, they greatly underestimated the risks from such diseases as diabetes, tuberculosis, and asthma, which often are not fatal and which are only rarely reported as causes of death in the news. In another study, a sample group consisting of members of the League of Women Voters, presumably educated, informed citizens, was asked to rank the risk of dying in the United States from thirty activities and technologies. Figure 7.12 shows their responses as compared with the rankings made by experts. Such results indicate that because our recollection of death from various hazards is affected by sensationalism and media coverage

(factors that are unrelated to actual mortality rates), reliance on the availability heuristic can cause serious misperceptions. This helps explain why heavy TV viewers are especially prone to overestimate the risk of violent crime (Gerbner and Gross, 1976). They do indeed witness much criminal violence, but it is happening in the world of television, not in the real world. Nevertheless, scenes of violence are readily available in the TV addict's memory, prompting him or her to conclude that violence must therefore be common.

Psychologists who stress such errors in probability judgments do not indict the use of heuristics per se. They acknowledge that these intuitive strategies can save us cognitive effort and often produce quite accurate estimates of odds. But when heuristics blind us to other relevant information, we become prone to systematic mistakes. And these mistakes can be irresistible. Even when people are offered rewards for correct judgments, they still continue to make the same mistakes. Nor are their oversights due strictly to lack

Figure 7.12 The availability heuristic affects our perception of the risk of death from various activities and technologies. The rankings of the League of Women Voters sample (with 1 representing a judgment of most risk and 30 of least risk) diverge from those of the experts—most notably on the topic of nuclear power, an issue that gets a great deal of sensational media coverage. *(From Slovic, Fischhoff, and Lichtenstein, 1980, p. 47.)*

League Members		Experts
1	Nuclear power	20
2	Motor vehicles	1
3	Handguns	4
4	Smoking	2
5	Motorcycles	6
6	Alcoholic beverages	3
7	General (private) aviation	12
8	Police work	17
9	Pesticides	8
10	Surgery	5
11	Firefighting	18
12	Construction work	13
13	Hunting	23
14	Spray cans	26
15	Mountain climbing	29
16	Bicycles	15
17	Commercial aviation	16
18	Electric power (nonnuclear)	9
19	Swimming	10
20	Contraceptives	11
21	Skiing	30
22	X rays	7
23	High school and college football	27
24	Railroads	19
25	Food preservatives	14
26	Food coloring	21
27	Power mowers	28
28	Prescription antibiotics	24
29	Home appliances	22
30	Vaccinations	25

of knowledge. Experienced research psychologists, extensively trained in statistics, are also prone to errors when they intuitively judge odds (Tversky and Kahneman, 1971, 1981). The factors that they, like everyone else, tend to overlook are simply not part of a person's normal set of intuitions, some psychologists conclude. According to this view, then, humans are generally earnest but rather error-prone judgers of probability, not perceptive enough to realize the limitations of their own heuristics (Fischhoff, 1981).

A More Positive Perspective. The problem with this view is that it contradicts the way we tend to see ourselves. Most of us do not have the sense that we muddle through uncertainty, repeatedly miscalculating our chances, seldom learning from our mistakes. Could we really be so consistently poor at judging probabilities and yet be totally oblivious of our own incompetence? A number of researchers strongly suspect that the answer is no.

But what are we to make of the decision-making errors demonstrated in the laboratory? Certainly the evidence documenting them is too extensive to be ignored. Some psychologists urge caution before we draw conclusions, however. For one thing, the findings are not completely consistent (Evans, 1982). People do not *always*, for example, ignore sample size in favor of the representativeness heuristic. In some studies many subjects *have* taken the size of a sample into account. Apparently it all depends on the situation (Evans and Dusoir, 1977; Bar-Hillel, 1979). Likewise, it is not *always* true that the vividness of what we witness distorts our later recall of the frequency of past events. Again it depends on the context (Taylor and Thompson, 1981). The principal challenge researchers now face is to pinpoint the kinds of circumstances that lead to good judgment and the kinds that lead to bad judgment.

One question that repeatedly comes up in research on human judgment is how similar to real-life circumstances the typical experiment on probability judgment is. Several psychologists have raised just this issue. Do laboratory subjects experience the same motivation to estimate odds correctly as people do in real life (Christensen-Szalanski, 1978)? Are they likely to become confused by the wording of an unusual question and so interpret it in an idiosyncratic way (Phillips, 1981)? How influenced are they by demand characteristics? Might they be telling the experimenter what they think he or she wants to hear (Kahneman and Tversky, 1982)? At the very least, one has to admit that the typical experimental setup differs from real-life settings in that the critical probability question is presented only once. Subjects have little chance to receive feedback about their misperceptions and modify their judgments accordingly (Hogarth, 1981). In real life, isn't a skilled squash player likely to deduce fairly quickly that a longer game gives her an added advantage over less skilled players? It is significant that when psychologists have studied probability judgments in real-life settings, people have often been found to perform reasonably well. In one study, for example, doctors appeared to consider prior probabilities routinely (such as the prevalence of pneumonia in their area) when estimating the chances that a particular patient had pneumonia. They did not just analyze how representative the person's symptoms were of those usually associated with this illness (Christensen-Szalanski and Bushyhead, 1981).

This more positive perspective on the quality of human probability judgments helps counterbalance the very negative one that often emerges from laboratory findings. On the one hand, the heuristics we use to estimate odds *can* lead to significant errors. On the other hand, we are far from totally inept at such judgments, nor do we fail repeatedly to learn from our mistakes (Loftus and Beach, 1982). Depending on the circumstances, we can be both intuitively perceptive and intuitively naive. This is what makes the study of human decision making so fascinating. It is hoped that further investigation into the way we go about judging probabilities will shed more light on both our strengths and our weaknesses. Such research could thus help us learn to avoid common pitfalls and develop strategies that would improve our skill at estimating odds.

Figure 7.13 Answers to problems

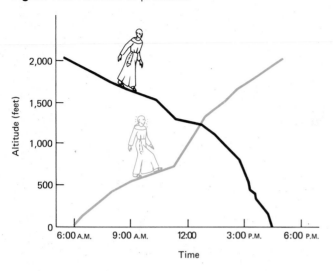

(A) The answer to the problem in Figure 7.4.

(B) The answer to the problem on page 192.

"Having recognized . . . that the symbols stood for letters, and having applied the rules which guide us in all forms of writing, the solution was easy enough. The first message was so short that it was impossible to do more than say that the symbol 𝗫 stood for E. As you are aware, E is the most common letter in the English alphabet . . . [so] it was reasonable to set this down as E . . . in some cases, [this] figure was bearing a flag, but it was probable, from the way in which [they were] distributed, that they were used to break the sentence up into words. I accepted this as a hypothesis. . . . I waited for fresh material. . . . [In message 4] I got the two E's coming second and fourth in a word of five letters. It might be 'sever' or 'level' or 'never'. . . . The latter as a reply to an appeal is far the most probable. . . . Accepting it as correct, we are now able to say that the symbols 𝕊 ⊣ 𝗫 stand respectively for N, V and R." And so on. The last fragment was a threat of murder against Mrs. Cubitt: "ELSIE PREPARE TO MEET THY GOD." (A. Conan Doyle, "The Adventure of the Dancing Men," in *The Return of Sherlock Holmes* [New York: Ballantine Books, © 1975.])

(C) The answer to the problem in Figure 7.5.

(D) The answer to the four-chain problem on page 196. Take one chain completely apart (for 6¢) and use its links to join the remaining three chains (for 9¢).

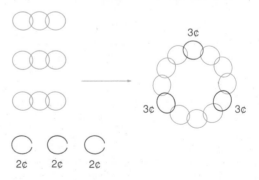

SUMMARY

1. **Cognition,** or thought, has become a major field of psychological investigation. It is the study of the way we organize information in our minds to achieve some desired end. Human cognition is difficult to study because **introspection,** the subjective description of one's own thought processes, is often faulty. Thus psychologists tend to focus on mental activities with observable and measurable results. Important among these activities are concept formation, problem solving, and decision making.

2. Our ability to form **concepts**—the mental constructs that classify together things with common traits—enables us to make generalizations and thus to engage in complex thought. Some psychologists argue that to form a new concept we test hypotheses regarding which of the many features of a stimulus define it as a member of a certain category. This is often called the **feature-based model** of concept formation. With a **global hypothesis,** for instance, we assume that all the salient features of a new stimulus define it as a member of the concept. Then we apply a **focusing strategy,** by which subsequent instances of the concept show us which features can be eliminated from our original definition. Alternatively, we can start with a limited hypothesis that picks out only one or two features as the defining traits. By a subsequent **scanning strategy** we then scan other examples of the concept for the same key features and revise our working hypothesis as the need arises.

3. Psychologist Eleanor Rosch, among others, has proposed another view of concept formation—the **prototype model,** which argues that we formulate a concept in terms of a best example or prototype, plus an implicit sense of how far a stimulus can vary from this prototype and still be an instance of the class. The prototype model helps account for the structure of **natural concepts,** those concepts we use every day.

4. A knowledge of concepts and relationships among them makes problem solving possible. To analyze problem solving, psychologists sometimes divide it into three stages: initially assessing the problem, devising solution strategies, and deciding when a satisfactory answer has been found.

5. Usually the best way to assess a difficult problem is to try to look at it from many angles. It is not always easy to change your initial perspective on a problem, however. Sometimes you get locked into focusing on irrelevant information. At other times you cannot break free of a perspective you have always held in the past. One example of this second obstacle is called **functional fixedness**—the tendency to see objects that could be used in novel ways to solve a problem as having only their customary uses.

6. When proper initial assessment alone will not solve a problem, we devise strategies to help us reach an answer. Some problems can best be solved by a strategy called an **algorithm,** a precisely stated set of rules that works for solving all problems of a particular type. When an algorithm is not available, we use a **heuristic,** or rule-of-thumb strategy. One general heuristic is **subgoal analysis,** in which a large problem is broken down into smaller problems of manageable size. Another is **means-end analysis,** by which one compares one's current position with a desired end point and then tries to find a means of closing the gap between the two. A third general heuristic is the **backward search,** by which one starts at a problem's end point and works backward to discover how to get there.

7. Just as flexibility is important when we initially assess a problem, it is also important when we select a problem-solving strategy. Unfortunately, there is a common tendency to stick with a solution that has worked in the past, and not to consider other options. This tendency is called a **mental set,** and it can make problem solving difficult. One way to achieve flexibility in the strategy stage of problem solving is to seek a period of **incubation**—get away from the problem for a while so it can later be approached with a fresh eye.

8. While the solution to some problems is clear-cut, it is not always easy to determine when you have found the best solution. People are often willing to settle for a less than perfect solution if continued search for the ideal one places too great a demand on cognitive capacity.

9. The problem-solving experiences of highly creative people seem to be much like those of the rest of us, except perhaps more intense. Solutions may come suddenly and unpredictably, often when the person is not actively working on the problem. This has led some investigators to suspect that many creative inspirations may be largely the products of unconscious thought. Other factors, however, also contribute to creativity, among them knowledge, strong motivation, persistence, and an appropriate environment.

10. Rational models of decision making generally hold that we systematically consider two basic factors in making choices: the **utility** or value of each potential outcome and the **probability** or likelihood that each of these outcomes will actually occur. Such rational approaches are restricted, however, by our persistent tendency to limit cognitive focus. When a decision is fairly complex and requires that we process and weigh substantial amounts of information, we tend to reduce our choices to simpler ones by concentrating on a few of the relevant factors and largely ignoring the others.

11. There is much debate over how good human beings are at estimating uncertain odds. One view holds that the heuristics we use to help us judge probabilities often lead us astray by diverting our attention from important pieces of information. One such heuristic is **representativeness,** according to which we judge probability by estimating how representative a particular stimulus is of a certain class of stimuli. Another is **availability,** by which we assess odds according to the ease with which instances of an event come to mind. An opposing view holds that we should not lose sight of our successes at judging probabilities. Although we sometimes make mistakes, according to this perspective, we are in general quite competent decision makers.

SUGGESTED READINGS

ELLIS, H. C., and HUNT, R. R. *Fundamentals of human memory and cognition,* 3d ed. Dubuque, Iowa: William Brown, 1983.

This paperback book not only provides extensive coverage of human memory, but also contains excellent chapters on concepts and categories and on problem solving.

HOWARD, D. V. *Cognitive psychology.* New York: Macmillan, 1983.

This is an excellent basic textbook in the field of cognition.

KAHNEMAN, D., SLOVIC, P., and TVERSKY, A. *Judgment under uncertainty.* New York: Cambridge University Press, 1982.

This book by experts in the field generally describes some of the biases that people display in judgment and decision making. These biases are observed not only in the laboratory, but in important social, medical, and political situations as well.

MATLIN, M. *Cognition.* New York: Holt, Rinehart and Winston, 1983.

This is another excellent basic textbook in the field of cognition.

THE PROCESS OF DEVELOPMENT

Human development is explored in Part
4: the unfolding of personality
throughout the life span in Chapter 8,
and the development of language—verbal
and nonverbal—in Chapter 9.

8

LIFE-SPAN
DEVELOPMENT

Barbara Hepworth. *Figure for Landscape*, 1960.

The development of a human being is a remarkable process. In just nine months a nearly microscopic fertilized egg cell is transformed into a human infant with heart, brain, muscle, lungs—all the biological systems needed for survival outside the mother's womb. A mere six years later this newborn has grown into an accomplished first-grader, as proficient in language as many adults and ready to begin mastering such complex skills as reading and arithmetic. From here it is a relatively short step to social and sexual maturation in adolescence, and then to such adult roles as worker, wife or husband, and parent. During the fifty or more years of adulthood remaining, a person continues to develop. With increased age come not just physical changes, but cognitive, social, and emotional ones as well. Development, in fact, is a never-ending process, from conception until death. The branch of psychology that seeks to comprehend the patterns of growth and change that occur during the life cycle is called **developmental psychology.**

THE PROCESS OF DEVELOPMENT

In investigating the process of human development, psychologists ask two closely related questions: *How* do people change—physically, intellectually, emotionally, and socially—as they grow older? And *why* do such changes occur? These questions, the how and the why of human development, are the subject of this chapter.

Developmental Sequences

Human development follows some broadly predictable patterns. Nowhere are these developmental sequences more apparent than in physical growth and change. At birth a human infant is, physically speaking, far from just a miniature adult. Aside from the newborn's relative weakness and lack of muscular coordination, its body is proportioned very differently from an adult's. The head is huge compared with the torso and the legs are bent and stubby. All this dramatically changes, however, over the next several years. By the time the child enters school, the body has taken on more mature proportions, in addition to increasing in strength, coordination, and height. Then, at puberty, further physical changes occur, usually quite rapidly. A boy's shoulders broaden; a girl's breasts and pelvis enlarge. Less sudden but equally predictable are the physical changes that occur throughout adulthood. With middle age the body generally thickens and the muscles begin to lose their tone. By old age, changes in the skeleton often cause the body to shorten, and posture may become slightly stooped.

Although the physical changes associated with development are probably the most apparent, they are not the only ones. Similar developmental sequences occur in other areas, from perceptual abilities to intellectual skills to styles of social interaction. Many developmental psychologists, in fact, focus their attention on identifying and describing such general patterns of change. These researchers certainly recognize that all people develop differently in many respects. Some people, for instance, reach puberty much sooner than others. Some age quite quickly, while others age only very gradually. All human beings, however, eventually undergo much the same sequences of developmental change. It is on these broadly shared developmental sequences that much of the research we will be discussing concentrates.

The Interaction of Heredity and Internal Environment

In addition to describing how people change as they grow older, developmental psychologists are also interested in the "why" of human development. They seek to know both why broad similarities in human development exist and why particular individuals differ (often markedly) from statistical norms. The answers to these questions lie in two interacting factors: heredity and a person's internal biochemical environment. But exactly how the two combine to produce a given developmental pattern is never easy to say.

Perhaps the best way to understand the complex interaction of heredity and environment is to begin at the moment of conception, when a male sperm penetrates a female egg cell. Both sperm and egg contain twenty-three **chromosomes,** structures within the cell nucleus that carry the organism's **genes,** its units of hereditary information. All other cells in the human body contain twenty-three *pairs* of chromosomes, or forty-six in all. The sperm and egg are different because toward the end of their development they undergo a form of cell division called **meiosis.** During meiosis, the twenty-three chromosome pairs are split, rearranged, and distributed to two "daughter" cells, each receiving twenty-three single chromosomes. The need for such a process is easy to understand. At the time of fertilization, the twenty-three chromosomes

in the father's sperm will combine with the twenty-three in the mother's egg to produce a complete set of genetic instructions for a new human being. And because meiosis involves a reshuffling of genes and chromosomes, it also guarantees variety in future generations.

But how exactly do chromosomes and the genes they carry influence development? It is only within the last several decades that scientists have begun to answer this question. Chromosomes are essentially long, spiral-shaped molecules of a complex substance called **DNA (deoxyribonucleic acid).** A gene is a small portion of a DNA molecule that contains the code for producing one of the many proteins from which the body is built. Genes, in other words, are the chemical "blueprints" for building and maintaining a living organism.

The end result is also shaped by the internal environment in which the blueprints are "read." The instructions in particular genes may or may not be followed, or they may be modified in any number of ways depending on the biochemistry of the individual in whom those genes operate. This can be seen clearly in the development of the male reproductive organs. (We know much less about how development of the female genitals is coordinated.) All genetically male embryos contain within their cells a so-called Y chromosome, which differentiates them from females. About six weeks after conception, some change in the embryo's internal environment activates the genes on a small portion of the Y chromosome to begin promoting the production of various proteins. Some of these proteins cause a part of the primitive reproductive structures (until then identical in genetic males and females) to differentiate into the male sex glands, or testes. Soon thereafter the cells in the testes start to produce the male sex hormone testosterone, which further changes the embryo's internal environment. It is this testosterone that finally stimulates embryonic tissue to form the remainder of the male genital organs. In fact, if something goes awry and *no* testosterone is secreted, a genetic male will be born who looks exactly like a female. Thus prenatal development is caused not just by our genes, but by a complex interplay of genes and internal environment.

Since internal environment is so critical to proper embryonic development, it is not surprising that the chemicals a woman ingests during pregnancy can greatly affect her baby. This was dramatically illustrated in the early 1960s when a sedative called thalidomide, sometimes prescribed to alleviate the "morning sickness" of pregnancy, was later found to inhibit the formation of embryonic arms and legs. Many other drugs are now known or suspected to be potentially harmful to an unborn child. As a result, many women today are advised to eliminate drugs during pregnancy except those that are absolutely necessary and approved by their physicians. By the same token, pregnant women are also advised to be careful with their diets so that all the nutrients needed for development will be present in their bodies. For instance, if the mother consumes inadequate amounts of vitamins B, C, or D or of calcium, phosphorus, or iodine, the genetic plan may go awry and birth defects may result.

The interaction of genes and environment continues after a person is born. People affect their internal environments through the food they eat, the water they drink, even the air they breathe. In addition, sensory information is constantly being stored in memory, a process that affects the physiology of the brain. And the things that people encounter can provoke a wide range of emotions, which are often associated with intense responses in various nerves and glands. All these forces can and do affect the ways in which genes are expressed. Consider, for instance, the impact of emotional deprivation on physical growth. When a baby is raised by indifferent caregivers, the child may be sickly and slow to mature. It is thought that the emotional barrenness is somehow linked to reduced secretions of the pituitary gland, including its growth hormone (Gardner, 1972). Thus a child with genes for normal body stature may end up stunted and frail if he or she grows up in an uncaring environment.

Because environments so vitally affect the ways in which genes are expressed, scientists have found that they can often change environments in ways that reduce the impact of defective genes. A striking example is seen in the case of the genetic abnormality called phenylketonuria, or PKU. PKU is caused by a defect in the gene that normally codes for an enzyme that converts the amino acid phenylalanine (primarily found in milk and egg whites) into another substance that the body can use. In a child with the PKU gene, this conversion is impossible. So phenylalanine and its by-products gradually build up, eventually damaging the central nervous system and causing severe mental retardation. Today most American newborns are screened for PKU, and those who have the defect are immediately placed on a diet low in phenylalanine. If this diet is maintained for the first six years of life (while critical features of the brain are forming), the child will develop normal intelligence. Thus a simple adjustment in the child's internal environment can prevent the devastating effects of this faulty gene.

Unfortunately, we do not yet know how to block the expression of a large number of other genetic defects. But we now realize that there is probably no trait that is completely impervious to environmental interventions. Consider recent research with children who have Down's syndrome, a condition caused by a defect in an entire chromosome. Children with Down's syndrome are usually retarded and lack normal physical coordination. In the past many people considered their cases to be hopeless. But recent studies show that when Down's-syndrome children are given intensive training in certain sensorimotor tasks, their performance on these tasks greatly improves (Rynders, 1975). Thus a change in the learning environment can make an enormous difference in the effects this abnormal chromosome has. Genetic makeup, in other words, should never be viewed in isolation. All human traits are influenced by both genes *and* environment.

The Competency of the Human Newborn

Human infants seem so weak and helpless at birth that it is hard to believe they are capable of much interaction with their external environments. Not too long ago, in fact, many people still wondered whether the newborn could even see or hear at all. In the last several decades, however, research on the newborn has expanded greatly, and a very different view of this period has emerged. We now know that human infants are born with sensory systems that are impressively able. They process information and learn about their surroundings from the very moment of birth.

Recent findings regarding the newborn's visual capabilities have done much to foster this view. Although babies do not develop 20/20 vision until sometime between the ages of six and twelve months (Cohen, De Loache, and Stauss, 1978), newborns are nevertheless quite capable of seeing things held at close enough range (their vision is sharpest at a distance of about seven to eight inches). What's more, even on the very day of birth most babies can visually fixate on objects and track slowly moving stimuli with their eyes (Greenman, 1963). These abilities enable infants to begin gathering visual information as soon as they enter the world.

Among the first things that babies see are other human faces, and from these they start to learn a great deal indeed. Judging from the way that newborns scan faces (focusing much more on the edges than on the internal features), it is unlikely that they perceive them the same way that older humans do (Haith, Bergman, and Moore, 1977). Nevertheless, there is evidence that on some level newborns detect changes in facial expressions. In one study, for instance, babies on average only thirty-six hours old were able to discriminate among happy, sad, and surprised expressions that an adult model displayed (Field et al., 1982). The researchers could tell this by the fact that the babies tended to look less and less at an expression that was repeatedly presented, as if they were growing bored with that particular face. Yet they showed renewed interest as soon as an "old" expression was replaced by a different one.

These same babies also showed a tendency demonstrated before in newborns: the tendency to imitate the facial expression of an adult (Meltzoff and Moore, 1977). As the accompanying photographs show, they often spread their lips and crinkled their eyes when they viewed a happy expression, often furrowed their brows and pouted their lips when they saw sadness displayed, and often opened their mouths and widened their eyes when they saw a surprised face. This is not to say that babies this young deliberately mimic others. As yet they have no sense of "self" and "other," no knowledge of the similarities between their own expressions and a model's. Their behavior in this case is akin to a reflex—an unpremeditated "matching" of their own facial movements with those of someone else (Kaye and Marcus, 1978). Yet the newborn's ability to attend so carefully to other human faces is undoubtedly an important foundation for future social and emotional development.

Adding to this foundation is the newborn's very

impressive ability to differentiate sounds. A baby can distinguish between speech sounds at an early age, even when those sounds are very similar. Peter Eimas and his colleagues demonstrated this with the English consonants *b* and *p*. If you say these sounds out loud while noting how you make them, you will realize how very alike they are. Yet even one-month-old babies can easily differentiate between them, as Eimas and

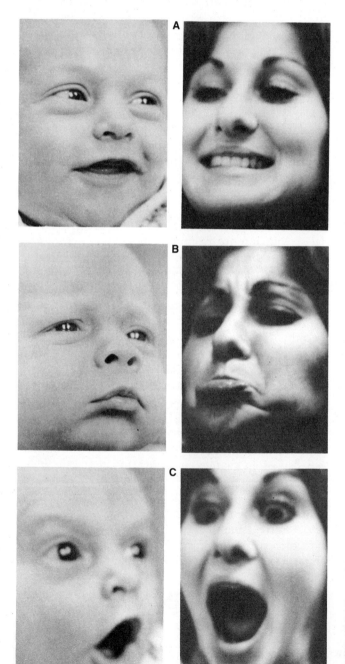

Human infants only 36 hours old seem to be able to imitate a model's expressions of (A) happiness, (B) sadness, and (C) surprise. The researchers who conducted this study believe that human infants have an innate ability to compare the visual information they receive about expressions with the movements they must make to match the expressions. *(Field et al., 1982, p. 180.)*

his coworkers showed (Eimas et al., 1971). They placed in each infant's mouth a pacifier wired to a tape recorder. A vigorous suck on the pacifier switched the tape on and played for the baby the sound of either "bah" or "pah." This sound was repeated as long as the infant kept sucking vigorously. The babies typically sucked hard and often upon first hearing the speech sound; then their sucking decreased as they grew bored with the stimulus. But if the first speech sound was then replaced by the second, the infants immediately showed renewed interest by increasing their rates of vigorous sucking. Apparently they were quite able to perceive the subtle difference between these two consonants. Given this remarkable ability, it is not surprising that babies as young as two weeks often respond differentially to the sound of their own name (Pines, 1982).

Babies also are able to differentiate smells. In one experiment, two-day-old babies were presented with a particular smell, which caused their activity, heart-rate, and breathing patterns to change. After a while the babies got used to the odor. When a different smell was presented to them, however, their activity, heart-rate, and breathing patterns again changed (Engen, Lipsitt, and Kaye, 1963). Similar experiments with five- and six-day-old infants showed that they are able to recognize their mother's scent as opposed to the smell of another woman (Macfarlane, 1977).

As if this were not enough, babies are also born with capacities that promote learning about the relationships between different sensations. This was shown in an early experiment by M. Wertheimer (1961), who made a soft clicking sound with a toy cricket near the ears of a baby girl only minutes after she was born. On the first click, near the child's right ear, she stopped crying, opened her eyes, and shifted her gaze to the right. The sound was then moved to the baby's left ear and the results were similar: she shifted her gaze to the left. Subsequent studies have shown that if properly supported, a newborn will turn its entire head in the direction of a sound (Muir and Field, 1979). A sound presented directly in front of a newborn, in contrast, will prompt the child to fixate its gaze forward for up to half a minute (Mendelson and Haith, 1976). Such innate coordination of auditory and visual processing is very important, for it increases the speed with which young babies learn associations between sights and sounds.

When we explore the perceptual capabilities of a newborn, then, we find surprisingly mature and well-integrated systems. With these systems a baby can interact with people and objects from the very first moments after birth. As we shall see, these interactions have a profound effect on both cognitive and social development.

COGNITIVE DEVELOPMENT

The amount of information people acquire in a lifetime is staggering. By the time most children enter school they have mastered the intricacies of language. They can count, recite the alphabet, narrate the plots of their favorite stories, and explain the rules of many games. They can also operate mechanical equipment such as TV sets, telephones, and video game machines. Upon graduation from high school twelve years later, they have probably learned more science and mathematics than their great-grandparents learned in a lifetime. As adults, they will find their way in a complex world that depends on sophisticated technology. They may choose an occupation that requires highly technical skills, such as programming a computer, performing brain surgery, or perhaps even piloting a spacecraft.

How does a person's intellect develop from the rudimentary abilities present at birth to the sophisticated skills exhibited in adulthood? Many psychologists see cognitive development as a series of *qualitatively different* stages. At each new stage the person constructs a more mature view of reality, which in turn changes the way he or she thinks about the world and assimilates new information. The most influential stage theory of cognitive development is that of the Swiss psychologist Jean Piaget (1896–1980). During his long and productive career, Piaget made detailed observations of many children, including his own three (Piaget, 1926, 1952, 1954, 1971). From these observations emerged insights that shaped the work of many other developmental psychologists. Piaget believed that intellectual development proceeds through four major stages: the **sensorimotor period,** which encompasses the first two years of life;

the **preoperational period,** which occurs during the preschool years; the **concrete-operational period,** which occupies the elementary school years; and the **formal-operational period,** which begins around adolescence and may continue to develop throughout adulthood (Piaget and Inhelder, 1969).

Not all psychologists agree with a stage approach to cognitive development, however. Some believe that many of the contrasts in cognitive ability between older and younger children can be largely explained by *quantitative differences* in their information-processing skills. From this perspective, the eight-year-old's ability to remember more than a four-year-old has little to do with qualitative differences in the way they construct reality. Instead, the eight-year-old, through greater experience, has acquired strategies for remembering information that the younger child still lacks. Undoubtedly both the qualitative and the quantitative approaches to cognitive development have some validity. We will consider evidence supporting each of them as we explore intellectual growth from infancy through adulthood.

Cognitive Development in Infancy

If you have ever met a child at age six months and then met the same child again two years later, you may have been astonished at the transformation that occurred. And this transformation was not simply physical. The cognitive changes that take place during the first several years after birth are perhaps the most remarkable of all. Two-and-a-half-year-olds are rapidly becoming skilled at language; they can interact socially in rather adult-like fashion and understand the meaning of most events around them. Six-month-olds, in contrast, can do none of these things. How does such enormous cognitive growth occur in such a short period?

The Infant's Capacity for Learning and Memory. Part of the answer lies in the fact that babies are capable of learning from the very moment of birth—probably even before. Infants only a few days old have been taught to turn their heads upon hearing a certain tone when a mouthful of sugary water awaits them as a reward (Siqueland and Lipsitt, 1966). Babies will even learn when the "reward" for doing so is

nothing more than a flash of light (Papousek, 1969). Suppose a nine-month-old boy is placed in a crib with a mobile above his head. A string is attached to each of his wrists and ankles, but only the string to the right ankle makes the mobile move. What does the baby do in this situation? Probably he starts to wave his arms and legs, as babies this age normally do. But suddenly he notices that the mobile is moving. The baby stops and observes the bobbing objects. Slowly he moves arms and legs until he discovers the relationship between a kick of the right leg and a flutter of the toy. The baby then gurgles with apparent delight, kicking the right leg repeatedly. If the contingency is then changed, so that the right arm now operates the mobile, the baby will again search for the solution and coo vigorously when he discovers it (Monnier, Boehmer, and Scholer, 1976). It is as if the child learns for the sheer fun of it. John S. Watson, one of the first researchers to notice this infant response to learning, suggests that babies derive a form of intellectual pleasure from solving a problem in

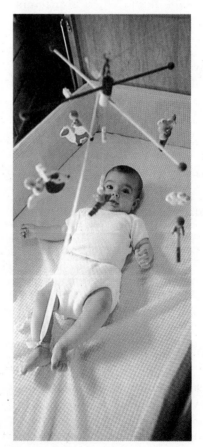

Babies can make their own fun. If a mobile is attached to an infant in such a way that the infant's movements activate the mobile, the infant soon discovers the relationship and seems to delight in making the appropriate kick to set the mobile in motion. *(Dr. Carolyn Ravel-Collier, Rutgers Department of Psychology.)*

much the same way that older children and adults do (Watson, 1972).

The fact that infants have this capacity for learning implies that they are also able to remember. But exactly how long do a baby's memories last? Do infants forget things as soon as they are distracted, much as adults forget an unfamiliar number as soon as they close the phone book? Many people assume that babies' memories *are* this fleeting, particularly given how little we remember about our own infancies. Yet recent research shows that this assumption greatly underestimates the baby's memory capabilities. In one study, for instance, four-week-olds were exposed for half an hour daily to the same stabile above their cribs (a stabile is like a mobile but without moving parts). After several weeks, the original stabile and a novel one were displayed together, twelve to twenty-four hours after the last presentation of the original stabile alone. The infants looked significantly longer at the novel stabile, suggesting that they recognized the other as old hat (Weizmann, Cohen, and Pratt, 1971). Older babies do even better at such recognition tasks, especially when remembering faces. Joseph Fagan (1976) has gathered evidence that five-month-olds can even recognize the picture of a person inspected for only minutes two weeks before. Such findings force us to conclude that very young infants can often remember for fairly long periods.

Development of the Object Concept.

Even very young babies can and do learn. But what do they learn about? As we have just seen, much of the information babies acquire has to do with the existence of objects (including other people), as well as with relationships between their own behavior and those objects' response. Piaget argued that constructing a view of the world which incorporates objects and causality is the central cognitive task of infancy. This the child does by exercising what Piaget called sensorimotor intelligence. The term *sensorimotor intelligence* implies that babies do not think abstractly, as older children do. They do not analyze problems, plan out strategies, and wonder what the consequences will be. Instead, babies come to know their worlds strictly by perceiving and acting. Their understanding is derived solely from what they sense and do.

After studying how infants use sensorimotor intelligence to construct an understanding of objects, Piaget proposed that the **object concept** develops in a series of stages. At first a baby has no awareness that objects have a permanent existence. When something can no longer be perceived by the senses, it ceases to exist for them. Piaget drew this conclusion after observing infants' reactions when an object "disappears." Suppose a toy that has captured a baby's attention is partially hidden from sight by a piece of paper, as shown in the photographs below. Piaget noticed that babies up to the age of about four months do not search for the "missing" toy either with their eyes or with their hands. They act as if it had vanished, suggesting that they lack any notion of the toy as an enduring whole. By the age of four to eight months, in contrast, infants *do* recognize and reach for partially covered objects. They also look downward to find an object they have dropped, implying that they expect it still to be there. By eight to twelve months a baby will also search for *totally* covered objects. The photographs on the next page show a child this age lifting up a "curtain" to retrieve an hourglass. In some ways, however, the child's concept of objects is still immature. Consider what would happen if during the "curtain" game the hourglass were suddenly hidden behind a second towel, still in the child's full view. A baby this age would continue to look for the object behind the *first* towel. He or she would simply repeat the action that had produced the

This infant of about six months has not yet developed the concept of object permanence. She looks intently at a toy elephant that is in front of her, but when the toy is blocked from her view, she gives no indication that she understands that the toy is still present. *(George Zimbel/Monkmeyer Press Photos.)*

This older infant realizes that the disappearance of an object does not necessarily mean that it is no longer present. When the object he sees is shielded from his view by a towel, he searches for it by crawling under the towel. *(George Zimbel/Monkmeyer Press Photos.)*

toy earlier, rather than look for it where it was last seen. It is only by the age of twelve to eighteen months that babies can deal with such displacements. And it is not until the age of eighteen to twenty-four months that children can conceive of displacements they have not actually seen (as when a toy hidden in one hand is surreptitiously passed to the other hand). This milestone marks the final stage in acquiring the object concept.

Piaget's stages describing infants' behavior toward objects have proved to be quite reliable. Babies all over the world have been found to pass through these developmental sequences, searching for hidden objects in predictable ways at different ages. But some researchers have questioned Piaget's conclusions about what these patterns mean. They wonder to what extent it is the child's construction of reality that is shaping his or her behaviors—whether failure to look for a hidden toy necessarily means that the baby sees objects as impermanent things that come and go at random. Some psychologists propose that infants' behavior in these situations may also reflect their memory powers (Kagan, Kearsley, and Zelazo, 1978). Although we saw earlier that very young babies can often recognize an object seen many times before, the memory requirements in Piaget's experiments may be more demanding. Imagine a three-month-old shown a toy, which is then hidden by a paper. The baby must hold in mind an image of this briefly viewed object after the paper covers it. The task is not simply to tell if something is familiar or unfamiliar. Instead, the child must actively recall what was previously present and coordinate this memory with a visual search. This is probably beyond the cognitive capabilities of someone so young. Of course, this explanation and Piaget's are not necessarily mutually exclusive. It could easily be that the two forces (object concept and memory ability) work together to bring about the developmental sequences regarding objects so reliably found in the first two years of life (Nelson, 1982).

Cognitive Development in the Preschool Years

Between the ages of two and three, children leave the cognitive world of infancy far behind. One of their key intellectual accomplishments is **representational thought**—the ability to represent things mentally when those things are not physically present. Children can now imagine, and by doing so, they expand their world far beyond the limits of their immediate perceptions. One sign that preschoolers can think representationally is their ability to imitate someone else's actions a long time after they have seen them. Another is their ability to play "make-believe," pretending, for example, that they are astronauts and that a large cardboard box is a spaceship. But the most important indication of representational thought is the ability to use language, an intellectual accomplishment that greatly expands the child's powers of reasoning and communication.

As impressive as the preschooler's cognitive advances are, however, children this age still have cognitive limitations. One is the fact that their thought is often egocentric. This means that preschool youngsters do not always understand that different people have different perspectives and that their own view is merely one among many. In one experimental demonstration of egocentrism Piaget and Inhelder (1969) showed preschoolers a large model composed of three mountains in a triangular arrangement (see Figure 8.1). After a child had walked around the model and become familiar with it, he or she sat in a chair facing one of the mountains. The experimenter sat in a chair facing another mountain and asked the child which of several pictures showed what the experimenter saw. Children this age repeatedly chose the picture depicting their own perspective.

While there is little doubt that preschool youngsters do show egocentrism, psychologists debate why this tendency occurs. Piaget believed it is because a pre-

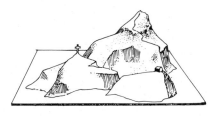

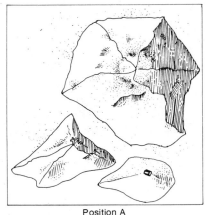

Position A

Figure 8.1 A model used to demonstrate egocentrism. Piaget and Inhelder first had children walk all around the model and look at it from all sides. Then they seated children of various ages at position A and asked them how the scene would appear to observers at other positions. Preoperational children regularly indicated that the scene would appear as it did from position A, no matter where the observer was located. Their thinking did not allow them to reconstruct the scene mentally from a point of view other than their own. *(After Piaget and Inhelder, 1956.)*

schooler's view of the world is subjectively structured. When asked to describe another person's viewpoint, Piaget argued, children this age cannot help but describe their own. But other psychologists answer that the cause of egocentrism may lie more in the preschooler's still limited information-processing capabilities. In one study, for instance, preschoolers were asked to hide a Snoopy doll behind a screen so that an experimenter could not see it from where she sat (Flavell, Shipstead, and Croft, 1978). Even two-and-a-half-year-olds were able to do this, suggesting that in certain situations they *can* adopt another person's perspective. Perhaps, then, failure on the mountain-range problem has more to do with the complexity of this particular task. The child, after all, must encode the entire landscape into memory, recall the experimenter's viewpoint, and retain this mental image while considering the various pictures (Huttenlocher and Presson, 1979). Faced with such difficult requirements, most preschool youngsters may simply fall back on what they see before them.

Cognitive Development in Middle Childhood

Around the time children enter school they begin to think in more logical ways than younger children do. Piaget felt that the major intellectual accomplishment of middle childhood was the ability to perform what he called **concrete operations.** This term refers to a variety of mental transformations (all of which can be reversed) that the child can carry out on concrete or tangible objects. The ability to perform concrete operations develops gradually between the ages of about six and twelve. An excellent example can be seen in the emergence of what are called **concepts of conservation**—the recognition that some characteristics of stimuli can remain the same (be conserved) despite changes in other features.

Development of Conservation Concepts. Suppose you show a four-year-old two identical short, wide beakers of water and ask the child to say whether beaker 1 or beaker 2 contains more. The child will probably answer correctly that the two beakers contain equal amounts. Now suppose you pour the water from beaker 2 into a third beaker, which is tall and thin. If you now ask the child which beaker contains more water, beaker 1 or beaker 3, the child is very apt to say that beaker 3 has more. The youngster seems to fixate on the general look of the two containers, concluding that the taller one is "bigger." On the basis of such experiments, Piaget and others have argued that preschoolers lack the concept of conservation of liquid quantity. Children of this age fail to understand that the amount of a liquid does not change simply because it is poured into a container of a different shape.

Nor have children this young grasped other concepts of conservation. For instance, if you show a preschooler two parallel rows of six identical-sized marbles, with the marbles in each row touching one another, the child will correctly say that both rows have an equal number. But if you then spread out the marbles in one row, as shown in Figure 8.2, the child will now say that the lengthened row has more, even though the number of marbles remains the same. Psychologists say that the child does not yet under-

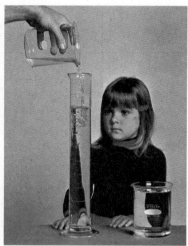

The girl taking part in this demonstration has not yet acquired the ability to understand the concept of conservation of liquid. She agrees that there is an equal amount of water in the two shorter beakers, but when the water from one of them is poured into the taller beaker, she incorrectly asserts that there is more water in the taller beaker than in the shorter. To develop an understanding of the principle of conservation, the child must be able to coordinate her thoughts about the length and width of the first container, the length and width of the second container, and the change or transformation brought about by pouring the liquid from the shorter beaker into the taller. (Steve Wells.)

stand conservation of number. He or she believes that number can vary with an irrelevant change in appearance, such as an increase in spacing. Parents sometimes take advantage of this error in reasoning. They may spread out a pile of candies, for example, so that preschoolers think they are getting more. Figure 8.2 shows two other conservation problems, conservation of mass and conservation of length, likewise beyond the grasp of children this young.

Older children gradually come to understand concepts of conservation. A girl of eight, for example, will probably be able to coordinate her thoughts

Figure 8.2 Examples of problems for which a child must acquire the concept of conservation. Concrete-operational children interiorize the possibility of making and unmaking the transformations for each task shown here. Thus, they come to see the lengths and quantities as unchanged in each case. Preoperational children, who are not able to imagine the transformations required, respond to perceptually striking but irrelevant aspects of the objects in attempting to answer the questions. For example, preoperational children will answer that there are more marbles in the bottom row than in the top one.

about the change in the height of a quantity of water with her thoughts about the width of each container, concluding that taller compensates for thinner. She will also be able mentally to picture the reverse operation: pouring the water back into the original beaker so that its surface is again even with that of the water in the other beaker of the same shape. As a result, she will answer correctly that the amount of water in both containers remains the same.

Do their differences in performance on conservation tasks mean that preschoolers and older children have qualitatively different views of reality—different ways of structuring the world? Piaget thought so, but other psychologists are not so sure.

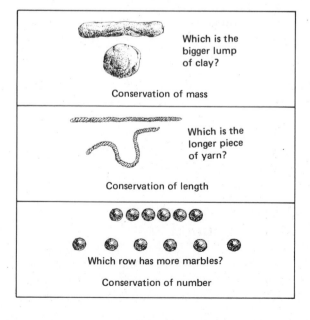

Which is the bigger lump of clay?

Conservation of mass

Which is the longer piece of yarn?

Conservation of length

Which row has more marbles?

Conservation of number

They wonder if preschoolers may sometimes be failing these experimental tests for reasons unrelated to an understanding of conservation. Consider the standard conservation-of-number test. Might some preschoolers say that there are more marbles in the longer row simply because they mistakenly assume that *more* is a synonym for *longer*? Alternatively, might the attention of some children be misdirected when they are instructed to watch as the experimenter spreads out the marbles in one of the rows? So later, when asked again, "Which row has more?" the child may conclude that this is a question about length. Both these explanations are certainly possible.

Psychologist Rochel Gelman (1972) designed an experiment to test whether preschoolers in fact were deceived by the language or conduct of typical conservation tests, though they could understand conservation concepts. She presented children aged three to six and a half with two plates. On one plate was a row of three toy mice fastened to a strip of Velcro. On the other plate was a row of two toy mice similarly fastened. The children were told that they were about to play a game in which they had to identify the "winning" plate. Gelman pointed to the plate with three mice and said that it would always be the winner. But she never described the plate in any way. The children had to decide for themselves which attributes—the number of mice, the length of the row, the spacing between the mice—made that plate the winner. This was Gelman's way to avoid using the words *more* and *less,* which might have meanings slightly different for preschoolers than for older children.

Now Gelman began her experiment. She covered each plate with a large lid and shuffled the plates. The child was then asked to pick the lid under which the "winning" plate lay. Whenever the child picked the three-mouse plate he or she was given a prize. After several rounds of shuffling and picking, Gelman made the critical transformation. She surreptitiously changed the three-mouse display, either by moving the mice closer together or farther apart or by removing one mouse entirely. The fact that these transformations were made covertly was Gelman's way of making sure that she did not call attention to the change and so bias the child's thinking.

Gelman's findings showed that most of the children, even the youngest ones, considered number the relevant attribute differentiating the two plates, rather than the length of the row or the spacing between the mice. Almost no child claimed that a change in the length of the three-mouse row disquali-fied it as a "winner." Many children, in fact, failed even to notice such a change. In contrast, almost all subjects noticed removal of a mouse from the previously "winning" plate. Many showed great surprise that one of the mice was missing, exclaiming, "Where is it?" "Where'd it go?" "Where'd ya put the threes?" Others searched for the vanished toy—under the lids, beneath the table, all around the room. Even more important, the overwhelming majority of children doubted whether a three-mouse plate with one of its mice missing could still be considered a "winner." Over two-thirds emphatically said that the plate had now become a "loser." The only way to fix things, they said, would be to add another mouse. Clearly these children understood that number can be changed only by addition or subtraction—the essence of the conservation concept.

The same results were obtained in another experiment that dealt with the possibility of linguistic confusion (McGarrigle and Donaldson, 1974–1975). As in the classic Piaget study, the experimenters asked preschoolers to judge whether two rows of counters were equal in number. Then, instead of deliberately rearranging one of the rows to be longer, the experimenters contrived to have one of the rows lengthened "accidentally." Most children who failed to make a correct number judgment in the conditions of the traditional experiment were able to judge correctly when the rearrangement was accidental. McGarrigle and Donaldson hypothesize that preschoolers seek linguistic clues in a person's actions. Thus, from the child's point of view, if an experimenter intentionally lengthens a row of counters and then asks a question, he or she must be asking something about that action. The child then focuses on length rather than number.

Perhaps the traditional conservation-of-number test is confusing to preschoolers for reasons that have nothing to do with a grasp of this basic notion. If this is the case, the intellectual differences between younger and older children may not be so qualitative as some psychologists maintain.

Development of Memory Capabilities. If you have ever asked a five-year-old to help remember a grocery list, you surely know how limited a preschooler's memory can be. The child may remember a few things that are especially appealing (cookies and ice cream, for instance), but the rest of the list will be entirely lost. Yet only six or seven years later the same child may be quite adept at memorization. Psychologists wonder what accounts for this marked improvement in memory. Does a preschooler's brain function more poorly than that of an older child? Or does the explanation lie in differences in the ways younger and older children process information?

Recent research suggests that the information-processing factor may be extremely important. Children of six, for instance, have been found to use far fewer deliberate strategies for storing and retrieving information than older children do (Flavell and Wellman, 1977). In one study, six-, eight-, and eleven-year-olds viewed pictures of three related objects along with a card that could serve as a memory cue (Kobasigawa, 1974). One group of pictures, for example, showed a bear, a monkey, and a camel, while the cue card showed a zoo with three empty cages. The experimenter explicitly related the card to the pictures by pointing out that the zoo is the place where these animals live. Later, some of the children were given the stack of cue cards and asked to recall the three pictures associated with each one. They were told that they could look at the cards if that would help them remember. Significantly, most of the six-year-olds virtually ignored the cards. They seemed not to grasp the relationship between these cues and the ability to retrieve information. The eleven-year-olds, in contrast, used the cues quite effectively, often recalling all three items associated with a card before moving on to the next one. The eight-year-olds were somewhere in between. They sometimes used the cue cards, but their strategy was more haphazard than that of the older children. Further testing provided insights into why these differences occurred. When all the children were *required* to use the cue cards, age differences in recall disappeared. Thus at least some of the improvements in memory we find as children grow older probably have to do with the learning of effective retrieval strategies.

Another factor that also contributes is greater familiarity with the items to be recalled. In general, the more familiar material is, the easier it is to remember, and the older children get, the more knowledge and experience they acquire. This link between familiarity and good memory was demonstrated in an experiment. Children who knew a great deal about the game of chess were better at remembering arrangements of pieces on the board than were adults who knew little about the game (Chi, 1978). The children's superiority in this situation may have also been tied to

their storage and retrieval strategies. The more one knows about a given topic, the easier it is to organize its data into meaningful units, thus greatly reducing the demands being placed on long-term memory.

Development of Metacognition.

If you asked some preschoolers to study a set of pictures until they were sure they could remember each and every one, you would probably find that they greatly overestimated their ability to remember the drawings. A quick look through the stack and a preschooler may announce, "I'm ready," only to make a dismal showing on the subsequent recall test. An older child, in contrast, is much more apt to *know* when he or she has fully memorized a list. This ability to monitor one's own thoughts—whether on a memory test, a problem-solving task, or some other cognitive activity—is called **metacognition.** It is another important intellectual capacity that emerges in middle childhood.

Recent experiments have shown how dramatic metacognitive differences can be. In one study, for instance, first-, second-, and third-graders were asked to evaluate a set of oral instructions about how to play a card game (Markman, 1977). The instructions were lacking a piece of information so vital that no one could possibly understand them. Yet most of the first-graders assured the experimenter that the instructions were perfectly clear. Only when they tried to play the game did they finally realize the problem. In contrast, most of the third-graders spotted the blatant gap in the instructions far sooner. Perhaps the younger children failed to process the instructions deeply enough—by trying to imagine them being carried out, for example. In any case, the fact that older children were much better than younger ones at gauging their own understanding demonstrates an important aspect of intellectual development.

What explains these age-related differences in metacognition? One answer may be younger children's limited exposure to such metacognitive techniques as self-testing, in which potential responses are mentally "checked" before they are actually given. Yet is is unlikely that differences in experience alone provide a full explanation. When very young children are deliberately taught metacognitive strategies, they often quickly forget them or fail to see their applicability to subsequent memory tasks. Thus there may be age constraints on the development of metacognition.

Cognitive Development in Adolescence

Around the beginning of adolescence a new set of cognitive capabilities, which Piaget called formal operations, start to emerge. Children are often able to carry out systematic tests to prove or disprove possible explanations. They also acquire the ability to think hypothetically and in abstract terms. As a result, they can solve new kinds of problems that would have been beyond their reach only a few years before.

Piaget created many tests to measure these emerging capacities. One involves four beakers of colorless, odorless liquids labeled 1, 2, 3, and 4, plus a smaller bottle, labeled *g*, also containing a colorless, odorless liquid (Piaget and Inhelder, 1969). The subjects are given some empty glasses and asked to find the liquid or combinations of liquids that will turn yellow when a few drops from bottle *g* are added. The combination that produces the yellow color is 1 plus 3 plus *g*. The liquid in 2 is plain water and has no effect on the reaction, and the liquid in 4 prevents the yellow from appearing. To make these discoveries and to be certain of them, the subjects must try all the possible combinations shown in Figure 8.3.

When presented with this task, elementary school children often begin by systematically trying out all the single possibilities. They may test 1 plus *g*, then 2 plus *g*, then 3 plus *g*, then 4 plus *g*. When none of these produces yellow, they are likely to say, "I tried them all and none of them works." With a little prompting from the experimenter, they may realize that more than one liquid can be combined with *g*. But they then mix the liquids haphazardly and often become confused. Most adolescents, in contrast, can systematically consider all possible combinations. They may need a paper and pencil to keep track of those they have tried, but they nevertheless understand how to generate the full set.

Although Piaget's conclusions about the cognitive skills emerging in adolescence seem reasonable enough, not all researchers have been able to demonstrate them—sometimes not even in adults. Consider, for instance, the problem in Figure 8.4. It is a task in logical reasoning that, according to Piaget, many adolescents should be able to solve. Yet research shows that only between 5 and 25 percent of adolescents, college students, and college-educated adults manage

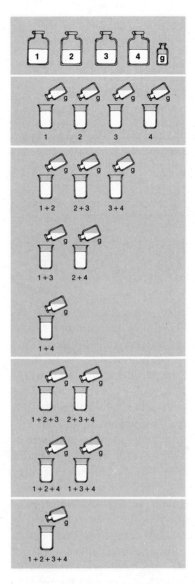

Figure 8.3 A problem that requires the systematic examination of hypotheses for its solution. The chemicals selected by Piaget and Inhelder for this problem have unexpected interactions. It is virtually impossible to determine how the color yellow is produced without trying every possible combination of the liquids, as shown here, and keeping track of the results. Not until children reach the formal-operational period can they conceive of such a procedure. *(After Piaget and Inhelder, 1969.)*

to give the right answer (Brainerd, 1978). Large proportions of teenagers and adults also fail on other formal operations (Wason and Johnson-Laird, 1972; Neimark, 1975). Piaget was aware of these negative findings, but he offered an explanation for them. He argued that the fact that a person has reached the stage of formal operations does not necessarily mean that he or she will always reason logically. A person may misunderstand the demands of a particular problem or find its solution too difficult. Many adults, in fact, may be capable of using formal thinking only in their own areas of expertise (Ault, 1983).

Premise 1:	If Rupert is a dog, then Rupert walks on four legs.
Premise 2:	Rupert is not a dog.
Conclusion:	Rupert does not walk on four legs.

Figure 8.4 When adults are asked to judge whether the reasoning displayed in arguments such as this one is correct, over 75 percent answer that it is. In fact, the conclusion is incorrect. One cannot say from the information given in the premises whether Rupert walks on four legs or not. Rupert may be a cat or a human, so the conclusion given here doesn't necessarily follow from the premises. *(Brainerd, 1978.)*

Cognitive Development in Adulthood

As any reader of this book knows, cognitive development does not end at adolescence. Most people proceed through broadly similar sequences of intellectual change from early to middle to later adulthood.

Early adulthood, from age 20 to roughly age 40, is a time of peak intellectual accomplishment. On any kind of learning or memory task, young adults usually perform better than they ever have before. And if success at a task depends on how fast one does it, they probably do a little better than they ever will again. Early adulthood also tends to be the time when people are most intellectually flexible. They can usually accept new ideas quite easily, and they can readily shift their strategies for solving problems.

Provided a person remains healthy, verbal skills and reasoning ability are likely to get even better during middle adulthood—roughly the years between ages 40 and 60. One long-term study of intellectual performance found that IQ generally increases into the middle years (Bradway, 1944; Kangas and Bradway, 1971). And since middle-aged adults continue to learn and store new information, they are often more knowledgeable than they were in their younger years. In addition, the ability to think flexibly, to shift one's mental set to solve a problem, is likely to be as good as it was in early adulthood. Only when people are asked to do a task involving hand-eye coordination do they tend to perform less well than they used to. This is because motor skills often decline in middle age (Baltes and Schaie, 1974). In all other ways, however, adults in their middle years remain in their intellectual prime.

What about cognitive skills after the age of 60? Do they decline in later adulthood, as many people assume? The most recent findings on this topic are extremely encouraging. Although some cognitive skills do diminish with advancing age, in many elderly people the losses experienced are not great enough to cause significant impairment. Certain cognitive abilities, in fact, hardly diminish at all with aging. Consider short-term memory. Most researchers now agree that the capacity of short-term memory—the amount of information it can hold—remains virtually the same as we grow older (Craik, 1977). When short-term memory decrements are found among the elderly, they are usually extremely slight.

A somewhat different picture emerges, however, when we consider long-term memory. Suppose you gave an elderly person a list of unrelated words to remember. He or she would probably recall fewer words from the beginning and middle of the list than would a younger person. As you may remember from Chapter 6, these are the items believed to be stored in long-term memory. Thus psychologists conclude that older people experience some decline in long-term memory performance. Yet this decline can frequently be compensated for. When subjects are given extra time to learn and recall information, for instance, the elderly perform much better than they do under pressure (Canestrari, 1963; Eisdorfer, Axelrod, and Wilkie, 1963; Monge and Hultsch, 1971). And when people are specifically advised to use mnemonic strategies, older subjects seem to profit more from this advice than younger ones, again narrowing the gap between old and young (Craik and Simon, 1980; Erber, Herman, and Botwinick, 1980; Perlmutter and Mitchell, in press).

Memory decline with aging, then, is nowhere near as extensive as many people believe. Those who study memory in the elderly are often impressed with the high levels of performance that most subjects achieve (Craik, 1977). In addition, research shows that none of the cognitive changes that generally accompany aging is inevitable. Some elderly people suffer no decline in cognitive functioning whatsoever. If there is one indisputable fact about aging, it is that its effects are widely varied. Psychologists, of course, are eager to learn why.

Biology certainly contributes to intellectual performance in later adult life. Identical twins are more

In laboratory experiments or on standardized tests of cognitive activity, older people sometimes do not score as high as younger adults, especially when speed of reaction is tested. But in real-life situations, where quality of intellectual response is more important than speed, age is a poor predictor of performance. *(Constantine Manos/Magnum.)*

alike in their cognitive functioning some forty or more years after finishing school than unrelated individuals or even fraternal twins are (Jarvik, 1975). Of course, these similarities do not necessarily mean that one's timetable for aging is genetically programmed (Fries and Crapo, 1981). It may be that what identical twins share is a predisposition toward, or resistance to, certain degenerative diseases, which in turn affects cognitive functioning. But whatever the specific link, biology appears to account for at least some of the wide variation in cognitive decline among the elderly.

Equally important, however, are environmental factors. An elderly person's response to his or her emotional environment, for instance, especially feelings of loneliness and depression, can contribute to cognitive deficits (Miller, 1975). So can mere expectations of intellectual decline with aging, for there is some evidence that actual performance often mirrors people's expectations (Perlmutter, 1983). Finally, the amount of stimulation in a person's environment also appears to be critical (DeCarlo, 1971; Spirduso, 1975). If older people keep active and involved in interesting and challenging activities—if, in short, they continue to *use* their minds—then there is a strong likelihood that their intellectual powers will not be blunted at all.

SOCIAL AND PERSONALITY DEVELOPMENT

We have seen how a person's cognitive capabilities develop from birth to old age. But equally important as we move through the life cycle are changes in our ways of responding to different situations and of interacting with other people—our social and personality development. Although we tend to stress the individual differences in these aspects of development, many shared patterns are also to be seen. Developmental psychologists try to understand these shared patterns, while still accounting for the wide diversity that exists among people.

One theory of social and personality development that does just this has been proposed by Erik Erikson, a psychoanalyst. Largely on the basis of his work with troubled patients, Erikson has described eight stages of psychosocial development through which all people presumably pass. These stages are summarized in Table 8.1. Each centers around an issue or challenge that becomes especially important at that particular time of life. How a person resolves these various issues critically affects the development of personality and social relationships. If an issue is resolved suc-

TABLE 8.1 ERIKSON'S EIGHT STAGES OF PSYCHOSOCIAL DEVELOPMENT

LIFE CRISIS	FAVORABLE OUTCOME	UNFAVORABLE OUTCOME
First Year		
Trust—mistrust	Hope. Trust in the environment and the future.	Fear of the future; suspicion.
Second Year		
Autonomy—shame, doubt	Will. Ability to exercise choice as well as self-restraint; a sense of self-control and self-esteem leading to good will and pride.	Sense of loss of self-control or sense of external overcontrol; the result is a propensity for shame and doubt about whether one willed what one did or did what one willed.
Third through Fifth Years		
Initiative–guilt	Purpose. Ability to initiate activities, to give them direction, and to enjoy accomplishment.	Fear of punishment; self-restriction or overcompensatory showing off.
Sixth Year through Puberty		
Industry—inferiority	Competence. Ability to relate to the world of skills and tools, to exercise dexterity and intelligence in order to make things and make them well.	A sense of inadequacy and inferiority.
Adolescence		
Identity—confusion about one's role	Fidelity. Ability to see oneself as a unique and integrated person and to sustain loyalties.	Confusion over who one is.
Early Adulthood		
Intimacy—isolation	Love. Ability to commit oneself, one's identity, to others.	Avoidance of commitments and of love; distancing of oneself from others.
Middle Age		
Generativity—stagnation	Care. Widening concern for what has been generated by love, necessity, or accident; for one's children, work, or ideas.	Self-indulgence, boredom, and interpersonal impoverishment.
Old Age		
Integrity—despair	Wisdom. Detached concern for life itself; assurance of the meaning of life and of the dignity of one's own life; acceptance that one will die.	Disgust with life; despair over death.

Source: H. Gardner, *Developmental psychology* (2d ed.). Boston: Little, Brown, 1982, p. 51.

cessfully, positive traits emerge, which in turn facilitate effective coping with all subsequent challenges. Poor resolution of a given issue, in contrast, leaves a person psychologically troubled and possibly in need of therapy. Although much of Erikson's theory remains to be tested, it has nevertheless been quite influential and we will return to it several times later in this chapter. The important point here is that many contemporary psychologists, following Erikson's example, tend to think of social and personality growth in terms of a series of developmental issues. A number of these issues provide the organizing themes for our own discussion of this topic.

Social and Personality Development in Infancy

Formation of Attachments. A baby begins to interact with other humans almost immediately after birth. Adults hold and cuddle the infant, smile and talk to him or her, and provide food, warmth, and other necessities. By the time the child is only six weeks old, a smiling adult face is likely to elicit a smile in return. Several months later, the infant shows signs of having formed a strong emotional bond to the principal caregiver. The baby smiles, gurgles, and coos when the caregiver approaches and cries loudly when that person departs. When the child is old enough to crawl, he or she usually tries to follow wherever the caregiver goes. Since the baby does not behave in this way toward strangers, psychologists infer that the child has formed a very specific **attachment.**

Researchers have wondered what attributes of the caregiver tend to encourage the baby's attachment. Is it the fact that the caregiver provides food and other necessities? Or is it more the emotional security and comfort that a caregiver offers? Some twenty years ago psychologist Harry Harlow and his colleagues set out to answer these questions by means of an ingenious experimental procedure. They separated newborn monkeys from their natural mothers and provided them instead with various kinds of "surrogate

mothers." In one set of studies, for instance, Harlow raised each baby monkey in a cage that contained two surrogate mothers, one made of stiff, bare wire and the other covered with soft terrycloth (Harlow, 1958; Harlow and Harlow, 1966, 1969). Even when the wire

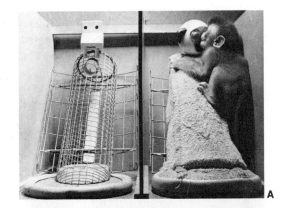

(A) One of Harlow's monkeys clings to its terrycloth surrogate mother. (B) A monkey stays in contact with the terrycloth mother even as it nurses from the wire mother.
(C) Typical posture of a monkey raised in isolation. *(Harry F. Harlow, University of Wisconsin Primate Laboratory.)*

mother was equipped with a milk dispenser, the babies still preferred the terrycloth mother. They spent a great deal of time clinging to its soft body, just as baby monkeys cling to their real mothers. And it was always the terrycloth mother to which the infant monkeys ran when alarmed. Thus it appears that the tactile sensations provided by a mother have something to do with attachment formation in monkeys. Such sensations seem related to the emergence of the mother as a security base from which the baby can explore.

In human infants the formation of attachment is undoubtedly more complex. The baby's emotional bond to the caregiver seems to grow not simply from the tactile experience of being held and cuddled but from many, many hours of social interaction as well. Since in most human families such repeated interactions occur with fathers as well as with mothers, it is not surprising that human infants typically become attached to *both* their parents at approximately the same age (Lamb, 1981). Fathers, in fact, seem to provide their infants with special kinds of stimulation, kinds that often complement those provided by the mother. Fathers are often inclined to engage in unpredictable, physical types of play with their babies, while mother-infant games are usually more rhythmic and less vigorous—such games as pat-a-cake and peek-a-boo, for instance (Lamb, 1976, 1977; Yogman et al., 1977). Such different interaction styles may be very early sources of sex-role learning for children (Lamb, 1981).

Although virtually all children form attachments of some kind during infancy, the quality of those attachments can vary greatly depending on the sensitivity of the caregiving received. This has been demonstrated in extensive research by Mary Ainsworth and her colleagues (1978). They have found that when the caregiver responds to the baby's needs promptly, appropriately, and consistently, the child tends to develop what Ainsworth calls a **secure attachment.** The infant seems to acquire the expectation that the caregiver will be available and responsive—that he or she will quickly and effectively remedy any distress the child may experience. In contrast, a baby who develops an **anxious attachment** typically has a caregiver who responds slowly to the infant's distress, and often with only partial effectiveness. The child seems to learn that the caregiver is not always accessible, and even when accessible may be unwilling to give all the comfort that the child needs.

Subsequent research has shown that the security of an infant's attachment can have important implications for future development. Children who were securely attached as infants, for instance, have been found to be generally less dependent and more socially competent as preschoolers than their anxiously attached peers (Stroufe, Fox, and Pancake, in press; Waters, Wippman, and Stroufe, 1979). Such findings are in keeping with Erik Erikson's theory that development of basic trust through early parent-child relationships is the single most important emotional task a person accomplishes during the first two years of life.

in depth Studying the Emotional Effects of Early Day Care

If formation of a secure attachment is so important in a young child's life, might not repeated separation of infant from parent jeopardize favorable development? This is precisely the question millions of Americans are currently asking because of a widespread change in the way we raise our preschoolers. Traditionally, American mothers have stayed at home and assumed responsibility for early childhood care. But as women have become more career-oriented, as the cost of living has spiraled, and as divorce has become more common, a growing number of American mothers have taken jobs outside the home. In 1980, for example, 42 percent of women with children under the age of three worked outside the home (Waite, 1981). And estimates are that by 1990 this proportion will have mushroomed to 75 percent—a large majority (Urban Institute, 1980). The children of these women are often placed in some kind of group care. This arrangement was at first such a departure from our traditional ideals that many working mothers wondered if they might not be doing their preschoolers harm. Is day care disruptive of sound emotional development? Psychologists' answers to this important question merit an in-depth look.

One of the first studies to examine the relationship between early day care and emotional development was conducted by psychologist Mary Blehar, a colleague of Mary Ainsworth. Blehar (1974) compared twenty two- and three-year-olds enrolled in full-time day care with twenty youngsters the same age cared for during the day by their mothers. She found that the day-care youngsters, as a group, seemed less secure in their maternal attachments. In a laboratory situation in which each mother repeatedly left her child alone with a stranger, the day-care children became more upset. They cried more, engaged in more oral behavior (thumb sucking, for instance), avoided the stranger more, and were more inclined to ignore or resist the mother each time she returned. Early day care, in short, seemed to be related to less emotional resiliency in children.

But many psychologists stressed the need for caution in interpreting Blehar's results. Some pointed out that many of those who had scored the children's behavior in the Blehar study knew beforehand to which group each youngster belonged. This could easily have biased their perceptions, inclining them to see what they *expected* to see. And, in fact, when researchers repeated Blehar's study with scorers who were unaware of the experiment's purpose and each child's background, they could not replicate her findings (Moskowitz, Schwarz, and Corsini, 1977). Instead, they found that children who had experienced day care were very similar emotionally to those who had not.

Still other psychologists argued that Blehar may have been observing only a *short-term* reaction to day care. Her day-care subjects had been enrolled in group care for only four and a half months. Perhaps they were still adjusting emotionally to this new experience. In support of this theory, one team of researchers found that children who had been in day care an average of nine and a half months seemed no different emotionally from home-reared youngsters (Portnoy and Simmons, 1978). Other investigators bolstered this conclusion by observing that the longer a child had been in day care, the fewer negative reactions he or she showed in a number of situations (Blanchard and Main, 1979). Thus the available data seemed to suggest that although children may go through a period of stressful adaptation to day care, regular care outside the home generally did not result in long-term emotional harm.

Some psychologists, however, were not satisfied with the data that had been gathered so far (Belsky and Steinberg, 1978). They argued that much of the research on day-care children had focused on those attending high-quality, university-affiliated centers with excellent staffs and programs. How comparable were such centers, these critics asked, to the kind of day care being experienced by most American youngsters with working mothers? Brian Vaughn and his colleagues were among those who set out to answer this question (Vaughn, Gove, and Egeland, 1980). They selected for study approximately one hundred economically disadvantaged mothers with an infant child. These mothers could ill afford top-quality day care. If they decided to take a job or to go back to school, they had to make do with whatever child-care arrangements were within their budgets—often a neighboring woman willing to babysit in her own home for a modest fee. Vaughn and his colleagues assessed the quality of the children's attachment to their mothers at ages twelve and eighteen months. They found a higher proportion of secure attachments among those youngsters who had been raised exclusively at home. Children who had been placed in day care before the age of one were especially likely to avoid the mother in stressful situations, a pattern that Ainsworth says arises when a mother is repeatedly inaccessible to her baby. This pattern has been found to be related to serious social and emotional maladjustment during later childhood (Sroufe, 1979, 1983). Thus poor-quality day care started at a very early age seems to be particularly harmful to children's development.

Other recent studies have drawn similar conclusions. Kathleen McCartney and her colleagues (1982), for instance, investigated day care on the islands of Bermuda, where 90 percent of children are tended by someone other than their mother by the time they are two years old. The McCartney team carefully evaluated the quality of ten day-care centers. They also assessed in numerous ways the developmental progress of children who had attended these centers for six months or more. The researchers found that early entry into day care (before the first birthday) coupled with low levels of verbal interaction between children and their caregivers was associated with emotional maladjustment. Children who had had these particular experiences were more likely than other youngsters to be anxious, hostile, and hyperactive.

Studies such as these seem to be saying that the quality of early day care is very important. Researchers are therefore trying to specify exactly what makes for good versus poor day-care experiences (Rutter, 1982; Belsky, in press). The Bermuda study suggests that caregiver involvement with the children is a critical factor. Day-care arrangements in which adults frequently talk to the youngsters, share discoveries with them, and show affection and concern appear to be the most conducive to favorable emotional development. This translates into settings with a low child-to-caregiver ratio and a generally small number of children overall (Travers and Ruopp, 1978; Howes and Rubenstein, 1981). Another significant factor seems to be continuity in caregiving. In the study Vaughn and his colleagues conducted of children from low-income homes, 80 percent of those in day care had experienced at least one change in their caregivers during the first eighteen months of life (Vaughn, Gove, and Egeland, 1980). Remember that in this study children exposed very early to such unstable care were likely to suffer insecure attachment relationships. This finding is echoed in another recent study in which toddlers were observed as they were dropped off each morning at day care (Cummings, 1980). Those who were left with an unfamiliar adult became much more distressed than those who were left with a familiar caregiver.

Thus it is not *where* children are raised that seems to make a difference in their emotional development. Instead, it is *how* they are cared for in a given setting that hampers or facilitates good adjustment (Belsky, in press). If our society can offer high-quality day care to the children of working mothers—day care that meets these youngsters' need for interaction, affection, and enduring relationships with adults—there is every reason to believe that adverse effects can be avoided. Setting minimum standards for day care has therefore become a high priority among developmental psychologists interested in this topic. Equally important is the challenge of providing good, quality day care at a cost that parents can afford.

Acquiring a Self-Concept. We have discussed emotional development during infancy in substantial detail because it appears to be an important element in the shaping of personality. But emotional adjustment is far from the only significant event that occurs during this period. In the course of interacting with the environment, especially with other people, an infant also begins to develop a sense of self.

How do researchers know that young children, who as yet have only rudimentary language skills, are gradually acquiring a self-concept? Primarily they observe how the youngsters respond to images of themselves. By the age of six months infants will reach out and touch their image in a mirror. By the

age of ten months infants can use a mirror to locate something on or about their bodies. At eighteen months infants whose noses have been daubed with rouge will note the discrepancy in their mirror image and will touch their noses. Evidently by this age the child has built up a schema of what his or her face should look like in a mirror (Bertenthal and Fischer, 1978). Thus it appears that by the end of the second year, at least, most children have developed a concept of self. With this awareness that their own thoughts and actions are distinct from those of others, two-year-olds begin to strive for greater autonomy. That striving helps mark their entry into the social world of childhood.

Social and Personality Development in Childhood

The role of the parents in a child's life gradually changes as the end of infancy approaches. To the baby parents are primarily caregivers—nurturing, loving figures. But as the child matures and becomes more active and more autonomous, the parents provide less physical care and more discipline. Their tasks now include teaching the child to act in ways consistent with society's notions of good and bad, acceptable and unacceptable. This process of instilling society's values in children is called **socialization.** It is one of the major learning experiences of childhood and has a profound effect on social and personality development. The basic goal of socialization is **internalization**—incorporation of society's values into the self or personality to such an extent that violation of these standards produces a sense of guilt. In this section we will discuss two areas of childhood development in which socialization plays an important part: the development of gender roles and the development of moral behavior and thought.

Acquiring Gender Roles. At a very early age most children begin to acquire the patterns of behavior generally associated with masculinity and femininity. One-year-old boys, for instance, tend to play more vigorously than girls of the same age (Maccoby and Jacklin, 1974), and by the age of about one and a half boys start to lean toward cars and trucks as playthings whereas girls lean more toward soft cuddly toys (Smith and Daglish, 1977). Psychologists say that such patterns are signs of incipient gender roles. The important question is why such sex-typed behaviors arise.

The Impact of Biology. It is not easy to assess the precise impact of biology on what we consider masculine and feminine behavior. But psychologists have been able to identify some behavioral differences that exist between males and females very early in life, before the social environment has a chance to exert much influence. They have found that newborn boys are generally more active than newborn girls (Phillips, King, and Du Bois, 1978), and as young infants boys also tend to cry more and sleep less than girls (Moss, 1967). What this means in terms of future personality and social development is difficult to say, for almost immediately after birth, biological tendencies begin to interact with experiences. Thus initial differences in level of activity may cause male and female babies to experience different kinds of caregiving and different patterns of social interaction. A very active, squirming infant, for example, may be played with more energetically, but hugged and cuddled less. Similarly, a high level of activity could prompt a baby to explore the physical environment more extensively, and this, in turn, could encourage certain patterns of personality development. In short, innate differences between boys and girls in activity level alone could interact with environmental factors to gradually produce a variety of behavioral differences.

Yet some psychologists now believe that biology may play an even greater role in male-female behavioral differences. As we mentioned in Chapter 3, the relative quantities of male and female sex hormones present in the body before birth seem to affect the inclination to react aggressively. Of course, learning experiences also have an influence on aggressive tendencies, helping to create wide variations in the amount of aggression individual men and women display. But in general, it appears that males may have a somewhat greater biologically based readiness to respond aggressively in certain circumstances than do females (Maccoby and Jacklin, 1974).

But though biological factors may produce some gender-related differences in behavior, it is extremely doubtful that biology alone is responsible for all the behavioral differences that generally exist between the sexes. If such differences were primarily genetic in origin, then males and females everywhere would exhibit the same gender-role patterns. This, however, is not the case. Anthropologists have observed marked differences among the world's cultures in the behavioral and personality traits ascribed to men and women (Mead, 1935, for example). Learning, therefore, seems to play a very important part in the acquisition of gender roles. The exact nature of this learning has been a subject of much debate.

The Freudian View. According to Freud, gender-role learning is the result of the **Oedipus conflict,** which presumably occurs between the ages of three and six. This is the time when most children discover the genital differences between the sexes, and this discovery, according to Freudian theory, prompts children to see themselves as rivals of the same-sex parent for the affection of the parent of the opposite sex. Eventually, however, the child comes to realize that this longing for the opposite-sex parent is not likely to be fulfilled. So the child compromises. Instead of trying to possess the opposite-sex parent, he or she tries to be like, or identify with, the parent of the same sex, adopting that parent's values, attitudes, gender role, and so forth. This process of **identification,** according to Freud, is crucial to the child's normal development, including the acquisition of appropriate sex-typed behaviors.

A number of researchers have tried to test Freud's notion that identification with the same-sex parent is brought on by the Oedipus conflict. Their findings have usually been inconclusive (Sears, Rau, and Alpert, 1965) or have not supported the theory. One noted anthropologist, for instance, reported that the Oedipus conflict does not occur among the Trobriand Islanders of the South Pacific (Malinowski, 1929). There the relationship between father and son is casual and protective throughout childhood. Still, identification with the same-sex parent is common among the Trobrianders, just as it is in most other cultures of the world. So whether or not the process is motivated by precisely the forces Freud described, identification remains an important part of gender-role learning and of personality development in general.

The Social Learning Perspective. Unlike Freudians, social learning theorists believe that the acquisition of sex-typed behavior is not initiated by a single event in a child's life, but rather is a gradual process of learning that begins even in infancy. Parents and other adults, social learning theorists argue, shape the child's behavior to conform with established gender roles by reinforcing "appropriate" responses and dis-

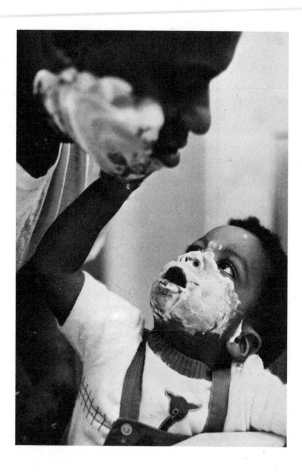

Learning sex-role behavior begins almost at birth. The ways adults respond to children, the toys they are given, and the models they see contribute to this learning process. (© *Burk Uzzle/Magnum.*)

couraging "inappropriate" ones. In addition, adults, as well as older brothers and sisters, provide numerous gender-role models for the child to imitate. The result is that the behavior expected of a boy or a girl has begun to emerge as early as the age of one and a half to two.

As logical as the social learning view seems, however, there has been some debate over the extent to which parents and others do shape children's behavior in accordance with traditional sex roles. One review of nearly two hundred published studies concluded that parents do not behave much differently toward their sons than toward their daughters (Maccoby and Jacklin, 1974). But social learning theorists argue that it is hard to trust the findings of studies in which parents are simply *asked* what their child-rearing practices are like. Mothers and fathers may be unaware of all the subtle differences in the ways they treat their sons and daughters. In recent studies in which family interaction has been observed in natural settings, some sex-role shaping has indeed been found. One researcher found, for instance, that par-

ents are more likely to react positively to a toddler girl who asks them for help or who follows at their heels than they are to a toddler boy who behaves similarly. A toddler boy, on the other hand, is more likely than a toddler girl to receive parental approval for manual skills, such as playing with blocks or manipulating objects (Fagot, 1978). These social influences seem to continue as children grow older, with nurturance and social skills being encouraged more in girls, and physical activity and achievement being reinforced more in boys (Frisch, 1977; Block, Block, and Harrington, 1974).

This sex-role channeling is not necessarily conscious and deliberate. Ironically, even parents who set out to treat their sons and daughters similarly may still end up responding in sex-typed ways. This was suggested in a recent study in which young adults were asked to evaluate a baby's emotional responses to four stimuli—a teddy bear, a jack-in-the-box, a doll, and a loud buzzer (Condry and Condry, 1976). Half the subjects were told they were watching a boy, while half were told they were watching a girl. In reality, they were all watching the same nine-month-old child, who had previously been filmed on videotape. When the infant cried after being presented with the jack-in-the-box several times, the subjects who believed they were observing a boy attributed the reaction to anger, whereas those who believed they were observing a girl attributed the same response to fear. In an ambiguous situation, the common stereotype that females are more fearful than males tended to influence the subjects' thinking. It is easy to imagine that as parents these same people might respond in very different ways to a crying son and a crying daughter—not because they think boys and girls merit different treatment, but because they perceive each child to be expressing a different emotion.

Once a child becomes old enough to play cooperatively with peers, sex-role shaping may intensify. Children, especially boys, are often staunch defenders of traditional sex roles. By the age of five or six most boys have firm ideas about sex-appropriate dress and behavior, and they expect social ostracism for deviating from the norm (Damon, 1977). These expectations are probably warranted. Observation of school-age children has shown that a boy who tries to enter a girls' game on the playground (jump rope, for instance) will be both shunned by the girls and ridiculed by other boys (Thorne, 1982). Thus, although psychologists still know relatively little about peer pressures in sex-role learning, what they do know suggests that this force is often powerful (Maccoby, 1980).

The Cognitive Developmental View. Researchers interested in the cognitive aspects of early childhood development have contributed yet another perspective on the way sex roles are acquired. They argue that it may not matter whether a child experiences external rewards and punishments for acting in what are deemed sex-appropriate and -inappropriate ways. According to their view, children have a "built-in" motivation to imitate the behaviors the society expects of their gender. Children, cognitive developmental theorists say, strive to be competent at all things—including the actions and attitudes associated with being a boy or a girl. Thus, once youngsters have the cognitive ability to understand the concepts of male and female and to recognize that one of these concepts applies to themselves, they will automatically want to adopt behaviors considered to be consistent with this newly discovered status (Kohlberg, 1969).

Note that according to the cognitive developmental view, a child should begin to show a preference for imitating the behavior of same-sex adults only *after* he or she has mastered the concept of gender identity (knowing one's own sex). Moreover, this preference should gradually grow stronger as the child comes to grasp the notions of gender stability over time (knowing that one has always been the same sex) and gender constancy given different situations and desires (knowing that one cannot change sex simply by changing hairstyle or by wanting to be the opposite sex). A number of psychologists have tried to test these predictions. In one study, for instance, researchers showed children a movie in which a man and a woman performed the same tasks at the same time (Slaby and Frey, 1975). In keeping with the cognitive developmental view, those with the best grasp of gender concepts spent the most time watching and learning from the actor whose sex was the same as their own. This suggests that some awareness of gender identity is necessary in order for sex-role learning through imitation to occur.

The cognitive developmental explanation of sex-role learning has received some support, but it has an important limitation. While children are able to identify themselves as "boy" or "girl" by the age of three (Thompson, 1975), it is not until age seven or so that they develop gender-identity constancy. Yet gender-related differences in behavior appear well before then. Kindergartners, for instance, have been shown consistently to prefer same-sex activities (Marcus and Overton, 1978). Even in late infancy children behave differently according to sex. It seems, then, that development of sex-typed behavior does not depend on a constant or stable gender identity (Shaklee, 1983). Many psychologists argue that a full explanation of gender-role acquisition must probably include elements from more than one theoretical perspective (Mussen, 1969).

Moral Development. Undoubtedly, several theoretical approaches are also needed to explain fully how children gradually acquire concepts of morality—that is, rules of proper conduct by which they judge their own and others' behavior. Remember that an infant enters the world as an amoral creature, bent on nothing more than the satisfaction of immediate needs and desires. How is this totally self-centered baby transformed over the years into a person keenly sensitive to the values, needs, and opinions of others? Three of the perspectives we discussed in exploring gender-role acquisition—the Freudian, the social learning, and the cognitive developmental views—also provide some answers to this question.

The Freudian View. According to Freud, a child internalizes the moral code of the same-sex parent during resolution of the Oedipus conflict. This process results in a dramatic change in the child's moral orientation. A strong sense of right and wrong emerges where previously there was none. The child, in other words, quite rapidly develops a conscience.

Research has not provided a great deal of support for Freud's view of moral development. The child does not seem to acquire a conscience as the result of a distinct developmental crisis, as the Freudian view suggests. Instead, moral development appears to be a gradual process that begins during the preschool years and continues into adulthood (Kohlberg, 1969; Hoffman, 1976).

The Social Learning Perspective. Unlike the Freudian view, the social learning perspective can accommodate the gradualness of moral development. Social learning theorists say that children act morally because over the years they are reinforced for "good" behavior and punished for "bad" behavior, and because they are also provided with moral models to imitate. Research has provided some support for these two contentions. Studies show, for example, that children often behave generously after observing an unselfish adult (Bryan, 1975), and they frequently behave aggressively after watching an aggressive model (Bandura, Ross, and Ross, 1961). Also in keeping with the social learning perspective, the degree to which a child is inclined to imitate such actions often depends on whether the model's behavior is observed to be rewarded or punished.

Research has also shown that parents' general approach to socializing their children can affect the extent to which the children internalize moral rules and

TABLE 8.2 MOTIVES FOR STEALING OR NOT STEALING THE DRUG AT VARIOUS LEVELS OF MORAL DEVELOPMENT

	FOR STEALING DRUG	AGAINST STEALING DRUG
Preconventional level		
Stage 1: obedience, or reward, orientation		
Action motivated by avoidance of punishment, and "conscience" is irrational fear of punishment.	If you let your wife die, you will get in trouble. You'll be blamed for not spending the money to save her and there'll be an investigation of you and the druggist for your wife's death.	You shouldn't steal the drug because you'll be caught and sent to jail if you do. If you do get away, your conscience would bother you thinking how the police would catch up with you at any minute.
Stage 2: Instrumental exchange, or marketplace, orientation		
Action motivated by desire for reward or benefit. Possible guilt reactions are ignored and punishment is viewed in a pragmatic manner.	If you do happen to get caught, you could give the drug back and you wouldn't get much of a sentence. It wouldn't bother you much to serve a little jail term, if you have your wife when you get out.	He may not get much of a jail term if he steals the drug, but his wife will probably die before he gets out so it won't do him much good. If his wife dies, he shouldn't blame himself, it wasn't his fault she has cancer.
Conventional level		
Stage 3: conformist, or "good boy, good girl," orientation		
Action motivated by anticipation of disapproval of others, actual or imagined.	No one will think you're bad if you steal the drug, but your family will think you're an inhuman husband if you don't. If you let your wife die, you'll never be able to look anybody in the face again.	It isn't just the druggist who will think you're a criminal; everyone else will too. After you steal it, you'll feel bad thinking how you've brought dishonor on your family and yourself; you won't be able to face anyone again.
Stage 4: "law and order" orientation		
Action motivated by anticipation of dishonor—that is, institutionalized blame for failure of duty—and by guilt over concrete harm done to others.	If you have any sense of honor, you won't let your wife die because you're afraid to do the only thing that will save her. You'll always feel guilty that you caused her death if you don't do your duty to her.	You're desperate and you may not know you're doing wrong when you steal the drug. But you'll know you did wrong after you're sent to jail. You'll always feel guilty for your dishonesty and lawbreaking

principles. Excessive use of power-assertive techniques of punishment (spankings, withdrawal of privileges, physical coercion and threats of force) tends to be associated with low levels of moral development (Hoffman, 1976). In contrast, reasoning with children about their behavior—explaining why a certain act is right or wrong, pointing out how the behavior affects others—appears to be associated with high levels of moral development, including consideration for others, capacity for moral reasoning, and feelings of guilt over wrongdoing (Hoffman and Saltzstein, 1967; Aronfreed, 1969; Hoffman, 1976).

The Cognitive Developmental View. The social learning view of moral development implicitly assumes that a child's acquisition of conscience depends more on the amount and type of training he or she receives than on the child's age and level of maturation. The cognitive developmental view, in contrast, reverses the importance of these two sets of factors. Its proponents (for example, Piaget, 1948) argue that a child progresses through distinct stages of moral reasoning, and that these stages reflect changes in the child's cognitive capabilities, which are broadly related to age.

The psychologist most closely associated with the cognitive developmental view of moral learning is Lawrence Kohlberg (1963, 1969). Kohlberg maintains that the stages of moral reasoning occur in an invariable sequence, each developing out of its predecessor and each cognitively more complex than the one before. He assesses a person's current level of moral thinking by presenting a series of moral dilemmas and asking how each should be resolved and why. Here is one example:

> In Europe a woman was near death from cancer. One drug might save her, a form of radium that a druggist in the same town had recently discovered. The druggist was charging $2,000, ten times what the drug cost him to make. The sick woman's husband, Heinz, went to everyone he knew to borrow the money, but he could only get together about half of what it cost. He told the druggist that his wife was dying and asked him to sell it cheaper or let him pay later. But the druggist said, "No." The husband got desperate and broke into the man's store to steal the

TABLE 8.2 MOTIVES FOR STEALING OR NOT STEALING THE DRUG AT VARIOUS LEVELS OF MORAL DEVELOPMENT (continued)

	FOR STEALING DRUG	AGAINST STEALING DRUG
Postconventional level		
Stage 5: social-contract, legalistic orientation		
Concern about maintaining respect of equals and of the community (assuming their respect is based on reason rather than emotions). Concern about own self-respect—that is, about avoiding judging self as irrational, inconsistent, non-purposive.	You'd lose other people's respect, not gain it, if you don't steal. If you let your wife die, it would be out of fear, not out of reasoning it out. So you'd just lose self-respect and probably the respect of others too.	You would lose your standing and respect in the community and violate the law. You'd lose respect for yourself if you're carried away by emotion and forget the long-range point of view.
Stage 6: universal ethical principle orientation		
Concern about self-condemnation for violating one's own principles.	If you don't steal the drug and let your wife die, you'd always condemn yourself for it afterward. You wouldn't be blamed and you would have lived up to the outside rule of the law but you wouldn't have lived up to your own standards of conscience.	If you stole the drug, you wouldn't be blamed by other people but you'd condemn yourself because you wouldn't have lived up to your own conscience and standards of honesty.

Source: Adapted from Lawrence Kohlberg, "Stage and sequence: The cognitive-developmental approach to socialization," in David A. Goslin (ed.), *Handbook of socialization theory and research*. Chicago: Rand-McNally, 1969.

drug for his wife. Should the husband have done that? Why?   [Kohlberg, 1969, p. 379]

What matters to Kohlberg is not the particular decision a subject makes (whether Heinz's behavior is right or wrong) but the person's explanation for that view. Table 8.2 presents typical explanations given at each of three major developmental levels, each of which has two stages. At the **preconventional** level, a child adheres to the rules of society out of fear of the consequences of breaking them. The child, in other words, acts "good" to avoid punishment. At the second major level, the **conventional,** the child is concerned about winning the approval of others and meeting their standards and expectations. He or she is often inclined to follow the dictates of established authority. The final level of moral reasoning, the **postconventional,** is not reached during childhood. In fact, it is attained by only a few adults (Shaver and Strong, 1976). A person at this level recognizes that universal ethical principles can transcend the laws of society. Failure to adhere to these principles brings self-condemnation.

When presented with moral dilemmas such as the story of Heinz, the overwhelming majority of seven-year-olds were classified at stage 1 of the first level. Ten-year-olds were more evenly distributed over the four stages of the first two levels. Virtually no seven- or ten-year-olds were classified at the highest level (Kohlberg, 1963). At levels 1 and 2, then, children tend either to view actions in terms of their consequences to themselves (reward or punishment) or to conform to rules in order to please others or obey an authority. Research confirms that a child's level of moral thinking is related to his or her level of cognitive development. In general, the more complex the intellectual tasks a youngster can perform, the higher the stage of moral reasoning that child tends to exhibit (Selman, 1976; Kuhn et al., 1977).

Kohlberg's cognitive theory of moral development has been criticized, however. Some have pointed out that a person's stage of moral reasoning does not always closely match his or her actual behavior (Kurtines and Greif, 1974). A person may talk about ethical principles, for instance, yet fail to adhere to them when faced with a moral dilemma. If this is the case, it is appropriate to ask how significant Kohlberg's stages of moral reasoning really are. Critics have also charged that Kohlberg's stages are biased because they fail to consider the values that people are taught

to emphasize (Simpson, 1974; Hogan, 1975; Sampson, 1978; Harkness, 1980; Holstein, 1976; Gilligan, 1977). It may not be fair, for instance, to apply these stages to people of other cultures—cultures that value social consequences more highly than abstract principles or stress obligations to family above all else. Similarly, Kohlberg's stages may be biased on the basis of sex. Women are socialized to accept the values of compassion, responsibility, and obligation, but moral reasoning based on these values restricts women to the conventional level of moral reasoning (Gilligan, 1977, 1982; Holstein, 1976). Such criticisms have helped to introduce well-deserved caution when the meaning of any given person's style of moral reasoning is assessed, especially an adult's. Nevertheless, many psychologists believe that Kohlberg's theory offers a useful way to think about changes in moral reasoning from early childhood to adulthood (Hoffman, 1977).

Social and Personality Development in Adolescence

The word *adolescence* comes from the Latin word *adolescere,* meaning "to grow into maturity." And so the beginning of adolescence is marked by the onset of **puberty,** the period of sexual maturation. This biological event transforms a child into a physical adult and carries with it important psychological and social consequences. The need to establish an independent identity, to gain a sense of oneself as a separate, autonomous person, becomes a major concern during this period. Erik Erikson has labeled the search for a secure, well-integrated personal identity *the* overriding challenge that adolescents face.

According to Erikson (1950), who introduced the concepts of identity and identity crisis to psychology, the physical, sexual, and social demands on the adolescent often produce internal conflict. To resolve this conflict successfully, adolescents must develop an inner sense of continuity between what they were in the past and what they will become. This they often attempt to do by temporarily trying out different roles. Thus one adolescent may try her hand at acting, throw herself into learning about computers, and become involved in politics. By experimenting with a variety of possible choices, adolescents acquire some idea of the lifestyles associated with various roles, yet do not commit hemselves irrevocably to any one. Erikson notes that these experiments with different identities are much more possible in some societies than others. While an American teenager has a prolonged period of adolescence during which to experiment, young people in societies that have either no period between socially defined childhood and adulthood or only a very short one are forced into permanent adult roles soon after puberty.

How stormy is the search for identity during adolescence? The term "identity crisis" has become so common that many young people assume that all adolescents must go through a difficult time to achieve this important goal. But such a crisis is unheard of in some cultures, where various initiation rites seem to reduce the strain of achieving an adult identity. Even in our own society, conflict and open rebellion against parents are not inevitable hallmarks of adolescent development (Lefrancois, 1976). Many high school and college students cope quite well with the developmental tasks of adolescence and make the passage through these years without major turmoil (King, 1973.)

Social and Personality Development in Adulthood

Many people assume that social and personality development slows and eventually ceases once a person has reached adulthood. In fact, Freud argued that basic personality traits are essentially fixed in childhood and that adult identity is established around the end of adolescence. As you will see in Chapter 13, however, there is much debate over this notion of a stable, highly predictable adult personality. At the very least, people face different challenges, have different concerns, and find different sources of satisfaction at various stages in their adult lives. Recent research suggests that these differences in life experiences make the attitudes and outlook of a man or woman of 25 significantly different from those of the same person twenty or forty years later.

If adolescence is a time of searching inward for personal identity, autonomy, and values, early adulthood is a time of looking outward to the external tasks of launching a career, a marriage, and perhaps a family. In one study of the feelings, concerns, and activities of more than five hundred men and women, those between the ages of 22 and 28 were found to be busy making commitments, taking on responsibilities, and focusing their energies on the attainment of goals (Gould, 1972, 1978). Thus, rather than being a period of deep introspection, the early and mid-twenties are usually a period of action.

The decade from age 20 to age 30 poses a special challenge to women. A young woman today is faced with a much wider range of choices concerning her life's work than was her grandmother or probably even her mother. Like generations of women before them, many women in their twenties today still see marriage and motherhood as major life goals. But a growing number are rejecting or postponing childbearing in favor of establishing a career. This means

Today women in their twenties and thirties have more options in choosing their life goals, often combining marriage and motherhood with full- or part-time work outside the home. *(Andrew Brilliant/The Picture Cube.)*

that the age at which many women start their families is becoming significantly older. In 1979, for instance, twice as many women between the ages of 30 and 34 gave birth for the first time as did so a decade earlier (Shreve, 1982). In addition, many other options are available between the two extremes of full-time wife and mother on the one hand and full-time member of the labor force on the other. As we saw in our discussion of day care, the majority of married women with children over the age of six now hold down paid jobs outside the home (Hacker, 1982). For these women, the balance between family and career is often adjusted several times during early and middle adulthood (Sheehy, 1976).

The attitudes and concerns of adults in their twenties gradually start to change as the thirtieth birthday approaches. Many of those between the ages of 28 and 34 begin to question the commitments they have made in the past decade, the values they have chosen, and the goals they have worked so hard to achieve. In short, this is a time of life when many people stop and ask themselves: "What is life all about now that I have done what I am supposed to do?" (Gould, 1972, 1978). Such misgivings, of course, can often lead to difficult and very painful reversals. Marriages may end, careers may be abandoned, and entire lifestyles may be changed. People in their early thirties sometimes feel that any unsatisfactory aspect of their lives must be rectified immediately because soon it will be too late. This period of life has been called the age-30 crisis (Levinson et al., 1978).

As the questioning and changes that accompany the age-30 crisis subside, a person enters a new period of adulthood. For working men and women, the years between 35 and 40 can be especially productive ones. In one recent study of both professional and working-class men, this was a time of "making it"—of establishing oneself in the adult world and of actively carving out a niche (Levinson et al., 1978). Usually this meant moving up the ladder of prestige and achievement in the person's chosen career.

Figure 8.5 A model of the developmental sequence of a man's life developed by Daniel Levinson. The major life eras are childhood and adolescence, early adulthood, middle adulthood, and later adulthood; within each era there are distinctive stages, and between eras a major transition occurs. This model emphasizes that development is a continuing process that requires continual adjustment. *(After Levinson, 1978.)*

At about the age of 40 the period of early adulthood comes to an end and a midlife transition begins. For the woman who has devoted her adult life to the role of wife and mother, a crisis may occur when her children begin to leave home. To adjust to these changes, the woman in midlife transition may search for satisfying work outside the home, returning to an interrupted career or perhaps starting a new one.

For men the midlife transition usually centers around questions about both personal life and career. Like women at this stage, they may wonder: "What have I done with my life? What have I accomplished? What do I still wish to do?" In the study of men conducted by Daniel Levinson and his colleagues (1978), which revealed the stages diagramed in Figure 8.5, fully 80 percent of the sample experienced the midlife transition as a moderate to severe crisis, characterized by a questioning of virtually every aspect of their lives.

Once a person emerges from the critical midlife transition, he or she is firmly entrenched in the middle adult years. For many people, this is a period of greater stability than they have ever known. Income is typically higher than at any time in the past. People usually have confidence in whatever skills they possess, and their productivity is often at its peak. But with middle age comes a new sense of time. People

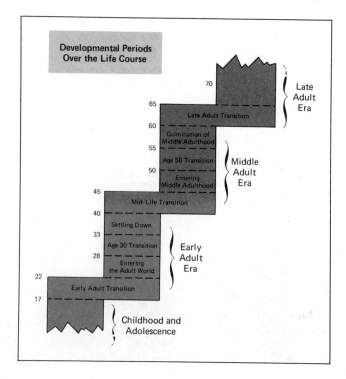

Developmental Periods Over the Life Course

Late Adult Era
70
65 Late Adult Transition
60 Culmination of Middle Adulthood
55 Age 50 Transition
50 Entering Middle Adulthood
Middle Adult Era
45 Mid-Life Transition
40
Settling Down
33 Age 30 Transition
28 Entering the Adult World
Early Adult Era
22 Early Adult Transition
17
Childhood and Adolescence

are increasingly aware that life is finite, and so they begin to think more in terms of priorities. Personal relationships may also become more important. Many people start to report greater satisfaction with their husband or wife, warmer ties with their children, and an increased value placed on friends. In many people these values and outlooks continue into later adult life (Gould, 1972, 1978).

We have seen that making the transition from one phase of adulthood to another is not always easy. But many people cope with major transitions—marriage, divorce, the birth of a baby, the departure of children from home, retirement, the death of a spouse, the approach of one's own death—without undue stress (Neugarten, 1976). Apparently these events are not necessarily traumatic. They become so only when they are not anticipated or when they occur at an unexpected time in the life cycle. Thus the death of a child is much more stressful than the death of a parent, and widowhood when a woman is 30 is often harder for her to accept than divorce at the same age. A study of men who had retired from their life's work found that nearly 70 percent of those who retired as planned were content with their new status, compared with less than 20 percent of those who retired unexpectedly as a result of layoffs or poor health (Barfield and Morgan, 1970). Similarly, a study of elderly people showed that those who were living in familiar and stable surroundings were less afraid of dying than those who were about to be admitted to an old-age home (Lieberman and Coplan, 1970). The prospect of dying in unknown circumstances understandably creates stress. But as long as the expected rhythms of the life cycle are not disrupted, most adults cope successfully with life, even in its final stages.

SUMMARY

1. The branch of psychology that seeks to describe and explain the regular patterns of growth and change that occur during the life cycle is called **developmental psychology.** Answers to the "why" of human development are generally sought in two interacting factors: heredity and environment.

2. Human infants are born with sensory systems that are impressively able. They process information and interact with their surroundings from the very first moments after birth. These early interactions in turn help to shape the child's cognitive and social development.

3. Psychologists tend to view cognitive development in two different ways. Some see it as a series of qualitatively different stages, with the child's construction of reality and related styles of thinking becoming more mature in each successive one. Others believe that quantitative differences in the knowledge children acquire as they grow older account for what appear to be qualitative differences in intellectual abilities.

4. Enormous cognitive changes take place during the first two years of life. Contributing to this remarkable advancement is the infant's substantial capacity for learning and memory. Babies can learn from the moment of birth and they can also remember for fairly long periods, even during the first year of life.

5. The Swiss psychologist Jean Piaget believed that infants exercise **sensorimotor intelligence**—they come to know the world strictly by perceiving and acting in it, not through any abstract kind of thinking. Using this intelligence, they gradually construct a view of the world which incorporates an understanding of objects (the **object concept**) as well as a grasp of the effects that their own actions have on things.

6. Unlike infants, preschool children are capable of **representational thought**—the ability to represent things mentally when those things are not physically present. But their intellect is still limited in some respects. In many circumstances, for instance, they are quite egocentric, failing to take into account the perspectives of others.

7. Piaget felt that the major intellectual accomplishment of middle childhood was the ability to perform **concrete operations**—a variety of reversible mental transformations carried out on tangible objects. One example is the **concept of conservation**—the recognition that some characteristics of stimuli remain the same (are conserved) despite changes in other features. But some psychologists have questioned

whether this general cognitive advance is as qualitative in nature as Piaget and others have claimed.

8. During middle childhood youngsters also become more adult-like in their memory capabilities, partly because they learn to use more effective strategies for storing and retrieving information and partly because they are more familiar with the items to be recalled. In addition, older children develop a capacity for **metacognition,** the ability to monitor their own thoughts.

9. Around the beginning of adolescence children begin to be able to carry out systematic tests and to think hypothetically and abstractly. Piaget said that they were now able to understand **formal operations.** In various tests of formal operations, however, teenagers and adults often fail to perform well, suggesting that logical reasoning is something that is not always attained.

10. Cognitive development continues throughout adulthood, as knowledge and experience expand. Recent research suggests that intellectual abilities do not usually decline sharply in old age, as many people fear. In fact, cognitive decline with aging is by no means inevitable. There is wide variation among individuals due to both biology and environment.

11. In addition to studying cognitive development, psychologists also study personality and social development—the emergence of characteristic ways of responding to situations and to people. Many see social and personality growth in terms of resolving a series of developmental issues that change quite predictably from one stage of life to the next.

12. A baby's formation of an emotional bond or **attachment** to its principal caregiver is a central developmental issue during infancy. Depending on how responsive the principal caregiver is, the child's attachment may be **secure** or **anxious.** The kind of attachment that forms can in turn affect later social and personality development. Another important developmental issue during infancy is the child's early formation of a self-concept—the beginning of recognition that one is distinct from others.

13. When children leave infancy, parents begin the process of **socialization**—instilling society's values into the child. The basic goal of socialization is **internalization**—incorporation of social values to such an extent that their violation produces guilt.

14. One area where socialization plays an important role is the acquisition of gender roles, the patterns of behavior generally associated with masculinity and femininity. Although biology may contribute to the behavioral differences that exist between the sexes, learning appears to play a very important role as well.

15. Like the learning of gender roles, the learning of rules of moral conduct has been explained in various ways. According to Freud, a child internalizes the moral code of the same-sex parent during resolution of the **Oedipus conflict.** Social learning theorists claim that children acquire morality gradually by being reinforced for good behavior and punished for bad. The cognitive developmental view holds that a child progresses through a number of distinct stages of moral judgment, each of which reflects the child's current cognitive capabilities.

16. Adolescence brings with it important psychological and social consequences because it marks the physical transition from childhood to adulthood. Erik Erikson proposed that adolescents go through an identity crisis, which they may try to resolve by temporarily trying out different roles.

17. Social and personality development continues throughout adulthood because people are continually facing new challenges and new concerns. Research shows that the major life transitions of adulthood need not be traumatic as long as they follow the expected pattern of the person's life cycle.

SUGGESTED READINGS

GALLAGHER, J. M., and REID, D. K. *The learning theory of Piaget and Inhelder.* Monterey, Calif.: Brooks/Cole, 1981.

    A good introduction to Piaget's theory, emphasizing the biological model and regulatory mechanisms as well as discussing stages of development.

GARDNER, H. *Developmental psychology.* 2d ed. Boston: Little, Brown, 1982.

    A general textbook that covers recent work on social development, cognitive development, and other important topics.

McKinney, J. P., Fitzgerald, H. E., and Strommen, E. A. *Developmental psychology: The adolescent and young adult.* Homewood, Ill.: Dorsey Press, 1982.

Serves as an introduction to the field of adolescent psychology. Contains chapters on theory and research on specific topics such as physical growth, family relations, and peer relations.

Reese, H. W., and Lipsitt, L. P. (Eds.) *Advances in child development and behavior.* New York: Academic Press, 1982.

Provides good reviews of current topics of interest written by leaders in the field.

9

LANGUAGE
AND ITS
DEVELOPMENT

David Smith, *Voltri XV*, 1962.

Language Without Words

What Is the Basis of Nonverbal Expression?
Biological Factors
The Role of Learning

Do Our Bodies Tell the Truth?

If you have ever tried to learn a foreign language, you know how complex and challenging that task can be. Now try to remember how you acquired your native language. Can you recall learning how to phrase a question? Or struggling with the verb forms for past, present, and future? Probably not. For one thing, you mastered these language skills when you were very young, probably before your fifth birthday. For another, people do not learn their native language in the same arduous way in which adults learn a foreign language. For children, learning a language is much more a process of trial and error, motivated by a desire to communicate their thoughts and feelings to others. Anyone who has ever observed a young child develop language is usually impressed with the apparent effortlessness of the process. Yet language proficiency is probably one of the most difficult skills most people ever acquire. It certainly rivals all others in importance.

That language is central to human existence becomes clear the moment you try to imagine a world without language of any kind. Even the most ordinary activities would be extremely difficult, if not impossible. How could you give directions, explain your feelings, make a promise, or ask a favor without language? Would you even be able to think without language? How could you deduce another person's motives, plan for the future, or puzzle over the meaning of life if language did not exist? Clearly, the ability we call language enables us to perform most of the activities that we consider uniquely human. And language underlies all of human culture, from commerce to games to literature.

We begin this chapter with a discussion of what language is—how it functions, how it is structured, and how speech is produced and understood. We then turn to the topic of human language and animal communication. If the ability to use language in infinitely flexible ways is a uniquely human trait, what is it about the human brain that makes this achievement possible? Language acquisition is also a topic of great interest to psychologists. So we next follow young children through the milestones of normal language development—from first words to first sentences to the mastery of complex grammatical rules and a grasp of how speech should be tailored to suit the social situation. From here we investigate the relationship between language and thought, asking whether language molds our thinking more than patterns of thinking mold our language. Finally, we conclude with the subject of nonverbal communication, considering how people express their emotions through facial expressions, gestures, and tones of voice.

THE NATURE OF LANGUAGE

Language functions as our principal means of communication. This statement is simple enough, but it does not begin to convey how rich a communication system human language is. There is almost nothing you might want to express that you cannot say with language. Why is language so remarkably flexible and efficient?

One reason is that language is *symbolic*—it involves the use of sounds to represent objects, events, and ideas. As a result, language is tied neither to the concrete nor to the present. You can talk about things removed in time and space as well as things that are immediately before you. When you utter the sounds that make up the word *book*, for example, you are symbolically referring to the collection of bound, printed pages in front of you or to any other book ever produced. Note that your use of these particular sounds to represent this object is completely arbitrary. A German conveys the same meaning with the word *Buch*, as does an Italian with the word *libro*. Language is simply a set of conventions that speakers agree to share.

Another reason why language is so versatile is that it is built up from numerous components (sounds, prefixes, suffixes, root words) that can be combined in an enormous variety of ways. Language, in other words, is based on a principle of combination, which makes virtually unlimited speech production possible. This is why precise sentence duplication is so rare in any language. Except for conventional forms, such as "How are you?" the vast majority of English sentences you hear or speak each day are in some way novel. To prove this to yourself, select any sentence in this book and then try to find another one just like it. Your chances of success are very low. The number of possible ways that the hundreds of thousands of words in the English language can be combined is staggering, making exact repetition highly unlikely. It has been estimated that it would take 10,000 billion years, nearly 2,000 times the estimated age of the earth, merely to utter all the possible twenty-word sentences in English.

How Language Is Structured

It is hard to discuss the function of language without also discussing language's structure. In this respect, language is like any other tool human beings might invent. The structure of a wrench, for instance, largely determines the purposes for which it can be used, just as the functions a wrench is to serve largely govern its structure. In much the same way, linguistic function and structure are intimately linked. Lin-

guists have consequently spent much time dissecting human languages into their component parts and trying to specify the rules for combining these parts into meaningful utterances. They have found that the structure of language can be analyzed at three basic levels: in terms of the sounds that make up the language (**phonology**); in terms of the rules by which these sounds are combined to form basic units of speech and by which these basic units of speech are combined to form complex words (**morphology**); and in terms of the rules by which words are combined into grammatical phrases and sentences (**syntax**).

Phonology. Human beings can produce a great number of vocal sounds, and each language uses a few of these sounds as its fundamental building blocks. Linguists divide the sounds a particular language uses into categories called **phonemes**. A phoneme is a class of slightly varying sounds that speakers of a language perceive as linguistically similar. In English, the sound of the *c* in *carrot* is a phoneme. The same phoneme may be represented by a different letter or group of letters, such as the *k* in *kite* or the *ch* in *character*. Most words are made up of several phonemes: *kite*, for example, has three—the sound of the *k*, of the long *i*, and of the *t*.

Most languages use some sounds that are completely meaningless in English. In the African language Xhosa, for example, a clicking sound made with the tongue is linguistically significant; so is a guttural *ch* in German, as in the word *Achtung!* English, in turn, uses some sounds that other languages do not. The sound of the *j* in the English word *jump*, for instance, is not used Spanish. Because of their distinctive ways of selecting and classifying sounds, different languages have different kinds and numbers of phonemes. English, for example, has about forty phonemes, the exact number depending on the regional dialect spoken. (These phonemes correspond to all our vowel and consonant sounds, plus indivisible sounds made by such combinations of letters as *ch*, *sh*, and *th*.) As languages go, English is neither scanty nor abundant in its number of phonemes. Some Polynesian languages have as few as fifteen phonemes; other languages use as many as eighty-five. All, however, are equally effective in expressing their speakers' thoughts.

To convey ideas, the sounds of a language must be combined into meaningful utterances. These combinations are not haphazard. Every language has rules that specify which groupings of sounds are acceptable and which are not. You know immediately, for instance, that the sequence of sounds *mfiydnu* cannot be an English word. It violates too many of our rules of proper sound ordering. The sequence of sounds *mundify*, however, is more plausible, although you may not know whether it is an actual English word without consulting a dictionary.

Morphology. The smallest combinations of speech sounds that have meaning in a given language are called **morphemes.** English has more than 100,000 morphemes, including *free morphemes* (words that can stand alone, such as *big, boat,* and *believe)* and *bound morphemes* (units such as the prefixes *un-* and *anti-* and the suffixes *-ly* and *-ing,* which must be combined with another morpheme to convey meaning). All languages have rules specifying how prefixes, suffixes, and root words can be combined. These rules are central to the language's morphology. We speakers of English know, for instance, that to describe something as "capable of having a certain action applied to it" we simply add the bound morpheme *-able* onto the end of the appropriate verb. Thus we form such words as *lovable, walkable,* and *disputable.* So implicit is your understanding of this morphological rule that even when presented with a nonsense word, such as *gorpable,* you immediately interpret it to mean "capable of being gorped." In fact, your very ability to form the nonsense word *gorped* shows your implicit understanding of yet another rule of English morphology. Can you specify what this rule is?

Syntax. Each language also has rules that govern the way words are combined to produce meaningful phrases and sentences. These rules constitute the language's syntax. The sentence "The old goat ate the rusty can" is a grammatical English statement because it adheres to our syntactic rules. In contrast, "The goat old ate the can rusty" violates our rule for the placement of adjectives and so sounds jumbled to us. In a language such as English, which uses many free morphemes, word order is particularly important. The sentence "Jane hit Jerry," for example, expresses a very different meaning from the simple rearrangement "Jerry hit Jane." Thus a single change in word order can drastically alter the meaning of an English sentence.

The syntactic rules of any language are numerous and complex. Yet at a very early age speakers of that language implicitly grasp and follow them. In fact, most speakers find the syntax of their native language so "natural" that they think it odd that speakers of other languages adhere to different rules. In Spanish, for example, adjectives usually *follow* the noun they modify, not precede it as in English. So in Spanish the sentence "El cabrón viejo comió la lata oxidada" ("The goat old ate the can rusty") is correct. Like all aspects of language, then, rules of syntax are arbitrary conventions.

Producing and Comprehending Speech

Our implicit understanding of the **grammar** of a language (its morphology plus its syntax) gives rise to what is called **linguistic competence** (Chomsky, 1965). Linguistic competence is a person's intuitive grasp of the rules for constructing grammatical sentences. But there is obviously much more to human language than knowledge of structural rules. These rules must somehow be applied whenever we speak or listen to others. This application of our implicit knowledge of grammar is known as **linguistic performance.**

From Strings of Words to Propositions. Some psychologists believe we can gain insight into the mental processes involved in linguistic performance by comparing a sentence's **surface structure** (the words and their organization) with its **underlying representation** (essentially its meaning). For example, the surface structure of the sentence "Hamlet bought Ophelia an anchovy pizza" can be described according to its grammatical elements. *Hamlet* is the subject of the sentence and *bought* the verb; *Ophelia* is the indirect object, *pizza* the direct object, and *an* and *anchovy* are modifiers of *pizza.* But although such an analysis specifies how the sentence is constructed, it does not tell us what the sentence means. This underlying representation can be summarized by units of meaning called **propositions.** The propositions contained in our sample sentence are listed in Figure 9.1. As you can see, each proposition is a unitary idea, and when these ideas are combined in a certain way, the meaning of our sentence emerges. Yet the propositions are not directly present in the surface structure. Instead, the surface structure transforms these three separate propositions into two phrases and a clause.

Hamlet bought Ophelia an anchovy pizza.
  a. Hamlet bought a pizza.
  b. The pizza is for Ophelia.
  c. The pizza is topped with anchovies.

Figure 9.1 The propositions, or units of meaning, of the sample sentence in the text.

When we speak, then, we transform an underlying representation (held in our mind) into the surface structure of a grammatical sentence. When we listen, we do essentially the opposite: we transform a sentence's surface structure into its underlying representation (the propositions it expresses) so that we can understand it.

If you pause to think about these processes, you will see that they are quite complex. Consider the sentences "I have no money" and "I don't have any money." They mean essentially the same thing, yet their surface structures are different. Since the same underlying representation can be expressed by many surface structures, speaking requires constant planning and decision making. Now consider the sentence "Visiting relatives can be tiresome." In this instance, a single surface structure has two possible underlying representations ("Relatives who visit can be tiresome" and "Going to visit relatives can be tiresome"). Such ambiguous sentences are common (Howard, 1983). They suggest that understanding speech also requires constant mental effort.

Psychologists who study language are interested in *how* we are able to perform the complex mental processes involved in interpreting speech. How are we able to understand what a string of words means? Most psycholinguists believe that as a person hears the surface structure of a sentence, he or she automatically divides it into phrases and subphrases called **constituents.** A constituent is a group of words that make sense together. Thus the sentence "My eccentric neighbor has twenty cats" naturally divides into two major constituents: the noun phrase "my eccentric neighbor" and the verb phrase "has twenty cats." These phrases in turn further divide into smaller constituents, as Figure 9.2 shows. It is from such constituents that listeners extract the underlying propositions, or units of meaning, that a sentence contains. And it is the gist of these propositions, not the sen-

tence verbatim, that people somehow represent in long-term memory (Kintsch and Glass, 1974; Kintsch and Keenan, 1974; Wanner, 1975; Ratcliff and McKoon, 1978).

How do psychologists know that listeners analyze sentences according to constituents? The evidence comes from several sources. For one thing, if a reader is shown a passage printed so that each line contains a separate constituent, he or she will comprehend the passage better than if the lines break in mid-constituent (Graf and Torrey, 1966). Dividing a sentence in the middle of its constituents seems to disrupt our usual mode of thought. Similarly, if a person listening to a sentence played into one ear hears a single unexpected click played into the other ear, he or she will tend to perceive the click as occurring near the boundary of a constituent even if the click actually occurred in mid-constituent (Fodor and Bever, 1965). Memory thus seems to preserve the integrity of each constituent by resisting interruptions of it.

Psychologists are not yet certain how listeners identify constituents, or how they build propositions from them. One line of reasoning (the so-called **syntactic approach**) holds that listeners rely heavily on syntactic clues when they analyze and interpret sentences. Consider the opening lines of Lewis Carroll's poem "Jabberwocky":

'Twas brillig, and the slithy toves
  Did gyre and gimble in the wabe:
All mimsy were the borogoves,
  And the mome raths outgrabe.

The words are nonsensical, yet somehow we feel they convey meaning. Why? We are probably using function words (articles, conjunctions, prepositions, and the like) plus prefixes and suffixes and an occasional English verb to divide this string of words into constituents and to identify the role that each constituent plays in the sentence. From here it is presumably a short step to extracting the intended meaning of a sentence when the content words are ones we know.

One problem with the syntactic approach, however, is that the function words, prefixes, and suffixes on which we are said to rely so heavily when dividing a sentence into its constituents are the very words that are most likely to be spoken quickly and enunciated poorly (Pollack and Pickett, 1964; Woods and Makhoul, 1973). Out of context, in fact, these words are often unintelligible. How, then, can they provide the only clues to the constituent structure of a sentence? The answer is that they cannot. Consider the sentence "The vase that the maid that the agency hired dropped broke on the floor" (Stolz, 1967). If we use a purely syntactic approach, this sentence is very difficult to interpret, for one relative clause ("that the agency hired") is confusingly embedded within another ("that the maid dropped"). Yet you can probably guess the meaning of this sentence just from hearing the major content words alone: *vase, maid, agency, hired, dropped, broke, floor*. According to the **semantic approach** to sentence interpretation, just by hearing key content words within a given context we can sometimes form plausible hypotheses about the underlying propositions a speaker is trying to convey. In actual conversations, of course, listeners undoubtedly use both syntactic and semantic clues to make sense of other people's speech.

The Importance of Linguistic Inferences. But our ability to understand language is not simply the

result of our grasp of the rules of syntax combined with our knowledge of the meaning of words. If these were the only tools we had for deciphering language, much of what we hear each day would be incomprehensible to us. To understand why, consider the following sentence: "The policeman held up his hand and stopped the car" (Schank and Abelson, 1977). At first glance, this statement seems simple enough. But stop for a moment and think how you managed to grasp it. Did you even consider the possibility that the policeman, in superhuman fashion, literally stopped the car with an upraised hand? Probably not. This is because part of our skill at understanding language comes from our ability to make inferences about what we hear.

Computer scientist Roger Schank (1983) was one of the first to call attention to this important process. He and his colleagues tried to program a computer to understand English by giving it a dictionary, a set of semantic rules, and the rules of English grammar. But they found that the machine was a hopeless failure at interpreting many sentences that people understand easily. The reason, they quickly discovered, was that the computer knew nothing about the world to which language refers. We humans, in contrast, have a large base of knowledge that we readily use to draw inferences. When presented with our sentence about the policeman, for example, we automatically make inferences on the basis of what we know about a police officer's work and how automobiles are driven. We infer that the policeman is directing traffic, that he holds up his hand as a signal to stop, and that the

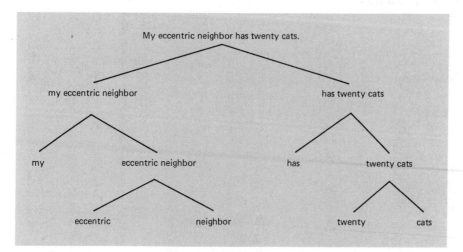

Figure 9.2 Tree diagram—so called because it resembles an upside-down tree—of the sample sentence in the text.

oncoming motorist applies the brakes that actually stop the car. If we did not make all these inferences we would miss the intended meaning of this sentence.

And it is not just a general knowledge of objects and events that promotes linguistic inferences. To see why, consider this bit of conversation:

A: I've got a headache. Do you have any aspirin?

B: There's a store around the corner.

What knowledge do you need to figure out the meaning of *B*'s reply? To a great extent you need an understanding of the implicit rules of English conversation. You need, for instance, an expectation that speaker *B* is trying to be cooperative—that he or she is not changing the subject by suddenly mentioning a store. You also need an expectation that *B*'s response is relevant—that the store being referred to is in fact one where aspirin is sold. Users of language are constantly making inferences on the basis of these and other implicit rules of conversation. In addition to our rules for cooperation and relevance, we also have expectations that speakers will be truthful to the best of their knowledge, that they will try to express their thoughts briefly and clearly, and that they will generally be polite (Miller, 1981; Howard, 1983).

The extent to which we depend on such rules to interpret language can be seen when we encounter someone who does not share our rules (usually because he or she was raised in a different language community). Speakers of German, for instance, are often more direct in making requests or voicing complaints than speakers of English are (House and Kasper, 1981). Thus, when a German who is speaking English tells us to "Open the door!" we will probably interpret the remark as domineering (even though it is not so intended) because it violates our implicit expectations concerning conversational politeness (Levinson, 1983). Identifying the implicit understandings people have about how language should be used in different social contexts is part of a growing field of study called **pragmatics.** Later in this chapter we will see how children begin to acquire such implicit knowledge at a very early age. But for now we simply want to stress that the meaning we assign to a sentence often derives from more than just its words and syntax. Meaning is also a product of the many inferences we make.

Our readiness to make inferences about language is often very helpful, for it spares us the need to communicate *everything* through explicit speech. But the ease with which we make such inferences also poses risks. If people want to mislead us, they can often do so simply by choosing sentences that make erroneous inferences likely. This was clearly demonstrated in a study in which subjects were presented with a series of commercials (Harris, 1977). Some of the subjects heard a version of each commercial that made a very explicit statement about what the product could do, while others heard a version that merely implied the same benefit. (Figure 9.3 gives an example of the two versions for a fictitious cold remedy.) When asked immediately afterward about the content of the commercial, the "implied version" subjects were almost as likely as the "explicit version" ones to say that the advertised claim had been made *explicitly.* They seemed to believe that their own inferences were actually part of what they had heard. This finding suggests that in real-life settings we must often be careful not to let the way we process language cloud the judgments we make.

Assertion Commercial	**Implication Commercial**	**Test Sentence**
Aren't you tired of the sniffles and runny noses all winter? Tired of always feeling less than your best? Taking Eradicold Pills as directed will get you through a whole winter without colds.	Aren't you tired of sniffles and runny noses all winter? Tired of always feeling less than your best? Get through a whole winter without colds. Take Eradicold Pills as directed.	If you take Eradicold pills as directed, you will not have any colds this winter.

Figure 9.3 A sample commercial excerpt and paired test sentence presented to college students by Harris (1977).

HUMAN LANGUAGE AND ANIMAL COMMUNICATION

Psychologists have long wondered what it is about the human mind that enables us to perform the highly complex tasks of producing and comprehending speech. Some have ventured into other parts of the animal kingdom in search of clues. Can other intelligent creatures also learn to use language? Or does language demand some special, uniquely human form of intelligence? Such questions have generated fascinating efforts to teach language to some of our closest animal relatives, especially the chimpanzee. Psychologists reason that if an ape can learn a communication system with many of the basic features of language, then we have evidence that the intellectual powers required for language are not unique to us.

Chimp Talk

Investigations of this kind began in the 1940s when two psychologists, Keith and Cathy Hayes, attempted to teach a young chimp named Viki to speak English words. The task proved arduous. The Hayeses had to shape Viki's mouth and lips in the correct positions to get her to say such simple words as *mama, papa,* and *cup.* After six years of painstaking training, Viki was able to make sounds that roughly approximated four words—hardly an impressive vocabulary (Hayes and Hayes, 1951).

Why was Viki so inept at language? Do chimps lack the cognitive ability to use sounds symbolically? This conclusion seemed questionable, for monkeys and apes in the wild appear to use a variety of calls, hoots, and grunts as forms of communication. As it turned out, the reason for Viki's incompetence at language was mainly physical: chimpanzees cannot learn spoken language because they lack the necessary vocal apparatus. They do not have the specially adapted tongue, palate, lips, teeth, and facial muscles that allow humans to produce such a wide variety of speech sounds.

This realization led to an interesting question. If chimpanzees could not learn spoken language, could they learn some visual form of language instead? Researchers were eager to find out. Psychologists Beatrice and R. Allen Gardner (1969, 1972), for example,

experimented with American Sign Language (or ASL), the language used by many deaf people in North America. ASL is based on a system of gestures, each corresponding to a word. Many, though by no means all, of these gestures visually suggest the word's meaning. Since chimpanzees are extremely nimble-fingered and spontaneously use gestures, they seemed ideally suited to learn ASL.

The Gardners began their research with a young female chimp named Washoe, whom they raised almost as though she were a human child. Washoe's training in ASL began when she was about one year old. The Gardners and their associates signed to Washoe and to one another just as deaf parents might. Whenever Washoe made a correct sign, she was rewarded. Sometimes her natural gestures were close enough to the correct signs to permit shaping. At other times the Gardners taught her signs by placing her fingers in the correct positions. Because Washoe was raised among her caretakers, she had rich opportunities to learn signs while interacting with her companions. After four years of training, Washoe had acquired about 160 signs. A few of the signs she learned are shown in Figure 9.4.

The Gardners saw many parallels between Washoe's progress and that of a young child learning spoken language. Once she had learned a particular sign, Washoe generalized its use to appropriate activities or objects. After learning the sign *more* to request more tickling, for example, she used the same gesture to request more swinging and more food. Many of her mistakes seemed to resemble those children commonly make, as when she applied the sign for flower to all kinds of smells—an apparent case of overgeneralization. Furthermore, as soon as she had learned her first eight or ten signs, Washoe spontaneously began to use some of them in combination, forming such statements as "More sweet" and "Roger come." Later she combined three or more signs: "Hurry gimme toothbrush" and "You me go there in." The Gardners felt that by the age of five Washoe's command of language in some ways resembled that of a three-year-old child.

Washoe's accomplishments were not unique. In another research project, psychologist David

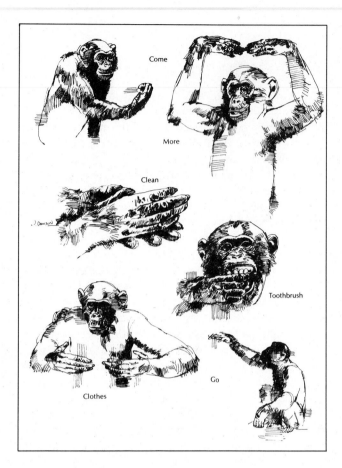

Come

More

Clean

Toothbrush

Go

Clothes

Figure 9.4 Hand signs used by the Gardners' chimpanzee Washoe within twenty-two months of the beginning of training. Signs are presented in order of their original appearance in her repertoire. Washoe not only used signs independently but combined them in sequences that suggest some capacity to employ a meaningful syntax. The most common combinations involved combining signals the Gardners called emphasizers (signals for "please," "come-gimme," "hurry," and "more"), with one other signal. She also used sequences of more than two signs involving names or pronouns, such as "you go gimme," "Roger you tickle," or "please Roger come."

Premack (1971a, 1971b) taught a chimpanzee named Sarah a language based on small arbitrary plastic symbols of varying colors and shapes, like those shown in Figure 9.5. Each piece of plastic stands for a word. Sarah has learned to construct simple sentences by arranging the symbols on a magnetized board. Premack's system is easier for the chimpanzee than ASL. Since the symbols are right in front of her, Sarah can use them as cues to recall the associated meanings. A major drawback, however, is that Sarah is "mute" when she does not have her symbols.

In yet another approach, Duane Rumbaugh, Timothy Gill, and E. C. von Glasersfeld (1963) have taught a chimp named Lana to operate a special typewriter linked to a computer. The machine has fifty keys, each displaying a geometric configuration that represents a word in a specially devised language called Yerkish (after the primatologist Robert M. Yerkes). When Lana types a configuration, it appears on a screen in front of her. She has learned to correct herself by checking the sequence of configurations as

they appear. Not only does Lana respond to humans who converse with her via her computer, she also initiates conversations. And when confronted with an object for which she has not been taught a word, Lana has been observed to create one. When she was shown a ring for the first time, for example, Lana identified it, using words she already knew, as a "finger bracelet."

Can chimpanzees be said to use language in the human sense of the word? This question is still being debated. Chimpanzees do use symbols meaningfully and accurately. And like humans, they are able to refer to things removed in time and space. This is an achievement that the chimpanzees' own call system, used in the wild, does not allow. Finally, there is some evidence that chimps can create novel and appropriate word combinations, such as Lana's "finger bracelet," based on simple grammatical rules. Such word combinations have led a number of researchers to conclude that chimps have at least some capacity for understanding elementary syntax.

But other researchers are not so certain. David Premack (1976) has wondered if the linguistic creativity of chimpanzees may not be limited to word substitutions in restricted sentence structures—"Mary eat apple," for example, transformed to "Mary wash apple." Psychologist Herbert Terrace, who spent nearly four years teaching sign language to a young male chimp named Nim Chimpsky, has expressed a similar reservation (Terrace, 1979).

While working with Nim, Terrace became convinced that his chimp was indeed combining words into grammatical utterances comparable to a child's first sentences. But on analyzing the data he had collected, Terrace began to doubt that Nim's achievements were really as sophisticated as a child's. For one thing, a child's sentences quickly grow in both length

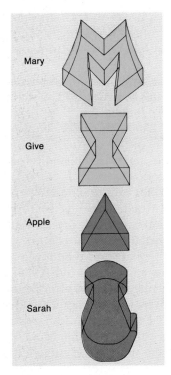

Figure 9.5 A sentence formed with the plastic symbols that David Premack and his associates (1971a, 1971b) used in their training regimen with the chimpanzee Sarah.

Mary

Give

Apple

Sarah

and complexity, incorporating correct rules of syntax. Nim did not progress in this way. Although he sometimes produced fairly lengthy sequences, his grasp of syntax did not expand. Furthermore, analysis of videotapes showing conversations with Nim revealed that many of his utterances were partial imitations of things a teacher had just said. This finding led Terrace to believe that subtle prompting by human trainers, coupled with the delivery of rewards, may play a primary role in a chimp's use of language.

Terrace believes that chimps may have the *potential* to create grammatical sentences, but indisputable evidence that they in fact do so has not yet been obtained. Moreover, there appear to be limits to the amount of language an ape can typically learn. One of the most impressive accomplishments so far has been that of a female gorilla named Koko, who after eight years of training in ASL acquired nearly 400 signs. Yet this achievement is tiny compared with that of a well-educated human, whose speaking vocabulary often encompasses tens of thousands of words. There are also definite limits to the kinds of things that apes can use language to communicate *about*. In discussing the intelligence of lower animals, Bertrand Russell once commented: "No matter how eloquent a dog is, he cannot tell me that his father was poor but

honest" (quoted in Hunt, 1982). Other animals, in short, do not seem capable of ever conveying the rich and complex thoughts that humans take for granted (Premack, 1983). This suggests that even though other animals may have some capacity to learn a communication system with many of the basic features of human language, the flexible, virtually unlimited use of such a system remains the domain of human beings.

The Human Adaptation for Language

Our discussion of efforts to teach language to chimpanzees makes it clear that a chimp's linguistic progress differs strikingly from that of a child. Children's acquisition of language seems amazingly effortless, given the complexity of the task. In contrast, it takes years of careful training to provide a chimp with a vocabulary of a few hundred words. Most psychologists believe that these differences may in part be due to differences between the chimp's and the human's brains.

Brain Lateralization. The human brain is larger and heavier than the brain of a chimpanzee, the cerebral cortex is more convoluted, and a larger proportion of the cortex is devoted to functions other than the control of sensorimotor activities. These are certainly significant differences, and they no doubt contribute to the greater intellectual capacity of humans. Probably just as important from the standpoint of language, however, is the fact that a human brain, unlike the brain of an ape or a monkey, is **lateralized.** By this we mean that control over different behaviors tends to be concentrated in one or the other side of the brain.

Hemispheric lateralization of the human brain was discussed at length in Chapter 3. There you learned that language, mathematics, and analytical thinking are primarily left-hemisphere activities, whereas the perception of spatial relationships, artistic abilities, and the ability to recognize faces are mainly within the right hemisphere's domain. Observations made of patients anaesthetized to undergo neurosurgery illustrate this asymmetrical functioning. In most people, including most left-handers, anaesthetizing the left hemisphere disrupts the ability to sing the words of a familiar song but does not interfere with the ability to produce the melody. Anaesthetizing the right hemisphere generally has the reverse effect: the patient loses the melody but is still able to recite the words (Gorden and Bogen, 1974).

Many researchers believe that lateralization of the brain in humans is the biological foundation of our capacity for language. Some see this foundation as a very general one. The left hemisphere, they say, is specialized for analytical thought, and it is this specialization that makes our linguistic ability possible. Others believe that parts of the brain are specialized *specifically* for language use. But how is specific specialization for the use of language possible when different languages (English, Russian, and Japanese, for example) vary so greatly? The well-known linguist Noam Chomsky (1972) believes that it is possible because the languages of the world have more in common structurally than is apparent at first glance. All languages have rules for combining sounds into words (morphology) and for combining words into sentences (syntax). These rules are similar in certain general respects. Chomsky maintains that these similarities reflect a universal grammar—basic ways of structuring speech that are a product of how the human mind works.

Exactly how the left hemisphere is organized to make language possible is still far from fully understood. Much of our current information comes from studies of people with left-hemisphere injuries due to tumors, accidents, or strokes. When a front (or anterior) portion of the left hemisphere is significantly damaged, the result is serious difficulty both in producing and in comprehending speech. This condition is known as **anterior aphasia,** *aphasia* being a general term referring to any language disorder caused by brain damage. The speech of a person with this problem is slow and labored, filled with stammers, hesitations, and frequent missing words. Particularly troublesome for the anterior aphasic are function words: conjunctions, prepositions, pronouns, articles, auxiliary verbs, and the like. When asked to repeat the sentence "Tom must be in class by ten," for example, such a person may reproduce "Tom . . . class . . . ten." Comprehension of function words is likewise impaired, making it difficult for many victims of anterior aphasia to do much more than guess at the meaning of a sentence on the basis of its nouns and verbs. Thus an anterior aphasic may correctly interpret the sentence "The bicycle that the boy is holding is broken" from the four content words—*bicycle, boy, holding, broken.* But he or she would fail to understand

"The lion that the tiger is chasing is fat," since an understanding of function words is essential before this sentence's meaning can be grasped (Caramazza and Zurif, 1976).

Recovered anterior aphasics often say that listening to language when one has this disorder is like listening to words that sound very familiar but that somehow can't be understood. This description implies that aphasia affects more than the use of function words alone. Producing verbs and concrete nouns can also be difficult for the anterior aphasic. If shown a saucer and asked to name it, for example, such a person may pause, appear confused, and then venture the word *cup.* Comprehension is similarly affected. If an anterior aphasic is instructed, say, to touch his or her elbow, the person may hesitate and then touch a shoulder instead (Goodglass and Geschwind, 1976).

It has been observed that children who suffer from anterior aphasia often recover, whereas adults so afflicted rarely regain normal speech. This suggests that in a young child who sustains left-hemisphere injury, the right hemisphere is still flexible enough to take over speech functions. Yet even with this "filling in" by the right hemisphere, there remain signs that all is not completely normal. Such a child's speech is simpler and less fluent than that of other youngsters (Miller, 1981). From this evidence researchers conclude that children are born with the *potential* for developing language specialization in either hemisphere, but with a strong predisposition toward developing it in the left.

Critical Period for Language Learning. Research into recovery from aphasia also suggests that there may be a **critical period** early in life during which a human being has a special facility for learning language. The classic example of a critical period in lower animals was first described by Konrad Lorenz (1965). Lorenz found that a newly hatched duckling or gosling will form an attachment, or **imprint,** to the first moving object it encounters. As a result, it will follow that object faithfully wherever the object goes. In the wild, of course, the first object a baby bird spots is almost always its mother, so this attachment is very useful. In the laboratory, however, a newly hatched bird can be exposed to some stimulus other than its mother and so become inappropriately imprinted. It can, for example, be made to follow a bird of a different species, a box on wheels, or even a human being. The length of the critical period dur-

Imprinting. A few hours after they were hatched (during a critical period), these goslings saw Konrad Lorenz instead of their mother. Thereafter they followed him around as though he were their real mother. *(Thomas McAvoy/Life Magazine.)*

ing which such imprinting can occur is always fairly restricted. A slightly older duckling or gosling, sometimes only a few hours older, will not form this attachment.

Some psychologists believe that a somewhat similar critical period is involved in the acquisition of human language. This period is said to begin at roughly the age of two and to extend until just before puberty. What is the evidence that such a period exists? If there is a critical period for language learning, then several predictions should hold true. First, children who lose their speech as a result of brain damage should be more likely to recover it than adults, for presumably they are still within the critical period. As we have already mentioned, this is in fact the case. Second, if there is a critical period in language development, then it should be difficult or even impossible to learn a first language (one's native tongue) after this period. Since almost everyone learns a first language well before puberty, it is difficult for psychologists to test this prediction. The study of people born deaf, however, does provide some evidence in favor of a critical period, as do studies of some severely deprived children. Deaf people readily acquire language when given the opportunity to do so during childhood. But if the opportunity is lacking, the deaf have difficulty learning language later in life. Cases of children brought up under conditions of severe isolation also suggest that permanent language deficits will result if a child does not learn to speak before

puberty (Mason, 1942; Curtiss, 1977). One such child spent her first thirteen years in a small room with a minimum of human contact. When discovered and removed from her disturbed parents, she was at the developmental level of a one-year-old. After five years of intensive treatment, the child had learned to speak, but her language was clearly abnormal (Curtiss, 1977; Franklin et al., 1974).

There also seems to be a measurable difference in the ease of acquiring a *second* language before and after puberty. Reviewing a number of pertinent studies, one researcher (Krashen, 1975) found that a child tends to acquire a second language with much less effort than does an adult. He or she may even do so without formal instruction. Moreover, a child often acquires a command of the phonology and grammar of a foreign language that eludes many older people. Yet the fact that adults *can* acquire a second (or third or fourth) language suggests that the years of childhood, although the most efficient time for language learning, may not be a true critical period.

If a critical period does exist, what is its biological basis? What is it about the human brain, at a time when most cognitive processes are relatively unsophisticated, that makes it capable of acquiring the complex grammar of a language? Eric Lenneberg (1967) has argued that a critical period for language may be related to the timing of brain lateralization. He believes that this lateralization takes place gradually between birth and adolescence—at about the same time that the ability to learn language is presumably at its peak. Other researchers, however, question Lenneberg's view. From the evidence of several studies, they conclude that brain lateralization is completed long before puberty. In one study, for example, researchers placed earphones on three-month-old babies and played different speech sounds (like *ba* and *da*) into the two ears. When a baby's rate of sucking on an electronically wired pacifier indicated that he or she was accustomed to the two sounds, one of them was changed. An infant was more likely to respond with vigorous sucking to a new sound played into the right ear (controlled by the left hemisphere) than to one played into the left ear (controlled by the right hemisphere). Thus, even in the earliest months of life, a baby's left hemisphere already appears to be specialized for processing language (Glanville, Best, and Levenson, 1977). Such findings raise some doubt as to whether brain lateralization alone can be the basis of a critical period for language learning extending over ten to twelve years.

LEARNING SPOKEN LANGUAGE

Two four-year-old children were heard to produce the following conversation when playing together:

GIRL: [*on toy telephone*] David!
BOY: [*not picking up second phone*] I'm not home.
GIRL: When you'll be back?
BOY: I'm not here already.
GIRL: But *when you'll be back?*
BOY: Don't you know if I'm gone already, I went *before* so I can't talk to you?

[Miller, 1981]

Children's struggles to express themselves in language often amuse their parents. In this case, besides grappling with the idea of past, present, and future, these two children are still learning to phrase questions. Soon they will learn that in an English question the auxiliary verb goes before the subject, and "When you'll be back?" will become "When will you be back?" Another rule of language will be mastered.

Although the human capacity for language begins to develop soon after birth, infants come into the world totally speechless. In fact, the very word *infant* comes from the Latin word *infans,* which means "without speech." Yet in a few years all children of normal intelligence are highly skilled speakers and listeners. How does a child progress in so short a period from meaningless babbling to the mastery of words and sentences? And what can psychologists tell us about why language learning takes place?

Milestones in Language Acquisition

Although children grow up in different cultures, they seem to go through a similar sequence in learning to speak their native language (Brown and Fraser, 1963; Bloom, 1970; Brown and Hanlon, 1970; Brown, 1973). One child may reach a particular stage slightly earlier than another does, or may express himself or herself more fluently, but all normal children learn the basic features of their language in a similar way.

Prespeech Communication. From the earliest weeks of life, the sounds that babies make attract the attention of others and communicate with them. Newborns quickly develop three patterns of crying: the basic rhythmical pattern (often erroneously called the hunger cry), the anger cry, and the pain cry. By playing a tape recording of a baby's cries on various occasions when the mother was out of the room, psychologist Peter Wolff (1969) discovered that a mother recognizes the differences in the cries of her own baby and responds appropriately. Whenever Wolff played the pain cry, for example, the baby's mother immediately rushed into the room with a worried expression on her face.

As babies grow older, they begin to produce more varied sounds. By three months they can coo. By six or seven months they can babble—that is, chant various syllabic sounds in a rhythmic fashion. Infants' early babbling, a type of motor play and experimentation, is not limited to the sounds used in their parents' language. Sometimes they also vocalize sounds that are phonemes in other languages (the baby of English-speaking parents, for instance, may be heard making a rolled *r* or a guttural German *ch*). For the first six months of life deaf babies babble like children who can hear, a further indication that these early vocalizations are spontaneous and relatively independent of what the child hears. It is only later that children develop the capacity to imitate the sounds made by others and to control the sounds they make themselves.

Although older prespeech babies communicate many things through actions and gestures, they may also express themselves through intonation. In one study, the patterns of pitch in the sounds babies made to convey frustration, satisfaction, a question, or a command corresponded closely to the typical adult patterns (Tonkova-Yampol'skaya, 1973). Babies at seven to ten months of age, for example, expressed commands with the same sharply rising and falling pitch that adults use: "Stop that!" Some months later, the children began to use the intonation that signifies a question, which is distinguished by a sharp rise in pitch at the end: "Are you going?" More research in the area of infant intonation is needed to determine whether this important part of language is indeed mastered so early.

First Words. By the end of the first year, children know the names of a few people and objects, and they begin to produce their first words. To reach this stage, babies must understand that sound can be used to express meaning. Simply pronouncing an English word in an appropriate context is not really enough. For instance, some prespeech babies, following prompting by adults, say what resembles *bye-bye* while waving at someone. But because they do not yet grasp the rather abstract meaning that this string of sounds conveys, it cannot be considered a genuine first word. Children's true first words usually refer to the immediately tangible and visible (Nelson, 1973, 1981). They label people, objects, and everyday actions (*dada, car, sit*) and issue simple commands (*down!*). What these words have in common is a focus on the here and now.

During this stage, infants often rely on intonation to give meaning to a single word. The one-word utterance *door,* for example, can be a declaration ("That's a door"), a question ("Is that a door?"), or a demand ("Open the door!"), depending on the intonation used (Menyuk and Bernholtz, 1969). In most cases, these utterances can be understood only in context. They succeed largely because other people are able to interpret the child's intentions from the gestures, intonation, and context that accompany the word.

This is also the stage when children tend to over- and underextend the meanings of words (Anglin, 1970). A girl who has learned the word *doggie* for the family pet, for instance, may apply it at first to any animal she sees. This is a case of overextension. Conversely, another child may correctly use the word *doggie* to label the neighbor's retriever but fail to apply it appropriately when she first encounters a chihuahua. This is a case of underextension. Through this process of over- and underextension a child gradually develops essentially the same mental representation of *doggie* as other speakers of the language possess.

First Sentences. Once children have acquired a basic vocabulary, they are ready for the momentous step of combining words into longer utterances. But just as the first step on their own two feet must await a

certain level of motor control, so the emergence of grammar must await a certain level of neurological maturation. Studies show that the numbers of interconnections among neurons of the cerebral cortex rapidly increase around the age of one and a half to two (Milner, 1976). Significantly, this is also the time when most children begin to put words together into elementary sentences.

At first children's sentences are primitive. They are short, usually two words long, and largely limited to concrete nouns and action verbs. Nonessential words, such as articles and conjunctions, are omitted, as are prefixes and suffixes (Brown, Cazden, and Bellugi-Klima, 1968). People who know the child can usually understand what he or she means, and they often respond by expanding the child's utterances into well-formed adult sentences. Here are examples of a young child's so-called **telegraphic speech** and his mother's interpretations (Brown and Bellugi, 1964):

Child	Mother
Baby highchair	Baby is in the highchair.
Eve lunch	Eve is having lunch.
Throw Daddy	Throw it to Daddy.
Pick glove	Pick the glove up.

Even at this early stage many children's speech appears to be quite structured. Oftentimes they combine words in an order that seems to follow adult syntax. While devouring a slice of birthday cake, for instance, a two-year-old may say, "Eat cake," correctly putting *cake* after *eat.* This tells the listener that the cake is the object being eaten rather than the actor doing the eating.

Not all children's sentences are simply reduced versions of adult sentences, however. The sentence "All gone sticky" (after washing hands) is just one example of the kind of utterances unique to children. But even though such sentences are not predictable from adult rules, they are predictable from the child's rules. In fact, psycholinguists have been able to specify rules that describe what is acceptable in a young child's linguistic system and what is not.

The range of meanings children express with two-word utterances is impressive. The basic categories of meanings shown in Table 9.1 are based on data gathered from children around the world. It seems that around their second birthday children start to put

TABLE 9.1 CATEGORIES OF MEANINGS EXPRESSED IN THE TWO-WORD STAGE

Category of Meaning	Description
Identification	Utterances such as "See doggy" and "That car" are elaborations on pointing, which emerged in the preverbal stage, and naming, which began in the one-word stage.
Location	In addition to pointing, children may use words such as *here* and *there* to signal location—as in "Doggy here" or "Teddy down." To say that something is in, on, or under something else, children juxtapose words, omitting the preposition—as in "Ball [under] chair" or "Lady [at] home."
Recurrence	One of the first things that children do with words is call attention to, and request, repetition—as in "More cookie" or "Tickle again."
Nonexistence	Children who pay attention to the repetition of experiences also notice when an activity ceases or an object disappears. Utterances such as "Ball all gone" and "No more milk" are common at this stage.
Negation	At about age two, children discover that they can use words to contradict adults (pointing to a picture of a cow and saying, "Not horsie") and to reject adults' plans (saying, "No milk" when offered milk to drink).
Possession	In the one-word stage children may point to an object and name the owner; in the two-word stage they can signal possession by juxtaposing words—as in "Baby chair" or "Daddy coat."
Agent, object, action	Two-word sentences indicate that children know that agents act on objects. But children at this stage cannot express three-term relationships. Thus, "Daddy throw ball" may be expressed as "Daddy throw" (agent-action), "Throw ball" (action-object), or "Daddy ball" (agent-object). Children may also talk of the recipient of an action by using similar constructions—saying, "Cookie me" or simply "Give me" instead of "Give me a cookie."
Attribution	Children begin to modify nouns by stating their attributes as in "Red ball" or "Little dog." Some two-word sentences indicate that children know the functions as well as the attributes of some objects—for example, "Go car."
Question	Children can turn types of sentences described here into questions by speaking them with a rising intonation. They may also know question words, such as *where*, to combine with others—as in "Where kitty?" or "What that?"

Source: Adapted from Roger Brown, *A first language: The early stages.* Cambridge, Mass.: Harvard University Press, 1973.

two words together to express the same universal range of concepts. These basic concepts form the core of all human language. Indeed, a large part of later language development is simply a matter of elaborating and refining basic ideas that are already present at this early stage.

Acquiring Complex Rules.
Two-word sentences are usually difficult to interpret out of context. "Baby chair," for example, could mean "This is the baby's chair" or "The baby is in the chair" or "Put the baby in the chair" or even "This is a little chair." Someone who knows the child has to be there when the sentence is spoken to know what he or she means. The

grammatical information contained in longer adult sentences reduces this dependence on context. The sentence "The baby is in the chair" is unambiguous because of the addition of the verb *is* and the locational preposition *in*. Thus the mastering of complex grammatical rules expands the child's ability to communicate beyond the immediate situation.

This stage in the acquisition of language occurs largely between the ages of two and five. By the time they enter school, most children have a good grasp of the grammar of their native language. This is not to say that children memorize a set of textbook rules. They do not. Indeed, many adults have trouble stating grammatical rules, although they are able to apply them correctly. What children do acquire during this period is an implicit sense of how to organize words into increasingly complex sentences. They also acquire vocabulary very rapidly at this age; as one expert put it, "Their minds are like little vacuum pumps designed by nature to suck up words" (Miller, 1981, p. 119). As their vocabulary expands, of course, children become more and more skilled at expressing themselves.

Children seem to learn grammatical rules in a fairly predictable order. There is some variation from child to child, but not as much as might be expected. Certain rules are apparently acquired in steps. A good example is the use of the negative (Bellugi, 1964). Two-year-olds have a very simple rule for forming negative sentences. They simply add *no* at the beginning (or occasionally the end) of a positive statement: "No get dirty." In fact, in every language studied so far, two-year-olds have been found to use this same rule of negation, even though it is never part of the more sophisticated adult grammar they hear (Slobin, 1973). This finding provides some support for Chomsky's view that all humans are born with certain innate rules for structuring language. As children's sentences grow more complex, however, this simple rule is often insufficient to express what they wish to say. So the child acquires more elaborate rules of negation, rules that build toward the appropriate ones for his or her native language. In English, for instance, a child's next step is to learn to place *no* or *not* just before the verb: "I not get it dirty." The last step is to add the required auxiliary verb: "I won't get it dirty."

Additional evidence supports the idea that children acquire grammatical rules in incremental steps. For example, psychologist Thomas Bever (1970) had children aged two to four act out the following sentences using a toy horse and a toy cow.

1. The *cow kisses* the horse.

2. It's the *cow that kisses* the horse.

3. It's the horse that the *cow kisses*.

4. The horse is kissed by the cow.

The two-year-olds nearly always acted out the first three sentences correctly, but their performance on the fourth sentence was random. The four-year-olds, in contrast, tended to make mistakes on both sentence 4 and sentence 3. Instead of the cow doing the kissing, they had the horse kissing the cow. Why did the older children make more mistakes than the younger ones? Bever suggested that two-year-olds have a simple strategy for interpreting sentences: if the noun and verb occur in sequence, the noun is the actor of the verb's action. If several words interrupt that sequence, as happens in sentence 4, two-year-olds get confused and make a random guess. Apparently four-year-olds have gone beyond this simple noun-verb strategy and have developed a rule that the first noun in the sentence is the actor. This is why they consistently misinterpret sentences such as 3 and 4, where the true actor is mentioned at the end.

One reason why learning grammar is so difficult is that there are exceptions to so many grammatical

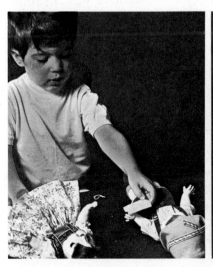 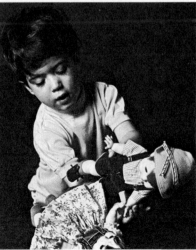

How can a researcher know for sure how a young child is interpreting adult sentences? One way is to have the child act the sentences out. This boy has been handed two dolls and a washcloth and asked by an experimenter to "Show me 'The boy is washed by the girl.'" The boy treats this sentence as though it were "The boy washes the girl." The grammatical rules that he has acquired so far are inadequate to process correctly a sentence in the passive voice. (Bill MacDonald.)

rules. As a result, young children tend to commit errors of **overregularization**—they overextend a grammatical rule to instances where it doesn't really apply (Bellugi, 1970; Slobin, 1972). Overregularizations, which are sometimes heard in the speech of three- and four-year-olds, are of much interest to researchers because they provide evidence that children have noticed and are trying to apply general rules of grammar. For this reason, overregularizations can be thought of as "smart" mistakes. These "smart" mistakes are committed by children around the world (Howard, 1983).

A good example of overregularization is the way in which children learn forms of the past tense in English. At first they correctly use certain irregular past-tense verbs such as *fell* and *came*, verbs that are very common in adult English. Each word probably enters the child's vocabulary as a separate item. But then children learn the general rule for forming the regular past tense by adding a *d* or *t* sound to the end of the base, as in *hugged* and *walked*. Once they have acquired this rule, they try to apply it to the irregular verbs as well, and such sentences as "He goed to the store" and "I falled down" begin to creep into their conversations. It may take a year or even longer before these exceptions are finally mastered (Ervin, 1964).

Such behavior cannot be explained as imitation. Most children that psycholinguists study come from homes in which incorrect verb forms are rarely used. Nor can it be explained as a lack of reinforcement, because most children practice, are reinforced for, and correctly use the irregular tenses before replacing them with the incorrect forms. The only explanation, then, is a predisposition among children to look for regularities in language and to impose these regularities on everything they say.

Speech in Social Context: Pragmatics. We have concentrated on how children acquire the phonology and grammar of their native language because these are such important parts of early language development. Yet, as we saw earlier, speaking a language involves more than just knowing proper word order and verb tense. People must also use language appropriately within a given social context (Nelson, 1978;

Dale, 1980). Studying how children acquire this ability is part of the field called pragmatics.

Researchers have found that children start to shape their use of language to suit the social context at quite an early age. In one study, for instance, four-year-olds showed marked differences in the way they went about describing a new toy to a two-year-old and to an adult (Shatz and Gelman, 1973). Figure 9.6 shows the descriptions that one child gave in these two situations. As you can see, they are quite different. For one thing, when addressing the two-year-old, the child uses many attention-getting words ("Look," "Watch," "Perry"—the younger child's name). Such attention-getters are not deemed necessary when the child is addressing the adult. Note, too, that the sentences directed to the two-year-old are shorter and simpler, assuming much less competence. Clearly, this four-year-old has learned that different listeners demand different kinds of speech. Although the child's ability to tailor speech to fit the situation will become more skilled in the years ahead, this important principle of language use is established in the preschool years.

Explaining Language Acquisition

Parents may believe that they get their children to master language by praising them for correct speech and by expressing disapproval of mistakes. In other words, they may think that they use reinforcement to shape language development. Yet our discussion of how children acquire irregular verbs suggests that, in this case at least, reinforcement is not particularly important. Does reinforcement play a central role in other aspects of language development? Or

Figure 9.6 Speech in social context in a four-year-old. (*Shatz and Gelman, 1973.*)

Four-year-old to two-year-old:...Watch, Perry. Watch this. He's backing in here. Now he drives up. Look, Perry. Look here, Perry. Those are marbles, Perry. Put the men in here. Now I'll do it.

Four-year-old to adult: You're supposed to put one of these persons in, see? Then one goes with the other little girl. And then the little boy. He's the little boy and he drives. And then they back up. And then the little girl has marbles....[Questions from adult and responses from child] And then the little girl falls out and then it goes backwards.

are parents' perceptions of its influence largely incorrect?

When one team of researchers studied tapes of actual parent-child interactions, they concluded that adults greatly overestimate the roles of praise and criticism in children's language learning (Brown, Cazden, and Bellugi-Klima, 1968). Parents do correct gross mistakes in a young child's choice of words, and they occasionally correct errors in pronunciation. But in most cases it is the truthfulness of a remark, not the correctness of the grammar, that elicits a parent's approval or rejection. For instance, when one child produced the grammatically perfect sentence, "There's the animal in the farmhouse," the mother corrected her because the building was, in fact, a lighthouse. Most parents pay little attention to grammar as long as they can understand what the child is trying to say and as long as the child's utterances conform to reality. Thus reinforcement alone cannot explain language development.

Neither can imitation. All children produce sentences they have never heard before. Children who say "All gone sticky" or "I seed two mouses" are not mimicking adults. Adults do not speak this way. Even when asked to reproduce exactly what an adult says, a child may make "mistakes." Consider, for example, the following dialogue between a little girl and her mother:

CHILD: Nobody don't like me.
MOTHER: No, say "Nobody likes me."
CHILD: Nobody don't like me.
(Eight repetitions of this dialogue)
MOTHER: No, now listen carefully; say *"Nobody likes me."*
CHILD: Oh! Nobody don't *likes* me.
[McNeill, 1966]

Clearly, the little girl is not directly imitating her mother. She is filtering what she hears through her own system of rules.

This is not to say that reinforcement and imitation have no impact on language development. Certainly they do. When children learn to say something that other people can understand, this experience in itself is reinforcing because it provides the child with a way of communicating needs and desires. Grammatically correct constructions tend to be repeated not because they are praised by adults but because they get results.

Similarly, although children do not imitate what adults say exactly, adult modeling does influence the development of grammar. One researcher (Nelson, 1977) was able to accelerate two-year-olds' acquisition of certain grammatical forms through repeated modeling. When a child asked, for example, "Where it go?" the experimenter provided a model for the use of future-tense verbs by responding to the child's question in slightly more complex form: "It will go there" and "We will find it." Soon the children began using the new forms in their own sentences—for example, picking up an object and saying "I will get up, hide it." To some extent, then, imitation is involved in learning linguistic rules. But this imitation is not mechanical. Language learning is part of a creative process in which children come to grasp the appropriate structure of speech by screening what others say to them through their own current levels of understanding.

One important question still remains, however. Why do children bother to go to all the trouble of learning the finer points of grammar? "I seed two mouses," for instance, although incorrect, is still understandable to virtually anyone who hears it. So what motivates the preschooler who makes these mistakes to master irregular verbs and plurals? The impetus seems to be a form of what is called intrinsic motivation—that is, motivation that arises from an inner need to deal effectively with things (White, 1959; De Charms, 1968; Deci, 1975). The simple realization that what one says is out of step with what one hears others say is apparently enough to encourage children to strive for greater language skill (Clark, 1982; Clark and Hecht, 1983).

m depth   Learning Written Language

As we have seen, simply by virtue of having others around who will talk to and informally guide them, most children learn to speak and understand their native language quite well by the time they reach school age. Children's next step, of course, is to make the connection between the language they hear and speak and a series of mysterious black marks on paper: in other words, to learn to read. This process is by no means as inevitable as learning to speak is. Some children, especially in parts of the world where schooling is short or unavailable altogether, never learn the correspondence between spoken and written language.

In our society, which places so much emphasis on formal education, reading is a crucial first skill. It is not surprising, therefore, that parents and teachers often become anxious if a child does not immediately catch on to the task of deciphering print. Today an entire industry is concerned with teaching reading, especially with helping the unfortunate child who has reading problems. It has been estimated that as many as 30 percent of American school-age children encounter some difficulty with reading, and for perhaps as many as 15 percent these difficulties are substantial (Cohen, 1973; Bee and Mitchell, 1980). Book publishers, special teachers, educational psychologists, and a host of other experts have joined forces to fight this problem, armed with all sorts of remedial teaching aids, from novel alphabets to computers. But why is all this effort necessary? If we learn to speak our language so readily, why should so many of us have trouble learning to read it?

Some people have tried to place much of the blame on the way reading is taught. Historically, there have been several approaches to the teaching of reading. One is the so-called **phonics approach.** It holds that children must first be taught the sounds that different letters stand for and then encouraged to see that spoken words are simply strings of sounds. The word *mat,* for instance, is formed by combining the sounds *m,* short *a,* and *t.* From here it is presumably a short step to "sounding out" words by blending the various sounds that letters and groups of letters stand for.

But others have argued that in English the phonics approach has limitations because the spellings of words often fail to correspond to their sounds. Consider the words *rough, bough, though, through,* and *trough,* for instance. They contain five different pronunciations of the letters *ou* and two different pronunciations of *gh.* Surely, critics have argued, such inconsistencies fill the phonics approach with stumbling blocks. Wouldn't it be easier to start children reading simply by getting them to associate a whole word with its meaning? A child might be shown the word *look,* for example, be told what it signifies, and through many repetitions come to remember it quite well. This so-called **whole-word approach** to reading became very popular in the 1930s, '40s, and early '50s. Textbook writers selected words familiar to young children and wove them into simple stories,

like the one from which the page reproduced here was taken. Proponents of this approach argued that it spared beginning readers from tedious drills in letter-sound associations. Instead, children could enjoy the pleasures of reading right from the start. Only later, when some competence at reading was established, would the connection between letters and sounds be gradually introduced.

Controversy over the merits of these two approaches came to public attention with the appearance of a book called *Why Johnny Can't Read* (1955). In it reading expert Rudolf Flesch pointed to the disturbing number of American children who were having difficulty reading. Believing that the problem lay in widespread use of the whole-word method, he advocated an immediate return to the use of phonics. Teachers who had adopted the whole-word method for what seemed like very good reasons were now given cause to doubt. Was traditional phonics really a superior tactic? Or would some children *still* have trouble reading no matter how they were taught?

In the past twenty years many researchers have tried to answer these questions. In 1967, for instance, Jeanne Chall published a book called *Learning to Read: The Great Debate.* She reviewed hundreds of studies on the teaching of reading and came to the conclusion that young children who received some instruction in phonics did seem to have an edge over other children, especially in word recognition and spelling. At the same time, Chall found that the phonics approach did *not* dampen children's intrinsic interest in reading, as critics had earlier feared. Even drills in letter-sound associations could be fun for youngsters if they were presented in enjoyable ways. Later studies have supported Chall's basic view that the early teaching of phonics can be beneficial (Stebbins et al., 1977; Guthrie, Martuza, and Seifert, 1979; Williams, 1979). But this is not the same as saying that the phonics approach to reading is a cure-all for reading problems. The extra help that a stress on phonics offers is often rather modest. For this reason, the whole-word approach to reading has not been discarded completely. Most contemporary reading programs sensibly try to combine the best of both methods, often in modernized forms.

Although large-scale evaluations of teaching methods have provided valuable insights into how reading problems may sometimes be avoided, many researchers have not been satisfied with this approach alone. They feel it is also important to try to discover in what ways those who have trouble with reading are approaching the task differently from those who find it easy. Obviously, a youngster with a very low IQ or very little motivation may have difficulty learning to read. But such a child also has difficulty mastering virtually every other subject taught in school. What intrigues many researchers is the fact that some children seem to have problems *strictly* with reading and not with other subjects, such as math and science (Crowder, 1982). What is it, cognitively speaking, that these children are doing wrong? The job of finding out has proved to be extremely difficult. In recent years, however, some promising leads have emerged.

Some investigators have found, for instance, that many children who have a hard time reading also have difficulty isolating the various sounds from which spoken words are built. Isabel Liberman, Donald Shankweiler, and their colleagues have explored this problem in detail by asking young children to listen for the number of sounds (or phonemes) that simple words possess. (*Eye*, for example, has one phoneme, *pie* two, *spy* three, and so forth.) They have found that preschoolers who have the greatest difficulty with this task also have the greatest trouble

Something Pretty

Mother said, "Look, look.
See this."

"Oh, oh," said Sally.
"It is pretty."

"Yes, yes," said Jane.
"Mother looks pretty."

21

A page from a typical reader based on the whole-word approach. The words here were chosen because they are very common in a child's vocabulary. But this book would be of little help to children learning to read by the phonics approach, since there is little consistency between letters and sounds in the words used. Notice the three different pronunciations of the *o* in the words "mother," "look," and "oh." *(From "Something Pretty" by Gertrude Warner, in* The New Fun with Dick and Jane. *Copyright © 1956 by Scott, Foresman and Company. Reproduced by permission.)*

learning to read when they are older (Liberman et al., 1976). Clearly, if someone finds it hard to isolate separate speech sounds within spoken words (persistently hearing words as unified wholes), he or she will probably have trouble using phonetic information to figure out the meanings of written words. One way to help overcome this problem may be to give children specific training in distinguishing phonemes *before* they are presented with letters. Then later, when they are introduced to written language, they need only make connections between the speech sounds they already know and the new visual symbol for each one. Educators in the Soviet Union are in fact experimenting with just this approach (Elkonin, 1973).

But it may not be only difficulty in isolating speech sounds that hinders youngsters who have trouble reading. Research also suggests that poor readers may process written language differently than skilled readers do. More specifically, some poor readers seem weak at mentally converting written words into their sound-related counterparts before they go on to retrieve the meanings from memory (Crowder, 1982). In one study, for instance, second-graders with varied reading abilities were presented with a series of twenty-eight written words (Mark et al., 1977). After reading these words, they were given another series, this one composed of the original words mixed in with twenty-eight new ones. Some of the new words were very similar in sound to words already seen. (If an old word was *good*, for example, a similar-sounding word might be *could*.) Other new words bore no relation to the old ones. The children were then asked to identify in the second series the words they had seen originally. The significant finding was that good and poor readers differed substantially in the kinds of new words that confused them—the kinds they were likely to identify mistakenly as "old." As Figure 9.7 shows, the good readers were far more easily confused than poor readers by words that *sounded* like ones they had heard previously. Poor readers were equally confused by *both* types of new words. The implication is that when poor readers

process a written word they do not mentally extract the spoken sound to the same extent that good readers do. This is one reason why specific training in phonics may provide some remedial help: by encouraging children to translate written words into sound-related representations, phonics may foster a cognitive process characteristic of skilled reading (Rubenstein, Lewis, and Rubenstein, 1971; McKay, 1972; Meyer, Schavaneveldt, and Ruddy, 1974).

This is not to say that answers to reading problems lie solely in teaching children skills for "decoding" letters into linguistic sounds. Some contemporary experts strongly believe that too much stress on "sounding out" everything one reads can make beginning reading a very tedious chore. Instead, they emphasize the need to make early reading a meaningful and enjoyable experience (Goodman, 1977; Smith, 1977, 1982). Providing interesting reading materials, stressing accomplishments instead of errors, and allowing children freedom to guess when they don't know the meaning of a word are all ways to help achieve this goal. In addition, beginning readers should be provided with many opportunities to practice reading in unpressured settings. Reading aloud to parents and siblings and enjoying the pleasures of writing a story or rereading a favorite book can help develop in children a sense of pride and satisfaction in acquiring this important new skill (Glover and Bruning, 1982).

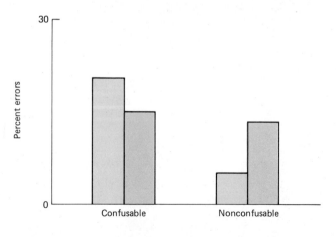

Figure 9.7 In a recognition test, good readers are more likely than poor readers to become confused by words that sound like those they have previously been exposed to in a reading test. This is one indication that poor readers need instruction in associating spoken sounds with written words—the phonics approach—to increase their skill. *(From data in Mark et al., 1977.)*

LANGUAGE AND THOUGHT

There is little doubt that language, both written and spoken, contributes to cognitive development, enabling children to express increasingly complex ideas. But some psychologists have argued that the impact of language on the developing child is even greater than this. According to this view, language determines *how* people think about objects and events, as well as *what* they are able to think about. "The limits of my language," wrote philosopher Ludwig Wittgenstein, "mean the limits of my world" (1963). Yet a moment's reflection quickly suggests that the relationship between language and thought cannot be strictly one-sided. If language is able to influence thought, thought must also be able to influence language. At the very least, human cognitive capabilities must impose some limit on how language can be structured and used. And since language is a means of communication, a way of conveying information about objects and events, it seems likely that language will be influenced by what people experience and learn. In the following sections we will trace these two important threads: the influence of language on thought and the influence of thought on language.

How Language Influences Thought

In the twentieth century, the strongest proponent of the idea that language shapes thought was the linguist Benjamin Lee Whorf. Whorf argued that the way people perceive the world is determined largely by the unique vocabulary and structural rules of their native language (Whorf, 1956). English, for example, has a single word *snow,* while Eskimo has more than twenty terms for various types of snow—fluffy, drifting, packed, and so forth. This difference has important implications, according to Whorf. He argued that when Eskimos gaze out across a winter landscape, their language forces them to perceive certain qualities of snow that the typical speaker of English is inclined to ignore. This tendency is often called *forced observation.* Whorf believed that the grammatical conventions of a language affect thought in a similar way. Consider one of the differences he noted between English grammar and the grammar of the language spoken by the Hopi Indians. Whorf called Hopi a

"timeless" language because, although it recognizes duration, it does not force a speaker to distinguish between the present, past, and future of an event. English, in contrast, always does so. Speakers must either inflect their verbs to show tense ("He talks," "He talked") or otherwise designate timing through their choice of words ("Tomorrow I talk"). Following Whorf's reasoning, this grammatical convention might be said to account in part for the care with which Americans keep track of time, their tendency to think of time in quantifiable terms, and their obsession with speed and efficiency. In other words, when an American child acquires language, he or she, according to Whorf, also acquires a particular world view. The notion that language heavily influences thought is called the **linguistic relativity hypothesis.** Some of its far-reaching implications are spelled out in George Orwell's chilling novel *1984,* in which a tyrannical government sets out to control all thought by removing certain words from the language, coining new ones, and redefining others (sometimes to mean their exact opposite).

Does language actually influence thought to the extent that Whorf believed? Recent evidence suggests that his claims were a bit too sweeping. Consider, for example, the perception of color. Although people tend to think of their own way of naming colors as the natural way, other languages have quite different systems, as Figure 9.8 shows. In fact, the number of basic color terms in a language (those terms that consist of one word and are not subsumed under another color) varies from two to eleven. Do people whose language has only a few basic color terms perceive the same distinctions in hue that people whose language has more basic terms perceive? According to Whorf's linguistic relativity hypothesis, they should not. Yet studies of actual perception show that they do.

Brent Berlin and Paul Kay (1969) demonstrated this by preparing a chart with 320 small squares of color, virtually all the colors that the human eye is capable of distinguishing. They then asked native speakers of dozens of languages to point out the best example of each of the basic color terms in their language. With the exception of languages that have only two basic color terms, the choices were virtually identical from one language to the next. The Navaho *lichi* is the same as the Japanese *aka,* the Eskimo *an-*

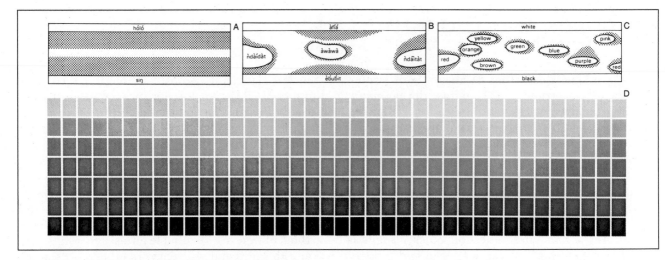

Figure 9.8 Some of Berlin and Kay's evidence that there is a universal cognitive basis for the naming of colors. The large color chart (D) shows most of the color chips Berlin and Kay presented to members of various cultures. (They also presented a black chip, a white chip, and several shades of gray chips.) The three small diagrams correspond to the large color chart, with the bands at the top and bottom of each diagram corresponding to the black and white not shown in the large chart. (Grays are not shown at all.) Each diagram shows the names that members of a particular culture applied to various chips. A name inside an outlined area indicates that it was applied to all the chips that correspond to that area in the large chart. The surrounding gray areas indicate chips to which that name was applied with less certainty. Thus, English speakers (C) designate as "green" a small set of chips that are included in a somewhat larger set of chips called "awawa" by South Nigerian speakers of Ibibio (B). These chips in turn are among an even larger set of chips for which the people of New Guinea who speak Jalé (A) have no name at all. (*After Berlin and Kay, 1969.*)

paluktak, and the English *red.* What varies is where the boundaries of basic color categories are drawn. Whether pink is included in red, for example, or is given a separate label depends on the number of basic color terms that a language has.

Berlin and Kay concluded that all people find certain basic colors more salient than others. These they called *focal colors.* Even when a language does not have a basic term for every focal color, speakers of that language can easily learn invented terms for the missing ones. Indeed, infants seem to categorize the color spectrum into the basic focal colors long before they learn labels for them (Bornstein, Kessen, and Weiskopf, 1976). Thus, although languages may categorize stimuli in different ways, people seem to perceive their physical surroundings in much the same way.

How Thought Influences Language

Such evidence as that obtained by Berlin and Kay has led most psychologists to conclude that Whorf overestimated the control of language over thought. The extent to which language actually limits thought appears to be small. Consequently, interest has now shifted to the opposite side of the relationship between language and thought—that is, the extent to which thought influences language.

One effort this shift has prompted is a search for **linguistic universals**—features found in *all* languages as a result of shared characteristics of thought. Color terms again provide a good example. Because of the structure of the human visual system, most people see the color spectrum in much the same way. (For a fuller discussion and some exceptions to the rule, see Chapter 4.) Studies show that this shared perceptual process leads to a rather startling regularity among cultures in their selection of basic color terms (Berlin and Kay, 1969). Regardless of the number of basic color terms a given language has, those terms always have their focal points in the colors that speakers of English call black, white, red, yellow, green, blue, brown, purple, pink, orange, and gray. Furthermore, color terms are generally incorporated into a language in a fairly set order. If a language has only two such terms, they are always the colors black and white (often more appropriately translated *dark* and *light.*) If a language has a third color term, that term will invariably be red. If a fourth color term exists, the choice is usually made from among the colors yellow, green, and blue. The complete sequence is illustrated in Figure 9.9. Thus there is a universal pat-

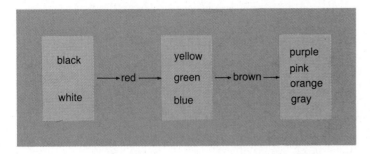

Figure 9.9 The sequence in which color terms are incorporated into a language.

tern to the ways in which languages select their basic color terms, a pattern that is due to perceptual processes that all humans tend to share. In much the same way, other universal aspects of human perception and thought appear to generate linguistic universals.

LANGUAGE WITHOUT WORDS

Consider this photograph. Not a word is being exchanged between these people. Does this mean that they are not communicating their emotions? Obviously not. The man's folded arms, the tilt of his head, his averted eyes all suggest a stubborn form of anger. The woman, in contrast, conveys resignation and despair by her bowed head, her stooped shoulders, and the way she has buried her face in her hand. We would be incredulous if someone tried to tell us that this domestic scene involved a casual conversation about a neighbor's new car. Powerful emotions are obviously being expressed here.

Words, then, are only one way in which we convey our thoughts and feelings to others. Spoken language is almost always accompanied by a diversity of nonverbal cues—facial expressions, body movements, pitch and tone of voice—that may reinforce, modify, or even reverse the meaning of what we express with words. In this concluding section we will investigate the subject of nonverbal communication.

People who live together can often "read" each other's nonverbal cues about their emotional states with lightning rapidity. (*Thomas Höpker/Woodfin Camp & Assoc.*)

What Is the Basis of Nonverbal Expression?

The ability to convey messages without the use of words appears to be based on a combination of biological and learned factors. People of widely diverse cultures show a great deal of similarity in the postures, gestures, and facial expressions they use to convey a variety of emotions, and this suggests a common biological foundation. However, there are also differences in nonverbal modes of expression among various cultural groups. Otto Klineberg (1938) pointed out, for example, that in Chinese literature the expression "He scratched his ears and cheeks" was supposed to let the reader know that the person was happy. In Western culture, this description might be interpreted as indicating that the person was anxious, even distraught. Thus learning, as well as biology, appears to play an important role in shaping the nonverbal ways in which people express their feelings.

Biological Factors. In his book *The Expression of the Emotions in Man and Animals* (1872), Charles Darwin asserted that many of our patterns of nonverbal expression are inherited—that they evolved because they had survival value. When we are enraged, for example, we commonly grimace and bare our teeth. Other animals also bare their teeth as a threat or when preparing to fight, thus warning their enemies that an attack is impending and perhaps preventing a violent encounter. According to Darwin, the baring of teeth served a similar communication function for our early ancestors. Although human aggression today seldom involves biting, this way of expressing a threat is still characteristic of our species.

One of the most frequently cited pieces of evidence supporting the proposition that nonverbal expression has biological underpinnings is the study of a ten-year-old girl who had been deaf and blind from birth (Goodenough, 1932). Obviously the little girl could not have learned nonverbal cues by observation, so her behavior was presumed to reflect primarily her innate tendencies. When the girl displayed pleasure on finding a doll hidden in her clothing, she "threw herself back in her chair. . . . Her laughter was clear and musical, in no way distinguishable from that of a normal child." The girl also showed anger in very characteristic ways. "Mild forms of resentment are shown by turning away her head, pouting the lips, or frowning. . . . More intense forms are shown by throwing back the head and shaking it from side to side, during which the lips are retracted, exposing the teeth which are sometimes clenched." Thus, despite some differences, the way this child expressed common emotions was remarkably similar to the patterns of emotional expression in most normal ten-year-olds. Later studies of disabled children have produced similar findings (Eibl-Eibesfeldt, 1970). A blind child will smile with pleasure without ever having seen a smiling face.

Finally, evidence that biological factors play a significant role in nonverbal expression also comes from cross-cultural research. In one study, people from different countries were asked to identify the emotions expressed in a series of photographs of faces, some of which are shown in Figure 9.10. Anger, fear, disgust, surprise, and happiness were consistently recognizable, regardless of the culture from which a subject came (Ekman and Friesen, 1974). Even members of New Guinea tribes, who had had little previous contact with Westerners and their characteristic patterns of expression, had little trouble labeling these basic emotions. Such evidence argues in favor of a strong biological component in certain aspects of nonverbal communication.

The Role of Learning. People of different cultures do vary, however, in their use of certain other nonverbal cues to convey emotion. Such differences have been suggested by the fact that people from different countries tend to vary consistently in the scores they receive on a test known as the Profile of Nonverbal Sensitivity, or PONS, which measures the ability to decode nonverbal messages. After administering the PONS to more than two thousand subjects from twenty nations, one group of researchers found that people from cultures similar to that of the United States (where the test was developed) performed best. Although all subjects did better on the test than would occur by chance, the differences obtained strongly suggest that some aspects of nonverbal expression are culturally learned (Hall et al., 1978).

Additional evidence for the role of learning in nonverbal expression is provided by the fact that men and women differ in their nonverbal display of emotion. When researcher Ross Buck (1976) showed the same series of emotion-arousing pictures to a group of men and women, observers could guess the content of the pictures much more easily from the faces

Photograph Judged						
Judgment	Happiness	Disgust	Surprise	Sadness	Anger	Fear
Culture			Percent Who Agreed with Judgment			
99 Americans	97	92	95	84	67	85
40 Brazilians	95	97	87	59	90	67
119 Chileans	95	92	93	88	94	68
168 Argentinians	98	92	95	78	90	54
29 Japanese	100	90	100	62	90	66

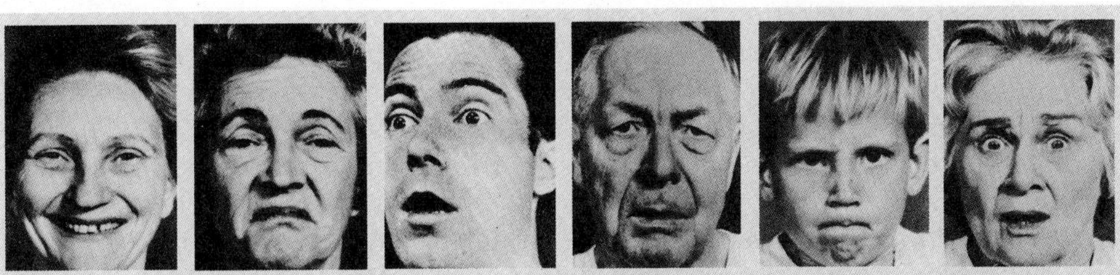

Figure 9.10 As this table indicates, there is a great deal of agreement among the members of different cultures about the meaning of facial expressions. This suggests that we are biologically programmed to recognize and produce the emotions conveyed by certain facial expressions. *(After Ekman, Friesen, and Ellsworth, 1972.)*

of the women than from those of the men. Even though the men often reacted with increased heart rate and sweating palms, they kept their faces "masked." Significantly, this sex-based difference in emotional expressiveness, according to Buck, does not exist in preschool children. Although young children vary in their responses to emotion-arousing pictures, their varied reactions are a function of personality, not of gender. In the process of growing up, boys apparently learn to control certain aspects of emotional expression. Thus adults' nonverbal response to emotion-arousing situations does not seem strictly a matter of biological makeup.

Finally, studies of nonhuman primates also support the conclusion that the nonverbal expression of emotion is to some extent learned. Experiments have shown that under normal circumstances monkeys and apes use facial expressions and body language to communicate emotion, just as humans do. One study disclosed that rhesus monkeys knew when to save a fellow monkey from an impending electric shock by watching the emotion of fear cross the other monkey's face (Miller, Caul, and Mirsky, 1967). It is significant that monkeys raised in social isolation were notably retarded in the nonverbal skills required by this task. They usually lacked the ability both to display an appropriate facial expression when shock was impending and to interpret the nonverbal signs of fear expressed by other monkeys. In rhesus monkeys, then, early social contact appears to be critical for the proper development of emotional expression. Some researchers believe that this may be true of people as well. It has been suggested that the damaging effects of early isolation from human contact may be partly the result of the isolated child's failure to develop basic nonverbal communication skills (Mason, 1961).

Do Our Bodies Tell the Truth?

It's not always a simple matter to decode another person's nonverbal messages, although apparently we can learn to do so. Adults are more adept at interpreting such messages than children because over the years they have observed people's body language in a variety of situations. Women, it is interesting to note, are generally better at detecting nonverbal cues than men are, perhaps because girls are socialized to be more sensitive to the feelings of others (Rosenthal et al., 1974). Whatever our skills in perceiving the nonverbal messages others send, how much faith can we put in the messages we get?

People tend to trust nonverbal messages (Mehrabian, 1972; Ekman and Friesen, 1969). When verbal and nonverbal information is contradictory—when, for example, a person denies that she is angry while repeatedly clenching and unclenching her fist—we generally conclude that the nonverbal message is the true one. This is because most people believe that body language is extremely difficult to control. Psychologists have shown that there may be some truth to this common assumption. Body movement is particularly difficult to disguise—more so than facial expressions. In one experiment designed to test our control over nonverbal cues (Ekman and Friesen, 1969, 1974), subjects watched a gory film showing amputations and burn victims. They were then asked to conceal the true nature of the film in describing it to others. When observers could see only a speaker's head and face, they could not distinguish the subjects,

who were lying, from the members of a control group, who were truthfully describing a pleasant film. But when given the opportunity to view the rest of the speaker's body, many of the observers could perceive deception. Apparently the liars managed to mask their feelings with a pleasant smile, but their anxiety showed in the movements of their bodies. Of course, whether the people we are trying to deceive do indeed notice such "leaks" through our nonverbal channels depends on a number of factors, including the strength of the emotions we are trying to conceal and how well our observers know us (Miller and Burgoon, 1982).

It is not difficult to imagine the problems in interpersonal communication that incongruous nonverbal cues can cause—not just cues that we hope others won't notice, but also nonverbal cues that we are totally unaware of producing. Unintended nonverbal messages can adversely affect many important relationships, such as those between doctors and patients, teachers and students, employers and employees, and husbands and wives. A better understanding of the ways in which we "speak" without words is clearly a vital step in improving our interactions with others.

SUMMARY

1. Language functions efficiently as our principal means of communication first because it uses arbitrary symbols that can refer to things removed in time and space, and second because its components can be combined in an almost endless variety of ways.

2. Language can be divided into three basic levels of structure. **Phonology** refers to the sounds that make up a language. The fundamental speech sounds used in a given language are called that language's **phonemes.** The rules by which those sounds are combined to form words make up the language's **morphology. Morphemes** are the smallest combinations of speech sounds that have meaning in a given language. Finally, the **syntax** of a language consists of the rules specifying how words are combined to produce phrases and sentences.

3. In the process of using language we exhibit both **linguistic competence**—our understanding of the **grammar** (morphology and syntax) of a language—and **linguistic performance**—the ability to apply this

knowledge in speaking and listening. One useful way of analyzing a sentence is to contrast its **surface structure** (the words and their organization) with is **underlying representation** or meaning, which in turn can be expressed by one or more **propositions.** When speaking we transform propositions through grammatical rules into surface structures.

4. Psychologists do not yet know how we extract the meaning of sentences we hear. The **syntactic approach** claims we rely mainly on syntactic clues to do this, while the **semantic approach** stresses our ability to guess at meaning from a knowledge of major content words. In addition, the meaning we derive from a sentence often depends on the many linguistic inferences we make. These inferences are based on both our general knowledge of the world and our implicit expectations about English conversations.

5. Efforts to teach language to apes have shown that chimpanzees and gorillas may be capable of learning a communication system that has several of the basic

features of human language. But even the smartest ape's aptitude for language is very limited compared with that of a normal human being.

6. Humans appear to be especially well equipped for the acquisition of language because their brains are **lateralized**—that is, different behavioral functions tend to be controlled largely by one or the other cerebral hemisphere. Language is primarily a left-hemisphere activity.

7. Psychologists disagree over whether there is a **critical period** early in life—roughly from toddlerhood until puberty—during which a person has a special facility for learning language. Of those who feel there is such a period, some argue that it corresponds to the time when the brain is becoming lateralized. Others doubt that brain lateralization alone can account for a critical period of such long duration.

8. Children of all cultures appear to go through similar sequences in acquiring language. Prespeech communication consists of different patterns of crying in newborns, and cooing, followed by babbling, in older babies. Older prespeech babies also learn to express themselves through gestures and intonation. By age one, most children produce their first words, often over- or underextending the meaning of a word until its underlying concept is fully grasped. Around age two, children begin to use what is known as **telegraphic speech**—short sentences made up of nouns and action verbs. The ability to organize words into increasingly complex sentences develops most prominently between ages two and five. Children seem to acquire an implicit knowledge of grammatical rules in fairly stable order. By the end of the preschool years children also display some understanding of how speech should be modified to suit different social situations.

9. Researchers have wondered why some children have difficulty learning to read their native language. Some have looked to the methods used to teach reading to children. They have found that reading programs that exclude early training in phonics are sometimes less effective than those that specifically teach beginning readers the associations between letters and sounds. Other researchers have tried to understand how children who are poor readers differ in their cognitive approaches to reading from children who are more successful at this task.

10. One of the aspects of language that interests psychologists is how language and thought interact. In the 1950s, linguist Benjamin Lee Whorf argued that the vocabulary and rules of a person's native language strongly influence the way that person perceives the world. But this notion—the **linguistic relativity hypothesis**—has been questioned by evidence that all humans seem to perceive their physical surroundings in much the same way regardless of differences in their languages. Researchers have also studied the opposite phenomenon—how thought influences language. They have found that broadly shared patterns of human thought and perception do sometimes give rise to **linguistic universals** (features common to all languages).

11. Nonverbal communication—consisting of facial expressions, body movements, and pitch and tone of voice—is a powerful force in human interaction. Our various patterns of nonverbal communication appear to be both inherited and learned. Because people believe that nonverbal cues are difficult to control intentionally, a nonverbal cue that conflicts with a spoken message is often considered the more truthful of the two. To some extent this greater trust in nonverbal messages is warranted, although not everyone is equally good at reading what nonverbal channels convey.

SUGGESTED READINGS

CLARK, H. H., and CLARK, E. V. *Psychology and language*. New York: Harcourt Brace Jovanovich, 1977.
   An excellent basic textbook on the psychology of language and language development.

CROWDER, R. G. *The psychology of reading*. New York: Oxford University Press, 1982.
   This introductory text examines the important principles of cognitive psychology that pertain to reading. It also presents the research behind these principles and shows the relationship between reading and such other cognitive activities as understanding spoken language, inference, and thought.

Foss, D. J., and HAKES, D. T. *Psycholinguistics: An introduction to the psychology of language.* Englewood Cliffs, N.J.: Prentice-Hall, 1978.

Another excellent basic textbook on the psychology of language and language development.

LLOYD, P., and BEVERIDGE, M. *Information and meaning in child communication.* New York: Academic Press, 1981.

This book is concerned with children's use of language to convey information and to influence the actions of others. A sizable body of empirical data on the ability of normal preschool children and retarded children is reported for the first time.

MILLER, G. A. *Language and speech.* New York: W. H. Freeman, 1981.

This highly readable book brings together information from several fields, including psychology, anthropology, and linguistics, covering topics that range from animal communication and speculations on the biological and social reasons for the development of language to the mechanics of conversation.

EMOTION, MOTIVATION, AND CONSCIOUSNESS

Part 5 covers three aspects of internal experience. Emotions, the subject of Chapter 10, are difficult to study, yet they hold the attention of psychologists nevertheless, as they give our experience its unique feeling and tone. What makes us behave? What makes our behavior characteristic of us? Motivation is considered in Chapter 11. Chapter 12 examines the nature of consciousness—its various states and the circumstances under which it is altered.

10

PERSPECTIVES ON EMOTION

Henry Moore. *Internal and External Forms,* 1953–54

He could not help but observe in his mother's actions a concealed nervousness, an irresolution as if under the strain of waiting. Unlike the fluent, methodical way in which she habitually moved about the kitchen, her manner now was disjointed, uncertain. In the midst of doing something or saying something, she would suddenly utter a curious, suppressed exclamation like a groan of dismay, or lift her hand in an obscure and hopeless gesture, or open her eyes as though staring perplexedly and brush back her hair. Everything she did seemed insecure and unfinished. She went from the sink to the window and left the water running and then remembering it with an odd overhastiness, turned, missed the handkerchief she was pegging to the clothesline and let it fall into the yard.

—HENRY ROTH, *Call It Sleep*

The world now looks remote, strange, sinister, uncanny. Its color is gone, its breath is cold. "It is as if I lived in another century. . . ."—"I see, I touch, but the things do not come near me, a thick veil alters the hue and look of everything."—"Persons move like shadows, and sounds seem to come from a distant world."—"There is no longer any past for me; people appear so strange; it is as if I could not see any reality, as if I were in a theatre; as if people were actors, and everything were scenery. . . . Everything floats before my eyes, but leaves no impression. . . . the things I see are not real things."

—WILLIAM JAMES, *The Varieties of Religious Experience*

Emotions are so much a part of our daily existence that it is difficult to imagine life without them. Try to imagine yourself standing in a two-hour line without annoyance, winning a $100,000 lottery without elation, learning of a loved one's death without grief. Such lack of emotion is almost inconceivable. Emotions set the tone of our experiences and give life its vitality. Without the ability to feel rage, grief, joy, and love, we would hardly recognize ourselves as human.

Yet as familiar as emotions are to us, it is not easy to frame a general definition of the term. Consider the passages at the beginning of this chapter. They clearly express anxiety and depression. But what do these two states have in common? What attributes do all emotions share?

Clearly, emotions involve a variety of feelings, feelings that are often aroused by external circumstances over which we have little control. In the second passage, for example, feelings of despondency are so overwhelming that the world seems colorless, dream-

like. Typically, emotions also entail physiological changes. Although such manifestations are not specifically described in the first passage, we can imagine the increased heartbeat, tightening of the throat, and slight hand tremors that often accompany acute anxiety. Finally, emotions may also affect behavior. The actions of the woman in the first passage—her odd, disjointed movements and apparent confusion of thought—are all the result of her emotional state. Thus, although no definition can ever capture the depth of many human emotions, we can define emotions in the following way. **Emotions** are states of feeling that can affect behavior; they often arise in response to social relationships and other external situations, and they are usually accompanied by physiological changes as well as by various thoughts about the emotion and its causes.

The first challenge psychologists face in studying emotions is that of identifying and measuring them. Some psychologists (Tomkins, 1963; Izard, 1977; Ekman, 1972) believe that distinct emotions can be labeled. For example, Robert Plutchik (1980) has proposed a general theory of emotions that includes these postulates: certain common elements, or prototypical patterns, can be identified in the emotions that different species exhibit; each emotion can vary in intensity from high to low; there is a small number of basic emotions, and all other emotions are combinations of these primary emotions. Underlying this theory is the evolutionary principle that emotions reflect the adaptations that animals (including humans) make to universal situations. For example, if a predator is attacking, the appropriate feeling is fear, the appropriate behavior is flight, and the purpose is self-preservation. The appropriateness of the emotional response determines whether the individual survives. According to Plutchik, millions of years of evolution have served to make evaluations of particular situations more accurate—and thus to make survival more likely. These situations, the primary emotions they evoke, the types of behavior they produce, and the implications for the individual's survival are summarized in Table 10.1.

Regardless of which scheme one uses for classifying emotions, it is still difficult to determine what emotions people are experiencing in a given situation and how strongly those emotions are being felt. One approach, of course, is simply to ask people—to solicit their self-reports. Silver and Wortman (1984) did this in interviews with young people who had recently

TABLE 10.1 UNIVERSAL SITUATIONS AND THE PRIMARY EMOTIONS THEY EVOKE

UNIVERSAL SITUATION	PRIMARY EMOTION	STIMULUS	INFERRED COGNITION	BEHAVIOR	EFFECT ON SURVIVAL
Flight	Fear, terror	Threat	"Danger"	Running, flying away	Protection
Attack	Anger, rage	Obstacle	"Enemy"	Biting, hitting	Destruction
Gain	Joy, ecstasy	Potential mate	"Possess"	Courting, mating	Reproduction
Loss	Sadness, grief	Loss of valued person	"Isolation"	Crying for help	Reintegration
Acceptance	Acceptance, trust	Group member	"Friend"	Grooming, sharing	Affiliation
Rejection	Disgust, loathing	Gruesome object	"Poison"	Vomiting, pushing away	Rejection
The expected	Anticipation	New territory	"What's out there?"	Examining, mapping	Exploration
The unexpected	Surprise	Sudden novel object	"What is it?"	Stopping, alerting	Orientation

Source: Adapted from R. Plutchik and H. Kellerman, *Emotion: Theory, research, and experience,* Vol. 1 (New York: Academic Press, 1980), p. 16. All the stimuli are important life events that are connected with survival. The inferred cognitions are probable interpretations made of these events.

been paralyzed as a result of serious accidents. The subjects reported that the most common emotion they had been feeling was anxiety, as you might well expect. But surprisingly, the second most common emotion was happiness, which typically arose in response to the kindness and concern expressed by other people. One problem with such self-reports, however, is that subjects may not always be willing to admit what they are really feeling, especially if doing so undermines the image of themselves they want to project (Plutchik, 1980). This is why careful interviewers usually try to emphasize the importance of honest responses. They assure their subjects that there is no right or wrong answer, thus encouraging them to express freely whatever emotions they feel (Wortman et al., 1980).

But despite researchers' assurances that no answer is bad or wrong, at times it is very hard to get accurate self-reports. Imagine that you harbor racial prejudices of which you are not particularly proud. If you suspect that an interviewer also disapproves of these feelings, how likely are you to admit to them? In such situations a researcher may use some other measurement technique—perhaps an assessment of the sub-

ject's physiological arousal (heart rate, respiration, blood pressure). Better still, the researcher may expose the subject to same-race and mixed-race situations while physiological reactions are being monitored. After the subject is hooked up to the experimental equipment, for example, a black or a white technician may come in to adjust the machines. Of course, one problem here is that even if the recording equipment shows an increase in physiological arousal when the subject is white and the technician black, we do not know for sure exactly what emotion the subject is feeling, for different emotions can be characterized by very similar physiological states.

One way around this limitation is for researchers to observe the subject's body language. As you may remember from our in-depth discussion of nonverbal communication in Chapter 9, nonverbal indicators of emotion are quite difficult to control consciously. Thus people who have negative feelings may be able to control their facial expressions, but their true feelings tend to show through in their posture, their hand gestures, their arm and leg movements (Ekman and Friesen, 1969, 1974).

Also revealing of a person's underlying feelings is

the number of speech errors he or she makes. Several speech faults have been found to increase significantly when a person is under stress (Kasl and Mahl, 1965). Such errors include abrupt sentence changes ("Well, she's . . . already she's lonesome") and stuttering ("It sort of l-l-leaves a memory"). You can probably remember many stressful circumstances in which you heard yourself or others making just these sorts of mistakes. Such observations can greatly enhance our ability to detect emotions in another person, even when that person is deliberately trying to conceal them. In this way they can help to compensate for limitations in both physiological assessments and self-reports. In fact, all three techniques for measuring emotions that we have mentioned tend to complement and bolster one another. For that reason many psychologists are now using them together in a single study.

Because emotions are such a central part of human existence, they are becoming an increasingly important area of psychological research. Studies of emotion have focused on a number of critical issues. What role do physiological changes play in emotional experience? If you are simply injected with a drug that creates physiological arousal, will you become emotional? Can a person with a severed spinal cord, who no longer experiences physiological change, still feel emotion? What types of emotional reactions accompany such life crises as rape and the death of a loved one, and how long do such reactions usually last? To what extent can intense or prolonged emotions lead to serious illness or even death? Why are some people able to take stress in stride, while others react by becoming seriously ill? Are some people more likely to experience happiness than others? Are people who have more money or more friends generally more happy than people who do not? These are some of the topics we will explore in this chapter.

THE PHYSIOLOGY OF EMOTION

The role that physiological factors play in human emotion has intrigued psychologists for nearly a century. Is physiological arousal the primary cause of emotion? Does arousal vary for different emotions? Although many answers to these questions have been proposed and a great deal of controversy has been generated, all psychologists agree on one point: strong emotion is in fact associated with changes in the autonomic nervous system.

Emotion and the Autonomic Nervous System

As we discussed in Chapter 3, the autonomic nervous system regulates the body's internal environment and usually functions without conscious control. It is composed of two divisions, the sympathetic and the parasympathetic, both of which connect to almost every muscle and gland. The two divisions have broadly opposite effects. Generally speaking, the sympathetic division dominates during emergency or stress and promotes energy expenditure. It encourages the increased blood sugar, heart rate, and blood pressure needed for sustained physical activity, and at the same time it inhibits digestion. The parasympathetic division, in contrast, dominates during relaxation and promotes energy conservation. It works to decrease heart rate and blood flow to the skeletal muscles, while also promoting digestion. Not surprisingly, most of the physiological changes associated with strong emotion, such as intense anger and fear, are caused by activation of the sympathetic division.

What exactly happens when the sympathetic nervous system is activated? Suppose it is 2:00 A.M. and you are walking to your car, which is parked on a deserted city street. Suddenly a man emerges from a dark alley. What physiological changes would occur in this fear-arousing situation?

1. The blood vessels leading to your stomach and intestines would constrict, and digestion would virtually stop. At the same time, the vessels leading to your larger skeletal muscles would expand, diverting the oxygen and nutrients carried in your blood to where they might be needed for fight or flight.

2. Your pancreas would secrete the hormone glucagon, which would stimulate your liver to re-

lease stored sugar into the bloodstream. The sugar would supply extra energy to your skeletal muscles should they need it. In addition, your adrenal glands would secrete the hormone epinephrine, which would help sustain many of the other physiological changes brought about by activation of the sympathetic nervous system.

3. Your breathing would become deeper and more rapid, and your bronchioles (the small air passages leading to your lungs) would expand. These changes would increase the supply of oxygen to your blood, oxygen that is needed to burn the sugar being sent to your skeletal muscles.

4. Your heartbeat would increase, perhaps more than doubling, thus speeding the circulation of your blood and hastening the delivery of oxygen and nutrients to your skeletal muscles.

5. The pupils of your eyes would dilate and your visual sensitivity would increase.

6. Your salivary glands might stop working, causing your mouth to become dry. The activity of your sweat glands, however, might increase, since sweating is one way to dissipate the heat generated by increased energy expenditure.

7. The muscles just beneath the surface of your skin would contract, causing hairs to stand on end. For our furry ancestors the erection of body hair may have been part of a threat display, but we relatively hairless humans simply break out in "goose bumps" (Lang, Rice, and Sternback, 1972).

These various changes prepare the body to deal with a potential threat—either by confronting it or by escaping. In fact, activation of the sympathetic nervous system has sometimes made possible feats of great strength or endurance. Cases have been reported in which a woman has managed to lift a car to free her child trapped beneath a wheel or a man somehow has swum against a powerful current in order to reach safety. This is not to say that arousal suddenly endows a person with superhuman powers. It is more accurate to say that physiological arousal enables a person to use the body's muscles more effectively and for a more prolonged period than would ordinarily be the case. Yet the effects of intense activation of the sympathetic nervous system may not all be positive. As

you will see later in this chapter, the physiological stress caused by intense and sustained emotional arousal can sometimes contribute to serious illness.

Once a threatening situation is over, diverse physiological changes again take place. Suppose that your would-be attacker turned out to be a police officer on patrol. Almost immediately the opposing effects of the parasympathetic nervous system would begin to reassert themselves. Your heartbeat, respiration, glandular secretions, blood flow, and muscular tension would all return to normal, and the body sensations associated with fear would subside. This general cycle of physiological arousal—caused by assertion of the sympathetic nervous system over muscles and glands, followed by reassertion of the parasympathetic division—is the cycle associated with most strong emotions.

Measuring the Physiology of Emotion

One way of monitoring the physiological changes that accompany emotion is by means of a machine called a **polygraph.** A polygraph examination is shown in the accompanying photograph. Electrodes attached to the subject's hand measure changes in the skin's conduction of electricity, also known as the galvanic skin response or GSR (the sweatier the palm, the greater the electrical conduction); a rubber tube (or pneumograph) around the subject's chest measures respiration; a band around the subject's upper arm measures blood pressure and heart rate. These measuring devices are all attached to a central monitor that automatically records changes in physiological response on rolling graph paper.

In addition to its use in psychological research, the polygraph is used to measure the truthfulness of statements made by persons who are suspected of crimes. Consequently, it is often called a lie detector. This use of the machine is based on the assumptions that people feel anxious when they lie and that this anxiety is accompanied by physiological changes. The first step in a lie-detector test is to monitor the subject's respiration, heartbeat, GSR, and so forth while he or she is relaxed in order to obtain a baseline for evaluating subsequent responses. The interrogator then asks a series of "routine" questions interspersed with "critical" ones. A person suspected of a bank robbery, for example, might first be asked routine

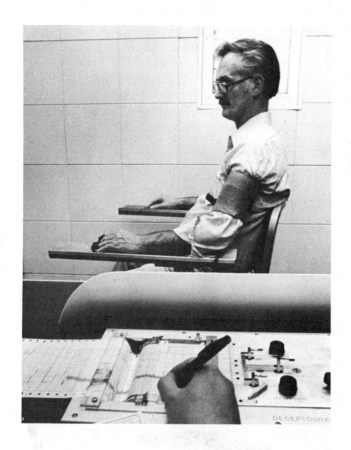

A demonstration of a polygraph examination. Sensors on the subject's hand, chest, and upper arm measure physiological changes that occur in response to the examiner's questions. These measurements are recorded on a moving graph by the monitoring machine in the foreground. *(Bill Powers/Tricorn Photos.)*

questions: "Is your name John Smith? Do you live at Forty-six Irving Place?" and then the critical question: "Were you at the First National Bank at two-fifteen last Thursday afternoon?" If the verbal response to this particular critical question is no, but involuntary autonomic responses show noticeable changes, the subject is presumed to be lying (Podlesny and Raskin, 1977).

Several problems with a lie-detector test make its use controversial. First, the act of lying does not necessarily promote physiological changes. Habitual liars may experience no strong emotion when they lie, and so their physiological changes will be slight or nonexistent. Or a knowledgeable suspect may practice lying in order to learn to control his or her "involuntary" responses. Second, physiological changes can be caused by factors other than lying. An innocent person may feel so anxious about being suspected of a crime that he or she may have a polygraph reading similar to a guilty person's. Such a reading may be triggered if the person is disturbed by the question for such reasons as embarrassment, uncertainty about how to answer, or fear (Gudjonsson, 1982). Alterna-

tively, a guilty person may surreptitiously induce psychological stress (by thinking about the crime, for instance) while being asked routine questions. In this way he or she may produce a high baseline and so make subsequent comparisons meaningless. For these reasons polygraph results are not considered admissible evidence in courts.

Nevertheless, use of the polygraph continues. Police still use it in preliminary phases of criminal investigation. A recent report (Office of Technology Assessment, 1983) found that the lie detector can be useful in such circumstances. This study reviewed research and field studies that noted accuracy rates averaging between 64 and 98 percent.

But the biggest consumer of lie-detection technology today is private industry. Every year an estimated half million American employees and job hunters take lie-detector tests. At this point almost no research substantiates the validity of lie-detection procedures for employment screening (Office of Technology Assessment, 1983). Still, nearly a third of the largest corporations in the country routinely use the polygraph (Bonner, 1983) to weed out "undesirable" job applicants (people who use hard drugs, are alcoholics, have stolen from past employers, or are lying about previous job experience), to test employees for honesty and trustworthiness, and to identify those responsible for "inside" thefts. The federal government is also beginning to use lie detectors with increasing frequency in order to single out employees who may be spies or may leak information to the press (Joyce, 1984).

Many corporate and government employees, however, feel that this practice invades their privacy and violates their civil rights. Refusal to submit to a polygraph test may in itself be grounds for dismissal or denial of a promotion, and those who have been falsely labeled "untrustworthy" feel that their careers have been ruined by an unreliable instrument. In fact, when the subject is being coerced, when the polygraph examiner is not well trained, and when the critical questions asked are very broad ("Have you ever used drugs? Stolen anything?"), some experts say that the accuracy of the device is hardly better than chance (Bonner, 1983). At best, reliance on this technology may net a few dishonest people, but many honest individuals may pay a heavy price (Joyce, 1984).

Emotion and the Structure of the Brain

Although it is the autonomic nervous system that triggers the physiological changes associated with emotion, this system is coordinated by the brain. In particular, the hypothalamus and certain areas of the limbic system (see Chapter 3) are involved in a number of emotional reactions, including anger, aggression, and fear (Pribram, 1981). This has been demonstrated by research on experimental animals in which different parts of these brain regions are mildly stimulated or surgically removed. Research with cats, for example, has shown that stimulation of particular areas of the hypothalamus can induce intense activation of the sympathetic nervous system and an emotional display that can be interpreted only as feline rage. The cat's pupils dilate; the fur on its back and tail stands erect; it flattens its ears, arches its back, unsheathes it claws, and hisses and snarls intensely (Flynn et al., 1970). In contrast, surgical lesions in areas of the amygdala (part of the limbic system) produce extremely docile behavior. For this reason, some of the "wild" animals that circus performers use have had part of the amygdala surgically removed.

Some researchers have found cases in which exaggerated emotional behavior in humans has accompanied damage to certain areas of the limbic system. Such damage can take place before, during, or after birth, and it can arise from a variety of causes, including diseases that affect the brain, drug abuse, and trauma due to auto accidents, athletic injuries, or gunshot wounds. A widely publicized case that occurred in 1966 involved a young man at the University of Texas. For months Charles Whitman had unsuccessfully sought psychiatric help for the irrational thoughts and violent impulses that periodically overcame him. A letter he wrote the evening before his death showed a deep concern about these sudden changes in his behavior, which he suspected might be due to a physical disorder. That night Whitman killed his wife and mother, and the next morning he climbed to the top of a campus tower carrying a high-powered rifle with a telescopic sight. From there he proceeded to fire at everything that moved. An hour and a half later, when Whitman was finally killed by police, he had shot thirty-eight people, killing fourteen of them. An autopsy revealed a malignant tumor on the amygdala (Sweet, Ervin, and Mark, 1969).

Documentation of other cases in which damage to the limbic system has been associated with uncontrollable violence has led some researchers to suggest that many extremely volatile people may be suffering from brain disease or injury of some sort (Mark and Ervin, 1970). This possibility has generated renewed interest in psychosurgery, the removal or destruction of parts of the brain, as a form of treatment. Al-

Stimulation of certain areas of the hypothalamus is inducing displays of aggression in these monkeys. *(Jim Amos/Photo Researchers.)*

though such a procedure may control violent behavior, it can also alter an individual's personality in very adverse ways. For this reason it is highly controversial and so is relatively rare. More will be said about psychosurgery in Chapter 16.

For a long time psychologists believed that the brain's control over emotion was exerted largely through such "primitive" structures as the hypothalamus and the amygdala. More recently, however, it has become clear that the cerebral cortex is intimately involved as well. And most fascinating of all has been the discovery that the cortex's role in emotion is asymmetrical: the left side contributes more to positive feelings, while the right side contributes more to negative ones. People who suffer extensive damage to the right cerebral hemisphere are often quite placid and carefree in mood. They may make inappropriate jokes or burst out laughing at inappropriate times.

The implication is that euphoric emotions are greatly influenced by *left*-brain activity, and that injury to the right brain may serve to disinhibit them. Conversely, people who suffer left-hemisphere damage often experience acute depression and periods of uncontrollable crying. These negative emotions seem to be heavily influenced by the *right* hemisphere, and extensive left-brain injury somehow turns them loose (Hécaen, 1972; Gainotti, 1972; Sackeim et al., 1982). Further evidence of right-hemisphere involvement in negative feelings comes from the finding that certain physical disorders believed to be linked to psychological stress (such as chronic pain, rheumatoid arthritis, and breast disease) seem to be more common on the left side of the body—the side controlled by the right hemisphere (Sackeim and Weber, 1982). We will say much more about the links between stress, negative emotions, and illness in a later section of this chapter.

THEORIES OF EMOTION

Whenever you encounter an emotion-provoking situation, such as the menacing figure in a dark alley imagined earlier, two things are likely to happen: (1) your brain triggers your sympathetic nervous system into action, causing physiological arousal, and (2) you subjectively experience a feeling known as fear, which is related to your awareness of potential danger. One of the oldest debates about human emotion concerns the sequence of these two events. Do you experience the feeling of fear because your heart is pounding and your hands are trembling? Or does your mind's appraisal of a particular set of circumstances induce the feeling you call fear, which is then followed by a set of physiological changes preparing you for fight or flight? Over the years psychologists have proposed different answers to these questions. Their theories, and the experiments conducted to test them, have greatly increased our understanding of exactly what emotions entail.

The Importance of Physiological Arousal

Our language suggests that the physiological changes that accompany each emotion are in some ways distinct. When we are frightened, we say we feel a "knot" in the stomach; when we are nervous we say we experience "butterflies." During intense anger we sometimes refer to a "pounding" in the temples; when we are embarrassed we often describe what we feel as a "blush." Is it possible that the diverse emotions we experience are simply the result of different sets of body changes? And if not, what role *do* physiological changes play in the experience of emotions?

The James-Lange Theory. William James was one of the first psychologists to propose that the ability to identify and label our own emotional states may be based on our ability to interpret the body changes associated with them. This proposal directly contradicted many of the theories of emotion popular in James's day. Most other writers in the late nineteenth century argued, quite logically, that events in the environment trigger a psychological state—the emotion—which in turn gives rise to physiological responses. But James disagreed:

My theory, on the contrary, is that *the bodily changes follow directly the perception of the exciting fact, and that our feeling of the same changes as they occur IS the emotion.* Common-sense says, we lose our fortune, are sorry

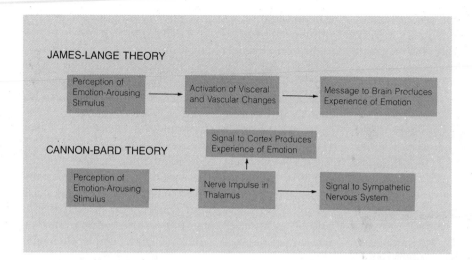

Figure 10.1 Comparison of the sequence of events outlined in the James-Lange and the Cannon-Bard theories of emotion.

and weep; we meet a bear, are frightened and run; we are insulted by a rival, are angry and strike. The hypothesis here to be defended says that this order of sequence is incorrect . . . and that the more rational statement is that we feel sorry *because* we cry, angry *because* we strike, afraid *because* we tremble. . . . Without the bodily states following on the perception, the latter would be purely cognitive in form, pale, colorless, destitute of emotional warmth. We might then see the bear, and judge it best to run, receive the insult and deem it right to strike, but we should not actually feel afraid or angry.   [James, 1890]

According to James, then, our perception of a certain stimulus in the environment triggers changes in the body. These changes cause sensory messages to be sent to the brain and produce the actual experience of emotion. Each emotional state is signaled by a unique physiological pattern. James emphasized patterns of response in the viscera, or abdominal organs, but another psychologist, Carl Lange, proposed a similar theory that emphasized vascular changes (changes in blood pressure). Because the work of James and Lange coincided in time, the view that the perception of body changes *is* the emotion came to be called the **James-Lange theory** (Lange and James, 1922).

Cannon's Critique. The James-Lange theory stimulated a great deal of research on emotions, much of it designed to disprove that theory's claims. In 1927 Walter Cannon published a powerful critique based on several arguments. First, the idea that body reac-

tions *cause* the experience of emotion is questionable on the basis of timing. Often we feel emotions quite rapidly. We feel the car skidding out of control and experience immediate panic; we spot an old friend and feel instantaneous joy. Changes in the viscera occur rather slowly. In addition, the internal organs are not very well supplied with nerves, so they are relatively insensitive structures. How, then, can the viscera be the source of sudden emotion, as James proposed?

Second, if James was right and physiological arousal causes emotion, then physiological changes induced artificially—by an injection of a drug, for example—should give rise to an emotion of some kind. But as Cannon noted, physiological arousal alone is not sufficient to induce emotion. As evidence, Cannon cited a study by Gregorio Marañón (1924). Marañón injected several hundred subjects with the hormone epinephrine and asked them to report the effects. About 71 percent said that they experienced only physical symptoms—rapid heartbeat, tightness in the throat—with no emotional overtones at all. The remainder reported emotional responses of some kind, but most described what Marañón called "as if" emotions. These subjects said, "I feel *as if* I were afraid" or "I feel *as if* I were happy." Their feelings, then, were similar to emotions but clearly not identical to them.

Third, in order to feel emotions by interpreting our body sensations, it would be necessary for each emotion to be characterized by a somewhat different set of physiological changes. Following the publica-

Although common sense may tell us that *first* we feel grief, and *then* we cry, the James-Lange theory maintains that *first* we cry, and *then* we feel grief—in other words, that feelings follow behavior. *(James H. Karales/Peter Arnold, Inc.)*

tion of James's theory, other psychologists tried to identify unique physiological responses for each emotional state, but their results were consistently negative, as Cannon pointed out. The evidence showed that many identical body changes occur in conjunction with very different emotions. How, then, could physiological arousal alone cause the wide diversity of emotions that people are capable of experiencing?

Subsequent Findings. Although Cannon's arguments were highly convincing at the time, more recent insights into the physiology of emotion force us to reconsider them. For one thing, there is now evidence that *some* physiological responses do vary in accordance with the emotions they accompany. Wolf and Wolff (1947), for example, located a subject with a gastric fistula—an opening in the stomach wall that made it possible to observe the stomach lining. They found that stomach movement, gastric secretion, and dilation of the blood vessels increased during anger and decreased during fear. But although they studied their subject for many months through a great variety of emotions, they were able to distinguish only two general patterns.

Albert Ax (1953) wondered if these findings might not be due to the unique response patterns of this particular person. So he designed an experiment in which he could measure the physiological correlates of anger and fear in a large number of subjects. Ax's procedure might raise ethical questions today. He connected his subjects to a polygraph under the pretext of recording their physiological responses during a period of relaxation. Then, at various points during the recording session, he provoked in his subjects both intense anger (by having the polygraph operator rudely insult them) and intense fear (by leading them to believe that the polygraph was short-circuited and might electrocute them). Ax found that certain responses, such as breathing rate and sweating, increased more during fear, and certain other responses, such as blood pressure, increased more during anger.

More recently scientists have also found significant differences in hormone secretions during various psychological states. In particular, such stress-producing factors as physical exertion, fasting, and exposure to intense heat and cold have been shown to be associated with their own distinctive patterns of hormone response (Mason, 1975; Mason et al., 1976). Researchers are still in the process of measuring hormone secretions associated with different emotions. Many believe that distinctive hormone patterns for specific emotions will eventually be found as new technology makes our measurement techniques more precise and accurate (Lazarus et al., 1980).

At the same time, techniques for studying the operation of neurotransmitters in the brain have opened up a whole new line of research regarding physiological changes and emotion. There is a good possibility that different emotions are associated with different brain chemicals, which in turn are secreted along distinctive neural pathways. Depression, for instance, is now known to be associated with reduced levels of the neurotransmitter norepinephrine. Drugs that deplete norepinephrine produce depression, while antidepressant drugs usually stimulate norepinephrine secretion (Schildkraut and Kety, 1967; Schildkraut and Freyhan, 1972). Moreover, anger, which is often provoked therapeutically to counteract depression, is also related to increased secretions of norepinephrine (Dienstbier, 1979). Granted, only a few such patterns have so far been discovered. But keep in mind the difficulty of studying this topic. It is only very recently that advances in technology have allowed scientists to trace neurotransmitters with any precision. Many suspect that in the future brain chemicals will be increasingly implicated in different kinds of emotions (Schmeck, 1982). In summary, then, it seems likely that a more important role may eventually be assigned to specific physiological patterns in the experience of different emotions than Cannon's early critique of the James-Lange theory allowed.

Despite the fact that we have much more to learn about the physiology of emotion, most researchers now agree that physiological arousal is not simply incidental to emotional experience. If it were, then people with damage to the sympathetic nervous system would still feel normal emotions, but research shows that they do not. Psychologist George W. Hohmann (1966), himself a paraplegic, interviewed twenty-five army veterans who had severed spinal cords. He found significant changes in the nature and intensity of certain emotions, especially anger and fear. Generally speaking, the higher the lesion on the spinal cord, the more extensive the disruption of sympathetic arousal and the greater the change in emotional experience. This is not to say that these men failed to perceive the significance of emotion-arousing situations, or even that they failed to display much of the behavior associated with strong emotion. But the

quality of their emotional experiences was often altered. As one man remarked, "Sometimes I get angry when I see some injustice. I yell and cuss and raise hell, because if you don't do it sometimes I've learned people will take advantage of you. But it just doesn't have the heat to it that it used to. It's a mental kind of anger." It seems that the physical correlates of anger—pounding heart, trembling hands, the sensation of being "heated up"—contribute to the full experience of the emotion.

The Role of Cognition

Hohmann's study suggests that physiological arousal is necessary to a complete experience of emotion. Yet the work of Marañón, discussed earlier, shows that physiological arousal alone is not enough. When subjects were artificially aroused by a shot of epinephrine they did not feel emotional. Something was missing from the experience that prevented it from being a true emotion. That something, according to Stanley Schachter, is an appropriate cognition that enables us to comprehend our stirred-up physiological state in emotional terms and so to label it joy, anger, jealousy, fear, or any other emotion. To Schachter, then, emotion involves two closely interacting factors: a state of physiological arousal and a cognitive interpretation of that arousal. Which comes first is not important to Schachter. What is important is that the cognitive interpretation enables us to label a *general* state of physiological arousal as a *specific* emotion (Schachter, 1964).

Schachter's Two-Factor Theory. It is difficult to isolate the role that cognition plays in the labeling of arousal as emotion, because in most cases arousal and a related cognition are closely linked. What is so intriguing about Schachter's approach, therefore, is that he invites us to consider an unusual situation—one in which the state of arousal and the explanatory cognition are to some extent independent. What would you do, he asks, if you felt the body sensations of emotion but could perceive no obvious reason for them? Schachter's answer is that you would experience a need to explain your feelings in some way and so would search your surroundings for a reasonable cause. As a result, you could label the very same state of arousal as joy, love, jealousy, or hate, depending on the cognitions available to you.

In trying to design an experiment to test this hypothesis, Schachter and his colleague Jerome Singer (1962) faced several problems. First, they had to find some nonemotional way to induce physiological arousal. They solved this problem by giving subjects an injection of the hormone epinephrine under the pretext that they wanted to study the effects of "vitamin injections" on vision. Subjects were randomly assigned to one of four conditions. In the *informed condition,* the experimenters announced that the injection would produce certain side effects, such as hand tremors and heart palpitations, which are real effects of epinephrine. In the *misinformed condition,* subjects were led to expect side effects unrelated to epinephrine, such as headache and itching. In the *ignorant condition,* subjects were incorrectly told that the injection would have no side effects at all. And finally, in the *placebo condition,* which served as a control, subjects received an injection of salt solution, which produced no side effects. Schachter and Singer predicted that, lacking an adequate explanation for their aroused state, subjects in both the misinformed and ignorant conditions would be likely to search their environments for information that could help explain what they felt.

But what might subjects find in their environments that could help them account for physiological arousal? Schachter and Singer solved this second problem by providing emotional cues. They had each subject wait for the "vision test" in a room with another person, who was actually a confederate in the experiment. In some cases the accomplice acted very happy and frivolous, throwing paper airplanes, laughing, and playing with a hula hoop. In other cases the accomplice acted increasingly incensed over a long and rather insulting questionnaire he and the subject had been asked to fill out, finally tearing up the questionnaire and storming out of the room. This was Schachter and Singer's way of creating two very different emotion-related cognitions: one of euphoria, the other of anger. They predicted that the subjects who had no explanation for their physiological arousal would label their feeling either euphoria or anger in accordance with the emotion expressed by the confederate to whom they were exposed. In short, Schachter and Singer believed that subjects in the misinformed and ignorant conditions would label the same unexplained state of arousal in very different ways, depending on environmental cues.

The results of the experiment (see Figure 10.2) gave qualified support to Schachter and Singer's theory. First let us consider the subjects in the misin-

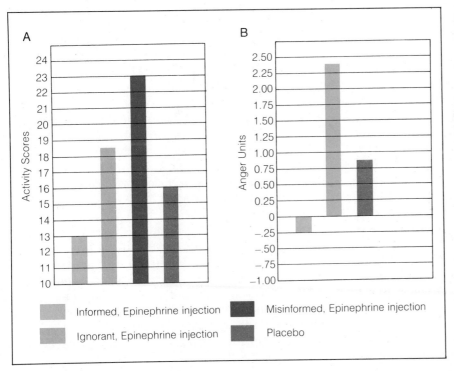

Figure 10.2 Comparison of the activities of the subjects in the euphoria and the anger conditions of the Schachter and Singer experiment. (A) Euphoria condition. (B) Anger condition. (The numbers on the vertical axis refer to scores on tests; they are only important in showing the relationship among the subjects' activities.) *(Schachter and Singer, 1962.)*

formed and ignorant conditions. These subjects did not expect the injection to produce arousal, and so presumably had no way to explain their physiological state. They did tend to show signs that they had adopted the mood of the confederate. Observed surreptitiously through a one-way window, they too threw paper airplanes in the euphoric condition and criticized the questionnaire in the angry one. In contrast, subjects in the informed condition, who were told to expect the side effects of epinephrine, were less likely to behave as the confederate did. Furthermore, subjects in both the misinformed and ignorant conditions who were exposed to the euphoric confederate tended to describe their own feelings as somewhat more "good or happy" than subjects in the informed condition.

Support for Schachter and Singer's theory was qualified, however, because not all the differences observed between the groups were precisely what the researchers had predicted. For one thing, subjects in the ignorant condition who were exposed to the angry confederate tended to describe their overall mood as slightly happy rather than as substantially annoyed. What's more, there were no statistically significant differences in self-reported emotion between the two unexplained arousal groups (the ignorant and misinformed conditions) and the placebo (control) group. This seems a direct contradiction of Schachter and Singer's theory, which proposes that a state of physiological arousal and a cognitive interpretation are needed for an emotion to be experienced. Since the placebo subjects were not physiologically aroused, they should have experienced significantly less emotion than the unexplained arousal subjects did.

Such problems prompted several other psychologists to examine Schachter and Singer's experiment more closely, and they found in it a number of methodological flaws (Plutchik and Ax, 1967; Zimbardo, Ebbeson, and Maslach, 1977; Kemper, 1978). Except for a brief measure of pulse rate before and after the epinephrine injection, for instance, Schachter and Singer failed to monitor their subjects' physiological responses. Because reactions to epinephrine are highly variable and sometimes very short-lived, it is not clear exactly how many subjects were physiologically aroused when they met the confederate. If only some of the subjects in the ignorant and misinformed conditions were actually aroused, this might explain why on average they felt little more emotion than pla-

cebo subjects did. In addition, although Schachter and Singer assumed that only the emotional cues provided by the confederate could plausibly explain unexpected arousal, this was not necessarily the case. When searching for an explanation, a person might look not only to the immediate environment but to memories of past events as well. For instance, subjects in the ignorant and misinformed conditions who suddenly found themselves with racing hearts and trembling hands might recall that they had always feared injections, and attribute their current sensations to that fear (Maslach, 1979). The possibility of such alternative explanations for arousal could certainly have confounded Schachter and Singer's results, once again reducing the differences between experimental and control subjects. These and other methodological problems may be part of the reason why subsequent researchers have not always been able to replicate Schachter and Singer's findings (Maslach, 1979; Marshall and Zimbardo, 1979). But Schachter and Singer answer that they never intended this one experiment to be the sole basis for their theory of emotion. They intended it rather as an intriguing starting point from which other investigators could explore further.

Extending Schachter's Research. And other investigators did just that, as Schachter's two-factor theory of emotion quickly captured widespread interest. It made intuitive sense that people would look to cues in the environment to explain their physiological sensations. Schachter and Singer's experiment had suggested that with clever structuring of available cognitions, subjects could be fooled into thinking that nonemotional states of arousal were really emotional in origin. But exactly how far could people's appraisals of their own feelings be manipulated?

Conversely, to what extent can the subjective experience of emotion be reduced by leading people to attribute their physiological arousal to some *non*emotional cause? Schachter and his colleague Richard Nisbett set out to investigate this issue (Nisbett and Schachter, 1966). They gave subjects a placebo pill and told half that the pill would cause physiological arousal (hand tremors, heart palpitations, butterflies in the stomach) and half that the pill might cause slight itching and other irrelevant symptoms. Then they asked the subjects to report how much pain and anxiety they experienced from a series of electric shocks. Naturally, the act of being shocked aroused the subjects, but to what should they attribute this arousal? When subjects had been told that the shocks would be mild and harmless, attributing the arousal to fear did not make much sense. A more plausible explanation available to half the subjects was to blame their physical symptoms on the "arousal-producing" pill. And this is apparently what they did, for subjects who were led to believe that the pill would cause arousal were willing to tolerate shocks four times as severe as the other subjects were. Thus, it appears that genuine emotions can sometimes be suppressed when people are given alternative explanations for their arousal.

Some psychologists have been intrigued by the possible applications of Nisbett and Schachter's findings to people with some emotional reaction that is making their lives difficult. Anxiety, for instance, often plays a key role in maintaining such problems as acute shyness, stuttering, and even impotence. Symptoms occur, the person becomes upset about them, and the symptoms consequently get worse. If a therapist could induce such a person to misattribute the initial emotional arousal to some nonemotional cause, this vicious cycle might be broken and the symptoms greatly reduced (Davison and Valins, 1972). For example, suppose you transfer to a new university in your sophomore year. Several months pass and you have not made a single real friend. You feel alone and dejected. You may well attribute your unhappiness to some shortcoming in yourself ("I can't seem to make friends. What's wrong with me?"). Such doubts about yourself could easily lead to excessive shyness, and shyness in turn to even more trouble forming friendships and greater unhappiness and self-blame. One way to help people out of such a cycle is to persuade them to attribute their unhappiness to legitimate situational factors ("It's always hard for a newcomer to break in") rather than to personal inadequacies (Valins and Nisbett, 1972).

In a later chapter we will discuss how this therapeutic approach is increasingly being used with people who are severely depressed and believe that the root of their problems lies in their own shortcomings. But for now the important point is that such therapy is essentially an application of Schachter's theory that cognitive appraisals are very important elements in all emotional experiences. If we can somehow undermine the cognitions supporting a negative emotional state, we can effectively reduce the emotion itself.

Are Cognitions Essential to Emotion? Schachter's conception of emotion has had substantial influence. In fact, it has helped to shift the entire field of social psychology toward a more cognitive orientation (Marshall and Zimbardo, 1979). But some psychologists ask if the cognitive aspects of emotion have not been overemphasized. In order to experience a true emotion, is it really essential that we think about the environmental factors that promote this response?

R. B. Zajonc is one psychologist who suspects that the answer is no. To help us understand why, he invites us to consider some of the emotions we experience in everyday life (Zajonc, 1980). When we meet a stranger, for example, we sometimes feel that we like or dislike the person instantly—long before we have a chance to evaluate the person's characteristics. How, Zajonc asks, could a cognitive appraisal be meaningfully involved in such a quick response?

Zajonc has gone on to compile empirical evidence in support of his belief that emotion and cognition are two separate psychological processes, so that a person may experience emotion *without* cognitive appraisal (Zajonc, 1980, 1984). One of the most striking pieces of evidence is the discovery that animals can acquire a strong aversion to a food paired with nausea even if they are unconscious when that pairing takes place (Garcia and Rusiniak, 1980). Now it is very difficult to argue that such an animal has made a cognitive appraisal leading to feelings of revulsion toward this particular food. It is more logical to surmise that the animal's brain is so constructed as to allow the learning of emotional responses with little cognitive processing except at a purely sensory level. Some studies of brain anatomy seem to support this conclusion (Goodale, 1982; Stephan, Berkley, and Moss, 1981).

Of course, the mere fact that it is possible for an emotional reaction to occur in the absence of much cognitive processing does not mean that this is what always, or even usually, happens. As we all know, elaborate thought processes are often intimately involved in emotion, and Zajonc acknowledges this. His goal is simply to determine whether such cognitive appraisals are *essential* to the experience of emotion, as Schachter's theory maintains. At this point we do not yet have all the evidence needed to answer Zajonc's question. Future research may shed more light on our understanding of exactly how human emotions are triggered.

EMOTIONAL REACTIONS TO CRISIS

At some point in our lives most of us will encounter tragedy of some kind. We or someone we love may be the victim of a violent crime, a disabling accident, or a life-threatening illness. How do people respond emotionally to such experiences? Do they progress through discrete stages in attempting to cope with misfortune? Do they eventually recover, or at least learn to live with their adversity? These are very important questions that some psychologists have recently begun to answer.

Variability in Responses to Crisis

One thing that has become increasingly clear is that popular expectations about the way people will react to adversity—expectations often shared by those in the medical and helping professions—are often incorrect (Silver and Wortman, 1980). Imagine a young woman who has just been raped. She arrives at the police station to fill out a report. How does she feel at the time? Filled with anger and hatred toward her assailant? Enraged enough to want him harshly punished? Such a reaction sounds appropriate to most people. It may therefore surprise you to learn that relatively few women feel anger immediately after being raped—in one recent study as few as 20 percent (McCombie, 1975).

And it is not just that we often misjudge how people will react to any given crisis. The very assumption that there is some "typical" response is itself a misconception. People respond with much variability to tragedy. In one survey of women who had recently lost their husbands, the initial emotional reaction to the husband's death ranged from intense shock and numbness to anxiety, depression, and anger (Parkes, 1972). There is even variation in whether or not *any* emotion is expressed. In a series of interviews with rape victims a few hours after their assaults, half the women showed intense emotions (crying, sobbing, severe tension and restlessness), while the other half appeared outwardly quite controlled (Burgess and Holmstrom, 1974). Unfortunately, a rape victim who appears controlled immediately after her attack is often judged more negatively by others, even viewed as less credible, than a victim who is more outwardly emotional (Calhoun et al., in press).

The idea that emotional response to crisis follows a predictable sequence of stages is also widespread, but it too is probably unwarranted. One of the best-known proponents of a stage model of coping is Elisabeth Kübler-Ross (1969). She has proposed that the terminally ill pass through five discrete stages. The first stage is denial, the second anger, the third bargaining (for example, promising to become a better person if given more time), the fourth depression, and the fifth peaceful acceptance of one's fate. Is there any evidence to support such a model? What evidence exists is very weak, mostly anecdotal accounts and researchers' subjective impressions. The few pertinent empirical studies that have been conducted do not seem to support a stage model. In a study of permanent paralysis from spinal cord injury, for instance, N. C. Lawson (1976) attempted to determine whether victims experienced a stage of depression. Multiple measures of depression were taken five times a week over an average of twenty-four weeks. Surprisingly, not a single patient was consistently depressed for even as short a period as one week. Such findings raise considerable doubt as to whether a stage model of response to crisis is valid.

Yet despite the scarcity of evidence in support of the stage model, most people continue to believe in it, even most people in the medical and helping professions. As a result, people who experience life crises are often told by well-meaning professionals how they *should* react. Worse still, when a person does not conform to these expectations, the people trying to help may lose patience. One researcher has reported that because of wide acceptance of Kübler-Ross's five stages of dying, terminally ill patients "who did not follow these stages were labeled 'deviant,' 'neurotic,' or 'pathological' diers. Clinical personnel became angry at patients who did not move from one stage to the next" (Pattison, 1977, p. 304). And if patients' emotional reactions are dismissed as "just a stage," legitimate complaints may be ignored. When one hospitalized cancer patient complained because she had been given the wrong tests, a nurse was overheard telling a co-worker: "Don't worry about Mrs. A.; she's just going through the anger stage" (Dunkel-Schetter and Wortman, 1982). Such responses from others may only compound the dying patient's problems.

Are Life Crises Always Overcome?

What about the prognosis for successfully overcoming a life crisis? Does "time heal all wounds," as many people believe? This common assumption, too, may not hold true for many people. There is considerable evidence that those who manage to recover from trauma do so less quickly and less completely than they or others expect. A large minority of people continue to be extremely upset long after their tragedy has occurred. In one study of women who had undergone mastectomies to remove malignant breast tumors, 39 percent experienced serious anxiety, depression, and/or sexual difficulties a year after the operation (Maguire et al., 1978). Another study found that fully 44 percent of widows and widowers continued to experience moderate to severe anxiety two to four years after their loss (Parkes, 1975). The sudden death of a loved one appears to produce the most severe and long-lasting distress (Parkes and Weiss, 1983). Even four to seven years after the loss of a spouse or child in an auto accident, for example, survivors have been found to exhibit depression and other psychiatric difficulties and to have problems functioning socially (Lehman, Wortman, and Williams, 1984). Similar slow recovery from adversity has been observed in many victims of rape. One survey found that 26 percent of rape victims still felt that they had not completely recovered four to six years after the assault (Burgess and Holmstrom, 1978). And even among those who seem to have overcome the worst of a trauma, the anguish can be retriggered by some sudden reminder—the anniversary of the day on which the tragedy occurred, the sight of a place somehow tied to the crisis, or even an encounter with a person or object that evokes memories of hap-

pier times. On these occasions, all the emotions felt at the time of the tragedy may come flooding back, with nearly the same intensity as before (Bornstein and Clayton, 1972; Wiener et al., 1975; Parkes, 1970).

Despite such findings, health-care professionals, as well as friends and relatives, often expect quite rapid emotional recovery from adversity. They urge the victims to "get back on their feet," to go on with their lives as soon as possible. Bereaved widows report that remarriage is often tactfully mentioned within a few days or weeks of the husband's death, especially when the widow is young (Maddison and Walker, 1967; Glick, Weiss, and Parkes, 1974). Similarly, parents who have lost a newborn baby are often immediately encouraged to "put the death behind them" and have another child (Helmrath and Steinitz, 1978). So strong is the expectation that victims of misfortune should bounce back rapidly that those who fail to do

Our culture accepts expressions of grief immediately after someone dies, but surviving spouses and close family members find that they are expected to recover quickly from their loss—even though they are actually likely to continue to feel depressed and anxious for months or years. (Mark Duncan/AP/Wide World Photos.)

so may be viewed in a negative light. Researchers have found that women who are still highly distressed six months after being raped are often viewed by others as maladjusted and generally less likable than more resilient rape victims (Coates, Wortman, and Abbey, 1979).

From the victim's or bereaved person's perspective, such attitudes are often upsetting. Widows invariably resent the early hints that they should date and remarry (Glick, Weiss, and Parkes, 1974). In addition, by encouraging the widow or victim to "get back on her feet," other people may subtly convey the message that her feelings and behaviors are inappropriate or even indicative of a psychological disorder. Ironically, victims who have such feelings may be reluctant to seek professional help. In one study, a third of the young women who had undergone a hysterectomy one year earlier were still extremely upset, yet they "were hesitant to seek medical or psychological help because they thought that they should be able to cope with this normal crisis" (Kaltreider, Wallace, and Horowitz, 1979, p. 1503).

The recent research on emotional reactions to crisis reminds us that our intuitions about human behavior are not always correct. We tend to emphasize the remarkable adaptability of people faced with adversity—their impressive ability to cope with the trauma and to recover emotionally. Although this highly resilient image may fit some victims of tragedy, it tends to divert attention from the many who experience distress much longer than is commonly expected. Outsiders should be sensitive to the fact that for many people a life crisis is never put entirely behind them. The emotional scar is carried with them for the rest of their lives (Silver and Wortman, 1980).

Much more needs to be learned about emotional reactions to crisis. The more information researchers obtain, the better able we will be to help people cope with tragedy. Of course, it is also important to examine the physical responses that often accompany the emotional responses to adversity. As you will see in the following section, highly stressful life events can have a marked effect on physical well-being, sometimes contributing to the onset of serious illness.

EMOTIONAL STRESS AND ILLNESS

Emotions—love, anger, joy, frustration—give texture and meaning to our lives. But emotional stress, if severe or prolonged, can take a harsh toll on the body. And stress is everywhere; it can scarcely be avoided. In fact, Hans Selye, the dean of stress researchers, has argued that the body can respond with stress to pleasure as well as to pain:

> Stress is the body's nonspecific response to *any* demand placed on it, whether that demand is pleasant or not. Sitting in a dentist's chair is stressful, but so is enjoying a passionate kiss with a lover—after all, your pulse races, your breathing quickens, your heartbeat soars. And yet who in the world would forgo such a pleasurable pastime simply because of the stress involved?   [Selye and Cherry, 1978, p. 60]

According to Selye, then, all unusual demands on the body tend to evoke a similar set of physiological responses. Selye calls these responses the **general adaptation syndrome.**

The Physiology of Stress: Selye's General Adaptation Syndrome

According to Selye (1956, 1982), the general adaptation syndrome involves three stages: alarm, resistance, and exhaustion. The alarm stage begins with activation of the sympathetic nervous system. The organism is made ready for action: glucose level rises, heartbeat and breathing accelerate—in short, the body pulses with energy. But this stage does not last indefinitely. If stress continues, the body soon responds with what Selye calls resistance. During the resistance stage the organism appears to be physiologically normal because heartbeat and breathing rate are no longer elevated. This appearance, however, is only superficial. Analysis of the blood shows that the body is under the influence of an increase in the pituitary hormone ACTH, as well as in the hormones of the adrenal cortex that ACTH stimulates. These elevated hormone levels, in turn, keep the level of blood glucose unusually high, thus providing a ready source of energy for any defensive actions the organism may need to take. However, the overabundance of ACTH and its related hormones also increases susceptibility to infection because it weakens the body's defenses against invading microorganisms. This is one reason why many students are prone to infectious diseases, from colds and flu to mononucleosis, during the stress of final exams. Like the alarm stage, the resistance stage cannot last forever. The pituitary and the adrenal cortex gradually lose their ability to produce elevated amounts of the hormones needed to sustain energy. If stress is intense and prolonged, Selye's final stage, exhaustion, begins to set in. Now the body's capacity to combat stress steadily declines as all physiological processes break down.

But other researchers have challenged Selye's notion of a general adaptation syndrome—the idea that physiological response to stress is the same in *all* stressful circumstances. Stress researcher John Lacey has found, for instance, that the reaction of the human sympathetic nervous system varies not only with the individual but also with the type of stress to which that person is exposed (Lacey and Lacey, 1962; Lacey, 1967). Moreover, cognitive and emotional factors also play an important part in the body's response to stress. Nervous system and hormone responses seem to increase the most when ordinarily predictable life events are suddenly thrown into turmoil, normal expectations are not met, and the per-

son feels that he or she can do little about the situation (Lazarus, 1977; Lazarus et al., 1980; Mason, 1971, 1974, 1975). Researchers suspect that it is in these situations, particularly when they are prolonged or repeated, that stress takes its greatest toll on the human body and may even contribute to the onset of disease.

Stress-Related Disease and Death

There is now abundant evidence that stress is related to certain serious illnesses (Miller, 1983). For example, people who have what is called a Type A personality—"people who are aggressively involved in a chronic, incessant struggle to achieve more and more in less and less time" (Friedman and Rosenman, 1974, p. 67)—are more prone to heart disease and other disorders than are Type B personalities, who are calmer and more relaxed. Specific psychological characteristics of a Type A personality include an excessive competitive drive, aggressiveness and hostility, impatience, and a chronic sense of time urgency. Type A's are also more likely than Type B's to suppress fatigue in an attempt to maintain their sense of performance and achievement (Glass, 1977). (Figure 10.3 allows you to gauge your own tendencies toward Type A or Type B behavior.)

The evidence linking Type A personality to heart disease is particularly strong (Friedman and Rosen-

Figure 10.3 Items from a self-test for Type A and Type B personalities. Circle the number of each statement that is true, or usually true, for you. The more starred items you agree with, the more you tend toward Type A behavior.

1. In comparison with most people, I know I'm not very involved in my work.

*2. I ordinarily work quickly and energetically.

*3. I hate giving up before I'm absolutely sure I'm licked.

*4. I am often in a hurry.

5. Being tailgated bothers me more than a car in front slowing me up.

*6. It is easy to make me angry.

*7. Sometimes I think I shouldn't work so hard, but something drives me on.

8. I usually speak softer than most people.

9. I prefer to linger over a meal and enjoy it.

*10. In general, I approach my work more seriously than most people I know.

11. I talk more slowly than most people.

12. I generally walk more slowly than most people.

*13. I eat rapidly even when there is plenty of time.

*14. I frequently set deadlines for myself.

*15. I can make myself angry about something in the past just by thinking about it.

man, 1959, 1974; Rosenman et al., 1975). In an important study of more than 3,500 men, twenty-two of the twenty-five who died from heart disease over a five-year period had been classified Type A (Western Collaborative Group Study, 1970). Moreover, autopsies of all the subjects who died showed that atherosclerosis (fatty buildup in the blood vessels) was six times more prevalent in Type A's than in Type B's. In another analysis of these data, Type A behavior posed an average twofold greater risk of heart disease among both men and women (Haynes, Feinlieb, and Kannel, 1980). Although one recent experiment has failed to confirm these findings (Multiple Risk Factor Intervention Trial, 1982), several new studies have found a correlation between Type A and heart disease (French-Belgian Collaborative Group, 1982; DeBacker et al., 1983).

What physiological mechanisms cause the Type A personality to be so susceptible to coronary disorders? No one knows. But scientists have recently found elevated secretions of certain hormones in Type A subjects who were performing only a mildly competitive mental arithmetic task (Williams et al., 1982). These elevated hormone levels may be early links in the chain leading to high rates of heart disease. Also unknown is the exact psychological component of the Type A personality pattern that is most likely to increase the risk of heart disease. This is an important problem because not every Type A personality necessarily exhibits all of the basic Type A characteristics. One individual, for example, may have a great sense of time urgency but not be especially hostile (Matthews, 1982). However, two recent studies (Barefoot, Dahlstrom, and Williams, 1982; Shekelle et al., 1983) suggest that hostility may be a particularly important factor in heart disease among Type A individuals. Work is continuing in this area to determine the precise way in which this behavioral pattern triggers coronary disorders.

High levels of stress are linked not only to heart disease but also to the onset of many other physical disorders, including diabetes, pneumonia, tuberculosis, stomach and intestinal problems, and a variety of more minor ailments, such as chronic headaches and flu (Miller, 1983; Institute of Medicine, 1981, 1982). There are even indications that stress may be related to the onset of cancer, although the evidence is still only suggestive (F. Cohen, 1979). And among people who have been diagnosed as having cancer, emotional expressiveness (which may help reduce stress) is asso-

ciated with longer survival rates (Rogentine et al., 1979; Derogatis et al., 1979). If this sounds hard to believe, remember the link that Hans Selye described between stress, increased hormone levels, and a weakening of the body's natural defenses. For reasons not yet fully understood, severe and prolonged stress tends to lead to suppression of the body's immune system, which normally fights off invading bacteria, viruses, and cancerous growths (Jemmott and Locke, 1984). One study (Bartrop et al., 1977), for example, found that bereaved spouses were more likely than a control group to suffer some reduction of immune-system functioning; loss of a spouse is a major stress-producing event.

Measuring Life Stress. The first attempt to quantify the degree of stress a person experiences was undertaken in 1967, when psychologists Thomas Holmes and Richard Rahe devised their Social Readjustment Rating Scale (SRRS). All of its forty-three common life events, listed in Table 10.2, require some degree of personal readjustment. The SRRS is based on the assumption, derived from Selye's work, that *any* major change in normal life routines is stressful, whether that change is pleasant or unpleasant. The birth of a much-wanted child, for instance, is thought to cause stress just as readily as the foreclosure of a mortgage or a fight with one's in-laws. Holmes and Rahe weighted their forty-three stressful life events according to the degree of readjustment a large sample of people felt each would require. The results are the "life-change units" listed in the right-hand column of Table 10.2. The death of a spouse ranks highest with 100 life-change units, while minor legal violations rank lowest with 11. Research shows that people who accumulate more than 150 life-change units in any one year tend to have more physical and psychological disorders than less stressed people do. These disorders include such major illnesses as heart disease, diabetes, and cancer and various kinds of accidents, even athletic injuries, as well as psychological problems ranging from poor performance in school to serious depression and schizophrenia (Rahe and Arthur, 1978; Perkins, 1982; Selzer and Vinokur, 1974; Bramwell et al., 1975; Lloyd et al., 1980; Paykel, 1979; Thoits, 1983).

The Holmes-Rahe Social Readjustment Rating Scale has had an enormous impact on the study of stress and illness. Only a decade or so after the scale was first developed, it had been used in more than

TABLE 10.2 SOCIAL READJUSTMENT RATING SCALE

RANK	LIFE EVENT	MEAN VALUE	RANK	LIFE EVENT	MEAN VALUE
1	Death of spouse	100	25	Outstanding personal achievement	28
2	Divorce	73	26	Wife begin or stop work	26
3	Marital separation	65	27	Begin or end school	26
4	Jail term	63	28	Change in living conditions	25
5	Death of close family member	63	29	Revision of personal habits	24
6	Personal injury or illness	53	30	Trouble with boss	23
7	Marriage	50	31	Change in work hours or conditions	20
8	Fired at work	47	32	Change in residence	20
9	Marital reconciliation	45	33	Change in schools	20
10	Retirement	45	34	Change in recreation	19
11	Change in health of family member	44	35	Change in church activities	19
12	Pregnancy	40	36	Change in social activities	18
13	Sex difficulties	39	37	Mortgage or loan less than $10,000	17
14	Gain of new family member	39	38	Change in sleeping habits	16
15	Business readjustment	39	39	Change in number of family get-togethers	15
16	Change in financial state	38	40	Change in eating habits	15
17	Death of close friend	37	41	Vacation	13
18	Change to different line of work	36	42	Christmas	12
19	Change in number of arguments with spouse	35	43	Minor violations of the law	11
20	Mortgage over $10,000	31			
21	Foreclosure of mortgage or loan	30			
22	Change in responsibilities at work	29			
23	Son or daughter leaving home	29			
24	Trouble with in-laws	29			

Source: Thomas H. Holmes and Richard H. Rahe, "The social readjustment rating scale," *Journal of Psychosomatic Research* (1967): 213–218.

The amount of life stress a person has experienced in a given period of time, say one year, is measured by the total number of life change units (LCUs). These units result from the addition of the values (shown in the right column) associated with events that the person has experienced during the target time period.

1,000 studies (Perkins, 1982). Physicians, as well as popular writers, have helped to publicize the findings by warning of the potential health risks posed by multiple life changes in the same year. Some health-maintenance organizations have even announced plans to advise patients who have already accumulated many life-change units in a given year to try to avoid additional changes if possible in order to protect against illness (F. Cohen, 1979). Such programs, however, although well intentioned, are probably premature.

Many researchers have recently questioned whether the Holmes-Rahe Scale is the best possible predictor of stress-related health problems that we might use.

One question is whether positive life changes, currently included on the SRRS, are very good indicators of stress. Recent evidence suggests that positive life changes (such as winning a sweepstakes or being promoted) are much less likely than negative life changes to lead to illness (Thoits, 1983; Perkins, 1982). Another question raised is whether the Holmes-Rahe scale is sensitive enough to the timing of life changes. People who experience many life changes in rapid succession appear to be at greater risk than those whose life changes are more widely spaced over the course of a year (Wainer, Fairbank, and Hough, 1978). Third, some psychologists have wondered whether all of the items on the SRRS are necessarily *causes* of illness. Might not some of them be consequences? People in the early stages of illness, before the condition is diagnosed, may have more sexual problems, more arguments with their spouses, more trouble with their bosses and in-laws, more changes in recreation and social activities than other people do. In fact, it has been argued that as many as half of the items listed on the SRRS might conceivably be the results of some disorder (Dohrenwend et al., 1982). If this is so, then it is no wonder that high scores on the SRRS often correlate with illness. Finally, some researchers have even questioned the basic assumption that major life changes are the most stressful factors in our lives. Richard Lazarus has argued that the little irritations, when they are frequent and intense, may be just as stress-inducing as the large-scale readjustments, if not more so. Lazarus and his colleagues call these minor irritations—the traffic jams, the lost car keys, the just-missed trains, the spilled coffee cups, the irritating co-worker, the boss's unreasonable demands, the child's temper tantrums—the "hassles" of everyday life. They have found that the frequency of hassles is a better predictor of both psychological and physical health problems than life-change units are (DeLongis, Coyne, and Lazarus, in press; Kanner et al., in press). This line of research seems to confirm what many of us have long believed: much stress is caused by those repeated little frustrations, none of which alone seems very significant.

Variability in Succumbing to Stress-Related Illness. We need to know much more about the kinds of life events that tend to promote stress and the circumstances in which they do so before we can predict with any accuracy who will succumb to stress-related illness. One major complication in trying to make such predictions is that people react so differently to the same potentially stressful events. One person who is fired from a job cheerfully sets out to find a new one, while another begins to suffer agonizing migraine headaches. Why do some people take stressful events in stride while others react by becoming ill?

One possible explanation involves differences in the emotional support that people under stress receive. Encouragement and understanding from others have been found to be related to the ability to cope with a variety of misfortunes, including the death of a loved one, paralysis, blindness, severe burns, cancer, and criminal assault. A study of rape victims, for example, found that nearly half of the women whose relatives and friends were supportive recovered within a few months. In contrast, none of the women who lacked social support recovered this quickly. Even four to six years later, 53 percent of the women without support from others were still psychologically scarred by the rape (Burgess and Holmstrom, 1978). And social support promotes not just psychological recovery but also physical well-being. One nine-year investigation showed that people who lacked close social ties were three to three hundred times more likely to die in the period studied than were people who enjoyed such ties (Berkman and Syme, 1979).

Another reason why some people are better able than others to cope with stress may have to do with their outlooks on life. Consider a study of two groups of male executives, one consisting of men who had experienced both high stress and a high incidence of illness and the other of men who had experienced equally high stress with few physical effects (Kobasa, 1979). Personality tests revealed that the stress-ridden executives who had avoided illness differed from their less healthy colleagues in what Suzanne Kobasa calls psychological "hardiness." The hardy executive, for instance, viewed a sudden transfer to an unfamiliar city as a challenging new opportunity. He threw himself into the job with enthusiasm, intent on using his capabilities to gain from the assignment. The executive low in hardiness, in contrast, viewed such a transfer as an imposition. Because he felt he had no choice, he went along with it, but with much resentment. In a subsequent study, Kobasa and her colleagues followed over a period of years a sample of subjects rated at the outset for their psychological hardiness (Kobasa, Maddi, and Kahn, 1982). As expected, hardy subjects tended to fare much better physically when they were exposed to potentially stressful circumstances. Their optimistic, "take-charge" outlooks apparently helped reduce the levels of anxiety and upset they might otherwise have felt.

A third, particularly provocative possibility in regard to individual differences in susceptibility to stress-related physical symptoms is that some of those who remain healthy despite adverse conditions simply care less than others do about the people and events around them. They are not strongly motivated to achieve any goals, have shallow attachments to others, lack involvement in life affairs, and are more concerned with their own well-being than are people who suffer frequent stress-related illness (Hinkle, 1974).

Clearly, such people would tend to be quite well insulated from many upsetting emotions. But much more research will have to be done before we can say to what extent this theory is correct.

Techniques for Reducing Stress

Although some people may be insulated from stress because of individual circumstances or personality traits, not everyone is so fortunate. Is there anything the more stress-prone person can do to reduce stress? Psychologists have developed techniques for just this purpose, some of which require little special training to undertake.

One technique involves the use of **biofeedback** to exert conscious control over internal processes. With biofeedback, a subject's physiological changes are electronically monitored, thus providing the person with constant feedback about the way his or her body is responding. Through trial and error the person then works at reducing any undesirable changes, hoping eventually to learn how to halt them at will.

There is now substantial evidence that, in the laboratory at least, biofeedback can indeed help people control a variety of physiological responses, including some related to stress. People can be taught to use biofeedback to control physiological responses that lead to particular symptoms, or taught to evoke a more general state of reduced arousal (Holroyd and Lazarus, 1982). One of the most well-established successes of biofeedback has been in helping people who suffer from tension and migraine headaches to reduce the incidence of these stress-related ailments (Blanchard et al., 1980). But it is not completely clear what is causing the improvement. Are these people, in their everyday lives, actually controlling the physiological responses that give rise to the headaches? Or are they simply learning to cope better *psychologically* with stress by being more assertive when something is bothering them, or by avoiding situations that previously elicited headaches? Answers to such questions will provide important data on the limits of biofeedback as a means of managing stress. We will explore other uses of biofeedback in Chapter 12, where we discuss human consciousness.

A second approach to managing stress is the one we just touched on when we proposed an alternative explanation for the way biofeedback works. The person under stress can try to control not his or her physiological reactions but the various cognitions that maintain and intensify those physiological responses. In the therapeutic setting, stress-prone people are encouraged to stop thinking of their circumstances in highly pessimistic ways, which can only increase their anxiety. They are taught cognitive skills for coping with adverse conditions. They might be taught, for instance, to (a) analyze the problem facing them; (b) generate a number of possible solutions; (c) evaluate the alternatives generated; (d) implement the most promising solution; and (e) assess the effectiveness of the solution implemented. They are then urged to use these newly acquired skills in real-life situations. This cognitive approach is being used quite successfully to help people at high risk of stress-related illnesses, as well as those suffering from acute anxiety and depression (Meichenbaum and Jeremko, 1982). In a sense therapists who employ it are trying to instill in stress-prone people psychological outlooks very similar to those held by Kobasa's "hardy" individuals. We will say much more about such cognitive interventions in Chapter 15, when we discuss the treatment of psychological disorders.

Another approach to reducing stress which focuses on cognitive factors involves the use of positive imagery. Stoyva and Anderson (1982) report on one early study in which people suffering from stomach ulcers, a stress-related illness, were asked to picture pleasant experiences whenever they felt anxious or upset (Chappel and Stevenson, 1936). This "imagery therapy" began soon after the patients had been medically treated for their ulcers, and so were temporarily symptom-free. In comparison with a control group of ulcer patients who were given no such instructions, the experimental patients were much less likely to show any recurrence of the disorder, even a full three years later. Unfortunately, we do not know the precise mechanisms by which this therapy worked. But presumably the pleasant imagery somehow undermined the fears and worries that tend to intensify stress reactions.

A final means of reducing stress, which holds much promise, is regular vigorous exercise. Investigators have found consistent links between physical fitness training and improvement in people's general emotional states. This is particularly true when a person is very unfit or feeling very anxious or depressed (Folkins and Sime, 1981; Folkins et al., 1972; Morgan et al., 1970). In a group of women with sedentary jobs who took part in a twenty-week physical fitness program, two-thirds showed reduced levels of anxiety as measured by both physiological assessments and self-reports (Popejoy, 1967). A recent experiment (McCaan and Holmes, in press) showed that exercise can have an equally dramatic effect on reducing depression. Forty-three depressed women were randomly assigned to one of three groups: an aerobics exercise class, a group that practiced relaxation exercises, and a control group that received no treatment. After ten weeks, those who participated in strenuous aerobics showed less depression than subjects in both of the other groups. These results provided the first controlled experimental evidence that exercise can help to relieve depression.

We must be cautious in drawing conclusions from some of the studies relating exercise to stress reduction, however. Many people who join the experimental groups volunteer to do so, and there may be something special about people who volunteer for fitness training which makes them less prone to anxiety or depression in the first place. Often, too, the experimental subjects are aware that they are "experimentals," and the feelings of importance that accompany this knowledge may alone tend to boost their morale (Folkins and Sime, 1981). Still, the evidence linking strenuous exercise to reduced levels of stress-related emotional symptoms is consistent enough to warrant further research.

One question that investigators seek to answer is how physical exercise manages to combat the emotional symptoms of stress. Some speculate that it may do so by reducing the physiological reactions to stressful life circumstances. We know that with prolonged fitness training a person's physiological responses to the stress of vigorous exercise gradually diminish. A physically fit person can engage in a strenuous workout with a smaller rise in heartbeat and respiration and lower outpourings of certain hormones than a physically unfit person experiences (Ledwidge, 1980). Perhaps this adaptation to physical stress carries over to psychological stressors. Perhaps when placed in psychologically stressful situations the physically fit person has significantly lessened bodily responses because he or she is accustomed to dealing with stress of a different kind. It has also been suggested that vigorous exercise may stimulate increased release of certain neurotransmitters, particularly norepinephrine and the morphine-like endorphins we talked about in Chapter 3. If so, then their effects on the brain may be counteracting the stress response

and promoting a sense of psychological well-being (Stein and Belluzzi, 1978; Howley, 1976). Another possibility is that people who exercise regularly feel good about themselves because they look better physically and feel a sense of accomplishment in achieving a difficult goal (Ismail and Trachtman, 1973; Solomon and Bumpus, 1978; Ledwidge, 1980). This alone might account for any reduced levels of anxiety and depression that physically fit people might show. It is hoped that future research will help to untangle this complex web of cause-and-effect relationships.

in depth Studying Happiness

A substantial part of this chapter has focused on negative emotions, particularly those related to adversity and stress. It therefore seems appropriate to conclude our discussion with an in-depth look at how psychologists have gone about studying human happiness.

When asked to define *happiness,* people emphasize different aspects of this elusive state (Brickman, 1978). Some see happiness as mainly passive contentment—the inner peace and tranquillity that come from deep satisfaction with one's surroundings, one's relationships with others, and oneself. Others see happiness primarily as active pleasures—stimulation, excitement, challenge, accomplishment, and involvement in rewarding activities. These differences in definition, however, are simply differences in emphasis. Most people agree that both these sides of happiness should be included in any complete definition of the term. **Happiness,** then, can be described as an enduring, positive emotional state that includes quiet contentment with one's life and self as well as active pleasures and achievements (Warr, 1978). Note that this definition refers to happiness as an *enduring* emotional state, as distinguished from the transient elevations of mood we often briefly experience. It is this more long-term kind of happiness, sometimes called positive well-being, that we will be emphasizing here.

THE PSYCHOLOGY OF HAPPINESS. One of the central questions in the study of happiness concerns the psychological factors that tend to make a person happy. Researchers have proposed several of them, some of which may surprise you. One is that happiness is primarily a matter of social comparison. If our present situation compares favorably with that of others who we perceive are broadly similar to us, we feel happy; if it compares unfavorably, we feel discontented. On the basis of this notion some people have argued that a utopian society in which people received everything they wanted would not foster happiness (Brickman, 1978). How in such a society of perpetual fulfillment could people ever judge themselves to be fortunate?

Empirical research has often supported the social comparison theory of happiness. One of the first pieces of evidence in its favor came from a survey of soldiers during the 1940s (Merton and Kitt, 1950). The survey revealed a number of puzzling paradoxes. Soldiers who lacked a high school diploma, for example, were much less likely to be promoted than were soldiers with a high school education or better. Yet the men with *less* education were generally *more* satisfied with the army's promotion policies than were their better-educated counterparts. The reason apparently had to do with each group's sources of comparison. In comparison with similarly educated men in the civilian world, the more educated soldiers were doing quite poorly, but the less educated soldiers were doing quite well. As a result, the former were very dissatisfied while the latter were reasonably content.

Such findings suggest that if we could only change the sources of comparison people use to gauge their degree of fortune, we might be able to change their self-perceived happiness. Advertisers, in fact, try to do this all the time. By bombarding us with pictures of people whose possessions are far more elegant than our own, they try to induce us to compare ourselves with these more fortunate others and so to feel discontented (Brickman, 1978). The reverse, of course, is also possible. If unfavorable sources of comparison are eliminated, people may be more satisfied with their lives. It has been argued that Cuban president Fidel Castro may have raised the satisfaction of his people considerably just by eliminating the rich American tourists who used to flock to Cuba each year (Brickman and Campbell, 1971). This ability to change people's perceived happiness simply by changing the sources of social comparison available to them has been demonstrated experimentally. In one study, for instance, Milwaukee residents who read vivid descriptions of how terrible life in their city was at the turn of the century reported more satisfaction

with their current circumstances than did residents who read a glowing description of Milwaukee's earlier years (Dermer, Cohen, and Anderson, 1978).

Outside the laboratory, however, the sources of comparison available to us are seldom so tightly controlled. As a result, people have a choice about which group of others they will compare themselves with. And research suggests that, when given such a choice, people are often strongly motivated to enhance their feelings of well-being by comparing themselves with *less* fortunate others (Wills, 1981). This has been clearly demonstrated in recent interviews with cancer patients, who have every reason to think of themselves as worse off than almost everyone else. But the remarkable thing is the extent to which these people find ways to think of themselves as relatively lucky (Taylor, Wood, and Lichtman, 1983). Women who have had a malignant tumor removed from one of their breasts compare themselves with less fortunate women who have undergone mastectomies (removal of the entire breast). The mastectomy patients, in turn, focus on others still worse off than themselves—perhaps those whose cancer is spreading despite the operation, or those whose surgical amputations are more disfiguring (loss of an arm or leg, for instance). Even those who are dying of their cancer often manage to find less fortunate others to compare themselves with. Some focus on the terminally ill who lack the comfort of friends and relatives, while others focus on dying patients who have failed to find inner peace.

As provocative as it is, the social comparison theory of happiness has limitations, however. One problem is its failure to explain why a person who is extremely fortunate in relation to others can still be unhappy. One study has shown, for instance, that winners of a million-dollar state lottery report no more satisfaction with life than less financially fortunate people (Brickman, Coates, and Janoff-Bulman, 1978). How could this be if happiness depends on social comparison alone? Clearly, some other psychological factors must be involved as well.

Adaptation theory provides one such set of factors (Helson, 1964; Brickman and Campbell, 1971). It argues that when something highly positive happens, we quickly adapt to our new level of fortune—that is, we accept it as an integral part of our lives. As a result, several things tend to happen. First, in the short run, simple things that once gave us pleasure tend to lose some of their appeal because they seem so much less

After their initial elation, most lottery winners are found to be no happier than other people of similar background who have not received such a windfall. For possible explanations of this paradoxical reaction, see the text. *(AP/Wide World Photos.)*

exciting than our recent windfall. This is called the "contrast effect." Second, in the longer run, the pleasure derived from the windfall itself tends to erode. What once seemed a thrilling stroke of fortune gradually loses its luster and becomes the status quo. This is called the "habituation effect."

Psychologists Philip Brickman and Dan Coates (1978) have gathered evidence that these two adaptation processes do indeed operate in everyday life. They interviewed twenty-two big winners in the Illinois state lottery and twenty-two other people with similar backgrounds who had never experienced such a financial windfall. Brickman and Coates found that, as predicted, the lottery winners described themselves as no more happy than the nonwinners did, and they also tended to derive less satisfaction from such simple pleasures as watching television and eating a good breakfast. Apparently winning a lottery is not nearly so rich a source of happiness as we might expect. Although winners may initially compare themselves with others and think how lucky they are, the contrast and habituation effects may eventually lessen the overall pleasure they experience.

Some people might interpret these findings in a very optimistic light: great wealth, great fame and power, all the fabulous things we will probably never acquire would not make us very happy anyway! But a far more pessimistic interpretation is also possible. These same findings can be used to argue that the pursuit of happiness is a kind of pleasure-seeking treadmill, whereby today's great joys tend to overshadow simpler pleasures and may eventually seem lackluster themselves. According to this perspective, great happiness can never be permanent unless our circumstances are *constantly* improving—something that is very unlikely.

Many psychologists take issue with this pessimistic outlook, however. They point out that in surveys a sizable number of people report being "very happy," and that those who are tend to stay that way over long periods of time (Gurin, Veroff, and Feld, 1960; Andrews and Withey, 1976; Palmore and Kivett, 1977). What could account for these chronically happy people if we assume that relatively few of them can have constantly improving life circumstances? One possibility, of course, is that they are simply more inclined than others to make favorable social comparisons—to see themselves as luckier than other people. But another possibility is that many of these people may possess certain personality traits associated with behaviors that typically bring pleasure and dissociated from behaviors that typically bring discontent.

This is what psychologists Paul Costa and Robert McCrae (1980) argue. On the basis of correlational studies of personality and subjective well-being, they propose that extroversive traits (sociability, warmth, involvement with other people) contribute to human pleasures, while neurotic traits (compulsiveness, hostility, feelings of guilt or anxiety) contribute to human discontent. Thus a person's overall potential for happiness can be thought of as the sum of these two personality dimensions. The person high in extroversion and low in neuroticism has the greatest potential for happiness, while the person high in neuroticism and low in extroversion has the greatest potential for misery. In between are those who have different mixes of these two basic tendencies, one drawing the person toward pleasures, the other encouraging negative feelings. But note that, according to this theory, people who are moderately happy may have vastly different kinds of emotional experiences. On the one hand is the superextrovert high in neurotic traits, who experiences great emotional highs but numerous lows as well, which average out to a moderate level of contentment. On the other hand is the introvert who is low in neurotic traits, and so has a life of emotional blandness with few positive or negative extremes.

Yet another way of explaining why some people are consistently happier than others invites us to define happiness in a rather unusual way. According to this definition, true happiness is found in the ability to abandon all concern about whether one is happy or not (Brickman and Campbell, 1971). Granted, this state of mind is difficult to achieve. But it is sometimes attained through total absorption in a challenging task that demands undivided attention. Dancers, composers, chess players, mountain climbers, and surgeons often report this kind of submergence in their profession or sport (Csikszentmihalyi, 1975). Here is how one young musician described the experience:

> All of a sudden nothing seemed to matter except the music. . . . The things I practiced seemed to just come out. I never thought about which fingering I would use or when I would breathe. It just came out naturally. All I thought about was expressing myself in the way that I thought the piece should sound. I never noticed there was an audience after the first eight bars of music. . . . Even now I don't remember their applause but only my feeling of satisfaction in playing the piece the way I actually felt it should be played. [Privette and Landsman, 1983, pp. 195–196]

When such states of total absorption occur, the person's self-consciousness fades and with it all thought of actively pursuing happiness. Perhaps some of the people who consistently describe themselves as "very happy" have a greater opportunity or capacity for this kind of experience.

HAPPINESS AND LIFE CIRCUMSTANCES.

The various theories we have been exploring focus on psychological processes that tend to encourage or dampen human happiness. But there is another side to the causes of happiness. Intuitively, most of us feel that life circumstances contribute more to human happiness than the theories so far discussed have acknowledged. We tend to believe, for instance, that the rural resident is happier than the city dweller, the prince happier than the pauper, the person of average intelligence happier than the genius. Is there any truth to such common assumptions? Are there particular life circumstances that tend to promote happiness?

The answer seems to be yes, but not always in the ways one might think. More money, for instance, does *not* necessarily mean more happiness (Duncan, 1975; Allardt, 1976). As long as people have enough to live on without financial worry, they would probably not be much happier if their incomes substantially increased. Brickman and Coates showed this tendency in their research on lottery winners, and several correlational studies confirm it (Larson, 1975; Brad-

A satisfying family life has been found to be the single best predictor of happiness. (Alan Carey/The Image Works.)

burn and Caplovitz, 1965). In contrast, the single most important life circumstance predictive of great happiness is a satisfying marriage and family life (Campbell, Converse, and Rodgers, 1976; Andrews and Withey, 1976; Glenn and Weaver, 1981). Love, in short, seems to contribute enormously to happiness, as does close friendship (Wessman and Ricks, 1966; Bradburn, 1969). Just as Costa and McCrae's theory of happiness suggested, some of the happiest people are those who, among other things, are actively involved in the world around them, especially with other people. Where a person lives does not seem to matter as far as happiness is concerned. City dwellers, in general, are just as happy as rural residents (Bull and Aucoin, 1975). A person's level of intelligence, however, may affect happiness—but not in the way the adage "ignorance is bliss" implies. If anything, more intelligent people are more satisfied with life and less likely to feel isolated from others (Campbell, Converse, and Rodgers, 1976; Sigelman, 1981).

INCREASING PERSONAL HAPPINESS. On the basis of the research we have covered so far, can any generalizations be made about how people can increase their levels of happiness? One key seems to

be strong and satisfying personal relationships. Friends, a good marriage, supportive family members all seem to contribute to personal happiness. So does a positive outlook on life, such as the ability to compare one's circumstances favorably with those of other people. In addition, happiness can be enhanced by some of the techniques for managing stress we talked about earlier. By reducing the stress-related emotions of anxiety and depression, people can raise their overall sense of well-being.

Another approach to increasing personal happiness is to get more involved in activities that provide short-run pleasures, in the hope that over time such involvement will boost our general morale. The first step is to find out just what everyday activities are most satisfying to us. The answers are not always obvious. Sometimes what people spend most of their free time doing is *not* what gives them the most pleasure. In one study, for instance, high school students were asked to write down what they were doing and how much they were enjoying it each time a small portable electronic signaling device beeped (between five and seven times a day). Although playing games and engaging in sports were most strongly associated with positive emotions, the students engaged in these

Figure 10.4 The perfectionist doctor who filled out this pleasure-prediction chart discovered that many activities he did only moderately well (recorded in the last column) could be rewarding (the third column). The exercise helped him relax and take chances in his professional life that he had been avoiding for fear of failure. If you draw up a list of activities you consider satisfying and rate them both before and after undertaking them, you may find a similar result. *(From Burns, 1980, p. 50.)*

Activity	Predict how satisfying the activity will be	Record how satisfying it actually was	Record how effectively you performed
Fix broken pipe in kitchen	20%	99% (I actually did it.)	20% (I took a long time and made a lot of mistakes.)
Give lecture to medical school class	70%	50% (I didn't feel particularly gratified about my performance.)	98% (As usual, I got a standing ovation.)
Play squash with Joe	75%	90% (Even though I didn't play especially well, we had a hell of a good time.)	40% (I played subpar. So what!)
Jog to store and get ice cream cone	60%	90% (It was fun!)	50% (I did not improve my time for jogging this distance.)

activities far less often than in watching TV, which they rated as much less pleasurable (Csikszentmihalyi, Larson, and Reed, 1977).

Some clinical psychologists suggest that one reason that many people refrain from activities that could make them feel happy is the widespread belief that things are fun only if they can be done extremely well. This belief is mistaken, as psychologist David Burnes (1980) demonstrated by asking clients to rate upcoming activities as to how pleasurable they were likely to be, on a scale of 0 to 100. After the activity was over the client once again rated it, this time in terms of how pleasurable it actually was and how well he or she performed it. Figure 10.4 shows such a pleasure-prediction sheet compiled by a doctor who strove for perfection in everything he did and complained of being frustrated and depressed. To the doctor's surprise, many of the things he had little aptitude for and expected to derive little pleasure from (such as fixing a leaky kitchen pipe) turned out to be far more satisfying than things he did outstandingly well. Apparently one need not perform an activity well in order to derive enjoyment from it. If you have a tendency toward perfectionism, you may want to compile your own pleasure-prediction sheet in order to find out if the things you consider your principal sources of happiness are really that pleasurable after all.

in depth

SUMMARY

1. All human beings experience **emotions,** states of feeling that can affect behavior, which often arise in response to social relationships and other external stimuli and are frequently accompanied by physiological changes as well as various cognitions.

2. The role of physiological arousal in emotion has long intrigued psychologists. Strong emotions, such as anger and fear, are often associated with activation of the sympathetic nervous system, which promotes such physiological changes as rapid breathing and an increased heartbeat. Psychologists can measure these changes by means of a **polygraph.** The polygraph is also used as a lie detector under the assumption that a person who lies will feel anxious and therefore undergo physiological changes. This use of the polygraph is controversial, however.

3. The brain coordinates the activities of the autonomic nervous system, and parts of the brain—the hypothalamus and the limbic system in particular—are involved in a number of emotions. Stimulation of or damage to these parts has been accompanied by exaggerated emotional behavior. The cerebral cortex, however, is also intimately involved in emotional experience.

4. Most theories of emotions have centered on the relationship between the two main aspects of emotion: (1) physiological arousal and (2) the subjective feelings we call fear, anger, and so on. At the turn of the century, William James and Carl Lange proposed that our perception of our body changes is itself the emotion, and that each emotional state is signaled by a unique physiological pattern. This view came to be known as the **James-Lange theory.** _1st we cry   2nd feel grief_

5. Subsequent researchers have tried to determine whether each human emotion is in fact associated with a unique set of physiological responses. For a while, many believed that the answer was probably no. Recently, however, improved physiological measurement techniques have reopened the question. Much research still needs to be done in this field.

6. The question of the distinctiveness of the physiology of each emotion aside, most psychologists agree that some kind of arousal is needed for a true emotion to be experienced. People with severed spinal cords who lack normal sympathetic nervous system responses no longer feel the full force of strong emotions, such as anger.

7. Stanley Schachter has proposed that emotion involves two closely interacting factors: a state of physiological arousal and a cognitive interpretation of that arousal. He attributes our capacity to comprehend emotional arousal to our ability to label _general_ sensations as _specific_ emotions. Schachter believes that arousal simply signals to us that an explanation of some kind is needed, and that we look to environmental cues to place a label on these physical sensations.

8. Although Schachter's theory of emotion has had widespread influence, R. B. Zajonc has recently questioned its basic assumption that cognitive appraisal is

essential to emotion. Zajonc believes that humans may be capable of experiencing emotion with only the most rudimentary kind of cognitive processing.

9. Three assumptions about emotional reactions to crisis characterize the beliefs of laymen and health-care professionals: that there are universal reactions that occur in response to crisis; that people go through stages as they cope with crisis; and that the crisis is ultimately resolved. Though widely held, these assumptions have not been experimentally supported.

10. Researcher Hans Selye has concluded from animal studies that the body responds to all types of emotional stress with a similar three-stage pattern—alarm, resistance, and exhaustion—which he calls the **general adaptation syndrome.** Other researchers believe the human response to stress may be more varied and complex than that outlined by Selye, particularly since different types of stress appear to cause different sympathetic reactions.

11. Many scientists are convinced that the onset of many (perhaps all) diseases involves emotional factors. Psychologists Thomas Holmes and Richard Rahe developed the Social Readjustment Rating Scale to measure the amount of stress a person is undergoing by assigning a certain number of "life-change units" to life events that require some personal readjustment. They found that the accumulation of many life-change units during a single year is associated with an increased risk of illness. Some psychologists have criticized the Holmes-Rahe scale, however, be-cause it assumes that both positive and negative life changes are stressful, because many of the items included could be signs of existing illness, and because life's small hassles (when numerous and intense) may be even more stressful than major life changes.

12. The prediction of stress-related illness is complicated by the differences in individual reactions to stress. One's personality and degree of social support are both influential in helping one cope successfully with stress.

13. Some psychologists have developed techniques for reducing stress. Current approaches include bio-feedback, cognitive therapies, and regular fitness training.

14. **Happiness** is a positive emotion that includes both inner contentment and active pleasure. Psychologists who have looked for the psychological roots of happiness have proposed several theories. One is that happiness lies in the tendency to make favorable comparisons between oneself and other people. A second is that the happiest people are those high in extroversive personality traits and low in neurotic qualities. A third is that happiness comes from the ability to "lose" oneself in some challenging task, so that the conscious pursuit of happiness is forgotten. Researchers have also found that happiness tends to be associated with certain life circumstances, the most important of which are close social relationships. Ironically, people are often unaware of the things in life that make them happiest.

SUGGESTED READINGS

EKMAN, PAUL, and FRIESEN, WALLACE V. *Unmasking the face.* Englewood Cliffs, N.J.: Prentice Hall, 1975.

A well-illustrated discussion of the facial expressions that are associated with various emotional states.

GOLDBERGER, LEO, and BREZNITZ, SHLOMO (Eds.). *Handbook of stress: Theoretical and clinical aspects.* New York: Free Press, 1982.

A useful collection of articles, including a discussion by Hans Selye of the history and present status of the stress concept.

JAMES, WILLIAM. The emotions. In *The principles of psychology.* Fredson Bowers and Frederick Burkhardt, eds. Cambridge, Mass.: Harvard University Press, 1983 (originally published 1890).

James's presentation and defense of what is now called the James-Lange theory of emotion.

KAPLAN, HOWARD B. (Ed.). *Psychosocial stress: Trends in theory and research.* New York: Academic Press, 1983.
 A valuable recent overview of the study of stress.

PLUTCHIK, ROBERT, and KELLERMAN, HENRY (Eds.). *Emotion: Theory, research, and experience.* New York: Academic Press, 1980.
 A two-volume compendium of papers on recent work in the area of emotions.

SCHACHTER, STANLEY. *Emotion, obesity, and crime.* New York: Academic Press, 1971.
 Articles related to Schachter's theory of emotion.

TAVRIS, C. *Anger: The misunderstood emotion.* New York: Simon & Schuster, 1982.
 An in-depth examination of anger that challenges many widely held assumptions about it.

11

THE DYNAMICS OF MOTIVATION

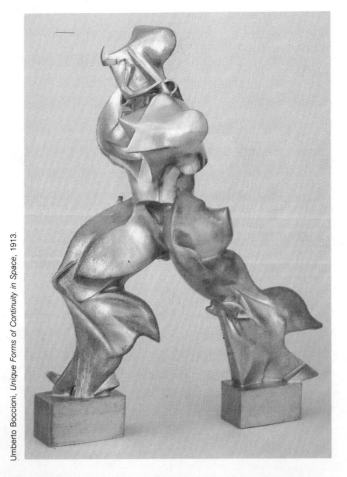

Umberto Boccioni, *Unique Forms of Continuity in Space*, 1913.

Learned Motivation: The Case of Achievement

Individual Differences in Achievement Motivation

Encouraging Achievement Behavior

Achievement Behavior among Women
Do Many Women Fear Success?
Sex Differences in Interpreting Failure
Sex Differences in Task Incentives

Why in the early 1950s did two men expose themselves to weeks of bitter wind and cold, scarcity of oxygen, and treacherous icy terrain in order to be the first humans to set foot on the summit of Mount Everest? Why, a decade earlier, did the Nazi regime in Germany systematically kill more than 6 million Jews in a manner so brutal it defies comprehension? Why in Nazi concentration camps did some prisoners risk their lives to steal food for a friend near death from starvation? The answers to all such questions are bound up in the complex web of human motivations.

Many contemporary psychologists define **motivation** as encompassing all the factors that arouse, sustain, and direct behavior toward attainment of some goal (Madsen, 1959). This definition leaves unanswered, however, exactly what these factors are. Which ones are most important? In which circumstances? And how do the various factors relate to one another? These are key questions that psychologists have long debated. Exploring some of the answers they have given over the years is an excellent way to introduce you to the fascinating topic of motivation.

THE DEVELOPMENT OF MOTIVATIONAL CONCEPTS

At the turn of this century, with the growing popularity of Darwin's theory of evolution, humans began to see themselves as part of nature, related through distant ancestry to every living creature. This was a radically new self-concept, and it prompted new perspectives on motivation. If the behavior of lower animals is controlled primarily by instincts, and if we humans are indeed kin to all other living things, might not some of our behavior also be instinctual? Such speculation launched a widespread effort to identify human **instincts**—innate, internal forces, characteristic of a species, which propel individuals to behave in broadly predictable ways (Weiner, 1972, 1980).

One of the most influential of the instinct theorists was psychologist William McDougall, who in 1908 proposed a list of human instincts which included curiosity, pugnacity, self-abasement, flight, repulsion, self-assertion, reproduction, gregariousness, acquisition, and parental care. Other investigators proposed different lists, and the number of instincts continued to grow as researchers tried to account for more and

305

more behaviors. One survey conducted in the 1920s found that more than 2,500 human instincts had so far been proposed (Bernard, 1924). One researcher facetiously suggested that we humans must also have an instinct to believe in instincts (Ayres, 1921).

Criticisms of the instinct concept were well founded. How do we know, critics asked, that all these behaviors are instinctive? The mere fact that they are common does not prove they are innate. Widespread behaviors could just as well be the products of cultural learning. Moreover, the concept of instincts does little to explain *why* behavior occurs. If we say that someone marries because of the "nesting" instinct, has children because of the "breeding" instinct, makes friends because of the "sociability" instinct, and so forth, what light have we really shed on any of these actions? For these reasons, a simple appeal to instincts fell out of favor with psychologists, and researchers began to develop more precise models of motivation.

Freud and Unconscious Motivation

One alternative was offered by the Viennese physician Sigmund Freud. He reduced the many human instincts that McDougall and others had proposed to two basic ones. The first was the urge toward life, procreation, and self-preservation, which included the drives for food, water, warmth, and above all sex. The second was the urge toward death and self-destruction, a return to the inanimate matter of which all living things are composed. Freud speculated that we often resolve the conflict between these two basic forces by turning our destructive energies outward, against others. Hence the human tendencies to compete, to conquer, and to kill.

Because many ways of satisfying sexual and aggressive urges are morally unacceptable, Freud believed that people push "forbidden" impulses deep into the unconscious. In Freudian terms, these impulses are **repressed.** But a repressed urge still has power; it demands some kind of outlet. Often it directs a person to engage in some substitute behavior that is more socially acceptable, a process called **sublimation.** Freud proposed, for example, that many of the beautiful nudes that Renaissance artists created on canvas and in marble were the products of sublimated sexual impulses. Similarly, we may unconsciously express anger toward our parents by losing or accidentally breaking one of their cherished possessions, or by showing up late for a special holiday dinner. The possibility that our behavior may be controlled by unconscious motives—motives that arise from deeply repressed urges—is one of Freud's most important contributions. Because Freud's primary aim was to explain abnormal behavior, we will postpone a detailed treatment of his viewpoints until Chapters 13 and 15.

Drive-Reduction Theory

At the same time that Freud's ideas were attracting interest in Europe, such American behaviorists as John B. Watson were stressing the need for a more scientific approach to motivation. These researchers rejected the mysterious realms of instinct and the unconscious in favor of the view that the way we act is the result of conditioning or learning. A person behaves aggressively, they argued, not because of an "aggressive instinct," but because he or she has been rewarded for such behavior in the past.

But as research accumulated, some problems emerged for those who tried to argue that *all* variations in goal-directed behavior could be explained simply by learning. Investigators found it difficult, for example, to condition the behavior of a dog that had just been fed. Should we therefore conclude that feeding produces some kind of learning deficit? Not likely. It makes more sense to say that learning is often encouraged when an animal is propelled by some biological need. Thus many psychologists interested in motivation began to focus on the role of physiological drives.

One such person was behaviorist Clark Hull, widely considered the most influential of all psychologists between 1930 and 1950. Hull (1943) argued that **drive** was the outcome of an animal's states of biological need. The result of drive was to make the animal more active, thus increasing the likelihood that it would perform a drive-reducing response. A hungry rat, for instance, would become agitated and soon hit upon the bar-press that delivered a pellet of food. When the rat ate, its drive state would decline and reinforcement would consequently occur. This, of course, would increase the likelihood that the same actions would be repeated when a similar drive was aroused. According to Hull, then, drive (a motivator of performance) and reinforcement (a key to learning) worked together to help an animal acquire adaptive responses.

But does the concept of drive, as Hull defined it, really provide a comprehensive theory of human motivation? Drives could certainly help explain why we eat, sleep, avoid pain, engage in sex, and so on. But how could they explain the large number of behaviors that seem unrelated to biological needs? Why, for example, do people seek out contact with other humans? Not because of any known biological need. What, then, motivates this behavior? To answer such questions Hullian theory proposed the distinction between primary and secondary drives. **Primary drives** were the most fundamental. They were the ones that arose from needs built into our physiological systems. **Secondary drives,** in contrast, were said to be learned through association with primary drives and their reduction. Thus when a child's contact with adults was repeatedly paired with reduction of hunger and pain, that contact itself soon became a secondary reinforcer, and the urge to obtain it a secondary drive. By appealing to the concept of secondary drives (a form of what are often called **learned motives**), drive-reduction theorists believed they could explain the impetus for a wide diversity of behaviors.

Beyond Drives and Drive Reduction

For many years drive-reduction theory was extremely popular. The concept of drive was something that researchers could study in the laboratory. They could deprive experimental animals of food and other biological necessities for specified lengths of time and then measure the behavioral outcomes, all in controlled environments. Many hundreds of such studies were performed by Hull and like-minded researchers, and the information gathered helped to refine their theories. But gradually it became apparent that the drive-reduction model had serious limitations. It simply could not account for certain facts that psychologists were uncovering.

For one thing, researchers were finding that animals of all kinds were strongly motivated to explore their environments and manipulate objects, even though no physiological needs were being served by doing so (Berlyne, 1950; Welker, 1956; Harlow, 1953). Rats, for instance, would endure electric shock in order to explore unfamiliar settings. And monkeys

would become engrossed in trying to solve puzzles, such as opening the clasp that fastened a door. These behaviors, moreover, occurred despite the fact that they had never been paired with food or other primary reinforcers, so that secondary drives were an inadequate explanation. Why, then, did animals so avidly engage in these activities? What was the source of motivation?

In a provocative paper psychologist Robert White (1959) suggested that humans and other animals have a basic need to deal effectively with their environments—to master and control things around them. We saw evidence of this in Chapter 8 when we described the reaction of human infants who figured out how to make a mobile move (Monnier, Boehmer, and Scholer, 1976). When the babies finally found the solution, they smiled and cooed vigorously, as if in apparent delight. White and others have argued that the great reward in performing such behaviors lies in the intrinsic satisfaction of acting competently. This kind of **intrinsic motivation,** many now believe, explains much of human behavior (De Charms, 1968; Deci, 1975).

An alternative approach to explaining why animals have a penchant for exploring unfamiliar things comes from the work of psychologist Donald Hebb and others. Hebb (1955) has proposed the simple but very intriguing idea that organisms are motivated to maintain an optimum level of arousal. Thus a bored and underaroused animal confined to a small cage may be motivated to raise its arousal by manipulating novel objects. Later in this chapter we will examine some of the findings in support of Hebb's view, as well as the implications of those findings.

But the urge to explore and manipulate the environment, or to increase one's arousal, was not the only factor that drive-reduction theory had trouble accounting for. Researchers were also finding that animals sometimes refuse to satisfy a biological need even though the means to do so are readily available. For instance, you may remember a time when you felt extremely hungry yet declined to eat when presented with a very unappetizing food. Hull's traditional model has no way to explain such behavior. It also has trouble explaining why you devour a delicious dessert at the end of a large meal, even though your need for food has already been fully satisfied. Contemporary psychologists say that in such cases the rewards and punishments available to you are acting as **incentives** and motivating your behavior.

This motivational role for rewards and punishments departs from the traditional perspective of drive-reduction theory. Hull argued in his early writings that reinforcement and punishment increase or decrease the likelihood of a response, but they do not in themselves *motivate* behavior. Instead, Hull saw primary drives as the great motivators of action. The growing recognition of incentives, however, demanded a different viewpoint. Rewards and punishments do not just stamp a behavior in or out; they also inform and energize people. Note how incentives differ from primary drives, which also serve to motivate. Incentives are a product of experience—of coming to learn which stimuli in the environment are pleasant or unpleasant. Thus you devour an ice cream sundae even though you have just eaten because you have learned in the past how good an ice cream sundae tastes. The sight of the sundae therefore works like a magnet, drawing you to eat once again. Primary drives, in contrast, are not dependent on experience. No learning is needed to feel hunger pangs, for instance. They arise automatically from changes within the body. Thus an animal's total motivation can be seen as resulting from two quite different forces—the external pull of incentives on the one hand and the internal push of primary drives on the other.

Although Hull eventually acknowledged a role for incentives in later versions of his theory, many psychologists felt that he had not gone far enough. Early cognitive psychologists such as Edward Tolman and Kurt Lewin argued that Hull's view of incentives was too mechanistic. Animals, they said, especially humans, are intelligent creatures. They are not simply drawn to rewards in a mindless, unthinking fashion.

Instead, they develop expectations about what their behaviors will lead to, and they attach subjective values to receiving or avoiding certain consequences. Out of these basic ideas emerged **expectancy-value models** of motivation (Tolman, 1959; Lewin, 1951). They explained motivated behavior by taking into account both the expectancy of achieving a particular goal and the value placed upon it. One of the many human motives to which expectancy-value theory has been applied is achievement motivation—the urge to succeed and excel (Atkinson, 1964). It is a topic that we will explore later in this chapter.

Because motivation touches on so many aspects of psychology, the subjects covered in this chapter will necessarily be diverse. They range from behaviors that are greatly influenced by our biological needs to behaviors that seem motivated purely by what we learn. First we discuss two motivations with strong biological components: the urge to eat and the urge to obtain sexual gratification. In the process of exploring eating we will also examine weight control, a very persistent problem for many Americans today. Next we return to the theory that Hebb originally proposed—the idea that organisms strive to maintain an optimum level of arousal. As you will discover, findings in this area help explain why our performance often drops when we are over- or understimulated. We then take up the related topic of high-arousal activities, such as hang gliding and parachuting. Here we examine the factors that could motivate people to risk their lives in such dangerous sports. Finally, we investigate the complex learned motives that often govern human behavior, with special emphasis on achievement motivation.

EATING AND WEIGHT CONTROL

A remarkable aspect of the motivational systems that underlie eating is their ability to balance energy intake (food consumed) against energy expenditure (calories burned away). Once most animals reach adulthood, their weight usually does not fluctuate widely. This relative stability in body weight is all the more impressive when you consider that an excess food intake of only one hundred calories a day—about the number in a handful of peanuts—could theoretically add a hundred pounds to body weight in just ten years! For most of us, fortunately, this does not happen. But how do we avoid such drastic long-term weight change? To understand the mechanisms we must look first at the physiological factors that regulate hunger.

Physiological Factors Regulating Hunger

What, physiologically speaking, makes us feel hungry? How do we determine when we have had enough to eat? Early researchers suspected that the answers might lie in the stomach contractions we call hunger pangs and in the feeling of a full stomach. To investigate the first of these factors, Walter B. Cannon persuaded his assistant to swallow a specially designed balloon, which he then inflated and used to measure stomach contractions. As expected, the contractions were highly correlated with subjective feelings of hunger (Cannon and Washburn, 1912). Later findings suggested that distention or stretching of the stomach likewise plays a role in the cessation of eating. When one team of researchers loaded a large bulk of nonnutritive material directly into a dog's stomach (via a surgical incision), the animal ate less than normal or not at all (Janowitz and Grossman, 1949, 1951). More recent evidence, however, indicates that cues from the stomach are of only secondary importance in the regulation of hunger and eating. Rats whose stomachs have been surgically removed still learn mazes to obtain food, so apparently they still experience the motivation to eat

(Penick et al., 1963). And humans who have had their stomachs removed because of ulcers or other diseases continue to report hunger pangs (Janowitz, 1976).

Other investigators have suggested that eating may also be regulated by changes in the sensation of taste. As Figure 11.1 shows, the hungrier a person is, the more likely he or she is to judge a sweet-tasting food as "pleasant." Once full, the person will rate the same food "unpleasant" (Cabanac, 1971). Thus the first bite of a food may taste better than the last, and intake is regulated accordingly.

But this decline in taste appeal appears to be counteracted if a new food is introduced. When a rat is given a diet with four different tastes, rather than just one, it may overeat by as much as 270 percent—nearly four times its normal intake (LeMagnen, 1971). You may recognize the same tendency in yourself. When you are served a meal of several courses, each with a different flavor, you may eat more overall than you would of a single food. This suggests that taste cues, like cues from the stomach, are of only secondary importance in controlling food intake (Woody et al., 1981). And in fact, when humans and other animals must press a lever to receive an injection of liquid food delivered through a tube directly into the stomach, they are able to control their body

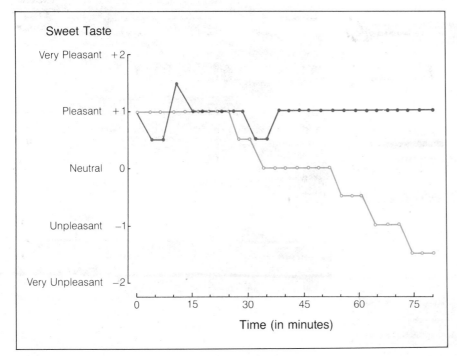

Figure 11.1 Graph of Cabanac's (1971) findings in his experiment on changes in the palatability of a sweet solution. The closed circles represent the response of a subject who sampled the solution without swallowing it. The open circles represent the response of a subject who swallowed the solution.

weight quite well despite the fact that they never taste what they are fed (Epstein and Teitelbaum, 1962; Jordan, 1969). An animal fed this way can maintain a stable weight even when the experimenter varies the amount of food delivered with each bar-press. Clearly some control system other than taste is at work.

The message in this other system may be carried in the blood. When the blood from a rat that has eaten from forty-five minutes to two hours earlier is transferred to the veins of a food-deprived rat, the latter no longer appears hungry. It nibbles indifferently at food it would otherwise devour (Davis et al., 1969). This finding clearly implies that something in the blood of the well-fed rat signals satiation. But what, exactly, is this signal? And how is the signal "read"? To answer these questions it is best to look first at a part of the brain that seems to play a special role in regulating eating. This is the hypothalamus.

Electrical or chemical stimulation of the lateral portion of the hypothalamus causes a previously satiated rat to eat voraciously (Epstein, 1960). Conversely, when the same area of the hypothalamus is surgically destroyed, a rat will refuse to eat. Because the rat spits out any food that is placed in its mouth and removes stray morsels from its fur, it appears to find eating aversive. In fact, a rat with lesions in the lateral hypothalamus will die of starvation unless it is force-fed (Anand and Brobeck, 1951). Such findings suggest that the lateral hypothalamus serves as a kind of feeding center that both initiates the hunger drive and helps sustain eating.

Another area of the hypothalamus—the ventromedial region—seems to have roughly opposite effects. When the ventromedial hypothalamus is artificially stimulated, a formerly hungry animal will refuse to eat (Hoebel and Teitelbaum, 1962). Conversely, surgical destruction of this area causes an animal to eat prodigious amounts of food and grow to incredible obesity (Hetherington and Ranson, 1940). Thus the ventromedial hypothalamus seems to serve as a kind of satiety center.

Although we have said that the lateral hypothalamus serves as a feeding center and the ventromedial hypothalamus as a satiety center, we use the term center in a very broad sense. Remember from Chapter 3 that control over a certain kind of behavior is never localized in one area of the brain. Almost everything that an animal does appears to involve activity in most or all of the brain. This is the principle of mass action. At the same time, a specific part of the brain is likely to be involved in the performance of many types of

behavior. This is the principle of multiple control. Eating behavior and the hypothalamus are no exceptions to these rules. The lateral and ventromedial regions of the hypothalamus do not maintain exclusive control over eating and satiety, respectively. Instead, they are important parts of much larger neural networks that radiate throughout many areas of the brain (Grossman, 1975). In addition, other neural pathways related to other motivational states also cross the hypothalamus. This is demonstrated by the fact that an animal with a lesioned ventromedial hypothalamus not only is a voracious eater but also is "irascible, emotional, and generally bitchy" (Schachter, 1971a). Apparently an intact ventromedial hypothalamus plays a role in restraining emotions as well as in restraining hunger.

But how does the brain, particularly the hypothalamus, receive information about the body's need for food? As we said earlier, this information is somehow carried in the blood. One blood-transported signal may derive from the amount of accumulated fat in the body. Each of the 30 billion or so fat cells in a normal human body is a warehouse for storing liquefied fat—microscopic droplets that look very much like the fat in a jar of cooking oil. As more fat accumulates, these fat cells swell, sometimes more than doubling in size. At the same time, every fat cell is continually spilling into the bloodstream a substance known as glycerol, which within the cell is attached to the fat molecules. Thus the more fat molecules crammed into a fat cell, the more glycerol discharged into the blood. It is this glycerol, some researchers suspect, that serves as the "eating" signal. According to this theory, when glycerol reaches the cells of the brain, it provides information about the size of the body's surplus energy stores. Depleted stores encourage additional eating, while overabundant stores curb the appetite. This theory is supported by the finding that rats injected with extra glycerol will virtually stop eating (Bennett and Gurin, 1982).

But there is more to the story. An injection of extra glycerol into the blood does not prompt an animal to stop eating indefinitely. Instead, the animal tends to limit its intake until part of its fat stores are burned away and it reaches a lower weight. It is as if the injected glycerol has fooled the brain into thinking that the body is fatter than it actually is, thus requiring a diet until "normal" fat levels are achieved (Bennett and Gurin, 1982). And what is "normal" seems to vary with the individual. For some individuals the brain seems to consider a pudgy profile normal, whereas for others the brain seems to be "set" to keep the body lean. In short, many researchers now believe that each of us has a **setpoint** for the amount of fat we carry in our bodies. When we are significantly over our setpoint, this theory goes, appetite tends to diminish and we lose weight. Conversely, when we are under our setpoint, we tend to feel constantly hungry and impelled to eat.

It is the setpoint that lesions in the hypothalamus appear to be altering. Consider the behavior of a rat with a lesion in the ventromedial hypothalamus. Such an animal typically gorges its way to colossal obesity, but this voracious eating does not last forever. After a number of weeks, the animal begins to eat only enough to maintain its new large size. It is as though the rat's behavior is directed toward achieving some new "optimum" higher weight set by the lesioned hypothalamus. In keeping with this idea, if an obese rat is forced to eat more than is needed to maintain its newly stabilized hefty weight, it will subsequently refrain from eating until its former hefty weight is restored (Teitelbaum, 1955). Conversely, if large portions of the rat's fat tissue are surgically removed, it will eat its way to precisely the same level of obesity as before (Liebelt, Bordelon, and Liebelt, 1973). What is intriguing here is that the "need" for food seems to be defined in terms not of the calories required to live on but of the calories needed to sustain a setpoint level of energy reserves in the form of fat. The setpoint concept—indeed, the entire topic of obesity and weight control—has such important implications in our society that we will explore it in depth.

in depth Studying Obesity and Weight Control

If we define obesity as being 20 percent above the average weight for one's height and sex, then a full 40 percent of Americans fall into the obese category. These extra pounds exact a price in terms of physical health. The mortality rate for people who are 20 to 30 percent overweight is 20 to 40 percent higher than normal. And when the scales tip at 50 to 60 percent over average weight, the chances of dying increase by an alarming 150 to 200 percent (Van Itallie, 1979). Why, then, do so many Americans allow themselves to be obese? The answer is that permanent weight loss

is often very difficult. Although opinions differ on how successful most dieters are (Schachter, 1982), a sizable number find it hard not to gain back the pounds they have lost. In recent years scientists have learned a great deal about why this may happen.

WHAT CAUSES OVEREATING AND OBESITY? Some contemporary scientists have begun their study of human obesity with the intriguing observation that many similarities exist between the behavior of an obese person and that of an animal with a surgical lesion in the ventromedial hypothalamus. Both eat more than subjects of normal weight, and they also eat more rapidly. Yet both tend to be rather choosy eaters. When enough quinine is added to food to make it slightly bitter, a lesioned rat will eat substantially *less* than a normal rat will. Similarly, when asked to drink milkshakes as part of a bogus taste test, obese subjects were more strongly influenced by the taste of the milkshakes than were normal-weight subjects; the obese subjects drank much more when the milkshake was good-tasting than when it was slightly bitter (Decke, 1971).

Both also tend to be reluctant to work to obtain food. For instance, if a rat with a lesion in the ventromedial hypothalamus is taught that it can press a lever to receive a pellet of food, it will press less and less often as the number of presses required to deliver the food increases (Teitelbaum, 1957). Compare this behavior with that of obese humans. In one study in which subjects were given the opportunity to eat from a bag of nuts while filling out questionnaires, only one out of twenty obese subjects bothered to indulge when the nuts had to be shelled, yet nineteen out of twenty ate the nuts when the shells had already been removed. For normal-weight subjects, in contrast, nut consumption was unrelated to the obstacle of a shell (Schachter and Friedman, 1974).

What do such parallels suggest? In the 1960s psychologist Stanley Schachter proposed that both a rat with a lesioned ventromedial hypothalamus and an obese human are extremely sensitive to environmental eating cues. This, Schachter argued, is why the overweight person is so affected by relatively modest changes in the availability, quality, or appearance of food—changes that the nonobese person may not even notice. In one study, for instance, when lights were focused on a dish of cashews, overweight people ate about twice as many nuts as they did when the cashews were under dimmed lights (Ross, 1974). Research has shown that this high responsiveness to food cues is present early in life (Costanzo and Woody, 1979). Overweight infants just a few days old tend to suck a sweet solution more rapidly than normal-weight babies (Nisbett and Gurwitz, 1970). Such findings led Schachter to suspect that heightened sensitivity to food-related cues may be built into the brain at birth.

According to Schachter's theory, then, people sometimes come equipped with heightened sensitivity to environmental food cues—perhaps because of heredity, perhaps because of early (even prenatal) nutrition. This heightened sensitivity encourages them to eat more when tempting food-related sights, smells, and tastes are present, and thus to grow obese. This theory generated widespread interest. But subsequent research revealed that not all fat people showed this heightened sensitivity to food cues, while many normal-weight people did (Rodin, 1980). What could explain these inconsistencies?

The insight that answered this question came from Richard Nisbett, a former student of Schachter's. Nisbett (1972) argued that heightened sensitivity to food cues was the *result* of the fat person's obesity rather than its cause. More specifically, he proposed that many fat people were starving from their brain's point of view. Thus they were in a constant state of hunger and highly responsive to the sight, smell, and taste of good food.

Nisbett came to this fascinating conclusion after reviewing many sources on the effects of prolonged hunger. Nisbett noticed some striking similarities between severely hungry people and the typical obese person who is eating as usual. Both are highly sensitive to environmental food cues and both are prone to emotional upset, excessive frustration, inactivity, and lack of interest in sex. In addition, both have abnormally high levels of free fatty acids in their bloodstreams, a sign that some body fat is being broken down to help meet energy needs. This led Nisbett to suspect that the obese person is in a state of chronic energy deficit, which gives rise to persistent hunger. Persistent hunger, in turn, causes both a tendency to overeat and a tendency toward overresponsiveness to food cues.

But how can an obese person be hungry when he or she eats more than enough to maintain a normal weight? Nisbett believes that the answer lies in the concept of setpoint. Biologically "normal" weight, he argues, varies from one person to the next. Some people have a setpoint for fat tissue which is well above the average. As a result, their bodies are constantly telling them that they are hungry and in need of food. Subsequent research suggests that a high setpoint may be partly related to an abnormally large number of fat cells (Knittle and Hirsch, 1968). The total number of fat cells in an adult body seems to be determined by some interaction of heredity and early nutrition. Although adults can increase their supply of fat cells by heavily overeating, they can never decrease the number that they have. Thus a large number of fat cells all clamoring to be filled with fats could help produce the chronic state of hunger that Nisbett talks about.

Nisbett has gone on to argue that some people respond to this chronic hunger by letting their bodies have their way. These are the people who eat until they are satisfied and grow to gargantuan proportions. But many other naturally obese people do not want to be fat. Obesity is considered unattractive in our society, so the fat person is under great pressure to lose weight. These people, according to Nisbett, find themselves in perpetual conflict. Their bodies tell them that they are hungry and need to eat more, while society tells them that they are fat and need to eat less.

Some intriguing evidence supports Nisbett's theory. Consider the fact that the *grossly* obese usually do not display the behavioral symptoms of hunger. Presumably these people have given up any effort to remain slender and so eat as much as they want. It is the person who is only moderately obese and who is constantly watching his or her weight that tends to display emotionalism, inactivity, and heightened responsiveness to food cues (Hibscher and Herman, 1977).

This finding raises an interesting possibility: some people who are of normal weight, or even very slim, may be "starving" themselves from their bodies' viewpoint in order to achieve their thinness. Psychologists C. Peter Herman and Janet Polivy (1975) call such people **restrained eaters.** Whether they are currently fat, slender, or somewhere in between, restrained eaters would gain a great deal of weight if they "let themselves go." Herman and Polivy have developed the scale in Table 11.1 to measure eating restraint. You can use it to assess your own eating behavior. If you score high on this test—totaling 14 or more points—you are apt to be frequently dieting. And when your eating restraint is for some reason broken, you may not just eat, you may binge.

TABLE 11.1 EATING RESTRAINT SCALE

1. How often are you dieting? Never; rarely; sometimes; often; always. (Scored 0–4)

2. What is the maximum amount of weight (in pounds) that you have ever lost within one month? 0–4; 5–9; 10–14; 15–19; 20+. (Scored 0–4)

3. What is your maximum weight gain within a week? 0–1; 1.1–2; 2.1–3; 3.1–5; 5.1+. (Scored 0–4)

4. In a typical week, how much does your weight fluctuate? 0–1; 1.1–2; 2.1–3; 3.1–5; 5.1+. (Scored 0–4)

5. Would a weight fluctuation of 5 pounds affect the way you live your life? Not at all; slightly; moderately; very much. (Scored 0–3)

6. Do you eat sensibly in front of others and splurge alone? Never; rarely; often; always. (Scored 0–3)

7. Do you give too much time and thought to food? Never; rarely; often; always. (Scored 0–3)

8. Do you have feelings of guilt after overeating? Never; rarely; often; always. (Scored 0–3)

9. How conscious are you of what you are eating? Not at all; slightly; moderately; extremely. (Scored 0–3)

10. How many pounds over your desired weight were you at your maximum weight? 0–1; 1–5; 6–10; 11–20; 21+. (Scored 0–4)

Herman's ideas about restrained eating received some support from an interesting experiment (Herman and Mack, 1975). Shortly after lunch or dinner, subjects were given either nothing to eat or one or two good-sized milkshakes as part of a bogus "taste test." Each subject was then left alone to taste and rate three flavors of ice cream. Subjects were told that after rating the flavors they could eat as much of the ice cream as they wanted. Enough ice cream was provided so that a subject could gorge without making an embarrassing dent. The researchers expected that the unrestrained eaters (those who rarely gave a thought to dieting) would unconsciously compensate for having previously consumed a milkshake or two by eating relatively little ice cream. As shown in Figure 11.2, this is exactly what they did. But what about the restrained eaters? Figure 11.2 shows that the restrained eaters ate very little ice cream when they had previously consumed *no* milkshakes, but they ate a substantial portion when they had previously downed *two* milkshakes! Why did overeating breed more overeating? Apparently, after indulging in the milkshakes, the restrained eaters reasoned that all hope of dieting for that day was lost. The consequence was a collapse of their normal restraint and a sizable eating binge. Many subsequent studies have replicated this tendency of restrained eaters to overeat once they have been induced to go off their diets (Herman and Polivy, 1980).

The combined concepts of setpoint and restrained eating go farther than Schachter's concept of heightened sensitivity to food cues to explain why some people are chronically obese. Many overweight people are indeed very responsive to the sight, smell, and

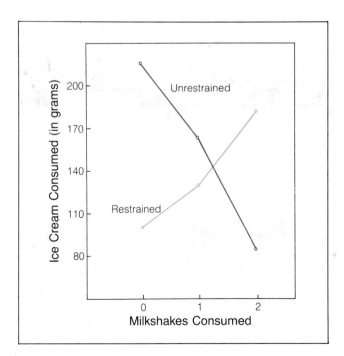

Figure 11.2 Unrestrained eaters, having consumed one or two milkshakes, show appropriate compensation when asked to taste and rate the flavors of three kinds of ice cream. Restrained eaters, however, eat more ice cream the more milkshakes they have already consumed. Herman and Polivy (1975) hypothesize that the suspensions of their self-imposed restraint (in this case, in the form of the milkshakes) causes dieters to capitulate to internal (hunger) and external (taste) cues.

taste of food, but Schachter himself admits that this is more often the result than the cause of their condition. The theories of Nisbett and Herman and Polivy, he says with good humor, are "really closer to the way God sees things. . . . They can incorporate far more data than any scheme I know of, including my own" (quoted in Bennett and Gurin, 1982, p. 44).

THE PROBLEM OF ACHIEVING WEIGHT REDUCTION.

What remedy do the recent findings on obesity leave for the overweight person? Many specific techniques have been tried, from special diets to "miracle" drugs to regular exercise regimes, and even, as a desperate last resort, digestive-tract surgery.

The diet is by far the most widely used weight-loss strategy. Almost every year a new best-seller announces some "breakthrough" diet, which claims to have found the secret weapon in the war against fat. The high-protein, low-carbohydrate "Calories Don't Count" diet swore that you could eat fried eggs and sausage, barbecued ribs and pastrami all to your heart's content, because none of these foods make you fat. Equally miraculous, the "Nine-Day Wonder Diet" suggested that you might be able to throw out your oversized wardrobe in just a little over a week. Sound impossible? It probably is. Most authorities on weight control contend that the only known way to lose a pound of fat through dieting is to consume roughly 3,500 fewer calories than you burn away. Thus about a half pound of shed fat daily (a 1,750-calorie deficit) is near the upper limit even for fairly heroic dieting. If you lose a great deal more than this on one of the fad diets, it is usually because you are losing water in addition to protein and fat. This is not to say that all fad diets are useless. Some do get you to eat less, often in subtle ways (T. Cohen, 1979). For instance, if you go on the high-protein, low-carbohydrate diet mentioned earlier, you will effectively eliminate many foods that are high in calories, such as cake and potato chips. Even carbohydrates that are not rich in calories (bread and potatoes, for instance) are often smothered in butter, gravy, or other fattening sauces. In addition, cutting out carbohydrates eliminates a great deal of snacking and bingeing. Similarly, diets that restrict a person to certain food categories, such as proteins or rice, can also subtly influence the amount consumed. Because these foods quickly become tiresome, the dieter tends to eat less.

Although popular diets that cut calorie intake may produce some weight loss, many have serious short-

comings. A few, if used without medical supervision, can actually cause severe harm by eliminating essential nutrients. For instance, the liquid protein diet, very popular several years ago, was linked to fifty-eight deaths. And even if fad diets cause no measurable harm, there is no evidence that they promote *long-term* weight control. The biggest problem with such diets is recidivism: an estimated 95 percent of the "successful" dieters regain their lost weight (Adler and Gosnell, 1982).

The concept of setpoint for fat tissue can help explain why people have trouble maintaining weight loss. Once fat has been lost, individuals with a high setpoint receive strong signals from the brain that they are extremely hungry. These signals will continue until the person eats enough to reach his or her setpoint again. Researchers have even identified specific physiological processes that seem to *ensure* that the obese person will have difficulty losing weight and will gain it back easily. For instance, a person who has lost a great deal of weight has elevated levels of a certain body chemical (lipoprotein lipase) that promotes the storage of fat (Adler and Gosnell, 1982). Any food such a person eats is likely to be stored as fat rather than being burned off as energy. In addition, the metabolism of a person on a semistarvation diet (only a few hundred calories a day) often shifts downward in an apparent effort to use meager food supplies frugally (Bray, 1970; Garrow, 1978; Wooley, Wooley, and Dyrenfurth, 1979). No wonder many crash dieters seem to reach a stubborn plateau of weight, beyond which they cannot manage to lose (Buskirk, 1974; Craddock, 1978). Then later, when the Spartan diet is finally replaced with more normal meals, the thrifty metabolism may not readjust quickly and rapid weight gain results. In one experiment, rats were forced to lose about 20 percent of their weight through dieting, then were placed on a week-long "maintenance" diet. Although the experimental animals ate *less* on the maintenance diet than did control rats who had not dieted, they gained 20 times more weight (Boyle, Storlien, and Keesey, 1978). The implication is that rapid weight loss can be counterproductive because it primes the body to restore quickly whatever fat is lost.

But if crash dieting won't do the trick, perhaps dieting plus something else will. For many people that something else is a medication—either a prescription or an over-the-counter drug. Americans spend millions of dollars annually on appetite suppressants and alleged miracle "fat-burners." Yet scientific evidence shows that these products do very limited good, and for only as long as the person continues to take them (Food and Drug Administration, 1972). Prolonged use, moreover, can have negative side effects. Most diet pills contain amphetamines, which are powerful stimulants, or some other chemically similar drug. They can produce hypertension and sleeplessness, and they can also become habit forming (Bennett and Gurin, 1982).

A more sensible approach is to combine dieting with behavior modification, the conscious use of learning principles to change human behavior (see Chapter 5). People who want to change their eating habits are encouraged to identify and try to avoid environmental cues (such as sitting down to watch a TV movie) which through years of being paired with recreational eating have come to elicit a strong tendency to snack. People who use eating as a kind of self-reward ("As soon as I finish studying for my exam I'll treat myself to an ice cream") are encouraged to substitute other pleasurable activities for snacking. There is evidence that such techniques can be effective. Still, many people continue to be fat despite efforts at behavior modification (Stunkard and Penick, 1979).

Anorexia and Bulimia. Although controlling what one eats is a popular approach to shedding unwanted pounds, this tactic imposes serious risks when carried to extremes. Some people become so obsessed with the desire to be slender that they literally starve themselves to death. This condition is known as **anorexia nervosa,** and it is far more prevalent in women than in men. About 95 percent of anorexics are females—most of them teenagers and young adults. These women have lost at least a quarter of their weight, and weight drops of two-thirds have been reported. Yet despite her emaciated, skeletal appearance, the anorexic's sense of body image has become so distorted that she continues to insist she must drastically restrict her diet (Bemis, 1978; Bruch, 1980). Table 11.2 lists the symptoms of this condition.

About half of all anorexics suffer from an additional eating disorder called **bulimia,** which involves periodic gorging. On a typical binge the average bulimic will consume 4,800 calories, or the equivalent of several days' worth of food, in an hour or two. Often such people will eat everything available—a loaf of bread, a jar of peanut butter, a half gallon of ice cream, a barrel of fried chicken, several bags of

cookies, a quart of potato salad—before the compulsive eating stops. Afterward most bulimics purge their systems by vomiting or taking laxatives, so as to avoid excessive weight gain. Although bulimia is often found in anorexics, it is certainly not confined to those who have starved themselves (Casper et al., 1980). In fact, most bulimics are of average or even above-average weight. For them the disorder usually begins after a period of stringent dieting. Some authorities think that the natural hunger caused by trying to stay well below setpoint may exacerbate an existing tendency toward binge eating (Abraham and Beaumont, 1982).

Exercise. As more and more has been learned about the negative side effects of stringent dieting, some people have looked to exercise as a way of losing excess weight. Correlational data suggest a link between

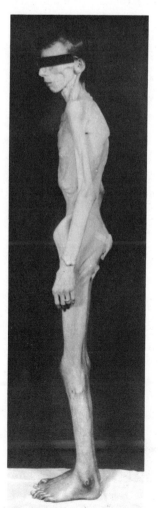

The extreme weight loss that is characteristic of anorexia nervosa is evident in this emaciated young woman, whose weight dropped to 47 pounds. *(Dr. A. J. Bachrach, Naval Medical Research Institute.)*

TABLE 11.2 CRITERIA FOR DIAGNOSIS OF ANOREXIA NERVOSA

A. Age at onset below 25.

B. Anorexia with accompanying weight loss of at least 25% of original body weight.

C. A distorted, implacable attitude toward eating, food, or weight that overrides hunger, admonitions, reassurance, and threats; e.g.:

1. Denial of illness with a failure to recognize nutritional needs.

2. Apparent enjoyment in losing weight with overt manifestations that food refusal is a pleasurable indulgence.

3. A desired body image of extreme thinness with overt evidence that it is rewarding to the patient to achieve and maintain this state.

4. Unusual hoarding or handling of food.

D. No known medical illness that could account for the anorexia and weight loss.

E. No other known psychiatric disorder.

F. At least two of the following manifestations:

1. cessation of menstrual cycle

2. growth of downy hair on body

3. slow heartbeat (persistent resting pulse of 60 or less)

4. periods of overactivity

5. episodes of bulimia

6. vomiting (may be self-induced)

After Bemis, 1978, p. 594. Based on information in Feighner et al., 1972.

lack of exercise and obesity. Many people, for instance, do not become fat until middle age, a time when exercise levels generally drop (Forbes and Reina, 1970; deVries, 1974). In all likelihood, a sedentary lifestyle contributes to this kind of creeping obesity. Many researchers have assumed that so much extra exercise would be needed to eliminate pounds of fat that it is not a practical solution for overweight people. But current evidence is challenging this view (Thompson et al., 1982). In addition to burning off calories in movement, exercise also seems to raise a person's metabolic rate, the effect often lasting for many hours after the exercise is over (deVries and Gray, 1963). This means that a person who engages in moderate, regular exercise may go on throughout the day to burn up more calories per pound of body weight than his or her sedentary peers. If a person is dieting as well as exercising, the increase in metabolic rate caused by the exercise may counteract the decline prompted by the restricted eating, thus making the diet more effective (Bray, 1979; Brownell and Stunkard, 1980). Furthermore, exercise increases the amount of lean muscle in the body while specifically decreasing stored fat (Parizkova, 1977). Dieting, in contrast, inevitably causes loss of lean tissue as well as

A sensible program of regular exercise coupled with restricted food intake is the most effective approach to weight reduction. (Richard Howard/Black Star.)

fat. With all these benefits it is not surprising that weight-loss programs that supplement dieting or behavior modification with exercise produce greater results than any of these strategies undertaken alone (Dahlkoetter, Calahan, and Linton, 1979; Stalonas, Johnson, and Christ, 1978).

New Approaches to Weight Reduction. Recently psychologists have started to look at the insights provided by people who eat heartily, but remain chronically thin. All of us know a few people who eat large quantities of food without ever noticeably gaining weight. In fact, research shows that some people can eat as much as 30 percent more than others of the same age, weight, height, occupation, and so forth, yet not gain a single pound (Garrow, 1978). How is this possible?

Some scientists now believe that an important part of the answer may lie in the body's small deposits of heat-producing fatty tissue, called **brown fat** because of its color. These cells are truly metabolic furnaces. Although they make up only 1 percent of all body tissue, they can produce as much heat as all the rest of the cells in the body combined. These are the cells that do much of the work to keep us warm in winter.

But they seem to have another role as well. When a person overeats for an extended period, the brown fat cells may rev up and even multiply, burning off some of the excess calories in the production of heat Rothwell and Stock, 1979). The implication is that some people may lack properly functioning brown fat tissue; having nothing else to do with excess calories, they store them away as fat. These may be the people who gain weight when they eat a single slice of pie. Brown fat may also help explain the creeping obesity of middle life, for the efficiency with which brown fat functions may decline with age (Elliott, 1980).

Not all the news is pessimistic, however. There are some indications that brown fat levels may be alterable by manipulation of the nutrients we eat (Elliott, 1980). If this is the case, then diets of the future may be geared as much to *in*creasing brown fat deposits as they are to *de*creasing stored fat. Of course, a great deal more research must be conducted before we know for sure whether raising human brown fat levels would have any significant weight-reducing effects. But many psychologists believe that this will be an exciting area for future research, one that could yield important new techniques for successful treatment of obesity.

in depth

SEXUAL BEHAVIOR

Incentives as well as drives are clearly involved in the motivation to eat. When it comes to sexual motivation, however, the role of incentives is even greater. Sexual stimuli of some kind (real or imagined) are essential for the process of sexual arousal to begin. Consider the behavior of a male rat that has lived alone for several weeks. The animal walks about his cage sniffing and exploring, occasionally nibbling at food or taking a sip of water. There are no external or internal signs that the rat is in a state of deprivation. But now suppose we introduce a female rat in heat. The male's behavior changes dramatically. He begins to court the female, seeking to mount her and copulate. Although the male's actions are strongly influenced by hormone changes within its body, these changes in turn are launched by the smell and behavior of the receptive female. In short, the animal's sexual behavior is under the interacting influence of two kinds of factors: on the one hand the presence of sexual stimuli, which tend to elicit certain physiological changes, and on the other those physiological changes that help to heighten and sustain sexual activities (Bolles, 1975). In this section we will be examining these interacting elements.

Hormones and Sexual Responsiveness

The role that hormones play in energizing sexual responses is still controversial. In lower animals hormones seem to be especially important. A female rat, for instance, is sexually responsive only when her ovaries secrete a high level of the female hormone estrogen, which in turn triggers release of egg cells for possible fertilization. This pattern has an obvious reproductive advantage, for it ensures that if copulation does occur, it will be at a time most likely to cause pregnancy. It is therefore not surprising that when the ovaries of a female rat are removed, she becomes totally unreceptive to a male. Significantly, injections of estrogen can completely restore her normal sexual responsiveness.

In humans, in contrast, sex hormones may help promote sexual activity but they certainly do not control it. Although many women's sexual responsiveness seems to increase during the middle of the menstrual cycle, when estrogen levels peak, most women can become sexually aroused *throughout* the normal rise and fall of estrogen levels (Adams, Gold, and Burt, 1978). In fact, even complete removal of the ovaries tends to have only a negligible effect on a woman's sexual responsiveness. It appears that the sex hormones secreted by the adrenal glands may have a greater impact on female arousal than those secreted by the ovaries. When diseased adrenals are surgically removed, a woman's sexual urge often drops appreciably. But even in the case of adrenal hormones, the effects are not clear-cut. Some women continue to be sexually responsive even after adrenal surgery. This suggests that although some degree of hormonal influence over sexual receptivity may exist in women, this influence is far from all-powerful.

In the human male the influence of hormones on sexual responsiveness is also less than in other species. If the testes (which produce the male hormone testosterone) are surgically removed in adulthood, a loss of sexual interest and responsiveness is not inevitable. Consider a study of over a hundred Scandinavian men who underwent castration either because of diseased testes or because they were chronic sex offenders (Bremer, 1959). In a third of these men sexual activity persisted for over a year, and in some it continued for as long as ten years (even though they all eventually lost their ability to ejaculate during orgasm). Castration *before* adolescence, however, seems to have a more predictably negative effect on humans. Although there are some exceptions, most boys who are castrated and who do not receive hormone therapy grow up to have little sexual interest or ability, nor do they develop secondary sex characteristics, such as facial hair and a deep-pitched voice (Money and Ehrhardt, 1972).

Hormones, of course, interact with the central nervous system. The hypothalamus, in particular, stimulates the anterior pituitary gland to release hormones that in turn stimulate both the gonads (the ovaries and testes) and the adrenal glands to secrete sex hormones. These sex hormones then travel in the bloodstream back to the hypothalamus, where they activate nerve networks involved in sexual arousal. One area of the hypothalamus that seems to play a key role in these nerve networks is the preoptic region (Giantonio, Lund, and Gerall, 1970). Electrical or chemical stimulation of the preoptic region greatly increases mating in both male and female rats (Malsbury, 1971; Fisher, 1956, 1967). Males so stimulated will mount other males if females are not available, and they can ejaculate at a rate of once every 27 seconds—over ten times faster than the normal rate.

The Role of Arousing Stimuli

But hormones reaching the hypothalamus serve only to prime sexual responses. As we said earlier, sexual stimuli are also needed for full-fledged sexual arousal. In humans, a wide variety of visual and tactile sensations—from the sight of a nude body to the touch of someone's lips—are widely acknowledged to serve this purpose. But what about less obviously sexual stimuli? Are humans affected by sexual signals they are not even aware of? To answer this question, researchers often look to sexual cues in lower animals, for similar cues may have been important in our own evolutionary past.

In many lower animals olfactory stimuli (those received by the sense of smell) serve as powerful sexual signals. The male silkworm moth, for instance, is strongly attracted by a chemical scent that the female exudes. So alluring is this odor that a male moth will attempt to mate with surgically removed scent glands in preference to a scentless but otherwise normal female (Kellogg, 1907). In mammals, too, various scents often serve as powerful sexual attractants. Male rats, dogs, horses, cattle, and sheep, among other species, have been observed to prefer the odor of a female in heat to the scent of a nonreceptive female (Carr and Caul, 1962; Michael and Keverne, 1968). Studies of dogs and monkeys have shown that it is the female's vaginal secretions that often provide a lure (Beach and Merari, 1970; Michael, Keverne, and Bonsall, 1971). Similarly, females of many mammalian species seem to show sexual interest upon smelling the urine of sexually potent males (Patterson, 1968; Michael and Keverne, 1968).

Some researchers think that humans, too, emit such sexually arousing odors, although we are seldom consciously aware of them (Wiener, 1966). It is believed that these scents may arise from the sweat glands and from secretions that accumulate in the genital region (Comfort, 1971). For instance, women have been found to be sensitive to a musky-smelling substance called exaltolide, found in unusually large amounts in the urine of adult males (Hassett, 1978). During the middle of the menstrual cycle, when an egg cell is released, a woman's ability to detect this odor tends to increase. Researchers have also isolated fatty acids in women's vaginal secretions which are identical to ones that seem to arouse sexual activity in male monkeys (Michael, 1971). But whether human males are also aroused by this odor is still an open question. In a recent attempt to answer it, researchers had married women dab one of four perfumes on their chests every night at bedtime (Morris and Udry, 1978). One of the perfumes contained the experimental fatty acids, often called copulins. Did the copulins sexually arouse the husbands more than the other scents did? Unfortunately, the answer was not clear. While some of the couples did increase their sexual activity when the copulins were applied, others did not. Thus much more research is needed to find out what role, if any, these substances normally play in human sexuality.

Other types of sexual arousers common in lower animals may likewise have some parallels in the human species. Consider the sexual incentive of novelty. Suppose a male rat is allowed to copulate with the same female until it reaches exhaustion and shows absolutely no further interest in its partner. If a new female partner is then introduced, the male undergoes a miraculous recovery. In fact, if that partner is replaced by another, and yet another, and so on through a bevy of receptive females, the male will continue copulating far longer than it will when only one female is available (Fowler and Whalen, 1961; Fisher, 1962; Wilson, Kuehn, and Beach, 1963).

This sexual attraction to novelty found in many mammals has been called the "Coolidge effect" in honor of President Calvin Coolidge. He and his wife were touring a farm, the story goes, when,

observing the vigor with which one particular rooster covered hen after hen, Mrs. Coolidge asked the guide to make certain that the President took note of the rooster's behavior. When President Coolidge got to the hen yard, the rooster was pointed out and his exploits recounted by the guide, who added that Mrs. Coolidge had requested that the President be made aware of the rooster's prowess. The President reflected for a moment and replied, "Tell Mrs. Coolidge that there is more than one hen."   [Walster and Walster, 1978]

Whether or not the Coolidge effect does indeed apply to humans has yet to be put to a scientific test.

The Mind's Role in Human Sexuality

The very fact that mammals process and interpret a variety of sexual cues implies that the brain's most advanced region—the cortex—is involved in directing sexual behavior toward appropriate goals. Experiments with lower species confirm this. When the temporal lobes of a male cat's cortex are surgically removed, the animal lacks all discrimination in its choice of sexual partners. It will attempt to mate with cats, dogs, furniture, stuffed toys, the experimenter's arm or leg—virtually anything it can conceivably mount (Schreiner and Kling, 1956; Bermant, Glickman, and Davidson, 1968).

As we move up the evolutionary ladder the involvement of the cortex in sexual behavior becomes even greater. In humans the cortex can clearly excite or inhibit the sexual responses mediated by lower brain structures. The fact that most of us do not make immediate and overt sexual advances toward every attractive man or woman we meet is evidence of the strong control that social learning exerts via the cortex. Similarly, the fact that both men and women can become highly aroused simply by sexual fantasies also testifies to the powerful role of the cortex in human sexuality. In one study of male sexual arousal, for instance, men were able both to increase and to decrease the vigor of their erections by means of various fantasies (Laws and Rubin, 1969).

Research also shows that erotic imagery plays an important role in most people's daily sex lives. In a study of nearly a hundred men, a large majority reported imagining various sexual acts during both intercourse and masturbation, and they also fantasized sexual scenes at least once daily *outside* any kind of overt sexual activity (Crépault and Couture, 1980). Such mental images seem to heighten erotic arousal and increase the motivation to engage in sexual behavior. The very same processes occur in women. Several surveys show that an equally large majority of women fantasize sexually both during and outside of the physical act of sex (Hariton and Singer, 1974; Crépault et al., 1977). And once again interviews indicate that such erotic images are often used to enhance sexual responsiveness.

Given that erotic fantasies have the power to increase sexual motivation, might there not be some basis to the often-heard fear that repeated exposure to hard-core pornography can breed unrestrained sexual urges? After all, viewing pornography may stimulate erotic fantasies, and those who view pornography do not always have access to willing sex partners. Might not the sex drive build up within such people and eventually find expression in such violent acts as rape? As logical as this reasoning may seem to many people, no scientific evidence supports it. In fact, studies of convicted sex offenders indicate that as adolescents these men often had *less* exposure to pornographic matter than other boys (Goldstein, Kant, and Hartman, 1974). Many psychologists now believe that rape and other acts of sexual violence are the product of deep-seated anger rather than of excessive sexual arousal (Gray, 1982). Such anger would continue to find expression in sex crimes even if pornography were banned.

STIMULUS SEEKING AND AROUSAL

At the beginning of this chapter we talked about some research that drive-reduction theories of motivation could not adequately explain. Studies show that animals often seek to raise their own states of physiological arousal by exposing themselves to stimulation of various kinds. For instance, if you give a monkey a mechanical puzzle, such as a metal clasp used to fasten a door, it will manipulate the object with great curiosity, searching diligently for the solution (Harlow, Harlow, and Meyer, 1950). We humans have a similar penchant for puzzles of various sorts. What makes a person stay up all night to finish a mystery novel? Why do people spend hours on end playing video games? One answer lies in the theory that people have an optimum level of arousal which they try to maintain.

The Optimum-Level-of-Arousal Concept

By the middle of this century psychologists had collected a wealth of information related to motivation. Among their data was a fascinating set of findings

Young monkeys become engrossed in a problem-solving situation. *(Harry F. Harlow, University of Wisconsin Primate Laboratory.)*

concerning arousal and the brain. In particular, scientists had learned that when sensory stimuli impinge on an organism, they activate not one, but two pathways in the brain. First there is the well-known pathway whereby sensory information travels from receptor cells through sensory nerves to the thalamus, and then to appropriate sensory areas of the cortex and beyond. But in addition, sensory input activates an area of the brainstem called the reticular formation, and from there the neural impulses travel upward, producing a very diffuse arousal of the entire cortex.

Most important for an understanding of motivation, this general state of cortical arousal seems to be essential if sensory signals are to activate a goal-directed response (Lindsley, 1951). When the diffuse cortical arousal induced by the reticular formation is very slight, the chains of neurons associated with goal-directed behaviors may be unable to fire effectively. Not surprisingly, therefore, very low activation of the reticular formation is associated with coma and deep sleep. Conversely, when a great deal of diffuse cortical arousal is induced by the reticular formation, the neural circuits associated with goal-directed behavior may be effectively blocked. As a result, the individual who is overaroused by the reticular formation may become temporarily paralyzed. No wonder, then, that at the height of battle only an estimated 15 to 25 percent of soldiers ever fire their rifles (cited in Hebb, 1955). The rest are immobilized by fear.

Figure 11.3 shows the general relationship between diffuse cortical arousal and efficiency of performance. As you can see, the relationship is U-shaped:

as arousal increases, performance first improves and then declines. These findings are what led psychologist Donald Hebb and others to suggest that organisms have an **optimum level of arousal**—a level at which their goal-directed behaviors will be most effective (Hebb, 1955; Duffy, 1957). According to Hebb, individuals automatically tend to maintain their own arousal within this optimum range. Others have argued that in humans, with their high levels of self-awareness, an optimum level of arousal is often consciously and actively sought (Berlyne, 1960).

Explaining Sensory Deprivation and Sensory Overload. The concept of an optimum level of arousal captured great interest, partly because it could help explain many of the findings that contradicted drive-reduction theory. Among these findings were the results of so-called **sensory deprivation** studies. In sensory deprivation research a subject's exposure to sensory stimuli is drastically reduced for a prolonged period in order to observe the effects on his or her functioning. Fascination with this topic ignited during the 1950s when Americans began to wonder whether their prisoners of war in Korea might become susceptible to "brainwashing" if they were kept long enough in solitary confinement. Sensory deprivation also had great relevance to our then-beginning space program. What would be the effect on astronauts of being isolated in space capsules, cut off completely from their normal environments? Researchers reasoned that they might begin to find the answers by subjecting volunteers to the most severe conditions of sensory deprivation possible. So people were asked to lie for days on soft mattresses in sound-proof rooms, with nothing to see or touch. Or they were suspended like giant fetuses in tanks of warm, still water, their eyes blindfolded, their ears blocked off from any sound. Needless to say, these novel experiments generated some provocative findings.

Consider the results of an experiment conducted just a few years before Hebb published his theory that organisms tend to maintain an optimum level of arousal. In this study, male college students were paid

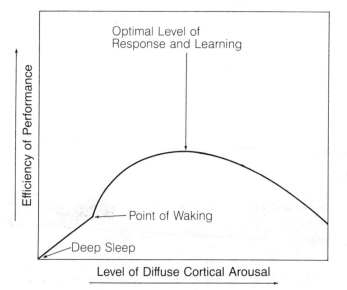

Figure 11.3 As the level of cortical arousal increases, performance increases to an optimal level and then decreases. Thus higher animals may be attracted by risk taking, or mild fear, and by problem solving, or mild frustration, since both serve to increase arousal. *(After Hebb, 1955.)*

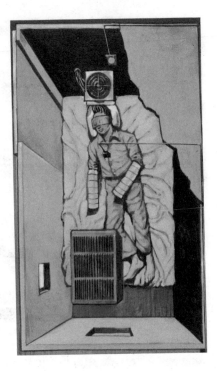

Figure 11.4 In a classic series of experiments on sensory deprivation conducted in the 1950s, subjects were isolated in sound-resistant cubicles. Gloves and cotton cuffs prevented input to their hands and fingers, a plastic visor diffused the light coming into their eyes; a foam pillow and the continuous hum of the air conditioner and fan made input to the ears low and monotonous. Except for eating and using the bathroom, the subjects did nothing but lie on the bed. Few chose to remain longer than three days. *(After Heron, 1957.)*

$20 a day to remain in an environment with very low levels of sensory stimulation (Bexton, Heron, and Scott, 1954). Each of the subjects lay on a bed in a small room, as illustrated in Figure 11.4. A hollowed pillow enveloped their ears, muffling the only sound— the low, monotonous hum of an electric fan. Their eyes were covered with translucent goggles that diffused light, so the few objects around them appeared blurred and indistinct. Because they were wearing loose-fitting pajamas, the subjects did not even feel the pressure of a belt or shoe. Cardboard tubes encased their arms from elbow to fingertips, cutting off the sense of touch. On demand, they received food or water and were allowed to use the bathroom. Otherwise, they heard almost nothing, saw almost nothing, and felt almost nothing. How do you think they responded to such conditions?

A drive-reduction theory of motivation would predict that they should remain happily quiescent. After all, their needs for food, water, relief from pain, and so forth were being admirably met. But this is not what happened. Many of the subjects quit the experiment after only a few days. Subsequent sensory deprivation studies have shown that about a third of all participants drop out before the experiment's official end (Goldberger, 1982). Why this negative reaction?

Part of the explanation probably has to do with the stress of social isolation (Suedfeld, 1975), but a less than optimum level of sensory stimulation seems to play a role as well. Subjects in such experiments tend to grow bored and apathetic. Their minds wander. They claim to have difficulty concentrating, and their brain waves sometimes show patterns more characteristic of sleep than of alert wakefulness. At the same time, they seem to develop a strong desire for sensory stimulation of *some* kind. When given the chance to listen to very boring recordings, such as a monotonous stock-market report or a lecture on the dangers of alcohol written at the six-year-old level, they ask to hear them repeatedly (Bexton, 1953). Such desire for stimulation is in keeping with an optimum-level-of-arousal theory, which postulates that very low levels of stimulation promote a quest for higher levels.

Also in keeping with an optimum-level-of-arousal theory is the fact that a person's performance on certain mental tasks often decreases with sensory deprivation (Goldberger, 1982). This is particularly true of complex mental activities—tasks that are novel and unstructured, that have no single solution, and that require some imagination and an integration of ideas (Suedfeld, 1975). In one study, for instance, subjects were given the complex task of thinking up as many uses as they could for common household objects. After thirty-six hours of sensory deprivation, their performance dropped markedly (Landon and Suedfeld, 1972).

The findings from sensory deprivation research have had many practical applications. They have guided those involved in providing workable environments for astronauts in space, scientists at arctic weather stations, laborers on assembly lines, and even truckers on long-distance hauls (Rasmussen, 1973). The common theme in all these applications is that severe and prolonged lack of variation in sensory stimulation should be avoided as much as possible if people are to function at their best. Note, however, that the point at which low levels of sensory input begin to impair performance varies with the person.

Each of us has his or her own optimum level of arousal, influenced by such factors as age, biological makeup, past learning experiences, and degree of sensory stimulation just encountered (Schultz, 1965). We will return to this important fact of human variation at several points later in this chapter.

If human functioning tends to be impaired when arousal levels fall too low, it seems logical that the opposite extreme should also cause problems. That is to say, excessively high levels of arousal should likewise be detrimental to human performance, making it harder for people to sustain goal-directed behavior. Researchers have investigated this subject in the laboratory by bombarding people with high-intensity sights and sounds for several hours. In a typical study, the subject lies down in a specially designed room where sounds blare from all directions and the walls are ablaze with rapidly changing and vividly colored patterns. As you might expect, most people find this kind of **sensory overload** even more aversive than sensory deprivation. They show signs of physiological arousal, become disoriented with regard to time and space, perform more poorly on many cognitive tasks, and sometimes even have hallucinations (Goldberger, 1982).

Similar reactions have been observed in real-life situations that involve sensory overload, especially those that also pose serious threats to life (Kaminoff and Proshansky, 1982). For instance, in one study of people's responses to such life-threatening disasters as fires and flash floods, at least 75 percent of the victims showed definite impairment in their ability to react rationally (Tyhurst, 1951). Many behaved in ways that simply did not make sense, such as wandering aimlessly rather than seeking a viable escape route. A full 12 to 25 percent were hopelessly disoriented. They screamed and cried hysterically or remained frozen to one spot. Apparently their extremely high levels of arousal, caused by sensory overload and intense emotion, made them unable to act in goal-directed ways.

Researchers are still trying to find out precisely what causes such functional impairment. As we said earlier, in cases of *extreme* overarousal, neural circuits controlling goal-directed responses may simply become blocked. But what about the milder impairments caused by lesser degrees of sensory overload? Some researchers think that part of the answer may lie in a narrowing of attention that tends to come with overarousal, especially when strong emotions are involved (Callaway and Dembo, 1958). When we are highly aroused we tend to focus on the central stimulus at hand, often the one that caused our arousal in the first place. This may be fine as long as flexible problem solving is not required of us. But when various alternatives must be perceived and weighed, choices made, and outcomes carefully evaluated, the person who is highly aroused may be at a real disadvantage. At the same time, overarousal may also impair short-term memory, causing us to have trouble retaining new information long enough to use it effectively (Humphreys et al., 1980). In keeping with both these explanations, researchers have found that the more complex the cognitive task, the more likely that high arousal will interfere with performance (Suedfeld, 1975). This is rather unfortunate, for arousal is often greatest when we face our most difficult challenges.

Individual Differences in Optimum Stimulation. Just as the degree of sensory deprivation that can be tolerated varies with the individual, so the degree of tolerable stimulation also varies from person to person. Psychologist Hans Eysenck (1967) first proposed a theory that could help explain these individual differences. He argued that people vary greatly in their need for stimulation as a result of differences in the way their brains function. Brain differences, Eysenck maintained, underlie the contrast between introverts (people who are generally withdrawn) and extroverts (those who are generally sociable and lively). The reticular formation of an introvert, according to Eysenck, is activated to a relatively high degree by sensory inputs. Consequently, the introvert has a high "natural" level of cortical arousal. This means that such a person needs very little external stimulation to achieve an optimum arousal level, and so prefers quiet, solitary activities. The extrovert, in contrast, has a reticular formation that is activated to a relatively low degree by sensory inputs and so has a naturally low level of cortical arousal. As a result, the extrovert requires a great deal of external stimulation to boost arousal to an optimum level. Hence the extrovert's preference for noise, excitement, and constant companionship.

If introverts and extroverts have different natural levels of arousal, they should perform quite differently under conditions of high stimulation. Introverts, with their normally high states of arousal, should be less tolerant than extroverts of high levels of stimulation and so consequently suffer a drop in performance. Such a drop should not occur for extroverts, however, for they *need* extra stimulation to help them perform their best. A striking experiment confirmed this hypothesis (Revelle, Amaral, and Turriff, 1976). Researchers asked college students to complete a section of the Graduate Record Exam under one of three conditions: a relaxed condition, a condition with time pressure, or a condition with both time pressure and caffeine. Since time pressure and caffeine are both arousing, the investigators predicted that these factors would raise extroverts from their natural low levels of arousal to a more optimum level, while they would raise introverts to a level of arousal too high for good performance. The results strongly supported this prediction. The extroverts did much better when they were stimulated by time pressure and caffeine than when they were relaxed, and the introverts did much worse.

Conversely, under conditions of reduced arousal, an introvert should outperform an extrovert. This, too, has been demonstrated through research. When deprived of sleep (an arousal-reducing condition), extroverts perform worse on a complex motor task, while introverts perform better (Corcoran, 1972). Presumably the lack of sleep reduces the naturally low arousal of the extroverts to a level of underarousal, but it reduces the naturally high arousal of the introverts to a more optimum level. Such findings emphasize that there is no single level of stimulation conducive to superior performance. The optimum level of arousal varies with both the person and the task.

Why People Take Risks

It was nearing noon that Sunday when a stiff, warm breeze suddenly materialized. Brent Hansen, a 29-year-old student . . . had been waiting for it most of the morning. Helmetless, he picked up the control bar of his multi-colored hang glider, fastened his harness, and ran 10 yards along the top of a 600-foot cliff. . . . But no sooner was he aloft than he got into serious trouble. Somehow he had become tangled in his harness. "I'm caught! I'm caught!" he screamed. But his friends below could only watch as he dove nose first into the ground at roughly 40 mph. After three days in the intensive-care unit . . . he recovered, only to hang glide again. [Greenberg, 1977, p. 17]

Although optimum-level-of-arousal theories help to explain the general tendency to seek some degree of stimulation, they cannot explain why some people risk their lives in high-arousal activities such as hang gliding. What makes Brent Hansen and many others like him return to a sport that has nearly killed them? What is it that draws the race-car driver back to the track and the sky diver back to the sky?

The Opponent Process Model. One theory that provides some insight has been proposed by Richard Solomon and J. D. Corbit (1974). Beginning with the assumption that organisms are designed to maintain a biological and psychological balance, Solomon and Corbit argue that when a strong emotional response disrupts this balance an **opponent process** is activated. By *opponent process* they simply mean an opposite response. If the initial emotion is negative, the opponent process will be positive, and vice versa. Usually the opponent process reduces and eventually cancels out the original emotion, thus returning the organism to a normal, emotionally neutral state. If, however, the stimulus that caused the initial emotion is suddenly removed, the opponent reaction can temporarily overwhelm the organism.

Applied to a high-arousal sport, such as sky diving, the opponent process theory says that on the sky diver's first leap from a plane he or she is likely to feel a moment of utter terror. Almost immediately, however, an opponent process begins to counteract this intense fear, and soon the jumper, though still highly anxious, is no longer terrified. Once the diver lands safely, fear evaporates and only the "pure" opposing emotion is left. The novice sky diver feels relieved and exhilarated.

It is this pleasurable sensation that coaxes the person back for another try. But this is not all. According to Solomon and Corbit, additional dives only serve to *intensify* the positive experience because an opponent process is strengthened every time it is elicited. Consequently, if a sky diver continues to jump, the opponent process that is activated becomes more and more powerful until eventually a jump provokes only mild anxiety. Furthermore, the exhilaration that follows landing can sometimes last for hours. It is this euphoria that presumably draws even the previously injured diver back jump after jump.

The opponent process model has been used to account for a wide variety of experiences, some of which might otherwise be hard to explain (Solomon, 1980). The pleasure of certain psychoactive drugs, for example, may decrease with increased use be-

The opponent process theory, described in the text, attempts to explain why sky divers enjoy an activity that other people find terrifying. (Edith G. Haun/Stock, Boston.)

come after the ordeal of donating blood is over. In keeping with opponent process theory, the anxiety felt before giving blood has been found to decrease with each subsequent donation, while the satisfaction afterward has been found to rise steadily (Piliavin, Callero, and Evans, 1982). Researchers have even collected evidence that the exhilaration that students sometimes feel after finishing a difficult exam may simply be the opponent emotion that has arisen to counteract their pre-exam anxiety (Craig and Siegel, 1979).

The opponent process model, then, has received substantial support in studies not only of humans but of laboratory animals as well (Mineka, Suomi, and De Lizio, 1981). Yet the theory is not without its critics. Some find it hard to believe that every emotion necessarily induces an equal and opposite response. If this were true, how could we explain cases in which an emotion such as grief endures for months or years? Clearly, more research is needed to determine the limits of Solomon and Corbit's theory and to shed more light on the physiological mechanisms that may underlie it.

Individual Differences in Sensation Seeking.

Solomon and Corbit's model provides one rationale for the drawing power of dangerous sports, but it does not explain why some people are more attracted to risks than others. One answer relates back to Eysenck's theory about "natural" levels of cortical arousal. High-sensation seekers may simply be Eysenck's extroverts—those people who need a great deal of external stimulation to attain an optimum arousal level.

Accordingly, psychologist Marvin Zuckerman has tried to assess the needs of high- and low-sensation seekers for other kinds of stimulation. He has developed a personality scale that includes items ranging from preferences for exotic vacations and spicy foods to the desire to try risky sports or hallucinogenic drugs. (A brief version of Zuckerman's Sensation-Seeking Scale is shown in Table 11.3.) More than ten thousand people have taken this test, and the results show that the drive for excitement and diversity is

cause a negative opponent process grows ever stronger. At the same time, withdrawal symptoms may become increasingly aversive, because the "pure" opponent process when the drug wears off is now so powerful (Siegel, Hinson, and Krank, 1978). Similarly, people generally find that running becomes less agonizing after a certain distance, as if an opponent process is counteracting their physical pain. And very experienced runners often report euphoria at the end of a run, again suggesting that what they are feeling is an intensified opponent process taking over when the stress of running ends. This post-run euphoria is said to be one reason why people can get "hooked" on running. Using the same logic, some psychologists have suggested that blood donors can gradually get "hooked" on the good feelings that

TABLE 11.3 SENSATION-SEEKING SCALE

1. A. I would like a job that requires a lot of traveling.
   B. I would prefer a job in one location.

2. A. I am invigorated by a brisk, cold day.
   B. I can't wait to get indoors on a cold day.

3. A. I get bored seeing the same old faces.
   B. I like the comfortable familiarity of everyday friends.

4. A. I would prefer living in an ideal society in which everyone is safe, secure, and happy.
   B. I would have preferred living in the unsettled days of our history.

5. A. I sometimes like to do things that are a little frightening.
   B. A sensible person avoids activities that are dangerous.

6. A. I would not like to be hypnotized.
   B. I would like to have the experience of being hypnotized.

7. A. The most important goal of life is to live it to the fullest and experience as much as possible.
   B. The most important goal of life is to find peace and happiness.

8. A. I would like to try parachute-jumping.
   B. I would never want to try jumping out of a plane, with or without a parachute.

9. A. I enter cold water gradually, giving myself time to get used to it.
   B. I like to dive or jump right into the ocean or a cold pool.

10. A. When I go on a vacation, I prefer the comfort of a good room and bed.
    B. When I go on a vacation, I prefer the change of camping out.

11. A. I prefer people who are emotionally expressive even if they are a bit unstable.
    B. I prefer people who are calm and even-tempered.

12. A. A good painting should shock or jolt the senses.
    B. A good painting should give one a feeling of peace and security.

13. A. People who ride motorcycles must have some kind of unconscious need to hurt themselves.
    B. I would like to drive or ride a motorcycle.

Scoring

Count one point for each of the following items that you have circled: 1A, 2A, 3A, 4B, 5A, 6B, 7A, 8A, 9B, 10B, 11A, 12A, 13B. Add up your total and compare it with the norms below.

1–3	Very low on sensation-seeking	10–11	High
4–5	Low	12–13	Very high
6–9	Average		

From Zuckerman, 1978.

seldom confined to one area of life, just as Eysenck's theory would predict. "The high-sensation seekers," Zuckerman writes, "are likely to have not just one but a number of adventurous tastes, from an eagerness to try risky sports such as sky diving to a desire for variety in sexual partners" (Zuckerman, 1978, p. 40). Whether such adventurous tastes can be explained entirely by naturally low cortical arousal is still a matter of debate. Zuckerman now suspects that the activities of certain neurotransmitters in the brain may play a role as well (Zuckerman, 1979; Carrol, Zuckerman, and Vogel, 1982). But regardless of cause, the fact remains that for certain people the quest for novel stimulation is virtually a way of life.

What are the implications of these findings for adjustment to life and to other people? Zuckerman suggests that high-sensation seekers may react badly if they feel trapped in unstimulating situations. They often do poorly in academic settings that lack creative exchange. And when tied down to dull, routine kinds of work, they may, according to Zuckerman, turn to excessive use of alcohol or drugs. Moreover, even when high-sensation seekers are able to select schools, jobs, and hobbies that answer their needs, they may still be misunderstood by low-sensation seekers, who consider some of their actions "reprehensible, foolish, and even crazy. The 'highs,' for their part, consider the caution of the 'lows' prudish, stuffy, timid, or inhibited. High- and low-sensation seekers do not understand one another, and this can be an unfortunate state of affairs if they are a therapist and patient, or a husband and wife" (Zuckerman, 1978, p. 99).

LEARNED MOTIVATION: THE CASE OF ACHIEVEMENT

The arousal of the cerebral cortex sheds much more light on some human actions than on others. Why are we willing to go out of our way to do a favor for a friend? Why does a student work weekends and abandon other interests to win acceptance to medical school? Why does a politician spend an entire lifetime and a personal fortune trying to become president of the United States? For answers to these and similar questions we must look to the motivations people learn in the course of growing up. These include the motives for achievement, power, social approval, and companionship, among many others. By concentrating on one learned motivation—achievement—we can explore the factors that underlie a learned motive and the benefits that scientific knowledge about those factors can bring.

Individual Differences in Achievement Motivation

To measure individual differences in achievement motivation, researchers typically use pictures from the Thematic Apperception Test (TAT), discussed in detail in Chapter 14 (McClelland et al., 1953; Atkinson, 1958). In this test subjects are presented with ambiguous pictures (such as a man standing by a machine or a boy apparently daydreaming) and are asked to write a brief story about each one. In these invented stories the subjects presumably express their own motivations. Stories that receive high scores for achievement motivation are those in which the major character performs at a high level or accomplishes something unique, is concerned with standards of excellence or pursuit of a long-term goal, expresses pride in success or shame at failure, or displays other achievement-related feelings and behaviors.

People who test high and low in achievement motivation differ in several important ways. Those with high so-called **need for achievement** persist longer and show better performance on exams than do those with low need for achievement (Atkinson and Raynor, 1974). They also tend to select occupations that require individual initiative, such as owning a business. People with low need for achievement, in contrast, tend to be attracted to such jobs as routine office work, which demand little individual initiative (McClelland, 1955). Interestingly, people with high need for achievement also tend to set challenging but realistic goals, whereas those with low need for achievement tend not to do so. In one study, for instance, researchers measured how far each subject chose to stand from the target when playing a ring-toss game. Those who scored high in achievement motivation stood at an intermediate distance, making the game challenging but not impossible. Those who scored low in achievement motivation, in contrast, usually stood either very close to the target or very far away from it (Atkinson and Litwin, 1960). Similarly, some psychologists have found that students with high need for achievement tend to seek challenge in their majors and future careers but also to be realistic in those choices. Students with low need for achievement, in contrast, tend to choose either very easy or extremely difficult majors (Isaacson, 1964).

Researchers have wondered what other factors, in addition to need for achievement, underlie achievement striving or its absence. They have found, for one thing, that people who avoid realistic challenge and fail to persist at difficult tasks tend to have a relatively high *fear of failure*. This fear helps explain the outcome of the ring-toss experiment and similar findings. Those who select very easy goals virtually assure their own success, while those who select very difficult goals provide a way of explaining failure that preserves their self-esteem ("No one could succeed at a task *this* hard!"). Anxiety about failure, then, is an important determinant of achievement behavior. People will seek challenge and accomplishment only if their motive to achieve success is stronger than their motive to avoid failure (Atkinson, 1964).

Another factor that helps explain differences in achievement strivings are the *expectations* that people hold regarding their own potential for success or failure. If people expect to do well on a task, they are likely to devote more effort to it than they will if they anticipate failure. But why do some people have confidence that they will ultimately prevail, while others are filled with doubts? One answer is that people differ in the ways in which they explain past performance (Weiner et al., 1971; Weiner, 1974; Dweck, 1975). When people attribute their successes to the stable factor of ability, they are likely to develop high expectations that they will succeed again and again. The same is true of people who attribute their failures to controllable factors, such as amount of effort. When people who fail are convinced that their failure was caused by too little effort, they develop the expectation that more effort will bring success. Now consider some explanations that tend to breed *lack* of confidence. When people attribute failure to an enduring lack of ability, they have every reason to expect many additional failures. And when they attribute success to variable factors, such as luck or the ease of the task, they have little reason to expect more successes in the future.

Yet a third factor that underlies achievement efforts is the positive or negative *value* that someone assigns to success or failure on a given task (Spenner and Featherman, 1978; Parsons and Goff, 1978). Will doing well or poorly on a particular activity affect the person's self-image or sense of self-worth? Will it facilitate or block the fulfillment of important future goals? Such questions are undoubtedly considered when people decide whether to strive for achievement or not. Raynor (1974) found, for instance, that students with a high need to achieve did better in a course they thought relevant to their long-term career goals, while students low in achievement motivation performed better in courses unrelated to their long-term goals. Figure 11.5 shows how incentive values fit into a broader model of achievement behavior.

Thus we see a complex relationship among the values people assign to specific successes and failures, the causes they attribute to them, their emotional reactions to doing well or poorly, and their tendencies to seek or avoid challenge. People who attribute achievements to their own abilities often place high value on success. Their self-esteem is raised by their accomplishments, so they tend to seek out challenges. People who attribute success to external causes and failure to themselves, in contrast, do not generally find accomplishment very rewarding, but they do find failure highly threatening. As a result, they tend

to avoid challenges. And because they believe that inability causes their lack of success, they seldom persist when failure threatens. Ironically, therefore, these people often give up in challenging situations, thereby ensuring the failure they so greatly fear (Heckhausen, 1977).

Encouraging Achievement Behavior

Clearly, a person's tendency to strive for achievement can have an enormous impact on his or her success in life. As we said earlier, such behavior seems to be heavily shaped in the course of growing up, especially by parents. One early study found that mothers of eight-to-ten-year-old boys who scored high in achievement motivation had long expected their children to be independent in a variety of ways—getting themselves ready for bed, earning their own spending money, choosing their own clothes, and so forth (Winterbottom, 1958). In addition, these mothers were more likely to control their children's behavior through rewards, such as affection and praise, rather than through punishment. Parents of boys with low achievement motivation, in contrast, seemed to relate to their children in a manner that was either aloof or domineering, and they tended to emphasize such

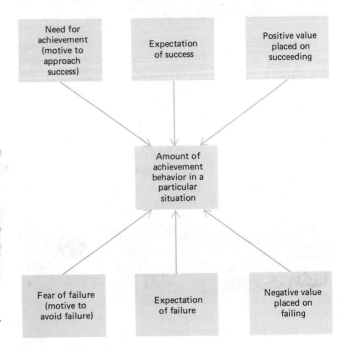

Figure 11.5 Factors affecting achievement behavior.

traits as good manners and obedience. Subsequent studies have tended to confirm these basic patterns (Rosen and D'Andrade, 1959).

Although parents help shape their children's achievement motivation, children's perception of themselves as the cause of their success or failure develops only gradually. Diane Ruble and her associates (1976) showed that while ten- and eleven-year-olds felt bad about their failures, four-year-olds didn't seem to care. The reason, she speculated, is that the young children did not associate the outcomes with their own behavior (Ruble, 1980). But the kinds of experiences children have may affect the *degree* to which they learn that they can make things happen. Some children are more likely than others to learn to assign responsibility to themselves for what happens at home or in the classroom. This, in turn, could affect their willingness to strive for goals.

If achievement strivings are strongly influenced by experiences in childhood, is it still possible to instill them when a person is an adult? Psychologist David McClelland and others believe that it is. In one study, for instance, McClelland and Winter (1969) encouraged and guided college students in the creation of success fantasies, and the students subsequently improved their academic performance. It is not entirely clear why this strategy worked. Perhaps just by making the rewards of success more salient, fantasies encourage people to try harder. Or perhaps the act of mentally "creating" successes makes people more likely to see themselves as in control.

In a far more ambitious study, called the Kakinada project, the same researchers tried to increase the achievement strivings of all of the businessmen in a village in India. The businessmen were encouraged to have high-achievement fantasies, to make plans that would help them realize their goals, and to communicate with one another about these goals and methods. McClelland does not know exactly why this program succeeded—whether one technique worked more than others or whether all contributed equally. But succeed it did. The businessmen became significantly more productive. They started several large industries, enlarged their existing businesses, and hired five thousand workers (McClelland and Winter, 1969). Moreover, unlike many other economic development projects, which succeed only in the short run, the Kakinada project appears to have had continuing impact for more than a decade (McClelland, 1978). McClelland suspects that this success may be due to the program's stress on achievement motivation, not just business knowledge.

Achievement Behavior among Women

In the many studies of achievement motivation that have been conducted, researchers found a peculiar but persistent pattern: a need for achievement did not predict the behavior of women as well as it predicted the behavior of men. Women who scored high in the need for achievement did not always set themselves challenging goals, nor did they always persist in achievement-oriented tasks. In fact, the performance of some women actually declined in certain competitive situations. Psychologists wondered why. One answer that generated a great deal of controversy was proposed by Matina Horner.

Do Many Women Fear Success? To explain the differences in behavior between men and women with high achievement motivation, Horner (1968) argued that achievement-oriented women are propelled in opposite directions by two very powerful forces. On the one hand, they are pushed toward achievement by their desire to obtain the psychological satisfaction associated with accomplishment. But on the other hand, they have learned from childhood that success for a woman is "unfeminine" and socially disapproved, especially by men. Consequently, they are also motivated to avoid success.

Horner devised an interesting way to measure this fear of success, as it came to be called. She gave male and female college students an opening sentence and then asked them to complete the "story." For the ninety women in the study, the opening sentence was: "After first-term finals, Anne finds herself at the top of her medical school class." For the eighty-eight men in the study, the sentence was the same except that the name "John" was substituted for the name "Anne." Horner reasoned that if a subject was fearful of success, that fear should be reflected in the story he or she wrote about a highly successful medical student of the same sex. Specifically, if a story contained references to social rejection, anxiety, or negative self-image as a result of success, if it linked success to abandonment of a medical career, or if it outright denied that such success was possible, the story was said to include fear-of-success imagery.

The results of this study confirmed Horner's predictions. The women showed significantly more evidence of fear of success than did the men. But the most striking feature of Horner's results was the sheer magnitude of the differences she found. More than 65 percent of the women wrote stories containing fear-of-success imagery, compared with fewer than 10 percent of the men. Some women's stories with fear-of-success imagery are seen in Figure 11.6, along with two typical achievement-oriented stories by men.

Horner's research and her provocative conclusions made headlines in the popular press, prompting many women to wonder if their slow climb in the business world might not be due to a deep-seated fear of success. This widespread interest helped to generate a wave of subsequent research. Later findings, however, did not always support Horner's original

conclusions. In sixty-one studies in which subjects were asked to write stories in response to an achievement cue (such as Anne at the top of her medical school class), the proportion of women expressing fear of success ranged from 11 to 88 percent, while the proportion of men expressing such a fear ranged from 14 to 86 percent. Fear of success, in other words, was not always dramatically greater in women. In fact, in seventeen of thirty-six studies that included men, the men expressed *more* fear of success than the women (Tresemer, 1974). If fear of success is a stable personality trait found primarily in women, how could these results be explained?

Important clues began to emerge when researchers looked for patterns in the circumstances surrounding fear-of-success imagery. Some psychologists, for instance, extended Horner's experimental design by having men write about Anne's success and women write about John's. Under these circumstances, the men envisioned many negative outcomes related to achievement, whereas the women envisioned relatively few (Monahan, Kuhn, and Shaver, 1974). These findings indicated that men were less able to envision favorable implications of success for a woman than for a man, and women found it easier to imagine positive outcomes for a successful man than

Figure 11.6 Stories written by subjects in Horner's (1970) research on the motive to avoid success. The first three stories, written by women, reflect the motive theorized by Horner. The other three stories, only one of which was written by a woman, do not. But were the subjects who wrote the first three stories really showing, not fear of success, but fear of social rejection of successful women who deviate from traditional sex roles? For a fuller discussion, see the text.

Anne has a boyfriend Carl in the same class and they are quite serious. Anne met Carl at college and they started dating around their sophomore years in undergraduate school. Anne is rather upset and so is Carl. She wants him to be higher scholastically than she is. Anne will deliberately lower her academic standing the next term, while she does all she subtly can to help Carl... His grades come up and Anne soon drops out of med school. They marry and he goes on in school while she raises their family.

Aggressive, unmarried, wearing Oxford shoes and hair pulled back in a bun, she wears glasses and is terribly bright.

Anne is really happy she's on top, though Tom is higher than she— though that's as it should be... Anne doesn't mind Tom winning.

Congrats to her! Anne is quite a lady —not only is she tops academically, but she is liked and admired by her fellow students. Quite a trick in a man-dominated field. She is brilliant —but she is also a lady. A lot of hard work. She is pleased—yet humble and her fellow students (with the exception of a couple of sour pusses) are equally pleased. That's the kind of girl she is—you are always pleased when she is—never envious. She will continue to be at or near the top. She will be as fine practicing her field as she is studying it. And—always a lady.

John is a conscientious young man who worked hard. He is pleased with himself. John has always wanted to go into medicine and is very dedicated. His hard work has paid off. He is thinking that he must not let up now, but must work even harder than

he did before. His good marks have encouraged him. (He may even consider going into research now.) While others with good first term marks sluff off, John continues working hard and eventually graduates at the top of his class. (Specializing in neurology.)

John is very pleased with himself and he realizes that all his efforts have been rewarded, he has finally made the top of his class. John has worked very hard, and his long hours of study have paid off. He spent hour after hour in preparation for finals. He is thinking about his girl Cheri whom he will marry at the end of med school. He realizes he can give her all the things she desires after he becomes established. He will go on in med school making good grades and be successful in the long run.

for a successful woman. In addition, the amount of negative or positive imagery a subject expressed could be increased or decreased simply by changing the achievement situation. Women, for example, wrote much less fear-of-success imagery about Anne when they were told that half of Anne's classmates were women (Katz, 1973) or that Anne was at the top of her *nursing* school class (Alper, 1974). Similarly, men wrote far more fear-of-success imagery when they discussed John's success in nursing school (Cherry and Deaux, 1975).

On the basis of such findings many researchers have concluded that Horner's original experiment may not have been measuring a fear of success at all. Instead, she may have been measuring women's assessments of the social rejection likely to be caused by deviation from traditional sex roles. And these assessments were probably warranted. In one study conducted shortly after Horner's, some men did indeed dislike being "outdone" by a girlfriend and so preferred to work alone rather than with the girlfriend on achievement tasks (Condry and Dyer, 1976). The message to the girlfriend was clear: "If you outperform me, I will be threatened and avoid you." Such social rejection may have been what women in Horner's study were fearing when they reacted ambivalently to Anne's success in a male-dominated field. Compounding this fear may have been the fact that many women at the time of Horner's study (about twenty years ago) were probably sex-role traditionalists. Subsequent research has shown that women who adhere to traditional sex-role values are more likely than other women to have lower career aspirations, to rate themselves as less intelligent, and to perform more poorly than otherwise when required to compete with a boyfriend (Peplau, 1976).

Sex Differences in Interpreting Failure.

But some researchers now suspect that a fear of deviating from traditional sex roles and being rejected by men may be only part of the reason why some women who score high in the need for achievement fail to persist at achievement tasks or refrain from setting challenging goals for themselves. Another possible explanation has emerged from recent research by psychologist Carol Dweck, one of whose studies we mentioned in Chapter 1. Dweck has found that some people are inclined to attribute failure to lack of ability rather than to a lack of effort, and as a result to stop trying to succeed. As it turns out, this tendency seems to be more prevalent in girls than in boys. Whereas girls are more likely than boys to view their academic failures as signs of low ability, boys are more likely than girls to see such failures as due to simple lack of effort. This is the case regardless of the fact that during the early school years girls equal or surpass their male classmates in all areas of academic work (Nichols, 1975; Dweck and Goetz, 1978; Dweck, Goetz, and Strauss, 1980). Certainly, if this negative way of interpreting failure came to undermine one's general sense of competence, it could easily prompt achievement-oriented women to behave in the puzzling ways they sometimes do.

Dweck has gone on to wonder just what it is in a young girl's experience that could encourage her to interpret failure in this negative fashion. One factor that she thinks may be important is the behavior of the average American teacher. Dweck and her colleagues (1978) have found that when most grade-school teachers criticize their girl students, they focus almost exclusively on the child's intellectual inadequacies. ("You spelled that word wrong"; "You forgot to carry the two.") Boys, of course, also receive this kind of negative feedback. But in addition, boys are very often criticized for *non*intellectual aspects of their work. ("You did this sloppily"; "You weren't trying very hard.") As a result, Dweck argues, when girls experience failure they are more apt than boys to conclude that their poor performance is caused by lack of ability. To demonstrate the power of these patterns, Dweck conducted a study in which she reversed the kind of criticisms boys and girls typically get. As expected, when the children were later confronted with failure, it was the boys that tended to act defeated, while the girls persevered and mastered.

Sex Differences in Task Incentives.

Psychologist Jacquelynne Eccles concedes that attributing failure to lack of ability may sometimes be a factor in the undermining of girls' achievement strivings. This may be particularly true early in life, when a girl's self-perception of competence is still forming. But Eccles disagrees with Dweck's view that a perception of lack of ability is the primary reason why girls sometimes fail to persist at achievement tasks. Eccles (1983) stresses the need for more complex models of achievement behavior. She points out that Dweck's theory focuses only on the expectations that people hold about their future chances for success or failure. Equally important, Eccles argues, are the incentive values of the tasks that people face. Some achievement tasks, according to Eccles, may simply not be worth the effort from the average female's point of view.

One such task is apparently higher mathematics. Eccles and her colleagues have extensively studied junior and senior high school students' attitudes and expectations toward current and future math courses (Eccles, Adler, and Meece, 1984). They have found that the value placed on mathematics is the single most important factor underlying the common decision among young women to stop taking math courses once math requirements are met. This is in keeping with the frequent finding that by the age of thirteen or fourteen boys are more likely than girls to regard math as important to their career goals (Dornbusch, 1974; Fennema and Sherman, 1977,

1978; Wise, Steel, and MacDonald, 1979). In a larger study that included younger children and parents, Eccles and her co-workers have tried to identify some of the forces that promote these sex-typed differences in values (Eccles et al., 1983). They have found that parents often reinforce the sex-stereotyped perception that higher math is more useful for men than it is for women. Thus we see that a complex set of factors can influence achievement choices. Actual achievement behavior in many settings is probably the result of inner needs, fears, and motives, self-concepts of ability and expectations for success, plus the incentive value of the task at hand, all interacting with one another.

SUMMARY

1. **Motivation** is what gives direction to our behavior by arousing, sustaining, and directing it toward the attainment of some goal.

2. Sigmund Freud proposed a theory of motivation according to which people are directed by two largely unconscious forces—one the urge toward life, procreation, and self-preservation, the other the urge toward death and self-destruction. Because people's ways of satisfying these impulses may conflict with society's moral standards, the impulses are often **repressed** and **sublimated** into more acceptable forms of behavior.

3. In the 1930s and 1940s, behaviorist Clark Hull and others developed **drive-reduction theories** of motivation. They saw biological needs (for food, water, relief from pain, and so forth) as the basic motivators of action. These needs were called **primary drives.** When the concept of **secondary drives** was added—that is, drives learned through association with a primary drive and its reduction—drive-reduction theories could account for a large number of behaviors.

4. But drive-reduction theories had limitations. They could not explain certain behaviors that seemed to involve **intrinsic motivation.** Nor could they account for actions that seemed to be as much the product of

incentives as of drives. Recognizing the need for a more cognitive approach to motivation, psychologists began to develop **expectancy-value models.**

5. Many researchers who study the motivations behind eating believe that humans regulate their food intake largely through chemical messengers released by fat cells and carried in the bloodstream to the brain. When the body has too little fat and these chemical messengers are scarce, the urge to eat seems to be activated. Recent thinking is that chronically obese people may have a high **setpoint** for fat tissue which the body is trying to defend. Thus when an obese person tries to become thin by being a **restrained eater,** the body may react as if it were underfed, giving rise to a constant state of hunger.

6. People use a variety of methods to shed unwanted pounds, among them dieting, medications, and behavior modification. Some researchers now believe that regular exercise may be one of the most effective keys to permanent weight loss because it tends to raise a person's metabolic rate, often for hours after the workout is through. Another key to weight loss in the future may be stimulation of activity by the body's heat-producing **brown fat** cells.

7. Hormones secreted by the ovaries, testes, and adrenal glands help to initiate and sustain sexual activ-

ity. But sexually arousing stimuli are also needed to activate sexual responses. In humans the cerebral cortex plays a crucial role in interpreting sexual signals and directing sexual behavior toward appropriate goals.

8. Psychologist Donald Hebb, among others, has proposed that there is an **optimum level of arousal** for effective behavior, and that organisms try to maintain that level. This notion can help explain why both **sensory deprivation** and **sensory overload** interfere with top performance on complex cognitive tasks. Psychologist Hans Eysenck believes that differences in the need for stimulation underlie the contrast between introverts (who need little stimulation to achieve an optimum arousal level) and extroverts (who need a great deal).

9. One intriguing question in motivation research is why people take risks. According to the **opponent process model,** a strong emotional response activates an opposite response, so that the anxiety associated with a high-risk activity triggers an exhilaration that draws the person back to the activity again and again. Another theory holds that individuals may have different levels of biological need for sensation seeking.

10. Many human motivations are learned, among them the urge to achieve. People who score high in **need for achievement** persist longer and do better on difficult tasks and are apt to set realistic but challenging goals for themselves. Other factors that underlie achievement strivings include a low fear of failure, a strong perception of one's own ability and high expectations of success, and a high value placed on accomplishing the task at hand.

11. Achievement strivings are heavily influenced by experiences in childhood, especially within the family. Affection, praise, and encouragement toward independence seem to be important factors, but much more research is needed before we can know why patterns of child rearing have the effects that they generally do.

12. Studies of achievement motivation have not been able to predict women's behavior as well as they have men's. One proposed reason is that achievement-oriented women suffer from a fear of success, but this theory has not been substantiated by recent research. Another possibility is that more women than men attribute failure to a lack of ability and so give up when challenges become great. A third alternative is that some achievement tasks simply do not have as high a subjective value for women as they do for men.

SUGGESTED READINGS

LURIA, ZELLA, and ROSE, MITCHEL D. *Psychology of human sexuality.* New York: Wiley, 1979.

A well-written survey of the psychological literature on sexuality.

PFAFF, D. W. (Ed.). *The physiological mechanisms of motivation.* New York: Springer-Verlag, 1982.

A consolidation of broad research data into an organized format that compares the constructs and mechanisms of motivation.

POLIVY, J., and HERMAN, C. P. *Breaking the diet habit.* New York: Basic Books, 1983.

A scientific analysis of the costs and consequences of dieting.

RAYNOR, J. O., and FONTIN, E. E. *Motivation, career striving, and aging.* New York: Hemisphere, 1982.

Application and expansion of achievement theory to areas such as personality, values, identity, perception, defenses, competence, and aging.

STEWART, A. J. (Ed.). *Motivation and society: A volume in honor of David C. McClelland.* San Francisco: Jossey-Bass, 1982.

A broad-based overview of motivation, including achievement motivation, measurement (Thematic Apperception Test), behavioral correlates of motivation, job skills, and affiliation.

STUNKARD, ALBERT J. (Ed.). *Obesity.* Philadelphia: W. B. Saunders, 1980.

A useful anthology of articles on various factors involved in overeating and obesity.

TAVRIS, CAROL, and OFFIR, CAROLE E. *The longest war.* 2d ed. New York: Harcourt Brace Jovanovich, 1984.

A witty, highly readable exploration of social-science findings about "the battle of the sexes," including research on gender differences in achievement motivation.

ZUCKERMAN, M. *Sensation seeking: Beyond the optimal level of arousal.* Hillsdale, N.J.: Erlbaum, 1979.

A look at the motivation to seek stimulation.

12

ALTERED STATES OF CONSCIOUSNESS

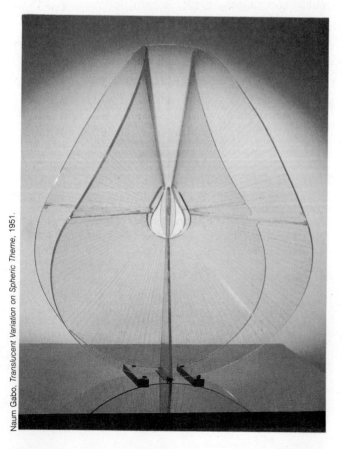

Naum Gabo. *Translucent Variation on Spheric Theme*, 1951.

What does it mean to be conscious? Is it simply to be clearly alert, as when you're following every play in an exciting football game? How about when you're daydreaming, or are only dimly aware of street scenes as you pass by on a bus? Or when you've stayed up all night at a party and you're feeling more than a little sluggish? Would you consider someone in a hypnotic trance or someone who is hallucinating or experiencing a nightmare as being in a conscious state? Actually, these are all examples of our rich states of consciousness, which are among the most inescapable aspects of human psychology. By **consciousness** psychologists mean our awareness of all the many thoughts, images, perceptions, and emotions that occupy the mind at any given time (Marsh, 1977). As we noted in Chapter 1, William James likened this conscious awareness to a river that perpetually flows. Stop reading for a moment and try to make your mind a complete void. Even if you close your eyes you will find it virtually impossible to do so, for sensations, thoughts, feelings, and fantasies keep intruding into consciousness. We hear, we feel, we analyze, we let our minds wander. Like William James's river, our mental stream keeps flowing on.

Because consciousness is such a subjective experience, early psychologists tended to ignore or bypass it. James (1904) even questioned whether there was any such thing as consciousness. He considered it to have no real existence and focused instead on the concrete reality of thoughts. The early behaviorists felt that the study of consciousness had no place within psychology. If we cannot objectively see into consciousness to measure and analyze its components, then it is not a proper subject for scientific inquiry, they argued. But most contemporary psychologists disagree with this view. They maintain that consciousness is far too important to human functioning to be completely ignored. Fortunately, modern technology is helping researchers to overcome some of the former barriers to eavesdropping on consciousness. Equipment for mapping electrical impulses and the activity of neurotransmitters in the brain is providing important new means of investigating some of what goes on physiologically during different states of consciousness.

Yet even with all our modern technology we still know virtually nothing about how the brain gives rise to conscious awareness in the first place. Are particular areas of the brain involved, and if so, which areas? Or is consciousness more the product of the way the whole brain functions as an integrated unit? One puzzling aspect of the problem is that the link between consciousness and brain activity appears to be interactional: brain activity is necessary for consciousness to emerge, yet consciousness seems to have a role in directing brain activity. How such a complex system might work baffles the imagination. According to Nobel Prize–winning psychologist Roger Sperry, the basis of human consciousness remains one of the most truly mystifying unknowns in all of science (Sperry, 1976).

But even though psychologists are still perplexed about the physiological roots of consciousness, they have extensively explored the subjective experience of consciousness. In doing so, they universally acknowledge that consciousness has many modes. You are surely aware of this yourself. Think of the differences in your conscious experiences during a typical day. Your states of consciousness vary from highly focused, systematic, and purposeful kinds of thinking—the kind you might do while taking an exam—to very loosely focused, unstructured, free-wandering images such as you might have during a dream. Psychologists describe this variation as the difference between normal waking consciousness on the one hand and so-called **altered states of consciousness** on the other. If this distinction seems fuzzy, that is because no hard-and-fast line can be drawn between the two states.

Though the two modes of consciousness cannot be differentiated clearly, researchers have found that altered states of consciousness can be induced in two basic ways (Fischer, 1971; Martindale, 1981). One is drastically to decrease sensory input, or to create a sensory environment that is highly repetitive and boring. We saw this in Chapter 11 when we discussed sensory deprivation and the marked changes in thought and attention that this condition brings. In everyday life, the altered state of consciousness called sleep is induced in much the same manner. We blot out external sights, sounds, and other sensory inputs until we drift away from normal waking consciousness. As we will see later in this chapter, certain types of meditation give rise to altered states in similar ways. Likewise, the altered state of consciousness called hypnosis is sometimes elicited by having a person focus attention on a very monotonous stimulus, such as a swinging pendulum. At the opposite extreme are altered states of consciousness induced by highly intense sensory inputs, or sensory overload.

The mentally confused, sometimes hallucinatory states produced in lab settings when people are persistently bombarded by intense sights and sounds provide one example, which we talked about in Chapter 11. In natural settings overarousal can occur as a result of emotional stress or physical trauma (such as an earthquake). Stimulant drugs, such as amphetamines and cocaine, which overarouse the central nervous system, also seem to induce altered states of consciousness. Figure 12.1 diagrams these two basic ways of altering consciousness from what we generally consider "normal."

As we will be discussing throughout this chapter, each of the various altered states of consciousness of which human beings are capable has its own distinctive characteristics. Nevertheless, all such states tend to have certain similarities. Psychologist Colin Martindale (1981) lists, among others, the following five shared features:

1. Thought during altered states of consciousness tends to involve rather "shallow" cognitive processing. We do not structure and analyze mental information as much as we normally do. Instead, we tend to remain on the level of concrete sights, sounds, and images. Since "deep" cognitive processing seems to aid retention, as we saw in Chapter 6, it is not surprising that memory

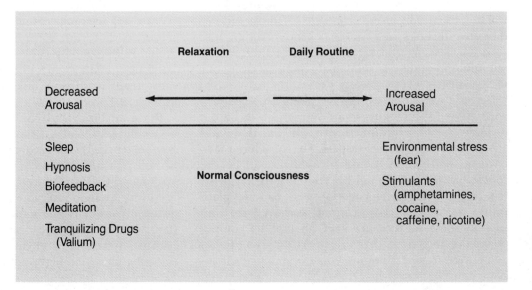

Figure 12.1 Altered states of consciousness are achieved by either increasing or decreasing arousal. Arousal can be decreased by any of the means shown at the left, though sleep and the use of such tranquilizers as Valium are the means most commonly used. Arousal can be increased either by the experience of stress or by the use of stimulants, such as amphetamines or even coffee and cigarettes.

Relaxation   Daily Routine

Decreased Arousal ← → Increased Arousal

Sleep

Hypnosis

Biofeedback   Normal Consciousness

Meditation

Tranquilizing Drugs (Valium)

Environmental stress (fear)

Stimulants (amphetamines, cocaine, caffeine, nicotine)

for what happened during an altered state of consciousness is often rather poor. The difficulty of remembering dreams is one familiar example.

2. Altered states of consciousness frequently involve a marked change in the way the self is experienced. Often the normally sharp demarcation between the self and the outside world becomes blurred. In extreme altered states, self and external reality may actually seem to blend. Some Eastern religions deliberately seek this change in self-awareness through meditation.

3. During altered states of consciousness people sometimes lose their normal inhibitions, while at the same time they become more susceptible to the suggestions of others. Some psychologists speculate that what is happening here is a dissociation of the mechanisms that control actions from those that control critical thought. As you will see later, this is one of the theories proposed to explain hypnosis.

4. Yet another unusual aspect of many altered states of consciousness is the extent to which perceptions may be divorced from external stimuli. During altered states we sometimes see, hear, and feel things that have no basis in reality. The perceptual hallucinations we call dreams are one example. Other instances may occur during drug-altered states, trance, and hypnosis.

5. Finally, the contents of consciousness may become more vivid during altered states. Colors may become brighter, sounds sharper, and emotions more acutely felt. Drugs are particularly well known for bringing about this effect, but other altered states of consciousness likewise seem to intensify our perceptions.

The rest of this chapter is devoted to a detailed exploration of various altered states of consciousness. We will be examining sleep and dreaming, hypnosis, meditation, and biofeedback, as well as drug-altered states. In doing so, we will focus mainly on the distinctive behavioral and physiological aspects of each of these changes in conscious awareness. But as you are reading, you should keep in mind the broad similarities to be found in many altered states of consciousness. Psychologists study altered states of consciousness because these states are fascinating in their own right. Perhaps, however, insights regarding them will someday provide pieces to the larger puzzle of the nature of consciousness itself.

SLEEP AND DREAMING

The transition from wakefulness to sleep and dreaming is an experience of entering an altered state of consciousness with which everyone is familiar. As we close our eyes and wait for sleep, our purposeful thoughts fade until we are just on the brink of losing awareness of the external world. This is the point at which people may enter what psychologists call the **hypnagogic state.** The term *hypnagogic* comes from Hypnos, the Greek god of sleep, and *agogos*, meaning "leading" or "inducing." The hypnagogic state, in other words, is that drowsy twilight between wakefulness and sleep. Some people experience vivid visual images during this altered state—images that intrude into consciousness suddenly and seem to have a life of their own (D. L. Schacter, 1976). Bright flashes of color may merge into geometric patterns, which in turn are replaced by faces and objects, often of extraordinary detail. Dramatic landscapes and even more complex scenes may follow, rather like a series of briefly displayed snapshots. Some people liken the experience to seeing a series of unrelated pictures projected on a screen. Others have auditory sensations, seeming to hear music or the sound of someone's voice. The sensation of falling is also common during the hypnagogic state. Some believe it is a concrete representation of the awareness of descending into sleep. Frequently, too, other abstract thoughts are transformed into concrete images. The formulas you have just been studying for a chemistry exam, for instance, may suddenly become animated, three-dimensional objects. This is what happened to the chemist Kekulé, whom we talked about in Chapter 7, when he "saw" the structure of the benzene molecule while drowsing before his fireplace. In his mind's eye the benzene atoms became transformed into a circular snake, thereby providing the answer he had been seeking: the benzene molecule is ring-shaped. Others have reported similar creative insights during the hypnagogic state. If you believe that you have never experienced hypnagogic images of any kind, it may simply be that by the time you awaken in the morning, all traces of these twilight sensations have faded from memory.

The same problem of recall often occurs with the thoughts and images that flood the mind during sleep itself. In fact, some people maintain that they hardly ever dream—that most of the time they spend sleeping is simply a mental void. Are these people right? During sleep does consciousness usually take time out? Research in the last several decades tells us the answer is definitely no. Despite our hazy recall of what happens during sleep, some mental activity goes on during all or most of it. What's more, a sizable portion of everyone's sleep is occupied by those strange, story-like fantasies we call dreams (Dement, 1976). Sleep, then, is a very rich reservoir of conscious thoughts and feelings, albeit very different ones from those of normal waking life.

Brain Activity from Wakefulness to Deep Sleep

The most revealing data concerning sleep as an altered state of consciousness come from use of the electroencephalograph, a device for recording the brain's electrical activity. The chart of brain-wave tracings that an electroencephalograph produces is called an **electroencephalogram,** or **EEG.** In a typical laboratory study of sleep, a volunteer subject is hooked up to an electroencephalograph by means of several electrodes attached to the scalp and face. The subject then settles down in bed to sleep away the night.

Figure 12.2 shows that the pattern of brain waves changes distinctively when a person drops from wakefulness into light sleep and then into deep sleep. Very noticeable are the reductions that occur in

brain-wave frequencies, measured in cycles per second. The EEG of a person who is fully awake and alert, eyes open, usually shows a predominance of so-called **beta waves.** These are rapid or high-frequency brain waves, measuring fourteen or more cycles per second. When the eyes close and the person relaxes, however, the brain-wave pattern begins to change. Now somewhat slower **alpha waves** start to appear in the record—waves that measure from eight to thirteen cycles per second. When a person begins to fall asleep (stage 1 in Figure 12.2), even slower **theta waves** (five to seven cycles per second) become mixed with the alphas, while every now and again a burst of betas is seen. As sleep becomes progressively deeper, the alpha pattern disappears (stage 2 in Figure 12.2). Then gradually very slow **delta waves** (four or fewer cycles per second) begin to dominate the record (stage 3 in Figure 12.2). In the deepest stage of sleep (stage 4 in the figure), delta waves occupy more than 50 percent of the EEG. This very deep sleep is

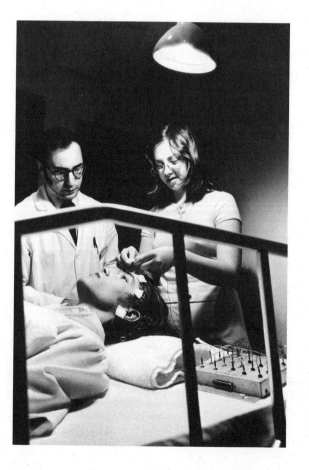

Measuring brain waves. *(James H. Karales/Peter Arnold, Inc.)*

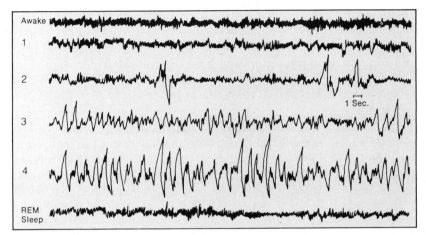

Figure 12.2 Records of the electrical activity of the brain (EEGs) in a person in various stages of sleep and in the relaxed waking state known as "alpha." Note that in the deeper stages of sleep the high-frequency, small-amplitude (small-sized) waves give way to lower-frequency, large-amplitude waves that are also more rhythmic (synchronized). This change is thought to reflect the fact that the neurons in the brain are all firing at about the same level and in about the same pattern. Note also that the EEG pattern in REM sleep is very similar to the waking pattern.

accompanied by marked relaxation of the muscles, very slow and regular breathing, and a significant drop in both body temperature and pulse rate.

Contemporary psychologists attribute substantial importance to deep, delta-wave sleep. The production of delta waves seems to be directly related to the amount of time a person has previously stayed awake. The longer the preceding period of wakefulness, the greater the number of delta waves emitted and the greater their amplitude or strength. This finding has led some researchers to suspect that the emission of delta waves may be associated with unknown physiological processes that are somehow compensating for physiological changes that took place during waking consciousness (Feinberg and Fein, 1982). Delta sleep, in other words, may be needed to restore a proper balance in the body, though precisely what that balance might entail remains a mystery.

The nature of consciousness during stage 4 sleep is also something of a puzzle. It is hard to awaken people from this deepest stage of sleep. They almost seem to be in a coma. As a result, by the time a subject is finally awakened and asked if any thoughts were occupying consciousness, the researcher cannot be sure *when* reported mental activity actually happened. Did it happen during deep sleep or during the waking-up process? Despite this obstacle, however, we know that some mental activity must occur during stage 4 sleep, because most episodes of sleepwalking, sleeptalking, and intense nightmares occur during this stage as well as during the neighboring stage 3.

REM Sleep

The nature of sleep is even more complex than our discussion so far implies. During a night's sleep you do not merely fall into progressively deeper sleep and then gradually awaken. Instead, your brain waves show a regular cyclical pattern that recurs about every ninety minutes, as shown in Figure 12.3. First you fall into deeper and deeper sleep, then gradually return to what superficially resembles a stage 1 or waking pattern. At this point, however, you do not actually

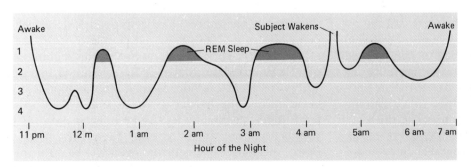

Figure 12.3 A typical night's sleep described in terms of the stages mentioned in the text and shown in Figure 12.2. Note that the depth of sleep increases and decreases in cycles and that sleep becomes shallower and REM sleep periods grow longer as the night wears on.

wake up. You remain sound asleep, although your eyes move rapidly back and forth under your closed eyelids. This stage is known as **REM** (rapid eye movement) **sleep.** The average person has about four or five episodes of REM sleep each night, which together consume roughly 25 percent of total sleep time, or between one and a half and two hours. Since the discovery of REM sleep some twenty-five years ago, psychologists have come to realize that the sharpest and most important distinction between the various stages of sleep is that between REM and all the other four stages, collectively referred to as non-REM sleep (Aserinsky and Kleitman, 1953; Kleitman, 1963; Dement, 1976).

REM Sleep and Dreaming.

When researchers first observed REM sleep, they suspected that it might be linked to dreaming. To explore this possibility, they woke subjects during the various stages of sleep and asked them to report any ongoing mental activity. The results were dramatic. During REM periods, dreams with vivid visual imagery, in which the dreamers felt they were actively participating, were reported about 80 percent of the time. During non-REM periods, in contrast, the story-like episodes that we typically label dreams occurred far less frequently, the exact percentage depending on exactly how "dream" was defined. Much of non-REM mental activity is apparently more like drifting, unstructured thinking than like dreaming.

With the discovery that rapid eye movements and dreams often go together, it was natural to speculate that these movements may occur as the dreamer "watches" the activity unfolding in the dream. This theory, called the **scanning hypothesis,** was first proposed by sleep researcher William Dement (1976) on the basis of data collected in his laboratory. When, for example, Dement awakened one subject who showed only horizontal eye movements during a particular REM period, the subject reported that he had been dreaming about a Ping-Pong match. The problem with the scanning hypothesis, however, is that the relationship between rapid eye movements and dream content is usually far less clear-cut. A complicated mixture of eye movements, with very few highly distinct patterns, occurs during most dreams. This finding has led some researchers to suspect that dreaming is not the cause of rapid eye movements, as the scanning hypothesis suggests. Instead, rapid eye movements and dreaming may be two parallel outcomes of the brain's unusually high state of activation during REM sleep. The rapid eye movements, in fact, may even come *first,* with the dream following as an effort to impose meaning on what normally are signs that visual information is being processed (Hobson and McCarley, 1977; McCarley, 1978).

The Paradoxes of REM Sleep.

One curious fact about REM sleep is that in some respects it seems similar to the waking state. The rapid, desynchronized brain waves that dominate the EEG record during REM periods look very much like those that occur when a person is wide awake. Other physiological signs likewise resemble those of a wide-awake person. Heartbeat, breathing, and blood pressure are irregular and varied, and there is evidence of sexual arousal. Usually these patterns would be observed in a person who is not only awake but also excited. It is therefore not surprising that certain medical catastrophes—heart attacks, acute ulcer pains, and attacks of emphysema—seem often to occur during REM periods of the night (Snyder, 1965; Armstrong, 1965; Trask and Cree, 1962).

Yet, paradoxically, the REM sleeper is *soundly* asleep, not just dozing lightly. He or she will often sleep on through the sound of a voice or the touch of a hand on the shoulder. Moreover, while all the many signs of arousal are present, the major muscles of the body lose their tone and become limp. The result is temporary paralysis. Unlike a person in stage 4 sleep, the REM sleeper is literally unable to move. Apparently activation of a specific area of the brain is responsible for this condition. When this small region was removed from the brain of a cat, REM sleep still occurred, but the animal no longer lay still. Instead, it jumped up and moved about—asleep all the while (Jouvet, 1967). This experiment suggests an odd possibility: if our muscles were not paralyzed during REM sleep, our bodies might act out our dreams.

Do We Need REM Sleep?

Suspecting that REM sleep may somehow be essential to psychological well-being, Dement (1960) deprived people of it for several nights in a row. Whenever he saw the beginnings of a REM period, he awakened the sleeper. With each successive REM episode, Dement found that it became harder and harder to arouse many of his subjects. A few eventually had to be hoisted onto their feet before they finally opened their eyes. What's more, the longer Dement denied REM sleep to his subjects, the more often they would start to enter REM periods. Whereas people normally have only four or five REM episodes during a night, Dement's subjects had to be awakened an average of ten or twelve times even on the first night of REM deprivation. By the third night Dement was running in and out of subjects' bedrooms so fast that he could hardly keep up the pace. Finally, on the fifth night, he let the sleepers go into REM sleep without interruptions. The result was a **REM rebound:** the subjects in general spent about double their normal times in REM sleep.

Although we apparently have a need for REM sleep, judging from the fact that our bodies automatically compensate for its loss, it is not clear what this kind of sleep actually does for us. Subjects in REM deprivation studies are perhaps tired or irritable as the result of the loss of sleep but do not display marked impairments during their waking hours. At most, they may be slightly more prone than normal to unconventional thoughts and behaviors (Dement, 1960; Kales et al., 1964; Sampson, 1965). Still, REM sleep may serve some special function that these relatively short-term experiments are unable to detect. What could this special function be?

There are several theories. Some evidence suggests that REM sleep may be a time when the brain adapts to disturbing or unusual life experiences. In one study, for example, subjects wore goggles with distorting lenses for several days. At night they slept in the laboratory. While becoming accustomed to the weird lenses, they showed a greater than usual amount of REM sleep. Once they had adapted, however, REM time dropped back to normal (Luce, 1971). In keeping with this theory, developmental research shows that REM time steadily decreases as people grow older. (See Figure 12.4.) Newborns spend about half their sleep in REM; infants under two years, 30 to 40 percent; adolescents and young adults, about 20 to 25 percent; and elderly people, less than 5 percent. REM sleep may allow key areas of

the brain to prepare for the enormous flood of stimulation from the outside environment during waking hours. Logically, the need for such "rehearsal" time would be greatest in the newborn and decrease with age, just as REM time does (Roffwarg, Muzio, and Dement, 1966).

There is also evidence that REM sleep may play some role in the consolidation of information into long-term memory. Consider a study in which pairs of subjects heard a tape-recorded string of nonsense phrases before going to bed (Empson and Clarke, 1970). During the night one of each pair was REM-deprived and the other was awakened at the same time whether or not the person was in a REM period. The REM-deprived subjects had significantly poorer recall of the nonsense phrases the next morning. This finding suggests that brain activation during REM somehow aids memory storage. Of course, other explanations are possible. It may be that lack of sleep caused REM-deprived subjects to be upset, which affected various behaviors, including recall.

Finally, several researchers have speculated that REM sleep may provide a way of reducing some of the energy built up when our biological needs go unfilled. Intriguing support for this notion comes from observations of laboratory animals deprived of REM sleep for long periods—far longer than those normally inflicted on human subjects. These animals tend to show an increased appetite for both food and sex. Laboratory cats, for instance, after long-term REM deprivation will often attempt to copulate with any available partner, even one that normally would not be sexually arousing (Dement, 1969). Prolonged loss of REM sleep seems to cause their basic drives to

Figure 12.4 The amount of time the average person spends each day in three states: awake, non-REM sleep, and REM (dreaming) sleep, as it changes over the years. In order to indicate the changes more clearly, the time intervals shown here are wider for younger people than for older people. As people get older, they tend to need less sleep. *(Adapted from Hartman, 1967.)*

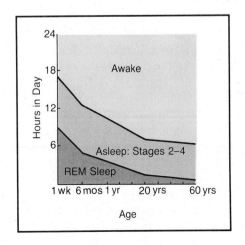

intensify. This finding suggests that ordinarily REM sleep may serve as a kind of physiological "release valve."

We do not know to what extent this function exists in humans. Some provocative clues, however, come from studies of people who naturally sleep unusually long or unusually little (nine or more hours each night versus six or fewer hours). Short sleepers, on average, experience only half the REM time nightly that long sleepers do. Significantly, they also tend to have higher energy levels and greater aggressive drive than long sleepers (Webb and Agnew, 1970; Hartman, Baekeland, and Zwilling, 1975). In view of this finding, some clinical researchers have tried prolonged REM deprivation as a treatment for the severely depressed, who are chronically tired and apathetic. In one study, half the depressed subjects deprived of REM and receiving no other treatment recovered enough to leave the hospital after about seven weeks (Vogel et al., 1975; Vogel, 1975). Future research may provide many more such fascinating clues to the possible functions of paradoxical REM sleep.

The Content of Dreams

One researcher estimates that by age seventy the average person will have had about 150,000 dreams (Snyder, 1970). Does this mean 150,000 fascinating adventures? No, not at all. When people are awakened randomly during REM sleep and asked what they have just been dreaming, the reports are often commonplace, even dull (Hall and Van de Castle, 1966). Under normal circumstances these uneventful dreams are experienced and forgotten. It is the more emotion-laden, bizarre, and sexy dreams that we remember and talk about (Webb, 1975). Still, some psychologists (especially psychoanalysts) find great symbolic meaning in even the most prosaic of dreams. Where does the stuff of dreams come from?

What Determines Dream Content? A papyrus in the British Museum dating from 1350 B.C. is about dream interpretation—evidence that one of the most ancient beliefs about dreams is that they contain great hidden truths about our lives. In modern times Sigmund Freud made this view famous. He argued that dreams reflect the repressed needs and desires of the unconscious, needs and desires that often arise from

unresolved psychosexual conflicts of childhood. In *The Interpretation of Dreams* (1900) Freud distinguished between the manifest and latent content of a dream. The **manifest content** is the readily perceived "story line"—the actors, the setting, the chain of events that take place. The **latent content,** in contrast, is the deeper meaning of the dream—the underlying, largely unconscious wishes it expresses. Through "dreamwork," Freud maintained, the manifest content veils the unconscious wishes in symbolic images more acceptable to the dreamer.

But other psychoanalysts have not always accepted Freud's view of dreams. Alfred Adler, for one, a close early colleague of Freud, broke away from Freudian doctrine on many issues, including the meaning of dreams. Adler (1936) argued that dreams do not embody our unconscious wishes, surfacing in symbolic form. Instead, he saw dreams as a continuation of whatever thoughts and feelings were dominating consciousness during waking hours. Many therapists share this perspective (Ullman, 1962; Foulkes, 1964). They say that the student who dreams about writing an exam in disappearing ink is not trying to resolve an infantile sexual conflict, as a strict Freudian might say, but is simply worried about failing an upcoming final.

Implicit in this view is the idea that during nighttime hours we continue to try to cope with our current concerns and problems. Psychologist Rosalind Cartwright (1979) has studied this process in the laboratory. In one study she had subjects identify a personality trait they particularly disliked in themselves. Then, as they were falling asleep, they repeated a wish to change that trait. Over and over they would say to themselves, "I wish I were not so sarcastic," "I wish I were not so hostile," or whatever. Thus the subjects went to sleep faced with a conflict. On the one hand, they acknowledged that they frequently displayed a certain characteristic; on the other, they were forced to admit that this characteristic was undesirable. Would dreams help them resolve the resulting tension? For some of the subjects, their dreams apparently did. They dreamed about the worrisome trait more than would be expected by chance. And when they did, they tended to fashion scenes in which the negative trait was entirely justified. Figure 12.5 gives two dreams reported by a subject who had wished upon falling asleep that she were not so sarcastic. These dreams seem to assert the view that sometimes the targets of our sarcasm richly de-

I was walking through a big department store and I had just come back from lunch. I was talking to this cop who must have had ten dollars worth of food for lunch and he said, "What does your mother think of all of this food?" and I said, "I don't know, she's not here with me. . . ." And the cop was—I wish I could swear—he was just a real mean guy, a real wise guy. I told him he ate like a pig. Except that I caught myself because you don't call a cop a pig, of course, but he was really eating a lot. . . . I was kinda *having a good time telling the cop what an animal he was.*

I was walking home . . . and all of a sudden I saw the whole sidewalk was covered with my bedspread and all of these people were walking on my bedspread, and all of a sudden this schoolteacher came out who was my neighbor, and I said, "Look, lady, that's kinda taking liberties on my bedspread. I ought to have you fired." And she said, "Well, I've got more brains than you," or something, and I called her a bitch or something, but she had ripped my bedspread. . . . This lady—*I really wasn't very diplomatic with her,* like I was immediately *very mean* to her—and she really snapped back and then I said something like, "Well, *at least my mother's not an old biddy like you."*

Figure 12.5 A woman who felt that she was too sarcastic with authority figures reported these two dreams. Psychologists might say that her dreams represented an attempt to resolve the conflict she felt over having a trait she considered undesirable or to assert her self-esteem in threatening circumstances. *(Reported in Cartwright, 1977.)*

serve what they get. Some psychologists would argue that this young woman might well wake up feeling less in conflict about her sarcasm than she had felt the night before.

Can We Control Our Dreams? Although psychologists debate where the basic material for our dreams comes from and what the meaning of particular dreams may be, they all agree that dreams have the power to arouse very strong emotions. Dreams can sadden or amuse us, cause us shame or pride, turn us into cowards or heroes, make us feel joy or fear. This is also true, of course, of our daytime fantasies—but with several important differences. Whereas we are always aware that our daytime fantasies are mere fabrications, our nighttime dreams seem real to us at the time. This may be one reason why emotions felt in nighttime dreams are often more intense than those experienced in daydreams. In addition, people can consciously select their daydreams, but usually not their nighttime fantasies. As a result, our waking reveries are overwhelmingly filled with themes of happiness and friendship, whereas our nighttime dreams are much more apt to evoke negative feelings, such as fear and hostility (Barrett, 1979). For a long time psychologists assumed that emotionally negative dreams that left us disturbed and unsettled were largely unavoidable. Recently, however, some researchers have begun to demonstrate that this common assumption may not be entirely true.

People in certain other cultures, most notably the Senoi of the Malay Peninsula, have long sought to control their dreams (Stewart, 1972). The management of dream content is part of every Senoi child's education. At the first meal of the day the elders of a household talk to the children about their dreams. Suppose a child has had a terrifying dream about a tiger, or about falling from a great height. The adult will instruct the frightened child to transform the dream into something pleasant should it ever occur again. A dream about falling might be transformed into a dream about being able to fly. A dream about a tiger might be transformed into a dream about being a courageous hunter. In this way the sleeper strives for control over dream life.

Some psychologists have tried to test whether such conscious control of dreams is really possible. Stephen La Berge (1981), for instance, began with the recognition that occasionally in our dreams we become fully aware that we are only dreaming, yet the dream continues. Such nighttime fantasies are called **lucid dreams,** because the dreamer is perceiving the true situation clearly. La Berge suspected that lucid dreams provide an excellent opportunity for people to take charge of their dreams. So he developed a technique for cultivating lucid dreaming in himself. Essentially, the technique involves telling oneself when wide awake at the end of a dream episode: "Next time I'm dreaming, I want to remember I'm dreaming." At the same time, one repeatedly pictures oneself dreaming and then realizing it is only a dream. La Berge reports that when he has used this method he has averaged over twenty lucid dreams a month, sometimes as many as four a night. More important, he claims that lucid dreams allow him to resolve many of his nighttime conflicts in ways that are emotionally satisfying.

Other psychologists are currently trying to develop similar dream-management techniques as therapy for situationally caused anxiety and depression. The theory is that if the troubled person can incorporate more constructive conclusions into dreams related to his or her present life crisis (divorce, loss of a job, failure at school, or whatever), that person's self-image and outlook may significantly improve. Lucid dreams, of course, are not essential for doing this. Sometimes just by talking about constructive solutions to problems before sleeping, people can apparently change the way they handle those problems in their dreams. Rosalind Cartwright has occasionally found this in recently divorced and depressed women who have volunteered for experimental dream therapy. Some have actually been able to insert better endings into recurring and emotionally disturbing dreams (Cartwright, 1978). We do not yet know to what extent such dream manipulations may influence one's behavior in real life. The possibilities, however, are intriguing. And the fascinating implication for the study of human consciousness is that people may have more capacity consciously to shape their nighttime fantasies than was ever before imagined.

Why Do We Sleep at All?

Sleep occupies roughly a third of our adult lives—even more of our lives when we are children. In view of the amount of time we spend in this altered state of consciousness, we know remarkably little about why we enter it at all. For years scientists have searched for some chemical in the body that periodically builds up and causes the onset of sleep. To date, however, no such chemical has been discovered. Although we have found that increased amounts of certain neurotransmitters (serotonin, for example) can sometimes promote sleep, there is as yet no evidence of any naturally occurring chemical changes in the brain that regularly bring about sleep. The physiological causes of sleep, like the causes of consciousness in general, remain a mystery.

But though we know almost nothing about the physiological causes of sleep, we do know that our sleep-wake cycle is part of a collection of naturally occurring daily rhythms in the body. These are often called **circadian rhythms** (the term *circadian* comes from the Latin *circa*, "about," and *dies*, "day"). Many biological factors, including blood pressure, body temperature, and various chemicals in the bloodstream, rise and fall predictably according to daily cycles.

The mechanisms that pace these cycles are believed to be internal, and thus are often called our **biological clocks.** The biological clock that times our sleep-wake cycle has been found to be set for a total period of about twenty-five hours (not the twenty-four hours it takes for the earth to rotate on its axis). This means that when experimental subjects are placed in windowless rooms with no indications of sunrise and sunset, they tend to go to bed about an hour later each day. Normally, of course, we "reset" our biological clock daily to stay in tune with the twenty-four-hour light-dark cycle. This relatively minor adjustment is easy. Larger adjustments, however, can be more difficult. This is why, when you fly across the country, it may take a while for your sleep patterns to adjust to the new time zone. It is also the reason workers placed on rapidly rotating work shifts (midnight to 8 A.M. one week, 4 P.M. to midnight the next week, 8 A.M. to 4 P.M. the following week) often complain of sleep disorders, health ailments, and drops in productivity. Work schedules that take circadian rhythms into account can help alleviate these problems. One team of researchers has found that increasing the time between rotations to at least three weeks makes a substantial difference (Czeisler, Moore-Ede, and Coleman, 1982). So does rotating shifts in a "forward" direction, so that workers who change shifts must stay up *past* their previous bedtimes rather than go to bed artificially early. Such a schedule takes advantage of the fact that the biological clock for sleeping and waking is longer than twenty-four hours, so that it is natural to stay up a little later today than yesterday. For the same reason, it is easier to adjust to jet lag between New York and San Francisco (where the traveler gains three hours) than to adjust to jet lag between San Francisco and New York (where three hours of the day are lost).

HYPNOSIS

The scene is a college classroom, with thirty students sitting in straight-back chairs. A professor is speaking to them in a soft, reassuring tone: "I want you to relax your body and become comfortable. Just relax and let yourself go limp. You will find yourself becoming warm, at ease, more comfortable. Now you are becoming drowsy and sleepy, drowsy and sleepy. . . ." One by one the students close their eyes and lower their heads. When everyone is still, the professor tells them: "Now clasp your hands together tightly, as though they were locked together by a steel band. Try as you might, you can't get them apart. Try to separate them. You can't!" The students strain to pry apart their hands, but their fingers remain interlocked. Finally the professor breaks the tension: "Stop trying and relax. Your hands are no longer locked together. You can take them apart now." The straining stops and everyone's hands easily separate. The entire class relaxes, awaiting the professor's next instruction.

Such demonstrations of hypnosis create the popular conception that a hypnotized person is like a sleepwalker—seemingly awake yet out of touch with normal waking awareness and self-control. Our language helps to give this impression, for as we mentioned earlier, Hypnos was the Greek god of sleep. There are substantial differences, however, between the sleepwalker and the hypnotized person. For one thing, their EEGs are very dissimilar. The sleepwalker's brain emits the slow delta waves typical of stages 3 and 4 of sleep. The hypnotic subject's brain waves, in contrast, are indistinguishable from those associated with a normal waking state. In addition, the sleepwalker pays no attention to other people and does not take instructions, whereas the hypnotized person does both. Finally, the sleepwalker usually does not remember sleepwalking, whereas it is normal for the hypnotized subject to recall everything that went on under hypnosis (Barber, 1975).

Clearly, sleep and hypnosis are in many ways quite different states. But what exactly is hypnosis if not a variant of sleep? After years of experimentation with hypnotism, psychologists still do not have a firm answer to this question. In fact, the difficulty of defining hypnosis except by describing the behavior of hypnotized people has caused some to doubt whether it represents a true altered state of consciousness at all. In the following sections we present the available evidence and invite you to judge for yourself.

Hypnotic Susceptibility

According to one estimate, about nineteen out of twenty people can by hypnotized to some degree if

At the hypnotherapist's suggestion, this young woman raises her arm. Psychologists are not yet certain whether hypnosis is truly an altered state of consciousness; nor do they agree about how or why hypnosis takes place. (© *Ken Robert Buck 1981/The Picture Cube.*)

they want to be and if they trust the hypnotist. But some people are more easily and deeply hypnotized than others. Psychologists measure the trait of hypnotic susceptibility by means of various standardized tests. Using the Stanford Hypnotic Susceptibility Scale, for instance, the hypnotist first attempts to bring the subject under hypnosis and then makes a series of suggestions, such as "Your left arm will become rigid" or "You will be unable to say your name when asked." If the subject is unable to bend the arm more than two inches in ten seconds, or is unable to say the name within ten seconds after being asked, he or she receives a positive rating. Positive ratings on the rest of a dozen suggestions earn the person classification as highly susceptible to hypnosis. In one study of more than 500 college students, about 10 percent were so classified (E. Hilgard, 1965).

What are people who score high in hypnotic susceptibility like? Many often become spontaneously absorbed in such experiences as reading a novel, listening to music, or appreciating the beauty of nature. Many also occasionally experience trancelike states in which they feel somehow separated from things as they usually experience them (K. Bowers, 1976). One researcher suggests that this ability to become deeply absorbed develops early in life. Her research shows that people who are highly susceptible to hypnosis are more likely to have had a history of daydreaming and imaginary companions when they were children (J. Hilgard, 1970, 1974). It seems that people who are easily hypnotized have developed in childhood the fantasy skills that make them more open to hypnotic suggestion as adults. Interestingly, these same fantasy skills may also make them very creative at certain tasks, for the ability to lose oneself in fanciful possibilities sometimes leads to imaginative problem solving (P. Bowers, 1979).

The Hypnotic State and Its Uses

In the past several decades hypnosis has been put to a growing number of uses. Medical practitioners are finding it useful as a way of relieving pain without resorting to drugs. In fact, on the battlefields of World War II, hypnosis was sometimes used to treat the wounded when anaesthetics and pain-killers were unavailable. Today, pregnant women who want to avoid artificial sedation despite a history of very painful childbirths sometimes seek out hypnosis as a way of relieving the pain of their pending delivery. Psychologically caused migraine headaches have also yielded to hypnosis (Harding, 1967). Even the intractable pain of terminal cancer has sometimes been alleviated by this intriguing process (J. Hilgard, 1974). The basis of these pain-killing effects still remains a puzzle. Some suggest the effects may simply be due to the deep relaxation associated with hypnosis, for anxiety, as we learned in Chapter 4, can greatly intensify pain. Others suspect that the hypnotized person may be induced to release some brain chemical that blocks the sensation of pain.

In addition to its role in alleviating pain, hypnotism is also attracting interest as a treatment for certain behavioral disorders. A long-time smoker, for instance, may seek the help of a hypnotist to break the cigarette habit. Under hypnosis the person is usually told that cigarette smoking will no longer be enjoyable, but he or she is also instructed to forget that this suggestion originally came from the hypnotist. For some people in some circumstances this approach has had positive results (Johnston and Donoghue, 1971; Spiegel, 1970). Similar posthypnotic suggestions have also been used with some success for a variety of other problems, including psychosomatic allergies, insomnia, and compulsive overeating.

The most controversial use of hypnosis is as a tool for probing human memory. Under hypnosis, subjects often recall events so clearly and fully that they seem to be tapping into memories unavailable to normal consciousness. Sigmund Freud was one of the first psychologists to be impressed by this phenomenon. Under hypnosis his troubled patients often reported shocking and vivid memories of being seduced in childhood, often by their fathers. So dramatic and emotion-laden were these "relived" episodes that Freud originally accepted them as factual, though later he came to believe that these hypnotized subjects were remembering childhood fantasies rather than real-life events.

Contemporary investigators of hypnosis echo this kind of interpretation. They believe that people under hypnosis often engage in confabulation, as described in Chapter 6. When such people are unable to retrieve a certain incident from memory, they manufacture something that seems appropriate in an effort to comply with the hypnotist's request. This process is believed to be related to the hypnotized person's sharp decline in critical judgment. Just as a decrease in critical judgment encourages acceptance of the hypnotist's instructions, so it also encourages acceptance of fabricated memories as accurate (Orne, 1979).

Several recent studies have tested for the accuracy of recalled material under hypnosis. In one study (Dywan and Bowers, 1983), subjects spent a week trying to recall sixty previously presented pictures. At the end of the week one group was hypnotized (a control group was not) before further recall was attempted. Although the hypnotized subjects were able to recall more new items than the control group, they committed three times as many errors. Why should this be? At least two explanations are possible. A hypnotized person may simply be more willing to report memories—whether correct ones or not. Or perhaps the vivid mental imagery hypnotized subjects experience gives them the mistaken impression of "recognizing" memories.

The realization that memories retrieved under hypnosis are not always reliable has led to great concern about the use of hypnosis in legal proceedings. In recent years more and more police officers and prosecutors have turned to hypnosis to refresh the memories of crime victims and witnesses. But are real memories being retrieved or are new memories being created? Laurence and Perry (1983) have shown how easily subjects under hypnosis incorporate false memories. They hypnotized twenty-seven subjects and through various suggestions induced seventeen of them to "remember" that they had been awakened by a loud noise the previous week. In posthypnotic sessions thirteen of the subjects reported the suggested memory as real. Psychologist Martin Orne, who has studied hypnosis extensively, cautions that hypnosis should be used for investigative purposes only when the information obtained from the hypnotized witness can be fully and independently verified (Orne, 1979; see also Smith, 1983). Courts in many states have banned "hypnotically refreshed" memory or restricted its admissibility as evidence.

Explaining Hypnosis

Psychologists are still uncertain as to the reason for hypnosis' strange effects on human behavior. No one yet has found a specific set of physiological changes that correlates with hypnotic trances. Some researchers, such as Ernest Hilgard, say this simply means we have yet to find the appropriate factors to measure.

Hilgard (1975) contends that anyone who has ever been deeply hypnotized will readily attest that this is a true altered state of consciousness, even though we lack the tools to monitor it objectively. But other researchers take a very different view. They argue that hypnosis may merely induce suggestible subjects to enact an elaborate role—that of a hypnotized person. To understand how far apart these two perspectives are, let us see how each would explain a dramatic change in behavior that once took place under hypnosis.

A Case of Hypnotic Blindness. Many years ago psychologist Frank Pattie (1935) wondered if he could make a hypnotized person blind in one eye. So he selected five subjects known to enter deep hypnotic trances and gave each one the hypnotic suggestion that sight in one eye would disappear. One woman, whom Pattie called E., did seem to become blind in one eye during this experiment. Throughout most of a long series of tests, E. consistently appeared to have no awareness of sensory impulses from that eye, although there were some signs that she might be cheating. For this reason, Pattie devised an extremely subtle test for blindness, one on which it was virtually impossible to cheat. He had E. look at the top line of Figure 12.6 with a red filter over her "seeing" eye and a green filter over her "blind" one. The two filters had the effect of blocking out different parts of the line. If E. had truly been blind in the green-filtered eye, she would have seen only what appeared through the red filter. But that was not what she reported seeing. Thus she was not really blind. Yet strangely enough, even when she failed this test E. insisted that she had not cheated and that she was in fact blind in one eye. According to every indication, she really believed what she was saying. How can we explain these curious results?

The Neodissociation View. One explanation, supported by Ernest Hilgard and others, is called the neodissociation view. Its central idea is most clearly demonstrated in studies conducted by Hilgard at Stanford University (Hilgard and Hilgard, 1975; E. Hilgard, 1978). In these experiments, hypnotized subjects were told to plunge one hand into a bucket of icy water with the instruction that they would feel no pain. When asked what they felt, the subjects reported that no pain was experienced. Yet at the same time their free hand told a different story. Covered

Figure 12.6 The technique used by Pattie to expose a suspected cheater in an experiment on hypnotically induced blindness. The subject was required to look at a line (top) of mixed colored letters and numbers with a red filter over her "seeing" eye and a green filter over her "blind" eye. The effect of the red filter is shown in the bottom line. If the subject had really been blind, she would have seen only a line of distinct letters and numbers. *(After Pattie, 1935.)*

by a box and out of the subject's sight, the free hand wrote that the experience was indeed painful, just what you would expect a person in a normal state of consciousness to say. According to Hilgard (1973, 1974), what occured here was a **dissociation**—a split in consciousness whereby certain thoughts, feelings, and behaviors operate independently from others.

"Automatic writing" that contradicts a verbal report is a very dramatic example of this split-consciousness phenomenon. But Hilgard and others contend it is far from unique. You may have experienced an instance of dissociation yourself. In everyday life it is not uncommon to be able to respond correctly to a message that you thought you did not hear. Similarly, people with severe phobias often insist they have no idea what incident caused the phobia to arise, yet their emotional reaction to the feared object is that of a person who remembers the traumatic event all too well. Dissociations, according to Hilgard and like-minded psychologists, routinely occur under hypnosis. Consider posthypnotic amnesia, for instance. A hypnotist can instruct a subject to forget all that happened during the hypnotic state until a cue to remember is given. The subject, upon coming out of the hypnotic trance, adamantly maintains that he or she remembers nothing—as if the memories were somehow split from normal conscious awareness. On cue, however, the person remembers everything. It seems as though the split in consciousness were somehow suddenly bridged. Similarly, E.'s insistence that she was blind in one eye, despite evidence to the contrary, could be explained by a split in consciousness between visual input to that eye and the part of her awareness that testified she was blind.

But perhaps hypnotized subjects like E. are just faking—going along to please the hypnotist, as sometimes happens in psychological experiments. Researchers such as Hilgard believe not. Although it is usually very difficult to distinguish between a truly hypnotized subject and one who is merely pretending, subtle differences in behavior do exist. In one experiment, for instance, subjects under hypnosis were given the answers to a list of esoteric questions ("What color does an amethyst turn when it is heated?" "What was the primary profession of the author Lewis Carroll?") and were then told to forget everything that had happened. Upon returning to normal consciousness, the subjects claimed to remember nothing about events while under hypnosis. Yet when they were asked the same esoteric questions, about a third of them immediately gave the correct responses even though they claimed to have no idea how they knew such things. This phenomenon is called **source amnesia** because the person remembers certain facts but fails to remember the context in which they were learned. Significantly, subjects who are asked to fake hypnosis and try to fool the hypnotist never display source amnesia when told to forget all that happened. Such a mistake is far too "dumb" for a person who is only play-acting to make (Evans, 1979).

The Role Enactment View. Other psychologists take a very different view. They maintain that the seemingly "impossible" things done under hypnosis are in fact perfectly possible in a normal state of consciousness. Theodore Barber (1965) has found, for instance, that when nonhypnotized people are merely exhorted to try their hardest and assured that the tasks to be performed are easy, they can accomplish the same "feats" as hypnotized subjects do. Nonhypnotized subjects can, for example, hold a heavy weight at arm's length for several minutes; they can lie rigid while supported only by a chair under their shoulders and another under their feet, with the rest of their bodies suspended in midair; they can even stick needles through their hands. If this is so, one cannot help wondering, is there anything special about the hypnotic state?

Proponents of **role enactment theory** contend there is not. They see hypnosis not as a special state of consciousness but as a special case of role playing. According to this view, the hypnotized person is simply acting as though he or she were hypnotized, just as an actor plays a role. The hypnotist prepares the subject to play the part of a hypnotized person by establishing expectations. The subject is given specific instructions about what is to happen, and the hypnotist reinforces those expectations by playing the role of competent hypnotist. Role expectations become more explicit during the induction of hypnosis, through such instructions as "You can enter a state of hypnosis by concentrating on my voice," "You will become relaxed," and so forth. In this way the hypnotist continually refines the subject's understanding of the role to be played. The transition to the role of hypnotized person is complete when the subject continues to meet the hypnotist's role demands as they change. The experiences that the subject reports, then, are determined by what he or she believes is appropriate and proper to report (Sarbin and Coe, 1972).

For the role enactment theorist, therefore, E.'s insistence that she was blind in one eye was typical of someone acting as though she had been hypnotized. So is insistence that one feels no pain or cannot remember what happened. As for the fact that people under hypnosis sometimes behave differently from people just pretending to be hypnotized, advocates of role enactment theory remain unconvinced. They argue that these differences result simply from the fact that two slightly different roles are being enacted: the role of a truly hypnotized person and the role of a person merely faking hypnosis.

It is impossible to reconcile these two interpretations of hypnosis. They are diametrically opposed. Nevertheless, hypnosis remains a remarkable phenomenon. That psychological instructions can "set" some people to tolerate severe pain, or to act in ways in which they would not otherwise act, is an extraordinary fact regardless of its explanation. Thus, even if the role enactment view were ultimately to be proved right, it should in no way diminish our interest in hypnosis and its potential uses.

SELF-REGULATED ALTERED STATES

A yogi sits in a laboratory in India with legs crossed and eyes closed, deep in meditation. From his head a forest of electrodes lead to an electroencephalograph. A team of psychologists watch intently as the yogi's brain waves are traced on paper. When the EEG shows that his brain is emitting a steady flow of slow, rhythmic alpha waves, the experiment begins. A psychologist strikes a tuning fork and holds it next to the yogi's ear. The alpha waves stream on, unbroken—a sign that the yogi is not aware of the sound at all. The test is repeated with a hand clap and even with a hot test tube applied to the yogi's arm, all with the same result: his brain, deep in meditation, registers no reaction to these disturbances. The yogi is in *samadhi,* a state in which his awareness appears to be separated from his senses through intense concentration on a single thought or object (Anand, Chhina, and Singh, 1961).

This investigation was one of the first attempts to study the ways people can regulate their own consciousness. Like hypnosis, self-regulation techniques have found a wide range of clinical uses, from the control of pain to the treatment of certain physical and psychological disorders. These techniques vary both in the altered states of consciousness they can (and cannot) produce and in the body changes they are able to create. Nevertheless, all are forcing us to revise our ideas about the degree of control people can exert over their minds and bodies. Two of the most widely studied techniques of self-regulation are meditation and biofeedback.

Meditation

Meditation is the most ancient technique for inducing an altered state of consciousness without the use of drugs. In one form or another, it has been incorporated into every major religion, including Judaism and Christianity. Vast differences are to be found among the many kinds of meditation practiced in the world today, but most share a common element: by requiring the meditator to focus attention on a single stimulus, they greatly restrict sensory input and ultimately produce an altered state (Goleman, 1977). In the form of meditation called *zazen,* for instance, practiced by a sect of Japanese Zen Buddhists, the meditators concentrate on the normal flow of their breathing, without trying to control it in any way. Other common stimuli on which people focus in order to enter a meditative state are short prayers, a sacred picture, a candle flame, or even a spot on the lower abdomen. Supporters of meditation claim that it neutralizes the stresses of daily life, enriches life experiences, and steadily expands one's happiness in life (Bloomfield and Kory, 1976).

The body of a meditator tends to undergo various changes that reflect a slowing of metabolism. In one study, two researchers recorded these changes in a group of experienced meditators (Wallace and Benson, 1972). Oxygen consumption fell markedly, breathing and heart rate slowed, skin resistance to electrical conduction rose abruptly, and blood pressure dropped. But a recent review of experimental evidence reported that the same changes could be found in subjects who were merely resting and there were no reliable differences between meditating and resting subjects (Holmes, 1984).

Although the physiological changes associated with meditation are similar to those that accompany relaxation, the meditator does have more pronounced changes in brain waves. Whereas the relaxed person shows only modest changes in brain-wave patterns compared with those during normal waking consciousness, the meditator's brain waves change markedly. The specific type of brain-wave activity during meditation depends to a large extent on the kind of meditation being done. One study, for instance, found that the EEGs of Buddhist monks who practiced *zazen* registered alpha waves as soon as the monks started meditating, even though their eyes were wide open (Kasamatsu and Hirai, 1966). Alpha waves are normally abundant only in people whose eyes are closed. As the meditation session progressed, the monks' alpha waves changed gradually to slower theta waves—very unusual in a person with open eyes.

How could a person with eyes open display such brain-wave patterns? The answer is still far from complete, but studies on the effects of restricted awareness have provided a fascinating insight. Remember from Chapter 4 that whenever you try to fix your gaze steadily on a single point, your eyes involuntarily move. This movement, you will recall, prevents your photoreceptor cells from adapting to constant stimulation and ceasing to respond at all. Ingenious researchers have managed to demonstrate the startling effect on visual perception that a truly steady gaze would have. One of their techniques involves a tiny projector attached to a contact lens. As the subject's eye moves, the contact lens moves with it, and so does the miniprojector. The result is that the projector steadily casts its image on one part of the retina. Subjects who have volunteered to wear this strange device report that the picture they see gradually disappears. And when it does, the person's visual cortex suddenly emits the preponderance of alpha waves generally found only when the eyes are closed (Lehmann, Beeler, and Fender, 1967). Meditation, then, may involve a similar loss of awareness of the outside world, precipitated by restricted focus on an unchanging stimulus (Ornstein, 1977).

Biofeedback

One reason that scientists are interested in meditation is that experienced meditators seem to be able to control certain body processes, such as blood pressure and heart rate, previously thought to be always involuntary. Indian and Tibetan yogis, for example, have been known to slow their respiration to such an extent that they can survive in airtight cubicles containing far too little oxygen to keep an average person alive for long. Similarly, on bitterly cold nights high in the Himalayas they have been observed to keep their body temperature high enough to melt surrounding ice (David-Neel, 1971). Such feats raise an intriguing question. Using modern electronic devices to monitor physiological responses, can Westerners unskilled in meditation also learn to control their internal processes? The technique of self-regulation called biofeedback has proved they can. **Biofeedback** is the use of monitoring instruments to give a person a continuous flow of information about his or her own biological state. A person can experiment with various ways of altering physiological function, check the data, and find out immediately which ways work. By trial and error, then, the person may gradually learn to control target responses at will.

Some researchers have reported that biofeedback has been very successful in helping people regulate a variety of physiological processes, including heart rhythms, body temperature, and muscle tension. In a therapeutic application involving, say, the control of cardiac arrhythmia (irregular heartbeat), the patient is connected to a machine that monitors heart rate (Marcus and Levin, 1977). When the heart beats too slowly, a green light goes on; when it beats too quickly, a red light flashes. An amber light signals that the heart is beating in the normal range. Slowly, through a process that often involves focusing on specific thoughts or feelings, the patient may learn to keep the amber light on. A subject in one study, for instance, said she slowed her heart rate by thinking about swinging slowly on a swing, while another claimed that she made her heart beat faster by picturing herself running down a street (Engel and Weiss, 1970). The precise role such mental imagery plays in controlling heartbeat is still not understood. But somehow successful patients seem to acquire the ability to control the firing rate of the major nerve leading to the heart (Jonas, 1979).

This same general procedure—using biofeedback to learn to control a specific physiological response and then controlling it without electronic feedback—has been tried successfully with a number of other disorders. Biofeedback appears to be quite effective, for instance, in helping people relax the tightened forehead muscles associated with tension headaches (Budzynski, 1979). It is also commonly used to help alleviate Raynaud's syndrome, a condition in which the blood vessels of the fingers and toes constrict, especially during stress, and so cause the extremities to turn exceedingly cold (Blanchard, 1979).

Psychologist Thomas Budzynski and his colleagues have demonstrated that biofeedback is also useful for encouraging and maintaining the hypnagogic state that precedes sleep (Budzynski et al., 1979). They used biofeedback to train people voluntarily to relax the muscles of the forehead. This relaxation, in turn, decreased arousal in the cerebral cortex, and the subjects became very drowsy. Soon their EEGs were displaying the theta waves characteristic of the twilight stage between wakefulness and deep sleep. At this point the researchers employed biofeedback again. The appearance of the theta waves caused a tape-recorded message to begin playing to the subjects. When brain waves began to change to alpha or beta, indicating that a subject was returning to wakefulness, the tape recorder would abruptly turn off. Conversely, when a subject began to drift into deep, delta-wave sleep, the volume of the message would inten-

sify and gently nudge the person back to the twilight zone. With practice, most subjects acquired the ability to keep themselves in the hypnagogic state.

But what is the value of this exercise? Budzynski and his colleagues believe that certain kinds of learning come more easily during the hypnagogic state. In particular, they suggest that people experiencing various emotional problems may be better able to confront the sources of their difficulties during hypnagogic consciousness, and thereby achieve better adjustment in waking life. To test this hypothesis they designed therapeutic messages to be played to subjects in the hypnagogic state. One man who was seriously troubled by a lack of assertiveness, for instance, listened over a three-week period to a hypnagogic message specifically written to probe the roots of his problem and to offer him constructive advice. Although the man had experienced little improvement in three years of conventional therapy, this unorthodox treatment seemed to help. He claimed that he was indeed becoming better able to assert himself in real-life situations.

It is very risky, of course, to make generalizations on the basis of a few such successes. Nevertheless, Budzynski (1979b) has ventured a tentative guess as to why this procedure may work. He believes that hypnagogic messages may be assimilated more readily than usual by the right hemisphere of the brain. Budzynski points to evidence that the right brain may function effectively over a wider range of cortical arousal than the left brain does. Thus as arousal drops and we begin to enter sleep, the right brain may start to dominate our thinking. Significantly, there is also evidence that the right hemisphere may be superior at processing emotional information (Springer and Deutsch, 1981). This is why Budzynski suspects that the hypnagogic state may be ideally suited to "reprogramming" deeply held emotional responses. Budzynski's hypothesis, we must emphasize, has not been proved. Nevertheless, it suggests an intriguing link between right- and left-brain specializations and an altered state of consciousness.

It is important to note that the potential of biofeedback is still being tested. Although some popular writers give the impression that biofeedback is a simple answer to many stress-related ailments, this is certainly very far from the case. Unless biofeedback training is supervised by a competent professional with access to good equipment, the results may be useless. And even when properly supervised, some people have much more difficulty than others learning to regulate a given physiological response. It is particularly difficult to learn to control a target response consistently over the long run. As a result, in most clinical applications biofeedback is used together with other forms of therapy. Still, many researchers in this field hope that biofeedback will someday offer a reliable alternative to drug treatment for a diversity of medical disorders, such as stomach and intestinal ailments and high blood pressure. In the more distant future, biofeedback may even be put to interesting nonmedical uses. It might, for example, find a role in education to help students maintain full concentration when learning difficult material (Ornstein, 1977). No one yet knows how many of these and other ambitious goals for biofeedback will ultimately be achieved (Gatchell and Price, 1979).

One reason why some psychologists are very cautious in accepting far-reaching claims for biofeedback is that some of the earliest claims for it have failed to hold up—most notably the claims concerning biofeedback's use for controlling alpha waves in the brain (Miller, 1974). It was once thought that with biofeedback people could greatly enhance their production of alpha waves and thus achieve an "alpha experience"—a state of calm, blissful euphoria. But subsequent research has shown that such an experience does not reliably accompany alpha activity (Plotkin and Cohen, 1976). Moreover, there is strong evidence that biofeedback cannot teach people to generate more alpha waves than they would simply by relaxing and closing their eyes (Lynch, Paskewitz, and Orne, 1974; Lindholm and Lowry, 1978). Thus there is currently much doubt as to whether biofeedback can be used to produce an altered state of consciousness similar to that created through meditation.

DRUG-ALTERED CONSCIOUSNESS

If a drug is any substance that can alter the functioning of a biological system, there is hardly a person alive who is not a drug user. Many substances fall within this broad definition, ranging from aspirin and antibiotics to vitamin C. The drugs of interest for the study of consciousness, however, are those that interact with the central nervous system to alter a person's mood, perception, mode of thinking, and behavior—the so-called **psychoactive drugs.** Here we will consider various psychoactive drugs that are taken specifically to alter consciousness.

The Effects of Certain Drugs on Consciousness

Alcohol. The most widely used mind-altering drug in this country is undoubtedly alcohol. Americans consume about 500 million gallons of alcoholic beverages each year. Alcohol, administered slowly and in small doses, is often regarded as a social wonder drug. It seems to relax inhibitions and makes many people gregarious. Under the influence of a moderate amount of alcohol, "the tongue-tied become eloquent, the shy grow bold, the awkward become graceful" (De Ropp, 1976, p. 122). How does alcohol produce these social lubricating effects?

Judging from its ability to transform a collection of ill-at-ease strangers into a laughing, boisterous group of friends, many people assume that alcohol must be a stimulant. It is not. In fact, alcohol is a **depressant,** a chemical that suppresses nerve impulses. One reason alcohol appears to stimulate is that, among other things, it slows down the brain's ability to think critically and exercise caution. As a result, people with as little as .05 percent alcohol in the bloodstream often say and do things they would never ordinarily do. As a person consumes more alcohol, a steady deterioration of all body functions occurs. Perception becomes distorted, speech begins to slur, and the drinker has trouble controlling simple movements of the arms and legs. How soon these and related symptoms arise depends on how rapidly alcohol enters the bloodstream and on how much alcohol is consumed in relation to body weight. When blood alcohol reaches a level of .3 or .4 percent, a person will lapse into a coma. At a blood alcohol level of about .5 percent, heartbeat and breathing stop and the drinker dies (Combs, Hale, and Williams, 1980).

Alcohol is a chemical depressant, but it acts as a social stimulant because it reduces inhibitions and because people *expect* alcohol to affect their behavior in certain ways. *(Rick Browne/Picture Group.)*

For a long while people assumed that all the behavioral changes typically associated with alcohol must be due entirely to the drug. Recently, however, research has called this assumption into question. It is now clear that people's expectations about the effects of alcohol can also influence their behavior. In one study, for instance, men were given either vodka and tonic or plain tonic to drink. (It is hard to taste any difference between the two.) Half of the vodka-and-tonic drinkers were correctly told that they were drinking an alcoholic beverage, while the others were incorrectly told that they were consuming a nonalcoholic drink. The same procedure was followed with the tonic drinkers: half were told truthfully that their drinks were nonalcoholic while the others were told untruthfully that they were drinking alcohol. At the end of the drinking session all the men were placed in a situation where they might express aggression. The results were surprising. Subjects who *believed* they had consumed alcohol, whether or not they actually had, were significantly more aggressive on average than those who believed they had simply been sipping tonic (Marlatt and Rohsenow, 1981). Such findings demand that we rethink our notions about the link between alcohol and a breakdown in social inhibitions. People's *expectations* that alcohol will loosen their social restraints are often partly responsible for this widely observed effect.

In regard to the nonsocial effects of alcohol, however, expectations play a much smaller role. The many deficits observed in the performance of complex motor and cognitive tasks are due almost entirely to the drug. Take memory, for instance. Alcohol seems to affect the transfer of information from short-term to long-term storage (Parker, Birnbaum, and Noble, 1976). For the person who has been drinking heavily, new information often evaporates as soon as attention shifts. This is one reason why drinkers may have great difficulty remembering the names of people they meet while under the influence of alcohol. It also helps explain the phenomenon called **alcoholic blackout:** fragmentary or even total memory loss for events that occurred while the person was drinking.

Another factor may also play a role in alcohol-related memory lapses. In some instances, information that a person manages to store while under the influence of alcohol may be more difficult to retrieve sober than drunk (Weingartner et al., 1976). This is another form of the state-dependent memory we talked about in Chapter 6. For maximum retrieval we seem to need to be in the same state we were in when we stored the information. A comic example of alcohol-dependent memory is depicted in the Charlie Chaplin film *City Lights*. Chaplin plays a tramp befriended by an alcoholic millionaire who invites him to live in his mansion. On the rare occasions when the millionaire is sober, he has no recollection of Chaplin and unceremoniously throws him out. But as soon as the millionaire gets drunk again, Chaplin is once more an honored guest. Of course, actual cases of alcohol-dependent memory are seldom this extreme. The differences in retrieval success from one state to the other are a matter of degree.

Given alcohol's adverse effects on memory, people sometimes wonder if alcohol can permanently affect the brain. For the person who drinks constantly, such dangers are very real. About 10 percent of those who seek help for alcoholism are discovered to have chronic brain damage and accompanying memory deficits. In severe cases the patient can remember almost nothing about events that occurred since the disorder set in. This acute condition is called **Korsakoff's syndrome,** and it is often irreversible. Fortunately, for those alcoholics who escape permanent brain damage, the prognosis for recovering normal memory is far more encouraging. One recent study showed that alcoholics tested four to five weeks after they stopped drinking performed remarkably well on a number of memory tests (Parsons and Prigatano, 1977).

What about those who are merely social drinkers? Need they worry about the long-term effects of alcohol on memory? Probably not. Research shows that many gallons of alcohol consumed over a lifetime have little, if any, effect on cognitive abilities—as long as the drinker does not regularly indulge in bouts of heavy drinking. Social drinkers who incur the greatest risk are those who may go for days without drinking but then consume large quantities in a single session. In terms of the impact on cognitive capabilities, it is apparently better to consume one drink every day for a week than to wait until Saturday night and splurge with seven drinks. Even though the amount of alcohol ingested is the same, the effects on the brain and memory are quite different (Parker and Noble, 1977).

Marijuana. Marijuana has been used as an intoxicant in Eastern cultures for centuries. In some societies it is legally and morally acceptable whereas alcohol is not. Before 1960 marijuana use in the United State was common only among members of certain subcultures, such as jazz musicians and artists living in big cities. By 1960, however, college students had discovered marijuana, and since then its rate of use has increased by a factor of perhaps ten thousand. According to government figures, more than 50 million Americans, perhaps many more, have tried marijuana (Maugh, 1982), and over 13 million consider themselves regular users. These figures suggest that marijuana, along with alcohol and the nicotine in tobacco, is one of America's top three recreational drugs.

Researchers are beginning to discover some therapeutic uses for marijuana. Apparently it can relieve the abnormal pressure on the optic nerve that results in glaucoma, a major cause of blindness in the elderly. It also appears to reduce the severe nausea and vomiting caused by chemotherapy (Cohen and Stillman, 1976). Since marijuana also seems mildly to suppress the body's immune system, however, some researchers think it could be dangerous to cancer patients, whose immune systems are already substantially suppressed (National Academy of Sciences, 1982). Thus many researchers recommend caution before the active ingredient in marijuana is put to widespread therapeutic use.

Just what that active ingredient is has been known for many years. It is a complex molecule called tetrahydrocannabinol (THC), which occurs naturally in the marijuana plant, a common weed with the Latin name *Cannabis sativa.* Marijuana is made by drying the plant; hashish is a gummy powder made from the resin exuded by the plant's flowering tops. Both marijuana and hashish are usually smoked, but they can also be cooked in food and eaten.

Effects of Marijuana on Consciousness. Although the effects of marijuana vary somewhat from person to person and depend partly on the setting in which the drug is taken, there is considerable consensus among regular users as to marijuana's effects on consciousness (Tart, 1970). For one thing, most sensory experiences are greatly enhanced or augmented. Music sounds fuller, colors are brighter, smells are richer, foods taste better, and sexual sensations are more intense. The sense of time may also be greatly distorted. A short sequence of events may seem to last for hours. A musical phrase of a few seconds' duration may seem to stretch out in time until it becomes isolated from the rest of the composition and the hearer perceives it as never before.

Elevations in mood are common, too, under the influence of marijuana. People may become elated. The world becomes somehow more meaningful, and even the most ordinary events may take on a kind of extraordinary profundity. Users may become so entranced with a common everyday object, for example, that they sit and stare at it for many minutes, marveling at its newly discovered qualities. Unfortunately, however, negative moods may also become heightened by marijuana. If a person is frightened or depressed to begin with, the chances are excellent that the drug will intensify these feelings. Cases have been reported in which marijuana appears to have helped bring on psychological disturbances in people who were already unstable before they used it.

Finally, marijuana tends to decrease a person's ability to direct thoughts at will. Ideas and perceptions extraneous to the person's current focus keep intruding into consciousness. As a result, users often have trouble sustaining goal-directed behavior because they cannot keep their minds on the task at hand (Melges et al., 1970, 1971). Their speech also shows that rather frequently they lose their train of thought (Weil and Zinberg, 1969).

Despite the obvious need for careful research on marijuana, the first well-controlled studies of human subjects did not appear until the late 1960s. One of the first was conducted with college students, some of whom had had experience with marijuana while others had not (Weil, Zinberg, and Nelson, 1968). All of the experienced subjects, but only one of the inexperienced ones, reported getting high. Yet on tests on intellectual and motor skills, the inexperienced subjects displayed impairment whereas the experienced users did not. Likewise, in a laboratory study of motor skills using a simulated driving test, inexperienced subjects showed greater impairment than experienced ones (Rafaelsen et al., 1973). Other studies, however, have found that experienced and inexperienced subjects suffer roughly similar impairment on certain kinds of intellectual tasks. How can these seemingly inconsistent results be reconciled?

Taken together, the findings to date suggest that marijuana does induce short-term cognitive and motor deficits, but regular users often learn to compensate for many of them. The degree of impairment marijuana produces, then, depends in part on how much prior experience with the drug a particular person has had. Some aspects of behavior are easier to control than others, however. This is why experienced and inexperienced users show equal impairment on certain tasks. Memory deficits are especially hard to compensate for completely. But exactly which aspects of memory does marijuana impair? Some of the experiments designed to answer this question are such fascinating examples of psychological detective work that we will examine them in depth.

in depth Studying Marijuana and Memory

In the early 1970s researchers at a California veterans' hospital recruited a group of volunteers willing to expose their marijuana highs to scientific scrutiny (Darley et al., 1973). Half of the volunteers were assigned to the experimental group, which was to be given marijuana, and half were assigned to the control group, which was to be given a placebo. Then all the subjects took a memory test consisting of ten lists of words. After each list was presented, the subjects were to recall as many of the words as possible in any order. As Figure 12.7A shows, there were no significant differences in performance between the experimental and control subjects. Both groups remembered virtually the same number of words, and the words they remembered most frequently were those at the beginning and the end of each list. This pattern of recall is typical of such tests. Remember from Chapter 6 that subjects have more time to rehearse the words at the beginning of a free-recall list. Consequently, these items are likely to become fixed in long-term memory and so be remembered quite well. Words at the end of the list are usually in short-term memory when recall begins. Hence they, too, have a high likelihood of being remembered.

Having determined that no differences in memory ability preexisted between experimental and control subjects, the researchers next gave each experimental subject a brownie generously laced with THC; the control subjects were given brownies that looked and tasted identical but contained no THC. An hour later, when the experimental subjects were high, the researchers requested that everyone attempt to recall the words included on the previous memory test. It may surprise you to learn that once again the two groups performed almost identically, as shown in Figure 12.7B. The marijuana, it seemed, had no measurable effect on retrieval of information already stored in long-term memory.

But what about memory for new information? Would marijuana disrupt it? About two hours after the subjects had eaten their brownies, and while the experimental subjects were still quite high, the researchers presented both groups with a new series of word lists. The percentage of words each group correctly remembered is shown in Figure 12.7C. As you can see, although recall of the last few words was

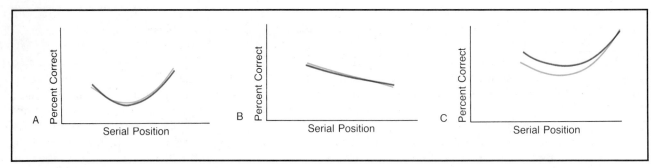

Figure 12.7 Comparison of the memories of volunteers who ate either placebo or marijuana-laced brownies. The serial position curve of the experimental subjects is shown in blue; that of the control subjects is shown in red. (A) Before eating the brownies, both groups were equally good at remembering lists of words. (B) An hour later, both groups were still equally proficient; marijuana did not affect their ability to remember the words they learned before eating the brownies. (C) But when both groups were tested for words learned while they were high, the experimental subjects did worse than the placebo subjects. *(After Darley et al., 1973.)*

equal, the drugged subjects forgot considerably more words from the beginning and the middle of each list than the nondrugged subjects did. These, of course, are items that would normally be recalled from long-term memory. Therefore, the marijuana must have affected long-term memory in some way. The previous test had shown that retrieval from long-term memory was not disrupted. Thus the researchers concluded that the drug must interfere with the *transfer* of information from short-term to long-term storage. In this respect marijuana acts much like alcohol. Also like alcohol, marijuana appeared to leave short-term memory (represented by words at the very end of a free-recall list) largely intact.

For several years many psychologists accepted these findings as gospel: marijuana disrupts the transfer of information to long-term storage but does not interfere with short-term memory. But then a puzzling contradiction emerged. Researchers at the University of Kentucky Medical Center conducted another investigation of the effects of marijuana on memory (Miller et al, 1977, 1978). As in the earlier California study, these researchers randomly assigned subjects to drug and placebo conditions and asked them to recall lists of words. As expected, marijuana impaired recall of words that had to be transferred to long-term memory. But it also impaired re-

call of words at the *end* of the lists—those presumably still held in short-term memory. How could this apparent contradiction be explained? Did marijuana affect short-term memory or didn't it?

The Kentucky researchers returned to the available data and compared the conflicting studies step by step. It was not long before they discovered a critical difference. The California subjects had eaten their marijuana in brownies, whereas the Kentucky subjects had smoked theirs. When you smoke marijuana it works more rapidly than when you eat it in food, so the Kentucky subjects were undoubtedly higher than their California counterparts had been when they took the memory tests. It may be, then, that low doses of marijuana do not usually impair short-term memory but high doses generally do. Further research is needed before we can know whether this answer is right.

Regardless of what future research shows, however, there is already little doubt that marijuana impairs the transfer of new information to long-term storage. Scientists have recently begun to piece together just how, physiologically speaking, this memory impairment comes about. Marijuana seems to reduce release of the neurotransmitter acetylcholine (ACh) in various neural pathways within the brain's limbic system (Miller and Branconnier, 1983). One structure within the limbic system—the hippocampus—seems to be particularly tied to memory performance. One theory is that it may help exclude extraneous stimuli from our attention (Douglas, 1967). If the functioning of the hippocampus is impaired, a person may have trouble processing new information thoroughly enough to get it firmly entrenched in long-term memory. So many distracting thoughts and perceptions may keep intruding into consciousness that the new information is simply lost. Some researchers suspect that the acute loss of memory found with alcohol-related Korsakoff's syndrome may sometimes be due to lesions in the hippocampus (Meissner, 1968). While the memory lapses induced by marijuana are far milder than those associated with chronic and severe alcoholism, the broad parallels between the two are intriguing.

There is evidence that some people who have smoked marijuana regularly for a substantial period of time are able to overcome part of its negative impact on memory performance. When, for instance, groups of regular marijuana users are created in the laboratory by administering the drug once a day for a month or more, performance on recall tests while under the drug's influence often gradually improves. Somehow the subjects seem to learn to compensate for the attention and memory deficits caused by marijuana. But exactly how they do this is not yet understood.

Of course, smoking marijuana once a day for one or two months is a far cry from smoking it many times a day year after year. What are the effects of marijuana on the habitual lifetime user? Does that person manage to function reasonably well? This is a difficult question to answer, for there are few sound data on the long-term effects of marijuana. Some studies of American teenagers suggest that those who use marijuana regularly do more poorly in school than nonusers do. This poorer performance, however, tends to *precede* the marijuana habit, so it is hard to say just what the effects of the drug are. Similarly, it is not clear whether the apathy, lack of ambition, and difficulty in carrying out long-term plans often observed in adolescents who use marijuana heavily may just be preexisting traits that predispose these youngsters to drug use in general (National Academy of Sciences, 1982; Maugh, 1982).

Some evidence suggests that marijuana may have little effect on the performance of chronic users. Consider a study of working-class men in Costa Rica (Carr, 1978). The *heaviest* users of marijuana generally had the highest incomes, the least unemployment, and the most stable job histories of all those surveyed. But before you jump to the conclusion that prolonged and regular marijuana use need not impair daily performance, remember that this is only one study of working-class subjects in a country far less industrialized than our own. Remember, too, that these results say nothing about other variables that may be influencing both marijuana use and steady employment. The psychological and physiological effects of marijuana use—especially in the long term—are not fully understood, so the possibility that marijuana may damage health cannot be ruled out.

in depth

Stimulants.

Stimulants are a class of drug that produces physiological and mental arousal. Specifically, they can decrease fatigue, increase talkativeness and physical activity, enhance endurance, diminish appetite, produce a state of alertness, and for a time elevate mood—often to the point of euphoria. Stimulants vary widely in their potency. Some, such as caffeine and nicotine, are relatively mild; others are extremely powerful. It is on two of the more powerful stimulants—cocaine and amphetamines—that we will focus here.

Cocaine is a substance obtained from the leaves of certain coca plants native to South America. Years ago it was one of the ingredients in Coca-Cola, originally sold as an invigorating tonic. (The leaf material, with the cocaine extracted, is still used as a flavoring in Coke.) As a recreational drug cocaine is currently both illegal and expensive. Nevertheless, its popularity is growing among middle-class professionals. Cocaine is usually taken in the form of a fine white powder inhaled, or "snorted," into the nostrils and absorbed into the bloodstream through the mucous membranes. It can also be taken orally, absorbed through the lungs by smoking, or injected into the body with a hypodermic needle.

Knowledge about the effects of cocaine on consciousness has usually come from interviews with users (Grinspoon and Bakalar, 1976). A moderate dose of cocaine produces a euphoria that can last from thirty minutes to an hour (Resnick, Kestenbaum, and Schwartz, 1977). Users have a sense that they are thinking more clearly than ever before, although often they overestimate their own capacities or the quality of their work under the drug. Like other stimulants, cocaine provides a short-term burst of energy. But because it does not replenish energy stores, users pay the price in physical exhaustion after the drug wears off and the body "comes down," or "crashes." Post-high depression and fatigue can be extreme when large doses of the drug are taken (Van Dyke and Byck, 1982).

Chronically heavy use of cocaine has more disturbing effects. The mucous membranes of the nose can be irreversibly damaged, and the user can suffer general mental deterioration, a loss of weight, persistent agitation, and feelings of paranoia. Cocaine taken frequently in large doses can also produce hallucinations, one of the most horrifying of which is the sensation of bugs crawling beneath the skin. This hallucination may be caused by drug-induced hyperactivity of the nerve cells embedded in the skin. In excessive doses, especially by injection, cocaine can produce headache, hyperventilation, nausea, convulsions, coma, and sometimes even death.

The amphetamines, commonly called "speed," "uppers," or "bennies," are also powerful stimulants. They increase release of the neurotransmitter dopamine, found in areas of the brain associated with arousal, motor activity, and emotion (Iversen, 1979). Before all the risks of amphetamines were known, they were sold by prescription under such trade names as Dexadrine and Benzedrine. Many people—truckers on long hauls, students studying for exams—used them to help stay awake. Others, particularly women, used them to suppress appetite and help "burn off" fat.

In addition to these more practical effects of amphetamines, however, these drugs significantly alter consciousness. Along with a boost in energy, arousal, and alertness comes a marked increase in confidence. People get the feeling that they can take on the world, solve any problem, achieve any goal. Are people really more capable under the influence of amphetamines? Not on intellectual tasks. Studies show that amphetamines improve neither problem-solving ability nor performance on any other complex cognitive task (Tinklenberg, 1971).

As long as they are taken irregularly and in low doses, amphetamines do not appear to cause any measurable harm. But the problem is that people develop a tolerance for amphetamines, so that they must take higher and higher doses to achieve the same effects. If intake of the drug becomes chronic and excessive, the user begins to develop ungrounded suspicions. The heavy user may imagine that people are staring in a peculiar fashion or talking behind his or her back. The person may also imagine objects on the skin and get caught up in meaningless meandering trains of thought. The symptoms are often strikingly similar to those found in certain kinds of schizophrenia, a psychological disorder also believed to be related to overactivity of dopamine pathways in the brain (Iversen, 1979). As a high dose of amphetamines begins to wear off, the chronic user typically sinks into a depression that may last for days

and sometimes be severe enough to provoke a suicide attempt. At its very worst, amphetamine abuse can cause serious brain damage.

Hallucinogens. Hallucinogens—so called because one of their main effects is to produce hallucinations—are found in plants that grow throughout the world and have been used for their effects on consciousness since earliest human history (Schultes, 1976). Among the most common hallucinogenic plants are henbane, mandrake, datura (Jimson weed), one species of morning-glory, peyote cactus, many kinds of mushrooms, and also marijuana, which we have already discussed. Other hallucinogens, such as LSD (lysergic acid diethylamide), are manufactured in the laboratory.

LSD is the most extensively studied of the hallucinogens and also the most potent. It is one hundred times stronger than psilocybin, which comes from certain mushrooms, and four thousand times stronger than mescaline, which comes from the peyote cactus. A dose of between 100 and 200 millionths of a gram (just a small speck) alters consciousness within thirty to sixty minutes, producing a "trip" that lasts from ten to twelve hours (Combs, Hales, and Williams, 1980). We do not yet know exactly how LSD produces its powerful effects. LSD does reduce the activity of serotonin, a neurotransmitter that may play a role in regulating sleep and emotion. But certain other drugs that also inhibit serotonin do not induce the hallucinations that LSD does (White and Appel, 1982). Thus the special ways that LSD affects the brain's pathways have yet to be discovered.

The hallucinations produced by LSD are very dramatic. Often visual hallucinations progress from simple geometric forms to complex images and then to dreamlike scenes (Siegel, 1977). The user may encounter such extreme perceptual distortions that familiar objects become almost unrecognizable. A wall, for example, may seem to pulsate and breathe. The senses, too, seem to intermingle. Sounds may be "seen" and sights "heard." A person may experience a dissociation of the self into one being who observes and another who feels. Distortions of time, either an acceleration or a slowing down, are also common. A single stimulus may become the focus of attention for hours, perceived as ever changing or newly beautiful and fascinating.

Thinking, as measured by the ability to perform simple tasks, is also impaired by LSD, even though the user may feel that he or she is thinking more clearly and logically than ever before. Lifelong problems may suddenly seem resolved, or the need to resolve them may seem absurd. The person often experiences the "great truth" phenomenon—that is, the sense that previously hidden and ultimate truths have suddenly been revealed. When the trip is over, however, the magnitude of these discoveries shrinks, and the solutions reached often turn out to be untenable.

During an LSD trip a person can experience any number of mood states, often quite intense and rapidly changing. The person's "set"—his or her pre-drug mood, expectations, and beliefs—and the circumstances under which the drug is taken can greatly affect the experience, making it euphoric or terrifying. Panic reactions are the most common of LSD's unpleasant side effects. Panic usually occurs when a person tries to ignore, change, or otherwise get rid of the effects of the drug, only to find that the task is impossible. Medical attention is sometimes needed for very intense panic reactions.

Powerful hallucinations can also be induced by another synthetic drug widely sold on the illegal market today. This is phencyclidine, or PCP, often called angel dust, among many other street names. PCP in small doses tends to produce depersonalization—a feeling of being cut off from one's normal self. Larger doses cause much more dramatic changes in consciousness. Heavy users experience insomnia, agitation, mental confusion, delusions and hallucinations, and the urge to behave violently. These negative effects often last for days. Studies of PCP in laboratory rats suggest that molecules of the drug bind to specific receptor sites within the brain, especially in the limbic system, which is known to be involved in motivation and emotion (Zukin and Zukin, 1979). But any naturally occurring neurotransmitter that normally binds to these sites has not yet been identified. One clue is that PCP was first introduced by medical researchers as a powerful pain-killer (only to be outlawed later when the disturbing side effects of higher doses were discovered). PCP may therefore act on some pain-reducing or pleasure system within the brain. Significantly, laboratory monkeys will administer PCP to themselves repeatedly, even when they are required to forgo eating in order to do so.

Drugs and Creativity

Some contemporary poets, novelists, and artists attribute creative insights to their use of drugs. Novelist Ken Kesey, for instance, used peyote and LSD while he wrote parts of *One Flew over the Cuckoo's Nest* (1962); poet Allen Ginsberg used LSD when he wrote *Kaddish and Other Poems* (1960); and the book *Psychedelic Art* (Masters and Houston, 1968) is a collection of paintings inspired by experience with hallucinogens. Can drugs really enhance creativity? Or is this effect at best very limited?

The evidence is by no means clear. On the one hand, the altered states of consciousness that certain drugs induce seem on the surface to be conducive to the creative process. Under the influence of certain drugs, for example, some people find free association easy, are relaxed and open, have heightened sensory awareness, and can fantasize freely. On the other hand, aspects of the drug state can hinder creative production. Users often experience a diminished capacity for logical thinking, a reduced ability to direct concentration or to control sequences that they imagine, and a tendency to become absorbed in the

Drawings done by a man under the influence of LSD. (A) Twenty minutes after the first dose, the drug had not yet taken effect. (B) Twenty-five minutes after the second dose was administered, the subject experienced the first alterations in perception. He saw the model correctly but could not control the sweeping movements of his hand. (C) Two hours and forty-five minutes after the first dose, the subject experienced the most intense effects of the drug. (D) After five hours and forty-five minutes, the effects of the drug began to wear off. (E) After eight hours, the effects were almost gone. *(Triangle, The Sandoz Journal of Medical Science, 1955, 2, 119–123.)*

A

B

C

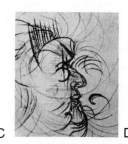
D

E

altered state of consciousness itself. Another problem is that during drug states a person's capacity for self-criticism is frequently blunted. Psychologist William James, for example, had several mystical revelations during experiments with nitrous oxide (laughing gas), but he was never able to record them before blacking out from the drug. One night, though, he managed to write down his monumental thoughts before losing consciousness. On returning to his normal state, James rushed to find out what he had written. It was:

Hogamous, higamous,
Man is polygamous.
Higamous, hogamous,
Woman monogamous.

There are as yet very few well-controlled studies of the effects of drugs on creativity. The best evidence to date suggests that while drugs can open new perspectives for almost anyone, it takes an already highly skilled person to translate these new ideas into a finished artistic product (Leavitt, 1974).

SUMMARY

1. **Consciousness** is our awareness of the many thoughts, images, sensations, and emotions that occupy the mind at any given time. Our conscious experiences vary from highly focused, systematic, and purposeful kinds of thinking to very loosely focused, unstructured, free-wandering fantasies and images. Psychologists describe this variation as the difference between normal waking consciousness on the one hand and **altered states of consciousness** on the other.

2. Altered states of consciousness can be induced in two basic ways. One is drastically to decrease sensory input; the other is to impose sensory overload. Regardless of how they are induced, many altered states of consciousness tend to have certain similarities. These common characteristics include shallow cognitive processing, a change in the way the self is experienced, a loosening of normal inhibitions, the possibility of hallucinations, and an intensification of emotions and perceptions.

3. Psychologists have distinguished several stages of sleep by monitoring people's brain waves on an electroencephalogram. Brain-wave frequencies steadily drop as a person falls from alert wakefulness through the **hypnagogic state** (a twilight period) and finally into deeper and deeper sleep stages. After a sleeper has been in the deepest stage of sleep for a while, he or she seems to return to a "waking" brain-wave pattern. Yet the person remains sound asleep, with eyes moving rapidly back and forth under closed eyelids. This stage is known as **REM** (rapid eye movement) **sleep,** and is closely associated with dreaming.

4. People will compensate for lost REM sleep on one night by entering REM more often during their next night's rest. This finding has led researchers to suspect that REM may serve some special biological function. What that function is, however, remains uncertain, although several theories exist. One is that REM helps the brain adapt to disturbing or unusual life experiences. Another is that REM plays a role in consolidating information into long-term memory. A third is that REM helps release pent-up energy associated with unfilled biological needs.

5. People have debated the meaning of dreams for centuries. Freud felt that dreams embodied our unconscious wishes and conflicts, disguised in symbolic form. Most contemporary therapists, in contrast, believe that most dreams are direct attempts to deal with the concerns and problems that dominate consciousness during waking hours. There is also evidence that occasionally people can control the content of their dreams, making the outcomes of dream episodes more emotionally satisfying.

6. The precise nature of the altered state of consciousness called hypnosis is uncertain. No set of physiological changes that correlates with hypnosis has yet been found. Nor is there any significant agreement over how hypnosis works, even though it has been put successfully to a wide variety of medical and therapeutic uses. Some researchers propose that when a person is hypnotized, a **dissociation,** or split in consciousness, occurs, such that certain thoughts, feelings, and behaviors operate independently of others. Proponents of **role enactment theory,** in contrast,

contend that hypnosis is simply a special case of role playing in which the subject, following increasingly specific cues from the hypnotist, merely acts *as though* he or she were hypnotized.

7. The various techniques of self-regulating consciousness challenge traditional concepts of the degree of control people can exert over their own minds and bodies. The most ancient and widespread of these techniques is **meditation,** an extreme restriction of sensory input that ultimately produces an altered state of consciousness. During meditation, a person's metabolism may undergo a measurable slowing, and brain-wave patterns may also slow. Exactly how and why these changes occur is a topic still being explored.

8. The technique of self-regulation called **biofeedback** involves the use of monitoring instruments to give a person a continuous flow of information about his or her own biological state. By experimenting with various ways of altering physiological function, many people can gradually learn to control target responses at will.

9. Altered states of consciousness involving changes in mood and thought can be induced by various **psychoactive drugs,** including the **depressant** alcohol, the **stimulants** cocaine and amphetamines, and the **hallucinogens** marijuana, LSD, and PCP. Each has its own distinctive effects, and each is suspected of working by altering the normal operation of neurotransmitters in the brain.

10. The altered states that certain drugs induce seem on the surface to be conducive to creativity. But drugs can also hinder creativity by diminishing one's capacity for controlled and well-ordered thought. The best evidence to date suggests that drugs can open new perspectives—good or bad—for almost anyone. But an already highly talented person is needed to turn these new perspectives into finished artistic products.

SUGGESTED READINGS

AULD, J. *Marijuana use and social control.* New York: Academic Press, 1981.

In addition to discussing the effects of the expectations of users on experience with marijuana, this book covers the impact and effectiveness of law-enforcement strategies and examines the social settings in which marijuana is used.

DEMENT, W. C. *Some must watch while some must sleep: Exploring the world of sleep.* New York: Norton, 1976.

Everything you ever wanted to know about sleep, written by a leading researcher in the field.

GOLEMAN, D., and DAVIDSON, R. J. (Eds.). *Consciousness: Brain, states of awareness and mysticism.* New York: Harper & Row, 1979.

A provocative collection of readings chosen from diverse areas. The book covers such topics as the brain and consciousness, ordinary states of consciousness, altered states of consciousness, and the politics of consciousness.

HILGARD, E. R. *Divided consciousness.* New York: Wiley, 1977.

This book discusses hypnosis in great detail. Hilgard is a well-known psychologist and highly respected researcher in the area of hypnosis.

JULIEN, R. M. *A primer of drug action.* 3d ed. San Francisco: Freeman, 1981.

This is an up-to-date sourcebook on the actions, uses, limitations, and side effects of drugs that affect the central nervous system. It thoroughly covers sedatives, tranquilizers, stimulants, opiates, alcohol, marijuana, and more powerful hallucinogens.

UNDERWOOD, G., and STEVENS, R. *Aspects of consciousness,* Vol. 2. New York: Academic Press, 1981.

The first volume of *Aspects of consciousness,* published in 1979, presented a selection of papers viewing consciousness from a cognitive viewpoint. In this volume, consciousness is viewed as the product of a biological mechanism.

WALLACE B., and FISHER, L. E. *Consciousness and behavior.* Boston: Allyn & Bacon, 1983.

This text offers a brief history of the psychology of consciousness, a superior chapter on biofeedback, and speculation on the future of the psychology of consciousness.

part 6

PERSONALITY AND INDIVIDUALITY

To many people, the chief concern of psychology *is* the study of personality: What makes each of us unique? What forms the stable, enduring constellation of qualities we each recognize as *me*? Chapter 13 surveys the four main approaches taken to the study of personality. Chapter 14 explores the area of testing: How are our strengths and abilities measured?

13

PERSONALITY THEORIES AND RESEARCH

Alexander Archipenko, *Walking Woman*, 1912.

We begin this chapter by asking you to describe yourself. Make sure that your description does *not* consist of the social roles you fill (I am a man or woman; I am a student; I am a member of a certain ethnic group). Instead, focus on your personal traits—your ways of responding to various situations. Are you thick-skinned or sensitive? Outgoing or shy? Aggressive or timid? Emotional or restrained? Try to list at least five or six traits that you think describe you quite well. Now answer this question: Do you think these traits will still describe you in ten or twenty years? Most people answer with a qualified yes. Although they recognize that ways of thinking and acting can and do change, they think of themselves as having certain fundamental features that will endure across the years. These features together form one's personality. More formally defined, **personality** consists of all the relatively stable and distinctive styles of thought, behavior, and emotional response that characterize a person's adaptations to surrounding circumstances (Maddi, 1976; Mischel, 1976).

Psychologists who study personality ask two key questions. The first concerns our individual differences. When several people encounter the same situation, why don't they all react alike? Why does one person confronted with a group of strangers find it easy to make conversation, while another feels uncomfortable and shy? Why does one student assigned a paper begin the research promptly, while another almost always puts it off to the last minute? Clearly people have different personalities, but why do these differences develop? As you will see later in this chapter, psychologists have given a variety of answers. Some have stressed the influence of our biological makeup, while others have stressed the influence of learning. Both factors undoubtedly play a role in shaping the traits that we display.

The second major question that personality theorists ask concerns the power of our individual differences. Do shyness, friendliness, punctuality, and other traits exert such a strong impact on behavior that they cause us to act with great predictability? Or are people often inclined to let the situation determine their response? Might a student be scrupulously honest in handling a campus club's funds, for instance, but be willing to cheat on exams if given the opportunity? Or would the student's honesty cause him or her to behave with integrity in both of these situations? Psychologists have come up with different answers to such questions, as this chapter will explain.

As you will also discover in reading this chapter, every personality theorist has stressed some factors more than others. Some have concentrated on specific traits, such as honesty and shyness, asking how each person's cluster of traits can best be measured and described. Others have stressed factors that integrate personality, such as the concept of the self. Still others have emphasized internal feelings (anxiety, conflict, self-fulfillment) that seem to be associated with various personality makeups. These diverse perspectives are what make the field of personality so challenging—and so frustrating. Just when you are convinced that one theory is correct, you may come upon another that seems equally persuasive. The best way to cope with this situation is to think of the theories you are about to encounter as complementary rather than competing. Each sheds valuable light on certain, but not all, aspects of the subject. Consequently, none is completely adequate in and of itself. Together, however, they paint a rich portrait of why individuals behave as they do.

In this chapter we will be discussing four major perspectives on personality. The first is a group of theories that adopt the so-called **psychoanalytic approach,** which began with Sigmund Freud. These theories emphasize childhood experiences as critically important in shaping adult personality. They also stress the role of the unconscious in motivating human actions. In contrast, the **behaviorist** and **social learning approaches** are based on principles of learning and reinforcement, discussed in Chapter 5. Behaviorists see personality as a set of learned responses, not as something that results from unconscious conflicts and urges. **Trait theories** take yet a different viewpoint. Trait theorists simply say that human personality can be described in terms of specific characteristics or traits (aggression, friendliness, emotional stability, and so forth). People differ in the extent to which they possess these various traits, all of which can be objectively measured. Finally, the **phenomenological approach** emphasizes the human potential for growth, creativity, and spontaneity. Those who adopt this perspective reject both the Freudian emphasis on irrational and sometimes destructive instincts and the behaviorist idea that people respond only to rewards and punishments. As you will see, despite their widely varying emphases, all these perspectives offer valuable insights into human behavior.

PSYCHOANALYTIC THEORIES

Although the concepts introduced by Sigmund Freud have been expanded and modified by later psychologists, sometimes substantially, all psychoanalytic theories have certain things in common. First, they are all concerned with powerful but largely unconscious motivations believed to exist in every human being. Second, most maintain that human personality is governed by conflict between opposing motives, anxiety over unacceptable motives, and defense mechanisms that develop to prevent anxiety from becoming too great. Freud, of course, provided the foundation for all later psychoanalytic writers. In fact, he is generally regarded as the single most important theorist in the field of personality. Some of Freud's concepts, such as Freudian slips, are widely referred to in everyday language, even if the average person has only a superficial understanding of them. Because of Freud's enormous importance in the history of twentieth-century thought and because of the heated controversy his ideas have generated, we will discuss his work in some detail.

Basic Concepts of Freudian Theory

Sigmund Freud was born in Moravia in 1856, the son of a Jewish wool merchant whose business failures prompted him to move his family to Vienna when Sigmund was still very young. In this important cultural and intellectual capital of Europe, Freud grew to maturity and spent nearly all of his long and productive adult life. At the age of seventeen, Freud entered medical school at the University of Vienna with the goal of becoming a professor of neurology. But opportunities for Jews in the Viennese academic world were extremely limited, so upon graduation Freud was reluctantly forced to set up private practice as a physician specializing in nervous disorders. The practice of medicine never greatly appealed to Freud. For him it was a financial necessity. Fortunately, however, his chosen field brought him many patients who were suffering not from neurological disease but from so-called hysterical disorders—that is, disorders

whose symptoms had no physiological cause. Freud's study of these patients and his innovative efforts to treat them marked the beginning of his far-ranging theories about the nature of the human psyche.

Freud's treatment of hysterical disorders was influenced by the "talking cure" that a fellow Viennese physician, Josef Breuer, had introduced. Breuer encouraged hysterical patients to talk about their emotional problems under hypnosis until their physical symptoms lessened. Freud developed the "talking cure" into a more elaborate procedure called **free association.** In free association, the unhypnotized patient is asked to relax on a couch and say out loud whatever comes to mind. When a topic arises about which the person appears to be resisting the spontaneous flow of ideas, this subject is presumed to be related to the patient's emotional problem and so becomes a focus of further inquiry. Through persistent probing, the patient is gradually led to recognize the nature of his or her conflicts.

On the basis of sessions with many patients, Freud came to believe that current problems could often be traced back to childhood experiences, especially those related to sexuality. Unfortunately, these early experiences were not usually available to consciousness. Only through great effort could they be coaxed into active memory. These beliefs led Freud to the core of his theory about the workings of the human mind. He proposed that neurotic anxiety, hysteria, and other psychological disorders often stemmed from early sexual conflicts that had been pushed deep into the mind's unconscious but were still capable of surfacing in disguised form. Thus hysterical paralysis of the hand might be explained in terms of a conflict between the desire to engage in some forbidden act— perhaps masturbation—and the requirement that sexuality be expressed only in socially acceptable ways. Freud coined the term **psychoanalysis** to describe the process by which he attempted to bring these repressed thoughts and desires out of the unconscious and into consciousness so that the patient could examine them rationally and break their power of control.

The concept of the unconscious is one of Freud's major contributions. Before Freud's time psycholo-

Freud's study in Vienna, with the famous couch. The couch, with its cushions and blankets, and the position of Freud's chair, at the head of the couch out of the patient's sight, were intended to help the patient relax and feel comfortable. The idea was to encourage free association by avoiding the inhibition that the patient might have felt as a result of sitting face-to-face with the analyst. (*Courtesy of Edmund Engelman.*)

gists were concerned only with people's conscious thoughts and feelings. Freud, however, likened the mind to an enormous iceberg, of which consciousness is only the small exposed tip. The massive structure of the iceberg that lies beneath the surface is the vast region of the unconscious. To Freud the unconscious was both a reservoir of instinctual drives and a storehouse of all the thoughts and wishes we conceal from conscious awareness because they cause us psychological conflict. In fact, Freud maintained that the unconscious is *the* major motivating force behind human behavior. According to him, much of what we say and do is either an effort to find some socially acceptable way of expressing unconscious impulses or an effort to keep those impulses under control.

One provocative aspect of Freud's view is that even seemingly trivial words and actions often have deeper meanings. Accidents, forgetfulness, the mislaying of objects, the mispronunciation of a name or an attempt at making a joke were to Freud all signs of unconscious drives, wishes, and conflicts. Even the most seemingly purposeless acts—doodling, twirling a button or lock of hair, humming a tune to oneself— had deeper significance to Freud. Each was believed to afford a glimpse into the subterranean world of the unconscious.

As fascinating as Freud's ideas were, his climb to international prominence was not an easy one. Freud's first book, *The Interpretation of Dreams* (1900), sold a mere six hundred copies in its first eight years in print. Why such staggering rejection of a man as brilliant as Freud? Much of the problem was that Freud's ideas collided sharply with turn-of-the-century morality. People were deeply shocked at Freud's view that the behavior of respectable people can often be traced to sexual conflicts in childhood. Many prospective patients simply refused to see him for fear that their sexual experiences would be probed. As a result, Freud's very livelihood was threatened by his unconventional theories. But still he persevered. Finally, around 1906, Freud began to attract a sizable following. Over the ensuing years, as he expanded and refined his theories, a full-fledged psychoanalytic school developed with Freud at its head. To understand the concepts around which this movement developed, it is helpful first to explore Freud's revolutionary notions about the structure of the human psyche.

Structure of the Human Psyche. On the basis of his work with troubled patients, Freud developed a comprehensive theory of the human mind that he believed applied to all people regardless of their psychological health. Freud divided the human psyche into three separate but interacting elements: the **id,** the **ego,** and the **superego.** As you read about these elements in the discussion that follows, do not make the mistake of viewing them as three distinct entities, locked in perpetual combat. True, Freud himself often suggested this very image in order to dramatize his points. But he did not intend to be taken literally. The id, the ego, and the superego are not entities, not physical divisions of the brain. Instead, they are names given to strong motivational forces, the existence of which is inferred from the ways that people behave.

Freud described the id as a reservoir of psychic energy, the pool of biological drives that arise from our basic physiological needs for food, water, warmth, sexual gratification, avoidance of pain, and so forth. Freud called these drives instincts, and he believed that they powered and directed all of human behavior. The id in Freud's scheme is an unconscious force. It has no link with objective reality. Consequently, the id seeks one thing only: the discharge of tension that accompanies satisfaction of bodily needs. This exclusive devotion of the id to satisfying bodily needs—without regard for logic or reason, reality or morality—is called the **pleasure principle.** The id is therefore like a demanding, impulsive, selfish child. It seeks only its own pleasure and cannot abide frustration or deprivation of any kind. In Freud's native German the word for id is *es,* which means "it," thus implying an alien force, something within a person that is not recognized as part of the self.

Although the id seeks satisfaction of biological needs, it has no way of determining which means of doing so are safe and which are dangerous. This task falls to the second structure of the human psyche, the ego. The ego, according to Freud, begins to develop soon after birth, but it does not become apparent until the age of about six months. The ego's role is to serve as a mediator between the id and reality (Freud, 1920, 1923). Unlike the id, much of the ego is conscious. In German the word for ego is *ich,* which means "I," signifying the part of the personality recognized as the self. By taking into account past experiences and outcomes, the ego tries to satisfy the desires of the id without inflicting personal harm. Thus, in contrast to the pleasure principle of the id, the ego operates on what is called the **reality principle,** the foundation of which is the concern for safety. Freud

believed that it is through this basic ego function of finding realistic means to satisfy the id that the mind develops and refines all its higher cognitive capacities: perception, learning, memory, problem solving, decision making, and planning.

As if the job of the ego were not difficult enough given the irrational, insistent nature of the id, there is yet another psychic component the ego must contend with. This is the superego, the part of the personality that represents the moral standards of society as conveyed to a person by his or her parents. The superego is approximately equivalent to what we call "conscience." This is why the German word for superego is *überich,* which means "over the I." Like the id, the superego is oblivious of reality. Instead of considering what is realistic or possible, it constantly commands that all sexual and aggressive impulses be stifled in service to lofty moral goals. The superego, then, is the great naysayer. Its function is to prohibit any thoughts and actions that express our instinctual drives. Thus, the superego puts the ego in an even more difficult position. On the one hand, the ego must find safe ways to satisfy the id, with its constant demands for pleasure. But on the other hand, it must do so without causing guilt or remorse to the superego, its highly moralistic watchdog. The very difficult role of the ego is illustrated in Figure 13.1.

Anxiety and Defense Mechanisms. Given the conflicting goals of the id and the superego, as well as the constant demands of reality, how does the ego ever manage to carry out its work? This important question brings us to a second part of Freud's theory—his ideas about anxiety and defense mechanisms.

According to Freud, the signal that the ego is losing its struggle to reconcile the divergent demands of the id, the superego, and reality comes in the form of **anxiety,** a state of psychic distress. Anxiety arises when the ego realizes that expression of an id impulse will lead to some kind of harm. The ego therefore inhibits the harmful action, and the resulting inner struggle is felt in anxiety. Anxiety, in turn, serves as an alarm signal that tells the ego that something must be done to resolve the conflict. That something is usually a **defense mechanism**—a mental strategy the ego uses to continue blocking the harmful behavior while at the same time reducing anxiety.

The most basic of the defense mechanisms is **repression,** a pushing back of unacceptable id impulses into the unconscious. Thus, repression is both a de-

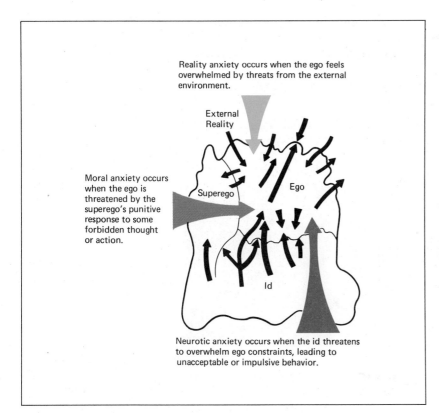

Reality anxiety occurs when the ego feels overwhelmed by threats from the external environment.

External Reality

Moral anxiety occurs when the ego is threatened by the superego's punitive response to some forbidden thought or action.

Superego

Ego

Id

Neurotic anxiety occurs when the id threatens to overwhelm ego constraints, leading to unacceptable or impulsive behavior.

Figure 13.1 A visual interpretation of the Freudian theory of personality structure. The id, which is entirely unconscious, is the source of all psychic energy. The superego and the ego, which are differentiated from the id during the development of the child, are partly conscious. The superego is an internalized version of the restrictions and demands placed on the child (that is, on the id) by the parents. The ego tries to balance the id's desires against the superego's demands and the realities of the world. In doing this it sometimes suppresses completely the irrational tendencies of the id, but it may also be able to deflect the id's energy (libido) into channels that are acceptable to both the superego and the outside world. These interactions and conflicts are represented by the arrows in the figure.

fense mechanism in its own right and the aim of all other defense mechanisms. For no matter what one's specific strategy for coping with anxiety may be, the ultimate goal is to make sure that the "forbidden" thoughts and feelings no longer intrude into consciousness. Throughout his writings Freud mentioned many different defense mechanisms, the hysterical disorders that plagued some of his patients being just one kind. But it was Freud's daughter Anna, herself a psychoanalyst, who actually discussed the ego's defenses in detail (A. Freud, 1946). Among the most important ones she described are denial, regression, reaction formation, projection, displacement, and sublimation.

Denial is a refusal to acknowledge some threat—a threat that may take the form of distressing feelings of concrete danger. Right before World War II, for instance, many German and Austrian Jews refused to acknowledge that the Nazi regime posed any real threat to them, even though Nazi intentions were plain enough to see. (Freud himself stayed in Vienna until 1938 and just managed to flee the country at the eleventh hour.) Psychoanalysts would say that this was a form of denial, a disavowal of reality.

Regression occurs when a person made anxious by threatening thoughts and feelings behaves in ways characteristic of an earlier stage in life, before the present conflict began. A middle-aged man who is having difficulties with his wife, for example, may resort to taking long afternoon naps on weekends, just as he did as a small child.

Reaction formation is the replacement of an anxiety-producing impulse or feeling by its direct opposite. A person who is strongly attracted to pornography, for instance, may vehemently insist that all sexually explicit material is filthy and disgusting. Thus many of those who lead crusades against pornography—those who "protest too much"—may in reality be displaying a reaction formation.

Projection occurs when people unknowingly attribute their own objectionable impulses to others. A man who has had many extramarital affairs, for example, may begin to accuse his wife of being unfaithful, thereby transferring his own shortcomings to her. Similarly, people who constantly accuse the young of being sexually promiscuous may simply be projecting their own sexual urges onto others.

Displacement is the transfer of unacceptable feel-

According to Freudian theory, members of groups such as the Ku Klux Klan are manifesting the defense mechanism known as projection, attributing undesirable characteristics and behavior to "scapegoat" groups such as blacks and Catholics. *(Ethan Hoffman/Archive Pictures.)*

ings from their appropriate target to a much "safer" one. A familiar example is the man who is constantly belittled by his boss and so vents his anger on his secretary, a store clerk, his children, or anyone else unlikely to retaliate. Thus wife beating and child abuse may sometimes be forms of displaced aggression.

Sublimation is a kind of displacement in which forbidden impulses are redirected toward the pursuit of socially desirable goals. In *Civilization and Its Discontents* (1930), Freud argued that civilization itself came about through such a rechanneling of primitive drives. He suggested, for example, that Leonardo da Vinci's urge to paint Madonnas was a sublimated expression of his longing for reunion with his mother, from whom he had been separated at an early age.

It is important to note that sublimation is not the only defense mechanism that can have positive outcomes. When used in moderation, almost any defense mechanism that does not injure others can help get us through distressing life events (Lazarus, 1980). Studies of people who have suffered misfortunes, such as devastating illnesses or accidents, suggest that a short-term use of denial may sometimes be beneficial. One such study found that heart attack victims who denied the severity of their conditions were less depressed and anxious and resumed their normal activities more rapidly than those who were more "realistic" (Stern, Pascale, and McLoone, 1976). Some researchers believe that denial and other defense mechanisms

may be especially helpful in getting people through an initial crisis period, thus buying them time to formulate more effective coping strategies (Hamburg and Adams, 1967). The problem is that defense mechanisms have a way of enduring. Instead of being temporary stopgaps, they may become a person's *only* way of handling the conflict being faced. When this happens, defense mechanisms cut off the person's chance of ever taking practical steps to reduce the *source* of anxiety. Such extreme reliance on defense mechanisms, to the point where they dominate a person's life or prevent healthy relationships with others, causes far more problems than it solves.

How Personality Develops. Because Freud learned from his work with troubled patients that psychological conflicts often begin in childhood, he developed an extensive theory about the shaping of adult personality by early life experiences. Freud argued that at each stage in a child's life, the drive for pleasure centers around a particular area of the body: first the mouth, then the anus, and finally the genitals. All these id urges he loosely labeled "sexual" to emphasize that the earlier strivings for sensual pleasure emanate from the same reservoir of psychic energy as does the striving for genital sex. Freud believed that adult personality is shaped by the way in which the conflicts between these early sexual urges and the requirements imposed by society (weaning, toilet training, prohibitions against masturbation, and so forth) are resolved. According to him, failure to resolve any of these conflicts can result in **fixation,** in which the person becomes perpetually "locked" in that particular psychological battle, forever expressing the conflict in symbolic ways. To understand these ideas more fully, let us consider each of Freud's five stages of psychosexual development.

The Stages of Psychosexual Development. Freud believed that during the first year of life—the **oral stage**—a child's sexual pleasure focuses on the mouth. Since sucking is the only means for a baby to obtain food, it is not surprising that this activity is an important aspect of the child's life. But Freud argued that to a baby the significance of sucking goes far beyond the basic satisfaction of hunger. Sucking, he maintained, is a source of intense pleasure in its own right, pleasure akin to that which genital sex holds for adults. According to Freud, this is why babies suck, lick, bite, and chew virtually anything they can get into the mouth. Fixation at the oral stage can occur for a variety of reasons. When, for example, a baby repeatedly experiences anxiety over whether food will be given or withheld, the child may come to learn that he or she is totally dependent on others. This lesson usually leads to a passive, overly dependent, unenterprising adult.

The next stage of development in Freud's scheme is the **anal stage.** It occurs during the second year of life, when the child begins to develop voluntary control over bowel movements. As a result, he or she comes to derive great sensual pleasure from holding in and expelling feces. But no sooner are these pleasures established than the demands of toilet training are imposed. Toilet training, according to Freudians, in a crucial event because it is the first large-scale conflict between the child's id impulses and society's rules. If this conflict is not satisfactorily resolved, fixation will again occur. The child who undergoes strict, punitive toilet training, for example, may repress the urge to defecate in a free and enjoyable manner. Repeated repression of this urge may result in personality traits that are very much the opposite of uninhibited defecation—such traits as fastidious orderliness and neatness.

Freud's third stage of development, the **phallic stage,** spans the years from about three to five or six. During this time the child's erotic pleasure focuses on masturbation—that is, on self-manipulation of the genitals. The phallic stage is said to be particularly important to a person's psychological development because this is the period when the Oedipus conflict presumably occurs. As we discussed in Chapter 8, this conflict involves an intense desire to take the place of the same-sex parent in the affections of the parent of the opposite sex. Freud saw this desire as explicitly sexual. He argued that "when the little boy shows the most open sexual curiosity about his mother, wants to sleep with her at night, or even attempts physical acts of seduction, the erotic nature of his attachment to her is established without a doubt" (Freud, 1935, p. 342). But the child naturally fears that the jealous same-sex parent will seek retribution for these incestuous longings. The child is therefore plagued by conflict—drawn toward the parent of the opposite sex, but fearful of being punished. The healthiest resolution, according to Freud, is for the child to recognize that he or she can never physically possess the opposite-sex parent. So instead the child tries to become like the person who does enjoy this privilege, striving to adopt the attitudes, behaviors, and moral values of the *same*-sex parent. This identification with the same-sex parent is believed to be crucial to development of the child's conscience, or superego. At the same time, striving to be like the same-sex parent is also a form of defense. By becoming like the powerful person who poses a potential threat, the child feels less likely to be the victim of punishment.

After the phallic stage, children presumably move into the fourth stage of psychosexual development, a period of **latency.** From the age of five or six until puberty, sexual impulses appear to remain in the background while the child is busy learning a range of social and cognitive skills. Finally, during adolescence, sexual feelings reemerge and the **genital stage** begins. The focus in this last period is on the pleasures of sexual intercourse. Feelings of dependency and Oedipal strivings that were not resolved earlier may resurface during this time. In fact, Freud maintained that the turmoil of adolescence may be partly due to such conflicts. With their successful resolution, however, a person is capable of forming deep and mature love relationships and of assuming a place in the world as a fully independent adult.

Freud's ideas about psychosexual development were the aspect of his theory that his contemporaries found most shocking. How perverse, they charged, to attribute sexual thoughts and actions to innocent little children! But in their indignation Freud's turn-of-the-century critics were largely missing his point. Freud was not seeking to uncover the "sins" of childhood. He was simply trying to emphasize that we are all born with biological drives, among them erotic ones. Human sexuality cannot suddenly emerge out of nowhere when a person reaches puberty, Freud reasoned. It is much more logical to think that erotic impulses are present all the time, but take different forms at different ages. Freud believed that if people persist in seeing children as totally asexual, it is only because that is what they *wish* children to be.

Freud on the Development of Women. As if Freud's theory of psychosexual development were not controversial enough, his ideas on the development of women have stirred even greater clamor, especially in the last decade. Freud has been accused of degrading women, and it is not difficult to see why. His writings are liberally sprinkled with passing references to female inferiority. The basis of this inferiority, and of female psychology in general, is the simple fact that women lack a penis. According to Freud, when little girls finally notice the absence of this fine piece of anatomical equipment, they "feel themselves heavily handicapped . . . and envy the boy's possession of it" (1925, p. 327). And this is the beginning of their long slide into inferiority. Freud reasoned that because a girl lacks a large and visible external genital organ, she cannot experience as intense an Oedipus conflict as does a boy. A boy, Freud argued, often comes to fear that his father will punish his Oedipal longings by cutting off his penis. This terrible dread, called **castration anxiety,** is presumably so powerful that it propels the boy strongly toward identification with his father and hence toward the development of a strong superego. As Freud wrote:

> I cannot evade the notion (though I hesitate to give it expression) that for women the level of what is ethically normal is different from what it is in men. Their superego is never so inexorable, so impersonal, so independent of its emotional origins as we require in men. Character traits which critics of every epoch have brought up against women—that they show less sense of justice than men, . . . that they are more often influenced in their judgments by feelings of affection or hostility—all these would be amply accounted for by the modification in the formation of their superego.   [Freud, 1925, p. 258]

According to Freud, then, women are morally inferior. And as a result, they are culturally inferior as well. Freud believed that the ability to contribute to the advance of civilization depends on the ability to sublimate our primitive urges, which in turn depends on a strong, mature superego—the very thing a woman lacks. According to Freud, women have made only one contribution to civilization, the art of weaving, a practice unconsciously motivated by woman's desire to conceal her "genital deficiency."

Opposition to Freud's penis-envy theory was first publicly voiced in 1926 by the psychologist Karen Horney. She argued that Freud, lacking exposure both to women in societies other than his own and to women without psychological problems, was in a poor position to know what normal, healthy girls think as they are growing up. According to Horney (1967), it is not little girls who perceive themselves as genitally deficient. Rather, it is little boys—and the men they eventually become—who see females as woefully castrated and have therefore created the self-fulfilling prophecy that dooms womankind to inferiority. More recent feminist writers have taken this argument several steps further, claiming that Freud's theory was merely the reflection of an age-old cultural bias against women and that it is nothing more than a devious attempt to justify male supremacy. We will say much more about prejudice and discrimination against women in Chapter 17, where we discuss the psychology of sexism.

Other Psychoanalytic Theorists

As we mentioned earlier, Freud's ideas about human personality eventually attracted many followers, and a psychoanalytic movement was born. From all over Europe and the United States, young people came to Vienna to study with Freud. Like Freud himself, some of these students were highly creative thinkers. So it is not surprising that a number of them began to expand and modify Freud's original theories.

Although it is difficult to summarize briefly all the different directions that later psychoanalytic thinking has taken, two trends in particular stand out. First, post-Freudian theorists have tended to give an increased importance to the ego and a decreased importance to the id. In Freud's view, the ego was simply the id's dutiful servant, trying as best it could to satisfy id instincts without neglecting reality or causing the superego remorse. Most later psychoanalytic thinkers, in contrast, have abandoned the idea that id drives are all-powerful and all-consuming. Instead, they have seen the ego as an important force in its own right, capable of much creativity, rational planning, and the formation of satisfying goals. Second, later psychoanalytic thinkers have emphasized the importance of social interaction in explaining how human personality develops. Instead of seeing a person's nature as solely the outcome of conflicts over id impulses, they have seen it as much more the product of a child's relationships with significant others in his or her life. Both these trends are reflected in a modern psychoanalytic approach called **object relations theory** (Klein, 1967; Kohut, 1971). It focuses on the human infant's social attachments, especially to the mother, and on the importance that the quality of these early attachments have for development of the child's ego, feelings about the self, and later interpersonal relationships. Thus objects relations theorists see early parenting as a critical factor shaping the direction that human personality takes.

Of all the deviations from orthodox Freudian theory that occurred during Freud's lifetime, the ones most personally distressing to him were those instigated by two of his closest colleagues, Carl Jung (1875–1961) and Alfred Adler (1870–1937). Jung strongly disagreed with Freud on several important issues (Jung, 1953). One was the nature of the unconscious. Jung believed that the unconscious was not simply a dark reservoir of "forbidden" urges and repressed memories. To him it was also the source of our strivings for pleasure and creativity. Jung also maintained that a struggle of opposing forces takes place in each of us. Every person, for example, has a passive "feminine" nature and an assertive "masculine" one. Similarly, every extrovert has an introvert lurking within, just as every introvert has a hidden extroverted side. There is a struggle as well between the face we present to others (our **persona**) and our private sense of self. Jung argued that each individual has the task of unifying these and other opposing forces and that failure to reconcile such opposites can lead to a stunted personality. Thus, an overemphasis on the persona may lead to a loss of sense of self and a doubting of who we really are. Striving for an integrated personality is a lifelong task, according to Jung.

Striving to fulfill our human potential was a theme that Alfred Adler also stressed. Unlike Freud, Adler believed that the great motivation in human life is not the striving for satisfaction of sexual urges, but rather the striving upward toward "superiority" (Adler, 1930). By this he did not mean social distinction or

prominence. He meant instead an inner quest for self-perfection. Adler proposed that all children are born with a deep sense of inferiority because of their small size, physical weakness, and lack of knowledge and power in the world of adults. In fact, it was Adler (1931) who coined the widely used term **inferiority complex.** Adler's views were probably related to his own frailty and illness as a child. Crippled with rickets at an early age, he suffered repeated bouts of pneumonia, a life-threatening disease in those days. Adler argued that the way parents interact with their children has a crucial effect on the children's ability to overcome feelings of inferiority and so to achieve competency later in life. Thus Adler saw personality as heavily influenced by the quality of early social relationships.

As we mentioned earlier, other psychoanalytic thinkers since Adler's time have elaborated this view of the self as a product of social relationships. The writings of the psychoanalyst Karen Horney (1885–1952) provide a good example. Horney was born in Germany, was trained in Europe by one of Freud's students, and emigrated to the United States shortly before World War II. Like Freud, Horney saw adult personality as largely shaped by childhood experiences. But unlike Freud, she focused on social relationships (especially with parents) rather than on the resolution of id-related conflicts (Horney, 1945). In particular, Horney argued that when parents' behavior toward a child is indifferent, disparaging, and erratic, the child feels helpless and insecure. Horney called this feeling **basic anxiety.** Accompanying basic anxiety, according to Horney, is a feeling of deep resentment toward the parents, or **basic hostility.** This hostility cannot be expressed directly, because the child needs and fears the parents and strongly wants their love. So the hostility is repressed, leading to increased feelings of unworthiness and anxiety. The conflict between basic anxiety and basic hostility leads the child, and later the neurotic adult, to adopt one of three modes of social interaction: moving *toward* others, moving *against* others, or moving *away* from others. Someone who moves toward others becomes compliant, always anxious to please in order to gain affection and approval. The person who moves against others is attempting to find security through domination. The goal of the person who moves away from others is to find security by becoming aloof and withdrawn, never allowing close relationships. Clearly all of these self-protective strategies give rise to many interpersonal problems.

Evaluating Psychoanalytic Approaches

Like all controversial views, psychoanalytic approaches to personality face forceful and persuasive criticisms. First is the charge that the data supporting them have not been collected and analyzed in rigorously scientific ways. Freud, for example, never attempted to quantify his findings, nor did he ever use standardized tests to assess his patients' behavior. Instead, he relied exclusively on his own subjective appraisals. Such lack of objective measurement suggests that Freud may inadvertently have biased his own observations by focusing on those aspects of behavior that tended to confirm his hypotheses and overlooking those that did not.

Contemporary researchers have tried to resolve some of these issues by putting some of Freud's notions to scientific tests. Two psychologists reviewed the many hundreds of such tests conducted over the years, with the goal of evaluating Freudian theory as a whole (Fisher and Greenberg, 1977). They found that the available scientific evidence gives fairly good support to some of Freud's notions. People who experience unusual anxiety over anal subjects, for instance, do tend to show the "anal" traits of orderliness, frugality, and obstinacy. In addition, there is evidence that arousal of erotic feelings may produce some anxiety in men and increase their concern about harm or attack to their bodies. This finding is in keeping with Freud's Oedipus theory and his concept of castration anxiety. In other cases, however, the available scientific evidence does not support Freud's views. There is absolutely no evidence, for instance, that women regard their bodies as inferior to men's because they lack a penis. If anything, women are generally more accepting of and comfortable with their bodies than men are.

In addition to criticisms about Freud's lack of scientific rigor, many psychologists have complained that a large number of Freud's concepts are too ambiguous to be pinned down and measured. In precisely what behaviors must a little boy engage, for example, to be considered embroiled in an Oedipus conflict? Are signs of strong attachment to the mother enough? Or must the boy's words and actions have explicitly sexual overtones? Freud never really specified. Furthermore, some of Freud's concepts are defined in ways that allow virtually *any* behavior to be used as evidence in their support. If a person acts in a blatantly sexual or aggressive manner, for instance, he or she can be said to be expressing an unbridled id instinct. But if the person acts the *opposite,* he or she may also be said to be driven by the very same impulse, only this time the impulse is surfacing as a reaction formation. In fact, many different actions can be interpreted as forms of compromise between a particular id impulse and the demands of conscience and reality. This looseness of Freudian theory prohibits its adherents from actually *predicting* behavior. Instead, the theory can be used only to explain behavior after the fact, and this is a serious weakness.

But despite these strong criticisms of Freud, his influence on twentieth-century thought has been profound. Such Freudian concepts as anxiety, repression, and defense mechanism are used by psychologists and lay people alike. The fact that we often analyze an individual's personality in terms of childhood experiences or worry about the way in which we toilet-train our children testifies to Freud's enduring impact on us. Although Freud may not have been a rigorous scientist, he was certainly a keen and meticulous observer of human behavior. The enormous originality of his thinking, his perseverance in the face of severe criticism, and the sheer comprehensiveness of his theories have earned him great distinction in the history of psychological thought.

BEHAVIORIST AND SOCIAL LEARNING APPROACHES

At approximately the same time that Freud was developing his theories of personality in Vienna, psychologists in the United States were formulating the doctrine of behaviorism, discussed in Chapters 1 and 5. Unlike psychoanalytic ideas and principles, which grew out of work with troubled patients, behaviorist theories were built on findings made within the laboratory. Behaviorists maintained that psychology must be limited solely to what can be observed and measured. As a result, they set about investigating how observable stimuli in the environment can, through learning, produce observable responses. Out of this intellectual heritage a number of approaches to personality emerged. One of the most influential has been that of B. F. Skinner.

Skinner's Radical Behaviorism

Skinner's approach is called **radical behaviorism** because it argues that what we call the "mind" is an unnecessary concept for explaining people's actions. According to Skinner, we do not need to infer that a man has some inner urge for power because he seeks to dominate others. Nor do we need to infer that a woman has an inner desire for achievement because she persists for hours at a challenging task. Instead, Skinner argues, such human actions can be largely explained by reference to the rewards and punishments that have been associated with them.

Research has shown that rewards and punishments are indeed powerful influences on human behavior. If a mother praises her child for acting independently, for instance, she increases the likelihood that the child will repeat such behavior. Similarly, if a husband showers his wife with concern and affection whenever she acts helpless, he certainly increases the chances that she will act this way again. Skinner and his followers have had success in deliberately modifying a variety of problem behaviors by altering the consequences that are related to people's responses. These problem behaviors include smoking, alcoholism, stuttering, nail biting, marital discord, classroom disciplinary problems, and even littering in public parks. The use of behavioral techniques to treat psychological disorders will be discussed in detail in Chapter 16.

While most psychologists acknowledge that rewards and punishments can shape human behavior, not all believe that these external consequences are central to personality development. What of inner fears, conflicts, wishes, and inclinations? Skinner's critics ask. Skinner answers that such inner thoughts and feelings certainly do exist. But he believes that they have often been greatly overemphasized in attempts to explain personality. To Skinner, what makes the saint different from the sinner is often the very different patterns of reinforcement that the two have experienced in life. Skinner does not deny that inherited biological traits can also influence behavior. But more than any other psychologists, Skinner and

his followers believe that the distinctive patterns of response we call personality are frequently acquired through operant conditioning (Skinner, 1974).

Skinner has been very outspoken about how operant conditioning principles might be used to solve pressing social problems (Skinner, 1971). He contends that behavior which is harmful to others is very often rewarded and thus encouraged in our society. Consider the slumlord, for instance. He can earn more profit by spending very little to maintain his property. So he lets his buildings deteriorate to the detriment of tenants. If we wish to change the slumlord's behavior, Skinner argues, we must associate a powerful reward not with property neglect but with slum renovation, perhaps through tax incentives. Skinner believes that such enlightened use of operant conditioning principles is our best hope for improving the world in which we live. In his novel *Walden Two* (1948) he has described how these principles could be applied to fashion his vision of a utopian society. Figure 13.2 contains passages from this thought-provoking book.

The idea of consciously controlling people with systematic rewards and punishments is disturbing to many, partly because it so openly downplays the importance of free will. Some doubt whether such total manipulation of human behavior would ever really be possible. As you will see later in this chapter, some

"After all, it's a simple and sensible program.... We set up a system of gradually increasing annoyances and frustrations against a background of complete serenity. An easy environment is made more and more difficult as the children acquire the capacity to adjust."

"But why?... What do [the children] get out of it?"

"What do they get out of it!... what they get is escape from the petty emotions which eat the heart out of the unprepared. They get the satisfaction of pleasant and profitable social relations.... They get new horizons, for they are spared the emotions characteristic of frustration and failure."

Figure 13.2 Can destructive or antisocial emotions be eliminated, or will such emotions always haunt us? In this dialogue from *Walden Two*, B. F. Skinner's novel about a utopian society, traits and emotions are seen not as inherent biological qualities or essences, but as learned and therefore *controllable* or *extinguishable* behaviors. Through principles of operant conditioning and reinforcement, Skinner argues, we can engineer a perfect society. Do you agree? *(From Skinner, 1948.)*

prominent personality theorists strongly argue that people are not just molded by rewards and punishments but are instead self-directed and free.

Social Learning Theory

As we have just seen, Skinner's radical behaviorism answers the question "Why do people behave as they do?" by focusing mainly on how events in the environment shape and control responses. Skinner does not deny the existence of subjective thoughts, perceptions, and feelings. He simply believes that such cognitive processes are incidental to learning and behavior. Not all learning theorists agree with him, however. In recent years social learning theorists have argued that cognition plays a critical role in determining how we act. While these researchers still believe that our actions are strongly influenced by rewards and punishments, they stress that we mentally interpret events in light of memories, beliefs, and expectations. Thus, when two men are approached by a very attractive woman, one may interpret the event as an occasion when his shortcomings are bound to be detected, while the other may see it as a lucky opportunity to get to know this woman better. Such differences in mental outlook help explain why people can behave so differently in the same objective situation.

This emphasis on cognitive processes has helped direct attention to the importance of so-called **observational learning.** Observational learning, as we discussed in Chapter 5, is the process of learning complex patterns of behavior simply by watching other people perform them. Through observational learning we acquire cognitive representations of behavior patterns we see, which may then serve as models for our own behavior. Social learning theorists argue that many of our habitual ways of responding in situations—our personality styles—have been influenced by observational learning.

And it is not just the potential for new actions that we acquire through observational learning. Consider what is being learned in the following incident:

Jim, age five, found a dead rat, picked it up by the tail, and brought it over to Rita, also age five, waving it in front of her, and evidently hoping to frighten her. Rita showed interest in the rat and wanted to touch it, much to Jim's apparent disappointment. He then took the rat to Dorothy, age seven, who reacted with apparent disgust and fear and ran away from Jim toward Rita, screaming. When Jim pursued Dorothy, Rita also ran away from Jim and the rat and began to scream. Later, when Jim showed up with his rat, Rita ran and showed fear even though Dorothy was not around any more. [Corsini, 1979, pp. 422–423]

Note that Rita has not only learned overt acts (running and screaming at the sight of a dead rat) through her observation of Dorothy. She has also learned a strong emotion (fear of dead animals) and a number of related cognitions (that dead animals are dirty, disgusting, and so forth). Social learning theorists argue that adults likewise acquire a whole range of thoughts, feelings, and actions through their observations of others. Thus, just by virtue of the models that are available to us, our personalities can develop in a variety of ways.

Of course, social learning theorists also see rewards and punishments as powerful factors in personality development. But unlike radical behaviorists they do not believe that these external consequences are essential for learning to occur. As we discussed in Chapter 5, social learning theorists see learning as a change in one's storehouse of information which can come about regardless of whether rewards or punishments are involved. When Rita watches Dorothy's fear of Jim's dead rat, she learns a potential way of responding to dead animals even though no apparent reward is involved in the learning process. Reinforcement operates, social learning theorists say, by encouraging people to *act* on what they have learned. Thus Rita may mimic Dorothy's fear of Jim's dead rat because she expects that this behavior will win the older girl's approval. In this way, Rita's observations of a particular style of behavior interact with her expectations concerning reinforcement to influence the way she behaves.

Another way in which the social learning view of personality development differs from the radical behaviorist one is in the stress it places on self-regulation of behavior. To social learning theorists, people do not respond to external events in mechanical, unreflective ways. Instead, they filter events through their own past experiences and develop expectations accordingly. Rita, for instance, isn't just automatically drawn toward mimicking Dorothy because of past rewards for imitation. Instead, she thinks about the present situation in light of past experiences and decides on her own course of action. Rita's cognitions, in other words, interact with external factors to motivate, direct, and sustain her behavior.

Thus, in answer to the question "Why do people behave differently in the same situation?" social learning theorists often try to look inside the actors' minds. How, they ask, have people's past experiences shaped their expectations about the consequences of various actions? In contrast to Rita, for instance, a boy might anticipate ridicule from other boys if he imitated Dorothy's behavior. So he would make every effort *not* to show fear when taunted with Jim's dead rat. Social learning theorists stress that it is the *expectations* here that matter, not just what objectively happens to the child. This is one reason why people seldom respond exactly the same even in what seem to be the same circumstances.

Another reason why people respond differently in the same situation is that they often have very different estimates of their own capabilities. This is an aspect of cognitive psychology that social learning theorist Albert Bandura has recently stressed (Bandura, 1977a, 1982). In Bandura's terms, when people believe they are capable of dealing effectively with a situation, they possess a sense of **self-efficacy** about it. Self-efficacy is important to personality development because it greatly affects whether or not a person will even *try* to behave in a certain manner. If a little girl is convinced, for instance, that she cannot touch a dead rat, she is likely to avoid dead animals, and such squeamishness may become characteristic of her. Bandura points out that our degree of self-efficacy in any given situation depends both on our own past experiences and on the experiences of others that we observe. In Chapter 16 we will see how instilling a sense of self-efficacy may help people to overcome a variety of maladaptive behaviors, from acute shyness to irrational fears.

To sum up, the social learning approach to personality stresses the interaction between a person's thoughts and expectations (shaped by past experiences) and factors in the external environment. People, it says, size up events in terms of possible outcomes, assess how valuable those outcomes are, judge their own abilities to deal with situations, and select their courses of action accordingly. "This conception of human functioning," Albert Bandura writes, "neither casts people into the role of powerless objects controlled by environmental forces nor free agents who can become whatever they choose" (Bandura, 1977a, p. vii). Behavior, in short, is determined by both external factors *and* inner ways of thinking. This is a central message of the social learning view.

Although social learning theory has been very influential and is becoming increasingly popular, it nevertheless has limitations as a comprehensive theory of personality. For one thing, social learning theory, like behaviorism, tends to focus on the reasons why people perform very specific responses. Why does John race motorcycles, for instance? A social learning theorist might say it is because he has developed an expectation that this sport will bring him status in the eyes of his friends. But the problem is that this perspective fails to provide a very coherent picture of John as an overall person. Which behaviors are most central to John's personality? And how do these behaviors relate to one another? Social learning theorists in general have not addressed these questions. What's more, social learning theorists leave us with the vague impression that a person's style of behavior could change suddenly and dramatically if expectations concerning rewards and punishments changed. Not all psychologists fully agree with this assumption. Prominent among those who have doubts are the so-called trait theorists.

TRAIT THEORIES

More than any other personality theorists, trait theorists emphasize and try to explain the *consistency* in human behavior. They believe that each person possesses broad and relatively stable personality traits that are part of that person's psychological makeup. As such, these traits predispose the person to act in characteristic ways in many different situations. The

same John who races motorcycles, for instance, is likely to seek excitement in many other areas, and is unlikely to take up a sedentary pastime like stamp collecting or needlepoint. Such preferences derive from his active, competitive, thrill-seeking nature, according to the trait theorist's view.

Trait theorists see their primary task as finding

ways of accurately identifying and measuring the various traits that people have. They define a **trait** as any "relatively enduring way in which one individual differs from another" (Guilford, 1959). Most traits can be thought of as dimensions of personality (dependency, timidness, friendliness, and so forth) in terms of which any person can be assessed. As you will see, many trait theorists believe that a few crucial traits provide the keys to virtually all others. John's high level of adventurousness, for instance, might be traced to the more basic trait of impulsiveness. A number of researchers have tried to pinpoint these important core characteristics so that each individual's nature can be more coherently described.

The trait approach to personality presents an interesting contrast with the Freudian approach. Freud recognized that each person has an individual constellation of traits, but his main concern was to explain those traits in terms of his overall theories. Stinginess, for example, was to Freud a displaced form of anal retentiveness, the infant's pleasure in retaining feces. Trait theorists, in contrast, do not start by seeking the origins of stinginess, or any other trait. Instead, they try to determine whether degree of stinginess is in fact a consistent quality in people. In other words, they try to find out whether people who are extremely stingy in one situation are extremely stingy in others. Then they may ask whether stinginess is a product of some more basic trait—perhaps possessiveness. Is the stingy person also very possessive in relationships? An important question for trait theorists, therefore, is which behaviors tend to go together. Note that trait theory, in and of itself, is not very good at *explaining* behavior. When people appeal to traits for this purpose, their reasoning often becomes circular. Why does Ann get angry so quickly? Because she is short-tempered. Why is she short-tempered? Because she has such a volatile nature. As an approach to personality, then, trait theory is more descriptive than explanatory.

Allport's Classification of Traits

One leading trait theorist, Gordon Allport, continually developed and refined his ideas for almost forty years (Allport, 1937, 1961, 1966). One of the first steps Allport took in his investigation of traits was to go through an unabridged dictionary and note all the terms that could be used to describe people (Allport and Odbert, 1936). He found almost eighteen thousand. Even after he eliminated words that simply evaluate a person's character (such words as *worthy* and *insignificant*) or that describe temporary states (*joyous* and *flustered,* for instance), there were still between four and five thousand items. How, Allport asked, could so many potential traits be organized to provide a coherent picture of a particular person's nature?

Allport ultimately proposed a scheme in which any given personality could be defined according to three types of traits, which together form a kind of hierarchy. A **cardinal trait** is one that directs a major portion of a person's behavior. Someone consumed by ambition or greed, for instance, would be described as dominated by a cardinal trait. But Allport believed that most people do not develop such single, overriding characteristics. Instead, they tend to develop a few so-called **central traits.** Central traits are not so all-consuming as cardinal traits, but they still influence much of a person's behavior. Honesty, lovingness, and gregariousness, for instance, would be considered central traits if they captured a person's characteristic ways of dealing with the world. Finally, Allport labeled much narrower characteristics (such as a fondness for children or an aversion to strenuous exercise) **secondary traits.** In everyday language, we often call such secondary traits "attitudes," and Allport often used this term as well.

Allport believed that traits unify and integrate a person's behavior by causing that person to approach different situations with similar goals or plans in mind. A person who is highly competitive, for instance, will view a variety of settings as chances to "beat" other people, to show that he or she is superior in strength, intelligence, or talent. As a result, the highly competitive person will display achievement strivings in a large number of circumstances. Allport believed that inner traits were the most important determinant of a person's behavior in a particular situation. Although acknowledging that external stimuli also have an influence, he saw such stimuli as interpreted in accordance with inner dispositions. For example, a highly competitive student might take pleasure in another's failure on an exam, while a highly cooperative person might respond to the situation by offering sympathy or help. "The same fire that melts the butter hardens the egg," wrote Allport, meaning that different people respond to the same situation in ways that are in accordance with their individual traits.

Allport also believed that any given trait manifests itself in different ways even in people who share it. Two women may both be ambitious, for instance, yet express their ambitiousness in noticeably different ways. In short, Allport saw each individual as having a unique personality profile, unlike that of any other person, regardless of any general traits that two people have in common. Consequently, he maintained that a person's traits can never be fully understood simply by administering a standardized test and comparing the results to group norms. Instead, he favored in-depth case studies of personalities in order to do justice to the uniqueness of each human being.

Eysenck's Dimensions of Personality

More recent trait theorists have relied more heavily than Allport on standardized tests and statistical tools for assessing and comparing personalities. One such theorist is the English psychologist Hans Eysenck (1970). On the basis of sophisticated statistical analyses, Eysenck initially concluded that personality can be essentially reduced to two major dimensions. One dimension is neuroticism versus emotional stability, the degree to which people have control over their feelings. At one extreme is the highly neurotic person—anxious, moody, touchy, restless, quick to fly out of control. At the other extreme is the very emotionally stable person—calm, even-tempered, reliable, almost never falling to pieces. The second of

Eysenck's major dimensions is extroversion versus introversion, the extent to which people are socially outgoing or socially withdrawn. On the one hand are those who are active, gregarious, impulsive, and excitement-oriented. On the other are those who are passive, quiet, cautious, and reserved. Figure 13.3 gives some of the items from Eysenck's questionnaires for measuring neuroticism and extroversion-introversion. More recently Eysenck has also proposed a third major personality dimension: what he calls psychoticism. Those who score high on psychoticism tend to be loners who have little concern for other people and who often violate social norms. Presumably, just by knowing where a person falls on each of these three major dimensions, we may predict a great deal about that person's behavior.

Eysenck believes there is a biological basis to how people score in terms of his three dimensions. Consider extroversion-introversion, for instance. As we saw in Chapter 11, Eysenck suggests that people who are extroverted have a naturally low level of arousal in the cortex of the brain. As a result, they seek high levels of external stimulation to raise cortical arousal to an optimum level. The introvert, in contrast, already has a naturally high level of cortical arousal and is easily overaroused by high external stimulation. So the introvert seeks out situations that minimize stimulation, thus preventing cortical arousal from becoming too great. Many observations have supported this basic theory. Introverts, for instance, take longer to fall asleep and are more sensitive to pain than extroverts, suggesting that their brains are somehow more alert. And alcohol, which lowers cortical arousal, makes introverts more extroverted. Conversely, when

	Yes	No
1. Do you usually take the initiative in making new friends?	___	___
2. Do ideas run through your head so that you cannot sleep?	___	___
3. Are you inclined to keep in the background on social occasions?	___	___
4. Are you inclined to be moody?	___	___
5. Do you very much like good food?	___	___
6. When you get annoyed do you need someone friendly to talk to about it?	___	___
7. Do you usually keep "yourself to yourself" except with very close friends?	___	___
8. Do you often make up your mind too late?	___	___

Figure 13.3 Sample items for extroversion and neuroticism from the Eysenck Personality Inventory. Questions 1, 3, 5, and 7 measure extroversion; questions 2, 4, 6, and 8 measure neuroticism.

extroverts take amphetamines, which increase cortical arousal, they become more introverted. Whether Eysenck's theory is actually correct remains to be determined. Nevertheless, it is an intriguing attempt to provide physiological explanations for what are essentially descriptive traits. Studies of identical twins add further evidence that Eysenck's speculations may be on the right track. Inherited biological factors *do* seem to make a major contribution to individual differences along the extroversion-introversion dimension of personality (Shields, 1976).

Recently, the extroversion-introversion dimension has been found to have interesting implications for college students. When trying to study, extroverts generally prefer more background noise and opportunities for socializing than introverts do. Extroverts are also inclined to take more study breaks than their introverted peers (Campbell and Hawley, 1982). These differences in study habits may be related to the fact that introverts usually do better in school than extroverts, particularly in higher-level subjects (Pervin, 1984). The introvert's preference for studying in quiet places with few interruptions may simply be more conducive to academic achievement. In addition, introverts have a tendency to be more thorough and careful than extroverts, which could also contribute to scholastic success (Wilson, 1978). Whatever the causes, extroverts are more likely to drop out of college for academic reasons than introverts are.

Is Behavior Really Consistent?

As we stressed earlier, the trait approach to studying personality makes an important assumption about human behavior. It assumes that people are relatively consistent in the ways they act. Granted, situational pressures can encourage or discourage the expression of any given trait. An aggressive person is more likely to display aggressiveness on a tennis court than in church. But in general, people's central traits, according to trait theorists, incline them to behave similarly in many different contexts.

This view of relative consistency in human behavior conforms to our intuitive perceptions, and a large number of psychologists accepted it for many years. But then, in the late 1960s, the social learning theorist Walter Mischel made a startling assertion in his book *Personality and Assessment* (1968). Reviewing study after study, Mischel showed that there was actually very little correlation among different behaviors

thought of as reflecting the same underlying trait. In one study, for instance, children were given a variety of opportunities to be dishonest, including lying to save face, cheating on a test, and stealing money (Hartshorne and May, 1928). These opportunities were also presented in a variety of contexts. The researchers found that only rarely did a child's degree of honesty in the face of one temptation in one context correspond with his or her degree of honesty in all other situations. A child who lied to save face when interacting with peers might refuse to steal money from one of the experimenters, and yet later steal money that belonged to a brother or sister. Mischel also found that there is often a low correlation between a person's score for a certain trait, as measured by a questionnaire, and that person's actual performance of behaviors related to the trait. Thus people who score high on a scale measuring generosity are often only slightly more willing than other people to give money to charity, to donate blood, or to perform other acts typically considered signs of a generous nature. If a person's behavior is so variable, Mischel argued, the concept of enduring personality traits may be of little practical value. Instead, it may be largely the context or situation, not an underlying disposition, that determines how we act.

But if behavior is not very consistent from one situation to the next, why do most of us believe that it is? Why are we convinced that fairly stable personality traits do indeed exist? The answer, Mischel and others say, is that the traits a particular person possesses lie as much in the eye of the beholder as in the psyche of the beheld. And beholders, they argue, are prone to many perceptual biases. One such bias is the so-called primacy effect—the tendency to maintain our first impression of a person even if he or she acts quite differently later. Thus, if your first impression of a particular woman is that she is selfish and cruel, it will be difficult for you to view her otherwise even after you see her perform several acts of kindness. Because we tend to want consistency in our beliefs and perceptions, we often discount information that doesn't fit our initial view. Another reason why we may see more consistency in behavior than actually exists is that we tend to see most people in only one role. If you see the head librarian only when she is sitting quietly at her desk, for instance, you may assume that she is in fact a very reticent person. What you fail to consider is that this demeanor is required by her job. In other contexts she may behave quite differently, but you never have a chance to see her do

The first impression formed of another person, in a situation such as a job interview, may persist—for better or worse—even when the other person subsequently behaves quite differently. Trait theorists refer to this perceptual bias as the primacy effect. *(Robert Eckert/EKM-Nepenthe.)*

so. Adding to these perceptual biases is the fact that our own behavior may conspire to produce the illusion of consistency in others. If you believe that a person is hostile, you may, by subtle cues of speech and body language—such as acting cold or unfriendly when he asks you something—elicit the very acts of hostility you expect to see. To the extent that our behavior toward another person consistently elicits the same responses, we may attribute to that person very stable traits that in reality are not so stable.

Mischel and others have pointed to a number of other factors—all supported by experimental data—that could cause us to see behavior as more consistent than it actually is (Mischel, 1973; Mischel and Peake, 1982). So persuasive were their arguments at the time they were proposed that many psychologists came to accept the view that situations generally exert a more powerful influence on human behavior than do inner dispositions. This view also made a great deal of sense in terms of human coping. The tendency to modify behavior according to situational demands seemed to offer a decided advantage in dealing with life's problems.

Other psychologists, however, viewed Mischel's perspective as a broadside attack on the concept of personality itself. How can personality have any real meaning, they asked, if inner dispositions are so weak? Not surprisingly, a number of researchers soon began to counter Mischel's claims. Daryl Bem and Andrea Allen (1974), although recognizing the validity of much of what Mischel said, cautioned that the concept of traits should not be discarded. Our intuition about the consistency of people's behavior, they argued, is not entirely wrong. Although no one is consistent in all areas of behavior, most people are relatively consistent in at least some areas. To demonstrate this fact, Bem and Allen asked students to rate their own consistency regarding "friendliness" and "conscientiousness." As predicted, those who described themselves as being quite consistent on one or the other of these traits did tend to show a high degree of consistency in behaviors related to that trait. Bem and Allen concluded that most of us do have some traits that we manifest fairly consistently, but those traits differ among people. As a result, when researchers study a large group of randomly selected people regarding an arbitrarily chosen trait, the behavior *on average* is bound to appear only slightly consistent.

Some studies used to support Mischel's view have

also been criticized for not observing the subjects in enough situations. How fair is it, critics ask, for a researcher to give a subject the chance to contribute spare change to a worthy cause and to donate blood to a blood bank and then, if the two responses are dissimilar, conclude that there is little evidence for a stable trait of generosity? Yet this is essentially what some psychologists have done: they have based their conclusions on a very small sample of behaviors. When other researchers have observed behavior across many situations, much greater consistency has been found (Epstein, 1980).

Evidence for behavioral consistency has also come from a number of other recent sources. Developmental psychologists have found that when people are rated by others along various personality dimensions, they often appear very consistent even over many years (Thomas, Chess, and Birch, 1970; Block, 1971; Block and Block, 1979, 1980). For example, Alexander Thomas and his colleagues (1970) have discovered that from birth through adolescence children can be remarkably stable in certain basic traits, such as activity level, attention span, adaptability to new situations, and general quality of mood. Thus the baby who is always bouncing and squirming often becomes the toddler who climbs all over the house, the kindergartner who runs incessantly, and the ten-year-old who has trouble sitting still long enough to finish homework. There are also signs that these relatively consistent behavior patterns may be partly genetic in origin, just as some trait theorists have proposed. Researchers studying identical twins have recently found some striking similarities between twins who have been raised apart, often in very different settings (Lykken, 1982; Holden, 1980). One pair of

identical twin brothers, for example, had been separated shortly after birth. One of the boys was raised by his Jewish father in the Caribbean and spent some of his time in an Israeli kibbutz, while the other, raised by his grandmother in Germany, had been a member of the Nazi Youth. When reunited and tested at age 47, they received very similar scores on personality scales. They also shared curious behavior patterns. Although no definite conclusions can as yet be drawn, the implication is that inner dispositions, partly shaped by heredity, often have a substantial influence on how we think and act.

When all the various evidence is taken into account, it becomes clear that both traits and situations play a role in directing human behavior. This is why our styles of responding are both coherent over time and capable of adapting to the demands of particular circumstances. The interaction of traits and situations, moreover, is often highly complex. Traits not only influence behavior directly by encouraging certain responses, but they also influence it *indirectly* by affecting the kinds of situations in which we choose to place ourselves (Bowers, 1973). A man with the trait of low self-confidence, for instance, may fail to strive for career advancement partly because he sees himself as low in ability. But at the same time his low self-confidence may prompt him to seek out jobs that are safe and unchallenging—jobs, in short, that place few demands on him.

The view that traits and situations interact is widely accepted today. A major task for contemporary psychologists is to unravel just how this interaction takes place in particular cases. Consider, for example, some recent investigations into the causes of child abuse. It has been found that a sizable minority of battered

These twins were separated soon after birth and raised apart by relatives. When reunited at age 47 through the efforts of the University of Minnesota's Study of Twins Reared Apart, they were found to be leading very different lives. Oskar Stöhr (left) is an industrial supervisor and devoted union member, married, and an avid skier. Jack Yufe (right) is a shop owner, separated from his wife, and a self-described "workaholic." Despite these differences, many intriguing similarities have emerged. Both men are domineering toward women, prefer the same kinds of clothing and food, and are absent-minded. Both wear mustaches, have a habit of falling asleep in front of the television, think it's funny to sneeze in a crowd of strangers, flush the toilet before using it, store rubber bands on their wrists, read magazines from back to front, and dip buttered toast in their coffee. *(Courtesy of Professor Thomas J. Bouchard, Jr., University of Minnesota.)*

children have traits that adults find annoying—hyperactivity, constant fussing, a particularly grating cry, and so forth (Gil, 1970). Obviously, this is insufficient reason for a normal adult to beat a child. But when these traits are presented to a parent who is emotionally unstable to begin with and under a great deal of stress, the result may be uncontrolled aggression. This theory is supported by the fact that many battered children have brothers or sisters who are *not* similarly abused, and some go on to be further abused by foster parents who have no past record of severely mistreating their children. The battered child, in turn, may intensify the original abrasive behavior in response to this abuse. So the parent responds with more abuse, and on its goes in a tragic interplay of traits and situations. It is hard to say which of these two factors is most important. Without either, the abuse might never occur. Many psychologists believe that much future research in personality is likely to focus on just such complex interactions between situations and traits.

PHENOMENOLOGICAL VIEWS

The current emphasis on the interaction between situations and traits is not the only negative reaction psychologists have had to the idea that people are controlled mainly by external forces. As we saw in Chapter 1, a number of psychologists began in the 1930s and 40s to shape a new vision of human personality—new at least in terms of the personality perspectives popular at the time. Although these thinkers differ substantially in the specific theories they propose, all share a broadly similar set of assumptions. They all believe that behavior is determined by a person's inner experiences—his or her unique ways of perceiving and thinking about the world, other people, and the self. Proponents of this **phenomenological approach** maintain that because subjective experiences are in many ways unique, we can understand another's personality only by trying to see the world through that person's eyes. Phenomenologists also share a strong belief in human self-determination and potential. All say that people are free to become what they want, to fulfill themselves, and to carve out their own destinies. This view contrasts sharply with certain earlier perspectives, especially the psychoanalytic and the behaviorist, both of which hold that our actions are largely molded by forces beyond our control. Two highly influential thinkers whose ideas are representative of the phenomenological perspective are Carl Rogers and Abraham Maslow.

The Self Theory of Rogers

Carl Rogers, a clinical psychologist, developed his theory of personality from observations he made while he practiced psychotherapy. He noticed that his clients (a term he prefers to "patients" because it does not imply illness) repeatedly expressed an organized set of perceptions, feelings, and attitudes about themselves. They made such statements as "I haven't been acting like myself; it doesn't seem like me" and "I don't have any emotional responses to situations; I'm worried about myself." Such statements led Rogers to believe that the *self*—the body of perceptions we think of as "I" or "me"—is a vital part of human experience. Furthermore, he found that most people are constantly struggling to become their "real" selves. Rogers concluded that the overriding human motivation is a desire to become all that one truly is—to fulfill one's capabilities and to achieve one's total potential. This powerful, lifelong motive Rogers called a striving toward **self-actualization** (Rogers, 1970, 1971).

But Rogers also discovered from his clients that self-actualization is often thwarted by an existing self-concept that is narrow and restricting. His clients seemed to have trouble accepting their true feelings and experiences as part of themselves. They seemed to have learned during childhood that in order to obtain the regard of others, they had to feel and act in ways that distorted or submerged what they were really like. In short, they had to deny certain feelings and inclinations in order to be accepted by parents, relatives, or peers.

Rogers explained this denial or distortion of feelings by arguing that almost every child is the victim of **conditional positive regard.** By this he meant that love and praise are often withheld until the child conforms to parental or social standards. If a boy dislikes rough-and-tumble play, for instance, he may be admonished not to be a "sissy." Or if he enjoys long walks in the woods by himself, he may be cautioned that it is not good to be a "loner." Contact sports and group activities, though, may be rewarded with smiles and compliments. According to Rogers, children incorporate into the self these so-called **conditions of worth**—strong ideas about which thoughts and behaviors will bring positive regard and so are desirable and "good." At the same time, they suppress, distort, or deny those feelings and experiences that prevent positive regard, even though they are genuine and would be intrinsically satisfying.

Rogers sees two possible outcomes from these early life experiences. When the conditions of worth a person learns are few and reasonable, the self will usually be flexible enough to allow a wide range of feelings and behaviors. Rogers describes such people as **fully functioning.** They are open, undefensive, realistic, creative, and self-determining, and have an underlying confidence in themselves. If, however, conditions of worth are severely restrictive, prohibiting many thoughts and actions in which the person would otherwise engage, self-actualization is blocked. The person is anxious, fearful, defensive, conforming, and unrealistic in self-demands, and feels manipulated rather than free.

To help such people back on the path toward self-actualization, Rogers (1951) has developed what he calls **person-centered therapy.** In this approach the therapist's role is not to judge the individual. Instead, the therapist tries to see the world from the person's point of view and to mirror whatever feelings he or she expresses. Most important, the therapist offers the person **unconditional positive regard:** the therapist gives support regardless of what the person says or does. In this warm, empathetic, and accepting environment, the individual is presumably released from the need to defend unrealistic conditions of worth. As a result, he or she can at last confront formerly suppressed feelings and experiences that are part of the true self. Rogers believes that as people become more fully functioning, they "live more intimately with their feelings of pain, but also more vividly with their feelings of ecstasy; anger is more clearly felt, but so also is love; fear is an experience they know more deeply, but so is courage" (Rogers, 1961, p. 195).

Some wonder whether a child who receives unconditional positive regard might not become selfish, even cruel and destructive. After all, how are we to inhibit a youngster's antisocial urges if we always accept what the child does? Rogers answers that in all his years as a therapist he has seen little evidence that people have aggressive, destructive instincts, as Freud proposed. When people are inclined to behave cruelly, he argues, it is largely because the culture in which they live has conspired to distort their true inner natures (Rogers, 1981). Rogers maintains that human beings naturally seek growth and positive relations with others. Consequently, a child who is raised in a warm and accepting atmosphere—where the need to follow social rules is based on reason, not on fear that love will be withheld—will grow up to be a happy, productive, self-actualizing adult.

Subsequent studies of parents and their children have provided mixed support for Rogers' view. On the one hand, there is evidence that parents who are warm and loving, who show interest in their children and respect their opinions, generally raise sons and daughters who are high in both self-esteem and self-reliance, just as Rogers would predict (Coopersmith, 1967; Baumrind, 1967, 1977). Also as Rogers would predict, children who are induced to comply with social standards because they are given persuasive reasons (*not* because they are threatened with withdrawal of love) are likely to develop mature moral outlooks and to think well of themselves (Hoffman, 1970; Conger, 1977). On the other hand, permissiveness on the part of parents is not generally associated with positive outcomes, even though it allows youngsters great freedom of action. The children of highly permissive parents are often *lower* in self-esteem and in self-reliance than the children of parents who enforce clearly defined limits without being domineering (Coopersmith, 1967; Baumrind, 1967, 1977). It may be that parental rules and limits, when not harshly imposed, help a child to develop a capacity for self-management and a sense of confidence in handling situations. It may also be that a child interprets parental guidelines as signs of the parents' interest and concern (Coopersmith, 1967). In any case, it is the warm, loving, responsive, *and* limit-setting parent who seems to encourage most reliably the personality traits found in Rogers' fully functioning adult. Interestingly, too, simply surrounding a child with positive regard may not always be enough to prevent selfishness from developing. To encourage children to be caring and helpful toward others, it seems, parents not only must be warm and loving, they also must model acts of kindness and altruism for their children to imitate (Mussen and Eisenberg-Berg, 1977; Yarrow, Scott, and Waxler, 1973).

Although Rogers has counseled many people whose self-actualization has presumably been thwarted by unreasonable conditions of worth, his theory is nevertheless a very optimistic one. He maintains that humans always have the potential to break free from any beliefs and feelings that are hampering their personal growth. This optimistic view is in keeping with recent findings by Ofria and Epstein (Epstein, 1979). These researchers asked college students to describe the experience in their lives that had the most positive impact on their self-concept. Significantly, a major boost in self-concept sometimes grew out of a situation in which a person was initially evaluated *negatively* by others. Rogers would not be the least surprised at this paradoxical finding. To him it would suggest that people originally oppressed by unreasonable conditions of worth were managing to reassert their true selves and become more fully functioning. Thus a young woman whose career choice is negatively greeted by parents and friends may be forced to reconsider her goals and values, eventually strengthening her career commitment, and ending up with a greater sense of self-reliance and self-worth.

Maslow's Self-Actualized Person

Like Carl Rogers, psychologist Abraham Maslow (1908–1970) began with the assumptions that people are free to shape their own lives and that their most important motivation is the desire to achieve self-actualization. A self-actualized person, as defined by Maslow, finds fulfillment in doing the best of which he or she is capable, not in competition with others, but in an effort to become "the best me I can be" (1971a, 1971b). Maslow criticized psychoanalysts and behaviorists for their pessimistic, negative, and limited conceptions of human beings. Where is the psychology, he asked, that takes account of gaiety, exuberance, love, and expressive art to the same extent that it deals with misery, conflict, shame, hostility, and habit (1966, 1968)? Accordingly, Maslow deliberately set out to create what he called a "third force" in psychology, one that would offer an appealing alternative to psychoanalysis and behaviorism.

One of Maslow's key concepts is what he called the **hierarchy of needs,** illustrated in Figure 13.4. Maslow believed that all humans face a series of needs in life, and that needs at more basic levels must be met before a person can go on to fulfill higher-level needs. At the bottom of Maslow's hierarchy are so-called **fundamental needs:** those associated with physical

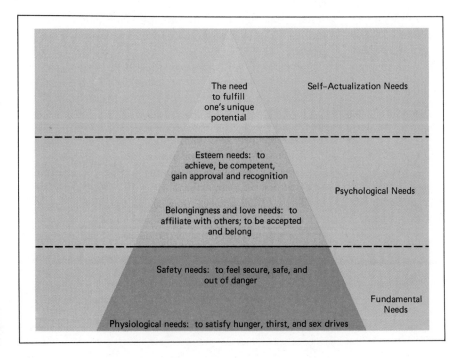

The need to fulfill one's unique potential — Self-Actualization Needs

Esteem needs: to achieve, be competent, gain approval and recognition

Belongingness and love needs: to affiliate with others; to be accepted and belong — Psychological Needs

Safety needs: to feel secure, safe, and out of danger

Physiological needs: to satisfy hunger, thirst, and sex drives — Fundamental Needs

Figure 13.4 This pyramid represents Maslow's hierarchy of needs. According to Maslow, fundamental needs must be satisfied before a person is free to progress to psychological needs, and these in turn must be satisfied before a person can turn to self-actualization needs. More recently, Maslow (1970) has added a need for transcendence—the experience of being able to see oneself in perspective—that is even higher than the need for self-actualization. *(After Maslow, 1971.)*

requirements, such as satisfying thirst and hunger, and those related to obtaining a safe and secure environment. Above these, Maslow identified a set of **psychological needs.** These include both the need to develop a sense of belonging and of being loved and the need to achieve competence, recognition, and high self-esteem. Finally, once all fundamental and psychological needs are met, a person can begin to fulfill the need for self-actualization—that is, the need to realize one's own unique potential. This includes not just excelling at one's lifework, but also devoting oneself to higher social goals, such as bringing about justice or stopping cruelty and exploitation. The self-actualized person, according to Maslow, does not seek fame and glory or the love and approval of everyone. Instead, he or she finds peace and contentment in the inner satisfaction that comes with being the best that one can be (Maslow, 1971a; Landsman, 1974).

Unlike Rogers, Maslow derived his theory of personality development largely from studies of healthy, creative, self-actualized people who made full use of their talents and capabilities. They included some historical figures—Abraham Lincoln, Henry David Thoreau, Ludwig van Beethoven, Eleanor Roosevelt, and Albert Einstein, for instance—as well as some of Maslow's own friends (Maslow, 1954). Their distinguishing personality traits are listed in Table 13.1. Maslow's critics point out that some self-actualized people do not seem to have scaled the hierarchy of needs in precisely the way Maslow predicted. Many writers and artists, for example, have created their masterpieces in spite of miserable childhoods, insecu-rity, social rejection, and poverty. To Maslow, however, these are the exceptions that prove just how strong the drive toward self-fulfillment is.

Evaluating Rogers and Maslow

Rogers and Maslow have been criticized, as we have already seen. Rogers' claims about the value of unconditional positive regard have been disputed. What's more, his enduring faith in the goodness of human nature has been described as overly optimistic, blind to the reality of the human potential for evil as well as for good (May, 1982). Maslow's list of self-actualized people has been called arbitrary and his hierarchy of needs too impressionistic. The ideas of both these theorists have been labeled vague and difficult to verify scientifically. Rogers, for example, has said that we cannot define what a fully functioning person is in hard and fast terms. Instead, we must always consider the particular individual. "Progress and maturity for one person," writes Rogers, "means developing sufficient autonomy to divorce himself from an unsuitable marriage partner; in another it means living more constructively with the partner he has. For one student it means working hard to obtain better grades; for another it means a lessened compulsiveness and a willingness to accept poorer grades" (Rogers, 1963, p. 9). Although we have an intuitive sense that this may in fact be true, such diversity makes Rogers' theory too slippery to prove or disprove.

Nevertheless, Rogers considered himself a scientist,

TABLE 13.1 CHARACTERISTICS OF SELF-ACTUALIZED PERSONS

They are realistically oriented.

They accept themselves, other people, and the natural world for what they are.

They have a great deal of spontaneity.

They are problem-centered rather than self-centered.

They have an air of detachment and a need for privacy.

They are autonomous and independent.

Their appreciation of people and things is fresh rather than stereotyped.

Most of them have had profound mystical or spiritual experiences, although not necessarily religious in character.

They identify with mankind.

Their intimate relationships with a few specially loved people tend to be profound and deeply emotional rather than superficial.

Their values and attitudes are democratic.

They do not confuse means with ends.

Their sense of humor is philosophical rather than hostile.

They have a great fund of creativeness.

They resist conformity to the culture.

They transcend the environment rather than just cope with it.

Source: Abraham Maslow, *Motivation and personality* (New York: Harper & Row, 1954).

and much of his behavior justifies this view. Rogers was the first clinical psychologist, for instance, to record all the communications that occurred in therapy sessions in order to make these data available for research and teaching purposes. Both the therapist's and the client's words and actions could then be classified and the effects of different types of exchanges systematically studied. Rogers himself conducted many such investigations (Rogers and Dymond, 1954). In fact, his very concept of the self, which lies at the heart of his theory, emerged from a thorough and quantitative analysis of the content of therapy interviews. In addition, Rogers' efforts prompted similar research by many other psychologists. Some, for instance, have specifically measured the degree to which warmth and empathy on the part of a therapist do in fact lead to positive outcomes for individuals, just as Rogers proposed (Truax et al., 1966). These scientific data-gathering methods stand in sharp contrast to the much more subjective techniques used by Sigmund Freud (Krasner, 1978).

However one evaluates the specific theories of Rogers and Maslow, there is little doubt that the basic questions they raised were important ones for the study of personality. Both theorists, for example, attacked the Freudian notion that adaptation to the demands of society is necessary for proper development. From the more humanistic viewpoint of Rogers and Maslow, excessive adaptation produces conforming, unimaginative, inhibited, and unfulfilled people. Although they recognized that some degree of adaptation is essential, Rogers and Maslow stressed the importance of transcending—going beyond—society's demands. Maturity, both believed, entails a certain willingness to defy social conventions and at times to take risks. And studies of creative people have in fact shown that their lives are often somewhat unconventional. A study that compared creative architects with randomly selected ones, for instance, found that the creative group socialized less, cared little for others' opinions, held unconventional beliefs, and had idiosyncratic work habits (MacKinnon, 1962, 1965). Thus total adaptation or "adjustment" to social conventions may not always be compatible with creative endeavors. Such humanists as Rogers and Maslow have done psychology a service by urging us to study such positive aspects of human potential.

Psychology also owes a debt to such people as Rogers and Maslow for bringing the concept of self back into the personality limelight. The concept of self was important to the early psychoanalysts, such as Freud, Jung, and Adler. But with the strong behaviorist reaction against the psychoanalytic perspective, and with the behaviorists' firm conviction that such concepts as the self were too vague and subjective to be scientifically explored, the notion of self fell out of favor during the 1920s and 1930s, especially in the United States, where behaviorism flourished. Then such thinkers as Rogers rescued the self from its many years of neglect. What we are like, Rogers argued, depends fundamentally on how we perceive the self. Since Rogers' initial writings, a great deal of empirical research has been conducted on the self. Because psychologists today see the concept as increasingly important, we have decided to examine it in depth. Space does not permit us to cover all aspects of this broad and complex subject. Consequently, we will limit our focus to the topic of self-esteem, the aspect of self that contemporary psychologists have studied more extensively than any other (Wylie, 1961, 1974; Rosenberg, 1979). This focus affords an excellent opportunity to observe the important interplay between personality theory and research.

in depth Studying Self-Esteem

Self-esteem can be defined as the general evaluation that a person makes about the self (Coopersmith, 1967). Do you see yourself as competent? Possessing many valuable traits? Worthy of others' respect? If so, you very likely have high self-esteem. Like other aspects of the self, self-esteem helps to integrate one's personality. Self-esteem provides a thread that runs through many thoughts and behaviors, weaving them together in a coherent whole. To see this more clearly, consider how one fourth-grade girl responded when asked to describe herself. The child's unedited statements are shown in Figure 13.5. She touches on many different feelings, thoughts, and actions. What is the unifying theme? Clearly, it is a tendency to view herself in very negative terms. This low level of self-esteem gives a sense of coherence to the girl's personality.

Psychologists from many different schools of thought consider a person's evaluation of the self vitally important. Carl Rogers, of course, is a prime example. Negative feelings about the self arising

I boss to much.	I fiddle around.
I get mad a my sisters.	I am careless at times.
I am a show off.	I forget.
I interupt to much.	Sometimes I don't do
I talk to much.	what mother tells
I wast time.	me to.
Sometimes I am a bad	I tattle on my sisters.
sport.	Sometimes I am unkind.

Figure 13.5 One child's answer to the question "Who am I?" Carl Rogers would say that the child's self-concept has been distorted by restrictive conditions of worth—conditions that make her impose unrealistic self-demands and that could hinder her from becoming an open, creative, fully functioning person. *(From Kuhn, 1960.)*

from others' unreasonable expectations is a major cause of psychological disturbance in Rogers' view. The crucial role of self-evaluations also appears in the social learning theory of Albert Bandura. As you may remember, Bandura has stressed the importance to people's behavior of a sense of self-efficacy—a feeling of being able to cope effectively with a given situation. Thus, regardless of the exact ways in which they express the idea, many psychologists believe that a person's view of the self has an enormous impact on both everyday behavior and psychological adjustment.

Since self-esteem is considered so important, many efforts have been made to measure it. One self-esteem scale is shown in Figure 13.6. Note that a person who scores high on this test should not be labeled arrogant or conceited. Instead, he or she simply possesses a strong sense of self-worth. In contrast, the person who scores low on this test tends to evaluate the self as generally unworthy, inadequate, and undeserving of respect (Rosenberg, 1979). And in most cases, these feelings are not just temporary. Studies suggest that a person's score on a self-esteem scale tends to be quite stable even over several years (Engel, 1959; Coopersmith, 1967).

One way to conceptualize what a self-esteem scale measures is in terms of the gap between what people *want* to be or think they *should* be and what they believe they actually are like. When the gap between the desired self and the perceived self is small, self-esteem is high. But when the gap between the desired

self and the perceived self is large, self-esteem is low. Carl Rogers used this measure of self-esteem to evaluate the effectiveness of his person-centered therapy. He found that during therapy the gap between a person's perceived self and idealized self narrowed quite significantly, as unrealistic conditions of worth were discarded. To Rogers and his followers this finding provided evidence that their approach to treatment was working.

Psychoanalyst Karen Horney (1945) also stressed the importance of achieving a close fit between the desired and the perceived selves. She believed that the child who develops "basic anxiety" because of indifferent or disparaging parents tries to establish a sense of security later in life by striving toward an image of the "perfect" self. The child strives to become so kind, so good, so generous that everyone

Figure 13.6 The New York State Self-Esteem Scale. Also known as the RSE (for Rosenberg Self-Esteem Scale, after its developer), this ten-item test measures an individual's sense of self-worth. Respondents are asked to indicate whether they strongly agree (SA), agree (A), disagree (D), or strongly disagree (SD) with each statement. Asterisks indicate low self-esteem responses. *(After Rosenberg, 1979, Appendix A.)*

1. On the whole, I am satisfied with myself.	SA A D* SD*
2. At times I think I am no good at all.	SA* A* D SD
3. I feel that I have a number of good qualities.	SA A D* SD*
4. I am able to do things as well as most other people.	SA A D* SD*
5. I feel I do not have much to be proud of.	SA* A* D SD
6. I certainly feel useless at times.	SA* A* D SD
7. I feel that I'm a person of worth, at least on an equal plane with others.	SA A D* SD*
8. I wish I could have more respect for myself.	SA* A* D SD
9. All in all, I am inclined to feel that I am a failure.	SA* A* D SD
10. I take a positive attitude toward myself.	SA A D* SD*

would have to love her. Or she strives to be so clever, so successful, so powerful that no one would dare to harm her. According to Horney, when such grossly idealized standards come to dominate a person's life, the person becomes driven to obtain the impossible and no amount of accomplishment will ever be enough. Such a person is also hypersensitive to criticism, for even the slightest negative appraisal will be seen as evidence that the real self is a pale copy of the great idealized model. Horney argued too that such a person is deeply vulnerable. Because the gap between the perceived and idealized selves is so enormous, low self-esteem is inevitable. Thus the person with low self-esteem in Horney's view is by definition anxious, depressed, and under tremendous strain.

Studies of people with low self-esteem tend to confirm Horney's basic view. Low self-esteem is generally related to anxiety, depression, vulnerability, and the tendency to seek psychiatric help (Rosenberg, 1965; Beck, 1967; Kaplan and Pokorny, 1969; Luck and Heiss, 1972). High self-esteem, in contrast, is often associated with good psychological adjustment—at least, up to a point. Some people who report *extremely* positive self-images tend to show signs of defensive denial regarding unfavorable traits (Block and Thomas, 1955). This finding is in keeping with the Freudian view that the defense mechanism of denial can become so powerful that a person is no longer able to see the self in terms even close to realistic. It is also in keeping with Rogers' theory that those who deny "unworthy" traits most vehemently are usually those who learned in childhood to view their true selves most negatively. Thus people whose self-opinions admit not the slightest flaw may in reality be those whose self-esteem is highly insecure.

Of course, not all of those with low self-esteem are troubled enough to seek out psychotherapy. Most manage to get on with the routine demands of life, even though they are often plagued by feelings of inadequacy. When situations require initiative, self-assurance, and persistence, however, the low-self-esteem person is often at a real disadvantage. Consider, for instance, a study of college students who were trying to find jobs (Ellis and Taylor, 1983). The researchers found that a student's level of self-esteem was *not* related to his or her grade point average or to other objective measures of ability. Yet level of self-esteem predicted quite well how many job offers that person would get in the four months before graduation. This link between level of self-esteem and suc-

cess in the job market seemed to be tied to a number of behavioral differences between low- and high-self-esteem people. For one thing, low-self-esteem students tended to rely on formal sources of job information, such as newspaper ads and employment agencies. These sources have been found to be generally less effective than those that require more personal initiative—following up a lead from a friend, for instance (Rosenfeld, 1975). Second, low-self-esteem students were less inclined to meet their own goals. Compared with high-self-esteem students, they ended up filing significantly fewer job applications than they had originally planned. Finally, low-self-esteem students had generally poorer social skills. This was revealed by the lower ratings they typically received in job interviews. All these factors together conspired to make the low-self-esteem students less successful job hunters.

Other studies have confirmed that people with low self-esteem often perform more poorly in a variety of situations than their high-self-esteem peers (Hamachek, 1971). Psychologists have wondered exactly why this happens. What is it about low self-esteem that causes people to act in self-defeating ways? One set of factors we touched on in Chapter 11. Low-self-esteem people tend to have low expectations regarding their own performance (Coopersmith, 1967; Kiesler and Baral, 1970). These low expectations often lead to lack of effort and persistence, which in turn, ironically, leads to a higher chance of failure (Diggory, Klein, and Cohen, 1964; Wattenberg and Clifford, 1964). And because these same people tend to attribute failure to lack of ability, they see their failures as "proof" that their low expectations are indeed deserved (Weiner et al., 1971).

A recent study has demonstrated clearly just how deeply ingrained these negative outlooks are (McFarlin and Blascovich, 1981). Female college students were assessed for their levels of self-esteem and were then given twenty analogy problems to solve. Some of the subjects were later told that they had done very poorly on these problems, while others were told that they had done very well. The experimenter then announced that a "spatial organization" test would be given the following week in order to complete his study. After briefly describing what this test entailed, he asked each subject to estimate her ability in regard to it and her future chances of success. Low-self-esteem subjects repeatedly downrated their own abilities and estimated that they would get relatively few of the problems right. This was true even of those who had just been told they had done very well on the analogies quiz. Low self-esteem, in short, seemed to overpower objective feedback, causing people to have chronically low expectations about themselves. These low expectations, in turn, could easily lead to lack of effort and hence to a high rate of failure.

Other factors may also be involved in this self-defeating cycle. Researchers have found, for instance, that people with low self-esteem are generally more self-conscious than other people (Turner et al., 1978). That is to say, they focus great attention on their own traits, thoughts, and actions, dwelling excessively on how others might evaluate these aspects of the self. It has been suggested that this higher level of self-consciousness may promote too much attention to one's own flaws, thus increasing anxiety and causing a drop in performance (Brockner and Hulton, 1978; Brockner, 1979a). Evidence in support of this theory comes from a study in which people previously assessed for their levels of self-esteem were asked to perform a complex cognitive task (Shrauger, 1972). Some of the subjects worked before an audience (a condition that raises self-consciousness), while others worked alone. Those with low self-esteem performed the task more poorly, *especially* when an audience was watching. Note that high self-consciousness (like low expectations) tends to be self-perpetuating. High self-consciousness leads to greater anxiety, which in turn leads to greater failure, which in turn provides additional reasons to disparage the self. This lowered self-regard then breeds more self-consciousness, and so on again and again.

Psychologists have offered several strategies for breaking such vicious circles. Joel Brockner has proposed, for instance, that if we can teach people with low self-esteem to focus their attention away from themselves and onto the task at hand, their performance may improve significantly. He has tested this approach in a series of experiments in which subjects were urged to give a task their undivided attention (Brockner and Hulton, 1978; Brockner, 1979b). Under this condition, those low in self-esteem often performed better than those whose self-esteem was high. The implication is that by training people low in self-esteem to direct their attention more productively, we may reduce their level of anxiety, allow them greater success, and slowly build their self-confidence.

Other approaches to breaking the link between low self-esteem and poor performance have likewise focused on changing the ways that victims of this pattern think. As we saw in Chapter 11, for instance, psychologist Carol Dweck (1975) has had success in raising self-perceptions of competence (and hence persistence at difficult tasks) by encouraging subjects to attribute their failures to lack of effort rather than to lack of ability. Social learning theorist Albert Bandura (1977b) has also stressed self-perceptions of competence in a therapeutic technique called participant modeling (to be discussed at length in Chapter 16). Bandura believes that by getting people who greatly fear a certain task to perform that task in small incremental steps, he can build in them a sense of self-efficacy which will help them to master the situation.

COMPARING APPROACHES TO PERSONALITY

Throughout this chapter we have discussed a range of personality theorists, often showing how the ideas of one either expanded or arose in reaction to the ideas of another. Now it is time to step back and take a broader look at personality theorizing. When we do, we can identify several important themes that tend to cut across theoretical viewpoints.

One such theme is *conflict,* first introduced to psychology by Sigmund Freud. To Freud, conflict was inherent in the human psyche. The best we could

hope for was an uneasy balance among competing forces. Although usually less pessimistic than Freud in their views on the inevitability and persistence of conflict, other psychoanalytic thinkers also incorporated the conflict theme in their work. In addition, Carl Rogers introduced a conflict theme when he argued that clashes between a person's true inclinations and the values of others can cause denial and distortion of reality.

A second recurring theme in personality research is

the importance of *external influences* on thought and behavior. You can see this theme in the work of the psychoanalytic thinkers Alfred Adler and Karen Horney, who stressed that early social environments have a crucial impact on our development. Carl Rogers also recognized the importance of social influences when he argued that a person's self-concept is partly shaped by the conditions of worth imposed by others. Radical behaviorism has taken the role of external forces even further, elevating them to a position of importance far above one's own thoughts, conflicts, and fears. In response, social learning theorists have tried to return the "person" to the behaviorist position by stressing our cognitive processing of external stimuli.

Continuity and consistency are a third theme we find in personality theories. They were certainly emphasized by Freud, who took the extreme view that personality is totally formed in the resolution of childhood conflicts and is thus very resistant to change in adulthood. The trait theorists also stress continuity and consistency—hence their efforts to identify and measure relatively enduring dispositions.

Finally, we come to the theme of *self-fulfillment*. It can be seen in the writings of Adler, who saw life as a kind of striving for self-perfection. But the fulfillment theme is most fully developed in the phenomenological approaches of Carl Rogers and Abraham Maslow. Here the striving to realize one's own potential becomes the overriding human motivation.

In summary, then, personality theorists often differ sharply in their views, sometimes engaging in heated debates over seemingly irreconcilable ideas. Yet a broader look shows that all seem to be touching in different ways on many of the same themes. Do these themes together begin to provide a unified picture of human behavior? To some extent, they do. Contemporary psychologists see human personality as an immensely complex subject, influenced by a host of factors, yet still susceptible to scientific study (Mischel, 1981). We are at once shaped by past experiences and responsive to new conditions, yet at the same time we have an enormous impact on the people and events around us. Sometimes we find ourselves driven by motivations that seem to arise from unconscious conflicts and needs. But we are also quite capable of creatively resolving those conflicts and of using our impressive cognitive powers to seek our own fulfillment.

SUMMARY

1. **Personality** consists of all the relatively stable and distinctive styles of thought, behavior, and emotional response that characterize a person's adaptations to surrounding circumstances.

2. The **psychoanalytic approach** to personality stresses the importance of childhood experience in shaping adult personality and focuses on the role of the unconscious in motivating human actions. Central to all psychoanalytic theories are the concepts of conflict between opposing motives, anxiety over unacceptable motives, and defense mechanisms to prevent anxiety from becoming too great.

3. Sigmund Freud was the founder of the psychoanalytic perspective. He originated the concept of the unconscious and considered it the motivating force behind all human behavior. Freud saw the human psyche as divided into three separate but interacting elements: the **id,** the **ego,** and the **superego.** The id, which is part of the unconscious, seeks only the satisfaction of bodily needs and is therefore said to operate on the **pleasure principle.** The ego, which serves as a mediator between the id and reality, is largely concerned with personal safety and thus is said to act according to the **reality principle.** The superego, which represents the moral standards of society, is equivalent to what we call "conscience."

4. When the demands of these three conflicting forces cannot be met, we experience **anxiety** and use **defense mechanisms** to try to reduce it. The most basic defense mechanism is **repression,** pushing unacceptable id impulses into the unconscious. Others are **denial, regression, reaction formation, projection, displacement,** and **sublimation.**

5. According to Freud, the child goes through five stages of psychosexual development—the **oral, anal, phallic, latency,** and **genital**—which are characterized by conflicts between the id and society. It is the resolution of these conflicts that presumably shapes

adult personality. A person who fails to resolve any one of these conflicts may become **fixated,** or locked in a psychological battle that is expressed symbolically throughout life.

6. Post-Freudian psychoanalysts have tended to give decreased importance to the id and increased importance to the ego, which they see as capable of creativity, planning, and the formation of self-fulfilling goals. They have also come to see personality development as less the result of conflicts over id impulses than the product of a child's relationships with significant others. Among the important psychoanalytic theorists besides Freud have been Carl Jung, Alfred Adler, and Karen Horney.

7. In contrast to the psychoanalytic perspective, the **behaviorist approach** to personality focuses on how rewards and punishments in the environment can, through learning, produce various responses in people. One such view is B. F. Skinner's **radical behaviorism.** It holds that internal thoughts and feelings are not essential to explaining human behavior.

8. In recent years learning theorists have begun to argue that our responses to external stimuli are greatly influenced by the way we cognitively interpret those stimuli. Moreover, **social learning theorists** stress that we learn not merely by repeated reinforcement, but also by observing the actions of people around us. Their research focuses heavily on such observational learning and its effects on personality.

9. Another approach to personality is called **trait theory.** A **trait** is any relatively enduring way in which one individual differs from another, and trait theorists focus on these various attributes to explain consistency in human behavior. Trait theorist Gordon Allport identified a hierarchy of three types of traits— **cardinal traits, central traits,** and **secondary traits**— according to which any given personality can presumably be defined. Trait theorist Hans Eysenck has used sophisticated statistical analyses to conclude that personality can be reduced to two major dimensions: neuroticism versus emotional stability and introversion versus extroversion.

10. In recent decades psychologists have been trying to determine just how much consistency there really is in human behavior. Walter Mischel has argued that our ability to predict future behavior on the basis of past behavior is almost negligible because people frequently modify their behavior according to the conditions of the moment. Other psychologists have answered that while no one is consistent in all areas of behavior, most people are relatively consistent in at least some areas. Many psychologists now agree that the constant interaction between traits and situations makes it very hard to identify one as more important than the other.

11. A final perspective on personality is offered by the **phenomenological approach,** which stresses the individual's unique perception of the world and a belief in human potential. Psychologist Carl Rogers has evolved a theory of the self according to which each person is engaged in a lifelong striving for **self-actualization.** Rogers found that many people were thwarted in this goal because, in order to receive approval from others, they had to deny their true selves and conform to those others' **conditions of worth.** Psychologist Abraham Maslow also saw self-actualization as an important human motive. But he proposed that one must fulfill a **hierarchy of needs** before reaching the goal of realizing one's own unique potential. Psychology owes a debt to such theorists as Rogers and Maslow for their renewed stress on the important concepts of the self and self-esteem.

12. While psychologists take many approaches to describing and explaining human personality, all have touched on at least some of the following four basic themes: conflict, external influences, continuity and consistency, and self-fulfillment.

SUGGESTED READINGS

FISHER, SEYMOUR, and GREENBERG, ROGER (Eds.). *The scientific evaluation of Freud's theories and therapy: A book of readings.* New York: Basic Books, 1978.

    A thorough overview of the research on Freud's theory of personality.

HALL, CALVIN, and LINDZEY, GARDNER. *Theories of personality.* 3rd ed. New York: Wiley, 1978.

    The classic secondary source, featuring a chapter on contemporary psychoanalytic theory and a chapter on Eastern psychology and personality theory.

HORNEY, KAREN. *Feminine psychology.* Harold Kelman, ed. New York: Norton, 1973.

A paperback edition of the classic discussion of the forces that influence the development and expression of personality in women.

MISCHEL, WALTER. *Introduction to personality.* 3rd ed. New York: Holt, Rinehart and Winston, 1981.

A survey of the research on a social learning approach to *aspects* of personality, such as frustration, aggression, and self-control.

NYE, R. D. *Three psychologies: Perspectives from Freud, Rogers, and Skinner.* 2d ed. Monterey, Calif.: Brooks/ Cole, 1981.

A very readable presentation of the major concepts in the work of these three prominent psychologists.

PERVIN, L. A. *Personality.* 4th ed. New York: Wiley, 1984.

An excellent overview of current developments in the field of personality, and a good discussion of the major personality theories.

14

ASSESSMENT AND INDIVIDUAL DIFFERENCES

Antoine Poncet, *Cororeol*, 1966.

Testing for Vocational Selection and Counseling

Interest Tests

Other Tests Used in Vocational Selection

The Ethics of Testing

In the spring of 1975 the mathematics department at Johns Hopkins University held a math contest for gifted eleventh-grade students in the Baltimore area. Math teachers in local high schools were invited to enter their most mathematically talented pupils. When educational psychologist Julian Stanley heard about the contest, he was tempted to try out a small experiment (Stanley, 1976). Stanley is the director of a program at Johns Hopkins for the study of mathematically gifted youth. He wanted to see if teenagers who showed exceptional math ability as measured by a standardized test would do better or worse in this math contest than students selected by their teachers. So Stanley received special permission to enter ten contestants of his own—all eleventh-graders who three years earlier had performed exceptionally well when given the math portion of a college entrance exam (the SAT). Only three of Stanley's ten choices had also been nominated by their teachers. In the eyes of school officials, therefore, Stanley's entrants were the dark horses. This is why the results of the contest were so surprising to many people. Three of Stanley's contestants came in first, second, and third, three more finished fifth, seventh, and eighth, and three were well within the top 40 percent. Thus high school teachers, even after months of personal interaction with students, were less capable of spotting exceptional math ability than a standardized test given three years earlier.

This incident is certainly striking. But before we conclude that standardized tests possess extraordinary assessment powers, let us reconsider the case more critically. The SAT did accurately identify those students who would do well in the university's math contest—but that "contest" was another test. Some critics would therefore argue that the talent the math SAT had spotted was simply the talent to take mathematics tests. Although most people would protest that something more than this must be involved, it has not always been easy to say what that "something more" is. Are those who do the best on written math exams necessarily those with the greatest talent for mathematical reasoning? Some people are not completely willing to say yes.

The accuracy with which such tests as the SAT measure what they claim to measure is of far more than academic interest. In our society a great deal often hinges on the results of standardized tests. We Americans are among the most extensively tested people in the world (National Academy of Sciences, 1982). Americans may take a dozen standardized tests before they graduate from high school. And if they want to go on to college, and later to professional schools, their scores on various entrance exams are an important factor in their acceptance. Even outside educational settings, testing pursues us. If one enters the military or the civil service, tests are required for job assignments and often for promotions. The same holds true in many large corporations: personnel offices across the country routinely select among applicants partly on the basis of test results.

Psychologists have stressed both the virtues of such testing and its inherent limitations. On the one hand, tests can tell us whether we have mastered a body of information. They can also help to diagnose a less than obvious problem—perhaps identifying a child who is so far ahead of the class that he or she daydreams constantly just to relieve the boredom. A proper test can help a teacher devise an instructional program to hold such a child's interest, or to give remedial help to others who are having trouble learning. Then, too, tests can help select people whose superior abilities warrant special rewards or consideration. On the other hand, so many criticisms have been raised against tests that they must be used with caution. Critics say, for instance, that many written tests place so much emphasis on language ability that it is hard for certain people to show what they really know. Tests have also been criticized for overlooking factors that are often important to success—such factors as creativity, motivation, and willingness to cooperate with others. Sometimes, too, people can be stigmatized by testing. They can come to be labeled "abnormal" or "retarded," and the label may stick with them for many years to come. Even the exceptionally bright may be unfairly judged by testing. Highly perceptive people can sometimes see ways of interpreting test questions that the test writers overlooked. As a result, their answers may be scored "incorrect" when in fact they are unusually insightful. Many of these pros and cons of testing will be explored in detail later in this chapter.

But first we begin with a look at what is involved in constructing and evaluating a good test. What characteristics, we ask, must a test have if it is to permit accurate measurement and be of practical value? We then turn to some of the specific tests in widespread use today, beginning with those that attempt to measure mental abilities. Chief among these are so-called intelligence tests—those that seek to assess a broad range of cognitive skills, reducing them to a single score (the intelligence quotient, or IQ). Here we also examine aptitude tests, designed to measure a person's potential for performing a certain task (the SAT, for example, is designed to assess a student's aptitude for college study). Of particular interest to us throughout these sections is why people's scores on such tests vary. What mix of genetic and environmental influences gives one person an IQ of 80 and another an IQ of 135? We then turn to tests intended to measure personality, discussing such topics as how the Rorschach inkblot test is scored and how written personality scales are developed. Next we consider tests used in vocational counseling and selection—those tests designed to steer people into jobs deemed appropriate for them. We conclude by discussing some of the ethical issues that surround the practice of testing.

CONSTRUCTING AND EVALUATING TESTS

Do you have a "PT" personality? To find out, take the brief PT profile test in Figure 14.1. Did you answer yes to most or even all of the questions? If so, you are far from alone. The overwhelming majority of people feel that this personality description fits them pretty well. The reason is simple. The test is composed entirely of what have been called "P. T. Barnum statements," after the famous circus impresario and astute judge of human nature. P. T. Barnum had a knack for presenting things in ways that would appeal to everyone, and this is just what our so-called personality test has done. Obviously, such a "test" cannot be considered a very good measure of

Figure 14.1 The PT profile test. Answer yes or no to each of the personality descriptions listed here. For an interpretation of test results, see the text. (After Price and Lynn, 1981, p. 125.)

1. I tend to be critical of myself and have a strong need to have other people like me.
2. Although I tend to be pretty well controlled on the outside, inside I frequently feel insecure.
3. At times my sexual adjustment has been a problem for me.
4. I like a certain amount of change in my life and become unhappy when I am hemmed in by restrictions and limitations.
5. Sometimes I feel sociable and extroverted, but at other times I feel very reserved and introverted.
6. Overall, I have some personality weaknesses, but I am generally able to compensate for them.

distinctive personality characteristics, for there is nothing distinctive about any of the traits listed. A good psychological test, in contrast, sets out to measure only those human traits or abilities in regard to which people are known to differ.

But the mere fact that a test attempts to measure genuine differences does not mean it will necessarily do so. Tests can be poor for a variety of reasons, as virtually every student knows. Psychologists use two major criteria to determine whether the tests they develop are adequate or deficient. These criteria are **reliability** and **validity.**

Reliability

A test is considered reliable if it consistently yields the same results. Our P. T. Barnum personality profile was certainly reliable, even though it did not measure anything of practical use. If you took this test over and over, you would probably answer the questions in much the same way each time. But not all tests share this characteristic. On some the scores that a person receives may fluctuate widely, from very high on one occasion to very low on another. This variation tells us that such a test is tapping more than just the relatively stable traits it is designed to measure. Instead, measurement of the target traits is being distorted by unwanted, variable influences (hence the fluctuations). Psychologists therefore say that the test is *unreliable.*

Various things about the way a test is written or conducted can promote unreliability. If test questions are ambiguous, for instance, respondents may be forced to guess, and guesswork increases the element of chance. The influence of chance may also be increased when care is not taken to standardize test settings. Suppose, for example, a team of researchers assesses the level of aggression in children by record-

ing their aggressive acts during a ninety-minute period. Some of the children are observed in their classrooms, others in extracurricular activities, still others at a local playground. Clearly, *where* each child happens to be assessed could greatly affect his or her opportunities for aggression. In such circumstances, the scores received will be unduly influenced by random variations in the setting and the test will be unreliable.

Unreliability can also be introduced when scoring methods are too vague. Suppose, for instance, our researchers assessing aggression are not given any criteria for deciding which behaviors are to be considered aggressive and *how* aggressive each one is. In these circumstances, the personal biases of different scorers will almost surely affect the results. Psychologists try to avoid such unwanted influences on scoring by making sure that two people trained in administering a particular test will independently make similar judgments about the same response. This is called **interjudge reliability.** In general, the more carefully defined the scoring criteria, the greater the chance that interjudge reliability will be high.

Researchers have developed several procedures for measuring reliability. One is called **test-retest:** a test is administered to the same people on more than one occasion, and if individual scores vary markedly, the test is deemed unreliable. Suppose, for example, that a group of boys is scored for aggression on one day, and then scored again the next. If individual ratings from one time to the other are only weakly correlated, we shall have to say that our method of assessment is low in reliability. Figure 14.2 diagrams the concepts of low and high test-retest reliability.

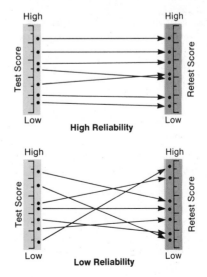

Figure 14.2 The concept of test reliability. On the left in each diagram the test scores obtained by seven individuals are ordered on a scale. On the right the corresponding scores on a second version of the same test, or on the same test given at a later time, are ordered. In the upper diagram the two sets of scores correspond very closely. This pattern of scores means that the test is highly reliable. In the lower diagram, there is little relationship between the two sets of scores. This scrambled pattern means that the test has low reliability: two different administrations of the same test got quite different results.

One problem with test-retest as a way of assessing reliability is that it is not always meaningful to administer a second test. Perhaps you are measuring something like emotion, which changes too rapidly. Or perhaps it is likely that your subjects will simply recall the answers they gave before. In such cases you can still judge reliability by using a procedure called **split halves.** The items that make up the test are randomly divided into two halves, and a subject's scores on both halves are compared. This measure of reliability is sometimes termed **internal consistency.** A test is internally consistent if a person responds the same way to items that presumably measure the same thing. If the math SAT were internally consistent, for instance, we would expect a person's total score on half the items to be similar to the total score he or she attains on the other half. But we would *not* expect a score on the math items to be highly similar to a score on the verbal items, for the two parts of the SAT are designed to measure different abilities.

Of course, few tests will ever be 100 percent reliable. People may perform differently on different occasions for any number of reasons. A person may feel alert one day and drowsy another, ill one week and healthy the next. These unwanted sources of variation are very hard to eliminate. A good test, however, will try to make sure that nothing about the test itself, how it is given, or how it is scored is contributing to individual inconsistencies in performance.

Validity

Test reliability assures us that we have established reasonably consistent measures—ones that will not be distorted by variable influences that are within our power to control. A very important aspect of test evaluation still remains, however. Are we sure our test is really measuring what we want it to measure? In other words, is the test valid?

To understand the concept of validity, imagine that a firm wants to test job applicants for typing ability,

but the personnel office has no spare typewriters available. So the interviewer draws up a diagram of a typewriter keyboard with a set of blank keys and asks each applicant to fill in the missing letters. It is assumed that those who do well on this test will also be the ones who can type. Is there anything wrong with this procedure? Clearly, there is. Since typing is something that people do automatically, an excellent typist may well be unable to reproduce a keyboard from memory. The correlation between scores on this test and actual typing performance may therefore be quite low. If it is, the test has been proved invalid. Figure 14.3 diagrams the concepts of high and low validity.

Because tests can differ so widely, researchers have developed a number of procedures to assess validity. One method (used in our typing example) considers what is called **criterion validity.** Criterion validity is important for tests that are trying to identify people who possess a specific trait or a specific kind of ability. The test validators determine the correlation between a person's score and some other yardstick of the factor that the test presumably measures. For example, a psychologist might validate a paper-and-pencil test of depression by comparing the scores obtained on that test with the judgments of trained clinicians. Or a researcher might validate a written test measuring aptitude for a particular job by comparing the scores of respondents with their actual job performance. The independent measure against which the test scores are compared is called the *criterion*—hence the term *criterion validity.*

Figure 14.3 The concept of test validity. A comparison of this figure with Figure 14.2 shows that reliability and validity are assessed in exactly the same way. The difference is that while assessment of reliability requires that a test be checked against itself, assessment of validity requires that the test scores be compared with some other measure of behavior.

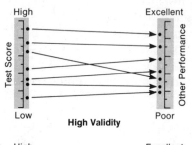

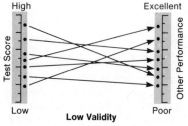

As the examples just given illustrate, two kinds of criteria may be used to validate a test: a criterion immediately available and a criterion measured in the future. If a test is validated by demonstrating a correlation with a criterion immediately available, it is said to have **concurrent validity.** A paper-and-pencil test of depression, for instance, would have concurrent validity if scores on the test correlated highly with the professional opinions of clinical psychologists who simultaneously observe the patients. But if other such criteria are available, why develop the test? One reason is that a short paper-and-pencil test is convenient and economical. If administrators in mental health facilities have such a test available, they can save hours of valuable staff time. Second, once a test has been validated, it can be used in settings where alternative criteria are *not* available. A researcher, for example, may want to study people who are depressed, but may lack the resources to have each prospective subject interviewed by one or more clinicians.

Sometimes, however, an investigator is interested less in whether test scores correlate with other currently available criteria than in whether the scores are related to people's *future* performance. What type of students are likely to be successful in a given college program? Which job applicants are likely to make an important contribution to the company? If test results can help to tell you, they are said to have **predictive validity.** It takes many years of research to demonstrate predictive validity. The developers of the SAT, for example, invested great time and effort to establish that test's predictive validity in regard to subsequent grades in college. Of course, when choosing a criterion such as this one, testers must be careful that it is truly meaningful. If, for instance, SAT scores predict grades in college but college grades show little relationship to subsequent success, people may justifiably complain that college administrators are placing too much stress on academic potential when they select among student applicants. As we will discuss later, just this criticism has in fact been raised against heavy reliance on the SAT by college admissions boards.

Standardization

Reliability and validity are characteristics that all good tests must have. But even if a particular test is both reliable and valid, it may still lack something needed to make it of practical use. That something is a set of standards by which to judge what individual scores mean. Suppose, for example, that a high school student receives a 600 on the math SAT. This fact alone is not very informative. To interpret it, we need to know the range of scores received by others and the percentage of test takers who earned scores at various levels.

Testers obtain these descriptive statistics—or **norms,** as they are called—through a process called **standardization.** Standardization is carried out before a test is put into general use. It involves giving the test under uniform conditions to a large group of people representative of those for whom that test is designed. This group is referred to as the **standardization group.** The mean, or arithmetic average, of the standardization group's scores then serves as a reference for interpreting other scores. Since it is important to make sure that the standardization group is representative of all those who will later be tested, many tests are developed with norms appropriate for people of different ages, races, and social classes.

THE MEASUREMENT OF MENTAL ABILITY

The most frequently used test of mental ability is the so-called intelligence test. Alfred Binet (1857–1911), a gifted and versatile French psychologist, was the first to develop a valid test of this type. Binet's research on the measurement of children's intelligence, the work for which he is best known today, came at the end of a career that included degrees in both law and medicine and the writing of plays, psychological treatises, and books on hypnotism, zoology, and chess (Miller, 1962). Binet's work is particularly significant because it departed so markedly from earlier methods of measuring intelligence. Before

Binet, some psychologists reasoned that because we come to learn everything we know by moving, sensing, and perceiving, people with high intelligence are likely to have very keen motor and sensory-perceptual skills. So they set about testing such things as people's ability to estimate the passage of time, the efficiency of their hand-eye coordination, and their speed at finger tapping, on the assumption that these attributes reflected intelligence. However, Binet was not sure that these skills differentiated between highly intelligent and less intelligent people. He felt that cognitive capacities, such as children's vocabulary, their recognition of familiar objects, their understanding of directions, and so forth, were likely to be important. To test his ideas, he and his assistants spent endless hours administering each test to a large number of schoolchildren. He found that cognitive tests worked better than tests of motor skills in differentiating students who were successful in the classroom from those who were not. Binet was also interested in determining which intellectual capacities change with age. He reasoned that if older children did better on these tests than younger ones did, then children whose performance surpassed that of others of their own age must be mentally older—more intelligent—than their agemates.

By the early twentieth century the French educational system had taken a turn that would put Binet's research to use. The Minister of Public Instruction for the Paris schools wanted to develop a test that could differentiate between normally intelligent children and those who required special help. In this way, all children would be given education suited to their abilities and needs. In collaboration with Théodore Simon, a psychiatrist, Binet introduced in 1905 the world's first standardized intelligence test, consisting of thirty items arranged in order of increasing difficulty.

Binet originally defined as retarded any child whose score was two or more years below the average score for all children of that age. One problem with this definition, however, was that children aged twelve who were two years behind their age group were considered just as retarded as children aged six who were two years behind their peers. The six-year-olds in this example would seem, intuitively, to be *more* retarded because the two-year disparity between them and their peers is a larger proportion of the children's total age. So a German psychologist, William Stern (1914), suggested that instead of using the absolute difference between mental age and chrono-

logical age, testers should use the *ratio* between these two ages. His idea resulted in the **intelligence quotient**, or **IQ.** It is computed by dividing a child's mental age (the average age of those who obtain this child's score) by the child's chronological age, and then multiplying by 100 to eliminate the decimal point. If, for example, a child has a mental age of twelve and a chronological age of ten, his or her IQ is $12/10 \times 100$, or 120.

Today many tests besides Binet's are used to measure mental abilities. Some require the examiner to give exclusive attention to one test taker at a time. Others are designed to be given to many people simultaneously. Some tests (like Binet's) are intended to measure general intelligence. Others (like the SAT) are intended to measure aptitudes for specific tasks. Still others assess achievement (what a person has learned in a particular subject area, such as calculus or American history). In the following sections we will explore examples of such tests, also examining some of the controversies that have arisen over their use.

Individual Intelligence Tests

Individual intelligence tests are given to only one subject at a time. As a result, the test taker can be given oral questions and performance tasks (in which objects must be manipulated) that would be hard to administer to a large number of people simultaneously. Two individual intelligence tests in wide use today are the current version of Binet's test and the intelligence scales developed by David Wechsler.

The Stanford-Binet Test. Binet's test of intelligence has been revised many times since he first developed it. The Stanford University revision was originally developed under the direction of Lewis Terman and is known as the **Stanford-Binet test** (Terman, 1916). The latest version of this test is widely used in the United States today. It contains a number of subtests—some of verbal ability and some of performance—that are grouped together by age level. The performance subtests include such activities as completing a drawing, reproducing a geometric pattern with colored blocks, arranging a set of pictures in a meaningful order, and assembling a designated object. The photographs opposite show two two-year-old-level tasks—one performance, one verbal—from the Stanford-Binet.

The examiner's goal is to find out the various age-

Two tests on the Stanford-Binet Intelligence Scale being administered to a little boy. Both are ones that he would easily pass unless he were severely retarded. (Top) The examiner has built a tower of four blocks and has told the child, "You make one like this." The average two-year-old is able to build the tower. Three-year-olds are asked to copy a three-block bridge. (Bottom) The examiner shows the child the card with six small objects attached to it and says, "See all these things? Show me the dog," and so on. The average two-year-old can point to the correct objects as they are named. *(Photos by John Oldenkamp with permission of the Houghton Mifflin Company, from Terman and Merrill* Stanford-Binet Intelligence Scale.*)*

level tasks that the subject can perform. The examiner begins by asking the subject some questions (often from the vocabulary test) in order to locate the proper level at which to start. When testing a nine-year-old who seems reasonably bright, for example, the examiner would probably begin with the tests for eight-year-olds, all of which most eight-year-olds can pass. If the child missed some of these questions, the examiner would then drop back to the tests for age seven. After locating the basal age—the highest age at which the child could pass all the items—the examiner would proceed with tests at older age levels. When the child reached the level at which he or she could pass no items, the testing session would end.

In the final scoring, the level of development a sub-

ject has reached is designated that person's mental age. If, for example, a child passes all the items at the twelve-year-old level but none of the items above it, he or she is said to have a mental age of twelve. If the child's chronological age is also twelve, that child's IQ is 100. If, however, the child's chronological age is lower (say, ten), his or her IQ is higher than 100 (in this case 120). If, on the other hand, chronological age is greater than twelve (say, fifteen), the subject's IQ is lower than 100 (in this case 80). Thus the Stanford-Binet IQ test provides an easy way of comparing one child's level of intellectual development with those of other children.

The original Binet tests were designed for school-age children, but successive revisions of the Stanford-Binet have extended the scales to both preschool and adult levels. The creation of the adult tests immediately presented a scoring problem: after early adolescence the pace of improvement on the test items slows, yet chronological age proceeds as always. Thus, if we applied the mental age ÷ chronological age formula to adult subjects, their IQs would inevitably decrease just by virtue of the fact that they were growing older. The solution to this problem fortunately was simple. Researchers assigned a score of 100 to the mean or average performance at any given age level. Then they used standard deviation as a yardstick for measuring just how much better or poorer than average a particular person did. Remember from Chapter 2 that the standard deviation indicates the average extent to which all the scores in a given distribution vary from the mean. In the case of such intelligence tests as the Stanford-Binet, the standard deviation is about 15. Consequently, a person who scores 1 standard deviation above the mean would receive an intelligence score of 115, someone who scores 1 standard deviation below the mean would receive an intelligence score of 85, and so on. Often these scores are still called IQs even though they are technically no longer "quotients." It is more accurate to think of them as "standard deviation from the mean" scores. Psychologists use the much shorter term *standard score.*

The Wechsler Scales. The other most frequently used individual intelligence tests are the **Wechsler scales.** They include the Wechsler Adult Intelligence Scale (WAIS); the Wechsler Intelligence Scale for Children (WISC), which is utilized with youngsters between the ages of six and sixteen; and the Wechsler Preschool and Primary Scale of Intelligence (WPPSI),

Figure 14.4 Items like these make up the performance subtests of the Wechsler Intelligence Scale for Children. In all of the tasks pictured here—picture arrangement, object assembly, and coding—speed and accuracy are of prime importance. It should be noted that maximum performance on these subtests does require familiarity with the general objects and situations depicted, and this familiarity is highly influenced by such factors as cultural, educational, and socioeconomic background. This, however, is true of the questions on most intelligence tests.

which is utilized with children aged four to six (Wechsler, 1949, 1955, 1967). Both the WAIS and the WISC have recently been revised and restandardized (1974, 1981).

Like the Stanford-Binet, the Wechsler scales are composed of verbal and performance sections, each with various subtests. In the "comprehension" subtest of the verbal section, for instance, a subject might be asked: "Why is it important to obey the stop signs on the street?" or "What makes an airplane fly?" In the "similarities" subtest, typical questions would be: "How are a ball and an apple alike?" and "In what way are a pencil and a typewriter similar?" Subtests in the performance section are likewise varied, as illustrated in Figure 14.4. The "picture arrangement" subtest requires that several pictures be arranged in an order that tells a story. The "picture completion" subtest asks the subject to identify the missing part in a drawing. The "object assembly" subtest requires the construction of a whole object from various pieces, much like putting together a jigsaw puzzle. And the "coding" subtest requires the subject to match digits with previously paired symbols.

The Wechsler tests differ from the Stanford-Binet in several ways. For one thing, the Wechsler tests have more performance tasks and are therefore less biased toward verbal skills. For another, the Wechsler tests do not have different items for different ages within any one of the three scales. Items on the WPPSI, for

instance, are the same for all the four- to six-year-olds who take it. Finally, the Stanford-Binet yields a single IQ score, whereas the Wechsler scales give separate scores for the various subtests, which are then combined into separate IQs for verbal and performance abilities. The scoring procedure for the WISC is summarized in Figure 14.5. This method of scoring treats intelligence as composed of several different abilities.

Group Tests

Most group tests are paper-and-pencil measures. There is no person-to-person interaction, as with individual tests. Thus group tests greatly simplify the role of the test administrator. The convenience and economy of group tests have led to their use in schools, employment offices, and many other mass testing situations. One of the primary purposes of group tests is to screen or classify large numbers of people. The Army Alpha and Army Beta tests, for example, were developed and used during World War I to classify American soldiers.

Despite their economy, group tests have disadvantages. It is difficult for the examiner to put the subjects at ease and to maintain their interest in the test. The examiner is also unlikely to detect illness, fatigue, anxiety, or other variable factors that may hinder test performance. As a result, most experts suggest that when important decisions about people are to be made, scores on group tests should be supplemented by individual testing or by information about personal abilities obtained from other sources (Anastasi, 1976).

This advice is generally heeded in regard to the group test that almost every college student has taken: the **Scholastic Aptitude Test,** or **SAT,** which measures some of the same abilities often included on IQ tests. Studies show that SAT scores are only one among several pieces of information that college admissions staffs consider, some of the others being high school grades, letters of recommendation, and personal interviews. One recent survey, in fact, found that only 2 percent of all colleges labeled aptitude scores the most important factor (Hargadon, 1981). But this has not prevented critics from attacking the SAT. What is it about this test that some observers find so objectionable?

One of the harshest recent attacks was launched by Allan Nairn and his associates (1980) in cooperation with Ralph Nader's consumer advocacy group. Nairn disparaged the validity of the SAT as a predictor of success in college. He maintained that for the vast majority of people, SAT scores do no better at predicting future grade point average than would a mere roll of the dice. Nairn also charged that the SAT discriminates against minorities. Success on this test, he argued, is more a product of an upper-middle-class background than a reflection of scholastic aptitude. Thus the SAT, in Nairn's view, is a class barrier that helps to channel white, upper-income youth into America's most prestigious colleges. The Nairn report therefore recommended that the current SAT be abandoned and that college boards of admission rely primarily on high school records, the single best predictor of performance in college.

Observers knowledgeable about statistics and the SAT say that Nairn's highly negative conclusions arise from serious misinterpretations of the available data (Kaplan, 1982; Linn, 1982). The relationship between SAT verbal and math scores and freshman grade point average yields a correlation coefficient in the range of .40—far from insignificant. Moreover, there is little convincing evidence that the SAT is unfairly biased against minorities. The predictive validity of the test has been shown to be quite consistent across income and ethnic groups (Linn, 1982). Historical data also suggest that use of the SAT may actually have *raised* the proportion of low-income students entering selective colleges (ETS, 1980; Kaplan, 1982). This is because the SAT gives those who attend academically inferior high schools the chance to demonstrate superior aptitude in comparison with *all* college applicants.

There are two other reasons why use of the SAT may be fairer than its elimination. First, when high school grades and SAT scores are used *together* to predict college performance, their combined power surpasses that of either yardstick alone (Linn, 1982; Kaplan, 1982). When you think about it, this makes a great deal of sense. Two methods of measurement—neither of which is 100 percent accurate—are bound to produce more accurate judgments than one of them alone. Second, the SAT provides a way of demonstrating the scholastic potential of people who believe that their high school grades are for some reason misleadingly low. If the college entrance exams

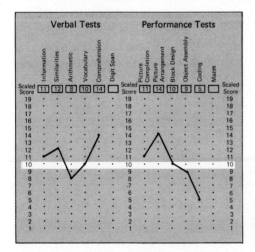

Figure 14.5 A simplified version of a WISC profile of a 13-year-old boy. (The optional digit span and mazes subscales were not administered.) Scores on the subscales within the verbal and performance groupings are first converted into special scaled scores and plotted accordingly on the chart. Then individual subtest scores are added together, yielding a total verbal and a total performance score. In turn, these scores are summed to reflect the full-scale score. Finally, the full-scale score is converted into the full-scale IQ score—in this case 103, or about average. The separability of scores on the subscales is sometimes useful in determining specific talents or deficits that might not have been apparent if only the overall IQ scores were reported. *(Adapted from WISC-R record form, © 1971, 1974, The Psychological Corporation.)*

	Scaled Score	IQ
Verbal Score	55	106
Performance Score	49	98
Full Scale Score	104	103

were abandoned, these applicants would lose an important second chance to prove themselves.

In recent years the development of private "coaching" services to raise SAT scores has added further controversy to this already hotly debated topic. Some people have reasoned that if coaching can improve results on the SAT, the test must be invalid, for this exam is supposed to measure a person's "innate" intelligence. This view reflects a total misunderstanding of what the SAT actually gauges. The SAT does not measure a "fixed" intellectual capacity, but rather skills in verbal comprehension and mathematical reasoning that develop gradually over many years of learning (Messick, 1980). These abilities *can* be improved by deliberate instruction. But it is very unlikely that the short-term coaching currently being offered can make a great deal of difference. Such efforts are simply too limited and brief. And studies confirm this suspicion. It has been estimated, for instance, that an increase in one's SAT score of just 30 points (about three more correct answers) would require 45 hours of coaching for the math section and 260 hours of coaching for the verbal (Messick and Jungeblut, 1981). Thus there is good reason to doubt that the average coaching service is having much of an impact on SAT results (Kulik, Bangert-Drowns, and Kulik, 1984).

Variations in Intelligence

When IQ tests are given to large numbers of people, the scores form close to "normal" distributions. That is, when plotted on a line graph, they produce the characteristic bell-shaped curve we talked about in Chapter 2. Such a curve is shown in Figure 14.6. As you can see, about 68 percent of all scores fall somewhere between the mean (100) and one standard deviation (15 points) to either side of it. This range of scores—85 to 115—is generally considered the "normal" range. If we move one more standard deviation to either side of the mean, we encompass all the scores between 70 and 130. More than 95 percent of a large population will fall within this range. Those who score between 70 and 85 are often considered "low normal," while those scoring between 115 and 130 are often classified "high normal." Beyond these scores is a small number of people of exceptionally low or exceptionally high intelligence. This tiny fraction of the population—just a little over 2 percent on either side of the mean—is the subject we turn to next.

The Mentally Retarded. A person whose general intelligence has from childhood been significantly below average and who chronically has trouble functioning in normal everyday settings is usually classified **mentally retarded** (Grossman, 1977). Traditionally, different levels of retardation have been associated with particular ranges of scores on standardized IQ tests. A score between 67 and 52 on the Stanford-Binet test, for example, has been said to indicate "mild" retardation, a score between 51 and 36 "moderate" retardation, and a score between 35 and 20 "severe" retardation. If the score is below 20, retardation is labeled "profound." These IQ ranges, however, should not be viewed as clear-cut categories. A person's ability to function in everyday life must also be considered. Thus children whose test scores suggest moderate retardation but who show evidence of adaptive skills (the abilities to communicate, interact socially, feed, clean, and dress themselves, for in-

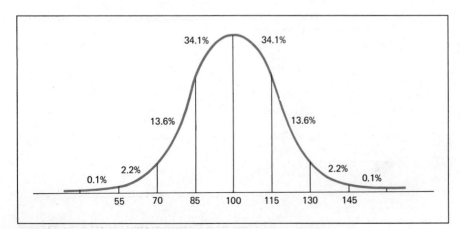

Figure 14.6 The normal distribution of IQ scores.

TABLE 14.1 CHARACTERISTICS OF MENTALLY RETARDED CHILDREN

AREA OF FUNCTIONING	MILD	MODERATE	SEVERE AND PROFOUND
Self-help skills	Feeds and dresses self and cares for own toilet needs.	Has difficulties and requires training but can learn adequate self-help skills.	No skills to partial, but some can care for personal needs on a limited basis.
Speech and communication	Receptive and expressive language are adequate. Understands communication.	Receptive and expressive language are adequate. Has speech problems.	Receptive language is limited to good. Expressive language is limited to poor.
Academics	Optimal learning environment—third to sixth grade.	Very few academic skills. First or second grade is maximal.	No academic skills.
Social skills	Has friends, can learn to adjust adequately.	Capable of friends but has difficulties in many social situations.	Not capable of having "real" friends. No social interaction.
Vocational adjustment	Can hold a job. Competitive to semi-competitive. Primarily unskilled work.	Sheltered work environment. Usually needs constant supervision.	No employment for the most part. May be in an activity center. Usually needs constant care.
Adult living	Usually marries, has children. Needs help during stress.	Usually does not marry or have children. Dependent.	Always dependent on others. No marriage or children.

From Van Osdol and Shane, 1977, p. 68.

stance) would more appropriately be classified as mildly retarded. The areas of functioning used to classify the retarded are shown in Table 14.1.

About 6 million people in the United States are mentally retarded (Gearheart, 1980). The causes of their retardation vary. They include such physical factors as chromosomal defects, metabolic disorders, and brain damage suffered at birth, as well as various kinds of environmental deprivation. Through a procedure known as amniocentesis, some forms of mental retardation can be predicted even before birth. During amniocentesis, a small amount of the fluid that surrounds the unborn fetus is withdrawn by means of a needle and carefully analyzed. This analysis can reveal a number of developmental abnormalities, including Down's syndrome (formerly called "mongolism"), which is caused by a chromosomal defect. In other cases, a child's retardation is detected at birth or shortly thereafter, when it becomes clear that the baby is not developing at the same rate as peers. Sometimes, however, despite slow development, a retarded child is not diagnosed until he or she enters school.

The stigma of being labeled "retarded" as children

enter school has led educators to plead for greater care in evaluating those youngsters who appear to have below-normal intelligence. In the past, children from non-English-speaking families, emotionally disturbed children, and children with hearing and vision problems were sometimes mistakenly classified as retarded on the basis of a single intelligence test that was poorly chosen and administered. Federal law now prohibits school officials from assigning children to special classes for the mentally retarded on the basis of an IQ score alone. Before such assignments are recommended, children must now be tested for normal hearing, vision, and general health. Each child's linguistic and cultural background must also be considered, as well as his or her ability to function in everyday surroundings. Only if the child exhibits both a low IQ and deficiencies in everyday adaptation, and only if these findings cannot be explained by linguistic or cultural barriers, physical handicaps, emotional problems, or ill health, can the child be classified as retarded.

The Mentally Gifted. In our culture the concept of genius has long been associated with negative stereo-

This newspaper portrait of child prodigy William James Sidis was made in 1911, when he was a 14-year-old senior at Harvard University. After graduating, Sidis dropped out of public view and began to drift from job to job. His main interest seemed to be his collection of streetcar transfers from around the world. Sidis' "burnout" has often been cited as evidence that most geniuses are misfits; but recent research indicates that most gifted children are well-adjusted individuals who can benefit from academic acceleration. *(Culver Pictures.)*

types. The brilliant person is expected to be eccentric, high-strung, and socially awkward, frail in physical appearance, and prone to poor health. In short, the genius is often seen as a bit of a misfit—someone who has trouble coping in the world beyond test tubes and books. As evidence, people sometimes cite the tragic case of William James Sidis, a remarkable young genius in the early part of this century.

Sidis was one of the most astonishing child prodigies ever to come to public attention (Montour, 1977). Born in 1898 in New York City to self-made Russian immigrant parents, he was reading at the age of two. To amuse himself young William, barely a toddler, would spell out the names of professional books in the library of his father, a prominent medical psychologist. By age five he could read four languages (English, Russian, French, and German), and at age six he knew enough about human anatomy to pass a medical student's exam. Required by law to enter grammar school, he astounded teachers by whizzing

through all seven grades in just six months. At age eleven he was admitted to Harvard, where he immediately made headlines by delivering a lecture on some of his original theories to the Harvard Mathematical Club. After he graduated from Harvard, however, problems of adjustment became apparent. Sidis dropped out of graduate school, failed at a teaching post, and spent the rest of his life in obscurity, working at low-paying clerical jobs. When he died at the age of 46, he was living alone in a rooming house, unemployed and penniless.

Is William Sidis' tragic decline typical of geniuses? In 1921 Lewis Terman, at Stanford University, launched a study of approximately 1,500 extremely gifted children which was intended to find out (Terman, 1916). All of Terman's subjects, who ranged in age from three to nineteen at the start of this research, had IQs above 135. Over the years, Terman followed the development of each subject to see how he or she fared. His findings disproved most of the common myths about unusually intelligent children (Terman and Oden, 1947; Oden, 1968). Not only were these gifted children generally superior to their peers in health, adjustment, and achievement, but their relative superiority continued as they moved through adulthood. Terman's subjects far exceeded persons with average IQs in educational attainment, occupational level, and income. In addition, their adult health and emotional adjustment were also well above average. As a group, they suffered fewer divorces, fewer cases of alcoholism and trouble with the law, and even fewer premature deaths than people with lower IQs.

Some have seized on Terman's findings as evidence that high intelligence tends to be a key to personal success and happiness. Arthur Jensen (1972) has argued that Terman's data show beyond a doubt that IQ tests are measuring something of great importance in our society. Others, however, have disputed Jensen's conclusion. It has been pointed out, for instance, that most of Terman's subjects were originally nominated by their teachers for inclusion in the study. As a result, we have no way of knowing whether high-IQ children overlooked by their teachers turned out to be equally successful. Certainly such reliance on teachers' recommendations could easily have produced a bias in favor of bright children who were especially well adjusted, socially skilled, and motivated.

David McClelland has also stressed that "Terman's studies do *not* demonstrate unequivocally that it is the kind of ability measured by intelligence tests that is responsible for . . . the greater success of the high-IQ children" (1973, p. 5). He bases this view primarily on the fact that Terman's sample of subjects was not representative of the population as a whole, but instead consisted heavily of middle- and upper-middle-class whites. Thus Terman's results may simply show that the privileged in our society have more opportunities than others and therefore do better in life. Lending some support to this interpretation is the finding that the 100 "most successful" men in Terman's sample (as measured by job status and income) were more likely to have had a professional father with a college education than were the 100 "least successful" men. In addition, the most successful tended to come from more intellectually stimulating home environments and more stable families that stressed initiative and achievement. All this suggests that high IQ is not the only factor contributing to the tendency to excel.

What, then, happened to William Sidis? He came from a middle-class professional family and his intellect was certainly "stimulated." In fact, William's father subjected him to a constant program of learning beginning in infancy. This was probably part of the problem. William's father exploited his son's intellectual abilities, seeing to it that the boy was often in the public limelight. At the same time, neither parent was warm or nurturing toward William, leaving him with few emotional resources to cope with his early fame. Thus it was not academic acceleration that thwarted Sidis' potential, but rather a combination of exploitation and emotional neglect (Montour, 1977).

Recently psychologist Julian Stanley has demonstrated that academic acceleration for gifted children is not only *not* harmful, it may even be beneficial, as long as the child's other needs are taken into account. Stanley, as you may remember from the beginning of this chapter, is the director of a program at Johns Hopkins University for the study of mathematically gifted youth. Over the last decade he has established various classes to teach mathematics to highly talented children at an extremely fast pace (Stanley, 1983). The results have been extraordinary. Consider, for instance, the first eleven youngsters to complete Stanley's precalculus program (which whisks twelve-year-olds from introductory algebra through analytic geometry in about a hundred hours of instruction). Ten of the eleven graduated from college one to five years before their peers, even though upon entering Stanley's program not one was above normal grade level. The most accelerated of these students entered the program in the sixth grade, subsequently skipped the seventh, also skipped the ninth, tenth, and twelfth grades, and enrolled in Johns Hopkins at the age of fifteen. He graduated just five semesters later, shortly after his seventeenth birthday, and by age 21 he was an assistant professor at a major university. Stanley admits that much more needs to be known about the long-term social and emotional consequences of such rapidly accelerated learning. But his preliminary findings seem to discredit the common belief that talented children who are allowed to progress a great deal faster than their agemates will almost always be harmed. The difficulty of adjusting appears to vary greatly with the child and the circumstances. For some brilliant youngsters, rapid acceleration offers a very desirable salvation from years of academic boredom.

Interestingly, Stanley's recent work also demonstrates something that Terman's research long ago suggested: impressive intellectual development doesn't just happen to people; it must be properly encouraged. But such encouragement is not always easy to come by. Often there are forces that work against intellectual achievement. For instance, a child may lack a home environment where academic learning is valued. Or a youngster may find that a reputation as a "brain" brings ridicule and rejection from peers. In recent years educators have become increasingly concerned about providing programs for gifted children that not only challenge their abilities but also give them pride in their unusual accomplishments (Rice, 1980). Gifted elementary school children are now being offered enrichment classes in such subjects as chemistry, astronomy, and computers. Talented junior high schoolers are tackling college-level courses in calculus and physics. Gifted high school students are participating in internship programs at local law offices and television stations. Such efforts help these youngsters fulfill their potential and maximize their future contributions to the world in which they live.

The challenge for psychologists who specialize in assessment is to find ways of identifying gifted children in the first place. Laws that provide funding for special programs for the gifted usually define these youngsters as children who because of their outstanding abilities are capable of exceptionally high performance. "High performance" may relate to *general* intellectual ability. But it may also be confined to a particular academic area (science or math, for instance), be related to creativity or leadership potential, or apply to the visual or performing arts. In short, educators have tried to broaden their definition of giftedness in order to make sure that no important intellectual resource is inadvertently neglected.

At the same time that educators have broadened their definition of giftedness, they have broadened their procedures for identifying gifted youngsters. The current trend is away from sole reliance on group intelligence test scores (Fox, 1981). Many gifted children will inevitably be overlooked when officials do their initial screening simply by setting a cutoff score of, say, 130 on some group test. One reason is that no group test is 100 percent valid. Another is that IQ tests in general often fail to spot those children who are highly talented in one specific area. IQ tests alone may also neglect creativity as a special type of giftedness. Paul Torrance, a leader in creativity research, stresses that children who score only moderately high on group intelligence tests may nevertheless score *very* high on tests of creativity and so be capable of some very impressive accomplishments (Torrance, 1965, 1977). Finally, group intelligence tests are often criticized for being biased against minority-group children whose cultural backgrounds differ from those of their white, middle-class peers.

The procedures currently used for identifying gifted children in the Flint, Michigan, school system provide just one example of how all these various factors can be taken into account (Fox, 1981). A child will be considered for special programs for the gifted if he or she meets any one of the following criteria: (1) scoring two or more years above grade level on either the math or the verbal section of a standardized achievement test; (2) scoring at or above the 90th percentile for the child's age level on a questionnaire about behavioral indications of giftedness filled out by parents; and (3) being nominated by a teacher as likely to be gifted in creativity, leadership, general intellectual ability, learning potential, motivation, or specific academic achievement. Encouragingly, these broad initial screening procedures have led to the discovery of an increased number of gifted children among black and other minority-group students (Lewis, 1980).

in depth | Explaining Differences in IQ

All the evidence we have discussed so far suggests that general intelligence (as measured by IQ tests) is not a fixed capacity, as some people mistakenly believe. One's level of intellectual development, or of any other quality, is always the product of genetically inherited potential (nature) in interaction with environmental circumstances and learning (nurture). Researchers often describe the genetic side of this equation as a person's *reaction range* in order to stress that what we inherit at birth is merely a range of developmental possibilities, any of which can be fulfilled or thwarted depending on our experiences. The reaction range related to intellectual development is usually quite broad. Provided a person is not subjected to severe deprivation in childhood (which would make almost anyone retarded), that person inherits the potential for an IQ that can vary by as much as 20 to 25 points, depending on environment (Scarr-Salapatek, 1971a; Cronbach, 1975).

But which of these two factors is *more* important— heredity or environment? When we look at the development of any one person, it is virtually impossible to say. Human development is always the product of heredity and environment in interaction; trying to pry the two apart is seldom very productive. What, then, are psychologists arguing about when they endlessly debate nature versus nurture? The answer is that they are debating the relative contributions of these two factors to human *differences*. Why did Jane score higher than Amy on the Stanford-Binet test? Is the difference in their scores due largely to genetic differences between them or to differences in their environments? This is a question to which we *can* hazard an answer if we know how similar the two girls are genetically and how alike or different their respective environments are. If Jane and Amy are identical twins raised apart in very different settings, we have reason to believe that the IQ difference between them is 100 percent attributable to environment (after all, they have identical genes). If, however, the two girls are adoptive sisters (sharing no genes) who have been raised from birth in the *same* home, we will suspect that their IQ difference may be partly genetic in origin.

Psychologists use much the same logic to estimate the causes of differences observed in large groups of people. Obviously, the more similar the environments of the group of people being studied, the higher the genetic contribution to whatever variations are found. This is why, when the American white middle class exclusively is considered, the genetic contribution to IQ differences (or *heritability factor,* as it is called) has been estimated to be as high as 60 to 80 percent (Scarr-Salapatek, 1971b).

JENSEN RENEWS THE RACIAL DEBATE.

It was just such statistics that prompted educational psychologist Arthur Jensen to renew a long-standing controversy with explosive implications. The year was 1969. Jensen was asked to write an article for the *Harvard Educational Review* on why many of our compensatory education programs for minority groups had so far produced disappointing results. In his article Jensen reviewed the data indicating that, among whites, individual differences in IQ can be heavily attributed to heredity. To a large extent he focused on studies conducted by a famous English psychologist, Sir Cyril Burt (1966, 1972). Partly on the basis of analyses of IQ differences found in identical and fraternal twins raised under varying circumstances, Burt had estimated the heritability factor for the white English population to be extremely high. Jensen reasoned that if individual IQ differences *within* white populations can be traced largely to heredity, then perhaps average IQ differences *between* whites and other races are also largely genetic in origin. Jensen pointed in particular to the well-known statistic that black Americans on average score 11 to 15 points lower on IQ tests than white Americans do. "It seems a not unreasonable hypothesis," Jensen concluded, "that genetic factors are strongly implicated in the average Negro-white intelligence difference" (Jensen, 1969, p. 82).

REACTIONS AND IMPLICATIONS.

The ink was barely dry on Jensen's article before the news media began to report highly simplified and sometimes inaccurate versions of it. A piece in *Newsweek,*

for instance, titled "Born Dumb?" summed up Jensen's theory as the belief that black intelligence is fixed at birth at a level far below that of whites—with the implication that no amount of compensatory schooling would ever make any difference (March 31, 1969). Although the vagueness of some of Jensen's claims left them open to such interpretations, Jensen had actually never made any such statement. Nearly every popular article on him drew this conclusion, however (Cronbach, 1975). Given the national political climate of the late 1960s, it was inevitable that Jensen would be widely attacked as a racist seeking to promote the idea of black genetic inferiority.

At the same time, some conservative policy makers in the newly elected Nixon administration welcomed Jensen's ideas (Blum, 1978). If black-white IQ differences were genetic, they reasoned, it made sense to dismantle compensatory programs aimed at helping largely black, disadvantaged children catch up to their more privileged peers. At one point, William Shockley, an extreme Jensen sympathizer, proposed a program of voluntary sterilization for those who are "born dumb"—at least those who also happen to be poor. Under his plan, which he detailed in a speech to the American Psychological Association, the government would pay welfare recipients with IQs under 100 $1,000 for every point below the mean if they would undergo sterilization (Chorover, 1979).

THE BURT DATA: FURTHER CONTROVERSY.

As if Jensen's article had not stirred up enough controversy, in 1976 a related furor erupted. Investigators charged that some of the data on which Jensen's original conclusions had been based were at best questionable and possibly fraudulent. An American psychologist, Leon Kamin (1974, 1976), and a reporter for the London *Sunday Times,* Oliver Gillie, carefully examined Sir Cyril Burt's data and discovered peculiarities in some of the figures. For one thing, identical correlations between twins' IQs kept showing up—the same to three decimal places—despite variations in the number of twins studied. The odds against this happening even once are many millions to one. Yet in twenty different places in Burt's data correlations remained the same while the size of the samples changed (Gillie, 1977). Further doubts were raised by the fact that it was impossible to locate two of Burt's alleged collaborators, Margaret Howard and Jane Conway. Gillie's search turned up no records of them. This is significant, for Burt claimed that these women were responsible for collecting many of the raw data used in his analyses. They were also listed as the authors of several articles praising Burt's research which were published in the journal Burt himself edited.

In response to these criticisms and allegations, Arthur Jensen quickly came to the late Sir Cyril's defense (Jensen, 1977). He argued that the errors detected in Burt's work were rather trivial and did not substantially change the basic thrust of his findings. What's more, Jensen reasoned that "even if all of Burt's findings were thrown out entirely, the picture regarding the heritability of IQ would not be materially changed" (p. 492). Other studies, conducted by independent psychologists, overwhelmingly supported Burt's basic view, Jensen asserted (Jensen, 1981).

GROWING OPPOSITION TO JENSEN.

Even before the Burt research was called into question, Jensen's critics had amassed powerful arguments against him. They very correctly stressed that Jensen had made an unwarranted leap in logic when he suggested that heritability factors within groups might provide some clues to the causes of variation between groups. In actual fact, the causes of differences *within* groups tell us nothing whatever about the causes of differences *between* groups. To understand why, consider a very simple example. Suppose you had two groups of 100 seeds, group *A* and group *B*, the individual seeds in each group being equally diverse genetically. You plant group *A* seeds in fertile soil, with plenty of sunlight and water, and group *B* seeds in poor soil, giving them little light or moisture. Six months later you measure the heights of all of your resulting plants. To what should you attribute any differences among them? Since all the plants within each group were exposed to exactly the same conditions, you would be tempted to attribute any within-group differences almost entirely to heredity. But what about the differences between the two groups? Should these also be attributed largely to heredity? Obviously not. Despite high heritability factors within groups, the differences between groups could quite plausibly be explained by the significant contrasts in their environments.

Critics of Jensen go on to point out that blacks and whites in this country likewise experience significant differences in their environments. At the most obvious level, a far higher proportion of blacks than whites live in conditions of poverty. As a result, they receive poorer prenatal care, poorer nutrition, inferior medical services, and so forth, all of which can significantly hinder development (Lederberg, 1969). In answer, Jensen has tried to argue that even when socioeconomic class is equated, blacks still score below whites on IQ tests. But in reasoning this way he is greatly underestimating the range of environmental factors that can affect test performance. Simply matching people for income level across the races does *not* make the environments of whites and blacks comparable. As N. J. Block and Gerald Dworkin have argued in their book *The IQ Controversy*, "Between United States blacks and whites there are systematic cultural differences and differences in psychological environment, both of which influence the development of cognitive skills in complex ways over long periods of time" (1976, p. 202). By this they mean that blacks in our society are systematically exposed to levels of prejudice and discrimination that even the poorest whites never experience. They also mean that black children, on average, are less exposed to the skills and knowledge required on a typical IQ test than white children are. This inherent white middle-class bias of most IQ tests is a topic we will return to later. The important point here is that when all environmental differences between white and black Americans are taken into account, they provide a powerful alternative to Jensen's genetic explanation of racial differences in IQ.

Psychologist Sandra Scarr and her colleagues have gathered interesting evidence that an environmental explanation of racial IQ differences is indeed much more likely than a genetic one (Scarr, 1979). In one study, for instance, Scarr and her associates found that the degree of white ancestry in people socially classified as "black" made no difference in their performance on tests of cognitive abilities (Scarr et al., 1977). Now if heredity largely accounted for the IQ differences between the races, American blacks of more mixed ancestry would be expected to score higher on average than blacks of more purely African lineage. This, however, is *not* what happened, suggesting that black-white differences in IQ scores can be attributed largely to environmental factors.

Finally, critics of Jensen stress another weakness in his genetic theory. They point out that even if we assume for the sake of argument that some of the average black-white difference in IQ scores *is* attributable to heredity, this in no way means that the IQ gap is somehow fixed and unchangeable. The *development* of intellectual abilities, as you remember, is always the product of heredity and environment in interaction. This would remain true even if an observed *difference* in intelligence were 100 percent genetic in origin. Thus changes in relevant aspects of the environment can always have a significant impact on the levels of performance we observe.

Scarr and Weinberg (1976) demonstrated this clearly in a study of black children adopted by white couples of higher-than-average socioeconomic status and above-average intelligence. These black youngsters were born to biological parents of about average intelligence. Yet their IQ scores were on average 6 points above the mean and 15 points above the average of other black children in that part of the country. Thus a black child's reaction range for intellectual development is at least as broad as, and probably even broader than, the current gap in IQ scores between blacks and whites. As anthropologist Sherwood Washburn (1976) has ironically commented:

> I am surprised to hear it stated that if [blacks] were given an equal opportunity, their IQ would be the same as whites'. If one looks at the degree of social discrimination against [blacks] and their relative lack of education, and also takes into account the tremendous amount of overlapping between the observed IQs of both [blacks and whites], one can make an equally good case that, given a comparable chance to that of whites, their IQs would test out ahead. Of course, it would be absolutely unimportant [if the mean IQ score of blacks *were* higher than that of whites,] because the vast majority of individuals of both groups would be of comparable intelligence.

in depth

Public Concerns About Intelligence Testing

The controversy sparked by Jensen's hypothesis about racial IQ differences in turn sparked heated debate over the fairness of IQ tests themselves. Blacks, Hispanics, and Native Americans (as well as economically disadvantaged whites) were being *over*represented in special classes for the mentally retarded and *under*represented in programs for the intellectually gifted. Some blamed the tests that were

assessing mental abilities. Use of these tests, they argued, was just another form of institutional discrimination—that is, discrimination that has become so built into the system that it is not necessarily even deliberate any more (Jones and Wilderson, 1976).

But exactly what is it about IQ tests that can be labeled unfair to minorities? Critics answer that the tests focus largely on language, knowledge, and skills prevalent in the white middle class. As a result, they are quite inappropriate for measuring the intelligence of children from other backgrounds, where different words and grammars are used and different knowledge and skills stressed. Vocabulary items from IQ tests provide a good example. A person who has never heard such words as *sonata* and *ingenuous* will perform poorly on the verbal portion of a typical IQ test. But isn't such knowledge as much a measure of one's cultural community as one's level of intelligence? What if the tables were turned, critics speculate, and urban blacks were in charge of developing IQ tests? Would the average middle-class white continue to score relatively well? To stress their point, some researchers have devised tests, like the one in Figure 14.7, with culturally loaded items alien to middle-class whites.

But the problem of developing a "culture-free" test has proved to be a difficult one. Nevertheless, efforts in this direction continue. One approach has been to build into the test adjustments for minority-group children. The best-known such effort is the **System of Multicultural Pluralistic Assessment,** or **SOMPA,** developed by sociologist Jane Mercer (1979). SOMPA includes three kinds of evaluation: a standard IQ test, which estimates the child's mental abilities as measured against the mainstream school culture; a one-hour interview with the child's parents, aimed at identifying the family's sociocultural background and the child's level of nonacademic performance; and a complete medical examination, intended to detect any physical impairments the child may have. Some have called SOMPA the first nondiscriminatory test of a child's intellectual development. But others oppose its reliance, even in part, on a standard IQ test. Additional efforts are being made to eliminate cultural bias from the test items themselves.

Although support for culture-free IQ tests has been enthusiastic, some psychologists wonder if the need to create them has not been exaggerated. These researchers stress that standard tests of mental abilities are just as valid for minority-group members as

The Dove Counterbalance Intelligence Test
by Adrian Dove

1. If they throw the dice and "7" is showing on the top, what is facing down?
   (a) "Seven"   (b) "Snake eyes"
   (c) "Boxcars"   (d) "Little Joes"
   (e) "Eleven"

2. Which word is most out of place here?
   (a) splib   (b) blood
   (c) gray   (d) spook
   (e) black

3. "Bird" or "yardbird" was the jacket jazz lovers from coast to coast hung on
   (a) Lester Young   (b) Peggy Lee
   (c) Benny Goodman   (d) Charlie Parker
   (e) Birdman of Alcatraz

4. Cheap "chitlings" (not the kind you purchase at the frozen-food counter) will taste rubbery unless they are cooked long enough. How soon can you quit cooking them to eat and enjoy them?
   (a) 15 minutes   (b) 2 hours
   (c) 24 hours
   (d) 1 week (on a low flame)
   (e) 1 hour

5. A "Handkerchief Head" is
   (a) A cool cat   (b) A porter
   (c) An "Uncle Tom"   (d) A hoddi
   (e) A "preacher"

Figure 14.7 The Dove Counterbalance Intelligence Test, devised by Adrian Dove, a black, to be culturally biased against whites, is an extreme example of how an intelligence test may depend on knowledge specific to one culture. A population of urban blacks would score high on this test, and a population of suburban whites would score low. Even when a test's items do not show this kind of obvious culture loading, a test may have validity problems. For example, many subcultures within Western society place great emphasis on competence in test taking. In a subculture where such emphasis is lacking, the validity of almost any test is likely to suffer.
(Answers: 1.a, 2.c, 3.d, 4.c, 5.c.)

are highly related to exceptional achievement later in life (Blum, 1978). Even among Lewis Terman's 1,500 or so IQ "geniuses," most of whom did well in their careers, there were still no winners of Nobel prizes or similarly prestigious awards. There were not even many millionaires in this high-IQ group (Goleman, 1980). Such findings have led some to conclude that IQ tests may miss certain factors very important to success—such factors as strong interests, powerful motivation, and unusual creativity. As David McClelland has noted regarding the SAT in particular, "no consistent relationships exist between scholastic aptitude scores in college students and their *actual accomplishments* in social leadership, the arts, science, music, writing, speech, and drama" (1973, p. 3).

A related problem is that intelligence tests are sometimes used to "weed out" applicants for certain kinds of jobs, even though the duties of the job have no apparent connection with the skills measured by the test. McClelland offers a telling example:

. . . suppose you are a ghetto resident in the Roxbury section of Boston. To qualify for being a policeman, you have to take a three-hour-long general intelligence test in which you must know the meaning of words like "quell," "pyromaniac," and "lexicon." If you do not know enough of these words or cannot play analogy games with them, you do not qualify and must be satisfied with some such job as being a janitor for which an "intelligence" test is not required by the Massachusetts Civil Service Commission. You, not unreasonably, feel angry, upset, and unsuccessful. Because you do not know those words, you are considered to have low intelligence, and since you consequently have to take a low status job and are unhappy, you contribute to the celebrated correlations of low intelligence with low occupational status and poor ad-

they are for members of the white majority (Schmidt and Hunter, 1981). By this they mean that test scores predict the criterion performance (school grades, success on the job, or whatever) of *all* test takers equally well. Those who do poorly on such tests, therefore, are said to lack skills that, like it or not, are important in our society. According to this view, then, it is wasted energy to try to make our tests "culture free." Instead, society should be concentrating its efforts on helping people improve their performance on the tests that already exist.

But others say the claim that IQ tests measure skills of importance to a person's future success simply doesn't conform to all the facts. Although IQ scores are good predictors of grades in school and college, there is little evidence that good grades themselves justment. Psychologists should be ashamed of themselves for promoting a view of general intelligence that has encouraged such a testing program, particularly when there is no solid evidence that significantly relates performance on this type of intelligence test with performance as a policeman. [1973, p. 4]

As a result of these kinds of criticisms, intelligence tests have come under something of a cloud. Some school systems have abandoned them entirely, and others no longer use them to "track" students into accelerated, average, and slow classes—a practice once followed extensively. Private industry's reliance on cognitive tests to select among job applicants also seems to be decreasing, a fact that many applaud. But others caution that to throw such tests out completely may do more harm than good. They stress that our current tests of cognitive abilities are the most valid tools we have for evaluating a person's current and future performance. Alternative tools (such as personal interviews for job placement or teachers' judgments in regard to assignment to special education classes) are even *more* likely to be inaccurate than a good standardized test (Tenopyr, 1981; Reschly, 1981). Thus, if all standardized tests were abolished tomorrow and we relied solely on the subjective opinions of teachers and employers to detect talent in others, we might end up with even more bias against minorities than we already seem to have. According to this view, then, our best option is to continue to use cognitive tests but to try to improve both the way we select and administer them and the quality of the items they include.

Recent research has pointed to several new directions that future intelligence tests might take. One is to include measures of "social intelligence"—that is, a person's ability to interact successfully with others. A test for entrance to medical school, for example, might ask each respondent to simulate an interview with a patient (Rice, 1979). Among other newly proposed yardsticks are those that measure a person's ability to perform several tasks at once (Hawkins, Rodriguez, and Reicher, 1979; Lansman and Hunt, 1980). In everyday life we are often called upon to do things simultaneously. When playing a game, for instance, we frequently need to think about what our next move will be before we finish our last one. It is reasonable to believe that those more adept at this common requirement may have a cognitive edge over their peers. Yet another new direction in intelligence testing is measurement of a person's capacity to handle novel and unexpected situations (Sternberg, 1981). Again, in everyday life, most of us consider people to be quite bright if they can deal quickly with unfamiliar problems (figuring out how to use public transportation in an unfamiliar city to get where they want to go, for instance). If this ability is part of what we generally mean by intelligence, why not include it in our tests of intellectual skills? New approaches such as these may one day change the way psychologists routinely assess intelligence, as they also broaden our understanding of exactly what intelligence is.

THE MEASUREMENT OF PERSONALITY

Although measuring mental abilities is an important part of assessing individuals, it is certainly not the whole story. Equally important is the capacity to assess objectively what people's personalities are like. Is a given person strongly motivated toward achievement? Is the person introverted or extroverted? Emotionally stable or unstable? Self-assured or low in confidence? To answer such questions psychologists turn to personality assessment tests.

Psychologists use personality assessment tests for a variety of reasons. Clinical psychologists, psychiatrists, and social workers use them to gain insight into clients' psychological and emotional problems, thereby aiding in diagnosis and treatment. School psychologists, industrial psychologists, and vocational counselors employ them to help people select careers, or to place them in jobs suited to their dispositions. Researchers interested in personality also use them to investigate some of the concepts and theories we talked about in Chapter 13. Self-esteem, for instance, could never be scientifically studied if we lacked a valid scale for measuring it.

As we discuss several methods of assessing personality, keep in mind that the particular method chosen often depends on a given psychologist's theoretical approach. Those who see personality as a set of fairly enduring characteristics administer personality tests developed to measure such traits. Behaviorists, in contrast, regard personality as much more variable, much more influenced by the immediate situation. As a result, they search for stimuli in the environment that reward and maintain particular responses. Their main tools for doing so are interviews, direct observations, and carefully compiled written self-reports, in which clients record problem behaviors and the situations in which they occur. Psychoanalytic theorists, as you would guess, take a different tactic. Because they believe that personality is often the outcome of unconscious conflicts within the human psyche, they favor techniques for probing personality that let these unconscious motives surface. A prime example is seen in so-called projective tests, the method of personality assessment we will examine first.

Projective Tests

In **projective tests** personality characteristics are assessed by the way a person responds to and interprets ambiguous material, such as an inkblot or a picture in which the motives and feelings of the characters are not clear. The subject is asked to describe or explain what the stimulus shows. He or she is allowed to respond in any way, using whatever words or ideas come to mind. As we said, these tests have been heavily influenced by the Freudian concept of the unconscious. It is presumed that people will unknowingly *project* their unconscious feelings and conflicts onto the test material. Thus a person who repeatedly sees peering eyes and threatening figures in abstract blotches of ink might be said to be projecting onto the inkblots the fears and suspicions typical of paranoia. As this example suggests, projective tests are most often used in clinical settings, where they originated as ways of "getting into the minds" of troubled patients.

The Rorschach Inkblot Test. Perhaps the best-known projective test for clinical diagnosis is the one developed in 1921 by Hermann Rorschach, a Swiss psychiatrist (Rorschach, 1942). In the **Rorschach Inkblot Test** the subject is handed one at a time a series of ten inkblots and is asked to report what each blot looks like. The examiner carefully notes not only what the subject says about the inkblots, but also *how* the person responds—quickly or cautiously, with what kind of emotion, and so forth. After the person has commented on all ten inkblots, the examiner presents the cards a second time and questions the subject about the initial responses. If the subject saw two elephant heads, for instance, the examiner may ask what part of the inkblot suggested that interpretation—the overall shape or protrusions that brought to mind tusks or trunks?

The method of scoring the Rorschach grew out of Rorschach's own observations after administering the test to people with various psychiatric symptoms that had already been diagnosed. Patterns in their responses were incorporated into the scoring system. Subsequent testing has broadened the number of characteristics (both normal and abnormal) that the Rorschach presumably can reveal. Although several systems for scoring are currently in use, at least three criteria are common to all of them. The first of these is *location*. What part of the blot does the subject respond to? The entire shape? The white space around it? Some particular detail? A second criterion consists of the qualities of the blot on which the subject focuses, its so-called *determinants*. Is the person reacting to the form of the inkblot? Its color? Its shading? (Several of the blots are brightly colored, while others are in shades of gray and black.) Does the person see movement in the pattern? (For example, "It's a man riding away on a motorcycle, and he's got his legs stretched out to keep from getting splashed as he goes through a puddle.") A third criterion is *content*. What does the subject see—human figures (such as our motorcycle rider), plants, animals, inanimate objects? Traditionally, certain patterns of response on the Rorschach have been interpreted to indicate certain personality characteristics. For instance, many responses to the entire form of the inkblots supposedly show conceptual thinking, many responses to color presumably indicate emotionality, and many responses involving descriptions of human movement are said to suggest strong imagination (Anastasi, 1976).

The usefulness of the Rorschach as a personality assessment tool depends greatly on one's perspective. Empirical researchers often accuse it of being unreliable and invalid (Aronow, Reznikoff, and Rauchway,

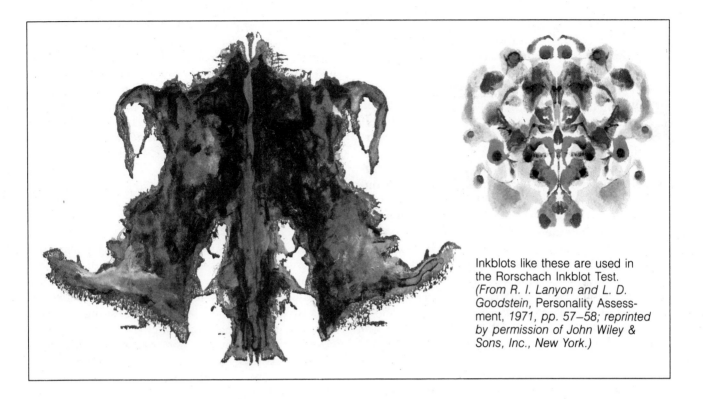

Inkblots like these are used in the Rorschach Inkblot Test. *(From R. I. Lanyon and L. D. Goodstein,* Personality Assessment, *1971, pp. 57–58; reprinted by permission of John Wiley & Sons, Inc., New York.)*

1979). Although there is evidence that the Rorschach may be useful for predicting the outcomes of psychotherapy, its value as a personality test is questioned (Korchin and Schuldberg, 1981). Some researchers have found, for instance, that the typical person's responses on the Rorschach are quite unstable over time, and that the test is not very good at diagnosing specific psychiatric disorders (Feshbach and Weiner, 1982). These criticisms are not surprising when you consider the vast freedom of response that Rorschach subjects are given, the extent to which their answers may be influenced by transitory feelings, and the fact that there is no single set of procedures for administering and scoring the test.

But these problems do not deter clinical psychologists from continuing to use the Rorschach—particularly as a way of obtaining an overall impression of their patients. Ironically, the same broad freedom of response that helps make the Rorschach so hard to validate also makes it a rich assessment tool in the minds of some clinicians (Aronow, Reznikoff, and Rauchway, 1979). From their perspective, the Rorschach is more an interview technique than a scientific test of personality. Psychologist Margaret

Singer (1977), for instance, considers the Rorschach a "bit of reality" around which a conversation can be structured. In her view, "communications deviances" in conversation—peculiarities in the use of language, odd disruptions in thought, sudden changes in focus—provide insights into the psyches of the speakers. Adopting this outlook, she has conducted studies into communication styles within the families of schizophrenics. Such innovative uses of the Rorschach suggest that clinical psychologists will probably be using it for many more years to come.

The Thematic Apperception Test. The **Thematic Apperception Test (TAT),** developed by Henry Murray in 1935, consists of a series of cards depicting ambiguous scenes that include one or two people. Usually the subject is shown twenty or fewer of these cards, chosen for their appropriateness to his or her age and sex. The subject is asked to tell a story about each picture, including what led up to the scene shown, what the characters are thinking and feeling, and how the situation will end.

In analyzing the stories the examiner first determines the character on whom the subject has apparently projected aspects of him- or herself. This is usually the central character of the story. Other characters are thought to reflect traits of people important in the subject's life. Murray originally suggested that the TAT be interpreted in terms of a person's "internal needs" and "environmental presses"—concepts from Murray's own theory of personality (Murray, 1938). Internal needs that Murray thought the TAT could indicate included the needs for achievement, affiliation, nurturance, aggression, dependency, power, and sex. By environmental presses, Murray meant factors in a person's environment that might help or block the satisfaction of needs. In the final scoring of the test, the strength and persistence of particular needs and presses are taken into account. If, for instance, the central character in several of a person's stories is constantly seeking to dominate others, that person is presumed to possess a marked need for power. Figure 14.8 shows a sample card from the TAT and one college student's description of it.

Today interpretation of the TAT involves analysis not only of needs and presses but also of other aspects of the subject's responses, somewhat in the manner of

Rorschach interpretation. The TAT is therefore open to one of the criticisms the Rorschach faces: that interpretation often depends on the skill of the examiner. In addition, some researchers fear that responses to the TAT, like responses to the Rorschach, will be unduly influenced by a subject's transitory feelings. Despite these criticisms, however, the TAT has gained wide acceptance as a personality test, and it is extensively used both in clinical settings and in research.

Self-Report Tests

The projective tests of personality we have just discussed strike some as being rather roundabout ways of discovering what people are like. Couldn't we just *ask* subjects what they feel and how they usually act? Do you feel awkward in most social settings? Do you often say things you immediately regret? Do you believe that most people can be trusted? On the whole, are you satisfied with yourself? If we asked enough such questions, wouldn't the answers provide relatively good insights into a person's psychological

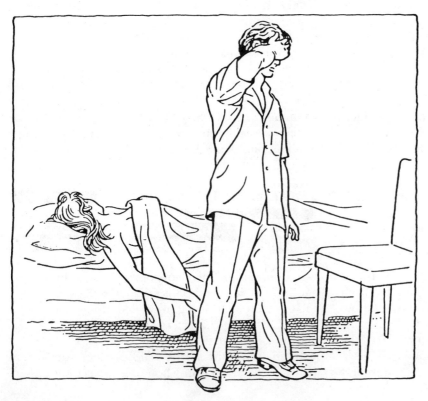

Figure 14.8 The TAT card shown here was interpreted as follows by a male college student, who seems to be distressed by sexual conflict:

This is a young boy who's never had any experience with girls, to any extent. For some reason he finds himself with a woman, a few years older than he is, who expects that he's gonna go to bed with her. He wants very much to prove to himself that he's a man . . . but still, he's afraid. He doesn't know what to do. His fear . . . turns into disgust, when he thinks of himself being unable to act like a boy his age he believes is supposed to act. . . . He'll probably run out of the room, and block off his mind, to sex and to women, for a long time. . . . He may never be able to develop normally . . . because of things that have happened to him in the past and are manifesting themselves in his immaturity and self-hate.

(From Lamberth, Rappaport, and Rappaport, 1978, p. 172.)

makeup? By the middle of this century psychologists had begun to develop just such **self-report tests** of personality.

Methods of Test Construction.

There have been two basic approaches to constructing self-report tests. One is to start with test items that seem, on the face of it, to be valid—that is, they have so-called **face validity.** Suppose, for instance, we want to develop a scale to measure dependency. We could begin by composing statements about the self that seem related to dependency, such as "I find it hard to make up my mind without consulting others" or "I don't think I would ever be able to live alone." It is reasonable to expect that those high in dependency would be more apt to agree strongly with such statements than those low in this trait. We could then administer our test several times to large samples of people. Analyzing their responses, we could retain those test items that have the highest amount of internal consistency and the highest correlation with any other measures of dependency we might have.

There are several difficulties with this approach to developing personality scales, however. For one thing, it is not always easy to come up with additional measures against which to validate such a test. And even if we do, those measures themselves must in turn be validated. And, even if we can demonstrate that this type of test is reasonably valid, how do we know we have hit upon the best measures of the trait being studied? After all, people are not always willing to answer direct questions about themselves, especially when truthful responses may seem to put them in an unfavorable light. Perhaps, then, there are more subtle questions that would provide better yardsticks. But how do we go about finding them?

A way that has proved quite effective is called the empirical approach to test construction. We begin by compiling a large number of test items without regard to their face validity as measures of any particular trait. Then we administer these items to an experimental group known to have the trait of interest. Suppose, for instance, we want to develop a scale to measure dependency in teenagers. We could observe a large number of teenagers in their homes and in their classrooms and select out those who are unusually dependent and those who are unusually independent. Both groups would be given the same self-report items to answer. Those items found to differentiate the two groups—that is, the items that elicit one answer from most of the dependent subjects and an entirely different answer from most of the independent ones—would be retained for inclusion on our test. We would then repeat this selection process several more times until our test was as reliable and valid as possible. Note that in this procedure it does not matter whether the content of an item *seems* closely related to dependency. If highly dependent people usually agree with the statement "I prefer team sports to individual sports," then that item will be considered a useful indicator of dependency. Of course, the groups of people we use to select our test items must be accurately assessed in the first place in order for this method to work. But if they are, the test we construct should be a good tool for future assessment.

The Minnesota Multiphasic Personality Inventory.

The **Minnesota Multiphasic Personality Inventory (MMPI)** is a widely used test developed by the empirical method. It was originally developed to aid in the diagnosis of psychiatric patients. A variety of possible test items were tried out on groups of patients suffering from various psychological disorders—schizophrenia, depression, paranoia, hypochondria, and so forth. The same items were also given to groups of normal subjects. Items that discriminated among the groups were incorporated in the test. Of the original pool of items, for instance, fifty-three were found to discriminate sharply between depressed and normal people. Later, a few more items were added to sharpen the discrimination between people who are severely depressed and those with other psychiatric conditions. The result is the D, or depression, scale of the MMPI. It is a highly sensitive indicator not only of psychotic depression but also of less severe depression and short-term slumps in mood.

The MMPI eventually came to contain 550 test statements, all of which can be answered true or false. Some items from it are shown in Figure 14.9A. A person's answers to the statements yield scores on each of the ten clinical scales listed in Table 14.2. Often these scores are presented graphically so that the assessment of a particular person can be readily compared with those of others. Figure 14.9B shows one such personality comparison between two groups of people.

You undoubtedly noticed in Figure 14.9B that the MMPI also provides scores on three other scales in addition to the ten clinical ones. The L, F, and K

TABLE 14.2 SCALES OF THE MMPI

CLINICAL SCALES

1. Hypochondriasis (Hs)	Items selected to discriminate people who persist in worrying about their bodily functions despite strong evidence that they have no physical illness.
2. Depression (D)	Items selected to discriminate people who are pessimistic about the future, feel hopeless or worthless, are slow in thought and action, and think a lot about death and suicide.
3. Hysteria (H)	Items selected to discriminate people who use physical symptoms to solve difficult problems or avoid mature responsibilities, particularly under severe psychological stress.
4. Psychopathic Deviate (Pd)	Items selected to discriminate people who show a pronounced disregard for social customs and mores, an inability to profit from punishing experiences, and emotional shallowness with others, particularly in sex and love.
5. Masculinity-Femininity (Mf)	Items selected to discriminate men who prefer homosexual relations to heterosexual ones, either overtly or covertly because of inhibitions or conflicts. Women tend to score low on this scale, but the scale cannot be interpreted as simply "upside down" for women.
6. Paranoia (Pa)	Items selected to discriminate people who have delusions about how influential and how victimized they are or how much attention is paid them by other people.
7. Psychasthenia (Pt)	Items selected to discriminate people with obsessive thoughts, compulsive actions, extreme fear or guilt feelings, insecurity, and high anxiety.
8. Schizophrenia (Sc)	Items selected to discriminate people who are constrained, cold, aloof, apathetic, and inaccessible to others, and who may have delusions or hallucinations.
9. Hypomania (Ma)	Items selected to discriminate people who are physically overactive and emotionally excited, and have rapid flights of disconnected, fragmentary ideas; these activities may lead to accomplishment but more frequently are inefficient and unproductive.
10. Social introversion (Si)	Items selected to discriminate people who are withdrawn from social contacts and responsibilities and display little real interest in people.

VALIDITY SCALES

Lie Scale (L)	Items that reflect socially desirable but unlikely behavior and are therefore likely to be marked true by a naive faker.
Infrequency Scale (F)	Items that are rarely marked true except by people who either are deliberately trying to give an exaggerated impression of their problems or are in fact highly deviant.
Correction Scale (K)	Items that reflect how defensive or how frank the person is being. The scale is sensitive to attitudes more subtle than those that affect the Lie Scale.

Source: Based on Dahlstrom, Welsh, and Dahlstrom, 1972.

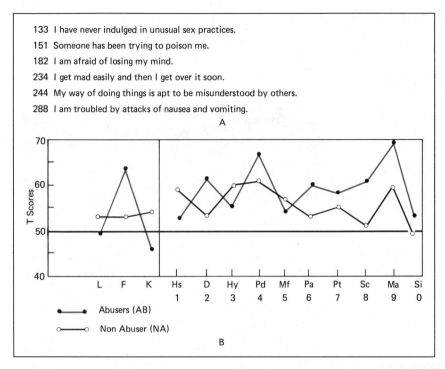

133 I have never indulged in unusual sex practices.

151 Someone has been trying to poison me.

182 I am afraid of losing my mind.

234 I get mad easily and then I get over it soon.

244 My way of doing things is apt to be misunderstood by others.

288 I am troubled by attacks of nausea and vomiting.

A

B

•——• Abusers (AB)

○——○ Non Abuser (NA)

Figure 14.9 (A) Sample MMPI items. (B) MMPI profiles for abusive and nonabusive fathers. The letters along the bottom of the graph correspond to the scales described in Table 14.2. Note that the two groups obtained different profiles: Fathers who abused their children scored much higher than nonabusive fathers on the depression (D), psychopathic deviate (Pd) and mania (Ma) scales. Although it appears that the MMPI can differentiate between abusive and nonabusive parents, further study would be necessary before a more conclusive profile of an abusive parent could be drawn. This research does offer some tentative hypotheses about important personality differences between abusers and nonabusers. *(Adapted from Paulson et al., 1974.)*

scales are designed to confront directly the problem of untruthful or careless responses, which can undermine a test's validity. The specific purposes of these so-called validity scales are summarized in Table 14.2. The L, or lie, scale helps identify those subjects who are faking their responses in order to appear better than they actually are. For instance, a person who answers "true" to the statement "I always tell the truth" is undoubtedly lying, for everyone tells a lie at one time or another. Agreement with many such statements will earn the person a high L score and cause the test results to be considered invalid. Invalidation will also result from a very high F, or infrequency, score. The F scale consists of items that are rarely marked "true" by normal subjects, such as the statement "I see things, animals, or people around me that others do not see." Even very disturbed people rarely agree with more than about a quarter of the F scale items because these statements do not describe symptoms normally found together. Thus agreement with many F scale items suggests that the person is either deliberately lying to give a bad impression or is not taking the test seriously and is simply answering at random. The K, or correction, scale is somewhat similar in content to the L scale, but the items are more subtle. The subject is presented with such state-ments as "At times I feel like swearing." Many "false" responses to such statements suggest that the person, although not blatantly lying, is being less than frank. As a result, a very high K score prompts the examiners to adjust scores on some of the clinical scales upward.

Over 6,000 studies have shown the MMPI to be a valid tool for diagnosing psychiatric problems (Dahlstrom et al., 1975). It is particularly helpful for the initial screening of large groups of people, especially now that computerized scoring is possible. Some of the clinical scales of the MMPI have also proved useful in predicting the effectiveness of various forms of psychotherapy. But note that the MMPI is not strong at assessing differences in normal personality. It is therefore unfortunate that some business firms inappropriately use it to try to identify job applicants with traits believed to be suitable for particular positions. Clearly, this is not the purpose for which the MMPI was developed.

Behavioral Assessment

We should not leave the topic of personality assessment without some mention of a newer approach to this general task: **behavioral assessment.** Behavioral assessment emerged during the 1960s and '70s with the advent of behavior modification as a method of psychological therapy. As you may remember from Chapter 5, behavior modification is the conscious use of learning and conditioning principles to change human behavior. It is closely related to B. F. Skinner's view that current behavior is greatly influenced by the consequences of past behavior—that is, by the rewards and punishments we have received. According to Skinner, it is needless effort to search for the causes of problem behavior *inside* a person's psyche, to look for underlying motives or dispositions that are somehow producing the undesirable response. Instead, we should concern ourselves with the problem behavior in its own right, and especially with the external conditions that are inadvertently maintaining it. Thus behavioral assessment is a way of objectively measuring two sets of factors: environmental contingencies (rewards and punishments) on the one hand and people's responses to such contingencies on the other.

Not surprisingly, behavioral assessment often involves direct observation of a problem behavior. For instance, psychologists may count the number of aggressive responses (shoving, punching, verbal attacks) that a disruptive child makes on the playground in a given period of time. Or they may record the unassertive behaviors (deferential postures, unnecessary apologies, unwarranted agreements with other people's opinions) that a person who has trouble with assertiveness makes in a role-playing situation. Of course, when such direct observations are impractical, therapists often request that clients keep their own written records of how often, in what forms, and in what circumstances their problem behaviors occur. These quantified records provide a baseline for assessing the effectiveness of subsequent treatment programs. They also provide insights into the environmental factors that may be maintaining the problem responses. The psychologists observing our disruptive child on the playground may note, for example, that teachers intervene whenever the boy acts aggressively. They may therefore hypothesize that this extra attention may be reinforcing the objectionable behavior.

The final step in behavior modification is to alter environmental consequences so as to reduce the frequency of old, unwanted responses and encourage new, more desirable ones. Here, too, assessment techniques may be needed to determine which rewards will be most effective in eliciting the new behaviors. When working with adults, behavior therapists sometimes use reinforcement checklists of various activities (MacPhillamy and Lewinsohn, 1974). The client indicates how pleasurable he or she considers each of the activities listed. Highly rated items may then be used as special rewards whenever the client behaves in the desired way (refrains from smoking cigarettes, for instance, or manages to do something previously feared). At the same time, the therapist continues to measure the overall frequency of the problem behavior, always comparing it against the baseline, in order to determine if the current treatment is working.

The behavioral approach to therapy is often quite effective, as we will see in Chapter 16. But because this approach is relatively new, reliable and valid methods of behavioral assessment are still being developed. Complicating this process is the fact that many behavior therapists no longer confine their attention solely to what clients say and do. Often today a client's thoughts, feelings, interpretations of events, and expectations are also considered important to understanding and changing that person's behavior. This is in keeping with the more cognitive view of human learning we have discussed at many points in this book. The end result is a broader definition of behavior therapy and a need for more diversified tools of behavioral assessment (Korchin and Schuldberg, 1981).

TESTING FOR VOCATIONAL SELECTION AND COUNSELING

A variety of tests are currently used in vocational selection. Intelligence tests and personality measures, for example, are sometimes used by employers to screen job applicants. And when a job requires very specific skills (the ability to program a computer or repair an engine, for instance), special performance tests are often given to select and evaluate workers. In addition, vocational counselors use tests to help guide people toward occupations suited to their interests. You may have taken a vocational interest test at some point yourself. What do such tests entail?

Interest Tests

Interest tests find their most important use in educational counseling. By the time a person is old enough to begin to consider future occupations seriously, that person has developed a definite pattern of interests. Measuring these interests can help direct a person toward a personally satisfying career, one in which the person has a reasonable chance of succeeding. But why do we need a formal test to identify interests? Aren't people aware of their own interests themselves? Not necessarily. Many people never analyze their interests deliberately. And even if they do, they may not know how those interests relate to the requirements of various jobs. A young woman with a strong interest in science, for instance, may think that she wants to be a doctor. But if she has no interest in dealing with other people's problems, she is overlooking an important part of a physician's work. Interest tests can help avoid such oversights by matching the full range of a person's interests with the demands of various types of work.

The **Strong-Campbell Interest Inventory (SCII)**, originally developed in the 1920s by E. K. Strong, Jr., consists of 325 items, most of which list particular occupations, school subjects, activities (repairing a clock, giving a speech, raising money for charity), amusements, and people one might associate with (old people, people who like to live dangerously, and so forth). The test taker is asked to mark each of these items "like," "indifferent," or "dislike." Other sets of items on the Strong-Campbell include pairs of activities to choose between ("Would you prefer to deal with things or to deal with people?") and simple self-descriptions that the person marks "yes" or "no" ("I make friends easily"; "I am always on time with my work"). All the subject's answers are then fed into a computer and analyzed in terms of three major scales.

The first of these scales is the so-called Occupational Scale. It tells the test taker how similar his or her answers are to those given by samples of successful people in specific occupations (psychologist, architect, advertising executive, musician, army officer,

and so on). A woman may discover, for instance, that her answers on the Strong-Campbell are highly similar to those given by a group of engineers but very dissimilar to those given by a group of social workers. Dissimilar answers are taken as more revealing than similar ones, and they can be used to eliminate career options—in this case, social work. To help provide some insight into why a particular person scores high in some occupations and low in others, a Basic Interest Scale is also included. It contains twenty-three interest areas, such as agriculture, military, science, art, sales, writing, and teaching. In each of these areas the test taker receives a score showing his or her degree of interest in working in that field. These scores are derived by comparing the test taker's responses with those of a large sample of other people in many walks of life. Finally, the Strong-Campbell also includes a General Occupational Themes Scale. It consists of six adjectives (realistic, conventional, enterprising, social, artistic, and investigative) which presumably capture different general styles of thinking and acting. Again the test taker receives a score in each of these six themes. Because the Strong-Campbell classifies all occupations in terms of the same six themes, the test taker gains additional insight into why particular vocations should or should not be considered. In general, since people cannot try out several occupations to see which they enjoy, the Strong-Campbell offers an acceptable alternative means of obtaining information relevant to making a career choice.

Other Tests Used in Vocational Selection

The Strong-Campbell helps to guide people toward careers suited to their interests. But what about the tests that employers use to select among job applicants? What do they involve? As we said earlier, tests for mental abilities are sometimes used in the process of vocational selection. This practice, however, has become controversial. On the one hand are those who argue that the abilities measured on such tests have little if anything to do with performance on many jobs. Where is the connection, these critics ask, between a test of verbal and mathematical abilities and the duties of, say, a fireman? But others answer that such tests, regardless of their apparent lack of face validity, are nevertheless relatively good predictors of future performance in a wide variety of fields. To abandon these tests completely, according to this view, would result in the hiring of less able workers and reduced productivity (Schmidt and Hunter, 1981). Given the strength of opinions on both sides of this issue, it is doubtful that the debate will be resolved in the near future.

Partly because of the heated controversy the use of cognitive abilities tests has raised, many employers have turned to other kinds of tests for screening job applicants. Some administer special aptitude tests designed to measure the potential to perform specific tasks. Factories seeking workers to assemble tiny electronic components, for example, often give applicants a manual dexterity test. Aptitude tests have also been developed to identify the potential to work with computers, various types of machinery, and so forth. Another kind of test often used to screen prospective employees is a current performance test. Applicants must demonstrate how well they can currently perform a given type of work. A typist, for example, may be asked to type a few pages or a proofreader to correct an actual proof. Finally, some corporations use personality tests to match candidates to jobs. To enter an executive training program, for instance, a person may have to rank exceptionally high in assertiveness and tolerance of stress, and moderately high in conformity.

Employers also assess job candidates by many means other than formal tests, of course. Application blanks, for instance, provide a summary of the applicant's schooling and employment history. The interview, another vocational assessment technique, is used almost universally. Employers often feel that interviewing has an advantage over other assessment methods in that it allows one to get a good "feel" for the kind of person the applicant is. When evaluated scientifically, however, interviewing does not fare well. Most validation studies on the interview have found it to be at best a rather random decision-making process and at worst an unfairly biased one (Tenopyr, 1981). Thus from the viewpoint of a company's future productivity, the best employee selection tools are those that have been carefully validated by identifying criteria that are in fact associated with long-term success in the firm.

THE ETHICS OF TESTING

Because Americans use standardized tests so extensively to differentiate and select among people, these tests have considerable power to affect people's lives. As a result, psychologists, government officials, and the general public have become concerned about the ethical standards that apply to such testing. The American Psychological Association has issued several documents on the subject; legislators have already enacted certain laws; and some corporations have voluntarily tightened their policies in regard to employee selection exams. What is it that all these groups are so concerned about? And what are the solutions, in the form of ethical guidelines, that they and others recommend?

One concern is that test users choose, administer, and evaluate tests properly (London and Bray, 1980). To this end, ethical guidelines stress that tests be employed only for appropriate purposes. If, for instance, a test is used to predict a person's future success at some task, that predictive power must be clearly and scientifically demonstrated. In addition, tests must be fair to members of all the social groups that take them. No test that discriminates unfairly should ever be employed. Those who use tests also have an obligation to keep in mind the limits of test results. Test scores never supply absolutely certain information. At best they provide only a good estimate of what they are designed to measure. Thus ethical guidelines suggest that no important decisions be made about a person on the basis of a test score alone. Such guidelines also recommend that those who are rejected partly on the basis of a test score at least be given the chance to take that test again.

Beyond the ethical issue of the proper use of tests is the ethical issue of the disclosure of test results. Exactly who should have access to people's test scores? The test takers themselves? Under all circumstances? This has been a difficult issue to resolve completely. The developers of tests argue that if questions and answers are disclosed to people who have taken a test, new test items must be constantly generated, some of which may eventually be inferior to those previously used. Overall, however, public opinion has sided with the rights of the test taker (Haney, 1981). In 1980, for example, New York State passed a law requiring that questions and answers on college entrance exams must be made available to those who have taken these tests. In addition, many organizations are setting their own ethical guidelines in regard to the disclosure of test scores to outside parties. In general, test takers are believed to have a right to confidentiality: their test results should not be released to others without their prior knowledge, and often their express consent (London and Bray, 1980).

Those concerned with testing sometimes emphasize that most tests, in and of themselves, are ethically neutral. It is how tests are *used* that influences people and raises questions of right and wrong. Careful attention to issues such as those raised in this section is a continuing necessity if tests are to be employed for the benefit of all involved.

SUMMARY

1. The value of a test is determined by its **reliability** and **validity**. A test is reliable if it yields essentially the same results over and over again. A test's reliability can be assessed by the **test-retest** method or, when this is impractical, by the **split-halves** method.

2. A test is valid if it measures what it is intended to measure. So-called **criterion validity** is assessed by determining the correlation between performance on the test in question and some other yardstick of the factor that the test is presumed to measure. Two kinds of criteria may be used to validate a test: a criterion immediately available, in which case the test is being assessed for **concurrent validity;** or a criterion to be measured in the future, in which case the test is being judged for **predictive validity.**

3. **Standardization** of a test is necessary to determine the significance of an individual's score relative to the scores of others. It involves the development of group **norms** based on the scores of a large **standardization group.**

4. Among the many types of tests used to measure mental abilities are so-called individual intelligence tests, which are administered to people individually (not in a group). One individual intelligence test in wide use today is the **Stanford-Binet,** an updated version of a test first developed by French psychologist Alfred Binet to measure **intelligence quotient,** or **IQ,** in children. The other most frequently used individual intelligence tests are the **Wechsler scales,** which differ from the Stanford-Binet in several important respects.

5. Although group intelligence tests have several disadvantages over individual tests, they are widely used in mass testing situations. One group test that measures some of the abilities often tested in IQ tests is the Scholastic Aptitude Test (SAT). It has recently been attacked as invalid and biased, but when used with discretion it is a reasonably good predictor of future grades in college.

6. At one extreme in the range of human intelligence are the **mentally retarded**—those whose general intelligence is significantly below average and who have trouble functioning in everyday settings. Because of the stigma of being labeled retarded, educators have become more careful in evaluating children of seemingly subaverage intelligence. Sociocultural, emotional, and health factors, among others, must be taken into account before such a classification is made.

7. At the other extreme of human intelligence are the mentally gifted. Contrary to common stereotypes, the mentally gifted as a group are not socially awkward, eccentric, or physically frail. But it is not clear that their generally high levels of success and adjustment in life should be attributed solely to their high IQs. Other factors, particularly family background and motivation, also contribute to the tendency to excel. In response to the needs of the gifted, many schools now offer special enrichment programs.

8. IQ scores reflect not only one's genetic potential for intellectual development (nature) but also one's environment and experience (nurture). Debate has continued over the years as to which of these factors is largely responsible for differences in intelligence. Educational psychologist Arthur Jensen has proposed that heredity may be strongly implicated in the IQ differences between groups—especially in the difference in average IQ scores between black and white Americans. But others have persuasively attacked Jensen's view.

9. The Jensen controversy sparked considerable criticism of IQ tests. Many argue that the tests reflect the language and culture of the white middle class too thoroughly to be valid for people from other backgrounds. Attempts have been made to create culture-free intelligence tests, the best known of which is the **System of Multicultural Pluralistic Assessment (SOMPA).**

10. Tests developed to assess human personality have grown out of several psychological traditions, including trait theory, psychoanalysis, and behaviorism. **Projective tests** are closely related to the psychoanalytic approach because they assume that subjects will project unconscious conflicts and needs into their interpretations of ambiguous test material. Examples include the **Rorschach Inkblot Test** and the **Thematic Apperception Test (TAT).**

11. **Self-report tests** of personality assume that we can find out much about a person's nature simply by asking that person questions about him- or herself. One such test widely used to help diagnose psychological disorders is the **Minnesota Multiphasic Personality Inventory (MMPI).** It contains 550 true-false statements that yield ratings on ten clinical scales.

12. **Behavioral assessment** is a relatively new approach to evaluating personality, which emerged with the advent of behavior modification as a method of psychological therapy. It involves objective measurement of both environmental contingencies (rewards and punishments) and people's responses to them. The most recent forms of behavioral assessment also take into account people's underlying thoughts and feelings.

13. A variety of tests are used for vocational selection and counseling. Interest tests, which attempt to identify a person's interest in the activities involved in various occupations, include the **Strong-Campbell Interest Inventory (SCII).** Companies use several kinds of tests to help screen job applicants. Among them are cognitive abilities tests, specific aptitude tests, and personality scales.

14. Psychologists, government officials, and the general public have become increasingly concerned about the ethical standards that apply to testing. Among their specific concerns are the uses to which standardized tests are put and the people to whom test results are disclosed. Several organizations are attempting to set guidelines in these and other areas.

SUGGESTED READINGS

ANASTASI, ANNE. *Psychological testing.* 5th ed. New York: Macmillan, 1982.

A survey of intelligence and personality tests, with useful discussions of test reliability and validity.

GOULD, STEPHEN JAY. *The mismeasure of man.* New York: Norton, 1981.

The history of misguided attempts to measure intelligence, written by a popular science writer and zoologist.

KLEINMUNTZ, B. *Personality and psychological assessment.* New York: St. Martin's, 1982.

Ability and aptitude testing and measurements of attitudes and values are addressed from a systematic and objective point of view.

LANYON, R. I., and GOLDSTEIN, L. D. *Personality assessment.* 2d ed. New York: Wiley, 1982.

Incorporates new developments in assessment methods and their applicability to a wide range of settings.

LOEHLIN, JOHN C., LINDZEY, GARDNER, and SPUHLER, J. N. *Race differences in intelligence.* New York: W. H. Freeman, 1975.

A thorough, though somewhat technical, examination of the research evidence on the issue of racial differences in IQ.

NATIONAL RESEARCH COUNCIL ASSEMBLY OF BEHAVIORAL AND SOCIAL SCIENCES. *Ability testing: Uses, consequences, and controversies.* 2 vols. A. K. Wigdor and W. R. Gardner (Eds.). Washington, D.C.: National Academy Press, 1982.

A valuable overview of the current status of the testing controversy.

PSYCHOLOGICAL DISORDERS

Part 7 is concerned with the clinical practice of psychology: How does mental illness manifest itself, and what strategies exist to improve it? Chapter 15 surveys abnormal behavior and Chapter 16, its treatment.

15

EXPLORING ABNORMAL BEHAVIOR

Alberto Giacometti, *Cubist Head*, 1934–35.

A twenty-four-year old man, armed with a .44-caliber revolver, cruises a New York neighborhood late at night, looking for "pretty girls" to shoot. When he is finally captured by police after a year-long search, he has killed six people and wounded seven others. He says that "demons" drove him to the crimes.

A middle-aged businessman, fed up with his stressful job, his hour-long commute, and the demands of his suburban lifestyle, packs a small bag of clothing and flees to the mountains, where he settles in an abandoned cabin, determined to live a life of isolation.

A young woman who showed great academic promise in high school begins to have difficulty with her studies in college. She believes that she is constantly behind in her work and will not be able to catch up, no matter how hard she tries. She feels lonely and becomes increasingly depressed and withdrawn.

A widely acclaimed young pianist, winner of many awards, begins to suffer inexplicable attacks of "nerves" whenever he must play before an audience. These feelings of anxiety become increasingly intense and develop into waves of panic. Eventually the very thought of performing in public becomes so terrifying that the pianist's career is jeopardized.

To what extent are these four people behaving "abnormally"? Are all in need of psychological help? How would trained professionals diagnose each of their conditions? And what kinds of therapy might be recommended? These are the questions we will be answering in this chapter and the next, which deal with psychological disorders and their treatments. We begin in this chapter by trying to define abnormality in human behavior—a task, as you will see, that is far from easy. We then explore the major theories that psychologists and others have proposed to explain why abnormal behavior arises. Finally, we describe the principal types of abnormal behavior, as well as the insights about them that current theories and research provide.

WHAT IS ABNORMAL BEHAVIOR?

Some patterns of behavior can clearly be labeled abnormal. The man who hears the voices of demons urging him to kill young women is unquestionably out of touch with reality and is acting in ways that most of us find incomprehensible. But would we be justified in applying the label "abnormal" to our hypothetical harried businessman or to our depressed college student? It is certainly more difficult to say. How, then, do psychologists go about defining what is normal and abnormal? Essentially, they judge a particular behavior according to several criteria, including deviation from statistical norms, lack of conformity to widely accepted social values, and deviation from some absolute standard of what is "healthy" and "good." Let's take a closer look at each of these criteria.

Ways of Defining Abnormality

The simplest approach to distinguishing normal from abnormal is to label "normal" whatever most people do. The "abnormal" then becomes whatever differs markedly from the statistical average. Consider, for example, a person who experiences anxiety after starting a new job. Because most people feel some anxiety in a stressful situation like this one, a therapist applying this standard would consider mild anxiety normal. Extreme anxiety—or no anxiety at all—would probably be considered abnormal. Of course, what is statistically frequent and infrequent is not always this clear-cut. Suppose a recently widowed woman told you that she had heard her dead husband speaking to her. You might well assume that this is very uncommon behavior and therefore should be classified as abnormal, but this assumption would be wrong. In fact, an estimated 50 to 90 percent of bereaved people experience such hallucinations (Coates and Wortman, 1980). What seems abnormal, therefore, is not always confirmed as such by statistical evidence.

Another way to define abnormality is to compare a person's behavior with widely accepted social expectations and values. A woman who walked around her neighborhood wearing a heavy winter coat in summer and screaming insults at strangers would, by this criterion, be considered abnormal. She would be violating the social rules governing dress and polite behavior. Such actions, of course, are also statistically uncommon. Thus the statistical approach can lend support to the social expectations approach when it comes to defining abnormality.

These two related yardsticks, however, while useful in defining abnormality, are not always sufficient. Sometimes behaviors that are statistically infrequent and in violation of social norms should not be considered abnormal. Studies show, for instance, that many college freshmen suffer serious bouts of loneliness and depression. Should we brush these episodes off by labeling them common and therefore not a problem? Most people would argue no. Conversely, what about the divorced father of thirty years ago who wished to have custody of his young children? At the time, his attitude would have been considered both statistically infrequent and opposed to social norms, but few people today would call his behavior abnormal. The same could be said about people throughout history who have pursued unconventional but worthwhile goals. Much of society's vitality comes from those who venture beyond the norms, striking out in new directions. Rigidly to label all such actions "abnormal" would be to discourage many valuable innovations.

One way around this problem is to assess abnormality in terms not of some statistical or socially accepted norm but of some absolute standard of what is psychologically "healthy." In theory this approach sounds reasonable enough. But in practice such standards are not easy to identify. Consider the criterion of freedom from emotional distress. It seems on the surface to be a valid yardstick for measuring mental health. But should the person who goes through life with little anxiety and upset *necessarily* be considered psychologically well adjusted? Probably not. For one thing, obviously there are times when great emotional distress is the psychologically expected reaction, as when a parent experiences the death of a child. The person who remains indifferent in such a situation can hardly be considered normal. In addition, some psychologists believe that people cannot grow and reach their full potentials without sometimes taking steps that will be distressing to them. From this perspective, painful choices are often a necessary part of becoming one's true self. Finally, freedom from distress, considered by itself, is not a broad enough criterion for determining what is normal. A man who is convinced that he is Jesus Christ may not be the least bit disturbed by his delusion. Yet few psychologists would want to say that he has no psychological problem. Other absolute standards for defining abnormality inevitably face similar limitations.

Thus no single approach to defining abnormality is adequate by itself. Nor is there universal agreement on where the line between normal and abnormal should be drawn. Most people have fears, anxieties, conflicts, and moments of depression. These feelings are considered abnormal only when they are persistent and tend to interfere with daily functioning. Mental health, therefore, might best be viewed as a continuum; at the extreme ends of the continuum, normality and abnormality can be clearly distinguished, but they are difficult to differentiate in the middle range.

The Neurotic-Psychotic Distinction

On the abnormal side of the normal-abnormal continuum, another distinction sometimes becomes useful. This is the difference between disorders that are often termed **neurotic** on the one hand and **psychotic** on the other.

Most people are familiar with the "neurotic." In everyday language it refers to a variety of behavior patterns that, while not what we would call truly bizarre, are nevertheless unusual and often infused with much anxiety. The woman who compulsively scrubs her house to rid it of every germ, the man who persistently checks his body for warning signs of cancer, and the person who becomes confused and distraught over the need to make the smallest decision are among those the average person would probably label neurotic. Many contemporary clinicians also use the term "neurotic," and the meaning they give it is very close to the everyday one. Today mental health professionals usually use "neurotic" to refer to disorders that are relatively mild—that is, disorders whose victims have not lost touch with reality. The neurotic person is still able to perceive the world with reasonable clarity, even though he or she is often troubled and unhappy.

In contrast, clinicians apply the term "psychotic" to very severe mental disorders—those whose victims *do* lose touch with reality. The woman who hears voices from outer space telling her what to do or the man who insists that he is Jesus Christ sent to save the world are among those who are called psychotic. Both suffer from profoundly irrational perceptions and beliefs. Such hallucinations and delusions are the hallmarks of psychotic disorders.

Later in this chapter we will sometimes be using the terms "neurotic" and "psychotic," for they provide simple, shorthand ways of conveying the severity of certain disorders. For instance, what are called the anxiety disorders (panic attacks, phobias, obsessions, and compulsions) are often labeled neurotic because they lie at the milder end of the abnormal continuum. Schizophrenia, in contrast, a disorder often marked by bizarre hallucinations, is appropriately labeled psychotic because the mental disturbance is so profound. Still other disorders can be thought of as having neurotic and psychotic subclasses. Depression, for instance, can vary from fairly mild but chronic dejection and apathy (what is sometimes called a depressive neurosis) to profound despair and delusions of worthlessness and vileness (psychotic depression). The neurotic-psychotic distinction does not apply so neatly to all mental disorders; but because it is useful in describing some, we have introduced it here.

APPROACHES TO ABNORMALITY

Over the years many theories have been proposed to explain abnormal behavior. The idea that madness results from possession by devils dates back to ancient times. Archeologists have found skulls of Stone Age people with surgical holes chipped in them—apparently to let the evil spirits out. Exorcism of demons by prayers, potions, and often physical torture was fairly common during the Middle Ages. Such practices survived in Europe and America until well into the seventeenth century, as the infamous Salem witch trials attest. These historical reminders clearly demonstrate that people's views about the causes of abnormal behavior largely determine how the mentally disturbed are treated.

In the following sections we will review six of today's major theories about the causes of abnormality. In each case we will explore the theory's underlying assumptions about the nature of psychological disorders, pointing out how these assumptions suggest particular kinds of treatment. We begin with the theory that first replaced the ancient notion linking abnormality to the work of devils. This is the biological perspective.

The Biological Perspective

According to the biological perspective, abnormal behavior arises from some physical dysfunction in the body which affects the central nervous system. The biological perspective gained great strength in the late nineteenth century when researchers began to discover that several kinds of previously baffling mental disorders could be traced to specific diseases of the brain. The most dramatic was the finding that **general paresis**—an irreversible deterioration of all mental and physical processes—was nothing more than the final stage in the venereal disease called syphilis (the stage at which the syphilitic microorganisms deeply penetrate the brain and other body organs). Optimism ran high that medical science would someday conquer all other kinds of psychological disturbance. Today biological researchers admit that they do not yet know the origins of all or even most mental disorders. Nevertheless, many firmly believe that physiological malfunctions will eventually be found to underlie many such disorders.

Contemporary biological researchers are using the most modern research techniques to explore the brain chemistries of mentally disturbed people. They suspect that changes in the workings of neurotransmitters may contribute to many psychological disorders. For example, abnormally low levels of the neurotransmitters norepinephrine and serotonin have been linked to depression, as we will see later in this chapter. In keeping with this line of thought, these investigators are also trying to develop new and more effective forms of drug treatment for the mentally disturbed. The successes they have had so far have helped to reinforce what is often called the **medical model** of psychological disturbance. This is the

Until well into the seventeenth century, ignorance and superstition about the causes of abnormal behavior gave rise to a variety of bizarre and sometimes cruel approaches to treatment. The contraptions shown in this 1596 German engraving are being used by quacks to drain harmful thoughts from one patient's abdomen and to distill them from another patient's brain. *(Historical Pictures Service.)*

view that psychological abnormality should be thought of as disease—a mental "illness"—to be "diagnosed" by a doctor, in an effort to "cure" the "patient."

The biological perspective on mental disorders has also encouraged the common belief that people who behave abnormally are not responsible for their actions. They are deemed to be mentally "sick," and therefore not in control of themselves. Some observers, however, strongly reject this notion, one of the most vocal being the psychiatrist Thomas Szasz (1961). Szasz believes that casting a disturbed person in the "sick" role may be the worst thing that we can do, for when we call people sick and treat them accordingly, they often learn to play the role all too well. Szasz urges us to think of abnormal behavior as a sign not of illness but rather of "problems in living"— problems that cannot be solved unless the sufferer gains a sense of control over him- or herself. As we will see later, however, Szasz's view is not widely shared.

Psychological Approaches

Despite the fact that the biological perspective has had much influence, few people believe that most mental disorders are strictly physiological in origin. A large number of mental health professionals place great stress on the psychological factors—strong emotional conflict, inappropriate learning—that also contribute to mental disturbance. The three main psychological theories of abnormal behavior parallel three of the theories of personality we discussed in Chapter 13. These are psychoanalytic theory, learning theory, and the phenomenological view.

The Psychoanalytic Perspective.
As you learned in Chapter 13, Sigmund Freud, the founder of psychoanalysis, believed that the human psyche consists of three interacting forces—the id (a pool of biological urges), the ego (which mediates between the id and reality), and the superego (which represents society's moral standards). Abnormal behavior, in Freud's view, is caused by conflict among these three components, especially conflict that arises from a failure to manage effectively the id's sexual impulses during childhood. Freud argued, for instance, that a child who fails to resolve the Oedipal conflict (a desire to possess the opposite-sex parent sexually) is unlikely to identify properly with the same-sex parent, and so

will inadequately incorporate that parent's moral standards. The result is a person with a weak superego who rarely experiences guilt. If, on the other hand, the superego becomes too great a naysayer— perhaps because of stern and moralistic punishment of masturbation during the phallic stage—the person may make exaggerated efforts to repress all sexuality.

Given this view of the causes of abnormal behavior, it is easy to understand the logic of the treatment Freud offered. Through psychoanalysis—a deep probing of people's current thoughts and feelings for clues to their past experiences and unconscious conflicts—Freud hoped his patients might gain critical insights into the roots of their problem behaviors, insights that might ultimately make them psychologically healthier. Note that the psychoanalytic perspective and the biological perspective, although very different, have an important belief in common. Both maintain that a disturbed person's external symptoms are merely clues to a deeper, underlying cause. For a "cure" to come about, that cause must be eliminated, or at least brought under control.

The Learning-Theory Perspective.
In sharp contrast to both the biological and psychoanalytic perspectives, learning theorists argue that most abnormality arises neither from physiological disorders nor from unresolved psychic conflicts. Instead, they see abnormality as largely the product of inadequate or inappropriate learning. Learning theorists believe that people acquire abnormal behaviors through the various kinds of learning we talked about in Chapter 5. For instance, a person may learn to be abnormally fearful of something through classical conditioning (as when a man who was once beaten and robbed in an elevator becomes terrified of all closed-in places). Or phobias may arise through observational learning—that is, simply by observation of intense fear in others (Rosenthal and Bandura, 1978). This is why the little girl whose mother is terrified of snakes will often learn to fear snakes herself. The rewards and punishments involved in operant conditioning can also shape abnormal behaviors. Consider the man who feels compelled to abuse and dominate women. When a woman he assaults shows fear and obedience, her responses may be a form of reinforcement for him, encouraging him to repeat the same behaviors another time. Note that learning theory shares with psychoanalytic theory a belief that abnormality is rooted in past experiences. But whereas psychoanalysts maintain that our most important learning expe-

According to learning theorists, abnormal or inappropriate behavior is learned in the same ways as normal behavior. Thus, children may learn that assaultive behavior is as effective as cooperative behavior—or even more effective—in getting attention from adults. *(Elizabeth Hamlin/ Stock, Boston.)*

riences take place during infancy and childhood, learning theorists argue that experiences continue to shape us throughout our adult lives.

The learning approach to abnormality also differs from the psychoanalytic one in the kinds of treatment prescribed. As we said earlier, psychoanalysts see abnormal behavior as symptomatic of deeper, unconscious conflicts. They therefore probe a patient's psyche to bring these conflicts to light. Learning theorists, in contrast, believe that abnormal behavior is not just a symptom; they see it as the problem itself. Thus learning therapies are designed either to "undo" past lessons that have instilled inappropriate behaviors or to provide new lessons that will foster desirable responses. Consider the learning approach to treating phobias, for instance. Learning theorists have found that many phobias are maintained because the phobic person scrupulously avoids the feared stimulus. A person with a dog phobia, for example, avoids all dogs and so never has a chance to learn that most dogs are perfectly harmless. Therapy for such a person is aimed at breaking this pattern of avoidance. The person is helped to approach dogs (perhaps in a series of steps, from looking at pictures of dogs to touching a real one) and thereby to learn that dogs usually pose no threat.

Historically, the learning approach to abnormality has confined itself to trying to change maladaptive *behavior*—hence the term "behavior therapy." Traditional behavior therapists were not particularly concerned about what went on inside the mind of the client, as long as that person's undesirable responses were reduced or eliminated. An increasing number of learning theorists, however, are now recognizing that people's interpretations of the events around them (their various *cognitions*) are also important. Consider two students who fail a difficult exam. One may interpret the failure as caused by lack of effort and so resolve to study harder. The other, in contrast, may attribute the failure to lack of personal ability, become depressed, and consider quitting school. These two cognitions ("I didn't try hard enough" versus "I don't have the brains for college") greatly influence the students' responses to the situation. Psychologists who take a cognitive view of learning argue that the quality of our internal dialogue—whether we accept or berate ourselves, build ourselves up or tear ourselves down—has a profound effect on our mental health. They believe that often people must change negative cognitions to break free of certain maladaptive behaviors. As you will see in Chapter 16, both this and the more traditional approach to behavior therapy are widely used today.

The Phenomenological Perspective. As we saw when we explored Carl Rogers' views in Chapter 13, those who adopt the phenomenological perspective argue that others often demand that we be different from what we feel are our "true" selves—that we conform to their expectations instead of following our own preferences. For instance, a young man's parents may ridicule his dream of becoming an actor, demanding that he pursue a more "serious" profession. And even today, the family and friends of a career-minded young woman may urge her instead to marry and "settle down." When such demands are many and unreasonable, acute anxiety can result. The person begins to feel that the true self is unworthy and so tries to be what others expect, only to find that such efforts thwart important opportunities for personal growth. These are the roots, in the phenomenological view, of psychological disturbance.

Like the psychoanalytic perspective, then, the phenomenological view sees the disturbed person as one in conflict, often trying to deny desires to think and act in certain ways. But these two perspectives differ markedly in the types of treatment they prescribe. Unlike the psychoanalyst, the phenomenologically oriented therapist spends relatively little time delving into a person's past and has no interest in probing for secrets hidden in the unconscious. Instead, the therapist concentrates on enabling the person to discover what he or she wants and to act in a way that will promote personal growth.

Note how much the phenomenological perspective differs from all the other approaches we have discussed in the degree to which it assigns responsibility to the individual. Other therapies often attribute a person's problems to such causes as biochemical imbalance, a neurotic parent, or a faulty learning experience. Phenomenologically oriented treatment seeks no such external source of responsibility. The therapist assumes that each individual is ultimately free to make the choices that shape the kind of person he or she becomes. For example, consider a woman who has been involved in an unsatisfying marriage for many years. According to the phenomenological view, she should attempt to understand why she has chosen to stay in the relationship as long as she has, instead of confronting the difficult question of whether to end the marriage. By the same token, phenomenologically oriented treatment assumes that the insights and impetus for change must come from the client, not from the therapist. It is the client that must ultimately bring about a "cure"; the therapist merely serves as an empathetic and supportive partner. Thus therapy becomes a natural extension of the perpetual human quest for meaning and self-fulfillment in life.

Other Approaches

The three psychological approaches to abnormality that we have just outlined—the psychoanalytic, the learning-theory, and the phenomenological—are extremely important ones. Each provides a comprehensive account of how psychological disturbance develops and how such disturbances can be treated and alleviated. But others concerned with abnormal behavior rightly argue that these three approaches plus the biological perspective do not explore *all* of abnormality's possible causes. They stress that we must also consider the social world in which the disturbed person lives. Two approaches that look beyond the individual to his or her important relationships and broad social context are the family, or systems, perspective on abnormality and the sociocultural perspective.

The Family, or Systems, Perspective. The family, or systems, perspective sees mental disorder as arising partly from the network of social relationships in which a person is involved. One of the most crucial of these networks—especially to a young child—is the family. The systems perspective, in fact, developed from the experiences of psychotherapists who treated children. These professionals were unable to ignore the role of the family in producing children's problems. As a result, they began to extend their search for causes beyond the young patient to the child's parents and siblings as well. Today this perspective includes a variety of viewpoints about how the family can disrupt normal development. All, however, share the central view that the interaction of family members is important in shaping and maintaining abnormal behavior.

Some systems theorists analyze the family as a set of interlocking roles (Minuchin, 1974, for example). In their view a family may have a disciplinarian, a scapegoat, a baby, and a peacemaker, among many other possible roles. While these roles may not always be good for family members, they allow the system to maintain a degree of predictability and equilibrium. Sometimes, however, a family identifies one member as a "patient" or "sick person." Other complementary roles (nurse, martyr, pillar of strength, chronic worrier) develop around this one, until the sick person's recovery may actually cause family turmoil.

Other systems theorists focus on faulty communications among family members (for example, Watzlawick, Beavin, and Jackson, 1967; Singer and Wynne, 1965; Haley, 1980). They suspect that when people habitually communicate in unsatisfactory ways, psychological disturbance may result. Consider the mother who often sends her son contradictory messages. Perhaps she repeatedly encourages him to speak his mind but then punishes him severely for "talking back." Some propose that such "double-bind" communications may contribute to the development of schizophrenia. Other deviant communication patterns have likewise been found in the families of schizophrenics. For instance, the emotional climate within the family may be characterized by hostility toward the schizophrenic person or overinvolvement with him or her (Brown et al., 1966). Or members of such families may fail to maintain a shared focus of attention. One person may begin talking about a particular subject, only to have another person pick up a different train of thought. In this way the family members fail to acknowledge one another's participation in a shared dialogue.

The Sociocultural Perspective. The sociocultural perspective, like the family perspective, looks beyond the individual for the causes of abnormality. The sociocultural approach argues, however, that the roots of mental disturbance often lie in such social ills as poverty, poor nutrition, inadequate housing, crime,

and discrimination. The primary evidence in support of this view is the generally higher rate of serious mental disorders (such as schizophrenia and alcoholism) among the lowest socioeconomic classes (Hollingshead and Redlich, 1958; Kolb, Bernard, and Dohrenwend, 1969; Redlich and Kellert, 1978).

Advocates of the sociocultural perspective have proposed several theories to account for the high incidence of serious abnormality in the lowest socioeconomic classes. First, the lives of the poor are generally more stressful than those of people with higher incomes (Pearlin and Schooler, 1978; Kessler, 1979; Kessler, Price, and Wortman, in press). Inadequate food and housing, frequent unemployment, and constant worries over sheer survival are enough to induce psychological disturbance in almost anyone, this argument holds. Second, people in the lowest social classes are generally less successful at warding off the stresses of hardship than people in higher social classes (Pearlin and Schooler, 1978). They are more inclined to use ineffective coping strategies (fretting, trying to ignore their problems, giving up to "fate") than are middle- and upper-class people. They are also more apt to lack the encouragement and support of others that can help people weather serious life crises (Liem and Liem, 1978). Finally, there is also the possibility that abnormal behavior is simply *labeled* more serious when the person comes from the lower social classes (Scheff, 1975). Many diagnosticians, themselves from the higher social classes, may find the characteristic styles of deviant behavior in the lower social classes more bizarre than those common in higher social strata. This may be one reason why a lower-class person who suffers a psychological disturbance is more likely to be placed in a state mental hospital than is a middle-class person (Hollingshead and Redlich, 1958; Myers and Bean, 1968).

Combining the Various Perspectives

Because each perspective on abnormal behavior looks to a different cause, therapists who subscribe to

The sociocultural perspective views social inequity as the primary cause of abnormal behavior. *(George Malave/ Stock, Boston.)*

a given view will ask their clients certain kinds of questions and offer them certain kinds of treatment. Consider the case of a woman who experiences severe and prolonged depression after the death of her elderly father. A psychoanalyst may question the woman closely about her childhood and her feelings about her parents, hoping to find a clue to some unconscious conflict that has turned normal grief into serious depression. A learning theorist, in contrast, may look for factors in the woman's immediate environment that are reinforcing her symptoms of depression. And a phenomenologist, after acknowledging the woman's need to mourn her father, may help her accept the fact that everyone is ultimately alone. Each approach thus attacks the problem from a different angle. As we consider various disorders in the sections that follow, we will examine the unique insights that various theoretical perspectives have to offer in regard to them.

But the fact that theoretical perspectives differ should not lead you to conclude that they are necessarily mutually exclusive. Often we get our richest insights into the causes of a particular psychological disturbance by combining several viewpoints. As you will see a little later, for instance, the biological perspective, the family perspective, and the sociocultural perspective, among others, all have something important to say about the possible causes of schizophrenia. Many clinicians today, in fact, are trying to develop even more complex models of abnormal behavior—models that incorporate elements from numerous theoretical approaches (Liem, 1980).

CLASSIFYING PSYCHOLOGICAL DISORDERS

Whatever model they may apply to abnormality, psychologists and psychiatrists must have some way of determining whether a person has a mental disorder, and if so, what kind of disorder it is. Their diagnosis is generally based on their observations of the person's problem behaviors.

In order to reach a diagnosis, however, some system of classification is needed. In all sciences classification is an essential foundation for the accumulation of knowledge. For one thing, it gives professionals a shorthand vocabulary for communicating among themselves. When a diagnosis of manic-depressive disorder is made, for instance, this single term provides a fairly accurate summary of what the person's disturbance is like. Classification also enables professionals to begin to build theories about the causes and possible treatments of various disorders. The common diagnostic categories actually contain information from a wide variety of experiences. Finally, a good classification system is important for accurate prediction. It can provide vital information about the likelihood of a given disorder, which people are most susceptible to it, how the condition is apt to progress once it has started, and what the chances of alleviating it are.

The *DSM-III* Classification System

The classification system on which virtually all mental health care professionals rely is the third edition of the *Diagnostic and Statistical Manual of Mental Disorders (DSM III)*, published by the American Psychiatric Association. It contains a detailed list of the major mental disorders and their characteristic symptoms. The disorders included in the manual are based on the current judgments of professionals, and so tend to change over time. In the first two editions of *DSM,* for example, homosexuality was listed as a disorder. In 1973, however, the American Psychiatric Association voted to strike it from the manual. *DSM III* (published in 1980) includes only a category called "ego-dystonic homosexuality," which applies exclusively to those homosexuals who are disturbed by their sexual orientation.

DSM III recommends a very thorough approach to the evaluation of psychiatric patients. It calls for assessment in terms of five dimensions, or "axes." Axes I and II include the psychological disorders from which the person suffers. Most serious disorders, such as major depression and schizophrenia, are on axis I. To ensure that a long-term personality disturbance is not overlooked after a current major disorder has been diagnosed on the basis of axis I, psychologists next use axis II. This axis is reserved for maladaptive personality traits (compulsiveness, overdependency, and so forth) as well as for certain developmental problems (language or reading difficulties, for instance). On axis III the patient is evaluated for physical conditions that may be related to his or her psychological symptoms. Axis IV specifies the level of stress in the person's current life, for stress is often directly linked to psychological problems. Finally, axis V provides an assessment of the highest level of functioning the patient has displayed in the last year—at work, at home, with friends, and in leisure-time pursuits. This highest level of functioning is often a good indication of the person's chances for recovery. It is hoped that this "multiaxial" system of evaluation will enable clinicians to avoid overlooking factors important to the treatment of particular patients.

The American Psychiatric Association has been responsive to requests that its descriptions of psychological disorders be made more specific. *DSM III* expanded *DSM II*'s relatively brief definitions into descriptions that often run for several pages. *DSM III* also provides straightforward lists of symptoms that *must* be present if a person is to receive a particular diagnosis. In addition, *DSM III* includes information on how to distinguish certain disorders from similar ones, estimates of the incidence of each disorder, data on whether a certain disorder occurs more frequently in one sex than in the other, data on the extent to which a disorder runs in families, and so forth. All this information is intended to make *DSM III* more useful than its predecessors.

in depth
Criticisms of Classification

No matter how hard the American Psychiatric Association has tried to expand and clarify its diagnostic system, classification still has its critics. Many argue that most attempts to categorize mental disorders do more harm than good. These so-called diagnoses, this argument goes, are simply labels devised for the convenience of psychologists and psychiatrists—labels that may obscure the real conditions of patients, while at the same time treating them like categories, not people.

A provocative paper expressing this anticlassification view was written by psychologist D. L. Rosenhan (1973) and titled "On Being Sane in Insane Places." In it Rosenhan described a study in which eight of his associates, who had never suffered any serious mental disorder, requested admission to psychiatric hospitals as patients. The group included three psychologists, a psychiatrist, a graduate student in psychology, a pediatrician, a painter, and a housewife. In their admission interviews they gave their personal histories truthfully, concealing only their identities. They also reported a single bogus symptom: hearing voices that seemed to be saying "empty," "hollow," and "thud." After being admitted to the hospital, all of the pseudopatients stopped faking any symptoms and behaved normally. Much of their time in the hospital wards was spent taking notes on what they observed.

The pseudopatients stayed in the hospital from seven to fifty-two days, with an average stay of nineteen days. Not one was recognized as normal by the professional staff, although several real patients suspected they were normal. Seven of the eight were diagnosed as schizophrenic and were discharged with the diagnosis of "schizophrenia in remission." In view of what happened to his pseudopatients, Rosenhan argued that psychiatric diagnosis is not valid. If mental health professionals cannot distinguish the sane from the insane, Rosenhan reasoned, of what real value is their diagnostic system?

Rosenhan also argued that the initial labeling of mental patients profoundly affects the way the hospital staff subsequently perceives them. Once the label of schizophrenic was applied to the pseudopatients, their normal behaviors were apparently overlooked or misinterpreted. Even note taking was seen as a psychiatric symptom. "Patient engages in writing behavior," one nurse wrote in the hospital record. Not even discharge from the hospital can erase the schizophrenic label, according to Rosenhan. As he described it:

> A psychiatric label has a life and an influence of its own. Once the impression has been formed that the patient is schizophrenic, he will continue to be schizophrenic. When a sufficient amount of time has passed, during which the patient has done nothing bizarre, he is considered to be in remission and available for discharge. But the label endures beyond dis-

charge, with the unconfirmed expectation that he will behave as a schizophrenic again.   [1973, p. 253]

One consequence of labeling patients, Rosenhan argued, is that they become stigmatized by the label. For the pseudopatients, this meant that staff members abused or avoided them. Family and friends may react the same way. Eventually, Rosenhan contended, "the patient himself accepts the diagnosis, with all of its surplus meanings and expectations, and behaves accordingly" (1973, p. 254). The diagnosis, in other words, becomes a self-fulfilling prophecy.

Rosenhan's study generated considerable controversy. One critic, Robert L. Spitzer, argued that the fact that the pseudopatients were able to lie their way into the hospital does not mean the diagnostic system is invalid (Spitzer, 1975, 1976). If a person swallowed a cup of blood, went to an emergency room, spat the blood up, and was then diagnosed as having a bleeding ulcer, would the diagnostic criteria for this disorder be invalidated? Spitzer maintained not, for the person would have convincingly faked a classic and serious symptom.

Spitzer also pointed out that the hospitals responded very quickly to the absence of symptoms. An average hospitalization of nineteen days is quite brief for someone who has initially complained of hearing nonexistent voices, a classic symptom of schizophrenia. Furthermore, the hospitals were justified in keeping the patients even though their behavior seemed to return to normal. The pseudopatients had reported a serious symptom, and the sudden absence of that symptom would not necessarily mean that no abnormality existed. Some truly schizophrenic patients have lucid intervals during which they seem quite normal. In addition, the discharge diagnosis "schizophrenia in remission" is rarely used, Spitzer noted, indicating that the hospital staff did recognize that these patients were symptom-free.

Finally, Spitzer noted that Rosenhan's study contains very little actual data. For example, Rosenhan stated that subjects' normal behavior was often seen as pathological by staff members. However, the only support offered for this claim was the nurse's comment on one patient's "writing behavior." Rosenhan erred further, Spitzer claimed, in not providing additional information about how the pseudopatients behaved in the hospital. Without a verbatim report of admission interviews, for example, we have no way of knowing exactly how the pseudopatients described their problems and thus how "sick" they seemed to the hospital staff.

Despite such criticisms, Rosenhan (1975) has maintained that his study illustrates the importance of context in psychiatric diagnosis. In the case of the pseudopatients, their very presence in the hospital almost guaranteed that some of their behavior would be viewed as a sign of disturbance. Even insistence that they were well was likely to be interpreted as evidence that they were truly "sick." One real patient advised a pseudopatient on how to negotiate this problem: "Don't tell them you're well. They won't believe you. Tell them you're sick, but getting better. That's called insight and they'll discharge you!" (Rosenhan, 1975, p. 472). Rosenhan believes that given the negative connotations of a diagnostic label and the fact that it may not be reliable, we are better off at this stage of our knowledge to eliminate diagnostic categories entirely.

Rosenhan's critics reply that some diagnosis is essential if our knowledge is ever to expand. How, such people as Spitzer ask, are we ever to study the effectiveness of treatments for such conditions as schizophrenia, depression, and alcoholism if we are prevented from using diagnostic labels? Without such labels we would be hard pressed even to identify a sample population to investigate. Thus, while recognizing the negative effects that diagnostic labeling can have, many clinicians are unwilling to abandon all attempts at psychiatric classification. For this reason, the rest of this chapter explores some of the major classes of disorders listed in *DSM III*.

in depth

ANXIETY DISORDERS

Anxiety disorders, as the name suggests, are characterized by anxiety—emotional distress caused by feelings of vulnerability, apprehension, or fear. The victims almost always try to defend against these feelings. Sometimes they engage in ritualized behaviors that may reduce the anxiety somewhat. At other times they try to escape from or avoid situations that tend to trigger the problem. Such strategies, of course, are only partly effective. The person remains troubled and ill at ease, clinging to defenses that have no chance of alleviating the cause of the anxiety. Because anxiety disorders are mild in comparison with other abnormal behaviors, they are often labeled neurotic. Nevertheless, the symptoms experienced are very upsetting to those who suffer them. Anxiety disorders also are fairly common. Three that afflict between 2 and 4 percent of the population are generalized anxiety and panic attacks, phobias, and obsessive-compulsive behaviors.

Generalized Anxiety and Panic Attacks

Generalized anxiety is characterized by diffuse fears that are impossible to manage through avoidance. The person is jumpy, irritable, and often upset. He or she expresses a great many worries, yet is unable to specify what is generating them—a condition Freud called **free-floating anxiety.** Sufferers may have nightmares in which things are closing in on them or in which they are lost or abandoned. Their daily functioning is also substantially impaired. They are so preoccupied by their worries that they cannot concentrate on their work, frequently becoming forgetful and disorganized.

Various physical symptoms often accompany generalized anxiety, as they do other anxiety disorders. Victims may complain of stiff, aching muscles, the result of sustained muscle tension. Their appetites tend to be poor, and they may be troubled by indigestion and a frequent need to urinate. Their sleeping patterns are also typically disturbed. They may have insomnia, or they may begin awakening suddenly in the night. In the morning they feel tired rather than refreshed. The following case illustrates several of these symptoms:

> Mr. Wright, a man of 35, was referred to hospital because of a "dizzy turn" which he had experienced during his work as a laborer. He had had similar attacks in the past but, with each one, the associated feelings of panic became more acute. . . .
> As the attacks developed, he began to sleep badly. He had difficulty in getting off to sleep because of worrisome thoughts that raced through his mind; fre-

quently his dreams had a menacing content and more and more they were only resolved by his awakening in a cold sweat, accompanied by frequent headaches. . . .
> [Later] he began to complain of pressure in the front of his head and uncontrollable trembling and palpitations. He became more and more dependent on his wife and would go nowhere without her. . . . This meant of course that he had to give up work. . . . The worries about his failure to support his family caused his anxiety to "spiral." [McCulloch and Prins, 1975, p. 54]

People who suffer generalized anxiety may also experience **panic attacks,** episodes in which an already heightened state of tension mounts to an acute and overwhelming level. The person may experience difficulty breathing, choking sensations, chest pain, heart palpitations, dizziness, faintness, hot or cold flashes, or fear of dying or going crazy. These terrifying sensations seem to come from nowhere. They may last for a minute or two or (more rarely) persist for an hour or more. When the panic attack subsides, the victim may feel exhausted.

Phobias

When a person's anxiety is focused irrationally on a particular object or situation, it is called a **phobia.** (The term comes from the Greek word for "fear.") Unlike those with generalized anxiety, people with phobias believe they know what triggers their feeling of dread. The case below is in many ways typical:

> The client was a 30-year-old male who reported intense fear of crossing bridges and of heights. The fear had begun 3 years earlier when he was driving over a large suspension bridge while feeling anxious due to marital and career conflicts. Looking over the side he had experienced intense waves of fear. From that time onward his fear of bridges had become progressively more severe. At first, only bridges similar to the original were involved, but slowly the fear generalized to all bridges. Concurrently, he developed a fear of heights. Just before he came for treatment, he had been forced to dine with his employer in a restaurant atop a 52-story building. He had developed nausea and diarrhea and had been unable to eat. This had decided him to seek treatment. [Hurley, 1976, p. 295]

Most people are somewhat afraid of heights, but for people who suffer from acrophobia the fear is so intense and terrifying that they will disrupt their lives in order to avoid the situations that trigger their panic—refusing, for instance, to live or work above the second floor of a building. *(Kevin Horan/ Picture Group.)*

A phobia, then, can be extremely disruptive to a person's life. Ironically, the person may recognize that the fear is irrational, yet still be unable to dismiss it. Only avoidance of the feared object relieves the anxiety. Table 15.1 lists some of the phobias clinicians have encountered.

Psychologists have proposed several theories to account for phobias. Freudians have argued that phobias develop as defense mechanisms against dangerous or unacceptable impulses. A man with a bridge phobia, for instance, may be defending against a suicidal urge to jump off a bridge. Learning theorists, in contrast, believe that many phobias result from classical conditioning. A child stung by a bee, for example, may thereafter fear bees because of their past association with pain. Firsthand contact with the feared object is not even needed for this type of classical conditioning to occur. A person may fear swimming in the ocean, for instance, after watching the movie *Jaws*. Here a previously neutral stimulus (ocean water) is repeatedly paired with a terrifying experience (watching people devoured by a shark) until eventually the water alone is enough to generate fear. Other phobias may be instilled through observational learning (Bootzin and Max, 1980). A girl who hears her mother express a terror of heights, for instance, may express the same fear later, even though heights have never been associated with any real danger to her.

Obsessions and Compulsions

An **obsession** is a recurring irrational thought, one that the victim realizes is senseless and tries to suppress but cannot. A **compulsion** is irrational behavior, again recognized as senseless but still beyond the victim's control. Obsessions and compulsions are closely related in that obsessive thinking often leads to compulsive behavior. A common example is the person who is obsessed by the idea of germs and feels compelled to wash her hands repeatedly in order to

TABLE 15.1 COMMON PHOBIAS

PHOBIA	FEARED OBJECT OR SITUATION
Acrophobia	High places
Agoraphobia	Open places
Claustrophobia	Enclosed places
Ergasiophobia	Work
Gamophobia	Marriage
Haphephobia	Being touched
Hematophobia	Blood
Monophobia	Being alone
Ocholophobia	Crowds
Taphophobia	Being buried alive
Xenophobia	Strangers

get rid of them. Below is a more extreme example:

Mr. B was unmarried, aged 45, and had a 30-year history of obsessive-compulsive problems. . . . [His] basic problem was a compulsion to be slow, meticulous, and ritualistic, especially when dressing, washing, shaving, cleaning his teeth and combing his hair. . . . For instance, cleaning his teeth involved 192 slow meticulous brush strokes for each application of toothpaste and for each rinse. . . . Bathing would take him up to three hours with half an hour spent in rinsing the bath before filling it and half an hour rinsing the bath afterwards. Every action was performed in a slow meticulous manner reminiscent of the care taken by a bomb disposal expert.   [Hodgson and Rachman, 1976, p. 29]

Obsessions without compulsions are experienced as ideas that cannot be dismissed from the mind. Sometimes the person with an obsession ruminates on the pros and cons of the same issue over and over in an exhausting pattern of perpetual uncertainty. Here is a case in point:

Eliot H., a college student, went to a telephone booth to call up a wealthy girl whom he had recently met, to ask her for a date. He spent an hour there, anxious and indecisive, unable to put the coin in the slot and unable to give up and go home. Each time his hand approached the telephone he anxiously withdrew it because he felt that telephoning her might ruin his chances with her. Each time he withdrew his hand he seemed to be throwing away a golden opportunity. . . .

His whole future seemed to Eliot to hang on the outcome of this little act. . . . He was helplessly caught in an obsessive dilemma, as he had been caught before hundreds of times.   [Cameron, 1963, p. 396]

Eliot's thinking is an exaggerated version of the doubt and indecisiveness we all feel from time to time. Many obsessions and compulsions, however, are much more remote from normal experience. People have been obsessed by the idea that they would kill a family member or disrobe on a busy street. Compulsive hand washers have been known to continue their repetitive scrubbing until their hands are raw. Other victims of compulsions have been unable to sleep at night, driven to get out of bed repeatedly and make sure that the doors are locked.

If you asked those who suffer from compulsions why they do these things, most would say that they feel uneasy unless they do them. The compulsive behaviors seem to avert anxiety. Unfortunately, however, the victims of compulsions often pay a high price. When every step must be counted or every doorknob touched twelve times before it can be turned, normal life becomes very difficult.

SOMATOFORM DISORDERS

The distinguishing characteristic of a **somatoform disorder** is the existence or fear of some physical (somatic) ailment, even though the ailment in this case has no organic cause. Whatever physical disorder the victim experiences or dreads is produced solely by that person's mind. Of the several types of somatoform disorder we will discuss two: hypochondriasis and conversion disorder. Because a person with either of these disorders remains lucid and generally in touch with reality, both are referred to as neurotic problems.

Hypochondriasis

People who suffer from **hypochondriasis** are persistently fearful that they have contracted some terrible, often fatal disease. The hypochondriac spends much of life scrutinizing bodily functions for signs of serious physical illness. The minor aches, pains, bumps, and bruises impossible to avoid in the course of normal living are immediately taken as signs of some dreaded malady now in its early stages. Thus a simple headache may be interpreted as a possible brain tumor, and an occasional cough as a sign of incipient lung cancer. You might think that when medical tests revealed the hypochondriac's fears to be groundless, his or her anxiety would end. But this is not what happens. The typical hypochondriac refuses to believe a doctor's reassurance that no disease exists. He or she is certain that the feared illness is lurking, and that the doctor has simply failed to recognize it. Many hypochondriacs go from doctor to doctor with the same minor ailments, always receiving the same reassurances yet never finding any relief from their irrational fears.

At present, little is known about the causes of hypochondriasis. For some people, reports of physical symptoms may be substitutes for expressions of emotional concerns: an aching shoulder may be easier to talk about than the pain of a son's failure to telephone.

Conversion Disorder

Hypochondriacs morbidly fear that they are very ill although no serious physical illness is present. The psychological distress of a person suffering a **conversion disorder,** in contrast, actually produces what appears to be a genuine physical dysfunction. The sufferer suddenly becomes blind, deaf, or paralyzed, or loses sensation in a part of the body, usually following some traumatic event. Yet no organic basis can be found for the condition. Moreover, the ailment often violates neurophysiological laws. A person's hand, for instance, may become completely numb, even insensitive to the stab of a pin, but inexplicably the person may feel normal sensations in a neurologically related area just above the wrist (see Figure 15.1). This is called glove anesthesia because the loss of sensation occurs in an area that would be covered by a glove rather than in an area corresponding to actual neurological pathways.

A conversion disorder often takes a form that makes it impossible for the victim to engage in some anxiety-provoking activity. The student who fears that she will fail a crucial exam becomes blind and can no longer study. The soldier who has had a brush with death on the battlefield develops a paralyzed arm and can no longer fire a rifle. These people are not faking or malingering. Their blindness and paralysis are real. But the cause is psychological, not organic. The role these afflictions play in reducing anxiety is revealed by the calm way in which many of the victims seem to accept their disabilities.

Conversion disorders often disappear as suddenly

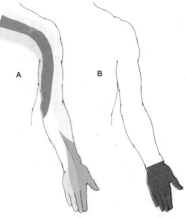

Figure 15.1 A person who complained of numbness in the hand might be diagnosed as suffering either from damage to the nervous system or from conversion disorder, depending on the exact pattern of the numbness. The skin areas served by different nerves in the arm are shown in A. The "glove anesthesia" shown in B could not result from damage to these nerves.

as they appeared. The blind student wakes up one morning able to see normally. Many so-called miracle cures in which the paralyzed suddenly leave their wheelchairs or the totally deaf suddenly hear may involve conversion disorders.

Several theories have been offered to explain conversion symptoms. Freud argued that conversion disorders develop as defenses against forbidden impulses. Guilt over masturbation or an urge to strike one's parents may result in paralysis of the arm, for instance. Learning theorists, in contrast, tend to see conversion symptoms as means both of escaping anxiety and responsibility and of gaining care and attention from others. Finally, family theorists broaden the search for causes to include relationships within the victim's family. They often try to discover whether the conversion disorder is serving some useful role in family life. Haley (1973) tells of a woman who developed conversion blindness when her husband retired. Her condition helped him cope with the difficult transition from his demanding job to a less active role at home. Caring for her and running the household made him feel useful. When she began to recover, he became depressed, and he felt better only after she suffered a relapse.

DISSOCIATIVE DISORDERS

The **dissociative disorders** affect psychological rather than physical functioning. A part of the personality is split-off, or dissociated, so that personal memory or identity is disturbed. Dissociative disorders include amnesia, fugue, and multiple personality.

Amnesia

Amnesia is the partial or total forgetting of past experiences after some stressful event. Some people accused of murder, for instance, maintain that they remember nothing about events surrounding the crime. Unlike amnesia that has an organic basis, dissociative amnesia appears suddenly in relation to some psychological trauma. What is forgotten is often highly selective and can sometimes be recovered under hypnosis. Interestingly, even when amnesia victims forget their former identities, they always retain *some* memories from the past. A woman may not recognize her family, for example, but remember how to knit.

Fugue

Victims of **fugue** ("flight") walk away from their homes and their identities for a period of time. That period may be hours, days, months, or even years. In rare cases, the person takes up an entirely new life. The recovered fugue victim usually recalls nothing of what happened during the fugue state. The following case is in many ways typical:

> A young married woman, chronically unhappy and in conflict over her marriage, occasionally wandered from her home in the daytime and got lost, much as unhappy little children do. She would suddenly "come to" far from home, and with no memory of having left it. [Cameron, 1963, p. 339]

Multiple Personality

In a more extreme form of dissociation, called **multiple personality,** an individual's personality structure divides into two or more complete identities, each well defined and distinct from the others. Two cases of this rare disorder have been widely publicized in the films *The Three Faces of Eve* and *Sybil.* Often the personalities contrast sharply. Eve, for example, expressed both the "good girl" personality of Eve White and the naughty, uninhibited Eve Black. Usually the personalities emerge and disappear suddenly and are generally unaware of one another.

AFFECTIVE DISORDERS

Affective disorders are characterized by disturbances of mood, or affect. All of us experience changes in mood, of course (Wessman and Ricks, 1966). Usually our moods are influenced by specific events in our lives. We become elated if we win a lottery and dejected if we fail an exam. At other times, however, we feel marvelous or miserable for no apparent reason. People with affective disorders experience much the same mood swings—but their swings are magnified and they tend to last for longer periods. As a result, these victims' emotional states come to distort their entire outlooks and to interfere greatly with their normal lives. Mental health professionals identify three major types of affective disorders: depression, mania, and manic-depressive (or bipolar) disorder. Each episode of mood disturbance is generally rated for its severity, ranging from a "mild" affective disorder to a "psychotic" one, in which the victim suffers hallucinations and delusions totally divorced from reality.

Depression

The most common affective disorder is **depression,** a dysphoric mood persisting for at least two weeks, during which time it tends to color all of the person's thoughts and behaviors. Depressed people usually describe themselves as sad, down, discouraged, and hopeless. The seriously depressed experience several other symptoms as well, at least half of which must be present before the label "major depression" is applied. One of these symptoms is a marked *loss of interest and pleasure* in activities. Nothing seems worth doing to the deeply depressed person. Even once enjoyable pastimes lose all their former appeal. Most seriously depressed people also experience a marked *loss of energy.* They feel perpetually tired, and even the slightest exertion exhausts them. In keeping with this chronic fatigue, depressed people frequently show a *slowing down of behavior.* Posture may become stooped, movements labored, and speech fragmented by pauses. Depressives also tend to experience *difficulties in thinking*. They cannot concentrate or remember well; they have great trouble making decisions. Frequently there is a *loss of appetite* too, as well as *problems in sleeping* (insomnia or a tendency to sleep for hours on end). And almost invariably the deeply depressed suffer exaggerated *feelings of worthlessness*. They see no virtues in themselves; they greatly magnify their failures; they are convinced that they are utterly hopeless cases. Such feelings can easily lead to a final symptom of depression: recurring *thoughts of death and suicide*.

Some of these symptoms, of course, are ones that many people experience when they are "low" or "blue." But for the seriously depressed person, these feelings, thoughts, and behaviors are far more intense than normal and also much more prolonged. One long-term study, for instance, found that 40 percent of seriously depressed patients had not recovered six months into the study, and 24 percent had *still* not recovered a full year after the study began. Even among the patients who recovered, the disorder had lasted a median of seven agonizing months (Shapiro and Keller, 1981; Keller and Shapiro, 1981). Relapses into depression after recovery are common, especially among those who report three or more prior episodes of depression and among first-episode patients who are older (Keller et al., 1983). Here is how one woman described what it is like to spiral downward into a major depression:

> I began not to be able to manage as far as doing the kinds of things that I really had always been able to do easily, such as cook, wash, take care of the children, play games, that kind of thing. . . . I think one of the most frightening aspects at the beginning was that time went so slowly. It would seem sometimes that at least an hour had gone by and I would look at my watch and it would only have been three minutes. And I began not to be able to concentrate. Another thing that was very frightening to me was that I couldn't read any more. And if awakened early . . . earlier than I needed to, I sometimes would lie in bed two hours trying to make myself get up because I just couldn't put my feet on the floor. Then when I did, I just felt that I couldn't get dressed. And then, whatever the next step was, I felt I couldn't do that.
> [From "Depression: The Shadowed Valley," from the series *The Thin Edge*, © 1975 by the Educational Broadcasting Corporation.]

Severe depression carries with it the danger of suicide. Overwhelmed with hopelessness, the sufferer may see suicide as "the only way out." *(Woodcut by Käthe Kollwitz; Courtesy of the National Gallery of Art, Washington, D. C., Rosenwald Collection.)*

Given the despair of a major depression and its typical long duration, it is not surprising that some of those who are seriously depressed eventually attempt suicide. Keller and Shapiro (1981) found, for instance, that of 101 depressed patients studied for a year, 10 made at least one suicide attempt. Exploring the relationship from another angle, other studies have shown that the majority of people who kill themselves have suffered serious depression (Robins et al., 1959; Barraclough et al., 1969).

But beyond a state of depression and a sense of hopelessness, what other traits do suicide victims tend to share? One thing is their marital status. Single, divorced, and widowed people are twice as likely as married ones to try to take their own lives. Suicide also tends to be age-related. The highest incidence of attempted suicides is in the 24-to-44 age bracket, and the highest incidence of successful ones is in the 55-to-65 age group (Shneidman and Farberow, 1970). However, suicide is also a problem among the young: teenagers account for an alarming 10 percent of all American suicides. College students have a relatively high suicide risk—almost twice that of their noncollege peers. Among college students in one study, almost 15 percent reported that they had attempted suicide, and another 65 percent reported that they had thought about attempting suicide (Mishara, Baker, and Mishara, 1976; Mishara, 1982). Finally, suicide patterns tend to vary between the sexes. Although about three times as many women as men *attempt* suicide, about four times as many men as women are successful at it (Shneidman, Farberow, and Litman, 1970). This pattern is partly linked to differences in suicide methods. While women frequently cut their wrists or swallow overdoses of pills, men often choose more lethal methods, such as shooting or hanging themselves.

Researchers have discovered that many common beliefs about suicide are nothing more than myths. There is no truth, for example, to the widespread notion that the person whose suicide attempt ends in failure is usually not "serious" about wanting to die. In fact, about 75 percent of those who successfully commit suicide have made at least one unsuccessful attempt previously (Cohen, Motto, and Seiden, 1966). Nor is there any truth to the common assumption that those who talk about committing suicide seldom go ahead and do it. One study found, for instance, that about 70 percent of suicide victims had communicated their intentions to others at least three months before their death (Stengel, 1964). About the same percentage of college students who attempted suicide reported telling others about their plans to do so (Mishara, 1982). Finally, the widespread belief that one should steer depressed people *away* from talk of suicide, for fear that it will only strengthen their resolve, is also invalid. Mental health professionals have found that letting despondent patients talk about their suicidal wishes may actually help them to overcome these thoughts. At the very least, such discussions can enable concerned others to estimate just how close to suicide a depressed person is. If someone has been through a recent crisis, talks about experiencing mood swings between elation and depression, and reports thinking about a plan for suicide, he or she should be considered at very serious risk. Providing reassurance and encouragement to find professional help can be critical in saving the person's life (Beck, Kovaks, and Weissman, 1979; Fawcett, n.d.).

Mania

In contrast to a depressed person, a person suffering from **mania** experiences exaggerated elation.

This emotional high is often mixed with intense irritability, especially when others try to impose some restraints. Another common symptom of mania is *hyperactivity*. The manic person may plunge headlong into a string of ambitious projects, often projects for which the person has never before shown any talent. The manic individual may suddenly begin to compose music, write film scripts, or plan to start a new business. None of these grandiose projects ever reaches completion. This behavior is related to the equally common manic symptom of a *decreased need for sleep*. Many manics carry on their feverish activities with only a few hours' rest each night. Typically, too, the manic displays *constant talkativeness*. Manics tend to talk rapidly, loudly, and endlessly. Often they are impossible to interrupt. This abnormality in speech may partly reflect the fact that many manics experience the sensation of "racing" thoughts, a sensation clinically referred to as *flight of ideas*. Not surprisingly, another common manic symptom is *great distractibility*. In conversation the typical manic leaps from topic to topic. Most manic people also show enormously *inflated self-esteem*. They are convinced that they are brilliant, irresistibly attractive, and superior to everyone they meet. This greatly distorted self-image is undoubtedly related to a final manic symptom: *reckless behavior*. Many manics go on extravagant buying sprees, invest the family savings in foolhardy business ventures, or commit sexual indiscretions, all without the slightest concern that these behaviors could have disastrous consequences for themselves and others.

You might think that from the victim's viewpoint mania is an exhilarating experience—a feeling of being invincible, all-powerful, and all-wise. In milder forms of the disorder, this is precisely how the person *does* feel. The problem is that mania often escalates to such feverish heights that the victim is totally and frighteningly out of control. Here is how one woman described the terrible transition from relatively mild mania (called hypomania) to much more psychotic symptoms:

[*Hypomania*] At first when I'm high it's tremendous . . . ideas are fast . . . like shooting stars you follow 'til brighter ones appear . . . all shyness disappears, the right words and gestures are suddenly all there . . . uninteresting people, things become intensely interesting. Sensuality is pervasive, the desire to seduce and be seduced is irresistible. Your marrow is infused with unbelievable feelings of ease, power, well-being, omnipotence, euphoria . . . you can do anything . . . But somewhere this changes . . . .

[*Mania*] The fast ideas become too fast and there are far too many . . . overwhelming confusion replaces clarity . . . you stop keeping up with it—memory goes. Infectious humor ceases to amuse—your friends become frightened . . . everything is now against the grain . . . you are irritable, angry, frightened, uncontrollable and trapped in the blackest caves of the mind—caves you never knew were there. It will never end. [Goldstein, Baker, and Jamison, 1980.]

Manic-Depressive (Bipolar) Disorder

So far we have talked about abnormal mood states separately—depression on the one hand, mania on the other. But the same person can suffer some combination of these two syndromes. When this happens, the condition is called **manic-depressive** or **bipolar disorder.**

Bipolar disorders take various forms. In some cases one or the other emotional extreme clearly predominates. The person may suffer many episodes of depression interspersed with a few of mania, or the pattern may be reversed. In rarer instances, mania and depression always alternate with one another. Cases have even been observed in which the moods switch regularly on a twenty-four- or forty-eight-hour basis, suggesting that in these cases the disorder may somehow be linked to the victim's physiological rhythms (Jenner et al., 1967; Bunney et al., 1972; Mendels, 1970). Another pattern, also rare, is the mixed bipolar disorder in which both manic and depressive symptoms occur simultaneously. The victim may weep uncontrollably and threaten suicide, for instance, yet at the same time display frantic hyperactivity. Usually with a bipolar disorder the periods of disturbed emotion are relatively short and are separated by intervals of normal mood and functioning.

Current Theories and Research on Depression

Space does not permit us to explore theories and research on all the affective disorders we have described. Consequently, we will focus on the possible causes of just one—depression, by far the most common of the three. Estimates are that about 20 percent of American women and 10 percent of American men will suffer a major depressive episode at some time during their lives. And in nearly a third of these cases the depression will be severe enough to require hospitalization (*DSM-III*). What insights into this serious problem do the perspectives on abnormality we outlined earlier provide?

The Psychoanalytic Perspective. Psychoanalytic thinkers have offered several theories as to why depression occurs. One was first expressed by a student of Freud, Karl Abraham (1911, 1916), and later elaborated by Freud himself (1917). It holds that depression is the product of hostility turned inward toward the self. More specifically, Freud believed that people often have both negative and positive feelings toward those to whom they are attached (a parent, a child, a spouse). Consequently, if the attachment figure dies or otherwise "abandons" the person, the negative feelings may turn to rage. Usually, however, conscious expression of rage would inflict too much guilt. So the person turns the powerful emotion inward, experiencing it as self-loathing. The end result is ultimately depression.

But although a link between depression and unexpressed anger frequently seems to exist, very little evidence supports Freud's explanation of this relationship. Many contemporary researchers therefore believe that a second line of psychoanalytic thinking on depression is more promising. This view holds that depression is a reaction to the loss of something deeply valued by a person whose need to be taken care of as an infant was not met for some reason (through neglect or the death of a parent, for instance). Such people presumably become fixated on the issues of dependency and the need for love. Thus, later in life, when something valued is taken from them, they feel unbearably vulnerable and are plunged into depression. In keeping with this theory, clinicians have found that many depressive episodes do seem to be triggered by critical losses in the victim's life, such losses as divorce, the death of a loved one, and being fired from a job (Paykel, 1979b). But exactly how these events are tied to depression— whether as psychoanalysts see it or in some other way—is still a matter of debate.

The Learning-Theory Perspective. Psychoanalysts are far from alone in their search for the causes of depression. Learning theorists have also offered several intriguing possibilities. Among them are the theories proposed by Peter Lewinsohn, Aaron Beck, and Martin Seligman.

Lewinsohn: Depression and Loss of Rewards.

Peter Lewinsohn (1974) has argued that depression can arise when a person's behavior no longer elicits the rewards it once did. This loss of rewards is often related to some change in the person's social environment—perhaps the death of a loved one, perhaps loss of or retirement from a job. Suddenly the person is placed in a new situation where he or she lacks the social skills to go about obtaining love and approval from others. So the person responds with depression and inactivity, which only worsen the problem. Withdrawing from social contacts virtually guarantees that few pleasures will be experienced. Both social participation and rewards decrease, in a vicious cycle. Lewinsohn has suggested that this cycle can be halted by helping depressed people get involved in activities that they find rewarding.

Beck: The Cognitive View.

The cognitive view of depression takes such speculations one step further. It holds that a major cause of depression lies not in what people do but in what they think. Psychologist Aaron Beck (1967, 1974) is a leading proponent of this view. He argues that errors in thinking lead depressed people to put self-critical interpretations on virtually everything. Consider one depressed patient's evaluation of her therapist's behavior. If the therapist arrived late, she quickly heaped the blame onto herself. ("He doesn't want to see me; I'm too hopeless.") Yet if the therapist was early, she also attributed his actions to her own shortcomings. ("I must be especially ill.") This kind of self-reproachful outlook, which often defies all logic, is common in the seriously depressed. At the very least, depressed people tend to "look on the dark side" or dwell on the negative in most situations (Lloyd and Lishman, 1975).

Such findings have important implications for the treatment of depression. They suggest that the provision of "rewarding" outcomes (as Lewinsohn recommends) may not be enough to improve the conditions of depressed people. The depressed can apparently find signs of their own inadequacies even in seemingly positive situations. What's more, when a person is despondent, what might otherwise be pleasant can become a matter of indifference, or even an aversive experience. It all depends on the person's mental outlook.

Seligman: "Learned Helplessness."

In an intriguing series of studies Martin Seligman and his colleagues have gathered further evidence that a person's interpretation of events may indeed be linked to depression. Seligman's research began with some unusual experiments on dogs (Seligman, Maier, and Greer, 1968). He strapped one group of dogs into a harness and exposed them to electric shocks from which they could not escape. Later, when these same dogs were placed in another experimental chamber where they *could* escape shocks just by jumping to one side, they tended not to do so. Instead, most stood there passively, enduring as many shocks as the experimenter chose to give. This was not true of a second group of dogs that had *not* received the earlier, uncontrollable shocks. Animals in this second group invariably managed to jump and escape the pain. Moreover, the two groups of dogs differed markedly in their postexperimental behavior. Those in the first group seemed to display long-term symptoms of depression: lethargy, inactivity, and loss of appetite. Seligman concluded that the differences between the groups stemmed from what they had learned. Animals in the first group had initially learned that they were helpless to control the shocks, and so continued to act helplessly in the second stage of the experiment, when the shocks *were* controllable. Such "learned helplessness," Seligman speculated, may be an important cause of depression in humans. When people are unable to influence a situation important to them, they may not only give up trying to change that situation, but also become depressed and show little initiative in new situations where success might be achieved.

Seligman's original theory and research generated much controversy. Critics charged that learned helplessness alone cannot explain the many variations seen in depression. Why do some depressed people constantly blame themselves while others are relatively free of this symptom? Why are some depressive episodes so severe and prolonged while others are much shorter and milder?

As a result of these and other criticisms, Seligman and his colleagues have modified their theory (Abramson, Seligman, and Teasdale, 1978). The revised version holds that uncontrollable outcomes alone do not determine the nature and magnitude of human depression. The way a person *explains* these outcomes also plays a crucial part. Consider three styles of explanation. People who attribute an undesirable outcome to their own inadequacies will probably experience depression accompanied by guilt and self-blame. Those who attribute an undesirable outcome to external causes, in contrast, may feel equally depressed but will not constantly reproach themselves. Finally, the severest depression may be experienced by those who not only attribute negative outcomes to their own shortcomings but also see those shortcomings as enduring traits that apply to all situations. The person who attributes business failure to innate stupidity, for instance, is apt to become much more depressed than one who attributes it to inexperience or sheer bad luck.

Seligman and his colleagues have developed a questionnaire to assess how people explain negative life events. When they administered this questionnaire to various subjects, they found that depressed people do indeed tend to attribute negative events to stable traits within themselves, traits that are applicable to many situations (Raps et al., 1982). This is not true of normal subjects or of people suffering from schizophrenia. What's more, the depressed person's way of explaining negative events has been found to *precede* depression; it is not just a result of the altered mood state. In one study, for instance, Seligman's questionnaire was administered to a group of women in the middle stages of pregnancy. Their responses proved to predict very well the degree of postpartum depression each woman would experience six to nine months later (O'Hara, Rehm, and Campbell, 1982).

But some psychologists have rightly asked why different people explain negative outcomes in such different ways (Wortman and Dintzer, 1978). Why, for example, does one student attribute a low grade to the teacher or to an unfair test, while another sees it as a sign of low intelligence? Seligman and his colleagues believe that the answer lies in what we learn as we grow up. Much of this learning seems to occur within the family, for a child's characteristic way of explaining bad events often matches that of the child's mother. Teachers may also influence the way youngsters learn to explain negative outcomes. Remember from Chapter 11 that teachers tend to criticize girls mainly for intellectual inadequacies, a tendency that may encourage girls to attribute failure to their own incompetence (Dweck et al., 1978; Dweck and Licht, 1980). This unfortunate learning process

may help explain why women are about twice as likely to experience depression as men.

The Biological Perspective.

But not all clinicians believe that the roots of most depressions lie in faulty learning experiences. A growing number are looking to biological factors that may induce depressive symptoms. In research similar to Seligman's experiments with dogs, for instance, Jay Weiss and his colleagues made an interesting discovery (Weiss, Stone, and Harrell, 1968, 1970; Weiss et al., 1979, 1980). They found that exposing rats to electric shocks from which they could not escape not only made them passive and "helpless," but also reduced the amount of the neurotransmitter norepinephrine in their brains. Perhaps, these researchers proposed, depression has a biological basis: low levels of norepinephrine brought about by stress.

Seligman (1975) has criticized this biological interpretation, noting that if the animals are allowed a rest period, during which their norepinephrine levels return to normal, they *still* behave helplessly when reexposed to shocks. Thus their behavior must be due to learning. But subsequent findings have cast some doubt on Seligman's argument. When animals are exposed to inescapable shocks and then allowed to rest, later shocks cause an unusually rapid decline in norepinephrine (Anisman and Sklar, 1979). Thus it appears that once an animal has been exposed to stress that induces norepinephrine depletion, this biochemical reaction occurs more readily under subsequent stress. Whether this physiological process is a major cause of depression, however, is still a matter of debate.

Other biological factors may be involved in depression. In addition to a depletion of norepinephrine, a deficiency of the neurotransmitter serotonin has been implicated (Berger, 1978). One theory about how this occurs involves the action of nerve cells, which prevent too much serotonin from circulating in the brain by reabsorbing it. If the nerve cells take up serotonin too quickly, the levels of this neurotransmitter drop, resulting in depression (Schildkraut, 1978).

Cobbin and his associates (1979) believe that the reason both norepinephrine and serotonin have been found to have a role is that depression is not a single disorder. Some depressed patients seem to respond best to a drug that increases the availability of norepinephrine, while others respond more favorably to one that decreases the absorption of serotonin. This suggests that there may be several types of depression. Several other possible biochemical bases for depression have been proposed (Depue and Evans, 1976; Brambilla et al., 1978). More research is needed to confirm these ideas.

The Family, or Systems, View. The family, or systems, perspective further broadens the search for causes of depression. James Coyne, for instance, has argued that depression is not just something that arises *within* a person; it also has important origins in interpersonal relationships (Coyne, 1976a, 1976b). Coyne believes that when someone begins to complain of depressive symptoms (sadness, tiredness, sleeplessness, and so on), others experience negative feelings. Although they may try to reassure the person and offer some support, their concern is not always genuine. Frequently their true feelings show in rejection and avoidance of the depressed person. The depressed person, of course, soon realizes this and responds with greater depression. This reaction adds to the frustration and aggravation experienced by family and friends, who are then likely to make more insistent demands on the depressed person to improve. A vicious circle has set in.

In an interesting experiment designed to test the theory that others are often hostile and rejecting toward a depressed person, forty-five normal subjects spoke by telephone to either a depressed or a nondepressed subject. Those who spoke to a depressed person reported feeling more depressed themselves after the conversation, and they also reported increased hostility. What's more, they expressed much less willingness than other subjects did to talk with the same person again (Coyne, 1976b). These findings contrast sharply with the view of many cognitive theorists that the depressed person's negative perceptions are largely distortions. Apparently, depressed people often do live in a world where others respond to them negatively. This could easily be a factor contributing to their disturbance, perhaps perpetuating a depression that originally arose for other reasons. Researchers are now attempting to determine why others react so negatively. One theory is that depressed people may turn others off because they are so involved with their own problems that they are unable to listen to and support others (Ziomek and Coyne, 1983).

An Integrated Approach. Given the many theories of depression that have been proposed, some researchers feel it is now time to try to integrate them (Akiskal and McKinney, 1973, 1975; Akiskal, 1979). These researchers stress the complex interaction between psychological responses to external events and biological changes within the body. Thus initial depressive symptoms may be caused by a biological factor and then maintained by learning or by other people's reactions. Or alternatively, the initial symptoms may be triggered by a negative life event, which in turn sets in motion a physiological reaction that intensifies the problem. In either case, the roots of depression are many and complex. Important future research into depression will probably adopt this kind of integrated approach.

In a recent study, Simons and her associates (1984) found some evidence to support an integrated perspective. They studied two groups of depressed patients, one that received daily doses of antidepressant drugs and one that received psychotherapy twice a week. Both treatments were effective in alleviating depression. Interestingly, the patients receiving medication showed a variety of positive changes in how they thought about themselves and the world, even though they had never discussed such matters with a therapist. Simon concluded that depression seems to involve a fusion of psychological and physiological processes, which therapy can reach in various ways. Improvement in any one process, she suggests, can generate improvement in the related processes.

SCHIZOPHRENIA

Schizophrenia is the diagnosis given to about one-half of all those who occupy our mental hospitals (Taube and Rednick, 1973). Estimates are that this disorder (or group of disorders) afflicts between 0.2 and 1 percent of the general population. Schizophrenia is considered a psychotic disorder because its symptoms are so severe. The condition is also very resistant to treatment. Even with modern drug therapy, little more than a third of all schizophrenics manage to recover (Stephens, 1978).

The name "schizophrenia" was coined by the Swiss psychiatrist Eugen Bleuler (1911) and comes from the Greek words *schizein,* "to split," and *phren,* "mind." Bleuler referred not to a splitting of personality into several parts, as occurs in the dissociative disorder multiple personality. Instead, Bleuler was attempting to describe a breaking of connections among various psychological functions. Emotions, for example, may be split from perception and thus be totally inappropriate to the situation. The victims of schizophrenia also experience profound disturbances of thought and are unable to function normally. The following case illustrates what an acute episode of schizophrenia is like:

> Six months before his admission Arnold began to scream while at work with no apparent provocation, turned off all the machinery, and continually interfered with the work of others. When his supervisor reprimanded him, Arnold told him to go to hell, and was fired. He claimed that he could see his mother's body floating in the air. . . . Four months before his admission he broke in the door of his home with an ax and threatened the members of his family. He was arrested for this, but released soon thereafter. On the day before his admission he threatened to burn the house, and then broke into his father's room and said,

"You have got to kill me or I will kill you. Tonight the time is up." Faced with this choice his father had Arnold arrested again. The next morning Arnold told the police, "I see a whole bunch of dead people sitting here now. They run about my cell at night like crazy men, pulling me around. I hear them whispering to me." He was then committed to the local state hospital.

> On admission he was quiet, and indifferent to his commitment. His conversation and behavior were childish and marked by foolish and inappropriate laughter. At first he thought it was "awful to be among so many crazy people" but shortly thereafter he realized that it was quite a joke, and laughed heartily about his fate. He felt that the attendants were going to kill him, but laughed foolishly while telling of his fears. . . . He experienced a series of vivid hallucinations, including feeling a man's claws on his throat, although he did not see or hear the man, feeling electricity jar him, seeing ghosts haunting him, seeing blue shadows going around and red shadows going up and down through the air, and seeing wingless female spirits flying through the air.   [Zax and Stricker, 1963, pp. 101–102]

Symptoms of Schizophrenia

The symptoms of schizophrenia tend to vary from one patient to the next. In fact, clinicians have distinguished several subtypes of schizophrenia according to the symptoms that predominate. Table 15.2 lists four of these subtypes and briefly describes each.

TABLE 15.2 SYMPTOMS OF FOUR SUBTYPES OF SCHIZOPHRENIA

SUBTYPE	SYMPTOMS
Disorganized (hebephrenic) schizophrenia	Most severe disintegration of personality. Most common symptoms are frequent or constant incoherent speech and odd affect, such as laughing or crying at inappropriate times. Disorganized hallucinations and delusions are present.
Catatonic schizophrenia	Characterized either by excessive, sometimes violent, motor activity or by a mute, unmoving, stuporous state. Some catatonic schizophrenics alternate between these two extremes, but often one or the other behavior pattern predominates.
Paranoid schizophrenia	Characterized by delusions of persecution, grandeur, or both. Paranoid schizophrenics trust no one and are constantly watchful, convinced that others are plotting against them. They may seek to retaliate against supposed tormentors.
Undifferentiated schizophrenia	Characterized by hallucinations, delusions, and incoherence without meeting the criteria for the other types or showing symptoms characteristic of more than one type.

Despite such differences, however, a number of symptoms are common to all forms of schizophrenia. These include severe abnormalities in attention, thought, perception, emotion, motor behavior, and social interaction.

Disorders of Attention. Although all of us are bombarded constantly by a mass of sensory stimuli, we are able to attend selectively to what we see, hear, and feel, filtering out the many bits of nonessential information. The schizophrenic seems to have lost this crucial "filtering" capability. Sensations flood the minds of schizophrenics. They speak of being totally helpless to control the many thoughts and perceptions that enter and leave their awareness. Some researchers believe that this severe loss of control over attention may underlie many other symptoms of schizophrenia.

Disorders of Thought. The schizophrenic's disorders of thought are clearly related to his or her attention deficits. Typically the patient exerts little control over the association of ideas. He or she will leap from one thought to another even though the two thoughts are only loosely related. As a result, the person's speech is very disjointed. Here is one example:

> I have just looked up "simplicity" and the dictionary says "sim—one, plicare—to fold, one fold." I told Dr. H. that I dreamed he returned to me the story I sent him which he had folded six times then I had folded it once making it double. Jesus said that the sheep he called would make one fold. I thought at the time that the Latin for six is sex, and that the number of the Beast is 666. Is sex then beastly? I think I will leave you to puzzle out the difference between 6 and 666 and 6 fold in substitution of one fold; for the number of the Beast is a mystery.   [Mayer-Gross, Slater, and Roth, 1969, p. 267]

In this case the speaker moves from a fold in a piece of paper to a sheepfold, from the number 6 to the Latin word for six (*sex*), and from there to the nature of sexual intercourse. Normal listeners unaccustomed to such rambling associations often find the schizophrenic's speech incomprehensible.

In addition to these abnormalities in the schizophrenic's style of associating ideas, the content of schizophrenic thought is also disturbed. Schizophrenics often suffer from **delusions**—that is, irrational beliefs held despite overwhelming evidence to the contrary. These delusions may take several forms. A person suffering delusions of grandeur believes that he or she is some famous person, such as Napoleon or Jesus Christ. Delusions of persecution involve the belief that others, often extraterrestrial beings or secret agents, are plotting against the patient, or controlling the patient's thoughts and actions. Schizophrenics often report that their thoughts are being stolen or broadcast aloud, or that "foreign" thoughts are being inserted into their heads.

Disorders of Perception. In addition to their delusions, schizophrenics also perceive the external world abnormally. They consistently report auditory, visual, olfactory, and sometimes tactile hallucinations. In our earlier case history, Arnold's visions of ghosts and spirits and his feelings of being jolted by electricity and choked are quite characteristic. Very often, too, schizophrenics hear voices commenting on their actions, repeating their thoughts aloud, or telling them what to do.

Disorders of Emotion. Like other aspects of functioning, the emotional responses of a schizophrenic are often disturbed as well. The emotions they express are either inappropriate or peculiarly blunted. A schizophrenic may laugh when told of a favorite relative's death, get angry when given a present, or show no emotion at all on either occasion.

Disorders of Motor Behavior. Schizophrenics may display bizarre behavior, such as banging their heads against a wall. More often, they simply act in ways that are inappropriate to the situation and repetitive beyond the norm. One patient may spend hours rubbing his forehead or slapping his leg; another may sit all day on a couch tracing the pattern of the fabric with her finger. In some cases there is no physical movement. The patient remains in one position for hours at a time, responding neither to people nor to things. This condition is called a catatonic stupor.

Social Withdrawal. The catatonic stupor is an extreme instance of the schizophrenic's frequent withdrawal from social interaction. Schizophrenics tend to become preoccupied with their own inner worlds and to avoid involvement with others. This social withdrawal has been measured in several ways. Schizophrenics prefer greater interpersonal distance than normal people—that is, they want more space between themselves and others (Duke and Mullins, 1973). Schizophrenics also look at others less than ordinary people do, and they tend to avert their gaze when others look at them (Harris, 1968). In acute cases schizophrenics often act as if other people did not exist at all.

Current Perspectives and Research on Schizophrenia

Schizophrenia puzzled people long before Eugen Bleuler gave the disorder a name. Today it remains one of the most disabling and also mysterious of all the common mental disorders. Researchers from different schools of thought have offered theories about its causes. Let us examine some of the most prominent ones.

The Biological Perspective. Studies of schizophrenics have consistently shown that this disorder tends to run in families—that is, blood relatives of schizophrenics are more likely to develop the condition than people from families free of schizophrenia (see, for example, Kallmann, 1953). The problem with interpreting such findings is the difficulty of separating the contributions of heredity and environment. Family members share not only genes but also attitudes, surroundings, and styles of interaction. How, then, can we tell if their shared susceptibility to

schizophrenia is genetic or environmental in origin?

Researchers have devised several ways to help answer this question. One is to compare the incidence of schizophrenia in pairs of identical twins (who have exactly the same genetic makeup) and in pairs of fraternal twins (who share on average only about 50 percent of their genes). If schizophrenia is even partly genetic in origin, an identical twin should be more likely than a fraternal twin to develop the disorder if his or her co-twin does. And studies show that this is precisely what happens. As Figure 15.2 illustrates, when one identical twin develops schizophrenia, the other is five times more likely than a fraternal twin to fall prey to the disorder as well (Ban, 1973).

But this fact alone does not necessarily prove that something genetic is at work here. It can be argued that identical twins are treated more alike by parents than fraternal twins are, and that this fact could account for their higher shared incidence of schizophrenia. Fortunately, a second method of exploring this issue has resulted in data very hard to explain in nongenetic terms. Children born to schizophrenic mothers and adopted as infants into normal families are more likely than other adopted children to develop schizophrenia. One study found that 18.8 percent of those born to schizophrenic parents and subsequently adopted by a normal couple showed some symptoms of schizophrenia. In contrast, among adopted children whose biological parents were *not* schizophrenic, only 10.1 percent displayed such symptoms. What's more, being raised by a schizo-

Paintings done by a schizophrenic man with paranoid tendencies. Both works are characterized by the consistent symbolism of watchful eyes, grasping hands, and the self as subject. Painting A, which reflects a subdued emotional state, shows a strong emphasis on the eyes, with a figure watching over the shoulder. The central figure is surrounded by hands, and the figure in the background is reaching out. Painting B, elaborately composed and vividly colored, reflects a more active emotional state. Again there is an emphasis on eyes and hands, represented by tentacles and claws. *(Courtesy Al Vercoutere, Camarillo State Hospital.)*

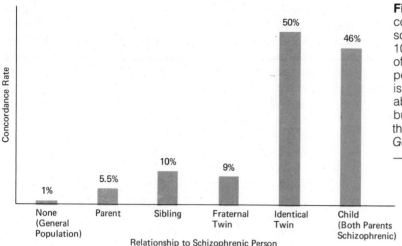

Concordance Rate

1%
5.5%
10%
9%
50%
46%

None (General Population)
Parent
Sibling
Fraternal Twin
Identical Twin
Child (Both Parents Schizophrenic)

Relationship to Schizophrenic Person

Figure 15.2 The concordance rates that accompany various degrees of relationship to a schizophrenic person. A concordance rate of 100 percent would mean that if one member of the related pair is schizophrenic, the other person will be, too. Note that if a fraternal twin is schizophrenic, the concordance rate is about the same as that for any other sibling, but that if an identical twin is schizophrenic, the concordance rate is far higher. *(After Gottesman and Shields, 1976.)*

phrenic does not carry as high a risk as being born to one. Among children of nonschizophrenic parents who were adopted by schizophrenics, the incidence of schizophrenic symptoms was only 10.7 percent. This is just slightly higher than the incidence among children born to nonschizophrenic parents and raised in *normal* homes (Wender et al., 1974).

Although this evidence clearly suggests that heredity is a factor in schizophrenia, it by no means rules out environmental influences. If schizophrenia were entirely a matter of heredity, the second in a pair of identical twins would *always* develop the disorder if the first twin did. This, however, is not the case. Studies show that only 40 to 50 percent of second twins succumb to the disorder. Thus environmental factors must also play an important part in the development of schizophrenia.

If schizophrenia is partly genetic in origin, as it seems to be, it makes sense to search for some biochemical abnormality that schizophrenics share. One factor that seems to be involved is the neurotransmitter dopamine (Valenstein, 1978). Drugs called phenothiazines, which are highly effective in reducing certain symptoms of schizophrenia, are known to block the uptake of dopamine at its receptor sites in the brain (Creese, Burt, and Snyder, 1975). Since many dopamine neurons branch into the limbic forebrain, an area intimately involved in attention and emotion, it is reasonable to surmise that overactivity of these neurons could produce schizophrenic symptoms. But exactly what is entailed in this overactivity is not yet known. One theory is that schizophrenics have an excess amount of dopamine; another is that their dopamine receptors in critical areas are unusually sensitive; and a third is that they have an abnormally large number of such receptors (Meltzer and Stahl, 1976; Lee and Seeman, 1977). The problem with all of these theories is that the data supporting them have not always been consistent. Researchers have not yet found a single abnormal trait related to dopamine activity that *all* schizophrenics share (*Schizophrenia Bulletin*, 1982).

This fact has led some investigators to suspect that what we label a single disorder—schizophrenia—may in fact encompass several disorders, each with its own set of causes. One researcher has recently proposed that there may be two common types of schizophrenia, occurring either separately or together (Crow et al., 1980). One type may involve "active" symptoms, such as hallucinations and disorders of thought. This type may be linked to dopamine overactivity, for it responds quite well to treatment with phenothiazines (Haracz, 1982). In contrast, the second type of schizophrenia may involve "passive" symptoms, such as flattened emotions and social withdrawal. Because it does not generally respond to phenothiazines, it seems to be *un*related to dopamine. It may, however, be tied to structural damage in the brain, which may be partly manifested in enlarged cerebral ventricles (fluid-filled areas of the brain). Studies show that many schizophrenics who do not improve with drug therapy have this brain defect. And the more enlarged the ventricles are, the more social isolation and other passive symptoms the patients tend to show

(Johnstone et al., 1978; Andreasen et al., 1982; Nasrallah et al., 1980).

Much more research needs to be done before we can draw any firm conclusions about the biological causes of schizophrenia. Today investigation proceeds along several fronts. In addition to studying dopamine, for instance, scientists are also exploring the possible involvement of other neurotransmitters, including serotonin, norepinephrine, and some of the neuropeptides. When the mystery of schizophrenia is finally solved, it may be found that many biochemical and structural factors can contribute to this disorder's varied and severe symptoms.

The Family, or Systems, View. Clinicians have long had indications that certain patterns of family life may contribute to schizophrenia. Some early studies showed, for instance, that the highest relapse rates, with the most severe recurring symptoms, often occurred among discharged patients who returned to the care of their families rather than living alone. It seemed as if the family might be aggravating the disorder. But what aspects of family life were involved in this relationship?

One factor seems to be a highly charged emotional atmosphere in the home. One study found that 55 percent of schizophrenics who returned to a hostile and intrusive home atmosphere suffered a relapse within nine months after their discharge from the hospital. In comparison, only 16 percent of those who returned to a more normal family environment suffered a relapse in the same time period (Brown, Birley, and Wing, 1972). Such evidence has led some to argue that the social withdrawal of the schizophrenic may be motivated in part by a need to protect the self (Leff, 1976).

Others have wondered exactly what kinds of emotionally charged relationships within the family are most closely related to schizophrenia. After studying the families of schizophrenics for several years, one group of researchers concluded that these families tend to fall into one of two types: the "schismatic family," which is split by intense parental conflict, and the "skewed family," in which one parent totally submits to the domineering, often disturbed behavior of the other (Lidz et al., 1957; Lidz, 1973). In either family the children tend to grow up feeling confused and uncertain, feelings that might contribute to a schizophrenic breakdown.

Another family trait that may contribute to schizophrenia is abnormal interpersonal communication. Various researchers have found that the close relatives of schizophrenics often communicate with one another in distinctively deviant ways. One group of researchers found, for instance, that the parents of young schizophrenics frequently send their children contradictory messages (Bateson et al., 1956). Here is one example:

> A young man who had fairly well recovered from an acute schizophrenic episode was visited in the hospital by his mother. He was glad to see her and impulsively put his arm around her shoulders, whereupon she stiffened. He withdrew his arm and she asked, "Don't you love me any more?" He then blushed, and she said, "Dear, you must not be so easily embarrassed and afraid of your feelings." The patient was able to stay with her only a few minutes more and following her departure he assaulted an aide. [Bateson et al., 1956, p. 251]

Such discrepancies between what parents say they feel and how they actually act places the child in a **double bind:** no matter which of the two contradictory messages the child responds to, the other message tells him he is wrong. It is not hard to imagine that someone repeatedly exposed to such conflicting communications might develop serious psychological problems, including disorders of thought, language, and emotion.

Researchers have studied still other patterns of deviant communication within the families of schizophrenics. Some have found that the members of such families frequently have trouble establishing and keeping a shared focus of attention (Singer and Wynne, 1963, 1965). Communication often shifts in midstream to an unrelated topic. Consider this example:

> A little boy of five runs to his mother holding a big fat worm in his hand, and says, "Mummy, look what a big fat worm I have got." She says, "You are filthy— go away and clean yourself immediately." (Laing, 1961, p. 85.)

Note that the mother doesn't respond to the boy's observations directly, expressing either approval or disapproval of his behavior. Instead, she goes off on a tangent, drawing attention to his dirtiness, which was not what he had in mind when he initiated the conversation.

It is tempting to think that such fragmented and confusing communications might contribute to schizophrenia. Thus far, however, the evidence points only to a link between such communication difficulties and relapses of the disorder. It is not clear that disturbed communication actually causes schizophrenia. In one recent long-term study, however, investigators have found that family communication problems tended to *precede* the onset of schizophrenia, thus suggesting that these problems may have been a cause (Doane et al., 1981). Much more research is needed before this issue can be fully resolved.

The Learning-Theory Perspective.
Learning theorists have also offered perspectives on schizophrenia. Some have argued that inadvertent rewards may shape some of the schizophrenic's bizarre behaviors (Ullmann and Krasner, 1975). Acting "crazy" may gain the person sympathy from family members and release from life's responsibilities. For some people these rewards can serve as powerful reinforcers. In the hospital this pattern of reinforcement may unwittingly continue. Indeed, the stranger the behavior, the more likely that schizophrenic patients will gain the attention of the hospital staff. Normal behaviors, in contrast, may gradually be extinguished because they are ignored.

In support of this view, some clinicians have noticed that "crazy" behavior does seem more pronounced when other people are around, suggesting that attention may be reinforcing it. Moreover, when schizophrenic symptoms are ignored and normal behaviors are reinforced by attention, some schizophrenics do seem to improve (Agras, 1967). Although none of this evidence shows that faulty learning *causes* schizophrenia, it does suggest that our reactions to schizophrenic patients may help to maintain their symptoms.

The Sociocultural Perspective.
As we mentioned earlier in this chapter, studies consistently show that schizophrenia is more common among members of the lower social classes. Those who take a sociocultural view suggest several reasons for this finding. One is the impact of marriage patterns on the distribution of genes. Since there are more schizophrenics in the lower classes, and since people usually marry within their own social class, any genes that might make a person more vulnerable to schizophrenia would tend to be passed on from one generation of low-income families to the next. A second factor is the stress of poverty itself (Kohn, 1973). Given enough stress, virtually anyone will begin to show marked disorders of thought, perception, and emotion. Soldiers in prolonged and intense combat sometimes show schizophrenic-like symptoms even though they have no past history of any mental disturbance. The chronic hardship of being poor could likewise take a serious toll on lower-class mental health. In addition, living in poverty can breed an attitude of fatalism that makes effective coping with stress all the more difficult (Kohn, 1973). According to the sociocultural perspective, then, low-income people are more vulnerable to schizophrenia than people at higher socioeconomic levels.

But others believe that this view has been overstated. They contend that in many cases lower-class status is not the cause but the *effect* of schizophrenia. Because schizophrenics can seldom cope with the demands of a good job, they tend to drift downward on the socioeconomic ladder, becoming concentrated in the ranks of the poor. In addition, one must consider the labeling bias of mental health professionals. Perhaps clinicians are more inclined to diagnose a lower-class person as schizophrenic because lower-class ways of expressing stress are more alarming to them.

The Phenomenological Perspective.
Some phenomenological theorists have also studied schizophrenia with the hope of identifying its causes. One has been the British psychiatrist R. D. Laing. Laing began by studying family interaction and its relationship to schizophrenia (Laing and Esterson, 1971). Eventually, however, he developed a more radical position. Laing argued that emotional disturbance is inherent in contemporary Western society, which forces people to suppress their true needs and feelings and to adopt distorted values. Schizophrenia, in Laing's view, is a retreat under stress from this masquerade that we call normality. It is simply "a special sort of strategy that a person invents in order to live in an unlivable situation" (Laing, 1964, p. 187). Not surprisingly, Laing has totally rejected the idea of "remolding" schizophrenics so that they may become again the kind of people their social worlds demand. Instead, he has tried to help them find a new authentic identity to replace the false identity society has imposed.

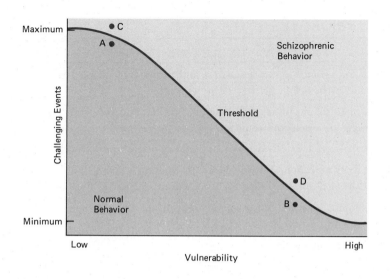

Figure 15.3 The vulnerability model of schizo-phrenia. A person remains below the threshold of schizophrenic behavior at point A, which repre-sents low vulnerability due to personal circum-stances but a high level of exposure to challenging events, and at point B, which repre-sents high vulnerability but a minimum exposure to challenging events. But at point C—low vul-nerability but a high level of challenging events—and point D—high vulnerability and a moderate level of challenge—a person passes the thresh-old and exhibits schizophrenic behavior. *(From Zubin and Spring, 1977.)*

Laing's view has been vehemently opposed by clini-cians from other schools of thought, most of whom deny his basic assertion that society is sicker than the schizophrenic. Nevertheless, Laing's perspective has made a contribution by emphasizing the importance of a disturbed person's own subjective experiences.

Vulnerability Theory: An Integrated Ap-proach. Many factors, both biological and environ-mental, apparently can increase a person's risk of developing schizophrenia. The approach to schizo-phrenia called **vulnerability theory** acknowledges this important diversity of causes. Proponents of this view hold that each of us is more or less vulnerable to schizophrenia depending on the number of contrib-

uting factors in our own personal histories (Zubin and Spring, 1977). These contributing factors include genes, family experiences, and the broader social context in which one lives. When people have many of these factors working against them, they can de-velop schizophrenia with relatively little current envi-ronmental stress. Less vulnerable people, in contrast, would have to be subjected to much greater stress before they succumbed to the disorder. In all cases, however, episodes of stress are what ultimately push the victims over the edge. Figure 15.3 diagrams these basic ideas of vulnerability theory. Proponents of the view argue that improving people's effectiveness at coping with stress may be one of the best defenses against schizophrenia, for it reduces basic vulnerabil-ity to schizophrenic breakdowns.

PERSONALITY DISORDERS

Although **personality disorders** may greatly im-pair the lives of those who suffer them, they do not cause the functional collapse and complete break with reality we saw in schizophrenia. Personality disorders, therefore, are not usually considered psychoses. In-stead they can be thought of as deep-seated mala-daptive patterns of relating to others. Unlike anxiety disorders, which are also maladaptive, personality disorders usually fail to produce high levels of guilt and anxiety. The disturbed person may not even rec-ognize that he or she has a disorder. The problem

behaviors are so deeply ingrained in the core person-ality that they are accepted as familiar character traits. Frequently the victims of personality disorders have little desire to change their ways, for they cause more distress to others than to themselves. Table 15.3 lists eleven personality disorders and gives the basic symp-toms of each. Space allows us to look at only one of these disorders in detail. We have chosen what is probably the most serious and among the most exten-sively studied: the antisocial personality.

TABLE 15.3 SYMPTOMS OF PERSONALITY DISORDERS

DISORDER	SYMPTOMS
Paranoid personality disorder	Pervasive and long-standing suspiciousness and mistrust of people; hypersensitivity and difficulty in getting along with others
Schizotypal personality disorder	Eccentricities of thinking, perception, communication, and behavior, not severe enough to be schizophrenic
Schizoid personality disorder	Social withdrawal and lack of normal emotional relationships with others
Avoidant personality disorder	Hypersensitivity to rejection and unwillingness to enter into relationships; social withdrawal despite a desire for interaction, and low self-esteem
Dependent personality disorder	Failure to assume responsibility for major areas of one's life; reliance on others to make important decisions; lack of self-esteem
Borderline personality disorder	Instability in behavior, mood, and self-image
Histrionic personality disorder	Overly reactive behavior; exaggerated expressions of emotion seemingly "performed" for an audience
Narcissistic personality disorder	Grandiose sense of self-importance; preoccupation with fantasies of unlimited success; exhibitionistic need for constant admiration
Compulsive personality disorder	Preoccupation with rules, order, organization, efficiency, and detail; rigidity and inability to express warm emotions or take pleasure in normally pleasurable activities
Passive-aggressive personality disorder	Indirectly expressed resistance to demands for adequate activity or performance in personal relations and on the job
Antisocial personality disorder	Chronic and continuous behavior that violates the rights of others; inability to form attachments or (often) to succeed in an occupation. Onset before age fifteen

Source: Bootzin and Acocella, 1984, p. 253.

The Antisocial Personality

The **antisocial personality,** or **sociopath,** follows his or her impulses without consideration for the rights or feelings of others and without experiencing guilt or remorse. Such people seem to have no conscience and to be untouched by a whole range of emotions shared by "normal" people. Yet their intellectual faculties and ability to reason are unimpaired.

The antisocial personality becomes apparent in early adolescence, if not before. The youngster begins to exhibit such problem behaviors as truancy, stealing, vandalism, picking fights, running away from home, and persistent lying. He or she may be suspended from school for misbehavior or arrested for some infraction of the law. Sexual promiscuity and drug abuse are also common. And the child's grades are typically far below what one would expect on the basis of IQ.

Similar problems continue in adulthood. The adult sociopath, like the adolescent, tends to have a flagrant disregard for truth. Antisocial personalities can lie unabashedly if it suits their purpose, and many think nothing of "conning" others for personal profit. Impulsiveness governs much of the antisocial personality's behavior. He or she may travel from town to town with no clear goal in mind. Sometimes this impulsiveness takes the form of random crime or vandalism. The antisocial personality may steal a car for a joyride or shoplift things never to be used. Some adopt a criminal lifestyle. Prostitution, pimping, and dealing in drugs or stolen goods are fairly common activities among sociopaths. Many are also unusually reckless. They are often arrested for speeding or for driving when drunk. Extreme aggressiveness is typical as well. The person who repeatedly assaults others on the slightest provocation may very well merit the label antisocial personality.

If asked to sum up the antisocial personality in just a few words, irresponsibility and lack of concern for others would have to be among them. Usually the person is unable to hold down a job for long. He or she either is fired for such offenses as chronic absenteeism or simply decides to quit with no other job prospects in sight. Often the antisocial personality is also very deficient as a parent. Severe neglect of children (leaving them alone for long periods or failing to get them proper medical attention) is quite common in people with this disorder. Typically, too, the antisocial personality has no regard for financial obligations. Many such people repeatedly default on debts or fail to support their dependents. This last trait is probably related to their common inability to form enduring attachments. Many are incapable of normal friendship or love. They view others as existing primarily to be used. Needless to say, the antisocial personality is difficult to treat because the person is often unperturbed by his or her own deviance. Children who show antisocial tendencies stand the best chance of leading normal adult lives when they manage to display some anxiety about their problem behaviors (Cass and Thomas, 1979).

Current Perspectives on the Antisocial Personality

Theorists of many persuasions have speculated on the causes of the antisocial personality. Psychoanalytic thinkers suggest that such people are products of rejecting parents. If there is no love between parent and child, the child is unlikely to adopt the parents' moral values and so develop a conscience. The goal of psychoanalytic treatment is therefore to create trust between the person and the therapist, a trust that can substitute for the one that never developed between parent and child. In this way the therapist hopes to win the person over to more responsible, humane values.

Learning theorists stress the importance of the child's learning history to the development of this disorder. The child may learn aggressive behavior from parents, peers, and the media. And the parents may fail to reinforce the youngster's prosocial responses. The parents may even punish the child no matter what he or she does, so the child has no incentive to adopt normal moral standards. Alternatively, deviant behavior may be the child's way of gaining from others the attention that does not seem obtainable in any other way. Treatment based on learning theory usually involves placing the antisocial personality in an environment—such as a residential community—where prosocial behavior will be consistently reinforced and antisocial behavior extinguished.

Biological theorists take a very different approach to antisocial disorders. They argue that such people may suffer from underarousal of the autonomic nervous system, which is greatly involved in emotional response (Hare, 1970). This could explain some of their puzzling behavior, such as the need to gratify impulses or commit crimes for thrills—all presumably to compensate for autonomic underarousal. Underarousal could also explain why many antisocial personalities seem so uncaring about the negative effects that their actions have on others. To date, however, no treatment for the antisocial personality based on this biological theory has been proposed.

ADDICTIVE DISORDERS

When a person becomes dependent on a psychoactive drug to the point where life revolves around the drug and interpersonal relationships suffer, that person is said to have an **addictive disorder.** People can develop addictive disorders with regard to any of the drugs we talked about in Chapter 12—marijuana, such hallucinogens as LSD, and such stimulants as cocaine and amphetamines. But by far the most widely abused psychoactive drug in our society is alcohol. That is why we have chosen to focus on it here.

Alcohol Abuse and Dependence

Clinicians generally distinguish between alcohol abuse and alcohol dependence, both of which are considered disorders. *DSM-III* says that for a diagnosis of **alcohol abuse** to apply, the person must display a pathological pattern of drinking. He or she must have a compelling psychological need for alcohol daily and must find it virtually impossible to cut down or to stop. The person may repeatedly try to "go on the wagon" but inevitably fails even though alcohol may be impairing his or her health. The person may also engage in drinking binges (remaining drunk for several days), may experience alcoholic blackouts, may occasionally drink a fifth of liquor in a single session, and may sometimes even turn to alcohol in forms not intended for consumption. In addition, the person diagnosed as an alcohol abuser experiences alcohol-related problems at home, on the job, or with the law. Such problems include arguments with family members about excessive drinking, frequent absences from work or a drop in productivity, and arrests for drunken driving or other illegal behavior while under the influence of alcohol. The person diagnosed as **alcohol dependent** also shows these symptoms, but in addiction he or she is physically addicted to the drug. This addiction manifests itself both in alcohol *tolerance* (a need for increasing amounts of alcohol in order to get high) and in alcohol *withdrawal symptoms* (profuse sweating, uncontrollable trembling, general disorientation) when use of alcohol is temporarily halted.

Abuse of alcohol in our society is widespread. One out of eleven adult Americans drinks heavily enough and regularly enough to be considered a "problem drinker" (Miller, 1979). In total, between 10 and 15 million Americans meet the definition of alcohol abuse or alcohol dependence. Perhaps as many as 35 million others experience negative effects as a result of these problem drinkers. A recent Gallup poll, for instance, indicated that fully a third of all American families have experienced difficulties related to alcohol use (Saxe et al., 1983).

Alcoholism takes a staggering toll economically, medically, and socially (Saxe et al., 1983). Our nation loses as much as $120 billion annually as a result of alcohol abuse, a large proportion of which comes from the sharp decline in the alcoholic's productivity on the job. In addition, an estimated 15 percent of all the dollars Americans spend on health care are used to treat medical problems related to alcohol abuse. Prolonged alcoholism can cause irreparable liver damage, serious brain dysfunctions, and cardiovascular disease. Not surprisingly, the life expectancy of an alcoholic is ten to twelve years shorter than that of the average person. Alcoholism is also frequently impli-

Alcohol is one of the few drugs with a high potential for dependence that are legally and readily available to the general adult population. *(Raoul Hackel/Stock, Boston.)*

cated in a long list of legal and social problems. It is estimated that 50 percent of all traffic accidents, 40 percent of all family court cases, 25 percent of all suicides, and sizable proportions of all assaults, rapes, and murders involve the use of alcohol. Yet, disturbingly, the vast majority of problem drinkers—an estimated 85 percent—receive no treatment.

Current Perspectives on Alcoholism

What are the causes of this widespread and harmful disorder? Some psychoanalysts have argued that alcohol abuse may arise in people who as babies develop a conflict over the need for oral gratification. These infants may be uncertain whether food will be given or withheld, and so come to feel abnormally dependent as well as highly anxious. As adults, they may reveal this fixation in such "oral behaviors" as drinking. Interestingly, alcoholics also tend to be heavier smokers than nonalcoholics, smoking presumably being another way to gratify oral needs (Maletzky and Klotter, 1974). Psychoanalytic thinkers have also suggested that heavy alcohol use may be a way of combatting low self-esteem and acquiring an illusion of mastery and power. The aggressiveness that intoxicated alcohol abusers sometimes show is said to be a direct expression of this quest for self-importance and control. But the psychoanalytic prediction that people prone to alcoholism will exhibit similar personality traits *before* the onset of the disorder has not always been supported by objective data (Saxe et al., 1983). Many kinds of people fall prey to alcoholism, suggesting that causes other than personality factors are at work here.

Many learning theorists argue that these causes lie in the rewards surrounding drinking. Alcohol use may result in peer approval, easier social relations, and a reduction in cares and anxieties. It is this last factor—a drop in psychological tension—that learning theorists emphasize. They say that in an effort to alleviate the stress arising from the problems of everyday living, many people take a drink. And for a while some of their worries *do* evaporate, so drinking is reinforced. But the more a person drinks, the greater the likelihood that his or her problems will increase. These problems naturally lead to even greater alcohol consumption and a vicious circle soon sets in. Laboratory research testing this theory has so far produced mixed results. While subjects under stress do sometimes drink more alcohol than nonstressed subjects do, at other times they drink the same amount or even significantly less (Higgins and Marlatt, 1973, 1975; Marlatt, Kosturn, and Lang, 1975; Holroyd, 1978). This finding suggests that while tension reduction may be a factor in alcohol use, it is not the only one.

Proponents of the sociocultural perspective point in addition to the attitudes that people learn in the process of growing up. They stress that the incidence of alcohol abuse is much higher in some social groups than in others, and that these patterns correspond to group values in regard to drinking. In social groups that frown on drinking (Muslims and Mormons, for instance), rates of alcoholism are very low, whereas in social groups that approve of drinking (the French, for example), alcoholism is quite common (Kinney and Leaton, 1978). People tend to behave, in other words, according to the norms of their society.

Most experts now acknowledge that there are probably many causes of alcohol abuse. No single theory is entirely satisfactory. No one treatment alone is associated with a high rate of success. Clinicians who deal with alcoholism usually approach the problem from several angles—the physical addiction itself, the victim's difficulties in handling stress, the rewards of alcohol use, and elements in the social environment that may be encouraging alcoholism. In this way they greatly increase their chances of permanently alleviating the disorder.

SUMMARY

1. Various criteria can be used to assess the normality or abnormality of any given behavior. Among them are deviation from statistical norms, conformity to social values, and comparison with an absolute standard of mental health.

2. Theories of psychological disorders are important because they suggest effective treatments, and treat-

ments in turn may yield evidence about the causes of disorders.

3. The biological perspective, probably the most influential view of mental illness, sees psychological disorders as forms of physical illness. In this view, mental disturbance is often considered the result of physical dysfunction.

4. The psychoanalytic perspective, pioneered by Sigmund Freud, sees psychological disturbances as the result of conflicts in a person's childhood development, particularly conflicts over the control of id impulses.

5. According to the learning-theory perspective, we learn abnormal behaviors much as we learn normal ones—through modeling, classical conditioning, operant conditioning, and so on. A recent extension of learning theory has gone beyond the focus on observable behavior to consider the role that patterns of thought—cognitions—play in abnormality.

6. The phenomenological perspective sees abnormal behavior as arising from distortion of a person's true inner self. This view stresses the freedom to make positive choices that will liberate one's potential for self-actualization.

7. The family, or systems, approach sees psychological problems as involving the network of human relationships important in a person's life. The family is considered to be among the most critical of these networks.

8. The sociocultural perspective sees the roots of mental disturbance in such social ills as poverty and discrimination. It looks beyond the individual and the family to focus on a person's broad social context.

9. A widely used system for classifying mental disorders is contained in the *Diagnostic and Statistical Manual of Mental Disorders (DSM)*, published by the American Psychiatric Association. Although classification has its critics, it is hard to imagine treatment of the mentally disturbed without it.

10. **Anxiety disorders** include generalized anxiety and panic attacks, phobias, and obsessive-compulsive behaviors. In **generalized anxiety,** the person is highly upset and apprehensive but is unable to specify why. The sufferer may also experience episodes of **panic,** often accompanied by chest pain, dizziness, difficulty in breathing, and intense fear and agitation. In a **phobia,** anxiety is aroused by one particular stim-

ulus only, such as dogs or high places. **Obsessions** are troubling, recurrent thoughts that seem irrational, while **compulsions** are senseless acts that the victim cannot control. Obsessions and compulsions often occur together, with obsessive thinking leading to compulsive behavior.

11. A **somatoform disorder** is characterized by some physical ailment with no organic cause. In **hypochondriasis,** the person is persistently fearful of having some terrible disease, despite doctors' assurances that no physical illness is present. In **conversion disorder,** the victim's psychological distress actually produces what appears to be a genuine physical dysfunction (paralysis or blindness, for instance) even though there is no organic impairment.

12. **Dissociative disorders** involve a splitting off (dissociation) of a part of one's personality, so that memory or identity is disturbed. The victim of **amnesia** forgets all or part of his or her personal past. The victim of **fugue** flees an existing identity for a period of time. The victim of **multiple personality** develops two or more distinct personalities, which may contrast sharply with one another.

13. **Affective disorders** are characterized by disturbances in mood, or affect. **Depression** is a state of despondency in which the person is apathetic and may see no worthwhile qualities in him- or herself, while **mania** is a condition of extreme elation, feverish activity, and hyperinflated self-esteem. **Manic-depressive disorder** is a disturbance whose victims suffer both of these mood extremes, usually at different times, but occasionally together.

14. **Schizophrenia** is characterized by a loss of the capacity to focus attention, associated disorders of thought, inappropriate emotional responses, disturbances in perception (including bizarre hallucinations), abnormal motor behavior, and extreme social withdrawal. Schizophrenia is a severe disorder that renders the victim unable to cope with most of life's ordinary demands.

15. **Personality disorders** are deeply ingrained maladaptive patterns of behavior that often distress those around the victims more than they do the victims themselves. The most serious of these disorders is the **antisocial personality.** Such a person acts impulsively and often destructively, lacks concern for others, and has a tendency not to learn from experience.

16. People have an **addictive disorder** when they become so involved with a drug that their lives center around its use and their interpersonal relationships suffer. The most widespread addictive disorders in our society are **alcohol abuse** and **alcohol dependence.** They take an enormous toll economically, socially, and medically.

SUGGESTED READINGS

BOOTZIN, RICHARD R., and ACOCELLA, JOAN ROSS. *Abnormal psychology.* 4th ed. New York: Random House, 1984.

A comprehensive textbook that describes the principal categories of psychological disorder and explains the major theoretical perspectives on abnormal behavior.

KAPLAN, BERT (Ed.). *The inner world of mental illness.* New York: Harper & Row, 1964.

First-person accounts of the experience of severe mental disorder, including excerpts from classic works of literature and the diaries of famous writers.

MEYER, R., and OSBORNE, Y. *Case studies in abnormal behavior.* Boston: Allyn and Bacon, 1982.

This collection of case studies provides examples of most major patterns of abnormal behavior. Each case discussion includes relevant diagnostic criteria and recommended forms of therapy.

RACHMAN, S., and HODGSON, R. *Obsessions and compulsions.* Englewood Cliffs, N.J.: Prentice-Hall, 1980.

Addresses the full range of obsessional thoughts and compulsive behaviors, from the experience of having lines of a song stay with us for days to irrational, time-consuming rituals that completely disrupt the person's life.

WYNNE, LYMAN C., CROMWELL, RUE L., and MATTHYSE, STEVEN W. *The nature of schizophrenia: New approaches to research and treatment.* New York: Wiley, 1978.

A survey of current theory and knowledge regarding all aspects of schizophrenia, from all modern perspectives.

ZILBOORG, GREGORY, and HENRY, GEORGE W. *A history of medical psychology.* New York: Norton, 1941.

A classic, fascinating discussion of the history of madness.

16

APPROACHES TO TREATMENT

David Smith, *Cubi XII*, 1963.

Anyone who has ever tried to calm a distraught person or bolster a friend who is feeling depressed has engaged in efforts akin to those practiced in psychotherapy. But the professional therapist comes armed with principles and tactics that the average person lacks. For the professional, intuitions about what might be helpful in easing psychological disturbance are replaced with treatment methods that grow out of articulated theories about the causes of various disorders. **Psychotherapy,** then, can be defined as a series of systematic interactions between one person who is trained in alleviating psychological problems and another who is suffering from them. These interactions are structured by both beliefs and scientific findings as to why such disturbances occur.

In recent years psychotherapy has rapidly expanded and diversified. Freudian psychoanalysis, which once dominated the field, has been challenged by newer schools of treatment—behavior therapies, phenomenologically oriented therapies, and family therapies. Each therapeutic school has spawned a host of specific approaches to treatment; today more than a hundred schools of psychotherapy exist. In the process of expanding, psychotherapy has gained increased acceptance, until most of the stigma once attached to it has disappeared.

The therapists who offer today's many forms of treatment vary widely in their training. **Clinical psychologists** have a doctorate in clinical psychology and have completed a one-year internship. **Psychiatrists** are physicians (M.D.s) who specialize in diagnosing and treating mental illness. **Psychoanalysts** are usually psychiatrists (though some are lay persons or psychologists) who have advanced training in psychoanalysis and have been psychoanalyzed as part of that training. **Psychiatric social workers** have a master's degree in social work and specialize in psychiatric problems. **Psychiatric nurses** are registered nurses who have specialized in psychiatric care and usually are employed in mental hospitals.

Therapists vary not only in their training but also in their theoretical approaches. This means that they make different assumptions about the causes of mental disorders, as we saw in Chapter 15. In this chapter we shall explore more fully how these various approaches shape the kinds of treatment therapists offer. We shall be covering psychoanalytically oriented treatments, treatments based on learning theory, phenomenologically oriented treatments, family therapies, and group therapies—all of which are different forms of psychotherapy. We shall also be examining various kinds of biological treatments, such as drug therapies and the use of electroconvulsive shock. These forms of treatment differ from psychotherapies in their attempt to change not the disturbed person's outlook or approach to handling problems, but rather the complex functioning of the individual's nervous system.

But note that most contemporary therapists do not adhere rigidly to one form of treatment or another.

Most are to some extent "eclectic," borrowing approaches and techniques from other schools of thought to supplement their own perspectives. Some family therapists, for instance, also use behavioral strategies, while some phenomenologically oriented therapists are sympathetic to certain Freudian ideas. This overlap should be kept in mind as you read the sections that follow.

PSYCHOTHERAPIES

Psychotherapeutic approaches to treatment are highly diverse. Some stress past conflicts in a person's development, while others focus on present obstacles and maladaptive ways of thinking. Some deal with the troubled person alone, as an individual, while others see the client's social relationships as the key to the disturbance. In some the therapist guides the client's progress in a structured step-by-step approach, while in others clients are expected to develop their own solutions to their problems. In all cases, however, psychotherapy aims at changing undesirable responses, improving the person's ability to handle stressful situations, and encouraging more adaptive ways of thinking, feeling, and behaving. Toward this end, clients discuss their thoughts, feelings, and behaviors freely

and in detail with the therapist. It is believed that through this important client-therapist interaction, the troubled person will begin to act in more psychologically healthy ways. Table 16.1 gives an overview of some of the therapies currently being used. In the following section we will examine each of these therapies in greater detail.

Psychoanalytically Oriented Therapies

The oldest form of psychotherapy still practiced today is Freudian psychoanalysis. For a variety of reasons, however, few contemporary practitioners follow

TABLE 16.1 A COMPARISON OF PSYCHOTHERAPIES

	PSYCHOANALYTIC THERAPY	BEHAVIOR THERAPY	PHENOMENOLOGICAL THERAPY	FAMILY THERAPY
Typical view of problem	Client's problems are symptoms of deep-seated, unresolved unconscious conflicts	Client has learned maladaptive habits	Client is not functioning at own optimum level of development	Client interacts with family members in maladaptive patterns
Emphasis of therapy	Identifying underlying causes	Focusing on specific behaviors or ideas identified as problems	Release of inherent growth potential	Improvement in communication
Nature of therapy	Psychoanalysis, including free association and dream analysis	Program designed to replace maladaptive behavior with adaptive behavior	Creation of climate to encourage self-appreciation, honest expression of feelings, and acceptance of responsibility	Paradoxical intervention

Source: Adapted from Sundberg, Taplin, and Tyler, 1983.

Freud's doctrines faithfully (Korchin, 1976). For one thing, traditional psychoanalysis is a very long and expensive process, one that most people cannot afford. Thus many psychoanalytically oriented therapists, while still striving for insights into unconscious conflicts and motives, have substantially shortened the total time a person spends in psychotherapy. But because the influence of Freudian psychoanalysis has been so profound, we shall examine it in some detail before describing the more modern approaches that have developed from it.

Freudian Psychoanalysis.

Freud's experiences with his patients led him to conclude that the source of most disorders was the anxiety felt when unconscious and unacceptable id impulses threatened to break into conscious awareness. To deal with this threat, the patient would resort to defense mechanisms, especially to repression—a pushing back of shameful thoughts and desires into the unconscious. But while id impulses could be temporarily hidden, they could not be banished entirely. As a result, other aspects of the psyche constantly had to expend energy in attempts to keep these impulses from surfacing. Freud believed that the best treatment was to coax the forbidden thoughts and desires into consciousness so that the patient could finally confront them. These thoughts and desires could then be "worked through," or explored rationally to facilitate understanding and change. According to Freud, this process should gradually reduce anxiety and free psychic energy for more constructive purposes.

Freud developed several techniques to draw troublesome urges and feelings out of the unconscious and into consciousness. One is **free association.** The patient lies on a couch and relaxes, thus helping to loosen conscious restraints. He or she then voices freely whatever thoughts come to mind. No thought is willfully censored; no logical structure is imposed on the flow of ideas. The therapist listens without interruption, keeping remarks to a minimum. Presumably, unconscious feelings and conflicts will eventually begin to surface.

Freud's second source of clues to the contents of the unconscious was **dream interpretation.** He believed that during sleep restraints are again loosened. But even in sleep, according to Freud, the unconscious is censored, with forbidden thoughts appearing only in symbolic form. Thus every dream has its **manifest content** (its plot or story line) and its **latent content** (its symbolic meaning), which exposes uncon-

scious conflicts. A woman who has just had a baby, for instance, might dream that she has given birth to two boys and that one has died (the manifest content). The symbolic meaning (latent content) might be that the new mother feels ambivalent toward her real child, whom she both wants and doesn't want. During psychoanalysis, free association is sometimes used to help a person gain insight into the hidden meaning of a dream. Here is one example of how this process works:

"Well," she said, "this is what I dreamed. . . . I was in what appeared to be a ballroom or a dance hall, but I knew it was really a hospital. A man came up to me and told me to undress, take all my clothes off. He was going to give me a gynecological examination. I did as I was told but I was very frightened. While I was undressing, I noticed that he was doing something to a woman at the other end of the room. She was sitting or lying in a funny kind of contraption with all kinds of levers and gears and pulleys attached to it. I knew that I was supposed to be next, that I would have to sit in that thing while he examined me. Suddenly he called my name and I found myself running to him. The chair or table—whatever it was— was now empty, and he told me to get on it. I refused and began to cry. It started to rain—great big drops of rain. He pushed me to the floor and spread my legs for the examination. I turned over on my stomach and began to scream. I woke myself up screaming."

Following the recital Laura lay quietly on the couch, her eyes closed, her arms crossed over her bosom.

"Well," she said after a brief, expectant silence, "what does it mean?"

"Laura," I admonished, "you know better than that. Associate, and we'll find out."

"The first thing I think of is Ben," she began. "He's an intern at University, you know. I guess that's the doctor in the dream—or maybe it was you. Anyhow, whoever it was, I wouldn't let them examine me."

"Why not?"

"I've always been afraid of doctors . . . afraid they might hurt me."

"How will they hurt you?"

"I don't know. By jabbing me with a needle, I guess. . . ."

"What about gynecological examinations?"

"I've never had one. I can't even bear to think of someone poking around inside me." Again silence; then, "Oh," she said, "I see it now. It's sex I'm afraid of. The doctor in the dream *is* Ben. He wants me to have intercourse, but it scares me and I turn away from him. That's true. . . ."

"But why, Laura?"

"I don't know," she cried, "I don't know. Tell me."

"I think the dream tells you," I said.

"The dream I just told you?"

"Yes. . . . There's a part of it you haven't considered. What comes to your mind when you think of the other woman in the dream, the woman the doctor was examining before you?"

"The contraption she was sitting in," Laura exclaimed. "It was like a—wheel chair—my mother's wheel chair! Is that right?"

"Very likely," I said.

"But why would he be examining her? What would that mean?"

"Well, think of what that examination signified for you."

"Sex," she said. "Intercourse—that's what it means. So that's what it is—that's what it means! Intercourse put my mother in the wheel chair. It paralyzed her. And I'm afraid that's what it will do to me. So I avoid it—because I'm scared it will do the same thing to me. . . ." [Lindner, 1954, pp. 93–95]

In fact, the mother's paralysis was totally unrelated to sex. But Laura had unconsciously connected her mother's condition with the muffled cries and moans that, as a child, she had heard through the walls during her parents' lovemaking.

Naturally, the conscious confrontation of thoughts such as these is not pleasant. As patients near exposure of particularly painful thoughts and feelings, they may show signs of **resistance,** or attempts to block treatment. They may avoid talking about certain topics, pause frequently, or report that their minds are blank. They may even launch into lengthy monologues about irrelevant subjects, such as world politics. The therapist's interpretation of resistance is an important part of treatment, for it helps the patient to see unconscious motives at work.

As psychoanalysis progresses, patients may transfer to the therapist the emotions they felt toward important others in their childhood development, particularly their parents. Thus the therapist may become the target of dependency, hostility, or whatever other feelings lie at the core of the person's problem. Through this process of **transference,** which essentially involves a reenactment of painful childhood conflicts, the therapist has a chance to see irrational fears and desires at first hand. With the therapist's help, the patient can then begin to acknowledge his or her own distorted perceptions, putting things ultimately into a more mature perspective. Such analysis of transference, in fact, is considered the key to successful psychoanalysis. Only in this way can the patient's unconscious conflicts be fully understood and resolved.

Psychoanalysis has many proponents, among them many "graduates" of analysis who feel their lives have been improved by the process. However, traditional psychoanalysis is invariably long and costly, often requiring years of analytic sessions several times a week, and an investment of thousands of dollars. In addition, since psychoanalysis is based on talk and insight, it tends to work best for those who are articulate and well educated (Luborsky and Spence, 1978). Thus, although traditional psychoanalysis may be of great help to those who can afford it, it is rather limited as a general treatment.

Other Psychoanalytic Treatments. Some of Freud's earliest associates, such as Carl Jung and Alfred Adler, began to modify psychoanalytic theory even as Freud was formulating it. As a result of their theoretical disagreements with Freud, these former disciples developed variations on Freud's therapeutic techniques. Later psychoanalytic thinkers carried these innovations still further. Unlike Freud, who maintained that all psychic energy originates in the id, many of the post-Freudian psychoanalytic theorists argued that the ego possesses substantial energy of its own. As therapists, they have therefore tried to help clients strengthen the ego and develop a firm, well-integrated, autonomous self-identity. Other post-Freudians have stressed the importance of the client's style of relating to other people. In this view, faulty relationships with others not only contribute to psychological problems but are the key defining features of all psychological disturbance.

The contrast between traditional psychoanalysis and more modern psychoanalytically oriented treatments can also be seen in the way therapy sessions are conducted. In the newer approaches, the general psychoanalytic framework still remains, with the therapist uncovering unconscious motives, breaking down defenses, and dealing with the client's resistance. But some of the classic Freudian procedures are missing. The couch is usually dispensed with; most clients now sit up and talk with the therapist face to face. The therapist also takes a more active role, advising, interpreting, and directing. Moreover, a modern analyst tends to place more emphasis on current situations than on events in the distant past. The therapy is briefer, less intensive, and typically aims for a less than complete restructuring of the client's personality (Zaiden, 1982).

Unlike traditional psychoanalysis, today's psychoanalytically oriented treatments are likely to dispense with the couch in favor of chairs, which facilitate face-to-face interaction between therapist and client. Clients may be individuals, groups of people with similar problems, or the members of a troubled family. *(Linda Ferrer/Woodfin Camp & Associates.)*

Behavior Therapies

Behavior therapy is the application of learning theories and other experimentally derived psychological principles to the task of changing problem behavior (Begelman, 1975; Bootzin, 1975). The term *behavior therapy* is used because this approach to treatment originally grew out of the behaviorist tradition, with its focus on the principles of classical and operant conditioning. But in recent years behavior therapies have diversified greatly. Today a broad range of therapeutic procedures fall into this category, including approaches based on observational, social, and cognitive learning principles.

Despite their diversity, however, behavior therapies share a number of basic features—features that distinguish them sharply from psychoanalytic therapies. For one thing, all behavior therapies are based on the assumption that psychological problems are *learned* responses. As such, these problems are believed to arise from the same learning principles that govern normal behavior. Clients' environments are deemed crucial to elimination of their problems. Behavior therapists believe that by changing people's environments in appropriate ways, one can effectively change their behavior. No deep probing of unconscious conflicts is thought to be needed. To the behavior therapist, problem behaviors are not merely symptoms of some deep psychic disturbance. Instead, the problems reported by the clients are themselves seen as the disturbance and the proper targets of therapy.

This is not to say that behavior therapists ignore what their clients are thinking and feeling. For many, changing maladaptive thoughts and feelings is central to effective treatment. But behavior therapists take clients' cognitions at face value rather than as defenses against unconscious urges. Behavior therapists also participate more actively in the therapeutic process than most traditional psychoanalysts do. Rather than spending long hours listening to clients recall their childhood experiences, describe their dreams, and free-associate, they often ask direct questions and give explicit advice and instructions (Sloane et al., 1975). They also focus on the *current* factors maintaining the problem behavior, not the past factors that may originally have encouraged it. Their treatment is also much more specific than the psychoanalyst's. They aim at eliminating *particular* problems, not at changing a person's overall way of perceiving the world.

In the following sections we shall explore a number of behavior therapies. First we will cover some treatments based on classical and operant conditioning. Then we will examine some approaches derived from social and cognitive learning principles.

Therapies Based on Classical Conditioning. As we learned in Chapter 5, classical conditioning involves the repeated pairing of a neutral stimulus with another stimulus that evokes some involuntary, reflex response. Gradually the formerly neutral stimulus by itself comes to elicit that same reflex. In John B. Watson's experiment with little Albert, for instance, a frightening noise was repeatedly paired with the presentation of a laboratory rat, until eventually the rat alone came to elicit fear. In most cases a classically conditioned response will become extinguished if the conditioned stimulus and the unconditioned stimulus are not paired at least occasionally. But in classically conditioned fears like little Albert's, the conditioned stimulus (in Albert's case, the rat) may be so terrifying that it is hard for the person to "unlearn" the deeply ingrained association. This is why behavior therapist Joseph Wolpe (1958, 1973, 1976) developed the technique for treating phobias called **systematic desensitization.**

Systematic Desensitization. Systematic desensitization is based on the principle that anxiety and relaxation are incompatible and that therefore people can be taught to be less anxious about something by learning to relax when confronting it. Suppose a par-

ticular client's anxiety centers on flying in airplanes. The therapist begins by asking the client to describe what part of the experience of flying is most frightening, what part is slightly less frightening, what part only moderately frightening, and so on. The therapist then arranges these situations in a hierarchy from most to least fear-arousing. Here is a hypothetical example:

1. Experiencing midair turbulence
2. Taking off
3. Taxiing down the runway
4. Boarding the plane
5. Waiting to get on the plane
6. Riding to the airport in a car
7. Buying an airline ticket

The client is next taught a technique of deep muscle relaxation. When he or she is thoroughly relaxed, the therapist asks the person to imagine the least frightening scene in the hierarchy while still remaining relaxed. When the client has done so, the procedure is repeated with the next highest item on the list. Eventually the client is able to imagine the most frightening scene without becoming afraid. Having learned to remain relaxed while progressively confronting the feared situation, the client ceases to fear it.

Systematic desensitization has been extensively tried and evaluated. It has been found to be effective not only for phobias, but also for a variety of other problems that involve stress and anxiety. These in-

The "graduation flight" of a group of people who have participated in a systematic desensitization program to overcome their fear of flying. Some are showing anxiety prior to takeoff—but before joining the program (conducted by a psychologist and former Pan Am pilot), they would not have been able to board the plane, or perhaps even to buy a plane ticket. *(Courtesy of Capt. T. W. Cummings, Freedom from Fear of Flying, Inc.)*

The Program For The Fearful Flyer

By Captain T. W. Cummings

clude recurrent nightmares, chronic alcoholism, and complex interpersonal problems, such as fears of intimacy and rejection (Kazdin and Wilson, 1978; Rimm and Masters, 1979).

Aversive Conditioning. Another therapeutic technique derived from classical conditioning principles is **aversive conditioning.** In this approach cues that are related to a deviant behavior are repeatedly paired with an aversive stimulus that elicits an unpleasant response. Eventually the deviant cues alone will evoke the unpleasant reaction, thus turning the person away from the old behavior patterns.

To understand aversive conditioning more fully, consider how it is applied to the treatment of alcoholism (Nathan, 1976). The presentation of alcohol, including its taste and smell, is repeatedly paired with a drug that causes vomiting and so evokes intense feelings of nausea and revulsion. Usually the drug is given immediately before the drink, or is mixed with it, so that the two stimuli occur close together in time. After a sufficient number of pairings, the person responds to alcohol alone as he or she does to the drug— with strong feelings of nausea at the very sight or smell of it.

Aversive conditioning is seldom used alone. Generally it is but one part of a comprehensive treatment program (Mahoney and Arnkoff, 1978). A client undergoing aversive conditioning for alcoholism, for instance, may also be given instructions on appropriate drinking behavior, explicit guidelines on how to refuse a drink, and videotaped feedback on how he or she behaves when drunk (Mills, Sobell, and Schaefer, 1971; Strickler et al., 1976). Although more research is needed, preliminary evidence suggests that

such techniques are effective in the treatment of alcoholism (Sherman, 1979).

Therapies Based on Operant Conditioning. In therapies based on operant conditioning, desirable behaviors are increased by reinforcement, and undesirable behaviors are decreased either by punishment or by withdrawal of rewards. This approach is often called **contingency management,** because the therapist is manipulating the consequences of a person's actions. Contingency management has been quite effective in institutional settings, where it is relatively easy to control the outcomes of behaviors. Severely retarded children, for instance, have been taught to dress and feed themselves by systematically rewarding them for successful attempts at tying their shoes, using a fork, and so on (Thompson and Grabowski, 1977). Similarly, the bizarre behaviors of schizophrenics have sometimes been reduced when hospital nurses simply refuse to pay attention to them (Sushinsky, 1970). Contingency management has also been successful with less severe problems. Overweight people have been helped to eat less, insomniacs to get to sleep, and couples experiencing marital difficulties to interact more effectively, all through careful application of operant conditioning principles (Stuart, 1967; Bootzin and Nicassio, 1978; Liberman et al., 1976).

Token Economies. The **token economy** is one way of systematically rewarding desired responses. In this system, specific behaviors immediately earn a person "tokens" (poker chips, slips of paper, or whatever) which can then be exchanged for desired rewards (candy, magazines, television privileges, and so forth).

A scene in a hallway of Camarillo State Hospital in California, where a token economy has been instituted. This room is a positive reinforcer; it is more private and more comfortable than the patients' regular sleeping quarters. (*John Oldenkamp.*)

Token economies have been used successfully in many settings: classrooms, residential programs for juvenile offenders, institutions for the mentally retarded, to name just a few (Fixsen, Phillips, and Wolf, 1976; Kazdin, 1977). One major study found that a token economy in combination with individual behavior therapy resulted in greater improvement in a group of chronic mental patients than did either of two alternative treatments (Paul and Lentz, 1977).

Although token economies do work well, some observers have questioned whether the gains patients make will be maintained when they leave the institution (Condry, 1977). To minimize such setbacks therapists employ a number of strategies (Ayllon and Arzin, 1968). First, they select target behaviors (those to be rewarded with tokens) that either are reinforcing in their own right (such as interaction with others) or will naturally be reinforced by social approval (such as improved personal hygiene). Second, as the patients acquire the desired behaviors, the hospital staff increasingly uses social approval rather than tokens to reward them. This strategy brings the reward structure closer to that found in the outside environment. Third, arrangements are often made to continue systematic reinforcement outside the hospital walls (by training family members to reward target behaviors, for instance). And fourth, people may be taught to provide their own reinforcement (such as treating themselves to a movie as a reward for looking for a job). These tactics seem to be effective. Compared with traditional hospital care, institutional programs that systematically reward positive behaviors not only *increase* patients' likelihood of being discharged, they also *decrease* their chances of being admitted again (Kazdin and Wilson, 1978).

Time Out. But sometimes rewarding desirable behavior does not seem enough. Some people with psychological problems may engage in actions that are highly offensive to those around them, or that may even endanger their own and others' safety. Behavior therapists again use operant conditioning principles to deter such behavior. One technique that is quite common, especially for treating problem children, is called **time out.** It simply involves following undesirable behavior with a period of time away from positive reinforcement. Gradually the unwanted responses should then be extinguished.

Time out is clearly related to the old-fashioned remedy of sending misbehaving children to their rooms. Several procedures that govern time out, however, make it more effective than the typical parent-imposed exile. First, the therapist sets clear rules as to when time out will be administered (when the child throws a tantrum, for instance, or bites another person). The child is carefully informed of these rules and they are always enforced. Second, the place to which the child is sent for a time-out session, while never intrinsically frightening, contains no rewards. There are no toys or books or records there, none of the pleasant distractions usually found in a child's own room. Third, the adult who imposes time out does so dispassionately, not with obvious annoyance. This is because some children find *any* attention—even attention provoked by anger—a form of reinforcement. Finally, the amount of time a child spends in a time-out room is carefully regulated. Generally it is quite brief, no more than five to fifteen minutes.

Stimulus Control. Another operant conditioning principle that behavior therapists use is that of **stimulus control.** Remember from Chapter 5 that operant responses tend to be governed by cues in the environment which signal that a reward may be available. A laboratory rat, for instance, may learn to associate the sight of a Skinner box, a lever, and a flashing light with the delivery of food, and so press the lever whenever these stimuli are present. The stimuli, in other words, may come to control its behavior.

Now suppose there is a behavior you want to decrease in frequency—say, overeating. One way to do this is to cut back drastically on the number of cues associated with eating. A behavior therapist might tell you to restrict your eating to one place only, usually the dining room or kitchen. All other settings where eating formerly occurred (in your car, at a movie, in front of the television set) are no longer to serve as cues for this behavior. In operant conditioning terms you are acquiring stimulus discrimination—the tendency to engage in eating only when very specific stimuli are present. Conversely, you can increase the frequency of a desired behavior by trying to ensure that the response you seek always occurs in the presence of certain stimuli. No other behaviors are allowed in this particular setting, until eventually the desired stimulus-response connection becomes automatic. Figure 16.1 describes how two psychologists were able to increase sleeping time for insomniacs by applying this approach (Bootzin and Nicassio, 1978).

Self-Control. Today it is increasingly popular for people to try to learn how to manipulate the conse-

1. Lie down intending to go to sleep *only* when you are sleepy.
2. Do not use your bed for anything except sleep; that is, do not read, watch television, eat, or worry in bed. Sexual activity is the only exception to this rule. On such occasions, the instructions are to be followed afterward when you intend to go to sleep.
3. If you find yourself unable to fall asleep, get up and go into another room. Stay up as long as you wish and then return to the bedroom to sleep. Although we do not want you to watch the clock, we want you to get out of bed if you do not fall asleep immediately. Remember the goal is to associate your bed with falling asleep *quickly!* If you are in bed more than about 10 minutes without falling asleep and have not gotten up, you are not following this instruction.
4. If you still cannot fall asleep, repeat Step 3. Do this as often as is necessary throughout the night.
5. Set your alarm and get up at the same time every morning irrespective of how much sleep you got during the night. This will help your body acquire a consistent sleep rhythm.
6. Do not nap during the day.

Figure 16.1 The technique of stimulus control has been applied to the treatment of insomnia. Researchers found that insomniacs often use their beds at night for activities unrelated to sleeping, such as watching television, eating, and worrying. To reestablish the connection between sleeping (response) and bed (the external stimulus), they recommended the regimen outlined here. Subjects in an experiment they conducted were able to reduce the time it took to fall asleep from an average of 85 minutes to an average of 36 minutes. *(From Bootzin and Nicassio, 1978.)*

quences and stimuli surrounding their own behaviors. Such efforts, which dispense with the need for a therapist's continual supervision, are part of what is called **self-control** (Williams and Long, 1983; Watson and Tharp, 1981). A qualified professional may advise the client on various strategies to set up a self-control program, but the responsibility for carrying out the program is the client's. Suppose, for example, that a client wants to improve her social relationships by becoming a better conversationalist. A professional counselor might advise her to tape her conversations in several situations and then analyze them on the basis of criteria such as those shown in Figure 16.2. The client's improvement would depend on how conscientious she was in evaluating her flaws (e.g., "I seem to complain a lot") and what she did to eliminate them. The great advantages of this approach are that it can be applied virtually anywhere, is quite inexpensive, and may help to ensure that therapeutic gains are not lost later.

Therapies Based on Social Learning. Although therapies based on operant conditioning are widely used today, it is important to remember that rewards and punishments are not always needed in order for learning to occur. Often we learn simply through observation—that is, through processing the stimuli around us—with no overt rewards or punishments being meted out. This is a central tenet of social learning theory, as we saw in Chapter 5. When we come to shape our own behavior on the basis of what others do, we are said to be acquiring new behavior through the process of **modeling.** Of course, we are far more likely to imitate, or model, behavior that we see resulting in reinforcement than behavior resulting in punishment.

Deliberate modeling has been successfully put to therapeutic uses. It has proved particularly effective in the treatment of phobias. Sometimes the client merely watches another person (either live or on film) interacting with the feared object. For instance, Albert Bandura and his co-workers have had much success eliminating dog phobias in children by having the phobic youngsters observe a fearless child who first approaches a dog, then touches and pets it, and finally engages the animal in active play (Bandura, Grusec, and Menlove, 1967). In a variation of this technique, called **participant modeling,** the therapist first models the feared activity for the client and then guides the client through a series of gradual steps culminating in the same behavior. In one study, for example, Bandura and others led people with snake phobias from first thinking about snakes, to looking at a snake in a cage, to approaching the snake, to touching it through the wires, and finally to holding it in their hands (Bandura, Blanchard, and Ritter, 1969). They found that participant modeling was more effective in ridding people of this fear than either symbolic modeling (watching a model on film) or systematic desensitization. Other research has yielded

I. Quantity of conversation

   A. Percentage of total time you were talking. Compute from a time duration assessment.

   B. Number of your responses that were 1 to 15 seconds, 16 to 30 seconds, 31 to 60 seconds, and more than 1 minute in duration. Compute from a frequency-count assessment.

II. Type of conversation

   A. Active listening. Record the number of instances in which you paraphrased or otherwise commented directly on what another person had just said.

   B. Questions
      1. Closed. Record the number of questions that called for a factual response.
      2. Open-ended. Record the number of questions that asked for an opinion or judgment from another person.

   C. Approval comments. Frequency-count assessment.

   D. Redundant expressions. Frequency count of verbalizations such as "uh," "you know," "well," "okay."

   E. Clichés. Frequency count of phrases such as "you're putting me on," "let it all hang out," "it turns me on."

   F. Complaints. Frequency count of negative comments about how you feel and how you're being treated.

   G. Cynical comments. Frequency count of critical comments about others' motives, ideas, and behavior.

   H. Defensive responses. Frequency count of times you responded to others' criticism by defending your own behavior and/or launching a counterattack on the other person.

   I. Sweeping generalizations. Frequency count of statements asserting that all people in a particular category behave in the same fashion, for example, "high school students just. . . ." "psychology students act as if. . . ." "women don't really. . . ."

   J. Circuitous responses. Frequency count of times you didn't answer others' questions immediately and directly.

   K. False starts. Frequency count of times you stopped in mid-sentence to begin a new sentence.

   L. Interruptions. Frequency count of times you broke in while another person was speaking.

   M. Garbled words. Frequency count of words not spoken audibly and clearly.

Figure 16.2 Analyzing conversation. A person who has problems communicating with others may benefit by evaluating his or her conversations in light of the criteria listed here. *(From Williams and Long, 1983.)*

similar results (Rimm and Mahoney, 1969; Thase and Moss, 1976).

Psychologists are not yet sure why participant modeling is so effective. Bandura (1977b) suspects that when people with phobias are led to engage in the feared activity themselves, they gain a sense of **self-efficacy,** a feeling of mastery over the situation. With each step in the treatment the person learns "I can do that," and thus acquires the confidence needed to try the next, bolder step. Since the therapy is slowly paced and carefully controlled, the client's success at each new challenge is virtually guaranteed. These repeated successes, in turn, not only are intrinsically rewarding but reinforce expectations of efficacy, thereby encouraging the person to persevere. Expectations of mastery, then, reinforced by actual demonstrations of competence, may explain much of participant modeling's impressive rate of success. This theory, however, is still only speculative. More re-

search is needed to identify the most important elements in participant modeling and to determine the limitations of this promising technique (Sherman, 1979).

Cognitive Behavior Therapy. Modeling therapies stress several cognitive events involved in behavior change (the disconfirmation of false beliefs, for instance, and the development of a sense of self-efficacy). But some forms of behavior therapy take this emphasis on cognitions even further. They are based on the assumption that the way people interpret events around them, perceive themselves, and judge their own abilities is central to their mental health. If people are having problems in living, proponents of this view hold, it is because they are caught in an insidious web of negative, self-defeating thoughts. It is believed that such thoughts are learned, just as maladaptive patterns of behavior are learned. Treatments that try to change these negative thought patterns are called **cognitive behavior therapies** and are becoming increasingly popular.

Perhaps the oldest such treatment is **rational-emotive therapy (RET),** developed by Albert Ellis (1962).

Ellis argues that thousands of people lead unhappy lives because of irrational beliefs that color their interpretation of events. Thus it is not failure itself that is psychologically damaging, but failure screened through the irrational belief that one must excel at everything. Likewise, it is not rejection by itself that causes depression, but rejection filtered through the irrational belief that one must be loved by everyone. Ellis' strategy is to make people aware of the irrationality of many of their views, and to replace these old problem-provoking outlooks with more realistic ones.

Similar in approach is Aaron Beck's **cognitive therapy,** discussed briefly in Chapter 15. Like Ellis, Beck holds that emotional problems are caused primarily by irrational thoughts. In analyzing the roots of depression, for instance, Beck argues that this disorder arises from three types of negative thoughts: (1) persistent self-devaluation, (2) negative interpretations of events, and (3) a pessimistic outlook on the future (Beck et al., 1979). When people interpret trivial setbacks as substantial, read disparagement into innocuous comments by others, and criticize themselves harshly for things they cannot possibly control, they are very probably on the road to a major depression, according to Beck.

To change such cognitions, Beck uses a Socratic approach—that is, he questions patients in such a way that they themselves discover the irrationality of their thinking. Here is one example:

Therapist: Why do you want to end your life?
Patient: Without Raymond, I'm nothing. . . . I can't be happy without Raymond. . . . But I can't save our marriage.
Therapist: What has your marriage been like?
Patient: It has been miserable from the very beginning. . . . Raymond has always been unfaithful. . . . I have hardly seen him in the past five years.
Therapist: You say that you can't be happy without Raymond. . . . Have you found yourself happy when you are with Raymond?
Patient: No, we fight all the time and I feel worse.
Therapist: You say you are nothing without Raymond. Before you met Raymond, did you feel you were nothing?
Patient: No, I felt I was somebody.
Therapist: If you were somebody before you knew Raymond, why do you need him to be somebody now?
Patient: [Puzzled] Hmmm. . . .
Therapist: If you were free of the marriage, do you think that men might be interested in you—knowing that you were available?

Patient: I guess that maybe they would be.
Therapist: Is it possible that you might find a man who would be more constant than Raymond?
Patient: I don't know. . . . I guess it's possible. . . .
Therapist: Then what have you actually lost if you break up the marriage?
Patient: I don't know.
Therapist: Is it possible that you'll get along better if you end the marriage?
Patient: There is no guarantee of that.
Therapist: Do you have a *real marriage?*
Patient: I guess not.
Therapist: If you don't have a real marriage, what do you actually lose if you decide to end the marriage?
Patient: [Long pause] Nothing, I guess. [Beck, 1976, pp. 289–291]

Research has shown that this kind of therapy can be extremely effective, particularly in the treatment of depression (Rush et al., 1977; Rush and Giles, 1982).

Donald Meichenbaum (1977) takes an even more active approach to helping people change their negative patterns of thought. Meichenbaum's version of cognitive behavior therapy is called **self-instructional training.** He thoroughly instructs his clients on how to think rational and positive thoughts in stressful situations instead of plunging into the old self-defeating patterns. For instance, a student who always becomes highly anxious when taking exams is very apt to think like this:

I'm so nervous, I'm afraid I'll forget the most important parts of the material. The teacher will read this test and lose all respect for me. If I get a D on this test, I'll have to get a B on the final just to get a C for the course. I *know* everybody here studied more than I did, which will shoot the curve way up. If I don't get an A in this course, I may as well forget about grad school. . . .

Of course, this pattern of thought makes the student even more nervous and so even less likely to do well on the exam. Meichenbaum's remedy is to teach the client new, more positive internal monologues to replace the negative ones. For our anxious student, the new monologue might be:

I'm going to take slow, deep breaths and keep myself calm. All I have to do is be calm and take my time . . . just consider the questions one by one. I spent a fair amount of time studying for this test and I'm going to take each question in turn and be calm while I'm thinking about the answer. I'm an intelligent, competent person, and that fact is not altered by whatever grade I get on this test.

Figure 16.3 Examples of statements that individuals rehearsed to manage the anger they anticipated before, during, and after a confrontation. *(Reprinted by permission of Dr. Ray Novaco, University of California, Irvine.)*

Preparing for a Provocation

This could be a rough situation, but I know how to deal with it.
I can work out a plan to handle this. Easy does it.
Remember, stick to the issues and don't take it personally.
There won't be any need for an argument. I know what to do.

Impact and Confrontation

As long as I keep my cool, *I'm* in control of the situation.
You don't need to prove yourself. Don't make more out of this than you have to.
There is no point in getting mad. Think of what you have to do.
Look for the positives and don't jump to conclusions.

Coping with Arousal

Muscles are getting tight. Relax and slow things down.
Time to take a deep breath. Let's take the issue point by point.
My anger is a signal of what I need to do. Time for problem-solving.
He probably wants me to get angry, but I'm going to deal with it constructively.

Subsequent Reflection

a. Conflict unresolved

Forget about the aggravation. Thinking about it only makes you upset.
Try to shake it off. Don't let it interfere with your job.
Remember relaxation. It's a lot better than anger.
Don't take it personally. It's probably not so serious.

b. Conflict resolved

I handled that one pretty well. That's doing a good job!
I could have gotten more upset than it was worth.
My pride can get me into trouble, but I'm doing better at this all the time.
I actually got through that without getting angry.

Self-instructional training can be applied to a variety of situations, including job interviews, achievement settings, and social events. The approach has been particularly effective in training people to manage their anger. Figure 16.3 lists some statements that people have used in practicing control over their anger. The self-instructional approach has gained adherents in recent years as research supporting it has accumulated (Meichenbaum and Jaemko, 1983).

Phenomenologically Oriented Therapies

The rise of phenomenologically oriented therapies was partly a reaction against the determinism implicit in both psychoanalysis and behaviorism. To Freud, a troubled person was the victim of childhood conflicts over which he or she could exert very little control. To B. F. Skinner, we are largely shaped by the external rewards and punishments that impinge upon us. Phenomenologically oriented therapists disagree strongly with these deterministic outlooks. To them, people are ultimately free to make the choices that affect the persons they become. From the phenomenological perspective, then, the goal of psychotherapy is to liberate the client's innate tendencies toward self-actualization and growth. Although there are many different kinds of phenomenologically oriented treatments, we will discuss just two: the person-centered therapy of Carl Rogers and gestalt therapy.

Person-Centered Therapy. The best known of the phenomenologically oriented treatments is Carl Rogers' **person-centered therapy.** It is also called nondirective counseling because clients are not led or directed toward goals that the *therapist* deems appropriate. Instead, the clients define their own problems and determine their own solutions. The therapist's role is to help them clarify their true feelings and to come to value who they really are.

A central assumption of person-centered therapy is that people have problems in living because others impose on them unreasonable **conditions of worth.** That is to say, parents, peers, and spouses withhold respect and affection until the person displays styles of behavior that depart from those of his or her true self. Thus a sensitive teenager may have to deny his sensitivity and behave in artificially aggressive ways in order to gain approval from his peers. The result is profound unhappiness and a stifling of self-actualization.

To free the person from unreasonable conditions of worth, the person-centered therapist establishes a warm and accepting environment. He or she never disapproves of what the client does or thinks. In fact, the therapist repeatedly supports the client, offering what Rogers calls "unconditional positive regard." This includes empathy for the client's feelings. The person-centered therapist tries to "mirror" the client's perspective, thereby helping the person to become more aware of what he or she feels. The following excerpt from a therapy session illustrates this technique. The client here is a college student plagued by feelings of inferiority:

Client: Well, it happened again yesterday. I got back that exam in American Lit.
Therapist: I see.
Client: Just like before. I got an A all right—me and eight others. But on the third question the instructor wrote a comment that I could have been a little clearer or else could have given more detail. The same old crap. I got an A all right, but it's pretty damn clear that I'm like a machine that can generate correct answers without ever understanding. That's it. I memorize, but there's no spark, no creativity. Boy! . . .
Therapist: Even though you got an A you are not satisfied.
Client: That's right. Never satisfied. I could get 42 A-pluses and never feel good. I hate myself. . . . I know I should be satisfied with an A. Other guys would be. They'd be glad to get an A. . . . A lot of

times I've tried to forget my lack of potential. Just go on and plug along.
Therapist: Yeah. I guess you really felt people put you down because of this lack of potential?
Client: Boy, did they! Especially my folks. They never really said so, but I could tell from the way they acted. . . .
Therapist: And this made you feel sort of worthless? . . .
Client: That's right. [Phares, 1979]

Presumably the client's heightened awareness of his feelings, encouraged by the therapist's "mirroring," will ultimately provide the basis for greater self-understanding. Notice also that the therapist expresses the client's feelings without disapproval. This nonjudgmental attitude is considered vital if the client is ever to break free of the unreasonable conditions of worth that currently entrap him.

Rogers was one of the first psychotherapists to publish transcripts of his therapy sessions, not just to illustrate how the process works, but also to encourage analysis of it. He has also conducted research showing that person-centered therapy improves self-image and helps people develop more realistic expectations of themselves. In addition, research has generally supported Rogers' belief that a client makes the most progress when he or she perceives the therapist as warm, sincere, and empathic (Mitchell, Bozarth, and Krauft, 1977).

Gestalt Therapy. Frederick (Fritz) Perls, who developed **gestalt therapy,** was originally trained as a psychoanalyst. From his Freudian roots, Perls derived the notion that psychological problems arise from repressed and unresolved conflicts—conflicts that must be uncovered and somehow worked through. But unlike traditional Freudians, Perls refuses to dwell on the past. Instead, he sees past conflicts as important only as they bear on a person's present. Like other phenomenologically oriented therapists, Perls also believes that people must take responsibility for their own feelings and actions. They cannot blame who they are on past traumas, as psychoanalysts permit, because the past no longer exists. He sees all humans as ultimately free to decide for themselves whether past conflicts will be allowed to hamper current interpersonal relationships.

Perls adopted the term *Gestalt* because in German it means "whole," and his gestalt therapy aims at making a person more integrated or psychologically whole. To this end, Perls tries to help his clients shed their old defenses, release their pent-up feelings, increase their self-awareness, and open their blocked potential for growth. He emphasizes being in touch with one's immediate feelings, expressing them honestly as they are felt, and accepting responsibility for them. Perls and other gestalt therapists employ a variety of tactics to accomplish these goals. For one thing, the client is supposed to use the first person singular ("I, me, mine") and the active voice ("I am, I do, I feel") to show that he or she takes responsibility for feelings and actions. The client says, for example, "I am angry" rather than "Don't you think I have a right to be annoyed?" (Levitsky and Perls, 1970). Sometimes, too, clients are asked to assume responsibility in no uncertain terms. After expressing some truth about themselves, they are to add the emphatic statement "and I take responsibility for that!"

Other gestalt exercises are designed to heighten awareness of important psychological conflicts. The client may be asked to voice a conversation between opposing parts of the self. The ambitious, competitive side of the self, for example, may talk with the side that lacks confidence. Each side is to express itself forcefully, as if arguing with the other. Out of such role-played dialogues an integration of opposing forces may emerge, one that is psychologically healthier than either of the original forces. Alternatively, the client may be asked to engage in a dialogue with some emotionally significant person who is not actually present. In this way the person can act out long-repressed emotions, with the aim of bringing them to some kind of resolution or closure. The following excerpt from a gestalt therapy session illustrates several of these strategies:

> *Therapist:* Tom, what are you experiencing now?
> *Patient:* Anger.
> *Therapist:* Where do you feel this anger?
> *Patient:* [indicating chest] Here, and [indicating hands] here.
> *Therapist:* Just stay with the feeling, and let it increase. And you may get more in touch with it if you breathe deeply, in your abdomen, and let a sound come out when you exhale. . . .
> *Patient:* [breathing abdominally] Ooooh! ooooh! ooooh!
> *Therapist:* What is that experience?
> *Patient:* Anger, resentment.
> *Therapist:* Will you address that resentment to somebody?

> *Patient:* Mother, I resent you . . . everything about you.
> *Therapist:* Specify your resentment.
> *Patient:* I . . . I resent you for making me dependent on you.
> *Therapist:* Tom, how is your voice?
> *Patient:* It's . . . it's a whine.
> *Therapist:* Will you own your voice? Take responsibility?
> *Patient:* I . . . I'm whining . . . I'm whining.
> *Therapist:* Do that. Whine to your mother, and experience yourself doing that.
> *Patient:* [whining voice; reaching out with hands] Mother . . . Please . . . please let me go . . . please turn me loose.   [Phares, 1979, p. 374]

This approach, with its emphasis on the expression of pent-up feelings, has had considerable influence on other therapies, particularly group therapies. The gestalt approach has also attracted many adherents, possibly because modern society discourages the expression of intense feelings in most contexts. Despite the impact of gestalt therapy, however, its effectiveness has not been supported by research data (Smith and Glass, 1977).

Family Therapies

Family approaches to psychotherapy grew out of the recognition that abnormal behavior seldom arises solely from a disturbance within the psyche of the person who is displaying the symptoms. Instead, its roots may lie in maladaptive patterns of interaction within that person's family. Changing these maladaptive patterns has therefore become an important area of treatment. Because family therapists must work with groups of intimately related people who have long-standing and emotion-laden ways of dealing with one another, their work is often very demanding:

> The family therapist is right there in the front lines, heaving and hauling his way through the clutter of disturbed transactions. He has to be actively involved, for it is only the force of his influence that can oppose the weight of the system. The family therapist can't wait around for a "family unconscious" to rise toward him; he has to introduce new energy into a system that will otherwise roll right along on the path it has carved for itself.   [Kovel, 1976, pp. 188–189]

Although there are many kinds of **family therapy,** a common perspective shapes them all. Family therapists see abnormal behavior as a form of communication. The person displaying the symptoms is indirectly conveying certain desires and needs to others in the household. One role of the family therapist, therefore, is to get family members to communicate with one another in more open and straightforward ways. Consider the case of a teenage girl named Laura who refused to eat (Aponte and Hoffman, 1973). After careful observation of relationships within the family, therapists determined that refusal to eat was an effective way for Laura to gain much-wanted attention from her father. When Laura and her parents were helped to express their needs to one another verbally, Laura's eating problems disappeared.

Unfortunately, however, simply explaining to family members why they act in certain ways is often not enough. Patterns of family interaction are deeply entrenched and very resistant to change. In fact, direct attempts to change an unwanted behavior may only increase resistance and intensify the problem. How, then, can a family therapist successfully intervene?

A very frequently used technique is called "paradoxical intervention." In one form of it the therapist demands that a person with negative symptoms go right on displaying those symptoms, perhaps even more forcefully than before. This seemingly absurd requirement is usually presented to the family as a necessary first step in gaining control over the problem ("If you can learn to turn the symptom on, you can learn to turn it off"). But the real reason for the tactic is to place the person exhibiting the symptoms in a very difficult bind (Stanton, 1981). Imagine a family that comes for treatment because of a teenage daughter's delinquent behavior (Haley, 1980). In the therapy session the daughter becomes so disruptive that no interaction is possible. The family therapist may then instruct her to go ahead and stage the worst disruption she can. Suddenly the girl is placed in a position where her uncooperative behavior no longer has its desired effect. If she is disruptive, she is following the therapist's orders and presumably working toward a "cure." If she quiets down and behaves normally, she is showing unwanted improvement and allowing the session to proceed. The confusion that results from this psychological dilemma can promote important insights into family relationships and lead to new, more effective means of communication.

Paradoxical intervention can also be used to change the ways in which other family members react to a member who is behaving abnormally. These changes are guided by the knowledge that what *seems* to be the right way to respond to a troubled person may sometimes only make matters worse. Consider a man who feels depressed. His family may respond by launching an all-out program to "cheer Daddy up." But their actions in a sense are telling him that his feelings are not acceptable and should be promptly stopped. If the man's depression persists, it may well be compounded by guilty feelings that he is letting his family down. In short, the family's well-intentioned actions may simply be encouraging the problem.

Family therapists Paul Watzlawick and James Coyne (1979) have reported just such a case. Mr. B was a middle-aged man who, following a stroke, lapsed into a depression so severe that he became, in the words of his family, a "vegetable." Mrs. B and the other family members made every effort to help him. They emphasized the positive and all he had to live for and repeatedly tried to involve him in family activities. But the more they encouraged him, the more depressed he appeared. A family therapist finally advised them to reverse their strategy. They were now to agree with Mr. B's gloomy outlook. They were to urge him to spend more time in bed and not to exert himself. At the same time, Mrs. B began to stage minor household emergencies and to pretend that she was having trouble coping. Mr. B, a proud and stubborn man, began to feel that he was needed. He also became determined to show his family that he could accomplish more than they thought. Soon he was once again taking part in family activities and the depression began to lift.

Some critics have called these paradoxical tactics unethical because they manipulate people, but family therapists disagree. Family members already manipulate one another, they argue. These therapeutic approaches simply allow them to do so in ways that are beneficial rather than harmful.

In recent years interest in family therapy has been increasing, as has research designed to evaluate its effectiveness (McPeak, 1979). There is some evidence that this approach may be particularly useful for treating disturbed adolescents, whose problems frequently center on poor relations with their parents (Haley, 1980). One study found that institutionalized adolescents who received family therapy were able to resume functioning in the community more rapidly than those who received individual therapy. What's more, these same youngsters were less likely to be institutionalized again (Ro-Trock, Wellisch, and Schoolar, 1977). Family therapy may also be superior to individual therapy for treating marital problems. One study found that about two-thirds of the couples receiving joint therapy experienced some improvement, compared to less than half the couples receiving individual therapy (Gurman and Kniskern, 1978). Family therapy, then, appears to be a relatively effective tool for treating a number of common problems.

Other Group Approaches

Family therapy is one kind of group approach to treatment: the therapist works not just with an individual, but with an interacting collection of people. There are, of course, many other kinds of **group therapy.** Such therapeutic groups often consist of people who initially are strangers to one another. Why, then, is treatment administered collectively to them? One reason is that people with similar problems often benefit from one another as well as from a therapist. From one another they learn that their disturbance is not unique, that there are others who understand and can provide emotional support. Group therapy is particularly useful in treating interpersonal problems, for it offers opportunities for people to interact and work toward building more effective relationships. Group therapy is also economical. Since the therapist's time is devoted to several clients at once, more people can be treated by a single therapist and at a lower fee per person. This

was an important factor in the spread of group therapy right after World War II, when thousands of people were suffering from psychological disturbances as a result of the enormous upheavals of the time. In those years some people believed that group treatments might completely replace more expensive individual therapies. Today, however, mental health professionals recognize that group and individual therapies have complementary roles. For some patients with certain kinds of problems, the two kinds of treatment are often used effectively together.

There are many kinds of group therapy, far more than we could possibly cover here. Each of the individual therapies we discussed earlier has produced one or more forms of group psychotherapy. Thus there are psychoanalytic therapy groups, behavior therapy groups, and phenomenologically oriented (especially gestalt) therapy groups. Many other kinds of group therapy draw their approaches from several theoretical schools of thought. In the following sections we will explore some of the most currently pop-

Figure 16.4 Eric Berne refers to interactions among people as transactions. He considers each personality to be capable of expressing itself as a Child (C), an Adult (A), or a Parent (P). Berne maintains that normal, or healthy, transactions can be represented in diagrams like these with arrows that run horizontally: Adult to Adult, Parent to Parent, Child to Child. It is not difficult to see that the kinds of transactions illustrated here, with their diagonal lines, are the ones that lead to trouble. *(After Berne, 1964.)*

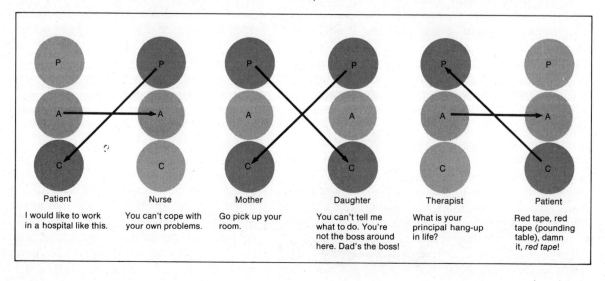

ular treatments of this kind: transactional analysis, encounter groups, and self-help groups. As you will see, the value of these approaches can vary considerably.

Transactional Analysis. Eric Berne developed **transactional analysis (TA)** in the 1950s and '60s, and popularized it with his book *Games People Play* (1964). TA is based on the idea that our relationships with one another can be seen as transactions between the more and less mature aspects of our personalities. According to Berne, everyone possesses within him or her a Child, a Parent, and an Adult. The Child is that part of the self shaped by our early relationships: the Child in us feels small and inferior and is oriented toward satisfying immediate wants and needs. The Parent in us represents the adoption of our own parents' rules and standards: it is the Parent who often dictates what to do and not to do. The Adult is the rational, mature part of the self that can see both sides of an issue, exercise empathy toward others, and behave in a responsible way. Figure 16.4 shows some typical "transactions" involving Child, Parent, and Adult. The relative strengths of the Child, Parent, and Adult within us show in our dealings with others. Are we sometimes pompous and authoritarian, issuing arbitrary orders? This is the Parent in us speaking, and it can cause problems with a spouse or with co-workers. Are we overly dependent on others, ready to interpret the slightest negative comment as rejection or criticism? Then we are acting the Child. TA tries to help people see these negative tendencies in their behavior, purposefully break them, and adopt more mature patterns by strengthening the Adult within themselves. Although TA has become extremely popular in recent years, it is hard to judge its effectiveness with various kinds of disorders because little sound empirical research has been conducted on it.

Encounter Groups. In contrast to most group therapies, the **encounter group** often aims not at overcoming some specific problem, but rather at helping people to "grow" and to experience more joy, warmth, and spontaneity in their lives. Various tactics are used to achieve these positive if somewhat vague goals. Often encounter-group participants engage in exercises designed to break down their defenses—such exercises as touching, yelling, or even weeping

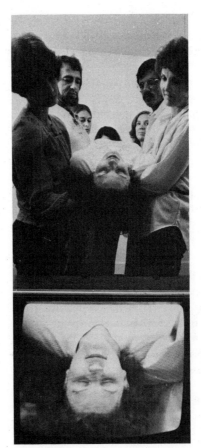

An encounter group at the Institute for Human Potential in Houston. This group is participating in a "trust exercise." The videotape is being made to provide the group with feedback. (© Watriss-Baldwin/ Woodfin Camp & Assoc.)

together. Nearly always, group members are encouraged to express emotions honestly and fully, sometimes to the point of criticizing one another in the bluntest terms. The effectiveness of such groups depends largely on the effectiveness of the group leader and that person's ability to guide the group and interpret its activities in nondestructive ways (Kaplan, Obert, and Van Buskirk, 1980).

Unfortunately, research suggests that a sizable minority of encounter-group leaders fail to perform their role well. In one study of several hundred encounter-group participants, 16 percent reported negative effects, and half of this number suffered significant psychological damage even months after their group disbanded. In contrast, 33 percent reported positive effects, so the ratio of positive to negative change was about 2 to 1—far from an impressive record (Lieberman, Yalom, and Miks, 1973). Further investigation revealed that serious casualties tended to occur when the leader misused his or her power either by being abusive toward group members or by failing to protect a person who was under undue attack. Here is how one man described the experience:

> The leader told me I was a dumb shit because I didn't know how to participate. I felt really outside and really hurt, alienated from other people in the group. I was an outsider: I was treated as the lowest thing on earth.   [Lieberman, Yalom, and Miks, 1973, p. 17]

Because of the possibility of negative reactions on the part of those attacked, people thinking about joining an encounter group should try to obtain information about the group leader's style and capabilities. Those who are insecure and unstable to begin with are especially prone to damage when the leader is poor.

Self-Help Groups. A fast-growing phenomenon in recent years has been the **self-help group**—a group of people who share a particular problem and meet to discuss it among themselves, without the active involvement of a professional therapist (Lieberman and Borman, 1979). The most familiar, and to some extent the inspiration for all such groups, is Alcoholics Anonymous. Many problems lend themselves to this kind of therapy, and groups have been formed by widows, single parents, cancer patients, overeaters, smokers, former drug addicts, child-abusing parents, and former mental patients, to name just a few. Following the lead of AA, these groups are organized so that members can appeal directly to one another for assistance and emotional support. A father tempted to explode at his child, for example, can telephone another member of his abusing-parents group for help in controlling his rage. Or a woman who has just had a mastectomy can confide her fears to other women who have undergone this operation. Because members of self-help groups have all had similar experiences, they can understand each other's problems and can reach out in ways that outsiders might find difficult.

There is evidence that self-help groups are very effective in facilitating adjustment to a variety of situations (see, for example, Spiegel, Bloom, and Yalom, 1981). A number of factors may contribute to these beneficial effects (Dunkel-Schetter and Wortman, 1982). One is the fact that self-help groups enable members to share their feelings openly with others who know at first hand what they are going through. Such open communication, understanding, and emotional support can help sustain people in times of

In the self-help approach to treatment, people who have a problem in common, such as alcoholism, meet regularly for mutual assistance, understanding, and support. *(AP/ Wide World Photos.)*

crisis. In addition, communication with others in the same situation provides other benefits. Members of self-help groups can model their behavior on those who are coping effectively. They can also exchange practical information; for example, former alcoholics can discuss how to cope with social pressure to drink, and cancer patients can discuss what they should tell their children or co-workers about their illness. In addition, members of self-help groups can learn that what they feel is normal in their situation; thus, for instance, widows can learn from one another that it is normal to feel angry at their spouse for "abandoning" them. All these factors can contribute to psychological improvement.

How Effective Are Psychotherapies?

Throughout the previous sections we have mentioned studies that suggest that particular therapeutic techniques are indeed effective. But what about the *overall* effectiveness of psychotherapies? Can more beneficial change be expected from a psychotherapy than would occur just with the passage of time? And if psychotherapy *is* generally effective, are some treatments better than others? Do some produce faster or more long-lasting results?

Much controversy was raised thirty years ago when psychologist Hans Eysenck (1952) reviewed two dozen studies on the effectiveness of various treatments, both psychoanalytic and eclectic (those that combine various approaches). Eysenck astonished therapists by concluding that psychotherapy was no more effective than no treatment at all. He argued that the average improvement rate shown in these twenty-four studies was 44 percent for psychoanalytic treatment and 64 percent for eclectic forms of therapy. In contrast, one study showed that 72 percent of a group of hospitalized neurotics improved when no treatment was given (Landis, 1937).

Needless to say, Eysenck's conclusion generated much debate. Allen Bergin (1971) pointed out that the treatment and control groups in Eysenck's analysis were not precisely comparable: they differed in education, socioeconomic background, motivation to improve, and other potentially important factors. Moreover, many members of the control population (those who presumably received no treatment) were in fact treated by general practitioners who listened sympathetically to the patients' problems and calmed them with sedatives. This constituted therapy of a sort.

Other reviews of published studies since Eysenck's analysis have supported Bergin's more positive assessment of psychotherapy (Luborsky, Singer, and Luborsky, 1975; Parloff, Waskow, and Wolfe, 1978). However, many of the early studies designed to evaluate psychotherapy contained serious methodological shortcomings. For example, many of them failed to assess psychological improvement in a rigorous way. Some simply accepted the therapist's opinion about whether patients had improved or not; others relied largely on the patients' own subjective reports, which might not be accurate. Suppose, for instance, a woman says she feels less depressed than she used to, but she continues to drink heavily and neglect her children. Should we take her word for it that therapy has worked? Similarly, a client entering therapy for treatment of a phobia may overcome that phobia but still remain withdrawn and dependent. Are we justified in declaring that person "cured"? The point is that evaluating psychotherapy is much more difficult than some studies have implied.

One study took special pains to measure psychotherapy outcomes in several different ways (Sloane et al., 1975). Ninety-four people with moderate ("neurotic") psychological disorders were assigned to one of three groups: behavior therapy, psychoanalytically oriented therapy, or a waiting list. After four months subjects were assessed by a combination of methods: personal interviews conducted by "blind" judges (those who did not know to which group each person had been assigned), reports from close associates of the patients, and several psychological tests. The results upheld the benefits of psychotherapy. Whereas 80 percent of those in both therapy groups improved, only 48 percent of those on the waiting list did so. After a year the subjects were evaluated again and members of all groups continued to improve. Eventually those on the waiting list tended to approach or equal the gains made by those in the therapy groups. This finding suggests that psychotherapy may not so much produce improvement as accelerate it.

Selecting adequate measurements, of course, is only one challenge in evaluating the effectiveness of psychotherapies. Another is the task of interpreting the results of many different studies. Eysenck and others have tackled this problem by sifting through large numbers of studies, discounting those that have crucial flaws and tallying up how many of the rest yield positive or negative results. One trouble with this approach, however, is its great subjectivity. Different researchers looking at the very same studies can draw quite different conclusions depending upon their pre-existing viewpoints. There is evidence that if a study contradicts a researcher's viewpoint, he or she is more likely to find methodological problems in the study (L. Ross, 1977). Another limitation of this approach is the difficulty of drawing sound conclusions from a large number of studies that may have very different results. In an effort to overcome such problems, psychologists Mary Lee Smith and Gene Glass have developed a sophisticated statistical method called **meta-analysis.** Meta-analysis enables researchers to combine the results of many studies, thus producing a single value showing the average size of a therapy's effects. In the meta-analyses they have conducted, Smith and Glass have found that psychotherapy is generally quite effective (Smith and Glass, 1977; Smith, Glass, and Miller, 1981). Their calculations suggest that the average person who receives psychotherapy is better off than a full 80 percent of those who remain untreated.

What about differences among psychotherapies? Is one form of treatment more effective than others? Smith and Glass identified 50 separate studies designed to compare the effectiveness of two or more psychotherapies. Performing a meta-analysis of these studies, they came to the conclusion that behavior therapies are only slightly more effective than psychoanalytic and phenomenologically oriented treatments, as Figure 16.5 indicates. Not surprisingly, some behavior therapists quickly protested. They argued that Smith and Glass's analysis failed to include a large number of studies that supported behavioral approaches (Rachman and Wilson, 1980). With these studies excluded, the critics charged, how can a meta-analysis be accurate? Meta-analyses conducted by other researchers have found that behavioral therapies, especially cognitive ones, have a modest but definite edge over psychoanalytic and phenomenologically oriented treatments (Shapiro and Shapiro, 1982; Andrews and Harvey, 1981).

The final verdict on the effectiveness of the various therapies is by no means in. Meta-analyses at this stage do not give definitive answers. Such analyses are only as good as the studies on which they are based, and unfortunately many of those studies have significant methodological flaws (Wilson and Rachman, 1983). More carefully designed research must be conducted if the data base for meta-analyses is to improve. In addition, there is a need for studies that seek to answer not just how effective a psychotherapy is in general, but which techniques work best for which kinds of problems under which sets of circumstances (Paul, 1967). From this point of view the assessment of psychotherapies has only just begun.

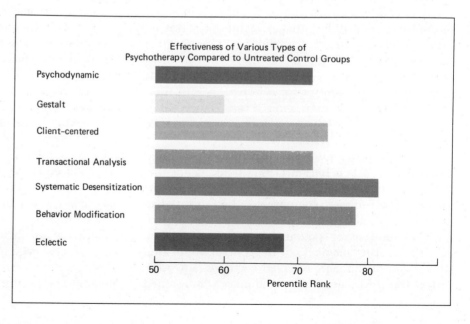

Figure 16.5 Is psychotherapy effective? Researchers Smith and Glass think the answer is yes. Clients who received each of the types of psychotherapy shown in this graph were compared with untreated control groups. The bars indicate the percentile rank that the average treated client attained on outcome measures for each type of therapy when compared with control subjects. Thus the average client who received psychoanalytic therapy scored more favorably on outcome measures than 72 percent of the untreated controls. *(Adapted from Smith and Glass, 1977.)*

Effectiveness of Various Types of Psychotherapy Compared to Untreated Control Groups

Psychodynamic
Gestalt
Client–centered
Transactional Analysis
Systematic Desensitization
Behavior Modification
Eclectic

50   60   70   80

Percentile Rank

BIOLOGICAL TREATMENTS

Psychotherapies try to alleviate disturbance by changing the ways in which people approach their environments. These forms of treatment stress talking, learning, improving mental outlooks and interpersonal relationships, resolving inner conflicts, and gaining insights into the self. Biological treatments, in contrast, take a very different tactic. They attempt to relieve psychological disorder by altering human physiology, in particular the workings of the central nervous system. Three forms of biological treatment in use today are drug therapies, electroconvulsive shock, and psychosurgery.

Drug Therapies

Psychotherapeutic drugs are the most common form of biological treatment. Drugs have been developed to treat anxiety, schizophrenia, depression, mania, and other disorders. Most of these drugs have been introduced in the past few decades, and their development offers an enormous advance in treatment. For example, the introduction of antipsychotic drugs markedly reduced the length of hospital stays for schizophrenic patients. **Drug therapy** is available to all patients, not just to those who have the time and money for extended psychotherapy or who are educated and articulate enough to benefit from it. Drugs have also proved useful in some cases where no other therapies have worked.

Antianxiety Drugs. Commonly known as minor tranquilizers, **antianxiety drugs** reduce excitability and cause drowsiness. Since most people experience anxiety and insomnia at one time or another, these drugs are widely used. Family doctors often prescribe them for people who, while not undergoing psychological treatment, are having trouble coping during difficult periods in their lives (Uhlenhuth, Balter, and Lipman, 1978). The most popular antianxiety drugs are Miltown (meprobamate), Librium (chlordiazepoxide hydrochloride), and Valium (diazepam). Until recently, Valium was the most widely prescribed drug in the United States. Researchers believe that it decreases anxiety by depressing the central nervous system (Caplan et al., 1983).

Although many people consider antianxiety drugs to be harmless, there are potential dangers surrounding them. Prolonged use can lead to dependency, and heavy doses taken along with alcohol can result in death. Furthermore, because anxiety can be a warning signal that something in a person's life needs changing, some researchers are concerned that antianxiety drugs may simply suppress that warning without addressing the fundamental problem (Schwartz, 1977).

Antipsychotic Drugs. **Antipsychotic drugs** are major tranquilizers used to alleviate extreme symptoms of agitation and hyperactivity in psychotic patients (Davis, 1975). The most popular of these drugs are the phenothiazines, including Thorazine (chlorpromazine) and Stelazine (trifluoperazine hydrochloride), which are widely used in the treatment of schizophrenia. When they were introduced about thirty years ago, antipsychotic drugs were viewed as major breakthroughs in the treatment of serious mental disorders. They were more humane, more effective, and more easily administered than psychosurgery and electroconvulsive shock, the other biological therapies of the time. Today it is estimated that 87 percent of all hospitalized psychiatric patients receive some such medication (MacDonald and Tobias, 1976).

At first doctors did not know how antipsychotic drugs worked. Only lately have scientists pieced together the data needed to devise theories about how these drugs produce their effects. Observation that the drugs produced good results with schizophrenics led to speculation that schizophrenia may be caused by some kind of chemical imbalance in the brain. Subsequent investigation into the drugs' effects on neurotransmitters led directly to the dopamine hypothesis, currently a promising theory about the causes of certain types of schizophrenia.

Antipsychotic drugs, however, are not without drawbacks, some of which have to do with the psychological state they cause. Although antipsychotics produce calm, they often create fatigue and apathy as well. As one patient described it:

On Thorazine everything's a bore. Not a bore, exactly. Boredom implies impatience. You can read

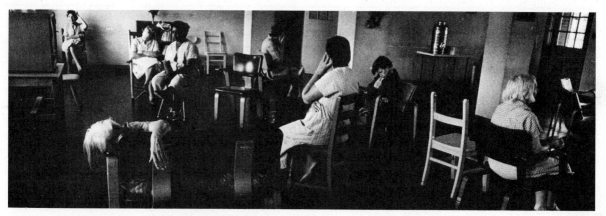

Antipsychotic drugs may not only calm patients but leave them in a constant state of drowsiness and fatigue. Scenes like this—patients nodding in front of a television set—are common in today's mental hospitals. *(© Ray Zalisky/Black Star.)*

comic books and *Reader's Digest* forever. You can tolerate talking to jerks forever. Babble, babble, babble. The weather is dull, the flowers are dull, nothing's very impressive. Musak, Bach, Beatles, Lolly and the Yum-Yums, Rolling Stones. It doesn't make any difference. . . . What the drug is supposed to do is keep away hallucinations. What I think it does is just fog up your mind so badly you don't notice the hallucinations or much else.   [Vonnegut, 1975, pp. 196–197]

Even more troubling is the fact that some hospitals have been known to use the drugs' calming effect in "patient management," giving stupor-inducing doses to troublesome patients.

Antipsychotic drugs can also have harmful physical side effects. Often they produce what is known as "pseudoparkinsonism," or a cluster of symptoms similar to those of Parkinson's disease. These symptoms, which include uncontrollable trembling, stiffening of the muscles, and drooling, may continue for up to a year after drug therapy is stopped (Parkes, 1976). Some patients also experience dizziness, fainting, nausea, diarrhea, blurred vision, sensitivity to sunlight, and other negative side effects. More serious still is an apparently irreversible condition called **tardive dyskinesia,** which develops in some patients who take the drugs for prolonged periods or in high doses. Symptoms include grotesque movements of the face—grimaces, lip smacking, and protrusions of the tongue. Some victims, acutely embarrassed by these uncontrollable behaviors, avoid all contact with

people, becoming social isolates (Widroe and Heisler, 1976). Permanent brain damage may also be associated with this distressing condition (MacDonald, Lidsky, and Kern, 1979). Estimates of the incidence of tardive dyskinesia range from 10 to 56 percent of those who take antipsychotic drugs (Jus et al., 1976).

Growing awareness of the harmful side effects of antipsychotic medications has led to controversy over their use. Although advocates of these drugs have argued that they immediately calm psychotic patients and help to prevent relapses, these claims have been disputed (MacDonald, Lidsky, and Kern, 1979). One study found the drugs to be no more effective than a placebo in calming agitated patients (Hamill and Fontana, 1975). Methodological flaws have also been found in many studies that suggest that maintenance doses are positively correlated with reduced relapse rates (Sulzbacher, 1973). After a careful review of all these findings, one team of researchers concluded that "psychoactive drug treatment, once thought to be the hope for the future, seems to have become the myth of the present" (MacDonald, Lidsky, and Kern, 1979, p. 437). The final verdict on these medications must await more definitive research.

Mood-Regulating Drugs. Widely used to regulate mood are drugs called **antidepressants,** discovered by accident in 1952. Irving Selikof and his colleagues were treating tuberculosis patients with a drug called Iproniazid when they noticed that it produced a mood elevation. Further experimentation led to the development of effective antidepressants, such as Tofranil and Elavil. These drugs are collectively called tricyclics because of their three-ringed molecular structure.

Tricyclics seem to work by increasing the levels of certain neurotransmitters in the brain, among them norepinephrine and serotonin. Studies have shown that these drugs often reduce depressive symptoms (Gelenberg, 1979). But the most effective program seems to be a combination of antidepressants and regular psychotherapy. Unfortunately, the tricyclics may sometimes cause negative side effects, including restlessness, faintness, trembling, blurred vision, constipation, and a dry mouth (Rosenbaum, Maruta, and Richelson, 1979).

Scientists have also discovered a drug that can be used to treat both mania and bipolar affective disorders. This is **lithium,** a metallic substance found in tiny amounts in water throughout the world. Even severely manic patients, who would otherwise be totally out of control, usually respond favorably to lithium treatment (Baldessarini, 1977). And for patients with bipolar conditions, a lithium maintenance program can substantially reduce the frequency of mood swings and make them less severe (Van Praag, 1978). But like other psychiatric drugs, lithium can have negative side effects, including restlessness, nausea, weight gain, and increased urination. It can even be fatal if its level in the bloodstream becomes too high. For this reason, patients who take the drug must have their dosage carefully monitored through regular blood tests (Branchey, Charles, and Simpson, 1976).

Electroconvulsive Therapy

"Shock treatment," as **electroconvulsive therapy (ECT)** is commonly called, has proven extremely effective in the treatment of severe depression. It seems particularly useful for endogenous depression—the kind apparently triggered by some physiological change, not by a negative event in the person's life (Scovern and Kilmann, 1980). One carefully designed study showed that shock therapy produced highly significant improvements, whether those improvements were rated by doctors, nurses, or the patients themselves (West, 1981). Yet, oddly enough, no one knows exactly how ECT works.

The procedure in ECT is quite simple. Over a period of several weeks, the patient receives a series of brief electrical shocks approximately 70 to 130 volts in intensity. This is enough to induce convulsions similar to epileptic seizures. It is the convulsion, not the electrical current, that produces the therapeutic effect. The purpose of the shock is merely to bring on the convulsion. Although it sounds painful, ECT as it is now administered entails very little discomfort. The patient is first given a sedative and is then injected with a muscle relaxant to alleviate involuntary movements and prevent physical injury. Shortly after the shock is given, the patient awakens with no memory of the treatment. In comparison with the tricyclic drugs, which normally take two weeks to begin to work, the beneficial effects of ECT begin almost immediately. These fast results can be very important, especially when a patient is suicidal. However, ECT is a drastic step that should be taken with great caution. One common side effect is temporary memory loss, which in rare cases may persist for several years.

Psychosurgery

The most extreme of all biological treatments is **psychosurgery.** This is a high-risk surgical procedure with irreversible effects. In 1935 Egas Moniz and Almeida Lima developed a procedure known as prefrontal lobotomy, in which a surgical cut is made between the brain's frontal lobes and the thalamus. They expected the interruption in communication between these two areas of the brain to reduce the impact of disturbing stimuli on patients who were agitated or violent. Over the next twenty years other methods of psychosurgery evolved and thousands of operations were performed. Some severely disturbed patients were helped by these procedures, but many were left in childlike and lethargic states, and others died on the operating table.

Today the surgical techniques of the 1940s and '50s have been abandoned in favor of "fractional operations," which destroy very small amounts of brain tissue in precise locations (Valenstein, 1973). Such operations are performed on about four hundred severely disturbed patients a year in the United States, and only after all other modes of treatment have been exhausted. Psychosurgery has been effective in treating severe depression, anxiety, and obsessions, but ineffective in treating schizophrenia (Bridges and Bartlett, 1977). For whatever purpose, psychosurgery should be considered an experimental procedure, to be used only under the most stringent safeguards of the rights and welfare of the patient.

COMMUNITY MENTAL HEALTH

By the early 1960s it had become apparent that a number of serious problems were associated with our mental health care system. First, the system was not providing adequate services to the poor—the very people who because of their stressful circumstances often needed psychological counseling and therapy the most. Second, even people of adequate means were often reluctant to seek out professional assistance in times of psychological distress. Surveys showed that having a "mental illness" was widely considered a social stigma, so most people experiencing problems turned instead to informal counselors—clergymen, family doctors, teachers, and the like (Gurin, Veroff, and Feld, 1960). Yet there were no programs to give these informal caregivers a background in psychology that might help them at their task. Finally, with the advent of antipsychotic drugs, many people formerly treated in mental institutions were now improved enough to leave the hospital. But most communities had few facilities where the newly discharged patients could receive much-needed outpatient care. It was in an effort to solve these critical problems that the community mental health movement was born.

Community Mental Health Centers

A milestone in this movement came in 1963 with the passage of the Community Mental Health Centers Act, a bill that reflected President John F. Kennedy's "bold new approach." This legislation mandated one mental health center for every 50,000 people, thus greatly decentralizing the provision of mental health care. These centers were to treat the mentally disturbed in their own local communities, not in large, isolated, state-run institutions. In addition, the centers would provide educational programs aimed at preventing psychological disorders, train paraprofessionals, and carry out research. Although a nationwide system of mental health care centers has not yet been achieved and funding for existing centers has been cut back in many cities, the centers that do operate provide important services.

One of these services is outpatient care. A person with a psychological problem can come to a center and receive therapy once, twice, or more times a week, without leaving school, job, or family, and without feeling stigmatized as a "mental patient." For those who *have* been hospitalized, the centers also provide a bridge between the sheltered world of the hospital and return to a normal, independent life. They accomplish this task by providing "aftercare" for newly discharged patients—regularly scheduled therapy or checkups, often conducted by the same people who treated the patient in the hospital. Treatment, therefore, is not abruptly ended when the patient leaves the hospital, and the patient is given a reassuring sense of continuing support.

Under the community mental health system, the nature of hospital care has changed as well. Many centers have arrangements for day hospitals, in which patients take advantage of the support systems and therapy offered by the hospital during the day and go home at night. Night hospitals work in a similar manner: patients work or go to school during the day and spend the night in the hospital.

Many community mental health centers also maintain storefront clinics that are open around the clock to deal with such emergencies as acute anxiety attacks, suicide attempts, and drug problems. Here troubled people can discuss their problems with a paraprofessional, a member of the community trained to deal with just such events. (The paraprofessional can be particularly useful in this kind of setting, because professional therapists, who often come from a higher social class than their clients, can be intimidating to some.)

Finally, community mental health centers provide qualified personnel to consult with those in the community who are often looked to for help in solving psychological problems—family doctors, members of the clergy, teachers, even police. These people often deal with as much mental disturbance as the average mental health professional. The professional, however, can help these informal caregivers by conveying to them psychological knowledge and therapy skills. In New York City, for instance, a program designed to teach police to intervene more effectively in family quarrels has had great success. Members of trained police intervention teams have substantially reduced the tendency of heated family arguments to escalate into physical violence (Bard, 1970). By helping the community's informal counselors in this fashion, mental health professionals can greatly expand the number of people they reach.

One example of the effectiveness of the community mental health movement can be seen in the response of mental health workers in Kansas City, Missouri, to the hotel disaster that occurred in July 1981. At a crowded dance in the lobby of the Hyatt Regency Hotel, two overhead walkways suddenly collapsed, trapping hundreds of victims for up to ten hours beneath ninety tons of steel and concrete. Psychologists feared that the incident would leave serious psychological scars not only for the 2,000 in attendance at the dance but for an estimated 3,000 others who were indirectly involved—including rescue workers, hotel employees and guests, medical personnel, media representatives, and the families and friends of the 111 dead and more than 200 injured.

To counter the possible adverse effects of the tragedy, community mental health workers immediately set up a three-pronged program. First, support groups were established in community mental health centers all over metropolitan Kansas City. The support groups would allow those who had been touched by the disaster to come together, express their personal reactions, and share their anguish. Second, training in how to counsel those in distress was provided for psychologists, ministers, doctors, and others who might be looked to for help. Finally, a campaign was begun to publicize where services could be obtained and what kinds of reactions people might expect to have following so large and unexpected a catastrophe.

The publicity campaign was successful in encouraging public acceptance of psychological counseling. Within a month more than 500 individuals had sought out the support groups. Nearly 200 people had attended training sessions to help others deal with their reactions. According to those directly involved in this community mental health effort, the program may well have succeeded in lessening the long-term psychological impact of this horrifying incident on the community by allowing people to express publicly and immediately their deeply felt emotions (Gist and Stolz, 1982).

Halfway Houses

Another result of the community mental health movement has been the development of halfway houses, so named because they provide an intermediate step between hospitalization and normal life in the community. In halfway houses, people with common problems who are newly discharged from a hospital live together and learn the skills needed to function independently. Although professional therapy is available to halfway house residents, the live-in staff typically consists of paraprofessionals who provide informal counseling and advice on handling practical matters (such as how to shop for groceries, cook, and do the laundry, how to talk to a store clerk or an employer, and other everyday procedures often foreign to people who have been hospitalized most of their lives). Many halfway houses also have money-making projects (small stores, cleaning and gardening services, and so forth) that help teach residents how to hold down a job. If a particular person has serious trouble making the adjustment, he or she can always return to the more protective world of the hospital. But studies show that people who are given the halfway house experience are less likely to require rehospitalization than those who are returned to the community "cold turkey" (Fairweather et al., 1969).

Halfway houses have proliferated in recent years. They are providing a useful transition not only for former mental patients, but also for former drug addicts, recovered alcoholics, and ex-convicts as well as those who are mentally retarded. Nevertheless, the halfway house concept continues to stir controversy. Some people are uncomfortable living near others who have histories of psychological disturbance. As a result, they often resist the establishment of halfway houses in their own neighborhoods.

In large urban centers, however, only a very small percentage of discharged mental patients reside in halfway houses. In 1978, for instance, New York City had an estimated 40,000 deinstitutionalized chronic mental patients living within its boroughs, only 424 of whom were in true halfway houses. Most of the rest were forced to shift for themselves in rundown residential hotels. Critics charge that these hotels are little more than mental hospital "back wards" located within the community (Jones, 1975). The residents there receive little or no therapy except their daily doses of psychiatric drugs. Most of their time is spent roaming the sidewalks or hanging about the lobby.

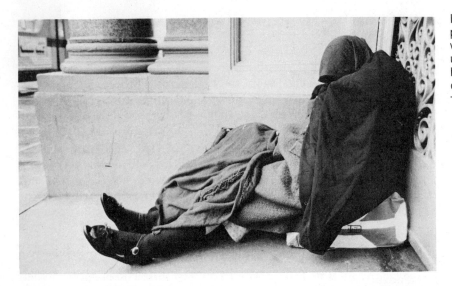

In recent years many chronic mental patients have been deinstitutionalized without adequate provision for follow-up care, and wander the streets as homeless "shopping bag ladies" or derelicts. *(Joel Gordon.)*

Others in the neighborhood avoid them and complain that these people have been "dumped" on their doorstep. Lacking adequate therapy or social support, the ex-patients have little hope of ever leading anything that approaches a normal life.

Crisis Intervention: The Hotline

We mentioned before that community mental health centers often maintain storefront clinics to deal with emergency situations. But many people facing a crisis are not in a frame of mind to travel some distance for help. One solution to this problem has been the crisis hotline. People in trouble can simply pick up a phone and receive immediate counseling, sympathy, and comfort. The best-known crisis hotline is run by the Los Angeles Suicide Prevention Center, established in 1958. Similar hotlines have been set up for alcoholics, rape victims, battered women, runaway children, habitual gamblers, and people who just need a shoulder to cry on. In addition to providing sympathy, hotline volunteers offer information on the community services available to handle each kind of problem.

Prevention

From its beginnings a major goal of the community mental health movement has been the prevention, not just the treatment, of psychological disorders.

Those involved in the movement seek to introduce measures that will help keep serious disturbances from arising. Given the number of factors that can contribute to psychological problems, this is clearly a very ambitious goal. Nevertheless, many such efforts have been initiated. Nutritional and genetic counseling are just two of the services that many community centers have offered for years. More recent efforts include the teaching of skills to help people cope with stress. Myrna Shure and George Spivack (1981, 1982), for instance, designed a program to teach interpersonal problem-solving skills to inner-city children in nursery school and kindergarten (ages four and five). The children were taught simple word concepts that would enable them to identify an interpersonal problem, generate a number of possible solutions, and identify the consequences of each solution. The children's teachers were helped to develop ways to talk with the children when real problems arose. This program helped inhibited children to become more outgoing, and impulsive children to become less disruptive. Effective coping, then, may be something that can be instilled at a very early age.

Programs like these are part of a growing focus on the active promotion of mental health. But some researchers argue that the best way to achieve this goal is not to treat the individual, but rather to eliminate the negative social conditions that generate stress and breakdown (Goodstein and Sandler, 1978). This, in fact, is one aim of the field called community psychology. Unfortunately, such a broad objective is not in itself enough. In a careful review of past efforts to prevent psychological disturbance, two researchers recently concluded that unless programs have very precise goals, they are unlikely to bring about much change (Lamb and Zusman, 1979).

Efforts to keep mental disorders from arising in the first place are often called primary prevention. If such programs work, they effectively eliminate the problem. Given the great difficulty of primary prevention, however, community mental health workers have other goals as well. One is secondary prevention, or efforts to detect and treat psychological problems early in order to prevent them from getting any worse. Troubled, lonely, or frightened people who seek help at outpatient clinics and crisis centers are appropriate subjects for secondary prevention. Tertiary prevention refers to efforts to keep already established mental disorders from having dire effects on the victims, their families, and society. An example of a tertiary prevention program would be treatment of schizophrenics in hospitals. Although secondary prevention and tertiary prevention are realistic goals, we still have a long way to go before fully achieving them.

in depth The Issue of Control Over Patients

The therapeutic treatments we have explored in this chapter have enormous potential to benefit patients. But a potential for misuse also exists. Drugs can be given to make people dull and drowsy, and thus easier to manage. Behavior techniques can be used to make people conform, sometimes to arbitrary rules. In short, the mental health profession has an enormous potential for power over people's lives. What guidelines exist to limit the exercise of this power? Do clinicians have the right to impose their definitions of "normal" on other people? Should they be allowed to administer a treatment "for the patient's own good," even though the patient opposes it? What rights do people with serious mental disorders retain? These are some of the complex ethical and legal issues surrounding the treatment of psychological disturbance. In this concluding section we will examine in depth those that revolve around the therapist's potential for control.

CONTROL IN PSYCHOTHERAPY. Just by virtue of trying to change people's behavior, a psychotherapist is striving for influence over those people's

lives. Such influence, in fact, is central to the psychotherapeutic process. But to what extent should therapists impose their own values on patients? Suppose, for example, that a married professor seeks out a therapist because of the enormous guilt he feels over an affair with one of his students. If the therapist believes that the man's moral standards are unduly restrictive, the cause of unnecessary remorse, is it right to try to change this person's traditional value system? Or imagine a woman who seeks help in breaking away from her husband and children to achieve her own identity. If the therapist repeatedly reminds her of her responsibility to her family, is this value judgment justified?

Many clinicians would answer that therapists should avoid imposing their values on clients in these and similar situations. But this is often easier said than done. For one thing, it is hard for anyone, even a trained psychotherapist, to set aside deeply held values. Despite his or her best efforts, values may still creep in. In addition, a therapist, like anyone else, can sometimes be unaware of the extent to which values are coloring perceptions, words, and actions.

CONTROL IN INSTITUTIONAL SETTINGS. Nowhere is the power of the mental health profession more far-reaching than in the area of involuntary commitment to mental hospitals. Not long ago, many institutionalized people were held for years simply because two psychiatrists were willing to declare them mentally ill and in need of treatment. Today, however, this situation is changing. Most states now require that some factor besides mental illness be present before a person can be committed involuntarily. Usually the person must also be considered dangerous, either to him- or herself or to others.

But how much proof must there be that a person is dangerous? If a mentally disturbed girl threatens to kill her father, is the threat enough to justify commitment? It is difficult to say. In the past, state courts often argued that as long as the likelihood of harm was greater than the likelihood of no harm, commitment was warranted. Under this standard, however, it was relatively common for harmless people to be institutionalized. Recognizing the possibilities for abuse, the Supreme Court has ruled that the standard of proof in commitment hearings must be more rigorous. This ruling was made in a Texas case in which a mother had petitioned to have her son committed (*Addington* v. *Texas*, 1979). The Court maintained that a person cannot be involuntarily committed without "clear and convincing" evidence that he or she is mentally ill and otherwise meets the legal requirements for commitment. But unfortunately this does not mean that unfair commitments will be largely eliminated. Mental health professionals have a poor record of predicting which patients will be dangerous. When asked to make such judgments, they tend to err on the side of safety, declaring many nondangerous people to be capable of inflicting harm (Kozol, Boucher, and Garofolo, 1972).

The power of the mental health establishment does not end with its role in determining who should be committed. Inside mental hospitals its control over patients' lives is also very great. Ken Kesey's novel *One Flew over the Cuckoo's Nest* (1962) offers a disturbing look at a hospital staff's absolute authority over committed mental patients twenty-odd years ago. In more recent times, such absolute power has increasingly been questioned. Today there is a strong trend toward guaranteeing mental patients certain basic rights.

An important step in this direction came in the case of *Wyatt* v. *Stickney* (1972). Ricky Wyatt was a resident in an Alabama institution for the mentally retarded. The conditions there were so deplorable that a class-action suit was filed, naming Ricky as the plaintiff. The state of Alabama was accused of grossly violating the rights of patients by confining them in filthy, dark, chaotically managed facilities with inadequate food and virtually no treatment. The Alabama court ruled that it is a contradiction in terms to confine people to an institution because they are in need of treatment and then to provide no treatment. All Alabama mental hospitals, the ruling stated, must offer treatment programs, as well as humane environments. After reviewing the *Wyatt* case, a federal court agreed that decent living conditions were a right of institutionalized persons. Not only must patients be given adequate meals, they must also have comfortable beds, the chance to have visitors, and access to recreational facilities and to regular outdoor activity.

These protections are certainly appropriate. But ironically, they may mean that many severely disturbed patients cannot be treated with certain behavior therapies known to be quite effective. The rewards that work best in token economies, for instance, are often the very things (food, recreation, outdoor privileges) which the courts have declared to

be patients' basic rights. As one proponent of behavior therapies has argued: "Here there is a direct conflict between the right to treatment and the right to enjoy basic privileges. By depriving some patients of an effective treatment, we may be condemning them to a lifetime of institutionalization" (Bootzin, 1975, p. 56). Others have suggested that perhaps behavior therapies could be modified to conform to the requirements of court decisions such as *Wyatt*. In one recent study, for instance, therapists were asked to judge the ethics of a procedure in which foods combined in a blender would be readily available, but patients who wanted normal meals would have to pay for them with earned tokens (Tymchuk et al., 1982). Sixty-eight percent of the therapists found this practice unacceptable even if it proved to be therapeutically effective. Thus the current trend is to place the rights to dignity and comfort above the demands of any particular therapeutic approach.

Another right of mental patients that is currently emerging is the right to refuse treatment—especially biological treatments that may cause negative side effects (Ennis and Emery, 1978). The courts of Massachusetts and New Jersey, for instance, have ruled that patients have a constitutional right to refuse treatment with psychiatric drugs (*Rogers* v. *Okin,* 1979; *Rennie* v. *Klein,* 1979). The only exceptions would be emergencies in which patients' condition threatened physical harm to themselves or to others. The courts reasoned that the right to refuse treatment is based both on the fundamental right to privacy in making personal decisions and on the First Amendment guarantee of freedom of thought and expression. "Whatever powers the Constitution has granted our government," declared the Massachusetts court, "involuntary mind control is not one of them" (*Rogers* v. *Okin,* 478 F. Supp. 1367).

But critics vehemently argue that such logic is faulty. They say that a psychiatric patient's very refusal to accept treatment is an irrational action—a symptom of the mental illness, not an exercise of civil rights (Appelbaum and Gutheil, 1980). Such irrational patients, these critics assert, should be given effective treatments for their own good. Others, however, point out that our very definition of mental illness is by no means clear-cut, so it is very difficult to distinguish between "rational" and "irrational" refusals of treatment (White and White, 1981).

Because the issues involved in patients' rights are so complex, institutions and organizations have established review boards to make sure that any grievances receive due consideration. One is the Committee on Scientific and Professional Ethics and Conduct of the American Psychological Association. It receives and reviews charges against professional psychologists and can discipline members found to have violated professional ethics. Thus, although a definite potential for abuse of power exists in the mental health profession, strong safeguards are being established. At the same time, the limits of a therapist's control over patients are increasingly being clarified.

in depth

SUMMARY

1. **Psychotherapy** may be defined as a systematic series of interactions between a person who is trained in alleviating psychological problems and another who is suffering from them. These interactions are structured by both beliefs and scientific findings as to why such disturbances occur.

2. In Freudian **psychoanalysis** the goal is to bring unconscious conflicts into consciousness, where they can be worked through and resolved. Various techniques are used to accomplish this aim, among them **free association** and **dream analysis.** Many other psychoanalytically oriented therapies have evolved as variants of Freud's approach.

3. **Behavior therapy** is the attempt to apply learning and other experimentally derived psychological principles to problem behavior. Behavior therapists use techniques based on classical conditioning principles (such as **systematic desensitization** and **aversive conditioning**), on operant conditioning principles (such as **token economies, time out,** and **stimulus control**), on social learning principles (such as **participant modeling**), and on cognitive learning principles (such as **rational-emotive therapy, cognitive therapy,** and **self-instructional training**). These techniques have been applied to a great many problems, including phobias, alcoholism, bed wetting, self-destructive behavior, and depression.

4. **Phenomenologically oriented therapies** are a diverse group of treatments that aim at liberating the client's innate tendencies toward self-actualization and growth. **Person-centered therapy** tries to free people from the unreasonable **conditions of worth** imposed by others. The therapist creates a warm and empathic environment in which the client can come to understand and to value the true self. **Gestalt therapy,** another phenomenologically oriented treatment, emphasizes the need to release pent-up emotions and to take responsibility for one's actions.

5. **Family therapy** stresses the importance of altering roles and communication patterns within the family which are maintaining maladaptive behavior. Family therapy seeks to involve all the members of the household, not just those who are displaying the troublesome symptoms.

6. Family therapy is just one form of treatment in which more than one client is involved. In recent decades other **group therapies** have become widely used. Among those currently most popular are **transactional analysis, encounter groups,** and **self-help groups.** Although these group therapies are widely practiced, little research has yet been done on their effectiveness.

7. Although the effectiveness of psychotherapy has sometimes been disputed, research indicates that such treatment does help patients to improve. It is not yet clear, however, to what extent one kind of therapy is more effective than others, and with which particular kinds of problems.

8. **Drug therapy** is now very commonly employed for many disorders. **Antianxiety drugs** are widely used by people who are having trouble coping with situational stress. **Antipsychotic drugs** are often prescribed for far more serious conditions, such as schizophrenia, although their overall value has been questioned. **Antidepressants,** especially in combination with psychotherapy, are quite effective in combating depression, and **lithium** works well for controlling both mania and bipolar affective disorders.

9. **Electroconvulsive therapy (ECT)** induces a brief convulsion similar to an epileptic seizure, which for reasons unknown relieves severe depression. Because

beneficial effects are often seen immediately, ECT is sometimes used on acutely suicidal patients.

10. **Psychosurgery,** a high-risk surgical cut in the brain with irreversible effects, is used only on severely disturbed patients after all other modes of treatment have failed.

11. The community mental health movement arose in an effort to decentralize the delivery of mental health care services in order to reach troubled people who were not being served by traditional facilities. The movement has brought about the establishment of community mental health centers, halfway houses, and crisis intervention services, such as hotlines. A major goal of the movement is prevention, not just treatment, of mental disorders.

12. Psychotherapies and biological treatments for the mentally ill raise many moral and legal issues. These include the extent to which therapists should impose their own values on clients, the conditions that justify involuntary commitment, and the rights of institutionalized patients. Because the potential for abuse of power exists, many safeguards to protect patients have emerged.

SUGGESTED READINGS

GUNTRIP, H. *Psychoanalytic theory, therapy, and the self.* New York: Basic Books, 1973.

An introduction to contemporary ego-analytic approaches.

JULIEN, R. M. *A primer of drug action.* 3rd ed. New York: W. H. Freeman, 1981.

An excellent introduction to the effects of drugs on human mood and behavior.

PERLS, F. S. *Gestalt therapy verbatim.* Lafayette, Calif.: Real People Press, 1969.

All you ever need to know about gestalt therapy.

REDD, W. H., PORTERFIELD, A. L., and ANDERSEN, B. L. *Behavior modification: Behavioral approaches to human problems.* New York: Random House, 1979.

Treats the varieties of behavior therapy and the problems to which it has been applied.

ROGERS, C. R. *Client-centered therapy.* Boston: Houghton Mifflin, 1951.

A classic work by one of the leaders of the phenomenological approach to psychotherapy.

SATIR, V. *Conjoint family therapy.* Rev. ed. Palo Alto, Calif.: Science and Behavior Books, 1969.

Sensitive coverage of the family approach to psychotherapy.

WATSON, D. L., and THARP, R. G. *Self-directed behavior: Self-modification for personal adjustment.* Monterey, Calif.: Brooks/Cole, 1981.

A useful guide to the self-control approach to behavior change.

YALOM, I. D. *The theory and practice of group psychotherapy.* 2d ed. New York: Basic Books, 1975.

Examines the various approaches to group psychotherapy.

part **8**

SOCIAL PSYCHOLOGY

Social psychology studies human behavior in its daily context—in constant interaction with others. The factors that affect our interpersonal relations are the subject of Part 8. How we evaluate other people is examined in Chapter 17, while Chapter 18 explores social influences and the human environment.

17

ATTITUDES AND SOCIAL PERCEPTION

John Storrs, *Composition Around Two Voids*, 1932.

The Psychology of Prejudice

The Nature of Prejudice

Some Common Prejudices
    Sexism
    Racism

**In Depth: A Psychological Look at Affirmative
    Action**

In 1969 social psychologist Philip Zimbardo and his colleagues (1972, 1973) began a seemingly innocent two-week simulation of life in a prison environment. They wanted to observe the effects such settings have on the ways people behave. Student volunteers were given extensive personality tests, and only those judged to be mature and emotionally stable were invited to participate in the study. By the flip of a coin, half were randomly assigned to the role of prisoner and half to the role of guard. The simulation then began, with the prisoners being jailed around the clock in the basement of a university building during summer session. After only six days, however, Zimbardo was forced to abandon the research because it had become too frighteningly real. The subjects acting as guards were using their power harshly and arbitrarily. Those acting as prisoners had either been reduced to servility or developed symptoms of severe anxiety. What had created this disturbing outcome? Why did otherwise perfectly normal college students begin to act in such abnormal ways?

The behavior of participants in this particular study, which we will discuss further in Chapter 18, dramatically illustrates the social-psychological perspective introduced in Chapter 1. How people think, feel, and act is not simply the result of their personalities and predispositions. Their behavior is also shaped to a large extent by the social situations in which they find themselves. What others around us are doing, thinking, and feeling, how they structure the environment, including its physical elements—all have a marked effect on the behaviors we display. Social psychologists seek to explore these fascinating situational forces. They seek to understand how the thoughts, feelings, and actions of people are influenced by the presence and behavior—either actual, imagined, or implied—of other people (Allport, 1968).

The subject of social psychology is so broad that we will devote two chapters to it. This chapter explores how people and the social environments they create often shape our innermost thoughts and feelings. We will discuss such topics as attitudes, first impressions, people's ideas about why other people behave as they do, interpersonal attraction, and prejudices. Then, in Chapter 18, we will examine how social forces influence overt actions. Here we look at pressures to conform to group norms, to obey those in authority, to adhere to social roles, and to follow others' behavior in a variety of circumstances. As you will see repeatedly in both chapters, human thoughts, feelings, and actions do not originate solely within us. They are also products of the social situations in which we find ourselves.

ATTITUDES

Why are some people staunch conservatives and others dedicated liberals? Why do some people abhor the bustle of city living, while others are dismayed by the prospect of country life? What makes you such a loyal fan of a certain type of music or a certain baseball team? Answers to these and similar questions are bound up in the psychological study of attitudes and their formation.

Briefly defined, **attitudes** are our affinities for and aversions to specific people, groups, objects, ideas, or situations. They are our likes and dislikes, our feelings for and against (Bem, 1970). This definition stresses the evaluative side of attitudes, which most psychologists would say is of central importance. Yet attitudes are more than this. Two psychologists who have studied attitudes extensively define them as learned, relatively enduring predispositions to respond to certain things in consistently favorable or unfavorable ways (Fishbein and Ajzen, 1975). Besides the evaluative aspect of attitudes, this definition points to three other attributes. First, an attitude is learned, not innate. Second, it persists for a relatively long time. And third, it motivates us to act, helping to shape and direct our behavior.

Another way of defining attitudes is to reduce the concept to its three basic components: (1) cognitions or beliefs about a particular person, idea, situation, or thing; (2) an emotional reaction toward that stimulus; and (3) a tendency to behave in a certain manner toward it (Insko and Schopler, 1976). When we adopt this approach, it is easy to see that attitudes can be measured in several different ways. The most common method is to administer a questionnaire that asks people to indicate both the direction and the strength of their opinion about an attitude object. (An **attitude object** is the target of an attitude, or that which we have an attitude about.) Questionnaires essentially tap the cognitive component of attitudes. Another way to measure attitudes is to assess the emotional component by seeing how physiologically aroused people become when they encounter an attitude object. This can be done by recording heart rate, galvanic skin response, or even pupil dilation (Katz et al., 1965; Rankin and Campbell, 1955; Hess, 1965; Hess and Polt, 1960, 1964). A third way of measuring attitudes is to look at the behavioral component. In one study, for instance, people's attitudes toward a museum exhibit were inferred by observing the amount of wear on the floor (Webb et al., 1966).

How Much Do Attitudes Influence Behavior?

Social psychologists have been interested in the study of attitudes largely because they have assumed that attitudes strongly influence behavior. But some researchers have wondered if this assumption is cor-

The process by which attitudes toward such topics as abortion are formed is seldom a clear-cut, completely rational one. Our attitudes are influenced by our emotions, expectations of rewards and punishments, desire for approval, need for consistency between beliefs and actions, and many other factors. *(Left, Owen Franken/Sygma; right, Christina Thomson/Woodfin Camp & Assoc.)*

rect. Consider, for instance, an early study we mentioned in Chapter 1. Psychologist Richard LaPiere (1934) traveled around the United States with a Chinese couple at a time when anti-Oriental feeling was relatively common. In 10,000 miles of travel the group was refused service in hotels and restaurants only once. Did this mean that most Americans were not prejudiced toward Chinese? Apparently not. When LaPiere subsequently wrote to the establishments he had visited and asked the owners if they would provide food or lodging to Orientals, more than 90 percent of those responding answered with a flat no. Of course, we cannot draw firm conclusions on the basis of this one study, especially as it is known to have methodological flaws. One obvious flaw is that the people who answered LaPiere's letter (that is, the owners or managers of the establishments) may not have been the same ones who encountered the Chinese couple (desk clerks or waiters). But even if we are cautious about LaPiere's findings, the fact remains that other researchers have sometimes obtained results quite similar to his. Often the correlation between an attitude and a related behavior is much lower than logic might predict (Wicker, 1969). Why should this be if attitudes are indeed powerful influences on behavior?

Those who argue for the importance of attitudes offer two basic answers to this question (Cooper and Croyle, 1984). One is that although attitudes *do* strongly influence behavior, so do a number of other powerful forces (Calder and Ross, 1973; Fishbein and Ajzen, 1975; Schuman and Johnson, 1976; Oskamp, 1977). These forces include social norms and values, as well as specific circumstances that pressure people to act in particular ways. Thus workers at some of the hotels and restaurants Richard LaPiere visited may well have been very prejudiced against Orientals. But a high value placed on politeness in dealing with people, or the simple embarrassment of turning someone away face to face, could easily have overridden a general inclination to deny service in such cases.

The second reason why the correlation between attitudes and behavior may sometimes be low is that researchers do not always use good measurement techniques (Ajzen, 1982). In the past some researchers have used a single behavioral measure as the test of whether a certain attitude affects a person's actions. It is much more accurate, however, to consider many different behaviors before drawing conclusions. And, in fact, when researchers have used such multiple measures, they have generally found the *overall* correlation between attitudes and behavior to be quite strong (Fishbein and Ajzen, 1974; Weigel and Newman, 1976). It has also been found that the more specifically an attitude is related to a particular behavior, the greater is the correlation between the two (Ajzen and Fishbein, 1977, 1980). This finding suggests that if LaPiere had framed his questions to proprietors more precisely ("How would you feel about serving a well-dressed Chinese couple in the company of a college professor?"), their attitudes would probably have been more in keeping with their actions. Attitudes and behaviors, in other words, *are* very often consistent, as long as measurements and comparisons are appropriately made.

Explaining Attitude Change

If attitudes do influence behavior to a substantial degree, it should be possible to alter people's behavior by changing their attitudes. This possibility has prompted psychologists to try to learn more about how existing attitudes can be weakened, so that people become more susceptible to alternative points of view. Some researchers in this area have taken what is referred to as the persuasive communications approach, while others have adopted the cognitive consistency view. Both perspectives have contributed much to our understanding of attitude change.

Persuasive Communications and Attitude Change. The **persuasive communications** approach to attitude change began during World War II, when the War Department asked psychologist Carl Hovland and his colleagues to help design persuasive messages to be used in the training and morale-boosting of troops. After the war Hovland continued his work at Yale University. There he tried to identify the major characteristics of persuasive communications that promote attitude change. In particular, he was concerned with characteristics that get people to attend to, comprehend, be swayed by, remember, and act on the basis of a message. Hovland and his co-workers explored many such features and inspired other psychologists to undertake similar research.

How the source of a message affects attitude change has been extensively studied. The basic question asked is: What characteristics make a source especially persuasive? One answer is the source's expertise. Research shows that people are most apt to be convinced by an argument from an expert than by the same argument from a nonexpert source (Kelman and Hovland, 1953; Hass, 1981). This is especially true when the position advocated is an extreme one. In one study, for example, subjects read a message that argued that people need X hours of sleep each night (Bochner and Insko, 1966). The exact number of hours ranged from eight to zero. When subjects believed that the source of the message was an expert (a Nobel prize-winning physiologist), the more radical the view he espoused, the more their attitude changed. Another factor often found to enhance persuasiveness is the trustworthiness of a source. Trustworthiness, in turn, is heavily influenced by the presence or absence of ulterior motives. That is why TV commercials often use the "hidden camera" technique. If a shopper who is unaware that she is being filmed extols a coffee's rich, full-bodied flavor, viewers are more likely to believe what she says. Similarly, researchers have found that most arguments are more persuasive when they are accidentally overheard than when they are addressed directly to us. The reason is that we tend to assume the overheard speaker is not purposely trying to deceive us (Walster and Festinger, 1962). Also found to be very persuasive are people who argue against their own vested interests (Walster, Aronson, and Abrahams, 1966). Thus if an Air Force general strongly argues in favor of a nuclear freeze, you would be quite likely to take his position to heart.

How the content of a message influences attitude change has also been widely studied. If you want to convince an audience of a certain view, how should you organize your statement? There is evidence that when your listeners are well educated and knowledgeable about the topic, and when they initially view your message *un*favorably, you should probably present not just your own position but the opposite one as well, pointing out its weaknesses as you go along (Hovland, Lumsdaine, and Sheffield, 1949). Such two-sided arguments are usually perceived as less biased than single-sided messages—a factor that would be especially important to an unsympathetic audience (Jones and Brehm, 1970). The advertisement repro-

duced here shows the two-sided approach to persuasive communication used effectively in advertising.

Another aspect of message content that psychologists have examined closely is the effectiveness of fear-inducing appeals. Imagine that your dentist is trying to influence your attitude toward oral hygiene. He begins by telling you that failure to floss your teeth daily may lead to serious gum infections. Then, to dramatize his message, he produces full-color photos of mouths in advanced stages of disease. How do you think you would react? Would you brush and floss your teeth with renewed diligence to prevent these terrible outcomes? Learning theory suggests that you would. As you saw in Chapter 5, people generally increase the frequency of any response that enables them to avoid unpleasant consequences.

Yet in a classic study of the impact of fear appeals, this prediction was not borne out (Janis and Feshbach, 1953). The researchers showed subjects one of three presentations on oral hygiene. The low-fear appeal simply stated that failure to brush can lead to tooth decay and gum disease; the moderate-fear ap-

Many advertisers seek to "inoculate" their audience against competing claims by overtly comparing their product to other brands. *(Courtesy of Amoco Oil Company.)*

peal illustrated the nature of these problems with pictures of mild infection and decay; and the high-fear appeal showed hideous color slides of rotting teeth and diseased gums—infections that, the experimenters warned, could spread throughout the body, causing "paralysis, kidney damage, or total blindness." Contrary to what the researchers expected, the appeal that aroused the *most* fear was the *least* effective in changing behavior. Subjects who viewed the high-fear appeal generally claimed immediately afterward that it had made a great impact on them; however, only 8 percent subsequently improved their oral hygiene. In contrast, 22 percent of those who viewed the moderate-fear appeal and 36 percent who viewed the low-fear one later improved their dental habits.

To make matters more puzzling, subsequent research yielded quite different results. One thorough review of many studies dealing with issues that ranged from smoking to the use of seat belts to the importance of regular chest X-rays concluded that the majority of fear-arousing appeals have positive effects (Higbee, 1969). How can these conflicting findings be reconciled?

One possibility is that fear promotes attitude change, but only up to a point. When fear reaches an extremely high level, people may attempt to reduce their anxiety by ignoring or discounting the message (McGuire, 1968). Another explanation is that fear alone is not enough to change behavior. People must also know what steps are needed to avoid the feared outcome, and they must believe that they are capable of taking those steps themselves. The importance of these additional factors has been demonstrated in research. Generally speaking, the more specific the recommendations for avoiding a feared consequence, the greater the response (Leventhal, Singer, and Jones, 1965; Leventhal and Nerenz, 1983). And the more people believe that their efforts will be effective, the more they will be motivated to take action (Rogers and Mewborn, 1976).

The persuasive communications approach to attitude change has provided much practical information about how to structure persuasive messages, from TV commercials to political speeches to recommendations concerning safety and health. (Table 17.1 summarizes some additional findings that researchers who adopt this view have made.) But the persuasive communications approach has also been criticized. One reason is its failure to specify interrelationships among all the many factors that influence the effectiveness of persuasive appeals. Thus the persuasive communications approach does not provide a general theory of attitude change. Another criticism is that the persuasive communications approach tends to concentrate on aspects of a message that listeners need not analyze carefully, if at all (Fishbein and Ajzen, 1981). For instance, you don't have to think about the novelty of an argument or the degree to which a source is attractive, even though those factors are likely to exert an influence on you. Petty and Cacioppo (1981) say that the persuasive communications approach deals largely with attitude change

TABLE 17.1 FACTORS THAT INFLUENCE THE PERSUASIVENESS OF A COMMUNICATION

FACTOR	FINDING
Credibility	High-credibility sources are more effective in changing attitudes than low-credibility sources.
Attraction	In general, liked sources are more persuasive than disliked sources.
Power	In general, powerful sources are more persuasive than sources without power.
Channel of communication	Face-to-face communication is generally more persuasive than indirect communication (e.g., through the media).
Conclusion drawing	Explicitly drawing the communication's conclusion is usually more persuasive than not doing so.
Repetition	Within limits, repeated arguments are more persuasive than one-time presentations.
Discrepancy	Communications that are moderately discrepant from the audience's views are more persuasive than either extremely or minimally discrepant communications.
Novelty	Novel arguments are more persuasive than familiar ones.

Source: Based on data from Middlebrook, 1980, pp. 200–212.

through the "peripheral route." Equally important, they argue, especially when an issue is personally relevant, is attitude change through the "central route," in which people carefully weigh the pros and cons (Petty, Cacioppo, and Goldman, 1981). Finally, persuasive communications researchers have been criticized for their failure to stress that attitude change alone may not induce change in behavior. The importance of this point was illustrated clearly in a study of efforts to get eighth-grade smokers to give up cigarettes (Evans, 1980). Messages on the dangers of smoking were seldom enough to change the youngsters' behavior. Information on how to handle peer pressure to smoke was a critical ingredient. Such findings remind us that no matter how cleverly structured a persuasive appeal may be, there are times when more is needed to change the way people ultimately act.

Cognitive Consistency and Attitude Change.
Another major approach to attitude change involves the concept of **cognitive consistency**—the tendency of people to keep their various cognitions in relative agreement with one another. Several cognitive consistency theories of attitude change have been proposed, each with certain distinctive features. All, however, are based on the belief that any perceived incompatibility among our thoughts and actions—any cognitive *in*consistency—makes us feel uncomfortable and motivates us to reduce this state of tension.

The Theory of Cognitive Dissonance. The most influential of all the cognitive consistency theories is the theory of **cognitive dissonance,** proposed more than twenty-five years ago by psychologist Leon Festinger (1957). Dissonance theory focuses primarily on discrepancies between attitudes and behavior. Such discrepancies, according to Festinger, produce a state of psychological distress. Take the case of a man who is president of a company that manufactures cigarettes. He will probably experience dissonance if he believes himself to be a moral person and also believes that smoking causes heart disease and cancer. His two inconsistent cognitions are: "I am a kind, well-intentioned person, yet by manufacturing cigarettes I am contributing to the premature death of thousands of people." To reduce this dissonance the man is not likely to convince himself that he is uncaring and ruthless, nor is he likely to give up his job. Instead, he

will probably modify his cognitions concerning the dangers of cigarettes or the effects of his producing them. He could minimize the link between smoking and fatal illness ("Most of those studies were done when cigarettes contained more tar and nicotine than they do now"). Or he could add positive cognitions to counterbalance his negative ones ("Cigarettes may create health problems, but these are more than compensated for by the fact that smoking reduces stress and makes life more enjoyable"). Or he could downplay the importance of the dissonance-arousing behavior ("It doesn't really matter whether I manufacture cigarettes because if smokers didn't buy my product they'd just buy someone else's").

In this example cognitive dissonance was aroused because a man engaged in an activity that violated his standards of right and wrong. But this is only one of many applications of dissonance theory. Dissonance theorists have also explored the effect of inducing people to behave in an attitude-discrepant way. Suppose one person is paid a great deal of money to say something he or she does not believe, while another person is paid very little to do so. Which one would you expect to experience cognitive dissonance? And how would this dissonance affect the person's attitudes? See if your answers agree with the findings in the following classic experiment conducted by Festinger and Carlsmith (1959).

Subjects were asked to perform an exceedingly boring task: either turning the pegs in a pegboard a quarter turn each and then repeating the procedure many times, or lining up spools in a tray, dumping them out, and lining them up again and again. When each subject finally finished, the experimenter confided that he was actually investigating the effects of preconceptions on performance. Would the subject help out by telling the next subject that the study had been fun and exciting? The researcher offered some of the subjects $1 and some of them $20 for telling this lie. (A third group, the control group, merely did the task and was not asked to do any persuading.) All of the experimental subjects voluntarily complied with the researcher's request. Then each subject was asked to evaluate the experimental task. Those who had been paid $20 for telling the lie (and those who had not had to lie at all) rated the job as boring—which by objective standards it certainly was. But those who had been paid only $1 to tell the same lie disagreed. They reported that the experimental task had in fact been fairly enjoyable!

Why did the $1 subjects rate an intrinsically boring task quite favorably? According to dissonance theory, saying something you do not believe causes psychological discomfort *unless* you have an adequate justification, such as a large fee—and $20 was a substantial sum in 1959. Thus, unlike the subjects offered $20, those offered only $1 had insufficient means to justify the lie to themselves. As a result, they experienced dissonance and responded by convincing themselves that the task had not been so boring after all.

These results have practical implications. They suggest that the *greater* the reward for engaging in a disliked behavior, the *less* the likelihood that attitudes will change to justify the act. Thus, when a little girl who hates schoolwork is offered $5 to bring home a good report card, she may decide that she is working for the money and continue to dislike studying. But a girl who is offered 50 cents for the same behavior may be induced to feel that studying is actually fun. The same logic can be applied to the use of punishment. If you want to convince a preschooler that it is wrong to play with the knobs on the stereo, threatening severe punishment is probably the wrong approach. It may temporarily produce the desired behavior out of fear of the consequences, but it may not produce lasting attitude change. A better tactic is to use only a mild threat. Then the child will have less external justification for avoiding the stereo and so be more apt to change his or her attitude toward the stereo as a desirable plaything.

The suggestion to parents, then, is never to threaten more than you have to. The validity of this advice has been demonstrated experimentally (Aronson and Carlsmith, 1963). Researchers showed preschoolers a very desirable toy but forbade them to play with it, threatening either severe or mild punishment. When left alone with the toy, none of the children played with it. When their attitudes toward the toy were reevaluated, however, over a third of those threatened with mild punishment devalued the toy to some extent, whereas none of those threatened with severe punishment did so. Presumably those who had been threatened with mild punishment experienced cognitive dissonance ("I didn't play with that toy even though I wouldn't have been punished much") and therefore decided that they didn't like the toy after all. Such attitude change, moreover, appears to be quite long-lasting. When children who participated in such an experiment were given complete freedom to play with the attractive toy several weeks later, many

of those previously exposed to the "mild punishment" condition continued to avoid the toy (Freedman, 1965). Apparently their feelings about playing with it underwent fairly long-term change.

Despite extensive evidence in support of cognitive dissonance, the theory has its critics. Some have argued that early cognitive dissonance experiments had serious methodological flaws (Chapanis and Chapanis, 1964; Rosenberg, 1965). If subjects are offered $20 simply to tell a lie, might not suspicion about the psychologist's motives make them resentful about the experimental task? Such criticisms have prompted better and more sophisticated studies. In fact, social psychologists have conducted nearly a thousand such studies since Festinger's theory was first introduced (Cooper and Croyle, 1984). Many of the findings continue to support the cognitive dissonance concept.

The extensive research into cognitive dissonance has also enabled psychologists to specify more precisely the conditions that cause dissonance. We now know, for instance, that cognitive dissonance tends to arise only when behavior is voluntary and when the person feels responsible for his or her actions (Linder, Cooper, and Jones, 1967; Collins and Hoyt, 1972; Pallak, Sogin, and Van Zante, 1974). If Festinger and Carlsmith's subjects had been *forced* to tell the lie (warned, for instance, that their psychology grade might be lowered if they failed to comply), then they would have had a perfectly good reason for doing what the experimenter asked. In this situation no dissonance or attitude change should result. Cognitive dissonance is also more likely when the consequences of an act are unpleasant either for the person who performs it or for someone else (Cooper and Worchel, 1970). Thus when people feel sorry or guilty for their behavior, they are apt to experience dissonance.

With such findings in mind, researchers have begun to explore factors that may contribute to the dissonance process. Some have argued that the attitude change that occurs in many cognitive dissonance experiments may be motivated in part by the need to maintain a positive self-image (Schlenker, 1980, 1982; Steele and Liu, 1983). Remember that in cognitive dissonance experiments people often find themselves behaving in ways that are reprehensible (lying to another person, for instance), or at least out of step with what they feel they should do. The desire to make such behavior seem less objectionable to oneself and to others could be a factor underlying subsequent attitude change. It also seems likely that a desire to reduce anxiety also motivates attitude change in many cognitive dissonance studies. As evidence, consider this finding: When people are induced to act in ways opposed to their true feelings, they are more inclined to accept a drink of alcohol than they normally would be (Steele, Southwick, and Critchlow, 1981). The implication is that alcohol is a way of reducing the uncomfortable anxiety that cognitive dissonance evokes. Significantly, after drinking the alcohol these subjects do not display the expected dissonance-reducing change in attitudes. It is as if their need to reduce anxiety has already been met by the effects of the drink.

Reassessing Dissonance: Bem's Self-Perception Theory. One problem with dissonance theory has been the difficulty of measuring the state of psychological tension that dissonance presumably creates. How do we know, some psychologists have asked, that such a state of tension necessarily arises? Couldn't attitude change be produced in cognitive dissonance experiments *without* such inner conflict? Daryl Bem (1967) is one researcher who maintains that it can be and often is.

Bem begins by asking how we come to know the attitudes of other people. The answer is often through inference. We observe people's behavior, interpret it in light of the current situation, and attribute attitudes accordingly. For instance, if we observe shoppers in a grocery store buying a certain brand of coffee and we see that the brand is not on sale, we are likely to conclude that these people must like the way this coffee tastes. If, however, we observe shoppers in a television commercial eagerly buying the same product, we are not likely to make the same inference about their attitudes. These paid actors have an ulterior motive (money) that ordinary shoppers do not. Both the observed behavior and the situation are therefore considered when the opinions of others are assessed.

Bem goes on to argue that we often use this same strategy to assess our *own* attitudes. At times, he says, we are not very sure of our own opinions. As a result, we must look to our behavior and the circumstances surrounding it to "know" what it is we feel. Suppose, for example, that someone asked you if you liked lamb stew. You might think to yourself: "I ate a large serving of lamb stew a few weeks ago even though I

wasn't very hungry. I guess I must like lamb stew quite a bit." In the same way, Bem argues, subjects in Festinger and Carlsmith's experiment who favorably rated the boring task had probably asked themselves: "What must my attitude toward this task be if, for only a dollar, I was willing to tell another subject it was fun? I guess my feelings must be *somewhat* positive."

Note that Bem's **self-perception theory** and the theory of cognitive dissonance make the same prediction about the outcome of the Festinger and Carlsmith study. Both say that subjects paid only $1 to lie will regard the peg-turning task more favorably than subjects paid $20. But the *explanations* proposed by these two theories are quite different. Dissonance theory argues that the low-paid subjects change their opinions because they experience inconsistency and psychological discomfort, while self-perception theory argues that no such discomfort occurs. According to self-perception theory, people faced with an ambiguous situation simply infer their own attitudes by examining their behavior and the surrounding circumstances. They do this in exactly the same dispassionate and untroubled manner as when they infer the feelings of another person.

Because dissonance theory and self-perception theory often make similar predictions, it has been difficult to determine which is correct. On the one hand, some researchers have shown that in certain situations where attitudes and behavior conflict, people *do* experience an uncomfortable state of arousal, just as dissonance theory suggests (Fazio and Cooper, 1983; Croyle and Cooper, in press). On the other hand, a number of psychologists have gathered evidence that self-perception also seems to affect our attitudes. The truth may be that both processes are valid, but in different circumstances (Fazio, Zanna, and Cooper, 1977).

One situation whose curious outcome can be accounted for very well by self-perception theory but not by dissonance theory is that in which people are rewarded for doing something they already like to do. It may surprise you to learn that in this situation people's interest in the activity may actually decline (Deci, 1971; Bates, 1979; Deci and Ryan, 1980). In one experiment, for instance, nursery school children who enjoyed drawing with felt-tip pens were told that they would be given a special prize for drawing the experimenter a picture. The children complied, but a week later their interest in the drawing materials had decreased markedly. This drop in interest did not occur among children who had been asked to draw a picture for *no* external reward (Lepper, Greene, and Nisbett, 1973). Why lose interest in something that gives you pleasure just because you are rewarded for it? Bem would argue that people reason: "If I'm being rewarded for doing *X*, perhaps I'm only doing it for the reward. Perhaps I don't really like *X* that much after all." Dissonance theory, in contrast, cannot explain this sudden change of heart, because doing something one likes, no matter how much one is paid, does not arouse dissonance.

This intriguing application of self-perception theory has stimulated much research into ways to maximize people's intrinsic motivation (Lepper and Greene, 1978). Will the satisfaction you derive from an enjoyable task *necessarily* decline just because you are rewarded for doing it? Psychologists have found that the answer is not always. The effect of rewards often depends on how they are delivered. If rewards are given as an acknowledgment of competence, they can actually increase intrinsic motivation by making the recipients feel good about their abilities (Deci and Ryan, 1980). Perhaps this is why verbal rewards, or praise, often lead to enhanced interest (Johnson, Greene, and Carroll, 1978; Anderson, Manoogian, and Reznick, 1976). But when rewards are given in a controlling way, the recipients are likely to view the reward merely as the reason for engaging in the behavior, and intrinsic motivation is likely to suffer (Deci and Ryan, 1980). Such findings highlight a central point of Bem's self-perception theory: people's interpretations of their own actions depend greatly on the circumstances surrounding those behaviors.

Resistance to Attitude Change

We have talked about some of the circumstances in which attitude change occurs. But such change is certainly not inevitable. People often resist changing their opinions for a variety of reasons. One important cause is **psychological reactance.** It occurs when a formerly available choice is eliminated or somehow threatened. The result is an increased desire to engage in that behavior (Brehm, 1966). If you have ever valued an activity more highly *after* it was forbidden, you have experienced psychological reactance.

Suppose, for example, that two similar groups of people read a speech arguing in favor of equal treatment for the American Communist party. The wording of both speeches is identical except that one includes such phrases as "You have no choice but to believe this" and "You cannot believe otherwise." How do you think the groups would react? Worchel and Brehm (1970) performed this experiment and found that subjects who encountered remarks that threatened their freedom of choice were much less likely to agree with the endorsed views. Moreover, a full 40 percent of those who read this kind of wording actually changed their attitudes *away* from those advocated in the speech. In contrast, only 15 percent of subjects in the "no threat" condition showed this boomerang effect.

The results of this and similar studies have ironic implications. It is when we are trying hardest to change a person's attitudes that our efforts may be *least* effective. When parents strenuously oppose the person a son or daughter is dating, for instance, their vehement objections may be viewed as a threat to freedom of choice and so be stubbornly resisted. In fact, the parents' approach can have an effect completely opposite to the one they intend. Research shows that parents' interference in a love relationship may only serve to intensify the couple's mutual attraction (Driscoll, Davis, and Lipetz, 1972). This process is often called the Romeo and Juliet effect, because it parallels the plot of Shakespeare's famous love story.

PERSON PERCEPTION AND ATTRIBUTION

Our attitudes toward other people are among the most important we form. What factors shape our perceptions of others? Imagine you are watching as a new neighbor moves into the vacant apartment next door. He is a young man about twenty-one, probably a student like yourself. But this fellow is so big and brawny that he looks like a bull in human clothing. His hair is cut short in a military style. His nose is large, his forehead narrow, his eyes close-set. As you watch him lifting a set of barbells up the front steps you step back from the window and think to yourself: "All brawn and no brains, that's for sure. Just my luck to get stuck with a moron next door." Not surprisingly, you ignore your new neighbor, except for a curt "Hi" when you meet by chance in the hall. Then six months later you are astounded to learn that your neighbor, a philosophy major, has been elected to Phi Beta Kappa.

Is it unusual to form opinions of others on the basis of so little evidence? No, not in the least. We constantly size up strangers on very scanty information. In the first of the following sections we will explore some of the factors that influence our first impressions. As we have just seen, the conclusions we arrive at can be critical to our future dealings with those we judge. If you hastily decide that your new neighbor is dull and shallow, you are likely to avoid him and to cut off all chances to learn otherwise. This is one reason why psychologists feel it is important to understand the bases on which first impressions are formed.

First Impressions

The Primacy Effect. The order in which we perceive traits has a definite impact on the initial impressions we form of others. Traits that we perceive first seem to count the most. If someone first strikes you as brash and unfeeling, it may be difficult to view him later as a sensitive musician when you learn that he plays the oboe in a chamber orchestra. This **primacy effect** has been demonstrated in many experiments. In one classic study, subjects were presented with the two paragraphs shown in Figure 17.1, which describe a young man named Jim (Luchins, 1957). Those who read only paragraph A saw Jim as extroverted and friendly. Those who read only paragraph B saw him as introverted and shy. How do you think subjects viewed Jim when they were asked to read both paragraphs? Generally the order of presentation governed their impressions. Most of those who read the "extroverted" paragraph first perceived Jim as basically outgoing, while most of those who read the "introverted" paragraph first saw Jim as essentially a loner.

A   Jim left the house to get some stationery. He walked out into the sun-filled street with two of his friends, basking in the sun as he walked. Jim entered the stationery store, which was full of people. Jim talked with an acquaintance while he waited for the clerk to catch his eye. On his way out, he stopped to chat with a school friend who was just coming into the store. Leaving the store, he walked toward school. On his way out he met the girl to whom he had been introduced the night before. They talked for a short while, and then Jim left for school.

B   After school Jim left the classroom alone. Leaving the school, he started on his long walk home. The street was brilliantly filled with sunshine. Jim walked down the street on the shady side. Coming down the street toward him, he saw the pretty girl whom he had met on the previous evening. Jim crossed the street and entered a candy store. The store was crowded with students, and he noticed a few familiar faces. Jim waited quietly until the counterman caught his eye and then gave his order. Taking his drink, he sat down at a side table. When he had finished his drink he went home.

Figure 17.1 How do first impressions strike us? Quite powerfully, suggests the Luchins experiment. How do you picture Jim after reading paragraph A, then paragraph B? Do you see him differently after reading the paragraphs in reverse order? *(From Luchins, 1957.)*

The reasons for the primacy effect are not completely clear. Perhaps once we have formed an impression of someone, we are less attentive to subsequent information about the person (Hendrick and Constantini, 1970). Or perhaps we strive for consistency in our perceptions of people. If we later observe behavior that contradicts our initial opinion, we may discount that behavior as an aberration, or interpret it in such a way that it fits our existing view. Once we have decided, for example, that Jim is basically friendly, we may assume that he is not feeling well if he avoids social contact (Anderson, 1968). A little later in this chapter we will examine evidence that such perceptual screening on the basis of first impressions does occur.

Expectations Based on Physical Attractiveness.

Although many people insist that physical attractiveness is not a factor in their evaluation of others, research shows conclusively that it is (Dion, 1980). Physical beauty or lack of it makes a critical difference to the first impressions we make. Elaine Walster and her colleagues (1966) demonstrated this in a well-known experiment. They assessed physical attractiveness, intelligence, and personality traits in more than seven hundred college freshmen who signed up for a computer-dating dance. But rather than use a computer to match participants by shared interests (as the dance advertised), the researchers simply paired them at random. It may disturb you to learn that neither intelligence nor personality had much of an impact on whether a date was later rated favorably by his or her partner. The only factor that consistently influenced a date's rating was that person's physical attractiveness. If beauty is only skin deep, as the old saying goes, so are first impressions.

What is it about beautiful people that so attracts us to them? Apparently we associate beauty with a whole set of desirable traits. When researchers show subjects pictures of men and women of various degrees of physical attractiveness and ask them to evaluate their personalities, the subjects often describe the beautiful ones more positively. Although they sometimes see them as more vain and sexually promiscuous, they also tend to view them as more sensitive, kind, interesting, strong, poised, and sociable, as well as more sexually responsive (Dermer and Thiel, 1975; Dion, Bersheid, and Walster, 1972). In addition, people are inclined to perceive a beautiful person as reasonably competent, even in the face of evidence to the contrary. When male college students were asked to read a very poorly written essay, they evaluated the author's ability more leniently when they were led to believe that she was beautiful than when they thought she was homely (Landy and Sigall, 1974).

The biases related to physical attractiveness also extend to children. Teachers who are led to believe that an attractive and a homely child received identical report cards still tend to view the attractive student as more intelligent and more likely to go to college (Clifford and Walster, 1973). Furthermore, an act of misbehavior is often rated less naughty when it is committed by an attractive rather than an unattractive child (Dion, 1972). Even children themselves take attractiveness into account when they judge their peers. Those as young as three have been found to prefer physically attractive youngsters as playmates (Dion, 1973).

Not only do we attribute many desirable traits to beautiful people, we also perceive people who merely associate with the beautiful in a more positive way. A man is admired, for instance, if he is romantically involved with an attractive woman (Sigall and Landy, 1973). Apparently people conclude that if a beautiful woman who could attract many men is interested in this one, he must be special indeed. One reason for our pursuit of beautiful people, therefore, may be our intuitive knowledge that association with them enhances our own social status.

The Effects of Schemas.

Why do we judge people on the basis of such scanty evidence? Part of the reason probably has to do with our limited information-processing capabilities. As we saw in Chapter 7, people must find ways to simplify their screening of the many pieces of information that bombard them about any given topic. As a result, they take shortcuts, focusing on some facts and largely ignoring others. This strategy allows them to avoid becoming so overwhelmed by information that no decision, solution, or judgment is possible.

Some psychologists have applied these findings to a general description of how people form first impressions. They say that when we meet a new acquaintance we develop a set of key cognitions about that person, cognitions collectively called a **schema** (Taylor and Crocker, 1980). A schema is compiled of selected pieces of information, typically pieces that strike us first and most strongly. These bits of data are organized into a logical, coherent whole. We may see someone as friendly, for example, and also as talkative, witty, and enthusiastic—in short, an extrovert. Once formed, such a schema is used to filter and help interpret additional information. If our schema for a certain woman is of an extrovert, for instance, we are likely to interpret her attendance at many parties as confirmation of this view. Psychologists sometimes say that our perceptions are "theory driven." Our schemas are our theories about what other people are like, and these theories shape our expectations about how those people will act. In this way schemas greatly simplify the job of understanding the complexities of human behavior.

But though schemas save us cognitive effort, they also pose some risks. For one thing, schemas are by nature sketchy. So when particular details are missing, we tend to fill them in on the basis of preconceptions (Cantor and Mischel, 1977; Bower, Black, and Turner, 1979). This is precisely what happened in our earlier example of the muscular new neighbor who was assumed to be unintelligent on the basis of his looks alone. The same process occurs when we assume that physically attractive people are also poised and sociable. We are using preconceptions to fill in the outlines of a schema, even though these preconceptions may have no basis in reality. Another danger in reliance on schemas is that once they are formed they tend to be quite resistant to change. People seem more inclined to mold the facts to fit an existing schema than to admit that the schema itself may be wrong (Snyder and Uranowitz, 1978). Schemas, in short, help to edit our subsequent perceptions. And unless we are faced with strong contradictory evidence, we may simply edit out any information that fails to conform to our schemas.

First Impressions and Self-Fulfilling Prophecies.

When forming first impressions, then, people sometimes make unjustified inferences. This in itself is unfortunate. But consider the further effects of incorrect first impressions. When you judge a person to be unfriendly, for example, you are likely to be somewhat stand-offish. Your demeanor, in turn, increases the likelihood that the person will respond in ways that confirm your evaluation. Through your own behavior, in other words, you have encouraged the very unfriendliness you initially expected. Your once erroneous belief has become a reality—a self-fulfilling prophecy.

That first impressions can become self-fulfilling prophecies has been demonstrated in a number of provocative experiments (for example, Rosenthal, 1966). In one study, researchers asked previously unacquainted college men and women to "get to know one another" through a ten-minute phone conversation (Snyder, Tanke, and Berscheid, 1977). Beforehand, each man was given a snapshot of a woman said to be his future "phonemate." In fact, however, the photo was of an entirely different woman—either a very attractive or a very unattractive one. As predicted, the men's expectations were based on physical appearance. If they received a snapshot of a beautiful woman, they imagined her to be outgoing, poised, humorous, and socially adept. If they received a snapshot of a homely woman, they assumed her to be exactly the opposite. How do you think these expectations influenced the men's behavior during their phone conversations? Not surprisingly, those who thought they were talking with an attractive partner were judged by unbiased listeners to be more friendly, interesting, sexual, humorous, and socially adroit than were those who thought they were talking with an unattractive partner. And the women responded in kind. Those presumed to be attractive by their phonemates acted friendly and sociable; those presumed to be unattractive acted aloof and withdrawn. Apparently each took her cue from her partner's behavior. She became the person he expected her to be.

Attributing Causes to Behavior

Evaluating other people certainly does not end with the formation of first impressions. Even when we know another person quite well, we often desire to find out *why* that person is acting in a certain way. This desire arises from more than curiosity alone. If we can attribute a given action to some enduring cause (a stable personality trait, for instance), we add a measure of predictability to our social world. We gain confidence that under similar conditions, this particular person will act much the same way again. Fritz Heider (1944, 1958), the first psychologist to study **causal attribution**—how people attribute causes to behavior—believed that all of us are constantly searching for relatively stable factors underlying other people's actions. Our ability to find such factors provides a sense of comfort by making our social environments seem less random and chaotic.

But the problem is that attributing causes to behavior is not always easy. Often we must decide among several very plausible explanations. When a student tells a professor how much he likes her organic chemistry course, does he really mean what he is saying or is he trying to wheedle a favorable recommendation for medical school? It may be difficult to say. Such ambiguity may even arise when we are assessing our own motives. As we saw earlier in regard to Daryl Bem's views, people are not always sure about their own attitudes. Sometimes they must infer their underlying feelings by analyzing their behavior and the context in which it occurs. Presumably we do the same when attributing causes to the behavior of others. It was Bem's work, in fact, that helped focus social psychologists' attention on the general process of making causal inferences.

In studying how people attribute causes to behavior, researchers have raised two main questions. First, what processes do people use to guide them in making causal inferences? If a man takes a woman out and at the end of the evening promises to call her tomorrow but doesn't, the woman can reach a number of conclusions. She may attribute the cause to her date ("He's forgetful or even inconsiderate"), to herself ("I must not be very attractive. What's wrong with me?"), or to situational factors ("Maybe he had a personal emergency and couldn't call"). Note that the conclusion the woman draws need not necessarily correspond to reality. It simply reflects her subjective view of the situation. This fact leads to a second major question about causal attribution: What kinds of errors do people typically make in assigning causes to behavior, and what impact do these errors have on people's dealings with others? Suppose our woman concludes that her date failed to call because he is inconsiderate, but the real reason is that he finds her self-centered and immature. As long as the woman continues to misattribute such actions, she may fail to make changes in herself that would improve her interpersonal relations. In the following sections we will explore some answers psychologists offer to both these intriguing questions.

Attribution Processes. There have been two influential theories about how people infer the causes of others' behavior. One, proposed by Jones and Davis (1965), focuses on the kinds of behaviors to which people attend when they make causal attributions. Not all behaviors are equally informative, Jones and Davis argue. Some behaviors are so common, so socially expected, that they reveal very little about a person. If, for example, a political candidate smiles broadly while shaking hundreds of hands, do you immediately assume that he is a genuinely warm and friendly person? Probably not, because these behaviors are widely expected of people who are seeking public office. According to Jones and Davis, it is behavior that is in some way *unexpected* that provides the greatest insight into a person's nature.

This theory has been tested through research. In one experiment, subjects listened to one of two tapes, both of a man being interviewed for a job (Jones, Davis, and Gergen, 1961). The interviewer specifically told the job candidate the personality traits required for the position, so the candidate had strong external pressure to conform to those characteristics. In one version of the tape the necessary traits were friendliness and cooperation, while in another version the necessary traits were independence and self-reliance. Half the subjects heard a candidate who described himself in accordance with the traits the interviewer listed. The other half heard a candidate who described himself as the exact opposite of what the interviewer sought. How do you think the subjects responded when they were later asked what they thought the job candidate was *really* like? Most were willing to make confident judgments only when they had heard an applicant who unexpectedly portrayed himself as the opposite of what the job demanded. Apparently, when someone's behavior is *consistent* with external pressures, we tend to discount those actions as a clue to personality ("He probably said that just to get the job"). It is behavior that is *inconsistent* with surrounding pressures that we tend to interpret as arising from inner dispositions.

We see this same screening of information in everyday life (Kelley, 1979). For example, if a woman constantly complains that her husband doesn't love her because he never tells her so, is she likely to conclude from a few "I love you's" that the husband has had a change of heart? Probably not. There is simply too much external pressure that could also be compelling this response. It is only when the husband says "I love you" in the absence of such pressures that the wife is likely to believe what he says.

A second influential theory of how people make causal attributions is that of Harold Kelley (1967, 1971). Kelley's theory is not incompatible with Jones and Davis's; it simply focuses on different aspects of the attribution process. Essentially, Kelley argues that when we infer the causes of behavior, we tend to compare people's present actions with their past performances, as well as with the responses that others make in similar circumstances.

To explain Kelley's theory more fully, suppose you see a classmate named Anne arguing angrily with the Psychology Department's secretary. Is Anne by nature argumentative and ill-tempered, or did an understandable set of circumstances provoke this outburst? Kelley suggests that you may find out by using the following strategy. First, you may consider the factor of *consistency*. Does Anne repeatedly lose her temper when she deals with this secretary? If not, you are likely to attribute this particular fit of anger to some unusual provocation, not to a stable personality trait. If consistency is high, however, you may proceed to a consideration of *distinctiveness*. Does Anne explode at other people with equal frequency? If you have seen her raging at professors, librarians, and fellow students alike, then the distinctiveness of this behavior is low, and you will be led to believe that her temper is perennially short. Finally, you may confirm your suspicions by considering the factor of *consensus*. Do other students frequently argue with this particular secretary? If not, then consensus is low and you have strong evidence that Anne's disposition is indeed feisty. Like Jones and Davis's view of how people attribute causes to behavior, this theory of Kelley's has been confirmed experimentally (McArthur, 1972).

An important difference between Jones and Davis's and Kelley's views of attribution is that Kelley assumes comparisons over time, whereas Jones and Davis do not. By using Kelley's strategy, people can base inferences on accumulated observations that by themselves may be insufficient to point to a firm conclusion. This makes Kelley's model somewhat broader than Jones and Davis's. Still, the two theories have similar notions about how people approach the problem of attribution. Both assume that people infer the causes of behavior in highly logical ways. We screen available evidence, eliminate that which is questionable, and conduct further tests to prove or disprove hypotheses. In these respects we behave very much like amateur scientists.

Attribution Biases. As amateurs, however, we have our limitations. Despite our frequent successes at attributing causes to behavior, we also make attribution errors. And the errors we make are seldom haphazard. We are prone to very systematic attribution biases (Ross, 1977; Nisbett and Ross, 1980).

Probably the most common attribution error is the tendency to see others' behavior as caused by their personalities rather than by external forces. If you see a woman acting in a rude, abrupt manner, you are much more inclined to infer that she is rude by nature than that her actions arise from unusual circumstances. This tendency is so powerful it can cause you to overlook even quite strong situational pressures. In one study, for instance, subjects read an essay that either praised or criticized Fidel Castro's leadership of Cuba (Jones and Harris, 1967). Most subjects inferred that the essay reflected the author's true attitude, even when they were specifically told that the writer had merely been instructed to take that position. The subjects, in short, tended to ignore situational constraints in favor of the theory that the writer himself was responsible for the view expressed. This tendency to attribute others' behavior to their inner dispositions is so pervasive that it has been called the **fundamental attribution error** (Ross, 1977).

What prompts us to attribute behavior so readily to inner dispositions? One answer is that our attention is usually drawn to whatever is most salient. By "salient" we mean distinctive in relation to the surroundings, and therefore tending to stand out. A Model T Ford is salient when you see it on a modern highway, just as a college student is salient in a group of eighty-year-olds (Fiske and Taylor, 1984).

Studies show that salience does indeed affect attributions. For instance, people have been found to perceive one of the participants in a group discussion as more influential than the others simply because that person is visually prominent (Taylor and Fiske, 1975). Visual prominence, in turn, can be manipulated by seemingly trivial factors. Being in a central location, moving while others remain stationary, or even being well lighted when others are slightly shadowed—all are enough to make a person stand out in the crowd (McArthur and Post, 1977). Thus, you are more likely to be perceived as influential relative to others in a group if you can make yourself more salient in some way (Taylor et al., 1979).

But one odd thing about the fundamental attribution error is that very often it is avoided with regard to our *own* behavior. We tend to attribute our own behavior to environmental causes, *not* to personality factors (Jones and Nisbett, 1971). Thus there is often a marked difference in the way actors and observers explain the same behavior. To the observer a behavior seems to arise from the actor's disposition, whereas to the actor the same behavior seems to be caused by the surrounding situation. This common difference in attributions is called the **actor-observer bias.** Sometimes it can cause problems in interpersonal relationships (Kelley, 1979). Parents, for example, may attribute a son's poor grades to sheer laziness on his part (a personality factor). But the son may be convinced that the real blame lies in a heavy course load (a situational cause). Awareness of the actor-observer bias might help both parties be more sensitive to the other's point of view.

Psychologists have offered several possible reasons for the actor-observer bias. One has to do with the different information that is salient to an actor and to an observer. Remember that as we act we do not see ourselves performing, as an observer does. Instead, our attention is drawn to the environment, making it likely that we will view environmental forces as the causes of our actions. Another contributing factor may be the actor's extensive knowledge of his or her own past behavior—especially knowledge of how that behavior has varied in different circumstances. If we act very rudely in a given situation, for example, but we know that we have seldom behaved this way before, it makes sense to look to environmental forces as the cause of this particular response. An observer, in contrast, has seen us acting in far fewer situations. As a result, the observer is more apt to conclude that rudeness is typical of our general behavior.

There are limits, however, to an actor's inclination to attribute causes to the environment. This inclination is strongest when the person's actions turn out badly—when they cause harm to others, for example, or when they appear to be bungled and incompetent. In these situations actors are often masters at finding excuses for what they have said or done. Did you get a D in English lit and nearly flunk biology? You would probably say it was because you had taken on too many outside activities. Did you make a dismal showing on the tennis court or collapse after jogging half a mile? You would probably lay the blame on a backache or on the very hot and humid weather. When the outcome of an action is favorable, in contrast, actors are often quick to attribute the cause to themselves. This tendency to take credit for successes and to find situational excuses for failures has been aptly called the **self-serving bias.**

Studies provide concrete evidence for the self-serving bias (Bradley, 1978). In experiments in which subjects play competitive games, winners usually attribute the results to skills, while losers usually attribute them to luck (Stephan, Rosenfield, and Stephan, 1976). People have also been found to overestimate their own contribution to a joint effort when that effort is successful. When a joint effort is a failure, in contrast, people are inclined to overestimate their co-workers' role in bringing about the failure (Ross and Sicoly, 1979). This is not to say that we never accept the blame for poor performance. Sometimes we do. But on such occasions we have a knack for making our failures seem like virtues (Markus, 1977). A woman who failed a typing test might be heard telling her friends: "Sure I failed. I'm a terrible typist. Guess it means I'm executive material, not the secretarial type." Thus even in defeat people may twist their causal attributions in self-serving ways.

The reason for the self-serving bias is still controversial. Many psychologists argue that it results from a desire to protect our self-esteem. This view is supported by the finding that people tend to ignore or forget about information that could be threatening to their self-images, while at the same time they take special note of things that can boost their self-esteem. In one study, for instance, people who underwent a personality assessment test had significantly better recall of their good traits than of their bad ones (Mischel, Ebbeson, and Zeiss, 1973). The implication is that when we attribute causes to our own behavior, we may be motivated to edit our perceptions in order to place ourselves in a favorable light.

Recently, however, some psychologists have challenged this motivational view (Miller and Ross, 1975; Nisbett and Ross, 1980). They suspect that avoiding disagreeable truths about ourselves may backfire in the long run. If people try to attribute all good outcomes to themselves, won't they eventually find it impossible to live up to their overblown self-images? And if people try to blame all bad outcomes on circumstances, denying any reason to make changes in themselves, won't they be destined to keep repeating the same mistakes and so lead very disappointing lives? According to these critics, a purely motivational explanation of the self-serving bias makes little sense.

An alternative explanation, proposed by Nisbett and Ross (1980), is that the self-serving bias may be partly cognitive in nature. People, they say, may unwittingly surround themselves with information that makes it hard to evaluate their own behavior accurately. Suppose a newly appointed sales manager's first year on the job is blessed with high sales—all of the success attributable to lucky circumstances and none of it to him. In fact, as a manager, the man is quite incompetent. What information might this person have to help him focus attention on the situational causes of the company's success rather than on himself? Realistically, he may have very little. The people who work for him are not likely to tell him of his ineptitude, though they may discuss it among themselves. Instead, some are probably motivated, for reasons of self-advancement, to inflate the sales manager's self-esteem. Then, too, the manager's friends undoubtedly view him in a very favorable light, which is part of the reason he chose them as friends. Their flattering views only help to convince him that he is right to attribute positive outcomes to himself. In short, this man is unwittingly being exposed to very one-sided evidence of his own talents. No wonder he feels responsible for the company's impressive sales!

Psychologists do not yet know whether a motivational or a cognitive explanation of the self-serving bias is more accurate. Very likely the two forces often interact. If so, our wishful thinking about ourselves seldom contradicts the evidence we see around us. Instead, such thinking is usually supported, even encouraged, by the "facts" we have available.

ATTRACTION, FRIENDSHIP, AND LOVE

Forming first impressions and attributing causes to behavior are processes that apply to virtually everyone we deal with. Liking and loving, in contrast, are much more selective. Not everyone we meet becomes a close friend. And fewer still are accorded that special, intense feeling we call romantic love. Yet forming friendships and falling in love are highly important to us. What light can social psychologists shed on these two processes?

Interpersonal Attraction and Friendship

If asked why you were attracted to your three closest friends, you would probably begin by listing all the things you have in common. One of the last things you would mention, if you mentioned it at all, would be the fact that your friends live or work close to you. It may therefore surprise you to learn that physical proximity or closeness, far from being incidental, is quite an important factor in friendship.

In a classic study of the effects of proximity on friendship, researchers surveyed married couples in a student housing complex at the Massachusetts Institute of Technology (Festinger, Schachter, and Back, 1950). All the residents were asked to name the three closest friends they had made in the complex. As Figure 17.2 illustrates, the results were clear-cut. The closer to each other two people lived, the more likely they were to identify each other as close friends. People who lived next door to each other were much more likely to have become friends than were people who lived two doors apart. Furthermore, people who were assigned an apartment near a heavily trafficked area—at the head or foot of the stairs, for example, or near the mailboxes—were much more likely to have a very active social life than those assigned an apartment in a relatively secluded corner. Unfair as it may seem, mere proximity to others can dramatically affect a person's popularity.

The impact of proximity on friendship is undoubtedly related to the frequency with which close neighbors see one another. Psychological research shows that merely being repeatedly exposed to someone can breed liking for that person. In one experiment designed to demonstrate this, subjects were told they were participating in a study on taste (Saegert, Swap, and Zajonc, 1973). They were shuttled in and out of several small cubicles, where they tasted and rated

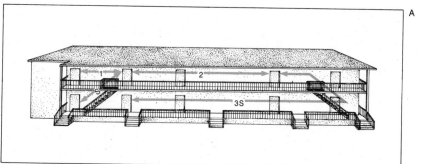

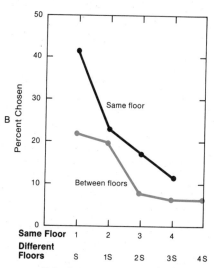

Figure 17.2 The results of the friendship study at MIT. The investigators studied the relationship between proximity and choice of friends in a housing development. (A) The illustration of one of the seventeen apartment buildings shows how proximity was measured: in roughly equal units of physical distance, with a special S unit indicating a flight of stairs. (B) The subjects' statements of where their three closest friends lived is given as a percentage of all the possible people who could have been chosen at a given distance. By far the largest proportion of friends were next-door neighbors. *(After Festinger, Schachter, and Back, 1950.)*

different liquids and in the process encountered a number of other people. The researchers arranged for each subject to see one person ten times, a second person five times, a third person twice, a fourth person once, and a fifth not at all. No talking or interaction was permitted during these encounters. After the bogus taste-testing was finished, all subjects were asked to fill out a lengthy questionnaire that included their reactions to the other people. Subjects generally expressed the greatest liking for those they had encountered the most.

Why do people tend to like those they see repeatedly? One possibility is that as we become more familiar with another person's ways, he or she becomes more predictable and less potentially threatening. Though we may never come to love another person solely through repeated exposure, we may at least feel comfortable in that person's presence. This feeling of comfortable familiarity is a basis on which we can begin to build a friendship.

But although familiarity and proximity may encourage friendship, they are seldom enough to form the basis of a strong relationship. You could probably name several people who live near you and whom you see often yet are not among your close friends. Clearly, something more than proximity and familiarity is needed to generate true friendship. That something more is mutual concern and understanding, a sense that one's personality harmonizes with another's. What causes these positive feelings to develop? Folk wisdom offers two very different answers.

One is captured by the old saying "Opposites attract," meaning that we are drawn to people whose personalities complement our own. But an equally common adage is "Birds of a feather flock together," suggesting that we make friends with those who are most like ourselves. Which of these two sayings, psychologists have wondered, is more accurate?

Research suggests that people who are alike are more attracted to each other than those who are opposites (Byrne and Clore, 1970; Byrne and Griffitt, 1973; Byrne and Lamberth, 1971). In one study, for instance, Donn Byrne and his colleagues asked a large number of college students to complete an attitude questionnaire (Byrne, Ervin, and Lamberth, 1970). They then paired up men and women who were either very similar in attitudes or very different. Each pair was invited to the laboratory, given a small amount of money, and sent to the student union to get a snack and become acquainted. As each couple returned to the lab, the researchers noted how close together they walked. Those who had been matched for similar attitudes tended to walk significantly closer, suggesting greater mutual attraction. And when the subjects were later asked how much they liked their partner, those paired with someone similar in attitudes expressed more positive feelings than those paired with someone with dissimilar opinions.

What explains our attraction to people similar to ourselves? One answer is that people who are like us in attitudes and outlook boost our self-image and provide reassurance that our view of the world is right (Arrowood and Short, 1973; Sanders, 1982). After all, few of us are 100 percent certain of all our opinions. It is pleasant to find someone who agrees with what we think. Thus the support and confirmation that similar-minded people offer one another can make friendship between them very rewarding.

Interpersonal Attraction and Love

In the early 1970s Senator William Proxmire made headlines by strongly questioning the value of many government-funded studies. Among his prime targets were several psychological investigations into the nature and causes of romantic love. As we mentioned in Chapter 1, Proxmire argued that falling in love is a mystery no scientist can possibly unravel. The subject, in his opinion, should be left strictly to song writers and poets. Psychologists, of course, disagree with Proxmire's view. They believe that all human behaviors, including romantic love, are valid topics for scientific inquiry. Let us explore some of the findings psychologists have made in the relatively few years since research on love began.

The Nature of Romantic Love. Twentieth-century Americans are repeatedly exposed to the notion of falling in love. So important is romance in our popular culture that by the time children reach adolescence they have come to believe that falling in love is an inevitable part of growing up. We also tend to think of love as something that comes suddenly, unavoidably, and without our conscious control. Is this a realistic view of how love develops?

The psychoanalyst Carl Jung so believed that love sometimes occurs in just such an explosive fashion that he devised a theory to explain "love at first sight." According to Jung, every man possesses an unconscious representation of the feminine side to his nature, and every woman possesses an unconscious image of the masculine side to herself. When a man or a woman meets a person who closely resembles this ideal image, the result is instantaneous attraction. But as much as Jung's theory may appeal to our romantic notions, there is no empirical evidence to support it. Instead, men and women seem to find, become attracted to, and fall in love with each other in much more mundane ways. In one survey of more than two hundred engaged college students, only 8 percent of

the men and 5 percent of the women reported feeling strong physical attraction for their partner within the first day or two after they met—a far cry from widespread love at first sight. For most of these couples, mutual attraction developed gradually over several months (Rubin, 1973).

Although love may seldom come as suddenly as romantic stories suggest, there are still measurable differences between liking and loving. Psychologist Zick Rubin (1970, 1973) investigated these differences by giving several hundred students a long list of statements that expressed feelings one might have toward a lover or toward a friend. Some of these statements were designed to assess liking; others, more emotional in tone, were designed to assess feelings of love. Some items from this "liking and loving" scale are given in Figure 17.3. The students were asked to indicate which statements expressed their feelings toward their current romantic partner and which ones expressed their feelings about a close friend of the same sex. Romantic partners were both liked and loved. Same-sex friends, however, received high "liking" but low "loving" scores. These results support the idea that the love scale measures something different from liking.

Why Do People Fall in Love? In addition to trying to define the experience of love, psychologists seek to explain *why* people fall in love. One provocative answer is based on Stanley Schachter's theory of emotion, discussed in Chapter 10. As you may recall, Schachter has proposed that the subjective experience of an emotion depends on a person's cognitive appraisal of the situation at the time he or she becomes aware of a racing heart, trembling hands, flushed face, and other bodily sensations of physiological arousal. When the true cause of arousal is unclear, a person may easily misattribute the inner upheaval to virtually any plausible factor in the environment. Applied to falling in love, Schachter's theory suggests that if a person is physiologically aroused for whatever reason but is unsure why that arousal has occurred, that person may search the surroundings to find a cause for these stirred-up feelings, spot an attractive other, and decide that the feelings must be due to the beginnings of love.

Some experiments have supported this **misattribution theory** of falling in love. In one of them, researchers arranged for male subjects to be approached by an attractive woman (a confederate in

Liking

1. *Favorable evaluation.* I think that _____ (my boyfriend or girlfriend) is unusually well-adjusted.

2. *Respect and confidence.* I have great confidence in _____ 's good judgment.

3. *Perceived similarity.* I think that _____ and I are quite similar to each other.

Loving

1. *Attachment.* If I could never be with _____ , I would feel miserable.

2. *Caring.* If _____ were feeling badly, my first duty would be to cheer him (her) up.

3. *Intimacy.* I feel that I can confide in _____ about almost anything.

Figure 17.3 Rubin's love scale items, some of which are shown here, were developed to distinguish between liking and loving in young opposite-sex student couples, but it is interesting to extend the analysis that these scale items make possible to same-sex relationships, relationships between very old people, and relationships between people of different ages. People form strong likes *and* loves outside the romantic context as well as within it. *(From Rubin, 1970.)*

the experiment) as they finished crossing one of two bridges. One bridge was a narrow, rickety structure that swayed in the wind several hundred feet above a rocky canyon. The other was a solid structure only a few feet above a shallow stream. The attractive confederate explained that she was doing a class project, and she wanted the subjects to compose a short story based on a picture she showed them. The men who met her after crossing the rickety bridge expressed more sexual imagery in their stories than did those who met her after crossing the solid bridge. The rickety-bridge subjects were also more likely to telephone the woman later, supposedly to get more information about the study. The researchers explained these results by arguing that the men were physiologically aroused by crossing the frightening bridge, and when they were then approached by an attractive woman, they relabeled their feelings as sexual attraction—a misattribution (Dutton and Aron, 1974).

This "adrenaline makes the heart grow fonder" theory has limitations, however (Kenrick and Cialdini, 1977). When the true reason for physiological arousal is fairly apparent, and when this reason remains salient even after a potential "love object" appears, then little if any misattribution is likely to occur (Kenrick, Cialdini, and Linder, 1979; White, Fishbein, and Rutstein, 1981). These findings tie in nicely with our earlier point that the most salient cues available to people are generally the ones to which they assign causes. When a man has safely crossed a rickety

bridge and becomes distracted by a beautiful woman, it is not surprising that he attributes his still racing heart to the woman rather than to the crossing now behind him. In contrast, if the man had met the woman in the middle of the rickety bridge, while it was swaying dangerously in the wind, it is likely that no misattribution would occur, for the true cause of his arousal would be quite salient.

When Does Love Endure? Once a romantic relationship has formed, can we predict with any accuracy whether it will last or not? Although many people find such predictions difficult, psychologists have found a number of factors that serve as fairly good indicators (Hill, Rubin, and Peplau, 1976). One is how well matched the lovers are in age, intelligence, educational plans, physical attractiveness, and so forth. Having certain things in common seems to help keep couples together. Another factor is the degree of closeness the partners feel toward each other, particularly in a romantic sense. (Scores on Rubin's love scale are better predictors of who will stay together than scores on Rubin's liking scale.) The strength of the woman's feelings are especially important. If the woman feels very much in love with her partner, and the relationship is not unusually one-sided, there is a good chance that the couple will not break up very quickly. Finally, contrary to what might be expected, neither having sexual intercourse nor living together seems to "cement" a love relationship. Couples who

Contrary to popular belief, few couples fall in love at first sight; more often, mutual attraction is a gradual process. *(Ellis Herwig/The Picture Cube.)*

have never had sex, much less lived together, are just as likely to stay together or to break up as their more sexually liberal peers. Apparently these behaviors depend as much on a couple's social attitudes as on the depth of their commitment.

Psychologists have also made some interesting findings regarding those love affairs that do eventually die. One is that in the vast majority of cases—85 percent—the partners see the breakup as being one-sided. Interestingly, too, in more cases than not it is the woman who brings about the split (Rubin, Peplau, and Hill, 1978). Men, apparently, are often more willing than women to hang on to a fading love relationship. Often, too, men are more troubled when an affair finally ends. They tend to report more depression, more loneliness, and more unhappiness than their former partners do. More often than women they cling to the hope that the love may somehow be rekindled. This finding suggests that, contrary to popular stereotypes, men may be in some ways more romantic than women (Hatfield, 1982).

THE PSYCHOLOGY OF PREJUDICE

We know that people are capable of forming strong attachments to each other, attachments of liking, friendship, and love. But humans are also capable of forming deep and intractable hatreds—some of them without any logical basis. Consider the following dialogue:

Mr. X: The trouble with Jews is that they only take care of their own group.
Mr. Y: But the record of the Community Chest campaign shows that they give more generously . . . to the general charities of the community than do non-Jews.

Mr. X: That shows that they are always trying to buy favor and intrude into Christian affairs. They think of nothing but money; that is why there are so many Jewish bankers.
Mr. Y: But a recent study shows that the percentage of Jews in the banking business is negligible. . . .
Mr. X: That's just it; they don't go in for respectable businesses; they are only in the movie business or run night clubs. [Allport, 1954]

Such negative and inflexible attitudes toward members of a minority group, attitudes based on erroneous or incomplete information, are called **prejudices.** Note that this definition stresses three things. First, prejudices involve hostile and negative opinions, usually toward an entire group of people. Second, these opinions are inaccurate; they are formed on faulty or partial information. And third, prejudices are peculiarly resistant to change even in the face of strong contradictory evidence. Because human prejudices are so widespread and can cause so much harm to their targets, psychologists believe it is critically important to study and understand them.

The Nature of Prejudice

Underlying prejudice toward any given group is a negative **stereotype**—a cluster of preconceived beliefs and expectations about how members of that group think and act. Stereotypes are very much like schemas, which we discussed earlier, except that they apply to groups rather than to individuals. To some extent stereotyping is an inevitable attempt to understand and simplify our complex social world. But stereotypes, unfortunately, can become so ingrained that they are accepted without question. Thus we can assume that anyone who has a particular trait (femaleness, for example) *necessarily* has a whole range of other traits (docility, emotionalism, lack of managerial skills) thought to be associated with the first. As a result, stereotypes blind us to individual differences. Even favorable stereotypes are unjust, because they ignore each person's uniqueness. Furthermore, stereotypes can easily become abusive when they are used to justify **discrimination** (the behavioral expression of prejudice). The stereotype of blacks as less intelligent than whites, for instance, has been used to justify denial of equal opportunities.

But how can stereotypes be maintained in the face of so much evidence that they are overgeneralizations? The answer lies partly in the way that human memory works. Remember from Chapter 6, and from our earlier discussion of schemas, that people filter new information through existing knowledge and beliefs. Anything that doesn't fit our preconceptions we often reinterpret or ignore. And anything that *does* confirm our expectations usually makes a strong impression on us. As a result, we tend to think our stereotypes are far more valid than they actually are. There is no truth, for instance, in the common assumption that women are unreliable employees

because they inevitably leave to marry or have children. Yet many people are convinced that this misconception is right partly because they selectively remember behavior that conforms to it (Nisbett and Ross, 1980).

Of course, some pieces of contradictory information are too obvious to ignore (the woman who stays with a company for many years and rises to a position of status and power, the black man who eventually becomes a Supreme Court justice). How does the prejudiced person explain these occurrences? The answer is often with "yes but" reasoning. In one study, male police officers who had been assigned a female partner were asked to evaluate that partner's performance (Milton, 1972). Although most of the men answered that their partner had done a good job, they nevertheless opposed the addition of more women to the police force. "*Yes,* my female partner was good," they admitted, "*but* she's the exception." Or "*Yes,* my female partner was effective on the job, *but* she had to work at it harder than a man would have to." The assumption here is that when a woman succeeds in a "masculine" occupation, the cause must be extraordinary effort, not innate ability. This attributional bias has been found to be quite common (Deaux, 1976; Fiske and Taylor, 1984). It helps prejudiced people to keep seeing the world in stereotyped ways.

Some Common Prejudices

Two of the most widespread prejudices in our society and throughout the world are **sexism** (prejudice directed toward one sex, almost always toward women) and **racism** (prejudice directed toward members of certain racial groups). Although sexism and racism have many things in common (Myrdal, 1944), they are distinctive enough to be considered separately.

Sexism. Throughout recorded history women have been viewed as weak and inferior creatures. Both the Bible and the Koran (the sacred book of the Muslims) are filled with references to man's moral and intellectual preeminence over woman. As the book of Genesis (3:13, 16) explains it:

And the Lord God said unto the woman, What is this that thou has done? And the woman said, The serpent beguiled me, and I did eat. . . . Unto the woman he [God] said, I will greatly multiply thy sorrow and thy conception; in sorrow thou shalt bring forth children; and thy desire shall be to thy husband, and he shall rule over thee.

Even men of the eighteenth-century Enlightenment, who advocated sweeping social reforms, were unwilling to view women as equals. Females, wrote Rousseau in *The Social Contract*, "must be trained to bear the yoke from the first, so that they may not feel it, to master their own caprices and to submit themselves to the will of others."

Today in the United States, despite the outlawing of many forms of discrimination against women, unequal treatment still persists. Men continue to monopolize most of the high-status, high-paying jobs in our society (Brown, 1979). Even when workers of the same age, education, skill, experience, and job tenure are compared, the women *still* earn significantly less than the men (Levitin, Quinn, and Staines, 1973; Treiman and Terrell, 1975). In many other countries the economic position of women is far worse than in the United States. Although women constitute one-half the world's population, they contribute two-thirds of the total working hours, earn one-tenth of the income, and own only one-hundredth of all the property, according to the United Nations Conference on Women.

Despite the fact that behavioral differences between the sexes are not very great (Maccoby and Jacklin, 1974), most people believe that they are. When asked to describe the personality of the "average" male, for instance, people tend to view him as active, aggressive, independent, dominant, competitive, ambitious, and a good decision maker, all traits we associate with competency. In addition, the "average" male is not seen as very tender or demonstrative. Like the John Wayne image, he is believed to be blunt, outspoken, and slow to perceive the feelings of others. The "average" woman, in contrast, is seen as much the opposite. She is believed to be unaggressive, uncompetitive, dependent, passive, submissive, low in ambition, and a generally poor decision maker. Emotionally she is viewed as caring and giving—tactful, quiet, sensitive to others, nurturant, and tender, although her need for security is thought to run high (Broverman et al., 1972). What is startling about these images is how widely held they are. Surveys of children, college students, older adults, clinical psychologists, women as well as men—all yield the same male and female stereotypes (Abramowitz et al., 1973).

How do these stereotypes develop? The process probably begins at the moment of birth, when a baby is proclaimed a boy or a girl. Even though male and female newborns are no different in size, muscle tone, or facial features, most parents and other adults perceive that they are. In one study, for instance, the parents of newborn girls described their infants as smaller, softer, weaker, more delicate, and more fine-featured than did the parents of newborn boys (Rubin, Provenzano, and Luria, 1974). Most parents soon begin to act on these stereotypes, as we saw in Chapter 8. Although sometimes unaware of what they are doing, they pass on to their children many traditional beliefs about what boys and girls are like.

Reinforcing these early learning experiences are the images of males and females portrayed in the mass media. In TV commercials, for instance, men are more likely than women to be the "experts" on the advertised products, whereas women are more likely to be the easily persuaded consumers. Psychologists Sandra and Daryl Bem (1970) believe that such images are so pervasive in our society that many people find it hard to conceive of the sexes in any other way. As a result, even when they try to create more egalitarian sex roles, the traditional sex-typed patterns continue to creep in. This may help explain why even after years of effort to make children's books less sex-role stereotyped, many of them still portray males and females in biased ways (Hoffman, 1982). And these biases have been found to affect the behavior of young readers (Ashby and Wittmaier, 1978). In one study, for instance, nursery school girls who heard a single story about a little girl who had worked hard to achieve were later observed to show more persistence and achievement orientation in their *own* activities (McArthur and Eisen, 1976). This response did *not* occur when the girls had heard a story about an achieving little boy, typical of the stories with which children's books are filled.

Psychologists maintain that as girls are bombarded with traditional female stereotypes, they gradually come to believe and to act upon them. The extent to which adult women are prejudiced against their own sex has been shown in a number of studies. In one, college students were asked to evaluate the course syllabus for a seminar (Linsenmeier and Wortman, 1979). When the seminar leader's expertise in the subject had not been established, women tended to make their evaluations on the basis of sex stereotypes. If the seminar leader was said to be a woman, they rated the syllabus less favorably than if the leader was said to be a man. Clearly, if women see themselves and other women as innately less competent than men, they may be reluctant to seek out challenging opportunities. The ironic result may be that women help to make female inferiority a self-fulfilling prophecy.

To make matters worse, even when women are very achievement-oriented and manage to gain footholds in male-dominated fields, traditional stereotypes about them may continue to hamper their progress. Studies suggest that when a solo woman is given a position of supposed equality within a group of men, the men's perceptions of her femaleness often become exaggerated (Kanter, 1977; Crocker and McGraw, 1984). This is because the solo woman's gender is so salient in such a group. And as happens with any salient feature on which people focus, "femaleness" in this instance comes to be seen as a major cause of the woman's behavior. Thus if the woman is perceptive enough to foresee some critical problem, her male colleagues may attribute her insight to "woman's intuition." Or if the woman delays for valid reasons in making a decision, her male co-workers may interpret her behavior as feminine lack of assertiveness. Such stereotyped perceptions make it hard for women who manage to break into male-dominated fields to be judged on their own personal merits. As a result, they face a serious obstacle to career advancement.

Racism. Evidence of prejudice against racial and ethnic minorities dates back nearly as far as evidence of prejudice against women. In the United States, some degree of prejudice and discrimination has existed against virtually every non-Anglo-Saxon Protestant group. The cost of such prejudice to those who suffer it has been enormous. It can be measured in the dramatically lower life chances among members of the discriminated groups—menial jobs, low incomes, poor housing, inferior education, poor nutrition and health care, high mortality rates. It can also be measured in reduced self-esteem. Not many years ago, for instance, one study found that North American Indians agreed with non-Indians on the adjectives that best described themselves: they selected such words as *lazy, drunkards, quiet,* and *superstitious* (Trimble, 1968).

Psychologists have tried to discover the causes of racial and ethnic prejudices. One theory is that such hatreds naturally result when groups find themselves in competition for valuable but scarce resources.

Thus, according to this view, Israeli Jews and Palestinian Arabs will inevitably despise each other, for they are in competition for the same small piece of land. Likewise, prejudice can be expected when groups compete for jobs but there are not enough positions for everyone. Some support for this prediction is suggested by the fact that, historically, racial bigotry has often increased when job markets have become unusually tight. When Chinese immigrants first came to the United States to help build the western railroads, for instance, construction jobs were plentiful and the Chinese were looked upon as hardworking and industrious. After the Civil War, however, when large numbers of ex-soldiers headed west and jobs became scarce, anti-Oriental sentiment in this country grew dramatically (Aronson, 1980).

Of course, in such real-life situations it is difficult to say whether it was greater economic competition or some other factor that caused racial hatred to increase. Isolating the role that competition plays in promoting prejudice requires a controlled experiment. One such experiment was designed by psychologists Muzafer and Carolyn Sherif (1953). They assigned twelve-year-old boys attending summer camp to one of two groups, the Red Devils or the Bulldogs. After fostering a period of friendly cooperation between the groups, the Sherifs began to pit them against each other in a series of intensely competitive games. The result was a great deal of intergroup hostility. Apparently, fierce competition can indeed initiate prejudice.

But not all psychologists have focused on the interpersonal dynamics that can foster racial bigotry. Others have turned their attention to those processes within the mind of a highly prejudiced person that generate such intense hatreds. One theory is that when people are frustrated by adverse conditions yet are powerless to make things better, they often vent their anger and aggression on the most readily available scapegoat. This tendency has been demonstrated experimentally (Miller and Bugelski, 1948). Researchers measured subjects' attitudes toward various minority groups and then placed them in a frustrating situation: they denied them the chance to see an interesting movie, requiring instead that they complete a long series of difficult tests. When asked again to express their attitudes toward the same minorities, most subjects showed significant increases in prejudice. No such increases were found among control subjects, who had not undergone the frustrating experience.

Some psychologists have wondered whether certain people in a population are more inclined than others to vent their frustrations on scapegoats. One such group of researchers set out after World War II to discover if those Germans who committed atrocities against the Jews had any significant personality traits in common (Adorno et al., 1950). They concluded that deeply prejudiced people are often authoritarian in nature, meaning that they tend to follow unquestioningly the commands of those in authority. The **authoritarian personality** is measured by a test called the Potentiality for Fascism, or F, scale, some items from which are shown in Figure 17.4. Those who score high on the F scale show rigid adherence to conventional values and a preference for strong, antidemocratic leaders. They also tend to hate and fear almost everyone different from themselves. How does such a negative personality develop? One finding is that authoritarian people often come from families with a domineering father and a mother who punishes disobedience harshly (Harris, Gough, and Martin, 1950). Threats, physical coercion, and fear of reprisals are used to maintain strict discipline. Parental love is almost always contingent on "good" behavior. As a result, children in such families presumably grow up to be hostile toward yet fearful of authority figures, and also highly insecure. These traits incline them to displace frustrations outward onto others less powerful than themselves.

But the problem with the authoritarian personality as a general explanation of prejudice is that it cannot explain why bigotry is more prevalent in certain geographic areas, even though scores on the F scale are quite evenly distributed throughout a population. In some instances prejudice cannot be explained by economic competition either, for it is sometimes high even when jobs are plentiful. Cultural learning theories of prejudice can shed much light in these cases. They argue that racial prejudice is often a cultural norm. As such, it is taught to children by parents, teachers, peers, and others in precisely the same fashion as any other socially prescribed standard. Children, for their part, internalize prevailing racial biases because in so doing they are rewarded with so-cial approval. The end result is that the same racial prejudices are passed on repeatedly, generation after generation. Evidence to support this view comes from the fact that children's racial attitudes *do* tend to match those of their parents (Ashmore and DelBoca, 1976). What's more, this cultural learning process appears to be strengthened by children's natural tendency to avoid those they are taught to dislike. In one study, for instance, white youngsters with highly prejudiced parents were less likely than peers to interact with black schoolmates. As a result, they had less of a chance to disconfirm their negative racial stereotypes than did youngsters from less prejudiced homes (Stephen and Rosenfield, 1978).

Undoubtedly, a full explanation of prejudice must include all three of the processes we have discussed here—unresolvable competition, frustration leading to aggression, and the learning of cultural norms. But no matter how prejudice arises, one question is central: How can racial bigotry and discrimination be reduced? Trying to change negative stereotypes simply by pointing out their errors very seldom works. As we saw earlier, people tend to ignore or distort new information that conflicts with their existing beliefs. In one study of junior high school students, for example, black youngsters were convinced that their white classmates were conceited and felt themselves superior to blacks (Schofield, 1981). As a result, when a white student offered assistance in a genuine display of friendship, a black student invariably took this as "proof" of white conceit. No matter what a target of prejudice does, therefore, *some* way can usually be found to cast those behaviors in an unflattering light. At the very least, the actions can be rationalized away

1. Sex crimes such as rape and attacks on children deserve more than mere imprisonment; such criminals ought to be publicly whipped, or worse.

2. Most people don't realize how much our lives are controlled by plots hatched in secret places.

3. Obedience and respect for authority are the most important virtues children should learn.

Figure 17.4 Items from the F scale. A person who agreed strongly with items such as these would be classified as a highly authoritarian personality. (*After Adorno et al., 1950.*)

with simple "yes but" reasoning. How, then, can prejudices be combatted?

One promising approach is to encourage interaction among the races in ways that foster mutual understanding and respect. For this purpose, not just any form of interaction will do. Before the civil rights movement, generations of blacks and whites interacted on a daily basis, yet little reduction in prejudice occurred. Psychologist Stuart Cook (1979) has identified five conditions of interracial contact that facilitate favorable attitude change. One is equal status. If whites encounter blacks only in the low-status roles of porter, janitor, domestic servant, and the like, traditional stereotypes will probably persist. A second favorable condition is the chance for people of different races to get to know each other as people. Simply living next door to a minority family will not often reduce prejudice unless mutual involvement is encouraged. Such involvement can sometimes be promoted by a third important condition: the existence of norms prescribing friendliness and courtesy. For instance, if the belief that neighbors should act "neighborly" overrides all others, a setting conducive to lessening prejudice exists. Fourth, prejudice is also likely to diminish when individuals repeatedly fail to conform to the stereotypes about their groups. Even better is for people of different races to find themselves quite similar in interests, backgrounds, values, and personality traits.

Finally, and most important, situations that encourage interdependence rather than competition are highly effective in decreasing prejudice. This is how the Sherifs eventually reduced hostility between their two groups of campers. They created incidents that required the boys to cooperate closely. Soon the youngsters were making friends across group boundaries. A similar tactic was used by psychologist Elliot Aronson and his colleagues in an effort to reduce interracial conflict in newly integrated fifth- and sixth-grade classrooms. Aronson set up special study groups in which each group member contributed part of the lesson. All group members therefore had to cooperate if they wanted to pass their exams. The results of Aronson's experiment were dramatic. Within about a week, most children had abandoned the old racial put-downs in favor of much more positive interactions (Aronson and Osherow, 1980). Thus, although overcoming racial prejudice is seldom easy, the right circumstances can make a big difference.

in depth: A Psychological Look at Affirmative Action

Recently the city of Detroit announced a new plan concerning employment in its police force. Historically the Detroit police department has been dominated by whites, even though the city's population is over 50 percent black. The new plan called for black and white officers to be hired and promoted in equal numbers until eventually the racial ratio—all the way up through the ranks—would be an evenly balanced 1:1.

The Detroit plan is an example of **affirmative action,** a program designed to compensate for years of discrimination by giving minority groups special consideration in hiring, job training, and school admissions. Affirmative action has its basis in the Civil Rights Act of 1964, which sought to eliminate biases based on race, ethnic background, or sex in both education and employment. The framers of the act realized that simply declaring discrimination illegal was not going to be enough. Decades of past discrimination made it very hard for minority members to outqualify whites. There were also emotional reactions that had to be dealt with. White employers considering equally qualified job candidates often felt more "comfortable" selecting a white applicant. Thus, in order to combat deeply held prejudices and a history of past injustice, it seemed that increased admission, hiring, and promotion of minorities should be made a national goal. Accordingly, the federal government has asked schools and businesses to survey their organizations, find areas where minorities are greatly underrepresented, and make efforts to rectify racial and sexual biases. No one is compelled to lower standards or to accept unqualified candidates. All that is required is a "good faith" effort to give minority members truly equal chances.

There is evidence that affirmative action has been successful. According to the U.S. Bureau of Labor Statistics, for example, in 1972 women constituted only 3.6 percent of all skilled craft workers and only 9.1 percent of all engineers. By 1982, however, these percentages had nearly doubled: women were filling 6.3 percent of skilled craft positions and 18.8 percent of engineering jobs. Similar patterns can be seen among racial minorities. In 1972, members of racial minorities made up only 4.3 percent of all computer specialists and a mere 3.4 percent of all engineers. By

1982, in contrast, 9.9 percent of computer specialists were members of racial minorities, as were 7.3 percent of all engineers. Although it is hard to say how much of this improvement was due *specifically* to affirmative action, it is clear that many occupations have become more open to minorities during the years when affirmative action has been in force.

It is likely that these gains are partly responsible for a recent wave of feeling against affirmative action among some members of dominant American groups. They question whether there is still a need for affirmative action programs. In one recent survey, 73 percent of those interviewed believed that blacks and members of other racial minorities already have an equal chance to get ahead in our society (Kluegel and Smith, 1982). Over half of white Americans also believed that affirmative action had resulted in "reverse discrimination." They felt that qualified whites are often passed over for desirable positions in favor of less qualified minority-group members. How do psychologists who see a continuing need for affirmative action answer these kinds of criticism?

One way is to point to employment statistics, which show that although important gains have been made toward equalized opportunities, minorities are by no means being given unfair advantages. In 1976, for example, blacks in professional and managerial positions had an average 16.6 years of education, whereas whites in similar jobs had only 15.8 years of schooling (Ryan, 1981). If blacks really enjoyed unfair preferential treatment, wouldn't we expect them to be *less* qualified than their white counterparts? Consider, too, the comparative rates of unemployment between the races. In 1960 (before affirmative action) the black unemployment rate was 85 percent higher than the white rate. By 1984, after two decades of affirmative action, the racial unemployment gap had not narrowed, but had widened. The black rate was now 157 percent higher than the white. If affirmative action had really created reverse discrimination, how could such figures be explained?

Psychologists also respond to the critics of affirmative action by pointing to the good that affirmative action can do in getting people of different races to change their negative opinions of each other. As we saw earlier, placing people in situations where cooperation makes sense is an excellent way to encourage them to see one another more favorably. Particularly effective should be situations in which people are not really *forced* to cooperate. This is in keeping with Daryl Bem's self-perception theory of attitude change (Bem, 1967). As you will remember, Bem argues that people often infer their own attitudes by observing their own behavior. Thus a prejudiced white man who observes himself cooperating freely with black and female co-workers may conclude to himself: "I'm treating these people in a reasonably friendly manner, so perhaps my feelings toward them are more positive than I thought." In contrast, if the company *insists* that the man be cooperative, on threat of demo-

Affirmative action programs give people of different races an opportunity to interact and perhaps to change their unfavorable views of each other. (Kevin Horan/Picture Group.)

tion or suspension, he is likely to attribute friendly behavior to these pressures and not to undergo any decrease in prejudice. The law's provision that allows organizations much freedom in establishing their own affirmative action goals and programs takes advantage of this common tendency to infer a change in attitudes on the basis of a voluntary change in behavior.

This is not to deny, however, that affirmative action can also have negative effects. For one thing, there is the danger that those in traditionally dominant groups will begin to view successful members of minorities as undeserving of what they achieve. Attribution theory predicts this result, as you may recall (Heider, 1958; Kelley, 1967). When members of a group perform in what we consider an uncharacteristic way (women or blacks rising to positions of wealth and status, for instance), we tend to attribute the cause to situational factors rather than to innate talents and traits (Fiske and Taylor, 1984). Affirmative action provides one obvious situational factor on which observers can focus in such instances. The tendency to do so has been demonstrated in a recent study (Garcia, Erskine, and Hawn, 1981). Subjects were given information about a graduate school candidate and asked to explain the school's response to that person's application. Sometimes the candidate was Mexican-American; at other times he was white. In some cases the school had an affirmative action program; in other cases it did not. Sometimes the school accepted the candidate; at other times he was rejected. As you might expect, personal qualifications tended to be discounted if a Mexican-American applicant was accepted at a school with an affirmative action program. In this condition only, the candidate's success was usually attributed to preferential treatment. This attribution bias is very distressing to members of minority groups. Thomas Sowell, a prominent black critic of affirmative action, has written, "What affirmative action has done is to destroy the legitimacy of what had already been achieved by making all black achievements look like questionable accomplishments, or even outright gifts" (Sowell, 1976, p. 64).

Others fear that affirmative action could do further damage by increasing white hostility toward racial minorities. The principle of psychological reactance we talked about earlier suggests why this might happen (Brehm, 1966). When a goal is blocked and we perceive that our freedom of choice is being limited, the unattainable goal becomes more attractive and we may respond with frustration and aggression (Worchel and Brehm, 1971). Thus psychological reactance helps explain the violence that sometimes erupts when schools are desegregated (Austin, 1979). The same response may inadvertently be sparked by affirmative action, critics say.

At the very least, whites hostile toward affirmative action may respond with "tokenism." They may provide minority members with a share of the better-paying jobs but fail to give them any real status or power within the company. Members of minority groups who complain of having "do-nothing" jobs that carry big titles are often victims of tokenism. The effects can be quite harmful to personal satisfaction and self-esteem. In one recent study, for example, women managers were asked how much the following factors had contributed to their being hired: ability, experience, education, and sex. Those who believed they were hired mainly because of their sex were less committed to their companies, less satisfied with their duties and co-workers, and more uncertain about what others expected of them (Chacko, 1982).

Thus we see that there are many complicated issues and problems associated with affirmative action, despite the enormous social benefits that such programs offer. The underlying goals of affirmative action conform to our democratic values. Affirmative action seeks to give all people fair access to educational and economic resources. It seeks to improve relations between mutually prejudiced groups by promoting equal-status, cooperative interactions among them. But these goals are not easily achieved. Mistaken assumptions, inaccurate perceptions, and halfhearted compliance with the law all impose obstacles. It is hoped that psychologists will continue to identify means by which these obstacles may be overcome.

in depth

SUMMARY

1. Social psychologists seek to understand how the presence and behavior of other people influence the ways we think and act. One area they investigate is **attitudes**—learned, relatively enduring predisposi-

tions to respond to given people, events, or objects in favorable or unfavorable ways.

2. How attitudes can be changed is a topic that has generated much research. One approach has been to study the important factors underlying **persuasive communications**—messages consciously intended to change opinions. Another approach has involved the concept of **cognitive consistency,** the assumption that people seek compatibility among their various thoughts and actions. When such compatibility is lacking (when attitudes and behaviors are discrepant), people presumably experience discomfort, which they then try to reduce, often by changing attitudes. The most influential cognitive consistency theory is the theory of **cognitive dissonance,** proposed by Leon Festinger. One alternative to it is Daryl Bem's **self-perception theory.** Bem argues that we sometimes infer our attitudes by observing our behavior and the circumstances surrounding it, much as we infer the attitudes of others.

3. People often resist attitude change. One important reason is **psychological reactance,** whereby a person who finds a particular line of action blocked feels increased motivation to engage in the blocked behavior.

4. Our perceptions of other people and the qualities we attribute to them have attracted the interest of psychologists for some time. First impressions are strong enough to influence our subsequent actions, which in turn can affect others' response to us. One factor that shapes a first impression is the **primacy effect,** whereby the traits we encounter first tend to dominate. Another factor that influences a first impression is physical attractiveness. We tend to attribute to attractive people a whole set of desirable traits. A major reason why we form first impressions on the basis of such scanty information is that our information-processing capacities are limited. As a result, we tend to form **schemas** of new acquaintances, which we then use to filter and help interpret additional information.

5. People are constantly trying to figure out the causes of others' behavior. According to Fritz Heider, the first to study **causal attribution,** behavior can be attributed either to a disposition or to a situational cause. Jones and Davis argue that behavior that is in some way unexpected provides the greatest insight into a person's nature. Psychologist Harold Kelley proposes that we can sometimes attribute meaning even to initially ambiguous behavior if we have time to consider consistency, distinctiveness, and consensus information.

6. Frequently we make errors in causal attributions. One, the **fundamental attribution error,** is the tendency when interpreting others' behavior to give too much weight to personality factors and not enough to situational ones. When it comes to assessing our own behavior, however, we are apt to attribute it to environmental causes. This common difference in attributions is called the **actor-observer bias.** One exception to it is the inclination to take credit for our good deeds while finding situational excuses for our bad ones. This is called the **self-serving bias.**

7. Social psychologists have also studied human friendships and love. Among the factors that can encourage two people to become friends are physical proximity, repeated exposure to one another, and the fact that they have many attitudes in common.

8. Contrary to popular images, psychologists have found that love is a feeling that seldom comes suddenly. Instead, it usually develops gradually over several months. One theory of why people fall in love is Stanley Schachter's **misattribution theory,** whereby physiological arousal due to another cause is mistaken for feelings of love. Other researchers, however, have pointed out that there are definite limits to the circumstances under which such a process can occur.

9. At the opposite pole from attachment to another person is **prejudice,** a negative and inflexible attitude based on erroneous or incomplete information. Prejudice, which is usually directed toward an entire group of people, involves an underlying negative **stereotype**—a cluster of preconceived beliefs and expectations about the way members of the disliked group think and act. Stereotypes are often used to justify **discrimination,** the behavioral expression of prejudice. Stereotypes are maintained in the face of much contradictory evidence partly because we tend to focus on information that supports existing beliefs.

10. One widespread form of prejudice is **sexism,** directed against members of one sex, almost always women. Influenced by early family learning experiences that are reinforced by images in the media, most people—including most women—come to accept on some level prevailing sex-role stereotypes.

11. **Racism** is prejudice against racial and ethnic minorities. One theory is that it arises from competition over scarce resources. Another is that frustration causes people in adverse conditions to vent their anger on a scapegoat. A third is that racism is simply the product of coming to learn the norms and values of one's society. Psychological research has provided some valuable insights into how racial prejudices might be reduced.

12. One of our national responses to sexism and racism consists of **affirmative action** programs, designed to compensate for years of discrimination by giving minorities some special consideration in hiring, job training, and school admissions. Although affirmative action offers many potential benefits to the targets of prejudice and to society as a whole, there have been some negative reactions to it, which psychologists can help us to understand.

SUGGESTED READINGS

ARONSON, E. *The social animal.* 3d ed. New York: W. H. Freeman, 1980.

This book, which won an American Psychological Association National Media award, is an engaging, easy-to-read introduction to social psychology.

BERSCHEID, E., and WALSTER, E. H. *Interpersonal attraction.* 2d ed. Reading, Mass.: Addison-Wesley, 1978.

The authors share, in an engaging way, what social psychology has learned about the causes of interpersonal attraction and the nature of love.

CIALDINI, R. *Influence: How and why people agree to things.* New York: Morrow, 1984.

This original and ground-breaking book acquaints readers with the fascinating ways in which people influence one another.

FISKE, S., and TAYLOR, S. *Social cognition.* Reading, Mass.: Addison-Wesley, 1984.

A scholarly yet readable discussion of such major topics in the field of social cognition as attribution, schemas, and social inferences.

SCHNEIDER, D. J., HASTORF, A. H., and ELLSWORTH, P. C. *Person perception.* 2d ed. Reading, Mass.: Addison-Wesley, 1979.

This discussion of how we perceive other people emphasizes attribution processes—that is, how we make judgments about the causes of behavior.

ZIMBARDO, P. G., EBBESEN, E. B., and MASLACH, C. *Influencing attitudes and changing behavior.* 2d ed. Reading, Mass.: Addison-Wesley, 1977.

An extremely accessible and interesting discussion of attitudes and attitude change.

18

SOCIAL INFLUENCE AND THE HUMAN ENVIRONMENT

Alexander Calder, *Large Spiny*, 1966.

On March 16, 1968, three platoons of American soldiers, collectively known as Charlie Company, swept into the South Vietnamese village of My Lai and proceeded to kill several hundred unarmed civilians—women, children, and old men. When reports of the massacre reached the United States, most citizens reacted with outrage and horror. How could these men, reportedly normal, decent "all-American boys," have committed such an atrocity? In the investigation that followed, it was revealed that the soldiers of Charlie Company, although arriving in Vietnam only a month earlier, had already sustained heavy casualties. Frightened by the dangers of entering My Lai, which was thought to be an enemy stronghold, upset by the loss of their comrades, and eager for revenge, the soldiers seemingly shot without thinking. Although the civilians offered no resistance, the Americans set fire to huts, drove the villagers into open areas, and began to shoot everyone. Some of the men reported that they had been following the orders of their leader, Lieutenant William Calley. Others said they had simply been following the example of others, who had started to shoot the peasants trying to flee. Most of the soldiers joined in the shooting, even firing upon children at close range. Of those who did not fire, not one attempted to stop the slaughter. They stood by without protest as bodies piled up in ditches and the village was burned to the ground.

The My Lai massacre was one of America's darkest moments in the long and controversial Vietnam war. As you will see later in this chapter, it is a disturbing illustration of the social psychological perspective we introduced earlier. How we think and act is not just a product of our inner dispositions. Although you may feel that the men of Charlie Company must have been cruel and without conscience, this most probably was not the case (remember the fundamental attribution error we talked about in Chapter 17). It is more accurate to say that these were basically ordinary people responding to very extraordinary circumstances. In fact, if you had been a member of Charlie Company, there is a good chance that you would have responded in much the same way. Hard to believe? Most people think so, but most people are not social psychologists. This chapter examines some of the powerful social forces that psychological research shows can sometimes make people behave in ways they would never expect to behave.

Whereas Chapter 17 focused primarily on how social circumstances shape our attitudes, perceptions, and feelings, this chapter focuses mainly on how social situations influence the way we *act*. Of course, it is difficult to make distinctions, because thoughts, emotions, and behaviors are all intimately interrelated; yet this chapter, in comparison with the previous one, looks at social forces that tend to affect people's overt actions. We begin with two behavioral patterns of major concern to social psychologists: conformity and obedience. Provocative findings in both these areas explain much about the events at My Lai. We then turn to the topic of human groups and their influence. If you have ever wondered how prisoners of war can be brainwashed, or what makes people join a religious cult, some of your questions will be answered here. Next we examine the diverse causes of human aggression and altruism. In these sections you will find that the many social forces that influence people can be harnessed for good or ill. Finally, we explore some aspects of environmental psychology, the study of people and their surroundings. Does the worker exposed to the constant drone of heavy machinery suffer any psychological effects from this noise? Does the person who lives in a densely populated city experience stress as a result of overcrowding? Environmental psychologists, as you will learn, provide some fascinating answers.

GOING ALONG WITH OTHERS

Most Americans insist that if they had lived in Germany during World War II, they would never have gone along with Adolph Hitler's policy of exterminating the Jews. Yet hundreds of Germans not only passively accepted this policy, they actively helped to carry it out. Could they all have been mentally deranged and sadistic, as our attributional biases lead us to suspect? As in the case of the My Lai massacre, the answer is, Probably not. There are social forces powerful enough to make average people publicly support a view they do not really believe in, or commit an act that in other circumstances would be morally out of the question. To understand what these powerful social forces are, we will investigate two behaviors—conformity and obedience.

Conformity to Prevailing Norms

Conformity is the tendency to shift one's opinions or actions to correspond with those of other people because of implicit or explicit social pressure (Kiesler and Kiesler, 1969). An extreme example of conformity occurred at My Lai. Under the enormous fear, stress, and confusion of battle, some of the men in Charlie Company simply followed the behavior of their fellow soldiers who had begun firing. As one soldier put it, "I looked around and saw everyone shooting. I didn't know what to do, so I started shooting" (*Time*, December 5, 1969). Although the consequences of conformity are seldom this devastating, essentially the same psychological process underlies many of the choices we make every day. Have you ever found yourself ridiculing someone who considers you a friend because others whom you admire were making fun of that person? If so, you have displayed conformity. Note that when you conform, you are not necessarily convinced that what you are saying or doing is right. You may even feel inside that your actions are wrong. But you outwardly behave in a certain manner because you believe that others prefer or even demand that you do so.

Social psychologist Solomon Asch (1951) revealed the power of conformity in a classic series of experiments. If you had been a subject in one of Asch's studies, this is what would have happened to you: You and seven other students report to a classroom for an experiment on visual judgment. The experimenter displays two large white cards like the ones shown in Figure 18.1. On one card is a single vertical line, which is to serve as a standard. On the other card are three vertical lines of different lengths. You are simply to determine which of the three lines is the same length as the standard line. The experiment opens uneventfully. The subjects give their answers in the order in which they are seated, you being next to last. On the first comparison everyone chooses the same line. The second set of cards is shown, and once again the choice is unanimous. The judgments seem very easy, and you settle in for what you expect will be a rather boring experiment.

On the third trial, however, something strange happens. The first person says that line 1 matches the standard, even though it is obvious to you that line 2 is the correct choice. The second person agrees with great certainty that line 1 is the right answer, and so do the third, fourth, fifth, and sixth subjects. Now it is your turn, and you are faced with a dilemma. Your own eyes unmistakenly tell you that line 2 is the correct response, but six other people have unanimously and confidently selected line 1. What should you do? Stand alone as a minority of one, or go along with the unanimous majority? If you think you would stick to your initial judgment, you may well be wrong. Actual

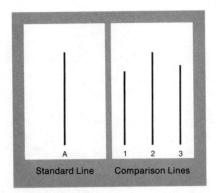

Figure 18.1 The stimuli in a single trial in Asch's experiment. The subject must state which of the comparison lines he or she judges to be the same length as the standard. The discrimination is easy to make: Control subjects (those who made the judgments without any group pressure) chose line 2 as correct more than 99 percent of the time. *(After Asch, 1951.)*

A

Standard Line   Comparison Lines

1   2   3

subjects in this experiment were presented with twelve "critical" trials (ones in which the majority agreed on an obviously wrong answer) interspersed with many trials in which the other participants (all confederates in the experiment) chose the correct line. Out of all the answers to critical trials given by a total of fifty subjects, about a third were conforming responses. A solid majority of subjects—roughly 75 percent—conformed at least some of the time. Note that this experiment contained situational factors that we might expect to *lower* the pressure to conform. The confederates were complete strangers to the subject (with no claim to personal loyalty), and they were the subject's peers in status and intelligence (not superiors whose opinions might carry special weight). For these and other reasons some psychologists suspect that Asch's work may reveal just the tip of the conformity iceberg.

What accounts for such frequent conformity? Part of the answer has to do with the way this experiment was designed. For one thing, the judgments of the confederates were unanimous. Not one gave even a hint that another answer might be possible. In variations of his original study, Asch found that the extent of group consensus was indeed an important factor. When just one confederate out of six gave the correct answer, the proportion of conforming responses on the part of subjects dropped dramatically to only 5 percent (Asch, 1956). In addition, the fact that Asch's subjects had to interact with the confederates face to face apparently made it more difficult for them to deviate from the group. When people are allowed to respond anonymously—when, for example, they sit in a private compartment and indicate their answer by pressing a button—they conform much less frequently (Deutsch and Gerard, 1955). Subsequent research has identified other factors (not present in

Asch's study) that also tend to increase conformity. For instance, being lower in status than other group members, or having generally low self-esteem, wanting to belong to a group but not feeling totally accepted, or knowing that you will have to interact with group members in the future can all make a person more likely to conform (Raven and French, 1958; Aronson and Osherow, 1980; Dittes and Kelley, 1956; Kiesler, Zanna, and De Salvo, 1966). Conformity likewise increases when the "right" way to answer or behave is very ambiguous. The less sure people are of what they should be doing, the more apt they are to follow the lead of others.

From the comments made by Asch's subjects in postexperiment interviews, it is clear that many realized their conforming answers had been wrong. One subject who conformed in eleven out of twelve trials opened the interview by saying: "If I'd been first I probably would have responded differently." This was his way of saying that he had known perfectly well what the correct answers were, but he was still unable to contradict the group. Such findings have relevance to the My Lai incident. The soldiers of Charlie Company knew that their actions violated guidelines they had learned during their training. But this knowledge did not prevent them from killing the villagers. The tendency to conform is not eliminated merely because the group response is known to be inappropriate.

The conformity of subjects in Asch's experiment is sometimes called **compliance**—an outward yielding to the group consensus, while inwardly retaining one's own opinions (Kelman, 1958, 1961). The major motivation for compliance is fear of negative consequences. Many of Asch's subjects probably feared looking foolish if they deviated from the group. Similarly, many Germans who complied with Hitler's policy of persecuting the Jews probably feared that protesting would endanger their own lives. You may be wondering, however, just how powerful such negative consequences normally are. After all, we do not live in Nazi Germany, where failure to comply might

By dressing alike, these business-men are demonstrating compliance with an occupational dress code; failure to comply might have negative consequences, such as loss of professional prestige or lack of career advancement. But this compliance does not necessarily indicate conformity to any other standard of behavior or belief. *(Abigail Heyman/ Archive Pictures.)*

be punished severely. Were Asch's nonconforming subjects really made to feel so psychologically uncomfortable? What actually happens to people who don't go along with the group?

The negative outcomes are often greater than many people think. Research shows that the nonconformer is usually ostracized in subtle and not-so-subtle ways. For instance, when conventionally and unconventionally dressed college students asked shoppers in a supermarket to change a dime for two nickels, the unconventional-looking students were much more likely to be shunned (Raymond and Unger, 1972). Far worse are the fates of nonconformers who deviate from the standards of those in positions of power. Hospital staffs, for example, expect their patients to be passive, cooperative, and unquestioning of their treatments (Taylor, 1979). Those who behave otherwise—who demand information and an active role in their own care—are often regarded as troublemakers. Frequently their complaints are not taken seriously, and sometimes they are tranquilized to make them easier to manage (Lorber, 1975). Thus, complying with group expectations in order to avoid unpleasant outcomes is often a very sensible path to take.

There are other types of conformity besides compliance, however, which makes an understanding of this subject even more complex (Kelman, 1958, 1961). A second pattern is conformity through **identification**—the tendency to go along with others because we admire and wish to be like them. A young German soldier who treats Jewish prisoners cruelly because he wants to be similar to officers he greatly respects is conforming through identification. Conformity can also involve **internalization,** or coming to accept others' views and actions as appropriate and right. If our young German soldier not only mimics his superiors' actions, but actually believes their cruelty toward Jews is justified, his conformity is partly a matter of internalized prejudices. These different types of conformity help us to predict how enduring a person's behavior is likely to be. For instance, the person who is merely complying will probably stop if the threat of negative consequences is lifted. In contrast, the person who is conforming because of internalization is much less likely to change his or her behavior.

Some social critics have argued that in modern society, with its large organizations that require great reliance on others, pressures to conform have increased (Riesman, 1950; Whyte, 1956). This trend, they maintain, is largely negative because it reduces individuality, personal initiative, and independence. Others, however, are not so quick to indict conformity.

Conformity, after all, can encourage people to perform socially valued acts. It can also fulfill such important personal needs as the need to be liked and accepted. As one social psychologist has commented, "The person who refused to accept anyone's word of advice on any topic whatsoever would probably make just as big a botch of life . . . as the person who always conformed" (Collins, 1970, p. 21).

in depth   Research on Obedience

After the My Lai massacre had been made public, the men of Charlie Company were asked to explain their brutal assault. A response familiar from the Nuremberg trials of Nazi war criminals some twenty years earlier was heard again and again: "I was simply following orders." As one young man remarked, "Well, hell, I was just following the orders of my officer like any good soldier—what's the good of having officers if they've nobody to obey them?" (*Time*, December 5, 1969). To many observers, however, such explanations are not acceptable. How, they ask, could anyone with a conscience have obeyed such a blatantly inhumane demand?

One social psychologist who has extensively studied why people follow orders to do cruel or immoral things is Stanley Milgram (1963, 1965b). Milgram's research has shown that many "average" people—people who would consider involvement in the My Lai massacre unthinkable—might nevertheless inflict severe pain on their fellow humans if an authority figure told them to do so. Milgram's area of research is the process called **obedience**—following the specific commands of a person in authority. (Obedience differs from conformity in that it is a response to explicit instructions, not just to implicit social pressures.) Sometimes obedience serves constructive purposes. Society could not function if most people disobeyed the laws requiring them to pay their taxes or to stop at traffic lights. But at other times obedience demands that we do things we feel are wrong. Such *destructive obedience* was the focus of Milgram's investigations.

Milgram's Initial Experiment. Milgram's subjects were men of different ages and occupations, but all had one thing in common: They had answered a request for people to participate in a study on learning at Yale University (Milgram, 1963). Upon arriving at the laboratory, each man was introduced to his supposed co-subject: a mild-mannered, likable man of about fifty, who was actually a confederate in the experiment. The two were asked to draw lots to determine who would be the "teacher" and who would be the "learner." The drawing, of course, was rigged. The real subject always became the teacher.

The experimenter, a rather stern man in a gray laboratory coat, then explained the study's purpose and procedure. The experiment, he said, was designed to investigate the effects of punishment on learning. The teacher was to read a list of word pairs to the learner, who was supposed to memorize them. Then the teacher was to give the first word in each pair, plus four possible second word choices from which the learner could select. Since the teacher and the learner would not be located in the same room, the learner was to indicate his choice of the correct word by pressing one of four buttons on a panel before him. This would activate a corresponding light on the teacher's control panel. Every time the learner made a mistake, the teacher was to punish him by administering electric shock from an authentic-looking shock generator. The generator had thirty clearly marked voltage switches, ranging from 15 to 450 volts. Beneath the switches, verbal labels indicated the intensity of the shock, beginning with slight shock and progressing through moderate, strong, very strong, intense, extremely intense, and severe (also marked "Danger"), and ending with the most severe of all, ominously labeled "XXX." With each additional mistake the learner made, the teacher was to increase the shock by one level, or 15 volts.

Everyone then proceeded to the room where the learner would sit. The teacher watched while the learner was securely strapped into a large chair and an electrode (presumably connected to the shock generator) was fastened to his wrist. The experimenter and teacher then returned to the generator room, where the teacher was given a mild "sample shock." Although the shock appeared to be produced by the generator, in actual fact it came from a 45 volt battery located nearby. The generator itself was an utter phoney, incapable of producing anything except buzzing and clicking sounds. In the mind of the teacher, however, the sample shock "proved" the machine's authenticity. The learning trials were now ready to begin.

The experimental plan called for the learner to

make many mistakes, requiring the teacher to administer increasingly severe shocks. If the teacher proceeded up to 300 volts (the highest level in the "intense shock" range), the learner would pound on the wall in protest. At 315 volts ("extremely intense shock") the learner would pound loudly again and then fall silent. After this, no more lights would flash on the teacher's panel in answer to his word-pair questions. If the teacher became puzzled as to how to proceed in this situation, the experimenter would instruct him to treat the absence of a response as a wrong response and continue raising the voltage. If at any point the teacher asked to stop the procedure, the experimenter would tell him to continue with a number of standardized commands ranging from a stern "Please go on" to an emphatic "You have no choice, you *must* go on." If the teacher still refused to obey, the experiment would immediately end.

How long do you think most subjects continued to deliver what they believed to be painful and increasingly dangerous electric shocks to a defenseless victim? When Milgram posed this same question to a group of psychology majors, they confidently predicted that few, if any, subjects would go beyond the "very strong shock" level—that is, they would never get to the point where the learner had to pound on the wall for release. A group of psychiatrists offered similar opinions. They felt that only 4 percent of the subjects would continue to shock the learner when he failed to respond (at 315 volts) and less than 1 percent

would administer the highest possible shock. Do you agree with these predictions? Most people do, which is why the true results are so disturbing. Out of a total of forty subjects, twenty-six, or 65 percent, obeyed the experimenter all the way to the very highest voltage level (see Figure 18.2).

These men were not sadists. In fact, most showed signs of severe emotional strain and psychological conflict during the experiment. They trembled, stuttered, groaned, perspired heavily, bit their lips, laughed nervously, and dug their fingernails into their palms. They frequently asked if they might please stop. But when the experimenter asked them to continue, they obeyed him. As one observer who watched the proceedings through a one-way mirror related:

> I observed a mature and initially poised businessman enter the laboratory smiling and confident. Within 20 minutes he was reduced to a twitching, stuttering wreck, who was rapidly approaching a point of nervous collapse. He constantly pulled on his earlobe and twisted his hands. At one point he pushed his fist into his forehead and muttered: "Oh God, let's stop it." And yet he continued to respond to every word of the experimenter and obeyed to the end (quoted in Milgram, 1963, p. 377).

Follow-Up Research: What Factors Influence Obedience? What could have prompted such an ex-

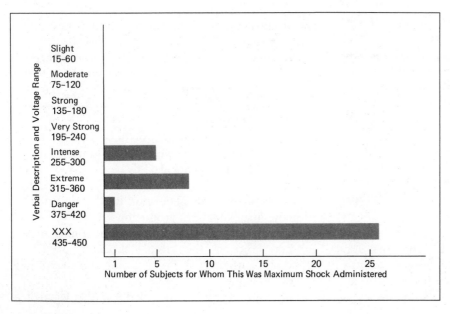

Figure 18.2 Results of Stanley Milgram's classic experiment on obedience. Subjects were told to administer increasing amounts of shock to a "learner" on the pretext that scientists were studying the effects of punishment on learning. Of forty experimental subjects, all administered shocks scaled "intense" or higher, and only fourteen refused to go all the way to the most severe, "XXX" shock level. *(After Milgram, 1963.)*

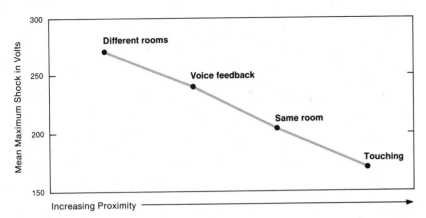

Figure 18.3 This graph of the results of some of Milgram's studies on obedience shows that the closer the subject was to the victim, the less the amount of shock he was willing to administer, despite the experimenter's demands that he continue. With increased proximity, there was a decrease in compliance. *(After Milgram, 1974.)*

traordinary degree of obedience? Milgram (1965b, 1974) designed a series of follow-up experiments in an effort to find out. In an early pilot study he had noticed that when the victim's outline was visible through an opaque glass partition, the subject always averted his eyes. Could it be that the remoteness of the victim in the experiment we just described made it easier for subjects to obey? Milgram investigated this possibility by setting up three new conditions. In one, the learner was again in a separate room from the subject, but this time the subject could hear groans escalating to agonized screams as he increased the shocks. In another arrangement, the victim was moved to the same room as the subject and seated only eighteen inches from him. In the final condition, the subject not only sat close to the victim but was also required to force the victim's hand onto a shock plate in order to administer the punishment. As Figure 18.3 shows, the maximum shock that subjects delivered decreased steadily as contact with the victim— auditory, visual, and physical—increased. Still, even in the final condition, a full 30 percent of the subjects delivered the highest possible voltage.

Milgram also explored the question of whether nearness to the experimenter would affect obedience by varying the experimenter's proximity to the subject as well as his degree of surveillance over the proceedings. Obedience dropped sharply when the experimenter, after giving his initial instructions, left the room and gave his subsequent orders by telephone. Whereas 65 percent of the subjects obeyed to the end when the experimenter was sitting just a few feet away, only 22 percent obeyed throughout when the experimenter was not physically present. Apparently, it is easier for people to disobey an authority they do not have to confront face to face.

It is also easier to disobey an authority when others provide models of defiance. Milgram demonstrated this by having two confederates act as co-teachers along with the real subject (Milgram, 1965a). After the shock reached 150 volts, one of the confederates refused to continue and took a seat in another part of the room. After 210 volts, the second confederate also refused to go further. Although the experimenter continued to order the true subject to carry on the procedure, only 10 percent obeyed until the end. The others announced their decision to stop shortly after one or the other confederate did. These encouraging results parallel what we saw in variations of Asch's experiment on conformity. When the illusion of unanimity is broken, people tend to stop going along with a response that is clearly wrong. This stresses the importance of speaking out when we observe some injustice. Not only may we help the victim in such cases, we may also prompt others to follow our lead (Hollander, 1975).

The Controversy over Milgram's Research.
Milgram's experiments raised an explosive controversy over the ethics of his procedures. Critics charged that without forewarning and prior permission Milgram knowingly exposed people to enormous stress and may have caused them long-term psychological harm (Baumrind, 1964). Any subject who followed the experimenter's commands to the very end learned a disturbing fact about himself: He was willing to obey an authority figure even if it meant performing a callous and inhumane act. Might not some subjects find this revelation difficult to live with? At the very least, might it not injure their self-concepts? According to Bem's self-perception theory, discussed in Chapter 17, people who observe themselves acting

cruelly in the absence of sufficient external pressures may conclude that they must be less sensitive than they formerly thought. In addition, might not participation in Milgram's experiments reduce a person's trust of legitimate authorities encountered in the future? After all, a Yale psychologist had duped them into acting immorally.

Milgram, however, flatly denies that his procedures caused any lasting harm (Milgram, 1964, 1968, 1974). He points out that all his sessions ended with a thorough "dehoaxing" in which the experimenter explained that shocks had never really been given and took care to reassure obedient subjects that their behavior had been entirely normal. As a result of these measures, Milgram argues, no subject left the laboratory in a continuing state of anxiety. Moreover, follow-up questionnaires indicated that most of the subjects (84 percent) were glad to have participated in Milgram's research because they learned something important about human behavior. And as for damaging subjects' ability to trust legitimate authorities in the future, Milgram argues that skepticism toward authorities who require us to act cruelly is a very valuable thing.

But Milgram's critics have not been satisfied with these arguments. They contend that the findings Milgram made were not important enough to justify the methods used to obtain them. In particular, critics doubt whether Milgram's results can be generalized to the world outside the laboratory. For example,

Milgram's subjects had volunteered to participate in an experiment; in such settings, people may be especially inclined to obey the commands of an authority (Orne and Holland, 1968). Moreover, the subjects were repeatedly prodded to continue with the shocks whenever they showed the slightest reluctance. In real life, Milgram's critics say, we seldom find ourselves in this position. In response, Milgram argues that complaints such as these arise more from the disturbing outcomes of his experiments than from the procedures used. "I am convinced," he writes, "that much of the criticism, whether people know it or not, stems from the results of the experiment. If everyone had broken off at slight shock or moderate shock, this would be a very reassuring finding and who would protest?" (Milgram, 1977, p. 98).

The fact that strong arguments have been raised on both sides of this controversy makes a key point: In psychological research, conflict between the need to answer important questions and the obligation to avoid causing subjects distress is not always easy to resolve. However, since the 1960s, when Milgram conducted his experiments, ethical standards governing human experimentation have become stricter. As we discussed in Chapter 2, ethical guidelines now require that subjects be informed about any stresses they will encounter in the course of an experiment. Thus, it would not be possible to perform experiments like Milgram's today.

THE SOCIAL SIGNIFICANCE OF GROUPS

In the mid-1970s Joan was a well-known political activist on her college campus. As she describes her life then: "I was into the radical feminist group at school; I was a political radical; I was trying to overthrow the system." Shortly thereafter, she became a member of a religious cult. Much to the surprise of her family and friends, who had always considered her strong-willed and independent, she began to grow meek and obedient. "In three months they recycled me," Joan explains, "and I was obeying everybody. . . . Any guy who asks me anything, I feel I should sacrifice for them; that's how I did for four years in the group" (Singer, 1979, pg. 79).

In 1957 automotive experts at the Ford Motor Company proudly announced the culmination of years of research and decision making. They had developed a brand new car that they were calling the Edsel, a car into which the company had invested a record-breaking quarter of a billion dollars. The Edsel was designed by a specially created committee at Ford, a committee that consisted of some of the "best minds" in the business. Yet somehow the group collectively produced one of the ugliest and least marketable cars ever to hit the highway. Within two years Ford had lost some $350 million on the venture, and company executives were wondering what went wrong.

Though supposedly the epitome of automotive design in the late 1950s, the Ford Motor Company's Edsel sold so poorly that it was discontinued after only two years. The major innovations made by the committee of experts formed to design the car—the vertical grille, low tailfins, and narrow horizontal taillights—were the very features that consumers objected to most strongly. *(United Press International.)*

Although these two events are very different, they both illustrate the profound influence that groups are capable of exerting on individual members. In the first example membership in a religious cult seemed to change a young woman's personality completely. In the second, a committee of automotive experts, backed by millions of dollars and reams of market research, collectively made one of the most disastrous decisions in marketing history. What processes underlie such far-reaching group effects?

Before answering this question, it is important to define what social psychologists mean by a **group.** In everyday language we often use the term to describe any collection of people who happen to be in the same place at the same time. In social psychology, however, the definition is more precise. To be a group, a collection of people must meet three criteria (De Lamater, 1974; Hare, 1976; Shaw, 1976). First, members must interact regularly in fairly structured and predictable ways. Second, they must be oriented toward one or more specific goals, which are aimed at satisfying certain shared needs. And finally, members must have a feeling of group identity and solidarity. They must see themselves as part of a whole, sharing to some extent a common fate.

Since this chapter could never attempt to cover all the influences groups can have on human behavior, we will focus on just a few. First, we look at how membership in a group can lead us to adopt ways of thinking and acting that we might never imagine ourselves capable of. Joan's dramatic transformation after joining a religious cult is just one example. We will be

discussing several others. Second, we examine how the very act of being in a group can often affect the quality of our performances and decisions. Ford's development of the Edsel is a case in point. We will explore some factors that shed light on such colossal group mistakes.

How Groups Shape Thought and Behavior

The Influence of Group Norms. One powerful way in which we are molded to the styles of thinking and acting that prevail within a group is through the existence of group norms. By **norms** we mean the unstated expectations and explicit standards for behavior that members of a group share. For example, the norms of a street gang include tough talk, "macho" behavior, and a refusal to yield to threats or intimidation. These, in short, are the rules by which gang members live.

The group that first presents us with a particular set of norms is the family. As we grow up, our parents expect us to adopt their standards of appropriate behavior. When we are old enough to develop friendships outside the home, however, we may reject our family's norms and adopt those of our peers instead. Or we may come to accept the norms of teachers, co-workers, and others we admire and respect. Social psychologists call the people to whom we look for guidance in formulating values, beliefs, and styles of behavior our **reference groups.** A positive reference

For each member of this VFW post, the other members serve as "reference others." In attempting to validate our beliefs, we generally turn to those individuals whose judgments we respect. (Neal Slavin.)

group is one whose outlooks and behaviors we generally accept, while a negative reference group is one whose outlooks and behaviors we generally reject.

How strong is the influence of reference groups other than the family? Consider, for example, how political beliefs are formed. Have your political views changed since your high school days? If so, why did this happen? Part of the answer undoubtedly lies in your changing reference groups.

In a classic five-year study of students attending Bennington College during the 1930s, Theodore Newcomb (1943) explored the power of reference groups. Many of the students at Bennington (then an expensive all-women's college) were born into wealthy, conservative families where labor unions were considered dangerous, Franklin Roosevelt was seen as a radical, and the welfare state was feared as an ever-encroaching threat. For these young women, the Bennington campus was a whole new world. Most of the faculty members were liberals who believed it their duty to inform an overprotected student body about the effects of the Great Depression and the implications of impending war. How did the Bennington women adapt to these new ideas? The majority gradually fell into step with the college community, becoming more liberal in their outlooks toward public affairs. For example, during the 1936 presidential election, 62 percent of the freshmen supported the conservative Republican candidate Alf Landon, whereas only 14 percent of the juniors and seniors did so.

Newcomb argued that the degree to which a particular student changed her attitudes was closely related to her reference groups. For the majority whose attitudes became more liberal, the college community as a whole, or a close circle of liberal friends, served as

an important positive reference group. Freshmen students were often influenced by junior and senior women, among whom liberals tended to be more outgoing and popular. Identification—or molding oneself to be like those one admires and respects—was often central to the process. "I was so anxious to be accepted," said one student, "that I accepted the political complexion of the community here." Similarly, the minority of students who did not become more liberal turned to family or conservative friends as positive reference groups. Explained one: "Every time I've tried to rebel against my family I've found how terribly wrong I am, and I've very naturally kept to my parents' attitudes."

Twenty-five years later Newcomb and several colleagues reinterviewed some of the women who had participated in the original study (Newcomb et al., 1967). They found that most of those who had been liberal in college had remained liberal. One reason was that many of these women had internalized liberal views—they had made them part of their own value systems (Kelman, 1958, 1961). Another reason was that these women tended to choose friends, husbands, and careers that reinforced liberal attitudes. In this way they continued to admire, respect, and identify with liberals like themselves.

Coercive Persuasion Within Groups. The process by which many Bennington women became more liberal was not one of force. In the absence of social pressures that we would call truly coercive, they gradually brought their attitudes in line with those of others at the college. But not all group-related changes in attitudes and behavior occur without duress. More coercive forms of persuasion within group settings are often called brainwashing.

The term **brainwashing** was coined by Edward Hunter, a journalist who published a book in 1951 describing the techniques that the Communist Chinese used to get the Nationalist Chinese to accept their point of view. One of the most extensive studies of brainwashing was done by Edgar H. Schein (1956, 1961), who detailed the procedures used by Chinese and North Koreans to "reform" the thinking of United Nations POWs during the Korean war. After conducting extensive interviews with a number of ex-POWs, Schein concluded that brainwashing is not as mysterious as many people think. Essentially, it is an extremely intense, determined effort to persuade people to change their opinions, backed by various types of hardship and punishment: social isolation, physical abuse, and relentless verbal attacks. People who are lonely, afraid, poorly housed, underfed, and subjected to constant pressures to adopt new opinions are good candidates for brainwashing.

The Cult Phenomenon. Brainwashing, ordinarily thought of in a wartime context, has become a subject of considerable interest lately in relation to the techniques that certain religious groups use to obtain new converts. Some of the groups suspected of using extreme methods of persuasion are the Unification Church of the Reverend Sun Myung Moon, the Hare Krishna sect, the Children of God, and the ill-fated People's Temple of the Reverend Jim Jones. Such religious cults rarely hold their followers through outright physical force, however. How, then, do they manage to attract and keep the estimated 3 million or more members they have acquired in the United States alone?

Many people think that the motivation to join must originate in the converts themselves. Eric Hoffer (1951) has taken the extreme position that such joiners are often social misfits; frustrated, rejected, deeply dissatisfied with life, they seek to "lose" themselves in a tightknit, highly purposeful group. But the problem with such theories is that they tend to ignore situational factors surrounding the decision to join a religious cult. This, once again, is the fundamental attribution error—the tendency to explain behavior largely in terms of inner dispositions, giving too little weight to external pressures that may contribute. Recent research suggests, in fact, that cult joiners are far from psychologically unique. Most are young, unmarried, white adults with some college education—people whose ways of thinking are not very different from others of this social background (Levine and Salter, 1976). Like many of their peers, young people who join cults are often experiencing certain developmental difficulties. Many are struggling to acquire a self-identity, to achieve idealistic goals, to cope with the first major loss in their lives, or to discover life's deeper "meaning" (Schwartz and Kaslow, 1981; Dean, 1982; Feinstein, 1980). These people seldom seek out cults deliberately as a way to resolve their problems. Instead, the cults simply find them at a time when they are particularly open to offers of friendship and "answers" (Bromley and Shupe, 1979; Schwartz and Kaslow, 1981; Stoner and Parke, 1977).

Once found by a cult, a person who seems a likely convert is sometimes invited to a rural retreat for a stay of a week or more. Many accept, partly to please the recruiting cult member who has approached them so warmly, and partly to satisfy their own curiosity. At the retreat the new prospects are cut off from contact with the outside world. Their activities are carefully scheduled from morning until night, including lectures, singing, meditation, and sometimes games and sports. This allows the prospective converts little time for critical evaluation of what they are experiencing, or even for informal talk among themselves. The end result is that the recruits are cast into an environment where only attitudes favorable to the cult are ever heard expressed. Like subjects in Solomon Asch's experiment they are faced with a situation in which the cult's views and behaviors are those of a unanimous majority. This creates powerful pressures to go along with the group, even if what they are doing initially seems silly. Consider the following incident reported by one young man who spent some time with a religious cult in order to visit his brother:

> I was in my sleeping bag on the floor of a room with about twenty other guys. At about 5:30 in the morning this guy comes in with a guitar and starts playing and singing "You Are My Sunshine" and I thought, "Oh, brother." I rolled over, buried my face and tried to go back to sleep. But all of a sudden I realized all the other guys were singing and rolling up their sleeping bags. . . . I thought, "They're crazy, a bunch of fanatics." But then I realized I was the only one in the room who wasn't singing . . . so I started to sing too. . . . I was behaving like a Moonie before I knew what hit me (Stoner and Parke, 1977, p. 155–156).

In addition to the process of compliance, illustrated in this example, prospective converts also experience

Cults typically require complete conformity and obedience from members. Here the Reverend Sun Myung Moon of the Unification Church joins 2,200 couples in the largest mass wedding in history in New York City's Madison Square Garden in July 1982. Most of the couples had not even met until shortly before the ceremony, but merely accepted the partner Reverend Moon assigned to them. *(Ethan Hoffman/Archive Pictures.)*

the powerful process of identification. Within the isolated group they are almost bound to find someone to become emotionally attached to—someone to admire and respect. That person's views and behaviors then serve as a model to be imitated at first and eventually internalized. The cult as a whole soon becomes a positive reference group, much like Bennington College became for many of its newly arrived freshman students. No wonder cult fledglings find it difficult to resist invitations to stay on with the group (Schwartz and Kaslow, 1981). They are no longer outsiders. They are now deeply involved.

Although many members find some meaning within a cult that was absent in their former lives, positive feelings are not universal. Some members eventually leave the cult due to discouragement, dissatisfaction, and doubt (Levine, 1980). Of those who leave, some apparently experience long-term negative effects (Singer, 1978; Singer, 1979; Levine, 1980; Schwartz and Kaslow, 1981). One is a lingering fear of harrassment by former cult comrades. Another is an inability to live independently. Once cut off from the cult community and its regular regimen of work and prayer, ex-members may feel lost and depressed. Many have difficulty returning to conventional lives at school, at work, within the family, and with the opposite sex. They seem mentally slower and more passive than they were before joining. Some end up drifting indecisively, unable to cope with a world that requires personal responsibility and initiative.

The Power of Group Roles. So far we have talked mainly about pressures to conform to norms within a group. But groups affect people's behavior in yet another powerful way. As we mentioned earlier, groups are not random collections of people; they are structured to accomplish goals. A university, for example, is organized into faculty, students, administrators, and so forth, all of whom are performing roles designed to carry out the goal of higher education. One thing that psychologists have noticed is that people often seem to "fit" their roles within a group. The clergyman, for instance, is frequently paternal; the drill sergeant, demanding; the bureaucrat, inflexible; the college professor, intellectual. Although you may think that people come to have the roles they do because these roles suit their inner natures, this is not always the case. Often, it is the role that shapes the individual, not the other way around. There is no better illustration of this fundamental fact than a study conducted by psychologist Philip Zimbardo and his colleagues (1972, 1973).

As described in the introduction to Chapter 17, Zimbardo set out to examine how the prison roles of inmate and guard affect how people act. Studying this subject in a real prison would have presented problems. For one thing, strict prison rules might mask some of the pressures being exerted by roles. For another, it is hard to say in a real-life setting whether observed behavioral differences arise from the roles that people are filling or from other differences between them (differences in personality or social background, for instance). So Zimbardo conducted his study in his own "mock" prison, set up in the basement of a Stanford University building during summer session. Over seventy-five young men, mostly college students on vacation, volunteered to participate in the paid, two-week simulation. Of these, Zimbardo selected twenty-one for their emotional stability and maturity. Completely at random he assigned ten to the role of prisoner and eleven to the role of guard. This random assignment to roles guaranteed that no consistent personality differences existed between the groups at the start of the project. The guards were given no instructions other than the general need to maintain "law and order." With this seemingly innocuous goal established, the study began.

To make the simulation as authentic as possible, prisoners were "arrested" at their homes and "booked" at the Palo Alto police station by actual police officers. They were then taken to the so-called Stanford County Prison. There they were issued uniforms and ushered into sparsely furnished cells. The first day passed without incident, but on the second day the prisoners staged a surprise revolt. This episode marked a critical turning point in the participants' behavior. After quelling the rebellion by threatening the prisoners with billy clubs and spraying them with fire extinguishers, the guards began to use their power harshly and arbitrarily. They created petty rules and demanded that the prisoners follow them to the letter. They made the inmates perform meaningless, exhausting, degrading chores and repeatedly ridiculed and demeaned them. The reaction of the prisoners was equally disturbing. Five of them developed such severe anxiety symptoms that they had to be released from the study. The other five were reduced to servile robots. After only six days, Zimbardo was forced to abandon the research because it had become too frighteningly real.

How can we explain such extraordinary behavior? Because the participants had been screened for emotional stability, we know they were not psychologically disturbed before the study began. In addition, each person was randomly assigned to the role of guard or prisoner, so there were no consistent personality differences between the groups initially. Zimbardo concluded that the outcome must have been caused by the power of prison roles. The demands of being an inmate or a guard became so dominant that subjects' personalities temporarily changed. As one ex-prisoner remarked: "I began to feel that I was losing my identity. The person I call [subject's real name] . . . was distant from me, was remote, until finally I wasn't that. I was #416—I was really my number." If a normal, well-adjusted young man can be this transformed by the part he is playing in a psychological study, it is likely that many roles in real life can also exert an enormous influence on us.

Zimbardo admits that his study, because of its effects on subjects, created an ethical dilemma similar to the one raised by Milgram's obedience research. In an effort to avoid any long-term harm to participants, he "debriefed" them extensively at the end of the

Life inside "Stanford County Prison." *(Courtesy, Professor Philip G. Zimbardo.)*

project, encouraging them to vent their feelings. Subsequent questionnaires, interviews, and group reunions suggest that subjects recovered reasonably well from the experience. Zimbardo argues that although the emotional price paid for this research was indeed high, the information gained was very important (Zimbardo et al., 1972). For one thing, it provided dramatic evidence that a prison environment can be socially destructive, regardless of the prior personalities of people who find themselves there. Zimbardo has made great effort to communicate his findings to a wide audience, including prison administrators and inmates, legislators, other government officials, and the public in general. In this way he hopes to make the high price paid for his data socially worthwhile (Zimbardo, 1975).

Group Effects on Problem Solving and Performance

Clearly, group norms and roles shape both our attitudes and actions. But what effects, if any, do groups have on our performance and problem-solving abilities? Does working within a group help us to produce a better product? Or do people usually do their best when working alone?

Social Facilitation. One of the earliest experiments in social psychology showed that people perform simple motor tasks faster when they compete with one another than when they merely race the clock (Triplett, 1898). Several decades later psychologist Floyd Allport made similar findings concerning simple cognitive tasks. People solving multiplication problems or generating word associations performed better in the presence of four or five others, even though they each worked independently (Allport, 1920, 1924). Allport called the tendency for the presence of others to improve people's performance **social facilitation.** Even lower animals were found to show this effect at times. For instance, in one experiment individual ants worked harder at digging tunnels (they moved more dirt) when they worked in groups of two or three than when they worked alone (Chen, 1937).

But the findings regarding social facilitation were not in complete agreement. People trying to learn complex mazes usually did better when alone. And in experiments with birds, performance on certain tasks seemed to be inhibited by the presence of other birds. Somehow these contradictory findings needed to be reconciled. But how could this be done?

One way was proposed by psychologist Robert Zajonc (1965, 1966). He argued that many of the contradictions could be eliminated if we assume that the presence of others increases a person's motivation, or drive. Studies had already demonstrated that when drive increases, subjects tend to perform the most well-learned, "automatic" responses they know—their so-called dominant responses. To this fact Zajonc simply added the observation that sometimes dominant responses are helpful and other times they are not. More specifically, when a person is confronted with very familiar tasks (such as simple arithmetic) to which the solutions are very well-known, increased drive should improve performance because the dominant responses are correct. In contrast, when people are faced with difficult tasks they have not yet mastered (such as solving a complex maze), increased drive should hinder performance because the dominant responses are usually inappropriate. Subsequent research has tended to support Zajonc's model of social facilitation (Geen and Gange, 1977).

Zajonc's model has many practical applications. People who are very familiar with and skillful at the tasks they are performing—professional musicians or actors, for example—are likely to do better in front of an audience than they are alone. Beginning pianists and actors, however, are in a different situation. They are likely to become rattled by the presence of others, fall back on their still undeveloped "instincts," and so perform more poorly than they would alone.

Today psychologists are still trying to determine just what it is about the presence of others that causes an increase in drive. One theory is that we simply have an innate reflex to become more alert and aroused when other people are around. Another possibility is that increased drive in the presence of others is a *learned* response. For instance, through learning we may come to expect that other people will evaluate our actions or provide us with competition. The resulting anticipation of positive or negative outcomes could in turn boost our level of drive. Alternatively, increased drive may result from a desire to overcome the distractions that other people create. When others are present they tend to divert our attention away from whatever task we have at hand.

Efforts to combat this diversion might lead to an increase in drive. Researchers are still conducting studies to determine which of these three mechanisms most accurately explains how the presence of others affects our drive level (Sanders, 1981; Geen, 1981; Marcus, 1981).

Decision Making in Groups. The theory of social facilitation attempts to explain the effects the presence of others has on people. Just because others are nearby and watching, your performance on a familiar task may significantly improve. Social facilitation, however, does not address a very important question: How is overall performance affected when members of a group work *together?*

As you learned in our earlier discussion of Solomon Asch's research, groups impose strong pressures to conform. Such pressures are especially powerful in small, close-knit groups (Blake and Mouton, 1979). When a small, cohesive group becomes so concerned with maintaining unanimity that it can no longer appraise alternatives realistically, it has fallen victim to a mode of decision making that social psychologist Irving Janis (1983) calls **groupthink.** The results can be disastrous, as the following example illustrates.

In the early months of 1961, a confident and tightly knit group, including men of outstanding intelligence, made what has come to be regarded as one of the worst decisions in recent history. The group, President John F. Kennedy's inner circle of foreign-policy advisers, met over the course of three months and reached the unanimous decision to invade Fidel Castro's Cuba, using an invasion force of Cuban exiles trained by the Central Intelligence Agency. Some 1,400 exiles took part in the attack at Cuba's Bay of Pigs, aided by the United States Navy and Air Force. Within three days, Cuban forces had sunk the ships that carried ammunition and supplies and had captured 1,200 of the invaders, killing the rest. Subsequent reflections on the blunder by President Kennedy and his staff revealed that the group had ignored many obvious and vital factors. It had failed to take into account available data on the size and strength of Castro's forces, the loyalty of his troops, and the deteriorating morale of the invaders. It had also failed to consider worldwide reaction to such a morally questionable military venture. "How," President Kennedy asked after the fiasco was over, "could we have been so stupid?"

Janis believes that the poor decision making arose because of several powerful conditions within the circle of Kennedy staff. For one thing the group was highly cohesive, as we have already said. In such groups, Janis argues, members often feel a strong compulsion to avoid disrupting group unity and the positive feelings it creates. As a result, they tend to convince themselves that all the group's decisions are sound. This is a major symptom of groupthink. Victims of it tend to suppress any objections they might have to policies being considered. Whenever doubts creep into their minds, they minimize the importance of them. As Kennedy adviser Arthur Schlesinger, Jr., wrote: "I can only explain my failure to do more than raise a few timid questions by reporting that one's impulse to blow the whistle on this nonsense was simply undone by the circumstances of the discussions" (Janis, 1983, p. 39). Such self-imposed censorship, in turn, has another important result. It fosters what Janis calls an "illusion of unanimity." Members of the Kennedy team mistakenly assumed that anyone who remained silent during policy talks must be in complete accord. This, of course, was incorrect. But once an illusion of unanimity was established, it helped convince the members that their existing plan *must* be right.

Strong cohesiveness can impair group decisions in yet another way. The close camaraderie that often arises within such groups can create feelings of euphoria and an "illusion of invulnerability." By this Janis means that close-knit groups sometimes come to believe that they will always be successful, no matter what the odds. As one member of Kennedy's inner circle recalled: "It seemed that, with John Kennedy leading us and with all the talent he had assembled, nothing could stop us" (Janis, 1983, p. 35). The other men around Kennedy shared this conviction, and it led them to underestimate many potential obstacles.

Janis does not argue that these negative tendencies occur in *all* close-knit groups. Only those that meet other conditions are likely to fall prey. According to Janis, a highly cohesive group that is insulated from other decision-making bodies, that lacks established procedures for searching out and appraising various options, and that is headed by a strong-minded, respected leader is the one most susceptible to groupthink. Although Janis's theory needs to be tested in controlled experiments, all the factors he lists did apply to Kennedy's decision-making staff (Moorhead, 1982).

How can groups that are vulnerable to groupthink avoid the dangers of it? Janis has offered several suggestions (Janis and Mann, 1977; Janis, 1982). First, the group leader should encourage members to express their doubts without fear of disapproval. If the leader has already formed an opinion, he or she should adopt an impartial stance while others are airing their views. Sometimes it helps to divide group members into separate units, each of which then considers the issues independently. This can increase the number of different options the group as a whole generates. Group members should also be encouraged to discuss deliberations with other colleagues whose opinions they value, and outside experts with differing views should be invited to address the group. In addition, at least one member at every group meeting should adopt the role of devil's advocate, challenging majority preferences. Finally, when the group has reached a preliminary decision, it should hold a "second chance" meeting in which everyone voices residual misgivings as forcefully as possible before making a final choice.

AGGRESSION AND ALTRUISM

In January 1978 a man in Phoenix, Arizona, walked up to a derelict sleeping outdoors in the city's skid row, doused him with gasoline, and set him on fire. Two other men met similar fates before the attacker was finally arrested. As far as authorities could tell, the victims had done nothing whatever to provoke the brutal assaults. In the same month, also in Phoenix, concerned citizens showered gifts and money on a desperately poor family, the father of which had been arrested for some minor offense. None of the donors knew the family personally. They had simply read about its plight in the local newspaper and responded with an outpouring of generosity.

These starkly different stories illustrate one of the central paradoxes of human nature: People can be aggressive and cruel, but they can also be generous and kind. What explains these opposing tendencies? In the next sections of this chapter we will examine the most important factors underlying each.

Factors Affecting Aggression

Every year about 1 million Americans are victims of reported violent crime, and probably hundreds of thousands of others suffer assaults that go unreported (FBI Uniform Crime Reports, 1977). It is estimated that between 1820 and 1945, 58 million people worldwide died at the hands of their fellow human beings. Murder, rape, beatings, and other forms of physical abuse are extreme examples of **interpersonal aggression**—behavior directed toward the goal of injuring another person who does not desire to be hurt (Baron, 1977). What accounts for the disturbingly high level of such aggression?

Biological Influences. The idea that human aggression is biologically based has taken several forms. Freud thought that aggression is part of our nature—"an innate, independent, instinctual disposition in man" (1930, p. 102). Aggressive energy, he argued, builds up within people and demands some form of release, often called a **catharsis.** This release can be direct, as when we shout in anger or hit someone. It can also be vicarious, as when we cheer contestants in a boxing match. In either case, however, Freud believed that such cathartic behaviors reduce aggressive drive.

More modern biological theories of aggression have appeared in recent years. The field of **sociobiology** seeks to discover the biological factors that underlie social behavior in all animal species, including human beings (E. O. Wilson, 1975, 1978). Sociobiologists believe that some of our behavioral inclinations—such as the tendency to respond aggressively when we are threatened—may be a direct outgrowth of the way the human brain and nervous system are structured. As such, these inclinations are part of our genetic inheritance, retained by natural selection because they helped our ancestors survive.

The Nobel Prize-winning ethologist Konrad Lorenz has described this evolutionary process in some detail. Lorenz argues that all animals have a "fighting instinct" directed toward members of their own species (Lorenz, 1974). This instinct, he maintains, has great survival value. For example, aggressive contests over mates ensure that the strongest males will father the most offspring, thus improving the species as a whole.

But Lorenz believes that violence has become a problem for humans partly because our ancestors never evolved the innate inhibition against killing members of their own species that many carnivorous animals acquired. Lorenz speculates that because our primitive ancestors were relatively harmless creatures (lacking sharp teeth, claws, and so forth) an innate inhibition against killing within the species was not essential to their survival. Today, however, all this has changed. Modern weapons now make us the most dangerous creatures on earth. To make matters worse, modern civilization often demands that we suppress our aggressive urges. Lorenz believes that if expression of the fighting instinct is repeatedly prohibited in any animal, aggressive impulses build up and may eventually be discharged in particularly vicious ways. This, Lorenz proposes, helps explain our periodic outbreaks of extreme violence.

However intriguing biological theories of aggression may be, they have some serious limitations. These theories propose that aggression stems largely from inborn tendencies that all humans share. But if this is the case, how can we explain the wide variation in degree of aggressiveness among different people? Most psychologists believe that the answer lies in the critical role of learning (Zillman, 1979). Research has shown that even in lower animals, many responses once considered purely "instinctive" are actually learned responses. For instance, young cats do not hunt rats solely through instinct. They learn this behavior by watching older cats (Kuo, 1930). In humans, of course, the influence of learning is even more extensive. This is why social learning theories of aggression have generated so much interest.

Social Learning Influences. According to social learning theories, people learn how to injure others through exposure to violent models and by having aggression positively reinforced (Bandura, 1976). The power of models to elicit aggressive behavior was demonstrated in a classic experiment (Bandura, Ross, and Ross, 1961). Nursery school children observed one of two adults: either an adult who ignored a five-foot inflated "Bobo" doll while playing quietly with a Tinker Toy set, or an adult who abused the doll. The violent model's attack was unlike anything that normal preschoolers would do spontaneously. Pinning

the doll to the floor, the model punched it in the face, yelling "Sock him in the nose!" He or she also beat the Bobo over the head with a mallet, tossed it angrily in the air, and kicked it about the room, punctuating these assaults with cries of "Throw him in the air!" . . . "Kick him!" . . . "Pow!" When the children were later given access to a Bobo doll under mildly frustrating conditions, those exposed to the violent model behaved much more aggressively than those exposed to the subdued model. Furthermore, the children who had witnessed the violent model tended to imitate that person's behavior. They punched, hammered, tossed, and yelled right down to the final kick and last emphatic "Pow!" Exposure to aggressive models, then, appears both to reduce inhibitions against aggression and to suggest specific aggressive acts.

What factors affect the degree to which a person is likely to imitate aggression? One important influence is the presence of rewards or punishments. In a follow-up study, Bandura (1965) found that children are much less likely to imitate a model who is punished for aggression. The inhibiting effect of punishment, however, has limitations. As soon as the threat of punishment is removed, a person may reenact observed aggression, especially if the potential rewards for doing so are great. And research shows that most aggression *is* extremely rewarding. In one study nearly 80 percent of children's physical and verbal assaults produced highly positive results for the aggressor (Patterson, Littman, and Bricker, 1967). Sometimes these rewards were tangible (such as obtaining a desirable toy), other times they were social (such as winning the admiration of peers), still other times they were internal (such as boosting the child's sense of power), and at times all three types of rewards were received.

One of the most controversial issues surrounding the social learning of aggression is the effect of widespread violence seen on television. Approximately 75 percent of the programs currently on TV depict some form of aggression. By the time the average child reaches the age of sixteen, he or she has witnessed over 13,000 dramatized murders and an even greater number of nonfatal assaults (Waters and Malamud, 1975). What happens to people who are bombarded by so much televised violence? Does it have any short-term or long-term effect on them?

Defenders of television programming argue that, for the most part, exposure to TV violence has a posi-

The debate continues over the effects of television violence on viewers, especially on young children. *(Mark Antman/The Image Works.)*

tive effect. They say it offers viewers a catharsis, a release of pent-up hostility, much as Sigmund Freud would have suggested. But others see TV violence far more negatively. They believe that popular programs provide people with models of destructive behavior. Young children, these critics charge, are especially vulnerable. They are likely to imitate the violent behavior of their TV heroes, whose acts of aggression are usually rewarded.

Although findings regarding the impact of TV violence have not always been in agreement, most studies to date support television's critics. It is clear that children who witness aggressive acts on television sometimes imitate them shortly thereafter (Liebert, Neale, and Davidson, 1973; Baron, 1977; Parke et al., 1977). A more important question, however, is whether exposure to TV violence has any *lasting* effects on children. Does a steady diet of televised aggression cause children to develop more aggressive ways of dealing with other people? On this issue research findings are less clear-cut. Nevertheless, the National Institute of Mental Health has recently drawn some conclusions based on a review of hundreds of studies published over the last decade (NIMH, 1982). First, the institute acknowledges that some well-conducted studies find no evidence of a causal link between heavy viewing of TV violence and the development of an aggressive nature (Milavsky et

al., 1982, for example). Such studies, however, are in the minority. Most researchers have found a small but consistent relationship between the amount of violence a child witnesses on television and the degree of aggressiveness he or she displays in dealing with other people. In one study, for instance, boys who reportedly watched a great deal of television at the age of eight were more aggressive at the age of eighteen than peers who had watched very little television as youngsters (Eron et al., 1972). Second, and equally important, the National Institute of Mental Health found not a single study of any merit supporting the viewpoint that televised violence reduces real-life aggression by providing a release for pent-up hostilities. Thus, all the evidence taken together suggests that the popular "shoot-em-ups" currently on TV are doing American children more harm than good.

Future research will undoubtedly probe the reasons for these harmful effects in more detail. For instance, there is now some evidence that children age eight and under are not yet fully able to follow the plots of many TV dramas (NIMH, 1982). Thus, when TV executives try to argue that their programs have prosocial lessons in them because the "good guys" always triumph over the bad, they are probably overestimating the cognitive capabilities of their youngest viewers. Very young children may be likely to focus, not on the story's moral, but on interest-grabbing behaviors performed in specific scenes—behaviors that are often violent and aggressive (Rubinstein, 1983). The *kind* of violence portrayed on television may also be a factor in explaining the negative effects on some young viewers. According to Goranson (1970), most television shows present "clean" violence—bloodless fist fights, car chases in which no one is injured, shoot-outs where the hero receives only a minor flesh wound. Because viewers see few negative consequences of aggressive acts, they are more likely to imitate them, Goranson argues. What is needed, then, are not just additional studies seeking to demonstrate a causal link between TV violence and real-life aggression; also essential are studies that look more deeply into the conditions that make this relationship more or less likely.

The Influence of Frustration.

Social learning theories provide great insight into how people acquire a repertoire of aggressive behaviors and how their performance of these behaviors is shaped by rewards and punishments. But social learning theories say nothing about the relationship between a person's emotional state and the amount of aggression that he or she shows. For instance, many highly aggressive acts seem to occur because of intense or prolonged frustration. Can we make any generalizations about the link between frustration and aggression?

Many years ago psychologist John Dollard and his colleagues took the extreme position that "aggression is *always* a consequence of frustration" and that "frustration *always* leads to some form of aggression" (Dollard et al., 1939, p. 1). By **frustration** they meant interference with any goal-directed behavior. Thus, when people are thwarted in their attempts to obtain food or shelter, sex or sleep, love or recognition, they become aggressive. This is not to say that they immediately lash out at the cause of their frustration. An aggressive response, Dollard argued, can be delayed, disguised, transferred to other people and objects (displaced), or otherwise deflected from its immediate and logical goal. Nevertheless, frustration in Dollard's view always leads to *some* kind of behavior aimed at releasing aggressive urges.

Critics, however, were quick to question Dollard's **frustration-aggression hypothesis.** Aggression, they said, is only one of many possible reactions to frustration. For example, some people withdraw when their efforts are thwarted, while others simply work harder

to achieve their goal. In response to this criticism Neal Miller, one of Dollard's colleagues, modified the original frustration-aggression hypothesis (Miller, 1941). He argued that frustration can produce a number of responses, *one* of which is aggression. But this modification raised a new and important question: Under precisely what circumstances would frustration lead to aggression?

Leonard Berkowitz proposed one answer (Berkowitz, 1962, 1965, 1969). He maintained that the immediate response to frustration is not aggression but the emotion of anger. Anger, however, can easily instigate aggression if suitable aggressive cues exist. If no such cues are present, then anger may give rise to some other reaction, such as withdrawal or renewed effort. Berkowitz tested his ideas by exposing frustrated subjects to aggressive cues, such as guns and violent films, and then providing them with an opportunity to display aggression if they wished. As predicted, such cues did increase the extent to which frustration led to aggression (Berkowitz and Geen, 1966; Berkowitz and Lepage, 1976).

Although Berkowitz's findings provide some insight into the link between frustration and aggression, they do not tell the whole story. Recent interviews with people about their real-life experiences of anger reveal several other pertinent facts (Averill, 1982, 1983). First, contrary to what Dollard originally suggested, frustration is not the only cause of anger and aggression. People report becoming angry for a variety of reasons, including injury to their pride or self-esteem and violation by others of accepted social norms. Second, although aggressive cues may sometimes encourage anger to be expressed as aggression, such cues are probably not essential. Aggressive urges and behaviors are quite common during anger. It is unlikely that in all these cases cues of the type Berkowitz has studied happen to be close at hand. Thus, in real life it remains hard to predict when anger will lead to aggression and when it will not.

Factors Affecting Altruism

Although they seldom make front-page headlines, acts of human **altruism** (unselfish concern for others) occur every day. At great risk to their own lives, bystanders sometimes rush into burning buildings to rescue children trapped inside. People give millions

Social psychologists have discovered many motives behind such altruistic acts as donating blood. *(Christopher Morrow/Stock, Boston.)*

of dollars to charities, donate blood, and volunteer their time to help those in need. Just as psychologists have tried to understand the causes of aggression, so have they also investigated the causes of altruistic behaviors.

The idea that human beings are genetically programmed to help one another—that we have altruistic instincts—has received much attention recently (Dawkins, 1975; Wilson, 1975). However, most social scientists reject this notion for the same reason they reject the instinct theory of human aggression: Biology alone seems insufficient to explain the great variations in altruistic tendencies that we repeatedly observe. It seems clear that both learning and situational pressures must also play a part. Social psychologists seek to discover the conditions in people's lives that encourage or inhibit the helping response.

Influences on Bystander Intervention in Emergencies.

At about 3 A.M. in a middle-class area of Queens, a borough of New York City, a young woman named Kitty Genovese was savagely attacked outside her apartment building as she arrived home from work. As the victim screamed for help, at least thirty-eight neighbors looked out their windows, but no one came to her aid. The attack continued for more than thirty minutes before Kitty Genovese died of multiple stab wounds.

The Genovese murder caused a sensation in the press. How could people be so apathetic, so indifferent to the fate of another human being? Many saw it as a classic illustration of urban callousness, of city dwellers' reluctance to "get involved." Yet investigation revealed that the witnesses to Kitty Genovese's murder had been far from indifferent. Her neighbors did not just close their blinds and go back to bed. They stood and watched transfixed, "unable to act but unwilling to turn away" (Latané and Darley, 1976, pp. 309–310). What prevented them from acting? Research on bystander intervention, inspired in part by the Genovese murder, indicates that a number of powerful social forces operate in any emergency situation, and some of these strongly inhibit helping.

John Darley and Bibb Latané, who have studied bystander intervention extensively, argue that the act of aiding the victim in an emergency is the result of many events and choices, all of which are *less* likely to occur in the presence of others (Darley and Latané, 1968). First, the bystander must notice that something unusual is occurring; the event must intrude on his or her private thoughts. But the problem here is that most people consider it bad manners to watch the actions of others closely, especially those of strangers. So in a crowd we tend to tune out sights and sounds and stare straight ahead. This decreases the likelihood that we, when immersed in a group, will even notice the signs of a possible emergency.

And noticing the signs of a possible emergency is not enough. A bystander must also determine whether this particular event is serious enough to warrant intervention. This decision is often far from easy, for most of the signs that suggest an emergency are ambiguous. Cries for help from the next apartment might be genuine, or they might be coming from your neighbor's television set. When other people are present, most of us think twice before rushing to the rescue because we are concerned about appearing foolish if no emergency exists. So we adopt an air of calm indifference while looking around to see how others are reacting. Unfortunately, everyone else may be trying to appear indifferent as well. The result is that each bystander is taken in by the others' nonchalance and led—or misled—to define the situation as a nonemergency (Latané, Nida, and Wilson, 1981).

Latané and Darley (1968) demonstrated the workings of both these social processes in an interesting experiment. Male college students, who had volunteered to be interviewed about the problems of life at an urban university, were directed to a waiting room to fill out a preliminary questionnaire. Some of the students were alone in the room. Others were in groups of three (the real subject plus two confederates). In either case, shortly after the subjects had started writing, the experimenters began to pump in smoke through a small vent in the wall. Each subject was observed through a one-way mirror in order to see how long it would take him to notice, evaluate, and report this emergency. Latané and Darley found that two-thirds of the subjects who were alone spotted the smoke immediately, whereas only one-quarter of the subjects in the group noticed it as quickly. Clearly, when others are present, people are much slower to perceive unusual events.

When others are present, people are also inclined to interpret unusual events as benign. In Latané and Darley's experiment, 75 percent of those who were alone in the room were concerned enough about the smoke to report it before the session ended, but only 12 percent of those who were not alone were worried enough to tell the experimenter. Instead, the typical subject in a group "would look at the other people, see them doing nothing, shrug his shoulders, and then go back to his questionnaire, casting covert glances first at the smoke and then at the others." What did he think was causing the smoke that made it safe to ignore? Steam or air-conditioning vapors were named by most subjects in postexperimental interviews, but some responses were much more imagina-

tive. A few subjects concluded that the smoke was artificial smog intended to simulate an urban environment, and two actually suggested that it was "truth gas" to induce accurate responses on the questionnaire! Note that all these answers, no matter how far-fetched, ruled out the possibility that the smoke indicated danger. In this way, those who failed to report the incident justified the appropriateness of their inaction.

But even if a bystander notices an event and correctly labels it an emergency, the presence of others may *still* decrease that person's chances of intervening. This is because being in a group tends to dilute our feelings of personal responsibility. Since others are present we tend to conclude that they have as much obligation to respond as we do. As a result, everyone hesitates, wondering who should step forward, and no one may take the initiative until it is too late. This diffusion of responsibility may have occurred among witnesses to the Kitty Genovese murder. Onlookers may have noticed that other people were also watching. If so, their own failure to act would seem far less reprehensible. After all, they probably reasoned, someone else had undoubtedly already summoned help.

To test whether diffusion of responsibility does indeed occur during emergencies, Darley and Latané (1968) staged another incident. This time, college students who had volunteered for an experiment were ushered into private rooms containing earphones and a microphone. The study was said to involve a group discussion about personal problems caused by life in a high-pressure urban environment. Subjects were told that the talk would take place over an intercom system, to preserve anonymity, and that the experimenter would not be listening in. Each subject was led to believe that one, two, or five other people were participating in the discussion, but in fact all voices except the true subject's were prerecorded.

The first speaker led off by saying that he was having difficulty adjusting to New York City and to his professors' academic demands. Then, very hesitantly and with some embarrassment, he added that he had even suffered nervous seizures, similar to epileptic attacks, when under severe stress. This young man was soon to be the victim. When it was again his turn to speak, he began to stutter and fumble for words, simulating very realistically the onset of a seizure. Within a few minutes he was choking and pleading for help. How do you think the subjects who overheard this performance reacted? As predicted by

Darley and Latané, the larger the perceived group, and therefore the greater the potential diffusion of responsibility, the less likely a subject was to summon help. Whereas 85 percent of those who thought they alone were hearing the victim reported his plight sometime during the faked attack, only 62 percent of those who thought there was one other bystander did so, and only 31 percent of those who thought there were four other bystanders. Thus, the tendency for feelings of personal responsibility to decline as groups grow larger seemed to be quite strong.

Darley and Latané have concluded from their various experiments that what people call bystander apathy is not really apathy at all. People who fail to act when they witness an emergency are very seldom indifferent to the victim's plight. In the experiment just described, those who failed to report the young man's epileptic seizure were anything but indifferent. Many showed symptoms of extreme anxiety as they considered what to do. Their failure to intervene seemed not so much a decision against responding as a state of *in*decision. The typical bystander in an emergency, Darley and Latané argue, is "an anguished individual in genuine doubt, concerned to do the right thing but compelled to make complex decisions under pressure of stress and fear. His reactions are shaped by the actions of others—and all too frequently by their inaction (Darley and Latané, 1968, p. 300).

Darley and Latané's findings are quite pessimistic about the prospects of receiving help when many bystanders are present. But do the social forces they describe *always* operate in groups that witness an emergency? Fortunately, the answer seems to be no. When the signs of an emergency are unambiguous and observers can see whether or not help is arriving, a victim may be more likely to receive aid in the presence of a sizable group than when few bystanders are watching (Solomon, Solomon, and Stone, 1978). This was demonstrated in an emergency staged on a New York City subway train (Piliavin, Rodin, and Piliavin, 1969). In 70 percent of the trials, bystanders immediately came to the aid of a young man who suddenly collapsed onto the floor. And the helping response was quicker when seven or more people were present than when only one, two, or three people were in the car. Note that in this case the emergency was unambiguous: The victim was sprawled on the floor directly in front of the bystanders. What's more, since all the bystanders were in clear view of one another, they could not justify inaction by telling themselves

that someone else was handling the matter. Why help was offered sooner with a larger number of observers is not completely clear, however. Perhaps once it is obvious that helping is the "right" reaction, a larger group increases the pressure to act on this ethical norm.

Other Influences on Helping Behavior.
In addition to studying the factors affecting bystander intervention in emergencies, social psychologists have studied the influences on other forms of helping, such as giving to charities or doing favors for people. Their research has shown that many things can promote or inhibit helping responses. We will explore just a few.

Mood and Level of Stress. Charity drives at Christmas seem to be based on the principle that when people are in a good mood their generosity increases. Social psychologists have confirmed this tendency in the laboratory. In one study, Alice Isen (1970) led teachers to believe that they had performed very well or very poorly on a series of tasks. She found that those who were basking in the "warm glow of success" donated more money to a school collection and were more inclined to help a woman struggling with an armload of books than were those who had experienced failure. But was it success *per se* that caused this effect or the general happiness associated with it? To find out, Isen and her colleague Paula Levin (1972) induced positive moods in other ways. For instance, they left change in the coin return of a public telephone and watched to see whether those who found the money would help a confederate who dropped a pile of papers outside the phone booth. Those who had been made to feel happy by this unexpected luck were indeed more likely to assist the confederate than were control subjects who had found no money. Subsequent studies have shown that even a mood raiser as simple as sunny skies and pleasant weather can increase a person's tendency to help others (Cunningham, 1979). The reasons for this effect are still unclear, however. One theory is that a good mood tends to make us remember how rewarding it is to help others, thus increasing the likelihood that we will behave altruistically to achieve those pleasant outcomes (Isen et al., 1978).

The effect of mood on helping may be related to another finding: City dwellers in general are less likely to help others than are small-town residents (House and Wolf, 1978). Could it be that urbanites, with all the noise and confusion of city living, are made more irritable than small-town residents and therefore less likely to help? Psychologist Stanley Milgram has suggested that cities, with their high densities of people, impose a sort of cognitive "overload" to which urbanites must adapt. This they do by paying less attention to what is going on around them, by developing blasé attitudes toward deviant, even bizarre, behavior, and by being highly selective in their responses to human demands. Milgram argues that without these very rational adaptations to crowded and stressful surroundings, city dwellers could hardly carry on their lives (Milgram, 1970). Some support for Milgram's theory comes from the research finding that urbanites who live in neighborhoods where stimulation levels are unusually high (very noisy, heavily trafficked, overcrowded) tend to be less helpful toward others than urbanites living elsewhere (Korte, Ypma, and Toppen, 1975).

Belief in a Just World. Another factor affecting altruism is belief in a just world—the conviction that, in the long run, wrong-doing will be punished and good deeds rewarded. Research suggests that this belief is very common among both children and adults (Lerner, Miller, and Holmes, 1976). (A few of the items from the Just-World Scale used to test the strength of people's convictions about a just world are shown in Figure 18.4.) Psychologist Melvin Lerner has argued that people with a strong belief in a just world may be motivated to try to restore justice when innocent people suffer. In addition, such people may also perform altruistic acts in anticipation of receiving some reward in return for their kindness. This was suggested in a series of experiments by Zuckerman (1975). He found that when students were asked two

days before a final exam to help a person with research or to serve as a reader for the blind, those who scored high on the Just-World Scale were more likely than others to comply with the request. According to Zuckerman these students reasoned that if they did something kind for another person, they would be repaid with success on their exam. Significantly, those with a strong belief in a just world were no more likely than others to perform a favor when final exams were five months away.

Belief in a just world, however, is a two-edged sword (Lerner, 1974). At times this conviction encourages people to behave altruistically, but at other times it prompts them to derogate the victims of misfortune. To understand why, suppose you saw people suffering through no fault of their own. Suppose further that there was nothing you could do to right this injustice. If you strongly believed that life was fair, such misfortune would be highly upsetting to your view of the nature of things. In order to eliminate this challenge to your belief in a just world, you might come to view the victims in a negative light, thus enabling you to conclude that they *deserve* their suffering.

Studies provide evidence that people do reason this way. Lerner and his colleagues have shown that subjects will derogate the personal qualities of a fellow subject who is assigned to receive painful electric shocks, even if it is made clear that the assignment occurred by chance (Lerner and Simmons, 1966; Lerner and Matthews, 1967; Lerner, 1970). Outside the laboratory, people have been found to blame, derogate, and shun those who are victims of violent crime or who suffer psychological disorders (Symonds, 1975; Farina et al., 1971). When a person has been raped or mugged, for example, she or he may receive censure from friends ("You should have known better than to walk in that neighborhood alone") instead of sympathy. An important goal of future research is to learn more about precisely when people will be kind to victims and when they will derogate victims and blame them for their problems.

---

1. Movies in which good triumphs over evil are unrealistic.
2. Students almost always deserve the grades they receive in school.
3. Although evil men may hold political power for a while, in the general course of history good wins out.

Figure 18.4 Items from the Just-World Scale. The scale is made up of two types of statements: those like item 1, with which people who believe in a just world tend to disagree; and statements like items 2 and 3, with which those holding just-world convictions would probably agree. (*From Rubin and Peplau, 1973, p. 79.*)

How Important Are Inner Dispositions? You may have wondered why we have failed to mention, throughout our discussion of factors affecting altruism, the importance of inner dispositions. Surely a primary reason for altruistic or selfish acts must be a person's underlying character traits. Yet research suggests that this common sense judgment is much less true than people think. The "Good Samaritan" is often more the product of circumstances than of inner dispositions. In fact, very few personality traits have been found to be consistently related to altruistic behaviors. Consider a recent study in which researchers compared people who had intervened to stop a crime (a robbery or assault, for instance) with people from similar backgrounds who had failed to do so (Huston et al., 1981). Tests measuring "humanitarianism" and "social responsibility" could not distinguish the helpers from the nonhelpers. What mattered was whether a person felt competent (because of size, strength, self-defense training, and so forth) to handle such a situation. Thus, the demands of a particular incident can overpower the tendency to act on the basis of one's "nature." This is the central message of social psychology: How we act is shaped to a large extent by the social situations in which we find ourselves.

The Consequences of Helping

People offer help with the expectation that their efforts will do some good. But how often is help actually successful? Are people who receive assistance always better off than those forced to "make it" on their own? Recent research has given us some thought-provoking answers. Studies show that not only do helping efforts often fail, they sometimes leave recipients worse off than they were initially (Coates and Wortman, 1980; Fisher, DePaulo, and Nadler, 1981; McCord, 1978; Rodin and Langer, 1977; Taylor, 1979; Wortman and Dunkel-Schetter, 1979). This is true not just of help given in institutions (prisons, nursing homes, welfare offices, and so forth), but also of help offered on a one-to-one level. Social psychologists wonder what it is about helping efforts that can sometimes cause more harm than good.

Why Helping Fails. Philip Brickman and his colleagues (1982) have proposed several answers. One is that help-givers often assume that the recipients of their help are far less competent than they really are. This assumption leads the help-givers to do things for the recipients that the recipients could learn to do themselves. As a result, the recipients are denied the opportunity to master useful skills. B.F. Skinner offers this example: "We watch a child tying a shoelace and grow jittery, and to escape from our jitteriness we 'help' the child tie the lace. In doing so we destroy one chance to learn to tie shoes" (Skinner, 1978). The same thing may happen when a well-meaning person leaps to assist someone physically disabled every time he or she seems to be having trouble. Although the help is well-intentioned, the disabled person has no chance to learn how to handle everyday problems alone.

A related difficulty is that when the help-giver does too much for the recipient, the recipient may come to assume that all the gains he or she makes are due to the help-giver's efforts. Suppose, for instance, that a welfare mother is having great difficulty finding a job. So a well-intentioned social worker assumes the major burden of tracking down possibilities and setting up interviews. If one of these interviews eventually leads to a short-term position, is it any wonder that the welfare mother would attribute this success to the social worker's skill? This simple attribution can be very self-defeating. Studies show that people are much more likely to continue working to overcome a problem when they believe that whatever gains they make are attributable to *themselves* (Brickman et al., 1982; Chambliss and Murray, 1979; Liberman, 1978). This is because attributing gains to the self tends to build a person's confidence that he or she can effectively deal with the problem (Coates, Renzaglia, and Embree, 1983). As a result, the person is much more apt to take the initiative, persevere, and overcome obstacles.

In extreme cases people who are not allowed to help themselves may come to believe that they have no ability to control their own lives. As a result, they think of themselves as helpless and increasingly act that way. This, in turn, only serves to reinforce the help-giver's perception that someone must "take charge." One instance of this process may occur in nursing homes (Langer, 1980). When staff members treat their elderly patients as capable of doing nothing for themselves, the patients may respond by becoming the helpless invalids they are expected to be.

Given all the negative side-effects that can accompany efforts to help, it is no wonder that help-givers often fail to bring about the lasting changes they seek. Unfortunately few are able to see their own contributions to this failure. As one observer of social workers has noted: "When staff complain about clients 'who cannot stand on their own two feet,' . . . they often fail to recognize that the source of these difficulties is the clients' passivity and dependence which the staff members themselves have done much to encourage" (Maslach, 1978, p. 119). Help-givers, in short, often commit the fundamental attribution error: They attribute people's failure to make progress to inner dispositions and overlook the role that situational factors play in this outcome.

The Helping Role: Burnout.
Recipients of help are not the only ones who may suffer from helping efforts. People who make helping their profession—doctors, nurses, social workers, teachers, and the like—sometimes reach the point of **burnout.** Burnout is a debilitating psychological state in which the help-giver emotionally withdraws from the job of helping. As motivation drops, the person becomes apathetic and may suffer a decline in self-esteem. Decreased concern for clients is another symptom of burnout, as help-givers lose their idealism and become pessimistic. Often they detach themselves from their clients as people, seeing them instead as "cases" to be treated in dehumanizing ways. Increased irritability and anger often accompany these changed outlooks. Burnout victims frequently rationalize their failures by attributing them to the people they are supposedly trying to help. Like the stereotype of the hardened bureaucrat, they also tend to become mechanical and very resistant to innovation (Maslach, 1976; Edelwich and Brodsky, 1980).

What causes burnout? In keeping with the social psychological perspective, burnout has less to do with personality factors than with situational ones. One obvious situational pressure is overwork. Help-givers with caseloads numbering into the hundreds and supported by very limited community resources may try to avoid feelings of guilt and frustration by distancing themselves from clients (Cherniss, Egnatios, and Wacker, 1976). Another contributing factor may be the unrealistic expectations with which many helping professionals begin their careers. They see the helping professions as offering interesting work with compassionate colleagues, work that benefits cooperative and grateful clients. The hard reality they discover once on the job can lead to early disillusionment

(Cherniss et al., in press). Finally, there are the emotional demands of being in a helping profession. People who are constantly exposed to the suffering of others may find that they cannot survive the situation if they repeatedly allow themselves to empathize with clients. One solution is to become emotionally detached, providing services in an uninvolved manner (Edelwich and Brodsky, 1980).

Clearly burnout has ill effects for professionals and clients alike. More troubling still, these ill effects tend to be self-perpetuating: Discouragement and withdrawal on the part of professionals lead to increased failure in their helping efforts and to more suffering on the part of clients. The professionals, in turn, react with even greater discouragement, and a vicious circle sets in. What can be done to break this disturbing pattern?

Since burnout results in part from exaggerated expectations, helping professionals should try to develop realistic outlooks toward their jobs. This involves accepting the fact that working conditions will probably never be perfect, that many clients will make progress only in very small steps, and that some will never make any progress at all (Edelwich and Brodsky, 1980). With these facts acknowledged, helping professionals can begin to set priorities for putting their limited resources to use. By giving more responsibility for improvements to their clients, they can often reduce their own workloads and emotional burdens. At the same time, the clients will be more apt to acquire a sense of confidence that they can control their own destinies and help solve their own problems. This, as we saw, can greatly increase a helping professional's success rate and so make his or her work more satisfying (Edelwich and Brodsky, 1980). Sometimes simple changes in work requirements can also boost job satisfaction. In one study, for instance, the outlooks of child-care workers improved significantly just by assigning each person a small number of children to look after rather than having the entire staff share responsibility for *all* the youngsters (Pines and Maslach, 1978). Finally, research shows that burnout is less likely among those professionals who can discuss their problems candidly with one another and who can voluntarily reduce interactions with clients when stress becomes too great (Maslach, 1976; Wortman and Dunkel-Schetter, 1979). Thus, maintaining a proper balance between concern for clients on the one hand and personal needs on the other seems to be an important factor in avoiding burnout.

ENVIRONMENTAL PSYCHOLOGY

The relatively new field of **environmental psychology** is an excellent illustration of the direction that psychology has been taking in recent years. Inspired by the concern for environmental quality that developed in the 1960s and early 1970s (Stokols, 1978), environmental psychology focuses on the interrelationships between people and their physical and social surroundings. Environmental psychologists ask questions such as: Does high population density in urban areas increase stress and contribute to crime? Are high-rise apartment buildings as suitable for people to live in as smaller-scale housing? Does constant exposure to noise from low-flying airplanes harm the people who live near major airports?

These questions reflect two trends emerging in psychology as a whole, but especially evident in environmental psychology. One is the tendency for psychologists to broaden their focus and to share information with professionals in other fields. The subject matter of environmental psychology is of interest not just to psychologists, but to sociologists, engineers, urban planners, physicians, and architects as well. In addition, research in environmental psychology reflects a growing concern among psychologists about the application of their findings to the world outside the laboratory.

Given a field as broad as environmental psychology, we cannot do justice here to all its major areas of research. Instead we will focus on just two topics of widespread interest: the effects of noise and the effects of crowding.

Noise

It has long been known that noise produces physiological arousal and can therefore be a source of stress. Laboratory studies show that noise can interfere with people's abilities to perform various kinds of tasks (Broadbent, 1978). Noise has also been shown to decrease our sensitivity to others. People in general are less likely to offer help in a noisy environment than they are in a quiet one (Mathews and Canon, 1975). Interestingly, however, such reactions are often determined by more than just the physical properties of the sound. To some extent, the impact of noise also depends on how predictable it is.

Glass and Singer (1972) demonstrated this in a laboratory study. They asked subjects to solve simple problems in arithmetic and verbal reasoning while being exposed to different noise conditions. One group heard loud bursts of noise regularly for a few seconds of each minute. Another group heard the same amount of loud noise, but the bursts were delivered for varying lengths of time at unpredictable intervals. A third group experienced no background noise. Glass and Singer found that all the groups were able to work effectively on the problems. But consider what happened immediately after this first part of the experiment was over. The researchers asked the same subjects to proofread a manuscript and to work on some puzzles in a quiet setting. Those who had previously been exposed to the unpredictable noise made more proofreading errors and gave up on puzzles more quickly than those previously exposed either to predictable noise or to no noise at all.

What is it about unpredictable noise that causes these negative effects? Glass and Singer suspected that unpredictable noise may heighten people's perception that a situation is beyond their control. When people cannot anticipate or prepare for a noise in any way, they may feel helpless and therefore give up quickly in the face of difficulty. To test this hypothesis, Glass and Singer conducted a variation of their original study, but this time adding another experimental condition. Some of the subjects exposed to the loud, unpredictable noise were told that while the experimenters preferred that they listen to it, they could stop the noise if they wanted simply by pressing a button. Very few of these subjects actually took advantage of the button, but their perception of control had an important effect. When later given the proofreading and puzzle-solving tasks, they performed just as well as those subjects who had previously heard *no* noise.

But laboratory studies such as Glass and Singer's can give us only limited information about how noise affects people in real-life situations. For instance,

Uncontrollable noise is a form of environmental pollution and can cause severe stress. *(Ken Levinson/International Stock.)*

briefly exposing subjects to noise during an experiment may not tell us much about exposure to noise over long periods of time. Researchers have therefore begun to measure the effects of noise in natural settings (Cohen, Glass, and Phillips, 1979). Such efforts, however, present problems of their own: Often it is difficult to isolate the effects of noise from the effects of other factors. Workers in a noisy factory, for example, might be influenced not just by the noise, but also by physical stress, noxious fumes, and many other variables. These other variables must be taken into account when conducting studies in a natural environment.

One such study that controlled extensively for other variables was done by Sheldon Cohen and his colleagues (Cohen et al., 1980). These researchers studied several hundred elementary school students in the Los Angeles area, some of whom attended noisy schools near the city's busiest airport and some of whom attended schools in quiet neighborhoods. The two groups of children were carefully matched by age, race, social class, and ethnic background, and those with hearing difficulties were excluded. The investigators even measured air quality around the schools to make sure that level of air pollution was not an influential factor. Cohen and his colleagues found that children attending the noisy schools had higher

blood pressure than those attending the quiet schools. In addition, children from the noisy schools were more easily distracted. Like subjects in Glass and Singer's study, they gave up more quickly when solving difficult problems than did the other children. And this higher level of distractibility was directly related to time spent in the noisy environment: The longer these children had been exposed to the noise, the more distractible they were. Even more disturbing were the results of a follow-up study conducted one year later (Cohen et al., 1981). Although 43 percent of the classrooms in the noisy schools had been modified to reduce noise levels, children in these classrooms showed no significant improvement. They were *still* more distractible than children from quiet schools. Further research is needed in order to determine if prolonged exposure to very loud noise causes permanent cognitive damage.

Crowding

Students of animal behavior have often observed the importance of space to many animal species—an observation that laboratory studies have confirmed. For instance, when colonies of rats are confined to overcrowded pens, the animals behave abnormally. Their mating patterns are disrupted, they fail to build their nests, they neglect their young markedly (as many as three-quarters of the babies die), and they fight among themselves (Calhoun, 1962). Psychologists naturally wonder if such findings have any implications for the effects of overcrowding on human beings.

Some have searched for answers in population statistics. They have looked to see if high-density living conditions correlate with high incidences of various social ills—disease, crime, family problems, and so forth. Many early studies of this kind did indeed indicate that overcrowding and social ills generally go together (Schmitt, 1957, 1966). But the problem was that these studies failed to separate the effects of crowding from the effects of other factors that often accompany crowding (poverty, for instance). What's more, the results of large-scale correlational studies were not always consistent (Winsborough, 1955; Schmitt, 1963). Researchers needed to use other methods to investigate this complex issue fully.

Some turned to laboratory experiments in which variables could be deliberately controlled. They exposed subjects to different degrees of crowding and assessed their reactions—primarily through performance tests and self-reports of stress. Some of these researchers did find that crowding seemed to cause greater stress and poorer performance (Evans, 1975; Stokols et al., 1973; Hutt and Vaizey, 1966), but others disagreed with this conclusion (Sundstrom, 1978; Freedman and Staff, 1975). Moreover, critics questioned whether short-term crowding in the laboratory really duplicated conditions of crowding that people experience in real life.

Recently, psychologists have attempted to overcome the limitations of laboratory research by conducting studies of crowding in natural environments. Some have looked at the effects of high-density housing. For instance, researchers have evaluated college freshmen who, because of large enrollments, were forced to triple up in dormitory rooms originally intended for only two. These overcrowded students in general had lower grade point averages than comparable students in normal living conditions (Glassman et al., 1978; Karlin, Rosen, and Epstein, 1979). Students in crowded housing may also be more vulnerable to various health problems. Studies have found that campus health centers are used more frequently by those who live in high-density arrangements than by those who live in more spacious accommodations

(Baron et al., 1976; Stokols, Ohlig, and Resnick, 1978).

And it is not just a large number of people per square footage that can have negative effects. Research suggests that living arrangements that merely give the impression of crowding and lack of privacy can adversely influence behavior. In one set of studies, for instance, psychologists compared college freshmen who had been randomly assigned to different kinds of dormitories (Baum and Valins, 1977; Baum, Aiello, and Calesnick, 1978). Some were in dorms with very long corridors, in which thirty-two to forty residents shared public areas (lounge, bathrooms, hallways). Others were in dorms with much shorter corridors, in which six to twenty residents were clustered together in their own suites (consisting of a living room and bedrooms) and shared only public areas of the building with other residents. Although the actual density in the two kinds of dorms did not differ greatly, the students experienced their living arrangements quite differently. Those in long-corridor dorms felt that their housing was more crowded, and they were less satisfied with it. They reported having more difficulty avoiding people when they did not want to see them and more problems regulating their social interactions. As a result, long-corridor residents tended to become withdrawn. They had fewer friends and belonged to fewer social groups in their dormitories than did suite-style residents. Students who lived in long-corridor dorms were also likely to feel it was useless to try to change dormitory conditions. They seemed, in short, to exhibit a degree of learned helplessness. These patterns appeared to generalize to other situations. When asked to play a two-person game in the laboratory, for instance, long-corridor residents were more passive and withdrawn, and less cooperative than suite-style residents (Baum, Aiello, and Calesnick, 1978; Baum and Gatchel, 1981).

Psychologists have proposed a number of reasons why human crowding has these harmful effects. One is that people find the close presence of many others overstimulating (Altman, 1975). According to this theory, even the mere perception of too much social contact (in the absence of genuine crowding) can be a source of stress. A second theory is that the negative effects of crowding are mediated by a sense that one has lost some control over the environment (Sherrod, 1974; Epstein, 1981). Long-corridor residents in the study just described, for instance, reported being troubled by the unpredictability of social encounters and the difficulty of regulating social interactions. It seemed that loss of control was a key factor making their dormitory life unpleasant. These two theories, of course, are not incompatible. It may well be that the two work together to produce the negative reactions to crowding that researchers have found.

PSYCHOLOGY AND THE FUTURE

Our discussion of research on noise and crowding points to a prominent trend in psychology, a trend that is very likely to continue. Psychologists today are less satisfied than many of their predecessors with the results obtained from laboratory experiments. Increasingly, they are combining laboratory research with "real world" investigations (Wortman et al., 1980; Cialdini, 1980). Working in real-life settings is often difficult, of course. The real world lacks the degree of control possible in the laboratory. But many psychologists believe that theories are enriched by attempts to test them in natural environments (McGuire, 1967a, 1967b).

One bonus of this trend is that research in natural environments often has direct implications for public policy. What we have discovered from studies of crowding, for instance, could prevent us from spending millions of taxpayer dollars on poorly designed public housing. Research in social psychology has an especially long record of influencing public policy. A prime example is the Supreme Court's landmark desegregation decision in *Brown* v. *Board of Education* (1954). In this case the Justices maintained that segregation deprived minority-group children of their right to equal educational opportunity. They argued that the so-called "separate but equal" school facilities prevalent at the time created in the minds of minority youngsters "a feeling of inferiority as to their status in the community that may affect their hearts and minds in a way unlikely ever to be undone." This judgment was influenced to a sizable extent by evidence social scientists provided. Particularly important were the research findings of psychologists Kenneth and Mamie Clark (1947). They concluded from projective tests given to black children that discrimination and segregation harmed these youngsters' self-esteem. Black children as young as three rejected black dolls in favor of white ones, which they judged to be pret-

tier and generally superior.

Many people have become enthusiastic about the prospect of using psychological research to formulate enlightened social policy. But the process of actually doing so may be more difficult than they think. There is evidence that people are not easily swayed by information that opposes their existing viewpoints. Consider, for instance, an experiment in which college students who had strong opinions about the value of capital punishment were asked to evaluate two studies on this subject (Lord, Ross, and Lepper, 1979). One study compared the murder rates in states before and after the adoption of capital punishment. The other compared murder rates during the same time period for states with or without the death penalty. Each subject was told that one or the other of these two studies supported his or her own viewpoint, while the other study was said to support the opposite point of view. Typically, the subjects declared whichever study was said to support their own position "more convincing" and "better conducted" than the other one. After reviewing the results of this and similar research Nisbett and Ross have come to a strong conclusion: "Supportive evidence," they say, "is handled with kid gloves; opposing evidence is mauled" (1980, p. 179). This tendency is not limited to college students. One team of researchers questioned several hundred government officials about how social science research was used in making public policy (Caplan, Morrison, and Stambaugh, 1975). They found that policy makers routinely dismissed findings that contradicted what they already believed. Clearly, ways must be found to encourage people to consider opposing viewpoints more fairly. We must also find ways to enhance people's awareness of how their values influence their judgments. Only then can we hope to realize the goal of using social science findings effectively in making policy choices.

SUMMARY

1. Social pressure often induces **conformity,** a shifting of our opinions and actions to correspond to those of others. There are degrees of conformity, however. Sometimes we merely **comply;** other times we actually embrace new values through **internalization** and **identification.**

2. Research on **obedience**—following the express commands of a person in authority—has shown that many of us are willing to obey orders even when our actions might harm other people. Although research on obedience remains controversial, Milgram's basic finding that we are susceptible to destructive obedience has not been refuted.

3. **Groups** often change our attitudes and actions by teaching us a new set of **norms,** or shared standards of behavior. In extreme cases, we may learn new values by being **brainwashed**—that is, subjected to intense efforts at persuasion, generally involving threat of force. Research shows that religious cults do not rely on brainwashing as often as many people believe. Instead, recruits become converted through less coercive processes like compliance and identification. The role we play within groups can also be very powerful in changing our behavior, as Zimbardo's mock prison study showed.

4. Being among others may enhance our ability to perform certain kinds of tasks, an effect known as **social facilitation.** But when people work together to come to a difficult decision, the results may not always be superior. Small, cohesive groups may fall victim to **groupthink,** a mode of thought characterized by suppression of alternative viewpoints and distorted appraisals of reality.

5. Excessive **interpersonal aggression** is a fundamental problem among human beings. Freud and Lorenz have argued that our aggressive drives are innate, but social learning theorists show that aggression can be learned through modeling. **Frustration** can also play a role in promoting aggression.

6. Whether we display **altruism** depends on many factors, including the nature of the event demanding our response, the number of other people present, our emotional state at the time, and the degree to which the situation seems just or unjust. Thus, acts of altruism often arise as much from external circumstances as from internal dispositions.

7. Many helping efforts have been found to be unsuccessful. The efforts of the professional helper, especially, may lead to passivity on the part of clients, who may then be blamed for their own misfortunes. One result may be the **burnout** that social service professionals sometimes suffer.

8. **Environmental psychology** focuses on the interrelationships between people and their surroundings. Environmental psychologists have studied such stresses of modern life as noise and crowding. In keeping with a trend in all of psychology, they often conduct their research in natural settings, not just in laboratories.

9. Social scientists have much to contribute to the formulation of public policy. But in order for social science research to be used for maximum benefit, people must be willing to consider alternative points of view.

SUGGESTED READINGS

ARONSON, E. *The social animal.* 3rd ed. New York: W. H. Freeman, 1980.

This book, which won an American Psychological Association National Media Award, is an engaging, easy-to-read introduction to the topics central to social psychology.

BARON, R. *Human aggression.* New York: Plenum, 1977.

This very readable introduction to research on aggression discusses social, environmental, and individual determinants of aggression and techniques for controlling or preventing aggression.

HEIMSTRA, N. W., and MCFARLING, L. H. *Environmental psychology.* Monterey, Calif.: Brooks/Cole, 1974.

This short book considers three central topics in environmental psychology: the relationship between behavior and built environments (ranging from single rooms to entire cities), the relationship between behavior and natural environments, and the relationship between behavior and environmental stressors (crowding, noise, and air and water pollution).

MILGRAM, S. *Obedience to authority.* New York: Harper & Row, 1974.

The reader is invited to observe as Milgram works methodically and creatively through his series of eighteen obedience experiments, searching for an explanation of destructive obedience.

RUSHTON, J., and SORRENTINO, R. (Eds.). *Altruism and helping behavior.* Hillsdale, N.J.: Lawrence Erlbaum, 1981.

This collection of chapters by researchers in the field of prosocial behavior discusses the ways in which prosocial behavior develops, the effects of various circumstances surrounding the helping incident, and the relationship of individual characteristics to helping behavior.

Glossary

The boldface number after each entry refers to the chapter in which the term is discussed.

absolute threshold   The minimum stimulus necessary to produce a detectable sensation. **4**

action potential   An abrupt change in a cell's polarity which temporarily makes the cell interior positive and the cell exterior negative. **3**

actor-observer bias   The tendency to attribute one's own behavior to environmental causes, rather than some enduring personality trait. **17**

addictive disorder   The psychological disorder of those who become dependent on drugs to the point where life revolves around the drugs and interpersonal relationships suffer. **15**

adrenals   A pair of endocrine glands located above the kidneys that affect the body's reaction to stress as well as producing sex hormones and numerous other hormonelike chemicals. **3**

affective disorders   Psychological disorders characterized by disturbances of mood, such as depression. **15**

affirmative action   A program designed to compensate for years of discrimination by giving minority groups special consideration in hiring, job training, and school admissions. **17**

afterimage   A visual impression that lasts after removal of the stimulus that caused it. **4**

alcohol abuse   A compelling psychological need for alcohol and inability to cut down or stop. **15**

alcohol dependency   Psychological and physical addiction to alcohol. **15**

alcoholic blackout   Fragmentary or even total loss of memory for events that occurred while drinking. **12**

algorithm   A precisely stated set of rules for solving problems of a particular kind. **7**

alpha waves   Moderately slow brain waves that occur when a person relaxes with eyes closed. **12**

altered state of consciousness   Any qualitative alteration in mental functioning, such that a person feels that his or her consciousness is distinctively different from the way it ordinarily functions. **12**

altruism   Unselfish concern for others. **18**

amnesia   The partial or total forgetting of past experience after a stressful experience. **15**

amplitude   The intensity of a sound wave, or amount of pressure it exerts, as measured by the distance of the wave's peaks and valleys from a baseline of zero. Amplitude determines loudness. **4**

amygdala   One of three interrelated structures of the limbic system; the others are the hippocampus and the septal area. **3**

anal stage   According to Freud, the second psychosexual stage (occurring during the second year of life) during which bowel control is accomplished and pleasure is focused on the function of elimination. **13**

androgens   Sex hormones secreted by the adrenal glands that are involved in the development of male sex characteristics. **3**

anorexia nervosa   The condition, affecting mainly teenage women, characterized by an obsession with extreme thinness and consequent rigid dieting. **11**

anterior aphasia   Difficulty in producing and comprehending speech, caused by damage to the front portion of the brain's left hemisphere. **9**

anterograde amnesia   A form of amnesia that affects memory only for new events; things that were learned before the condition started are recalled perfectly. **6**

antianxiety drugs   Commonly known as "minor" tranquilizers, these drugs reduce excitability and cause drowsiness. **16**

antidepressant drugs   Mood-regulating drugs effective in treating certain types of depression; known as the tricyclics because of their three-ringed molecular structure. **16**

antipsychotic drugs   Major tranquilizers, used to alleviate extreme symptoms of agitation and hyperactivity in psychotic patients. **16**

antisocial personality (sociopath)   A person who follows his or her impulses without consideration for the rights or feelings of others, and who does so without guilt. **15**

anvil   One of a set of three tiny, interconnected bones in the middle ear that transmit sound from the eardrum to the cochlea. **4**

anxiety   A state of psychic distress which, according to Freud, occurs when the ego loses its struggle to reconcile the divergent demands of the id, the superego, and reality. **13**

anxiety disorders   The group of mental disorders characterized by emotional distress caused by feelings of vulnerability, apprehension, or fear. **15**

anxious attachment   The type of bond between infant and caregiver characterized by the expectation that the caregiver will be inaccessible at times and somewhat unresponsive and ineffective. **8**

aphasia   Language disorder caused by brain damage. **9**

applied science   The deliberate use of research findings to solve some practical problem, or to improve the quality of human life. **1**

association cortex   The area, constituting about three quarters of the cortex, which participates in abstract mental processes. **3**

associative learning   Learning that certain events are associated with one another. **5**

attachment   The emotional bond of an infant to the mother or other caregiver. **8**

attitude object   The target of an attitude; that which we have an attitude about. **17**

attitudes   Learned, relatively enduring predispositions to respond to certain things in consistently favorable or unfavorable ways. **17**

auditory canal   The passageway that extends from the opening of the outer ear to the eardrum. **4**

authoritarian personality   The personality of an individual who shows rigid adherence to conventional values about authority and morality, as well as a preference for strong, antidemocratic leaders. **17**

autonomic nervous system   The division of the peripheral nervous system that controls the visceral muscles (blood vessels, heart, intestines) and the glands. **3**

availability   A heuristic involving the assessment of the probability of an event by the ease with which instances come to mind. **7**

aversive conditioning   A therapeutic technique which attempts to reduce the frequency of deviant behavior by pairing an aversive stimulus, such as a loud noise, with the cues related to the deviant behavior, thereby making the cues themselves become aversive. **11**

axons   The long extensions of a neuron that usually transmit impulses away from the cell body. **3**

backward conditioning   Presenting the unconditioned stimulus before the conditioned stimulus, thereby reversing the usual order. **5**

backward search   A heuristic that involves working backward from the end point of a problem in order to discover the steps involved in getting there. **7**

basic anxiety   According to Horney, the helplessness and insecurity a child feels when parents' behavior is indifferent, disparaging, and erratic. **13**

basic hostility   According to Horney, a child's feeling of deep resentment toward parents who arouse basic anxiety in him or her. **13**

basic science   A quest for understanding a subject without regard for whether that understanding will have immediate physical effects. **1**

basilar membrane   A membrane in the cochlea whose motion stimulates hair cells, thus aiding in the passing of sound waves to the auditory nerve. **4**

behavioral assessment   A type of personality assessment that seeks to objectively measure both environmental contingencies and people's responses to them. **14**

behavioral measures   Objective, quantifiable measures of a subject's behavior. **2**

behavioristic and social learning approaches   The methods of understanding personality that view the development and functioning of the personality as a set of learned responses, not as something that results from unconscious conflicts and urges. **13**

behaviorists   Psychologists who stress the study of observable behavior and account for such behavior in terms of an association that the organism has learned in the past. **1**

behavior modification   The conscious use of operant conditioning principles to change human behavior. **5**

behavior therapy   The application of learning theory and other experimentally derived psychological principles to the task of changing problem behavior. **16**

beta waves   Rapid or high-frequency brain waves common when a person is fully awake and alert. **12**

binocular disparity   The difference between the retinal images of the two eyes. **4**

biofeedback   The use of monitoring instruments to give a person a continuous flow of information about his or her own physiological responses in order to control them. **10, 12**

biological clocks   The internal mechanisms that pace circadian rhythms. **12**

bipolar cells   Cells in the eye that are stimulated by rods or cones and in turn stimulate ganglion cells. **4**

blind spot   The area of the retina where the optic nerve leaves the eye and that is devoid of rods and cones. It is insensitive to light. **4**

brain stem   The knobby extension that the spinal cord forms at the point where it enters the skull. **3**

brainwashing   An intense and determined effort, backed by the infliction of hardship and punishment, to persuade people to change their opinions. **18**

brown fat   Heat-producing fatty tissue that functions to keep people warm and burn off excess calories. **11**

bulimia   Eating disorder which involves periodic gorging alternating with purging to avoid weight gain. **11**

burnout   A syndrome among some service professionals characterized by apathy and a decline in self-esteem, loss of concern for clients, rationalizing failure by attributing it to clients, irritability and anger, and resistance to change. **18**

cardinal trait   According to G. Allport, a trait that directs a major portion of a person's behavior. **13**

case study   Intensive investigation and in-depth analysis of a single individual. **2**

castration anxiety According to Freud, the fear a young boy experiences that his father will punish him for his Oedipal longings by cutting off his penis. **13**

catharsis Release of built-up aggressive energy. **18**

causal attribution How people attribute causes to behavior. **17**

cell body Region of the neuron which contains the cell nucleus and all other life-sustaining systems of the cell. **3**

central fissure The separation between the frontal lobe and the parietal lobe of the brian. **3**

central nervous system (CNS) The ultimate control center of all human behavior, consisting of the brain and the spinal cord. **3**

central tendency A middle value of a set of scores. **2**

central traits According to G. Allport, an individual's characteristic ways of dealing with the world. **13**

cerebellum Located to the rear of the brain stem, it coordinates voluntary movement of the skeletal muscles and regulates physical balance. **3**

cerebral hemispheres The two large structures lying above the brain's central core that are involved in learning, speech, reasoning, and memory. **3**

chaining Learning a sequence of operant behaviors which eventually ends in a primary reward. **5**

chromosomes Thread-shaped structures within the cell nucleus that carry the organism's genes. **8**

ciliary muscles Muscles in the eye that change the shape of the lens for focus. **4**

circadian rhythms Naturally occurring daily cycles of the body. **12**

classically conditioned response Behavior that results when a neutral stimulus is repeatedly paired with another stimulus that evokes a nonvoluntary response, such as fear. **5**

clinical psychologists Those with doctorates in clinical psychology who specialize in the diagnosis and treatment of behavior disorders. **1, 16**

cochlea The spiral-shaped part of the inner ear containing the receptors for hearing. **4**

cognition The process of organizing information in our minds to help accomplish some desired end. **7**

cognitive approach The psychological theory that in almost any learned association, important thought processes intervene between the stimulus and the response. **5**

cognitive behavior therapies Therapies that try to change clients' negative thought patterns. **16**

cognitive consistency The tendency of people to keep their various cognitions in relative agreement with one another. **17**

cognitive dissonance The theory advanced by Leon Festinger that people are motivated by the need to achieve consistency between their attitudes and their behavior. **17**

cognitive learning Learning that involves the formation of concepts, schemes, theories, and other mental abstractions. **5**

cognitive therapy A variation of cognitive restructuring therapy developed by Aaron Beck in which patients are questioned in such a way that they themselves discover the irrationality of their thoughts. **15, 16**

compliance Seeming to outwardly yield to pressure while actually maintaining one's own opinions. **15**

compulsion An act of irrational behavior that the person seems unable to control. **15**

concepts Mental constructs that enable a person to classify objects by the characteristics they share with other objects. **7**

concepts of conservation The understanding that some characteristics of stimuli can stay the same despite changes in other features. **8**

concrete-operational period The third of Piaget's periods of intellectual development (which usually comprises the elementary-school years), during which a child begins to deal with specific systems of operations but cannot think abstractly. **8**

concrete operations Logical operations that involve reversible transformations of concrete objects and events. **8**

concurrent validity The type of validity a test has if results can be correlated with another criterion that is immediately available. **14**

conditional positive regard According to Rogers, the withholding of love and praise from a child unless he or she conforms to parental and social standards. **13**

conditioned response (CR) A response to a previously neutral stimulus learned through association in the process of conditioning. **1, 5**

conditioned stimulus (CS) The stimulus which elicits a new response as a result of the conditioning process. **5**

conditions of worth Rogers' term for the strong ideas children hold about which thoughts and behaviors will bring positive regard and so are desirable and "good." **13, 16**

cones Cells in the retina that are sensitive to color and that are used primarily for daytime or high-light-intensity vision. **4**

confabulation The manufacture of an item in memory to replace one that cannot be retrieved. **6**

conformity The tendency to shift one's opinions or actions to correspond with those of other people because of implicit or explicit social pressure. **18**

consciousness   An awareness of the many thoughts, images, sensations, and emotions that occupy one's mind at any given time. **12**

consolidation hypothesis   The idea that a series of solidifying events occurs when a memory is acquired enabling it to become fixed in long-term memory. **6**

constituent   A group of words that make sense together. **9**

contingency   A relationship between two stimuli such that the occurrence of one seems to depend on the occurence of the other. **5**

contingency management   An operant-conditioning therapy that seeks to increase desirable behaviors by reinforcement and decrease undesirable ones by punishment or withdrawal of rewards. **16**

continuity   A gestalt principle of organization proposing that items will be perceived as belonging together if they appear to form a single, continuous pattern. **4**

continuous reinforcement schedule   The providing of reinforcement each time an organism exhibits the desired behavior. **5**

control group   In an experiment, subjects who experience all the same conditions as experimental subjects except the key factor that is being evaluated. **2**

conventional stage   According to Kohlberg, the stage in moral development during which a child adheres to rules to win the approval of others, and is inclined to follow the dictates of established authority. **8**

conversion disorder   The loss of a sensory or motor function without organic impairment, usually following some traumatic event. **15**

cornea   The tough, transparent outer covering of the front of the eyeball which admits light into the interior of the eye. **4**

correlational research   A research design used to find out the extent to which two variables are related when a true experiment is not feasible. **2**

correlation coefficient   A numerical value that indicates the strength and direction of the relationship between two variables. **2**

cortex   The covering of gray matter of the cerebral hemispheres, in which much of the "higher-order" processing that occurs in the cerebral hemispheres is carried out. **3**

counseling psychologists   Those who help individuals deal with mild problems of social and emotional adjustment. **1**

criterion validity   The type of validity a test has if a person's score on it can be correlated with some other yardstick of what is being measured. **14**

critical period   A relatively restricted period of development in which an animal is especially susceptible to particular influences that may bring about enduring behavior changes or effects; in relation to language learning, a pe-

riod early in life during which a human being has a special facility for language learning. **9**

cross-sectional study   A study in which the population is divided into subgroups on the basis of certain criteria, the subgroups are randomly sampled, and the members of each sample are then surveyed, tested, or observed. **2**

decay theory   The view that memories simply fade away with the passage of time if they are not renewed through periodic use. **6**

defense mechanisms   According to Freudian theory, a mental strategy that the ego uses to block harmful behavior and thus reduce anxiety. **13**

defensive avoidance   The tendency of people to rationalize, procrastinate, pass the buck, or engage in other such behavior in order to avoid making difficult decisions. **7**

delta waves   Very slow brain waves that predominate in deep sleep. **12**

delusions   Irrational beliefs held despite overwhelming evidence to the contrary. **15**

demand characteristics   In an experiment, clues felt by the subject to demand certain "correct" responses. **2**

dendrites   The short, branched extensions of a neuron that usually carry neural impulses toward the cell body. **3**

denial   According to psychoanalytic theory, a defense mechanism which involves a refusal to acknowledge some threat. **13**

dependent variable   A factor that is expected to change when the independent variable is manipulated. **2**

depressant   A chemical that suppresses nerve impulses. **12**

depression   A dysphoric mood, persisting for at least two weeks, which tends to color all of a person's thoughts and behaviors. **15**

depth of processing view   The theory that we have only one memory system and that the observed differences between short-term and long-term memory are due to how shallowly or deeply we process information. **6**

depth perception   The brain's tendency to see the world in three dimensions although the images that strike our retinas are in two dimensions. **4**

descriptive statistics   Statistical methods used to summarize a vast amount of data in forms that are brief, meaningful, and easy to grasp. **2**

developmental psychology   The branch of psychology that seeks to comprehend the patterns of growth and change that occur in human beings throughout the life cycle, from conception to death. **1, 8**

dichotic listening   A technique, developed by E. C. Cherry, involving the simultaneous input of different information into each ear. **6**

dichromat A person who is partially color blind because of the lack or loss of one of the three forms of iodopsin normally found in the cones. **4**

discrimination The behavioral expression of prejudice. **17**

discrimination training A procedure used to teach an animal to respond to only a specific stimulus by presenting similar stimuli which will not elicit a reward. **5**

discriminative stimuli The stimuli which elicit rewards in discrimination training. **5**

dispersion The degree of scatter among the individual numbers of a set of numbers. **2**

displacement According to psychoanalytic theory, a defense mechanism that involves the transfer of unacceptable feelings from their appropriate target to a "safer" object. **13**

dissociation A split in consciousness whereby certain thoughts, feelings, and behaviors operate independently from others; an explanation of what happens in hypnosis. **12**

dissociative disorders Psychological disorders that involve the splitting off of a part of the personality so that the victim's memory or identity is disturbed. **15**

DNA (deoxyribonucleic acid) An organic molecule composed of subunits of chemical structures whose sequence determines the genetic information carried by the chromosome. **8**

double bind A state of confusion that occurs when an individual is exposed to contradictory communications simultaneously. **15**

double-blind technique A procedure in which neither the experimenter nor the subjects know who has been assigned to the experimental group or who is acting as a control. **2**

dream interpretation A technique used in psychoanalytically oriented therapy in which the hidden meaning of a dream can be brought to light, and unconscious wishes, fantasies, and conflicts can be explored. **16**

drive State of biological need that motivates an animal to act to reduce tension. **11**

drug therapy The treatment of psychological disorders through the administration of drugs. **16**

dual control The control that the autonomic nervous system exercises over visceral muscles and glands by the exercise of its sympathetic and parasympathetic subsystems. **3**

dual memory view The theory that there exists a separate long-term and short-term memory. **6**

eardrum A membrane between the outer and inner ear that responds to changes in air pressure by moving in and out, thus amplifying sound. **4**

educational psychologists Researchers who study all psychological aspects of the learning process. **1**

effector cells Cells specialized for contracting muscles and for stimulating glandular secretions. **3**

ego According to Freud, the part of the psyche that handles transactions between the external environment and the demands of the id and the superego based on the reality principle. **13**

eidetic imagery Visual images that persist with incredible clarity and detail for a minute or two before they fade. **6**

electroconvulsive therapy (ECT) A form of biological therapy used to treat depression in which an electric current is passed through the brain, causing a convulsion which is therapeutic. **16**

electroencephalogram (EEG) A device that records the electrical activity of brain waves by electrodes placed on the skull. **12**

emotions States of feeling that can affect behavior, that often arise in response to social relationships and other external situations, that are usually accompanied by physiological changes and various thoughts about the emotion and its causes. **10**

empiricist viewpoint The notion that perceptual processes are largely learned. **4**

encounter group A form of group therapy emphasizing personal growth and improved interpersonal interactions through intensive experience in a small group that encourages honest expression of emotion. **16**

endocrine glands Those glands that produce hormones and secrete them into the bloodstream. **3**

endorphins Morphinelike neurotransmitters whose role in schizophrenia is being studied. **3**

enkephalins Morphinelike neurotransmitters that serve as the body's natural pain fighters. **3**

environmental psychology The study of the relationship between human beings and their physical and social surroundings. **1, 18**

epinephrine Also called adrenalin, this hormone prepares the body to deal with stress by producing various physiological changes. **3**

estrogen A sex hormone secreted by the ovaries that is involved in the development of female sex characteristics and the onset of menstruation. **3**

event-related potentials Patterns of electrical activity that accompany mental processes. **3**

evoked potential The pattern of electrical activity in the brain caused by a stimulus. **3**

expectancy-value model The explanation of motivation that takes into account both the expectancy of achieving a particular goal and the value placed upon it. **11**

experiment A situation in which the researcher can control conditions and so rule out all influences on people's behavior except the factors being examined. **2**

experimental group   In an experiment, subjects who experience the experimental condition. **2**

experimental psychologists   Psychologists who use experimentation to gather data on those behavioral processes shared by many animal species. **1**

extinction   The slow weakening and eventual disappearance of a conditioned response. **20**

face validity   The characteristic of a test item that commonsensically seems to measure what it is supposed to. **14**

family therapy   Psychotherapy which stresses the importance of altering family roles and patterns of communication that maintain maladaptive behavior. **16**

feature-based model   The model of concept formation which holds that we test hypotheses regarding which features of a stimulus define it as a member of a category. **7**

figure   The section of the perceptual field which represents objects. **4**

first-order conditioning   Classical conditioning in which a conditioned stimulus is followed by a primary reinforcer. **5**

fixation   In psychoanalysis, a state of arrested development where an individual remains "locked" in a particular psychological battle and expresses this conflict symbolically. **13**

fixed-interval schedule   A partial reinforcement schedule in which a reward is given for the first correct response after a certain time interval. **5**

fixed-ratio schedule   A partial reinforcement schedule in which a reward is given after a specified number of responses. **5**

focusing strategy   The approach to concept formation which states that we start with a global hypothesis and gradually, with experience, eliminate features that can vary and thus cannot be defining characteristics. **7**

forensic psychology   The application of psychological principles to problems of law enforcement and the courts. **1**

formal-operational period   The last of Piaget's periods of intellectual development (from adolescence through adulthood), during which a person learns to think simultaneously about many systems of operations and to think hypothetically. **8**

fovea   A pitlike depression near the center of the retina, containing cones but no rods, that is the point of highest visual acuity. **4**

free association   A psychoanalytic technique for exploring the unconscious through a patient's unrestrained expression of thoughts that occur spontaneously. **1, 16**

free-floating anxiety   Freud's term for worries for which the sufferer is unable to specify a cause. **15**

free recall   The recounting of memorized material in no particular order. **6**

frequency   The number of compression-rarefaction cycles that occur per second. The frequency of a soundwave corresponds to the pitch we hear. **4**

frequency distribution   The number of instances of each score. **2**

frequency theory   The theory of pitch that argues that the basilar membrane vibrates in exactly the same frequency pattern as the original sound wave, thus causing neural impulses to fire in that pattern too. **4**

frontal lobe   The portion of each cerebral hemisphere that is concerned with motor activities and speech. **3**

frustration   Interference with any goal-directed behavior. **18**

frustration-aggression hypothesis   Dollard's theory that aggression is always a consequence of frustration, and frustration always leads to some form of aggression. **18**

fugue   A total abdication of one's home and identity. People suffering from this disorder may be absent from their home for hours or years, and recall nothing of what happened in the fugue state. **15**

fully functioning   Rogers' term for people who, because they have learned conditions of worth that are few and reasonable, are open to a wide range of feelings and behaviors. **13**

functional fixedness   The tendency to overlook novel uses for things. **7**

functionalism   The view, influenced by Darwin's theories and expounded chiefly by William James, that psychological processes have adaptive functions that allow the human species to survive and that these processes are more important to investigate than the mind's structure. **1**

fundamental attribution error   The tendency to overestimate the role of dispositional rather than situational factors in judging the behavior of others. **17**

fundamental needs   In Maslow's hierarchy, those needs associated with physical requirements, such as satisfying thirst and hunger, and those related to obtaining a safe environment. **13**

ganglion cells   Cells that form the fibers of the optic nerve. **4**

gate-control theory   The theory asserting that the sensation of pain depends on the balance of activity between large- and small-diameter (A and C) nerve fibers within the spinal cord. **4**

general adaptation syndrome   As outlined by Hans Selye, the set of physiological responses that is evoked by unusually demanding stress. **10**

generalization gradient   The graph of responses from a discrimination training exercise, showing the number of responses per each stimulus. **5**

generalized anxiety Diffuse fears that are impossible to manage through avoidance. **15**

general paresis The final stage of syphilis characterized by irreversible deterioration of all mental and physical processes. **15**

genes Ultramicroscopic particles within the cell nucleus that are the basic units for the transmission of hereditary characteristics. **8**

genital stage According to Freud, the fifth psychosexual stage (occurring from puberty on), during which the sexual focus shifts from autoeroticism to sexual intercourse. **13**

gestalt psychology The approach to psychology that maintains that what emerges from perception of individual pieces of information is a whole that is greater than the sum of its parts. **1**

gestalts Meaningful patterns that the brain constructs from sensory information. **4**

gestalt therapy Psychotherapy that emphasizes the present and attempts to make a client whole by ridding him or her of defenses, increasing awareness, and releasing pent-up feelings. **16**

glia Cells that hold neurons in place, carry nutrients to them, repair and protect them, and aid in the propagation of impulses. **3**

global hypothesis The assumption we make, upon first encountering a stimulus that is an instance of an unfamiliar concept, that all of its features are defining characteristics. **7**

gonads Glands that secrete sex hormones. The female gonads are the ovaries, which secrete estrogen and progesterone. The male gonads are the testes, which secrete testosterone. **3**

grammar The structural rules (morphology plus syntax) that speakers of a language share. **9**

gray matter The nonmyelinated axons, dendrites, and cell bodies of the nervous system. **3**

ground The part of the perceptual field that represents space between objects. **4**

group A collection of people who regularly interact with one another in a structured way, are oriented toward specific goals, and who have a feeling of group identity and solidarity. **18**

group therapy The type of treatment in which therapists work with an interacting collection of people rather than with individuals. **16**

groupthink The mode of decision making whereby a small, cohesive group becomes so concerned with maintaining unanimity that it can no longer appraise alternatives realistically. **18**

growth hormone The hormone produced by the pituitary gland which plays a key role in a child's physical development. **3**

habituated Accustomed to a stimulus, so that it no longer produces an orienting reflex. **5**

hair cell A cell, containing hairlike projections, that is a receptor for hearing in the inner ear. **4**

hallucinogens Drugs that produce hallucinations and impaired thinking. **12**

hammer One of a set of three tiny, interconnected bones in the middle ear that transmit sound from the eardrum to the cochlea. **4**

happiness An enduring, positive emotional state that includes quiet contentment with one's life as well as active pleasures and achievements. **10**

health and health care A field in which psychologists' roles are expanding due to the increased recognition of psychological factors in illness. **1**

heuristic A rule-of-thumb strategy in problem solving. **7**

hierarchy of needs Maslow's concept that all humans face a series of needs in life, and that needs at more basic levels must be met before the person can go on to fulfill higher-level needs. **13**

hippocampus One of three interrelated structures of the limbic system; the others are the septal area and the amygdala. **3**

histogram A graph arranged so as to show frequency distribution, the number of instances of each score. **2**

hormones Chemical substances produced by the endocrine system which travel through the bloodstream and regulate physiological activities. **3**

hypnagogic state The drowsy altered state of consciousness between wakefulness and sleep. **12**

hypochondriasis Psychological disorder characterized by irrational fear of contracting a disease and continuous search for reassurance from doctors. **15**

hypothalamus The structure located below the thalamus which regulates the body's internal environment and acts to maintain balance within the body. **3**

hypothesis A proposition or belief that one sets out to test. **2**

id According to Freud, the impulsive and unconscious part of the psyche which operates via the pleasure principle towards the gratification of instinctual drives. **13**

identification According to Freud, a method of reducing the anxiety produced by the Oedipus conflict by categorizing oneself as psychologically similar to the parent of one's own sex, and therefore adopting the parent's gender role as one's own. In social psychology, the tendency to go along with others because we admire and wish to be like them. **8, 18**

illusion decrements Decreases in the strength of illusions with longer exposure to the illusion-producing stimuli. **4**

imprint   The attachment birds form to other organisms or objects during an early critical period. This attachment is somewhat resistant to later modification. **9**

incentives   Expectations of receiving a reward that stimulate or maintain goal-directed behavior. **11**

incubation   A period of rest from problem solving, which encourages mental flexibility. **7**

independent variable   A factor that an experimenter deliberately manipulates. **2**

industrial psychologists   Psychologists who study the relationship between people and their work. **1**

inferential statistics   Statistical methods used to conclude whether the data clearly support one's original hypothesis. **2**

inferiority complex   Adler's theory that all children are born with a deep sense of inferiority because of their small size, physical weakness, and lack of knowledge and power in the adult world. **13**

insight   A sudden understanding of the critical relationships of a problem. **7**

instincts   Innate, internal forces, characteristic of a species, which propel individuals to behave in broadly predictable ways. **11**

intelligence quotient (IQ)   A measure of an individual's mental development obtained by dividing a person's mental age (the average age of children who obtain a particular score on an intelligence test) by a person's chronological age and multiplying the quotient by 100. **14**

intensity   In light, how densely photons of light are packed. In sound, the amount of pressure a sound wave exerts. **4**

interference   The fading of memory due to the inevitable confusion caused by the subsequent encountering of similar experiences. **6**

interjudge reliability   The characteristic of a test that yields the same results when administered independently by two or more trained people. **14**

internal consistency   The characteristic of a test that yields the same responses from people to items that measure the same thing. **14**

internalization   Incorporation of society's values into the self or personality to such an extent that violation of these standards produces a sense of guilt. **8, 18**

interneurons   The neurons that connect neurons to each other and integrate the activities of the sensory and motor neurons. **3**

interpersonal aggression   Behavior directed toward the goal of injuring another person who does not desire to be hurt. **18**

intrinsic motivation   The internal satisfaction of acting competently that explains human behavior. **11**

intrinsic reinforcement or punishment   Self-reactions such as self-esteem or self-reproach that affect a person's learning and behavior. **5**

introspection   Wundt's technique of investigating consciousness by precise, systematic, detached observation of one's mental experiences. Also, a method of exploring thought processes by asking subjects to describe in detail how they arrived at an answer or solved a problem. **1, 7**

iodopsin   The purple pigment, contained in various forms in the cones of the eye, that responds to different bands of light waves. **4**

iris   A ring of pigmented tissue that gives the eye its color and expands and contracts to control the amount of light that enters the retina. **4**

James-Lange theory   The view of William James and Carl Lange that the perception of bodily changes produces the actual experience of emotion. **10**

key word system   A mnemonic device involving the association of items to be learned with simple words that can be visualized easily. **6**

Korsakoff's syndrome   Irreversible brain damage and accompanying memory loss suffered by alcoholics. **12**

latency stage   According to Freud, the fourth stage of psychosexual development (occurring from age five or six until the start of puberty), during which sexual impulses are repressed while the child learns social and cognitive skills. **13**

latent content   In psychoanalysis, the symbolic meanings of dreams that expose unconscious conflicts. **12, 16**

latent learning   Learning in which knowledge of a new behavior is not demonstrated until an incentive to do so arises. **5**

lateral fissure   The top boundary of the temporal lobe of the brain. **3**

lateralized   The term used to describe the human brain, in which different sides control different behavioral functions. **9**

law of effect   Thorndike's theory that responses that lead to satisfying consequences will be strengthened and are therefore likely to be repeated, whereas responses that lead to unsatisfying consequences will be weakened and are unlikely to be repeated. **5**

learning   A relatively permanent change in performance potential that arises from experience. **5**

lens   In vision, a transparent, elastic structure that allows the eye to adjust focus in accordance with an object's distance. **4**

lesion   An alteration of the brain produced by surgical destruction or removal of a small area. **3**

limbic system   The innermost of the cerebral hemispheres which is important in emotion, motivation, and sexual and feeding behavior. **3**

linear perspective   The impression of depth created by the convergence of parallel lines as they recede into the distance. **4**

linguistic competence   A person's intuitive grasp of the rules for constructing grammatical sentences. **9**

linguistic performance   The application of implicit knowledge of grammar during speaking or listening. **9**

linguistic relativity hypothesis   Whorf's notion that language heavily influences thought. **9**

linguistic universals   Features found in all languages as a result of shared characteristics of thought. **9**

lithium   A drug used to treat both mania and bipolar affective disorders. **16**

localization of function   The principle that different parts of the brain are involved in different behaviors. **3**

longitudinal study   A study in which the same group of people is examined over a number of years. **2**

long-term memory   The storage of information for an indefinite period of time to be used over and over again. **6**

lucid dreams   Nighttime fantasies in which the dreamer clearly perceives that he or she is only dreaming, yet the dream continues. **12**

mania   A prolonged state of elation and feverish activity often mixed with intense irritability. **15**

manic-depressive (bipolar) disorder   A psychological disorder characterized by the episodic nature of extremes of mood. **15**

manifest content   In psychoanalysis, dream material that is recalled and reported by the dreamer; the plot or story line of the dream. **12, 16**

maze   A complex path leading to food or water; used to carry out operant conditioning in animals. **5**

mean   The arithmetic average of a set of numbers. **2**

means-end analysis   A heuristic by which means are sought that will move the problem solver closer to the goal. **7**

measures of variability   Statistical techniques for expressing the spread of numbers in a frequency distribution. **2**

median   The number that falls in the exact middle of a distribution of numbers arranged from highest to lowest. **2**

medical model   The theoretical perspective on abnormal behavior that considers psychological disorders to be similar to physical illnesses. **15**

meditation   A focusing of attention on a single stimulus, thus restricting sensory input and producing an altered state of consciousness. **12**

medulla   The part of the brain stem that controls autonomic activities, chewing, salivation, and facial movements. **3**

meiosis   The process of sperm and egg cell division during which chromosome pairs are split, rearranged, and distributed to two daughter cells. **8**

mentally retarded   The term applied to a person whose general intelligence has from childhood been significantly below average and who chronically has trouble functioning in normal everyday settings. **14**

mental set   The inclination to repeat a solution that has worked in the past. **7**

meta-analysis   A sophisticated statistical method by which the results of many studies are combined to give the average size of a therapy's success. **16**

metacognition   The ability to monitor one's own thoughts. **8**

method of loci   A mnemonic device involving the association of items to be remembered with a series of places, or loci, that are already firmly fixed in memory. **6**

midbrain   A small structure of the brain stem that contains centers for visual and auditory reflexes. **3**

Minnesota Multiphasic Personality Inventory (MMPI) An objective personality test, designed to provide a detailed list of a subject's personality traits based on his or her answers to a series of over 550 statements. **14**

misattribution theory   Schachter's theory that feelings of love can be mistaken for physiological arousal due to another cause. **17**

mnemonic devices   Various techniques that improve recall ability, including method of loci, key word system, and eidetic imagery. **6**

mode   The number that is most frequently obtained in a distribution. **2**

modeling   The process by which someone learns a new behavior by observing other people perform that behavior. **16**

monochromat   A person whose cones contain only one form of iodopsin and who thus cannot distinguish colors. **4**

morphemes   The smallest combinations of speech sounds that have meaning in a given language. **9**

morphology   The study and description of how sounds form basic units of speech, and how these basic units form complex words. **9**

motion parallax   The differences in apparent movement between near and far objects. **4**

motivated forgetting   The forgetting of information because we want to, either consciously or unconsciously. **6**

motivation   Those factors that arouse, sustain, and direct behavior toward attainment of some goal. **11**

motor cortex   The area of the brain's frontal lobe next to the central fissure which is concerned primarily with the regulation of voluntary movements. **3**

motor neurons   The neurons that carry signals from the brain and spinal cord to the muscles and glands. **3**

multiple personality   An extreme form of dissociation in which a person's personality structure divides into two or more complete identities, each well defined and distinct from the others. **15**

myelin sheath   A fatty, whitish substance that wraps around an axon. **3**

nativist viewpoint   The notion that perceptual processes are accounted for partly by learning and partly by the ways in which sensory systems work. **4**

natural concepts   Categories used in daily thought to classify objects. They are thought to be encoded through prototypes, not a list of defining features. **7**

naturalistic observation   The study of subjects in a natural setting without interference or distraction from the investigator. **2**

need for achievement   The motivation to achieve; those high in this need persist longer and do better on difficult tasks and are apt to set realistic and challenging goals. **11**

negative correlation   The relationship between two variables in which a high rank on one is accompanied by a low rank on the other. **2**

negative reinforcement   Reinforcement that strengthens a response because the response removes some painful or unpleasant stimulus or enables the organism to avoid it. **5**

nerves   Bundles of neurons that transmit electrochemical impulses from one part of the body to another. **3**

network theory   The notion that when information is stored in long-term memory it becomes linked to whatever strong emotion a person may be feeling at the time. **6**

neurons   Cells specialized for conducting signals from one part of the body to another; they connect receptor cells to effector cells and integrate their activities. They are also called nerve cells. **3**

neuropeptides   A class of brain chemicals first identified as hormones that are now considered neurotransmitters. **3**

neurotic   The term used by mental health professionals to refer to relatively mild disorders whose victims do not lose touch with reality. **15**

neurotransmitters   Chemical substances which diffuse across synapses and activate receptor sites on adjacent cells. **3**

noise   Irrelevant, competing stimuli that serve to limit our sensory capacities. **4**

norepinephrine   Also called noradrenalin, this hormone plays a role in adapting the body to stress. **3**

norm   An unstated expectation or explicit standard for behavior that members of a group share. In testing, the range of scores on a test and percentage of test takers who earned scores at various levels. **14, 18**

normal curve   A line graph of a distribution having a bell-shaped curve. **2**

normal distribution   A distribution showing a normal curve. **2**

obedience   Following the explicit commands of a person in authority. **18**

object concept   According to Piaget, the capacity, which develops during the sensorimotor period, to understand that an object exists even when it is no longer perceived. **8**

objects relation theory   A modern psychoanalytic approach that focuses on an infant's social attachments, especially to the mother, and on the importance that the quality of these attachments have for development of the child's ego, feelings about the self, and later interpersonal relations. **13**

observational learning   The process of learning how to act by watching the behavior of others. **5, 13**

obsession   A recurring irrational thought, one that the victim recognizes as senseless and tries to suppress but cannot. **15**

occipital lobe   A rear portion of each cerebral hemisphere, concerned with the reception and analysis of visual information. **3**

Oedipus conflict   According to Freud, the tendency of children to see themselves as rivals of the same-sex parent for the affection of the parent of the opposite sex. When resolved, the conflict leads to adoption of the values of the same-sex parent. **8**

olfaction   The sense of smell. **4**

olfactory bulbs   The part of the brain at the forward base of the cerebral hemispheres that receives nerve impulses concerning smell from the nose and relays them to other parts of the brain. **4**

olfactory membranes   Membranes that line the roof of the nasal passages and contain many receptor cells. **4**

operant behaviors   Actions that an organism emits spontaneously, of its own accord. **5**

operant conditioning   Learning to either make or withhold a particular response because of its positive or negative consequences. **5**

operantly conditioned response   A response resulting from a learned association between a particular action and a desirable consequence. **5**

opponent process model   The model of emotional response which holds that a negative emotion triggers a positive emotion, and vice versa. If the original emotion is removed, the opposite emotion will temporarily overwhelm the organism. **11**

opponent-process theory   The theory that three different systems, composed of three types of cells, are responsible for color vision: In one system, some cells are stimulated by red and inhibited by green and others are stimulated by green and inhibited by red. In another system, yellow and blue similarly act in opposition to each other. The other system is achromatic and sensitive to brightness. **4**

optic chiasma   The point at which the nerves from each retina meet and then split to opposite sides of the cerebral cortex. **4**

optic nerve   The nerve that carries visual information from the eye to the brain for interpretation. **4**

optimum level of arousal   The level of cortical arousal at which an organism's goal-directed behaviors are most effective. **11**

oral stage   According to Freud, the first psychosexual stage (occurring during the first year of life) in which sexual pleasure is focused on the mouth's activities. **13**

organizational psychologists   Psychologists who study the relationship between the behavior of individuals in large organizations, such as businesses, and the efficiency of the organization. **1**

orienting reflex   A response that involves a whole chain of activities—looking, listening, touching, sniffing—designed to ascertain what a new stimulus is about. **5**

oval window   A membrane between the middle ear and the inner ear that transmits sound to the cochlea. **4**

overregularization   The erroneous extension of a grammatical rule to instances where it does not apply. **9**

panic attacks   Episodes of acute and overwhelming tension experienced by those with generalized anxiety. **15**

papillae   The bumpy projections on the top surface of the tongue that contain the taste buds. **4**

parasympathetic nervous system   The division of the autonomic nervous system that dominates under conditions of relaxation and tends to conserve the body's energy. **3**

parietal lobe   A portion of the cerebral hemisphere concerned with skin senses and the sense of body position. **3**

partial overlap   The illusion, created when one object partially covers another, that the covered object is farther away. **4**

partial reinforcement schedule   Reinforcing a desired behavior only part of the time. **5**

participant modeling   A therapeutic technique which has the therapist serve as a model by performing activities feared by a patient and then guiding the client through a series of steps culminating in the same activity. **16**

participant observation   A form of naturalistic observation in which an investigator joins an existing group in order to record thoughts and feelings accessible to only group members. **2**

perception   The process whereby the brain gives order and meaning to the sensations it receives. **4**

perceptual constancy   The tendency of the brain to perceive objects with stable properties even though the images received are constantly changing. **4**

perceptual grouping   The concept by which gestalt psychologists explain relationships among sensory stimuli. The chief principles of grouping are proximity, continuity, and similarity, which may all be integrated by another principle— simplicity. **4**

perceptual illusions   Perceptions not in accord with the true characteristics of objects. **4**

peripheral nervous system   The part of the nervous system that conveys signals from the body's sensory receptors to the central nervous system and transmits messages back out to the muscles and glands. **3**

persona   The self that we present to others. **13**

personality   The set of relatively stable and distinctive styles of thought, behavior, and emotional response that characterize a person's adaptations to surrounding circumstances. **13**

personality disorders   Deep-seated maladaptive patterns of relating to others that cause distress either to the victim, those around the victim, or both. **15**

personality psychologists   Psychologists who measure and explain individual differences in behavior. **1**

person-centered therapy   Carl Rogers' system of psychotherapy, based on the belief that the client is responsible for his or her own potential and self-actualization and which creates an atmosphere of acceptance and feedback to aid the client. **13, 16**

personnel psychology   A subfield of industrial psychology that is concerned with hiring, assigning, and promoting employees. **1**

persuasive communications   Messages consciously intended to persuade or to promote attitude change. **17**

phallic stage   According to Freud, the third psychosexual stage (occurring during the third to fifth or sixth year of life), during which a child struggles with identification with the same-sex parent. **13**

phenomenological approach   Method of understanding personality that emphasizes the human potential for growth, creativity, and spontaneity, and that stresses the importance of an individual's subjective experience of the world. **1, 13**

phobia   An excessive and irrational fear of particular objects or situations. **15**

phonemes   A class of slightly varying sounds that speakers of a language perceive as linguistically similar. **9**

phonics approach   The method of teaching reading which holds that children must first be taught the sounds that letters stand for and then encouraged to see spoken words as strings of these sounds. **9**

phonology   The study and description of the sounds that make up a language. **9**

phrenology   The study of behavior by assessing the shape of the skull, which, according to nineteenth-century anatomist Franz Joseph Gall, conformed to the shape of the brain beneath. **3**

physiological measures   Measures that provide objective, quantitative data on phenomena associated with particular psychological states, such as sleep, that are difficult to assess in other ways. **2**

physiological psychologists   Those psychologists concerned with the underlying biological bases of behavior. **1, 3**

pinna   The projection of skin-covered cartilage visible on the outside of the head, through which sound enters the outer ear. **4**

pituitary gland   A small endocrine gland at the base of the brain which controls a wide range of bodily functions, and which has been called the "master gland." **3**

placebo   A substance that has no physiological effect. **2**

place theory   The theory, proposed by Hermann von Helmholtz, that the pitch we hear depends on which part of the basilar membrane a sound wave vibrates the most. **4**

pleasure principle   According to psychoanalytic theory, the principle of mental functioning of the id whereby physical tensions are reduced by gratification of instinctual drives without regard for logic, reality, or morality. **13**

polarized   Describing cells that are negatively charged inside and positively charged outside. **3**

polygraph   Often called a lie detector, this instrument monitors the physiological changes (blood pressure, heart rate, and the like) that accompany emotion. **10**

pons   The structure of the brain which transmits motor information from the higher brain areas and spinal cord to the cerebellum, and is vital in integrating movements between the right and left sides of the body. **3**

positive correlation   The relationship between two variables in which a high rank on one is accompanied by a high rank on the other. **2**

positive reinforcement   Reinforcement that strengthens a response because the response is followed by a positive or pleasant stimulus. **5**

postconventional stage   According to Kohlberg, the final stage in moral development, during which a person recognizes that universal ethical principles can transcend specific societal laws. Failure to adhere to these principles brings self-condemnation. **8**

pragmatics   The field that studies the implicit understandings people have about how language should be used in different social contexts. **9**

preconventional stage   According to Kohlberg, the early stage in moral development during which a child adheres to the rules of society because he or she fears the consequences of breaking them. **8**

predictive validity   The type of validity a test has if results can be correlated with people's future performance. **14**

prejudice   A negative and inflexible attitude toward members of a minority group based on erroneous or incomplete information. **17**

preoperational period   The second of Piaget's periods of intellectual development (from age two through six) during which a child understands complex events but cannot use mental operations or coordinate thoughts into logical systems. **8**

primacy effect   The principle that information received early in a series tends to outweigh later information. **17**

primary drive   A state of physiological tension that arises from needs built into the body's system. **11**

primary reinforcer   A reinforcer that satisfies some basic biological need and can thus be used to establish and maintain a conditioned response. **5**

principle of mass action   Karl Lashley's term for the fact that almost all activity involves many parts of the brain. **3**

principle of multiple control   The fact that a specific part of the brain is likely to be involved in the performance of many types of behavior. **3**

proactive interference   The fading of memory that occurs when material learned earlier interferes with recall of material learned later. **6**

probability   The likelihood of a particular event or response occurring, calculated mathematically. **2, 7**

progesterone   A sex hormone secreted by the ovaries that is involved in the development of female sex characteristics and the onset of menstruation. **3**

program evaluation   A field of psychology that involves the measuring of the variables that go into particular programs, especially in government, and the results they bring about. **1**

programmed instruction   Instruction which emphasizes reinforcement by providing the student with immediate feedback for every response, and by not allowing the student to proceed until each subject has been fully understood. **5**

projection   According to psychoanalytic theory, a defense mechanism that involves the unknown attribution of one's own objectionable impulses to other people. **13**

projective tests   Tests in which personality characteristics are revealed by the way a subject responds to and interprets ambiguous material, such as an inkblot or ambiguous scene in a picture. **14**

propositions Unitary ideas that combine to yield the meaning of a sentence. **9**

prospective studies Studies that follow subjects forward through time. **2**

prototype An example that best illustrates a concept; the means by which natural concepts are thought to be encoded in memory. **7**

proximity The principle of gestalt psychology that stimuli close to each other will tend to be perceived as a group. **4**

psychiatric nurses Registered nurses who have specialized in psychiatric care as part of the nursing degree and are usually employed in a mental hospital. **16**

psychiatric social workers Those who have a master's degree in social work and have specialized in psychiatric social work. **16**

psychiatrists Medical doctors who specialize in the diagnosis and treatment of mental disorders. **1, 16**

psychoactive drugs Drugs that interact with the central nervous system to alter a person's mood, perception, mode of thinking, and behavior. **12**

psychoanalysis Freudian psychotherapy which employs techniques such as analysis of dreams and free association to unlock the thoughts and feelings of the unconscious and break their power to control behavior. **1, 13**

psychoanalyst Usually a psychiatrist (although sometimes a lay person or psychologist) who has had advanced training in psychoanalysis and who has been psychoanalyzed as part of that training. **1, 16**

psychoanalytic approach Method of understanding personality initiated by Freud that emphasizes childhood experiences as critically important in shaping adult personality. **13**

psychological needs In Maslow's hierarchy, all higher-level needs, including the needs to belong, to be loved, to achieve competence and recognition, and to attain self-actualization. **13**

psychological reactance The tendency of people to increase their support for an activity or idea when they feel threatened by attempts to change that idea or behavior. **17**

psychology The study of behavior and mental processes. **1**

psychopharmacology The study of the relationship between drugs and behavior. **1**

psychosurgery The removal or destruction of parts of the brain for the purpose of altering behavior. **16**

psychotherapy A series of systematic verbal and emotional interactions between a person who is trained to aid in alleviating psychological problems and someone who is suffering from them. **16**

psychotic The term used by mental health professionals to describe very severe mental disorders whose victims lose touch with reality. **15**

puberty The period marking the start of adolescence during which a person's reproductive organs become capable of functioning and secondary sex characteristics develop. **8**

punishment A consequence that produces suppression (decrease in frequency) of the behavior that caused it. **5**

pupil The opening in the center of the eye through which light enters and travels to the retina. **4**

quasi-experiment A research design that approximates, but does not meet, the requirements of a true experiment because the investigator has far less control over variables or subjects cannot be randomly assigned to conditions. **2**

racism Prejudice directed toward members of certain racial groups. **17**

radical behaviorism Skinner's approach which argues that human actions can largely be explained by reference to rewards and punishment rather than to the concept of "mind." **13**

random sample A sample in which every member of the population has an equal chance of being included. **2**

range The difference between the highest and lowest scores of a set of scores. **2**

rational-emotive therapy (RET) Ellis's method of therapy, which seeks to replace irrational, problem-provoking outlooks with more realistic ones. **16**

reaction formation According to psychoanalytic theory, a defense mechanism that involves the replacement of an anxiety-producing impulse or feeling with its direct opposite. **13**

reality principle The operating principle of the ego according to which the need for gratification of instinctual drives is curbed by the realistic demands of the environment; gratification is thereby modified or delayed based on a concern for the safety of the individual. **13**

recall The retrieval of specific pieces of information from long-term memory, usually guided by retrieval cues. **6**

receptor cells Cell embedded in the sense organs that are sensitive to various types of stimulation from the environment. **3**

recognition Consideration of a given stimulus and decision about whether it matches something stored in long-term memory. **6**

reference group A group with which a person associates or identifies himself or herself, and to which that person turns for guidance in formulating values, beliefs, and attitudes. **18**

reflex arc The simplest set of connections between neurons that links a sensory input to a motor response. **3**

regression   According to psychoanalytic theory, a defense mechanism whereby a person made anxious by threatening thoughts and feelings behaves in ways characteristic of an earlier period of life. **13**

rehearsal   The conscious repetition of information in an effort to retain it in short-term memory, usually involving speech. **5**

reinforcement (reward)   A consequence that produces repetition (increase in frequency) of the behavior that caused it. **5**

relative size   Of two objects thought to be the same size, the one that casts the smaller retinal image is perceived to be farther away; a monocular depth cue. **4**

reliability   An essential criterion in determining the value of a test. A test is reliable if it yields, upon repetition, similar results for different parts of the test, for scoring by different judges, and for the same test administered to the same person at two different times. **14**

REM rebound   Compensation for lost REM sleep on one night by more REM sleep the next night. **12**

REM sleep   The stage of sleep where a person experiences rapid eye movement. Vivid dreaming appears to take place primarily during this stage. **12**

replication   Reconstruction of the basic features of a study to see if the results are similar. **2**

representational thought   The ability to recognize things mentally when they are not physically present. **8**

representativeness   A heuristic by which given information is matched with a stereotype. **7**

representative sample   A sample in which critical subgroups are represented according to their incidence in the population as a whole. **2**

repression   The psychological defense mechanism, first described by Freud, by which people push unacceptable, anxiety-provoking thoughts and impulses into their unconscious so as to avoid confronting them directly. **6, 11, 13**

resistance   Attempts by a client in therapy to block treatment. **16**

resting potential   The electrical imbalance that occurs across the cell membrane when a cell is polarized. **3**

restrained eater   A person who must constantly watch his or her diet to maintain normal weight and avoid obesity. **11**

reticular formation   A complex network of neural fibers and cell bodies which extends from the spinal cord to the thalamus, acting as a sentry system to the higher brain and also affecting the sleep-waking cycle. **3**

retina   The light-sensitive, innermost coat of the eyeball. The retina is a predominantly neural structure consisting of several layers, including a layer of rods and cones. **4**

retroactive interference   The fading of memory that oc-

curs when information learned later interferes with information learned earlier. **6**

retrograde amnesia   A form of amnesia in which the memory deficit involves only a specific segment of the past and does not affect the recollection of new events. **6**

rhodopsin   The deep red pigment contained in the rods of the eye. **4**

rods   Long, thin cells in the periphery of the retina that are sensitive to light of low intensity and that function in low-light intensity and nighttime vision. **4**

role enactment theory   The view that hypnosis is not a special state of consciousness, but a special case of role playing. **12**

Rorschach Inkblot Test   During this test, which was developed in 1921 by Hermann Rorschach, a subject's responses to ambiguous inkblots are studied for their emotional expression, their focus, and their recurring patterns. **14**

sample   A selected segment of the available data, representative of the whole. **2**

scanning hypothesis   The theory, proposed by William Dement, that rapid eye movements accompanying dreams may be due to the dreamer's "watching" the activity in the dream. **12**

scanning strategy   The approach to concept formation which states that we start with a limited hypothesis (a few key features as defining traits) and subsequently revise this hypothesis as we scan examples for defining features. **7**

schedule of reinforcement   The way in which rewards are given for appropriate behavior. **5**

schema   A set of key cognitions about a person, gathered from first impressions, which forms a logical and coherent whole and which is used to filter and help interpret additional information. **17**

schizophrenia   Any of a group of psychoses characterized by disorders of attention or perception, profound disturbances in thinking, inappropriate emotional reactions, disturbed motor behavior, and social withdrawal. **15**

Scholastic Aptitude Test (SAT)   A verbal and mathematical test developed by the College Entrance Examination Board and designed to measure "aptitude for college studies." **14**

school psychology   An applied field of psychology which is concerned with behavior in the school environment. **1**

secondary drive (learned motive)   A state of physiological tension learned through association with primary drives and their reduction. **11**

secondary (conditioned) reinforcer   A stimulus that signals that the primary reinforcer is on its way and thus by association has the power to reinforce a learned response. **5**

secondary traits   G. Allport's term for attitudes. **13**

second-order conditioning   Classical conditioning in which a second conditioned stimulus is repeatedly paired with the first so that it eventually produces by itself the conditioned response. **5**

secure attachment   The type of bond between infant and caregiver characterized by the expectation that the caregiver will be available and responsive. **8**

selective attention   The brain's ability to damp down some information entering a given sensory channel while directing attention to other information entering the same channel. **6**

self-actualization   According to Rogers, the striving for the fulfillment of one's own capabilities and potential. **13**

self-control   An operant-conditioning therapy that allows a person to increase or decrease the frequency of one of his or her own behaviors by manipulating the consequences and stimuli surrounding them. **16**

self-efficacy   The feeling people have of being able to deal effectively with a situation. **13**

self-fulfilling prophecy   The phenomenon whereby investigators' expectations influence their findings. **2**

self-help groups   Groups of people who share a particular problem and meet to discuss it among themselves, without the active involvement of professional therapists. **16**

self-instructional training   Donald Meichelbaum's version of cognitive therapy in which clients make a conscious effort to think rational and positive thoughts in stressful situations. **16**

self-perception theory   Bem's theory that people infer their attitudes by observing their own behavior and the circumstances surrounding it, much as they infer the attitudes of others. **17**

self-reports   A method of measuring variables by recording and tallying the responses of subjects to questions about how they thought, felt, or were inclined to act in a given situation. **2, 14**

self-serving bias   The tendency of an individual to take credit for successes and to find situational excuses for failures. **17**

semantic approach   The theory that listeners form hypotheses about the meaning of sentences by hearing key content words in a given context. **9**

sensation   The process whereby stimulation of receptor cells in various parts of the body sends nerve impulses to the brain. **4**

sensorimotor period   The first of Piaget's periods of intellectual development (from birth to about two years), during which an infant learns through overt action to function in his or her environment but lacks an understanding of what he or she is doing. **8**

sensory adaptation   Reduced ability of a sensory system to provide information after prolonged, constant stimulation. **4**

sensory deprivation   Drastic reduction of exposure to stimuli for a prolonged period. **11**

sensory gating   The selective control over sensory imputs the mind exerts in order to focus attention on the most important sensory information. **6**

sensory memory   The momentary lingering of sensory information we experience after a stimulus has been removed. **6**

sensory neurons   The neurons that carry information from the sense organs to the brain and spinal cord. **3**

sensory overload   Intense bombardment of the senses with stimuli. **11**

sensory ratios   The relationship between the intensity of a stimulus and the intensity of its resulting sensation. **4**

septal area   One of three interrelated structures of the limbic system; the others are the hippocampus and amygdala. **3**

serial position curve   A graph showing the results of a free recall experiment. **6**

setpoint   The level of fat that the brain considers normal. When weight goes above setpoint, loss of appetite sets in; when weight falls below it, hunger takes over. **11**

sexism   Prejudice directed toward one sex, almost always toward women. **17**

shaping   A method developed by B. F. Skinner in which an animal is reinforced for displaying closer and closer approximations of a desired behavior. **5**

short-term memory   Our conscious retention of recently encountered things or information retrieved from long-term storage for very short periods. **6**

signal detection theory   Theory that summarizes the factors that influence ability to detect sensory stimuli. **4**

similarity   A gestalt principle of organization proposing that similar items will be perceived as belonging with each other more than with equally near but different items. **4**

simplicity   The concept that simple patterns are more easily perceived than complex ones. **4**

single-blind technique   A procedure in which the experimenter knows who is in the experimental group and who is in the control group but the subjects do not. **2**

Skinner box   A box that provides a controlled setting in which an animal may be trained to press a bar or peck a disk for a reward, such as food. **5**

social facilitation   The phenomenon that occurs when a person's performance improves because of the presence of others. **18**

socialization   The process of instilling society's values in children. **8**

social learning theory   The belief of cognitive psychologists that a great deal of learning is accomplished by observation of other people's behavior, often in the absence of reinforcement. **5**

social psychologists   Psychologists who study how individual perception, belief, motivation, and behavior is influenced by environmental factors, especially the actions of others. **1**

sociobiology   The field that seeks to discover the biological factors that underlie social behavior in all animals, including human beings. **18**

somatic nervous system   The division of the peripheral nervous system that controls the skeletal muscles. **3**

somatoform disorder   A physical ailment, or fear of such ailment, that has no organic cause. **15**

somatosensory cortex   The part of the parietal lobe that is the primary receiving area for the skin senses and for the sense of body position. **3**

source amnesia   The recall of certain facts without remembering the context in which they were learned. **12**

split halves   A procedure for randomly dividing a test into two halves and comparing subjects' scores on both halves to measure a test's reliability. **14**

spontaneous recovery   The reappearance of an extinguished response when an animal is returned to an experimental chamber. **5**

standard deviation   The average extent to which all the numbers in a particular set vary from the mean. **2**

standardization   The administering of a test to a group which is considered representative of those for whom the test is designed, to determine the normative distribution of the test. **14**

standardization group   A large, representative group of people to whom a psychological test is given prior to general distribution in order to establish norms. **14**

Stanford-Binet test   The Stanford University revision of Binet's test; currently employed, usually with children, to judge intelligence by verbal and performance tests grouped according to the subjects' age levels. **14**

state-dependent memory   A memory that is retrievable only in the psychological state in which it was originally stored. **6**

statistical significance   The level of probability that the results of an experiment occurred solely by chance; a convention for deciding when to reject chance as the explanation of results. **2**

statistics   Mathematical methods for assessing and presenting data in summary form. **2**

stereotype   A cluster of preconceived beliefs and expectations about the way members of a group think and act. **17**

Stevens' power law   The law, formulated by S. S. Stevens, that the magnitude of a sensation is equal to the intensity of the stimulus producing the sensation raised to some power (exponent). The exponent varies, depending on the sense that is being measured. **4**

stimulants   Drugs that produce physiological and mental arousal. **12**

stimulus   Any form of energy to which an organism is capable of responding. **4**

stimulus control   A condition where an animal has been so well trained that whenever the stimuli associated with the learning situation are present the learned response will occur. The technique is used as a way to decrease behaviors such as overeating or increase behaviors such as falling asleep quickly at night. **5, 16**

stimulus discrimination   The expression of a learned response to only a particular stimulus. **5**

stimulus generalization   The performance of a learned response in the presence of similar stimuli. **5**

stimulus substitution   The tendency to react to a previously neutral stimulus as though it were an unconditioned stimulus. **5**

stirrup   One of a set of three tiny, interconnected bones in the middle ear that transmit sound from the eardrum to the cochlea. **4**

Strong-Campbell Interest Inventory (SCII)   A test designed to measure a subject's pattern of interests in order to aid in occupational choices. **14**

structuralism   Developed by Wilhelm Wundt, it is the study of how the constituent elements of the human consciousness form the organization, or structure, of the mind. **1**

subgoal analysis   A heuristic by which a problem is analyzed into a set of manageable smaller problems called subgoals. **7**

subjective contour   A line or shape that appears to be present but which is not physically there. **4**

sublimation   According to psychoanalytic theory, a defense mechanism that involves the redirecting of forbidden impulses toward socially desirable goals. **11, 13**

subliminal perception   The brain's ability to register a stimulus presented so briefly or weakly that it cannot be consciously perceived. **4**

superego   According to Freud, the partially unconscious part of the psyche that incorporates parental and social standards of morality and that acts to prohibit thoughts and actions that express instinctual drives. **13**

superstitious behavior   Behavior that is strengthened or weakened because by chance it happens to precede reinforcement or punishment. **5**

surface structure   The words and organization of a sentence. **9**

survey   An attempt to estimate the opinions, characteristics, or behaviors of a particular population by investigation of a representative sample. **2**

sympathetic nervous system   The division of the autonomic nervous system that mobilizes the body's resources in an emergency or stress situation. **3**

synapses   Tiny gaps that separate axons from adjacent cells. **3**

syntactic approach   The theory that listeners derive meaning by relying on syntactic clues when they analyze and interpret sentences. **9**

syntax   The rules of a language which determine how words are to be combined into grammatical phrases and sentences. **9**

systematic desensitization   A behavior-therapy technique for reducing anxiety or removing phobias by pairing muscle relaxation with the presentation of potentially threatening objects or situations in hierarchical order, from least to most feared. **5, 16**

System of Multicultural Pluralistic Assessment (SOMPA)   A "culture-free" intelligence test developed by Jane Mercer for minority-group children. It consists of a standard IQ test, a one-hour interview with a child's parents, and a complete medical examination for the test taker. **14**

tardive dyskinesia   A condition, characterized by grotesque facial movements and sometimes associated with brain damage, which develops in some patients who take antipsychotic drugs. **14**

target organs   Organs that particular hormones will act on exclusively. **3**

taste buds   Tiny organs located in the surface layer of the tongue that are the receptors for taste. **4**

tectorial membrane   A relatively rigid membrane in the inner ear which helps transmit sound waves to the auditory nerve. **4**

telegraphic speech   A child's short, usually two-word, sentence consisting of a concrete noun and action verb. **9**

temporal lobe   A portion of each cerebral hemisphere, concerned with hearing and visual processing. **3**

testosterone   Sex hormone, secreted by the testes, which is involved in the development of male sex characteristics and the regulation of sperm production. **3**

test-retest   A procedure for administering a test to the same people on more than one occasion to measure its reliability. **14**

texture gradient   The impression of depth created by the graduated differences of texture that occur as distance increases. **4**

thalamus   The structure at the top of the brain stem which relays information from the sensory organs to the cerebral cortex. **3**

Thematic Apperception Test (TAT)   A projective psychological test in which a subject's responses to a series of cards with ambiguous scenes are analyzed on an individual basis. **14**

theta waves   Slow brain waves that occur at the beginning of sleep. **12**

thyroid gland   Located in the neck, this endocrine gland secretes hormones that help regulate the body's metabolism. **3**

thyroxin   A hormone secreted by the thyroid gland which plays an important role in regulating the body's metabolism. **3**

time out   An operant-conditioning therapy technique that involves following undesirable behavior with a period of time away from positive reinforcement. **16**

time-series   A design in which the researcher repeatedly observes or measures the dependent variable both before and after the independent variable changes. **2**

tip-of-the-tongue phenomenon   The experience of feeling as though something is stored somewhere in our memory but cannot be located quickly. **6**

token economies   Structured environments in which objects such as poker chips are used as rewards that may be exchanged by patients for desired activities or objects; a technique used in operant-conditioning therapies. **5, 16**

trait   According to Guilford, any relatively enduring way in which one individual differs from another. **13**

trait theories   Methods of understanding personality that organize human behavior according to characteristics, or traits, that distinguish a person and can be objectively measured. **13**

transactional analysis (TA)   A therapeutic approach that is based on the belief that each relationship with others can be seen as a dominance of either a mature or immature part of an individual, and that a growth of the Adult, or mature, part of an individual can help interactions to run more smoothly. **16**

transference   The transfer to the analyst of feelings of love and hostility that were originally directed toward a client's parents or other authority figures; a basic feature of psychoanalysis. **16**

trichromat   A person whose cones contain three distinct forms of iodopsin and thus has normal color vision. **4**

trichromatic theory   The theory that there are three different types of color receptors in the eye for detecting all colors. **4**

unconditional positive regard Acceptance and support that a therapist following Carl Rogers' approach would give to a client, regardless of what he or she said or did. **13**

unconditioned response (UCR) A response elicited by an unconditioned stimulus without any form of training. **5**

unconditioned stimulus (UCS) A stimulus that elicits an unconditioned response without any form of training. **5**

underlying representation The meaning of a sentence. **9**

utility The value one places on potential outcomes in a decision-making situation. **7**

validity An essential criterion in determining the value of a test. A test is valid if it measures what it is supposed to measure. **14**

variable-interval schedule An unpredictable and irregular partial reinforcement schedule in which there is no perceived relationship between the time elapsed and the frequency of rewards. **5**

variable-ratio schedule An unpredictable and irregular partial reinforcement schedule in which there is no perceived relationship between the number of responses and the number of rewards. **5**

variables Factors capable of change. **2**

vicarious reinforcement and punishment Environmental consequences following the behavior of others that affect how an observer will behave. **5**

volley principle The theory that explains why we can hear high-frequency sound by assuming that the frequency of neural firing which the brain detects is determined not by the rate of firing of single neurons but rather by groups of neurons. **4**

vulnerability theory The theory of schizophrenia which holds that the disorder is triggered by a combination of personal factors and environmental stress. Only a little stress may set off the disorder in those predisposed by genes, family history, and unfavorable social conditions. **15**

wavelength The distance between the crest of one light wave and the crest of the next; the determinant of color. **4**

Weber's law Formulated by Gustav Fechner, this law states that the amount by which a stimulus must be increased to produce a "just noticeable difference" in sensation is always a constant proportion of the initial stimulus intensity. **4**

Wechsler Intelligence Scales These are the Wechsler Adult Intelligence Scale (WAIS), the Wechsler Intelligence Scale for Children (WISC), and the Wechsler Preschool and Primary Scale of Intelligence (WPPSI). Along with the Stanford-Binet, they are the most frequently used individual intelligence tests; they differ from the Stanford-Binet in several ways, primarily in yielding not a single IQ score but separate scores for each subtest. **14**

white matter The myelinated axons of the nervous system. **3**

whole-word approach The method of teaching reading that exposes beginning readers to selected words in simple stories and only later stresses the connection between letters and sounds. **9**

References

The number in brackets at the end of each entry refers to the chapter of the text in which that work is cited.

Abraham, K. Notes on psychoanalytic investigation and treatment of manic-depressive insanity and allied conditions (1911). In D. Bryan and A. Strachey (Trans.), *Selected Papers of Karl Abraham, M.D.* London: The Hogarth Press, 1948. [15]

Abraham, K. The first pregenital stage of the libido (1916). In D. Bryan and A. Strachey (Trans.), *Selected Papers of Karl Abraham, M.D.* London: The Hogarth Press, 1948, [15]

Abraham, S. F., and **Beaumont, P. J. V.** How patients describe bulimia or binge eating. *Psychological Medicine*, 1982, *12*, 625–635. [11]

Abramowitz, S. I., Abramowitz, C. V., Jackson, C., and **Gomes, B.** The politics of clinical judgment: What nonliberal examiners infer about women who don't stifle themselves. *Journal of Consulting and Clinical Psychology*, 1973, *41*, 385–391. [17]

Abramson, L. Y., Seligman, M. E. P., and **Teasdale, J. D.** Learned helplessness in humans: Critique and reformulation. *Journal of Abnormal Psychology*, 1978, *87*, 49–74. [15]

Adams, D. B., Gold, A. R., and **Burt, A. D.** Rise in female-initiated sexual activity at ovulation and its suppression by oral contraceptives. *New England Journal of Medicine*, 1978, *299*, 1145–1150. [11]

Adams, J. A. *Learning and Memory: An Introduction* (rev. ed.). Homewood, Ill.: Dorsey Press, 1980. [6]

Adler, A. Individual psychology, In C. A. Murchison (Ed.), *Psychologies of 1930*. Worcester, Mass.: Clark University Press, 1930. Pp. 395–405. [13]

Adler, A. *What life should mean to you.* Boston: Little, Brown, 1931. [13]

Adler, A. On the interpretation of dreams. *International Journal of Individual Psychology*, 1936, *1*, 3–16. [12]

Adler, J., and **Gosnell, M.** What it means to be fat. *Newsweek*, December 13, 1982, 84–90. [11]

Adorno, T. W., Frenkel-Brunswick, E., Levinson, D. J., and **Sanford, R. N.** *The authoritarian personality.* New York: Harper & Row, 1950. [17]

Agras, W. S. Behavior therapy in the management of chronic schizophrenia. *American Journal of Psychiatry*, 1967, *124*, 240–243. [15]

Ainsworth, M., Bleher, M., Waters, E., and **Wall, S.** *Patterns of attachment.* Hillsdale, N.J.: Lawrence Erlbaum, 1978. [8]

Ajzen, I. On behaving in accordance with one's attitudes. In M. P. Zanna, E. T. Higgins, and C. P. Herman (Eds), *Consistency in social behavior: The Ontario symposium* (Vol. 2). Hillsdale, N.J.: Lawrence Erlbaum, 1982. [17]

Ajzen, I., and **Fishbein, M.** Attitude-behavior relations: A theoretical analysis and review of empirical research. *Psychological Bulletin*, 1977, *84*, 888–918. [17]

Ajzen, I., and **Fishbein, M.** *Understanding attitudes and predicting social behavior.* Englewood Cliffs, N.J.: Prentice-Hall, 1980. [17]

Akiskal, H. S. A biobehavioral approach to depression. In R. A. Depue (Ed.), *The psychobiology of the depressive disorders.* New York: Academic Press, 1979. [15]

Akiskal, H. S., and **McKinney, W. T., Jr.** Depressive disorders: Toward a unified hypothesis. *Science*, 1973, *182*, 20–29. [15]

Akiskal, H. S., and **McKinney, W. T., Jr.** Overview of recent research in depression. *Archives of General Psychiatry*, 1975, *32*, 285–305. [15]

Allardt, E. Dimensions of welfare in the comparative Scandinavian study. *Acta Sociologica*, 1976, *19*, 227–239. [10]

Allport, F. H. The influence of the group upon association and thought. *Journal of Experimental Psychology*, 1920, *3*, 159–182. [18]

Allport, F. H. *Social Psychology.* Boston: Houghton Mifflin, 1924. [18]

Allport, G. W. *Personality: A psychological interpretation.* New York: Holt, Rinehart and Winston, 1937. [13]

Allport, G. W. *The nature of prejudice.* Cambridge, Mass.: Addison-Wesley, 1954. [17]

Allport, G. W. *Pattern and growth in personality.* New York: Holt, Rinehart and Winston, 1961. [13]

Allport, G. W. Traits revisited. *American Psychologist*, 1966, *21*, 1–10. [13]

Allport, G. W. The historical background of modern social psychology. In G. Lindzey and E. Aronson (Eds.), *Handbook of social psychology* (Vol. 1) (2d ed.). Reading, Mass.: Addison-Wesley, 1968. Pp. 1–80. [17]

Allport, G. W., and **Odbert, H. S.** Traitnames: A psycho-texical study. *Psychological Monographs*, 1936, *47*, Whole No. 211. [13]

Allport, G. W., and **Postman, L. J.** *The psychology of rumor.* New York: Holt, 1947, [6]

Alper, T. G. Achievement motivation in college women: A now-you-see-it-now-you-don't phenomenon. *American Psychologist*, 1974, *29*, 194–203. [11]

Altman, I. *The environment and social behavior: Privacy, personal space, territory, and crowding.* Monterey, Calif.: Brooks/Cole, 1975. [18]

American Psychological Association. Bylaws of the American Psychological Association. *1968 Directory.* Washington, D.C.: American Psychological Association, 1968. [1]

American Psychological Association. *Ethical principles of psychologists.* Washington, D.C.: American Psychological Association, 1981. [2]

Amoore, J. E., Johnston, J. W., Jr., and **Rubin, M.** The stereochemical theory of odor. *Scientific American*, 1964, *210*, 42–49. [4]

Amoore, J. E., and **Venstrum, D.** Correlations between stereochemical assessments and organoleptic analysis of odorous compounds. In T. Hayashi (Ed.), *Olfaction and taste.* Oxford: Pergamon, 1967. Pp. 3–17. [4]

Anand, B. K., and **Brobeck, J. R.** Localization of a "feeding center" in the hypothalamus of the rat. *Proceedings of the Society for Experimental Biological Medicine*, 1951, *77*, 323–324. [11]

Anand, B. K., Chhina, G. S., and **Singh, B.** Some aspects of electroencephalographic studies in yogis. *Electroenecephalography and Clinical Neurophysiology*, 1961, *13*, 452–456. [12]

Anderson, N. H. A simple model of information integration. In R. P. Abelson, E. Aronson, W. J. McGuire, T. M. Newcomb, M. J. Rosenberg, and P. H. Tannenbaum (Eds.), *Theories of cognitive consistency: A sourcebook.* Chicago: Rand McNally, 1968. Pp. 731–743. [17]

Anderson, R., Manoogian, S. T., and **Reznick, J. S.** The undermining and enhancing of intrinsic motivation in preschool children. *Journal of Personality and Social Psychology*, 1976, *34*, 915–922. [17]

Andreasen, N. C., Smith, M. R., Jacoby, C. G., Dennert, J. W., and **Olsen, S. A.** Ventricular enlargement in schizophrenia: Definition and prevalence. *American Journal of Psychiatry*, 1982, *139*(3), 292–302. [15]

Andrews, E. A., and **Braveman, N. S.** The combined effects of dosage level and interstimulus interval on the formation of onetrial poison-based aversions in rats. *Animal Learning and Behavior*, 1975, *3*, 287–289. [5]

Andrews, F. M. Social and psychological factors which influence the creative process. In I. A. Taylor and J. W. Getzels (Eds.), *Perspectives in creativity.* Hawthorne, N.Y.: Aldine, 1975, [7]

Andrews, F. M., and **Withey, S. B.** *Social indicators of well-being: Americans' perceptions of life quality.* New York: Plenum Press, 1976. [10]

Andrews, G., and **Harvey, R.** Does psychotherapy benefit neurotic patients? *Archives of General Psychiatry*, 1981, *38*, 1203–1208. [16]

Anglin, J. A. *Word, object, and conceptual development.* New York: Norton, 1977. [7]

Anglin, J. M. *The growth of word meaning.* Cambridge, Mass.: MIT Press, 1970. [9]

Anisman, H., and **Sklar, L. S.** Catecholamine depletion in mice upon reexposure to stress: Mediation of the escape deficits produced by inescapable shock. *Journal of Com-*

parative and Physiological Psychology, 1979, *93*, 610–625. [15]

Aponte, H., and **Hoffman, L.** The open door: A structural approach to a family with an anorectic child. *Family Process*, 1973, *12*, 1–44. [16]

Appelbaum, P. S., and **Gutheil, T. G.** Drug refusal: A study of psychiatric inpatients. *American Journal of Psychiatry*, 1980, *137*, 340–346. [16]

Armstrong, R. H. *Gastric secretion during sleep and dreaming.* Paper presented at the annual meeting of the Association for the Psychophysiological Study of Sleep, March 1965. [12]

Aronfreed, J. The concept of internalization. In D. A. Goslin (Ed.), *Handbook of socialization theory and research.* Chicago: Rand McNally, 1969. [8]

Aronow, E., Reznikoff, M., and **Rauchway, A.** Some old and new directions in Rorschach testing. *Journal of Personality Assessment*, 1979, *43*, 227–234. [14]

Aronson, E. *The social animal* (3rd ed.). New York: W. H. Freeman, 1980. [17, 18]

Aronson, E., and **Carlsmith, J. M.** The effect of the severity of threat on the devaluation of forbidden behavior. *Journal of Abnormal and Social Psychology*, 1963, *66*, 584–588. [17]

Aronson, E., and **Osherow, N.** Cooperation, prosocial behavior, and academic performance: Experiments in the desegregated classroom. In L. Bickman (Ed.), *Applied social psychology annual* (Vol. 1). Beverly Hills, Calif.: Sage Publications, 1980. [17]

Aronson, E., Willerman, B., and **Floyd, J.** The effect of a pratfall on increasing interpersonal attractiveness. *Psychonomic Science*, 1966, *4*, 227–228. [2]

Arrowood, J., and **Short, J. A.** Agreement, attraction, and self-esteem. *Canadian Journal of Behavioral Science*, 1973, *5*, 242–252. [17]

Asch, S. E. Effects of group pressure upon the modification and distortion of judgments. In H. Guetzkow (Ed.), *Groups, leadership, and men.* Pittsburgh: Carnegie Press, 1951. [18]

Asch, S. E. Studies of independence and conformity: A minority of one against a unanimous majority. *Psychological Monographs*, 1956, *70*(9), Whole No. 416. [18]

Aserinsky, E., and **Kleitman, N.** Regularly occurring periods of eye motility and concomitant phenomena during sleep. *Science*, 1953, *178*, 273–274. [12]

Ashby, M. S., and **Wittmaier, B. C.** Attitude changes in children after exposure to stories about women in traditional or nontraditional occupations. *Journal of Educational Psychology*, 1978, *70*, 945. [17]

Ashmore, R. D., and **Del Boca, F. K.** Psychological approaches to understanding intergroup conflicts. In P. A. Katz (Ed.), *Towards the elimination of racism.* Elmsford, N.Y.: Pergamon Press, 1976. [17]

Atkinson, J. W. (Ed.). *Motives in fantasy, action, and society.* New York: Van Nostrand Reinhold, 1958. [11]

Atkinson, J. W. *An introduction to motivation.* Princeton, N.J.: Van Nostrand Reinhold, 1964. [11]

Atkinson, J. W., and **Litwin, G. H.** Achievement motive and test anxiety conceived as motive to approach success and motive to avoid failure. *Journal of Abnormal and Social Psychology*, 1960, *60*, 52–63. [11]

Atkinson, J. W., and **Raynor, J. O.** (Eds.). *Motivation and achievement.* Washington, D.C.: Winston, 1974. [11]

Attneave, F. Some information aspects of visual perception. *Psychological Review*, 1954, *61*, 183–193. [4]

Ault, R. L. *Children's cognitive development* (2d ed.). Oxford: Oxford University Press, 1983. [8]

Austin, W. Justice, freedom, and self-interest in intergroup conflict. In G. Austin and S. Worchel (Eds.), *The social psychology of intergroup relations.* Monterey, Calif.: Brooks/Cole, 1979. [17]

Averill, J. R. *Anger and aggression: An essay on emotion.* New York: Springer-Verlag, 1982. [18]

Averill, J. R. Studies on anger and aggression: Implications for theories of emotion. *American Psychologist*, November 1983, 1145–1160. [18]

Ax, A. F. The physiological differentiation between fear and anger in humans. *Psychosomatic Medicine*, 1953, *15*, 433–442. [10]

Ayllon, T., and **Azrin, N. H.** *The token economy: A motivational system for therapy and rehabilitation.* New York: Appleton-Century-Crofts, 1968. [16]

Ayres, C. E. Instinct and capacity: I. The instinct of belief in instincts. *Journal of Philosophy*, 1921, *18*, 561–566. [11]

Azrin, N. H., and **Foxx, R. M.** *Toilet training in less than a day.* New York: Simon & Schuster, 1974. [5]

Baddeley, A. *Your memory: A user's guide.* New York: Macmillan, 1982. [6]

Baldessarini, R. J. *Chemotherapy in psychiatry.* Cambridge, Mass.: Harvard University Press, 1977. [16]

Baltes, P. B., Reese, H. W., and **Nesselroade, J. R.** *Life-span developmental psychology: Introduction to research methods.* Monterey, Calif.: Brooks/Cole, 1977. [2]

Baltes, P. B., and **Schaie, K. W.** Aging and IQ: The myth of the twilight years. *Psychology Today*, 1974, *7*, 35–40. [8]

Ban, T. *Recent advances in the biology of schizophrenia.* Springfield, Ill.: Charles C. Thomas, 1973. [15]

Bandura, A. Influence of models' reinforcement contingencies on the acquisition of imitative responses. *Journal of Personality and Social Psychology*, 1965, *1*, 589–595. [18]

Bandura, A. Vicarious processes: A case of no-trial learning. In L. Berkowitz (Ed.), *Advances in experimental social psychology* (Vol. 2). New York: Academic Press, 1966. Pp. 1–55. [13]

Bandura, A. *Aggression: A social learning analysis.* Englewood Cliffs, N.J.: Prentice-Hall, 1973. [5]

Bandura, A. Social learning analysis of aggression. In E. Ribes-Inesta and A. Bandura (Eds.), *Analysis of delinquency and aggression.* Hillsdale, N.J.: Lawrence Erlbaum, 1976. Pp. 202–232. [18]

Bandura, A. Self-efficacy: Toward a unifying theory of behavioral change. *Psychological Review*, 1977a, *84*, 191–215. [5, 16]

Bandura, A. *Social learning theory.* Englewood Cliffs, N.J.: Prentice-Hall, 1977. [5]

Bandura, A. Self-efficacy mechanism in human agency. *American Psychologist*, 1982, *37*, 122–147. [13]

Bandura, A., Blanchard, E. B., and **Ritter, B.** Relative efficacy of desensitization and modeling approaches for inducing behavioral, affective, and attitudinal changes. *Journal of Personality and Social Psychology*, 1969, *13*, 173–199. [5, 16]

Bandura, A., Grusec, J. E., and **Menlove, F. L.** Vicarious extinction of avoidance behavior. *Journal of Personality and Social Psychology*, 1967, *5*, 16–23. [16]

Bandura, A., Ross, D., and **Ross, S.** Transmission of aggression through imitation of aggressive models. *Journal of Abnormal and Social Psychology*, 1961, *63*, 575–582. [8, 13, 18]

Banks, M. S., Aslin, R. N., and **Letson, R. D.** Sensitive period for the development of human binocular vision. *Science*, 1975, *190*, 675–677. [4]

Barber, T. X. Measuring "hypnotic-like" suggestibility with and without hypnotic induction: Psychometric properties, norms, and variables influencing response to the Barber suggestibility scale (BSS). *Psychological Reports*, 1965, *16*, 809–844. [12]

Barber, T. X. Responding to "hypnotic" suggestions: An introspective report. *American Journal of Clinical Hypnosis*, 1975, *18*, 6–22. [12]

Bard, M. *Training police as specialists in family crisis intervention.* Washington, D.C.: U.S. Government Printing Office, 1970. [16]

Barefoot, J. C., Dahlstrom, W. G., and **Williams, R. B., Jr.** Rapid communication: Hostility, CHD incidence, and total mortality: a 25-year follow-up study of 225 physicians. *Psychosomatic Medicine*, 1983, *45*, 59–63. [10]

Barfield, R. A., and **Morgan, J. N.** *Early retirement: The decision and the experience.* Ann Arbor, Mich.: Institute for Social Research, University of Michigan, 1970. [8]

Bar-Hillel, M. The role of sample size in sample evaluation. *Organizational Behavior* *and Human Performance*, 1979, *24*, 245–257. [7]

Barlow, H. B., and **Mollon, J. D.** (Eds.). *The senses*. Cambridge: Cambridge University Press, 1982. [4]

Baron, R. A. *Human aggression*. New York: Plenum, 1977. [18]

Baron, R. M., Mandel, D. R., Adams, C. A., and **Griffen, L. M.** Effects of social density in university residential environments. *Journal of Personality and Social Psychology*, 1976, *34*, 434–446. [18]

Barraclough, B. M., Nelson, B., Bunch, J., and **Sainsbury, P.** The diagnostic classification and psychiatric treatment of 100 suicides. Proceedings of the Fifth International Conference for Suicide Prevention, London, 1969. [15]

Barrett, D. The hypnotic dream: Its relation to nocturnal dreams and waking fantasies. *Journal of Abnormal Psychology*, 1979, *88*, 584–591. [12]

Barron, F. H. The psychology of imagination. *Scientific American*, 1958, *199*, 150–170. [7]

Barron, F. H. Behavioral decision theory: A topical bibliography for management scientists. *Interfaces*, 1974, *5*, 56–62. [7]

Bartlett, F. C. *Remembering: A study in experimental and social psychology*. London: Cambridge University Press, 1932. [6]

Bartoshuk, L. M. Taste illusions: Some demonstrations. *Annals of the New York Academy of Sciences*, 1974, *237*, 279–285. [4]

Bartrop, R. W., Lazarus, L., Luckhurst, E., Kiloh, L. G., and **Penny, R.** Depressed lymphocyte function after bereavement. *Lancet*, 1977, *1*, 834–836. [10]

Bates, J. A. Extrinsic reward and intrinsic motivation: A review with implications for the classroom. *Review of Educational Research*, 1979, *49*, 557–576. [17]

Bateson, G., Jackson, D., Haley, J., and **Weakland, J.** Toward a theory of schizophrenia. *Behavioral Science*, 1956, *1*, 251–264. [15]

Baum, A., Aiello, J., and **Calesnick, L.** Crowding and personal control: social density and the development of learned helplessness. *Journal of Personality and Social Psychology*, 1978, *36*, 1000–1011. [18]

Baum, A., and **Gatchel, R. J.** Cognitive determinants of reaction to uncontrollable events: Development of reactance and learned helplessness. *Journal of Personality and Social Psychology*, in press. [18]

Baum, A., and **Valins, S.** *Architecture and social behavior: Psychological studies of social density*. Hillsdale, N.J.: Lawrence Erlbaum, 1977. [18]

Baumrind, D. Some thoughts on the ethics of research: After reading Milgram's "Behavioral study of obedience." *American Psychologist*, 1964, *19*, 421–423. [18]

Baumrind, D. Child care practices antecedating three patterns of preschool behavior.

Genetic Psychology Monographs, 1967, *75*, 43–88. [13]

Baumrind, D. *Socialization determinants of personal agency*. Paper presented at the biennial meetings of the Society for Research in Child Development, New Orleans, 1977. [13]

Beach, F., and **Merari, A.** Coital behavior in dogs: V. Effects of estrogen and progesterone on mating and other forms of social behavior in the bitch. *Journal of Comparative and Physiological Psychology Monograph*, 1970, *70*(1) Part 2, 1–22. [11]

Beach, L. R., Campbell, F. L., and **Townes, B. D.** Subjective utility and the prediction of birth-planning decisions. *Organizational Behavior and Human Performance*, 1979, *24*, 18–28. [7]

Beck, A. T. *Depression: Clinical, experimental and theoretical aspects*. New York: Hoeber, 1967. [13, 15]

Beck, A. T. The development of depression: A cognitive model. In R. J. Friedman and M. M. Katz (Eds.), *The psychology of depression: Contemporary theory and research*. Washingon, D.C.: Winston-Wiley, 1974. [15]

Beck, A. T. *Cognitive therapy and the emotional disorders*. New York: International Universities Press, 1976. [16]

Beck, A. T., Kovacs, M., and **Weissman, A.** Assessment of suicidal intention: The scale for suicide ideation. *Journal of Clinical and Consultant Psychology*, 1979, *47*, 243–252. [15]

Beck, A. T., Rush, A. J., Show, B. F., and **Emery, G.** *Cognitive therapy of depression*. New York: Guilford Press, 1979. [16]

Bee, H. L., and **Mitchell, S. K.** *The developing person: A life-span approach*. New York: Harper & Row, 1980. [9]

Beebe-Center, J. G., Rogers, M. S., and **O'Connell, D. N.** Transmission of information about sucrose and saline solutions through the sense of taste. *Journal of Psychology*, 1955, *39*, 157-160. [4]

Begelman, D. Ethical and legal issues of behavior modification. In M. Hersen, R. Eisler, and P. Miller (Eds.), *Progress in behavior modification* (Vol. 1). New York: Academic Press, 1975. [16]

Behrens, M., Rosenthal, H., and **Chodoff, P.** Communication in lower class families of schizophrenics. *Archives of General Psychiatry*, 1968, *18*, 689–696. [15]

Bekerian, D. A., and **Bowers, J. M.** Eyewitness testimony: Were we misled? *Journal of Experimental Psychology: LMC*, 1983, *9*, 139–145. [6]

Bekesy, G. von. Synchronism of neural discharges and their demultiplication in pitch perception on the skin and in learning. *Journal of the Acoustical Society of America*, 1959, *31*, 338–349. [4]

Bellugi, U. *The emergence of inflections and negative systems in the speech of two children*. Paper presented at the meeting of the New

England Psychological Association, 1964. [9]

Bellugi, U. Learning the language. *Psychology Today*, 1970, *4*, 32–35ff. [9]

Belsky, J. Two waves of day care research: Developmental effects and conditions of quality. In R. Ainslie (Ed.), *The child and the day care setting*. New York: Praeger, in press. [8]

Belsky, J., and **Steinberg, L. D.** The effects of day care: A critical review. *Child Development*, 1978, *49*, 929–949. [8]

Bem, D. J. *Beliefs, attitudes, and human affairs*. Monterey, Calif.: Brooks/Cole, 1970. [17]

Bem, D. J. Self-perception: An alternative interpretation of cognitive dissonance phenomena. *Psychological Review*, 1976, *74*, 183–200. [17]

Bem, D. J., and **Allen, A.** On predicting some of the people some of the time: The search for cross-situational consistencies in behavior. *Psychological Review*, 1974, *81*, 506–520. [13]

Bem, S. L. The measurement of psychological androgyny. *Journal of Consulting and Clinical Psychology*, 1974, *42*, 155–162. [1]

Bem, S. L. Sex-role adaptability: One consequence of psychological androgyny. *Journal of Personality and Social Psychology*, 1975, *31*, 634–643. [1]

Bem, S. L., and **Bem, D. J.** Case study of a nonconscious ideology: Training the woman to know her place. In D. J. Bem, *Beliefs, attitudes, and human affairs*. Monterey, Calif.: Brooks/Cole, 1970. Pp. 89–99. [17]

Bemis, K. M. Current approaches to the etiology and treatment of anorexia nervosa. *Psychological Bulletin*, 1978, *85*, 593–617. [11]

Bennett, W., and **Gurin, J.** *The dieter's dilemma*. New York: Basic Books, 1982. [11]

Berger, P. A. Medical treatment of mental illness. *Science*, 1978, *200*, 974–981. [15]

Bergin, A. E. The evaluation of therapeutic outcomes. In A. E. Bergin and S. L. Garfield (Eds.), *Handbook of psychotherapy and behavior change: An empirical analysis*. New York: Wiley, 1971. [16]

Berkman, L. F., and **Syme, S. L.** Social networks, host resistance, and mortality: A nine-year follow-up of Alameda County residents. *American Journal of Epidemiology*, 1979, *109*, 186–204. [10]

Berkowitz, L. *Aggression: A social psychological analysis*. New York: McGraw-Hill, 1962. [18]

Berkowitz, L. The concept of aggressive drive: Some additional considerations. In L. Berkowitz (Ed.), *Advances in experimental social psychology* (Vol. 2). New York: Academic Press, 1965. [18]

Berkowitz, L. (Ed.). *Roots of aggression: A reexamination of the frustration-aggression hypothesis*. New York: Atherton, 1969. [18]

Berkowitz, L., and **Geen, R. G.** Film violence and cue properties of available targets. *Journal of Personality and Social Psychology,* 1966, *3,* 525–530. [18]

Berkowitz, L., and **Lepage, A.** Weapons as aggression-eliciting stimuli. *Journal of Personality and Social Psychology,* 1976, *7,* 202–207. [18]

Berlin, B., and **Kay, P.** *Basic color terms: Their universality and evolution.* Berkeley: University of California Press, 1969. [9]

Berlyne, D. E. Novelty and curiosity as determinants of exploratory behaviour. *British Journal of Psychology,* 1950, *41,* 68–80. [11]

Berlyne, D. E. *Conflict, arousal, and curiosity.* New York: McGraw-Hill, 1960. [11]

Bermant, G., Glickman, S., and **Davidson, J.** Effects of limbic lesions on copulatory behavior of male rats. *Journal of Comparative and Physiological Psychology,* 1968, *65,* 118–125. [11]

Bernard, L. L. *Instinct.* New York: Holt, 1924. [11]

Berne, E. *Games people play.* New York: Grove Press, 1964. [16]

Bernstein, I. L. Learned taste aversions in children receiving chemotherapy. *Science,* 1978, *200,* 1302–1303. [5]

Bernstein, I. L. Webster, M. M., and **Bernstein, I. D.** Food aversions in children receiving chemotherapy for cancer. *Cancer,* 1982, *50,* 2961–2963. [5]

Bertenthal, B. I., and **Fischer, K. W.** The development of self-recognition in the infant. *Developmental Psychology,* 1978, *14,* 44–50. [8]

Bevan, W. Subliminal stimulation: A pervasive problem for psychology. *Psychological Bulletin,* 1964, *61,* 89–99. [4]

Bever, T. G. The cognitive basis for linguistic structures. In J. R. Hayes (Ed.), *Cognition and the development of language.* New York: Wiley, 1970. Pp. 279–362. [9]

Bexton, W. H. *Some effects of perceptual isolation in human beings.* Unpublished doctoral dissertation, McGill University, 1953. [11]

Bexton, W. H., Heron, W., and **Scott, T. H.** Effects of decreased variation in the sensory environment. *Canadian Journal of Psychology,* 1954, *8,* 70–76. [4, 11]

Birch, H. G., and **Rabinowitz, H. S.** The negative effect of previous experience on productive thinking. *Journal of Experimental Psychology,* 1951, *41,* 121–125. [7]

Birnbaum, I. M., Parker, E. S., Hartley, J. T., and **Noble, E. P.** Alcohol and memory: Retrieval processes. *Journal of Verbal Learning and Verbal Behavior,* 1978, *17,* 325–335. [12]

Blake, R., and **Hirsch, H. V. B.** Deficits in binocular depth perception in cats after alternating monocular deprivation. *Science,* 1975, *190,* 1114–1116. [4]

Blake, R. R., and **Mouton, J.** Intergroup problem solving in organizations: From theory to practice. In W. Austin and S. Worchel (Eds.), *The social psychology of intergroup relations.* Monterey, Calif.: Brooks/Cole, 1979. [18]

Blakemore, C., and **Cooper, G.** Development of the brain depends on the visual environment. *Nature,* 1970, *228,* 477–478. [1, 4]

Blanchard, E. B. Biofeedback and the modification of cardiovascular dysfunctions. In R. J. Gatchel and K. P. Price (Eds.), *Clinical applications of biofeedback: Appraisal and status.* Elmsford, N.Y.: Pergamon Press, 1979. [12]

Blanchard, E. B., Andrasik, F., Ahles, T. A., Teders, S. J., and **O'Keefe, D.** Migraine and tension headache: A meta-analytic review. *Behavior Therapy,* 1980, *11,* 613–631. [10]

Blanchard, M., and **Main, M.** Avoidance of the attachment figure and social-emotional adjustment in day-care infants. *Developmental Psychology,* 1979, *15,* 445–446. [8]

Blehar, M. C. Anxious attachment and defensive reactions associated with day care. *Child Development,* 1974, *45,* 683–692, [8]

Bleuler, E. *Dementia praecox or the group of schizophrenias* (1911). J. Sinkin (Trans.) New York: International Universities Press, 1950. [15]

Block, J. *Lives through time.* Berkeley, Calif.: Bancroft Books, 1971. [13]

Block, J., and **Block, J.** The role of ego-control and ego resiliency in the organization of behavior. In W. A. Collins (Ed.), *The Minnesota symposium on child psychology* (Vol. 13). Hillsdale, N.J.: Lawrence Erlbaum, 1980. [13]

Block, J., and **Thomas, H.** Is satisfaction with self a measure of adjustment? *Journal of Abnormal and Social Psychology,* 1955, *51,* 254–259. [13]

Block, J. H. *Another look at sex differentiation in the socialization behaviors of mothers and fathers.* Paper presented at the Conference on New Directions for Research on Women, Madison, Wisconsin, May 1975. [8]

Block, J. H., Block, H., and **Harrington, D. M.** *The relationship of parental teaching strategies in preschool children.* Paper presented at the meeting of the Western Psychological Association, San Francisco, California, April 1974. [8]

Bloom, L. M. *Language development: Form and function in emerging grammars.* Cambrige, Mass.: MIT Press, 1970. [9]

Bloomfield, H. H., and **Kory, R. B.** *Happiness: The TM program, psychiatry and enlightenment.* New York: Dawn Press/Simon & Schuster, 1976. [12]

Blum, J. M. *Pseudoscience and mental ability.* New York: Monthly Review Press, 1978. [14]

Bochner, S., and **Inske, C.** Communicator discrepancy, source credibility, and influence. *Journal of Personality and Social Psychology,* 1966, *4,* 614–621. [17]

Bolles, R. C. *Theory of motivation* (2nd ed.). New York: Harper & Row, 1975. [11]

Bolles, R. C., and **Fanselow, M. S.** Endorphins and behavior. *Annual Review of Psychology,* 1982, *33,* 87–101. [3]

Bonner, R. Lie detectors as corporate tools. *The New York Times,* February 13, 1983. [10]

Bootzin, R. R. *Behavior modification and therapy.* Boston: Winthrop, 1975. [16]

Bootzin, R. R., and **Acocella, J. R.** *Abnormal psychology: Current perspectives* (4th ed.). New York: Random House, 1984. [15]

Bootzin, R. R., and **Max, D.** Learning and behavioral theories of anxiety and stress. In I. L. Kutash and L. B. Schlesinger (Eds.), *Pressure point: Perspectives on stress and anxiety.* San Francisco: Jossey-Bass, 1980. [15]

Bootzin, R. R., and **Nicassio, P. M.** Behavioral treatments for insomnia. In M. Hersen, R. M. Eisler, and P. M. Miller (Eds.), *Progress in behavior modification* (Vol. 6). New York: Academic Press, 1978. [16]

Boring, E. G. *A history of experimental psychology* (2d ed.). New York: Appleton-Century-Crofts, 1957. [1]

Bornstein, M. H. The psychological component of cultural difference in color naming and illusion susceptibility. *Behavior Science Notes,* 1973, *8,* 41–101. [4]

Bornstein, M. H., Kessen, W., and **Weiskopf, B.** The categories of hue in infancy. *Science,* 1976, *191,* 201–202. [4, 9]

Bornstein, P. E., and **Clayton, P. J.** The anniversary reaction. *Diseases of the Nervous System,* 1972, *33,* 470–472. [10]

Bourne, L. E., Dominowski, R. L., and **Loftus, E. F.** *Cognitive processes.* Englewood Cliffs, N.J.: Prentice-Hall, 1979. [7]

Bower, G. H. A selective review of organizational factors in memory. In E. Tulving and W. Donaldson (Eds.), *Organization of memory.* New York: Academic Press, 1972. [6]

Bower, G. H. Mood and memory. *American Psychologist,* 1981, *36,* 129–148. [6]

Bower, G. H., Black, J., and **Turner, T.** Scripts in text comprehension and memory. *Cognitive Psychology,* 1979, *11,* 177–220. [17]

Bower, G. H., and **Clark, M. C.** Narrative stories as mediators for serial learning. *Psychonomic Science,* 1969, *14,* 181–182. [6]

Bower, G. H., and **Gilligan, S. G.** Remembering information related to one's self. *Journal of Research in Personality,* 1979, *13,* 420–432. [6]

Bower, G. H., Monteiro, K. P., and **Gilligan, S. G.** Emotional mood as a context of learning and recall. *Journal of Verbal Learning and Verbal Behavior,* 1978, *17,* 573–585. [6]

Bowers, K. S. Situationism in psychology: An analysis and critique. *Psychological Review,* 1973, *80,* 307–336. [13]

Bowers, K. S. *Hypnosis for the seriously curious.* Monterey, Calif.: Brooks/Cole, 1976. [12]

Bowers, P. Hypnosis and creativity: The search for the missing link. *Journal of Abnormal Psychology,* 1979, *88,* 564–572. [12]

Boyle, P. C., Storlien, L. H., and **Keesey, R. E.** Increased efficiency of food utilization following weight loss. *Physiology and Behavior,* 1978, *21,* 261–264. [11]

Bradburn, N. M. *The structure of psychological well-being.* Chicago: Aldine, 1969. [10]

Bradburn, N. M., and **Caplovitz, D.** *Reports on happiness.* Chicago: Aldine, 1965. [10]

Bradley, G. W. Self-serving biases in the attribution process: A re-examination of the fact or fiction question. *Journal of Personality and Social Psychology,* 1978, *35,* 56–71. [17]

Bradway, K. I.Q. constancy on the revised Stanford-Binet from the preschool to the junior high school level. *Journal of Genetic Psychology,* 1944, *65,* 197–217. [8]

Brainerd, C. J. The stage question in cognitive-developmental theory. *The Behavioral and Brain Sciences,* 1978, *1,* 173–213. [8]

Brambilla, F., Smeraldi, E., et al. Deranged anterior pituitary responsiveness of hypothalamic hormones in depressed patients. *Archives of General Psychiatry,* 1978, *35,* 1231. [15]

Bramwell, S. T., Masuda, M., Wagner, N. N., and **Holmes, T. H.** Psychosocial factors in athletic injuries. *Journal of Human Stress,* 1975, *1,* 6–20. [10]

Branchey, M. H., Charles, J., and **Simpson, G. M.** Extrapyramidal side effects in lithium maintenance therapy. *American Journal of Psychiatry,* 1976, *133,* 444–445. [16]

Bray, G. A. The myth of diet in the management of obesity. *American Journal of Clinical Nutrition,* 1970, *23,* 1141–1148. [11]

Bray, G. A. *Obesity in America* (U.S. Department of Health, Education and Welfare, National Institutes of Health Publication No. 79-359). Washington, D.C.: U.S. Government Printing Office, 1979. [11]

Bray, G. A., and **Gallagher, T. F., Jr.** Manifestations of hypothalamic obesity in man: A comprehensive investigation of eight patients and a review of the literature. *Medicine,* 1975, *54,* 301–330. [11]

Brehm, J. W. *A theory of psychological reactance.* New York: Academic Press, 1966. [17]

Bremer, J. *Asexualisation: A follow-up study of 244 cases.* New York: Macmillan, 1959. [11]

Brickman, P. *Happiness: Can we make it last?* Paper, Northwestern University, April 1978. [10]

Brickman, P., and **Campbell, D. T.** Hedonic relativism and planning the good society. In M. H. Appley (Ed.), *Adaptation level theory.* New York: Academic Press, 1971. [10]

Brickman, P., Coates, D., and **Janoff-Bul-**

man, R. Lottery winners and accident victims: Is happiness relative? *Journal of Personality and Social Psychology,* 1978, *36,* 917–927. [10]

Brickman, P., Rabinowitz, V. C., Coates, D., Cohn, E., Kidder, L., and **Karuza, J.** *Helping.* Unpublished paper, Institute for Social Research, University of Michigan, 1979. [18]

Brickman, P., Rabinowitz, V. C., Karuza, J., Coates, D., Cohn, E., and **Kidder, L.** Models of helping and coping. *American Psychologist,* 1982, *37,* 368–384. [18]

Bridges, P. K., and **Bartlett, J. R.** Psychosurgery: Yesterday and today. *British Journal of Psychiatry,* 1977, *131,* 249–260. [16]

Broad, W. J. What happens when heroes of science go astray? *The New York Times,* January 25, 1983, C1-C2. [3]

Broadbent, D. E. *Perception and communication.* London: Pergamon Press, 1958. [6]

Broadbent, D. E. The current state of noise research: Reply to Poulton. *Psychological Bulletin,* 1978, *85,* 1052–1067. [18]

Brockner, J. The effects of self-esteem, success-failure, and self-consciousness on task performance. *Journal of Personality and Social Psychology,* 1979a, *37,* 1732–1741. [13]

Brockner, J. Self-esteem, self-consciousness, and task performance: Replications, extensions, and possible explanations. *Journal of Personality and Social Psychology,* 1979b, *37,* 447–461. [13]

Brockner, J., and **Hulton, A. J. B.** How to reverse the vicious cycle of low self-esteem: The importance of attentional focus. *Journal of Experimental Social Psychology,* 1978, *14,* 564–578. [13]

Bromley, D. G., and **Shupe, A. D.** "Just a few years seems like a lifetime": A role theory approach to participation in religious movements. In L. Kriesberg (Ed.), *Research in social movements, conflict and change.* Greenwich, N.Y.: JAI Press, 1979. [18]

Broverman, I. K., Vogel, S. R., Broverman, D. M., Clarkson, F. E., and **Rosenkrantz, P. S.** Sex-role stereotypes: A current appraisal. *Journal of Social Issues,* 1972, *28,* 59–78. [17]

Brown, B. W., Jr. Statistics, scientific method, and smoking. In J. M. Tanur et al. (Eds.), *Statistics: A guide to the unknown.* San Francisco: Holden-Day, 1978. Pp. 59–70. [2]

Brown, G. W., Birley, J. L. T., and **Wing, J. K.** Influence of family on the course of schizophrenic disorders: A replication. *British Journal of Psychiatry,* 1972, *121,* 241–258 [15]

Brown, G. W., Bone, M., Dalison, B., and **Wing, J. K.** *Schizophrenia and social care.* London: Oxford University Press, 1966. [15]

Brown, J. (Ed.). *Recall and recognition.* London: Wiley Interscience, 1976. [6]

Brown, L. K. Women and business man-

agement. *Signs: Journal of Women in Culture and Society,* 1979, *5,* 266–288. [17]

Brown, R. *A first language: The early stages.* Cambridge, Mass.: Harvard University Press, 1973. [9]

Brown, R., and **Bellugi, U.** Three processes in the child's acquisition of syntax. *Harvard Educational Review,* 1964, *34,* 133–151. [9]

Brown, R., Cazden, C., and **Bellugi-Klima, U.** The child's grammar from I to III. In J. P. Hill (Ed.), *Minnesota Symposium on Child Development* (Vol. 2). Minneapolis: University of Minnesota Press, 1968. Pp. 28–73. [9]

Brown, R., and **Fraser, C.** The acquisition of syntax. In C. N. Cofer and B. S. Musgrave (Eds.), *Verbal behavior and learning problems and processes.* New York: McGraw-Hill, 1973. [9]

Brown, R., and **Hanlon, C.** Derivational complexity and order of acquisition in child speech. In J. R. Hayes (Ed.), *Cognition and the development of language.* New York: Wiley, 1970. [9]

Brown, R., and **McNeill, D.** The "tip of the tongue" phenomenon. *Journal of Verbal Learning and Verbal Behavior,* 1966, *5,* 325–337. [1, 6]

Brownell, K. D., and **Stunkard, A. J.** Physical activity in the development and control of obesity. In A. J. Stunkard (Ed.), *Obesity.* Philadelphia: W. B. Saunders, 1980. [11]

Bruch, H. *The golden cage: The enigma of anorexia nervosa.* New York: Random House, 1980. [11]

Bruner, J. S., Goodnow, J. J., and **Austin, G. A.** *A study of thinking.* New York: Wiley, 1956. [7]

Bry, A. *EST: 60 hours that transform your life.* New York: Harper & Row, 1976. [16]

Bryan, J. H. Children's cooperation and helping behaviors. In E. M. Hetherington (Ed.), *Review of child development research* (Vol. 5). Chicago: University of Chicago Press, 1975. [8]

Buck, R. A test of nonverbal receiving ability: Preliminary studies. *Human Communication Research,* 1976, *2,* 162–171. [9]

Budzynski, T. H. Biofeedback strategies in headache treatment. In J. V. Basmajian (Ed.), *Biofeedback—principles and practice for clinicians.* Baltimore: Williams & Wilkins, 1979a. [12]

Budzynski, T. H. Biofeedback and the twilight states of consciousness. In D. Goleman and R. Davidson (Eds.), *Consciousness: Brain, states of awareness and mysticism.* New York: Harper & Row, 1979b. Pp. 161–165. [12]

Bull, C. N., and **Aucoin, J.** Voluntary association, participation, and life satisfaction: A replication note. *Journal of Gerontology,* 1975, *30* 73–76. [10]

Bunney, W. E., Jr., Murphy, D. L., Goodwin, F. K., and **Borge, G. F.** The "switch process" in manic-depressive illness: A systematic study of sequential behavior changes." *Archives of General Psychiatry,* September 1972, *27,* 295–302. [15]

Burgess, A. W., and **Holmstrom, L. L.** Rape trauma syndrome. *American Journal of Psychiatry,* 1974, *131,* 981–986. [10]

Burgess, A. W. and **Holmstrom, L. L.** Recovery from rape and prior life stress. *Research in Nursing and Health,* 1978, *1,* 165–174. [10]

Burns, D. D. The perfectionist's script for self-defeat. *Psychology Today,* November 1980, 34–52. [10]

Burt, C. The genetic determination of differences in intelligence: A study of monozygotic twins reared together and apart. *British Journal of Psychology,* 1966, *57,* 137–153. [14]

Burt, C. Inheritance of general intelligence. *American Psychologist,* 1972, *27,* 175–190. [14]

Burkirk, E. R. Obesity: A brief overview with emphasis on exercise. *Federation Proceedings,* 1974, *33 (8),* 1948–1951. [11]

Bryne, D., and **Clore, G. L.** A reinforcement model of evaluative responses. *Personality: An Interactional Journal,* 1970, *2,* 103–128. [17]

Bryne, D., Ervin, C. R., and **Lamberth, J.** Continuity between the experimental study of attraction and "real life" computer dating. *Journal of Personality and Social Psychology,* 1970, *16,* 157–165. [17]

Byrne, D., and **Griffitt, W.** Interpersonal attraction. *Annual Review of Psychology,* 1973, *24,* 317–336. [17]

Byrne, D., and **Lamberth, J.** Reinforcement theories and cognitive theories as complementary approaches to the study of attraction. In B. I. Murstein (Ed.), *Theories of love and attraction.* New York: Springer, 1971. [17]

Cabanac, M. The physiological role of pleasure. *Science,* 1971, *173,* 1103–1107. [11]

Calder, B. J., and **Ross, M.** *Attitudes and behavior.* Morristown, N.J.: General Learning Press, 1973. [17]

Calhoun, J. B. Population density and social pathology. *Scientific American,* 1962, *206,* 139–148. [18]

Calhoun, L. G., Kahn, A., Selby, J. W., and **Magee, D. L.** Victim emotional response: Effect on social reaction to victims of rape. *British Journal of Social and Clinical Psychology,* in press. [10]

Callaway, E., III, and **Dembo, D.** Narrowed attention: A psychological phenomenon that accompanies a certain physiological change. *AMA Archives of Neurology and Psychiatry,* 1958, *79,* 74–80. [11]

Cameron, N. *Personality development and psychopathology.* Boston: Houghton Mifflin, 1963. [15]

Campbell, A., Converse, P. E., and **Rogers, W. L.** *The quality of American life: Perceptions,* *evaluations and satisfactions.* New York: Russell Sage Foundation, 1976. [10]

Campbell, A. M. G., Evans, M., Thomson, J. L., and **Williams, M. J.** Cerebral atrophy in young cannabis smokers. *Lancet,* 1971, *2,* 1219–1224. [1]

Campbell, D. T. Reforms as experiments. In F. G. Caro (Ed.), *Readings in evaluation research.* New York: Russell Sage Foundation, 1971. [2]

Campbell, D. T. Measuring the effects of social innovations by means of time series. In J. M. Tanur et al. (Eds.), *Statistics: A guide to the unknown.* San Francisco: Holden-Day, 1978. Pp. 159–169. [2]

Campbell, D. T., and **Ross, H. L.** The Connecticut crackdown on speeding: Time-series data in quasi-experimental analysis. *Law and Society Review,* 1968, *3* 33–53. [2]

Campbell, D. T., and **Stanley, J. C.** Experimental and quasi-experimental designs for research on teaching. In N. L. Gage (Ed.), *Handbook of research on teaching.* Chicago: Rand McNally, 1963. Pp. 171–246. (Reprinted as *Experimental and quasi-experimental designs for research.* Chicago: Rand·McNally, 1966.) [2]

Campbell, J. B., and **Hawley, C. W.** Study habits and Eysenck's theory of extroversion-introversion. *Journal of Research in Personality,* 1982, *16,* 139–146. [13]

Campos, J., Langer, A., and **Krowitz, A.** Cardiac responses on the visual cliff in premotor human infants. *Science,* 1970, *170,* 195–196. [4]

Canestrari, R. E., Jr. Paced and self-paced learning in young and elderly adults. *Journal of Gerontology,* 1963, *18,* 165–168. [8]

Cannell, C. G., and **Kahn, R. L.** Interviewing. In G. Lindzey and E. Aronson (Eds.), *The handbook of social psychology* (2nd ed.). Vol. 2: Research methods. Reading, Mass.: Addison-Wesley, 1968. [6]

Cannon, W. B., and **Washburn, A. L.** An explanation of hunger. *American Journal of Physiology,* 1912, *29,* 441–454. [11]

Cantor, N., and **Mischel, W.** Traits as prototypes: Effects on recognition memory. *Journal of Personality and Social Psychology,* 1977, *35,* 38–48. [17]

Caplan, N., Morrison, A., and **Stambaugh, R. J.** *The use of social science knowledge in policy decisions at the national level.* Ann Arbor: University of Michigan, 1975. [18]

Caplan, R. D., Abbey, A., Abramis, D. J., Andrews, F. M., Conway, T. L., and **French, J. R. P.** *Tranquilizer use and well-being: A longitudinal study of social and psychological effects.* Ann Arbor, Mich.: Institute for Social Research, University of Michigan, 1983. [16]

Caramazza, A., and **Zurif, E. B.** Dissociation of algorithmic and heuristic processes in language comprehension: Evidence from aphasia. *Brain and Language,* 1976, *3,* 572–582. [9]

Carmichael, L., Hogan, H. P., and **Walter,**

A. A. An experimental study of the effect of language on the reproduction of visually perceived form. *Journal of Experimental Psychology,* 1932, *15,* 73–86. [6]

Carr, R. What marijuana does (and doesn't do). *Human Behavior,* January 1978. [12]

Carr, W. J., and **Caul, W. F.** The effect of castration in rats upon the dissemination of sex odors. *Animal Behavior,* 1962, *10,* 20–27. [11]

Carrol, E. N., Zuckerman, M., and **Vogel, W. H.** A test of the optimal level of arousal theory of sensation seeking. *Journal of Personality and Social Psychology,* 1982, *42,* 572–575. [11]

Cartwright, R. D. *Night life: Explorations in dreaming.* Englewood Cliffs, N. J.: Prentice-Hall, 1977. [12]

Cartwright, R. D. Happy endings for our dreams. *Psychology Today,* December 1978, 66–76. [12]

Cartwright, R. D. The nature and function of repetitive dreams: A survey of speculation. *Psychiatry,* 1979, *42,* 131–137. [12]

Casper, R. C., Eckert, E. D., Halmi, K. A., Goldberg, S. C., and **Davis, J. M.** Bulimia: Its incidence and clinical importance in patients with anorexia nervosa. *Archives of General Psychiatry,* 1980, *37,* 1030–1035. [11]

Cass, L. K., and **Thomas, C. B.** *Childhood pathology and later adjustment.* New York: Wiley, 1979. [15]

Chacko, T. I. Women and equal opportunity: Some unintended effects. *Journal of Applied Psychology,* 1982, *67,* 119–123. [17]

Chall, J. S. *Learning to read: The great debate.* New York: McGraw-Hill, 1967. [9]

Chambliss, C. A., and **Murray, E. J.** Efficacy attribution, locus of control, and weight loss. *Cognitive Therapy and Research,* 1979, *3,* 349–353. [18]

Chapanis, N. P., and **Chapanis, A. C.** Cognitive dissonance: Five years later. *Psychological Bulletin,* 1964, *61,* 1–22. [17]

Chen, S. C. Social modification of the activity of ants in nest-building. *Physiological Zoology,* 1937, *10,* 420–436. [18]

Cherniss, C., Egnatios, E. S., and **Wacker, S.** Job stress and career development in new public professionals. *Professional Psychology,* 1976, *7,* 428–436. [18]

Cherniss, C., Egnatios, E. S., Wacker, S., and **O'Dowd, B.** The professional mystique and burnout in public sector professionals. *Social Policy,* in press. [18]

Cherry, E. C. Some experiments on the recognition of speech with one and two ears. *Journal of the Acoustical Society of America,* 1953, *25,* 975–979. [6]

Cherry, F., and **Deaux, K.** *Fear of success vs. fear of gender-inconsistent behavior: A sex similarity.* Paper presented at the meeting of the Midwestern Psychological Association, Chicago, May 1975. [11]

Chi, M. T. H. Knowledge structures and

memory development. In R. S. Siegler (Ed.), *Children's thinking: What develops?* Hillsdale, N. J.: Lawrence Erlbaum, 1978. [8]

Chomsky, N. *Aspects of the theory of syntax.* Cambridge, Mass.: MIT Press, 1965. [9]

Chomsky, N. *Language and mind.* New York: Harcourt Brace Jovanovich, 1972. [9]

Chorover, S. L. *From genesis to genocide.* Cambridge, Mass.: MIT Press; 1979. [14]

Christensen-Szalanski, J. J. J. Problem-solving strategies: A selection mechanism, some implications, and some data. *Organizational Behavior and Human Performance,* 1978, 22, 307–323. [7]

Christensen-Szalanski, J. J. J., and **Bushyhead, J. B.** Physicians' use of probabilistic information in a real clinical setting. *Journal of Experimental Psychology,* 1981, 7, 928–935. [7]

Cialdini, R. B. Full-cycle social psychology. In L. Bickman (Ed.), *Applied social psychology.* Beverly Hills, Calif.: Sage Publications, 1980. Pp. 21–47. [18]

Clark, E. V. What's in a word? On the child's acquisition of semantics in his first language. In T. E. Moore (Ed.), *Cognitive development and the acquisition of language.* New York: Academic Press, 1973. Pp. 65–110. [9]

Clark, E. V. Language change during language acquisition. In M. E. Lamb and A. L. Brown (Eds.), *Advances in child development.* Hillsdale, N. J.: Lawrence Erlbaum, 1982. [9]

Clark, E. V., and **Hecht, B. F.** Comprehension, production, and language acquisition. *Annual Review of Psychology,* 1983, 34, 325–349. [9]

Clark, K. B., and **Clark, M. P.** Racial identification and preference in Negro children. In T. M. Newcomb and E. L. Hartley (Eds.), *Readings in social psychology.* New York: Holt, 1947. [18]

Clifford, M., and **Walster, E.** The effect of physical attractiveness on teacher expectations. *Sociology of Education,* 1973, 46, 248–258. [17]

Coates, D., Renzaglia, G. J., and **Embree, M. C.** When helping backfires: Help and helplessness. In J. D. Fisher, A. Nadler, and B. DePaulo (Eds.), *New directions in helping* (Vol. 1). New York: Academic Press, 1983. [16]

Coates, D., and **Wortman, C. B.** Depression maintenance and interpersonal control. In A. Baum, J. E. Singer, and Y. Epstein (Eds.), *Advances in environmental psychology* (Vol. 2). Hillsdale, N. J.: Lawrence Erlbaum, 1980. [15]

Coates, D., Wortman, C. B., and **Abbey, A.** Reactions to victims. In I. H. Frieze, D. Bar-Tal, and J. S. Carroll (Eds.), *New approaches to social problems.* San Francisco: Jossey-Bass, 1979.

Cobbin, D. M., Requin-Blow, B., Williams, L. R., and **Williams, W. O.** Urinary MHPG

levels and tricyclic antidepressant drug selection. *Archives of General Psychiatry,* 1979, 36, 1111–1115. [15]

Cohen, D. H. *The learning child.* New York: Vintage, 1973. [9]

Cohen, E., Motto, J. A., and **Seiden, R. H.** An instrument for evaluating suicide potential: A preliminary study. *American Journal of Psychiatry,* 1966, 122, 886–891. [15]

Cohen, F. Personality, stress, and the development of physical illness. In G. Stone, F. Cohen, N. Adler, and associates (Eds.), *Health psychology—A handbook.* San Francisco: Jossey-Bass, 1979. [10]

Cohen, L. B., DeLoache, J. S., and **Stauss, M. S.** Infant visual perception. In J. Osofsky (Ed.), *Handbook of infancy.* New York: Wiley, 1978. [8]

Cohen, S., Evans, G. W., Krantz, D. S., and **Stokols, D.** Physiological, motivational, and cognitive effects of aircraft noise on children: Moving from the laboratory to the field. *American Psychologist,* 1980. [18]

Cohen, S., Evans, G. W., Krantz, D. S., Stokols, D., and **Kelly S.** Aircraft noise and children: Longitudinal and cross-sectional evidence on adaptation to noise and the effectiveness of noise abatement. *Journal of Personality and Social Psychology,* in press. [18]

Cohen, S., Glass, D. C., and **Phillips, S.** Environment and health. In H. E. Freeman, S. Levine, and L. G. Reeder (Eds.), *Handbook of medical sociology.* Englewood Cliffs, N.J.: Prentice-Hall, 1979. [18]

Cohen, S., and **Stillman, R. C.** (Eds.), *The therapeutic potential of marijuana.* New York: Plenum, 1976. [12]

Cohen, T. Why diets don't work. *New York,* May 1979, 45–51. [11]

Collias, N. E. The analysis of socialization in sheep and goats. *Ecology,* 1956, 37, 228–239. [2]

Collins, A. M., and **Quillan, M. R.** Retrieval time from semantic memory. *Journal of Verbal Learning and Verbal Behavior,* 1969, 8, 240–247. [7]

Collins, B. E. *Social psychology.* Reading, Mass.: Addison-Wesley, 1970. [18]

Collins, B. E., and **Hoyt, M. F.** Personal responsibility-for-consequences: An integration and extension of the forced compliance literature. *Journal of Experimental Social Psychology,* 1972, 8, 558–593. [17]

Collins, R. L., and **Marlatt, G. A.** Social modeling as a determinant of drinking behavior: Implications for prevention and treatment. *Addictive Behaviors,* in press. [2]

Combs, B. J., Hales, D. R., and **Williams, B. K.** *An invitation to health.* Menlo Park, Calif.: Benjamin/Cummings, 1980. [12]

Comfort, A. Likelihood of human pheromones. *Nature,* 1971, 230, 432–433. [11]

Condry, J. Enemies of exploration: Self-initiated versus other-initiated learning.

American Psychologist, 1977, 35, 459–477. [16]

Condry, J., and **Condry, S.** Sex differences: A study of the eye of the beholder. *Chid Development,* 1976, 47, 812–819. [8]

Condry, J., and **Dyer, S.** Fear of success: Attribution of cause to the victim. *Journal of Social Issues,* 1976, 32, 63–83. [11]

Cook, S. *Social science and school desegregation: Did we mislead the Supreme Court?* Boulder, Colo.: Institute of Behavioral Science, University of Colorado, 1979. [17]

Coon, C. S. The taxonomy of human variation. *Annals of the New York Academy of Sciences,* 1966, 134, 516–523. [4]

Cooper, J., and **Croyle, T.** Attitudes and attitude change. *Annual Review of Psychology,* 1984, 35, 395–426. [17]

Cooper, J., and **Worchel, S.** Role of undesired consequences in arousing cognitive dissonance. *Journal of Personality and Social Psychology,* 1970, 16, 199–206. [17]

Coopersmith, S. *The antecedents of self-esteem.* New York: W. H. Freeman, 1967. [13]

Coren, S., and **Girgus, J. S.** Differentiation and decrement in the Mueller-Lyer illusion. *Perception & Psychophysics,* 1972, 12, 466–470. [4]

Coren, S., and **Girgus, J. S.** *Seeing is deceiving: The psychology of visual illusions.* Hillsdale, N.J.: Lawrence Erlbaum, 1978. [4]

Coren, S., Porac, C., and **Ward, L.** *Sensation and perception.* New York: Academic Press, 1978. [4]

Corsini, R. J., (Ed.), *Current personality theories.* Itasca, Ill.: Peacock, 1977. [13]

Corteen, R. S., and **Wood, B.** Autonomic responses to shock-associated words in an unattended channel. *Journal of Experimental Psychology,* 1972, 94, 308–313. [6]

Costa, P. T., and **McCrae, R. R.** Influence of extraversion and neuroticism on subjective well-being: Happy and unhappy people. *Journal of Personality and Social Psychology,* 1980, 38, 668–678. [15]

Costanzo, P. R., and **Woody, E. Z.** Externality as a function of obesity in children: Persuasive style or eating-specific attribute? *Journal of Personality and Social Psychology,* 1979, 37, 2286–2296. [11]

Coyne, J. Toward an interactional description of depression. *Psychiatry,* 1976a, 39, 14–27. [15]

Coyne, J. Depression and the response of others. *Journal of Abnormal Psychology,* 1976b, 85, 186–193. [15]

Craddock, D. *Obesity and its management.* London: Churchill-Livingstone, 1978. [11]

Craig, R. L., and **Siegel, P. S.** Does negative affect beget positive affect? A test of the opponent-process theory. *Bulletin of the Psychonomic Society,* 1979, 14, 404–406. [11]

Craik, F. I. M. Age differences in human memory. In J. E. Birren and K. W. Schaie (Eds.), *Handbook of the psychology of aging.*

New York: Van Nostrand Reinhold, 1977. Pp. 384–420. [8]

Craik, F. I. M., and **Lockhart, R. S.** Levels of processing: A framework for memory research. *Journal of Verbal Learning and Verbal Behavior,* 1972, *11,* 671–684. [6]

Craik, F. I. M., and **Simon, E.** Age differences in memory: The roles of attention and depth of processing. In L. W. Poon et al. (Eds.), *New directions in memory and aging.* Hillsdale, N.J.: Lawrence Erlbaum, 1980. [8]

Craik, F. I. M., and **Tulving, E.** Depth of processing and the retention of words in episodic memory. *Journal of Experimental Psychology: General,* 1975, *104,* 268–294. [6]

Creese, I., Burt, D. R., and **Snyder, S. H.** Brain's dopamine receptor—labeling with [dopamine-H$_3$] and [H$_{21}$ operidol-H$_3$]. *Psychopharmacology Communications,* 1975, *1,* 663–673. [15]

Crépault, C., Abraham, G., Porto, R., and **Couture, M.** Erotic imagery in women. In R. Gemme and C. C. Wheeler (Eds.), *Progress in sexology.* New York: Plenum, 1977. Pp. 267–283. [11]

Crépault, C., and **Couture, M.** Men's erotic fantasies. *Archives of Sexual Behavior,* 1980, *9,* 565–582. [11]

Crocker, J., and **McGraw, K. M.** What's good for the goose is not good for the gander: Solo states as an obstacle to occupational achievement for males and females. *American Behavioral Scientist,* 1984, *27,* 357–369. [17]

Cronbach, L. J. Five decades of public controversy over mental testing. *American Psychologist,* 1975, *30,* 1–14. [14]

Crow, T. J., Cross, A. J., Johnstone, E. C., Longden, A., Owen, F., and **Ridley, R. M.** Time course of the antipsychotic effect in schizophrenia and some changes in postmortem brain and their relation to neuraleptic medication. *Advances in Biochemical Psychopharmacology,* 1980, *24,* 495–503. [15]

Crowder, R. G. *The psychology of learning.* New York: Oxford University Press, 1982. [9]

Croyle, R. T., and **Cooper, J.** Dissonance arousal: Physiological evidence. *Journal of Personality and Social Psychology,* in press. [17]

Csikszentmihalyi, M. *Beyond freedom and anxiety.* San Francisco: Jossey-Bass, 1975. [10]

Czikszentmihalyi, M., Larson, R., and **Prescott, S.** The ecology of adolescent activity and experience. *Journal of Youth and Adolescence,* 1977, *6,* 281–294. [10]

Cummings, E. M. Caregiver stability and day care. *Developmental Psychology,* 1980, *16,* 31–37. [8]

Cunningham, M. R. Weather, mood, and helping behavior: Quasi-experiments with the Sunshine Samaritan. *Journal of Personality and Social Psychology,* 1979, *37,* 1947–1956. [18]

Curtiss, S. *Genie: A psycholinguistic study of a modern-day "wild child."* New York: Academic Press, 1977. [9]

Czeisler, C. A., Moore-Ede, M. C., and **Coleman, R. M.** Rotating shift work schedules that disrupt sleep are improved by applying circadian principles. *Science,* 30 July 1982, *217,* 460–463. [12]

Dahlkoetter, J., Callahan, E. J., and **Linton, J.** Obesity and the unbalanced energy equation: Exercise vs. eating habit change. *Journal of Consulting and Clinical Psychology,* 1979, *47,* 898–905. [11]

Dahlstrom, W. G., Welsh, G. S., and **Dahlstrom, L. E.** *An MMPI handbook, Vol. I: Clinical interpretation.* (Rev. ed.) Minneapolis: University of Minnesota Press, 1972. [14]

Dahlstrom, W. G., et al. *An MMPI handbook, Vol. 2: Research applications.* (Rev. ed.) Minneapolis: University of Minnesota Press, 1975. [13]

Dale P. Is early pragmatic development measurable? *Journal of Child Language,* 1980, *1,* 1–12. [9]

Damon, W. *The social world of the child.* San Francisco: Jossey-Bass, 1977. [8]

Darley, C. F., Tinklenberg, J. R., Roth, W. T., Hollister, L. E., and **Atkinson, R. C.** Influence of marihuana on storage and retrieval processes in memory. *Memory and Cognition,* 1973, *1,* 196–200. [12]

Darley, J. M., and **Latané, B.** Bystander intervention in emergencies: Diffusion of responsibility. *Journal of Personality and Social Psychology,* 1968, *8,* 377–383. [1, 18]

Darwin, C. *On the origin of species by means of natural selection* (1859). Cambridge, Mass.: Harvard University Press, 1964. [1]

Darwin, C. *The descent of man and selection in relation to sex* (1871). New York: Modern Library. [1]

Darwin, C. *The expression of the emotions in man and animals.* London: Murray, 1872. [9]

David-Neel, A. *Magic and mystery in Tibet.* Baltimore: Penguin, 1971. [12]

Davidson, P. *Ethics and social science research.* Englewood Cliffs, N.J.: Prentice-Hall, 1982. [2]

Davis, J. D., Gallagher, R. J., Ladove, R. F., and **Turausky, A. J.** Inhibition of food intake by a humoral factor. *Journal of Comparative and Physiological Psychology,* 1969, *67,* 407–414. [11]

Davis, J. M. Overview: Maintenance therapy in psychiatry: I. Schizophrenia. *American Journal of Psychiatry,* 1975, *132,* 1237–1245. [16]

Davison, G. C., and **Valins, S.** Maintenance of self-attributed and drug-attributed behavior change. *Journal of Personality and Social Psychology,* 1969, *11,* 25–33. [10]

Daw, N. W. Colour-coded ganglion cells in the goldfish retina: Extension of their receptive fields by means of new stimuli. *Journal of Physiology* (London), 1968, *197,* 567–592. [4]

Dawkins, E. *The selfish gene.* New York: Oxford University Press, 1975. [18]

Dean, R. A. Youth: Moonies' target population. *Adolescence,* 1982, *17,* 567–574. [18]

Deaux, K. Sex: A perspective on the attribution process. In J. H. Harvey, W. J. Ickes, and R. F. Kidd (Eds.), *New directions in attribution research* (Vol. 1). Hillsdale, N.J.: Lawrence Erlbaum, 1976. [17]

DeBacker, G., et al. Behavior, stress, and psychosocial traits as risk factors. *Preventative Medicine,* 1983, *12,* 32–36. [10]

De Carlo, T. J. *Recreational participation patterns and successful aging: A twin study.* Unpublished doctoral dissertation, Columbia University, 1971. [8]

deCharms, R. *Personal causation: The internal affective determinants of behavior.* New York: Academic Press, 1968. [9,11]

Deci, E. L. Effects of externally mediated rewards on intrinsic motivation. *Journal of Personality and Social Psychology,* 1971, *18,* 105–115. [17]

Deci, E. L. *Intrinsic motivation.* New York: Plenum, 1975. [11]

Deci, E. L., and **Ryan, R. M.** The empirical exploration of intrinsic motivational processes. In L. Berkowitz (Ed.), *Advances in experimental social psychology* (vol. 13). New York: Academic Press, 1980. [17]

Decke, E. Effects of taste on the eating behavior of obese and normal persons. Cited in S. Schacter, *Emotion, obesity, and crime.* New York: Academic Press, 1971. [1, 11]

De Groot, A. D. *Thought and choice in chess.* The Hague: Mouton, 1965. [6]

De Lamater, J. A definition of "group." *Small Group Behavior,* 1974, *5,* 30–44. [18]

Delgado, J. M. R. *Physical control of the mind.* New York: Harper & Row, 1969. [1]

De Longis, A. M., Coyne, J. C., and **Lazarus, R. S.** Daily hassles, uplifts, and major life events in the prediction of health status. *Psychosomatic Medicine,* in press. [10]

Dement, W. C. Dream deprivation. *Science,* 1960, *132,* 1420–1422. [12]

Dement, W. C. The biological role of REM sleep. In A. Kales (Ed.), *Sleep physiology and pathology.* Philadelphia: Lippincott, 1969. [12]

Dement, W. C. *Some must watch while some must sleep: Exploring the world of sleep.* New York: Norton, 1976. [12]

Denton, G. G. *The influence of visual pattern on perceived speed.* Crowthorne, England: Road Research Library, 1971. [4]

Depue, R. A., and **Evans, R.** The psychobiology of depressive disorders. In B. H. Maher (Ed.), *Progress in experimental personality research* (Vol. 8). New York: Academic Press, 1976. [15]

Dermer, M., Cohen, S. J., and **Anderson, E. A.** *Evaluative aspects of life as a function of* *vicarious exposure to hedonic extremes.* Unpublished paper, University of Wisconsin-Milwaukee, 1978. [10]

Dermer, M., and **Thiel, D. L.** When beauty may fail. *Journal of Personality and Social Psychology,* 1975, *31,* 1168–1176, [17]

Derogatis, L. R., Abeloff, M. D., and **Melisaratos, N.** Psychological coping mechanisms and survival time in metastatic breast cancer. *Journal of the American Medical Association,* 1979, *242,* 1504–1508. [10]

De Ropp, R. S. *Drugs and the mind.* New York: Dell, 1976. [12]

Deutsch, M., and **Gerard, H. B.** A study of normative and informational influences on social judgment. *Journal of Abnormal and Social Psychology,* 1955, *51,* 629–636. [18]

De Valois, R. L., Abramov, I., and **Jacobs, G. H.** Analysis of response patterns of LGN cells. *Journal of the Optical Society of America,* 1966, *56,* 966–977. [4]

de Vries, H. A. *Physiology of exercise.* Dubuque, Iowa: William C. Brown, 1974. [11]

de Vries, H. A., and **Gray, D. E.** Aftereffects of exercise upon resting metabolism rate. *Research Quarterly,* 1963, *34,* 314–321. [11]

Diamond, B. Interview regarding Sirhan Sirhan. *Psychology Today,* September 1969, pp. 48–55. [6]

Diamond, S. (Ed.). *The roots of psychology.* New York: Basic Books, 1974. [1]

Diamond, S. Pigeon pilots. *Omni,* November 1979, p. 37. [5]

Dienstbier, R. A. Emotion-attribution theory: Establishing roots and exploring future perspectives. In S. Murray and R. Levine (Eds.), *Nebraska Symposium on Motivation,* 1978, *26.* [10]

Diggory, J. C., Klein, S. J., and **Cohen, N. M.** Muscle action potentials and estimated probability of success. *Journal of Experimental Psychology,* 1964, *68,* 448–456. [13]

Dion, K. Physical attractiveness and evaluations of children's transgressions. *Journal of Personality and Social Psychology,* 1972, *24,* 207–213. [17]

Dion, K. Young children's stereotyping of facial attractiveness. *Developmental Psychology,* 1973, *9,* 183–188. [17]

Dion, K. Physical attractiveness, sex roles and heterosexual attraction. In M. Cook (Ed.), *The bases of human sexual attraction.* London: Academic Press, 1980. [17]

Dion, K., Berscheid, E., and **Walster, E.** What is beautiful is good. *Journal of Personality and Social Psychology,* 1972, *24,* 285–290. [17]

Dittes, J., and **Kelley, H.** Effects of different conditions of acceptance upon conformity to group norms. *Journal of Abnormal and Social Psychology,* 1956, *53,* 100–107. [18]

Dixon, N. F. *Subliminal perception: The nature of a controversy.* London: McGraw-Hill, 1971. [4]

Doane, J. A., West, K. L., Goldstein, M. J., Rodnick, E. H., and **Jones, J. E.** Parental communication deviance and affective style as predictors of subsequent schizophrenia spectrum disorders in vulnerable adolescents. *Archives of General Psychiatry,* 1981, *38,* 679–685. [15]

Dohrenwend, B. S., Krasnoff, L., Askenasy, A. R., and **Dohrenwend, B. P.** The psychiatric epidemiology research interview life events scale. In Leo Goldberger and Shlomo Breznitz (Eds.), *Handbook of stress: Theoretical and clinical aspects.* New York: Free Press, 1982. Pp. 332–363. [10]

Doll, R., and **Hill, A. B.** Lung cancer and other causes of death in relation to smoking: A second report on the mortality of British doctors. *British Medical Journal,* 1956, *2,* 1071–1081. [2]

Dollard, J., Doob, L. W., Miller, N. E., Mowrer, O. H., and **Sears, R. R.** *Frustration and aggression.* New Haven: Yale University Press, 1939. [18]

Dornbusch, S. M. To try or not to try. *Stanford Magazine,* 1974, *2,* 51–54. [11]

Douglas, R. J. The hippocampus and behavior. *Psychological Bulletin,* 1967, *67,* 416–442.[12]

Driscoll, R., Davis, K. E., and **Lipetz, M. E.** Parental interference and romantic love: The Romeo and Juliet effect. *Journal of Personality and Social Psychology,* 1972, *24,* 1–10. [17]

Duffy, E. The psychological significance of the concept of "arousal" or "activation." *Psychological Review,* 1957, *64,* 265–275. [11]

Duke, M. P., and **Mullins, M. C.** Preferred interpersonal distance as a function of locus of control orientation in chronic schizophrenics, non-schizophrenic patients, and normals. *Journal of Consulting and Clinical Psychology,* 1973, *41,* (2), 230–234. [15]

Duncan, C. P. The retroactive effect of electroshock on learning. *Journal of Comparative and Physiological Psychology,* 1949, *42,* 32–44. [6]

Duncan, O. D. Does money buy satisfaction? *Social Indicators Research,* 1975, *2,* 267–274. [10]

Duncker, K. On problem-solving (1935). L. S. Lees (Trans.). *Psychological Monographs,* 1945, *58,* Whole No. 270. [7]

Dunkel-Schetter, C., and **Wortman, C. B.** The interpersonal dynamics of cancer: Problems in social relationships and their impact on the patient. In H. Freedman (Ed.), *Interpersonal issues in health care.* New York: Academic Press, 1982. Pp. 69–100. [10, 16]

Dutton, D. G., and **Aron, A. P.** Some evidence for heightened sexual attraction under conditions of high anxiety. *Journal of Personality and Social Psychology,* 1974, *30,* 510–517. [17]

Dweck, C. S. The role of expectations and attributions in the alleviation of learned

helplessness. *Journal of Personality and Social Psychology,* 1975, *31,* 674–685. [1]

Dweck, C. S., Davidson, W., Nelson, S., and **Enna, B.** Sex differences in learned helplessness: II. The contingencies of evaluative feedback in the classroom; and III. An experimental analysis. *Developmental Psychology,* 1978, *14,* 268–276. [11]

Dweck, C. S., and **Goetz, M.** Attributions and learned helplessness. In J. Harvey, W. Ickes, and R. F. Kidd (Eds.), *New directions in attribution research* (Vol. 2). Hillsdale, N.J.: Lawrence Erlbaum, 1978. [11]

Dweck, C. S., Goetz, T. E., and **Strauss, N.** Sex differences in learned helplessness: IV. An experimental and naturalistic study of failure generalization and its mediators. *Journal of Personality and Social Psychology,* 1980, *38,* 441–452. [11]

Dweck, C. S., and **Licht, B. G.** Learned helplessness and intellectual achievement. In J. Garber and M. E. P. Seligman (Eds.), *Human helplessness: Theory and applications.* New York: Academic Press, 1980. [15]

Dweck, C. S., and **Reppucci, N. D.** Learned helplessness and reinforcement responsibility in children. *Journal of Personality and Social Psychology,* 1973, *25,* 109–116. [1]

Dywan, J., and **Bowers, K.** The use of hypnosis to enhance recall. *Science,* 1983, *222,* 184–185. [12]

Ebbinghaus, H. *Memory: A contribution to experimental psychology* (1885). H. A. Roger and C. E. Bussenius (Trans.). New York: Teachers College, 1913. [6]

Eccles, J. C., Ito, M., and **Szentágotnai, J.** *The cerebellum as a neuronal machine.* New York: Springer, 1967. [3]

Eccles, J. E. Attributional processes as mediators of sex differences in achievement. *Journal of Educational Equity and Leadership,* 1983, *3,* 19–27. [11]

Eccles, J. E., Adler, T., and **Meece, J. L.** Sex differences in achievement: A test of alternative theories. *Journal of Personality and Social Psychology,* 1984, *46,* 26–43. [11]

Eccles, J. E., and **Goff, S. B.** Achievement and motivation: Dual modalities. *Journal of Educational Psychology,* 1978, *13,* 93–96. [11]

Edelson, E. Scanning the body magnetic. *Science 83,* July–August 1983, pp. 60–65. [3]

Edelwich, J., and **Brodsky, A.** *Burnout: Stages of disillusionment in the helping professions.* New York: Human Sciences Press, 1980. [18]

Educational Testing Service. *Test scores and family income.* Princeton, N.J.: Educational Testing Service, 1980. [14]

Ehrhardt, A. A., and **Baker, S. W.** *Hormonal aberrations and their implications for the understanding of normal sex differentiation.* Paper presented at the meeting of the Society for Research in Child Development, Philadelphia, 1973. [3]

Eibl-Eibesfeldt, I. *Ethology: The biology of behavior.* E. Klinghammer (Trans.). New York: Holt, Rinehart and Winston, 1970. [9]

Eimas, P. D., Siqueland, E. R., Jusczyk, P. and **Vigorito, J.** Speech perception in infants, *Science,* 1971, *171,* 303–306. [8]

Eisdorfer, C., Axelrod, S., and **Wilkie, F.** Stimulus exposure time as a factor in serial learning in an aged sample. *Journal of Abnormal and Social Psychology,* 1963, *67,* 594–600. [8]

Ekman, P. Universal and cultural differences in facial expression of emotion. In J. R. Cole (Ed.), *Nebraska symposium on motivation, 1971.* Lincoln: University of Nebraska Press, 1972. [10]

Ekman, P., and **Friesen, W. V.** The repertoire of nonverbal behavior categories, origins, usage, and coding. *Semiotica,* 1969, *1,* 49–98, [9]

Ekman, P., and **Friesen, W. V.** Constants across culture in the face and emotion. *Journal of Personality and Social Psychology,* 1971, *17,* 124–129. [9]

Ekman, P., and **Friesen, W. V.** Detecting deception from body or face. *Journal of Personality and Social Psychology,* 1974, *29,* 288. [9]

Ekman, P., and **Friesen, W. V.** *Unmasking the face: A guide to recognizing emotions from facial expressions.* Englewood Cliffs, N.J.: Prentice-Hall/Spectrum, 1975. [10]

Ekman, P., Friesen, W. V., and **Ellsworth, P.** *Emotion in the human face: Guidelines for research and an integration of findings.* Elmsford, N.Y.: Pergamon Press, 1972. [9]

Elkonin, D. B. U.S.S.R. In J. Downing (Ed.), *Comparative reading.* New York: Macmillan, 1973. [9]

Elliott, J. Blame it all on brown fat now. *Journal of the American Medical Association,* 1980, *243,* 1983–1985. [11]

Ellis, A. *Reason and emotion in psychotherapy.* Secaucus, N.J.: Lyle Stuart, 1962. [16]

Ellis, R. A., and **Taylor, M. S.** Role of self-esteem within the job search process. *Journal of Applied Psychology,* 1983, *68,* 632–640. [13]

Engel, M. The stability of the self-concept in adolescence. *Journal of Abnormal and Social Psychology,* 1959, *58,* 211–215. [13]

Engen, T., Lipsitt, L. P. and **Kaye, H.** Olfactory responses and adaptation in the human neonate. *Journal of Comparative and Physiological Psychology,* 1963, *56,* 73–77. [8]

Ennis, B. J., and **Emery, R. D.** *The rights of mental patients.* New York: Avon, 1978. [16]

Epstein, A. N. Water intake without the act of drinking. *Science,* 1960, *131,* 497–498. [11]

Epstein, A. N. The lateral hypothalamic syndrome: Its implications for the physiological psychology of hunger and thirst. In E. Stellar and J. M. Sprague (Eds.), *Progress in physiological psychology* (Vol. 4). New York: Academic Press, 1971. [3]

Epstein, A. N., and **Teitelbaum, P.** Regulation of food intake in the absence of taste, smell and other oropharyngeal sensations. *Journal of Comparative and Physiological Psychology,* 1962, *55,* 753–759. [11]

Epstein, S. The ecological study of emotions in humans. In K. Blankstein (Ed.), *Advances in the study of communication and affect.* New York: Plenum, 1979. [13]

Epstein, S. The stability of behavior: II. Implications for psychological research. *American Psychologist,* 1980, *35,* 790–806. [13]

Epstein, Y. M. Crowding, stress, and human behavior. *Journal of Social Issues,* 1981, *37,* 126–144. [18]

Erber, J.T., Herman, J., and **Botwinick, J.** The effects of encoding instructions on recall and recognition memory. *Experimental Aging Research,* 1980, *6,* 341–348. [8]

Ericsson, K. A., Chase, W. G., and **Faloon, S.** Acquisition of a memory skill. *Science,* 1980, *208,* 1181–1182. [6]

Ericsson, K. A., and **Simon, H. A.** Verbal reports as data. *Psychological Review,* 1980, *87,* 215–251. [7]

Erikson, E. H. *Childhood and society.* New York: Norton, 1950. [8]

Eron, L. D., Huesman, L. R., Lefkowitz, M. M., and **Walder, L. O.** Does television violence cause aggression? *American Psychologist,* 1972, *27,* 253–263. [18]

Ervin, S. Imitation and structural change in children's language. In E. H. Lenneberg (Ed.), *New directions in the study of language.* Cambridge, Mass.: MIT Press, 1964. [9]

Evans, F. J. Contextual forgetting: Posthypnotic source amensia. *Journal of Abnormal Psychology,* 1979, *88,* 556–563. [12]

Evans, G. *Behavioral and physiological consequences of crowding in humans.* Unpublished doctoral dissertation, University of Massachusetts, Amherst, 1975. [18]

Evans, J. St. B. T. On statistical intuitions and inferential rules: A discussion of Kahneman and Tversky. *Cognition,* 1982, *12,* 319–323. [7]

Evans, J. St. B. T., and **Dusoir, A. E.** Proportionality and sample size as factors in intuitive statistical judgement. *Acta Psychologica,* 1977, *41,* 129–137. [7]

Evans, R. Behavioral medicine: A new applied challenge to social psychologists. In L. Bickman (Ed.), *Applied social psychology annual* (Vol. 1). Beverly Hills, Calif.: Sage Publications, 1980. [17]

Eysenck, H. J. The effects of psychotherapy: An evaluation. *Journal of Consulting Psychology,* 1952, *16,* 319–324. [16]

Eysenck, H. J. *The biological basis of personality.* Springfield, Ill.: Charles C. Thomas, 1967. [11]

Eysenck, H. J. *The structure of human personality.* London: Methuen, 1970. [13]

Fagan, J. F. Infants' delayed recognition memory and forgetting. *Journal of Experimental Child Psychology,* 1976, *21,* 425–455. [8]

Fagot, B. I. The influence of sex of child on parental reactions to toddler children, *Child Development,* 1978, *49,* 459–465. [8]

Fairweather, G. W., Sanders, D. H., Maynard, H., and **Cressler, D. L.** *Community life for the mentally ill: An alternative to institutional care.* Chicago: Aldine, 1969. [16]

Farina, A., Gliha, D., Boudreau, L. A., Allen, J. G., and **Sherman, M.** Mental illness and the impact of believing others know about it. *Journal of Abnormal Psychology,* 1971, *77,* 1–5. [18]

Fawcett, J. *Before it's too late: What to do when someone you know attempts suicide.* American Association of Suicidology, prepared in cooperation with Merck, Sharp & Dohne Health Information Services, West Point, Pa. [15]

Fazio, R. H., and **Cooper, J.** Arousal in the dissonance process. In J. T. Cacioppo and R. E. Petty (Eds.), *Social psychophysiology.* New York: Guilford, 1983. [17]

Fazio, R. H., Zanna, M. P., and **Cooper J.** Dissonance and self-perception: An integrative view of each theory's proper domain of application. *Journal of Experimental Social Psychology,* 1977, *13,* 464–479. [17]

Fechner, G. T. *Elemente der psychophysik.* Leipzig: Breitkopf und Härtel, 1860. [7]

Feinberg, I., and **Fein, G.** Computer-detected patterns of electroencephalographic delta activity during and after extended sleep. *Science,* 26 February 1982, *215,* 1131–1133. [12]

Feinstein, S. C. The cult phenomenon: Transition, repression, and regression. *Adolescent Psychiatry,* 1980, *8,* 113–122. [18]

Fennema, E., and **Sherman, J.** Sex-related differences in mathematics achievement, spatial visualization and affective factors. *American Educational Research Journal,* 1977, *14,* 51–71. [11]

Fennema, E., and **Sherman, J.** Sex-related differences in mathematics achievement and related factors: A further study. *Journal for Research in Mathematics Education,* 1978, *9,* 189–203. [11]

Fenz, W. D., and **Epstein, S.** Gradients of physiological arousal in parachutists as a function of an approaching jump. *Psychosomatic Medicine,* 1967, *29,* 33–51. [2]

Feshbach, S., and **Weiner, B.** *Personality.* Lexington, Mass.: D. C. Heath, 1982. [14]

Festinger, L. *A theory of cognitive dissonance.* Stanford, Calif.: Stanford University Press, 1957. [17]

Festinger, L., and **Carlsmith, J. M.** Cognitive consequences of forced compliance. *Journal of Abnormal and Social Psychology,* 1959, *58,* 203–210. [17]

Festinger, L., Schachter, S., and **Back, K.** *Social pressures in informal groups: A study of human factors in housing.* New York: Harper & Row, 1950. [17]

Field, T. M., Woodson, R., Greenberg, R., and Cohen, D. Discrimination and imitation of facial expressions by neonates. *Science*, 1982, *218*, 179–181. [8]

Fields, H. L. Secrets of the placebo. *Psychology Today*, November 1978, *12*, 172. [3]

Fischer, R. A cartography of ecstatic and meditative states. *Science*, 1971, *174*, 898. [12]

Fischhoff, B. Debiasing. In D. Kahneman, P. Slovic, and A. Tversky (Eds.), *Judgment under uncertainty: Heuristics and biases*. New York: Cambridge University Press, 1981. [7]

Fishbein, M., and Ajzen, I. Attitudes toward objects as predictors of single and multiple behavioral criteria. *Psychological Review*, 1974, *81*, 58–74. [17]

Fishbein, M., and Ajzen, I. *Belief, attitude, intention, and behavior: An introduction to theory and research*. Reading, Mass.: Addison-Wesley, 1975. [17]

Fishbein, M., and Ajzen, I. Acceptance, yielding, and impact: Cognitive processes in persuasion. In R. Petty, T. Ostrom, and T. Brock (Eds.), *Cognitive responses in persuasion*. Hillsdale, N.J.: Lawrence Erlbaum, 1981. [17]

Fisher, A. E. Maternal and sexual behavior induced by intracranial chemical stimulation. *Science*, 1956, *124*, 228–229. [3, 11]

Fisher, A. E. Effects of stimulus variation on sexual satiation in the male rat. *Journal of Comparative Physiological Psychology*, 1962, *55*, 614–620. [11]

Fisher, A. E. Chemical stimulation of the brain. In *Psychobiology: The biological bases of behavior*. San Francisco: W. H. Freeman, 1967. [11]

Fisher, J. D., DePaulo, B. M., and Nadler, A. Extending altruism beyond the altruistic act: The mixed effects of aid on the help recipient. In J. P. Rushton and R. M. Sorrentino (Eds.), *Altruism and helping behavior: Social, personality, and developmental perspectives*. Hillsdale, N.J.: Lawrence Erlbaum, 1981. [18]

Fisher, S., and Greenburg, R. P. *The scientific credibility of Freud's theories and therapy*. New York: Basic Books, 1977. [13, 15]

Fiske, S. T., and Taylor, S. E. *Social cognition*, Reading, Mass.: Addison-Wesley, 1984. [17]

Fixsen, D. L., Phillips, E. A., and Wolf, M. M. The teaching-family model of group home treatment. In W. E. Craighead, A. E. Kazdin, and M. J. Mahoney (Eds.), *Behavior modification: Principles, issues, and applications*. Boston: Houghton Mifflin, 1976. [16]

Flavell, J. H., Shipstead, S. G., and Croft, K. Young children's knowledge about visual perception: Hiding objects from others. *Child Development*, 1978, *49*, 1208–1211. [8]

Flavell, J. H., and Wellman, H. M. Metamemory. In R. V. Kail, Jr., and J. W. Hagen (Eds.), *Perspectives on the development of mem-ory and cognition*. Hillsdale, N.J.: Lawrence Erlbaum, 1977. Pp. 3–33. [8]

Flesch, R. *Why Johnny can't read*. New York: Harper, 1955. [9]

Flynn, J. P., Vanegas, H., Foote, W., and Edwards, S. Neural mechanisms involved in a cat's attack on a rat. In R. E. Whalen (Ed.), *Neural control of behavior*. New York: Academic Press, 1970. Pp. 135–173. [10]

Fodor, J. A., and Bever, T. G. The psychological reality of linguistic segments. *Journal of Verbal Learning and Verbal Behavior*, 1965, *4*, 414–420. [9]

Folkins, C. H., Lynch, S., and Gardner, M. M. Psychological fitness as a function of physical fitness. *Archives of Physical Medicine and Rehabilitation*, 1972, *53*, 503–508. [10]

Folkins, C. H., and Sime, W. E. Physical fitness training and mental health. *American Psychologist*, 1981, *36*, 373–389. [10]

Food and Drug Administration. Anorectics have limited use in treatment of obesity. *FDA Drug Bulletin*, December 1972. [11]

Forbes, G., and Reina, J. C. Adult lean body mass declines with age: Some longitudinal observations. *Metabolism*, 1970, *19*, 653–663. [11]

Foulkes, D. Theories of dream formation and recent studies of sleep consciousness. *Psychological Bulletin*, 1964, *62*, 236–247. [12]

Fowler, H., and Whalen, R. Variation in incentive stimulus and sexual behavior in the male rate. *Journal of Comparative and Physiological Psychology*, 1961, *54*, 68–71. [11]

Fowler, O. S., and Fowler, L. N. *Phrenology: A practical guide to your head*. New York: Chelsea House, 1969. [3]

Fox, L. H. Identification of the academically gifted. *American Psychologist*, 1981, *36*, 1103–1111. [14]

Fraser, A., and Wilcox, K. J. Perception of illusory movement. *Nature*, 1979, *281*, 565–566. [4]

Freedman, J. L. Long-term behavioral effects of cognitive dissonance. *Journal of Experimental Social Psychology*, 1965, *1*, 145–155. [17]

Freedman, J. L., and Fraser, S. C. Compliance without pressure: The foot-in-the-door technique. *Journal of Personal and Social Psychology*, 1966, *4*, 195–202. [2]

Freedman, J. L., and Staff, I. Crowding, aggressiveness, and external or internal crowding as an intensifier of internal vs. external pleasantness. In J. L. Freedman (Ed.), *Crowding and behavior*. New York: W. H. Freeman, 1975. [18]

French-Belgian Collaborative Group. Ischemic heart disease and psychological patterns: Prevalence and incidence in Belgium and France. *Advances in Cardiology*, 1982, *29*, 25–31. [10]

Freud, A. *The ego and mechanisms of defense*. New York: International Universities Press, 1946. [13]

Freud, S. Mourning and melancholia (1917). In *Collected papers* (Vol. 4). London: Hogarth Press, 1924. [15]

Freud, S. *Civilization and its discontents*. James Strachey (Ed. and Trans.). London: Hogarth Press, 1930. [13, 18]

Freud, S. *A general introduction to psychoanalysis*. New York: Washington Square Press, 1935. [13]

Freud, S. *The ego and the id* (1923). London: Hogarth Press, 1947. [13]

Freud, S. Beyond the pleasure principle (1920). In James Strachey (Ed. and Trans.), *The standard edition of the complete psychological works of Sigmund Freud* (Vol. 18). London: Hogarth Press, 1953. [13]

Freud, S. *The interpretation of dreams* (1900). James Strachey (Ed. and Trans.). New York: Basic Books, 1955. [12, 13]

Freud, S. Some physical consequences of the anatomical distinction between the sexes (1925). In *The standard edition of the works of Sigmund Freud* (Vol. 19). London: Hogarth Press, 1961. [13]

Friedman, M., and Rosenman, R. H. Association of a specific overt behavior pattern with blood and cardiovascular findings. *Journal of the American Medical Association*, 1959, *169*, 1286. [10]

Friedman, M., and Rosenman, R. H. *Type A behavior and your heart*. New York: Knopf, 1974. [10]

Fries, J. F., and Crapo, L. M. *Vitality and aging: Implications of the rectangular curve*. San Francisco: W. H. Freeman, 1981. [8]

Frisch, H. L. Stereotypes in adult–infant play. *Child Development*, 1977, *48*, 1671–1675. [8]

Fromkin, V., Krashen, S., Curtiss, S., Rigler, D., and Rigler, M. The development of language in Genie. *Brain and Language*, 1974, *1*, 81–107. [9]

Gainotti, G. Emotional behavior and hemispheric side of the lesion. *Cortex*, 1972, *8*, 41–55. [10]

Gallup, G. Opinion polling in a democracy. In J. M. Tanur et al. (Eds.), *Statistics: A guide to the unknown*. San Francisco: Holden-Day, 1978. Pp. 187–194. [2]

Garcia, J., Ervin, F. R., and Koelling, R. A. Learning with prolonged delay of reinforcement. *Psychonomic Science*, 1966, *5*, 121–122. [5]

Garcia, J., Hankins, W. G., and Rusiniak, K. W. Behavioral regulation of the milieu interne in man and rat. *Science*, 1974, *185*, 824–831. [6]

Garcia, J., Kimeldorf, D. J., and Hunt, E. L. The use of ionizing radiation as a motivating stimulus. *Psychological Review*, 1961, *68*, 383. [5]

Garcia, J., Kimeldorf, D. J., Hunt, E. L., and Davies, B. P. Food and water consumption of rats during exposure to gamma radiation. *Radiation Research*, 1956, *4*, 33–41. [5]

Garcia, J., and **Koelling, R. A.** Relation of cue to consequence in avoidance learning. *Psychonometric Science*, 1966, *4*, 123–124. [1, 5]

Garcia, J., and **Rusiniak, K. W.** What the nose learns from the mouth. In D. Muller-Schwarze and R. M. Silverstein (Eds.), *Chemical signals.* New York: Plenum, 1980. [10]

Garcia, L. T., Erskine, K., and **Hawn, K.** The effect of affirmative action on attributions about minority group members. *Journal of Personality*, 1981, *49*, 427–437. [17]

Gardner, B. T., and **Gardner, R. A.** Two-way communication with an infant chimpanzee. In A. M. Schrier and F. Stollnitz (Eds.), *Behavior of nonhuman primates* (Vol. 4). New York: Academic press, 1972. [9]

Gardner, E. *Fundamentals of neurology.* Philadelphia: W. B. Saunders, 1975. [3]

Gardner, H. *Art, mind, and brain.* New York: Basic Books, 1982. [3, 7]

Gardner, L. I. Deprivation dwarfism. *Scientific American*, 1972, *227*, 76–82. [8]

Gardner, R. A., and **Gardner, B. T.** Teaching sign language to a chimpanzee. *Science*, 1969, *165*, 664–672. [9]

Garrow, J. S. *Energy balance and obesity in man.* Amsterdam: Elsevier/North Holland Biomedical Press, 1978. [11]

Gatchel, R. J., and **Price, K. P.** (Eds.). *Clinical applications of biofeedback: Appraisal and status.* Elmsford, N.Y.: Pergamon Press, 1979. [12]

Gazzaniga, M., and **Ledoux, J.** *The integrated mind.* New York: Plenum, 1978. [3]

Gearheart, B. R. *Special education for the '80s.* St. Louis: C. V. Mosby, 1980. [14]

Geen, R. G. Evaluation apprehension and social facilitation: A reply to Sanders. *Journal of Experimental Social Psychology*, 1981, *17*, 252–256. [18]

Geen, R. G., and **Gange, J. J.,** Drive theory of social facilitation: Twelve years of theory and research. *Psychological Bulletin*, 1977, *84*, 1267–1288. [18]

Geldard, F. A. *The human senses* (2nd ed.). New York: Wiley, 1972. [4]

Gelenberg, A. J. The rational use of psychotropic drugs: Prescribing antidepressants. *Drug Therapy*, 1979, *9*, 95–112. [16]

Gelman, R. Logical capacity of very young children: Number invariance rules. *Child Development*, 1972, *43*, 75–90. [8]

Gerbner, G., and **Gross, L.** Living with television: The violence profile. *Journal of Communications*, Spring 1976, *26*, 172–199. [5, 7]

Geschwind, N. Specialization of the human brain. *Scientific American*, 1979, *241*, 180–199. [3]

Ghiselin, B. (Ed.). *The creative process.* Berkeley: University of California Press, 1952. [7]

Gholson, B., Levine, M., and **Phillips, S.** Hypotheses, strategies, and stereotypes in discrimination learning. *Journal of Experimental Child Psychology*, 1972, *13*, 423–446. [7]

Giantonio, G. W., Lund, N. L., and **Gerall, A. A.** Effects of diencephalic and rhinencephalic lesions on the male rat's sexual behaviour. *Journal of Comparative Physiological Psychology*, 1970, *73*, 38–46. [11]

Gibson, E. J., and **Walk, R. D.** The "visual cliff." *Scientific American*, 1960, *202*, 64–71. [8]

Gibson, J. J. *The Perception of the visual world.* Boston: Houghton Mifflin, 1950. [4]

Gibson, J. J. *The senses considered as perceptual systems.* Boston: Houghton Mifflin, 1966. [4]

Gibson, J. J. *The ecological approach to visual perception.* Boston: Houghton Mifflin, 1979. [4]

Gil, D. G. *Violence against children.* Cambridge, Mass.: Harvard University Press, 1970. [13]

Gillie, O. Did Sir Cyril Burt fake his research on heritability of intelligence?—Part I. *Phi Delta Kappan*, February 1977, 469–471. [14]

Gilligan, C. In a different voice: Women's conceptions of self and of morality. *Harvard Educational Review*, 1977, *47*, 481–517. [8]

Gilligan, C. *In a different voice: Psychological theory and women's development.* Cambridge, Mass.: Harvard University Press, 1982. [8]

Gist, R., and **Stolz, S. B.** Mental health promotion and the media: Community response to the Kansas City hotel disaster. *American Psychologist*, 1982, *37*, 1136–1139. [16]

Glass, A. L., Holyoak, K. J., and **Santa, J. L.** *Cognition.* Reading, Mass.: Addison-Wesley, 1979. [7]

Glass, D. C. *Behavior patterns, stress, and coronary disease.* Hillsdale, N.J.: Lawrence Erlbaum, 1977. [10]

Glass, D. C., and **Singer, J. E.** *Urban stress: Experiments on noise and social stressors.* New York: Academic Press, 1972. [18]

Glassman, J. B., Burkhart, B. R., Grant, R. D., and **Vallery, G. G.** Density, expectation, and extended task performance: An experiment in the natural environment. *Environment and Behavior*, 1978, *10*, 299–316. [18]

Glenn, N. D., and **Weaver, C. N.** The contribution of marital happiness to global happiness. *Journal of Marriage and the Family*, 1981, *43*, 161–168. [10]

Glick, I. O., Weiss, R. S., and **Parkes, C. M.** *The first year of bereavement.* New York: Wiley, 1974. [10]

Globus, A., Rosenzweig, M. R., Bennett, E. L., and **Diamond, M. C.** Effects of differential experience on dendritic spine counts in rat cerebral cortex. *Journal of Comparative Physiological Psychology*, 1973, *82*, 175–181. [6]

Glover, J. A., and **Bruning, R. H.** *Educational psychology: Principles and applications.* Boston: Little, Brown, 1982. [9]

Glucksburg, S., and **Danks, J. H.** Effects of discriminative labels and of nonsense labels upon availability of novel function. *Journal of Verbal Learning and Verbal Behavior*, 1968, *7*, 12–16. [7]

Goldberger, L. Sensory deprivation and overload. In L. Goldberger and S. Breznitz (Eds.), *Handbook of stress: Theoretical and clinical aspects.* New York: Free Press, 1982. [11]

Goldstein, M. J., Baker, B. L., and **Jamison, K. R.** *Abnormal psychology: Experiences, origins and interventions.* Boston: Little, Brown, 1980. [15]

Goldstein, M. J., Kant, H. S., and **Hartman, J. J.** *Pornography and sexual deviance.* Berkeley, Calif.: University of California Press, 1973. [11]

Goleman, D. *The varieties of the meditative experience.* New York: Dutton, 1977. [12]

Goleman, D. 1,528 little geniuses and how they grew. *Psychology Today*, February 1980, pp. 28–53. [14]

Goodale, M. A. Vision as a sensorimotor system. In T. E. Robinson (Ed.), *A behavioral approach to brain research.* New York: Oxford University Press, 1982. [10]

Goodenough, F. L. Expression of the emotions in a blind-deaf child. *Journal of Abnormal and Social Psychology*, 1932, *27*, 328–333. [9]

Goodglass, H., and **Geschwind, N.** Language disorders (aphasia). In E. C. Carterette and M. Friedman (Eds.), *Handbook of perception* (Vol. 8). New York: Academic Press, 1976. [9]

Goodman, K. S. Acquiring literacy is natural: Who killed Cock Robin? *Theory into Practice*, 1977, *16*, 309–314. [9]

Goodstein, L., and **Sandler, I.** Using psychology to promote human welfare: A conceptual analysis of the role of community psychology. *American Psychologist*, 1978, *33*, 882–891. [16]

Goranson, R. E. Media violence and aggressive behavior. In L. Berkowitz (Ed.), *Advances in experimental and social psychology* (Vol. 5). New York: Academic Press, 1970. [18]

Gorden, H. W., and **Bogen, G. E.** Hemispheric lateralization of singing after intracarotid sodium amylobarbitone. *Journal of Neurology, Neurosurgery, and Psychiatry*, 1974, *37*, 727–738. [9]

Gotlib, I. H., and **Robinson, L. A.** Responses to depressed individuals: Discrepancies between self-report and observer-related behavior. *Journal of Abnormal Psychology*, 1982, *91*, 231–240. [15]

Gottesman, I., and **Shields, J.** A critical review of recent adoption, twin and family studies of schizophrenia: Behavioral genetics perspectives. *Schizophrenia Bulletin,* 1976, *2* (3), 360–398. [15]

Gould, R. L. The phases of adult life: A study in developmental psychology. *American Journal of Psychiatry,* 1972, *129,* 521–531. [8]

Gould, R. L. *Transformations.* New York: Simon & Schuster, 1978. [8]

Graf, R., and **Torrey, J. W.** Perception of phrase structure in written language. *American Psychological Association Convention Proceedings,* 1966, 83–84. [9]

Graham, S. The sociological approach to epidemiology. *American Journal of Public Health,* 1974, *64,* 1046–1049. [10]

Gray, S. H. Exposure to pornography and aggression toward women: The case of the angry male. *Social Problems,* 1982, *29,* 387–398. [11]

Green, D. M., and **Swets, J. A.** *Signal detection theory and psychophysics.* New York: Wiley, 1966. [4]

Greenberg, P. F. The thrillseekers. *Human Behavior,* 1977, *6,* 17–21. [11]

Greene, E., Flynn, M. S., and **Loftus, E. F.,** Inducing resistance to misleading information. *Journal of Verbal Learning and Verbal Behavior,* 1982, *21,* 207–219. [6]

Greenman, G. W. Visual behavior of newborn infants. In A. J. Solnit and S. A. Provence (Eds.), *Modern perspectives in child development.* New York: International Universities Press, 1963. [8]

Gregory, R. L. *The intelligent eye.* New York: McGraw-Hill, 1970. [4]

Greist, J. H., Klein, M. H., Eischens, R. R., Faris, J., Gurman, A. S., and **Morgan, W. P.** Running as treatment for depression. *Comprehensive Psychiatry,* 1979, *20,* 41–53. [10]

Grinker, J. Behavioral and metabolic consequences of weight reduction. *Journal of the American Dietetic Association,* 1973, *62,* 30–34. [11]

Grinspoon, L., and **Bakalar, J. G.** *Cocaine: A drug and its social evolution.* New York: Basic Books, 1976. [12]

Grossman, H. J. (Ed.). *Manual on terminology and classification in mental retardation* (3rd ed.). Washington, D.C.: American Association on Mental Deficiency, 1977. [14]

Grossman, S. P. Eating or drinking elicited by direct adrenergic, or cholinergic stimulation of hypothalamus. *Science,* 1960, *132,* 301–302. [3]

Grossman, S. P. Role of the hypothalamus in the regulation of food and water intake. *Psychological Review,* 1975, *82,* 200–224. [11]

Gruber, H. *Darwin on man.* (2nd ed.) Chicago: University of Chicago Press, 1981. [7]

Gudjonsson, G. H. Electrodermal responsivity to interrogation questions and its relation to self-reported emotional disturbance. *Biological Psychology,* 1982, *14,* 213–218. [10]

Guilford, J. P. *The nature of human intelligence.* New York: McGraw-Hill, 1967. [7]

Guilford, J. P., and **Hoepfner, R.** *The analysis of intelligence.* New York: McGraw-Hill, 1971. [14]

Gurin, G., Veroff, J., and **Feld, S.** *Americans view their mental health: A nationwide interview survey.* New York: Basic Books, 1960. [10, 16]

Gurman, A. S. and **Kniskern, D. P.** Research on marital and ˙ family therapy: Progress, perspective, and prospect. In S. L. Garfield and A. E. Bergin (Eds.), *Handbook of psychotherapy and behavior change: An empirical analysis* (2d ed.). New York: Wiley, 1978. [16]

Gustavson, C. R., Garcia, J., Hawkins, W. G., and **Rusiniak, K. W.** Coyote predation control by aversive conditioning. *Science,* 1974, *184,* 581–583. [5]

Guthrie, J. T., Martuza, V., and **Seifert, M.** Impacts of instructional time in reading. In L. B. Resnick and P. A. Weaver (Eds.), *Theory and practice of early reading.* Hillsdale, N.J.: Lawrence Erlbaum, 1979. [9]

Haber, R. N. Eidetic images. *Scientific American,* 1969, *220,* 36–44. [6]

Haber, R. N. Twenty years of haunting eidetic imagery: Where's the ghost? *The Behavioral and Brain Sciences,* 1979, *2,* 583–629. [6]

Haber, R. N., and **Standing, L. G.** Direct measures of short-term visual storage. *Quarterly Journal of Experimental Psychology,* 1969, *21,* 43–45. [6]

Hacker A. Farewell to the family? *The New York Review,* March 18, 1982, pp. 37–44. [8]

Haith, M. M., Bergman, T., and **Moore, M. J.** "Eye contact and face scanning in early infancy," unpublished manuscript, University of Denver, 1977. [8]

Haley, J. *Uncommon therapy.* New York: Norton, 1973. [15, 16]

Haley, J. *Leaving home: The therapy of disturbed young people.* New York: McGraw-Hill, 1980. [15, 16]

Hall, C. S., and **Van de Castle, R. L.** *The content analysis of dreams.* New York: Appleton-Century-Crofts, 1966. [12]

Hall, E. T., interviewed by **Kenneth Friedman.** Learning the Arab's silent language. *Psychology Today,* 1979, *13,* 45–54. [3]

Hall, J. A., Rosenthal, R., Archer, D., Di Matteo, M. R., and **Rogers, P. L.** Decoding wordless messages. *Human Nature,* May 1978, pp. 68–75. [9]

Hamachek, D. *Encounters with the self.* New York: Holt, Rinehart and Winston, 1971. [13]

Hamburg, D. A., and **Adams, J. E.** A perspective on coping behavior: Seeking and utilizing information in major transitions. *Archives of General Psychiatry,* 1967, *17,* 277–284. [13]

Hamill, W. T., and **Fontana, A. F.** The

immediate effects of chlorpromazine in newly admitted schizophrenic patients. *American Journal of Psychiatry,* 1975, *132,* 1023–1026. [16]

Hammond, E. C., and **Horn, D.** The relationship between human smoking habits and death rates. *Journal of the American Medical Association,* 1954, *155,* 1316–1328. [2]

Haney, W. Validity, vaudeville, and values: A short history of social concerns over standardized testing. *American Psychologist,* 1981, *36,* 1021–1034. [14]

Haracz, J. H. The dopamine hypothesis: An overview of studies with schizophrenic patients. *Schizophrenia Bulletin,* 1982, *8,* 438–469. [15]

Harding, H. C. Hypnosis in the treatment of migraine. In J. Lassner (Ed.), *Hypnosis and psychosomatic medicine.* New York: Springer-Verlag, 1967. [12]

Hare, A. P. *Handbook of small group research.* New York: Free Press, 1976. [18]

Hargadon, F. Tests and college admissions. *American Psychologist,* 1981, *36,* 1112–1119. [14]

Hariton, E. B., and **Singer, J. L.** Women's fantasies during sexual intercourse: Normative and theoretical implications. *Journal of Consulting and Clinical Psychology,* 1974, *42,* 313–322. [11]

Harkness, S. The cultural context of child development. In C. M. Super and S. Harkness (Eds.), *New directions for child development.* No. 8. *Anthropological perspectives on child development.* San Francisco: Jossey-Bass, 1980. Pp. 7–13. [8]

Harlow, H. F. Mice, monkeys, men, and motives. *Psychological Review,* 1953, *60,* 23–32. [11]

Harlow, H. F. The nature of love. *American Psychologist,* 1958, *13,* 673–685. [8]

Harlow, H. F., and **Harlow, M. K.** Learning to love. *American Scientist,* 1966, *54,* 244–272. [8, 11]

Harlow, H. F., and **Harlow, M. K.** Effects of various mother–infant relationships on rhesus monkey behaviors. In B. M. Foss (Ed.), *Determinants of infant behavior* (Vol. 4). London: Methuen, 1969. Pp. 15–36. [8]

Harlow, H. F., Harlow, M. K., and **Meyer, D. R.** Learning motivated by a manipulation drive. *Journal of Experimental Psychology,* 1950, *40,* 228–234. [11]

Harris, B. Whatever happened to Little Albert? *American Psychologist,* 1979, *34,* 151–160. [5]

Harris, D. B., Gough, H. G., and **Martin, W. E.** Children's ethnic attitudes related to methods of child rearing. *Child Development,* 1950, *21,* 169–181. [17]

Harris, J. E. Memory aids people use: Two interview studies. *Memory & Cognition,* 1980, *8,* 31–38. [6]

Harris, R. J. Comprehension of pragmatic implications in advertising. *Journal of Applied Psychology,* 1977, *62,* 603–608. [9]

Harris, S. E. Schizophrenics' mutual glance patterns. *Dissertation Abstracts*, 1968, *29B*, 2202. [15]

Hartman, E. *The biology of dreaming.* Springfield, Ill.: Charles C. Thomas, 1967. [12]

Hartmann, E., Baekeland, F., and Zwilling, G. Psychological differences between long and short sleepers. *Archives of General Psychiatry*, 1975, *32*, 765–777. [12]

Hartshorne, H., and May, M. A. *Studies in the nature of character, Vol. 1: Studies in deceit.* New York: Macmillan, 1928. [13]

Hass, R. G. Effects of source characteristics on cognitive responses in persuasion. In R. E. Petty, T. M. Ostrom, and T. C. Brock (Eds.), *Cognitive responses in persuasion.* Hillsdale, N.J.: Lawrence Erlbaum, 1981. [17]

Hassett, J. Sex and smell. *Psychology Today*, March 1978, pp. 40–45. [11]

Hatfield, E. Gender differences in love and sexual behavior. In E. R. Allgeier and N. B. McCormick (Eds.), *Gender roles and sexual behavior: Changing boundaries.* Palo Alto, Calif.: Mayfield, 1982. [17]

Hawkins, H. L., Rodriguez, G., and Reicher, G. M. Is timesharing a general ability? (NR150-407 ONR Technical Report No. 3). Eugene: University of Oregon, 1979. [14]

Hayes, J. R. *Cognitive psychology: Thinking and creating.* Homewood, Ill.: Dorsey Press, 1978. [7]

Hayes, K. J., and Hayes, C. The intellectual development of a home-raised chimpanzee. *Proceedings of the American Philosophical Society*, 1951, *95*, 105–109. [9]

Haynes, S. G., Feinlieb, M., and Kannel, W. B. The relationship of psychosocial factors to coronary heart disese in the Framingham study: III. Eight-year incidence of coronary heart disease. *American Journal of Epidemiology*, 1980, *111*, 37–58. [10]

Hebb, D. Drives and the CNS. *Psychological Review*, 1955, *62*, 243–253. [11]

Hécaen, H. Clinical symptomatology in right and left hemispheric lesions. In V. B. Mountcastle (Ed.), *Interhemispheric relations and cerebral dominance.* Baltimore: Johns Hopkins University Press, 1962. [10]

Heckhausen, H. Achievement motivation and its constructs: A cognitive model. *Motivation and Emotion*, 1977, *1*, 283–329. [11]

Heider, F. Social perception and phenomenal causality. *Psychological Review*, 1944, *51*, 358–374. [17]

Heider, F. *The psychology of interpersonal relations.* New York: Wiley, 1958. [17]

Held, R., and Hein, A. Movement-produced stimulation in the development of visually guided behavior. *Journal of Comparative and Physiological Psychology*, 1963, *56*, 872–876. [4]

Helmrath, T. A., and Steinitz, E. M. Death of an infant: Parental grieving and the failure of social support. *Journal of Family Practice*, 1978, *6*, 785–790. [10]

Helson, H. *Adaptation-level theory.* New York: Harper & Row, 1964. [10]

Hendrick, C., and Costantini, A. F. Effects of varying trait inconsistency and response requirements on the primacy effect in impression formation. *Journal of Personality and Social Psychology*, 1970, *15*, 158–164. [17]

Herman, C. P. *Possible costs of successful weight control.* Paper presented at the ninth annual meeting of the Association for the Advancement of Behavior Therapy, 1975. [11]

Herman, C. P., and Mack, D. Restrained and unrestrained eating. *Journal of Personality*, 1975, *43*, 647–660. [11]

Herman, C. P., and Polivy, J. Restrained eating. In A. J. Stunkard (Ed.), *Obesity.* Philadelphia: W. B. Saunders, 1980. [11]

Heron, W. The pathology of boredom. *Scientific American*, 1957, *196*, 52–56. [11]

Hess, E. H. Attitude and pupil size. *Scientific American*, 1965, *212*, 46–54. [3, 17]

Hess, E. H., and Polt, J. M. Pupil size as related to interest value of visual stimuli. *Science*, 1960, *132*, 349–350. [17]

Hess, E. H., and Polt, J. M. Pupil size in relation to mental activity during simple problem solving. *Science*, 1964, *143*, 1190–1192. [17]

Hetherington, A. W., and Ranson, S. W. Hypothalamic lesions and adiposity in the rat. *The Anatomical Record*, 1940, *78*, 149–172. [3, 11]

Hibscher, J. A., and Herman, C. P. Obesity, dieting, and the expression of "obese" characteristics. *Journal of Comparative and Physiological Psychology*, 1977, *91*, 374–380. [11]

Higbee, K. L. Fifteen years of fear arousal: Research on threat appeals: 1953–1968. *Psychological Bulletin*, 1969, *72*, 426–444. [17]

Higgins, R. L. and Marlatt, G. A. Effects of anxiety arousal on the consumption of alcohol by alcoholics and social drinkers. *Journal of Consulting and Clinical Psychology*, 1973, *41*, 426–433. [15]

Higgins, R. L., and Marlatt, G. A. Fear of interpersonal evaluation as a determinant of alcohol consumption in male social drinkers. *Journal of Abnormal Psychology*, 1975, *84*, 644–651. [15]

Hilgard, E. R. *Hypnotic susceptibility.* New York: Harcourt Brace Jovanovich, 1965. [12]

Hilgard, E. R. A neodissociation interpretation of pain reduction in hypnosis. *Psychological Review*, 1973, *80*, 396–411. [12]

Hilgard, E. R. Hypnosis. *Annual Review of Psychology*, 1975, *26*, 19–44. [12]

Hilgard, E. R. Hypnosis and consciousness. *Human Nature*, 1978, *1*, 42–49. [12]

Hilgard, E. R., and Hilgard, J. R. *Hypnosis in the relief of pain.* Los Altos, Calif.: William Kaufmann, 1975. [12]

Hilgard, J. R. *Personality and hypnosis: A study of imaginative involvement.* Chicago: University of Chicago Press, 1970. [12]

Hilgard, J. R. Imaginative involvment: Some characteristics of the highly hypnotizable and the nonhypnotizable. *International Journal of Clinical and Experimental Hypnosis*, 1974, *22*, 128–156. [12]

Hill, C. T., Rubin, Z., and Peplau, L. A. Breakups before marriage: The end of 103 affairs. *Journal of Social Issues*, 1976, *32*, 147–168. [17]

Hinkle, L. E., Jr. The effect of exposure to culture change, social change, and changes in interpersonal relationships on health. In B. S. Dohrenwend and B. P. Dohrenwend (Eds.), *Stressful life events: Their nature and effects.* New York: Wiley, 1974. [10]

Hirst, W., Neisser, U., and Spelke, E. Divided attention. *Human Nature*, June 1978, 54–61. [6]

Hobson, J. A. and McCarley, R. W. The brain as a dream state generator: An activation-synthesis hypothesis of the dream process. *American Journal of Psychiatry*, 1977, *134*, 1335–1348. [12]

Hochberg, J. E. *Perception.* Englewood Cliffs, N.J.: Prentice-Hall, 1964. [4]

Hodgson, R., and Rachman, S. The modification of compulsive behavior. In H. J. Eysenck (Ed.), *Case studies in behaviour therapy.* Boston: Routledge and Kegan Paul, 1976. [15]

Hoebel, B. G., and Teitelbaum, P. Hypothalamic control of feeding and self-stimulation. *Science*, 1962, *135*, 375–377. [11]

Hoffer, E. *The true believer: Thoughts on the nature of mass movements.* New York: Harper & Row, 1951. [18]

Hoffman, L. Empirical findings concerning sexism in our schools. *Corrective and Social Psychiatry and Journal of Behavior Techniques, Methods, and Therapy*, 1982, *28*, 100–108. [17]

Hoffman, M. L. Conscience, personality, and socialization techniques. *Human Development*, 1970, *13*, 90–126. [13]

Hoffman, M. L. Empathy, role-taking, guilt, and development of altruistic motives. In T. Lickona (Ed.), *Moral development and behavior: Theory, research and social issues.* New York: Holt, Rinehart and Winston, 1976. [8]

Hoffman, M. L. Personality and social development. *Annual Review of Psychology*, 1977, *28*, 295–321. [8]

Hoffman, M. L., and Saltzstein, H. D. Parent discipline and the child's moral development. *Journal of Personality and Social Psychology*, 1967, *5*, 45–57. [8]

Hoffman, P. J., Slovic, P., and Rorer, L. G. An analysis-of-variance model for the assessment of configural cue utilization in clinical judgment. *Psychological Bulletin*, 1968, *69*, 338–349. [7]

Hogan, R. Theoretical egocentrism and the

problem of compliance. *American Psychologist*, 1975, *30*, 533–540. [8]

Hogarth, R. Beyond discrete biases: Functional and dysfunctional aspects of judgmental heuristics. *Psychology Bulletin*, 1981, *90*, 197. [7]

Hohmann, G. W. Some effects of spinal cord lesions on experienced emotional feelings. *Psychophysiology*, 1966, *3*, 143–156. [10]

Holden, C. Identical twins reared apart. *Science*, 1980, *207*, 1323–1328. [13]

Hollander, E. P. Independence, conformity, and civil liberties: Some implications from social psychological research. *Journal of Social Issues*, 1975, *31*, 55–67. [18]

Hollingshead, A. B., and **Redlich, F. C.** *Social class and mental illness: A community study.* New York: Wiley, 1958. [15]

Holmes, D. S. Meditation and somatic arousal reduction: A review of the experimental evidence. *American Psychologist*, 1984, *39*, 1–10. [12]

Holmes, T. H., and **Rahe, R. H.** The social readjustment rating scale. *Journal of Psychosomatic Research*, 1967, *11*, 213–218. [10]

Holroyd, K. A. Effects of social anxiety and social evaluation on beer consumption and social interaction. *Journal of Studies on Alcohol*, 1978, *39*, 737–744.

Holroyd, K. A., and **Lazarus, R. S.** Stress, coping, and somatic adaptation. In Leo Goldberger and Shlomo Breznitz (Eds.), *Handbook of stress: Theoretical and clinical aspects.* New York: Free Press, 1982. Pp. 21–35. [10]

Holstein, C. B. Irreversible, stepwise sequence in the development of moral judgment: A longitudinal study of males and females. *Child Development*, 1976, *47*, 31–61. [8]

Horner, M. S. *Sex differences in achievement motivation and performance in competitive and non-competitive situations.* Unpublished doctoral dissertation, University of Michigan, 1968. [11]

Horner, M. S. Femininity and successful achievement: A basic inconsistency. In J. M. Bardwicks et al., *Feminine personality and conflict.* Monterey, Calif.: Brooks/Cole, 1970. [11]

Horney, K. *Our inner conflicts.* New York: Norton, 1945. [13]

Horney, K. *Feminine psychology.* New York: Norton, 1967. [13]

House, J., and **Kasper, G.** Politeness markers in English and German. In F. Coulmas (Ed.), *Conversational routine: Explorations in standardized communication situations and prepatterned speech.* The Hague: Mouton, 1981. Pp. 157–185. [9]

House, J. S., and **Wolf, S.** Effects of urban residence on interpersonal trust and helping behavior. *Journal of Personality and Social Psychology*, 1978, *36*, 1029–1043. [18]

Howard, D. *Cognitive psychology: Memory,*

language and thought. New York: Macmillan, 1983. [9]

Howes, C., and **Rubenstein, J. L.** Determinants of toddler experience in day care: Social-affective style of age of entry and quality of setting. Unpublished manuscript, University of California at Los Angeles, 1981. [8]

Howley, E. T. The effect of different intensities of exercise on the excretion of epinephrine and norepinephrine. *Medicine and Science in Sports*, 1976, *8*, 219–222. [10]

Hubel, D. H. The brain. *Scientific American*, 1979, *241*, 45–53. [3]

Hubel, D. H., and **Wiesel, T. N.** Receptive fields of single neurons in the cat's striate cortex. *Journal of Physiology*, 1959, *148*, 574–591. [4]

Hubel, D. H., and **Wiesel, T. N.** Receptive fields and functional and architecture in two non-striate visual areas (18 and 19) of the cat. *Journal of Neurophysiology*, 1965a, *28*, 229–289. [4]

Hubel, D. H., and **Wiesel, T. N.** Binocular interaction in striate cortex of kittens reared with artificial squint. *Journal of Neurophysiology*, 1965b, *28*, 1041–1059. [4]

Hubel, D. H., and **Wiesel, T. N.** Receptive fields and functional architecture of monkey striate cortex. *Journal of Physiology*, 1968, *195*, 215–243. [4]

Hubel, D. H., and **Wiesel, T. N.** Brain mechanisms of vision. *Scientific American*, 1979, *241*, 150–162. [4]

Hull, C. L. *Principles of behavior.* New York: Appleton, 1943. [11]

Humphreys, M., Revelle, W. R., Simon, L., and **Gilliland, K.** The interactive effect of personality, time of day and caffeine: A test of the arousal model. *Journal of Experimental Psychology: General*, 1980, *109*, 1–31. [11]

Hunt, M. *The universe within.* New York: Simon & Schuster, 1982. [9]

Hunter, E. *Brainwashing in Red China: The calculated destruction of men's minds.* New York: Vanguard, 1951. [18]

Hurley, A. D. Unsystematic desensitization using pleasurable images to inhibit anxiety. *Journal of Behavior Therapy and Experimental Psychiatry*, 1976, *7*, 295. [15]

Hurvich, L. M., and **Jameson, D.** An opponent-process theory of color vision. *Psychological Review*, 1957, *64*, 384–404. [4]

Huston, T. L., Ruggiero, M., Conner, R., and **Geis, G.** Bystander intervention into crime: A study based on naturally occurring episodes. *Social Psychology Quarterly*, 1981, *44*, 14–23. [18]

Hutt, C., and **Vaizey, M. J.** Differential effects of group density on social behavior. *Nature*, 1966, *209*, 1371–1372. [18]

Huttenlorher, J., and **Presson, C. C.** The coding and transformation of spatial information. *Cognitive Psychology*, 1979, *11*, 375–394. [8]

Huxley, A. *Brave new world.* New York: Harper & Row, 1932. [13]

Hydén, H., and **Egyhazi, E.** Nuclear RNA changes of nerve cells during a learning experiment in rats. *Proceedings of the United States Academy of Natural Science*, 1962, *48*, 1366–1373. [6]

Hynes, K. Innovative career opportunities and job placement mechanisms in psychology. In P. J. Woods (Ed.), *Career opportunities for psychologists: Expanding and emerging areas.* Washington, D.C.: American Psychological Association, 1976. [1]

Iggo, A. Cutaneous sensory mechanisms. In H. B. Barlow and J. D. Mollon (Eds.), *The senses.* Cambridge: Cambridge University Press, 1982. [4]

Inhelder, B., and **Piaget, J.** *The growth of logical thinking from childhood to adolescence.* New York: Basic Books, 1958. [8]

Insko, C. A., and **Schopler, J.** Triadic consistency: A statement of affective-cognitive-conative consistency. *Psychological Review*, 1967, *74*, 361–376. [17]

Institute of Medicine. *Research on stress and human health.* Washington, D.C.: National Academic Press, 1981. [10]

Institute of Medicine. *Health and behavior: A research agenda.* Washington, D.C.: National Academic Press, 1982. [10]

Isaacson, R. L. Relation between achievement, test anxiety, and curricular choices. *Journal of Abnormal and Social Psychology*, 1964, *68*, 447–452. [11]

Isen, A. M. Success, failure, attention and reactions to others: The warm glow of success. *Journal of Personality and Social Psychology*, 1970, *15*, 294–301. [18]

Isen, A. M., and **Levin, P. F.** Effect of feeling good on helping: Cookies and kindness. *Journal of Personality and Social Psychology*, 1972, *21*, 384–388. [18]

Isen, A. M., Shalker, T. E., Clark, M., and **Karp, L.** Affect, accessibility of material in memory, and behavior: A cognitive loop? *Journal of Personality and Social Psychology*, 1978, *36*, 1–12. [18]

Ismail, A. H., and **Trachtman, L. E.** Jogging the imagination. *Psychology Today*, March 6, 1973, pp. 78–82. [10]

Iversen, L. L. The chemistry of the brain. *Scientific American*, 1979, *241*, 134–149. [3]

Izard, C. E. Emotions as motivations: An evolutionary-developmental perspective. *Nebraska Symposium on Motivation*, 1978, *26*, 163–200. [1]

Izard, C. E. *Human emotions.* New York: Plenum, 1977. [10]

James, W. *The principles of psychology* (Vol. 2). New York: Holt, 1890. [10, 12]

James, W. Does "consciousness" exist? *Journal of Philosophy, Psychology, and Scientific Methods*, 1904, *1*, 477–491. [12]

Janis, I. L. *Victims of groupthink: A psychological study of foreign policy decisions and fiascoes.* Boston: Houghton Mifflin, 1972. [1, 18]

Janis, I. L. Counteracting the adverse effects of concurrence-seeking in policy-planning groups: Theory and research perspectives. In H. Brandstatter and J. Davis (Eds.), *Group decision making* (European Monographs in Social Psychology, No. 25), 1982. [18]

Janis, I. L. *Groupthink: Psychological studies of policy decisions and fiascoes* (2d ed.), Boston: Houghton Mifflin, 1983. [18]

Janis, I. L., and **Feshbach, S.** Effects of fear-arousing communication. *Journal of Abnormal and Social Psychology,* 1953, *48,* 78–92. [17]

Janis, I. L., and **Mann, L.** *Decision making: A psychological analysis of conflict, choice, and commitment.* New York: Free Press, 1979. [7, 18]

Janis, I. L., and **Wheeler, D.** Thinking clearly about career choices. *Psychology Today,* May 1978, pp. 67ff. [7]

Janowitz, H. D. Role of gastrointestinal tract in the regulation of food intake. In C. F. Code (Ed.). *Handbook of physiology: Alimentary canal 1.* Washington, D.C.: American Physiological Society, 1967. Pp. 219–224. [11]

Janowitz, H. D., and **Grossman, M. I.** Some factors affecting the food intake of normal dogs and dogs with esophagostomy and gastric fistula. *American Journal of Physiology,* 1949, *159,* 143–148. [11]

Janowitz, H. D., and **Grossman, M. I.** Effect of prefeeding, alcohol and bitters on food intake of dogs. *American Journal of Physiology,* 1951, *164,* 182–186. [11]

Jarvik, L. F. Thoughts on the psychobiology of aging. *American Psychologist,* 1975, 576–583. [12]

Jemmott, J. B., and **Locke, S. E.** Psychosocial factors, immunologic mediation, and human susceptibility to infectious diseases: How much do we know? *Psychological Bulletin,* 1984, *95,* 78–108. [10]

Jenkins, J. G., and **Dallenbach, K. M.** Oblivescence during sleep and waking. *American Journal of Psychology,* 1924, *35,* 605–612. [6]

Jenner, F. A., Gjessing, L. R., Cox, J. R., Davies-Jones, A., and **Hullin, R. P.** A manic-depressive psychotic with a 48-hour cycle. *British Journal of Psychiatry,* 1967, *113,* 859–910. [15]

Jensen, A. R. How much can we boost I.Q. and scholastic achievement? *Harvard Educational Review,* 1969, *39,* 1–123. [14, 18]

Jensen, A. R. The heritability of intelligence. *Saturday Evening Post,* 1972, *244,* pp. 9ff. [14]

Jensen, A. R. Did Sir Cyril Burt fake his research on heritability of intelligence?—Part II. *Phi Delta Kappan,* February 1977, 471. [14]

Jensen, A. R. Raising the IQ: The Ramey and Haskins study. *Intelligence,* 1981, *5,* 29–40. [14]

John, E. R. How the brain works—a new theory. *Psychology Today,* May 1976, pp. 50–52. [3]

Johnson, E. J., Greene, D., and **Carroll, J. S.** Reasons and overjustification: A test of the means-end hypothesis. Unpublished manuscript, Carnegie-Mellon University, 1978. [17]

Johnston, E., and **Donoghue, J. R.** Hypnosis and smoking: A review of the literature. *American Journal of Clinical Hypnosis,* 1971, *13,* 265–272. [12]

Johnstone, E. C., Crow, T. J., Frith, C. D., Stevens, M., Kreel, L., and **Husband, J.** The dementia of dementia praecox. *Acta Psychiatrica Scandinavica,* 1978, *57,* 305–324. [15]

Jonas, G. Biofeedback. In D. Goleman and R. Davidson (Eds.), *Consciousness: Brain, states of awareness, and mysticism.* New York: Harper & Row, 1979. [12]

Jones, E. E., and **Davis, K. E.** From acts to dispositions: The attribution process in person perception. In L. Berkowitz (Ed.), *Advances in experimental social psychology* (Vol. 2). New York: Academic Press, 1965. Pp. 219–266. [17]

Jones, E. E., Davis, K. E., and **Gergen, K. J.** Role playing variations and their informational value for person perception. *Journal of Abnormal and Social Psychology,* 1961, *63,* 302–310. [17]

Jones, E. E., and **Harris, V. A.** The attribution of attitudes. *Journal of Experimental Social Psychology,* 1967, *3,* 1–24. [17]

Jones, E. E., and **Nisbett, R. E.** *The actor and observer: Perceptions of the causes of behavior.* New York: General Learning Press, 1971. [17]

Jones, M. Community care for chronic mental patients: The need for a reassessment. *Hospital and Community Psychiatry,* 1975, *26,* 94–98. [16]

Jones, M. C. The elimination of children's fears. *Journal of Experimental Psychology,* 1924, 383–390. [5]

Jones, M. C., Albert, Peter, and **John B. Watson.** *American Psychologist,* August 1974, 581–583. [5]

Jones, R. and **Wilderson, F.** Mainstreaming and the minority child: An overview of issues and a perspective. In R. Jones (Ed.), *Mainstreaming and the minority child.* Reston, Va.: Council for Exceptional Children, 1976. [14]

Jones, R. A., and **Brehm, J. W.** Persuasiveness of one- and two-sided communications as a function of awareness there are two sides. *Journal of Experimental Social Psychology,* 1970, *6,* 47–56. [17]

Jonides, J., Kahn, R., and **Rozin, P.** Imagery instructions improve memory in blind subjects. *Bulletin of the Psychonomic Society,* 1975, *5,* 424–426. [6]

Jordan, H. A. Voluntary intragastric feeding: Oral and gastric contributions to food intake and hunger in man. *Journal of Comparative and Physiological Psychology,* 1969, *68,* 498–506. [11]

Jouvet, M. The stages of sleep. *Scientific American,* 1967, *216,* 62–72. [12]

Joyce, C. Lie detector. *Psychology Today,* February 1984, pp. 6–8. [10]

Judd, D. B., and **Wyszecki, G.** *Color in business, science, and industry.* New York: Wiley, 1963. [4]

Jung, C. G. *Collected works.* H. Read, M. Fordham, and G. Adler (Eds.). R. F. C. Hull (Trans.). Princeton, N. J.: Princeton University Press, 1953. [13]

Jus, A., Pineau, R., Lachance, R., Pelchat, G., Jus, K., Pires, P., and **Villeneuve, R.** Epidemiology of tardive dyskinesia. Part I. *Diseases of the Nervous System,* 1976, *37,* 210–214. [16]

Kagan, J., Kearsley, R. B., and **Zelazo, P. R.** *Infancy: Its place in human development.* Cambridge, Mass.: Harvard University Press, 1978. [8]

Kahneman, D., and **Tversky, A.** On the psychology of prediction. *Psychological Review,* 1973, *80,* 237–251. [7]

Kahneman, D. and **Tversky, A.** A reply to Evans. *Cognition,* 1982, *12,* 325–326. [7]

Kaiser, R. B. *R.F.K. must die: A history of the Robert Kennedy assassination and its aftermath.* New York: Dutton, 1970. [6]

Kalat, J. W., and **Rozin, P.** Role of interference in taste-aversion learning. *Journal of Comparative and Physiological Psychology,* 1971, *77,* 53–58. [5]

Kales, A., Hoedemaker, F., Jacobson, A., and **Lichtenstein, E.** Dream deprivation: An experimental reappraisal. *Nature,* 1964, *204,* 1337–1338. [12]

Kallmann, F. J. *Heredity in health and mental disorder.* New York: Norton, 1953. [15]

Kaltreider, N. B., Wallace, A., and **Horowitz, M. J.** A field study of the stress response syndrome: Young women after hysterectomy. *Journal of the American Medical Association,* 1979, *242,* 1499–1503. [10]

Kamin, L. *The science and politics of IQ.* New York: Wiley, 1974. [14]

Kamin, L. Heredity, intelligence, politics, and psychology: 1. In N. J. Block and G. Dworkin (Eds.), *The IQ controversy.* New York: Pantheon, 1976. [14]

Kaminoff, R. D., and **Proshansky, H. M.** Stress as a consequence of the urban physical environment. In L. Goldberger and S. Breznitz (Eds.), *Handbook of stress: Theoretical and clinical aspects.* New York: Free Press, 1982. [11]

Kandel, E. R. Small systems of neurons. *Scientific American,* 1979, *241,* 67–76. [6]

Kangas, J., and **Bradway, K.** Intelligence at middle age: A thirty-eight-year follow-up. *Developmental Psychology,* 1971, *5,* 333–337. [8]

Kanizsa, G. Subjective contours. *Scientific American*, 1976, *234*, 48–52. [4]

Kanner, A. D., Coyne, J. C., Schaefer, C., and Lazarus, R. S. Comparison of two modes of stress measurement: Daily hassles and uplifts versus major life events. *Journal of Behavioral Medicine*, in press. [10]

Kanter, R. M. Some effects of proportion on group life: Skewed sex ratios and responses to token women. *American Journal of Sociology*, 1977, *82*, 965–990. [17]

Kaplan, H. B., and Pokorny, A. D. Self-derogation and psycho-social adjustment. *Journal of Nervous and Mental Disease*, 1969, *149*, 421–434. [13]

Kaplan, R. E., Obert, S. L., and Van Buskirk, W. R. The etiology of encounter group casualties: Second facts. *Human Relations*, 1980, *33*, 131–148. [16]

Kaplan, R. M. Nader's raid on the testing industry: Is it in the best interest of the consumer? *American Psychologist*, 1982, *37*, 15–23. [14]

Karlin, R. A., Rosen, L. S., and Epstein, Y. M. Three into two doesn't go: A follow-up on the effects of overcrowded dormitory rooms. *Personality and Social Psychology Bulletin*, 1979, *5*, 391–395. [18]

Kasamatsu, A., and Hirai, T. An electroencephalographic study on the Zen meditation (Zazen). *Folia Psychiatrica et Neurologica Japonica*, 1966, *20*, 315–366. [12]

Kasl, S. V., and Mahl, G. F. Disturbance and hesitation in speech. *Journal of Personality and Social Psychology*, 1965, *1*, 425–433. [10]

Katz, H., Cadoret, R., Hughes, K., and Abbey, D. Physiological correlates of acceptable and unacceptable attitude statements. *Psychological Reports*, 1965, *17*, 78. [12]

Katz, M. L. *Female motive to avoid success: A psychological barrier or a response to deviancy?* Princeton, N.J.: Educational Testing Service, 1973. [11]

Kaye, K., and Marcus, J. Imitation over a series of trials without feedback: Age six months. *Infant Behavior and Development*, 1978, *1*, 141–155. [8]

Kazdin, A. E. *The token economy: A review and evaluation.* New York: Plenum, 1977. [16]

Kazdin, A. E., and Wilson, G. T. *Evaluation of behavior therapy: Issues, evidence, and research strategies.* Cambridge, Mass.: Ballenger, 1978. [16]

Keller, M. B., Lavori, P. W., Lewis, C. E., and Klerman, G. L. Predictors of relapse in major depressive disorder. *Journal of the American Medical Association*, 1983, *250*, 3299–3304. [15]

Keller, M. B., and Shapiro, R. W. Major depressive disorder: Initial results from a one-year prospective naturalistic follow-up study. *The Journal of Nervous and Mental Disease*, 1981, *169*, 761–768. [15]

Kelley, H. H. Attribution theory in social psychology. In D. Levine (Ed.), *Nebraska Symposium of Motivation*, 1967 (Vol. 15). Lincoln: University of Nebraska Press, 1967. Pp. 192–238. [17]

Kelley, H. H. *Attribution in social interaction.* Morristown, N.J.: General Learning Press, 1971. [17]

Kelley, H. H. *Personal relationships.* Hillsdale, N.J.: Lawrence Erlbaum, 1979. [17]

Kelling, S. T., and Halpern, B. P. Taste flashes: Reaction times, intensity, and quality. *Science*, 1983, *219*, 412–414. [4]

Kellogg, V. Some silkworm moth reflexes. *Biology Bulletin*, Woods Hole, 1907, *12*, 152–154. [11]

Kelman, H. C. Compliance, identification, and internalization: Three processes of attitude change. *Journal of Conflict Resolution*, 1958, *2*, 51–60. [18]

Kelman, H. C. Processes of opinion change. *Public Opinion Quarterly*, 1961, *25*, 57–78. [18]

Kelman, H. C., and Hovland, C. I. "Reinstatement" of the communicator in delayed measurement of opinion change. *Journal of Abnormal and Social Psychology*, 1953, *48*, 327–335. [17]

Kemper, T. D. *A social interaction theory of emotions.* New York: Wiley, 1978. [10]

Kennell, J. H., Jerauld, R., Wolfe, H., Chesler, D., Kreger, N.C., McAlpine, W., Steffa, M., and Klaus, M. H., Maternal behavior one year after early and extended post-partum contact. *Developmental Medicine and Child Neurology*, 1974, *16*, 172–179. [2]

Kenrick, D. T., and Cialdini, R. B. Romantic attraction: Misattribution versus reinforcement explanations. *Journal of Personality and Social Psychology*, 1977, *35*, 381–391. [17]

Kenrick, D. T., Cialdini, R. B., and Linder, D. E. Misattribution under fear-producing circumstances: Four failures to replicate. *Personality and Social Psychology Bulletin*, 1979, *5*, 329–334. [17]

Kessler, R. C. Stress, social status, and psychological distress. *Journal of Health and Social Behavior*, 1979, *20*, 259–272. [15]

Kessler, R. C., Price, R. M., and Wortman, C. B. Psychopathology: Social approaches. *Annual Review of Psychology*, in press. [15]

Kety, S. S. Disorders of the human brain. *Scientific American*, 1979, *241*, 202–214. [3]

Kiesler, C. A., and Kiesler, S. B. *Conformity.* Reading, Mass.: Addison-Wesley, 1969. [18]

Kiesler, C. A., Zanna, M. P., and DeSalvo, J. Deviation and conformity: Opinion change as a function of commitment, attraction, and presence of a deviate. *Journal of Personality and Social Psychology*, 1966, *3*, 458–467. [18]

Kiesler, S. B., and Baral, R. L. The search for a romantic partner: The effects of self-esteem and physical attractiveness on romantic behavior. In K. J. Gergen and D. Marlowe (Eds.), *Personality and social behav-*ior. Reading, Mass.: Addison-Wesley, 1970. [13]

Kimble, G. A. *Hilgard and Marquis conditioning and learning* (2d ed.). New York: Appleton-Century-Crofts, 1961. [5]

Kimmel, A. J. Ethics and human subjects research: A delicate balance. *American Psychologist*, 1979, *34*, 633–635. [2]

King, S. H. Coping mechanisms in adolescents. *Psychiatric Annuals*, 1973, *1*, 10–46. [8]

Kinney, J., and Leaton, G. *Loosening the grip: A handbook of alcohol information* (2d ed.). St. Louis: Mosby, 1978. [15]

Kinsbourne, M. Hemispheric specialization and the growth of human understanding. *American Psychologist*, 1982, *37*, 411–420.[3]

Kinsey, A. C., Pomeroy, W. B., and Martin, C. E. *Sexual behavior in the human male.* Philadelphia: W. B. Saunders, 1948. [2, 11]

Kinsey, A. C., Pomeroy, W. B., Martin, C. E., and Gebhard, P. H. *Sexual behavior in the human female.* Philadelphia: W. B. Saunders, 1953. [2, 11]

Kintsch, W., and Glass, G. Effects of propositional structure upon sentence recall. In W. Kintsch (Ed.), *The representation of meaning in memory.* Hillsdale, N.J.: Lawrence Erlbaum, 1974. [9]

Kintsch, W., and Kennan, J. The psychological reality of text bases. In W. Kintsch (Ed.), *The representation of meaning in memory.* Hillsdale, N.J.: Lawrence Erlbaum, 1974. [9]

Klaus, M. H., Jerauld, R., Kreger, N. C., McAlpine, W., Steffa, M., and Kennell, J. H. Maternal attachment: Importance of the first post-partum days. *New England Journal of Medicine*, 1972, *286*, 460–463. [2]

Klaus, M. H., and Kennell, J. H. *Maternal–infant bonding.* St. Louis: C. V. Mosby, 1976. [2]

Klein, G. S. Peremptory ideation: Structure and force in motivated ideas. In R. Jessor and S. Feshback (Eds.), *Cognition, personality, and clinical psychology.* San Francisco: Jossey-Bass, 1967. [13]

Kleinginna, P. R., Jr., and Kleinginna, A. M. A categorized list of emotion definitions, with suggestions for a consensual definition. *Motivation and Emotion*, 1981, *5*, 355. [10]

Kleiter, G. D., Gachowetz, H., and Huber, D. *Bibliography: Decision making.* Salzburg: Psychology Institute, University of Salzburg, 1976. [7]

Kleitman, N. *Sleep and wakefulness* (rev. ed.). Chicago: University of Chicago Press, 1963. [12]

Klineberg, O. Emotional expression in Chinese literature. *Journal of Abnormal and Social Psychology*, 1938, *33*, 517–520. [9]

Kluegel, J. R., and Smith, E. R. Whites' beliefs about blacks' opportunity. *American Sociological Review*, 1982, *47*, 518–532. [17]

Klüver, H., and **Bucy, P. C.** Preliminary analysis of function of the temporal lobes in monkeys. *Archives of Neurology and Psychiatry,* 1939, *42,* 979–1000. [3]

Knittle, J. L., and **Hirsch, J.** Effect of early nutrition on the development of rat epididymal fat pads: Cellularity and metabolism. *Journal of Clinical Investigation,* 1968, *47,* 2091. [11]

Kobasa, S. C. Stressful life events, personality, and health: An inquiry into hardiness. *Journal of Personality and Social Psychology,* 1979, *37,* 1–11. [10]

Kobasa, S. C., Maddi, S. R., and **Kahn, S.** Hardiness and health: A prospective study. *Journal of Personality and Social Psychology,* 1982, *42,* 168–177. [10]

Kobasigawa, A. Utilization of retrieval cues by children in recall. *Child Development,* 1974; *45,* 127–134. [8]

Kohlberg, L. The development of children's orientation toward a moral order: 1. Sequence in the development of moral thought. *Vita Humana,* 1963, *6,* 11–33. [8]

Kohlberg, L. Stage and sequence: The cognitive-developmental approach to socialization. In D. A. Goslin (Ed.), *Handbook of socialization and research.* Chicago: Rand McNally, 1969. Pp. 347–480. [8]

Kohler, I. Experiment with goggles. *Scientific American,* 1962, *206,* 62–72. [4]

Köhler, W. *The mentality of apes.* New York: Harcourt, Brace, 1925. [7]

Kohn, M. L. Social class and schizophrenia: A critical review and a reformulation. *Schizophrenia Bulletin,* 1973, *7,* 60–79. [15]

Kohut, H. *The analysis of the self: A systematic approach to the psychoanalytic treatment of narcissistic personality disorders* (Monograph Series of the Psychoanalytic Study of the Child, No. 41). New York: International Universities Press, 1971. [13]

Kolata, G. Grafts correct brain damage. *Science,* 1982, *217,* 342–344. [3]

Kolb, B., and **Whishaw, T. Q.** *Fundamentals of human neuropsychology.* San Francisco: W. H. Freeman, 1980. [3]

Kolb, L. C., Bernard, V. W., and **Dohrenwend, B. S.** (Eds.), *Urban challenges to psychiatry: The case history of a response.* Boston: Little, Brown, 1969. [15]

Korchin, S. J. *Modern clinical psychology.* New York: Basic Books, 1976. [16]

Korchin, S. J., and **Schuldberg, D.** The future of clinical assessment. *American Psychologist,* 1981, *36,* 1147–1158. [14]

Korte, C., Ypma, I., and **Toppen, A.** Helpfulness in Dutch society as a function of urbanization and environmental input level. *Journal of Personality and Social Psychology,* 1975, *32,* 996–1003. [18]

Kovel, J. *A complete guide to therapy.* New York: Pantheon, 1976. [16]

Kozol, H., Boucher, R., and **Garofolo, R.** Diagnosis and treatment of dangerousness.

Crime and Delinquency, 1972, *18,* 371–392. [16]

Krashen, S. D. The critical period for language acquisition and its possible basis. In D. Aaronson and R. W. Rieber (Eds.), *Developmental Psycholinguistics and Communication Disorders.* Annals of the New York Academy of Sciences, Vol. 263, 1975, 211–244. [9]

Krasner, L. The future and the past in the behaviorism–humanism dialogue. *American Psychologist,* 1978, *33,* 799–804. [13]

Kübler-Ross, E. *On death and dying.* New York: Macmillan, 1969. [10]

Kuhn, D., Langer, J., Kohlberg, L., and **Haan, N. S.** The development of formal operations in logical and moral judgment. *Genetic Psychology Monographs,* 1977, *95L,* 97–188. [8]

Kuhn, M. H. Self-attitudes by age, sex and professional training. *Sociological Quarterly,* 1960, *9,* 39–55. [13]

Kulik, J. A., Bangert-Drowns, R. L., and **Kulik, C. C.** The effectiveness of coaching for aptitude tests. *Psychological Bulletin,* 1984, *95,* 179–188. [14]

Kulik, J. A., and **McKeachie, W. J.** The evaluation of teachers in higher education. In F. N. Kerlinger (Ed.), *Review of research in education.* Itasca, Ill.: Peacock, 1975. [1]

Kunst-Wilson, W., and **Zajonc, R.** Affective discrimination of stimuli that cannot be recognized. *Science,* 1980, *207,* 557–558. [4]

Kuo, Z. Y. The genesis of the cat's responses to the rat. *Journal of Comparative Psychology,* 1930, *11,* 1–35. [18]

Kurtines, W., and **Greif, E. B.** The development of moral thought: Review and evaluation of Kohlberg's approach. *Psychological Bulletin,* 1974, *81,* 453–470. [8]

La Berge, S. P. Lucid dreaming: Directing the action as it happens. *Psychology Today,* January 1981, pp. 48–57. [12]

La Breque, M. On making sounder judgments. *Psychology Today,* June 1980, pp. 33–42. [7]

Lacey, J. I. Somatic response patterning and stress: Some revisions of activation theory. In M. H. Appley and R. Trumbull (Eds.), *Psychological stress.* New York: Appleton-Century-Crofts, 1967. Pp. 14–42. [10]

Lacey, J. I., and **Lacey, B. C.** The law of initial value in the longitudinal study of autonomic constitution: Reproducibility of autonomic responses and response patterns over a four-year interval. *Annuals of the New York Academy of Science,* 1962, *98,* 1257–1326. [10]

Laing, D. G., Characterisation of human behaviour during odour perception. *Perception,* 1982, *11,* 221–230. [4]

Laing, R. D. *Self and others.* New York: Pantheon, 1961. [15]

Laing, R. D. Is schizophrenia a disease? *International Journal of Social Psychiatry,* 1964, *10,* 184–193. [15]

Laing, R. D., and **Esterson, A.** *Sanity, madness, and the family* (2d ed.). New York: Basic Books, 1971. [15]

Lamb, H. R., and **Zusman, J.** Primary prevention in perspective. *American Journal of Psychiatry,* 1979, *136,* 12–17. [16]

Lamb, M. E. Interactions between eight-month-old children and their fathers and mothers. In M. E. Lamb (Ed.), *The role of the father in child development.* New York: Wiley, 1976. [8]

Lamb, M. E. Father–infant and mother–infant interaction in the first year. *Child Development,* 1977, *48,* 167–181. [8]

Lamb, M. E. The development of father–infant relations. In M. E. Lamb (Ed.), *The father's role in child development* (rev. ed.). New York: Wiley, 1981. [8]

Lamb, M. E., and **Hwang, C. P.** Maternal attachment and mother-neonate bonding: A critical review. In M. E. Lamb and A. L. Brown (Eds.), *Advances in developmental psychology* (Vol. 2). Hillsdale, N.J.: Lawrence Erlbaum, 1982. Pp. 1–39. [2]

Lamberth, J. L., Rappaport, H., and **Rappaport, M.** *Personality: An introduction.* New York, Knopf, 1978. [14]

Landis, C. A. A statistical evaluation of psychotherapeutic methods. In L. E. Hinsie (Ed.), *Concepts and problems of psychotherapy,* New York: Columbia University Press, 1937. Pp. 155–165. [16]

Landon, P. B., and **Suedfeld, P.** Conplex cognitive performance and sensory deprivation: Completing the U-curve. *Perceptual and Motor Skills,* 1972, *34,* 601–602. [11]

Landsman, T. The humanizer. *American Journal of Orthopsychiatry,* 1974, *44,* 345–352. [13]

Landy, D., and **Sigall, H.** Beauty is talent: Task evaluation as a function of the performer's physical attractiveness. *Journal of Personality and Social Psychology,* 1974, *29,* 299–304. [17]

Lang, P. J., Rice, D. G., and **Sternbach, R. A.** The psychophysiology of emotion. In N. S. Greenfield and R. A. Sternbach (Eds.), *Handbook of psychophysiology.* New York: Holt, Rinehart and Winston, 1972. [10]

Lange, C. G., and **James, W.** *The emotions.* I. A. Haupt (Trans.). Baltimore: Williams & Wilkins, 1922. [10]

Langer, E. J. Old age: An artifact? In *Biology, behavior, and aging.* National Research Council Publication, 1980. [18]

Lansman, M., and **Hunt, E.** *Individual differences in secondary task performance* (NR154-398 ONR Technical Report No. 7). Seattle: University of Washington, 1980. [14]

Lanyon, R. I., and **Lanyon, B.** *Behavior therapy: A clinical introduction.* Reading, Mass.: Addison-Wesley, 1978. [5]

LaPiere, R. T. Attitudes vs. actions. *Social Forces,* 1934, *13,* 230–237. [1, 17]

Larson, R. Is satisfaction with life the same

in different subcultures? Unpublished manuscript, 1975. [10]

Lashley, K. S. *Brain mechanisms and intelligence.* Chicago: University of Chicago Press, 1929. [3]

Lassen, N. A., Ingvar, D. H., and Skinhoj, E. Brain function and blood flow. *Scientific American*, 1978, *239*, 62–71. [3]

Latane, B., and Darley, J. M. Group inhibition of bystander intervention in emergencies. *Journal of Personality and Social Psychology*, 1968, *10*, 215–221. [1, 18]

Latané, B., and Darley, J. M. *Help in a crisis: Bystander response to an emergency.* Morristown, N.J.: General Learning Press, 1976. [18]

Latané, B., Nida, S. A., and Wilson, D. W. The effects of group size on helping behavior. In J. P. Rushton and R. M. Sorrentino (Eds.), *Altruism and helping behavior: Social, personality, and developmental perspectives.* Hillsdale, N.J.: Lawrence Erlbaum, 1981. [18]

Laurence, J. R., and Perry, Campbell. Hypnotically created memory among highly hypnotizable subjects. *Science*, 1983, *222*, 523–524. [12]

Lawson, N. C. *Depression after spinal cord injury: A multimeasure longitudinal study.* Unpublished doctoral dissertation, University of Houston, 1976. [10]

Lazarus, R. S. The costs and benefits of denial. In S. Breznitz (Ed.), *The denial of stress.* New York: International Universities Press, 1983. [13]

Lazarus, R. S., Cohen, J. B., Folkman, S., Kanner, A., and Schaefer, C. Psychological stress and adaptation: Some unresolved issues. In H. Selye, (Ed.), *Guide to stress research.* New York: Van Nostrand Reinhold, 1980. [10]

Leavitt, F. *Drugs and behavior.* Philadelphia: W. B. Saunders, 1974. [12]

Lederberg, J. Racial alienation and intelligence. *Harvard Educational Review*, 1969, *39*, 611–615. [14]

Ledwidge, B. Run for your mind: Aerobic exercise as a means of alleviating anxiety and depression. *Canadian Journal of Behavioral Science*, 1980, *12*, 126–140. [10]

Lee, T., and Seeman, P. Dopamine receptors in normal and schizophrenic human brains. *Society for Neuroscience Abstracts* (Vol. 3). Bethesda, Md.: Society for Neuroscience, 1977, 443. [15]

Leff, J. P. Schizophrenia and sensitivity to the family environment. *Schizophrenia Bulletin*, 1976, *2 (4)*, 566–574. [15]

Lefrancois, G. R. *Of children: An introduction to child development.* Belmont, Calif.: Wadsworth, 1976. [8]

Lehman, D. R., Wortman, C. B., and Williams, A. F. Long-term effects of losing a spouse or child in a motor vehicle crash. Submitted for publication, 1984. [10]

Lehmann, E., Beeler, G. W., and Fender, D. H. EEG responses during the observation of stabilized and normal retinal images. *Electroencephalograph and Clinical Neurophysiology*, 1967, *22*, 136–142. [12]

LeMagnen, J. Advances in studies on the physiological control and regulation of food intake. In E. Stellar and J. M. Sprague (Eds.), *Progress in physiological psychology* (Vol. 4). New York: Academic Press, 1971. [11]

Lenneberg, E. *The biological foundations of language.* New York: Wiley, 1967. [9]

Lepper, M. R., and Greene, D. (Eds.). *The hidden cost of reward.* Hillsdale, N.J.: Lawrence Erlbaum, 1978. [17]

Lepper, M. R., Greene, D., and Nisbett, R. E. Undermining children's intrinsic interest with extrinsic reward: A test of the "overjustification" hypothesis. *Journal of Personality and Social Psychology*, 1973, *28*, 129–137. [17]

Lerner, M. J. The desire for justice and reaction to victims. In J. R. Macaulay and L. Berkowitz (Eds.), *Altruism and helping behavior.* New York: Academic Press, 1970. [18]

Lerner, M. J. Social psychology of justice and interpersonal attraction. In T. Huston (Ed.), *Foundations of interpersonal attraction.* New York: Academic Press, 1974. [18]

Lerner, M. J., and Matthews, G. Reactions to suffering of others under conditions of indirect responsibility. *Journal of Personality and Social Psychology*, 1967, *5*, 319–325. [18]

Lerner, M. J., Miller, D. T., and Holmes, J. Deserving and the emergence of forms of justice. In L. Berkowitz and E. Walster (Eds.), *Advances in experimental social psychology.* New York: Academic Press, 1976. [18]

Lerner, M. J., and Simmons, C. H. Observer's reaction to the "innocent victim": Compassion or rejection? *Journal of Personality and Social Psychology*, 1966, *4*, 203–210. [18]

Lettvin, J. Y. What the frog's eye tells the frog's brain. *Proceedings of the Institute of Radio Engineers*, 1959, *47*, 1940–1951. [3]

Leventhal, H., and Nerenz, D. R. A model for stress research with some implications for the control of stress disorders. In D. Meichenbaum and M. E. Jaremko (Eds.), *Stress reduction and prevention.* New York: Plenum, 1983. [17]

Leventhal, H., Singer, R., and Jones, S. The effects of fear and specificity of recommendation upon attitudes and behavior. *Journal of Personality and Social Psychology*, 1954, *2*, 20–29. [17]

Levine, S. V. The role of psychiatry in the phenomenon of cults. *Adolescent Psychiatry*, 1980, *8*, 123–137. [18]

Levine, V., and Salter, N. E. Youth and contemporary religious movements. *Canadian Psychiatric Association Journal*, 1976, *21*, 411–420. [18]

Levinson, D. J., with Darrow, C. N., Klein, E. B., Levinson, M. H., and McKee, B. *The seasons of a man's life.* New York: Knopf, 1978. [8]

Levinson, S. C. *Pragmatics.* New York: Cambridge University Press, 1983. [9]

Levitin, T. E., Quinn, R. P., and Staines, G. L. A woman is 58% of a man. *Psychology Today*, 1973, *6*, pp. 89–92. [17]

Levitsky, A., and Perls, F. S. The rules and games of gestalt therapy. In J. Fagan and I. L. Sheperd (Eds.), *Gestalt therapy now.* Palo Alto, Calif.: Science and Behavior Books, 1970. [16]

Levy, J. Psychobiological implications of bilateral asymmetry. In S. Dimond and G. Beaumont (Eds.), *Hemispheric function in the human brain.* New York: Halstead Press, 1974. [3]

Levy, J., and Trevarthen, C. Metacontrol of hemispheric function in human split-brain patients. *Journal of Experimental Psychology: Human Perception and Performance*, 1976, *2*, 299–312. [3]

Levy, J., Trevarthen, C., and Sperry, R. W. Perception of bilateral chimeric figures following hemispheric disconnection. *Brain*, 1972, *95*, 61–78. [3]

Lewin, K. *Field theory in social sciences.* New York: Harper, 1951. [11]

Lewinsohn, P. M. A behavioral approach to depression. In R. J. Friedman and M. M. Katz (Eds.), *The psychology of depression: Contemporary theory and research.* Washington, D. C.: V. H. Winston, 1974. [15]

Lewis, A. J. (Ed.). New vistas in special education. In *Focus 8*. Princeton, N. J.: Educational Testing Service, 1980. [14]

Lewis, M., and Brooks, J. Self-knowledge and emotional development. In M. Lewis and L. Rosenblum (Eds.), *The development of affect.* New York: Plenum, 1978. Pp. 205–226. [8]

Liberman, B. L. The role of mastery in psychotherapy: Maintenance of improvement and prescriptive change. In J. D. Frank, R. Hoehn-Saric, D. D. Imber, B. L. Liberman, and A. R. Stone (Eds.), *The effective ingredients of successful psychotherapy.* New York: Brunner-Mazel, 1978. [18]

Liberman, I. Y., Schenkweiler, D., Liberman, A. M., Fowler, C., and Fisher, F. W. Phonetic segmentation and recoding in the beginning reader. In A. S. Reber and D. Scarborough (Eds.), *Reading: Theory and Practice.* Hillsdale, N.J.: Lawrence Erlbaum, 1976. [9]

Liberman, R. P., Levine, J., Wheeler, E., Sanders, N., and Wallace, C. J. Marital therapy in groups: A comparative evaluation of behavioral and interactional formats. *Acta Psychiatrica Scandinavica*, 1976, Supplementum 266, 1–34. [16]

Lidz, T. *The origin and treatment of schizophrenic disorders.* New York: Basic Books, 1973. [15]

Lidz, T., Cornelison, A., Fleck, S., and Terry, D. The intrafamilial environment of schizophrenic patients: II. Martial schism and marital skew. *American Journal of Psychiatry*, 1957, *114*, 241–248. [15]

Liebelt, R. A., Bordelon, C. B., and **Liebelt, A. G.** The adipose tissue system and food intake. In E. Stellar and J. M. Sprague (Eds.), *Progress in physiological psychology*. New York: Academic Press, 1973. [11]

Lieberman, M. A., and **Borman, L.** *Self-help groups for coping with crisis.* San Francisco: Jossey-Bass, 1979. [16]

Lieberman, M. A., and **Coplan, A. S.** Distance from death as a variable in the study of aging. *Developmental Psychology*, 1970, 71–84. [8]

Lieberman, M. A., Yalom, I. D., and **Miks, M. B.** *Encounter groups: First facts.* New York: Basic Books, 1973. [16]

Liebert, R. M., Neale, J. M., and **Davidson, E. S.** *The early window: Effects of television on children and youth.* Elmsford, N. Y.: Pergamon Press, 1973. [18]

Liem, R., and **Liem, J. V.** Social class and mental illness reconsidered: The role of economic stress and social support. *Journal of Health and Social Behavior*, 1978, *19*, 139–156. [15]

Linder, D. E., Cooper, J., and **Jones, E. E.** Decision freedom as a determinant of the role of incentive magnitude in attitude change. *Journal of Personality and Social Psychology*, 1967, *6*, 245–254. [17]

Lindholm, E., and **Lowry, S.** Alpha production in humans under conditions of false feedback. *Bulletin of the Psychonomic Society*, 1978, *11*, 106–108. [12]

Lindner, R. *The fifty-minute hour.* New York: Holt, Rinehart and Winston, 1954. [16]

Lindsay, P. H., and **Norman, D. A.** *Human information processing: An introduction to psychology* (2d ed.). New York: Academic Press, 1977. [6]

Lindsley, D. B. Emotion. In S. S. Stevens (Ed.), *Handbook of experimental psychology*. New York: Wiley, 1951. [11]

Linn, R. L. Admissions testing on trial. *American Psychologist*, 1982, *37*, 279–291. [14]

Linsenmeier, J. A., and **Wortman, C. B.** Attitudes toward workers and toward their work: More evidence that sex makes a difference. *Journal of Applied Social Psychology*, 1979, *4*, 320–324. [17]

Linton, M. I remember it well. *Psychology Today*, July 1978, pp. 81–86. [6]

Linton, M. Transformations of memory in everyday life. In Ulric Neisser (Ed.), *Memory observed*. New York: W. H. Freeman, 1982. Pp. 77–91. [6]

Lips, Hilary. Hormones, cycles, and the adult experience. In H. M. Lips and N. L. Colwill (Eds.), *The psychology of sex differences*. Englewood Cliffs, N.J.: Prentice-Hall, 1978. [3]

Lloyd, C., Alexander, A. A., Rice, D. G., and **Greenfield, N. S.** Life events as predictors of academic performance. *Journal of Human Stress*, 1980, *6*, 15–25. [10]

Lloyd, G. G., and **Lishman, W. A.** Effect of depression on the speed of recall of pleasant and unpleasant experiences. *Psychological Medicine*, 1975, *5*, 173–180. [15]

Loftus, E. F. Leading questions and the eyewitness report. *Cognitive Psychology*, 1975, *7*, 560–572. [2, 5]

Loftus, E. F. Shifting human color memory. *Memory and Cognition*, 1977, *5*, 696–699. [6]

Loftus, E. F. *Eyewitness testimony.* Cambridge, Mass.: Harvard University Press, 1979a. [6]

Loftus, E. F. Reactions to blatantly contradictory information. *Memory and Cognition*, 1979b, *7*, 368–374. [6]

Loftus, E. F., and **Beach, L. R.** Human inference and judgment: Is the glass half empty or half full? *Stanford Law Review*, 1982, *34*, 901–918. [7]

Loftus, E. F., and **Burns, T. E.** Mental shock can produce retrograde amnesia. *Memory and Cognition*, 1982, *10*, 318–323. [6]

Loftus, E. F., and **Loftus, G. R.** On the permanence of stored information in the human brain. *American Psychologist*, 1980, *35*, 409–420. [6]

Loftus, E. F., Miller, D. G., and **Burns, H. J.** Semantic integration of verbal information into a visual memory. *Journal of Experimental Psychology*, 1978, *4*, 19–31. [6]

Loftus, G. R., and **Loftus, E. F.** *Human memory: The processing of information.* Hillsdale, N.J.: Lawrence Erlbuam, 1976. [6]

Loftus, G. R., and **Loftus, E. F.** *Mind at play: The psychology of video games.* New York: Basic Books, 1983. [5]

London, M., and **Bray, D. W.** Ethical issues in testing and evaluation for personnel decisions. *American Psychologist*, 1980, *35*, 890–901. [14]

Lorber, J. Good patients and problem patients: Conformity and deviance in a general hospital. *Journal of Health and Social Behavior*, 1975, *16*, 213–225. [18]

Lord, C. G., Ross, L., and **Lepper, M. R.** Biased assimilation and attitude polarization: The effects of prior theories on subsequently considered evidence. *Journal of Personality and Social Psychology*, 1979, *37*, 2098–2109. [18]

Lorenz, K. *Evolution and modification of behavior.* Chicago: University of Chicago Press, 1965. [9]

Lorenz, K. *The eight deadly sins of civilized man.* Marjorie Kerr-Wilson (Trans.). New York: Harcourt Brace Jovanovich, 1974. [18]

Lowry, R. *The evolution of psychological theory: A critical history of concepts and presuppositions* (2d ed.). Hawthorne, N.Y.: Aldine, 1982. [1]

Luborsky, L., Singer, B., and **Luborsky, L.** Comparative studies of psychotherapies. *Archives of General Psychiatry*, 1975, *32*, 995–1008. [16]

Luborsky, L., and **Spence, D. P.** Quantitative research on psychoanalytic therapy. In S. L. Garfield and A. E. Bergin (Eds.), *Handbook of psychotherapy and behavior change: An empirical analysis* (2d ed.). New York: Wiley, 1978. [16]

Luce, G. G. *Body time.* New York: Random House, 1971. [12]

Luchins, A. S. Classroom experiments on mental set. *American Journal of Psychology*, 1946, *59*, 295–298. [7]

Luchins, A. S. Primacy-recency in impression formation. In C. I. Hovland (Ed.), *The order of presentation in persuasion*. New Haven: Yale University Press, 1957. Pp. 33–61. [17]

Luck, P. W., and **Heiss, J.** Social determinants of self-esteem in adult males. *Sociology and Social Research*, 1972, *57*, 69–84. [13]

Luria, A. *The mind of a mnemonist.* Lynn Solotaroff (Trans.). New York: Basic Books, 1968. [6]

Lykken, D. T. Research with twins: The concept of emergenesis. *Psychophysiology*, 1982, *19*, 361–373. [13]

Lynch, J. J., Paskewitz, D. A., and **Orne, M. T.** Some factors in the feedback control of human alpha rhythm. *Psychosomatic Medicine*, 1974, *36*, 399–410. [12]

McArthur, L. A. The how and what of why: Some determinants and consequences of causal attribution. *Journal of Personality and Social Psychology*, 1972, *22*, 171–193. [17]

McArthur, L. A., and **Post, D.** Figural emphasis and person perception. *Journal of Experimental Social Psychology*, 1977, *13*, 520–535. [17]

McArthur, L. Z., and **Eisen, S. V.** Television and sex-role stereotyping. *Journal of Applied Social Psychology*, 1976, *6*, 329–351. [17]

McCaan, I. L., and **Holmes, D.** Influence of aerobic exercise on depression. *Journal of Personality and Social Psychology*, in press. [10]

McCardell, J., and **Murray, E. J.** Nonspecific factors in weekend encounter groups. *Journal of Consulting Clinical Psychology*, 1974, *42*, 337. [16]

McCarley, R. W. Where dreams come from: A new theory. *Psychology Today*, December 1978, pp. 54–65+. [12]

McCartney, K., Scarr, S., Phillips, D., Grajek, S., and **Schwarz, J. C.** Environmental differences among day care centers and their effect on children's development. In E. F. Zigler and E. W. Gordon (Eds.), *Day care: Scientific and social policy issues*. Boston: Auburn House, 1982. [8]

McClelland, D. C. Some social consequences of achievement motivation. In M. R. Jones (Ed.), *Nebraska symposium on* *motivation 1955.* Lincoln: University of Nebraska Press, 1955. [11]

McClelland, D. C. Testing for competence rather than for "intelligence." *American Psychologist*, 1973, 1–14. [14]

McClelland, D. C. Managing motivation to expand human freedom. *American Psychologist*, 1978, 201–210. [11]

McClelland, D. C., Atkinson, J. W., Clark, R. W., and **Lowell, E. L.** *The achievement motive.* New York: Appleton-Century-Crofts, 1953. [11]

McClelland, D. C., and **Winter, D. G.** *Motivating economic achievement.* New York: Free Press, 1969. [11]

McCloskey, M., and **Watkins, M. J.** The seeing-more-than-is-there phenomenon: Implications for the locus of iconic storage. *Journal of Experimental Psychology,* 1978, *4,* 553–565. [6]

Maccoby, E. E. *Social development: Psychological growth and the parent-child relationship.* New York: Harcourt Brace Jovanovich, 1980. [8]

Maccoby, E. E., and **Jacklin, C. N.** *The psychology of sex differences.* Stanford, Calif.: Stanford University Press, 1974. [3, 8, 17]

McCombie, S. L. Characteristics of rape victims seen in crisis interviewing. *Smith College Studies in Social Work,* 1975, *46,* 137–158. [10]

McConnell, J. V. *New evidence for "transfer of training" effect in planarians: Symposium on the biological bases of memory traces.* Paper read at the Eighth International Congress of Psychology, Moscow, 1966. [6]

McCord, J. A thirty-year follow-up of treatment effects. *American Psychologist,* 1978, *33,* 284–289. [18]

McCulloch, J. W., and **Prins, H. A.** *Signs of stress.* London: Collins, 1975. [15]

MacDonald, M. L., Lidsky, T. I., and **Kern, J. M.** Drug instigated effects. In A. P. Goldstein and F. H. Kanfer (Eds.), *Maximizing treatment gains: transfer enhancement in psychotherapy.* New York: Academic Press, 1979. Pp. 429–444. [16]

MacDonald, M. L., and **Tobias, L. L.** Withdrawal causes relapse? Our response. *Psychological Bulletin,* 1976, *83,* 448–451. [16]

McDougall, W. *Social psychology.* New York: Putnam's, 1908. [11]

Macfarlane, A. *The psychology of childbirth.* Cambridge, Mass.: Harvard University Press, 1977. [8]

Macfarlane, D. A. The role of kinesthesis in maze learning. *University of California Publications in Psychology,* 1930, *4,* 277–305. [5]

McFarlin, D. B., and **Blascovich, J.** Effects of self-esteem and performance feedback on future affective preferences and cognitive expectations. *Journal of Personality and Social Psychology,* 1981, *40,* 521–531. [13]

McGarrigle, J., and **Donaldson, M.** Conservation accidents. *Cognition,* 1974–1975, *3,* 341–350. [8]

McGaugh, J. L. Time-dependent processes in memory storage, *Science.* 1966, *153,* 1351–1358. [6]

McGuire, W. J. Some impending reorientations in social psychology: Some thoughts provoked by Kenneth Ring. *Journal of Experimental Social Psychology,* 1967a, *3,* 124–139. [18]

McGuire, W. J. *Theory-oriented research in natural settings: The best of both worlds for social psychology.* Symposium paper presented at Pennsylvania State University, May 1967b. [18]

McGuire, W. J. Theory of the structure of human thought. In R. Abelson, E. Aronson, W. J. McGuire, T. Newcomb, M. Rosenberg, and P. Tannenbaum (Eds.), *Theories of cognitive consistency: A sourcebook.* Chicago: Rand McNally, 1968. Pp. 140–162. [17]

McKay, D. G. Input testing in the detection of misspellings. *American Journal of Psychology,* 1972, *85,* 121–127. [9]

McKee, S. P., McCann, J. J., and **Benton, J. L.** Color vision from rod and long-wave cone interactions: Conditions in which rods contribute to multicolored images. *Vision Research,* 1977, *17,* 175–185. [4]

McKinney, F. Fifty years of psychology. *American Psychologist,* 1976, *31,* 834–842. [1]

MacKinnon, D. W. The nature and nurture of creative talent. *American Psychologist,* 1962, *17,* 484–495. [13, 14]

MacKinnon, D. W. Personality and the realization of creative potential. *American Psychologist,* 1965, *20,* 273–281. [13, 14]

MacLean, P. D. Contrasting function of limbic and neocortical systems of the brain and their relevance to psychophysiological aspects of medicine. *American Journal of Medicine,* 1958, *25,* 611–626. [3]

McNeill, D. Developmental psycholinguistics. In F. L. Smith and G. A. Miller (Eds.), *The genesis of language: A psycholinguistic approach.* Cambridge, Mass.: MIT Press, 1966. [9]

MacNichol, E. F., Jr. Three-pigment color vision. *Scientific American,* 1964, *211,* 48–56. [4]

McPeak, W. R. Family therapies. In A. P. Goldstein and F. H. Kanfer (Eds.), *Maximizing treatment gains: transfer enhancement in psychotherapy.* New York: Academic Press, 1979. Pp. 155–181. [16]

MacPhillamy, D. J., and **Lewinsohn, P. M.** Depression as a function of levels of desired and obtained pleasure. *Journal of Abnormal Psychology,* 1974, *83,* 651–657. [14]

Maddi, S. *Personality theories: A comparative analysis* (3rd ed.). Homewood, Ill.: Dorsey Press, 1976. [13]

Maddison, D., and **Walker, W. L.** Factors affecting the outcome of conjugal bereavement. *British Journal of Psychiatry,* 1967, *113,* 1057–1067. [10]

Madsen, K. B. *Theories of motivation: A comparative study of modern theories of motivation.* Copenhagen: Munksgaard, 1959. [11]

Maier, N. R. F. Reasoning in humans. *Journal of Comparative Psychology,* 1931, *12,* 181–194. [7]

Maletzky, B. M., and **Klotter, J.** Smoking and alcoholism. *American Journal of Psychiatry,* 1974, *131 (4),* 445–447. [15]

Malinowski, B. *The sexual life of savages in northwestern Melanesia.* New York: Eugenics Press, 1929. [8]

Malsbury, C. W. Facilitation of male rat copulatory behaviour by electrical stimulation of the medial preptic area. *Physiology and Behavior,* 1971, *7,* 797–805. [11]

Marañon, G. Contribution à l'etude de l'action emotive de l'adrenaline. *Revue Francaise d'Endocrinologie,* 1924, *2,* 301–325. [10]

Marcus, D. E., and **Overton, W. F.** The development of cognitive gender constancy and sex role preferences. *Child Development,* 1978, *49,* 434–444. [8]

Marcus, H. The drive for integration: Some comments. *Journal of Experimental Social Psychology,* 1981, *17,* 257–261. [18]

Marcus, N., and **Levin, G.** Clinical applications of biofeedback: Implications for psychiatry. *Hospital and Community Psychiatry,* 1977, *28 (1),* 21–25. [12]

Mark, L. S., Schenkweiler, D., Liberman I. Y., and **Fowler, C. A.** Phonetic recoding and reading difficulty in beginning readers. *Memory and Cognition,* 1977, *5,* 623–629. [9]

Mark, V. H., and **Ervin, F. R.** *Violence and the brain.* New York: Harper & Row, 1970. [10, 18]

Markman, E. Realizing that you don't understand: A preliminary investigation. *Child Development,* 1977, *48,* 986–992. [8]

Markus, H. Self-schemata and the processing of information about the self. *Journal of Personality and Social Psychology,* 1977, *35,* 63–78. [17]

Marlatt, G. A., Kosturn, C. F., and **Lang, A. R.** Provocation to anger and opportunity for retaliation as determinants of alcohol consumption in social drinkers. *Journal of Abnormal Psychology,* 1975, *84,* 652–659. [15]

Marlatt, G. A., and **Nathan, P. E.** (Eds.). *Behavioral approaches to alcoholism.* New Brunswick, N.J.: Rutgers Center for Alcohol Studies, 1978. [2]

Marlatt, G. A., and **Rohsenow, D. J.** The think-drink effect. *Psychology Today,* December 1981, pp. 60–70. [12]

Marlowe, D., Frager, R., and **Nuttall, R. L.** Commitment to action taking as a consequence of cognitive dissonance, *Journal of Personality and Social Psychology,* 1965, *2 (6),* 864–868. [2]

Marsella, A. J. Cross-cultural studies of depression: A review of the literature. Paper presented at the Symposium on Cross-Cultural Aspects of Depression, International Association of Cross-Cultural Psychology, Tilburg, Netherlands, 1976. [10]

Marsh, C. A framework for describing subjective states of consciousness. In N. E. Zinberg (Ed.), *Alternate states of consciousness.* New York: Free Press, 1977. Pp. 145–157. [12]

Marshall, G. D., and **Zimbardo, P. G.** Affective consequences of inadequately explained physiological arousal. *Journal of Personality and Social Psychology,* 1979, *37,* 970–988. [10]

Martindale, C. *Cognition and consciousness.* Homewood, Ill.: Dorsey Press, 1981. [12]

Maslach, C. Burned-out. *Human Behavior,* 1976, *5,* 16–22. [18]

Maslach, C. The client role in staff burnout. *Journal of Social Issues,* 1978, *34,* 111–124. [18]

Maslach, C. Negative emotional biasing of unexplained arousal. *Journal of Personality and Social Psychology,* 1979, *37,* 359–369. [10]

Maslow, A. H. *Motivation and personality.* New York: Harper & Row, 1954. [13]

Maslow, A. H. *The psychology of science: A reconnaissance.* New York: Harper & Row, 1966. [13]

Maslow, A. H. *Toward a psychology of being* (2d ed.). New York: Van Nostrand Reinhold, 1968. [13]

Maslow, A. H. *Motivation and personality* (2d ed.). New York: Harper & Row, 1970. [13]

Maslow, A. H. *The farther reaches of the human mind.* New York: Viking, 1971a. [13]

Maslow, A. H. Some basic propositions of a growth and self-actualization psychology. In S. Maddi (Ed.), *Perspectives on personality.* Boston: Little, Brown, 1971b. [13]

Mason, J. W. A re-evaluation of the concept of "non-specificity" in stress theory. *Journal of Psychiatric Research,* 1971, *8,* 323–333. [10]

Mason, J. W. Specificity in the organization of neuroendocrine response profiles. In P. Seeman and G. M. Brown (Eds.), *Frontiers in neurology and neuroscience research.* First International Symposium of the Neuroscience Institute. Toronto: University of Toronto, 1974. [10]

Mason, J. W. Emotion as reflected in patterns of endocrine regulation. In L. Levi (Ed.), *Emotions: Their parameters and measurement.* New York: Raven Press, 1975. [10]

Mason, J. W., Maher, J. T., Hartley, L. H., Morigey, E., Perlow, M. J., and **Jones, L. G.** Selectivity of corticosteroid and catecholamine response to various natural stimuli. In G. Serban (Ed.), *Psychopathology of human adaptation.* New York: Plenum, 1976. Pp. 141–171. [10]

Mason, M. K. Learning to speak after years of silence. *Journal of Hearing and Speech Disorders,* 1942, *7,* 295–304. [9]

Mason, W. A. The effects of social restriction on the behavior of rhesus monkeys: III. Tests of gregariousness. *Journal of Comparative and Physiological Psychology,* 1961, *54,* 287–290. [9]

Mathews, K. E., and **Canon, L. K.** Environmental noise level as a determinant of helping behavior. *Journal of Personality and Social Psychology,* 1975, *32,* 571–577. [18]

Matthews, K. A. Psychological perspectives on the Type A behavior patterns. *Psychological Bulletin,* 1982, *91,* 293–323. [10]

Matlin, M. *Cognition.* New York: Holt, Rinehart and Winston, 1983. [7]

Maugh, T. H., II. Marijuana "justifies serious concern." *Science,* 19 March 1982, *215,* 1488–1490. [12]

May, R. The problem of evil: An open letter to Carl Rogers. *Journal of Humanistic Psychology,* 1982, *22,* 10–21. [13]

Mayer, R. E. *Thinking, problem solving, cognition.* New York: W. H. Freeman, 1983. [7]

Mayer-Gross, W., Slater, E., and **Roth, M.** *Clinical psychiatry.* Baltimore: Williams & Wilkins, 1969. [15]

Mead, M. *Sex and temperament in three primitive societies.* New York: Morrow, 1935. [8]

Mehrabian, A. *Nonverbal communication.* Hawthorne, N.Y.: Aldine-Atherton, 1972. [9]

Meichenbaum, D. H. (Ed.). *Cognitive behavior modification: An integrative approach.* New York: Plenum, 1977. [16]

Meichenbaum, D. H., and **Jaemko, M.** (Eds.). *Stress prevention and management: A cognitive behavioral approach.* New York: Plenum, 1982. [10]

Meichenbaum, D. H., and **Jaemko, M. E.** (Eds.). *Stress reduction and prevention.* New York: Plenum, 1983. [16]

Meissner, W. W. Learning and memory in the Korsakoff syndrome. *International Journal of Neuropsychiatry,* 1968, *4,* 6–20. [12]

Melges, F. T., Tinklenberg, J. R., Hollister, L. E., and **Gillespie, H. K.** Marihuana and temporal disintegration. *Science,* 1970, *168,* 1118–1120. [12]

Melges, F. T., Tinklenberg, J. R., Hollister, L. E., and **Gillespie, H. K.** Marihuana and the temporal span of awareness. *Archives of General Psychiatry,* 1971, *24,* 564–567. [12]

Meltzer, H. Individual differences in forgetting pleasant and unpleasant experiences. *Journal of Educational Psychology,* 1930, *21,* 399–409. [6]

Meltzer, H. Y., and **Stahl, S. M.** Dopamine hypothesis of schizophrenia—Review. *Schizophrenia Bulletin,* 1976, *2,* 19–76. [15]

Meltzoff, A. N., and **Moore, M. K.** Imitation of facial and manual gestures by human neonates. *Science,* 1977, *198,* 75–78. [8]

Melzack, R., and **Woll, P. D.** Pain mechanisms: A new theory. *Science,* 1965, *150,* 971–979. [4]

Mendels, J. *Concepts of depression.* New York: Wiley, 1970. [15]

Mendelson, M. J., and **Haith, M. M.** The relation between audition and vision in the human newborn. *Monographs of the Society for Research in Child Development,* 1976, *41 (4),* serial no. 167. [8]

Menyuk, P., and **Bernholtz, N.** Prosodic features and children's language production. *M.I.T. Research Laboratory of Electronics Quarterly Progress Reports,* 1969, *93,* 216–219. [9]

Mercer, J. *Technical manual: SOMPA: System of multicultural pluralistic assessment.* New York: Psychological Corporation, 1979. [14]

Merskey, H. The perception and measurement of pain. *Journal of Psychosomatic Research,* 1973, *17,* 251–255. [4]

Merton, R. K., and **Kitt, A. S.** Contributions to the theory of reference group behavior. In R. K. Merton and P. F. Lazarsfeld (Eds.), *Continuities in social research: Studies in the scope and method of "The American Soldier."* New York: Free Press, 1950. [10]

Mervis, C. B., Catlin, J., and **Rosch, E.** Relationships among goodness-of-example, category norms, and word frequency. *Bulletin of the Psychonomic Society,* 1976, *7,* 283–284. [7]

Messick, S., and **Jungeblut, A.** Time and method in coaching for the SAT. *Psychological Bulletin,* 1981, *89,* 191–216. [14]

Meyer, D. E., Schavaneveldt, R. W., and **Ruddy, M. G.** Functions of graphemic and phonemic codes in visual word recognition. *Memory and Cognition,* 1974, *2,* 309–321. [9]

Meyer, V., Gross, C. G., and **Teuber, H.** Effect knowledge of site of stimulation on the threshold for pressure sensitivity. *Perception and Motor Skills,* 1963, *16,* 637–640. [4]

Michael, R. P. Hormonal factors and aggressive behaviour in the rhesus monkey. In D. H. Ford (Ed.), *Influence of hormones on the nervous system.* Basel: Karger, 1971. [11]

Michael, R. P., and **Keverne, E. B.** Pheromones in the communication of sexual status in primates. *Nature,* 1968, *218,* 746–749. [11]

Michael, R. P., Keverne, E. B., and **Bonsall, R. W.** Pheromones: Isolation of male sex attractants from a female primate. *Science,* 1971, *172,* 964–966. [11]

Middlebrook, P. N. *Social psychology and modern life.* New York: Knopf, 1980. [17]

Milavsky, J. R., Kessler, R., Stipp, H., and **Rubens, W. S.** Television and aggression: Results of a panel study. In National Institute of Mental Health, *Television and behavior: Ten years of scientific progress and implications for the eighties* (Vols. 1 and 2). D. Pearl, L. Bouthilet, and J. Lazar (Eds.). Washington, D. C.: U. S. Government Printing Office, 1982. [18]

Milgram, S. Behavioral study of obedience. *Journal of Abnormal and Social Psychology,* 1963, *67,* 371–378. [1, 2, 18]

Milgram, S. Issues in the study of obedience: A reply to Baumrind. *American Psychologist*, 1964, *19*, 848–852. [18]

Milgram, S. Liberating effects of group pressure. *Journal of Personality and Social Psychology*, 1965a, *1*, 127–34. [18]

Milgram, S. Some conditions of obedience and disobedience to authority. In I. D. Steiner and M. Fishbein (Eds.), *Current studies in social psychology*. New York: Holt, Rinehart and Winston, 1965b. Pp. 243–262. [18]

Milgram, S. Some conditions of obedience and disobedience to authority. *Human Relations*, 1968, *18*, 56–76. [18]

Milgram, S. The experience of living in cities: A psychological analysis. *Science*, 1970, *167*, 1461–1468. [18]

Milgram, S. *Obedience to authority.* New York: Harper & Row, 1974. [18]

Milgram, S. *The individual in a social world.* Reading, Mass.: Addison-Wesley, 1977. [18]

Miller, D. T., and **Ross, M.** Self-serving biases in the attribution of causality: Fact or fiction? *Psychological Bulletin*, 1975, *82*, 213–225. [17]

Miller, G. A. The magical number seven, plus or minus two: Some limits on our capacity for processing information. *Psychological Review*, 1956, *63*, 81–97. [6]

Miller, G. A. *Psychology.* New York: Harper & Row, 1962. [1, 14]

Miller, G. A. *Language and speech.* New York: W. H. Freeman, 1981. [9]

Miller, G. R., and **Burgoon, J. K.** Factors affecting assessments of witness credibility. In N. L. Kerr and R. M. Bray (Eds.), *The psychology of the courtroom*. New York: Academic Press, 1982. [9]

Miller, L. L. and **Branconnier, R. J.** Cannabis: Effects on memory and the cholinergic limbic system. *Psychological Bulletin*, 1983, *93*, 441–456. [12]

Miller, L. L., Cornett, T. L., Brightwell, D. R., McFarland, D. J., Drew, W. G., and **Winkler, A.** Marijuana: Effects on storage and retrieval of prose material. *Psychopharmacology*, 1977, *51*, 311–316. [12]

Miller, L. L., Cornett, T. L., and **McFarland, D. J.** Marijuana: An analysis of storage and retrieval deficits in memory with the technique of restricted reminding. *Pharmacology Biochemistry and Behavior*, 1978, *8*, 327–332. [12]

Miller, N. E. The frustration-aggression hypothesis. *Psychological Review*, 1941, *48*, 337–342. [18]

Miller, N. E. Experiments on motivation. *Science*, 1957, *126*, 1271–1278. [3]

Miller, N. E. Biofeedback: Evaluation of a new technic. *New England Journal of Medicine*, 1974, *290*, 684–685. [12]

Miller, N. E. Behavioral medicine: Symbiosis between laboratory and clinic. *Annual Review of Psychology*, 1983, *34*, 1–31. [10]

Miller, N. E., and **Bugelski, R.** Minor studies of aggression: II. The influence of frustrations imposed by the in-group on attitudes expressed toward out-groups. *Journal of Psychology*, 1948, *25*, 437–452. [17]

Miller, R. E., Caul, W. F., and **Mirsky, I. A.** Communication of affects between feral and socially isolated monkeys. *Journal of Personality and Social Psychology*, 1967, *7*, 231–239. [9]

Miller, W. Psychological deficit in depression. *Psychological Bulletin*, 1975, *82*, 238–260. [8]

Miller, W. R. Problem drinking and substance abuse: Behavioral perspectives. NIDA Research Monograph No. 25, *Behavioral analysis and treatment of substance abuse*, 1979, Chapter 11. [15]

Mills, K. C., Sobell, M. B., and **Schaefer, H. H.** Training social drinking as an alternative to abstinence for alcoholics. *Behavior Therapy*, 1971, *2*, 18–27. [16]

Milner, B. Some effects of frontal lobectomy in man. In J. M. Warren and K. Arent (Eds.), *The frontal granular cortex and behavior*. New York: McGraw-Hill, 1964. [3]

Milner, B. Amnesia following operation on the temporal lobes. In C. W. M. Whitty and O. L. Zangwill (Eds.), *Amnesia*. London: Butterworth, 1966. [2, 6]

Milner, B. CNS maturation and language acquisition. In H. Whitaker and H. A. Whitaker (Eds.), *Studies of Neurolinguistics* (Vol. 1). New York: Academic Press, 1976. [9]

Milton, K. Women in policing. *Police Foundation*, 1972. [17]

Mineka, S., Suomi, S. J., and **DeLizio, R.** Multiple separations in adolescent monkeys: An opponent-process interpretation. *Journal of Experimental Psychology*, 1981, *110*, 56–85. [11]

Minuchin, S. *Families and family therapy.* Cambridge, Mass.: Harvard University Press, 1974. [15]

Mischel, W. *Personality and assessment.* New York: Wiley, 1968. [13]

Mischel, W. *Introduction to personality* (2d ed.). New York: Holt, Rinehart and Winston, 1976. [13]

Mischel, W. Toward a cognitive social learning reconceptualization of personality. *Psychological Review*, 1973, *80*, 252–283. [13]

Mischel, W. *Introduction to personality* (3rd ed.). New York: Holt, Rinehart and Winston, 1981. [13]

Mischel, W., Ebbesen, E., and **Zeiss, A. R.** Selective attention to the self: Situational and dispositional determinants. *Journal of Personality and Social Psychology*, 1973, *27*, 129–142. [17]

Mischel, W., and **Peake, P. K.** Beyond *déjà vu* in the search for cross-situational consistency. *Psychological Review*, 1982, *89*, 730–755. [13]

Mishara, B. L. College students' experiences with suicide and reactions to suicidal verbalizations: A model for prevention. *Journal of Community Psychology*, 1982, *10*, 142–150. [15]

Mishara, B. L., Baker, A. H., and **Mishara, T. T.** The frequency of suicide attempts: A retrospective approach applied to college students. *American Journal of Psychiatry*, 1976, *113*, 841–844. [15]

Mitchell, K. M., Bozarth, J. D., and **Krauft, C. C.** A reappraisal of the therapeutic effectiveness of accurate empathy, nonpossessive warmth, and genuineness. In A. S. Gurman and A. M. Razin (Eds.), *Effective psychotherapy: A handbook of research*. Elmsford, N.Y.: Pergamon Press, 1977. [16]

Mollon, J. D. Color vision. *Annual Review of Psychology*, 1982, *33*, 41–85. [4]

Monahan, L., Kuhn, D., and **Shaver, P.** Intrapsychic versus cultural explanations of the "fear of success" motive. *Journal of Personality and Social Psychology*, 1974, *29*, 60–64. [11]

Moncrieff, R. W. *Odor preferences.* New York: Wiley, 1966. [4]

Money, J., and **Ehrhardt, A. A.** *Man and woman, boy and girl.* Baltimore: Johns Hopkins University Press, 1972. [11]

Monge, R., and **Hultsch, D.** Paired associate learning as a function of adult age and the length of anticipation and inspection intervals. *Journal of Gerontology*, 1971, *26*, 157–162. [8]

Monnier, M., Boehmer, A., and **Scholer, A.** Early habituation, dishabituation, and generalization induced in visual center by color stimuli. *Vision Research*, 1976, *16*, 1497–1504. [8]

Montour, K. William James Sidis, the broken twig. *American Psychologist*, 1977, *32*, 265–279. [14]

Moore, D. S. *Statistics: Concepts and controversies.* New York: W. H. Freeman, 1979. [2]

Moore, T. E. Subliminal advertising: What you see is what you get. *Journal of Marketing*, 1982, *46*, 38–47. [4]

Moorhead, G. Groupthink: Hypothesis in need of testing. *Group and Organization Studies*, 1982, *7*, 429–444. [18]

Moray, N. Attention in dichotic listening: Affective cues and the influence of instructions. *Quarterly Journal of Experimental Psychology*, 1959, *11*, 56–60. [6]

Morgan, W. P., Roberts, J. A., Brand, F. R., and **Feinerman, A. D.** Psychological effect of chronic physical activity. *Medicine and Science in Sports*, 1970, *2*, 213–217. [10]

Morrell, P., and **Norton, W. T.** Myelin. *Scientific American*, 1980, *242*, 88ff. [3]

Morris, N. M., and **Udry, J. R.** Pheromonal influences on human sexual behavior: An experimental search. *Journal of Biosocial Science*, 1978, *10*, 147–157. [11]

Morse, R. C., and **Stoller, D.** The hidden message that breaks habits. *Science Digest,* September 1982, 28. [4]

Moskowitz, D. S., Schwarz, J. C., and **Corsini, D. A.** Initiating day care at three years of age: Effects on attachment. *Child Development,* 1977, *48,* 1271–1276. [8]

Moss, H. A. Sex, age, and state as determinants of mother–infant interaction. *Merrill-Palmer Quarterly of Behavior and Development,* 1967, *13,* 19–36. [8]

Mowrer, O., and **Mowrer, W.** Enuresis: A method for its study and treatment. *American Journal of Orthopsychiatry,* 1938, *8,* 436–459. [5]

Mueller, C. G. Some origins of psychology as science. *Annual Review of Psychology,* 1979, *30,* 9–29. [1]

Muir, D., and **Field, J.** Newborn infants orient to sound. *Child Development,* 1979, *50,* 431–436. [8]

Murray, H. A. *Explorations in personality.* New York: Oxford University Press, 1938. [11, 14]

Murray, H. A. Vicissitudes of creativity. In H. H. Anderson (Ed.), *Creativity and its cultivation.* New York: Harper & Row, 1959. [7]

Mussen, P. H. Early sex role development. In D. A. Goslin (Ed.), *Handbook of socialization theory and research.* Chicago: Rand McNally, 1969. Pp. 707–731. [8]

Mussen, P. H., and **Eisenberg, N.** *The roots of caring.* New York: W. H. Freeman, 1977. [13]

Muter, P. Very rapid forgetting. *Memory & Cognition,* 1980, *8,* 174–179. [6]

Myers, D. G., and **Ridl, J.** Can we all be better than average? *Psychology Today,* 1979, *13,* pp. 89–98. [6]

Myers, J. K., and **Bean, L. L.** *A decade later: A follow-up of social class and mental illness.* New York: Wiley, 1968. [15]

Myrdal, G. *An American dilemma.* New York: Harper, 1944. [17]

Naftulin, D. H., Ware, J. E., Jr., and **Donnelly, F. A.** The Doctor Fox lecture: A paradigm of educational seduction. *Journal of Medical Education,* 1973, *48,* 630–635. [1]

Nairn, A., and Associates. *The reign of ETS: The corporation that makes up minds.* Washington, D.C.: Nader, 1980. [14]

Nasrallah, H. A., Kleinman, J. E., Weinberger, D. R., Gillin, J. C., and **Wyatt, R. J.** Cerebral ventricular enlargement and dopamine synthesis inhibition in chronic schizophrenia (letter to editor). *Archives of General Psychiatry,* 1980, *37,* 1427. [15]

Nathan, P. E. Alcoholism. In H. Leitenberg (Ed.), *Handbook of behavior modification and behavior therapy.* Englewood Cliffs, N. J.: Prentice-Hall, 1976. [16]

National Academy of Sciences. *Ability testing: Uses, consequences, and controversies.* A. K. Wigdor and W. R. Gardner (Eds.).

Washington, D.C.: National Academy Press, 1982a. [14]

National Academy of Sciences. *Marijuana and health.* Washington, D.C.: National Academy Press, 1982b. [12]

National Institute of Mental Health (NIMH), *Television and behavior: Ten years of scientific progress and implications for the eighties* (vols. 1 and 2). D. Pearl, L. Bouthilet, and J. Lazar (Eds.). Washington, D.C.: U.S. Government Printing Office, 1982. [18]

National Science Foundation funded projects controversy: Senator William Proximire vs. social scientists. *Wisconsin Sociologist,* 1975, *12,* 72–86. [1]

Neimark, E. D. Longitudinal development of formal operations thought. *Genetic Psychology Monographs,* 1975, *91,* 171–225. [8]

Neisser, U. *Cognition and reality: Principles and implications of cognitive psychology.* New York: W. H. Freeman, 1976. [6]

Nelson, K. E., Structure and strategy in learning to talk. *Monographs for the Society for Research in Child Development,* 1973, *38* (serial no. 149). [9]

Nelson, K. E. Concept, word, and sentence: Interrelations in acquisition and development. *Psychological Review,* 1974, *81,* 267–285. [9]

Nelson, K. E. Facilitating children's syntax acquisition. *Developmental Psychology,* 1977, *13,* 101–107. [9, 13]

Nelson, K. E. *Children's language* (Vol. 1). New York: Gardner Press, 1978. [9]

Nelson, K. E. Individual differences in language development: Implications for development and language. *Psychological Bulletin,* 1981, *17,* 170–187. [9]

Nelson, K. E. Cognitive development in the first years of life. *Behavioral and Social Science Research,* Part II. Washington, D.C.: National Academy Press, 1982. [8]

Nelson, K. E., and **Ross, G.** The generalities and specifics of long-term memory in infants and young children. *New Directions for Child Development,* 1980, *10,* 87–101. [1]

Neugarten, B. L. Adaptation and the life cycle. *The Counseling Psychologist,* 1976, *6,* 16–20. [8]

Newcomb, T. M. *Personality and social change.* New York: Dryden Press, 1943. [18]

Newcomb, T. M., Koening, K., Flacks, R., and **Warwick, D.** *Persistence and change: Bennington College and its students after 25 years.* New York: Wiley, 1967. [18]

Newell, A., Shaw, J. C., and **Simon, H. A.** The process of creative thinking. In H. E. Gruber, G. Terrell, and M. Wertheimer (Eds.), *Contemporary approaches to creative thinking.* New York: Atherton, 1963. [7]

Newell, A., and **Simon, H. A.** *Human problem solving.* Englewood Cliffs, N.J.: Prentice-Hall, 1972. [7]

Nichols, J. G. Causal attributions and other achievement-related cognitions: Effects of task outcomes, attainment value and sex.

Journal of Personality and Social Psychology, 1975, *31,* 379–389. [11]

Nisbett, R. E. Taste, deprivation, and weight determinants of eating behavior. *Journal of Personality and Social Psychology,* 1968, *10,* 107–116. [11]

Nisbett, R. E. Hunger, obesity, and the ventromedial hypothalamus. *Psychological Review,* 1972, *79,* 433–453. [11]

Nisbett, R. E., and **Gurwitz, S.** Weight, sex, and the eating behavior of human newborns. *Journal of Comparative and Physiological Psychology,* 1970, *73,* 245–253. [11]

Nisbett, R. E., and **Ross, L.** *Human inference: Strategies and shortcomings of social judgment.* Englewood Cliffs, N.J.: Prentice-Hall, 1980. [7, 17]

Nisbett, R. E., and **Schachter, S.** Cognitive manipulation of pain. *Journal of Experimental Social Psychology,* 1966, *2,* 227–236. [10]

Nisbett, R. E., and **Wilson, T.** Telling more than we know. *Psychological Review,* 1977, *84,* 231–259. [7, 12]

O'Brien, D. F. The chemistry of vision. *Science,* 1982, *218,* 961–966. [4]

Oden, M. H. The fulfillment of promise: Forty-year follow-up of Terman gifted group. *Genetic Psychology Monographs,* 1968, *7,* 3–93. [14]

Office of Technology Assessment. *Scientific validity of polygraph testing: A research review and evaluation.* Washington, D.C.: Office of Technology Assessment, 1983. [10]

O'Hara, M. W., Rehm, L. P., and **Campbell, S. B.** Predicting depressive symptomatology: Cognitive-behavioral models and post-partum depression. *Journal of Abnormal Psychology,* 1982, *91,* 457–461. [15]

Orne, M. T. On the social psychology of the psychological experiment: With particular reference to demand characteristics and their implications. *American Psychologist,* 1962, *17,* 776–783. [2]

Orne, M. T. The use and misuse of hypnosis in court. *The International Journal of Clinical and Experimental Hypnosis,* October 1979, *27,* 311–322. [12]

Orne, M. T., and **Holland, C. C.** On the ecological validity of laboratory deceptions. *International Journal of Psychiatry,* 1968, *6,* 282–293, [18]

Ornstein, R. *The psychology of consciousness* (2d ed.). New York: Harcourt Brace Jovanovich, 1977. [3, 12]

Oskamp, S. *Attitudes and opinions.* Englewood Cliffs, N.J.: Prentice-Hall, 1977. [17]

Paivio, A., *Imagery and verbal process.* New York: Holt, Rinehart and Winston, 1971. [6]

Pallak, M. S., Sogin, S. R., and **Von Zante, A.** Bad decisions: Effect of volition, locus of causality, and negative consequences on attitude change. *Journal of Personality and Social Psychology,* 1974, *30,* 217–227. [17]

Palmore, E., and **Kivett, V.** Change in life

satisfaction: A longitudinal study of persons aged 46–70. *Journal of Gerontology,* 1977, *32,* 311–316. [10]

Papert, S. *Mindstorms.* New York: Basic Books, 1980. [5]

Papousek, H. Individual variability in learned responses in human infants. In R. J. Robinson (Ed.), *Brain and early behavior: Development in the fetus and infant.* London: Academic Press, 1969. Pp. 251–266. [8]

Parizkova, J. *Body fat and physical fitness.* The Hague: Martinus Nijhoff, 1977. [11]

Parke, R. D., Berkowitz, L., Leyens, J. P., West, S. G., and **Sebastian, R. J.** Some effects of violent and nonviolent movies on the behavior of juvenile delinquents. In L. Berkowitz (Ed.), *Advances in experimental social psychology* (Vol. 10). New York: Academic Press, 1977. Pp. 135–172. [18]

Parker, E. S., Birnbaum, I. M., and **Noble, E. P.** Alcohol and memory: Storage and state dependency. *Journal of Verbal Learning Behavior,* 1976, *15,* 691–702. [12]

Parker, E. S., and **Noble, E. P.** Alcohol consumption and cognitive functioning in social drinkers. *Journal of Studies on Alcohol,* 1977, *36,* 1224–1232. [12]

Parkes, C. M. The first year of bereavement: A longitudinal study of the reactions of London widows to the death of their husbands. *Psychiatry,* 1970, *33,* 444–467. [10]

Parkes, C. M. Components of the reaction to loss of a limb, spouse, or home. *Journal of Psychosomatic Research,* 1972, *16,* 343–349. [10]

Parkes, C. M. Unexpected and untimely bereavement: A statistical study of young Boston widows and widowers. In B. B. Schoenberg, I. Gerber, A. Wiener, A. H. Kutscher, D. Peretz, and A. C. Carr (Eds.), *Bereavement: Its psychosocial aspects.* New York: Columbia University Press, 1975. [10]

Parkes, C. M., and **Weiss, R. S.** *Recovery from bereavement.* New York: Basic Books, 1983. [10]

Parkes, J. D. Clinical aspects of tardive dyskinesia. In H. F. Bradford and C. D. Marsden (Eds.), *Biochemistry and neurology.* New York: Academic Press, 1976. [16]

Parloff, M. B., Waskow, I. E., and **Wolfe, B. E.** Research on therapist variables in relation to process and outcome. In S. L. Garfield and A. E. Bergin (Eds.), *Handbook of psychotherapy and behavior change: An empirical analysis* (2d ed.). New York: Wiley, 1978. [16]

Parsons, J. E., Adler, T. F., Futterman, R., Goff, S. B., Kaczala, C. M., Meece, J. L., and **Midgley, C.** Expectancies, values, and academic behavior. In J. Spence (Ed.), *Achievement and achievement motivation.* New York: W. H. Freeman, 1983. [11]

Parsons, O. A., and **Prigatano, G. P.** Memory functioning in alcoholics. In I. M. Birnbaum and E. S. Parker (Eds.), *Alcohol and*

human memory. Hillsdale, N.J.: Lawrence Erlbaum, 1977. Pp. 185–194. [12]

Patterson, G. R., Littman, R. A., and **Bricker, W.** Assertive behavior in children: A step toward a theory of aggression. *Monographs of the Society for Research in Child Development,* 1967, *32,* Serial No. 113. [18]

Patterson, R. L. S. Identification of 3-hydroxy-5-androst-16-ene as the mask odour component of boar submaxillary salivary gland and its relationship to the sex odour taint in pork meat. *Journal of the Science of Food and Agriculture,* 1968, *19,* 434. [11]

Pattie, F. A. A report of attempts to produce uniocular blindness by hypnotic suggestion. *British Journal of Medical Psychology,* 1935, *15,* 230–241. [12]

Pattison, E. M. *The experience of dying.* Englewood Cliffs, N.J.: Prentice-Hall, 1977. [10]

Paul, G. L. Outcome research is psychotherapy. *Journal of Consulting Psychology,* 1967, *31,* 109–118. [16]

Paul, G. L., and **Lentz, R. J.** *Psychosocial treatment of chronic mental patients: Milieu versus social-learning programs.* Cambridge, Mass.: Harvard University Press, 1977. [16]

Pavlov, I. P. *Conditioned reflexes.* G. V. Anrep (Trans.). London: Oxford University Press, 1927. [5]

Paykel, E. S. Causal relationships between clinical depression and life events. In J. E. Barrett, R. M. Rose, and G. L. Klerman (Eds.), *Stress and mental disorder.* New York: Raven, 1979a. [10]

Paykel, E. S. Recent life events in the development of depressive disorders. In R. A. Depue (Ed.), *The psychology of the depressive disorders: Implications for the effects of stress.* New York: Academic Press, 1979b. [10]

Pearlin, L. I., and **Schooler, C.** The structure of coping. *Journal of Health and Social Behavior,* 1978, *19,* 2–21. [15]

Penfield, W. Consciousness, memory, and man's conditioned reflexes. In K. H. Pribram (Ed.), *On the biology of learning.* New York: Harcourt Brace Jovanovich, 1969. Pp. 127–168. [6, 12]

Penfield, W., and **Rasmussen, T.,** *The cerebral cortex of man.* New York: Macmillan, 1950. [3]

Penick, S., Smith, G., Wienske, K., and **Hinkle, L.** An experimental evaluation of the relationship between hunger and gastric motility. *American Journal of Physiology,* 1963, *205,* 421–426. [11]

Peplau, L. A. Impact of fear of success and sex-role attitudes on women's competitive achievement. *Journal of Personality and Social Psychology,* 1976, *34,* 561–568. [11]

Perkins, D. The assessment of stress using life events scales. In Leo Goldberger and Shlomo Breznitz (Eds.), *Handbook of stress: Theoretical and clinical aspects* New York: Free Press, 1982. Pp. 320–331. [10]

Perlmutter, M., Learning and memory

through adulthood. In M. W. Riley, et al. (Eds.), *Aging in Society.* Hillsdale, N. J.: Lawrence Erlbaum, 1982.

Perlmutter, M., and **Mitchell, D. B.** The appearance and disappearance of age differences in adult memory. In I. M. Craik and S. Trehub (Eds.), *Aging and cognitive processes.* New York: Plenum, in press. [8]

Pervin, L. A. *Personality: Theory, assessment, and research.* (4th ed.). New York: Wiley, 1984. [13]

Peterson, L. R., and **Peterson, M.** Short-term retention of individual verbal items. *Journal of Experimental Psychology,* 1959, *58,* 193–198. [6]

Petty, R. E., and **Cacioppo, J. T.** *Attitudes and persuasion: Classic and contemporary approaches.* Dubuque, Iowa: William C. Brown, 1981. [17]

Petty, R. E., Cacioppo, J. T., and **Goldman, R.** Personal involvement as a determinant of argument-based persuasion. *Journal of Personality and Social Psychology,* 1981, *41,* 847–855. [17]

Phares, E. J. *Clinical psychology: Concepts, methods, and profession.* Homewood, Ill.: Dorsey Press, 1979. [16]

Phillips, L. *A theoretical perspective on heuristics and biases in probabilistic thinking.* Paper delivered at the Eighth Research Conference on Subjective Probability, Utility, and Decision Making, Budapest, Hungary, August 1981. [7]

Phillips, S., with **King, S.,** and **Du Bois, L.** Spontaneous activities of female versus male newborns. *Child Development,* 1978, *49,* 590–597. [8]

Piaget, J. *The language of the child.* M. Warden (Trans.). New York: Harcourt, 1926. [8]

Piaget, J. *The moral judgment of the child* (1932). New York: Free Press, 1948. [1, 8]

Piaget, J. *The origins of intelligence in children.* M. Cook (Trans.). New York: International Universities Press, 1952. [8]

Piaget, J. *The construction of reality in the child.* M. Cook (Trans.). New York: Basic Books, 1954. [8]

Piaget, J. *Biology and knowledge.* B. Walsh (Trans.). Chicago: University of Chicago Press, 1971. [8]

Piaget, J., and **Inhelder, B.** *The psychology of the child.* New York: Basic Books, 1969. [8]

Piliavin, I. M., Rodin, J., and **Piliavin, J. A.** Good Samaritanism: An underground phenomenon? *Journal of Personality and Social Psychology,* 1969, *13,* 289–299. [18]

Piliavin, J. A., Callero, P. L., and **Evans, D. E.** Addiction to altruism? Opponent-process theory and habitual blood donation. *Journal of Personality and Social Psychology,* 1982, *43,* 1200–1213. [11]

Piliavin, J. A., and **Piliavin, I. M.** Effect of blood on reactions to a victim. *Journal of Personal and Social Psychology,* 1972, *23,* 353–361. [2]

Pines, A., and **Maslach, C.** Characteristics of staff burnout in mental health settings. *Hospital and Community Psychiatry,* 1978, *29,* 233–237. [18]

Pines, M. The civilizing of Genie. *Psychology Today,* September 1981, pp. 28–34. [2]

Pines, M. Baby, you're incredible. *Psychology Today,* February 1982, pp. 48–53. [8]

Plotkin, W. B., and **Cohen, R.** Occipital alpha and the attributes of the "alpha experience." *Psychological Physiology,* 1976, *13,* 16–21. [12]

Plutchik, R. A general psychoevolutionary theory of emotion. In R. Plutchik and H. Kellerman (Eds.), *Emotion: Theory, research, and experience* (Vol. 1). New York: Academic Press, 1980. [10]

Plutchik, R., and **Ax, A. F.** A critique of "determinants of emotional state" by Schachter and Singer (1962). *Psychophysiology,* 1967, *4,* 79–82. [10]

Podlesny, J. A., and **Raskin, D. C.** Physiological measures and the detection of deception. *Psychological Bulletin,* 1977, *84,* 782–799. [10]

Pollack, I., and **Pickett, J. M.** Intelligibility of excerpts from fluent speech: Auditory vs. structural context. *Journal of Verbal Learning and Verbal Behavior,* 1964, *3,* 79–84. [9]

Popejoy, D. I. The effects of a physical fitness program on selected psychological and physiological measures of anxiety. Doctoral dissertation, University of Illinois, 1967. [10]

Portnoy, F., and **Simmons, C.** Day care and attachment. *Child Development,* 1978, *49,* 239–242. [8]

Posner, M. I. *Cognition: An introduction.* Glenview, Ill.: Scott, Foresman, 1973. [7]

Premack, D. Language in the chimpanzee? *Science,* 1971a, *172,* 808–822. [9]

Premack, D. On the assessment of language competence in the chimpanzee. In A. M. Schrier and F. Stollnitz (Eds.), *Behavior of nonhuman primates.* New York: Academic Press, 1971b. Pp. 185–228. [9]

Premack, D. Language and intelligence in ape and man. *American Scientist,* 1976, *64,* 674–683. [9]

Premack, D. Animal cognition. *Annual Review of Psychology,* 1983, *34,* 351–362. [9]

Pribram, K. H. Emotions. In S. B. Filskov and T. J. Boll (Eds.), *Handbook of clinical neuropsychology.* New York: Wiley, 1981. [10]

Price, R. H. and **Lynn, S.** *Abnormal psychology in the human context.* Homewood, Ill.: Dorsey Press, 1981. [14]

Privette, G., and **Landsman, T.** Factor analysis of peak performance: The full use of potential. *Journal of Personality and Social Psychology,* 1983, *44,* 195–200. [10]

Public Health Service. *Smoking and health: Report of the Advisory Committee to the Surgeon General of the Public Health Service.* Washing-

ton, D.C.: U.S. Government Printing Office, 1964. [2]

Rachman, S., and **Wilson, G. T.** *The effects of psychological therapy.* Oxford: Pergamon Press, 1980. [16]

Rafaelsen, L., Christup, A., Bech, P., and **Rafaelsen, O. J.** Effects of cannabis and alcohol on psychological tests, *Nature,* 1973, *242,* 117–118. [12]

Rahe, R. H., and **Arthur, R. J.** Life change and illness studies: Past history and future directions. *Journal of Human Stress,* 1978, *4,* 3–15. [10]

Rankin, R. E., and **Campbell, D. T.** Galvanic skin response to Negro and white experimenters. *Journal of Applied Social Psychology,* 1955, *51,* 30–33. [17]

Raps, C. S., Peterson, C., Reinhard, K. E., Abramson, L. Y., and **Seligman, M. E. P.** Attributional style among depressed patients. *Journal of Abnormal Psychology,* 1982, *91,* 102–108. [15]

Rasmussen, J. (Ed.). *Man in isolation and confinement.* Hawthorne, N. •Y.: Aldine, 1973.

Ratcliff, R., and **McKoon, G.** Priming in item recognition: Evidence for the propositional structure of sentences. *Journal of Verbal Learning and Verbal Behavior,* 1978, *17,* 403–417. [9]

Raven, B. H., and **French, J.** Legitimate power, coercive power, and observability in social influence. *Sociometry,* 1958, *21,* 83–97. [18]

Raymond, B. J., and **Unger, R. K.** "The apparel oft proclaims the man": Cooperation with deviant and conventional youths. *Journal of Social Psychology,* 1972, *87,* 75–82. [18]

Raynor, J. O. Future orientation in the study of achievement motivation. In J. W. Atkinson and J. O. Raynor (Eds.), *Motivation and achievement.* Washington, D.C.: Winston, 1974. [11]

Redlich, F., and **Kellert, S. R.** Trends in American mental health. *American Journal of Psychiatry,* 1978, *135,* 22–28. [15]

Reed, E. W. Genetic anomalies in development. In F. D. Horowitz (Ed.), *Review of child developmental research.* Chicago: University of Chicago Press, 1975. [3]

Renault, B., Ragot, R., LeSevere, N., and **Remond, A.** Onset and offset of brain events as indices of mental chronometry. *Science,* 1982, *215,* 1413–1415. [3]

Reschly, D. J. Psychological testing in educational classification and placement. *American Psychologist,* 1981, *36,* 1094–1102. [14]

Rescorla, R. A. Pavlovian conditioning and its proper control procedures. *Psychological Review,* 1967, *74,* 71–80. [5]

Resnick, R. B., Kestenbaum, R. S., and **Schwartz, L. K.** Acute systemic effects of cocaine in man: A controlled study by intranasal and intravenous routes of administration. *Science,* 1977, *195,* 696–698. [12]

Restak, R. *The brain: The last frontier.* Garden City, N.Y.: Doubleday, 1979. [3]

Revelle, W., Amaral, P., and **Turriff, S.** Introversion/extraversion, time stress, and caffeine: The effect on verbal performance. *Science,* 1976, *192,* 149–150. [11]

Revusky, S. H., and **Bedarf, E. W.** Association of illness with prior ingestion of novel foods. *Science,* 1967, *155,* 219–220. [5]

Rice, B. Brave new world of intelligence testing. *Psychology Today,* 1979, *13,* pp. 27–41. [14]

Rice, B. Going for the gifted gold. *Psychology Today,* 1980, *13,* pp. 55ff. [14]

Richards, M., Richardson, K., and **Spears, D.** Conclusion: Intelligence and society. In K. Richardson, D. Spears, and M. Richards (Eds.), *Race and intelligence.* Baltimore: Penguin, 1972. [14]

Riesman, D. (in association with **N. Glazer** and **R. Denny**). *The lonely crowd: A study of the changing American character.* New Haven, Conn.: Yale University Press, 1950. [18]

Rimm, D. C., and **Mahoney, M. J.** The application of reinforcement and participant modeling procedures in the treatment of snake-phobic behavior. *Behavior Research and Therapy,* 1969, 7, 369–376. [16]

Rimm, D. C., and **Masters, J. C.** *Behavior therapy: Techniques and empirical findings.* New York: Academic Press, 1979. [16]

Risberg, J., Halsey, J. H., Wills, E. L., and **Wilson, E. M.** Hemispheric specialization in normal man studied by bilateral measurements of the regional cerebral blood flows: A study with the 133 Xe inhalation technique. *Brain,* 1975, *98,* 511–524. [3]

Ritter, W., Simson, R., Vaughan, H. G., Jr., and **Macht, M.** Manipulation of event-related potential manifestations of information processing stages. *Science,* 1982, *218,* 909–910. [3]

Robins, E., Gassner, J., Kayes, J., Wilkinson, R., and **Murphy, G. E.** The communication of suicidal intent: A study of 134 successful (completed) suicides. *American Journal of Psychiatry,* 1959, *115,* 724–733. [15]

Robinson, F. P. *Effective study* (4th ed.). New York: Harper & Row, 1970. [6]

Rodgers, J. E. The malleable memory of eyewitnesses. *Science Digest,* 1982, *3,* 32–35. [6]

Rodgers, J. E. Brain triggers: Biochemistry and behavior. *Science Digest,* January 1983, pp. 60–65. [3]

Rodin, J. The externality theory today. In A. J. Stunkard (Ed.), *Obesity.* Philadelphia: W. B. Saunders, 1980, Pp. 226–239. [11]

Rodin, J., and **Langer, E. J.** Long-term effects of a control-relevant intervention with the institutionalized aged. *Journal of Personality and Social Psychology,* 1977, *35,* 897–902. [18]

Roe, A. The personality of artists. *Educa-*

tional Psychology Measurement, 1946, *6*, 401–408. [7]

Roe, A. *The making of a scientist.* New York: Dodd, Mead, 1953. [7]

Roffwarg, H. P., Muzio, J. N., and **Dement, W. C.** Ontogenetic development of the human sleep-dream cycle. *Science*, 1966, *152*, 604–619. [12]

Rogentine, G. N., Jr., Fox, B. H., and **Boyd, S. C.** Psychological factors in the prognosis of malignant melanoma: A prospective study. *Psychosomatic Medicine*, 1979, *41*, 647–655. [10]

Rogers, C. R. *Client-centered therapy: Its current practice, implications, and theory.* Boston: Houghton Mifflin, 1951. [13, 16]

Rogers, C. R. *On becoming a person: A therapist's view of psychotherapy.* Boston: Houghton Mifflin, 1961. [13]

Rogers, C. R. The actualizing tendency in relation to "motives" and to consciousness. In M. R. Jones (Ed.), *Nebraska symposium on motivation.* Lincoln: University of Nebraska Press, 1963. Pp. 1–24. [13]

Rogers, C. R. *On becoming a person: A therapist's view of psychotherapy* (2d ed.). Boston: Houghton Mifflin, 1970. [13, 15]

Rogers, C. R. A theory of personality. In S. Maddi (Ed.), *Perspectives on personality.* Boston: Little, Brown, 1971. [13]

Rogers, C. R. Rollo May: Man and philosopher. *Perspectives*, 1981, *2(1)*. [13]

Rogers, C. R., and **Dymond, R. F.** (Eds.). *Psychotherapy and personality change.* Chicago: University of Chicago Press, 1954. [13]

Rogers, R. W., and **Mewborn, C. R.** Fear appeals and attitude change: Effects of a threat's noxiousness, probability of occurrence, and the efficacy of coping responses. *Journal of Personality and Social Psychology*, 1976, *34*, 54–61. [17]

Rorschach, H. *Psychodiagnostik: Methodik und ergebnisse eines wahrnehmungs-diagnostichen experiments* (2d ed.). P. Lemkau and B. Fronenberg (Trans.). Berne and Berlin: Huber, 1932. (Republished: New York: Grune & Stratton, 1942.) [14]

Rosch, E. Principles of categorization. In E. Rosch and B. B. Lloyd (Eds.), *Cognition and categorization.* New York: Wiley, 1978. [7]

Rosen, B. C., and **D'Andrade, R.** The psychological origins of achievement motivations. *Sociometry*, 1959, *22*, 185–218. [11]

Rosenbaum, A. H., Maruta, T., and **Richelson, E.** Drugs that alter mood: 1. Tricyclic agents and monoamine oxidase inhibitors. *Mayo Clinic Proceedings*, 1979, *54*, 335–344. [16]

Rosenberg, M. *Society and the adolescent self-image.* Princeton, N.J.: Princeton University Press, 1965. [13]

Rosenberg, M. *Conceiving the self.* New York: Basic Books, 1979. [13]

Rosenberg, M. J. When dissonance fails: On eliminating evaluation apprehension from attitude measurement. *Journal of Personality and Social Psychology*, 1965, *1*, 28–42. [17]

Rosenfeld, C. Job seeking methods used by American workers. *Monthly Labor Review*, 1975, *98*, 39–42. [13]

Rosenhan, D. L. On being sane in insane places. *Science*, 1973, *179*, 250–258. [1, 15]

Rosenhan, D. L. The contextual nature of psychiatric diagnosis. *Journal of Abnormal Psychology*, 1975, *84*, 462–474. [15]

Rosenman, R. H., Brand, R. J., Jenkins, C. D., Friedman, M., Straus, R. and **Wurm, M.** Coronary heart disease in the Western Collaborative Group Study: Final follow-up experience of 8.5 years. *Journal of the American Medical Association*, 1975, *223*, 872–877. [10]

Rosenthal, D., Wender, P. H., Kety, S. S., Welner, J., and **Schulsinger, F.** The adopted-away offspring of schizophrenics. *American Journal of Psychiatry*, 1971, *128*, 307–311. [15]

Rosenthal, R. *Experimenter effects in behavioral research.* New York: Appleton-Century-Crofts, 1966. [2, 9, 17]

Rosenthal, R., Archer, D., Di Matteo, M. R., Koivumaki, J. H., and **Rogers, P. L.** Body talk and tone of voice: The language without words. *Psychology Today*, September 1974, pp. 64–68. [9]

Rosenthal, R., and **Rosnow, R. L.** *The volunteer subject.* New York: Wiley, 1975. [2]

Rosenthal, T., and **Bandura, A.** Psychological modeling: Theory and practice. In S. L. Garfield and A. E. Bergin (Eds.), *Handbook of psychotherapy and behavior change: An empirical analysis* (2d ed.). New York: Wiley, 1978. [15, 16]

Rosenzweig, M. R., Bennett, E. L., and **Diamond, M. C.** Brain changes in response to experience. *Scientific American*, 1972, *226*, 22–29. [3]

Ross, A. *Child behavior therapy.* New York: Wiley, 1981. [5]

Ross, L. Obesity and externality. In S. Schachter and J. Rodin (Eds.), *Obese humans and rats.* Hillsdale, N.J.: Lawrence Erlbaum, 1974. [11]

Ross, L. The intuitive psychologist and his shortcomings: Distortions in the attribution process. In L. Berkowitz (Ed.), *Advances in experimental social psychology.* New York: Academic Press, 1977. [16, 17]

Ross, M., and **Sicoly, F.** Egocentric biases in availability and attribution. *Journal of Personality and Social Psychology*, 1979, *37*, 322–336. [17]

Rothwell, N., and **Stock, M.** A role for brown adipose tissue in diet-induced thermogenesis. *Nature*, 1979, *281*, 31–35. [11]

Ro-Trock, G., Wellisch, D., and **Schoolar, J. A.** A family therapy outcome study in an inpatient setting. *American Journal of Orthopsychiatry*, 1977, *47*, 514–522. [16]

Roueché, B. All I could do was stand in the woods. *New Yorker*, September 12, 1977, pp. 97–117. [4]

Rubenstein, H., Lewis, S. S., and **Rubenstein, M. A.** Evidence for phonemic recoding in visual word recognition. *Journal of Verbal Learning and Verbal Behavior*, 1971, *10*, 645–657. [9]

Rubin, J. L., Provenzano, F. J., and **Luria, Z.** The eye of the beholder: Parents on sex of newborns. *American Journal of Orthopsychiatry*, 1974, *44*, 512–519. [17]

Rubin, Z. Measurement of romantic love. *Journal of Personality and Social Psychology*, 1970, *16*, 265–273. [17]

Rubin, Z. *Liking and loving: An invitation to social psychology.* New York: Holt, Rinehart and Winston, 1973. [17]

Rubin, Z., and **Peplau, A.** Belief in a just world and reactions to another's lot: A study of participants in the national draft lottery. *Journal of Social Issues*, 1973, *29*, 73–93. [18]

Rubin, Z., Plplau, L. A., and **Hill, C. T.** *Loving and leaving: Sex differences in romantic attachments.* Unpublished manuscript, Brandeis University, 1978. [17]

Rubinstein, E. A. Television and behavior: Research conclusions of the 1982 NIMH report and their policy implications. *American Psychologist*, July 1983, pp. 820–825. [18]

Ruble, D. N. A developmental perspective on theories of achievement motivation. in L. J. Fyans (Ed.), *Achievement motivation: Recent trends in theory and research.* New York: Plenum, 1980. [11]

Ruble, D. N., Parsons, J. E., and **Ross, J.** Self-evaluative responses of children in an achievement setting. *Child Development*, 47 (1976), 990–997. [11]

Rumbaugh, D. M., Gill, T. V., and **von Glasersfeld, E. C.** Reading and sentence completion by a chimpanzee. *Science*, 1963, *182*, 731–733. [9]

Rush, A. J., and **Giles, D. E.** Cognitive therapy: Theory and research. In A. J. Rush (Ed.), *Short-term psychotherapies for depression.* New York: Guilford Press, 1982. Pp.143–181. [16]

Rush, J., Beck, A., Kovacs, M., and **Hollon, S.** Comparative efficacy of cognitive therapy and pharmacotherapy in the treatment of depressed outpatients. *Cognitive Therapy and Research*, 1977, *1*, 17–38. [16]

Russell, W. R., and **Nathan, P. W.** Traumatic amnesia. *Brain*, 1946, *69*, 280–300. [6]

Russo, J. E., Krieser, G., and **Miyashita, S.** An effective display of unit price information. *Journal of Marketing*, 1975, *39*, 11–19. [7]

Rutter, M. Social-emotional consequences of day care for preschool children. In E. F. Zigler and E. W. Gordon (Eds.), *Day care: Scientific and social policy issues.* Boston: Auburn House, 1982. [8]

Ryan, W. *Equality.* New York: Random House, 1981. [17]

Rynders, J. *Annual report of the University of Minnesota Institute of Child Development,* 1975. [8]

Sackeim, H. A., Greenberg, M. S., Weiman, A. L., Gur, R. C., Hungerbuhler, J. P., and **Geschwind, N.** Hemispheric asymmetry in the expression of positive and negative emotions: Neurological evidence. *Archives of Neurology,* 1982, *39,* 210–218. [10]

Sackeim, H. A., and **Weber, S. L.** Functional brain asymmetry in the regulation of emotion: Implications for bodily manifestations of stress. In Leo Goldberger and Shlomo Breznitz (Eds.), *Handbook of stress: theoretical and clinical aspects.* New York: Free Press, 1982. Pp. 183–199. [10]

Saegert, S., Snap, W. C., and **Zajonc, R. B.** Exposure, context, and interpersonal attraction. *Journal of Personality and Social Psychology,* 1973, *25,* 234–242. [17]

Sakitt, B. Locus of short-term visual storage. *Science,* 1975, *190,* 1318–1319. [6]

Sakitt, B. Iconic memory. *Psychological Review,* 1976, *83,* 257–276. [6]

Samelson, F. J. B. Watson's Little Albert, Cyril Burt's twins, and the need for a critical science. *American Psychologist,* 1980, *35,* 619–625. [5]

Sampson, E. E. Scientific paradigms and social values: Wanted—a scientific revolution. *Journal of Personality and Social Psychology,* 1978, *36,* 1332–1343. [8]

Sampson, H. Deprivation of dreaming sleep by two methods. *Archives of General Psychiatry,* 1965, *13,* 79–86. [12]

Sandberg, M. A., Berson, E. L., and **Effron, M. H.** Rod–cone interaction in the distal human retina. *Science,* 1981, *212,* 829–830. [4]

Sanders, G. S. Driven by distraction: An integrative review of social facilitation theory and research. *Journal of Experimental Social Psychology,* 1981, *17,* 227–251. [18]

Sanders, G. S. Social comparison as a basis for evaluating others. *Journal of Research in Personality,* 1982, *16,* 21–31. [17]

Sarbin, T. R., and **Coe, W. C.** Hypnosis: A social psychological analysis of influence communication. New York: Holt, Rinehart and Winston, 1972. [12]

Saxe, L., Dougherty, D., Esty, K., and **Fine, M.** Health technology case study 22: The effectiveness and costs of alcoholism treatment. Washington, D.C.: Office of Technology Assessment, 1983. [15]

Scarf, M. Brain researcher José Delgado asks—"What kind of humans would we like to construct?" *New York Times Magazine,* November 15, 1970, pp. 54–62. [1]

Scarr, S. *Toward a more biological psychology.* Paper delivered at the meetings of the American Association for the Advancement of Science, Houston, Texas, January 5, 1979. [14]

Scarr, S., Pakstis, A. J., Katz, S. H., and **Barker, W. B.** Absence of relationship between degree of white ancestry and intellectual skills within a black population. *Human Genetics,* 1977, 857, 1–18. [14]

Scarr, S., and **Weinberg, R. A.** IQ test performance of black children adopted by white families. *American Psychologist,* 1976, *3,* 726–739. [14]

Scarr, S., and **Weinberg, R. A.** The Minnesota adoption studies: Genetic differences and malleability. *Child Development,* 1983, *54,* 260–267. [14]

Scarr-Salapatek, S. Unknowns in the IQ equation. *Science,* 1971a, *174,* 1223–1228. [14]

Scarr-Salapatek, S. Race, social class, and IQ. *Science,* 1971b, *174,* 1286–1295. [14]

Schachter, S. *The psychology of affiliation.* Stanford, Calif.: Stanford University Press, 1959. [2]

Schachter, S. The interaction of cognitive and physiological determinants of emotional state. In L. Berkowitz (Ed.), *Advances in experimental social psychology.* New York: Academic Press, 1964. Pp. 48–81. [10]

Schachter, S. *Emotion, obesity, and crime.* New York: Academic Press, 1971a. [1, 11]

Schachter, S. Some extraordinary facts about obese humans and rats. *American Psychologist,* 1971b, *26,* 129–144. [11]

Schachter, S. Recidivism and self-cure of smoking and obesity. *American Psychologist,* 1982, *37,* 436–444. [11]

Schachter, S., and **Friedman, L. N.** The effects of work and cue prominence on eating behavior. In S. Schachter and J. Rodin (Eds.), *Obese humans and rats.* Hillsdale, N. J.: Lawrence Erlbaum, 1974. [11]

Schachter, S., and **Singer, J. E.** Cognitive, social, and physiological determinants of emotional state. *Psychological Review,* 1962, *69,* 379–399. [10]

Schacter, D. L. The hypnagogic state: A critical review of the literature. *Psychological Bulletin,* 1976, *83,* 452–481. [12]

Schaefer, H. H. Twelve-month follow-up of behaviorally trained ex-alcoholic social drinkers. *Behavior Therapy,* 1972, *3,* 286–289. [16]

Schank, R., interviewed by **Frank Kendig.** A conversation with Roger Schank. *Psychology Today,* April 1983, pp. 28–36. [9]

Schank, R., and **Abelson, R.** *Scripts, plans, goals, and understanding.* Hillsdale, N. J.: Lawrence Erlbaum, 1977. [9]

Schaps, E. Cost, dependency, and helping. *Journal of Personality and Social Psychology,* 1972, *21,* 74–78. [2]

Scharf, B. Critical bands. In J. V. Tobias (Ed.), *Foundations of modern auditory theory* (Vol. 1). New York: Academic Press, 1970. [4]

Scheerer, M. Problem-solving. *Scientific American,* 1963. *208,* 118–128. [7]

Scheff, T. J. *Labeling madness.* Englewood Cliffs, N. J.: Prentice-Hall, 1975. [15]

Schein, E. H. The Chinese indoctrination program for prisoners of war: A study of attempted "brainwashing." *Psychiatry: Journal for the Study of Interpersonal Processes,* 1956, *19,* 149–172. [18]

Schein, E. H. *Coercive persuasion.* New York: Norton, 1961. [18]

Scherer, K. R., Summerfield, A. B., and **Wallbott, H. G.** Cross-national research on antecedents and components of emotion: A progress report. *Social Science Information,* 1983. [10]

Schildkraut, J. J. The biochemistry of affective disorders: A brief summary. In A. M. Nicholi, Jr. (Ed.), *The Harvard guide to modern psychiatry.* Cambridge, Mass.: Harvard University Press, 1978. [15]

Schildkraut, J. J., and **Freyhan, F. A.** Neuropharmacological studies of mood disorder. In J. Zubin (Ed.), *Disorders of mood.* New York: Grune & Stratton, 1972. [10]

Schildkraut, J. J., and **Kety, S. S.** Biogenic amines and emotions. *Science,* 1967, *156,* 21–30. [10]

Schlenker, B. R. *Impression management: The self-concept, social identity, and interpersonal relations.* Monterey, Calif.: Brooks/Cole, 1980. [17]

Schlenker, B. R. Translating actions into attitudes: An identity analytic approach to the explanation of social conduct. *Advances in Experimental Social Psychology,* 1982, *15,* 193–247. [17]

Schmeck, H. M., Jr. The biology of fear and anxiety: Evidence points to chemical triggers. *The New York Times,* September 7, 1982, pp. C1, C8. [10]

Schmidt, F. L. and **Hunter, J. E.** Employment testing: Old theories and new research findings. *American Psychologist,* 1981, *36,* 1128–1137. [14]

Schmitt, R. C. Density, delinquency, and crime in Honolulu. *Sociology and Social Research,* 1957, *41,* 274–276. [17]

Schmitt, R. C. Implications of density in Hong Kong. *American Institute of Planners Journal,* 1963, *29,* 210–217. [17]

Schmitt, R. C. Density, health, and social disorganization. *American Institute of Planners Journal,* 1966, *32,* 38–40. [17]

Schofield, J. W. Complementary and conflicting identities: Images and interaction in an interracial school. In S. Asher and J. Gottman (Eds.), *The development of children's friendships: Description and intervention.* Cambridge: Cambridge University Press, 1981. [17]

Schreiner, L., and **Kling, A.** Rhinencephalon and behavior. *American Journal of Physiology,* 1956, *184,* 486–490. [11]

Schuessler, K. F. The deterrent influence of the death penalty. *Annals of the American Academy,* 1952, *284,* 54–62. [2]

Schultes, R. E. *Hallucinogenic plants.* New York: Golden Press, 1976. [12]

Schultz, D. P. *Sensory restriction: Effects on behavior.* New York: Academic Press, 1965. [11]

Schuman, H., and **Johnson, M. P.** Attitudes and behavior, *Annual Review of Sociology,* 1976, *2,* 161–207. [17]

Schwartz, G. E. Psychosomatic disorders and biofeedback: A psychobiological model of disregulation. In J. D. Maser and M. E. P. Seligman (Eds.), *Psychopathology: Experimental models.* New York: W. H. Freeman, 1977. [16]

Schwartz, L. L. and **Kaslow, F. W.** The cult phenomenon: Historical, sociological, and familial factors contributing to their development and appeal. *Marriage and Family Review,* 1981, *4,* 3–30. [18]

Scovern, A. W., and **Kilmann, P. R.** Status of electroconvulsive therapy: Review of the outcome literature. *Psychological Bulletin,* 1980, *87,* 260–303. [16]

Sears, R. R., Rau, L., and **Alpert, R.** *Identification and child rearing.* Stanford, Calif.: Stanford University Press, 1965. [8]

Segall, M. H., Campbell, D. T., and **Herskovitz, M.** *The influence of culture on visual perception.* Indianapolis: Bobbs-Merrill, 1966. [4]

Sekuler, R., and **Ball, K.** Mental set alters visibility of moving targets. *Science,* 1977, *198,* 9960–9962. [4]

Seligman, M. E. P., Maier, S. F., and **Geer, J.** The alleviation of learned helplessness in the dog. *Journal of Abnormal Psychology,* 1968, *78,* 256–262. [15]

Selman, R. L. Toward a structural analysis of developing interpersonal relations concepts. In A. Pick (Ed.), *Minnesota symposia on child psychology* (Vol. 10). Minneapolis: University of Minnesota, 1976. [8]

Selye, H. *The stress of life.* New York: McGraw-Hill, 1956. [10]

Selye, H. History and present status of the stress concept. In Leo Goldberger and Shlomo Breznitz (Eds.), *Handbook of stress: Theoretical and clinical aspects.* New York: Free Press, 1982. Pp. 7–17. [10]

Selye, H., and **Cherry, L.** On the real benefits of eustress. *Psychology Today,* March 1978, pp. 60–63, 69–70. [10]

Selzer, M. L., and **Vinokur, A.** Life events, subjective stress, and traffic accidents. *American Journal of Psychiatry,* 1974, *131,* 903–906. [10]

Senden, M. von. *Space and sight: The perception of space and shape in the congenitally blind before and after operation.* Peter Heath (Trans.). New York: Free Press, 1960. [4]

Shaklee, H. Sex differences in children's behavior. In M. Wolraich and D. Routh (Eds.), *Advances in developmental and behavioral pediatrics* (Vol. 3). Greenwich, Conn.: JAI Press, 1983. [8]

Shapiro, D. A., and **Shapiro, D.** Meta-analysis of comparative therapy outcome studies: A replication and refinement. *Psychological Bulletin,* 1982, *92,* 581–594. [16]

Shapiro, R. W., and **Keller, M. B.** Initial six-month follow-up of patients with major depressive disorder: A preliminary report from the NIMH Collaborative Study of the Psychobiology of Depression. *Journal of Affective Disorders,* 1981, *3,* 205–220. [15]

Shashova, V. E. RNA metabolism in goldfish brain during acquistion of new behavioral patterns. *Proceedings of the National Academy of Science,* 1970, *65,* 160–167. [6]

Shatz, M., and **Gelman, R.** The development of communication skills: Modifications in the speech of young children as a function of listener. *Monographs of the Society for Research in Child Development,* 1973, *38,* 1–37. [9]

Shaver, J. P., and **Strong, W.** *Facing value decisions: Rationale-building for teachers.* Belmont, Calif.: Wadsworth, 1976. [8]

Shaw, M. E. *Group dynamics: The psychology of small group behavior* (2d ed.). New York: McGraw-Hill, 1976. [18]

Sheehy, G. *Passages: Predictable crises of adult life.* New York: Dutton, 1976. [8]

Shekelle, R. B., Gale, M., Ostfeld, A. M., and **Paul, O.** Hostility, risk of coronary heart disease, and mortality. *Psychosomatic Medicine,* 1983, *45,* 109–114. [10]

Sherif, M., and **Sherif, C. W.** *Groups in harmony and tension.* New York: Harper & Row, 1953. [17]

Sherman, A. R. *In vivo* therapies for phobic reations, instrumental behavior problems, and interpersonal and communication problems. In A. P. Goldstein and F. H. Kanfer (Eds.), *Maximizing treatment gains: Transfer enhancement in psychotherapy.* New York: Academic Press, 1979. Pp. 25–86. [16]

Sherrod, D. R. Crowding, perceived control, and behavioral after effects. *Journal of Applied Social Psychology,* 1974, *4,* 171–186. [18]

Shields, J. Heredity and environment. In H. J. Eysenck and G. D. Wilson (Eds.), *A textbook of human psychology.* Baltimore: University Park Press, 1976. [13]

Shneidman, E. S., and **Farberow, N. L.** Attempted and completed suicide. In E. S. Shneidman, N. L. Farberow, and R. E. Litman (Eds.), *The psychology of suicide.* New York: Science House, 1970. [15]

Shneidman, E. S., Farberow, N. L., and **Litman, R. E.** (Eds.). *The psychology of suicide.* New York: Science House, 1970. [15]

Shrauger, J. S. Self-esteem and reactions to being observed by others. *Journal of Personality and Social Psychology,* 1972, *23,* 192–200. [13]

Shreve, A. Careers and the lure of motherhood. *The New York Times Magazine,* November 21, 1982. [8]

Shure, M. B., and **Spivack, G.** The problem-solving approach to adjustment: A competency-building model of primary prevention. *Prevention in Human Services,* 1981, *1,* 87–103. [16]

Shure, M. B., and **Spivack, G.** Interpersonal problem-solving in young children: A cognitive approach to prevention. *American Journal of Community Psychology,* 1982, *10* (3), 341–356. [16]

Siegel, R. K. Hallucinations. *Scientific American,* 1977, *237,* 132–140. [12]

Siegel, S., Hinson, R. E., and **Krank, M. D.** The role of pre-drug signals in morphine analgesic tolerance: Support for a Pavlovian conditioning model of tolerance. *Journal of Experimental Psychology: Animal Behavior Processes,* 1978, *4,* 188–196. [11]

Sigall, H., and **Landy, D.** Radiating beauty: The effects of having a physically attractive partner on person perception. *Journal of Personality and Social Psychology,* 1973, *28,* 218–224. [17]

Sigelman, Lee. Is ignorance bliss? A reconsideration of the folk wisdom. *Human Relations,* 1981, *34,* 965–974. [10]

Silvar, S. D., and **Pollack, R. H.** Racial differences in pigmentation of the fundus oculi. *Psychonomic Science,* 1967, *7,* 159–160. [4]

Silveira, J. *Incubation: The effect of interuption timing and length on problem solution and quality of problem processing.* Unpublished doctoral dissertation, University of Oregon, 1971. [7]

Silver, R. L., and **Wortman, C. B.** Coping with undesirable life events. In J. Garber and M. E. P. Seligman (Eds.), *Human helplessness: Theory and application.* New York: Academic Press, 1980. [10]

Silver, R. L., and **Wortman, C. B.** Emotional reactions to spinal cord injury: Is happiness relative or relevant? Paper presented at the American Psychological Association meeting, Washington, D. C., 1983. [10]

Silverman, P. R. Mutual help groups. *Sage human services guide* (Vol. 16). Beverly Hills, Calif.: Sage Publications, 1980. [16]

Simmons, F. B., Epley, J. M., Lummis, R. C., Guttman, N., Frishkopf, L. S., Harmon, L. D., and **Zwicker, E.** Auditory nerve: Electrical stimulation in man. *Science,* 1965, *148,* 104–106. [4]

Simon, H., and **Gilmartin, K.** A simulation of memory for chess positions. *Cognitive Psychology,* 1973, *5,* 29–46. [6]

Simpson, E. L. Moral development research: A case study of scientific cultural bias. *Human Development,* 1974, *17,* 81–106. [8]

Singer, M. T. The Rorschach as a transaction. In M. A. Rickers-Orsiankina (Ed.), *Rorschach psychology.* Huntington, N. Y.: Krieger, 1977. [14]

Singer, M. T. Therapy with ex-cult members. *National Association of Private Psychiatric Hospitals Journal,* 1978, *9,* 14–18. [18]

Singer, M. T. Coming out of the cults. *Psychology Today,* 1979, *12,* 72–82. [18]

Singer, M. T. and **Wynne, L. C.** Differentiating characteristics of the parents of childhood schizophrenics, childhood neurotics, and young adult schizophrenics. *American Journal of Psychiatry*, 1963, *120*, 234–243. [15]

Singer, M. T., and Wynne, L. C. Thought disorder and family relations of schizophrenics, III: Methodology using projective techniques. *Archives of General Psychiatry*, 1965, *12*, 187–200.

Singular, S. A memory for all seasonings. *Psychology Today*, October 1982, pp. 54–63. [6]

Siqueland, E. R. and Lipsitt, L. P. Conditioned head-turning in human newborns. *Journal of Experimental Child Psychology*, 1966, *3*, 356–376. [8]

Skinner, B. F. *The behavior of organisms: An experimental analysis.* New York: Appleton-Century-Crofts, 1938. [1, 5]

Skinner, B. F. Superstitious behavior in the pigeon. *Journal of Experimental Psychology*, 1948a, *38*, 168–172. [5]

Skinner, B. F. *Walden Two.* New York: Macmillan, 1948b. [1, 13]

Skinner, B. F. *Science and human behavior.* New York: Macmillan, 1953. [5]

Skinner, B. F. *Beyond freedom and dignity.* New York: Knopf, 1971. [13]

Skinner, B. F. *About behaviorism.* New York: Knopf, 1974. [13]

Skinner, B. F. The ethics of helping people. In L. Wispe (Ed.), *Sympathy, altruism, and helping behavior.* New York: Academic Press, 1978. [18]

Skinner, B. F. Utopia or disaster. (Interview conducted by L. Rosenthal.) *Science Digest*, January 1983, pp. 14–15, 103–104. [5]

Slaby, R. G. and Frey, K. S. Development of gender constancy and selective attention to same-sex models. *Child Development*, 1975, *46*, 849–856. [8]

Sloane, R. B., Staples, F. R., Cristal, A. H., Yorkston, W. J., and Whipple, K. *Psychotherapy vs. behavior therapy.* Cambridge, Mass.: Harvard University Press, 1975. [16]

Slobin, D. I. Children and language: They learn the same way all around the world. *Psychology Today*, 1972, *6*, pp. 71–74ff. [9]

Slobin, D. I. Cognitive prerequisites for the development of grammar. In C. A. Ferguson and D. I. Slobin (Eds.), *Studies of child language development.* New York: Holt, Rinehart and Winston, 1973. [9]

Slovic, P., Fischhoff, B., and Lichtenstein, S. Cognitive processes and societal risk taking. *Oregon Research Institute Monograph*, 1976, *15*. [7]

Slovic, P., Fischhoff, B., and Lichtenstein, S. Risky assumptions. *Psychology Today*, June 1980, pp. 44–48. [7]

Slovic, P., Kunreuther, H., and White, G. F. Decision processes, rationality, and adjustment to natural hazards. In C. F. White (Ed.), *Natural hazards, local, national and global.* New York: Oxford University Press, 1974. Pp. 187–205. [7]

Slovic, P., and Lichtenstein, S. Relative importance of probabilities and payoffs in risk taking. *Journal of Experimental Psychology*, 1968, *78*, 1–18. [7]

Smith, E. E., and Medin, D. L. *Categories and concepts.* Cambridge, Mass.: Harvard University Press, 1981. [7]

Smith, E. E., Shoben, E. J., and Rips, L. J. Structure and process in semantic memory: A feature model for semantic decisions. *Psychological Review*, 1974, *81*, 214–224. [7]

Smith, F. Making sense of reading—and of reading instruction. *Harvard Educational Review*, 1977, *47*, 386–395. [9]

Smith, M. C. Hypnotic memory enhancement of witnesses: Does it work? *Psychological Bulletin*, 1983, *94*, 387–407. [12]

Smith, M. L., and Glass, G. V. Meta-analysis of psychotherapy outcome studies. *American Psychologist*, 1977, *32*, 752–760. [16]

Smith, M. L., Glass, G. V., and Miller, R. L. *The benefits of psychotherapy.* Baltimore: Johns Hopkins University Press, 1981. [16]

Smith, P. K., and Daglish, L. Sex differences in parent and infant behavior in the home. *Child Development*, 1977, *48*, 1250–1254. [8]

Snyder, F. Sleep and dreaming: Progress in the new biology of dreaming. *American Journal of Psychiatry*, 1965, *122*, 377–391. [12]

Snyder, F. The phenomenology of dreaming. In L. Madow and L. H. Snow (Eds.), *The psychodynamic implications of the physiological studies on dreams.* Springfield, Ill.: Charles C. Thomas. 1970. [12]

Snyder, M., Tanke, E. D., and Berscheid, E. Social perception and interpersonal behavior: On the self-fulfilling nature of social stereotypes. *Journal of Personality and Social Psychology*, 1977, *35*, 656–666. [17]

Snyder, S. H. *Biological aspects of mental disorder.* New York: Oxford University Press, 1980. [3]

Solomon, E. G., and Bumpus, A. K. The running meditation response: An adjunct to psychotherapy. *American Journal of Psychotherapy*, 1978, *32*, 583–592. [10]

Solomon, L. Z., Solomon, H., and Stone, R. Helping as a function of number of bystanders and ambiguity of emergency. *Personality and Social Psychology Bulletin*, 1978, *4*, 318–321. [18]

Solomon, R. L. The opponent-process theory of acquired motivation: The costs of pleasure and the benefits of pain. *American Psychologist*, 1980, *35*, 691–712. [11]

Solomon, R. L., and Corbit, J. D. An opponent-process theory of motivation. *Psychological Review*, 1974, *81*, 119–145. [11]

Sowell, T. "Affirmative action" reconsidered. *Public Interest*, 1976, *42*, 47–65. [18]

Spenner, K., and Featherman, D. L. Achievement ambitions. *Annual Review of Sociology*, 1978, *4*, 373–420. [11]

Sperling, G. The information available in brief visual presentation. *Psychological Monographs*, 1960, *74*, Whole No. 498. [6]

Sperry, R. W. Some effects of disconnecting the cerebral hemispheres. *Science*, 1982, *217*, 1223–1226. [3]

Sperry, R. W. Changing concepts of consciousness and free will. *Perspective in Biology and Medicine*, 1976, *20*, 9–19. [12]

Spiegel, D., Bloom, J., and Yalom, I. Group support for patients with metastatic cancer. *Archives of General Psychiatry*, 1981, *38*, 527–533. [16]

Spiegel, H. A single-treatment method to stop smoking using ancillary self-hypnosis. *International Journal of Clinical Hypnosis*, 1970, *18*, 235–250. [12]

Spirduso, W. W. Reaction and movement time as a function of age and physical-activity level. *Journal of Gerontology*, 1975, *30*, 435–440. [8]

Spitzer, R. L. On pseudoscience in science, logic in remission, and psychiatric diagnosis: A critique of D. L. Rosenhan's "On being sane in insane places." *Journal of Abnormal Psychology*, 1975, *84*, 442–452. [15]

Spitzer, R. L. More on pseudoscience in science and the case for psychiatric diagnosis: A critique of D. L. Rosenhan's "On being sane in insane places" and "The contextual nature of psychiatric diagnosis." *Archives of General Psychiatry*, 1976, *33*, 459–470. [15]

Spitzer, R. L., and Fleiss, J. L. A reanalysis of the reliability of psychiatric diagnosis. *British Journal of Psychiatry*, 1974, *125*, 341–347. [15]

Spivack, G., and Shure, M. B. *Social adjustment of young children: A cognitive approach to solving real life problems.* San Francisco: Jossey-Bass, 1974. [16]

Springer, S., and Deutsch, G. *Left brain, right brain.* New York, W. H. Freeman, 1981. [3]

Sroufe, L. A. The coherence of individual development. *American Psychologist*, 1979, *34*, 834–841. [8]

Sroufe, L. A. Infant-caregiver attachment and patterns of adaptation in preschool: The roots of maladaptation and competence. In M. Perlmutter (Ed.), *Development and policy concerning children with special needs, Minnesota symposium in child psychology series* (Vol. 16). Hillsdale, N. J.: Lawrence Erlbaum, 1983. [8]

Sroufe, L. A., Fox, N., and Pancake, V. Attachment and dependency in developmental perspective. *Child Development*, in press. [8]

Stalonas, P. M., Johnson, W. G., and Christ, M. Behavior modification for obesity: The evaluation of exercise, contingency management, and program adherence. *Journal of Consulting and Clinical Psychology*, 1978, *46*, 463–469. [11]

Stanley, J. C. Test better finder of great math talent than teachers are. *American Psychologist*, 1976, *31*, 313–314. [14]

Stanley, J. C. Education in the fast lane: Methodological problems of evaluating its effects. *Evaluation News*, February 1983, pp. 28–46. [14]

Stanton, M. D. Strategic approaches to family therapy. In A. Gurman and D. P. Kniskern (Eds.), *Handbook of family therapy*. New York: Brunner/Mazel, 1981. P. 361. [16]

Stapp, J., and **Fulcher, R.** The employment of 1979 and 1980 doctorate recipients in psychology. *American Psychologist*, 1982, *37*, 1159–1185. [1]

Stebbins, L. B., St. Pierre, R. G., Proper, E. C., Anderson, R. B., and **Cerva, T. R.** *Education as experimentation: A planned variation model, Vol. IV-A: An evaluation of Follow Through.* Cambridge, Mass.: Abt Books, 1977. [9]

Steele, C. M., and **Liu, T. J.** Dissonance processes as self-affirmation. *Journal of Personality and Social Psychology*, 1983, *45*, 5–19. [17]

Steele, C. M., Southwick, L. L., and **Critchlow, B.** Dissonance and alcohol: Drinking your troubles away. *Journal of Personality and Social Psychology*, 1981, *41*, 831–846. [17]

Stein, L., and **Belluzzi, J. D.** Brain endorphine and the sense of well-being: A psychobiological hypothesis. *Advances in Biochemical Psychopharmacology*, 1978, *18*, 299–311. [10]

Stein, M. I. A transactional approach to creativity. In. C. W. Taylor (Ed.), *The 1955 University of Utah Research Conference on the Identification of Creative Scientific Talent.* Salt Lake City: University of Utah Press, 1956. [7]

Stengel, E. *Suicide and attempted suicide.* Baltimore, Md.: Penguin, 1964. [15]

Stephan, F. K., Berkley, K. J., and **Moss, R. L.** Efferent connections of the rat suprachiasmatic nucleus. *Neuroscience*, 1981, *6*, 2625–2641. [10]

Stephan, W. G., and **Rosenfield, D.** Effects of desegregation on racial attitudes. *Journal of Personality and Social Psychology*, 1978, *36*, 795–804. [17]

Stephan, W. G., Rosenfield, D., and **Stephan, C.** Egotism in males and females. *Journal of Personality and Social Psychology*, 1976, *34*, 1161–1167. [17]

Stephens, J. H., Long-term prognosis and followup in schizophrenia. *Schizophrenia Bulletin*, 1978, *4*, 25–46. [15]

Stern, M. J., Pascale, L., and **McLoone, J. B.** Psychosocial adaptation following an acute myocardial infarction. *Journal of Chronic Diseases*, 1976, *29*, 513–526. [13]

Stern, W. *The psychological methods of testing intelligence.* G. W. Whipple (Trans.). Baltimore: Warwick & York, 1914. [14]

Sternberg, R. J., Intelligence and nonentrenchment. *Journal of Educational Psychology*, 1981, *73*, 1–16. [14]

Sternberg, R. J., and **Davidson, J. E.** The mind of the puzzler. *Psychology Today*, June 1982, pp. 37–44. [7]

Stevens, C. F., The neuron. *Scientific American*, 1979, *241*, 55–65. [3]

Stevens, S. S. On the psychophysical law. *Psychological Review*, 1957, *64*, 153–181. [4]

Stevens, S. S. The surprising simplicity of sensory metrics. *American Psychologist*, 1962, *17*, 29–39. [4]

Stewart, K. Dream theory in Malaya. In C. T. Tart (Ed.), *Altered states of consciousness.* Garden City, N.Y.: Doubleday, 1972. [12]

Stokols, D. Environmental psychology. *Annual Review of Psychology*, 1978, *29*, 253–295. [18]

Stokols, D., Ohlig, W., and **Resnick, S. M.** Perception of residential crowding, classroom experiences, and student health. *Human Ecology*, 1978, *6*, 233–252. [18]

Stokols, D., Rall, M., Pinner, B., and **Schopler, J.** Physical, social, and personal determinants of the perception of crowding. *Environment and Behavior*, 1973, *5*, 87–115. [18]

Stolz, W., A study of the ability to decode grammatically novel sentences. *Journal of Verbal Learning and Verbal Behavior*, 1967, *6*, 867–873. [9]

Stoner, C., and **Parke, J. A.** *All God's Children.* Radnor, Pa.: Chilton, 1977. [18]

Stoyva, J., and **Anderson, C.** A coping-rest model of relaxation and stress management. In Leo Goldberger and Shlomo Breznitz (Eds.), *Handbook of stress: Theoretical and clinical aspects.* New York: Free Press, 1982. Pp. 745–763. [10]

Strickler, D., Bigelow, G., Lawrence, C., and **Liebson, I.** Moderate drinking as an alternative to alcohol abuse: A nonaversive procedure. *Behavior Research and Therapy*, 1976, *14*, 279–288. [16]

Stromeyer, C. F., III. Eidetikers. *Psychology Today*, November 1970, pp. 76–80. [6]

Stuart, R. B. Behavioral control of overeating. *Behavior Research and Therapy*, 1967, *5*, 357–365. [16]

Stunkard, A. J. (Ed.), *Obesity.* Philadelphia: W. B. Saunders, 1980. [11]

Stunkard, A. J., and **Penick, S. B.** Behavior modification in the treatment of obesity. *Archives of General Psychiatry*, 1979, *36*, 801–806. [11]

Suedfeld, P. The benefits of boredom: Sensory deprivation reconsidered. *American Scientist*, 1975, *63*, 60–69. [11]

Sulzbacher, S. Psychotropic medication with children: An evaluation of procedural biases in results of reported studies. *Pediatrics*, 1973, *51*, 513–517. [16]

Sundberg, N. D., Taplin, J. R., and **Tyler, L. E.** *Introduction to clinical psychology: Perspectives, issues, and contributions to human service.* Englewood Cliffs, N.J.: Prentice-Hall, 1983. [16]

Sundstrom, E. Crowding as a sequential process: Review of research on the effects of population density on humans. In A. Baum and Y. Epstein (Eds.), *Human response to crowding.* Hillsdale, N.J.: Lawrence Erlbaum, 1978. [18]

Sushinsky, L. An illustration of a behavioral therapy intervention with nursing staff in a therapeutic role. *Journal of Psychiatric Nursing and Mental Health Services*, 1970, *8* (5), 24–26. [16]

Sweet, W. H., Ervin, F., and **Mark, V. H.** The relationship of violent behavior to focal cerebral disease. In S. Garattini and E. Sigg (Eds.), *Aggressive behavior.* New York: Wiley, 1969. [10]

Swets, J. A. Is there a sensory threshold? *Science*, 1961, *134*, 168–177. [4]

Swets, J. A., and **Sewall, S.** Stimulus vs. response uncertainty in recognition. *Journal of Acoustical Society of America*, 1961, *33*, 11, 1586–1592. [4]

Sylvester, J. D., and **Liversedge, L. A.** Conditioning and the occupational cramps. In H. J. Eysenck (Ed.), *Behavior therapy and the neuroses.* Elmsford, N.Y.: Pergamon Press, 1960. Pp. 334–348. [5]

Symonds, M. Victims of violence: Psychological effects and aftereffects. *American Journal of Psychoanalysis*, 1975, *35*, 19–26. [18]

Synder, M., and **Uranowitz, S.** Reconstructing the past: Some cognitive consequences of person perception. *Journal of Personality and Social Psychology*, 1978, *36*, 941–85. [17]

Syverson, P. D. *Summary report 1981: Doctorate recipients from United States universities.* Washington, D.C.: National Academy Press, 1982. [1]

Szasz, T. S. *The myth of mental illness: Foundations of a theory of personal conduct.* New York: Harper & Row, 1961. [15]

Tart, C. T. Marijuana intoxication: Common experiences. *Nature*, 1970, *226*, 701–704. [12]

Taube, C. A., and **Rednick, R.** *Utilization of mental health resources by persons diagnosed with schizophrenia.* DHEW Publication No. (HSM) 72–9110. Rockville, Md.: National Institute of Mental Health, 1973. [15]

Tavris, C. *Anger: The misunderstood emotion.* New York: Simon & Schuster, 1982. [5]

Taylor, S., and **Thompson, S.** *Stalking the elusive "vividness" effect.* Unpublished manuscript, University of California at Los Angeles, 1981. [7]

Taylor, S. E. Hospital patient behavior: Reactance, helplessness, or control? *Journal of Social Issues*, 1979, *35*, 156–184. [18]

Taylor, S. E., and **Crocker, J.** Schematic bases of social information processing. In E. T. Higgins, P. Hermann, and Z. P. Zanna (Eds.), *Social cognition: Cognitive structure and* *processes underlying person perception.* Hillsdale, N.J.: Lawrence Erlbaum, 1980. [17]

Taylor, S. E., Crocker, J., Fiske, S. T., Sprinzen, M., and **Winkler, J. D.** The generalizability of salience effects. *Journal of Personality and Social Psychology,* 1979, *37,* 357–368. [17]

Taylor, S. E., and **Fiske, S. T.** Point of view and perceptions of causality. *Journal of Personality and Social Psychology,* 1975, *32,* 439–445. [17]

Teasdale, J. D., and **Fogarty, F. J.** Differential effects of induced mood on retrieval of pleasant and unpleasant events from episodic memory. *Journal of Abnormal Psychology,* 1979, *88,* 248–257. [6]

Teitelbaum, P. Sensory control of hypothalamic hyperphagia. *Journal of Comparative and Physiological Psychology,* 1955, *48,* 156–163. [11]

Teitelbaum, P. Random and food-directed activity in hyperphagic and normal rats. *Journal of Comparative and Physiological Psychology,* 1957, *50,* 486–490. [11]

Teitelbaum, P. The encephalization of hunger. In E. Stellar and J. M. Sprague (Eds.), *Progress in physiological psychology* (Vol. 4). New York: Academic Press, 1971. [3]

Tenopyr, M. L. The realities of employment testing. *American Psychologist,* 1981, *36,* 1120–1127. [14]

Terman, L. M. *The measurement of intelligence.* Boston: Houghton Mifflin, 1916. [14]

Terman, L. M., and **Oden, M. H.** *The gifted child grows up.* Stanford, Calif.: Stanford University Press, 1947. [14]

Terrace, H. S. How Nim Chimpsky changed my mind. *Psychology Today,* November 1979, pp. 65–76. [9]

Thase, M. E., and **Moss, M. K.** The relative efficacy of covet modeling procedures and guided participant modeling on the reduction of avoidance behavior. *Journal of Behavior Therapy and Experimental Psychiatry,* 1976, *7,* 7–12. [16]

Thoits, P. A. Dimensions of life events as influences upon the genesis of psychological distress and associated conditions: An evaluation and synthesis of the literature. In Howard B. Kaplan (Ed.), *Psychosocial stress: Trends in theory and research.* New York: Academic Press, 1983. [10]

Thomas, A., Chess, S., and **Birch, H.** The origin of personality. *Scientific American,* 1970, *223,* 102–109. [13]

Thomas, L. *The lives of a cell.* New York: Viking Press, 1974. [3]

Thompson, J. K., Jarvie, G. J., Lahey, B. B., and **Cureton, K. J.** Exercise and obesity: Etiology, physiology, and intervention. *Psychological Bulletin,* 1982, *91,* 55–79. [11]

Thompson, L. C. The spectral sensitivity of the central fovea. *Journal of Physiology,* 1951, *112,* 114–132. [4]

Thompson, S. K. Gender labels and early sex role development. *Child Development,* 1975, *46,* 339–347. [8]

Thompson, T., and **Grabowski, J.** *Behavior modification of the mentally retarded* (2d ed.). New York: Oxford University Press, 1977. [16]

Thompson, W., Reyes, R. and **Bower, G.** *Delayed effects of availability on judgment.* Unpublished manuscript, Stanford University, 1979. [7]

Thorndike, E. L. *The fundamentals of learning.* New York: Teachers College, 1932. [6]

Thorne, B. Girls and boys together . . . but mostly apart: Gender arrangements in elementary schools. Paper presented to the Social Science Research Council Conference on "Social Relationships: Their Role in Children's Development," Harwichport, Mass., June 1982. [8]

Tinklenberg, J. R. A clinical view of the amphetamines. *American Family Physician,* 1971, *4,* 82–86. [12]

Tolman, E. C. Principles of purposive behavior. In S. Koch (Ed.), *Psychology: A study of science* (Vol. 2). New York: McGraw-Hill, 1959. [11]

Tolman, E. C., and **Honzik, C. H.** *Introduction and removal of reward and maze performance in rats.* University of California Publications in Psychology, 1930, *4,* 257–275. [5]

Tomkins, S. *Affect, imagery, consciousness.* New York: Springer, 1963. [10]

Tonkova-Yampol'skaya, R. V. Development of speech intonation in infants during the first two years of life. In C. A. Ferguson and D. I. Slobin (Eds.), *Studies of child language development.* New York: Holt, Rinehart and Winston, 1973. Pp. 128–138. [9]

Torrance, E. P. *Gifted child in the classroom.* New York: Macmillan, 1965. [14]

Torrance, E. P. Creatively gifted and disadvantaged gifted students. In J. C. Stanley, W. C. George, and C. H. Solano (Eds.), *The gifted and the creative: A fifty-year perspective.* Baltimore: Johns Hopkins University Press, 1977. [14]

Trask, C. H., and **Cree, E. M.** Oximeter studies on patients with chronic obstructive emphysema, awake and during sleep. *New England Journal of Medicine,* 1962, *266,* 639–642. [12]

Travers, J., and **Ruopp, R.** *National day care study: Preliminary findings and their implications.* Cambridge, Mass.: Abt Books, 1978. [8]

Treiman, D., and **Terrel, K.** Sex and the process of status attainment: A comparison of working women and men. *American Sociological Review,* 1975, *40,* 174–200. [17]

Treisman, A. M. Contextual cues in selective listening. *Quarterly Journal of Experimental Psychology,* 1960, *12,* 242–248. [6]

Treisman, A. M. Verbal cues, language and meaning in selective attention. *American Journal of Psychology,* 1964, 77, 206–219. [6]

Tresemer, D. Fear of success: Popular, but unproven. *Psychology Today,* March 1974, pp. 82–85. [11]

Trimble, J. E. *The consonance of agreement of stereotypic descriptions of the American Indian.* Unpublished manuscript, Oklahoma City University, 1968. [17]

Triplett, N. The dynamogenic factors in pacemaking and competition. *American Journal of Psychology,* 1898, *9,* 507–533. [18]

Truax, C. B., Wargo, D. G., Frank, J. D., Imber, S. D., Battle, C. C., Hoehn-Saric, R., Nash, E. H., and **Stone, A. R.** Therapist empathy, genuineness, and warmth and patient therapeutic outcome. *Journal of Consulting Psychology,* 1966, *30,* 395–401. [13]

Tulving, E., and **Pearlstone, Z.** Availability versus accessibility of information in memory for words. *Journal of Verbal Learning and Verbal Behavior,* 1966, *5,* 381–391. [6]

Turner, R. G., Scheier, M. F., Carver, C. S., and **Ickes, W. J.** Correlates of self-consciousness. *Journal of Personality Assessment,* 1978, *42,* 285–289. [13]

Tversky, A., and **Kahneman, D.** Belief in the law of small numbers. *Psychological Bulletin,* 1971, *76,* 105–110. [7]

Tversky, A., and **Kahneman, D.** Availability: A heuristic for judging frequency and probability. *Cognitive Psychology,* 1973, *5,* 207–232. [7]

Tversky, A., and **Kahneman, D.,** The framing of decisions and the psychology of choice. *Science,* 1981, *211,* 453–458. [7]

Tyhurst, J. S. Individual reactions to community disaster. *American Journal of Psychiatry,* 1951, *10,* 746–769. [11]

Tymchuk, A. J., Drapkin, R., Major-Kingsley, S., Ackerman, A. B., Coffman, E. W., and **Baum, M. S.** Ethical decision making and psychologists' attitudes toward training in ethics. *Professional Psychology,* 1982, *13,* 412–421. [16]

Uhlenhuth, E. H., Balter, M. B., and **Lipman, R. S.** Minor tranquilizers: Clinical correlates of use in an urban population. *Archives of General Psychiatry,* 1978, *35,* 650–655. [16]

Ullman, L. P., and **Krasner, L.** *A psychological approach to abnormal behavior* (2d ed.). Englewood Cliffs, N.J.: Prentice-Hall, 1975. [15]

Ullman, M. Dreaming, life-style, and physiology: A comment on Adler's view of the dream. *Journal of Individual Psychology,* 1962, *18,* 18–25. [12]

Ungar, G. Role of proteins and peptides in learning and memory. In G. Ungar (Ed.), *Molecular mechanisms in memory and learning.* New York: Plenum, 1970. [6]

Urban Institute, *The subtle revolution: Women at work.* Washington, D.C.: The Urban Institute, 1980. [8]

Valenstein, E. S. *Brain control: A critical examination of brain stimulation and psychosurgery.* New York: Wiley, 1973. [3, 16]

Valenstein, E. S. Science-fiction fantasy and the brain. *Psychology Today,* 1978, *12,* pp. 28–39. [15]

Valins, S., and Nisbett, R. E. Attribution processes in the development and treatment of emotional disorders. In E. E. Jones et al. (Eds.), *Attribution: Perceiving the causes of behavior.* Morristown, N.J.: General Learning Press, 1972. [10]

Van Dyke, C., and Byck, R. Cocaine. *Scientific American,* March 1982, *44,* 132–141. [12]

Van Itallie, T. B. Obesity: Adverse effects on health and longevity. *American Journal of Clinical Nutrition,* 1979, *32,* 2723–2733. [11]

Van Osdol, W. R., and Shane, D. G., *An introduction to exceptional children.* Dubuque, Iowa: William C. Brown, 1977. [14]

Van Praag, H. M. *Psychotropic drugs: A guide for practitioners.* New York: Brunner/Mozel, 1978. [16]

Vaughan, E. Misconceptions about psychology among introductory psychology students. *Teaching of Psychology,* 1977, *4,* 138–141. [1]

Vaughn, B. E., Gove, F. L., and Egeland, B. The relationship between out-of-home care and the quality of infant–mother attachment in an economically disadvantaged population. *Child Development,* 1980, *51,* 1203–1214. [8]

Vogel, G. A review of REM deprivation. *Archives of General Psychiatry,* 1975, *32,* 749–761. [12]

Vogel, G., Thurmond, A., Gibbons, D., Sloan, K., Boyd, M., and Walker, M. Sleep reduction effects on depressive syndromes. *Archives of General Psychiatry,* 1975, *32,* 765–777. [12]

Vonnegut, M. *The Eden express.* New York: Praeger, 1975. [16]

Wainer, H., Fairbank, D. T., and Hough, R. L. Predicting the impact of simple and compound life change events. *Applied Psychological Measurement,* 1978, *2,* 311–320. [10]

Waite, L. U. S. women at work. *Population Bulletin,* 1981, *36* (2). [8]

Wald, G. The receptors of human color vision. *Science,* 1964, *145,* 1007–1017. [4]

Wald, G. Molecular basis of visual excitation. *Science,* 1968, *162,* 230–239. [4]

Wall, P. D., and Sweet, W. H. Temporary abolition of pain in man. *Science,* 1967, *155,* 108–109. [4]

Wallace, R. K., and Benson, H. The physiology of meditation. *Scientific American,* 1972, *226,* 84–90. [12]

Walster, E., Aronson, E., and Abrahams, D. An increasing the persuasiveness of a low-prestige communicator. *Journal of Experimental Social Psychology,* 1966, *2,* 325–342. [17]

Walster, E., Aronson, V., Abrahams, D., and Rottman, L. Importance of physical attractiveness in dating behavior. *Journal of Personality and Social Psychology,* 1966, *4,* 508–516. [17]

Walster, E., and Festinger, L. The effectiveness of "overheard" persuasive communications. *Journal of Abnormal and Social Psychology,* 1962, *65,* 395–402. [17]

Walster, E., and Walster, W. G. *A new look at love.* Reading, Mass.: Addison-Wesley, 1978. [10]

Wanner, E. *On remembering, forgetting, and understanding sentences.* The Hague: Mouton, 1975. [9]

Ward, C. H., Beck, A. T., Mendelson, M., Mock, J. E., and Erbaugh, J. K. The psychiatric nomenclature: Reasons for diagnostic disagreement. *Archives of General Psychiatry,* 1962, *7,* 198–205. [15]

Warner, K. E. Cigarette smoking in the 1970's: The impact of the antismoking campaign on consumption. *Science,* 1981, *211,* 729–730. [2]

Washborn, S. L. Presidential address to the American Anthropological Society. Quoted in D. Layzer, Science or superstition? A physical scientist looks at the IQ controversy. In N.J. Block and G. Dworkin (Eds.), *The IQ controversy.* New York: Pantheon, 1976. Pp. 194–241. [14]

Wason, P., and Johnson-Laird, P. N. *Psychology of reasoning: Structure and content.* Cambridge, Mass.: Harvard University Press, 1972. [8]

Waters, E., Wippman, J., and Sroufe, L. A. Attachment, positive affect, and competence in the peer group: Two studies in construct validation. *Child Development,* 1979, *50,* 821–829. [8]

Waters, H. F., and Malamud, P. Drop that gun, Captain Video. *Newsweek,* March 10, 1975, *85,* pp. 81–82. [18]

Watkins, L. R., and Mayer, D. J. Organization of endogenous opiate and nonopiate pain control systems. *Science,* 1982, *216,* 1185–1192. [3]

Watson, D. L. and Tharp, R. G. *Self-directed behavior: Self-modification for personal adjustment.* Monterey, Calif.: Brooks/Cole, 1981. [16]

Watson, J. B. *Behaviorism.* New York: People's Institute, 1924. [1,5]

Watson, J. B., and Rayner, R. Conditioned emotional reactions. *Journal of Experimental Psychology,* 1920, *3,* 1–14. [5]

Watson, J. S. Smiling, cooing, and "the game." *Merrill-Palmer Quarterly of Behavior and Development,* 1972, *18,* 323–339. [8]

Wattenberg, W. W., and Clifford, C. Relation of self-concept to beginning achievement in reading. *Child Development,* 1964, *35,* 461–467. [13]

Watzlawick, P., Beavin, J., and Jackson, D. *Pragmatics of human communication: A study of interaction patterns, pathologies, and paradoxes.* New York: Norton, 1967. [15]

Watzlawick, P., and Coyne, J. C. Depression following stroke: Brief, problem-focused family treatment. *Family Process,* 1980, *19,* 13–18. [16]

Webb, E. J., Campbell, D. T., Schwartz, R. D., and Sechrest, L. *Unobtrusive measures: Nonreactive research in the social sciences.* Chicago: Rand McNally, 1966. [2]

Webb, W. B. *Sleep: The gentle tyrant.* Englewood Cliffs, N. J.: Prentice-Hall, 1975. [12]

Webb, W. B., and Agnew, H. Sleep characteristics of long and short sleepers. *Science,* 1970, *168,* 146–147. [12]

Weber, D. J., and Castleman, J. The time it takes to imagine. *Perception and Psychophysics,* 1970, *8,* 165–168. [6]

Wechsler, D. *Wechsler Intelligence Scale for Children.* New York: Psychological Corporation, 1949. [14]

Wechsler, D. *Wechsler Adult Intelligence Scale manual.* New York: Psychological Corporation, 1955. [14]

Wechsler, D. *Wechsler Preschool and Primary Scale of Intelligence.* New York: Psychological Corporation, 1967. [14]

Wechsler, D. *Wechsler Intelligence Scale for Children—Revised.* New York: Psychological Corporation, 1974. [14]

Wechsler, D. *Wechsler Adult Intelligence Scale—Revised.* New York: Psychological Corporation, 1981. [14]

Weigel, R. H., and Newman, L. S. Increasing attitude–behavior correspondence by broadening the scope of the behavioral measure. *Journal of Personality and Social Psychology,* 1976, *33,* 793–802. [17]

Weil, A. T. and Zinberg, N. E. Acute effects of marijuana on speech. *Nature,* 1969, *222,* 434–437. [12]

Weil, A. T., Zinberg, N., and Nelsen, J. M. Clinical and psychological effects of marijuana in man. *Science,* 1968, *162,* 1234–1242. [12]

Weiner, B. *Theories of motivation: From mechanism to cognition.* Chicago: Markham, 1972. [11]

Weiner, B. (Ed.). *Achievement motivation and attribution theory.* Morristown, N. J.: General Learning Press, 1974. [11]

Weiner, B. *Human motivation.* New York: Holt, Rinehart and Winston, 1980. [11]

Weiner, B., Frieze, I. Kukla, A., Reed, L., Rest, S., and Rosenbaum, R. M. *Perceiving the causes of success and failure.* Morristown, N. J.: General Learning Press, 1971. [11,13]

Weingartner, H., Adefris, W., Eich, J. E., and Murphy, D. L. Encoding-imagery specificity in alcohol state-dependent learning. *Journal of Experimental Psychology: Human Learning and Memory,* 1976, *2,* 83–87. [12]

Weingartner, H., Gold, P., Ballenger, J. C., Smallberg, S. A., Summers, R., Rubinow, D. R., Post, R. M., and Goodwin, F. K. Effects of vasopressin on human memory function. *Science*, 1981, *211*, 601–603. [6]

Weisenberg, T., and McBride, K. E. *Aphasia: A clinical and psychological study.* New York: Commonwealth Fund, 1935. [3]

Weiss, J. M., Glazer, H. I., Pohorecky, L. A., Bailey, W. H., and Schneider, L. H. Coping behavior and stress-induced behavioral depression: Studies of the role of brain catecholamines. In R. A. Depue (Ed.), *The psychobiology of the depressive disorders: Implications for the effects of stress.* New York: Academic Press, 1979. [15]

Weiss, J. M., et al. Behavioral depression produced by an uncontrollable stressor: Relationship to norepinephrine, dopamine, and serotonin levels in various regions of rat brain. *Brain Research Reviews*, 1981, *3*, 167–205. [15]

Weizmann, F., Cohen, L. B., and Pratt, J. Novelty, familiarity, and the development of infant attention. *Developmental Psychology*, 1971, *4*, 149–154. [1, 8]

Wender, P. H., Rosenthal, R., Kety, S., Schulsinger, S., and Welner, J. Cross fostering: A research strategy for clarifying the role of genetic and experimental factors in the etiology of schizophrenia. *Archives of General Psychology*, 1974, *30*, 121–128. [15]

Wessells, M. G. *Cognitive psychology.* New York: Harper & Row, 1982. [7]

Wessman, A. E., and Ricks, D. F. *Mood and personality.* New York: Holt, Rinehart and Winston, 1966. [10,15]

West, E. D. ECT in depression: A double-blind controlled trial. *British Medical Journal*, 1981, *31*, 355–357. [16]

Wetheimer, M. Psychomotor coordination of auditory and visual space at birth. *Science*, 1961, *134*, 1692. [8]

Wever, E. G., and Bray, C. W. The perception of low tones and the resonance-volley theory. *Journal of Psychology*, 1937, *3*, 101–114. [4]

White, B. L. *Human infants.* Englewood Cliffs, N. J.: Prentice-Hall, 1971. [4]

White, F. J., and Appel, J. B. Lysergic acid diethylamide (LSD) and lisuride: Differentiation of their neuropharmacological actions. *Science*, 30 April 1982, *216*, 535–537. [12]

White, G. L., Fishbein, S., and Rutstein, J. Passionate love and the misattribution of arousal. *Journal of Personality and Social Psychology*, 1981, *41*, 56–72. [17]

White, M. D., and White, C. A. Involuntarily committed patients' constitutional right to refuse treatment: A challenge to psychology. *American Psychologist*, 1981, *36*, 953–962. [16]

White, R. W. Motivation reconsidered: The concept of competence. *Psychological Review*, 1959, *66*, 297–333. [9,11]

Whitehouse, P. J., Price, D. L., Struble, R.

G., Clark, A. W., Coyle, J. T., and DeLong, M. R. Alzheimer's disease and senile dementia: Loss of neurons in the basal forebrain. *Science*, 1982, *215*, 1237–1239. [3]

Whorf, B. L. Science and linguistics. In J. B. Carroll (Ed.), *Language, thought, and reality: Selected writings of Benjamin Lee Whorf.* Cambridge, Mass.: MIT Press, 1956, Pp. 207–219. [9]

Whyte, W. H., Jr. *The organization man.* New York: Simon & Schuster, 1956. [18]

Wicker, A. W. Attitudes versus action: The relationship of verbal and overt behavioral responses to attitude objects. *Journal of Social Issues*, 1969, *25*, 41–43. [17]

Widroe, H. J., and Heisler, S. Treatment of tardive dyskinesia. *Diseases of the Nervous System*, 1976, *37*, 162–164. [16]

Wiener, A., Gerber, I., Battin, D., and Arkin, A. M. The process and phenomenology of bereavement. In B. B. Schoenberg, I. Gerber, A. Wiener, A. H. Kutscher, D. Peretz, and A. C. Carr (Eds.), *Bereavement: Its psychosocial aspects.* New York: Columbia University Press, 1975. [10]

Wiener, H. External chemical messengers, 1: Emission and reception in man. *New York State Journal of Medicine*, 1966, *66*, 3153–3170. [11]

Wiesel, T. N., and Hubel, D. H. Comparison of the effects of unilateral and bilateral eye closure on cortical unit responses in kittens. *Journal of Neurophysiology.* 1965, *28*, 1029–1040. [4]

Williams, J. Reading instruction today. *American Psychologist*, 1979, *34*, 917–922. [9]

Williams, M. D. *Retrieval from very long-term memory.* Unpublished doctoral dissertation, University of California at San Diego, 1976. [6]

Williams, P. L., and Warwick, R. *Functional neuroanatomy of man.* Philadelphia: W. B. Saunders, 1975. [3]

Williams, R. B., Jr., Barefoot, J. C., and Skekelle, R. B. The health consequences of hostility. In M. A. Chesney, S. E. Goldston, and R. H Rosenman (Eds.), *Anger, hostility, and behavioral medicine.* New York: McGraw-Hill/Hemisphere, in press. [10]

Williams, R. L., and Long, J. D. *Toward a self-managed lifestyle.* 3rd ed. Boston: Houghton Mifflin, 1983. [16]

Wills, T. A. Downward comparison principles in social psychology. *Psychological Bulletin*, 1981, *90*, 245–271. [10]

Wilson, E. O. *Sociobiology: The new synthesis.* Cambridge, Mass.: Harvard University Press, 1975. [18]

Wilson, E. O. *On human nature.* Cambridge, Mass.: Harvard University Press, 1978. [18]

Wilson, G. Introversion/extroversion. In H. London and J. E. Exner (Eds.), *Dimensions of personality.* New York: Wiley, 1978. Pp. 217–261. [13]

Wilson, G. T. From experimental research

to clinical practice: Behavior therapy as a case study. In R. M. Adams, N. J. Smelser, and D. J. Treiman (Eds.), *Behavioural and social science research: A national resource.* Part II. Washington, D. C.: National Academy Press, 1982. [5]

Wilson, G. T. and Rachman, S. J. Meta-analysis and the evaluation of psychotherapy outcome: Limitations and liabilities. *Journal of Consulting and Clinical Psychology*, 1983, *51*, 54–64. [16]

Wilson, J., Kuehn, R., and Beach, F. A. Modification in the sexual behavior of male rats produced by changing the stimulus female. *Journal of Comparative Physiological Psychology*, 1963, *56*, 636–644. [11]

Winsborough, H. The social consequences of high population density. *Law and Contemporary Problems*, 1955, *30*, 120–126. [18]

Winterbottom, M. R. The relation of need for achievement to learning experiences in independence and mastery. In J. W. Atkinson (Ed.), *Motives in fantasy, action and society.* New York: Van Nostrand, 1958. [11]

Wise, L, Steel, L., and MacDonald, C. *Origins and career consequences of sex differences in high school mathematics achievement.* Prepared for the National Institute of Education, Washington, D. C., 1979. [11]

Wittgenstein, L. *Tractatus logico-philosphicus* (2d ed.). New York: Humanities Press, 1963. [9]

Wolf, S., and Wolff, H. G. *Human gastric function.* New York: Oxford University Press, 1947. [10]

Wolfe, J. B. Effectiveness of token-rewards for chimpanzees. *Comparative Psychological Monographs*, 1936, *12*, Whole No. 5. [5]

Wolff, P. The natural history of crying and other vocalizations in early infancy. In B. M. Foss (Ed.), *Determinants of infant behavior* (Vol. 4). London: Methuen, 1969. Pp. 81–109 [9]

Wolpe, J. *Psychotherapy by reciprocal inhibition.* Stanford, Calif.: Stanford University Press, 1958. [16]

Wolpe, J. *The practice of behavior therapy* (2d ed.). Elmsford, N. Y.: Pergamon, Press, 1973. [16]

Wolpe, J. *Theme and variations: A behavior therapy casebook.* Elmsford, N. Y.: Pergamon Press, 1976. [16]

Wong, E., and Weisstein, N. A new perceptual context-superiority effect: Line segments are more visible against a figure than against a ground. *Science*, 1982, *218*, 587–589. [4]

Wood, G. *Cognitive psychology: A skills approach.* Monterey, Calif.: Brooks/Cole, 1983. [7]

Woods, P. J. (Ed.). *Career opportunities for psychologists: Expanding and emerging areas.* Washington, D. C.: American Psychological Association, 1976. [1]

Woods, W. A., and Makhoul, J. Mechanical inference problems in continuous speech understanding. *Proceedings of the Third In-*

ternational Joint Conference on Artificial Intelligence. Stanford, Calif.: Stanford Research Institute, 1973. Pp. 200–207. [9]

Woody, E. Z., Costanza, P. R., Liefer, H., and Conger, J. The effects of taste and caloric perceptions on the eating behavior of restrained and unrestrained subjects. *Cognitive Therapy and Research,* 1981, *5*(4), 381–390. [11]

Wooley, S. C., Wooley, O. W., and Dyrenfurth, S. R. Theoretical, practical, and social issues in behavioral treatment of obesity. *Journal of Applied Behavior Analysis,* 1979, *12,* 3–25. [11]

Woolsey, C. N. Organization of the cortical auditory system. In W. A. Rosenblith (Ed.), *Sensory communication.* New York: Wiley, 1961. [3]

Worchel, S., and Brehm, J. W. Effect of threats to attitudinal freedom as a function of agreement with the communicator. *Journal of Personality and Social Psychology,* 1970, *14,* 18–22. [17]

Worchel, S., and Brehm, J. W. Direct and implied social restoration of freedom. *Journal of Personality and Social Psychology,* 1971, *18,* 294–304. [17]

Wortman, C. B., Abbey, A., Holland, A. E., Silver, R. L., and Janoff-Bulman, R. Transitions from the laboratory to the field: Problems and progress. In L. Bickman (Ed.), *Applications in social psychology* (Vol. 1). Beverly Hills, Calif: Sage Publications, 1980. [2,10]

Wortman, C. B., and Dintzer, L. Is an attributional analysis of the learned helplessness phenomenon viable? A critique of the Abramson, Seligman, and Teasdale reformulation. *Journal of Abnormal Psychology,* 1978, *87,* 75–90. [15]

Wortman, C. B., and Dunkel-Schetter, C. Interpersonal relationships and cancer: A theoretical analysis. *Journal of Social Issues,* 1979, *35,* 120–154. [10,16]

Wylie, R. *The self-concept: A critical survey of pertinent research Literature.* Lincoln: University of Nebraska Press, 1961. [13]

Wylie, R. *The self-concept* (Rev. ed.). Vol 1: *A review of methodological considerations and measuring instruments.* Lincoln: University of Nebraska Press, 1974. [13]

Yarkin, K., Harvey, J. L., and Bloxom, B. M. Cognitive sets, attribution, and social interaction. *Journal of Personality and Social Psychology,* 1981, *41,* 243–252. [15]

Yarmey, A. D. I recognize your face but I can't remember your name: Further evidence on the tip-of-the-tongue phenomenon. *Memory and Cognition,* 1973, *1,* 287–290. [6]

Yarrow, M. R., Scott, P., and Waxler, C. Z. Learning concern for others. *Developmental Psychology,* 1973, *8,* 240–260. [13]

Yogman, M. W., Dixon, S., Tronick, E., Als, H., Adamson, L., Lester, B., and Brazelton, T. B. The goals and structures of face-to-face interaction between infants and fathers. Paper presented to the Society for Research in Child Development, New Orleans, March 1977. [8]

Young, W. C., Goy, R. W., and Phoenix, C. H. Hormones and sexual behavior. *Science,* 1964, *143,* 212–218, [3]

Zaiden, J. Psychodynamic therapy: Clinical applications. In A. J. Rush (Ed.), *Short-term psychotherapies for depression.* New York: Guilford Press, 1982. Pp. 251–310. [16]

Zajonc, R. B. Social facilitation. *Science,* 1965, *149,* 269–274. [18]

Zajonc, R. B. *Social psychology: An experimental approach.* Belmont, Calif.: Wadsworth, 1966. [18]

Zajonc, R. B. Feeling and thinking: Preferences need no inferences. *American Psychologist,* 1980, *35,* 151–175. [10]

Zajonc, R. B. On the privacy of affect. *American Psychologist,* 1984, *39* (2), 117–123. [10]

Zax, M., and Stricker, G. *Patterns of psychopathology.* New York: Macmillan, 1963. [15]

Zillmann, D. *Hostility and aggression.* Hillsdale, N. J.: Lawrence Erlbaum, 1979. [18]

Zimbardo, P. G. Transforming experimental research into advocacy for social change. In M. Deutsch and H. Hornstein (Eds.), *Applying social psychology: Implications for research, practice, and training.* Hillsdale, N. J.: Lawrence Erlbaum, 1975. [18]

Zimbardo, P. G., Ebbesen, E. B., and Maslach, C. *Influencing attitudes and changing behavior* (2d ed.). Reading, Mass.: Addison-Wesley, 1977. [10]

Zimbardo, P. G., Haney, C., and Banks, W. C. A Pirandellian prison. *The New York Times Magazine,* April 8, 1973, pp. 38–60. [17, 18]

Zimbardo, P. G., Haney, C., Banks, W. C., and Jaffe, D. *The psychology of imprisonment: Privation, power, and pathology.* Unpublished paper, Stanford University, 1972. [17,18]

Ziomek, M., and Coyne, J. C. *Depression and supportive behavior.* Unpublished manuscript, University of California at Berkeley, 1983. [15]

Zubin, J., and Spring, B. Vulnerability—a new view of schizophrenia. *Journal of Abnormal Psychology,* 1977, *86,* 103–126. [15]

Zuckerman, M. The effects of subliminal and supraliminal suggestions on verbal productivity. *Journal of Abnormal and Social Psychology,* 1960, *60,* 404–411. [4]

Zuckerman, M. Belief in a just world and altruistic behavior. *Journal of Personality and Social Psychology,* 1975, *31,* 972–976. [18]

Zuckerman, M. The search for high sensation. *Psychology Today,* 1978, *11,* pp. 30–46, 96–99. [11]

Zuckerman, M. *Sensation seeking: Beyond the optimal level of arousal.* Hillsdale, N. J.: Lawrence Erlbaum, 1979. [11]

Zukin, S. R. and Zukin, R. S. Specific phencyclidine-3 binding in rat central nervous system. *Proceedings of the National Academy of Sciences,* 1979, *10,* 5372–5376. [12]

Credits and Acknowledgments

Chapter 2

Page

35 *Figure 2.3* Reprinted by permission of *Law and Society Review*. Copyright © 1968 by the Law and Society Association.

41 *Figure 2.4* Used by permission of Elsevier Science Publishing Company, Inc.

44 *Figure 2.5* Copyright 1981 by the American Association for the Advancement of Science.

51 *Figure 2.9* Used by permission of Robert Rosenthal.

Chapter 3

65 *Figure 3.5* After P. L. Williams and R. Warwick, *Functional Neuroanatomy of Man*, 1st ed. (1975), Churchill Livingstone, Edinburgh.

66 *Figure 3.6* After Ernest Gardner, *Fundamentals of Neurology*, 6th ed. (1976), W. B. Saunders, Philadelphia. Reprinted by permission.

78 *Figure 3.12* Reprinted with permission of Macmillan Publishing Company from *The Cerebral Cortex of Man* by Wilder Penfield and Theodore Rasmussen. Copyright 1950 by Macmillan Publishing Company, renewed 1978 by Theodore Rasmussen.

82 *Figure 3.13* Copyright © 1980 by The New York Times Company. Reprinted by permission.

85 *Figure 3.14* From *Left Brain, Right Brain* by S. Springer and G. Deutsch. W. H. Freeman and Company. Copyright © 1981.

87 *Figure 3.16* From *Left Brain, Right Brain* by S. Springer and G. Deutsch. W. H. Freeman and Company. Copyright © 1981.

87 *Figure 3.17* Copyright © 1976 by the American Psychological Association. Reprinted by permission.

Chapter 4

96 *Figure 4.1* Reprinted by permission of Academic Press, Inc.

113 *Figure 4.11* From G. Kanisza, "Subjective Contours," *Scientific American*, 1976, *234*, 48–52. W. H. Freeman and Company. Copyright © 1976.

119 *Figure 4.15* Center photos, Philip Clark; photo at right, Bob Ward. From *The Intelligent Eye* by R. L. Gregory, McGraw-Hill Book Company, © 1970. Used by permission.

120 *Figure 4.16* Reprinted by permission of Richard Held.

Chapter 5

134 *Figure 5.1* From *Psychonomic Science* Journal.

Chapter 6

159 *Figure 6.3* © 1978 American Psychological Association.

162 *Figure 6.4* After L. R. Peterson and M. G. Peterson, "Short-Term Retention of Experimental Verbal Items," *Journal of Experimental Psychology*, 58, 193–198, © 1959 by the American Psychological Association. Reprinted by permission of Lloyd R. Peterson.

Page

171 *Figure 6.9* Redrawn from *The Psychology of Rumor* by Gordon W. Allport and Leo Postman. Copyright © 1947, renewed 1975 by Holt, Rinehart and Winston, Inc. Reprinted by permission of CBS College Publishing.

171– *Figure 6.10* After L. Carmichael, H. P. Hogan, and
172 A. A. Walter, "An Experimental Study of the Effect of Language on the Reproduction of Visually Perceived Form," *Journal of Experimental Psychology*, 1932, *15*, 73–86.

176 *Figures 6.11 and 6.12* Reprinted by permission of Lawrence Erlbaum Associates, Inc.

Chapter 7

190 *Figure 7.1*

192 *Figure 7.4*

199 *Figure 7.9* From *Cognition* by Margaret Matlin. Copyright © 1983 by Holt, Rinehart and Winston. Reprinted by permission of CBS College Publishing.

191 *Figure 7.3*

197 *Figure 7.8* Adapted from *The Task of Gestalt Psychology* by Wolfgang Köhler, with an introduction by Carroll C. Pratt, copyright © 1969 by Princeton University Press.

194 *Figure 7.6* From *Psychology Today* Magazine. Copyright © 1982 American Psychological Association.

195 *Figure 7.7* Reprinted by permission of University of Illinois Press.

202 *Figure 7.10* With permission of The Free Press, a division of Macmillan, Inc., from *Decision Making* by Irving Janis and Leon Mann. Copyright © 1979 by The Free Press and *Psychology Today* Magazine.

203 *Figure 7.11* Used by permission of Paul Slovic.

206 *Figure 7.12* Reprinted from *Psychology Today* Magazine. Copyright © 1980 American Psychological Association.

Chapter 8

221 *Figure 8.1* After J. Piaget and B. Inhelder, *The Child's Conception of Space*, © 1956 by Humanities Press and Routledge & Kegan Paul Ltd.

236– *Table 8.2* Adapted from Lawrence Kohlberg, "Stage
237 and Sequence: The Cognitive-Developmental Approach to Socialization," in David A. Goslin (ed.), *Handbook of Socialization Theory and Research*. Copyright © 1969 Houghton Mifflin Company.

240 *Figure 8.5* From *The Seasons of a Man's Life*, by Daniel J. Levinson et al. Copyright © 1978 by Daniel J. Levinson. Reprinted by permission of Alfred A. Knopf, Inc.

Chapter 9

250 *Figure 9.3* Reprinted by permission of Richard Jackson Harris.

258 *Table 9.1* Reprinted by permission of Harvard University Press.

260 *Figure 9.6* © 1973 The Society for Research in Child Development, Inc.

Page
269   *Figure 9.10* Reproduced from P. Ekman (Ed.), *Darwin and Facial Expressions*, Academic Press, 1973, with permission from Paul Ekman and Silvan Tomkins.

Chapter 10
276   *Table 10.1* Reprinted by permission of Robert Plutchik and Academic Press, Inc.
285   *Figure 10.2* Reprinted by permission of Stanley Schachter.
291   *Figure 10.3* Reprinted by permission of Lawrence Erlbaum Associates, Inc.
293   *Table 10.2* From *Journal of Psychosomatic Research, 11,* from Thomas H. Holmes and Richard H. Rahe, "The Social Readjustment Rating Scale," copyright © 1967, Pergamon Press, Inc. Reprinted by permission of Thomas H. Holmes and Pergamon Press, Inc.
300   *Figure 10.4* Reprinted from *Psychology Today* Magazine. Copyright © 1980 American Psychological Association.

Chapter 11
309   *Figure 11.1* Copyright 1971 by the American Association for the Advancement of Science.
313   *Table 11.1* From C. P. Herman and J. Polivy, "Restrained Eating," in A. J. Stunkard (Ed.), *Obesity,* Philadelphia, W. B. Saunders Co. (1980). Reprinted by permission.
316   *Table 11.2* Copyright © 1972 by the American Medical Association. Reprinted by permission.
326   *Table 11.3* Reprinted from *Psychology Today* Magazine. Copyright © 1978 American Psychological Association.
330   *Figure 11.6* From M. S. Horner, "Femininity and Successful Achievement: A Basic Inconsistency," in J. M. Bardwick et al., *Feminine Personality and Conflict.* Copyright © 1970 by Wadsworth, Inc. Reprinted by permission of the publisher, Brooks/Cole Publishing Company, Monterey, California.

Chapter 12
341   *Figure 12.4* After E. Hartman, *The Biology of Dreaming,* 1976. Courtesy of Charles C Thomas, Publisher, Springfield, Illinois.

Chapter 13
379   *Figure 13.3* From H. J. Eysenck, *The Structure of Human Personality,* 1970, reprinted by permission of Methuen & Co.
386   *Table 13.1* Data (for table) based on Hierarchy of Needs in "A Theory of Human Motivation" in *Motivation and Personality,* 2d ed., by Abraham H. Maslow. Copyright © 1970 by Abraham H. Maslow.
388   *Figure 13.5* Reprinted by permission of the Midwest Sociological Society.

Chapter 14
402   *Figure 14.4*
403   *Figure 14.5* Adapted from WISC-R record form, © 1971, 1974, The Psychological Corporation.

Page
405   *Table 14.1* Text from Max L. Hutt and Robert G. Gibby, *The Mentally Retarded Child: Development, Education, and Treatment,* 3rd ed. Copyright © 1976 by Allyn and Bacon, Inc., Boston. Used with permission. As compiled in William R. Van Osdol and Don G. Shane, *An Introduction to Exceptional Children,* 2d ed., © 1974, 1977 Wm. C. Brown Company, Publishers, Dubuque, Iowa. Reprinted by permission.
412   *Figure 14.7* Copyright, 1968, by Newsweek, Inc. Reprinted by permission. All rights reserved.
416   *Figure 14.8* Used by permission of Alfred A. Knopf, Inc.
418   *Table 14.2* © 1972 University of Minnesota.
419   *Figure 14.9* MMPI copyright 1943, © renewed 1970 University of Minnesota. Reprinted by permission.

Chapter 15
443   Quotation reprinted by permission of the Educational Broadcasting Corporation.
452   *Figure 15.2* Used by permission.
455   *Figure 15.3* Reprinted by permission of Joseph Zubin.
456   *Table 15.3* From *Abnormal Psychology: Current Perspectives,* 4th ed., by Richard R. Bootzin and Joan Ross Acocella. Copyright © 1972, 1977, 1980, 1984 by Random House, Inc. Reprinted by permission of Random House, Inc.

Chapter 16
465–   Quotation from R. Lindner, *The Fifty-Minute Hour.*
466   Copyright 1954 by Robert Lindner. Reprinted by permission of Holt, Rinehart and Winston, Publishers.
471   *Figure 16.1* Reprinted by permission of Michael Hersen and Academic Press, Inc.
472   *Figure 16.2* Copyright © 1983 by Houghton Mifflin Company. Used by permission.
474   *Figure 16.3* Reprinted by permission of Dr. Raymond W. Novaco.
478   *Figure 16.4* Used by permission of Random House, Inc.

Chapter 17
499   *Table 17.1* Used by permission of Alfred A. Knopf, Inc.
504   *Figure 17.1* Copyright 1957 Yale University Press. Reprinted by permission.
511   *Figure 17.2* Adapted from L. Festinger, S. Schachter, and K. Back, *Social Pressures in Informal Groups,* © 1950 by the Board of Trustees of the Leland Stanford Junior University. By permission of the Stanford University Press.
513   *Figure 17.3* Reprinted by permission of Zick Rubin.
518   *Figure 17.4* Three items from "F-Scale Clusters" (pp. 255–257) in *The Authoritarian Personality* by T. W. Adorno, Else Frenkel-Brunswik, Daniel J. Levinson, and R. Nevitt Sanford. Copyright 1950 by the American Jewish Committee.

Chapter 18
530   *Figure 18.2* Reprinted by permission of Stanley Milgram.
531   *Figure 18.3* Adapted from Figure 6 (p. 36) in *Obedience to Authority: An Experimental View* by Stanley Milgram. Copyright © 1974 by Stanley Milgram.

Name Index

Subject Index

abnormal behavior, *see* psychological disorders and abnormal behavior
absolute thresholds, 94–95, 123
  influences on, 95
  measurement of, 94–95
abstract mental processes, association cortex and, 78
academic performance, IQ correlated with, 36
acetylocholine, 68, 69, 356
achievement motivation, 327–32, 333
  encouragement of, 328–29, 333
  individual differences in, 328–29, 333
  of women, 329–32, 333
acromegaly, 71
ACTH (adrenocorticotrophic hormone), 290–91
action potentials, 67, 68, 90
actor-observer bias, 509, 522
acupuncture, pain relief with, 111
adaptation theory, 297–98
addictive disorders, 325, 457–59, 461
adolescence:
  cognitive development in, 225, 242
  social and personality development in, 238–39, 242
adrenal glands, 71, 72, 290, 291, 318
adrenalin (epinephrine), 72, 282, 285
adulthood:
  cognitive development in, 226–27, 242
  language acquisition in, 255
  midlife transition in, 240
  social and personality development in, 239–41, 242
affective disorders, 442–48, 460
affiliation studies, 31, 32–34, 40
affirmative action, 519–21, 523
A fibers, 110–11
afterimages, 104, 105
aggression, 540–43
  biological influences on, 76, 540–41
  brain stimulation therapy for, 80
  frustration and, 543
  gender roles and, 233
  as rewarded behavior, 306
  social learning influences on, 541–43
aging:
  intellectual performance and, 189, 226–27, 242
  visual acuity lost in, 100
alcohol, 352–54, 361, 458–59, 461
  abuse vs. dependence, 458
  blackouts induced by, 353
  cognitive dissonance reduced by, 502
  memory impairment arising from, 353–54, 356, 357
  social inhibitions reduced by, 352–53, 379

Alcoholics Anonymous (AA), 480
alcoholism, 354, 406, 458–59, 461, 469, 480
alexia, 79
algorithms, 193–94, 209
alpha waves, 338, 349, 350, 351, 352
altered states of consciousness, 334–61
  drug-induced, 352–60, 361
  hypnotic, 336, 337, 345–49, 360–61
  self-regulated, 349–52, 361
  shared features of, 336–37, 360
  sleep as, 336, 337–44, 360
  see also consciousness
altruism, 540, 543–48
Alzheimer's disease, 69
ambiguity, in surface structure, 248
American Psychiatric Association, 435–36
American Psychological Association, 7, 409
  ethical guidelines of, 55, 422, 491
American Sign Language (ASL), 251, 252, 253
Ames room, 118
amnesia:
  anterograde, 177
  as dissociative disorder, 442
  retrograde, 176
  source, 348
  see also forgetting
amphetamines, 315, 358, 361, 380
amplitude, 107
amygdala, 76, 90, 280, 281
anal retentiveness, 378
anal stage, 371, 391
androgens, 72, 73
androgyny, 16–17
angel dust (PCP), 359, 361
angina pectoris, pain associated with, 110
anorexia nervosa, 315, 316
anterior aphasia, 254
anterograde amnesia, 176
antisocial personality disorder, 456–57, 460
anvil (bone), 107, 123
anxiety, 287, 288, 289, 437–39, 460, 485
  basic, 373, 388
  castration, 372
  drug therapy for, 483, 491
  free-floating, 438
  Freudian view of, 366, 368–70, 372, 391, 438
  generalized, 438, 460
  phobic, *see* phobias
  see also stress
aphasia, 254
applied science, psychology as, 7–8, 24
aqueous humor, 100, 101
Army intelligence tests, 402
ASL, *see* American Sign Language
association cortex, 78
associative learning, 128–50, 154–55
  classical conditioning as, 129–37, 146–50, 154
  cognitive view of, 150–51
  operant conditioning as, 129, 137–50, 154
ataxia, 75

attachments, formation of, 229–30, 242, 254
attitude objects, 496
attitudes, 496–503, 521–22
  defined, 496
  influence of cognitive consistency on, 500–503
  influence of persuasive communications on, 497–500
  repeated exposure and, 510–11
  resistance to change in, 503
  as secondary traits, 378
  willingness to act on, 5, 496–97
  see also social perception
attribution retraining, 3–4
auditory canal, 107, 123
auditory cortex, 108
authoritarian personality, 518
authority, obedience to, 17–18, 40, 52, 529–32
autonomic nervous system, 63–64, 74, 89, 277–78, 280
  biofeedback control of, 63, 295, 302, 350–52, 361
  dual control of, 63
  emotions and, 277–78, 290–91
  parasympathetic division of, 63–64, 89, 277, 278
  sympathetic division of, 63–64, 89, 277–78, 280, 290–91
availability heuristic, 204, 205–6, 210
aversive conditioning, 469, 491
avoidant personality disorder, 456
axons, 64, 65, 67, 68, 89–90

backward conditioning, 132
backward search, 195, 209
basal age, 401
basic anxiety, 373, 388
basic hostility, 373
basic science, psychology as, 7–8, 24
basilar membrane, 108, 109
behavior:
  attitudes vs., 5, 496–97
  attributing causes to, 506–10, 522
  biological foundations of, 60–91
  compulsive, 439–40, 456, 460
  consistency of, 380–83, 392
  in groups, 37–38, 532–40
  isolating variables in, 4–5
  learning inferred from, 128
  operant, 138
  predicting patterns of, 36
  self-regulation of, 376–77
  traits of, 365, 377–83, 392
  unlearned influences on, 128
  see also brain–behavior relationships; psychological disorders and abnormal behavior; performance
behavioral assessment, 419–20, 424
behavioral measures, 40, 56
behaviorism, 10–12, 24–25, 365, 374–76, 392
  early resistance to, 8
  Freudian psychology vs., 14
  learning–performance link in, 127–28